מסורה

ArtScroll Mesorah Series

Rabbi Nosson Scherman/Rabbi Meir Zlotowitz
General Editors

באור על התורה לרבי עובדיה ספורנו

COMMENTARY ON THE TORAH

Published by

Mesorah Publications, ltd

SFORNO

Translation and explanatory notes
by Rabbi Raphael Pelcovitz

FIRST EDITION
First Impression . . . December 1987

Published and Distributed by
MESORAH PUBLICATIONS, Ltd.
Brooklyn, New York 11223

Distributed in Israel by
MESORAH MAFITZIM / J. GROSSMAN
Rechov Harav Uziel 117
Jerusalem, Israel

Distributed in Europe by
J. LEHMANN HEBREW BOOKSELLERS
20 Cambridge Terrace
Gateshead, Tyne and Wear
England NE8 1RP

THE ARTSCROLL MESORAH SERIES®
SFORNO — COMMENTARY ON THE TORAH
Volume I: Bereishis/Sh'mos

1969 Coney Island Avenue / Brooklyn, N.Y. 11223 / (718) 339-1700

ISBN: 0-89906-238-5 (hard cover)
0-89906-239-3 (paperback)

Typography by CompuScribe at ArtScroll Studios, Ltd., Brooklyn, NY

Printed by Moriah Offset U.S.A.
Bound by **Sefercraft, Inc.,** Brooklyn, NY

Volume I:

ספר בראשית

Bereishis/Genesis

ספר שמות

Sh'mos/Exodus

מוקדש לזכר נשמת אשת נעורי

״מנשים באהל תבורך״

פרומא בת יצחק ליב ע״ה

י״ג תשרי תשמ״ז

Dedicated to the everlasting memory of

My Beloved Wife

FRUMI PELCOVITZ

Who encouraged me to undertake this project

and whose blessed memory inspired me

to complete it.

תנצב״ה

☙ Preface

This project was begun in תשכ"ו (1966), although my interest in the *Sforno* dates back to my earlier years when I was studying and teaching *Chumash* and commentaries. Since my background is also one which was steeped in the *Mussar* movement, whose teachers quoted the *Sforno* constantly, it is understandable that this 16th-century Torah commentator attracted and intrigued me. The idea of translating the *Sforno* and writing explanatory notes, although started in 1966 in Jerusalem, was set aside due to the many demands on my time and the varied pressures associated with my rabbinical position.

When my congregation granted me a sabbatical in תשמ"ו (1985-86), I decided to resume this project and dedicate my time and energy to it, spurred on by the willingness of Mesorah Publications to publish this work.

The Mosad HaRav Kook edition of the *Sforno's Chumash* commentary, published in תש"מ (1980), edited and annotated by Avrohom Darom ז"ל and Zev Gottlieb ז"ל, served as an invaluable source and guide to this work. It should be noted that their version is a most definitive one, based as it is on nine different manuscripts. The perceptive reader will note that there are certain commentaries of the *Sforno* found in their work, and in this translation, which do not appear in the מקראות גדולות (the standard *Chumash* with commentaries) edition.

This translation of the *Sforno* is basically a literal one, retaining the original flavor and also permitting the reader to refer to it while studying the *Sforno* in the original Hebrew. Parenthesized words and phrases are inserted by the translator to enhance the grammatical flow, and for the purpose of clarification, recognizing that an English translation of Medieval Hebrew, were it totally a literal one, would at times be obscure, awkward and even incomprehensible. The explanatory notes will, hopefully, elucidate, explain and clarify the meaning, sense and intent of the author.

This work is dedicated to the memory of my beloved wife Frumi ע"ה. The translation of the first three books — *Bereishis, Sh'mos* and *Vayikra* — were completed during our Sabbatical in the States and Jerusalem, a period of tranquility, contentment and fulfillment with her at my side. Her sudden passing caused me to put aside this work for a period of time, but I was determined to resume and finish it לזכר נשמתה — in her beloved memory, as a tribute to a most outstanding and special woman.

Our Sages, who were extremely sensitive to the unique worth and value of a true *Aishes Chayil,* and profoundly understood the vital role she plays in her husband's life, state: "A man who has no wife lives without joy, without blessing, without good, without Torah and without peace" (Tractate *Yevamos* 62). My wife's passing indeed left me deprived of these many blessings, save one. I learned that the study of Torah can, and must, be salvaged, and only through it can one's equilibrium and clarity of mind be retained. King David, in his great wisdom, summed it up beautifully when he said: *Had Your Torah not been my pursuit, I would have perished in my affliction* (*Psalms* 119:92).

Let it be recorded that the total support of my children, grandchildren, friends and congregants gave me much needed encouragement and strength, enabling me to fulfill my manifold duties, and above all, to proceed with the completion of this work on the *Sforno*.

It is my sincere hope and prayer that the students and scholars who will read and study this *sefer*, will come to appreciate the פשטות ועמקות (the reasoned logic and profound depth) of the *Sforno's* commentary on the Torah. If this English translation and explanatory notes will help them better understand and appreciate the *Sforno*, that will be my greatest source of satisfaction and fulfillment.

ACKNOWLEDGMENTS

The author wishes to express his heartfelt thanks and appreciation to the editors of the ArtScroll series, Rabbi Nosson Scherman and Rabbi Meir Zlotowitz, for their invaluable assistance; to Rabbi Sheah Brander, who was in charge of the beautiful design and layout of this work; and to Rabbi Avie Gold for his painstaking proofreading and most helpful suggestions.

During my stay in Israel, Rabbi Samuel Stern and Rabbi Heshie Leiman were most helpful in supplying me with the necessary *seforim* not available to me in my temporary residence in Jerusalem. I am also most thankful to my assistant, Rabbi David Weinberger, to Rabbi Aaron Brafman, and to my daughter, Ethel Gottlieb, for their careful reading of the galley proofs, and their valuable suggestions and corrections. I am especially appreciative to Eleanor Klein for the many hours spent in preparing the manuscript of the Introductory Essay.

A special *yasher koach* is extended to my congregation, Knesseth Israel of Far Rockaway, N.Y., for giving me the opportunity to spend so much time on this work. May we all merit to attain חלקנו בתורתך, *our portion in Your Torah*.

Raphael Pelcovitz

Tammuz, 5747

INTRODUCTION

Ovadiah ben Yaacov Sforno

◆§ Biographical Data and Historical Period

Ovadiah Sforno (referred to respectfully as "the *Sforno*") was born in Cesena, Italy, in the year 5230 (1470) or 5235 (1475) the records regarding the date are unclear. He received his Jewish education in the city of his birth and, from his prestigious works on the Torah as well as the Talmudic knowledge for which he was famous, one can assume that his Torah education was most thorough. From Cesena he moved to Rome where he attended the university, and studied philosophy, mathematics and medicine, receiving his medical degree in 1501. For thirty years the *Sforno* lived in Rome, where he was a great *marbitz Torah* (a teacher and disseminator of Torah), as well as the author of many works on Jewish philosophy and commentaries on *Tanach*. A number of rabbis consulted with him regarding halachic problems and we find him quoted in their responsa, including a responsum of the Torah luminary, Maharam of Padua (Rabbi Meir Katzenellenbogen).

While living in Rome, the *Sforno* came into contact with the Christian community and, apparently, moved with ease and comfort in high society. For example, he was retained by Johann Reuchlin, the well-known German scholar and humanist, to teach him the Hebrew language. Indeed, the *Sforno* had a marked influence on Reuchlin who, during the critical period when Jews were under attack by the Church, became a spirited defender of the Talmud and the Jews.

The *Sforno* dedicated his commentaries on *Shir Hashirim* (Song of Songs) and *Koheles* (Ecclesiastes) to Henry II of France, and after writing his famous philosophical work *Or Amim* (Light of Nations), he translated it into Latin and sent it to King Henry, indicating that there was a close relationship between them.

This was a relatively peaceful period, thanks to the liberal climate fostered by the popes who headed the Church at that time. The fact that the *Sforno* was able to attend the university and associate with prominent men and even kings, indicates that it was a period of intellectual openness and tolerance. As usually happens, such freedom also proved detrimental to the loyalties and commitments of the Jewish community, which we can deduce from the *Sforno's* introduction to his commentary on Torah. In this introduction, he explains that he was motivated to undertake this commentary

> ... because our people dwell in an alien land and concentrate their efforts on the accumulation of wealth, feeling that this will protect them from the exigencies of their time. This in turn results in a condition where they have no proper time to consider the wonders and wisdom of our Torah, and even brings them to question the importance of our holy Torah, becoming critical of its teachings for they do not understand it properly.

From these words of the *Sforno*, we detect the Jewish intellectual and spiritual poverty of his fellow Jews, which prompted him to write his commentary on the Torah in the hope that he would be able to arouse their interest and develop in them an appreciation for the word of *Hashem*.

In addition to his major work on the Five Books of Moses, and his philosophical treatise, *Or Amim*, the *Sforno* also wrote commentaries on the books of *Psalms, Job, Jonah, Zechariah* and *Habakuk*, as well as a commentary on *Avos* (Ethics of the Fathers). He later moved from Rome and lived for a time in Reggio, prior to settling in Bologna where his banker brother, Hananel, supported him financially and urged him to complete his commentary on the Torah. In Bologna the *Sforno* apparently practiced medicine, for we find him described as the *Abir Harofim* (the mightiest physician) in various records of that time. He established a Beth Medrash in Bologna, where he taught Torah until the end of his life, in 1550.

Although the early period of his life was, as we have noted, a relatively peaceful one, wherein Jews in Italy were able to enter the professions and participate in the business and banking world, nonetheless, the clouds gathering in other countries would also affect Italian Jewry. The Expulsion from Spain 1492 affected the Jews in Sicily and Sardinia as well, for these islands were under the rule of the Aragonese. In addition to Spanish Jews who were expelled from their native land, a large number of Sicilian Jews emigrated to Italy. This had an impact upon the *Sforno*, who was a witness to these persecutions and, no doubt, he sensed the beginnings of a deteriorating Christian-Jewish relationship even in Italy. As early as 1510, the kingdom of Naples, under Spanish rule, expelled the Jews, and the Venice ghetto was established in 1516.

Indeed, the *Sforno* lived at a critical juncture in Jewish history, a period of volatile change. Although the serious persecution of Jews in Italy did not begin until after his death, his later years were clouded by the many difficulties that confronted the Jewish population. The popes who headed the Church from 1549 to 1559 were particularly antagonistic to the Jews. Among the anti-Jewish measures instigated during this period was the burning of the Talmud in 1553. The Counter Reformation also had a deleterious effect upon Jews who were suspected of sympathizing with the Protestants against the Catholics. Many of these events were brewing in the *Sforno's* later years and are reflected in his writings, where he alludes to the difficult conditions of his fellow Jews and strives to encourage and strengthen them with words of hope and faith in the ultimate triumph of Israel over Esau (Edom), which is synonymous with Rome, as every Jewish reader of that time understood. See his commentary on *Genesis* 25:26 and 32:29 regarding the names of Jacob and Israel.

◆§ Method and Style of the Sforno's Exegesis

The *Sforno's derech* (method) of commentary is that which is known as *pshat* — the interpretation of a verse in accordance with the grammatical and linguistic connotation of the words. However, he often goes beyond the simple, straightforward meaning of a verse, offering expositions that are scientific or philosophical and often ethical. He usually avoids philological analyses of individual words and is more interested in elucidating the sense of a complete passage. Rather than spelling out the difficulties inherent in a verse, he resolves them through a comment that anticipates the questions and problems that may trouble the student. He also emphasizes the inner connection between different but similar parts of a verse, and thus removes the problem of *kaphel lashon* (duplication in phraseology). He is not averse at times to interpret sections of the Torah allegorically or mystically, based upon the *Zohar*. See, for example, *Exodus* 13:15, *Numbers* 12:2, and *Exodus* 12:22.

His approach is in keeping with his motivation and intent as spelled out in his Introduction, namely to demonstrate that the Torah is reasoned, logical, ordered and not redundant, and also to refute the argument that our Torah speaks only of material rewards while remaining silent regarding the World to Come, immortality of the soul and eternal reward, as opposed to the Christian faith which stresses these latter elements so strongly.

In addition to the general introduction to his commentary on the Torah, the *Sforno* wrote a lengthy introduction to Torah, which he entitled *Kavanos HaTorah* (the intent and meaning of Torah). In that essay, he explains that the reason the Torah was given to Israel was to sanctify them as an eternal people, a goal that would be realized

> . . . by their being like unto Him in thought and deed . . . and to attain this exalted level, the Almighty gave us in His Torah, a theoretical section called "Torah" and a second section dealing with practical, pragmatic actions called "Mitzvah." The portion of the Torah which is theoretical has as its primary purpose, to understand, comprehend and find proof of the existence of God, Who is non-corporeal, Creator of all, Omniscient and Omnipotent. This knowledge of God's greatness will bring man to revere and fear Him while also accepting the concept of reward and punishment.

This section of the Torah is also meant

> . . . to bring man to an appreciation of God's mercy and kindness, His concern for all creation and especially for the human race, which He created in His image and after His likeness. Through the knowledge of these two fundamentals — recognition of God's existence and of His goodness and kindness — the Torah grants us life in this world and eternal life in the world to come. By studying Torah, one learns to strive to emulate *Hashem* in all His ways, to imitate His goodness and kindness to others and to be holy as He is holy. By so doing, we attain the goal meant for all mankind and especially for Israel, His people, whom He created in His image and after His likeness.

This *hashkafah* (point of view) of the *Sforno* is found time and again in his commentary. He is committed to the concept of universal man, which in no way however diminishes his fierce faith in the status of Israel as God's chosen people. Many, therefore, have referred to the *Sforno* as a humanist, but this lends itself to misinterpretation. Humanism, the attitude of mind which attaches primary importance to man and which was a characteristic attitude of the Renaissance, was in many ways a reaction to the Church's belittling of man's natural condition. The *Sforno's* commitment, however, to the dignity of man is drawn totally from our Torah and our Sages. The verse, *Let us make man in our image and our form* (*Genesis* 1:26) is of sufficient import to cause him to accept universal man — his role in the world, his importance and his place in the divine pattern of this world. The expression, "Precious is man who was created in the Divine image" (*Avos* 3:18) buttresses this belief and is a theme which is repeated time and again in the *Sforno's* commentaries. Nonetheless, he fully recognizes Israel's special role: that although the Almighty had hoped originally to realize His purpose through mankind in general, this hope was ultimately shattered and *Hashem* therefore chose Abraham and his seed to realize the original intent of *Hashem* in the creation of man.

Toward that end the Torah also contains the second section of which the *Sforno* speaks in his *Kavanos HaTorah,* the one dealing with deeds and actions that are meant "to prepare man, especially the people of Israel, toward the goal of God's original intent." To explain this section the *Sforno* submits that the *mitzvos* are built upon seven pillars, among them *mitzvos* that are meant to create a pure heart in man, others which are meant as deterrents, and some that have as their purpose the regulation of man's reproductive behavior. Another section of *mitzvos* concerns dietary disciplines, while other observances serve as signs and symbols teaching us that we are *Hashem's* people — such as circumcision and Sabbath, which are signs of the Covenant. The last two pillars consist of 'reminders' that we are servants of God, which include *tzitzis, tefillin* and *mezuzah;* and *mitzvos* that are meant to correct and control domestic, social and political behavior, such as the ordinances and laws. It is interesting to note that Samson Raphael Hirsch's *Horeb* in many ways follows this order.

We see that the *Sforno*, in order to refute the argument of those who felt that the Torah was unclear and disorganized, applied himself to explain and clarify the intent and purpose of the Torah. As for the second argument that the Torah speaks only of material and not eternal reward, he stresses, in his *Kavanos HaTorah,* the concepts that "the reward of a *mitzvah* is not given in this world" *(Kiddushin* 39b) and that "the reward of a *mitzvah* is another *mitzvah*" *(Avos* 4:2). He emphasizes that the treasures awaiting the righteous in the next world have never been revealed to man and, therefore, remain a mystery to which the Torah does not address itself, but he reassures us that the soul of man is immortal. He also vigorously defends the eternal character and obligation of *mitzvos* and the everlasting viability, vitality and legitimacy of the covenant between God and Israel, which was never supplanted by a 'new covenant' or a 'new Israel' as claimed by the Church. Of course, it was extremely important to convey this message to sixteenth century Italian Jewry.

The literary style of the *Sforno*, who was famed for his proficiency in the Hebrew language, is succinct, precise and clear. It is simple yet elegant, and at times poetic. He paraphrases many expressions from the *Tanach* and the Talmud, often quoting directly from these sources, while drawing parallels from verses in *Tanach* to the verse at hand. It is for this reason that the phrase *k'inyan* (similar to) appears very frequently.

Although the *Sforno's* knowledge of *Tanach* and Talmud is all-encompassing, nonetheless there are times when he deviates from the interpretation of our Sages or other commentators who preceded him, and offers an original, fresh approach. However, this is always done in the spirit of tradition and never negates the accepted principles of Torah, nor questions the discipline and authority of Torah. The *Sforno* is known for his brevity, but there are times when he deviates from this style and presents a lengthy discourse on a subject that he feels is important for his readers to understand, especially if it represents a fundamental and critical aspect of Torah *hashkafah.* Some examples are: *Genesis* 1:27 regarding man's creation in the image of God; *Exodus* 19:9 regarding the prophetic spirit granted to the people of Israel at Sinai; *Leviticus* 13:27 regarding נִגְעֵי בְגָדִים *(plague of garments); Leviticus* 18:6 regarding forbidden sexual unions; *Numbers* 19:2 regarding the red cow and *Numbers* chapter 20 regarding the episode of the waters of Meribah.

He often draws a moral lesson from an episode and underscores the ethical teachings underlying an event, a law, a commandment or an ordinance of the Torah. A few examples are in *Genesis* 2:9, 33:11 and 35:1. There are many more, which will be apparent to the reader of his Torah commentary. It is for this reason that the masters of *Mussar* in the nineteenth and twentieth centuries looked to the *Sforno* as a classical source for their moral and ethical discourses. The method of the *Mussar* masters is to delve deeply into every episode related in the Torah and Prophets in an attempt to detect the motivation of the personae who are meant to serve as our models, and also to analyze the nuances and subtleties of expression used in the Torah, which reveal a much more profound meaning than one can gain through a superficial reading. This is precisely what the *Sforno* does time and time again. He is sensitive to every moral and ethical lesson which one can derive from events recorded in the Torah, as well as the underlying purpose and goal of various *mitzvos*, which the masters of *Mussar* incorporated into their teachings as well.

Through his commentary on the Torah the *Sforno* stresses themes that are at the heart of the *Mussar* approach: the paramount importance of man; the purpose of man; the complexity of his emotions and motivations; and the major role of *teshuvah* (repentance) in man's experience. These themes represent the core of *Mussar* teachings, hence it is no wonder that the Lithuanian School of *Mussar*, in particular, drew from the *Sforno* so extensively.

The *Sforno* was familiar with, and often reflects, the commentaries of the *Ramban, Rashi, Ibn Ezra, Rashbam, Chizkuni* and, especially, *Abarbanel*, whose commentary he very often parallels. He was also well versed in the writings of *Rambam*, especially his *Guide for the Perplexed*. Strangely, the *Sforno* does not quote any of these great commentators or attribute any interpretation to his predecessors by name. This failure to quote or attribute was apparently an accepted practice of his time. He also was knowledgeable in the teachings of *Kabbalah* and the *Zohar*, which he incorporates in his commentary. See, for example, his commentary on *Exodus* 12:22. His genius lies in his ability to digest and distill the essence of these great classic commentators while adding his own distinct, unique flavor to them.

◆§ Major Recurrent Themes

These are the major recurring themes that the careful reader and serious student will find in the *Sforno's* commentary:

1. *Universal Man and Israel.*

Man plays an extremely important role in the *hashkafah* of the *Sforno*. In addition to the concept of universal man — without denying the special role played by Israel — the *Sforno* stresses the concept of יִשְׂמַח ה׳ בְּמַעֲשָׂיו *(God rejoices in His creations)*. God's greatest delight is to rejoice with His creation and especially with man, the crown of His creation, and, of course, with Israel who represents the most precious jewel in this crown. Hence, it is our duty to conduct ourselves in a manner that will afford God this *simchah*. As he states in *Kavanos HaTorah*, "When we fulfill His will and are worthy to be rewarded, God rejoices for He desires to do kindness. Conversely, when we sin, God is brought to עַצְבוּת *(sorrow)*, as it is written, וַיִּתְעַצֵּב אֶל לִבּוֹ *(and it grieved Him at his heart)*, for He does not desire the death of the sinner."

This latter expression, that God does not desire the sinner's death, is based on

Ezekiel 18:23, and is repeated time and again in the *Sforno's* commentary, to emphasize God's love, compassion and kindness, and His readiness to accept man's repentance. Man is frail and is prone to transgress and sin. God's desire is for man to repent, for His desire is not to punish the wicked, but rather that they return to Him. This is found in the *Sforno's* commentary on the Ten Plagues in Egypt as well as in the story of the Golden Calf.

The greatness of the human being, according to him, lies in the fact that 'he alone among all creatures is predisposed to be like the Creator in intellect and deed' (*Leviticus* 13:47). Nonetheless, not all people are privileged to be subject to God's Divine Providence [הַשְׁגָּחָה פְּרָטִית] in a particular, individualistic fashion. As the *Sforno* explains in his commentary on the aforementioned verse in *Leviticus*, "Mankind as a whole is controlled by the natural order and heavenly forces ... similar to the destiny of other living creatures who are not subject to God's providence individually but only as a species." Israel, the chosen people, on the other hand, is distinctive and as such is under the Almighty's direct, personal supervision. However, not all Jews are worthy of this special Divine Providence in a particular sense. Indeed, "the majority of Israel, except for chosen individuals, are doubtless controlled by the natural order similar to all gentiles" (ibid.).

In the view of the *Sforno*, בְּחִירָה חָפְשִׁית (freedom of choice) and Divine Providence are interwoven. The man who strives to imitate God and attempts to adopt His will as his own has utilized the gift of free will as intended by God and therefore deserves to be under His protection and providence. In *Or Amim* the *Sforno* presents this theory succinctly and clearly:

> Being that Israel is more readily prepared for this (i.e., to fulfill God's intent and purpose here on earth) because they are children of the covenant, therefore God is referred to as "the God of Israel," meaning that He watches over them in a particular, personal fashion ... (but) when the nations will ultimately call in the Name of Hashem and serve Him in unison, He will be called "the God of the entire world."

In other words, universal man has the potential to realize God's purpose in His creation of mankind. Until that time, however, Israel is the people chosen to reach this goal more readily and, as such, is worthy of special Divine consideration and concern. The *Sforno* expresses this thought in *Deuteronomy* 26:18: "You (Israel) have been granted the advantage of being chosen to observe His commandments, through which you will find favor in His eyes, whereas the other nations are not worthy or prepared to do so." He perceives that the purpose of man is to imitate God, i.e., to imitate His *ways*. As the Talmud (*Shabbos* 133b) states: "Abba Shaul says: *V'anvayhu* (וְאַנְוֵהוּ), be like Him. As He is merciful and gracious so shall you be merciful and gracious."

In *Or Amim* the *Sforno* writes, "The intended purpose of the human race is that man shall be like his Creator in his behavior and intelligence, to the extent possible, as the Torah attests, *Let us make man in our image and after our likeness, (Genesis* 1:26). [Therefore man] must choose to walk in His path and follow the well-ordered ways of His conduct in this world, to the extent possible." In his commentary on *Genesis* 1:26 the *Sforno* develops this theme. He points out that, unlike the angels, man has freedom of choice, which is a power equal to that of the Creator Himself, Who is the ultimate Master of Free Will. On the other hand, unlike God, man does not always choose well. Nonetheless, man is entitled to be called one who is 'in His likeness and image.' Hence the mission and purpose of man is to strive to emulate God's *ways,* for it is impossible to imitate God Himself.

The charge given to Israel to be holy (קְדוֹשִׁים תִּהְיוּ) is explained by the *Sforno* in a similar vein: "The purpose of all these laws (i.e., regarding sexual morality, purity and impurity, dietary disciplines, etc.) is that [the Jewish people] be holy, in order to become like their Creator, to the extent possible. This was indeed the Divine intent in creating man as it says, *Let us make man in our image and our likeness; For I, your God, am holy (Leviticus* 19:2), therefore it is fitting that you be like Me in thought and deed."

2. *Israel Among the Nations*

To some extent the *Sforno's* own life reflected the general state of Israel in exile, a most difficult and perilous condition in his time, including as it did the expulsion of Jews from Spain and the establishment of ghettos in Italy. Consequently, he injects in his commentary words of comfort and encouragement to his fellow Jews. He stresses this topical theme in his commentary on various verses, especially when he explains the reason for the names Yaakov and Yisrael. The former name refers to the end of time, indicating that Jacob will survive and exist even after all others have disappeared from the stage of history, while the latter indicates the status of our people in the Messianic period. He attempts to combat the sense of despair which doubtless enveloped many of his co-religionists at that time and reassures them that God's providence has never been removed and that He cares and is concerned for them. See, for example, *Exodus* 12:42. However, in spite of his great faith in the ultimate victory of Israel, he is doubtful whether statehood is for Israel's optimum benefit. In his commentary on *Genesis* 27:29, he makes the interesting suggestion that it may be more beneficial for Jacob to live under the protection of Esau, lest by becoming involved in the demands of statehood, Jacob will have to forsake his pursuit of the spiritual!

This theme of the interrelationship between brothers is expressed in a different manner regarding the interaction and relationship between Issachar and Zevulun, wherein the former pursues the study of Torah and is supported by the latter. This, no doubt, is a reflection of his own warm relationship with his brother, Hananel, and mirrors the economic problems which confronted him, preventing his exclusive pursuit of Torah scholarship, before Hananel stepped in. This is also mirrored in his commentary on *Genesis* 28:20 and 49:13.

3. *Medicine and the Natural Sciences*

The *Sforno's* medical knowledge is reflected in a number of his commentaries and, at times, is extremely original and advanced for his period. For example, regarding Sarah's and Rachel's difficulty in conceiving, which caused each of them to offer her handmaiden to her husband as a co-wife, the *Sforno* comments that, by involving themselves in the rearing of the children of Hagar and Bilhah respectively, they hoped that their own fertility and reproductive capabilities would be enhanced. This concept is accepted even today and has been proven to be beneficial. Many women who adopt a baby, eventually are able to conceive their own. The *Sforno's* grasp of this psychosomatic factor is most impressive.

At times he includes the opinion of medical experts in his interpretation of Biblical verses such as *Leviticus* 13:19, regarding skin ailments, and *Numbers* 13:18, regarding the effect of climate on population growth. He cites the importance of climate in other verses as well, for example regarding Jethro's reluctance to join Moses and Israel in their journey to the Promised Land, as well as in *Numbers* 10:30 where the spies speak of the climate of *Eretz Yisrael* in a disparaging manner. His knowledge of the natural sciences is apparent in his discussion regarding the rainbow (*Genesis* 9:13), as well as in his commentary on *Exodus* 35:20 regarding the spinning the goat's hair for use in the construction of the Sanctuary. His pharmaceutical skills are demonstrated in his commentary on *Exodus* 30:34.

4. *Aesthetics*

In a number of places, the *Sforno* points out the aesthetic dimension of Torah. A prime example is in *Genesis* 2:9 regarding the Tree of Knowledge, which the Torah describes as being "pleasant to look at." The *Sforno* comments that this would expand man's heart and sensitize his mind to receive the "intellectual flow" emanating from on High. Similarly, in the episode when Jacob enters the room of his blind father Isaac, wearing Esau's clothes, the Torah tells us that Isaac *smelled the aroma of his clothes, which was the aroma of the fields* (*Genesis* 27:27). The *Sforno* comments that this pleasant experience enhanced Isaac's spiritual capacity, and he quotes the statement of our Sages that man's soul gains pleasure and enjoyment from the sense of smell. Scripture's description of Isaac's enjoyment of the aroma is followed immediately by the words, *and he blessed him*, implying that Isaac was divinely inspired by this aesthetic experience. The *Sforno* adds that Isaac urges his son to consider carefully the ability of man to smell the aroma of a field, and thereby enjoy God's gifts of nature. The sense of smell provides an added dimension to the practical benefit derived by man from the produce of the field. The latter satisfies his material needs while the former nurtures his spirit of life and his soul (רוּחַ חִיּוּנִי וְנֶפֶשׁ).

It is important to remember that the *Sforno* lived at the time of the Renaissance, a period when people were exposed to great art, classical music and literature, all of which appeal to man's aesthetic sense. It is understandable therefore that in addressing his contemporaries he considered it important to demonstrate that the Torah was sensitive to man's emotions, sensitivities and feelings. The *Sforno* was writing for the readers of his time, just as *Rambam* in his *Guide For The Perplexed* spoke to his contemporaries in their language, attempting to resolve their problems and answer their questions in a manner to which they could relate, thereby more effectively conveying to them the truth of Torah. R' Samson Raphael Hirsch did the same in the nineteenth century in his *Horeb* and so the *Sforno* in the sixteenth century. All great commentators and teachers must gear their style and approach to the audience at hand, for they must be relevant and reasonable in order to appeal to the minds and hearts of their students. It is amazing that even though *Sforno* spoke to his contemporaries four centuries ago, his comments are as fresh, engaging and modern as if they had been written today.

We detect in the introduction to his commentary that there were many commentators who preceded him, who, in his opinion, did not address themselves to the needs of the time. He expresses this criticism in a frank and open fashion. "Their attempts were, at times, not sufficiently clear and at times insufficient to resolve doubts, thereby resulting in the embarrassment of these authors." He was determined to avoid these pitfalls and engage the minds and hearts of his readers, by using the tools of his time, while always remaining steadfast in his loyalty to Torah and reverence for the Almighty.

5. *Biblical Narratives*

Ramban explains that Biblical narratives serve a most important purpose. As he puts it, מַעֲשֵׂה אָבוֹת סִימָן לַבָּנִים, (*The events of our fathers are a portent and guide for their children*). The *Sforno* similarly stresses this idea in his *Kavanos HaTorah* and in the body of his Bible commentary. In *Kavanos HaTorah* he states,

> The purpose of the [narrative] section of the Torah, which relates various events and episodes is to instruct us in the ways of the righteous ones among the ancients — their tests, trials, and actions that found favor in God's eyes — so that we, in turn, shall strive to emulate them. The Torah also relates how tests were accepted and passed by individuals and by Israel as a people, thereby establishing their superiority even over the angels, as the angel himself admits to Abraham after the binding of Isaac (the *Akeidah*), and the exalted position of Israel attested to by God, when He stated that Israel was put to the test of wandering in the wilderness so that His angels might know that Israel is superior to them. (See *Deuteronomy* 13:4 and the *Sforno's* interpretation of the phrase *to know.*)
>
> We are also told the reverse: the evil deeds of wicked ones serve as a warning to us to avoid and reject such actions, which resulted in terrible and destructive consequences, such as the sin of Adam which brought the decree of death in its wake; the sins of the generation of the Flood which caused major disruptions in nature and decreased man's longevity; the sin of the generation of dispersion which resulted in the Babel of tongues and further shortened man's longevity; the sins of Sodom, which was the choicest of all areas at that time and became desolate and a wasteland; and the sin of the Golden Calf which thwarted the intent of God, Who, through the giving of Torah, meant to return us to the level of Adam before the sin.

This theme of *maaseh avos* (the events of our forefathers) and their symbolism for the future, repeats itself quite frequently in the *Sforno's* commentary on the Torah. For example, see *Genesis* 16:6, 21:12; 32:25, 32; 33:4, 41:14 and 46:5; and *Exodus* 12:42.

6. *Leadership and Authority*

As mentioned above, the *Sforno* moved in circles of leadership and power. He had frequent contact with royalty and Church personalities. This exposure no doubt impacted on his attitude toward authority and made him sensitive to the important role leadership plays in the security and stability of society. It is understandable that among Jews there was always a fear of general unrest and resultant anarchy in the host society, which would have a deleterious effect upon the Jewish community. The *Sforno*, therefore, emphasizes in his commentary the impact a leader has on his people (see *Genesis* 26:10); the influence of his behavior and conduct upon society (see *Genesis* 45:14 and 47:17); and above all, the great responsibility which the leader bears and cannot evade (see *Genesis* 21:26). In general, he emphasizes that just as God "establishes the earth with justice," so everyone who is in a position of authority and power must emulate the Almighty and strengthen the foundation of justice in his society.

Given this attitude, one can understand why the *Sforno* stresses the obligation of those who live under the authority of a leader to show him respect as indicated in his commentary on *Exodus* 22:27, where he states, "The evil which befalls the king will, in most cases, cause great evil and harm to the community as well." This echoes his comment in *Genesis* 26:10 regarding Abimelech, where he states, "When the leader of the generation is punished, great harm befalls those who find protection under his wings."

It is interesting to note that the *Sforno's* high regard for leadership qualities is also incorporated in his definition of what he calls the completeness and perfection of the truly wise man *(chacham hashalem)*. In *Genesis* 49:14, he speaks of Issachar as one who symbolizes the wise man embodying completeness and perfection in his intellectual and personal qualities. "Issachar shall carry the yoke of Torah, the yoke of earthly pursuits *(derech eretz)* and that of community leadership." This may well be his definition, informed by Torah teaching, of the ideal state of what his gentile contemporaries called Renaissance Man.

◌§ Fundamentals of Faith in The Sforno's Hashkafah

There are a number of fundamental principles of Judaism that are reflected in the *Sforno's* commentary on the Torah and that serve as an index to his basic *hashkafos*. Among them are:

1. *Freedom of Choice and Ability to Repent*

Belief in man's freedom of choice is inexorably linked to the concept of repentance in Judaism. In *Sefer Bamidbar* (the Book of Numbers) the Torah records various sins and transgressions committed by the people of Israel, which the *Sforno* uses as a springboard for his philosophy regarding sin and repentance. For example, in *Numbers* 11:23 he stresses that God will never deny man his freedom of choice, for if this were to happen, he would also automatically be denied the ability to repent. The *Sforno* also cites these episodes as revealing the frailty of man. In *Numbers* 5:28 he comments regarding the *sotah*, a wife who is suspected of being unfaithful, that God desires to clear her of such unfounded accusations, for "He knows man's evil inclinations and man's weakness."

Very often the *Sforno* quotes from the Prophet Ezekiel that God does not desire the death of the wicked, but rather that he turn away from evil and return to Him. Even regarding Israel's bondage and suffering in Egypt, he is careful to point out that the plagues visited upon the Egyptians were not meant as punishment for their cruel deeds, but as an inducement for them to repent. This, he submits, is the symbolism of the burning bush *(Exodus* 3:7) which is not consumed. According to his interpretation, the bush is meant to represent Egypt (not the Jews!) who will be subjected to the fire of divine punishment but will not be consumed thereby.

The theme of repentance is also found in his commentary regarding the episode of the Golden Calf *(Exodus* 32:15), where the *Sforno* explains the reason why Moses brought down the Tablets of Testimony, even though he had already been told by God that Israel had sinned. Moses, thought that if he returned to them, they would repent, and if not, he would shatter the tablets of stone in their presence so as to shock them into repenting.

2. *The Power of Prophecy*

Regarding the gift of prophecy that God has granted man, the *Sforno* stresses that the epitome of the prophetic spirit in man is found in Moses our Teacher. Although others were granted this power of prophecy, none attained the special level reached by Moses, who communicated with God 'face to face' and who was in a state of total awareness when the Almighty spoke to him. Other prophets received

God's message in a dream or in a trance but not while in command of their senses. Only one other person came close to Moses' powers of prophecy and that, strangely, was Balaam. However, there was a time in history when, according to the *Sforno*, an entire people reached the level of Moses in their ability to prophesy and receive the spirit of *Hashem*. That people was the people of Israel, and the time and place was when God descended on Mt. Sinai to give the Ten Commandments to Israel and, through them, to mankind at large.

The *Sforno* is of the opinion, as stated in *Exodus* 19:9, that the people of Israel were granted this unique gift of prophecy, if only for a brief period of time, so that their own experience would convince them that God spoke to Moses, not through a vision or a dream, but indeed "face to face." The sin of the Golden Calf, however, caused this power of Israel's prophecy to become dissipated, and from that moment forward only select individuals were granted this power of prophecy, and even then on a much lower level than the one which Israel experienced at Sinai.

3. *The Shechinah* (Divine Presence)

Just as God's communication with Israel was adversely affected when they sinned with the Golden Calf, the nature of His Presence (the *Shechinah*) in their midst was also altered. The *Sforno* submits that God's original intent was to dwell in our midst without the need for a Sanctuary, priestly services or sacrifices. This original intent was thwarted as a result of Israel's sin. According to the *Sforno*, the Sanctuary is not a sign of God's forgiveness for the sin of the Golden Calf, as explained by other commentators, but it is an imperfect substitute for what was originally meant to be a far greater gift — namely His Presence in Israel's midst without need for a special structure.

In *Kavanos HaTorah* he expresses this idea as follows:

> It is important to note that prior to the sin of the Golden Calf, it was unnecessary to have a Sanctuary, priestly services or sacrifices in order to merit *Hashem's* Presence in their midst. No intermediary was needed, nor any special structure, nor any mandatory offerings. When they would wish to bring a peace offering, it could be brought on an altar of earth and wherever God's Name would be mentioned, including houses of study, He would come. However, after the sin of the Golden Calf, although Moses intervented with his prayers and was successful to the extent that the Divine Presence did not depart from the camp of Israel, nonetheless it was now necessary to build a sanctuary and appoint priests to offer sacrifices, since Israel had descended from their exalted, unique status and God no longer was willing to have a direct relationship with them as had been His initial intent.

4. *The Centrality of Kedushah*

Although Israel had fallen from their "exalted, unique status," as the *Sforno* puts it, nonetheless the *Shechinah* still came to rest in their midst through the medium of the *Mishkan* (Sanctuary), for God still desired to keep Israel as His people and was willing to dwell with them even *in the midst of their uncleanliness (Leviticus* 16:16). This was, no doubt, due to the fact that they were still a holy people, as God had stated when He gave the Torah. The concept of *kedushah* (holiness) is a very important one. The Torah commands us to be holy for God is holy. This is indeed our primary mission and from it flow all of our other responsibilities toward mankind.

The *Sforno* adds a most interesting and unique dimension to the concept of *kedushah* as it applies to God and to Israel. The added dimension is that of eternity. In *Exodus* 15:11 he states, "The ultimate in holiness is everlasting and eternal," a concept which is taught to us by our Sages in *Sanhedrin* 92a, and which they base upon a verse in the Prophets (*Isaiah* 4:3). Since the Almighty states that the people of Israel shall be unto Him *a kingdom of priests and a holy people* (*Exodus* 19:6), the nation will never perish for it possesses the force of eternity, which is an integral aspect of *kedushah*. See the *Sforno's* commentary on *Exodus* 19:6, where he posits this idea and also his commentary on *Leviticus* 11:42 and *Deuteronomy* 26:19. By linking the eternity of Israel to its sanctity, the *Sforno* once again gave encouragement to his people at a time when they needed it desperately, thereby strengthening their faith in God and confidence in their future as a people.

☙ The Sforno as an Eclectic Exegete

As one studies the commentary of the *Sforno* on the Torah, one finds a treasure house of original and unusual interpretations of verses. It is worthwhile for the student to examine carefully a number of these commentaries which reflect his knowledge of the natural sciences, of the Kabbalah, and also his willingness to interpret verses and events in a most original and unique manner.

For example, his commentary regarding the rainbow in *Genesis* 9:13 is in keeping with the scientific teachings of the twentieth century as well as that of the sixteenth century. In *Exodus* 12:22, the *Sforno* explains the sprinkling of the blood of the *pesach* lamb on the lintel and doorpost in accordance with the teachings of the *Zohar*. In the following chapter (13:14-15), the *Sforno* offers a most unique explanation of the commandment of the Torah regarding the redemption of a firstborn donkey. Many find this *mitzvah* inexplicable since the ass is an unclean animal and, therefore, should not have the sanctity that would necessitate redemption. He explains this in a most original and brilliant allegorical manner.

Other examples of his originality of approach can be found in *Exodus* 32:29, regarding the call of Moses to the Levites to rally around him on behalf of God in the aftermath of the sin of the Golden Calf. There the *Sforno* explains the words *each one against his son and his brother* as referring to the willingness of the Levites to circumcise their children even while they were in the Wilderness! In *Exodus* 6:14-25, the *Sforno* explains that the development of the character of Moses and Aaron was due to a great extent to the longevity of their great-great grandfather, Levi. He thereby instructs us in the influence that older generations can wield on grandchildren and even great-grandchildren.

☙ Olam Haba and Eternal Reward

Toward the end of *Kavanos HaTorah*, the *Sforno* addresses himself to a definition of what our Sages mean when they speak in terms of "the life of the world to come" (*chaye olam haba*). He bases his explanation upon numerous statements of our Sages regarding *the world which is all Sabbath* (*Rosh Hashanah* 31a). It is a purely spiritual world, in which there is "neither food nor drink, but where the righteous sit with crowns on their heads and enjoy the radiance of the *Shechinah*" (*Berachos* 17a). The *Sforno* tells us that regarding *Olam Haba*, we really have no way to grasp or comprehend it, for no eye has seen it, not even that of a prophet, nor has anyone been granted the power to envision it. This, however, we do know, he continues: that all the promised rewards and punishments found in the Torah are not experienced in this life as a direct result of our actions, for indeed our Sages have taught us "today to perform them, but it is not today that you receive their reward" *(Avodah Zarah* 3a). Rather, the immediate result of our good deeds is that the condition and quality of our life is of such a nature that one is afforded the opportunity to live the good life of Torah without hindrance or obstacles, while the consequence of deviation is one's vulnerability to the nations and הֶסְתֵּר פָּנִים (the concealment of God's face). This concealment may well spur us to repent, which will ultimately redound to our own benefit. In respect of performance of *mitzvos* and study of Torah, the *Sforno* stresses that each of us acts on a different level, for each person is granted different powers of intellect and spirit, and each of us develops his potential differently, so that even among the righteous in the world to come, there are levels and gradations. As our Sages tell us in *Baba Basra* 75a: "The Holy One, blessed is He, will make for everyone a canopy corresponding to his rank (of honor and glory), and everyone one will be burnt by reason of the (superior) canopy of his friend." From this saying of our Sages, the *Sforno* proves that honor in the World to Come is contingent upon one's superior rank, which in turn depends upon what he has accomplished in this world — the only world where a man can prepare for the world to come, as our Sages say, "Happy is he who comes here with his Torah knowledge in his hands" *(Pesachim* 50a).

The *Sforno* also discusses, in addition to man's quest for ultimate honor, his desire to attain joy *(simchah).* As the *Sforno* sees it, *simchah* is realized when one attains that which he truly desires and wants, whereas *atzvus* (melancholy) results when his desires are frustrated. Hence, when mankind fulfills God's will, they bring joy to Him, as it were: *Let HASHEM rejoice in His works (Psalms* 104:31), because God wants man to serve Him. The opposite occurred when mankind rebelled against God causing Him to *grieve at His heart (Genesis* 6:6), for then God brought retribution upon mankind, which He did not desire to do, since He *does not desire the death of the wicked.*

Since, according to this definition, joy is the attainment of one's desire and is comparable to the attainment of superior rank, the ultimate honor in *Olam Haba,* it therefore follows that in *Olam Haba* where there is no eating or drinking, enjoyment will be derived from "the brightness of the Divine Presence"; and this represents man's ultimate joy in the world to come. The *Sforno* views *Olam Haba* as a world where man will enjoy the rewards of honor and joy to the degree that he has prepared himself for this eternal reward by his actions in this world.

He concludes by stating, "Lest we find ourselves cast into despair when we consider that even the righteous will be ashamed of one another in *Olam Haba* due to their deeds and shortcomings," nonetheless he urges us not to lose hope, but to consider that as long as we have done our best and striven to realize our potential, even though we may have fallen short, "HASHEM in His kindness will grant us favor and honor. As our Sages relate, when Rabbi Yochanan visited Rabbi Eleazar, who had fallen ill, Rabbi Yochanan noticed him weeping and said to him, 'Why do you weep? Is it because you did not study enough Torah? Surely we learn: the one who sacrifices much and the one who sacrifices little have the same merit provided that the heart is directed to heaven' *(Berachos* 5b)." On this note, the *Sforno* completes *Kavanos HaTorah.*

❦ ❦ ❦

The appeal of the *Sforno* has not diminished with the passage of time. Each generation has come to appreciate his unique contribution to Torah commentary. As mentioned above, his concise style, penetrating analysis of Torah phraseology, the major themes that he develops, and his original, unique interpretations have captured the imagination of Bible scholars, students, and learned laymen for the past four centuries. The excellence of his commentary motivated editors and publishers to include his commentary in most editions of *Mikraos Gedolos*, together with the classical commentaries of *Rashi*, *Ramban* and other early and later masters of Bible commentary.

In spite of this popularity and although the *Sforno* is basically an adherent of *p'shat*, nonetheless serious students have often found his commentary difficult to comprehend. As they read it, they sense that there are nuggets of wisdom buried in his words, but, confronted by the imponderable, they often skip his commentary, thereby depriving themselves of his great elucidation and clarification of Biblical verses. Also, with the passage of time, a new group of Bible students has appeared on the American scene whose proficiency in Hebrew is inadequate to grasp the meaning, and certainly the nuances and allusions of the *Sforno* in the original.

This present work attempts to overcome both of these obstacles. The English translation will, it is hoped, open the door to the masterful work of one of the great Bible exegetes of the Middle Ages, while the explanatory notes will prove to be of considerable assistance, even to those who are conversant with the original Hebrew text.

Many exegetes of the early sixteenth century do not appeal to the twentieth century reader and student. Not so the *Sforno*. His intellectual clarity, philosophical insights, and the religious fervor and profound faith that forms his commentary are as fresh, meaningful and stimulating today as they were 420 years ago, when his commentary was first published in Venice. His purpose in writing the commentary, as he explains in his introduction, is also relevant to our time. Considering that it was meant to demonstrate the truth of Torah and its timeless message for all ages, and to encourage Israel to adhere to its eternal teachings, it is of paramount importance to introduce this remarkable commentary to a wider audience, especially to those who have in recent years manifested a thirst for Torah knowledge.

The Five Books of Moses represent the foundation of our Torah. A classic commentary such as the *Sforno's* grants us profound understanding and brilliant insights, while affording us a valuable aid to our comprehension of *Chumash*. This work will hopefully provide many serious students of Bible with an opportunity to expand their knowledge and appreciation of the eternal wisdom and inspiring message of God's Torah.

Raphael Pelcovitz

סיון תשמ״ז
Sivan, 5747

באור על התורה לרבי עובדיה ספורנו

SFORNO

COMMENTARY ON THE TORAH

Sforno's Introduction

I Ovadiah, the young one,[1] may my Rock and Redeemer watch over me[2] son of my honored master and teacher Jacob Sforno, may his memory be unto the life of the World to Come[3] (hearkening) to the voice (and) words of my honored teacher, my brother Rav Chananel, may his Rock and Redeemer watch over him, who in his zeal to defend the Torah from insult (inflicted by) irresponsible heretics, 'children in whom there is no faithfulness'[4] who discredit and give blemished explanations to the reasoned words, stories and order of Torah, (which in reality is) a wholly precious treasure, straightforward to all who discern (and understand) and there are none to say, Restore![5] (did) awaken and convince me to find desirable words which would relate (Torah) in a straightforward manner, removing all obstacles so that its righteousness might shine forth brightly. Then I said, I will present a particle[6] of what I have attained toward that end. Behold, the little I will present may arouse many more honorable than I, to present pleasing words as 'a memorial in the book'[7] to enlarge Torah and ennoble it.

For indeed (as a result) of impatience of the spirit, bondage and the preoccupation of our people in a land which is not theirs, confronted by oppressors who pressure them daily to incapacitate and destroy them, they all as one have concentrated their attention, eyes and hearts to (amass) wealth, (which will) shelter and protect them from the daily alien stream which envelops them as bees, so that there is no proper place or time to consider the wonders of our Torah. Therefore they have become like 'dreamers' (deluded) in the midst of the nations, drawing nigh as disputors saying: "What profit and gain is there in the promise of our holy Torah, considering that it (deals) only with the material (i.e., this world) devoid of hope for eternal life? And to what avail its many stories, which at times are without chronological order?"

The 'myriad holy ones then came forth,'[8] a remnant of Torah scholars (to defend and explain the Torah). (However) at times the commentary of these early scholars is not sufficiently clear and at times (their) answers are inadequate to resolve the doubts, resulting in their humiliation.

1. The Hebrew term הַצָּעִיר, *the young one,* is used by many authors as an expression of 'diminishment,' which is another meaning of צָעִיר. It is meant to indicate one's sense of humility.

2. The abbreviation used is יצ״ו which represents יִשְׁמְרֵנִי צוּרִי וְגוֹאֲלִי, *may my Rock, etc.* The term 'Rock' as a name for God is based on *Deut.* 32:18.

3. The Hebrew expression זִכְרוֹנוֹ לְחַיֵּי הָעוֹלָם הַבָּא is written in its abbreviated form זלה״ה.

4. Based on *Deut.* 32:20.

5. An expression based on *Isaiah* 42:22.

6. Based on *Job* 4:12.

7. Based on *Exodus* 17:14.

8. Based on *Deut.* 33:2.

As for us, how shall we justify ourselves to God when He will hold us accountable for the honor of His name? (Only) by relating the wonders of His Torah, which illuminate the eyes of every intelligent (person) through its tales and order, its division of books and their conclusions, demonstrating the great righteousness and goodness of *Hashem*, the blessed One, through telling of His supreme kindness when He granted salvation after total despair. For indeed He commanded His covenant forever, to understand and teach through pure words which are established on a foundation (lit., 'sockets') of analysis and deed, as He, blessed is He, testified, saying "The Torah and the commandments which I have written to teach them" (*Exodus* 24:12). For through it He told us the purpose and intent of existence in general, and the choice of His people, and the time to give His Torah, (all of which are matters) over which many have marveled; 'they have seen and wondered.'

Now, being that the goal of contemplation is to understand and know the greatness of the Holy God, whereby His reverence will be experienced by all discerning people, and by knowing His ways of goodness and kindness, especially toward the human race, for which there is (the greatest) love — as it becomes clear that God, blessed is He, indeed attempts through the generations to elevate man and correct what he has distorted — every intelligent person will then love to make God's will his will[1] and with these two (attributes), reverence and love (of God) he will perfect the area of observance[2] intended (for him) by God.

Therefore, He the blessed One, undertook (consented) to explain through reasoned evidence, in His first book which is *Genesis*, (the story of Creation etc.).

1. *Aboth*, Chapter 2, Mishnah 4.

2. Love of God will bring man to perform the positive commandments. Reverence will insure the observance of the negative commandments.

ספר בראשית

Bereishis/Genesis

Sforno's Introduction

(This book relates) the story of Creation and the general and individual providence (of God). (It also relates) the existence of (angels) who are 'separated from matter' (i.e., totally spiritual) and among them are those who move the spheres; man's power of intellect; (and) that all emanates from Him with intent and will for a specific purpose.

(The Torah) then explains how precious is His loving-kindness toward the human race, for indeed He remedies their needs in each generation to the extent possible, but (man's sins) increased thereby bringing destruction upon himself.

(The Torah) first relates how the Blessed One created man in His image after His likeness,[1] that he might choose to imitate his Maker to the extent possible, for in this manner he will perfect himself, and his deeds will be more perfect and more honored than all other creatures, as is the intent of the Blessed One, that man be superior to all other (living) creatures. God in His mercy and compassion granted man his needs without any pain, placing him in the Garden of Eden, until "he perverted his ways and destroyed his livelihood,"[2] whereupon God, the Blessed One, drove him forth from there to work the earth and to occupy himself with many labors in order to earn bread for himself.[3]

The second story relates that in spite of all this, God did not choose to destroy him. The produce of the earth was beneficial and sufficient for his food needs to the extent that man lived close to a thousand years, until the wickedness of the generation increased and they were sentenced to be destroyed with the earth (6:13). (In turn) the nature of earth's elements was corrupted, its vegetation and that of all living creatures, resulting in an insufficiency of food to sustain man, as it did originally.[4]

The third story (tells us) that in spite of all the above He took pity on the remnant (of the human race) and permitted them to eat the flesh of all living creatures, save that of humans. He ordained that (control of) the earth be given to man, to the extent that the dread of man should be upon every beast of the earth.[5] In spite of all these radical changes, man's lifespan was four hundred years or more, until they gathered together to call upon the name of a certain strange god, chosen by them, and to place his image in a tower so that all the people would seek him out (for worship). This would have caused the Name of God, the Blessed One, to no longer be remembered among them.[6] Conse-

1. "In His image after His likeness" — 1:26. The image of God means the intelligence of man who can understand and discern, thereby meriting the designation of "His likeness," to be like God though not equal to Him.

2. This expression is based upon Tractate *Kiddushin* 82b.

3. See Tractate *Berachos* 58a.

4. The effect of the deluge upon the longevity of man was most radical. The reduction first was from one thousand to four hundred and then two hundred after which it diminished further with the passage of time.

5. *Genesis* 9:2,3.

6. *Genesis* 11:1-6.

quently, (God) dispersed them, and their lifespan was halved to about two hundred years — diminishing even further with the passing of time. The Torah then tells us that when it was apparent that there was no longer any hope that the human race as a whole would repent, having thwarted the divine plan on their behalf on two and three different occasions, God then chose a pious man from among the entire species (of man), Abraham[1] and his seed, to attain through them the goal intended by Him from the moment man had been placed on earth, as explained above.

Now this three-ply cord, Abraham, his son (Isaac) and grandson (Jacob) who filled the earth with God's glory, by proclaiming His Name, found favor in His eyes, (so that) He entered into a covenant with them to be a God to them and their descendants after them eternally, and to give a place[2] (i.e., *Eretz Yisrael*) to their seed, when they would become a people of sufficient size to warrant a state in which they would unite to serve Him with common accord.

Because of the perfection of these three (patriarchs), the episodes regarding them related in the Torah serve to instruct (later) generations through these principal happenings (for they are symbolic lessons) augmented by some other (events) such as the use of the rod[3] (of Moses and Aaron) with which the signs and wonders in Egypt were performed and the episode of (Elisha and Yoash): יְרֵה וַיּוֹר, *"Shoot!" And he shot* (II *Kings* 13:17).[4]

Thus, the history of Israel is (divided into three periods). (The first) from the time they left Egypt until the building of the First Temple, during which time four altars were constructed — namely, the Sanctuary in the Wilderness, Shiloh, Nov, and Givon, which mirror the events of Abraham from the time he left Ur Casdim to go to Canaan where he (also) built four altars.[5] (The second being) the events of the period of the First Temple which mirror the events of Isaac who built only one altar.[6] The events of the First Temple period, and the subsequent exile followed by the future redemption, during which time the Second Temple was built and the future (one) may it be built 'speedily in our days', are similar to the events of Jacob, our Father, who built two altars[7] and is the third period. After despair, he merited at the end to witness 'good' [8]. Thus, the first Book concludes.

1. *Genesis* 12.

2. *Genesis* 15:18.

3. *Exodus* 4:17.

4. The prophet Elisha tells Yoash, the king of Israel, to take a bow and arrow and shoot the arrow through the window. He tells him that this is the arrow of salvation, symbolizing victory over Aram. The *Sforno* uses this episode, in various sections of his commentary (*e.g. Genesis* 16:9, 32:25) to demonstrate that episodes and events of our ancestors are symbolic of future events. Indeed these symbolic acts often prepare the way for the future.

5. *Genesis* 12:7, 12:8, 13:18, 22:9.

6. *Genesis* 26:25.

7. *Genesis* 33:20, 35:7.

8. Jacob lived through many troubles and was confronted by a myriad of problems both external and internal. However after many years of pain, sorrow and frustrations, his life ends in honor and a sense of fulfillment. This also is symbolic of the history of the people of Israel.

פרשת בראשית
Parasháš Bereishis

א א בְּרֵאשִׁ֖ית בָּרָ֣א אֱלֹהִ֑ים אֵ֥ת הַשָּׁמַ֖יִם וְאֵ֥ת הָאָֽרֶץ׃ וְהָאָ֗רֶץ הָיְתָ֥ה תֹ֙הוּ֙ וָבֹ֔הוּ

I

1. בְּרֵאשִׁית — *In the beginning.* (This means) at the beginning of time, the very first moment which could not be a part of time, since time did not exist prior to it (i.e., that moment).

בָּרָא — *Of God's creating.* He made 'something' from 'nothing,' hence the concept of time cannot apply (to this) at all.

אֱלֹהִים — *Elohim.* The term אֱלוֹהַּ, *Eloha,* denotes the eternal and everlasting. That is why the שֵׁדִים *(demons)* who are mortal like human beings, as our Sages testify (*Chagigah* 16a), are called לַשֵּׁדִים לֹא אֱלוֹהַּ, *to demons, no-gods (Deut.* 32:17), whereas God, the Blessed One, is called אֱלוֹהַּ for He is surely (definitively) eternal as it says, וַיִּטֹּשׁ אֱלוֹהַּ עָשָׂהוּ, *and he forsook God Who made him* (ibid. verse 15). He is called אֱלֹהִים, *Elohim,* in the plural form to teach us that He is 'the form of all forms,' be they everlasting or otherwise, as it says, מְלֹא כָל הָאָרֶץ כְּבוֹדוֹ, *the whole earth is full of His glory (Isaiah* 6:3), for nothing can exist except that which is reserved from His existence; and there can be no being without His Being, as it says, וְאַתָּה מְחַיֶּה אֶת כֻּלָּם, *and You preserve them all (Nehemiah* 9:6). In a similar sense, all who are separated from matter (i.e., the angels) are called *Elohim.* Expert judges are also called *Elohim,* when they judge (guided by) the 'image of God.' To indicate God's superior Being as the Eternal, from Whom emanates the everlasting power of others who are separated from matter (i.e., the angels), we read in *Deuteronomy* 10:17, הוּא אֱלֹהֵי הָאֱלֹהִים, *He is the God of gods.*

NOTES

In the first chapter of the Torah, the *Sforno* reflects, to a great extent, the teachings of the *Rambam* (Maimonides) in his *Guide of the Perplexed* (מוֹרֵה נְבוּכִים). These notes will often refer to the *Guide* in explaining the commentary of the *Sforno.*

I

1. בְּרֵאשִׁית – *In the beginning.* The *Rambam (Guide* II:30) states that the world was not created in 'a temporal beginning' for 'time belongs to the created things.' There are, of course, many philosophers — Aristotle among them, and even some of our Sages *(Genesis Rabbah* III) — who believe that time existed before the creation of the world. This doctrine of the 'eternity of the world,' however, is vigorously rejected by the *Rambam.* Judaism asserts that just as the Almighty created the world *ex nihilo,* something out of nothingness, so must one accept that there was no concept of time until creation. As mentioned above, time itself was *created,* and did not exist before. It is to this that the *Sforno* alludes when he states that בְּרֵאשִׁית means *at the beginning of time,* the first instant, not a point in time separate from what previously existed. It is this idea which the *Sforno* is referring to in his interpretation of the phrase בָּרָא *(created),* where he uses the Hebrew phrase אֵינוֹ יֶשְׁנוֹ which is the equivalent of the more common term יֵשׁ מֵאַיִן, both meaning *something (that which is) from nothing.* By rejecting the doctrine of the existence of prior matter one also rejects the doctrine of the eternity of the world. This in turn compels us to accept the idea of time itself being one of the created things, as has already been explained (see the *Guide* II:13).

אֱלֹהִים – *Elohim.* The phrase צוּרַת כֹּל הַצּוּרוֹת, *the form of all forms,* is used by the *Rambam (Guide* I:69) and the concept presented here by the *Sforno* in explaining the plural form אֱלֹהִים, *Elohim,* is developed by the *Rambam* there. '(God) is that One upon Whom the existence and stability of every form in the world ultimately reposes and by which they are constituted.' What the *Sforno* calls הַנֶּאֱצָל, *that which is separated and shared by God,* the *Rambam* calls שֶׁפַע, *the overflowing.* The existence of all things, both the everlasting and the perishable (mortal), flows from God and is dependent upon Him not only as the 'Maker' but as the 'Cause,' in an ongoing

אֵת הַשָּׁמַיִם — *The heavens.* The word שָׁם, *there,* denotes a far, distant place. Whenever a word is changed from the singular to the plural (i.e., by adding the letters י and ם) preceded by a *pasach,* it indicates two that are equal. Therefore, the word שָׁמַיִם indicates an object far removed from our point of perspective, on two sides, both equidistant from all sides. This can only be true of a sphere which revolves in a perfect circle. Therefore, (the Torah states) that (God) created this object which is now equidistant (to our naked eye) from all sides. This is the גַּלְגַּל, *the celestial sphere* (the sphere of the Zodiac) and that is why it does not say בָּרָא שָׁמַיִם, *He created heaven* (rather אֵת הַשָּׁמַיִם) for (the term שָׁמַיִם) is not one that can be expressed independently by itself but only in relationship to our place (i.e., the earth). The Torah then says וְאֵת הָאָרֶץ, *and the earth,* i.e., the central point which is fitting for the celestial sphere.

2. וְהָאָרֶץ הָיְתָה תֹהוּ וָבֹהוּ — *And the earth was desolate and void.* That earth, which was created, was an amalgam of primeval matter called תֹהוּ and primeval form called בֹּהוּ, for it would not be suitable (possible) for primeval matter to exist without being clothed in some form. This then, was the first amalgam perforce, of matter and substance (form). The Torah is explaining that primeval matter was a totally new creation (there being no 'matter' preceding the world's creation). The matter in this initial amalgam is called תֹהוּ for it only possesses potential but no actuality, as it says כִּי תֹהוּ הֵמָּה, *for they are vain (I Samuel* 12:21), that is, something not existing in reality, only in the imagination. The form of that initial amalgam is called בֹּהוּ for *in it* the תֹהוּ is found, in actuality. The prophet calls אַבְנֵי בֹהוּ, *stones sunken in the primeval mire (Isaiah* 34:11), any object which does not remain in a given form for an appreciable period of time, just as we call the initial form בֹּהוּ which immediately clothed itself in a variety of forms (namely the four elements).

NOTES

sense. Without His continuous will they would cease, unlike the carpenter and his handiwork, which exists even after he departs. This is what the *Sforno* is referring to when he quotes the verses from *Isaiah* and *Nehemiah.* The former verse establishes the idea that (as the *Rambam* puts it in the *Guide* I:19): 'The whole earth bears witness to His perfection' for without Him the earth, and all which is in it, could not exist. The latter verse supports this thesis by emphasizing that God is the חַי עוֹלָמִים, *Living of the World,* meaning that He is the life of the world, for all life and existence emanates from Him, not only as the original cause but as the ongoing one.

The *Sforno,* however, also adds an important explanation of the term *Elohim.* As he explains, the source of this word is אֱלוֹהַּ, *Eloha,* signifying the eternal and everlasting, as well as that which is separated from matter, and is perfect (see the *Sforno* on verse 27). This term can then be applied to the angels and even judges when they reflect Divine intelligence. In this manner the *Sforno* explains the difficult term אֱלֹהֵי הָאֱלֹהִים, *God of gods,* for it is not praiseworthy or proper to speak of Hashem in relationship to other gods! Rather it is to be understood as God being the source of the eternal and everlasting, as well as of Divine intelligence, from which emanate similar qualities to others (compare this to the *Rambam's Guide* II:6).

אֵת הַשָּׁמַיִם — *The heavens.* The *Sforno* derives the word שָׁמַיִם from שָׁם, *there.* The heaven above, from our perspective on earth, is *there.* To us everything in heaven *appears* to be the same distance away, even though in reality it is not so. Now since this thing called שָׁמַיִם, *heaven,* is so named, only in relationship to man on earth, the Torah cannot state *He created heaven,* but must precede it with the indefinite article אֵת, thereby indicating that it is so called relative to our perception. In keeping with this interpretation the *Sforno* explains הָאָרֶץ, written with the definite article ה as indicating that *this* earth is to be considered as the center of the sphere of the Zodiac, so destined to be, by God's will. The *Sforno* is proposing the theory that the world is geocentric.

2. וְהָאָרֶץ הָיְתָה תֹהוּ וָבֹהוּ — *And the earth was*

ג וְחֹשֶׁךְ עַל־פְּנֵי תְהוֹם וְרוּחַ אֱלֹהִים מְרַחֶפֶת עַל־פְּנֵי הַמָּיִם׃ וַיֹּאמֶר אֱלֹהִים
ד יְהִי אוֹר וַיְהִי־אוֹר׃ וַיַּרְא אֱלֹהִים אֶת־הָאוֹר כִּי־טוֹב וַיַּבְדֵּל אֱלֹהִים בֵּין

וְחֹשֶׁךְ עַל פְּנֵי תְהוֹם — *With darkness upon the surface of the deep.* The dark air which emanated from the first amalgam was on the surface of the two lower elements (water and earth) which also emanated from the first amalgam; these encircled one another.

וְרוּחַ אֱלֹהִים מְרַחֶפֶת עַל פְּנֵי הַמָּיִם — *And the Divine Presence hovered upon the surface of the waters.* The (angels) that moved the spheres who are called רוּחַ, *wind,* as it says, עֹשֶׂה מַלְאָכָיו רוּחוֹת, *Who makes wind His angels (messengers) (Psalms* 104:4) moved the dark air over the surface of the water, which then encompassed the foundation of the earth. As a result, the inner part (of the dark air) close to the orb overheated through the friction of its movement and that became the element of fire, while that part (of the dark air) close to the water was cooled by the water, except for a small portion thereof which became heated, thereby forming sparks which gave forth light.

3. יְהִי אוֹר — *Let there be light.* This is the light of the seven days (of Creation) for the purpose of generating growth without the benefit of seed. This (phenomenon) will also come to pass at the end of days (lit., 'the future') for our Sages tell us that this hidden light will be used for the purpose of bringing forth cakes and woolen robes without the medium of planted seed (*Shabbos* 30b).

4. וַיַּרְא אֱלֹהִים אֶת הָאוֹר כִּי טוֹב — *God saw that the light was good.* And so it was, for God *saw* (comprehended) (that light was good) and He chose its existence toward the end of the achievement of *good,* and He brought it (light) into being through His knowledge which is the 'efficient cause' (that alone brought it into actuality).

NOTES

desolate and void. The *Sforno* explains the two words תֹהוּ *(tohu)* and בֹהוּ *(bohu)* in the following manner. All matter had to be created by God since we reject the theory of the eternity of matter. Matter, as such, only had potential (כֹּחַ) and was not actual. This is called תֹהוּ in the Hebrew language. An idol is called תֹהוּ because it has no substance. The phrase בֹהוּ is a combination of two words, בוֹ and הוּא, *it is in it.* Hence the word בֹהוּ means the form which contains within it בֹהוּ, *primeval matter.* This in turn is comprised of the four primeval elements of fire, air, water, and dust. The potential of תֹהוּ became actual through the בֹהוּ — the initial form. Said form did not remain inflexible but kept changing until it eventually reached its final state, on the subsequent days of creation. At the beginning of creation, heaven, earth and all which is in them, was created at one time, בְּכֹחַ, *in potentia*; afterward, this potential was formed into the substantive, each on its day, as chosen by God.

וְחֹשֶׁךְ עַל פְּנֵי תְהוֹם – *With darkness upon the surface of the deep.* The sequence of events recorded in this verse, as interpreted by the *Sforno,* is to be understood as follows: *Darkness* is not to be understood as the absence of light but as a specific object of God's creation. It was composed of fire and air, two of the fundamental elements. The תְּהוֹם, *the deep,* contained the other two elements, water and dust. These four elements emanated from the first amalgam. Now there were two intersecting circles, the outer being fire and the inner air, which hovered over the surface of the deep, which was composed of water and dust. The light mentioned in the next verse resulted from the sparks created by the movement of the sphere, said movement being caused by the angels, i.e., the wind sent by God. As the *Rambam* says (*Guide* II:6), 'All forces (of God) are (called) angels.'

3. יְהִי אוֹר – *Let there be light.* The statement of our Sages in Tractate *Shabbos* that *Eretz Yisrael,* the Land of Israel, in future time will bring forth 'cakes and woolen robes,' is explained by the *Sforno* as resulting from the unique powerful light of the seven days of Creation, which was capable of generating

ה הָאוֹר וּבֵין הַחֹשֶׁךְ: וַיִּקְרָא אֱלֹהִים ׀ לָאוֹר יוֹם וְלַחֹשֶׁךְ קָרָא לָיְלָה וַיְהִי־עֶרֶב
וַיְהִי־בֹקֶר יוֹם אֶחָד:
ו־ז וַיֹּאמֶר אֱלֹהִים יְהִי רָקִיעַ בְּתוֹךְ הַמָּיִם וִיהִי מַבְדִּיל בֵּין מַיִם לָמָיִם: וַיַּעַשׂ
אֱלֹהִים אֶת־הָרָקִיעַ וַיַּבְדֵּל בֵּין הַמַּיִם אֲשֶׁר מִתַּחַת לָרָקִיעַ וּבֵין הַמַּיִם

וַיַּבְדֵּל אֱלֹהִים בֵּין הָאוֹר וּבֵין הַחֹשֶׁךְ — *And God separated between the light and the darkness.* During those days that the primeval light served the world, there were periods of light and periods of darkness without the revolution of the spheres. It was so only through Divine Will which separated between the 'time' of light and the 'time' of darkness.

5. וַיִּקְרָא אֱלֹהִים לָאוֹר יוֹם — *God called to the light, 'Day.'* Although the periods of light and darkness did not function at that time in the same manner as they do today, when we call (these periods) by their names of day and night, nonetheless . . .

וַיְהִי עֶרֶב וַיְהִי בֹקֶר — *And there was evening and there was morning.* Although God separated light and darkness so that they might serve at different times, without benefit of the revolution of the spheres, nonetheless He separated (these periods of light and darkness) in a gradual manner so that there was a time called 'evening' as night arrived and a time called 'morning' as day came.

6. יְהִי רָקִיעַ בְּתוֹךְ הַמָּיִם — *Let there be a firmament in the midst of the waters.* Let the nature of the elemental waters become as though the form of a wheel is girdling it, separating one part from the other, in such a manner that a portion of the upper waters adjacent to the air mass change once again to the nature of vapor. In this manner, they will be elevated to a (higher) area of the elemental air. This air will now perforce somehow be made into a place for that portion (of water) which changed to vapor. It will expand considerably into a larger area than it was originally (and become the firmament).

7. וַיַּעַשׂ אֱלֹהִים אֶת הָרָקִיעַ — *So God made the firmament.* Now, since the rest of the foundation waters which remained below those waters that vaporized, gathered

NOTES

growth without the benefit of seed, and which will shine again in future time. According to tradition, this special light was deemed fit only for the righteous and was therefore 'stored' away by God, to be used at the end of days. It is this unique generative light that our Sages refer to in the above-cited passage of the Talmud.

4. וַיַּרְא אֱלֹהִים אֶת הָאוֹר כִּי טוֹב — *God saw that the light was good.* One cannot say of God, as one would say of a human being, that after an object is formed or a certain matter fashioned, it is examined and found to be good. Hence the expression וַיַּרְא אֱלֹהִים, *and God saw,* does not mean He saw His handiwork, i.e., light, and found it to His liking, for it was good. Rather וַיַּרְא means: because God knew that light was good for the world and its inhabitants, therefore He created it. As the *Rambam* says (*Guide* II:30), 'The meaning of the words "that it was good," is that the thing in question is externally visible and of manifest utility for the existence and permanence of that which exists.' The expression יְדִיעָתוֹ הַפּוֹעֶלֶת, *His knowledge which is the efficient cause,* means that God does not have to order something to happen through a command, but as soon as He 'knows,' in the sense of the 'potential,' it becomes 'actual.'

5. וַיִּקְרָא אֱלֹהִים לָאוֹר יוֹם — *God called to the light, 'Day.'* Although the periods of light and darkness functioned arbitrarily, by the will of God, and were separated by His decree — not as a result of the revolution of the spheres — nonetheless the changeover from light to darkness and darkness to light did not occur abruptly but happened gradually, as it does now; evening leading into darkness and dawn into the light of day. This, also, was due to the kindness of Hashem for the benefit of the

ח אֲשֶׁר מֵעַל לָרָקִיעַ וַיְהִי־כֵן: וַיִּקְרָא אֱלֹהִים לָרָקִיעַ שָׁמָיִם וַיְהִי־עֶרֶב
וַיְהִי־בֹקֶר יוֹם שֵׁנִי:
ט וַיֹּאמֶר אֱלֹהִים יִקָּווּ הַמַּיִם מִתַּחַת הַשָּׁמַיִם אֶל־מָקוֹם אֶחָד וְתֵרָאֶה הַיַּבָּשָׁה

---

together, as it says, יִקָּווּ הַמַּיִם מִתַּחַת הַשָּׁמַיִם, *let the waters beneath the heaven be gathered*, it should follow that the upper waters which became vapor would have filled the vacuum left by the departure of the waters. However, He made the רָקִיעַ which separated (the higher and lower waters), in such a manner that it (the רָקִיעַ) was given the power of restraint, preventing the vapor portion — that is, the water which was above the firmament — from descending; in a manner that the (newly) fashioned atmosphere did fill the void while the vapor remained in its initial position. Now, when the moist vaporized water becomes dense, it brings forth rain, snow and hail as it becomes laden heavily (with water) and descends (to the earth), as it says, לְקוֹל תִּתּוֹ הֲמוֹן מַיִם בַּשָּׁמַיִם, *At the sound of His giving a multitude of waters in the heavens (Jeremiah* 10:13). What is meant by the term הַשָּׁמַיִם *(the heavens)* is the firmament which holds back the vapor portion, as it says, *And God called the firmament heaven* (verse 8). And when the smoke-laden mist comes there, it results in thunder and lightning as it says, וַיַּעֲלֶה נְשִׂאִים מִקְצֵה הָאָרֶץ בְּרָקִים לַמָּטָר עָשָׂה, *He causes the clouds to ascend from the ends of the earth, He makes lightning for the rain (Jeremiah* 10:13). Since the elemental waters, which are denser, are above the light air, this condition is contrary to nature, indicating that it is an act performed by God's Will, directed without a doubt toward a (good) purpose and end, as it says, וּמַעֲשֵׂה יָדָיו מַגִּיד הָרָקִיעַ, *the firmament shows His handiwork (Psalms* 19:2).

וַיְהִי כֵן — *And it was so.* It remained so contrary to its (own) nature.

8. וַיִּקְרָא אֱלֹהִים לָרָקִיעַ שָׁמָיִם — *God called to the firmament, 'Heaven' . . .* because the heavenly functionings reach the earth through the medium (of the רָקִיעַ), as it says: *And God set them in the firmament of the heaven to give light upon the earth, to dominate by day and by night, and to separate, etc.* (verses 17, 18).

9. יִקָּווּ הַמַּיִם אֶל מָקוֹם אֶחָד — *Let the waters be gathered into one area.* This drying (process) by which the exposed (dry) land occurred, was not due to the effect of the constellations (מַעַרְכוֹת הַשָּׁמַיִם), as many may think, rather (God) commanded that (the waters) be gathered in order that they not transgress (their bounds). Therefore, though they are higher than the earth they do not descend upon it, as our senses testify, as it says, גְּבוּל שַׂמְתָּ בַּל יַעֲבֹרוּן בַּל יְשׁוּבוּן לְכַסּוֹת הָאָרֶץ, *You set a bound which they do not pass over, that they may not return to cover the earth (Psalms* 104:9).

NOTES

world — even before there was man or living creatures.

7. וַיַּעַשׂ אֱלֹהִים אֶת הָרָקִיעַ – *So God made the firmament.* Since the lower waters gathered into one area leaving a vacuum, by right the upper waters should have come down to fill that void. The firmament, however, held them back, and instead, the air, replaced by the upper waters which had become vapor, came down and filled the void with atmosphere. The vapor is heavier than air, still it remains above (restrained by the firmament) except when it rains or snows. This is one of the great wonders of the Creator, done for the benefit of the world and its inhabitants.

8. וַיִּקְרָא אֱלֹהִים לָרָקִיעַ שָׁמָיִם – *God called to the firmament, 'Heaven.'* The *Sforno* is explaining why the רָקִיעַ, *firmament*, is called שָׁמַיִם, *heaven.* Since the light of the luminaries, which are *heavenly* bodies, reach the earth *through* the firmament, it is called שָׁמַיִם, *heaven.*

9. יִקָּווּ הַמַּיִם . . . – *Let the waters be gathered.* The ocean waters do not go beyond the boundary of sand on the shore. God estab-

י וַיְהִי־כֵן׃ וַיִּקְרָא אֱלֹהִים ׀ לַיַּבָּשָׁה אֶרֶץ וּלְמִקְוֵה הַמַּיִם קָרָא יַמִּים וַיַּרְא
יא אֱלֹהִים כִּי־טוֹב׃ וַיֹּאמֶר אֱלֹהִים תַּדְשֵׁא הָאָרֶץ דֶּשֶׁא עֵשֶׂב מַזְרִיעַ זֶרַע עֵץ
יב פְּרִי עֹשֶׂה פְּרִי לְמִינוֹ אֲשֶׁר זַרְעוֹ־בוֹ עַל־הָאָרֶץ וַיְהִי־כֵן׃ וַתּוֹצֵא הָאָרֶץ
דֶּשֶׁא עֵשֶׂב מַזְרִיעַ זֶרַע לְמִינֵהוּ וְעֵץ עֹשֶׂה־פְּרִי אֲשֶׁר זַרְעוֹ־בוֹ לְמִינֵהוּ וַיַּרְא
יג אֱלֹהִים כִּי־טוֹב׃ וַיְהִי־עֶרֶב וַיְהִי־בֹקֶר יוֹם שְׁלִישִׁי׃
יד וַיֹּאמֶר אֱלֹהִים יְהִי מְאֹרֹת בִּרְקִיעַ הַשָּׁמַיִם לְהַבְדִּיל בֵּין הַיּוֹם וּבֵין הַלָּיְלָה
טו וְהָיוּ לְאֹתֹת וּלְמוֹעֲדִים וּלְיָמִים וְשָׁנִים׃ וְהָיוּ לִמְאוֹרֹת בִּרְקִיעַ הַשָּׁמַיִם
טז לְהָאִיר עַל־הָאָרֶץ וַיְהִי־כֵן׃ וַיַּעַשׂ אֱלֹהִים אֶת־שְׁנֵי הַמְּאֹרֹת הַגְּדֹלִים

---

10. וַיִּקְרָא אֱלֹהִים לַיַּבָּשָׁה אֶרֶץ — *God called to the dry land, 'Earth'.* He called that specific area (i.e., dry land) by its (original) general name (i.e., אֶרֶץ, *earth),* since that area was the principal intended part of the entire earth, as it states: לָשֶׁבֶת יְצָרָהּ, *He formed it to be inhabited (Isaiah* 45:18).

וַיַּרְא אֱלֹהִים כִּי טוֹב — *And God saw that it was good.* He so wanted it, toward the intended end (which was) *good.*

11. דֶּשֶׁא — *Vegetation.* This refers to a variety of herbage fit for animals, as it says: כִּי דָשְׁאוּ נְאוֹת מִדְבָּר, *For the pastures of the wilderness spring forth abundant growth (Joel* 2:22).

עֵשֶׂב מַזְרִיעַ זֶרַע — *Herbage yielding seed.* For man to eat.

עֵץ פְּרִי עֹשֶׂה פְּרִי לְמִינוֹ — *Fruit trees yielding fruit after its kind.* A hybrid of two kinds will not reproduce.

וַיְהִי כֵן — *And it was so.* So it was established (and remained) that it not (be able) to accept less (than its inherent nature) or more (of a different species) so that if perchance there be a hybrid from two kinds, it will not reproduce.

14. יְהִי מְאֹרֹת בִּרְקִיעַ הַשָּׁמַיִם — *Let there be luminaries in the firmament of the heaven.* Let there be the spark of light from the luminaries in that firmament created on the second day, and let it increase and refract so as to work upon the lower (terrestrial) land, as related in this chapter. We see through our (own) senses that there is an increase of light when it passes through clear (pure) water.

15. לְהָאִיר עַל הָאָרֶץ — *To shine upon the earth.* That blended (filtered) light shall shine (upon the earth in a manner) suitable for its inhabitants.

NOTES

lished this border to protect the integrity of the dry land.

10. וַיִּקְרָא אֱלֹהִים לַיַּבָּשָׁה אֶרֶץ – *God called to the dry land, 'Earth'.* The name אֶרֶץ was already given to the earth, in the first verse of this chapter. This verse, which states that *dry land* was called אֶרֶץ, *earth,* signifies that although earth is a general term incorporating the totality of the planet Earth, it is the dry land which represents the primary purpose for which the earth was created, as we see from the verse of *Isaiah* quoted by the *Sforno.*

וַיַּרְא אֱלֹהִים כִּי טוֹב – *And God saw that it was good.* As explained in verse 4, the word וַיַּרְא, *He saw,* does not mean He saw *after* the creation of dry land but signifies the *reason* for God's decision to gather the waters and expose dry land, namely, to realize His original intent of bringing 'good' to the world and its inhabitants.

14-15. יְהִי מְאֹרֹת בִּרְקִיעַ הַשָּׁמַיִם ... לְהָאִיר עַל הָאָרֶץ – *Let there be luminaries in the firmament ... to shine upon the earth.* The source of the light emanating from the luminaries is in the higher heavens. However, it comes to earth through the firmament, thereby radiating and refracting and increas-

אֶת־הַמָּאוֹר הַגָּדֹל לְמֶמְשֶׁלֶת הַיּוֹם וְאֶת־הַמָּאוֹר הַקָּטֹן לְמֶמְשֶׁלֶת הַלַּיְלָה
יז וְאֵת הַכּוֹכָבִים: וַיִּתֵּן אֹתָם אֱלֹהִים בִּרְקִיעַ הַשָּׁמָיִם לְהָאִיר עַל־הָאָרֶץ:
יח וְלִמְשֹׁל בַּיּוֹם וּבַלַּיְלָה וּלְהַבְדִּיל בֵּין הָאוֹר וּבֵין הַחֹשֶׁךְ וַיַּרְא אֱלֹהִים
יט כִּי־טוֹב: וַיְהִי־עֶרֶב וַיְהִי־בֹקֶר יוֹם רְבִיעִי:
כ וַיֹּאמֶר אֱלֹהִים יִשְׁרְצוּ הַמַּיִם שֶׁרֶץ נֶפֶשׁ חַיָּה וְעוֹף יְעוֹפֵף עַל־הָאָרֶץ עַל־פְּנֵי

וַיְהִי כֵן — *And it was so.* That blend (of light filtered through the firmament), which came about perforce by God's command, was established and remained (for all time).

16-18. וַיַּעַשׂ . . . וַיִּתֵּן . . . לְהָאִיר . . . וְלִמְשֹׁל . . . וּלְהַבְדִּיל . . . כִּי טוֹב — *And He made . . . And He set . . . to give light . . . to dominate . . . and to separate . . . that it was good.* Regarding the luminaries and other stars (the phrase used) is וַיַּעַשׂ, *And He made,* for they were already (created) as part of the spheres, or of the heavens, the creation of which the Torah already related (in verse 1), therefore the verb *create* is not used, but *make.*

Now, the reason why they were made (different than the other spheres and orbs) in round forms and as shining ones, is because, כִּי טוֹב, *that it was good,* i.e., God's intent was for the good (of mankind) which was the proper ultimate purpose of His act.

וְלִמְשֹׁל בַּיּוֹם וּבַלַּיְלָה — *To rule by day and by night.* (They rule by) generating existences (creatures) in the (terrestrial) lower world. This (light) was necessary to function with the primeval light to bring living creatures into being, for they are more important (and complex) than the plant (world).

וּלְהַבְדִּיל בֵּין הָאוֹר וּבֵין הַחֹשֶׁךְ — *And to separate between the light and between the darkness.* (This means) to separate, in the lower (terrestrial) world, through its rising and setting, between the period of light which was called day and the period of darkness which was called night, as it says above *to separate between the day and the night* (verse 14).

20. יְעוֹפֵף עַל הָאָרֶץ עַל פְּנֵי רְקִיעַ הַשָּׁמָיִם — *(And fowl) that fly about over the earth across the expanse of the heavens.* (They) cleanse the air (atmosphere) of the earth, on behalf of its inhabitants, of extraneous moisture coming from the firmament, which was created on the second day, through the medium of the sparks which worked upon it.

NOTES

ing its efficacy. That is why both terms are used — רָקִיעַ and שָׁמַיִם.

16-18. This commentary of the *Sforno* does not appear in the *Mikraos Gedolos* edition, but does appear in the *Mosad Harav Kook* edition which is based on a number of different manuscripts.

20. יְעוֹפֵף עַל הָאָרֶץ עַל פְּנֵי רְקִיעַ הַשָּׁמָיִם — *(And fowl) that fly about over the earth across the expanse of the heavens.* The *Sforno* is of the opinion that there was a residue of mist and vapor generated by the heat working on the moisture of the firmament. The birds' wings act as fans circulating these vapors and clear the air for the benefit of mankind.

21-22. וַיִּבְרָא אֱלֹהִים אֶת הַתַּנִּינִם — *And God created the great sea-giants.* The phrase וַיִּבְרָא, *He created,* is used here for the first time since the first day. It denotes that a new כֹּחַ, *potential force,* had to be introduced into the waters to produce such huge sea-creatures. A special blessing was also necessary, so as to realize the end purpose for which they were created.

כא רְקִיעַ הַשָּׁמָיִם: וַיִּבְרָא אֱלֹהִים אֶת־הַתַּנִּינִם הַגְּדֹלִים וְאֵת כָּל־נֶפֶשׁ הַחַיָּה ׀
הָרֹמֶשֶׂת אֲשֶׁר שָׁרְצוּ הַמַּיִם לְמִינֵהֶם וְאֵת כָּל־עוֹף כָּנָף לְמִינֵהוּ וַיַּרְא
כב אֱלֹהִים כִּי־טוֹב: וַיְבָרֶךְ אֹתָם אֱלֹהִים לֵאמֹר פְּרוּ וּרְבוּ וּמִלְאוּ אֶת־הַמַּיִם
כג בַּיַּמִּים וְהָעוֹף יִרֶב בָּאָרֶץ: וַיְהִי־עֶרֶב וַיְהִי־בֹקֶר יוֹם חֲמִישִׁי:
כד וַיֹּאמֶר אֱלֹהִים תּוֹצֵא הָאָרֶץ נֶפֶשׁ חַיָּה לְמִינָהּ בְּהֵמָה וָרֶמֶשׂ וְחַיְתוֹ־אֶרֶץ
כה לְמִינָהּ וַיְהִי־כֵן: וַיַּעַשׂ אֱלֹהִים אֶת־חַיַּת הָאָרֶץ לְמִינָהּ וְאֶת־הַבְּהֵמָה לְמִינָהּ
כו וְאֵת כָּל־רֶמֶשׂ הָאֲדָמָה לְמִינֵהוּ וַיַּרְא אֱלֹהִים כִּי־טוֹב: וַיֹּאמֶר אֱלֹהִים נַעֲשֶׂה

---

21. וַיִּבְרָא אֱלֹהִים אֶת הַתַּנִּינִם — *And God created the great sea-giants.* The generative potential which was present in the water (as endowed by God), was not sufficient (in power) to bring forth the first sea-giants without seed, until (God) created at that time sufficient potential (power) to do so.

22. וַיְבָרֶךְ אֹתָם אֱלֹהִים — *God blessed them.* Their end purpose would not be realized unless they were numerous.

24. תּוֹצֵא הָאָרֶץ נֶפֶשׁ חַיָּה — *Let the earth bring forth living creatures.* A living soul in addition to the (living) plants which grow.

וַיְהִי כֵן — *And it was so.* Nothing was added or diminished; and if a new hybrid be crossbred from two species it will not be capable of reproducing.

25. וַיַּעַשׂ אֱלֹהִים אֶת חַיַּת הָאָרֶץ לְמִינָהּ — *God made the beast of the earth after its own kind.* He endowed each species with whatever senses and faculties were required by that species.

26. וַיֹּאמֶר אֱלֹהִים נַעֲשֶׂה — *And God said, 'Let us make (man).'* He then endowed His פַּמַלְיָא, *His heavenly host,* with the power to impart the (heavenly) image to the subject which was prepared for it (i.e., man).

NOTES

24. תּוֹצֵא הָאָרֶץ נֶפֶשׁ חַיָּה —*Let the earth bring forth living creatures.* Beyond the דּוֹמֵם, *inanimate, mineral,* and the צוֹמֵחַ, *growing plants,* are חַי, *living,* i.e., creatures which possess the spark of life, free, living, breathing beings. This characteristic, which makes them superior to the two lower categories, is called נֶפֶשׁ, a *soul,* by the Torah. It is to this that the *Sforno* alludes when he states, 'a living soul in addition to the (living) plants which grow.'

וַיְהִי כֵן — *And it was so.* The expression וַיְהִי כֵן, *and it was so,* is used here and above in verse 11, as it is used in verses 7, 9, 15 and 30; however, the *Sforno* apparently feels the need to comment only here and in verse 11, where the Torah speaks of *according to its kind.* It is his opinion that כֵן implies something that is immutably set, firmly established in the nature of the plant and animal kingdoms, regarding their reproductive capacity. What is common to both is the exactness and absolute preciseness of each species and kind created by the Almighty — neither too little or too much. Hence, if an attempt is made to graft or crossbreed, though a hybrid may result, it will not be able to reproduce!

26. וַיֹּאמֶר אֱלֹהִים נַעֲשֶׂה — *And God said, 'Let us make (man).'* The phrase נַעֲשֶׂה, *let us make,* is in the plural, which obviously presents a great difficulty, considering the 'oneness' and 'unity' of the Almighty. Rashi's explanation, based upon the interpretation of our Sages, is well known, namely, to teach us a great lesson in humility, that a superior consult with his inferiors. The *Sforno,* however, follows the interpretation of the *Rambam* in his *Guide* (II:6) based on the Talmud (*Sanhedrin* 38b) which states that 'The Holy One, Blessed is He, does nothing without consulting the "famalya" *(host* or *families)* above.' This does not mean that God consults or asks the opinion of His 'Heavenly household.' The meaning is rather that God acts and

אָדָם בְּצַלְמֵנוּ כִּדְמוּתֵנוּ וְיִרְדּוּ בִדְגַת הַיָּם וּבְעוֹף הַשָּׁמַיִם וּבַבְּהֵמָה
כז וּבְכָל־הָאָרֶץ וּבְכָל־הָרֶמֶשׂ הָרֹמֵשׂ עַל־הָאָרֶץ: וַיִּבְרָא אֱלֹהִים | אֶת־הָאָדָם

אָדָם — *Man.* (Man is) a species of the 'living being' species, which I (already) formed (verse 24), whose name is 'Adam,' as it says, *And man became a living creature.* Let us make him . . .

בְּצַלְמֵנוּ — *In our image.* (Who shall be) one (lit., 'an object') that is everlasting (נִצְחִי) and (endowed with) reason (שִׂכְלִי); and thus God, the Blessed One, gave man an opening in His Torah to acquire knowledge regarding those separated from matter (i.e., the angels) through the (intuitive) knowledge of our souls.

כִּדְמוּתֵנוּ — *As our likeness* . . . indeed — that he be in a small way like the 'Heavenly host,' insofar as they function with knowledge and recognition (understanding). However, their actions (i.e., the angels) are (performed) without (freedom) of choice, and in this sense man is not like them. In a limited manner, man is (also) like God, the Blessed One, Who acts with choice. However, God's choice is always (to do) good, but man's choice is not (always) so. In this (area) the Divine (freedom of choice) is far superior to man's (freedom of) choice. Therefore it says, כִּדְמוּתֵנוּ, *'as' our likeness,* not בִּדְמוּתֵנוּ, *'in' our likeness* (which would mean it is so) in truth.

NOTES

governs through the intermediary vehicle of angels, 'for all forces are angels' (the words used by the *Rambam).* Angels are 'intellects separate from matter' (*Guide* I:49) and these separate intellects are God's intermediaries. This then explains the plural form of נַעֲשֶׂה אָדָם, *Let 'us' make man,* i.e., God creates through His intermediaries (angels) as explained. By *image* (צֶלֶם) the *Sforno* means the power of 'intellectual apprehension' (intuitive understanding) imparted to man through the angels, as the *Rambam* explains in his *Guide* I:1.

אָדָם — *Man.* Included in the general species of *living beings* was a species called 'Adam.' This is clearly stated in 2:7. What this species was is not yet clarified or described. The vessel (his body) was in existence waiting for further development. When God says, 'Let us make this species called Adam, *in our image, after our likeness,*' the identity of 'Adam,' his special unique character and position in the scheme of Creation, becomes clear. This interpretation of the *Sforno* reconciles this verse with that of 2:7, in a manner which demonstrates the two are not redundant.

בְּצַלְמֵנוּ — *In our image.* To understand what the *Sforno* is saying regarding the term צֶלֶם in relation to man, one must examine the Rambam's *Guide* I:1. There Maimonides explains that the term צֶלֶם (image) in Hebrew does not denote the shape and configuration of a thing. The proper term designating that form is תּוֹאַר. Image, on the other hand, 'is applied to the natural form.' In man this refers to his 'intellectual apprehension.' This is what the *Sforno* means by שִׂכְלִי, *reason* or *intellect.* Through this power of the intellect, man now possesses an 'image' similar to that of the angels — hence בְּצַלְמֵנוּ, *in our image.*

The term נִצְחִי means that which has eternal existence, enduring and immutable. In connection with Adam it refers to his immortal soul.

כִּדְמוּתֵנוּ — *After our likeness.* Whereas צַלְמֵנוּ, *our image,* refers to man's intellectual apprehension, כִּדְמוּתֵנוּ, *after our likeness,* refers to the actions of men and the angels. The reason why the expression used is כִּדְמוּתֵנוּ, *as our likeness,* and not בִּדְמוּתֵנוּ, *in our likeness,* is because man is only 'similar to' the angels in his actions, but not 'the same,' for man is tempted by his evil inclination and has freedom of choice in fulfilling God's commandments, whereas the angels do not, being compelled by their nature and essence to obey the Almighty. In this respect man is 'higher than the angels.' This freedom of choice granted to man is a reflection of God Himself, Who is the ultimate in רָצוֹן, *will* — for all that He does is by His choice. In this respect also man is only 'similar' but certainly not 'the same,' for God's choices are always טוֹב, *good,* whereas man chooses both good and evil. Hence man is *as our likeness,* i.e., כִּדְמוּתֵנוּ but not בִּדְמוּתֵנוּ, considering that he is similar to

כח בְּצַלְמוֹ בְּצֶלֶם אֱלֹהִים בָּרָא אֹתוֹ זָכָר וּנְקֵבָה בָּרָא אֹתָם: וַיְבָרֶךְ אֹתָם
אֱלֹהִים וַיֹּאמֶר לָהֶם אֱלֹהִים פְּרוּ וּרְבוּ וּמִלְאוּ אֶת־הָאָרֶץ וְכִבְשֻׁהָ וּרְדוּ

---

27. בְּצֶלֶם אֱלֹהִים — *In the image of God.* The term *Elohim* used in a comparable sense (or as a counterpart) can be applied to every intelligent force (object) separated from matter which is perfect (complete) and (can function) in actuality and as such, is perforce everlasting. Therefore (this term) is used regarding God, the Blessed One, and His angels. It is also applied to judges (reflecting) their power of reason which is suitable for them. However, even though human reasoning functions without any material medium, expanding to the extrasensory and to a limited extent, even into the future, nor does (this power) weaken through much use or with age but increases in strength, which demonstrates that man's reason is also without a doubt separated from matter — seeing that the opposite is true of all physical material powers — nonetheless, before man contemplates and thinks deeply, lacking the perfection and completeness prepared for him, he cannot be called *Elohim,* but can only be called the *image* of *Elohim* — until he attains perfection. (This is) especially (so until he attains) the wisdom which brings to the love and awe of God. Only then will he become one who is intellectually apprehensive in deed (action); perfect and separated from matter, resulting in immortality, existing even after the death of his body. Now since man can choose to attain this perfection, by striving to delve into the aforementioned wisdom (it follows) that if he restrains himself from (this perfection) his intellectual powers will remain (only) potential, deprived of all perfection in the actual (as it was in the beginning), resulting in his desolation and destruction, as it says: אָדָם בִּיקָר וְלֹא יָבִין נִמְשַׁל כַּבְּהֵמוֹת נִדְמוּ, *Man is in his splendor (honor) but does not understand, he is like the beasts that perish (Psalms* 49:21). All this, God, the Blessed One, taught us in these two words, saying בְּצֶלֶם אֱלֹהִים, *in the image of Elohim.*

28. וְכִבְשֻׁהָ וּרְדוּ — *And subdue it and rule . . .* to protect it with your intelligence,

NOTES

God — but not in every respect; and he is similar to the angels — but not the same.

27. בְּצֶלֶם אֱלֹהִים — *In the image of God.* The *Sforno* is explaining why the term *Elohim* is not applied to man, only that of the image of *Elohim,* considering that this term *(Elohim)* is not reserved for God alone, but is applied to angels and judges as well. After all, if man is similar to God and the angels, having been created in their 'image and likeness,' why then is he only an 'image' of *Elohim?* The argument can even be strengthened, as the *Sforno* does here, by pointing out the reasoning power and intellectual capacity of man which is comparable to the angels, to the extent that these qualities function, akin to theirs, without benefit of any physical limb or organ, as the *Rambam* states in his *Guide* and in the *Mishnah Torah (Yesodei HaTorah* 4:8). However, all this is true only in man's potential but does not become actual, unless he chooses to attain perfection, separate himself from matter (as such) and translate his intellectual apprehension into action — all of these being the three characteristics of angels, i.e., separation from matter, perfection, and actuality (force). Until this comes to pass, man can only be called צֶלֶם אֱלֹהִים, an *image* of *Elohim,* having not as yet merited the name *Elohim* itself! The *Sforno* also underlines the tragic consequences resulting from the squandering of these great potential forces and abilities, with which man was endowed, the ultimate goal being the attainment of the greatest wisdom of all — the love and fear (reverence) of the Almighty, which insures man's immortality. To ignore and reject his spiritual and intellectual potential is to reject the noble, unique status of אָדָם, *Man* — as opposed to בְּהֵמָה, *animal* — and makes of him a mere physical being, no different than an animal.

28. וְכִבְשֻׁהָ וּרְדוּ — *And subdue it and rule.* The

כט בִּדְגַת הַיָּם֙ וּבְע֣וֹף הַשָּׁמַ֔יִם וּבְכָל־חַיָּ֖ה הָרֹמֶ֣שֶׂת עַל־הָאָ֑רֶץ: וַיֹּ֣אמֶר אֱלֹהִ֗ים
הִנֵּה֩ נָתַ֨תִּי לָכֶ֜ם אֶת־כָּל־עֵ֣שֶׂב | זֹרֵ֣עַ זֶ֗רַע אֲשֶׁר֙ עַל־פְּנֵ֣י כָל־הָאָ֔רֶץ
ל וְאֶת־כָּל־הָעֵ֛ץ אֲשֶׁר־בּ֥וֹ פְרִי־עֵ֖ץ זֹרֵ֣עַ זָ֑רַע לָכֶ֥ם יִֽהְיֶ֖ה לְאָכְלָֽה: וּֽלְכָל־חַיַּ֣ת
הָאָ֡רֶץ וּלְכָל־עוֹף֩ הַשָּׁמַ֨יִם וּלְכֹ֣ל | רוֹמֵ֣שׂ עַל־הָאָ֗רֶץ אֲשֶׁר־בּוֹ֙ נֶ֣פֶשׁ חַיָּ֔ה
לא אֶת־כָּל־יֶ֥רֶק עֵ֖שֶׂב לְאָכְלָ֑ה וַֽיְהִי־כֵֽן: וַיַּ֣רְא אֱלֹהִים֮ אֶת־כָּל־אֲשֶׁ֣ר עָשָׂה֒
וְהִנֵּה־ט֖וֹב מְאֹ֑ד וַֽיְהִי־עֶ֥רֶב וַֽיְהִי־בֹ֖קֶר י֥וֹם הַשִּׁשִּֽׁי:

---

and prevent the beasts from entering your limits (boundaries), for you will rule over them with nets and snares, to subject them to your service.

29. הִנֵּה נָתַתִּי לָכֶם — *Behold I have given to you . . .* for human consumption.

30. וּלְכָל חַיַּת הָאָרֶץ — *And to every beast of the earth.* But for all the beasts of the earth, and the animals and birds I have given . . .

אֶת כָּל יֶרֶק עֵשֶׂב לְאָכְלָה — *Every green herb for food.* Species of herbs which are not planted by seeds.

31. אֶת כָּל אֲשֶׁר עָשָׂה וְהִנֵּה טוֹב מְאֹד — *All that He had made and behold it was very good.* The end (result) of existence *in toto* was far greater than the end result of each particular part which was intended for the general purpose.

יוֹם הַשִּׁשִּׁי — *The sixth day.* The first (sixth day) which was the beginning of all *sixth days (Erev Shabbos)* when all deeds are completed so as to rest on Shabbos, as it says, וְעָשִׂיתָ כָּל מְלַאכְתֶּךָ, *And do all your work (Exodus* 20:9) (followed by), וְיוֹם הַשְּׁבִיעִי שַׁבָּת, *But, the seventh day is a Sabbath* (ibid. verse 10).

NOTES

two expressions *to subdue* and *to rule* refer to two separate areas of man's dominion over the animal kingdom. One is the power to prevent the beasts from overrunning man's domain, thanks to the special fear of man implanted by God in the beasts. The second is man's ability to subject animals, and channel their strength into his service.

29-30. הִנֵּה נָתַתִּי לָכֶם . . . וּלְכָל חַיַּת הָאָרֶץ — *Behold I have given to you . . . And to every beast of the earth.* For human food consumption, God gave herbage yielding seed and seed-yielding fruit, whereas the beasts of the earth and the fowl of the heaven were confined to green herbage, which grows wild, independent of the need to be planted by man.

31. אֶת כָּל אֲשֶׁר עָשָׂה וְהִנֵּה טוֹב מְאֹד — *All that He had made and behold it was very good.* The *Rambam (Guide* III:13) explains the expression 'And God saw that it was good,' which is repeated a number of times in the Creation chapter (verses 10, 12, 18, 21, 25), as meaning that the existence of every *part* in the world 'conformed to its purpose.' He stresses that the expression טוֹב, *good,* is applied to whatever

conforms to its purpose, said expression being used about man as well. The expression טוֹב מְאֹד, *very good,* used in this verse, regarding the whole of Creation, comes to teach us that whereas 'sometimes a thing is good by itself and conforms for a time to our purpose,' nonetheless 'afterwards the goal is missed.' Not so with the process of Creation where all things made 'conformed to His intention and purpose,' and continue so 'without ceasing to correspond to what was intended.' The *Sforno* in his commentary on this verse is expressing the same thought, adding a succinct summary, namely, that the whole represents more than the sum of its parts, and that is characterized as being *very good.*

יוֹם הַשִּׁשִּׁי — *The sixth day.* The prefix ה at the beginning of the word הַשִּׁשִּׁי, *the sixth,* is explained by our Sages *(Shabbos* 88a) as alluding to *the* sixth day of Sivan when the Torah was given, indicating that the existence of the world depends upon Israel's acceptance of the Torah. The *Sforno,* however, explains the use of the definite article as an allusion to all subsequent 'sixth days,' i.e., the sixth day of the week, *Erev Shabbos,* for this day will for

ב

א־ב וַיְכֻלּוּ הַשָּׁמַיִם וְהָאָרֶץ וְכָל־צְבָאָם: וַיְכַל אֱלֹהִים בַּיּוֹם הַשְּׁבִיעִי מְלַאכְתּוֹ
ג אֲשֶׁר עָשָׂה וַיִּשְׁבֹּת בַּיּוֹם הַשְּׁבִיעִי מִכָּל־מְלַאכְתּוֹ אֲשֶׁר עָשָׂה: וַיְבָרֶךְ
אֱלֹהִים אֶת־יוֹם הַשְּׁבִיעִי וַיְקַדֵּשׁ אֹתוֹ כִּי בוֹ שָׁבַת מִכָּל־מְלַאכְתּוֹ אֲשֶׁר־
בָּרָא אֱלֹהִים לַעֲשׂוֹת:

II

1. וַיְכֻלּוּ — *Were finished . . .* having reached the end purpose of existence (Creation) in general.

2. וַיְכַל אֱלֹהִים בַּיּוֹם הַשְּׁבִיעִי — *By the seventh day God completed.* God completed all creative activity at the (exact) beginning of the seventh day, at the indivisible moment which marked the inception of the future time, but yet was not part of it, as our Sages said, 'He entered into it by a hair's-breadth' *(Bereishis Rabbah).*

וַיִּשְׁבֹּת בַּיּוֹם הַשְּׁבִיעִי — *And He rested (abstained) on the seventh day.* That entire day was distinguished from the first six days by abstention (from creative activity).

3. וַיְבָרֶךְ אֱלֹהִים אֶת יוֹם הַשְּׁבִיעִי — *God blessed the seventh day.* Every future seventh day was blessed with an 'added soul' so that it be more prepared than any other day to be *illuminated by the light of life* (based on *Job* 33:30) as our Sages state, כיון ששבת ווי אבדה נפש, *'When Shabbos ends, woe! The (additional) soul is lost'* (*Beitzah* 16a).

NOTES

all times carry a special character. On this day each week a Jew must feel that all his work is done so that he may rest, with ease and tranquility, on Shabbos. This echoes the statement of the *Mechilta*, quoted by *Rashi* in *Exodus* 20:9: 'When Shabbos arrives, let it be in your eyes as though *all* your work is done, and put any thoughts of labor out of your mind.' The end of verse 9 and the beginning of verse 10 in *Exodus* 20 are thus linked.

II

1. וַיְכֻלּוּ – *Were finished.* The expression *were finished* does not mean to imply the material completion of the creation of heaven and earth. Rather it indicates that just as every aspect and part of Creation has its purpose, so too the totality of Creation met the goal set for it by the Almighty. At the end of six days, the process of creation was 'finished' in the sense that it had achieved the general purpose of Creation, as the *Sforno* puts it.

2. וַיְכַל אֱלֹהִים בַּיּוֹם הַשְּׁבִיעִי –*By the seventh day God completed.* The expression רֶגַע בִּלְתִּי מִתְחַלֵּק, *an indivisible moment*, was used by the *Sforno* in the first verse of *Bereishis* and is repeated here. The implication is a precise, exact moment in time which is compared by our Sages to a 'hair's breadth.' In the case of the Seventh Day — Shabbos — it teaches us that the six days of Creation were total and complete, while the seventh day was total and complete in its character of rest and cessation of labor. Both are perfect and whole with total integrity. This is the meaning of the verse in *Exodus* 20:11: *In six days God made it . . . and He rested on the seventh day.* Six *complete* days God made the heavens and the earth and the *entire* seventh day He rested. This also explains the expression *And He rested on the seventh day* in our verse; it implies the entire seventh day, since no part of the six days impinged upon the seventh day, nor did the seventh day impinge upon the six days.

3. וַיְבָרֶךְ אֱלֹהִים אֶת יוֹם הַשְּׁבִיעִי — *God blessed the seventh day.* The definite article ה is used before the word שְׁבִיעִי, *seventh*, to indicate that every seventh day, for all time, is blessed with an 'added soul' (נְשָׁמָה יְתֵרָה). The Talmud explains this as being the reason for lamenting the end of the Shabbos, for then one loses this great gift — until the following Shabbos.

שני ד אֵלֶּה תוֹלְדוֹת הַשָּׁמַיִם וְהָאָרֶץ בְּהִבָּרְאָם בְּיוֹם עֲשׂוֹת יְהֹוָה אֱלֹהִים אֶרֶץ
ה וְשָׁמָיִם׃ וְכֹל ׀ שִׂיחַ הַשָּׂדֶה טֶרֶם יִֽהְיֶה בָאָרֶץ וְכָל־עֵשֶׂב הַשָּׂדֶה טֶרֶם יִצְמָח
כִּי לֹא הִמְטִיר יְהֹוָה אֱלֹהִים עַל־הָאָרֶץ וְאָדָם אַיִן לַֽעֲבֹד אֶת־הָֽאֲדָמָה׃
ו-ז וְאֵד יַֽעֲלֶה מִן־הָאָרֶץ וְהִשְׁקָה אֶֽת־כָּל־פְּנֵֽי־הָֽאֲדָמָה׃ וַיִּיצֶר יְהֹוָה אֱלֹהִים

---

4. אֵלֶּה תולְדות הַשָּׁמַיִם וְהָאָרֶץ בְּהִבָּרְאָם — *These are the generations (products) of the heaven and the earth when they were created.* These plants and living creatures which we have already mentioned, were the products of heaven and earth *in potentia*, and (were) contained within them from the time of their creation, from which time (all) active and passive, eternal and perishable powers were present, as it says (verse 1) אֵת הַשָּׁמַיִם, *the heavens* (preceded by the indefinite article אֵת). This is to be understood as an amplification, i.e., including its 'offspring' (heavenly bodies and constellations). וְאֵת הָאָרֶץ, *and the earth*, which similarly is an amplification including its 'offspring' (the trees, herbage and living creatures). However, all these only became actual . . .

בְּיוֹם עֲשׂות ה׳ אֱלֹהִים אֶרֶץ וְשָׁמָיִם — *In the day that* HASHEM *God made earth and heaven.* On that day He set in order, from heaven, the permanent natural laws of the earth and its 'offspring.' This was after the six days of Creation. He is then called ה׳ אֱלֹהִים, *HASHEM, Elohim*, for by setting this order, He made its existence permanent.

5. טֶרֶם יִהְיֶה בָאָרֶץ — *Was not yet on the earth.* The reason that the trees were only in their potential and not actual state when they were created, in such a manner that there were as yet no tree of the field, and so also . . .

וְכָל עֵשֶׂב הַשָּׂדֶה — *No herb of the field* . . . had as yet sprouted.

כִּי לֹא הִמְטִיר — *For (Hashem) had not sent rain.* Hence the 'material' was not prepared to realize its complete potential, for it lacked rain and work of the soil (by man).

6. וְאֵד יַעֲלֶה מִן הָאָרֶץ — *A mist ascended from the earth.* When (God) established (lit., 'set in order') as a continual order (plant life), a mist (vapor) came up from the earth which (caused) dew, as a blessing, to water the earth, bring forth and bud, without benefit of rain or (man's) working of the soil.

NOTES

4. אֵלֶּה תולְדות הַשָּׁמַיִם וְהָאָרֶץ בְּהִבָּרְאָם בְּיוֹם עֲשׂות ה׳ אֱלֹהִים אֶרֶץ וְשָׁמָיִם — *These are the generations (products) of the heaven and the earth when they were created in the day that* HASHEM *God made earth and heaven.* As *Rashi* points out in 1:14, everything in heaven and on earth was created *in potentia* on the first day, following which, on their appropriate days, they were brought from the potential to the actual. To this theory the *Sforno* adds that the permanent order of all these things in heaven and earth were established as laws of nature, after the six days of Creation. The reason this twofold name of God is used, i.e., ה׳ אֱלֹהִים, is explained by the *Sforno* as reflecting God's overflowing powers of eternal existence with which He endows all living matter and creatures. As the *Sforno* explained in 1:1, the name *Elohim* implies precisely that, while the name ה׳ (which in Hebrew is called הֲוָיָ׳, *to be)* indicates the ongoing permanent order of living nature — its existence flowing from the Eternal 'Being.'

6. וְאֵד יַעֲלֶה מִן הָאָרֶץ — *A mist ascended from the earth.* The *Sforno* is of the opinion that the mist ascended after the six days of Creation. The *Rambam (Guide* II:6), however, interprets this verse as being a description of 'the first state of matters obtaining before the command of "Let the earth bring forth grass" ' (I:11). *Onkelos* also is of the same opinion,

אֶת־הָאָדָם עָפָר מִן־הָאֲדָמָה וַיִּפַּח בְּאַפָּיו נִשְׁמַת חַיִּים וַיְהִי הָאָדָם לְנֶפֶשׁ
ח חַיָּה: וַיִּטַּע יהוה אֱלֹהִים גַּן בְּעֵדֶן מִקֶּדֶם וַיָּשֶׂם שָׁם אֶת־הָאָדָם אֲשֶׁר יָצָר:
ט וַיַּצְמַח יהוה אֱלֹהִים מִן־הָאֲדָמָה כָּל־עֵץ נֶחְמָד לְמַרְאֶה וְטוֹב לְמַאֲכָל וְעֵץ

7. וַיִּיצֶר ה׳ אֱלֹהִים — *And HASHEM God formed.* However, to bring forth living creatures, it was not sufficient (to use the earlier method and powers). The Creator utilized different ways and methods (to create all living creatures). To form man He chose (to use) . . .

עָפָר מִן הָאֲדָמָה — *Dust from the ground.* A distinguished part (of the ground).

וַיִּפַּח בְּאַפָּיו נִשְׁמַת חַיִּים — *And He blew into his nostrils the soul of life* . . . a vivifying soul ready to receive the 'image of God,' as it says: וְנִשְׁמַת שַׁדַּי תְּבִינֵם, *And the breath of the Almighty that gives them understanding (Job* 32:8), nonetheless . . .

וַיְהִי הָאָדָם לְנֶפֶשׁ חַיָּה — *And the man became a living being.* In spite of all this (his special forming by God), he was still only a living creature, unable to speak, until he was created in (God's) image and likeness.

8. אֲשֶׁר יָצָר — *Whom he had formed.* After He formed him in the distinguished manner already mentioned, He placed him there (in the garden), being a place suitable for man to receive God's image and acquire intellectual reasoning (functioning) powers, (through) its atmosphere and food.

9. וַיַּצְמַח ה׳ — *And HASHEM caused to grow* . . . his food, without toil (lit., 'suffering').

נֶחְמָד לְמַרְאֶה — *Pleasing to the sight* . . . gladdening and broadening the heart, preparing it (and) making it receptive to the flow of intelligence, as it says, וְהָיָה כְּנַגֵּן הַמְנַגֵּן, וַתְּהִי עָלָיו יַד ה׳, *And it came to pass when the minstrel played that the hand of HASHEM came upon him (II Kings* 3:15).

NOTES

translating our verse, *And there had gone up a mist, etc.* The preceding verse, however, seems to bear out the *Sforno's* interpretation for it states *no tree of the field was yet on the earth,* nor any herb of the field until rain fell, and rain in turn was caused by the vapor ascending. Hence all this occurred at the end of the six days of Creation, not at the beginning as the *Rambam* states.

7-8. וַיִּיצֶר ה׳ אֱלֹהִים ... אֲשֶׁר יָצָר — *And HASHEM God formed . . . Whom he had formed.* All living creatures, as compared to the mineral and plant kingdom, needed a special 'forming' by God to be brought into being. This was especially true of man. Each, according to the *Sforno,* was fashioned in a different manner by God, with man's raw material, (dust) chosen carefully from a special part of the earth, namely the eventual place of the altar on Mt. Moriah. Now, the process of man's creation was in two phases. First man was formed as a higher, more advanced living creature, granted a 'soul of life.' However, he was not as yet endowed with the 'image of God' until God placed him in the Garden of Eden, a place conducive for Adam to receive this image thanks to its unique character. The *Sforno* interprets this 'image' as meaning the flow of reason and intelligence emanating from God.

9. נֶחְמָד לְמַרְאֶה — *Pleasing to the sight.* The spirit of prophecy, according to our Sages, can only come to rest upon one who is in a state of *simchah,* happiness and contentment. God's intention was for man to dwell in the Garden, where his material needs would be taken care of and he would be able to occupy himself with the pursuit of דַּעַת ה׳, *the knowledge of God.* The *Sforno* therefore explains the reason for God's planting trees in the garden pleasant to the sight, as being for the purpose of preparing Adam to receive the spirit of *Hashem*, since by appealing to his aesthetic sense Adam would be more receptive to the

י הַחַיִּים בְּתוֹךְ הַגָּן וְעֵץ הַדַּעַת טוֹב וָרָע׃ וְנָהָר יֹצֵא מֵעֵדֶן לְהַשְׁקוֹת אֶת־הַגָּן
יא וּמִשָּׁם יִפָּרֵד וְהָיָה לְאַרְבָּעָה רָאשִׁים׃ שֵׁם הָאֶחָד פִּישׁוֹן הוּא הַסֹּבֵב אֵת
יב כָּל־אֶרֶץ הַחֲוִילָה אֲשֶׁר־שָׁם הַזָּהָב׃ וּזֲהַב הָאָרֶץ הַהִוא טוֹב שָׁם הַבְּדֹלַח
יג־יד וְאֶבֶן הַשֹּׁהַם׃ וְשֵׁם־הַנָּהָר הַשֵּׁנִי גִּיחוֹן הוּא הַסּוֹבֵב אֵת כָּל־אֶרֶץ כּוּשׁ׃ וְשֵׁם
הַנָּהָר הַשְּׁלִישִׁי חִדֶּקֶל הוּא הַהֹלֵךְ קִדְמַת אַשּׁוּר וְהַנָּהָר הָרְבִיעִי הוּא פְרָת׃
טו־טז וַיִּקַּח יְהוָה אֱלֹהִים אֶת־הָאָדָם וַיַּנִּחֵהוּ בְגַן־עֵדֶן לְעָבְדָהּ וּלְשָׁמְרָהּ׃ וַיְצַו

וְעֵץ הַדַּעַת — *And the tree of knowledge. Knowledge* to give one's attention to and focus one's heart on (what is) good and evil. From this (source of the word דַּעַת) we also find, *And Adam knew* (4:1), i.e., he became aware and concentrated his heart on her. (This is also) why we call a relative מוֹדַע, as it says מוֹדַע לְאִישָׁהּ, *a relative of her husband (Ruth* 2:1), for it is natural that one concerns himself for the needs of his relative, as it says וְאָח לְצָרָה יִוָּלֵד, *And a brother is born for adversity (Proverbs* 17:17).

טוֹב וָרָע — *Good and bad.* To choose the sweet even when it is harmful and reject the bitter even when it is beneficial.

10. וְנָהָר יֹצֵא מֵעֵדֶן — *And a river issues forth from Eden . . .* without need (lit., pain) of rain or the toil (labor) of man.

11. שֵׁם הָאֶחָד פִּישׁוֹן — *The name of the first is Pishon.* The (Torah) tells us how praiseworthy was the river that watered the garden, (the name of) which is unknown to us, by informing us of (the names of) the rivers branching out from it, which are well known to us as commendable for their size and the quality of their waters and fruits.

15. לְעָבְדָהּ — *To work it.* To work (to perfect) his *soul of life,* as it says: *And He blew into his nostrils the soul of life* (verse 7).

וּלְשָׁמְרָהּ — *And to guard it . . .* that it (i.e., his *soul of life)* not be diminished through the impact of nature's heat upon his fundamental vitality; this (therapeutic aid) coming from the esteemed fruits which constantly replaced what man's constitution lost, for (these fruits) never rotted.

NOTES

overflow of the intellect emanating from God. The quote from *Kings* refers to Elisha who was unable to receive prophecy until his mood was changed, and his spirit elevated by the music of the minstrel which dispelled his gloom and gladdened his heart.

טוֹב וָרָע — *Good and bad.* The *Rambam* in his *Guide* (I:2) explains that man was originally granted an 'overflow of the intellect' allowing him 'to distinguish between truth and falsehood.' Only after the sin of eating from the tree of knowledge did man develop a taste for good and evil, or 'fine and bad' as Maimonides puts it. The term 'good and evil,' however, does not mean good and evil in the moral sense. Rather, that which is sweet and pleasant to man's physical senses he now considers 'good,' even though, as the *Sforno* says, it is harmful; and what is bitter, or difficult, is rejected by man, and considered 'evil,' even though it is really beneficial for him. It is in this sense that the forbidden fruit of this prohibited tree caused man to give his heart, not to truth and falsehood, but to good and bad. As Onkelos translates, it was a tree "of the knowledge of good and bad" *not* a "tree of knowledge."

15. לְעָבְדָהּ וּלְשָׁמְרָהּ — *To work it and to guard it. To work it* does not refer to the garden, for it was not necessary for man to *work it* as explained by the *Sforno* in verses 9-10. Rather *it* refers to man's *soul of life* mentioned in verse 7. In the Garden of Eden man was meant to develop himself, expanding his spirit and broadening his knowledge of Hashem, thereby receiving the 'image of God' for

יז יְהוָה אֱלֹהִים עַל־הָאָדָם לֵאמֹר מִכֹּל עֵץ־הַגָּן אָכֹל תֹּאכֵל: וּמֵעֵץ הַדַּעַת
יח טוֹב וָרָע לֹא תֹאכַל מִמֶּנּוּ כִּי בְּיוֹם אֲכָלְךָ מִמֶּנּוּ מוֹת תָּמוּת: וַיֹּאמֶר יְהוָה
יט אֱלֹהִים לֹא־טוֹב הֱיוֹת הָאָדָם לְבַדּוֹ אֶעֱשֶׂה־לּוֹ עֵזֶר כְּנֶגְדּוֹ: וַיִּצֶר יְהוָה

---

16. מִכֹּל עֵץ הַגָּן — *Of every tree of the garden* . . . according to the changing seasons, as affected by the stars, as it says, לָחֳדָשָׁיו יְבַכֵּר, *It shall bring forth new fruit every month* (*Ezekiel* 47:12).

17. וּמֵעֵץ הַדַּעַת — *But of the tree of knowledge* . . . which was situated in the midst of the garden near the tree of life mentioned above, as it says, *a tree of life in the midst of the garden* (verse 9). (This is) in keeping with, הַחַיִּים וְהַמָּוֶת נָתַתִּי לְפָנֶיךָ, *I have set before you life and death* (*Deut.* 30:19).

18. לֹא טוֹב הֱיוֹת הָאָדָם לְבַדּוֹ — *It is not good that man be alone.* The (goal and) purpose intended in his being in the likeness and image (of God) will not be realized if (man) will have to occupy himself alone, to supply the needs of life.

עֵזֶר כְּנֶגְדּוֹ — *A helper corresponding to him.* (This means) a helper that will be, as it were, equal to him in image and likeness. This was mandatory so that (the helper) would appreciate his needs and meet them at the proper time. The word כְּנֶגְדּוֹ, *opposite him,* implies that when an object is placed on one side of a scale it will be even with the object on the other side providing they are both equal in weight. Only then is it נֶגְדּוֹ, *opposite,* on a straight line. However, if they are unequal in weight, they will not be opposite one another on a straight line, rather, one will go up and the other down (higher and lower). This is what is meant by our Sages when they state, 'Moshe was equal to all of Israel' (*Mechilta*). It would, however, not have been proper for the helper to be completely equal to him for then one would not be properly able to work for and serve the other.

19. וַיִּצֶר ה' אֱלֹהִים מִן הָאֲדָמָה כָּל חַיַּת הַשָּׂדֶה — *HASHEM God formed out of the ground every beast of the field.* He gave them a complete form as feeling (creatures); the

NOTES

which he was destined. The expression *to guard it* is also interpreted by the *Sforno* as referring to man's 'soul of life.' Through the precious, unusual fruits of the garden, man's well being would be guarded and preserved.

16. מִכֹּל עֵץ הַגָּן —*Of every tree of the garden.* The expression *Of 'every' tree of the garden* is interpreted by the *Sforno* as implying a variety of fruits in different seasons, thereby satisfying man's inherent desire for variety.

17. וּמֵעֵץ הַדַּעַת — *But of the tree of knowledge.* In verse 9 the Torah implies that not only was the tree of life *in the midst of the garden* but also the *tree of the knowledge of good and bad,* for these two are placed in juxtaposition, following one another in the same verse. 3:3 also states that the tree was *in the center of the garden.* The *Sforno* sees in this a great moral lesson; that man was given the choice between life and death, for he alone has been granted freedom of choice. Had man chosen to eat from the tree of life, rather than the tree of the knowledge of good and bad, he apparently would have been granted eternal life. Because he chose the sweet and pleasant, which was forbidden to him, he also chose death over life, as the verse in Deuteronomy states.

18. עֵזֶר כְּנֶגְדּוֹ — *A helper corresponding to him.* Were the Torah to have said נֶגְדּוֹ, without the prefix כ, it would have meant that woman was to be fully equal to man. This was not God's intent, for then she could not be his עֵזֶר, *helper.* Rather she was meant to be like him, similar but not completely equal. Still, since both of them fulfill the roles destined for them, they are 'equal in weight,' on a straight line, striking a proper balance for their mutual benefit.

19. וַיִּצֶר ה' אֱלֹהִים — *HASHEM God formed.* The *first* beasts had to be formed by Hashem's

אֱלֹהִים מִן־הָאֲדָמָה כָּל־חַיַּת הַשָּׂדֶה וְאֵת כָּל־עוֹף הַשָּׁמַיִם וַיָּבֵא אֶל־
הָאָדָם לִרְאוֹת מַה־יִּקְרָא־לוֹ וְכֹל אֲשֶׁר יִקְרָא־לוֹ הָאָדָם נֶפֶשׁ חַיָּה הוּא
שלישי כ שְׁמוֹ: וַיִּקְרָא הָאָדָם שֵׁמוֹת לְכָל־הַבְּהֵמָה וּלְעוֹף הַשָּׁמַיִם וּלְכֹל חַיַּת הַשָּׂדֶה
כא וּלְאָדָם לֹא־מָצָא עֵזֶר כְּנֶגְדּוֹ: וַיַּפֵּל יהוה אֱלֹהִים ׀ תַּרְדֵּמָה עַל־הָאָדָם
כב וַיִּישָׁן וַיִּקַּח אַחַת מִצַּלְעֹתָיו וַיִּסְגֹּר בָּשָׂר תַּחְתֶּנָּה: וַיִּבֶן יהוה אֱלֹהִים ׀ אֶת־
כג הַצֵּלָע אֲשֶׁר־לָקַח מִן־הָאָדָם לְאִשָּׁה וַיְבִאֶהָ אֶל־הָאָדָם: וַיֹּאמֶר הָאָדָם
זֹאת הַפַּעַם עֶצֶם מֵעֲצָמַי וּבָשָׂר מִבְּשָׂרִי לְזֹאת יִקָּרֵא אִשָּׁה כִּי מֵאִישׁ

---

heavenly force not being sufficient to do so without the help of the natural reproductive (lit., 'seed') force.

וַיָּבֵא אֶל הָאָדָם — *And brought (them) to the man* ... so that he (man) might recognize (appreciate) that he needed a new creation (as a mate) seeing that there was none among the living creatures to serve him suitably.

לִרְאוֹת מַה יִּקְרָא לוֹ — *To see what he would call each one* ... so that he might see and discern what name was proper for each one of them, according to the function most suitable to its form (essential being).

נֶפֶשׁ חַיָּה הוּא שְׁמוֹ — *Living creature, that remained its name.* The particular name by which it was called indicated the form of that living creature, i.e., the essence of its living soul which represents its actuality in existence.

21. וַיַּפֵּל ה׳ אֱלֹהִים תַּרְדֵּמָה עַל הָאָדָם — *So* HASHEM *God cast a deep sleep upon the man* ... so he should not be afraid or experience pain.

וַיִּקַּח אַחַת מִצַּלְעֹתָיו — *And He took one of his sides.* Since the choicest dust had been gathered and all proper material (matter) went into man's living form, therefore, when God wanted to fashion the female form, which was almost similar to him (Adam), it was fitting to take some of his material being (body), namely one of his sides.

22. וַיִּבֶן ה׳ אֱלֹהִים אֶת הַצֵּלָע ... לְאִשָּׁה — *Then* HASHEM *God fashioned the side ... into a woman* ... that she may have the form of man and his faculties (qualities), differing from him only in 'the physical vessels' (i.e., sex) — this being the difference between them, (otherwise) both have the possibility for (the attainment of) perfection, (be the measure) abundant or meager.

23. זֹאת — *This.* This female.

הַפַּעַם — *Time.* This time it is ...

NOTES

direct intervention, after which they could reproduce themselves, from the seed within them.

לִרְאוֹת מַה יִּקְרָא לוֹ — *To see what he would call each one.* God did not need Adam to decide which name to give to each of these living creatures. This was meant as an object lesson for Adam to understand the essential form of each animal and beast to better discern its purpose. By so doing man also came to recognize that none of these creatures could be his mate and helper and would thereby appreciate the loving-kindness of God in creating a new person, and yet taken from him, as his helper who (as the *Sforno* states in verse 18) would appreciate his needs and fulfill them.

23. זֹאת הַפַּעַם עֶצֶם מֵעֲצָמַי — *This time bone of my bone.* The *Sforno* interprets and explains the repetition of the word זאת — in this verse. Before she was called אִשָּׁה — woman — she is referred to as זאת — the feminine form of *this*. Therefore the words זאת and הַפַּעַם are not linked, rather we connect הַפַּעַם to עֶצֶם מֵעֲצָמַי,

כד לֻקְחָה־זֹּאת׃ עַל־כֵּן֙ יַֽעֲזָב־אִ֔ישׁ אֶת־אָבִ֖יו וְאֶת־אִמּ֑וֹ וְדָבַ֣ק בְּאִשְׁתּ֔וֹ וְהָי֖וּ
כה לְבָשָׂ֥ר אֶחָֽד׃ וַיִּֽהְי֤וּ שְׁנֵיהֶם֙ עֲרוּמִּ֔ים הָֽאָדָ֖ם וְאִשְׁתּ֑וֹ וְלֹ֖א יִתְבֹּשָֽׁשׁוּ׃
א וְהַנָּחָשׁ֙ הָיָ֣ה עָר֔וּם מִכֹּל֙ חַיַּ֣ת הַשָּׂדֶ֔ה אֲשֶׁ֥ר עָשָׂ֖ה יהוה אֱלֹהִ֑ים וַיֹּ֙אמֶר֙ אֶל־ ג

עֶצֶם מֵעֲצָמַי וּבָשָׂר מִבְּשָׂרִי — *Bone of my bone and flesh of my flesh.* Henceforth, however, the female of the human species will not be so (she will be formed separately from man).

לְזֹאת — *This.* Every female woman, in the future . . .

יִקָּרֵא אִשָּׁה — *Shall be called woman* . . . even though she will not be a part of man.

כִּי מֵאִישׁ לֻקֳחָה זֹּאת — *For from man was she taken* . . . the first one of all (women).

24. עַל כֵּן — *Therefore* . . . since the first woman was intended by God to be similar to man as much as possible (to such an extent) that He formed her from (man's) body.

יַעֲזָב אִישׁ אֶת אָבִיו וְאֶת אִמּוֹ וְדָבַק בְּאִשְׁתּוֹ — *Shall a man leave his father and his mother and cling to his wife.* It is proper that a man should attempt to marry a woman suitable for him and suitable to cleave to him. (This he shall do) even though it may be necessary to leave his father and mother; there can be no authentic cleaving among those who are not alike; it can only be among those who are similar, for only then can they be of one mind.

וְהָיוּ לְבָשָׂר אֶחָד — *And they shall become one flesh.* In all their actions they will aim to attain the perfection intended by man's creation, as though the two were as only one (flesh).

25. עֲרוּמִּים . . . וְלֹא יִתְבֹּשָׁשׁוּ — *Naked . . . and they were not ashamed.* At that time, all their organs, limbs and actions were (used for the purpose) of fulfilling God's will exclusively, not to attain physical pleasure at all. (Consequently) the act of sexual congress was to them as normal as that of eating and drinking; therefore their reproductive organs were regarded by them as we regard our mouth, face and hands.

III

1. וְהַנָּחָשׁ — *And the serpent.* 'He is Satan, he is the evil prompter' (*Baba Basra* 16a). Although he is small in appearance he does much damage. (The Torah) describes things figuratively by (various names) which are similar to them, just as a king is called 'lion,' as it says, עָלָה אַרְיֵה מִסֻּבְּכוֹ, *A lion is gone up from his thicket (Jeremiah*

NOTES

bone of my bone. The sense of the verse is as follows: Only this time is 'this' female literally 'flesh of my flesh' and therefore rightfully called אִשָּׁה, having been taken from אִישׁ. In the future, however, she will still be called אִשָּׁה since the first one was taken from him.

24. עַל כֵּן יַעֲזָב . . . — *Therefore shall leave* . . . The *Sforno* submits that only those who are alike can cleave to one another. Since woman was once actually part of man, she is certainly like him, and when man and woman marry they come together once again. The motivation to do so is stronger than the natural desire of man to remain close to his parents. This commentary echoes the words of our Sages who liken man's search for a wife to one who seeks something he has lost. Man lost one of his sides, which God fashioned into woman, so he looks for it until he finds a wife, thereby becoming 'whole' once again.

III

1. וְהַנָּחָשׁ — *And the serpent.* The *Sforno* is of the opinion that the serpent is not to be

ב הָאִשָּׁה אַף כִּי־אָמַר אֱלֹהִים לֹא תֹאכְלוּ מִכֹּל עֵץ הַגָּן: וַתֹּאמֶר הָאִשָּׁה
ג אֶל־הַנָּחָשׁ מִפְּרִי עֵץ־הַגָּן נֹאכֵל: וּמִפְּרִי הָעֵץ אֲשֶׁר בְּתוֹךְ־הַגָּן אָמַר אֱלֹהִים

4:7), or enemies who do harm, 'serpents, adders', as it says, הִנְנִי מְשַׁלֵּחַ בָּכֶם נְחָשִׁים צִפְעֹנִים אֲשֶׁר אֵין לָהֶם לָחַשׁ, *For behold I will send serpents, adders, among you which will not be charmed (Jeremiah* 8:17). In this manner the evil inclination which tempts man is called 'serpent,' for he is similar to a serpent, which is (an animal) with limited utility but great potential to do harm, though small in appearance. Our Sages have told us that Samael (the accuser; Angel of Death) rode on him (the serpent), meaning that the power of lust, bringing to sin, accomplishes its end through the medium of the power of imagination which brings to man visions of physical, material pleasures, which lead him astray (turning him away) from the way of perfection intended by God, the Blessed One. This power of desire (and base appetites) with the images of pleasure accompanying it are present in the functional physical powers (of man), causing him to frustrate God's will and intent unless the power of reason rises up to combat it, as our Sages state, 'the heart and the eye are the two agents of sin' (Jerusalem Talmud, *Berachos* 1:8). This is what the Torah cautions against, saying, וְלֹא תָתוּרוּ אַחֲרֵי לְבַבְכֶם וְאַחֲרֵי עֵינֵיכֶם, *Go not after your own heart and your own eyes (Numbers* 15:39).

הָיָה עָרוּם מִכֹּל חַיַּת הַשָּׂדֶה — *Was cunning beyond any beast of the field.* For the imaginative powers (in man) which project the image of pleasures to the powers of his base desire is stronger (in man) than in other living creatures as our Sages say, 'He who is greater than his fellow, his evil inclination is greater than his' (*Succah* 52a).

וַיֹּאמֶר אֶל הָאִשָּׁה — *And he said to the woman.* For her weaker intellect was too indolent to delve deeply to discern (the truth) and could not withstand the false image (of temptation). Rather she pictured in her imagination that even though ...

אַף כִּי אָמַר אֱלֹהִים — *Although God had said.* Although God had said not to eat from the tree of knowledge *lest you die,* nonetheless it will not come to pass, and therefore when the serpent, which means her imaginative powers, began to plant a doubt (in her mind), the woman with her weak intellect (first) said — from all ...

2. עֵץ הַגָּן נֹאכֵל — *Of the fruit of any tree of the garden we may eat.* And there is no need to expose ourselves to danger by eating from the tree which God, the Blessed One, cautioned us not to eat from, lest we die. However, her imagination overpowered her (reason) thereby attributing jealousy and falsehood (God forbid) to

NOTES

interpreted literally, but figuratively. Just as a lion is used by the prophet to represent King Nebuchadnezzar and adders to represent the enemies of Israel, so the serpent represents Satan and the יֵצֶר הָרַע (the evil inclination) which is within man, leading him astray. This 'evil prompter' works through the heart of man (his desires) and his eyes, which see and arouse man's base appetites. Since the evil inclination, Satan and the Angel of Death are one and the same, the imagery used by our Sages when they depict the Angel of Death (Samael) riding on the serpent (*Pirkei Eliezer* 13; *Zohar Chadash)* is an apt one. The original sin of man was caused by his inherent weakness and inability to withstand temptation which ultimately resulted in his death.

1-5. וַיֹּאמֶר ... אַף כִּי אָמַר ... כִּי יֹדֵעַ אֱלֹהִים — *And he said ... Although God had said ... For God knows.* The *Sforno* depicts the internal struggle within Eve between her reason and

ד לֹא תֹאכְלוּ מִמֶּנּוּ וְלֹא תִגְּעוּ בּוֹ פֶּן תְּמֻתוּן׃ וַיֹּאמֶר הַנָּחָשׁ אֶל־הָאִשָּׁה לֹא־
ה מוֹת תְּמֻתוּן׃ כִּי יֹדֵעַ אֱלֹהִים כִּי בְּיוֹם אֲכָלְכֶם מִמֶּנּוּ וְנִפְקְחוּ עֵינֵיכֶם
ו וִהְיִיתֶם כֵּאלֹהִים יֹדְעֵי טוֹב וָרָע׃ וַתֵּרֶא הָאִשָּׁה כִּי טוֹב הָעֵץ לְמַאֲכָל וְכִי
תַאֲוָה־הוּא לָעֵינַיִם וְנֶחְמָד הָעֵץ לְהַשְׂכִּיל וַתִּקַּח מִפִּרְיוֹ וַתֹּאכַל וַתִּתֵּן גַּם־
ז לְאִישָׁהּ עִמָּהּ וַיֹּאכַל׃ וַתִּפָּקַחְנָה עֵינֵי שְׁנֵיהֶם וַיֵּדְעוּ כִּי עֵירֻמִּם הֵם וַיִּתְפְּרוּ

God, the Blessed One, (falsely) picturing (God) as prohibiting the fruit so that they would not attain the purpose of being as *Elohim* (divine beings), but not because it would result in (their) death. Therefore he said to the woman . . .

4-5. לֹא מוֹת תְּמֻתוּן כִּי יֹדֵעַ אֱלֹהִים כִּי בְּיוֹם אֲכָלְכֶם מִמֶּנּוּ וְנִפְקְחוּ עֵינֵיכֶם — *You will not surely die. For God knows that on the day you eat of it then your eyes shall be opened.* He did not prohibit this fruit at all because it would cause your death. Rather it was because He knows that by eating from it, you will gain added knowledge, and (as a result) be as *Elohim* (divine beings) perfect in knowledge.

6. וַתֵּרֶא הָאִשָּׁה כִּי טוֹב הָעֵץ לְמַאֲכָל — *And the woman perceived that the tree was good for eating.* She perceived that it was pleasant (sweet) to eat, because of the nature of its place, atmosphere and the aroma of its fruit.

וְנֶחְמָד הָעֵץ לְהַשְׂכִּיל — *And the tree was desirable as a means of wisdom.* As God Himself said, that it was *a tree of knowledge of good and evil* (2:9).

גַּם לְאִישָׁהּ עִמָּהּ — *Also to her husband with her.* He was receptive to her request, because he was אִישָׁהּ, *her husband,* and because he was עִמָּהּ, *with her* (in an intimate sense).

7. וַתִּפָּקַחְנָה עֵינֵי שְׁנֵיהֶם — *Then the eyes of both of them were opened.* They turned their attention to what was sweet (pleasant) and pleasurable, even though it was harmful. Attending to and inspecting any matter is called פְּקִיחַת עֵינַיִם, *opening of the eyes,* as it says, אַף עַל זֶה פָּקַחְתָּ עֵינֶךָ, *And you open your eyes upon such a one* (*Job* 14:3).

וַיֵּדְעוּ כִּי עֵירֻמִּם הֵם — *And they realized that they were naked.* They perceived that it was proper to conceal their private organs inasmuch as their major function had now become for pleasure that was degrading and harmful.

NOTES

desire. At first she reasoned correctly that since there is such a plentiful variety of permitted fruits, why should they expose themselves to the danger of death? But she then was overcome by her appetite and desire, succumbing to the wiles of the 'evil prompter,' rationalizing that death would not occur, and justifying her action by convincing herself that God's motivation in prohibiting this tree was to protect His exclusive monopoly of knowledge, Divine wisdom and perfection.

6. גַּם לְאִישָׁהּ עִמָּהּ — *Also to her husband with her.* The two words אִישָׁהּ, *her husband,* and עִמָּהּ, *with her,* are interpreted by the *Sforno* as representing two reasons for Adam's willingness to listen to Eve. First because he was her husband and felt a certain sense of responsibility to accommodate her, and second because he was *with her,* a euphemism for marital intimacy.

7. וַתִּפָּקַחְנָה עֵינֵי שְׁנֵיהֶם וַיֵּדְעוּ — *Then the eyes of both of them were opened and they realized.* Obviously the expression פְּקִיחַת עֵינַיִם, *opening of the eyes,* cannot be understood in a literal sense. Also the expression וַיֵּדְעוּ, *they knew* — or *realized* — rather than וַיִּרְאוּ, *they saw,* is significant. The *Rambam* in his *Guide* (I:2) observes that the choice of words ('knew' rather than 'saw') as well as the expression *'opening of the eyes'* indicates that man

ח עֲלֵה תְאֵנָה וַיַּעֲשׂוּ לָהֶם חֲגֹרֹת: וַיִּשְׁמְעוּ אֶת־קוֹל יהוה אֱלֹהִים מִתְהַלֵּךְ
בַּגָּן לְרוּחַ הַיּוֹם וַיִּתְחַבֵּא הָאָדָם וְאִשְׁתּוֹ מִפְּנֵי יהוה אֱלֹהִים בְּתוֹךְ עֵץ הַגָּן:
ט־י וַיִּקְרָא יהוה אֱלֹהִים אֶל־הָאָדָם וַיֹּאמֶר לוֹ אַיֶּכָּה: וַיֹּאמֶר אֶת־קֹלְךָ
יא שָׁמַעְתִּי בַּגָּן וָאִירָא כִּי־עֵירֹם אָנֹכִי וָאֵחָבֵא: וַיֹּאמֶר מִי הִגִּיד לְךָ כִּי עֵירֹם
יב אָתָּה הֲמִן־הָעֵץ אֲשֶׁר צִוִּיתִיךָ לְבִלְתִּי אֲכָל־מִמֶּנּוּ אָכָלְתָּ: וַיֹּאמֶר הָאָדָם
יג הָאִשָּׁה אֲשֶׁר נָתַתָּה עִמָּדִי הִוא נָתְנָה־לִּי מִן־הָעֵץ וָאֹכֵל: וַיֹּאמֶר יהוה

---

8. מִתְהַלֵּךְ בַּגָּן — *Moving about (manifesting itself) in the garden.* To and fro, according to the intended end (purpose), similar to, הִתְהַלֵּךְ בָּאָרֶץ, *walk through the land* (13:17) and, וַיִּתְהַלְּכוּ מִגּוֹי אֶל גּוֹי, *they went about from nation to nation (Psalms* 105:13).

לְרוּחַ הַיּוֹם — *In the wind of the day.* According (to His) will that day, to do the desirable things for that day, just as He did during the other days of Creation, and as He did that day (as well) before they sinned.

וַיִּתְחַבֵּא — *And he hid.* As it says, וְלֹא יִרְאֶה בְךָ עֶרְוַת דָּבָר, *that He see no unseemly thing in you (Deut.* 23:15).

9. אַיֶּכָּה — *Where are you?* That you are no longer visible in the garden as heretofore, having now hidden yourself — something you did not do before.

10. וָאִירָא — *And I was afraid.* This also happened to Israel after the sin (of the golden calf) as it says, וַיִּירְאוּ מִגֶּשֶׁת אֵלָיו, *and they were afraid to come near to Him (Exodus* 34:30).

11. מִי הִגִּיד לְךָ — *Who told you.* The knowledge of good and evil.

כִּי עֵירֹם אָתָּה — *That you are naked.* That because you are naked it is proper to cover yourself (i.e., that nakedness is shameful).

12. הִיא — *She* . . . whom You gave (to me) as a helper, to be useful . . .

נָתְנָה לִּי מִן הָעֵץ — *She gave me of the tree.* (She) was an obstacle (stumbling block). And thus he attributed his guilty act to his 'Owner' (Hashem) instead of repenting,

NOTES

'entered upon another state in which he considered as bad things that he had not seen in that light before.' The *Sforno* explains this verse in a manner similar to his interpretation of 2:9, where he explains the word דַּעַת, *knowledge*, as pertaining to the concentration of one's attention and concern toward a person, object or issue. He explains the 'opening of one's eyes' in similar fashion, i.e., the concentration of their thoughts away from truth and spirituality to the pleasurable and physical. This change in their priorities, in turn, causes them to perceive their bodies in a different light, and they *recognize* (וַיֵּדְעוּ) the need to conceal their private parts. The *Sforno*, therefore, to a certain extent, reflects the *Rambam's* comments in the *Guide*.

8. מִתְהַלֵּךְ בַּגָּן לְרוּחַ הַיּוֹם — *Moving about (manifesting itself) in the garden in the wind of the day.* God's will is supreme; naught can control it. There can also be no aimless movement on His part. Hence the *Sforno* interprets this difficult verse as follows: God's movements in the garden were with purpose, motivated by His will, just as they were during the six days of Creation. However, when Adam and Eve sinned, He paused in His activities and addressed Himself to them.

וַיִּתְחַבֵּא — *And he hid.* Although man had sinned, still this noble creation of God is sensitive to the requirements of modesty in the presence of God. This sensitivity is also underscored in verse 10 (see the *Sforno's* comment there).

9. אַיֶּכָּה — *Where are you?* God is not asking Adam where he is. All is known to Him. Rather He is asking Adam to explain the reason for his strange, new behavior. By so

אֱלֹהִים לָאִשָּׁה מַה־זֹּאת עָשִׂית וַתֹּאמֶר הָאִשָּׁה הַנָּחָשׁ הִשִּׁיאַנִי וָאֹכֵל׃
יד וַיֹּאמֶר יהוה אֱלֹהִים ׀ אֶל־הַנָּחָשׁ כִּי עָשִׂיתָ זֹּאת אָרוּר אַתָּה מִכָּל־הַבְּהֵמָה
טו וּמִכֹּל חַיַּת הַשָּׂדֶה עַל־גְּחֹנְךָ תֵלֵךְ וְעָפָר תֹּאכַל כָּל־יְמֵי חַיֶּיךָ׃ וְאֵיבָה ׀
אָשִׁית בֵּינְךָ וּבֵין הָאִשָּׁה וּבֵין זַרְעֲךָ וּבֵין זַרְעָהּ הוּא יְשׁוּפְךָ רֹאשׁ וְאַתָּה

---

which would have been proper for him, as David did, when he said to Nathan (the prophet), 'חָטָאתִי, *I sinned*' (*II Samuel* 12:13).

13. מַה זֹּאת עָשִׂית — *What is this that you have done?* He said this to urge her also toward repentance, *For He does not desire that (the wicked) die but rather that he should return* (based on expressions in *Ezekiel* 18:23 and 32).

14. אָרוּר אַתָּה מִכָּל — *Accursed are you beyond all.* (The serpent) would attain his desires and needs with pain and less pleasure than all other living creatures, as our Sages say, 'Have you ever seen a beast or bird with a craft, yet they are sustained without anxiety' (*Kiddushin* 82a), and this He explains, saying . . .

עַל גְּחֹנְךָ תֵּלֵךְ — *Upon your belly shall you go.* You will attain your food through suffering, as our Sages say, 'Because I have acted evilly and destroyed my livelihood' (ibid.), and (they have also stated), 'What labors Adam had to carry out before he obtained bread to eat' (*Berachos* 58a).

וְעָפָר תֹּאכַל — *And dust shall you eat.* You will no longer attain the enjoyment of food, drink and sexual congress, that you experienced before the sin. This also happened to the people of Israel when they sinned, as our Sages say, '(The cessation of) purity has removed taste and fragrance (from the fruits) and (the cessation of) tithes has removed the fatness of corn' (*Sotah* 49a).

15. וְאֵיבָה אָשִׁית — *And I will put enmity.* Woman will be abhorrent in the (mind's) eye of one's imagination, even her own, as our Sages say: 'A woman (is like) a pitcher full of filth and her mouth is full of blood' (*Shabbos* 152a). This will be so among males and females (alike).

וּבֵין זַרְעֲךָ וּבֵין זַרְעָהּ — *And between your offspring and her offspring.* This (enmity) will not be between Adam and Eve alone.

הוּא יְשׁוּפְךָ רֹאשׁ — *He will pound your head.* The power of imagination will diminish pleasure at the very outset of its attainment, due to (man's) mental image and apprehension of harm (resulting from) the quality, quantity and (arrangement) procedure of his pleasure.

NOTES

doing he will hopefully be led to repent. Unfortunately, Adam blames both Eve and God instead of confessing his guilt and repenting.

14. אָרוּר אַתָּה מִכָּל — *Accursed are you beyond all.* Our Sages were of the opinion that unlike man, all creatures sustain themselves without undue hardship. The curse of the serpent is that he, unlike other creatures, will attain his needs with pain, as a punishment for his sin. Since the *Sforno* interprets the serpent figuratively, as the evil inclination within man, he quotes the saying of our Sages regarding the difficulties of man in obtaining his bread. Apparently, he is linking the cause of man's suffering in finding his sustenance, as do the Sages, with his spiritual shortcomings which in turn are caused by his succumbing to the blandishments of the serpent — i.e., the evil inclination.

15. וְאֵיבָה אָשִׁית — *And I will put enmity.* The *Sforno*, apparently, interprets this enmity as referring to the relationship of Adam and Eve *after* the sin. Adam's attitude toward his wife

טז תְּשׁוּפֶנּוּ עָקֵב: אֶל־הָאִשָּׁה אָמַר הַרְבָּה אַרְבֶּה עִצְּבוֹנֵךְ וְהֵרֹנֵךְ
יז בְּעֶצֶב תֵּלְדִי בָנִים וְאֶל־אִישֵׁךְ תְּשׁוּקָתֵךְ וְהוּא יִמְשָׁל־בָּךְ: וּלְאָדָם
אָמַר כִּי־שָׁמַעְתָּ לְקוֹל אִשְׁתֶּךָ וַתֹּאכַל מִן־הָעֵץ אֲשֶׁר צִוִּיתִיךָ לֵאמֹר לֹא

וְאַתָּה תְּשׁוּפֶנּוּ עָקֵב — *And you will bruise his heel* . . . for the lustful (person) whose (lust) will overpower him, will bring harm (to himself) at the culmination of his pleasure.

16. הַרְבָּה אַרְבֶּה עִצְּבוֹנֵךְ — *I will greatly increase your suffering* . . . (This refers to) menstrual blood, which is called נִדַּת דּוֹתָהּ, *the impurity of her sickness* (*Leviticus* 12:2), for (during this period) she is, כָּל הַיּוֹם דָּוָה, *faint all the day* (*Lamentations* 1:13).

וְהֵרֹנֵךְ — *And your childbearing.* This was the reverse of their condition prior to the sin, as our Sages tell us, 'On the very same day they were created, they cohabited and (she) gave birth' (*Bereishis Rabbah* 22:3), and so it shall be in the future, as our Sages say, 'In the future a woman will give birth daily' (*Shabbos* 30b), for at that time Israel will find favor with God, the Blessed One, as Adam originally did before he sinned.

בְּעֶצֶב תֵּלְדִי בָנִים — *In pain shall you bear children.* You will rear them with greater pain (trouble) than other living creatures. The word לֵידָה, *to bear*, is (also) used to denote 'raising' (children), as it says, חֲמֵשֶׁת בְּנֵי מִיכַל בַּת שָׁאוּל אֲשֶׁר יָלְדָה לְעַדְרִיאֵל בֶּן בַּרְזִלַּי הַמְּחֹלָתִי, *the five sons of Michal, the daughter of Saul, whom she bore to Adriel the son of Barzillai the Meholti* (*II Samuel* 21:8).

17. כִּי שָׁמַעְתָּ לְקוֹל אִשְׁתֶּךָ — *Because you listened to the voice of your wife* . . . when she imputed to God falsehood and jealousy.

וַתֹּאכַל מִן הָעֵץ — *And ate of the tree.* You disobeyed and therefore deserve the death penalty, since you were warned. (Yet) you listened to her voice and accepted her opinion that God misled you.

NOTES

had changed, and hers toward him as well. The sin created tension, not only between the first man and woman, but left a legacy for future generations as well.

הוּא יְשׁוּפְךָ רֹאשׁ וְאַתָּה תְּשׁוּפֶנּוּ עָקֵב — *He will pound your head and you will bruise his heel.* The *Sforno*, consistent with his interpretation of the serpent as the evil inclination, interprets the word רֹאשׁ as *beginning* and עָקֵב as *end*. God is depicting man's ongoing confrontation with his יֵצֶר (inclination-prompter). Even at the *beginning*, before he gives in to his desires and passions, he anticipates the problems that may beset him, thereby diminishing his intensity of pleasure. And afterward, at the *end*, his indulgence may well bring him harm.

16. הַרְבָּה אַרְבֶּה עִצְּבוֹנֵךְ . . . בְּעֶצֶב תֵּלְדִי בָנִים — *I will greatly increase your suffering* . . . *In pain shall you bear children.* The *Sforno* follows the interpretation of our Sages (*Erubin* 100b) regarding the discomfort of woman's menstrual periods, but whereas the Talmud applies the difficulties associated with rearing children to the word עִצְּבוֹנֵךְ, *your suffering*, the *Sforno* applies the area of childraising to the phrase בְּעֶצֶב תֵּלְדִי, consistent with his interpretation in various places (see 25:2) that the word לֵידָה denotes rearing of children, as well as its common meaning of bearing and giving birth to a child.

17. כִּי שָׁמַעְתָּ לְקוֹל אִשְׁתֶּךָ וַתֹּאכַל מִן הָעֵץ — *Because you listened to the voice of your wife and ate of the tree.* God chastises Adam for two transgressions. First, for accepting Eve's false claim that God's intention in prohibiting the fruit of the tree of knowledge was to prevent mankind from attaining added knowledge, thereby becoming as *Elohim*. Sec-

תֹּאכַל מִמֶּנּוּ אֲרוּרָה הָאֲדָמָה בַּעֲבוּרֶךָ בְּעִצָּבוֹן תֹּאכֲלֶנָּה כֹּל יְמֵי חַיֶּיךָ׃
יח־יט וְקוֹץ וְדַרְדַּר תַּצְמִיחַ לָךְ וְאָכַלְתָּ אֶת־עֵשֶׂב הַשָּׂדֶה׃ בְּזֵעַת אַפֶּיךָ תֹּאכַל
לֶחֶם עַד שׁוּבְךָ אֶל־הָאֲדָמָה כִּי מִמֶּנָּה לֻקָּחְתָּ כִּי־עָפָר אַתָּה וְאֶל־עָפָר
כ־כא תָּשׁוּב׃ וַיִּקְרָא הָאָדָם שֵׁם אִשְׁתּוֹ חַוָּה כִּי הִוא הָיְתָה אֵם כָּל־חָי׃ וַיַּעַשׂ יהוה
אֱלֹהִים לְאָדָם וּלְאִשְׁתּוֹ כָּתְנוֹת עוֹר וַיַּלְבִּשֵׁם׃
רביעי כב וַיֹּאמֶר | יהוה אֱלֹהִים הֵן הָאָדָם הָיָה כְּאַחַד מִמֶּנּוּ לָדַעַת טוֹב וָרָע וְעַתָּה

אֲרוּרָה הָאֲדָמָה — *Accursed is the ground.* It will no longer yield up its strength (crop) to you without toil; and because you were disobedient and transgressed His command . . .

19. וְאֶל עָפָר תָּשׁוּב — *And to dust shall you return . . .* as I forewarned you when I commanded and said, *For on the day you eat of it, you shall surely die* (2:17), i.e., you will become mortal (and *ultimately* die).

20. חַוָּה — *Eve.* Because of her sin, she must sustain (nurture) and raise her children.

כִּי הִיא הָיְתָה אֵם כָּל חָי — *Because she had become the mother of all the living.* Although other women will also be mothers, nonetheless she alone is called by this name, because she was the first of them all.

21. וַיַּעַשׂ . . . כָּתְנוֹת עוֹר — *Made . . . garments of skin . . .* without the efforts of man, as it will come to pass in the future, as our Sages say, *'Eretz Yisrael* will bring forth cakes and woolen garments, in the future' (*Shabbos* 30b).

וַיַּלְבִּשֵׁם — *And He clothed them.* He did not drive them out naked, lest they dress themselves later through their own efforts and thereby think they had an added attainment (of knowledge).

22. כְּאַחַד מִמֶּנּוּ לָדַעַת טוֹב וָרָע — *As one of us to know good and evil.* He knows good and evil since he is formed in our (the Divine) image. Should he also be immortal, he will pursue (earthly) pleasures all his days and cast aside all intelligent (spiritual) concepts and good deeds, and never attain that spiritual bliss which God intended for him in making him in His image and likeness.

NOTES

ond, for the overt act of eating the fruit of the prohibited tree. This eliminates any question of redundancy in this verse.

19. וְאֶל עָפָר תָּשׁוּב — *And to dust shall you return.* The punishment of death, if man were to eat of the tree, was never meant to be immediate. Rather, the consequence of this act was that man would now become a mortal being, destined eventually and inevitably to die.

20. חַוָּה — *Eve.* The word חַיָּה, in connection with a person's relationship to a child, means to sustain, nurture — *give life* — to the dependent infant. Regarding Yocheved and Miriam, the Torah says וַתְּחַיֶּיןָ, *they 'gave life to,'* (i.e., *they sustained) the infants (Exodus* 1:17). *Rashi* comments on that verse, 'they provided them with water and food.' The *Sforno* interprets Eve's name accordingly — חַוָּה derived from חַיָּה — her task now being to sustain, nurture and raise her children.

21. וַיַּלְבִּישֵׁם — *And He clothed them.* Although God's clothing of Adam and Eve is considered by our Sages as an act of *chesed* (kindness) on His part, the *Sforno* gives an additional reason. Since they had eaten of the tree of knowledge they might well delude themselves into thinking, were they to clothe themselves on their own, that they had indeed gained a new, higher status of wisdom as the serpent had suggested. Therefore God clothed them before they left the garden, to dispel such an assumption.

כג | פֶּן־יִשְׁלַח יָדוֹ וְלָקַח גַּם מֵעֵץ הַחַיִּים וְאָכַל וָחַי לְעֹלָם: וַיְשַׁלְּחֵהוּ יְהוָה
כד אֱלֹהִים מִגַּן־עֵדֶן לַעֲבֹד אֶת־הָאֲדָמָה אֲשֶׁר לֻקַּח מִשָּׁם: וַיְגָרֶשׁ אֶת־הָאָדָם
וַיַּשְׁכֵּן מִקֶּדֶם לְגַן־עֵדֶן אֶת־הַכְּרֻבִים וְאֵת לַהַט הַחֶרֶב הַמִּתְהַפֶּכֶת לִשְׁמֹר
ד א אֶת־דֶּרֶךְ עֵץ הַחַיִּים: וְהָאָדָם יָדַע אֶת־חַוָּה אִשְׁתּוֹ וַתַּהַר וַתֵּלֶד
ב אֶת־קַיִן וַתֹּאמֶר קָנִיתִי אִישׁ אֶת־יְהוָה: וַתֹּסֶף לָלֶדֶת אֶת־אָחִיו אֶת־הָבֶל
ג וַיְהִי־הֶבֶל רֹעֵה צֹאן וְקַיִן הָיָה עֹבֵד אֲדָמָה: וַיְהִי מִקֵּץ יָמִים וַיָּבֵא קַיִן מִפְּרִי

---

23. וַיְשַׁלְּחֵהוּ — *And He sent him forth.* He commanded them to leave from there (the garden), similar to, לְמַהֵר לְשַׁלְּחָם מִן הָאָרֶץ, *to send them out of the land in haste* (*Exodus* 12:33).

הָאֲדָמָה אֲשֶׁר לֻקַּח מִשָּׁם — *The soil from which he was taken* . . . for that place and its atmosphere was suitable to (man's) temperament, food (source) and his needs, more so than other parts of the earth.

24. וַיְגָרֶשׁ אֶת הָאָדָם — *And He drove out the man* . . . that neither he nor his descendants should ever return there.

וַיַּשְׁכֵּן — *And He stationed* . . . before they had departed.

לִשְׁמֹר אֶת דֶּרֶךְ עֵץ הַחַיִּים — *To guard the way to the tree of life* . . . so they should not detour to the tree of life and partake of it on their way out.

IV

2. וַיְהִי הֶבֶל רֹעֵה צֹאן — *And Abel became a shepherd.* This was a more skilled occupation than that of agriculture.

וְקַיִן הָיָה עֹבֵד אֲדָמָה — *And Cain became a tiller of the ground* . . . therefore, each brought (an offering to God) from that which came to his hand.

NOTES

22-23. כְּאַחַד מִמֶּנּוּ . . . וַיְשַׁלְּחֵהוּ — *As one of us . . . and He sent him forth.* Man was granted freedom of choice. In that sense he is 'as one of us' (i.e., Divine beings), still he has physical appetites and desires. Were he to live forever he would pursue his bodily pleasures and reject the spiritual blessings which God intended for him. However, his mortality encourages him to attain knowledge and spiritual perfection in the brief time allotted to him. That is why God sends them out of the garden and guards the key to the tree of life, lest they partake of it *prior* to their departure (see verse 24).

23. הָאֲדָמָה אֲשֶׁר לֻקַּח מִשָּׁם — *The soil from which he was taken.* The *Sforno* (2:7,8) explains that man was formed from the earth outside the garden and then placed therein. Now, he is sent back to the place of his origin for his own benefit. Even as God punishes him He is compassionate, and places him in an environment to which he can readily adjust.

IV

2. וַיְהִי הֶבֶל רֹעֵה צֹאן וְקַיִן הָיָה עֹבֵד אֲדָמָה — *And Abel became a shepherd and Cain became a tiller of the ground.* Since Cain was older than Abel, his occupation should have been mentioned first. The reason Abel's occupation as a shepherd is given precedence is explained by the *Sforno* as reflecting its relative importance, compared to agriculture. The tending of sheep, cattle and animals in general is established at this early stage as a preferred occupation for those who are concerned with spiritual excellence and reaching out to God. The patriarchs, Moshe, David and many other great men of our people were shepherds. Apparently it is a way of life that frees man to come closer to God and meditate on His ways, attaining eventually heightened knowledge of Him. The expression used by the *Sforno,* מְלֶאכֶת חָכְמָה, *skilled occupation,* literally, *occupation of wisdom,* may well imply not only the skill required, but the higher wisdom eventually

ד הָאֲדָמָה מִנְחָה לַיהוָה: וְהֶבֶל הֵבִיא גַם־הוּא מִבְּכֹרוֹת צֹאנוֹ וּמֵחֶלְבֵהֶן וַיִּשַׁע
ה יהוה אֶל־הֶבֶל וְאֶל־מִנְחָתוֹ: וְאֶל־קַיִן וְאֶל־מִנְחָתוֹ לֹא שָׁעָה וַיִּחַר לְקַיִן
ו מְאֹד וַיִּפְּלוּ פָּנָיו: וַיֹּאמֶר יהוה אֶל־קָיִן לָמָּה חָרָה לָךְ וְלָמָּה נָפְלוּ פָנֶיךָ:
ז הֲלוֹא אִם־תֵּיטִיב שְׂאֵת וְאִם לֹא תֵיטִיב לַפֶּתַח חַטָּאת רֹבֵץ וְאֵלֶיךָ

---

4. אֶל הֶבֶל וְאֶל מִנְחָתוֹ — *To Abel and to his offering.* Abel, himself, was pleasing and acceptable, and his offering was also pleasing, for it came from a species worthy to be accepted.

5. וְאֶל קַיִן וְאֶל מִנְחָתוֹ לֹא שָׁעָה — *But to Cain and to his offering He did not turn.* He did not turn to Cain, himself, who was not pleasing, nor to the offering, which also was not worthy to be accepted (by God).

וַיִּחַר לְקַיִן מְאֹד — *And Cain was very annoyed (wroth)* ... jealous of his brother (whose offering) was accepted (by God).

וַיִּפְּלוּ פָּנָיו — *And his countenance fell* ... in shame, for God had shamed him by not accepting it (his offering).

6. לָמָּה חָרָה לָךְ — *Why are you annoyed (angry).* Why are you jealous of your brother, and concerned that I accepted his offering with good will? This was not an arbitrary decision nor an unjust one.

וְלָמָּה נָפְלוּ פָנֶיךָ — *And why has your countenance fallen?* When a fault can be remedied it is not proper to grieve over what has passed, but rather to try to amend and improve (matters) for the future.

7. הֲלוֹא אִם תֵּיטִיב — *Surely, if you improve (yourself).* (Improve) yourself, and strive that you should also be acceptable (to God).

שְׂאֵת — *You will be lifted.* Exalted heights and elevated position await you, and will be yours.

וְאִם לֹא תֵיטִיב לַפֶּתַח חַטָּאת רֹבֵץ — *But if you will not improve yourself, sin rests at the door.* Then sin also awaits you, and you will add iniquity to your sins, for such is the way of the evil inclination.

NOTES

attained.

The expression מִן הַבָּא בְיָדוֹ, *from that which came to his hand,* is taken by the *Sforno* from 32:14. It implies that which one possesses and can legitimately give as a gift or offering.

4. אֶל הֶבֶל וְאֶל מִנְחָתוֹ — *To Abel and to his offering.* Since the Torah mentions both the name of the one who brings the sacrifice, as well as his offering, the implication is that God examined the character and motivation of the person bringing the sacrifice, not only the animal or produce brought. Abel measured up well on both counts, while Cain failed to do so on both.

5-6. וַיִּחַר לְקַיִן מְאֹד וַיִּפְּלוּ פָּנָיו ... לָמָּה חָרָה לָךְ וְלָמָּה נָפְלוּ פָנֶיךָ — *And Cain was very annoyed (wroth) and his countenance fell ... Why are you annoyed (angry) and why has your countenance fallen?* The *Sforno* interprets the phrase וַיִּחַר, *he was wroth,* as referring to Cain's jealousy of his brother, while וַיִּפְּלוּ פָּנָיו *(his countenance fell)* implies shame. It therefore follows that God's questions to Cain are twofold. You have no reason to be jealous since My decision was a just one, and if you are ashamed, let that be channeled into the positive act of self-improvement rather than dwelling on the failure of the past.

7. ... וְאִם לֹא תֵיטִיב — *But if you will not improve yourself* ... The expression used by the *Sforno* — 'for such is the way of the evil inclination' — refers to the saying of our Sages (*Shabbos* 105b) regarding the יֵצֶר (the evil tempter): 'Today he tells you to do thus and

ח תְּשׁוּקָתוֹ וְאַתָּה תִּמְשָׁל־בּוֹ: וַיֹּאמֶר קַיִן אֶל־הֶבֶל אָחִיו וַיְהִי בִּהְיוֹתָם
ט בַּשָּׂדֶה וַיָּקָם קַיִן אֶל־הֶבֶל אָחִיו וַיַּהַרְגֵהוּ: וַיֹּאמֶר יהוה אֶל־קַיִן אֵי הֶבֶל
י אָחִיךָ וַיֹּאמֶר לֹא יָדַעְתִּי הֲשֹׁמֵר אָחִי אָנֹכִי: וַיֹּאמֶר מֶה עָשִׂיתָ קוֹל דְּמֵי

וְאֵלֶיךָ תְּשׁוּקָתוֹ — *Its desire is toward you.* If you turn to him (the evil inclination) and succumb to your evil desires, as our Sages say, יִצְרוֹ שֶׁל אָדָם מִתְגַּבֵּר עָלָיו בְּכׇל יוֹם, *The evil inclination within man grows stronger from day to day (Succah* 52a).

וְאַתָּה תִּמְשָׁל בּוֹ — *Yet you can conquer it.* You can overpower it (the evil inclination) through the Divine Image (within you) as our Sages say (ibid.), וְאִלְמָלֵא הקב״ה עוֹזְרוֹ אֵינוֹ יָכוֹל לוֹ שֶׁנֶּאֱמַר: ה׳ לֹא יַעַזְבֶנּוּ בְיָדוֹ, *Were it not that the Holy One, Blessed is He, helps him, he would not be able to withstand it, as it says: 'HASHEM will not leave him in his hand' (Psalms* 37:33).

8. וַיֹּאמֶר קַיִן אֶל הֶבֶל אָחִיו — *Cain spoke with his brother Abel.* (He told him) how annoyed he was, and how his countenance fell, because of his brother.

וַיְהִי בִּהְיוֹתָם בַּשָּׂדֶה — *And it happened when they were in the field* . . . away from the presence of their father and mother.

וַיָּקָם קַיִן — *That Cain rose up* . . . without any prior argument, as (we find), וְאָרַב לוֹ וְקָם עָלָיו, *And lie in wait for him, and rise up against him (Deut.* 19:11).

9. אֵי הֶבֶל אָחִיךָ — *Where is Abel your brother?* Where did you bury him? (God) asked this, so that he (Cain) might repent, for He does not desire the death (of the wicked).

לֹא יָדַעְתִּי — *I do not know.* He thought that the question meant 'what happened to him (Abel)?' Since Cain had not sought out God to attain prophecy or acceptance, as he had originally done, he thought (was convinced) that God, the Blessed One, was not aware of (all) human details, except of those who cleaved to Him.

NOTES

tomorrow thus . . . until he eventually tells you to become an idolater!' The Almighty cautions Cain, and through him all mankind, that the evil tempter lies in wait, 'crouching at the door,' ready to capitalize on man's weakness and vulnerability. Yet man is in reality stronger, and can conquer the יֵצֶר because he possesses the strength of the Divine image within him. The *Sforno* seems to interpret the saying of our Sages (*Succah* 52a), 'and were it not for the Holy One, Blessed is He,' as referring not only to God Himself, but to the Divine image within man as well.

8. וַיֹּאמֶר קַיִן אֶל הֶבֶל אָחִיו – *Cain spoke with his brother Abel.* The Torah does not tell us what Cain said. The *Sforno* surmises it was the baring of his heart, sharing his deep hurt with Abel.

וַיְהִי בִּהְיוֹתָם בַּשָּׂדֶה – *And it happened when they were in the field.* Although Cain is prepared to harm his brother, he is not so callous and cruel as to do so in the presence of his parents!

וַיָּקָם קַיִן – *That Cain rose up.* The *Sforno* is drawing a parallel from the word וַיָּקָם, *rose up,* to קָם, *rise up,* where the Torah explicitly states that one ambushed his victim without any warning.

9. אֵי הֶבֶל אָחִיךָ – *Where is Abel your brother?* Since God knows all and all is revealed to Him, the question posed to Cain, 'Where is your brother?' cannot be interpreted literally. It is only a subtle opening given to Cain, to confess and repent.

לֹא יָדַעְתִּי – *I do not know.* Cain is convinced that God is close to those who are close to Him. As such His providence is extended to them alone, not to those who have distanced themselves from Him. It therefore follows that God is not concerned or aware of the detailed actions of those who transgress. The truth

יא אָחִיךָ צֹעֲקִים אֵלַי מִן־הָאֲדָמָה: וְעַתָּה אָרוּר אָתָּה מִן־הָאֲדָמָה אֲשֶׁר
יב פָּצְתָה אֶת־פִּיהָ לָקַחַת אֶת־דְּמֵי אָחִיךָ מִיָּדֶךָ: כִּי תַעֲבֹד אֶת־הָאֲדָמָה
יג לֹא־תֹסֵף תֵּת־כֹּחָהּ לָךְ נָע וָנָד תִּהְיֶה בָאָרֶץ: וַיֹּאמֶר קַיִן אֶל־יהוה גָּדוֹל
יד עֲוֹנִי מִנְּשֹׂא: הֵן גֵּרַשְׁתָּ אֹתִי הַיּוֹם מֵעַל פְּנֵי הָאֲדָמָה וּמִפָּנֶיךָ אֶסָּתֵר וְהָיִיתִי
טו נָע וָנָד בָּאָרֶץ וְהָיָה כָל־מֹצְאִי יַהַרְגֵנִי: וַיֹּאמֶר לוֹ יהוה לָכֵן כָּל־הֹרֵג קַיִן

---

11. אָרוּר אָתָּה מִן הָאֲדָמָה — *You are cursed more than the ground* . . . cursed and deprived of the earth's goodness.

אֲשֶׁר פָּצְתָה אֶת פִּיהָ — *Which opened wide its mouth.* You used the earth to cover (the traces) of the murder of your brother; as punishment you will be unable to use (its strength) as you did heretofore, for your life's needs. (The Torah) does not find it necessary to describe the punishment of the murderer, for the law is clearly defined in nature itself, regarding anyone who inflicts injury, that, כַּאֲשֶׁר עָשָׂה כֵּן יֵעָשֶׂה לוֹ, *as he has done, so shall it be done to him (Leviticus* 24:19).

13. גָּדוֹל עֲוֹנִי מִנְּשֹׂא — *My iniquity is too great to be borne.* After (Cain) realized that God, the Blessed One, observes absolutely every (human) detail, he thought that (God) would surely know that he is (really) not repenting his sin, since his regret was due only to (the fear) of punishment, and even then, only after God entreated him to repent, which he (at first) refused (to do). Therefore, he felt that there was no hope for (true) repentance of his sin which would atone and protect him from the present punishment, as we find by Saul in the episode of Amalek, when he said to Samuel, חָטָאתִי, *I sinned (I Samuel* 15:24), (only) after Samuel pleaded and entreated him to repent of his sin, (and so) was punished, as it says, וַיִּמְאָסְךָ מִמֶּלֶךְ, *He has rejected you as king (ibid. 23).*

14. וְהָיָה כָל מֹצְאִי יַהַרְגֵנִי — *Whoever meets me will kill me* . . . hence, my punishment will be greater than what You decreed.

NOTES

however is that the Almighty oversees, supervises and knows the actions of every human being. This is one of the major lessons taught to us through this episode.

11. אָרוּר אָתָּה מִן הָאֲדָמָה — *You are cursed more than the ground.* The concept of 'curse' is one of diminishment and lack, just as that of 'blessing' (בְּרָכָה) implies increase and plenty. Because Cain used and abused the earth to conceal his victim, it will no longer be a blessing to him but will withhold its strength from him, thereby depriving Cain of his sustenance. This is what is meant by אָרוּר אָתָּה, *you will be cursed* — not *you* as a person, but your productive relationship to the earth will now be diminished.

אֲשֶׁר פָּצְתָה אֶת פִּיהָ — *Which opened wide its mouth.* Cain murdered his brother and then used the earth to conceal his crime. For the initial crime the Torah finds no need to spell out his punishment. Since the dawn of human history, the enormity of a crime such as murder would perforce bring with it consequences commensurate with the crime — *as he has done so shall it be done to him.* As for the misuse of the earth by Cain, who had heretofore drawn his sustenance from it, God utters the phrase אָרוּר, *cursed.*

13. גָּדוֹל עֲוֹנִי מִנְּשֹׂא — *My iniquity is too great to be borne.* According to *Rashi*, this is a question, 'Is my iniquity too great to bear?' However, the *Sforno* interprets Cain's words as a statement, not a question. Since God had admonished and cautioned him before his murderous act (verse 7) to no avail, then his repentance will surely not atone for his sin nor protect him from punishment. Were he to have repented on his own there would have been hope, but now that he does so only because of God's importuning, as Saul did after Samuel pleaded and pressured him to repent, it is meaningless. In both cases it is too late to avert the punishment.

טו שִׁבְעָתַיִם יֻקָּם וַיָּשֶׂם יְהוָה לְקַיִן אוֹת לְבִלְתִּי הַכּוֹת־אֹתוֹ כָּל־מֹצְאוֹ: וַיֵּצֵא
יז קַיִן מִלִּפְנֵי יְהוָה וַיֵּשֶׁב בְּאֶרֶץ־נוֹד קִדְמַת־עֵדֶן: וַיֵּדַע קַיִן אֶת־אִשְׁתּוֹ וַתַּהַר
יח וַתֵּלֶד אֶת־חֲנוֹךְ וַיְהִי בֹּנֶה עִיר וַיִּקְרָא שֵׁם הָעִיר כְּשֵׁם בְּנוֹ חֲנוֹךְ: וַיִּוָּלֵד
לַחֲנוֹךְ אֶת־עִירָד וְעִירָד יָלַד אֶת־מְחוּיָאֵל וּמְחִיָּיאֵל יָלַד אֶת־מְתוּשָׁאֵל
חמישי יט וּמְתוּשָׁאֵל יָלַד אֶת־לָמֶךְ: וַיִּקַּח־לוֹ לֶמֶךְ שְׁתֵּי נָשִׁים שֵׁם הָאַחַת עָדָה וְשֵׁם
כ־כא הַשֵּׁנִית צִלָּה: וַתֵּלֶד עָדָה אֶת־יָבָל הוּא הָיָה אֲבִי יֹשֵׁב אֹהֶל וּמִקְנֶה: וְשֵׁם
כב אָחִיו יוּבָל הוּא הָיָה אֲבִי כָּל־תֹּפֵשׂ כִּנּוֹר וְעוּגָב: וְצִלָּה גַם־הִוא יָלְדָה
אֶת־תּוּבַל קַיִן לֹטֵשׁ כָּל־חֹרֵשׁ נְחֹשֶׁת וּבַרְזֶל וַאֲחוֹת תּוּבַל־קַיִן נַעֲמָה:
כג וַיֹּאמֶר לֶמֶךְ לְנָשָׁיו עָדָה וְצִלָּה שְׁמַעַן קוֹלִי נְשֵׁי לֶמֶךְ הַאְזֵנָּה אִמְרָתִי כִּי
כד אִישׁ הָרַגְתִּי לְפִצְעִי וְיֶלֶד לְחַבֻּרָתִי: כִּי שִׁבְעָתַיִם יֻקַּם־קָיִן וְלֶמֶךְ שִׁבְעִים

---

15. כָּל הֹרֵג קַיִן שִׁבְעָתַיִם יֻקָּם — *Whoever slays Cain, twice sevenfold shall he be avenged.* I (i.e., Hashem) say to whoever is to kill Cain, 'I decree that the revenge for his sin is "twice sevenfold." ' Whoever is (only) 'prepared to kill' is (also) referred to as a 'killer,' as it says, וְאֶפְרַיִם לְהוֹצִיא אֶל הֹרֵג בָּנָיו, *Ephraim must bring out his children to slayers (Hosea* 9:13), and the word שִׁבְעָתַיִם implies seven times doubled, as we find וְנִמְצָא יְשַׁלֵּם שִׁבְעָתָיִם, *If caught he must pay twice sevenfold (Proverbs* 6:31). The decree therefore was that for this murder, where the blood of his brother represented one half or one third of mankind, the revenge (punishment) for the murderer shall be 'twice sevenfold,' in such a manner that for six generations (Cain) will be a 'vagrant and wanderer,' (which is) a bad life equal to death, or even more severe, as it says, אַל תַּהַרְגֵם פֶּן יִשְׁכְּחוּ עַמִּי הֲנִיעֵמוֹ בְחֵילְךָ, *Do not kill them lest my people be unmindful; with Your power make wanderers of them (Psalms* 59:12). In the end, he (Cain) will be killed, in the seventh generation, as (indeed) happened through Lemech, as is brought in traditional sources (*Tanchuma* 10).

23. שְׁמַעַן קוֹלִי נְשֵׁי לֶמֶךְ — *Hear my voice, wives of Lemech . . .* as I cry out in sorrow.

אִמְרָתִי — *My speech.* As I relate my pain.

הָרַגְתִּי לְפִצְעִי — *A man have I slain by my wound.* I actually wounded myself, since the victim was my father.

וְיֶלֶד לְחַבֻּרָתִי — *And a child by my bruise.* I actually bruised myself, since the victim was my son.

24. וְלֶמֶךְ שִׁבְעִים וְשִׁבְעָה — *Then Lemech at seventy-seven.* The pain that I will suffer for these (deaths) all my days will be greater than the pain experienced by

NOTES

15. כָּל הֹרֵג קַיִן שִׁבְעָתַיִם יֻקָּם — *Whoever slays Cain, twice sevenfold shall be avenged.* The punishment of wandering and exile is greater than the eventual one of death. Therefore God cautions anyone who may plan to execute Cain to refrain from doing so, since God's decree of banishment and wandering is a far more severe punishment, justified by the enormity of this murder of Abel who represented one half of humankind, if you consider their generation, or one third if you also include Adam. After seven generations the final stage of Cain's punishment will occur, namely, his death at the hands of Lemech.

23. שְׁמַעַן קוֹלִי נְשֵׁי לֶמֶךְ . . . אִמְרָתִי — *Hear my voice, wives of Lemech . . . My speech.* Two expressions are used by Lemech; *my voice* and *my speech.* The first refers to his cry of sorrow while the second refers to his tale of woe.

כה וְשִׁבְעָה: וַיֵּדַע אָדָם עוֹד אֶת־אִשְׁתּוֹ וַתֵּלֶד בֵּן וַתִּקְרָא אֶת־שְׁמוֹ שֵׁת כִּי
כו שָׁת־לִי אֱלֹהִים זֶרַע אַחֵר תַּחַת הֶבֶל כִּי הֲרָגוֹ קָיִן: וּלְשֵׁת גַּם־הוּא יֻלַּד־בֵּן
ה ששי א וַיִּקְרָא אֶת־שְׁמוֹ אֱנוֹשׁ אָז הוּחַל לִקְרֹא בְּשֵׁם יהוה: זֶה
סֵפֶר תּוֹלְדֹת אָדָם בְּיוֹם בְּרֹא אֱלֹהִים אָדָם בִּדְמוּת אֱלֹהִים עָשָׂה אֹתוֹ:
ב זָכָר וּנְקֵבָה בְּרָאָם וַיְבָרֶךְ אֹתָם וַיִּקְרָא אֶת־שְׁמָם אָדָם בְּיוֹם הִבָּרְאָם:
ג וַיְחִי אָדָם שְׁלֹשִׁים וּמְאַת שָׁנָה וַיּוֹלֶד בִּדְמוּתוֹ כְּצַלְמוֹ וַיִּקְרָא אֶת־שְׁמוֹ

Cain when he was a vagrant and a wanderer. The reason is that Lemech suffered all his days for having killed his grandfather Cain and his son Tubal-Cain, as we learn from our traditional sources (ibid.).

26. אָז הוּחַל לִקְרֹא בְּשֵׁם ה׳ — *Then they began to publicly expound the name of* H*ASHEM*. The righteous of the generation began to expound the name of *HASHEM* to the public, similar to, וַיִּקְרָא שָׁם בְּשֵׁם ה׳ אֵל עוֹלָם, *And called there in the name of* H*ASHEM the everlasting God* (21:33). This was necessary to refute the beliefs of the idolaters, who then began (to spread their heresy) as our Sages tell us (*Shabbos* 188b).

V

1. זֶה סֵפֶר תּוֹלְדֹת אָדָם — *This is the book of the descendants of man.* This is the history of the events which befell the human race.

בִּדְמוּת אֱלֹהִים עָשָׂה אֹתוֹ — *He made him in the likeness of G-d* ... as one who has freedom of choice. Therefore when (future) generations angered G-d, the Blessed One, (by their sins), He punished them.

3. וַיּוֹלֶד בִּדְמוּתוֹ כְּצַלְמוֹ — *He begot in his likeness and his image.* He (Seth) was more righteous than those who preceded him (i.e., Cain and Abel), for even Abel did not bring a sacrifice until Cain did so first.

NOTES

According to tradition, Lemech killed Cain (accidentally) as well as his own son, Tubal-Cain (see *Rashi*).

24. וְלֶמֶךְ שִׁבְעִים וְשִׁבְעָה — *Then Lemech at seventy-seven.* Lemech bemoans the fact that he killed two relatives, one his forefather (an ancestor) and the second his own son (a descendant). His pain and regret will therefore be greater than that experienced by Cain who killed one person — his brother.

26. אָז הוּחַל לִקְרֹא בְּשֵׁם ה׳ — *Then they began to publicly expound the name of* H*ASHEM*. The word הוּחַל can be translated *began* or *profane* (from the word חוּלִין, *secular, non-sacred). Rashi,* based on the Midrash, translates *that the name of* H*ASHEM became profaned,* for idolatry had begun. The *Sforno* translates *began to proclaim the name of* H*ASHEM*. The righteous ones, observing how idolatry was developing, realized the need to counteract this rejection of God's truth by publicly expounding the name of HASHEM. This is precisely what Abraham did later, in his generation, for the same reason.

V

1. זֶה סֵפֶר תּוֹלְדֹת אָדָם — *This is the book of the descendants of man.* The word תּוֹלְדוֹת lends itself to various translations. The *Sforno* consistently interprets it as the events or 'offspring' of one's life activities. See 6:9, 25:19 and 37:2.

The Torah uses the expression סֵפֶר אָדָם, *Book of Man,* at this point in the narrative, because with the death of Abel and the eventual decimation of Cain's offspring, the human race is descended from Seth (verse 3).

3. וַיּוֹלֶד בִּדְמוּתוֹ כְּצַלְמוֹ — *He begot in his likeness and his image. Sforno* bases his contention that Seth was more righteous than his brothers on the fact that the Torah does not use the expression *in his likeness and his*

ד שֵׁת: וַיִּהְיוּ יְמֵי־אָדָם אַחֲרֵי הוֹלִידוֹ אֶת־שֵׁת שְׁמֹנֶה מֵאֹת שָׁנָה וַיּוֹלֶד בָּנִים
ה וּבָנוֹת: וַיִּהְיוּ כָּל־יְמֵי אָדָם אֲשֶׁר־חַי תְּשַׁע מֵאוֹת שָׁנָה וּשְׁלֹשִׁים שָׁנָה
ו וַיָּמֹת: וַיְחִי־שֵׁת חָמֵשׁ שָׁנִים וּמְאַת שָׁנָה וַיּוֹלֶד אֶת־
ז אֱנוֹשׁ: וַיְחִי־שֵׁת אַחֲרֵי הוֹלִידוֹ אֶת־אֱנוֹשׁ שֶׁבַע שָׁנִים וּשְׁמֹנֶה מֵאוֹת שָׁנָה
ח וַיּוֹלֶד בָּנִים וּבָנוֹת: וַיִּהְיוּ כָּל־יְמֵי־שֵׁת שְׁתֵּים עֶשְׂרֵה שָׁנָה וּתְשַׁע מֵאוֹת
ט שָׁנָה וַיָּמֹת: וַיְחִי אֱנוֹשׁ תִּשְׁעִים שָׁנָה וַיּוֹלֶד אֶת־קֵינָן:
י וַיְחִי אֱנוֹשׁ אַחֲרֵי הוֹלִידוֹ אֶת־קֵינָן חֲמֵשׁ עֶשְׂרֵה שָׁנָה וּשְׁמֹנֶה מֵאוֹת שָׁנָה
יא וַיּוֹלֶד בָּנִים וּבָנוֹת: וַיִּהְיוּ כָּל־יְמֵי אֱנוֹשׁ חָמֵשׁ שָׁנִים וּתְשַׁע מֵאוֹת שָׁנָה
יב וַיָּמֹת: וַיְחִי קֵינָן שִׁבְעִים שָׁנָה וַיּוֹלֶד אֶת־מַהֲלַלְאֵל:
יג וַיְחִי קֵינָן אַחֲרֵי הוֹלִידוֹ אֶת־מַהֲלַלְאֵל אַרְבָּעִים שָׁנָה וּשְׁמֹנֶה מֵאוֹת שָׁנָה
יד וַיּוֹלֶד בָּנִים וּבָנוֹת: וַיִּהְיוּ כָּל־יְמֵי קֵינָן עֶשֶׂר שָׁנִים וּתְשַׁע מֵאוֹת שָׁנָה
טו וַיָּמֹת: וַיְחִי מַהֲלַלְאֵל חָמֵשׁ שָׁנִים וְשִׁשִּׁים שָׁנָה וַיּוֹלֶד
טז אֶת־יָרֶד: וַיְחִי מַהֲלַלְאֵל אַחֲרֵי הוֹלִידוֹ אֶת־יֶרֶד שְׁלֹשִׁים שָׁנָה וּשְׁמֹנֶה
יז מֵאוֹת שָׁנָה וַיּוֹלֶד בָּנִים וּבָנוֹת: וַיִּהְיוּ כָּל־יְמֵי מַהֲלַלְאֵל חָמֵשׁ וְתִשְׁעִים
יח שָׁנָה וּשְׁמֹנֶה מֵאוֹת שָׁנָה וַיָּמֹת: וַיְחִי־יֶרֶד שְׁתַּיִם וְשִׁשִּׁים
יט שָׁנָה וּמְאַת שָׁנָה וַיּוֹלֶד אֶת־חֲנוֹךְ: וַיְחִי־יֶרֶד אַחֲרֵי הוֹלִידוֹ אֶת־חֲנוֹךְ שְׁמֹנֶה
כ מֵאוֹת שָׁנָה וַיּוֹלֶד בָּנִים וּבָנוֹת: וַיִּהְיוּ כָּל־יְמֵי־יֶרֶד שְׁתַּיִם וְשִׁשִּׁים שָׁנָה
כא וּתְשַׁע מֵאוֹת שָׁנָה וַיָּמֹת: וַיְחִי חֲנוֹךְ חָמֵשׁ וְשִׁשִּׁים שָׁנָה
כב וַיּוֹלֶד אֶת־מְתוּשָׁלַח: וַיִּתְהַלֵּךְ חֲנוֹךְ אֶת־הָאֱלֹהִים אַחֲרֵי הוֹלִידוֹ אֶת־
כג מְתוּשֶׁלַח שְׁלֹשׁ מֵאוֹת שָׁנָה וַיּוֹלֶד בָּנִים וּבָנוֹת: וַיְהִי כָּל־יְמֵי חֲנוֹךְ חָמֵשׁ
כד וְשִׁשִּׁים שָׁנָה וּשְׁלֹשׁ מֵאוֹת שָׁנָה: וַיִּתְהַלֵּךְ חֲנוֹךְ אֶת־הָאֱלֹהִים וְאֵינֶנּוּ
כה כִּי־לָקַח אֹתוֹ אֱלֹהִים: וַיְחִי מְתוּשֶׁלַח שֶׁבַע וּשְׁמֹנִים שָׁנָה שביעי
כו וּמְאַת שָׁנָה וַיּוֹלֶד אֶת־לָמֶךְ: וַיְחִי מְתוּשֶׁלַח אַחֲרֵי הוֹלִידוֹ אֶת־לֶמֶךְ שְׁתַּיִם
כז וּשְׁמוֹנִים שָׁנָה וּשְׁבַע מֵאוֹת שָׁנָה וַיּוֹלֶד בָּנִים וּבָנוֹת: וַיִּהְיוּ כָּל־יְמֵי
כח מְתוּשֶׁלַח תֵּשַׁע וְשִׁשִּׁים שָׁנָה וּתְשַׁע מֵאוֹת שָׁנָה וַיָּמֹת: וַיְחִי־
כט לֶמֶךְ שְׁתַּיִם וּשְׁמֹנִים שָׁנָה וּמְאַת שָׁנָה וַיּוֹלֶד בֵּן: וַיִּקְרָא אֶת־שְׁמוֹ נֹחַ
לֵאמֹר זֶה יְנַחֲמֵנוּ מִמַּעֲשֵׂנוּ וּמֵעִצְּבוֹן יָדֵינוּ מִן־הָאֲדָמָה אֲשֶׁר אֵרְרָהּ יהוה:

---

22. וַיִּתְהַלֵּךְ חֲנוֹךְ אֶת הָאֱלֹהִים — *Chanoch walked with God.* He walked in His ways, doing good on behalf of others, (through) charitable acts and admonition.

29. זֶה יְנַחֲמֵנוּ — *This one will bring us comfort (rest).* He (Lemech) prayed that this one (Noah) will comfort us by bringing us rest (relief) from our labors. The word נוֹחַ indicates rest, similar to וְנוֹחַ מֵאֹיְבֵיהֶם, *and they rested from their enemies (Esther* 9:16).

NOTES

image regarding Cain and Abel, as it does regarding Seth.

22. וַיִּתְהַלֵּךְ חֲנוֹךְ אֶת הָאֱלֹהִים – *Chanoch walked with God.* The *Sforno* is of the opinion that to emulate God, one must be kind to others and still admonish them.

29. זֶה יְנַחֲמֵנוּ – *This one will bring us comfort (rest).* The name נֹחַ does not seem to be correctly derived from the word נֶחָמָה, as the Torah implies. Indeed the Midrash comments,

ל וַיְחִי־לֶמֶךְ אַחֲרֵי הוֹלִידוֹ אֶת־נֹחַ חָמֵשׁ וְתִשְׁעִים שָׁנָה וַחֲמֵשׁ מֵאֹת שָׁנָה
לא וַיּוֹלֶד בָּנִים וּבָנוֹת: וַיְהִי כָּל־יְמֵי־לֶמֶךְ שֶׁבַע וְשִׁבְעִים שָׁנָה וּשְׁבַע מֵאוֹת
לב שָׁנָה וַיָּמֹת: וַיְהִי־נֹחַ בֶּן־חֲמֵשׁ מֵאוֹת שָׁנָה וַיּוֹלֶד נֹחַ אֶת־שֵׁם
ו א אֶת־חָם וְאֶת־יָפֶת: וַיְהִי כִּי־הֵחֵל הָאָדָם לָרֹב עַל־פְּנֵי הָאֲדָמָה וּבָנוֹת יֻלְּדוּ
ב לָהֶם: וַיִּרְאוּ בְנֵי־הָאֱלֹהִים אֶת־בְּנוֹת הָאָדָם כִּי טֹבֹת הֵנָּה וַיִּקְחוּ לָהֶם נָשִׁים
ג מִכֹּל אֲשֶׁר בָּחָרוּ: וַיֹּאמֶר יהוה לֹא־יָדוֹן רוּחִי בָאָדָם לְעֹלָם בְּשַׁגַּם הוּא
ד בָשָׂר וְהָיוּ יָמָיו מֵאָה וְעֶשְׂרִים שָׁנָה: הַנְּפִלִים הָיוּ בָאָרֶץ בַּיָּמִים הָהֵם וְגַם
אַחֲרֵי־כֵן אֲשֶׁר יָבֹאוּ בְּנֵי הָאֱלֹהִים אֶל־בְּנוֹת הָאָדָם וְיָלְדוּ לָהֶם הֵמָּה
הַגִּבֹּרִים אֲשֶׁר מֵעוֹלָם אַנְשֵׁי הַשֵּׁם:
מפטיר ה וַיַּרְא יהוה כִּי רַבָּה רָעַת הָאָדָם בָּאָרֶץ וְכָל־יֵצֶר מַחְשְׁבֹת לִבּוֹ רַק רַע

VI

3. לֹא יָדוֹן רוּחִי בָאָדָם לְעֹלָם בְּשַׁגַּם הוּא בָשָׂר — *My spirit shall not contend evermore concerning man since he is but flesh.* It is not appropriate that there should forever be contention within Me (concerning man) or that an opportunity be given to those who would dispute Me, saying, 'Although man is worthy to be greatly punished for his rebellion (against God) since he is (created) in His image and likeness, nonetheless it is proper to show him mercy since he is, after all, *flesh,* not only (Divine) image and likeness, therefore he is brought to sin . . .'

וְהָיוּ יָמָיו — *His days shall be.* He will be granted time to repent.

מֵאָה וְעֶשְׂרִים שָׁנָה — *A hundred and twenty years* . . . during which time Noah constructed the ark, admonished them and warned them, as our Sages tell us (*Sanhedrin* 108a).

4. הַנְּפִלִים הָיוּ בָאָרֶץ בַּיָּמִים הָהֵם — *The Nephilim were on the earth in those days.* God gave them this period of time for the purpose of repentance.

וְגַם אַחֲרֵי כֵן — *And also afterward.* They did not repent at all.

5. כִּי רַבָּה רָעַת הָאָדָם — *The wickedness of man was great* . . . in the past.

וְכָל יֵצֶר מַחְשְׁבֹת — *And every product of the thoughts of his heart* . . . for the future — they did not hearken to the (words) of the admonisher, since there was no hope that they would repent.

NOTES

'The name does not correspond to its interpretation nor does the interpretation correspond to the name.' The *Sforno,* however, reconciles this difficulty, linking the words מְנוּחָה, *rest,* and נֶחָמָה, *comfort,* by interpreting Lemech's 'saying' as a prayer: 'May this child *comfort* us by bringing us *rest* (relief).' Hence the name נֹחַ is appropriate. Indeed this hope was fulfilled when Noah fashioned agricultural tools, relieving mankind from the toil of farming by hand.

VI

3. לֹא יָדוֹן רוּחִי בָאָדָם לְעֹלָם בְּשַׁגַּם הוּא בָשָׂר — *My spirit shall not contend evermore concerning man since he is but flesh.* The meaning of this verse, according to the *Sforno,* is that since man is comprised of both physical and spiritual elements, the former causing him to pursue the demands and pleasures of the flesh, while the latter makes him vulnerable to God's anger when he fails to attain his spiritual

ו כָּל־הַיּוֹם: וַיִּנָּחֶם יהוה כִּי־עָשָׂה אֶת־הָאָדָם בָּאָרֶץ וַיִּתְעַצֵּב אֶל־לִבּוֹ:
ז וַיֹּאמֶר יהוה אֶמְחֶה אֶת־הָאָדָם אֲשֶׁר־בָּרָאתִי מֵעַל פְּנֵי הָאֲדָמָה מֵאָדָם
ח עַד־בְּהֵמָה עַד־רֶמֶשׂ וְעַד־עוֹף הַשָּׁמָיִם כִּי נִחַמְתִּי כִּי עֲשִׂיתִם: וְנֹחַ מָצָא חֵן
בְּעֵינֵי יהוה:

---

6. וַיִּתְעַצֵּב אֶל לִבּוֹ — *And He had heartfelt sadness* (or: *He grieved to His heart*)... for He does not desire the death of the wicked, on the contrary יִשְׂמַח ה׳ בְּמַעֲשָׂיו, *HASHEM rejoices in His works* (*Psalms* 104:31).

8. וְנֹחַ מָצָא חֵן — *But Noah found grace.* (Sufficient) to save his sons and daughters; not that they were worthy (to be saved in his merit). It was (only) because of God's grace that he merited it, as it says, ... וְהָיוּ שְׁלֹשֶׁת הָאֲנָשִׁים הָאֵלֶּה בְּתוֹכָהּ נֹחַ דָּנִאֵל וְאִיּוֹב ... חַי אָנִי, נְאֻם ה׳ אֱלֹהִים, אִם בָּנִים וְאִם בָּנוֹת יַצִּילוּ, הֵמָּה לְבַדָּם יִנָּצֵלוּ, *Even if these three men, Noah, Daniel and Job, be in it ... as I live, declares HASHEM God, they would save neither sons or daughters, they alone would be saved* (*Ezekiel* 14:14,15). The reason is that they did not teach their generations to know God, as Abraham, Moshe and Samuel did (and others as well). As our Sages say, 'Elam (i.e., Daniel and his colleagues) merited to study but not to teach' (*Pesachim* 87a). Noah, also, even though he admonished them regarding their corrupt deeds (which were) harmful to the welfare of society, did not teach them to know God, the Blessed One, (and) to walk in His ways, although he (himself) was a righteous and perfect man in thought and practice. A righteous man who perfects himself alone is worthy to rescue himself alone, but one who perfects others as well, merits to save others, because there is then hope that they will repent, as our Sages say, 'If you see a Torah scholar who has committed an offense by night, do not cavil at him by day, for he certainly has repented' (*Berachos* 19a).

NOTES

potential, hence, conflict and tension is now present within God (as it were) and within man. This state of affairs is unacceptable to God. The solution is to hold man accountable for his sins, but also to give him the opportunity to repent. The time allotted would be 120 years, during which time Noah would admonish and caution them of the impending destruction unless they mended their ways. Unfortunately, they did not heed his words.

6. וַיִּתְעַצֵּב אֶל לִבּוֹ – *And He had heartfelt sadness.* The *Sforno*, in this verse as well as 12:2 and 28:3, stresses that God's desire is to rejoice in His works. This will only be if man perfects his deeds and pursues the knowledge of God. When this goal is thwarted by man's evil ways it causes God 'heartfelt sadness.'

8. וְנֹחַ מָצָא חֵן – *But Noah found grace.* God's grace is necessary when man is unworthy of His providence and protection. Noah, although worthy to be saved in his own merit, did not merit to have his family saved, for he failed to teach his generation the knowledge of God. Had he done so, many of them would have repented and been saved. Therefore the salvation of Noah's family is only due to God's grace and compassion. The selection from *Berachos* quoted by the *Sforno* indicates that a scholar, though he may sin, will certainly repent quickly and not postpone his *teshuvah*. Had Noah, and the others mentioned by Ezekiel, taught and trained their generation, many of their disciples would have become scholars and therefore repented. By failing to do so, these three great men saved only themselves but not their contemporaries. Hence, even Noah needed Divine grace to save his immediate family.

פרשת נח
Parashas Noach

ט אֵלֶּה תּוֹלְדֹת נֹחַ נֹחַ אִישׁ צַדִּיק תָּמִים הָיָה בְּדֹרֹתָיו אֶת־הָאֱלֹהִים
י־יא הִתְהַלֶּךְ־נֹחַ׃ וַיּוֹלֶד נֹחַ שְׁלֹשָׁה בָנִים אֶת־שֵׁם אֶת־חָם וְאֶת־יָפֶת׃ וַתִּשָּׁחֵת
יב הָאָרֶץ לִפְנֵי הָאֱלֹהִים וַתִּמָּלֵא הָאָרֶץ חָמָס׃ וַיַּרְא אֱלֹהִים אֶת־הָאָרֶץ וְהִנֵּה
יג נִשְׁחָתָה כִּי־הִשְׁחִית כָּל־בָּשָׂר אֶת־דַּרְכּוֹ עַל־הָאָרֶץ׃ וַיֹּאמֶר

---

9. תּוֹלְדֹת נֹחַ — *The toldos* (lit., *offspring*) *of Noah* . . . the events and history of his life.

צַדִּיק — *A righteous man* . . . in deeds.

תָּמִים — *Perfect* . . . in intellectual understanding.

בְּדֹרֹתָיו — *In his generations* . . . according (relative) to his generations. These were the generations of Methuselah, Lemech, his own (Noah's) and the descendants of his contemporaries during the six hundred years (prior to the Deluge).

אֶת הָאֱלֹהִים הִתְהַלֶּךְ נֹחַ — *Noah walked with God.* He walked in His ways, doing good to others and reproving his contemporaries, as our Sages tell us. Barusi the Chaldean also writes so, regarding him (Noah).

10. וַיּוֹלֶד נֹחַ — *Noah had begotten.* When he began admonishing his contemporaries, he was rewarded with children.

12. וְהִנֵּה נִשְׁחָתָה — *And behold it was destroyed (corrupted)* . . . on its own; even without (Divine) punishment it was on the way to destruction, through the corruption of their ways (immorality) which damages (corrupts) one's progeny, and violent robbery which corrupts the social order, similar to וְטַחֲנִי קָמַח, *and grind meal* (*Isaiah* 47:2).

NOTES

9. תּוֹלְדֹת נֹחַ– *The toldos* (lit., *offspring*) *of Noah.* Regarding the phrase תּוֹלְדוֹת, see note to 5:1. Various explanations are given by the commentators to explain the seeming digression in this opening section of Noah, where the Torah begins with the genealogy of Noah (continued in verse 10) only to interject a description of Noah's character. However, the *Sforno's* translation of תולדות as *events* and *history* obviates the difficulty. The Torah's description of Noah as being a *righteous* and *perfect* man, *walking with God,* is an integral part of his life story, hence not a digression at all.

בְּדֹרֹתָיו — *In his generations.* Generations in the plural is explained most logically by the *Sforno* as referring to the various generations that Noah's first 600 years spanned.

. . . אֶת הָאֱלֹהִים — . . . *With God.* Barusi the Chaldean (Berosus the Babylonian) was a historian who lived in the third century B.C.E. He is mentioned a number of times in the works of Josephus, and is purported to have deciphered events recorded by the ancient Mesopotamians on stone tablets. Since every culture has a 'Flood story,' the *Sforno* feels it is important to cite the writings of a Chaldean historian, who supports the words of our Sages. The *Sforno* cites him again in 9:22.

10. וַיּוֹלֶד נֹחַ — *Noah had begotten.* Noah had no children until a late age. Whatever the reason may have been, he is now blessed with three sons, as a reward for reproving his contemporaries. The concept of מִדָּה כְּנֶגֶד מִדָּה, *measure for measure,* may well be that if one demonstrates his willingness and ability to admonish and instruct, he can also be an effective parent to his children; as Solomon says, *'My son, listen to the* מוּסַר, *admonishment, of your father'* (*Proverbs* 1:8).

12. וְהִנֵּה נִשְׁחָתָה — *And behold it was destroyed (corrupted).* The *Sforno* interprets the phrase וְהִנֵּה נִשְׁחָתָה as meaning *behold it was on the path to (self-) destruction,* translating נִשְׁחָתָה as *destruction* rather than *corruption.* His proof from the verse in *Isaiah* is based on the use of the word קֶמַח instead of דָּגָן — *flour* rather than grain. Flour is the *end* product of

אֱלֹהִים לְנֹחַ קֵץ כָּל־בָּשָׂר בָּא לְפָנַי כִּי־מָלְאָה הָאָרֶץ חָמָס מִפְּנֵיהֶם וְהִנְנִי
יד מַשְׁחִיתָם אֶת־הָאָרֶץ: עֲשֵׂה לְךָ תֵּבַת עֲצֵי־גֹפֶר קִנִּים תַּעֲשֶׂה אֶת־הַתֵּבָה
טו וְכָפַרְתָּ אֹתָהּ מִבַּיִת וּמִחוּץ בַּכֹּפֶר: וְזֶה אֲשֶׁר תַּעֲשֶׂה אֹתָהּ שְׁלֹשׁ מֵאוֹת
טז אַמָּה אֹרֶךְ הַתֵּבָה חֲמִשִּׁים אַמָּה רָחְבָּהּ וּשְׁלֹשִׁים אַמָּה קוֹמָתָהּ: צֹהַר ׀
תַּעֲשֶׂה לַתֵּבָה וְאֶל־אַמָּה תְּכַלֶּנָּה מִלְמַעְלָה וּפֶתַח הַתֵּבָה בְּצִדָּהּ תָּשִׂים
יז תַּחְתִּיִּם שְׁנִיִּם וּשְׁלִשִׁים תַּעֲשֶׂהָ: וַאֲנִי הִנְנִי מֵבִיא אֶת־הַמַּבּוּל מַיִם עַל־

---

13. קֵץ כָּל בָּשָׂר — *The end of all flesh* . . . the period of 120 years which I stipulated for them.

בָּא לְפָנַי — *Has come before me* . . . which I set for their repentance.

כִּי מָלְאָה הָאָרֶץ חָמָס מִפְּנֵיהֶם — *For the earth is filled with robbery through them.* Each robs the other; the landowners rob the sharecroppers forcibly, while the sharecropper robs the landowner through deceit. Thus the earth is producing all its fruit for robbers!

וְהִנְנִי מַשְׁחִיתָם אֶת הָאָרֶץ — *And behold, I am about to destroy them with the earth.* I will destroy them *with* the earth. I will destroy (alter) the climate of the earth and air, i.e., after the deluge the angle of the earth to the sun was altered, (whereas before) the equinox was constant (day and night being of equal length) — as God explained to Job in His rejoinder. As a result, immediately after the Flood, the span of human life was shortened, since weather conditions and fruits were no longer perfect (complete) as before. It is for this reason that man was permitted to eat the meat of living creatures after the Flood.

14. עֲשֵׂה לְךָ תֵּבַת — *Make yourself an ark.* During the time stipulated for them, so that they may observe and repent.

16. בְּצִדָּהּ תָּשִׂים — *Put (the entrance) in its side.* Along the breadth (of the ark) for that is referred to as צַד; the long side is called צֶלַע.

תַּחְתִּיִּם — *Lower (deck).* Customary in (all) ships (boats).

שְׁנִיִּם וּשְׁלִשִׁים — *Second and third (decks).* Similar to the usual lower one (of the average boat).

NOTES

grinding; still the prophet speaks of grinding *flour!* The answer is that he 'calls' it flour עַל שֵׁם סוֹפוֹ, by its eventual, ultimate name. And so in our instance: the earth may seem secure and stable, but it is already on the path to destruction.

13. וְהִנְנִי מַשְׁחִיתָם אֶת הָאָרֶץ – *And behold, I am about to destroy them with the earth.* See Verse 3, the *Sforno's* commentary and explanatory notes.

וְהִנְנִי מַשְׁחִיתָם – *And behold, I am about to destroy.* See the *Sforno's* commentary to 8:22. At the time of Creation it was always springtime. The ideal climate, and the equal length of day and night, created a perfect balance which affected man's well being and the quality of the earth's productivity. The Flood disrupted this balance and as a result adversely affected man and the produce of the land. The *Sforno* interprets the word אֶת in this verse as meaning *with,* i.e., man together with the earth is 'destroyed.' His reference to Job alludes to God's retort in Chapter 38, where He begins, *'Where were you when I laid the earth's foundations?'* and then proceeds to describe the wonders of nature.

14. עֲשֵׂה לְךָ תֵּבַת – *Make yourself an ark.* As our Sages say in *Sanhedrin* 108b, the Almighty could have saved Noah without

הָאָרֶץ לְשַׁחֵת כָּל־בָּשָׂר אֲשֶׁר־בּוֹ רוּחַ חַיִּים מִתַּחַת הַשָּׁמָיִם כֹּל אֲשֶׁר־
יח בָּאָרֶץ יִגְוָע: וַהֲקִמֹתִי אֶת־בְּרִיתִי אִתָּךְ וּבָאתָ אֶל־הַתֵּבָה אַתָּה וּבָנֶיךָ
יט וְאִשְׁתְּךָ וּנְשֵׁי־בָנֶיךָ אִתָּךְ: וּמִכָּל־הָחַי מִכָּל־בָּשָׂר שְׁנַיִם מִכֹּל תָּבִיא אֶל־
כ הַתֵּבָה לְהַחֲיֹת אִתָּךְ זָכָר וּנְקֵבָה יִהְיוּ: מֵהָעוֹף לְמִינֵהוּ וּמִן־הַבְּהֵמָה לְמִינָהּ
כא מִכֹּל רֶמֶשׂ הָאֲדָמָה לְמִינֵהוּ שְׁנַיִם מִכֹּל יָבֹאוּ אֵלֶיךָ לְהַחֲיוֹת: וְאַתָּה קַח־
כב לְךָ מִכָּל־מַאֲכָל אֲשֶׁר יֵאָכֵל וְאָסַפְתָּ אֵלֶיךָ וְהָיָה לְךָ וְלָהֶם לְאָכְלָה: וַיַּעַשׂ
ז שני א נֹחַ כְּכֹל אֲשֶׁר צִוָּה אֹתוֹ אֱלֹהִים כֵּן עָשָׂה: וַיֹּאמֶר יהוה לְנֹחַ בֹּא־אַתָּה וְכָל־
ב בֵּיתְךָ אֶל־הַתֵּבָה כִּי־אֹתְךָ רָאִיתִי צַדִּיק לְפָנַי בַּדּוֹר הַזֶּה: מִכֹּל ׀ הַבְּהֵמָה
הַטְּהוֹרָה תִּקַּח־לְךָ שִׁבְעָה שִׁבְעָה אִישׁ וְאִשְׁתּוֹ וּמִן־הַבְּהֵמָה אֲשֶׁר לֹא

---

17. וַאֲנִי הִנְנִי מֵבִיא אֶת הַמַּבּוּל — *And as for Me — Behold I am about to bring the Flood-waters.* You complete the ark, and I will immediately bring on the Flood (מַבּוּל). This word (i.e., *mabul*) is a term meaning downfall and loss (catastrophe), similar to the term נְבָלָה, *wither, decay.* (The verse is) saying: I will bring about (by means of water) the downfall and loss (i.e., catastrophe) which I (already) said, *And behold, I am about to destroy them from the earth* (verse 13).

18. וַהֲקִמֹתִי אֶת בְּרִיתִי — *But I will establish My covenant* . . . (which I will make) *after* the Flood.

21. וְאַתָּה — *And as for you* . . . now!

קַח . . . מִכָּל מַאֲכָל — *Take . . . of every food* . . . various foods for the various species.

VII

1. כִּי אֹתְךָ רָאִיתִי צַדִּיק — *For it is* you *that I have seen to be righteous.* You, not your household. Nonetheless, 'You and all your household' I will save only for your sake.

2. הַטְּהוֹרָה — *Clean (animal).* All (clean animals) were then fit for sacrifice, as our Sages mention to us (*Zevachim* 115b). (These) were also suited for food, as opposed to, וְנִטְמֵתֶם בָּם, *And you will be defiled by them (Vayikra* 11:43).

NOTES

imposing upon him the lengthy difficult process of constructing an ark. However the real purpose was to arouse the people to question, contemplate and repent.

17. וַאֲנִי הִנְנִי מֵבִיא אֶת הַמַּבּוּל — *And as for Me — Behold I am about to bring the Flood-waters.* In the *Sforno's* opinion, the word מַבּוּל does not mean 'flood' but any catastrophic event which causes a sudden and widespread disaster. In this particular instance the medium used by God was water. Therefore when He promises that there will never again be a מַבּוּל to destroy the earth (9:11) it is all inclusive, not only a flood but through any medium.

18. וַהֲקִמֹתִי אֶת בְּרִיתִי — *But I will establish My covenant.* Many commentators interpret this covenant as one now being made. The *Sforno* is of the opinion, however, that it refers to the covenant which God will establish later, after the Flood (9:9-11).

21. קַח . . . מִכָּל מַאֲכָל — *Take . . . of every food.* The *Sforno* interprets these words as emphasizing that it is Noah's responsibility to make provision for each and every species in his ark.

VII

1. כִּי אֹתְךָ רָאִיתִי צַדִּיק — *For it is you that I have seen to be righteous.* The *Sforno* interprets the verse in reverse order. The end of the verse, Noah's personal righteousness, is the reason for the beginning of the verse, where Hashem tells Noah to enter the ark *with* his household. They were not worthy on their own to be saved, and even Noah's merit was insufficient were it not for God's grace, as the *Sforno* explained above, in 6:8.

2. הַטְּהוֹרָה — *Clean (animal).* (a) The phrase טְהוֹרָה, *clean,* when applied to an animal or

ג טְהֹרָה הוּא שְׁנַיִם אִישׁ וְאִשְׁתּוֹ: גַּם מֵעוֹף הַשָּׁמַיִם שִׁבְעָה שִׁבְעָה זָכָר וּנְקֵבָה
ד לְחַיּוֹת זֶרַע עַל־פְּנֵי כָל־הָאָרֶץ: כִּי לְיָמִים עוֹד שִׁבְעָה אָנֹכִי מַמְטִיר עַל־
הָאָרֶץ אַרְבָּעִים יוֹם וְאַרְבָּעִים לָיְלָה וּמָחִיתִי אֶת־כָּל־הַיְקוּם אֲשֶׁר עָשִׂיתִי
ה־ו מֵעַל פְּנֵי הָאֲדָמָה: וַיַּעַשׂ נֹחַ כְּכֹל אֲשֶׁר־צִוָּהוּ יהוה: וְנֹחַ בֶּן־שֵׁשׁ מֵאוֹת שָׁנָה
ז וְהַמַּבּוּל הָיָה מַיִם עַל־הָאָרֶץ: וַיָּבֹא נֹחַ וּבָנָיו וְאִשְׁתּוֹ וּנְשֵׁי־בָנָיו אִתּוֹ
ח אֶל־הַתֵּבָה מִפְּנֵי מֵי הַמַּבּוּל: מִן־הַבְּהֵמָה הַטְּהוֹרָה וּמִן־הַבְּהֵמָה אֲשֶׁר
ט אֵינֶנָּה טְהֹרָה וּמִן־הָעוֹף וְכֹל אֲשֶׁר־רֹמֵשׂ עַל־הָאֲדָמָה: שְׁנַיִם שְׁנַיִם בָּאוּ
י אֶל־נֹחַ אֶל־הַתֵּבָה זָכָר וּנְקֵבָה כַּאֲשֶׁר צִוָּה אֱלֹהִים אֶת־נֹחַ: וַיְהִי לְשִׁבְעַת
יא הַיָּמִים וּמֵי הַמַּבּוּל הָיוּ עַל־הָאָרֶץ: בִּשְׁנַת שֵׁשׁ־מֵאוֹת שָׁנָה לְחַיֵּי־נֹחַ בַּחֹדֶשׁ
הַשֵּׁנִי בְּשִׁבְעָה־עָשָׂר יוֹם לַחֹדֶשׁ בַּיּוֹם הַזֶּה נִבְקְעוּ כָּל־מַעְיְנוֹת תְּהוֹם רַבָּה
יב וַאֲרֻבֹּת הַשָּׁמַיִם נִפְתָּחוּ: וַיְהִי הַגֶּשֶׁם עַל־הָאָרֶץ אַרְבָּעִים יוֹם וְאַרְבָּעִים
יג לָיְלָה: בְּעֶצֶם הַיּוֹם הַזֶּה בָּא נֹחַ וְשֵׁם־וְחָם וָיֶפֶת בְּנֵי־נֹחַ וְאֵשֶׁת נֹחַ וּשְׁלֹשֶׁת
יד נְשֵׁי־בָנָיו אִתָּם אֶל־הַתֵּבָה: הֵמָּה וְכָל־הַחַיָּה לְמִינָהּ וְכָל־הַבְּהֵמָה לְמִינָהּ
וְכָל־הָרֶמֶשׂ הָרֹמֵשׂ עַל־הָאָרֶץ לְמִינֵהוּ וְכָל־הָעוֹף לְמִינֵהוּ כֹּל צִפּוֹר
טו כָּל־כָּנָף: וַיָּבֹאוּ אֶל־נֹחַ אֶל־הַתֵּבָה שְׁנַיִם שְׁנַיִם מִכָּל־הַבָּשָׂר אֲשֶׁר־בּוֹ רוּחַ
טז חַיִּים: וְהַבָּאִים זָכָר וּנְקֵבָה מִכָּל־בָּשָׂר בָּאוּ כַּאֲשֶׁר צִוָּה אֹתוֹ אֱלֹהִים וַיִּסְגֹּר
שלישי יז יהוה בַּעֲדוֹ: וַיְהִי הַמַּבּוּל אַרְבָּעִים יוֹם עַל־הָאָרֶץ וַיִּרְבּוּ הַמַּיִם וַיִּשְׂאוּ
יח אֶת־הַתֵּבָה וַתָּרָם מֵעַל הָאָרֶץ: וַיִּגְבְּרוּ הַמַּיִם וַיִּרְבּוּ מְאֹד עַל־הָאָרֶץ וַתֵּלֶךְ
יט הַתֵּבָה עַל־פְּנֵי הַמָּיִם: וְהַמַּיִם גָּבְרוּ מְאֹד מְאֹד עַל־הָאָרֶץ וַיְכֻסּוּ כָּל־הֶהָרִים
כ הַגְּבֹהִים אֲשֶׁר־תַּחַת כָּל־הַשָּׁמָיִם: חֲמֵשׁ עֶשְׂרֵה אַמָּה מִלְמַעְלָה גָּבְרוּ הַמָּיִם
כא וַיְכֻסּוּ הֶהָרִים: וַיִּגְוַע כָּל־בָּשָׂר | הָרֹמֵשׂ עַל־הָאָרֶץ בָּעוֹף וּבַבְּהֵמָה וּבַחַיָּה
כב וּבְכָל־הַשֶּׁרֶץ הַשֹּׁרֵץ עַל־הָאָרֶץ וְכֹל הָאָדָם: כֹּל אֲשֶׁר נִשְׁמַת־רוּחַ חַיִּים
כג בְּאַפָּיו מִכֹּל אֲשֶׁר בֶּחָרָבָה מֵתוּ: וַיִּמַח אֶת־כָּל־הַיְקוּם | אֲשֶׁר | עַל־פְּנֵי

---

18. וַתֵּלֶךְ הַתֵּבָה — *And the ark drifted (went).* Pushed by the strong gush (of water) which came from below.

23. וַיִּמַח אֶת כָּל הַיְקוּם — *And He blotted out all existence.* Living creatures; but not herbage, plants or vegetation, as the verse clearly explicates, saying: מֵאָדָם עַד בְּהֵמָה עַד רֶמֶשׂ וְעַד עוֹף הַשָּׁמַיִם, *from man to animal to creeping things and to the bird of the heavens.*

NOTES

fowl, refers to its acceptability as a sacrifice as well as being fit halachically for consumption by man. In this particular instance it would only be applicable to the former, since man was not permitted to eat the flesh of living creatures until after the Flood. Nonetheless, the *Sforno* is of the opinion that since Noah was familiar with the animals and birds of prey, he also discerned which would eventually be טְהוֹרָה, *clean,* for food, when the flesh of animals and birds would be permitted, since the reason certain flesh is prohibited is because it defiles man and makes him dull and insensitive, as our Sages tell us (*Yoma* 39a).

(b) Before the giving of the Torah, all the animals were qualified as sacrifices. It is only later that the Torah limits and restricts it to specific species and kinds. Hence, at the time of the Flood, the quota of seven applied to *all* clean creatures.

23. וַיִּמַח אֶת כָּל הַיְקוּם — *And He blotted out all existence.* The phrase *blotted out* appears twice in this verse (וַיִּמַח-וַיִּמָּחוּ). According to

הָאֲדָמָה מֵאָדָם עַד־בְּהֵמָה עַד־רֶמֶשׂ וְעַד־עוֹף הַשָּׁמַיִם וַיִּמָּחוּ מִן־הָאָרֶץ
כד וַיִּשָּׁאֶר אַךְ־נֹחַ וַאֲשֶׁר אִתּוֹ בַּתֵּבָה: וַיִּגְבְּרוּ הַמַּיִם עַל־הָאָרֶץ חֲמִשִּׁים וּמְאַת
ח א יוֹם: וַיִּזְכֹּר אֱלֹהִים אֶת־נֹחַ וְאֵת כָּל־הַחַיָּה וְאֶת־כָּל־הַבְּהֵמָה אֲשֶׁר אִתּוֹ
ב בַּתֵּבָה וַיַּעֲבֵר אֱלֹהִים רוּחַ עַל־הָאָרֶץ וַיָּשֹׁכּוּ הַמָּיִם: וַיִּסָּכְרוּ מַעְיְנֹת תְּהוֹם
ג וַאֲרֻבֹּת הַשָּׁמָיִם וַיִּכָּלֵא הַגֶּשֶׁם מִן־הַשָּׁמָיִם: וַיָּשֻׁבוּ הַמַּיִם מֵעַל הָאָרֶץ הָלוֹךְ
ד וָשׁוֹב וַיַּחְסְרוּ הַמַּיִם מִקְצֵה חֲמִשִּׁים וּמְאַת יוֹם: וַתָּנַח הַתֵּבָה בַּחֹדֶשׁ
ה הַשְּׁבִיעִי בְּשִׁבְעָה־עָשָׂר יוֹם לַחֹדֶשׁ עַל הָרֵי אֲרָרָט: וְהַמַּיִם הָיוּ הָלוֹךְ וְחָסוֹר
ו עַד הַחֹדֶשׁ הָעֲשִׂירִי בָּעֲשִׂירִי בְּאֶחָד לַחֹדֶשׁ נִרְאוּ רָאשֵׁי הֶהָרִים: וַיְהִי מִקֵּץ
ז אַרְבָּעִים יוֹם וַיִּפְתַּח נֹחַ אֶת־חַלּוֹן הַתֵּבָה אֲשֶׁר עָשָׂה: וַיְשַׁלַּח אֶת־הָעֹרֵב
ח וַיֵּצֵא יָצוֹא וָשׁוֹב עַד־יְבֹשֶׁת הַמַּיִם מֵעַל הָאָרֶץ: וַיְשַׁלַּח אֶת־הַיּוֹנָה מֵאִתּוֹ

וַיִּמָּחוּ מִן הָאָרֶץ — *And they were blotted out from the earth* ... children, relatives, grandchildren and great-grandchildren.

24. וַיִּגְבְּרוּ ... חֲמִשִּׁים וּמְאַת יוֹם — *And (the waters) prevailed ... a hundred and fifty days.* The water increased in intensity from the start of the rain until it ceased, 150 days from its beginning on the seventeenth day of the second month (Cheshvan), ending on the seventeenth of the seventh month (Nissan) — the 150 days (comprising) a full (complete) five months. The ark then came to rest since there was (no longer) a strong upsurge to propel it, for from the day the rains commenced the waters began to surge strongly from below, as it says: *All the fountains of the great deep burst forth* (v. 11). In truth, the ark did not move on the surface of the water until the waters were so high that the ark was lifted up over the earth. Even when the days of rain were finished and there was only the upsurge of water from below, which continued until the completion of the 150 days (the ark continued to move). When this upsurge which had propelled the ark ceased, the ark (also) came to rest.

VIII

7. וַיְשַׁלַּח אֶת הָעֹרֵב — *He sent out the raven* ... to see whether, after the tops of the mountains were seen, the atmosphere was dry enough for the raven to accept (endure) it.

וַיֵּצֵא יָצוֹא וָשׁוֹב — *And it kept going and returning* ... for he could not endure it.

8. וַיְשַׁלַּח אֶת הַיּוֹנָה — *Then he sent out a dove* ... the complete species of doves, which were seven pairs.

NOTES

many commentators this is to indicate total obliteration; everything was wiped away. The *Sforno* interprets the verse differently. He feels that the balance of the verse qualifies the word וַיִּמַח, when it specifies men, animals, creeping things and birds — thereby excluding plants and vegetation. He therefore explains the repetition of the word *blotted out* as meaning the total annihilation of the human race — except for Noah and his family.

VIII

8. וַיְשַׁלַּח אֶת הַיּוֹנָה — *Then he sent out a dove.* The sending forth by Noah of all seven pairs is brought in certain manuscripts. It does not appear in our *Mikraos Gedolos* editions. It is difficult to understand why it was necessary for Noah to do so, hence it would seem that our version of the *Sforno* is correct. Nonetheless, since the *Sforno's* commentary regarding the nesting of doves appears in every version,

ט לִרְאוֹת הֲקַלּוּ הַמַּיִם מֵעַל פְּנֵי הָאֲדָמָה: וְלֹא־מָצְאָה הַיּוֹנָה מָנוֹחַ לְכַף־
רַגְלָהּ וַתָּשָׁב אֵלָיו אֶל־הַתֵּבָה כִּי־מַיִם עַל־פְּנֵי כָל־הָאָרֶץ וַיִּשְׁלַח יָדוֹ
י וַיִּקָּחֶהָ וַיָּבֵא אֹתָהּ אֵלָיו אֶל־הַתֵּבָה: וַיָּחֶל עוֹד שִׁבְעַת יָמִים אֲחֵרִים וַיֹּסֶף
יא שַׁלַּח אֶת־הַיּוֹנָה מִן־הַתֵּבָה: וַתָּבֹא אֵלָיו הַיּוֹנָה לְעֵת עֶרֶב וְהִנֵּה עֲלֵה־זַיִת
יב טָרָף בְּפִיהָ וַיֵּדַע נֹחַ כִּי־קַלּוּ הַמַּיִם מֵעַל הָאָרֶץ: וַיִּיָּחֶל עוֹד שִׁבְעַת יָמִים
יג אֲחֵרִים וַיְשַׁלַּח אֶת־הַיּוֹנָה וְלֹא־יָסְפָה שׁוּב־אֵלָיו עוֹד: וַיְהִי בְּאַחַת וְשֵׁשׁ־
מֵאוֹת שָׁנָה בָּרִאשׁוֹן בְּאֶחָד לַחֹדֶשׁ חָרְבוּ הַמַּיִם מֵעַל הָאָרֶץ וַיָּסַר נֹחַ אֶת־
יד מִכְסֵה הַתֵּבָה וַיַּרְא וְהִנֵּה חָרְבוּ פְּנֵי הָאֲדָמָה: וּבַחֹדֶשׁ הַשֵּׁנִי בְּשִׁבְעָה
טו וְעֶשְׂרִים יוֹם לַחֹדֶשׁ יָבְשָׁה הָאָרֶץ: וַיְדַבֵּר אֱלֹהִים רביעי
טז אֶל־נֹחַ לֵאמֹר: צֵא מִן־הַתֵּבָה אַתָּה וְאִשְׁתְּךָ וּבָנֶיךָ וּנְשֵׁי־בָנֶיךָ אִתָּךְ:
יז כָּל־הַחַיָּה אֲשֶׁר־אִתְּךָ מִכָּל־בָּשָׂר בָּעוֹף וּבַבְּהֵמָה וּבְכָל־הָרֶמֶשׂ הָרֹמֵשׂ
יח עַל־הָאָרֶץ °הוֹצֵא אִתָּךְ וְשָׁרְצוּ בָאָרֶץ וּפָרוּ וְרָבוּ עַל־הָאָרֶץ: וַיֵּצֵא־נֹחַ °הַיְצֵא ק׳
יט וּבָנָיו וְאִשְׁתּוֹ וּנְשֵׁי־בָנָיו אִתּוֹ: כָּל־הַחַיָּה כָּל־הָרֶמֶשׂ וְכָל־הָעוֹף כֹּל רוֹמֵשׂ
כ עַל־הָאָרֶץ לְמִשְׁפְּחֹתֵיהֶם יָצְאוּ מִן־הַתֵּבָה: וַיִּבֶן נֹחַ מִזְבֵּחַ לַיהוָה וַיִּקַּח
כא מִכֹּל ׀ הַבְּהֵמָה הַטְּהֹרָה וּמִכֹּל הָעוֹף הַטָּהֹר וַיַּעַל עֹלֹת בַּמִּזְבֵּחַ: וַיָּרַח
יהוה אֶת־רֵיחַ הַנִּיחֹחַ וַיֹּאמֶר יהוה אֶל־לִבּוֹ לֹא־אֹסִף לְקַלֵּל עוֹד

לִרְאוֹת הֲקַלּוּ — *To see whether the waters had subsided.* If (the waters) had subsided, they would nest on the mountains and towers instinctively (lit., 'according to its way').

9. כִּי מַיִם עַל פְּנֵי כָל הָאָרֶץ — *For water was upon the surface of all the earth.* The tops of the mountains which had appeared were still saturated so that even there ... *the dove could not find a resting place for the sole of its foot.*

13. וַיָּסַר נֹחַ אֶת מִכְסֵה הַתֵּבָה — *Noah removed the covering of the ark.* He thought that the excessive moisture of the air had dried.

וְהִנֵּה חָרְבוּ פְּנֵי הָאֲדָמָה — *And behold, the surface of the ground had dried.* But not dry enough to enable him to leave.

21. אֶת רֵיחַ הַנִּיחֹחַ — *The pleasing aroma* ... for at that time, they (i.e., *all* clean animals and birds) were acceptable for sacrifice.

וַיֹּאמֶר ה׳ אֶל לִבּוֹ — *And HASHEM said in His heart.* He did not reveal it to Noah and his sons until they accepted His commandments and established a covenant.

NOTES

we can speculate that this test would be negated if the doves refused to nest without their mates or even without their fellow doves, since their species is known for loyalty one to another. For this reason Noah had to send *all* of them, to determine whether the waters had subsided.

21. אֶת רֵיחַ הַנִּיחֹחַ – *The pleasing aroma.* The *Sforno* stresses that all clean animals were acceptable as sacrifices (see 7:2). However, in *Leviticus* 1:2 he seemingly retreats from his original position (that at that time *all* clean animals were suitable to be brought as sacrifices) and he interprets this particular verse to mean 'the pleasing aroma of those animals that would eventually be deemed worthy as sacrifices.'

וַיֹּאמֶר ה׳ אֶל לִבּוֹ – *And HASHEM said in His heart.* The expression 'said in His heart' is not anthropomorphic. As the *Sforno* explains, it is to be understood as a decision of the Almighty which He does not reveal to others.

אֶת־הָאֲדָמָה֙ בַּעֲב֣וּר הָֽאָדָ֔ם כִּ֠י יֵ֣צֶר לֵ֧ב הָאָדָ֛ם רַ֖ע מִנְּעֻרָ֑יו וְלֹֽא־אֹסִ֥ף ע֛וֹד
כב לְהַכּ֥וֹת אֶת־כָּל־חַ֖י כַּאֲשֶׁ֥ר עָשִֽׂיתִי׃ עֹ֖ד כָּל־יְמֵ֣י הָאָ֑רֶץ זֶ֡רַע וְקָ֠צִיר וְקֹ֨ר וָחֹ֜ם
ט א וְקַ֧יִץ וָחֹ֛רֶף וְי֥וֹם וָלַ֖יְלָה לֹ֥א יִשְׁבֹּֽתוּ׃ וַיְבָ֣רֶךְ אֱלֹהִ֔ים אֶת־נֹ֖חַ וְאֶת־בָּנָ֑יו
ב וַיֹּ֧אמֶר לָהֶ֛ם פְּר֥וּ וּרְב֖וּ וּמִלְא֥וּ אֶת־הָאָֽרֶץ׃ וּמוֹרַאֲכֶ֤ם וְחִתְּכֶם֙ יִֽהְיֶ֔ה עַ֚ל
כָּל־חַיַּ֣ת הָאָ֔רֶץ וְעַ֖ל כָּל־ע֣וֹף הַשָּׁמָ֑יִם בְּכֹל֩ אֲשֶׁ֨ר תִּרְמֹ֧שׂ הָֽאֲדָמָ֛ה
ג וּבְכָל־דְּגֵ֥י הַיָּ֖ם בְּיֶדְכֶ֥ם נִתָּֽנוּ׃ כָּל־רֶ֙מֶשׂ֙ אֲשֶׁ֣ר הוּא־חַ֔י לָכֶ֥ם יִהְיֶ֖ה לְאָכְלָ֑ה
ד־ה כְּיֶ֣רֶק עֵ֔שֶׂב נָתַ֥תִּי לָכֶ֖ם אֶת־כֹּֽל׃ אַךְ־בָּשָׂ֕ר בְּנַפְשׁ֥וֹ דָמ֖וֹ לֹ֥א תֹאכֵֽלוּ׃ וְאַ֨ךְ

כִּי יֵצֶר לֵב הָאָדָם רַע מִנְּעֻרָיו — *Since the imagery (lit., formation) of man's heart is evil from his youth.* Since the climate (of the earth) and the temperament (of mankind) will from now on be inferior to conditions prior to the Flood, their intellectual powers will not illuminate them from their youth, as it did before, in a manner (that they might) overcome the base desires which overpower one from his youth.

22. עֹד כָּל יְמֵי הָאָרֶץ זֶרַע וְקָצִיר וְקֹר וָחֹם וְקַיִץ וָחֹרֶף וְיוֹם וָלַיְלָה לֹא יִשְׁבֹּתוּ — *While the earth remains, seedtime and harvest, cold and heat, summer and winter, day and night, shall not cease.* (They will not cease) from continuing in this unnatural fashion, which I set for them after the Flood: that the sun shall revolve spherically, tilted from the equator (hence the equinox will not be constant) and this turning will cause the change of all these seasons. Before the Flood the (angle of the earth) to the sun was such that the equinox was constant, and therefore it was always springtime, which was a general betterment for the elements, vegetation and the span of life of living creatures. (Now, the Torah) says that this will be 'while the earth remains,' (meaning) until (such time) that God, the Blessed One, will ameliorate the damage caused by the Flood, as He says, הָאָרֶץ הַחֲדָשָׁה אֲשֶׁר אֲנִי עֹשֶׂה, *The new earth which I will make (Isaiah 66:22)*, for then the sun will return, once again, to the (permanent) equinox, and there will be a general improvement of the elements, vegetation and living creatures, (including) their length of days. This is the way it was before the Flood, as it says, כִּי הַנַּעַר בֶּן מֵאָה שָׁנָה יָמוּת וְהַחוֹטֶא בֶּן מֵאָה שָׁנָה יְקֻלָּל, *He who dies at a hundred years shall be reckoned a youth, and he who fails to reach a hundred shall be reckoned accursed* (ibid. 65:20); and this is what is meant by, מוֹצָאֵי בֹקֶר וָעֶרֶב תַּרְנִין, *The lands of sunrise and sunset (will) shout for joy* (*Psalms* 65:9).

IX

4. אַךְ בָּשָׂר בְּנַפְשׁוֹ — *But flesh with its soul.* However, the flesh of a living (animal) while it is still with its soul, i.e., alive.

NOTES

כִּי יֵצֶר לֵב הָאָדָם רַע מִנְּעֻרָיו – *Since the imagery of man's heart is evil from his youth.* A basic transformation occurred within man spiritually following the Flood, as it did physically. The evil inclination was now present from birth, whereas the good inclination only develops later in life as one reaches adulthood.

22. עֹד כָּל יְמֵי הָאָרֶץ ... לֹא יִשְׁבֹּתוּ – *While the earth remains ... shall not cease.* See the *Sforno's* commentary on 6:13 and the notes. The *Sforno* submits that the various seasons and the ever-changing climate is the result of the Flood, which disrupted the perfect balance of nature that earth and man enjoyed from the time of Creation until the Flood. These ideal conditions will, however, be renewed at the 'end of days.'

אֶת־דִּמְכֶם לְנַפְשֹׁתֵיכֶם אֶדְרֹשׁ מִיַּד כָּל־חַיָּה אֶדְרְשֶׁנּוּ וּמִיַּד הָאָדָם מִיַּד
ו אִישׁ אָחִיו אֶדְרֹשׁ אֶת־נֶפֶשׁ הָאָדָם: שֹׁפֵךְ דַּם הָאָדָם בָּאָדָם דָּמוֹ יִשָּׁפֵךְ כִּי
ז בְּצֶלֶם אֱלֹהִים עָשָׂה אֶת־הָאָדָם: וְאַתֶּם פְּרוּ וּרְבוּ שִׁרְצוּ בָאָרֶץ וּרְבוּ־

דָּמוֹ — *Its blood* . . . similarly, the blood drawn from a living (animal) . . .

לֹא תֹאכֵלוּ — *You shall not eat.* However, (blood) drawn from a dead animal is permitted to Noachides.

5. וְאַךְ אֶת דִּמְכֶם לְנַפְשֹׁתֵיכֶם אֶדְרֹשׁ — *However your blood which belongs to your souls I will demand.* Although I will not demand the blood of other living creatures from your hands, nonetheless I will demand your blood because of your souls which are more precious to Me than the lives of other living creatures. Now, this 'demanding' will be in various ways; if the person (the intended victim) is worthy then . . .

מִיַּד כָּל חַיָּה אֶדְרְשֶׁנּוּ וּמִיַּד הָאָדָם — *Of every beast will I demand it; and of the hand of man* . . . to save him. (This is) comparable to, וְדָרַשְׁתִּי אֶת צֹאנִי מִיָּדָם . . . וְהִצַּלְתִּי צֹאנִי מִפִּיהֶם, *I will demand a reckoning for My flock . . . for I will rescue My flock from their mouths (Ezekiel* 34:10).

מִיַּד אִישׁ אָחִיו אֶדְרֹשׁ אֶת נֶפֶשׁ הָאָדָם — *Of the hand of every man for that of his brother I will demand the soul of man.* If he is not worthy to be saved and is slain by another, I will avenge the victim by punishing the slayer — but not the beast (who kills him).

6. בָּאָדָם דָּמוֹ יִשָּׁפֵךְ — *By man shall his blood be shed* — by the court (here on earth).

כִּי בְּצֶלֶם אֱלֹהִים — *For in the image of God.* The reason I demand (punishment) for the shedding of man's blood but not for the blood of other living creatures is because *in the image of God He made,* i.e., in the image of those who are separated (from material; i.e., angels) who are called *Elohim,* some of the (humans) were made. From the moment that God, the Blessed One, said *Let us make man* (1:26), he gave the power to the 'forms separated (from material),' or one of them, to endow with intellectual power, every subject prepared (to receive this power), which includes every human. Now since man (is created) in the image of *Elohim,* which is the human soul by which he becomes a 'rational living being' (based on the *Rambam's Guide* I:51), it is proper that his blood and living soul, which serve that image, be considered precious, and (if shed) be demanded of his murderers, more so than the (taking of the) life of all other living creatures.

NOTES

IX

4. אַךְ בָּשָׂר בְּנַפְשׁוֹ – *But flesh with its soul. Sforno* is of the opinion (as is *Rashi)* that the sense of the verse is: There are two prohibitions; both the flesh and the blood taken from a living animal (דַּם מִן הַחַי and אֵבֶר מִן הַחַי) are prohibited to a Noachide. This follows the view of Rav Chaninah ben Gamliel in *Sanhedrin* 59. However, the blood drawn from a dead animal was permitted to them.

5-6. מִיַּד כָּל חַיָּה אֶדְרְשֶׁנּוּ . . . כִּי בְּצֶלֶם אֱלֹהִים . . . – *Of every beast will I demand it . . . For in the image of God.* The sense of these two verses, according to the *Sforno,* is thus: Man, who is created in the image of *Elohim,* is far more important and precious than any other living creature. As such, if he is worthy God will save him from his attacker, be he beast or man. If he is not worthy, God will punish the murderer (if he is a man) but preferably, the court should execute justice. The reason given by

חמישי ח בָּהּ׃ וַיֹּאמֶר אֱלֹהִים אֶל־נֹחַ וְאֶל־בָּנָיו אִתּוֹ לֵאמֹר׃
ט־י וַאֲנִי הִנְנִי מֵקִים אֶת־בְּרִיתִי אִתְּכֶם וְאֶת־זַרְעֲכֶם אַחֲרֵיכֶם׃ וְאֵת כָּל־נֶפֶשׁ
הַחַיָּה אֲשֶׁר אִתְּכֶם בָּעוֹף בַּבְּהֵמָה וּבְכָל־חַיַּת הָאָרֶץ אִתְּכֶם מִכֹּל יֹצְאֵי
יא הַתֵּבָה לְכֹל חַיַּת הָאָרֶץ׃ וַהֲקִמֹתִי אֶת־בְּרִיתִי אִתְּכֶם וְלֹא־יִכָּרֵת כָּל־בָּשָׂר
יב עוֹד מִמֵּי הַמַּבּוּל וְלֹא־יִהְיֶה עוֹד מַבּוּל לְשַׁחֵת הָאָרֶץ׃ וַיֹּאמֶר אֱלֹהִים זֹאת
אוֹת־הַבְּרִית אֲשֶׁר־אֲנִי נֹתֵן בֵּינִי וּבֵינֵיכֶם וּבֵין כָּל־נֶפֶשׁ חַיָּה אֲשֶׁר אִתְּכֶם
יג לְדֹרֹת עוֹלָם׃ אֶת־קַשְׁתִּי נָתַתִּי בֶּעָנָן וְהָיְתָה לְאוֹת בְּרִית בֵּינִי וּבֵין הָאָרֶץ׃

---

7. וְאַתֶּם פְּרוּ וּרְבוּ — *And you, be fruitful and multiply* . . . and do not shed the blood of men.

9. וַאֲנִי הִנְנִי מֵקִים אֶת בְּרִיתִי — *And as for Me, behold I establish My covenant.* On the condition that you not shed innocent blood do I *establish My covenant* not to destroy the earth again, but if there will be innocent blood shed, the earth will be destroyed, as it says, . . . כִּי הַדָּם הוּא יַחֲנִיף אֶת הָאָרֶץ וְלָאָרֶץ לֹא יְכֻפַּר, *For blood pollutes the land, and no expiation can be made for the land, etc. (Numbers* 35:33). However, for all other sins, only the sinner will be punished, but the earth shall not be destroyed.

11. וְלֹא יִהְיֶה עוֹד מַבּוּל לְשַׁחֵת הָאָרֶץ — *And never again shall there be a flood to destroy the earth.* There will not be any sort of catastrophe (lit. downfall and loss) to destroy the substance of the earth.

13. אֶת קַשְׁתִּי נָתַתִּי בֶּעָנָן — *I have set My bow in the cloud.* I set it (originally) that it be part of nature.

וְהָיְתָה לְאוֹת בְּרִית — *And it shall be a sign of the covenant* . . . since the bow is double; for indeed scholars and researchers have tried in vain to give a reason for the order of colors of the second bow, which is opposite of the color order of the normal first bow. (The bow) will be a sign to the righteous in (each generation), that their generation is guilty, as our Sages say, *'Did the rainbow appear in your days?' (Ketuboth* 77b), so that they (the righteous) might pray, admonish and teach the people knowledge (of God).

NOTES

the *Sforno* for the importance and value of the physical body of man is that it houses and gives life to the soul and intellect of man, which is called צֶלֶם אֱלֹהִים, the *Divine image.*

7. וְאַתֶּם פְּרוּ וּרְבוּ – *And you, be fruitful and multiply.* The phrase פְּרוּ וּרְבוּ, *Be fruitful and multiply,* appears in verse 1 and is repeated here. *Rashi* explains that the former is a blessing, while this is a command to procreate. The *Sforno* resolves this difficulty (i.e. why the Torah repeats this phrase) by explaining that the command in this verse is not to procreate but to *preserve* human life. By refraining from shedding blood the human race will be *fruitful and multiply.*

9-11. וַאֲנִי הִנְנִי מֵקִים אֶת בְּרִיתִי . . . וְלֹא יִהְיֶה עוֹד מַבּוּל לְשַׁחֵת הָאָרֶץ – *And as for Me, behold I establish My covenant . . . And never again shall there be a flood to destroy the earth.* A covenant involves two parties; in this instance God and mankind. A condition is now being made by the Almighty: if man refrains from shedding innocent blood, God in turn will not destroy the inhabitants of the earth again. This pledge, however, is a conditional one, and the covenant demands mutual, reciprocal responsibility. In addition to this promise of God (verse 9) there is another *unconditional* statement made by Him (verse 11) that regardless of man's conduct, the *substance* of the earth will never again be destroyed by a total catastrophe.

13. אֶת קַשְׁתִּי נָתַתִּי בֶּעָנָן וְהָיְתָה לְאוֹת בְּרִית – *I have set My bow in the cloud and it shall be a*

יד־טו וְהָיָה בְּעַנְנִי עָנָן עַל־הָאָרֶץ וְנִרְאֲתָה הַקֶּשֶׁת בֶּעָנָן׃ וְזָכַרְתִּי אֶת־בְּרִיתִי
אֲשֶׁר בֵּינִי וּבֵינֵיכֶם וּבֵין כָּל־נֶפֶשׁ חַיָּה בְּכָל־בָּשָׂר וְלֹא־יִהְיֶה עוֹד הַמַּיִם
טז לְמַבּוּל לְשַׁחֵת כָּל־בָּשָׂר׃ וְהָיְתָה הַקֶּשֶׁת בֶּעָנָן וּרְאִיתִיהָ לִזְכֹּר בְּרִית עוֹלָם
יז בֵּין אֱלֹהִים וּבֵין כָּל־נֶפֶשׁ חַיָּה בְּכָל־בָּשָׂר אֲשֶׁר עַל־הָאָרֶץ׃ וַיֹּאמֶר אֱלֹהִים
אֶל־נֹחַ זֹאת אוֹת־הַבְּרִית אֲשֶׁר הֲקִמֹתִי בֵּינִי וּבֵין כָּל־בָּשָׂר אֲשֶׁר
עַל־הָאָרֶץ׃
ששי יח־יט וַיִּהְיוּ בְנֵי־נֹחַ הַיֹּצְאִים מִן־הַתֵּבָה שֵׁם וְחָם וָיָפֶת וְחָם הוּא אֲבִי כְנָעַן׃ שְׁלֹשָׁה

---

14. בְּעַנְנִי עָנָן — *When I place a cloud* . . . for the rainbow will not be visible without a thick, heavy cloud, following the moisture and the clearing.

16. וּרְאִיתִיהָ לִזְכֹּר בְּרִית עוֹלָם — *And I will look upon it to remember the everlasting covenant.* I will regard the result of the bow, which is the prayers of the righteous as they stand in the breach to turn away My wrath from destroying (the earth) — similar to, *He remembers the everlasting covenant.*

17. וַיֹּאמֶר אֱלֹהִים אֶל נֹחַ זֹאת אוֹת הַבְּרִית — *And God said to Noah, 'This is the sign of the covenant.'* This second rainbow is the sign of the covenant, and it is incumbent upon you, and those like you, to bestir yourselves when you see it, to rouse the people to repent and understand to better (themselves).

18. וְחָם הוּא אֲבִי כְנָעַן — *And Ham was the father of Canaan.* Akin in his ways to Canaan who is well known for degradation, in such a manner that he (Ham) was truly the *father of Canaan,* and similar to him as well; (this is) comparable to אָבִיךְ הָאֱמֹרִי, *Your father was an Emorite (Ezekiel* 16:3).

NOTES

sign of the covenant. There is a difference of opinion among the early Torah commentators as to whether the rainbow was brought forth by God after the Flood, or it was part of original Creation. *Saadiah Gaon* and the *Ramban* are of the latter opinion, to which the *Sforno* also subscribes. However, the *Sforno* submits that since a rainbow shows two bands of colors, the inner brighter one (called the *primary* bow) and the outer, less distinct one (known as the *secondary* bow), both theories as to the time of the rainbow's origin may be correct. At the time of Creation there was only the primary bow, but after the Flood the secondary one appeared, made visible by God as a 'sign of the covenant,' for the purpose of alerting the righteous to pray on behalf of their generation and arouse the people to repent. He feels that this interpretation regarding the double bow explains the phenomena of the reverse order of the rainbow's colors. The primary bow has the red coloring on the outside and the violet on the inside of the arch, while in the secondary bow the colors appear just the opposite. The passage from the Tractate *Kesubos* (77b) which he cites alludes to the exchange between Rabbi Shimon Bar Yochai and Rabbi Yehoshua ben Levi. The former asks Rabbi Yehoshua whether the rainbow appeared in his generation. When he answers affirmatively, Rabbi Shimon questions his righteousness, for a truly great *tzaddik* protects his generation so that it is unnecessary for God to give the rainbow as a sign to the righteous to pray and intercede.

14. בְּעַנְנִי עָנָן – *When I place a cloud.* The *Sforno's* observation is scientifically sound. Rainbows vary, some are brighter and others lighter. If the rain has been heavy, the bow will spread all the way across the sky and be more pronounced. This is the meaning of the phrase, *When I place a cloud,* interpreted by the *Sforno* as a thick, heavy cloud which produces heavy rain that is a prerequisite for a full rainbow.

18. וְחָם הוּא אֲבִי כְנָעַן – *And Ham was the father of Canaan.* Ham had other sons in addition to Canaan. The Torah singles him out to indicate that father and son were strikingly similar in their wickedness. The quote cited by the *Sforno* from *Ezekiel* is to prove that ethnic

כ אֵלֶּה בְּנֵי־נֹחַ וּמֵאֵלֶּה נָפְצָה כָל־הָאָרֶץ: וַיָּחֶל נֹחַ אִישׁ הָאֲדָמָה וַיִּטַּע כָּרֶם:
כא־כב וַיֵּשְׁתְּ מִן־הַיַּיִן וַיִּשְׁכָּר וַיִּתְגַּל בְּתוֹךְ אָהֳלֹה: וַיַּרְא חָם אֲבִי כְנַעַן אֵת עֶרְוַת
כג אָבִיו וַיַּגֵּד לִשְׁנֵי־אֶחָיו בַּחוּץ: וַיִּקַּח שֵׁם וָיֶפֶת אֶת־הַשִּׂמְלָה וַיָּשִׂימוּ עַל־
שְׁכֶם שְׁנֵיהֶם וַיֵּלְכוּ אֲחֹרַנִּית וַיְכַסּוּ אֵת עֶרְוַת אֲבִיהֶם וּפְנֵיהֶם אֲחֹרַנִּית

---

19. שְׁלֹשָׁה אֵלֶּה בְּנֵי נֹחַ — *These three were the sons of Noah.* Although a wicked one was among them, since they were the *sons of Noah,* God blessed all of them, saying, *'Be fruitful and multiply and fill the land'* (9:1), the result being that מֵאֵלֶּה נָפְצָה כָל הָאָרֶץ, *from these the whole world was spread out.*

20. וַיָּחֶל נֹחַ — *And Noah (the man of the earth) began.* He began with an unsuitable project, therefore unsavory deeds resulted from it, for indeed, a small fault at the beginning will cause many more at the end, as (often) happens in (the pursuit of) wisdom (sciences) which (are based) on an incorrect premise. This is taught to us (when the Torah) says, וַיָּחֶל הָעָם לִזְנוֹת, *And the people began to commit harlotry (Numbers* 25:1).

22. וַיַּרְא חָם אֲבִי כְנַעַן אֵת עֶרְוַת אָבִיו — *Ham, the father of Canaan, saw his father's nakedness.* He saw the degradation inflicted on him (Noah) by his son Canaan, i.e., emasculation, as some of our Sages say (*Sanhedrin* 70a). Barusi the Chaldean wrote that he emasculated him through sorcery. Ham, in his wickedness, saw (this happening) and did not protest. Truly, shame is termed עֶרְוָה, *nakedness,* as it says, וְעַרְוַת מַלְכָּא לָא אֲרִיךְ לָנָא לְמֶחֱזֵא, *It is improper for us to see the shame (nakedness) of the king (Ezra* 4:14). Also, (the term) עֶרְוַת דָּבָר, *unseemly thing,* is applied to an ugly thing (or act).

וַיַּגֵּד לִשְׁנֵי אֶחָיו — *And told his two brothers outside.* He rejoiced at the act of his son.

23. וּפְנֵיהֶם אֲחֹרַנִּית — *Their faces were turned away.* Even when they were covering (him) at which time there was a need to turn toward him, (nonetheless) they did not turn to look, for that would have increased their pain (sadness).

NOTES

names are not always used literally but at times figuratively. In that verse the prophet is alluding to their deeds, not their origin; their *actions* were those of Emorites. In our case, the name Canaanite represents degradation and immorality.

19. שְׁלֹשָׁה אֵלֶּה בְּנֵי נֹחַ — *These three were the sons of Noah.* The previous verse enumerates the sons of Noah; why is it necessary to repeat again, *These three were the sons of Noah* from whom the new world spread out? The *Sforno's* answer is that although a wicked one was among them (Ham) since they were the *sons of Noah,* God blessed them, with the result that from all three of them *the whole world was spread out.*

20. וַיָּחֶל נֹחַ — *And Noah began.* The *Sforno* stresses the moral lesson to be learned from Noah's first agricultural project following the flood. The planting of a vineyard and drinking of the wine produced by its grapes may seem innocent, yet this inappropriate act led to far more serious consequences. The proof brought by the *Sforno* from *Numbers* is most telling. The tragic episode of Shitim begins with harlotry, but leads to idolatry, the most serious transgression of all.

22. וַיַּרְא חָם אֲבִי כְנַעַן אֵת עֶרְוַת אָבִיו — *Ham, the father of Canaan, saw his father's nakedness.* Contrary to the interpretation of some of our Sages, and the literal meaning of the verse, the *Sforno* (as *Rashi)* is of the opinion that it was Canaan, not Ham, who inflicted this indignity upon his grandfather. Ham's sin was that he did not prevent or protest; on the contrary — he rejoiced and joyfully told his brothers.

כד וְעֶרְוַת אֲבִיהֶם לֹא רָאוּ: וַיִּיקֶץ נֹחַ מִיֵּינוֹ וַיֵּדַע אֵת אֲשֶׁר־עָשָׂה לוֹ בְּנוֹ
כה־כו הַקָּטָן: וַיֹּאמֶר אָרוּר כְּנָעַן עֶבֶד עֲבָדִים יִהְיֶה לְאֶחָיו: וַיֹּאמֶר בָּרוּךְ יהוה
כז אֱלֹהֵי שֵׁם וִיהִי כְנַעַן עֶבֶד לָמוֹ: יַפְתְּ אֱלֹהִים לְיֶפֶת וְיִשְׁכֹּן בְּאָהֳלֵי־שֵׁם וִיהִי
כח כְנַעַן עֶבֶד לָמוֹ: וַיְחִי־נֹחַ אַחַר הַמַּבּוּל שְׁלֹשׁ מֵאוֹת שָׁנָה וַחֲמִשִּׁים שָׁנָה:
כט וַיְהִי כָּל־יְמֵי־נֹחַ תְּשַׁע מֵאוֹת שָׁנָה וַחֲמִשִּׁים שָׁנָה וַיָּמֹת:

---

24. בְּנוֹ הַקָּטָן — *His small son.* Grandchildren are considered as children, and Canaan was the youngest of Ham's sons. Perhaps he (also) was the youngest grandson of Noah; also in his conduct (behavior), קָטֹן . . . בַּגּוֹיִם בָּזוּי . . . מְאֹד, (*He was*) *least among the nations, most despised* (*Obadiah* 1:2).

25. עֶבֶד עֲבָדִים יִהְיֶה לְאֶחָיו — *A slave of slaves shall he be to his brothers.* Under normal circumstances he should be a slave to his brothers, since he was the least in (moral) stature and the (most) degraded of them all, as it says, וְעֶבֶד אֱוִיל לַחֲכַם לֵב, *A fool shall be slave to the wise hearted* (*Proverbs* 11:29), therefore when he sinned, the *added* (punishment) was *slave of slaves.*

26. וִיהִי כְנַעַן — *And let Canaan* ... his offspring, be ...

עֶבֶד לָמוֹ — *A slave to them* ... to the God of Shem and the descendants of Shem, as it says, חֹטְבֵי עֵצִים וְשֹׁאֲבֵי מַיִם לָעֵדָה וּלְמִזְבַּח ה׳, (*And they became*) *choppers of wood and hewers of water for the congregation and the altar of* HASHEM (*Joshua* 9:27).

27. בְּאָהֳלֵי שֵׁם — *In the tents of Shem.* (This refers to the) houses of study, besides the Temple (lit. 'Chosen House').

עֶבֶד לָמוֹ — *A slave to them.* This is repeated (a second time) to indicate both Shem and Japheth, even not at the time of the Temple.

29. וַיָּמֹת — *And he died.* Prior to the major historical event of that era, namely, the awakening of Abraham to call in the name of Hashem.

NOTES

24. בְּנוֹ הַקָּטָן – *His small son.* The *Sforno* suggests three reasons for calling him, *his small son.* Consistent with his interpretation that Canaan was the perpetrator of this gross act, the *Sforno* submits that he was (a) the youngest of Ham's sons; (b) Noah's youngest grandson; (c) the Torah does not call him small in a chronological sense but refers to his inferior, deficient status.

26-27. וִיהִי כְנַעַן עֶבֶד לָמוֹ . . . בְּאָהֳלֵי שֵׁם . . . עֶבֶד לָמוֹ – *And let Canaan be a slave to them ... In the tents of Shem a slave to them.* The word לָמוֹ, *to them,* is in the plural. In verse 26 it refers to Canaan's relationship to Shem, therefore the plural term is interpreted by the *Sforno* as alluding to the double duty imposed by Joshua on the Givonim (who were descendants of Canaan), i.e., to do the menial labor for the Sanctuary and to serve Israel as well. The repetition of the phrase לָמוֹ in verse 27 is meant to teach us that Canaan will be a slave to both Shem and Japheth. The *Sforno* is constrained to explain the second לָמוֹ in this manner, since this verse speaks of a time when the Temple no longer exists, hence the initial interpretation of the plural form לָמוֹ is not applicable.

27. בְּאָהֳלֵי שֵׁם – *In the tents of Shem.* The *Sforno* agrees with Rashi that the subject of *and dwell in the tents of Shem* is God. Therefore he explains the plural form (tents) as referring to the Temple and all Houses of Study, where God's presence is found.

29. וַיָּמֹת – *And he died.* The phrase וַיָּמֹת, *and he died,* is used to indicate finality and culmination. In 11:11 the *Sforno* points out that the Torah does not use the term *he died* for the generations mentioned in that chapter, i.e., from Noah to Abraham. He states that the reason is that they were all alive when

י א-ב וְאֵלֶּה תּוֹלְדֹת בְּנֵי־נֹחַ שֵׁם חָם וָיָפֶת וַיִּוָּלְדוּ לָהֶם בָּנִים אַחַר הַמַּבּוּל: בְּנֵי
ג יֶפֶת גֹּמֶר וּמָגוֹג וּמָדַי וְיָוָן וְתֻבָל וּמֶשֶׁךְ וְתִירָס: וּבְנֵי גֹּמֶר אַשְׁכְּנַז וְרִיפַת
ד-ה וְתֹגַרְמָה: וּבְנֵי יָוָן אֱלִישָׁה וְתַרְשִׁישׁ כִּתִּים וְדֹדָנִים: מֵאֵלֶּה נִפְרְדוּ אִיֵּי
ו הַגּוֹיִם בְּאַרְצֹתָם אִישׁ לִלְשֹׁנוֹ לְמִשְׁפְּחֹתָם בְּגוֹיֵהֶם: וּבְנֵי חָם כּוּשׁ וּמִצְרַיִם
ז וּפוּט וּכְנָעַן: וּבְנֵי כוּשׁ סְבָא וַחֲוִילָה וְסַבְתָּה וְרַעְמָה וְסַבְתְּכָא וּבְנֵי רַעְמָה
ח-ט שְׁבָא וּדְדָן: וְכוּשׁ יָלַד אֶת־נִמְרֹד הוּא הֵחֵל לִהְיוֹת גִּבֹּר בָּאָרֶץ: הוּא־הָיָה
י גִבֹּר־צַיִד לִפְנֵי יהוה עַל־כֵּן יֵאָמַר כְּנִמְרֹד גִּבּוֹר צַיִד לִפְנֵי יהוה: וַתְּהִי
יא רֵאשִׁית מַמְלַכְתּוֹ בָּבֶל וְאֶרֶךְ וְאַכַּד וְכַלְנֵה בְּאֶרֶץ שִׁנְעָר: מִן־הָאָרֶץ הַהִוא

X

6. וּפוּט וּכְנָעַן — *And Phut and Canaan.* His children are not mentioned (i.e., Phut's) because all his children formed one people called by his name, as it says, פָּרַס כּוּשׁ וּפוּט אִתָּם, *Among them shall be Persia, Cush and Phut (Ezekiel* 38:5).

7. וּבְנֵי כוּשׁ סְבָא וַחֲוִילָה — *The children of Cush; Seba and Havilah.* Each became the founder of a people, besides those who are called by his name, as it says: כּוּשׁ וּסְבָא תַּחְתֶּיךָ, *Cush and Seba in exchange for you (Isaiah* 43:3).

8. וְכוּשׁ יָלַד אֶת נִמְרֹד — *And Cush begot Nimrod.* Among those who are called by his name he begot an individual known as a mighty man.

9. לִפְנֵי ה׳ — *Before Hashem.* Exceedingly mighty, similar to, עִיר גְּדוֹלָה לֵאלֹהִים, *(Nineveh) an enormously large city (Jonah* 3:3).

עַל כֵּן יֵאָמַר כְּנִמְרֹד גִּבּוֹר צַיִד — *Therefore it is said: 'Like Nimrod a mighty hunter.'* And because of his reputation as a mighty man he ruled over nations, as it says . . .

10. וַתְּהִי רֵאשִׁית מַמְלַכְתּוֹ בָּבֶל — *The beginning of his kingdom was Babel.* This is to tell (us) that because of his kingdom, it came to pass that various nations came to dwell in Shinar and (consequently) the city and tower were built (11:4) for the purpose of expanding his (Nimrod's) kingdom over the human race through the

NOTES

Abraham sought to lead man to the worship of God, as opposed to the ten generations from Adam to Noah who died by the time of the Flood (hence the Torah does use the term *and he died* in *Parashas Bereishis*). Whenever there is a *culmination* of a unit of the Torah's narrative, i.e., 'the major historical event of that era,' as the *Sforno* phrases it, the word וַיָּמֹת is used. If, however, the central feature of a unit is still in process, the word וַיָּמֹת is not used. This explains the *Sforno's* interpretation here. Although Abraham was 58 years old when Noah died, he had as yet not become known or begun his mission of leading man to God. Therefore, the death of Noah represented the culmination of an era, the central feature of which was the Flood. That is why וַיָּמֹת, *and he died*, is used here.

X

8. וְכוּשׁ יָלַד אֶת נִמְרֹד — *And Cush begot Nimrod.* In the previous verse (7) the children of Cush are listed. The singling out of Nimrod in this verse is explained by the *Sforno* as indicating his unique position among the offspring of Cush.

9. לִפְנֵי ה׳ — *Before* HASHEM. The expression לִפְנֵי ה׳ *(before* HASHEM*)* cannot be translated literally here as meaning 'before God' or 'in His presence.' It is an idiom for anyone or anything which is exceedingly *mighty*, as in the case of Nimrod, or *large*, as in the case of the city Nineveh.

10. וַתְּהִי רֵאשִׁית מַמְלַכְתּוֹ בָּבֶל — *The beginning of his kingdom was Babel.* The plan of Nimrod

יב יָצָא אַשּׁוּר וַיִּבֶן אֶת־נִינְוֵה וְאֶת־רְחֹבֹת עִיר וְאֶת־כָּלַח׃ וְאֶת־רֶסֶן בֵּין נִינְוֵה
יג וּבֵין כָּלַח הִוא הָעִיר הַגְּדֹלָה׃ וּמִצְרַיִם יָלַד אֶת־לוּדִים וְאֶת־עֲנָמִים
יד וְאֶת־לְהָבִים וְאֶת־נַפְתֻּחִים׃ וְאֶת־פַּתְרֻסִים וְאֶת־כַּסְלֻחִים אֲשֶׁר יָצְאוּ מִשָּׁם
טו פְּלִשְׁתִּים וְאֶת־כַּפְתֹּרִים׃ וּכְנַעַן יָלַד אֶת־צִידֹן בְּכֹרוֹ וְאֶת־חֵת׃
טז־יז וְאֶת־הַיְבוּסִי וְאֶת־הָאֱמֹרִי וְאֵת הַגִּרְגָּשִׁי׃ וְאֶת־הַחִוִּי וְאֶת־הַעַרְקִי וְאֶת־
יח הַסִּינִי׃ וְאֶת־הָאַרְוָדִי וְאֶת־הַצְּמָרִי וְאֶת־הַחֲמָתִי וְאַחַר נָפֹצוּ מִשְׁפְּחוֹת
יט הַכְּנַעֲנִי׃ וַיְהִי גְּבוּל הַכְּנַעֲנִי מִצִּידֹן בֹּאֲכָה גְרָרָה עַד־עַזָּה בֹּאֲכָה סְדֹמָה
כ וַעֲמֹרָה וְאַדְמָה וּצְבֹיִם עַד־לָשַׁע׃ אֵלֶּה בְנֵי־חָם לְמִשְׁפְּחֹתָם לִלְשֹׁנֹתָם
כא בְּאַרְצֹתָם בְּגוֹיֵהֶם׃ וּלְשֵׁם יֻלַּד גַּם־הוּא אֲבִי כָּל־בְּנֵי־עֵבֶר אֲחִי

---

medium of a universal strange god whom all would worship, similar to the strategy of Jeroboam when he feared the (magnetic) call of the Temple (*I Kings* 12:26).

11. מִן הָאָרֶץ הַהִיא יָצָא אַשּׁוּר — *From that land Ashur went forth.* He rejected (both) the rulership of Nimrod and his wicked vulgar plan, as our Sages tell us (*Midrash*).

וַיִּבֶן אֶת נִינְוֵה — *And built Nineveh* ... and therefore he merited to build all these cities, as it says, אֶל פָּנָיו יְשַׁלֶּם לוֹ, *He will repay him to his face* (*Deut.* 7:10).

21. וּלְשֵׁם יֻלַּד — *And to Shem was born* ... a man, virtuous like him, namely Eber.

גַּם הוּא אֲבִי כָּל בְּנֵי עֵבֶר — *He also was the ancestor (father) of all the descendants (children) of Eber.* Although those who hold fast to the belief in God's existence, His power and providence, are called עִבְרִים, *Ivrim,* after עֵבֶר, *Eber,* (their teacher) who endeavored to understand and teach this (belief) as it says, *And he told Abram the Ivri* (14:13), nonetheless *he also,* namely Shem, was the father and teacher of *all the children of Eber.* (This is so) because one who teaches and guides is called *father,* as we find, *He was the 'father' of all who handle the harp and flute* (4:21); also, וּמִי אֲבִיהֶם, *And who are their fathers?* (*I Samuel* 10:12); and the students are called *sons,* as it says, בְּנֵי הַנְּבִיאִים, *The disciples (sons) of the Prophets* (*I Kings* 20:35).

NOTES

and his advisors was to consolidate the rulership of Nimrod not only through political allegiance but also through a common religious commitment. The *Sforno* cites the case of Jeroboam, the first king of the northern kingdom — Israel — who feared the effect of the festival pilgrimage to Jerusalem on his people, who might transfer their allegiance to the kingdom of Judah, so he proceeded to erect golden calves in Bethel and Dan to rally his people around these idols, using their commitment to a new faith to buttress their allegiance to him.

11. מִן הָאָרֶץ הַהִיא יָצָא אַשּׁוּר — *From that land Ashur went forth.* Since Ashur refused to support Nimrod in his nefarious plan, although he was not that worthy himself, God rewards him for this one proper act of defiance. The verse cited from *Deuteronomy,* where the expression *to his face* is used, is to be understood as referring to the reward given by God to the wicked in this world, during their lifetime, for any good deed performed by them. Punishment for their sins, on the other hand, will be meted out in the next world.

21. וּלְשֵׁם יֻלַּד גַּם הוּא אֲבִי כָּל בְּנֵי עֵבֶר — *And to Shem was born, he also was the ancestor (father) of all the descendants (children) of Eber.* Since it does not say *And Shem begot* but, *and to Shem was born,* which implies a child whose character reflected his father Shem, the *Sforno* interprets this as referring to Eber who possessed the qualifications to transmit the teachings of his great father Shem. The *Sforno* also links the phrase גַּם הוּא — *(he also)* to the latter part of the verse, to emphasize the pedagogic role played by Shem in teaching and influencing the followers of Eber. Indeed, in our tradition reference is always made to the 'school of Shem and Eber.'

כב־כג יֶפֶת הַגָּדוֹל: בְּנֵי שֵׁם עֵילָם וְאַשּׁוּר וְאַרְפַּכְשַׁד וְלוּד וַאֲרָם: וּבְנֵי אֲרָם עוּץ
כד־כה וְחוּל וְגֶתֶר וָמַשׁ: וְאַרְפַּכְשַׁד יָלַד אֶת־שָׁלַח וְשֶׁלַח יָלַד אֶת־עֵבֶר: וּלְעֵבֶר
יֻלַּד שְׁנֵי בָנִים שֵׁם הָאֶחָד פֶּלֶג כִּי בְיָמָיו נִפְלְגָה הָאָרֶץ וְשֵׁם אָחִיו יָקְטָן:
כו־כז וְיָקְטָן יָלַד אֶת־אַלְמוֹדָד וְאֶת־שָׁלֶף וְאֶת־חֲצַרְמָוֶת וְאֶת־יָרַח: וְאֶת־הֲדוֹרָם
כח־כט וְאֶת־אוּזָל וְאֶת־דִּקְלָה: וְאֶת־עוֹבָל וְאֶת־אֲבִימָאֵל וְאֶת־שְׁבָא: וְאֶת־אוֹפִר
ל וְאֶת־חֲוִילָה וְאֶת־יוֹבָב כָּל־אֵלֶּה בְּנֵי יָקְטָן: וַיְהִי מוֹשָׁבָם מִמֵּשָׁא בֹּאֲכָה
לא סְפָרָה הַר הַקֶּדֶם: אֵלֶּה בְנֵי־שֵׁם לְמִשְׁפְּחֹתָם לִלְשֹׁנֹתָם בְּאַרְצֹתָם לְגוֹיֵהֶם:
לב אֵלֶּה מִשְׁפְּחֹת בְּנֵי־נֹחַ לְתוֹלְדֹתָם בְּגוֹיֵהֶם וּמֵאֵלֶּה נִפְרְדוּ הַגּוֹיִם בָּאָרֶץ
אַחַר הַמַּבּוּל:

יא שביעי א־ב וַיְהִי כָל־הָאָרֶץ שָׂפָה אֶחָת וּדְבָרִים אֲחָדִים: וַיְהִי בְּנָסְעָם מִקֶּדֶם וַיִּמְצְאוּ
ג בִקְעָה בְּאֶרֶץ שִׁנְעָר וַיֵּשְׁבוּ שָׁם: וַיֹּאמְרוּ אִישׁ אֶל־רֵעֵהוּ הָבָה נִלְבְּנָה
לְבֵנִים וְנִשְׂרְפָה לִשְׂרֵפָה וַתְּהִי לָהֶם הַלְּבֵנָה לְאָבֶן וְהַחֵמָר הָיָה לָהֶם
ד לַחֹמֶר: וַיֹּאמְרוּ הָבָה ׀ נִבְנֶה־לָּנוּ עִיר וּמִגְדָּל וְרֹאשׁוֹ בַשָּׁמַיִם וְנַעֲשֶׂה־לָּנוּ

---

25. פֶּלֶג כִּי בְיָמָיו נִפְלְגָה הָאָרֶץ — *Peleg, for in his days the earth was divided.* (The Torah) tells us Eber's virtue, that he correctly divined through the holy spirit what was to come to pass in the days of his son. He called his son by the name Peleg to tell (everyone) the cause for the reduced human longevity beginning from Peleg and beyond; the cause being the sin of the generation of Dispersion and their (consequent) punishment, for their vitality (was affected) by the sudden change of climates.

XI

2. בְּנָסְעָם מִקֶּדֶם — *When they traveled from the east* ... as is the custom of shepherds who travel from place to place in search of suitable pasture.

3. הָבָה נִלְבְּנָה לְבֵנִים — *Come, let us make bricks* ... to construct houses and sheepfolds; this was the counsel of individuals among the populace, as it says, *They said to one another.*

4. וַיֹּאמְרוּ הָבָה נִבְנֶה לָּנוּ עִיר — *And they said, 'Come, let us build us a city.'* This was the counsel of the princes of the generation, (their goal being) to make Nimrod king over the whole human race.

NOTES

The *Sforno* stresses that the relationship between a teacher and pupil is akin to that of a father and son, which accounts for the term 'the *father* (אֲבִי) of the descendants of Eber,' a term used in other instances as well, as cited by the *Sforno*.

25. פֶּלֶג כִּי בְיָמָיו נִפְלְגָה הָאָרֶץ — *Peleg, for in his days the earth was divided.* The word פֶּלֶג means *half.* The name given by Eber to his son פֶּלֶג was meant to indicate, as *Rashi* states in *Chronicles,* that in his days the lifespan of man was cut in half. The *Sforno* adds that the reason for this reduced longevity was because through man's dispersal, the dislocation and resultant climate changes had a deleterious effect upon his lifespan.

XI

3-4. וַיֹּאמְרוּ הָבָה — *And they said, 'Come ...'* The introductory phrase, *And they said, 'Come,'* (וַיֹּאמְרוּ הָבָה) appears in both verses. The *Sforno* explains that it is not redundant: the first refers to the masses, who are interested in building homes and sheepfolds — the

ה שֵׁם פֶּן־נָפוּץ עַל־פְּנֵי כָל־הָאָרֶץ: וַיֵּרֶד יהוה לִרְאֹת אֶת־הָעִיר וְאֶת־
ו הַמִּגְדָּל אֲשֶׁר בָּנוּ בְּנֵי הָאָדָם: וַיֹּאמֶר יהוה הֵן עַם אֶחָד וְשָׂפָה אַחַת לְכֻלָּם

וּמִגְדָּל וְרֹאשׁוֹ בַשָּׁמַיִם וְנַעֲשֶׂה לָּנוּ שֵׁם — *And a tower with its top in the heavens, and let us make a name for ourselves.* 'Let us make a name,' an idol which will be situated in the tower. The fame of its height, and the huge size of the city, will spread among the whole human race in such a manner that this deity will be considered as the 'deity of deities' among mankind, and all will seek it out. The one who would rule over that city would rule over the entire human race, since everyone would seek it out — and this was (indeed) their intent.

5. וַיֵּרֶד ה׳ לִרְאֹת — *And* HASHEM *came down to see.* The idiom 'descending to see' said of God, the blessed One, is used when the action (of the sinner) does not in itself merit punishment. but will inevitably lead to a (more serious) deterioration, (as we find by) בֵּן סוֹרֵר וּמוֹרֶה, *a rebellious, gluttonous son* (*Deut.* 21:18-21) where our Sages explain, 'The Torah descended to the depths of his intention' (*Sanhedrin* 72a). The same (is true) of Sodom, where it is written, *I will go down now and see* (18:21), for indeed their wickedness was no greater than that of other people to merit punishing them (so severely) in this world — except in the area of cruelty against poor people, from which total deterioration would eventually result, as it says, הִנֵּה זֶה הָיָה עֲוֹן סְדֹם אֲחוֹתֵךְ ... וְיַד עָנִי וְאֶבְיוֹן לֹא הֶחֱזִיקָה, *Behold this was the iniquity of Sodom, your sister (city) ... she did not support the poor and the needy* (*Ezekiel* 16:49). This was also (true) of the punishment of Israel in their exile, as it says, אֶרְאֶה מָה אַחֲרִיתָם, *I will see what their end shall be* (*Deut.* 32:20).

6. הֵן עַם אֶחָד — *Behold they are one people.* (Normally) the counsel of nations and their plans are thwarted and nullified as a result of divisions which occur between them, caused by (differences) regarding faith, or (lack of a common) language.

NOTES

necessities of life; and the second to the princes and leaders who are interested in a base of power for Nimrod, who according to our Sages (*Hullin* 89a) was the initiator of this plan. They also realized that by combining physical grandeur with religious fervor they would insure the success of this grand plan.

4. וְנַעֲשֶׂה לָּנוּ שֵׁם — *And let us make a name for ourselves.* The *Sforno* interprets the word שֵׁם, *name,* as meaning idolatry, in keeping with the interpretation of our Sages (*Sanhedrin* 109a) and the *Zohar* which explains it as meaning, 'let us make an *object of worship.*'

5. וַיֵּרֶד ה׳ לִרְאֹת — *And* HASHEM *came down to see.* The Almighty has no need to 'descend and see'; all is known to Him. The word וַיֵּרֶד, *He descended,* is meant to imply that He sees the *ultimate* consequences of a present act or condition. In the case of the rebellious son cited by the *Sforno,* although the present actions of this son are not serious enough to warrant such severe punishment, God however knows that ultimately he will murder and steal to satisfy his appetites. Even Sodom, wicked and evil as they were, would not have deserved destruction were it not for the ultimate evil which would inevitably result from their present behavior. In the case of the tower, He examines the inevitable results of this project, and determines that it must be prevented through dispersion (see verse 6). The verse cited from *Deuteronomy* is perhaps the key to his interpretation. He does not interpret the phrase *what their end shall be* as meaning the vulnerability of the Jewish people when God will *hide His face from them,* which is the beginning of that particular verse (*Deut.* 32:20). Rather it is the *reason* for God's decision to 'hide His face' (to remove His providence). Because He sees what their actions will eventually lead to, He turns away from them — now!

6. הֵן עַם אֶחָד — *Behold they are one people.* The *Sforno,* in his reference to the Sabians,

ז וְזֶה הַחִלָּם לַעֲשׂוֹת וְעַתָּה לֹא־יִבָּצֵר מֵהֶם כֹּל אֲשֶׁר יָזְמוּ לַעֲשׂוֹת: הָבָה
ח נֵרְדָה וְנָבְלָה שָׁם שְׂפָתָם אֲשֶׁר לֹא יִשְׁמְעוּ אִישׁ שְׂפַת רֵעֵהוּ: וַיָּפֶץ יְהוָה
ט אֹתָם מִשָּׁם עַל־פְּנֵי כָל־הָאָרֶץ וַיַּחְדְּלוּ לִבְנֹת הָעִיר: עַל־כֵּן קָרָא שְׁמָהּ
בָּבֶל כִּי־שָׁם בָּלַל יְהוָה שְׂפַת כָּל־הָאָרֶץ וּמִשָּׁם הֱפִיצָם יְהוָה עַל־פְּנֵי
כָּל־הָאָרֶץ:
י אֵלֶּה תּוֹלְדֹת שֵׁם שֵׁם בֶּן־מְאַת שָׁנָה וַיּוֹלֶד אֶת־אַרְפַּכְשָׁד שְׁנָתַיִם אַחַר
יא הַמַּבּוּל: וַיְחִי־שֵׁם אַחֲרֵי הוֹלִידוֹ אֶת־אַרְפַּכְשָׁד חֲמֵשׁ מֵאוֹת שָׁנָה וַיּוֹלֶד
יב בָּנִים וּבָנוֹת: וְאַרְפַּכְשַׁד חַי חָמֵשׁ וּשְׁלֹשִׁים שָׁנָה וַיּוֹלֶד אֶת־שָׁלַח:

They, however, were 'one people' in the area of religion, for they all agreed (to accept) the philosophy of the Sabians, and they also accepted (one) language.

וְזֶה הַחִלָּם לַעֲשׂוֹת — *And this they begin to do.* They also now have this beginning, which they have all agreed to . . .

וְעַתָּה לֹא יִבָּצֵר מֵהֶם — *And now nothing will be withheld from them.* Therefore there is no deterrent to prevent them from completing their intentions, and the religion (deity) they choose will become universal for the whole human race so that no man will turn to (seek) the knowledge of the Creator, the blessed One, or to understand that He formed all. The opposite of this will happen when there will be division between the nations, regarding their strange gods, for each one of them does believe that there is a 'god of gods' with whom all other gods agree, and through him their governance and the governance of all existence reaches perfection, as it says, כִּי מִמִּזְרַח שֶׁמֶשׁ וְעַד מְבוֹאוֹ גָּדוֹל שְׁמִי בַּגּוֹיִם, *From where the sun rises to where it sets, My Name is honored among the nations* (*Malachi* 1:11).

11. וַיּוֹלֶד בָּנִים וּבָנוֹת — *And he begot sons and daughters.* The phrase וַיָּמֹת, *and he died*, is not mentioned by any one of these ten generations, as it is mentioned of the ten generations from Adam to Noah. (The reason is) that they all died prior to the major historical event of that era, namely, the Flood. These generations, however,

NOTES

follows the *Rambam's* approach in his *Guide* (III:29). He explains that their doctrine was 'that there is no deity but the stars,' and that the 'sun is the greatest deity.' The *Rambam* always refers, in his *Guide*, to the pagan philosophers of early times as 'Sabians' (צאבי׳ה). The *Sforno* interprets the phrase עַם אֶחָד as meaning one, both in language and religion, their faith being that of the Sabians.

וְעַתָּה לֹא יִבָּצֵר מֵהֶם — *And now nothing will be withheld from them.* The *Sforno* understands the reason for the Dispersion thus: When people worship deities other than God, such as stars, luminaries, spirits, or even inanimate objects that symbolize, or reflect, these deities, as the *Rambam* explains 'in respect of its being an *image* of a thing that is an intermediary between ourselves and God' (*Guide* I:36), they still accept the concept of a אֱלֹהֵי הָאֱלֹהִים, a *god of gods*, i.e., a supreme being. Hence, the possibility exists that some day they will come to the knowledge of God, the Blessed One. The Sages in *Menachos* 110a express this thought in their interpretation of the verse in *Malachi* cited here by the *Sforno*. However, if universal man would have accepted the religion fostered by Nimrod, this monolithic idolatry would have closed the door to further inquiry and speculation, thereby barring mankind's way to return to the true God. The dispersion was meant to disrupt the acceptance of an exclusive false deity, for through dispersion would come diverse religions which would result in a more favorable religious climate, leading ultimately to the day of ה׳ אֶחָד וּשְׁמוֹ אֶחָד, when *God would be One and His Name one* (*Zechariah* 14:9).

11. וַיּוֹלֶד בָּנִים וּבָנוֹת — *And he begot sons and*

יג וַיְחִי אַרְפַּכְשַׁד אַחֲרֵי הוֹלִידוֹ אֶת־שֶׁלַח שָׁלֹשׁ שָׁנִים וְאַרְבַּע מֵאוֹת שָׁנָה
יד־טו וַיּוֹלֶד בָּנִים וּבָנוֹת׃ וְשֶׁלַח חַי שְׁלֹשִׁים שָׁנָה וַיּוֹלֶד אֶת־עֵבֶר׃ וַיְחִי־
שֶׁלַח אַחֲרֵי הוֹלִידוֹ אֶת־עֵבֶר שָׁלֹשׁ שָׁנִים וְאַרְבַּע מֵאוֹת שָׁנָה וַיּוֹלֶד בָּנִים
טז־יז וּבָנוֹת׃ וַיְחִי־עֵבֶר אַרְבַּע וּשְׁלֹשִׁים שָׁנָה וַיּוֹלֶד אֶת־פָּלֶג׃ וַיְחִי־
עֵבֶר אַחֲרֵי הוֹלִידוֹ אֶת־פֶּלֶג שְׁלֹשִׁים שָׁנָה וְאַרְבַּע מֵאוֹת שָׁנָה וַיּוֹלֶד בָּנִים
יח־יט וּבָנוֹת׃ וַיְחִי־פֶלֶג שְׁלֹשִׁים שָׁנָה וַיּוֹלֶד אֶת־רְעוּ׃ וַיְחִי־פֶלֶג אַחֲרֵי
כ הוֹלִידוֹ אֶת־רְעוּ תֵּשַׁע שָׁנִים וּמָאתַיִם שָׁנָה וַיּוֹלֶד בָּנִים וּבָנוֹת׃ וַיְחִי
כא רְעוּ שְׁתַּיִם וּשְׁלֹשִׁים שָׁנָה וַיּוֹלֶד אֶת־שְׂרוּג׃ וַיְחִי רְעוּ אַחֲרֵי הוֹלִידוֹ אֶת־
כב שְׂרוּג שֶׁבַע שָׁנִים וּמָאתַיִם שָׁנָה וַיּוֹלֶד בָּנִים וּבָנוֹת׃ וַיְחִי שְׂרוּג
כג שְׁלֹשִׁים שָׁנָה וַיּוֹלֶד אֶת־נָחוֹר׃ וַיְחִי שְׂרוּג אַחֲרֵי הוֹלִידוֹ אֶת־נָחוֹר מָאתַיִם
כד שָׁנָה וַיּוֹלֶד בָּנִים וּבָנוֹת׃ וַיְחִי נָחוֹר תֵּשַׁע וְעֶשְׂרִים שָׁנָה וַיּוֹלֶד
כה אֶת־תָּרַח׃ וַיְחִי נָחוֹר אַחֲרֵי הוֹלִידוֹ אֶת־תֶּרַח תְּשַׁע־עֶשְׂרֵה שָׁנָה וּמְאַת
כו שָׁנָה וַיּוֹלֶד בָּנִים וּבָנוֹת׃ וַיְחִי־תֶרַח שִׁבְעִים שָׁנָה וַיּוֹלֶד
כז אֶת־אַבְרָם אֶת־נָחוֹר וְאֶת־הָרָן׃ וְאֵלֶּה תּוֹלְדֹת תֶּרַח תֶּרַח הוֹלִיד
כח אֶת־אַבְרָם אֶת־נָחוֹר וְאֶת־הָרָן וְהָרָן הוֹלִיד אֶת־לוֹט׃ וַיָּמָת הָרָן עַל־פְּנֵי
מפטיר כט תֶּרַח אָבִיו בְּאֶרֶץ מוֹלַדְתּוֹ בְּאוּר כַּשְׂדִּים׃ וַיִּקַּח אַבְרָם וְנָחוֹר לָהֶם נָשִׁים
שֵׁם אֵשֶׁת־אַבְרָם שָׂרָי וְשֵׁם אֵשֶׁת־נָחוֹר מִלְכָּה בַּת־הָרָן אֲבִי־מִלְכָּה וַאֲבִי
ל־לא יִסְכָּה׃ וַתְּהִי שָׂרַי עֲקָרָה אֵין לָהּ וָלָד׃ וַיִּקַּח תֶּרַח אֶת־אַבְרָם בְּנוֹ וְאֶת־לוֹט
בֶּן־הָרָן בֶּן־בְּנוֹ וְאֵת שָׂרַי כַּלָּתוֹ אֵשֶׁת אַבְרָם בְּנוֹ וַיֵּצְאוּ אִתָּם מֵאוּר
לב כַּשְׂדִּים לָלֶכֶת אַרְצָה כְּנַעַן וַיָּבֹאוּ עַד־חָרָן וַיֵּשְׁבוּ שָׁם׃ וַיִּהְיוּ יְמֵי־תֶרַח
חָמֵשׁ שָׁנִים וּמָאתַיִם שָׁנָה וַיָּמָת תֶּרַח בְּחָרָן׃

---

were all still alive when the major historical event began, i.e., when Abraham our father, more so than all the righteous ones of the previous generations, endeavored to call in the Name of Hashem, לְהוֹדִיעַ לִבְנֵי הָאָדָם גְּבוּרֹתָיו וּכְבוֹד הֲדַר מַלְכוּתוֹ, *to make His mighty acts known among men, and the majestic glory of His kingship* (*Psalms* 145:12), and to draw them with cords of loving-kindness, to serve Him with one accord.

31. לָלֶכֶת אַרְצָה כְּנַעַן — *To go to the land of Canaan.* (This land) was predisposed to bring about intellectual elevation, and was more desirable (spiritually) than all other lands, as it says, אֶרֶץ אֲשֶׁר ה׳ אֱלֹהֶיךָ דֹּרֵשׁ אֹתָהּ, *A land which HASHEM your God cares for* (*Deut.* 11:12). Its climate had not been adversely affected by the Flood's rains as was that of other lands, as it says, לֹא גֻשְׁמָהּ בְּיוֹם זָעַם, *not to be washed with rain on the day of indignation* (*Ezekiel* 22:24), and our Sages (also) have said, 'The air of *Eretz Yisrael* makes one wise' (*Baba Basra* 158b).

NOTES

daughters. See the explanatory note to 9:29. The expression *cords of loving-kindness* is derived from *Hosea* 11:4 and that of *one accord* from *Zephaniah* 3:9.

31-32. לָלֶכֶת אַרְצָה כְּנַעַן — *To go to the land of Canaan.* Terach senses that the Land of Canaan represented the potential for spiritual excellence and a place which could cause revolutionary change in the history of mankind. He sets out to go there but never reaches his destination. His son Abraham,

32. וַיָּמָת תֶּרַח בְּחָרָן — *And Terach died in Charan.* And he did not endeavor to achieve what he intended to achieve by journeying from Ur Casdim, (nor) did he come, at all, to (visit) Abraham when he lived in the land of Canaan, calling there *in the name of HASHEM* and (even when) his reputation became widespread. The reverse of this was done by Lot, who for a time (did accompany Abraham) and therefore he and his descendants merited to (share) a portion of Abraham's gifts, whereas the other offspring of Terach, who were as closely related to Abraham, if not more so, did not merit (to share in these gifts).

NOTES

however, is destined to realize Terach's dream. Strangely, once Terach's initial plan is frustrated, he loses all desire to go to that special land, even after his son has become 'a prince' in the land and his fame as teacher and man of righteousness has spread far and wide. The fact that Lot, of all Abraham's family, does accompany Abraham, is most commendable, and as a result he is rewarded with wealth, while his offspring, Ammon and Moab, are granted an inheritance of the land that was once Canaan.

פרשת לך לך
Parashas Lech Lecha

יב

א וַיֹּאמֶר יהוה אֶל־אַבְרָם לֶךְ־לְךָ מֵאַרְצְךָ וּמִמּוֹלַדְתְּךָ וּמִבֵּית אָבִיךָ אֶל־
ב הָאָרֶץ אֲשֶׁר אַרְאֶךָּ: וְאֶעֶשְׂךָ לְגוֹי גָּדוֹל וַאֲבָרֶכְךָ וַאֲגַדְּלָה שְׁמֶךָ וֶהְיֵה
ג בְּרָכָה: וַאֲבָרְכָה מְבָרְכֶיךָ וּמְקַלֶּלְךָ אָאֹר וְנִבְרְכוּ בְךָ כֹּל מִשְׁפְּחֹת הָאֲדָמָה:
ד וַיֵּלֶךְ אַבְרָם כַּאֲשֶׁר דִּבֶּר אֵלָיו יהוה וַיֵּלֶךְ אִתּוֹ לוֹט וְאַבְרָם בֶּן־חָמֵשׁ שָׁנִים
ה וְשִׁבְעִים שָׁנָה בְּצֵאתוֹ מֵחָרָן: וַיִּקַּח אַבְרָם אֶת־שָׂרַי אִשְׁתּוֹ וְאֶת־לוֹט
בֶּן־אָחִיו וְאֶת־כָּל־רְכוּשָׁם אֲשֶׁר רָכָשׁוּ וְאֶת־הַנֶּפֶשׁ אֲשֶׁר־עָשׂוּ בְחָרָן וַיֵּצְאוּ
ו לָלֶכֶת אַרְצָה כְּנַעַן וַיָּבֹאוּ אַרְצָה כְּנָעַן: וַיַּעֲבֹר אַבְרָם בָּאָרֶץ עַד מְקוֹם

XII

1. אֶל הָאָרֶץ אֲשֶׁר אַרְאֶךָּ — *To the land that I will show you . . .* to a particular place in the land which I will show to you through a Godly vision. He therefore passed through the land but did not pitch his tent until (he came to the) place where God appeared to him, as it says, *Abram passed onto the land as far as the site of Shechem . . . HASHEM appeared to Abram and said, 'To your offspring I will give this land'* (verses 6-7).

2. וֶהְיֵה בְּרָכָה — *And you shall be a blessing.* The blessing of God is that He should rejoice in His creation, as our Sages have said, יִשְׁמָעֵאל בְּנִי בָּרְכֵנִי, אָמַרְתִּי לוֹ: יְהִי רָצוֹן מִלְּפָנֶיךָ . . . וְיָגֹלּוּ רַחֲמֶיךָ עַל מִדּוֹתֶיךָ, "(God said to me,) *'Ishmael, My son, bless Me.' I replied, 'May it be Your will . . . and Your mercy may prevail over Your other attributes' " (Berachos* 7a). Therefore He (God) says, 'Become a blessing to Me by (your) deep understanding (whereby) you will acquire perfection, and teach knowledge (of God) to the people.'

5. וַיֵּצְאוּ לָלֶכֶת אַרְצָה כְּנַעַן — *And they embarked for the land of Canaan . . .* which was widely known to them as a land conducive to deep understanding and service of God, the Blessed One.

וַיָּבֹאוּ אַרְצָה כְּנָעַן — *And they came to the land of Canaan . . .* unlike Terach's departure *to go to the land of Canaan* (11:31) when he only came as far as Charan.

6. וַיַּעֲבֹר אַבְרָם בָּאָרֶץ — *Abram passed into the land.* He did not stop (for any

NOTES

XII

1. אֶל הָאָרֶץ אֲשֶׁר אַרְאֶךָּ —*To the land that I will show you.* Terach, Abram's father, had set out from Ur Kasdim to go to the Land of Canaan because people already knew that this land was conducive to spiritual and intellectual elevation and excellence (see the *Sforno* 11:31). Hence, the Almighty's command to Abram, *to the land that I will show you,* cannot mean that the land was unknown to Abram at the time he set out on his journey. Therefore, the *Sforno* interprets this phrase to mean a particular place in Canaan, which God would *show to him.* Only when this place was revealed to Abram by God, would he pitch his tent there.

2. וְהָיֵה בְּרָכָה — *And you shall be a blessing.* Many find it difficult to comprehend a 'blessing' as applied to God. Still we see from the Talmudic statement (*Berachos* 7a) cited by the *Sforno* in this verse, that the Almighty asks to be blessed! The *Sforno,* therefore, interprets this to mean that God's greatest 'desire' is to rejoice in His creation and above all with mankind. When this happens He is 'blessed.' This concept is established here in the phrase וְהָיֵה בְּרָכָה, and is repeated again in 14:20, 28:4, and a number of other places.

5. וַיָּבֹאוּ אַרְצָה כְּנָעַן — *And they came to the land of Canaan.* These three Hebrew words are missing from 11:31. They are the key words which differentiate Abram's journey from his father's.

6. וַיַּעֲבֹר אַבְרָם בָּאָרֶץ — *Abram passed into the land.* See note on verse 1.

ז שְׁכֶם עַד אֵלוֹן מוֹרֶה וְהַכְּנַעֲנִי אָז בָּאָרֶץ: וַיֵּרָא יהוה אֶל־אַבְרָם וַיֹּאמֶר
לְזַרְעֲךָ אֶתֵּן אֶת־הָאָרֶץ הַזֹּאת וַיִּבֶן שָׁם מִזְבֵּחַ לַיהוה הַנִּרְאֶה אֵלָיו:
ח וַיַּעְתֵּק מִשָּׁם הָהָרָה מִקֶּדֶם לְבֵית־אֵל וַיֵּט אָהֳלֹה בֵּית־אֵל מִיָּם וְהָעַי
ט מִקֶּדֶם וַיִּבֶן־שָׁם מִזְבֵּחַ לַיהוה וַיִּקְרָא בְּשֵׁם יהוה: וַיִּסַּע אַבְרָם הָלוֹךְ וְנָסוֹעַ
הַנֶּגְבָּה:
י וַיְהִי רָעָב בָּאָרֶץ וַיֵּרֶד אַבְרָם מִצְרַיְמָה לָגוּר שָׁם כִּי־כָבֵד הָרָעָב בָּאָרֶץ:
יא וַיְהִי כַּאֲשֶׁר הִקְרִיב לָבוֹא מִצְרָיְמָה וַיֹּאמֶר אֶל־שָׂרַי אִשְׁתּוֹ הִנֵּה־נָא יָדַעְתִּי
יב כִּי אִשָּׁה יְפַת־מַרְאֶה אָתְּ: וְהָיָה כִּי־יִרְאוּ אֹתָךְ הַמִּצְרִים וְאָמְרוּ אִשְׁתּוֹ זֹאת
יג וְהָרְגוּ אֹתִי וְאֹתָךְ יְחַיּוּ: אִמְרִי־נָא אֲחֹתִי אָתְּ לְמַעַן יִיטַב־לִי בַעֲבוּרֵךְ

---

period) in any one place until God, the Blessed One, appeared to him as He had instructed him when He said, *'To the land that I will show you.'*

8. בֵּית אֵל מִיָּם וְהָעַי מִקֶּדֶם — *Bethel on the west and Ai on the east* . . . between two large cities, so that many people would come to listen when he called in the name of *HASHEM.*

9. הָלוֹךְ וְנָסוֹעַ הַנֶּגְבָּה — *Journeying steadily toward the south.* As he journeyed from place to place, as is the custom of shepherds, he did not turn eastward or westward so as not to turn away from these two cities (Bethel and Ai) because a number of its inhabitants had begun to follow him.

10. לָגוּר שָׁם — *To sojourn there* . . . but not to settle there permanently.

11. כַּאֲשֶׁר הִקְרִיב — *As he came near* . . . close to the necessary time (of arrival) lest she forget (his instructions).

לָבוֹא מִצְרָיְמָה — *To enter Egypt.* Egypt was a place known for its immorality, as it is said of them, אֲשֶׁר בְּשַׂר חֲמוֹרִים בְּשָׂרָם וְזִרְמַת סוּסִים זִרְמָתָם, *Whose flesh is as the flesh of asses, and whose issue is like the issue of horses (Ezekiel* 23:20).

12. וְהָרְגוּ אֹתִי — *Then they will kill me* . . . for they cannot hope that I would consent to give you to them.

13. לְמַעַן יִיטַב לִי — *That it may go well with me.* When you will tell them that you are my sister, each one will have hopes of marrying you (with my consent) thereby preventing them from killing me. (On the contrary) it will go well for me as a result of the dowry and gifts (they will give to me), as was the custom at that time, to induce the father of the bride through a dowry and the (bride's) relatives through gifts, to gain their consent to give her in marriage to her suitor. As the Torah tells us, מָהֹר יִמְהָרֶנָּה, *he shall surely pay a dowry* . . . אִם מָאֵן יְמָאֵן אָבִיהָ . . . כֶּסֶף יִשְׁקֹל, *if her father utterly refuses (to give her) he shall pay money (according to the dowry of virgins) (Exodus* 22:15,16). In the interim, Abram thought, he (and Sarai) would depart from there.

NOTES

13. לְמַעַן יִיטַב לִי — *That it may go well with me.* This concluding comment of the *Sforno* explains how Abram, who rejects riches offered to him by man (see his response to the king of Sodom 14:23), can allow himself to say לְמַעַן יִיטַב לִי, *that it may go well with me.* As the *Sforno* sees it, this was only a strategy to forestall an overt act of force to take Sarai, by having her 'brother' negotiate for an acceptable dowry, thereby buying time, in the hope

שני יד וְחִיְתָה נַפְשִׁי בִּגְלָלֵךְ: וַיְהִי כְּבוֹא אַבְרָם מִצְרָיְמָה וַיִּרְאוּ הַמִּצְרִים
טו אֶת־הָאִשָּׁה כִּי־יָפָה הִוא מְאֹד: וַיִּרְאוּ אֹתָהּ שָׂרֵי פַרְעֹה וַיְהַלְלוּ אֹתָהּ
טז אֶל־פַּרְעֹה וַתֻּקַּח הָאִשָּׁה בֵּית פַּרְעֹה: וּלְאַבְרָם הֵיטִיב בַּעֲבוּרָהּ וַיְהִי־לוֹ
יז צֹאן־וּבָקָר וַחֲמֹרִים וַעֲבָדִים וּשְׁפָחֹת וַאֲתֹנֹת וּגְמַלִּים: וַיְנַגַּע יהוה ׀
יח אֶת־פַּרְעֹה נְגָעִים גְּדֹלִים וְאֶת־בֵּיתוֹ עַל־דְּבַר שָׂרַי אֵשֶׁת אַבְרָם: וַיִּקְרָא
פַרְעֹה לְאַבְרָם וַיֹּאמֶר מַה־זֹּאת עָשִׂיתָ לִּי לָמָּה לֹא־הִגַּדְתָּ לִּי כִּי אִשְׁתְּךָ
יט הִוא: לָמָה אָמַרְתָּ אֲחֹתִי הִוא וָאֶקַּח אֹתָהּ לִי לְאִשָּׁה וְעַתָּה הִנֵּה אִשְׁתְּךָ

---

14. וַיִּרְאוּ הַמִּצְרִים — *The Egyptians saw.* As Abram had foreseen, they all gazed at her (beauty, and were attracted to her).

15. וַיִּרְאוּ אֹתָהּ שָׂרֵי פַרְעֹה — *The officials of Pharaoh saw her.* And thwarted the plans of the masses (to take Sarai).

וַתֻּקַּח הָאִשָּׁה — *And the woman was taken . . .*

16. וּלְאַבְרָם הֵיטִיב — *And Abram was treated well.* Contrary to the accepted custom, they did not consult with (Abram) first or attempt to induce him (to agree to the match) for they thought it was unnecessary, since it was the king who was marrying her. Now since she claimed to be Abram's sister and marriageable, there could certainly be no better match for her than the king, as he himself attested when he said, *'So that I would take her as my wife'* (verse 19). Therefore, they brought her to the king first, and afterwards the king treated (Abram) well, on her behalf, by giving a dowry and gift, as was the custom.

צֹאן וּבָקָר . . . וַעֲבָדִים — *Sheep, oxen . . . slaves.* Many . . . as befits a king.

17. וַיְנַגַּע ה׳ אֶת פַּרְעֹה נְגָעִים גְּדֹלִים — *HASHEM afflicted Pharaoh with severe plagues.* Only Pharaoh (was afflicted) with 'severe plagues.'

וְאֶת בֵּיתוֹ — *along with his household.* His household was also afflicted with plagues, but not as severe as those of Pharaoh's. This demonstrated that only this pious woman (Sarai) was saved (from the plagues) so that all would recognize that this plague was brought on her account, and (hopefully) they would repent of their evil.

18. לָמָּה לֹא הִגַּדְתָּ לִּי — *Why didn't you tell me?* For even if you suspected the masses you should not have suspected the king who establishes justice in the land (of harming you).

19. לָמָה אָמַרְתָּ אֲחֹתִי הִיא — *Why did you say, 'She is my sister'?* (You said this) even after she was brought to my palace.

וָאֶקַּח אֹתָהּ לִי לְאִשָּׁה — *So that I would take her as my wife . . .* not as a concubine! (True) I did it without your permission, (but that was) because I thought you would be pleased to have your sister marry the king.

NOTES

that they would be able to leave before anything happened to them. This plan was only effective, however, when dealing with the people, but not with Pharaoh, who took her first and negotiated later (see verses 15-16).

17. וַיְנַגַּע ה׳ אֶת פַּרְעֹה נְגָעִים גְּדֹלִים — *HASHEM afflicted Pharaoh with severe plagues.* The reason the *Sforno* interprets the word גְּדֹלִים, *severe,* as referring only to Pharaoh is because if it is an adjective describing נְגָעִים, *plagues,*

כ קַח וָלֵךְ: וַיְצַו עָלָיו פַּרְעֹה אֲנָשִׁים וַיְשַׁלְּחוּ אֹתוֹ וְאֶת־אִשְׁתּוֹ וְאֶת־כָּל־
יג א אֲשֶׁר־לוֹ: וַיַּעַל אַבְרָם מִמִּצְרַיִם הוּא וְאִשְׁתּוֹ וְכָל־אֲשֶׁר־לוֹ וְלוֹט עִמּוֹ
ב-ג הַנֶּגְבָּה: וְאַבְרָם כָּבֵד מְאֹד בַּמִּקְנֶה בַּכֶּסֶף וּבַזָּהָב: וַיֵּלֶךְ לְמַסָּעָיו מִנֶּגֶב
וְעַד־בֵּית־אֵל עַד־הַמָּקוֹם אֲשֶׁר־הָיָה שָׁם אָהֳלֹה בַּתְּחִלָּה בֵּין בֵּית־אֵל וּבֵין
ד הָעָי: אֶל־מְקוֹם הַמִּזְבֵּחַ אֲשֶׁר־עָשָׂה שָׁם בָּרִאשֹׁנָה וַיִּקְרָא שָׁם אַבְרָם בְּשֵׁם
שלישי ה-ו יְהוָה: וְגַם־לְלוֹט הַהֹלֵךְ אֶת־אַבְרָם הָיָה צֹאן־וּבָקָר וְאֹהָלִים: וְלֹא־נָשָׂא
אֹתָם הָאָרֶץ לָשֶׁבֶת יַחְדָּו כִּי־הָיָה רְכוּשָׁם רָב וְלֹא יָכְלוּ לָשֶׁבֶת יַחְדָּו:
ז וַיְהִי־רִיב בֵּין רֹעֵי מִקְנֵה־אַבְרָם וּבֵין רֹעֵי מִקְנֵה־לוֹט וְהַכְּנַעֲנִי וְהַפְּרִזִּי אָז
ח יֹשֵׁב בָּאָרֶץ: וַיֹּאמֶר אַבְרָם אֶל־לוֹט אַל־נָא תְהִי מְרִיבָה בֵּינִי וּבֵינֶךָ וּבֵין

XIII

2. וְאַבְרָם כָּבֵד מְאֹד בַּמִּקְנֶה — *Now, Abram was very laden with cattle.* He was forced to lead (his flocks) slowly even though he was anxious to return quickly to the place of (his) altar, in that place to understand (God) and teach (others) as before. Therefore . . .

3. וַיֵּלֶךְ לְמַסָּעָיו — *He proceeded on his journey.* A shepherd's journey, traveling from place to place; leaving the first place (for a second) when the pasture was exhausted.

6. וְלֹא נָשָׂא אֹתָם הָאָרֶץ — *And the land could not support them.* There was insufficient pasture for both, therefore . . .

7. וַיְהִי רִיב בֵּין רֹעֵי מִקְנֵה אַבְרָם וּבֵין רֹעֵי מִקְנֵה לוֹט — *And there was quarreling between the herdsmen of Abram's flocks and the herdsmen of Lot's flocks.* The quarrel was to see who would be forced out by whom from the pasture available.

וְהַכְּנַעֲנִי וְהַפְּרִזִּי אָז יֹשֵׁב בָּאָרֶץ — *And the Canaanite and the Perizzite were then dwelling in the land.* The quarrel between two relatives who were strangers in the land was odious in the eyes of the native dwellers who would consider them as argumentative men, and would assume that if they quarrel among themselves how much more so will they quarrel with the native dwellers.

8. אַל נָא תְהִי מְרִיבָה בֵּינִי וּבֵינֶךָ — *Let there be no quarrel between me and you* . . . in the future, when one chooses a piece of ground for pasture which the other also wants.

NOTES

the words נְגָעִים גְּדֹלִים, *severe plagues*, should be placed after וְאֶת בֵּיתוֹ, *and his household*, not following פַּרְעֹה. This then indicates that *severe* plagues refers *only* to Pharaoh.

XIII

7. וְהַכְּנַעֲנִי וְהַפְּרִזִּי אָז יֹשֵׁב בָּאָרֶץ — *And the Canaanite and the Perizzite were then dwelling in the land.* This phrase is seemingly added to this verse unnecessarily. The commentators suggest various explanations. The *Sforno* offers his interpretation, that since Abram and Lot were dwelling in the midst of other people, who were in the majority, the quarrel between them would expose them to the contempt and eventual enmity of the inhabitants of the land.

8. אַל נָא תְהִי מְרִיבָה בֵּינִי וּבֵינֶךָ — *Let there be no quarrel between me and you* . . . The argument was between the herdsmen, not Lot and Abram. Why then does Abram say *between me and you?* The answer is that he is anticipating a future argument, which he would like to avoid.

ט רֹעַי וּבֵין רֹעֶיךָ כִּֽי־אֲנָשִׁים אַחִים אֲנָֽחְנוּ׃ הֲלֹא כָל־הָאָ֙רֶץ֙ לְפָנֶיךָ הִפָּרֶד נָא
י מֵֽעָלָי אִם־הַשְּׂמֹאל וְאֵימִנָה וְאִם־הַיָּמִין וְאַשְׂמְאִֽילָה׃ וַיִּשָּׂא־לוֹט אֶת־עֵינָיו
וַיַּרְא֙ אֶת־כָּל־כִּכַּר הַיַּרְדֵּן כִּי כֻלָּהּ מַשְׁקֶה לִפְנֵי ׀ שַׁחֵת יהוה אֶת־סְדֹם֙
יא וְאֶת־עֲמֹרָה כְּגַן־יהוה֙ כְּאֶרֶץ מִצְרַיִם בֹּאֲכָה צֹֽעַר׃ וַיִּבְחַר־לוֹ לוֹט אֵת
יב כָּל־כִּכַּר הַיַּרְדֵּן וַיִּסַּע לוֹט מִקֶּדֶם וַיִּפָּֽרְדוּ אִישׁ מֵעַל אָחִֽיו׃ אַבְרָם יָשַׁב
יג בְּאֶֽרֶץ־כְּנָעַן וְלוֹט יָשַׁב֙ בְּעָרֵי הַכִּכָּר וַיֶּאֱהַל עַד־סְדֹֽם׃ וְאַנְשֵׁי סְדֹם רָעִים

וּבֵין רֹעַי וּבֵין רֹעֶיךָ — *And between my herdsmen and your herdsmen* . . . also now, while we are still here together.

9. הֲלֹא כָל הָאָרֶץ לְפָנֶיךָ — *Is not all the land before you?* You can choose the place you want, therefore . . .

הִפָּרֶד נָא מֵעָלָי — *Please, separate from me.* You separate yourself to the side you choose, and I will journey in the opposite direction.

אִם הַשְּׂמֹאל — *If you go left.* If you choose to seek out pasture on the left.

וְאֵימִנָה — *Then I will go right.* I will seek on the right.

11. וַיִּבְחַר לוֹ לוֹט אֵת כָּל כִּכַּר הַיַּרְדֵּן — *So Lot chose for himself the whole plain of the Jordan.* He chose a place where only he and his herdsmen would have the right to seek out pasture, while Abram and his herdsmen would not be permitted to do so.

וַיִּסַּע לוֹט מִקֶּדֶם — *And Lot journeyed from the East.* He did not turn to the right or the left, which would have been the north or south, but he journeyed from east to west, so as to distance himself from Abram whose dwelling place was in eastern *Eretz Yisrael* close to Ai. (This is) where the tribes came up into the land initially, upon crossing over from the east of the Jordan.

וַיִּפָּרְדוּ אִישׁ מֵעַל אָחִיו — *And they parted, one from another* not only insofar as pasture, but also (insofar as) their dwelling places.

12. אַבְרָם יָשַׁב בְּאֶרֶץ כְּנָעַן — *Abram remained in the land of Canaan.* Although Sodom and its neighboring towns were also part of Canaan, nevertheless its inhabitants at that time were not Canaanites. (The Torah tells us) Abram chose to dwell in that part of the land where the Canaanites lived, since they were not as wicked as the Sodomites; and (Abram) did not come close to the environs of Sodom.

NOTES

9. הֲלֹא כָל הָאָרֶץ לְפָנֶיךָ – *Is not all the land before you?* Neither Abram or Lot had a legal claim to the land at that time — hence the suggestion, made by Abram, that each choose a place for their flocks and herds to graze, could only apply to the accepted right of nomadic shepherds to seek out pastureland. That is why the *Sforno* stresses here 'to seek out pasture,' and in verse 11 explains that the agreement between Lot and Abram was regarding the exclusive right to seek out pasture in a given area.

11. וַיִּסַּע לוֹט מִקֶּדֶם – *And Lot journeyed from the East.* When Abram and Lot discussed their decision to separate, they were in the east facing westward. Right would then be north and left, south. Lot, however, chose neither direction and opted instead to journey west, which the Torah interprets as being motivated by Lot's desire to distance himself from Abram *totally*, not only regarding the issue of pasture, but a separation in spirit as well.

12. אַבְרָם יָשַׁב בְּאֶרֶץ כְּנָעַן – *Abram remained in the land of Canaan.* The expression *Abram remained in . . . Canaan* implies that Lot did not. However, this is not so since Sodom is also part of Canaan. The answer must perforce be that the Torah is referring to the *residents* of

יד וְחַטָּאִים לַיהוָה מְאֹד: וַיהוָה אָמַר אֶל־אַבְרָם אַחֲרֵי הִפָּרֶד־לוֹט מֵעִמּוֹ
שָׂא־נָא עֵינֶיךָ וּרְאֵה מִן־הַמָּקוֹם אֲשֶׁר־אַתָּה שָׁם צָפֹנָה וָנֶגְבָּה וָקֵדְמָה וָיָמָּה:
טו־טז כִּי אֶת־כָּל־הָאָרֶץ אֲשֶׁר־אַתָּה רֹאֶה לְךָ אֶתְּנֶנָּה וּלְזַרְעֲךָ עַד־עוֹלָם: וְשַׂמְתִּי
אֶת־זַרְעֲךָ כַּעֲפַר הָאָרֶץ אֲשֶׁר | אִם־יוּכַל אִישׁ לִמְנוֹת אֶת־עֲפַר הָאָרֶץ
יז גַּם־זַרְעֲךָ יִמָּנֶה: קוּם הִתְהַלֵּךְ בָּאָרֶץ לְאָרְכָּהּ וּלְרָחְבָּהּ כִּי לְךָ אֶתְּנֶנָּה:
יח וַיֶּאֱהַל אַבְרָם וַיָּבֹא וַיֵּשֶׁב בְּאֵלֹנֵי מַמְרֵא אֲשֶׁר בְּחֶבְרוֹן וַיִּבֶן־שָׁם מִזְבֵּחַ
לַיהוָה:

יד רביעי א וַיְהִי בִּימֵי אַמְרָפֶל מֶלֶךְ־שִׁנְעָר אַרְיוֹךְ מֶלֶךְ אֶלָּסָר כְּדָרְלָעֹמֶר מֶלֶךְ עֵילָם
ב וְתִדְעָל מֶלֶךְ גּוֹיִם: עָשׂוּ מִלְחָמָה אֶת־בֶּרַע מֶלֶךְ סְדֹם וְאֶת־בִּרְשַׁע מֶלֶךְ
°צְבוֹיִם ק׳ עֲמֹרָה שִׁנְאָב | מֶלֶךְ אַדְמָה וְשֶׁמְאֵבֶר מֶלֶךְ °צביים וּמֶלֶךְ בֶּלַע הִיא־צֹעַר:
ג־ד כָּל־אֵלֶּה חָבְרוּ אֶל־עֵמֶק הַשִּׂדִּים הוּא יָם הַמֶּלַח: שְׁתֵּים עֶשְׂרֵה שָׁנָה עָבְדוּ

---

14. אַחֲרֵי הִפָּרֶד לוֹט — *After Lot had parted.* This (renewed promise of the land) was not given while Lot was still with them, lest Lot and his herdsmen expropriate Abram's honored role and with arrogant pride be encouraged to rob (land for pasture).

17. לְךָ אֶתְּנֶנָּה — *To you will I give it.* Even in your days the inhabitants of the land will consider you as an honored prince of God.

18. וַיֶּאֱהַל אַבְרָם — *And Abram moved his tent.* He arranged the tents (for his) cattle here and there (on different sites).

וַיָּבֹא וַיֵּשֶׁב בְּאֵלֹנֵי מַמְרֵא — *And he came to dwell in the plains of Mamre* . . . and later he came and established his own dwelling place in the plains of Mamre.

XIV

1. וַיְהִי בִּימֵי אַמְרָפֶל מֶלֶךְ שִׁנְעָר — *And it happened in the days of Amraphel king of Shinar.* He was a great, prominent king in that generation, as well as later. In his days, Arioch, Chedorlaomer and Tidal arose and waged war with Bera and his allies. Afterward . . .

3. כָּל אֵלֶּה — *All these* . . . Amraphel and the two contending forces.

חָבְרוּ אֶל עֵמֶק הַשִּׂדִּים — *Joined in the Valley of Sidim* . . . entering into an alliance (made a compromise) as a result of which the five kings who were losing the war . . .

NOTES

the land, not the land per se.

14. אַחֲרֵי הִפָּרֶד לוֹט – *After Lot had parted. Rashi,* quoting the *Midrash,* tells us that Lot's herdsmen justified their grazing on other people's pastures, basing their right to do so on the fact that some day the land would belong to Lot as the only heir of Abram. Therefore, God does not renew His promise of the land to Abram while Lot is still with him, for then Lot's herdsmen would be encouraged all the more so to engage in the robbery of private pastures.

17. לְךָ אֶתְּנֶנָּה – *To you will I give it.* The expression, *to you will I give it,* implies that this will be fulfilled in Abram's lifetime. The *Sforno* therefore explains it to mean that Abram will gain recognition and honor from the inhabitants of Canaan.

XIV

1. וַיְהִי בִּימֵי אַמְרָפֶל מֶלֶךְ שִׁנְעָר – *And it happened in the days of Amraphel king of Shinar.* The episode related here involves many kings; still, the opening statement, setting the histori-

ה אֶת־כְּדָרְלָעֹמֶר וּשְׁלֹשׁ־עֶשְׂרֵה שָׁנָה מָרָדוּ׃ וּבְאַרְבַּע עֶשְׂרֵה שָׁנָה בָּא
כְדָרְלָעֹמֶר וְהַמְּלָכִים אֲשֶׁר אִתּוֹ וַיַּכּוּ אֶת־רְפָאִים בְּעַשְׁתְּרֹת קַרְנַיִם
ו וְאֶת־הַזּוּזִים בְּהָם וְאֵת הָאֵימִים בְּשָׁוֵה קִרְיָתָיִם׃ וְאֶת־הַחֹרִי בְּהַרְרָם שֵׂעִיר
ז עַד אֵיל פָּארָן אֲשֶׁר עַל־הַמִּדְבָּר׃ °וַיָּשֻׁבוּ וַיָּבֹאוּ אֶל־עֵין מִשְׁפָּט הִוא קָדֵשׁ
ח וַיַּכּוּ אֶת־כָּל־שְׂדֵה הָעֲמָלֵקִי וְגַם אֶת־הָאֱמֹרִי הַיֹּשֵׁב בְּחַצְצֹן תָּמָר׃ וַיֵּצֵא
°צְבוֹיִם ק׳ מֶלֶךְ־סְדֹם וּמֶלֶךְ עֲמֹרָה וּמֶלֶךְ אַדְמָה וּמֶלֶךְ °צביים וּמֶלֶךְ בֶּלַע הִוא־צֹעַר
ט וַיַּעַרְכוּ אִתָּם מִלְחָמָה בְּעֵמֶק הַשִּׂדִּים׃ אֵת כְּדָרְלָעֹמֶר מֶלֶךְ עֵילָם וְתִדְעָל
מֶלֶךְ גּוֹיִם וְאַמְרָפֶל מֶלֶךְ שִׁנְעָר וְאַרְיוֹךְ מֶלֶךְ אֶלָּסָר אַרְבָּעָה מְלָכִים
י אֶת־הַחֲמִשָּׁה׃ וְעֵמֶק הַשִּׂדִּים בֶּאֱרֹת בֶּאֱרֹת חֵמָר וַיָּנֻסוּ מֶלֶךְ־סְדֹם וַעֲמֹרָה
יא וַיִּפְּלוּ־שָׁמָּה וְהַנִּשְׁאָרִים הֶרָה נָּסוּ׃ °וַיִּקְחוּ אֶת־כָּל־רְכֻשׁ סְדֹם וַעֲמֹרָה
יב וְאֶת־כָּל־אָכְלָם וַיֵּלֵכוּ׃ וַיִּקְחוּ אֶת־לוֹט וְאֶת־רְכֻשׁוֹ בֶּן־אֲחִי אַבְרָם וַיֵּלֵכוּ
יג וְהוּא יֹשֵׁב בִּסְדֹם׃ וַיָּבֹא הַפָּלִיט וַיַּגֵּד לְאַבְרָם הָעִבְרִי וְהוּא שֹׁכֵן בְּאֵלֹנֵי

---

4. עָבְדוּ אֶת כְּדָרְלָעֹמֶר — *They served Chedorlaomer.* As a result of the compromise (treaty) they (served) for twelve years, and then rebelled.

5. וְהַמְּלָכִים אֲשֶׁר אִתּוֹ — *And the kings who were with him . . .* those who had joined the alliance in the Valley of Sidim, among them being Amraphel.

וַיַּכּוּ אֶת רְפָאִים . . . וְאֶת הַזּוּזִים . . . וְאֵת הָאֵימִים — *And smote the Rephaim . . . and the Zuzim . . . and the Eimim.* These all served the five kings and fought on their side. (The Torah) is telling us how great these five kings were, and how powerful were the four kings who defeated them. Now we can know (judge) the great might of Abram and his military skill, as well as the great kindness shown to his relative (Lot), by his willingness to sacrifice himself to overcome them (the four kings) so as to save his nephew and his possessions from them, wresting the prey from their jaws and achieving even more than he had hoped for, thanks to the mercy of God.

10. וַיָּנֻסוּ מֶלֶךְ סְדֹם וַעֲמֹרָה — *The kings of Sodom and Amorah fled.* This would explain why Abram had no faith in them (in his effort to) rescue Lot.

וְהַנִּשְׁאָרִים הֶרָה נָּסוּ — *And those who remained fled to the mountain . . .* i.e., the three remaining kings.

12. וַיִּקְחוּ אֶת לוֹט וְאֶת רְכֻשׁוֹ בֶּן אֲחִי אַבְרָם — *And they captured Lot, Abram's nephew, and his possessions.* They tried especially to capture Lot, because he was Abram's nephew, and being aware of Abram's wealth they hoped to receive a huge ransom.

13. וַיַּגֵּד לְאַבְרָם הָעִבְרִי — *And told Abram the Ivri.* The fugitive did not know that Abram was Lot's relative. He knew only that he was a believer in the religion of Eber, as was Abram.

NOTES

cal time frame, calls it יְמֵי אַמְרָפֶל, *the days of Amraphel.* The reason given by the *Sforno* is that being the most prominent of all these leaders, this age is called by his name. Following this reasoning, the *Sforno* singles out Amraphel when he explains the compromise (alliance) in verse 3 and again in verse 5.

13. וַיַּגֵּד לְאַבְרָם הָעִבְרִי — *And told Abram the Ivri.* The *Sforno* interprets this verse thus because it does not say, *Abram, the relative of Lot,* which would account for the fugitive seeking him out to relate the capture of Lot. Apparently, Og (who was the fugitive) did not know of their relationship, but did know

יד מַמְרֵא הָאֱמֹרִי אֲחִי אֶשְׁכֹּל וַאֲחִי עָנֵר וְהֵם בַּעֲלֵי בְרִית־אַבְרָם: וַיִּשְׁמַע
אַבְרָם כִּי נִשְׁבָּה אָחִיו וַיָּרֶק אֶת־חֲנִיכָיו יְלִידֵי בֵיתוֹ שְׁמֹנָה עָשָׂר וּשְׁלֹשׁ
טו מֵאוֹת וַיִּרְדֹּף עַד־דָּן: וַיֵּחָלֵק עֲלֵיהֶם ׀ לַיְלָה הוּא וַעֲבָדָיו וַיַּכֵּם וַיִּרְדְּפֵם
טז עַד־חוֹבָה אֲשֶׁר מִשְּׂמֹאל לְדַמָּשֶׂק: וַיָּשֶׁב אֵת כָּל־הָרְכֻשׁ וְגַם אֶת־לוֹט
יז אָחִיו וּרְכֻשׁוֹ הֵשִׁיב וְגַם אֶת־הַנָּשִׁים וְאֶת־הָעָם: וַיֵּצֵא מֶלֶךְ־סְדֹם לִקְרָאתוֹ
אַחֲרֵי שׁוּבוֹ מֵהַכּוֹת אֶת־כְּדָרְלָעֹמֶר וְאֶת־הַמְּלָכִים אֲשֶׁר אִתּוֹ אֶל־עֵמֶק
יח שָׁוֵה הוּא עֵמֶק הַמֶּלֶךְ: וּמַלְכִּי־צֶדֶק מֶלֶךְ שָׁלֵם הוֹצִיא לֶחֶם וָיָיִן וְהוּא
יט כֹהֵן לְאֵל עֶלְיוֹן: וַיְבָרְכֵהוּ וַיֹּאמַר בָּרוּךְ אַבְרָם לְאֵל עֶלְיוֹן קֹנֵה שָׁמַיִם

וְהוּא שֹׁכֵן בְּאֵלֹנֵי מַמְרֵא — *And he dwelt in the plains of Mamre.* Therefore, Aner, Eshkol and Mamre joined him (Abram) in battle, as it says: *Aner, Eshkol and Mamre — they will take their portion* (verse 24).

14. וַיִּרְדֹּף עַד דָּן — *And he pursued them as far as Dan . . .* in great haste, so as to attack them suddenly.

15. וַיֵּחָלֵק עֲלֵיהֶם — *And deployed against them.* As part of his strategy, so that they would think they were being attacked from all sides, as Aram thought when they said, הִנֵּה שָׂכַר עָלֵינוּ מֶלֶךְ יִשְׂרָאֵל, *The king of Israel has hired against us . . . (II Kings* 7:6).

לַיְלָה — *At night.* This was also part of his strategy, that they should not see how few they were in number, just as Achitofel advised, when he said, וְאֶרְדְּפָה אַחֲרֵי דָוִד הַלָּיְלָה, *And I will rise and pursue David at night (II Samuel* 17:1).

וַיַּכֵּם — *And struck them . . .* a blow which caused them to flee.

וַיִּרְדְּפֵם — *He pursued them.* 'Flight is the beginning of defeat' *(Sotah* 44a).

16. וְגַם אֶת הַנָּשִׁים — *As well as the women.* Lot's (wives) whom he had to ransom.

וְאֶת הָעָם — *And the people . . .* the Sodomites who were taken captive. These are the ones to whom the king of Sodom was referring when he said to Abram, *'Give me the people'* (verse 21).

18. הוֹצִיא לֶחֶם וָיָיִן — *Brought out bread and wine . . .* to the returning battle-weary.

וְהוּא כֹהֵן — *He was a priest . . .* and thus, it was proper (fitting) for him to give a blessing.

19. וַיְבָרְכֵהוּ וַיֹּאמַר בָּרוּךְ אַבְרָם לְאֵל עֶלְיוֹן — *He blessed him saying, Blessed is Abram of God the Most High.* First he blessed him. Afterward he said: even without my blessing, Abram is *blessed of God the Most High,* as it is said, וַאֲבָרֶכְךָ, *I will bless you* (12:2).

קֹנֵה שָׁמַיִם וָאָרֶץ — *Possessor of heaven and earth.* Heaven and earth are God's possessions (acquisitions) to do with them as He wills, for they did not come into

NOTES

they shared the same religious beliefs. This the verse indicates by saying *Abram the Ivri.*

15. וַיַּכֵּם – *And struck them.* The word וַיַּכֵּם normally means to smite one and kill him. In our case it cannot be translated thus, for then how could a dead person flee and be pursued (וַיִּרְדְּפֵם)? For this reason the *Sforno* interprets וַיַּכֵּם as a blow, instilling fear followed by flight.

כ וָאָֽרֶץ׃ וּבָרוּךְ֙ אֵ֣ל עֶלְי֔וֹן אֲשֶׁר־מִגֵּ֥ן צָרֶ֖יךָ בְּיָדֶ֑ךָ וַיִּתֶּן־ל֥וֹ מַעֲשֵׂ֖ר מִכֹּֽל׃
חמישי כא־כב וַיֹּ֥אמֶר מֶֽלֶךְ־סְדֹ֖ם אֶל־אַבְרָ֑ם תֶּן־לִ֣י הַנֶּ֔פֶשׁ וְהָרְכֻ֖שׁ קַֽח־לָֽךְ׃ וַיֹּ֥אמֶר אַבְרָ֖ם
אֶל־מֶ֣לֶךְ סְדֹ֑ם הֲרִימֹ֨תִי יָדִ֤י אֶל־יהוה֙ אֵ֣ל עֶלְי֔וֹן קֹנֵ֖ה שָׁמַ֥יִם וָאָֽרֶץ׃
כג אִם־מִחוּט֙ וְעַ֣ד שְׂרוֹךְ־נַ֔עַל וְאִם־אֶקַּ֖ח מִכָּל־אֲשֶׁר־לָ֑ךְ וְלֹ֣א תֹאמַ֔ר אֲנִ֖י
כד הֶעֱשַׁ֥רְתִּי אֶת־אַבְרָֽם׃ בִּלְעָדַ֗י רַ֚ק אֲשֶׁ֣ר אָכְל֣וּ הַנְּעָרִ֔ים וְחֵ֙לֶק֙ הָאֲנָשִׁ֔ים
טו א אֲשֶׁ֥ר הָלְכ֖וּ אִתִּ֑י עָנֵר֙ אֶשְׁכֹּ֣ל וּמַמְרֵ֔א הֵ֖ם יִקְח֥וּ חֶלְקָֽם׃ אַחַ֣ר ׀

---

existence through any natural cause (as some philosophers and scientists believe) but (it is only) He who dictates their existence through His will, and works them as He wills.

20. וּבָרוּךְ אֵל עֶלְיוֹן — *And Blessed is God the Most High.* This act which He wrought, i.e., the mighty victory of Abram over his enemies, is a blessing for Him, the Blessed One, for He rejoices with His creations when the wicked are destroyed; and the righteous rejoice (exult) as we find, שַׁבְּחוּהוּ כָּל הָאֻמִּים כִּי גָבַר עָלֵינוּ חַסְדּוֹ, *Laud Him all you people, for His mercy is great toward us* (*Psalms* 117:1-2).

23. אִם מִחוּט וְעַד שְׂרוֹךְ נַעַל — *If so much as a thread or a shoestrap.* Throughout the Torah, the word אִם, *if*, where it is not followed by a condition, replaces the phrase, *I will not*. Therefore, the meaning is: 'I lift up my hand to Hashem, that I cannot give you so much as a thread or shoestrap' for I have nothing (of the booty). And, also, 'I will not take anything of yours.' Similarly, אִם יִרְאוּ אֶת הָאָרֶץ, *If they will see the land* (*Numbers* 14:23), meaning *they will* not *see;* אִם אַתֶּם תָּבֹאוּ, *If you will come* (*Numbers* 14:30), meaning *they will* not *come;* חַי ה׳ אִם יוּמָת, *As* H*ASHEM lives if he will die* (*I Samuel* 19:6), meaning *he will* not *die;* חַי ה׳ אֲשֶׁר עָמַדְתִּי לְפָנָיו אִם אֶקָּח, *As* H*ASHEM lives, before whom I stand, if I will take* (*II Kings* 5:16), meaning *I will* not *take*, and many more (such examples).

24. בִּלְעָדַי — *Far from me (without me).* You said, *'Give me the people.'* Even without my permission you can take them, for I am keeping nothing for myself.

רַק אֲשֶׁר אָכְלוּ הַנְּעָרִים וְחֵלֶק הָאֲנָשִׁים — *Only what the young men have eaten, and the share of the men.* Only this will I accept from you: the expenses incurred in feeding the young men. I will also take the share of the men who accompanied me, but ...

עָנֵר אֶשְׁכֹּל וּמַמְרֵא הֵם יִקְחוּ חֶלְקָם — *Aner, Eshkol and Mamre, they will take their portion.* I will not (be the one) to give them a share, nor will I take a portion for them, rather they themselves shall take (their portion) as (befits) leaders.

NOTES

23. אִם מִחוּט וְעַד שְׂרוֹךְ נַעַל — *If so much as a thread or a shoestrap.* Based upon the *Sforno's* general principle that the word אִם, if not followed by a condition, has the implication of an oath, the meaning being *I will not*, it follows that (unlike the simple interpretation) the phrase *so much as a thread or a shoestrap*, is not connected to אִם אֶקַּח, *if I should take*, but means *I cannot* give *to* you (the king of Sodom) anything — not even a small item such as a thread or a shoestrap. The phrase אִם אֶקַּח begins a new thought, i.e., I will also take nothing *from* you.

24. רַק אֲשֶׁר אָכְלוּ הַנְּעָרִים וְחֵלֶק הָאֲנָשִׁים ... עָנֵר אֶשְׁכֹּל וּמַמְרֵא הֵם יִקְחוּ חֶלְקָם — *Only what the young men have eaten, and the share of the men ... Aner, Eshkol and Mamre, they will take their portion.* Abram is willing to act as intermediary on behalf of his young men and those men who accompanied him, to collect their share and apportion it among them. He will not do so, however, on behalf of his friends, Aner, Eshkol and Mamre, for this

הַדְּבָרִים הָאֵלֶּה הָיָה דְבַר־יהוה אֶל־אַבְרָם בַּמַּחֲזֶה לֵאמֹר אַל־תִּירָא
ב אַבְרָם אָנֹכִי מָגֵן לָךְ שְׂכָרְךָ הַרְבֵּה מְאֹד: וַיֹּאמֶר אַבְרָם אֲדֹנָי יֱהוִה מַה־
ג תִּתֶּן־לִי וְאָנֹכִי הוֹלֵךְ עֲרִירִי וּבֶן־מֶשֶׁק בֵּיתִי הוּא דַּמֶּשֶׂק אֱלִיעֶזֶר: וַיֹּאמֶר
ד אַבְרָם הֵן לִי לֹא נָתַתָּה זָרַע וְהִנֵּה בֶן־בֵּיתִי יוֹרֵשׁ אֹתִי: וְהִנֵּה דְבַר־יהוה
ה אֵלָיו לֵאמֹר לֹא יִירָשְׁךָ זֶה כִּי־אִם אֲשֶׁר יֵצֵא מִמֵּעֶיךָ הוּא יִירָשֶׁךָ: וַיּוֹצֵא

XV

1. אַל תִּירָא אַבְרָם — *Fear not, Abram.* Fear not that the four kings will seek revenge from you (for their defeat at your hand).

שְׂכָרְךָ— *Your reward.* Not only have your merits not been diminished by the victory granted to you (by God), but you have earned a reward for the act of kindness shown to your relative and others, by saving these victims from their oppressors.

הַרְבֵּה מְאֹד — *Very great.* In this world, and the world to come (lit., 'eternal life'), as our Sages say, אֵלּוּ דְבָרִים שֶׁאָדָם אוֹכֵל פֵּרוֹתֵיהֶם בָּעוֹלָם הַזֶּה וְהַקֶּרֶן קַיֶּמֶת לָעוֹלָם הַבָּא, *These are the things, the fruits of which a man enjoys in this world and the stock remains for him in the world to come (Peah* 1:1), and among these we find acts of loving-kindness (as Abram demonstrated to Lot and the others).

2. מַה תִּתֶּן לִי — *What can you give me?* In this world.

עֲרִירִי — *Childless.* I have no son to succeed me and be in charge of my affairs, as it says, כִּתְבוּ אֶת הָאִישׁ הַזֶּה עֲרִירִי גֶּבֶר לֹא יִצְלַח בְּיָמָיו כִּי לֹא יִצְלַח מִזַּרְעוֹ אִישׁ יֹשֵׁב עַל כִּסֵּא דָוִד, *Write this man childless, a man that shall not prosper in his days, for no man of his seed shall prosper sitting upon the throne of David (Jeremiah* 22:30).

וּבֶן מֶשֶׁק בֵּיתִי הוּא דַּמֶּשֶׂק אֱלִיעֶזֶר — *And the steward of my house is Damascus Eliezer* . . . who is a slave known only by the name of his city, without a (true) name of his own, and without a doubt there is a vast difference between a servant conducting the affairs of a household motivated by fear, as compared to a son's conducting (these affairs) motivated by love.

3. בֶּן בֵּיתִי יוֹרֵשׁ אֹתִי — *My steward is my heir.* Even were You to grant me offspring eventually, as You said, *'To your offspring I will give this land'* (12:7), he will be young after my demise and unprepared to conduct (financial) affairs. (Therefore) my steward will be in charge and (in effect) be the heir — as often happens.

4. לֹא יִירָשְׁךָ זֶה כִּי אִם אֲשֶׁר יֵצֵא מִמֵּעֶיךָ — *That one will not inherit you, but he who comes forth from within you.* Your son will successfully conduct your affairs even in your lifetime, as it says, *And Abraham gave all that he had to Isaac* (25:5); *and he sent them* (i.e., the sons borne to him by Keturah) *away from his son Isaac, while he yet lived* (25:6).

NOTES

would be insulting to them. They are respected and honored men who should be dealt with directly, as befits their status and position.

XV

1. שְׂכָרְךָ הַרְבֵּה מְאֹד — *Your reward is very great.* The *Sforno* interprets הַרְבֵּה, *great,* as referring to reward in this world, while the adverb 'very' is added, to indicate reward in the world to come. He bases this upon the Mishnah in *Peah,* which he quotes, where we find that the reward for גְּמִילַת חֲסָדִים, acts of loving-kindness, such as that of Abram in the rescue operation, is both in this world and the next.

אֹתוֹ הַחוּצָה וַיֹּאמֶר הַבֶּט־נָא הַשָּׁמַיְמָה וּסְפֹר הַכּוֹכָבִים אִם־תּוּכַל
ו לִסְפֹּר אֹתָם וַיֹּאמֶר לוֹ כֹּה יִהְיֶה זַרְעֶךָ: וְהֶאֱמִן בַּיהוָה וַיַּחְשְׁבֶהָ לּוֹ צְדָקָה:
ששי ז וַיֹּאמֶר אֵלָיו אֲנִי יהוה אֲשֶׁר הוֹצֵאתִיךָ מֵאוּר כַּשְׂדִּים לָתֶת לְךָ אֶת־הָאָרֶץ
ח-ט הַזֹּאת לְרִשְׁתָּהּ: וַיֹּאמַר אֲדֹנָי יֱהוִה בַּמָּה אֵדַע כִּי אִירָשֶׁנָּה: וַיֹּאמֶר אֵלָיו
י קְחָה לִי עֶגְלָה מְשֻׁלֶּשֶׁת וְעֵז מְשֻׁלֶּשֶׁת וְאַיִל מְשֻׁלָּשׁ וְתֹר וְגוֹזָל: וַיִּקַּח־לוֹ

---

6. וְהֶאֱמִן בַּה׳ — *And he trusted in* HASHEM. He believed without a doubt that (God) would do as He said, even though it was highly improbable according to the laws of nature.

וַיַּחְשְׁבֶהָ לוֹ צְדָקָה — *He reckoned it to him as righteousness.* God, the Blessed One, reckoned this trust in Him as righteousness and to the merit of Abram. We are, then, being told that when Abram later asked, 'בַּמָּה אֵדַע כִּי אִירָשֶׁנָּה', *Whereby shall I know that I am to inherit it?'* (verse 8), he did not lose his faith (in this promise) at all, for if he had, his (original) faith would not have been considered as righteousness, as it says, וּבְשׁוּב צַדִּיק מִצִּדְקָתוֹ וְעָשָׂה עָוֶל כְּכֹל הַתּוֹעֵבוֹת אֲשֶׁר עָשָׂה הָרָשָׁע יַעֲשֶׂה וָחָי כָּל צִדְקֹתָו אֲשֶׁר עָשָׂה לֹא תִזָּכַרְנָה, *But when the righteous turns away from his righteousness and commits iniquity ... none of his righteous deeds that he has done shall be remembered* (*Ezekiel* 18:24).

7. אֲשֶׁר הוֹצֵאתִיךָ מֵאוּר כַּשְׂדִּים לָתֶת לְךָ אֶת הָאָרֶץ הַזֹּאת — *Who brought you out of Ur Kasdim to give you this land* ... that you, yourself, should take possession of it (the land) through חֲזָקָה (an act of acquisition).

לְרִשְׁתָּהּ — *To inherit it* ... so that your children will inherit it from you as an inheritance which is never ending.

8. בַּמָּה אֵדַע — *Whereby shall I know.* Perhaps my children will sin and not merit to inherit it.

9. קְחָה לִי עֶגְלָה מְשֻׁלֶּשֶׁת — *Bring me three heifers* ... to enter a covenant, so that my word become a decree with the status of an irrevocable oath, as our Sages teach us (*Rosh Hashanah* 18), (it was to this that) Moses our Teacher referred when he said, *'It is not for your righteousness ... but because of the wickedness of these nations* HASHEM *is driving them out, and in order to fulfill the oath that He swore* (based on *Deut.* 9:5).

NOTES

6. וְהֶאֱמִן בַּה׳ — *And he trusted in* HASHEM. Faith and trust in God, to be considered as righteousness, must be abiding. Therefore the *Sforno* stresses that Abram's question, *'How shall I know, etc.'* is to be understood, as he later explains in his commentary on verse 8, that perhaps his children will sin and not be worthy to inherit the land. At no time, however, does Abram doubt God's promise.

7. אֲשֶׁר הוֹצֵאתִיךָ מֵאוּר כַּשְׂדִּים לָתֶת לְךָ אֶת הָאָרֶץ הַזֹּאת — *Who brought you out of Ur Kasdim to give you this land.* One of the methods of חֲזָקָה, *acquisition,* is to walk through the length and breadth of a newly purchased field (*Baba Basra* 100). God had already commanded Abram (13:17) to *walk about the land* for this purpose. This is what the *Sforno* is referring to. God had taken Abram out of Ur Kasdim, brought him to *Eretz Yisrael,* and commanded him to perform an act of possession in the land thereby acquiring it, after which he can transmit it to his children as an eternal inheritance.

9. קְחָה לִי עֶגְלָה מְשֻׁלֶּשֶׁת — *Bring me three heifers.* The Talmud (*Rosh Hashanah* 18), establishes the principle that when a final sentence is pronounced it can still be rescinded, unless it is accompanied by an oath.

אֶת־כָּל־אֵלֶּה וַיְבַתֵּר אֹתָם בַּתָּוֶךְ וַיִּתֵּן אִישׁ־בִּתְרוֹ לִקְרַאת רֵעֵהוּ וְאֶת־
יא־יב הַצִּפֹּר לֹא בָתָר: וַיֵּרֶד הָעַיִט עַל־הַפְּגָרִים וַיַּשֵּׁב אֹתָם אַבְרָם: וַיְהִי הַשֶּׁמֶשׁ
לָבוֹא וְתַרְדֵּמָה נָפְלָה עַל־אַבְרָם וְהִנֵּה אֵימָה חֲשֵׁכָה גְדֹלָה נֹפֶלֶת עָלָיו:
יג וַיֹּאמֶר לְאַבְרָם יָדֹעַ תֵּדַע כִּי־גֵר ׀ יִהְיֶה זַרְעֲךָ בְּאֶרֶץ לֹא לָהֶם וַעֲבָדוּם וְעִנּוּ
יד אֹתָם אַרְבַּע מֵאוֹת שָׁנָה: וְגַם אֶת־הַגּוֹי אֲשֶׁר יַעֲבֹדוּ דָּן אָנֹכִי וְאַחֲרֵי־כֵן
טו יֵצְאוּ בִּרְכֻשׁ גָּדוֹל: וְאַתָּה תָּבוֹא אֶל־אֲבֹתֶיךָ בְּשָׁלוֹם תִּקָּבֵר בְּשֵׂיבָה
טז־יז טוֹבָה: וְדוֹר רְבִיעִי יָשׁוּבוּ הֵנָּה כִּי לֹא־שָׁלֵם עֲוֹן הָאֱמֹרִי עַד־הֵנָּה: וַיְהִי
הַשֶּׁמֶשׁ בָּאָה וַעֲלָטָה הָיָה וְהִנֵּה תַנּוּר עָשָׁן וְלַפִּיד אֵשׁ אֲשֶׁר עָבַר בֵּין

---

13. יָדֹעַ תֵּדַע — *Know with certainty.* He told him the reason for the delay in the inheriting (of the land) by his children, which is: כִּי לֹא שָׁלֵם עֲוֹן הָאֱמֹרִי, *Because the iniquity of the Emorite is not yet full* (v. 16), and it is not right to expel a nation from its land until its 'measure (of wickedness) is full.' Therefore (God) says, 'Know with certainty' that even though I have sworn to give this land to your children, it will not be immediately.

כִּי גֵר יִהְיֶה זַרְעֲךָ בְּאֶרֶץ לֹא לָהֶם — *For your offspring shall be aliens in a land not their own . . .* until the time that the iniquity of the Emorites will be full. (Abram) is being told the future events of servitude and affliction which will befall some of his offspring in their burdensome state. This will (however) not occur during the generation of the righteous, for as long as one of the tribes (Jacob's sons) was alive the servitude did not begin, until they (the Israelites) corrupted their ways, as the Prophet testifies, וַיַּמְרוּ בִי וְלֹא אָבוּ לִשְׁמֹעַ אֵלַי, אִישׁ אֶת שִׁקּוּצֵי עֵינֵיהֶם לֹא הִשְׁלִיכוּ, וְאֶת גִּלּוּלֵי מִצְרַיִם לֹא עָזָבוּ, וָאֹמַר לִשְׁפֹּךְ חֲמָתִי עֲלֵיהֶם, לְכַלּוֹת אַפִּי בָּהֶם בְּתוֹךְ אֶרֶץ מִצְרָיִם, וָאַעַשׂ לְמַעַן שְׁמִי, *But they rebelled against Me, and would not hearken to Me; they did not, every man, cast away the detestable things of their eyes, neither did they forsake the idols of Egypt; then I said I would pour out My fury upon them in the midst of the land of Egypt* (*Ezekiel* 20:8-9). All this He revealed (to Abram) so that the last generation should know, through tradition, that this is (because of) God's word, and not attribute it to other causes, as the Prophet says, וָאַגִּיד לְךָ מֵאָז בְּטֶרֶם תָּבוֹא הִשְׁמַעְתִּיךָ פֶּן תֹּאמַר עָצְבִּי עָשָׂם, *I have already from the beginning told it to you; announced things to you before they happened; lest you say, 'My idol has caused them'* (*Isaiah* 48:5).

14. וְגַם אֶת הַגּוֹי אֲשֶׁר יַעֲבֹדוּ דָּן אָנֹכִי — *But also upon the nation which they shall serve will I execute judgment.* Just as I shall judge your children for their wickedness, (visiting upon them) affliction and servitude, so shall I execute judgment upon the nation, Egypt, that will enslave them.

NOTES

The *Sforno* paraphrases this Talmudic statement, applying it to the covenant God entered into with Abram. The ritual followed here, as described in this chapter, is the equivalent of an oath, therefore the promise made to give Abram's children *Eretz Yisrael* is irrevocable. Even if they will be unworthy, the covenant is unbroken, and the promise remains. It is this oath that Moses alludes to in the verse quoted by the *Sforno.*

13. כִּי גֵר יִהְיֶה זַרְעֲךָ בְּאֶרֶץ לֹא לָהֶם — *For your offspring shall be aliens in a land not their own.* The *Sforno* points out that the status of aliens in a strange land is not always a precarious and difficult one. The Israelites lived in Egypt quite securely and prospered, even though they were aliens. God's statement, therefore, must be understood as being applicable only to a number of generations, and even after the death of the שְׁבָטִים *(the*

יח הַגְּזָרִים הָאֵלֶּה: בַּיּוֹם הַהוּא כָּרַת יהוה אֶת־אַבְרָם בְּרִית לֵאמֹר לְזַרְעֲךָ
יט נָתַתִּי אֶת־הָאָרֶץ הַזֹּאת מִנְּהַר מִצְרַיִם עַד־הַנָּהָר הַגָּדֹל נְהַר־פְּרָת: אֶת־
כ הַקֵּינִי וְאֶת־הַקְּנִזִּי וְאֵת הַקַּדְמֹנִי: וְאֶת־הַחִתִּי וְאֶת־הַפְּרִזִּי וְאֶת־הָרְפָאִים:
טז כא־א וְאֶת־הָאֱמֹרִי וְאֶת־הַכְּנַעֲנִי וְאֶת־הַגִּרְגָּשִׁי וְאֶת־הַיְבוּסִי: וְשָׂרַי
ב אֵשֶׁת אַבְרָם לֹא יָלְדָה לוֹ וְלָהּ שִׁפְחָה מִצְרִית וּשְׁמָהּ הָגָר: וַתֹּאמֶר שָׂרַי
אֶל־אַבְרָם הִנֵּה־נָא עֲצָרַנִי יהוה מִלֶּדֶת בֹּא־נָא אֶל־שִׁפְחָתִי אוּלַי אִבָּנֶה
ג מִמֶּנָּה וַיִּשְׁמַע אַבְרָם לְקוֹל שָׂרָי: וַתִּקַּח שָׂרַי אֵשֶׁת־אַבְרָם אֶת־הָגָר
הַמִּצְרִית שִׁפְחָתָהּ מִקֵּץ עֶשֶׂר שָׁנִים לְשֶׁבֶת אַבְרָם בְּאֶרֶץ כְּנָעַן וַתִּתֵּן אֹתָהּ
ד לְאַבְרָם אִישָׁהּ לוֹ לְאִשָּׁה: וַיָּבֹא אֶל־הָגָר וַתַּהַר וַתֵּרֶא כִּי הָרָתָה וַתֵּקַל
ה גְּבִרְתָּהּ בְּעֵינֶיהָ: וַתֹּאמֶר שָׂרַי אֶל־אַבְרָם חֲמָסִי עָלֶיךָ אָנֹכִי נָתַתִּי שִׁפְחָתִי

XVI

2. הִנֵּא נָא עֲצָרַנִי ה׳ מִלֶּדֶת — *See now,* H*ASHEM* *has restrained me from bearing.* Although He promised you offspring, as it says, *'To your offspring I will give this land'* (12:7), He has not said that this offspring will issue from me.

אוּלַי אִבָּנֶה מִמֶּנָּה — *Perhaps I will be built up through her.* Perhaps my jealousy of her will stimulate (my) potential powers of reproduction into functioning, and I will be able to have offspring.

לְקוֹל שָׂרָי — *To the voice of Sarai.* He considered that her suggestion was correct; therefore he complied with her wish, not because he wanted to consort with (enjoy) another woman.

5. חֲמָסִי עָלֶיךָ — *My violence is upon you.* You should have admonished her, since she is (now) your wife, when she treated me so lightly once she became pregnant.

NOTES

tribes, i.e., the sons of Jacob) the offspring of Abram could have been spared the pain of exile, had they not sinned! It was important for God to reveal all this to Abram, so that future generations would know that the bondage in Egypt was ordained by God and that it was so severe because of their transgressions. Indeed, our Sages tell us that the Israelites were not redeemed from Egypt until they had repented of their sins.

XVI

2. הִנֵּה נָא עֲצָרַנִי ה׳ מִלֶּדֶת — *See now,* H*ASHEM* *has restrained me from bearing.* Sarai, whose faith was perfect, never questioned God's promise to Abram that he would have children. She merely points out that these children were not promised specifically through her. This thought is echoed by Rivkah in 25:22. See the *Sforno's* commentary on that verse.

אוּלַי אִבָּנֶה מִמֶּנָּה — *Perhaps I will be built up through her.* When Sarai says, 'Perhaps I will be built up through her,' she does not mean to say that she will rear the child born to Hagar. She is expressing the hope that the jealousy she will experience may serve as a powerful catharsis awakening her potential to conceive. Rachel expresses a similar hope in chapter 30:3. In both cases the word מִמֶּנָּה, *from her,* is to be understood literally, i.e., *from* Hagar's conception Sarai may ultimately conceive, and 'from' Bilhah's, Rachel may also conceive.

לְקוֹל שָׂרָי — *To the voice of Sarai.* In Hebrew the difference between בְּקוֹל and לְקוֹל is that the former means 'to obey,' whereas the latter means 'to understand and agree.' Since the phrase used here is וַיִּשְׁמַע אַבְרָם לְקוֹל — the *Sforno* interprets it to mean the latter.

5. חֲמָסִי עָלֶיךָ — *My violence is upon you.* Had Sarai freed Hagar, she would no longer have control over her. Since she had not, Abram correctly said to her, 'Even though she is now my wife, she is still your maidservant, hence under your authority.' Leah and Rachel, how-

ו בְּחֵיקֶךָ וַתֵּרֶא כִּי הָרָתָה וָאֵקַל בְּעֵינֶיהָ יִשְׁפֹּט יְהוָה בֵּינִי וּבֵינֶיךָ: וַיֹּאמֶר
אַבְרָם אֶל־שָׂרַי הִנֵּה שִׁפְחָתֵךְ בְּיָדֵךְ עֲשִׂי־לָהּ הַטּוֹב בְּעֵינָיִךְ וַתְּעַנֶּהָ שָׂרַי
ז וַתִּבְרַח מִפָּנֶיהָ: וַיִּמְצָאָהּ מַלְאַךְ יְהוָה עַל־עֵין הַמַּיִם בַּמִּדְבָּר עַל־הָעַיִן
ח בְּדֶרֶךְ שׁוּר: וַיֹּאמַר הָגָר שִׁפְחַת שָׂרַי אֵי־מִזֶּה בָאת וְאָנָה תֵלֵכִי וַתֹּאמֶר
ט מִפְּנֵי שָׂרַי גְּבִרְתִּי אָנֹכִי בֹּרַחַת: וַיֹּאמֶר לָהּ מַלְאַךְ יְהוָה שׁוּבִי אֶל־גְּבִרְתֵּךְ

---

6. שִׁפְחָתֵךְ בְּיָדֵךְ — *Your maidservant is in your hand.* She has not been set free by you.

וַתְּעַנֶּהָ שָׂרַי — *And Sarai dealt harshly with her* . . . so she should recognize her subordinate position and cease insulting her mistress. This (incident) is symbolic of all who demean Israel, as it says, וְהִשְׁתַּחֲווּ עַל כַּפּוֹת רַגְלַיִךְ כָּל מְנַאֲצָיִךְ, *And all who despised you will bow down at the soles of your feet (Isaiah* 60:14).

7. וַיִּמְצָאָהּ מַלְאַךְ ה׳ — *An angel of* HASHEM *found her.* He found her ready for the Divine vision and therefore appeared to her.

עַל עֵין הַמַּיִם — *At the spring of water.* (She was) praying, as implied in verse 11, *for* HASHEM *has heard your prayer.*

עַל הָעַיִן — *At the spring.* At the crossroad. When there are two roads, it is called עֵינַיִם (in Hebrew). Where the two roads start, it is called פֶּתַח עֵינַיִם; while our Sages refer to it as פָּרָשַׁת דְּרָכִים, *the dividing (forking) of the roads.*

בְּדֶרֶךְ שׁוּר — *On the road to Shur.* (Shur) is identical to חַגְרָא, as Onkelos translates. It is a town on the border of *Eretz Yisrael*, or across the border, as our Sages tell us (*Gittin* 2a). We are being told (by the Torah) that her intention was to leave *Eretz Yisrael.*

8. אֵי מִזֶּה בָאת וְאָנָה תֵלֵכִי — *Where have you come from, and where are you going?* The meaning is: Consider well 'from where you are traveling,' a holy place and a house of the righteous; and you are going outside the Land, to an unclean place of wicked people!

אָנֹכִי בֹּרַחַת — *I am running away.* I have no particular destination. I am merely fleeing.

NOTES

ever, did free their maidservants Zilpah and Bilhah when they urged Jacob to take them as wives (see the *Sforno* 30:6).

6. וַתְּעַנֶּהָ שָׂרַי — *And Sarai dealt harshly with her.* Both in this verse and in verse 9, the *Sforno* sees the incident of Sarai and Hagar as mirroring the eventual roles and relationship of Israel with the Ishmaelites. Ultimately, the latter will have to subjugate themselves to the former, as Hagar did to Sarai.

7. וַיִּמְצָאָהּ מַלְאַךְ ה׳ — *An angel of* HASHEM *found her.* One cannot translate the word וַיִּמְצָאָהּ, *and he found her*, literally, for that would be an inappropriate statement to make regarding an angel of God, who needs not *search* for someone. Therefore the word must be understood as finding Hagar in a certain condition and frame of mind. He *found* her ready for Divine vision. And the reason she was ready was because she had prepared herself through prayer.

עַל הָעַיִן — *At the spring.* The phrase עַיִן in this verse connotes purity of mind and heart, while the word עַיִן means a road. Normally a different word for road may have been used but here it is a play on words — עַיִן and עַיִן.

8. אָנֹכִי בֹּרַחַת — *I am running away.* Hagar answers the angel succinctly and sharply. He admonishes her for leaving a holy place for an impure one. She retorts, 'I am not making a free choice. I am simply fleeing my mistress and have no destination in mind.'

י וְהִתְעַנִּי תַּחַת יָדֶיהָ: וַיֹּאמֶר לָהּ מַלְאַךְ יהוה הַרְבָּה אַרְבֶּה אֶת־זַרְעֵךְ וְלֹא
יא יִסָּפֵר מֵרֹב: וַיֹּאמֶר לָהּ מַלְאַךְ יהוה הִנָּךְ הָרָה וְיֹלַדְתְּ בֵּן וְקָרָאת שְׁמוֹ
יב יִשְׁמָעֵאל כִּי־שָׁמַע יהוה אֶל־עָנְיֵךְ: וְהוּא יִהְיֶה פֶּרֶא אָדָם יָדוֹ בַכֹּל וְיַד כֹּל
יג בּוֹ וְעַל־פְּנֵי כָל־אֶחָיו יִשְׁכֹּן: וַתִּקְרָא שֵׁם־יהוה הַדֹּבֵר אֵלֶיהָ אַתָּה אֵל רֳאִי
יד כִּי אָמְרָה הֲגַם הֲלֹם רָאִיתִי אַחֲרֵי רֹאִי: עַל־כֵּן קָרָא לַבְּאֵר בְּאֵר לַחַי רֹאִי
טו הִנֵּה בֵין־קָדֵשׁ וּבֵין בָּרֶד: וַתֵּלֶד הָגָר לְאַבְרָם בֵּן וַיִּקְרָא אַבְרָם שֶׁם־בְּנוֹ
טז אֲשֶׁר־יָלְדָה הָגָר יִשְׁמָעֵאל: וְאַבְרָם בֶּן־שְׁמֹנִים שָׁנָה וְשֵׁשׁ שָׁנִים בְּלֶדֶת־

---

9. וְהִתְעַנִּי — *And submit yourself (be afflicted).* This indicates future events, similar to יְרֵה וַיּוֹר, *'Shoot!' and he shot (II Kings* 13:17), for so the king has decreed.

12. פֶּרֶא אָדָם — *A wild ass of a man.* פֶּרֶא is a wild ass. He will be as an ass, in temperament, (acquired) from his mother the Egyptian, as it is said of the Egyptians, אֲשֶׁר בְּשַׂר חֲמוֹרִים בְּשָׂרָם, *Whose flesh is as the flesh of asses (Ezekiel* 23:20). (He will be) a wild ass, dwelling in the desert, as it says, *And he grew up and he dwelt in the desert* (21:20). (However) he will also be an אָדָם, *a man,* (acquiring this) from his father (Abram), as our Sages tell us, 'Ishmael repented' (*Baba Basra* 16).

13. וַתִּקְרָא שֵׁם ה׳ — *And she called the name of* HASHEM. Calling the name of HASHEM signifies prayer, (for one should first) praise the Holy One, Blessed is He, in thought or words (before praying) as our Sages teach us: 'A man should always first recount the praise of the Holy One, Blessed is He, and then pray' (*Berachos* 32). In this manner the worshiper will concentrate on God, as we find, שִׁוִּיתִי ה׳ לְנֶגְדִּי תָמִיד, *I have set* HASHEM *before me always (Psalms* 16:8). (We find this phrase, *calling the name of* HASHEM*)* also in, קָרָאתִי שִׁמְךָ ה׳, *I have called upon Your Name,* HASHEM *(Lamentations* 3:55); also in, וּשְׁמוּאֵל בְּקֹרְאֵי שְׁמוֹ, *And Samuel among them that call upon His Name (Psalms* 99:6); also in, כִּי שֵׁם ה׳ אֶקְרָא, *for I will proclaim the name of* HASHEM *(Deut.* 32:3*)*. (The Torah) is then telling us that when she prayed, she (first) recounted the praises of God, Who had spoken to her; this she did by stating . . .

13. אַתָּה אֵל רֳאִי — *You are the God of vision.* You are the God Who sees everywhere, not only in the house of Abram, as our Sages tell us, 'All gates are locked, except the gates (through which pass the cries) of wrongdoing' (*Baba Metzia* 59a).

15. שֵׁם בְּנוֹ אֲשֶׁר יָלְדָה הָגָר יִשְׁמָעֵאל — *(Abram) named his son that Hagar bore him, Ishmael.* This name was appropriate for both (i.e., Abram and Hagar) — on account

NOTES

9. וְהִתְעַנִּי — *And submit yourself.* The quote from the Book of *Kings* is from an episode wherein the prophet Elisha commands King Yoash to shoot an arrow through the window (*'Shoot!' and he shot)* which he calls 'the arrow of salvation,' symbolizing Israel's victory over Aram. The *Sforno* is bringing proof from this episode that a seemingly simple act can have great historical significance. And so the one (Heb.) word spoken to Hagar — וְהִתְעַנִּי, *submit yourself* — will one day be fulfilled on a vast scale when the descendants of Ishmael will submit to the children of Israel, just as Hagar is told to submit to Sarai.

15. שֵׁם בְּנוֹ אֲשֶׁר יָלְדָה הָגָר יִשְׁמָעֵאל — *(Abram) named his son that Hagar bore him, Ishmael.* The name יִשְׁמָעֵאל is comprised of two words — יִשְׁמַע, *to hear,* and אֵל, *God.* The angel of God tells Hagar specifically to name her son יִשְׁמָעֵאל, for God had listened to her prayer. Later Abram prays for his son, and God

יז א הָגָר אֶת־יִשְׁמָעֵאל לְאַבְרָם: וַיְהִי אַבְרָם בֶּן־תִּשְׁעִים שָׁנָה וְתֵשַׁע
שָׁנִים וַיֵּרָא יְהוָה אֶל־אַבְרָם וַיֹּאמֶר אֵלָיו אֲנִי־אֵל שַׁדַּי הִתְהַלֵּךְ לְפָנַי וֶהְיֵה

---

of Abram, who later prayed on his behalf, and (God answered), וּלְיִשְׁמָעֵאל שְׁמַעְתִּיךָ, *As for Ishmael, I have heard you* (17:20); and also on account of Hagar, as the angel had told her (verse 11).

XVII

1. וַיֵּרָא ה׳ — *HASHEM appeared.* The phrase מַרְאָה — *vision* or *appearance* — always denotes a lower degree of prophecy. This is what (God) said (to Moses), וּשְׁמִי ה׳ לֹא נוֹדַעְתִּי לָהֶם, *But My Name, HASHEM, I made not known to them (Exodus* 6:3).

אֲנִי אֵל שַׁדַּי — *I am El-Shaddai.* I am He, that has sufficiency in My existence, to uniquely create (all Creation) even though there was no other prior matter or substance — implying that the Creator needs naught (in existence) to act (and create). The reverse is true of all others, except the Creator, who can perform no act without a recipient, nor can they be the objects of an action unless there is some being (or force) to act upon them. From all this, perforce, there is clear proof to all thorough thinkers of the existence of the Creator, His uniqueness and the perfection of His work, as compared to all other creative acts. All this, God taught to the Patriarchs. However, He did not make known the (mysterious) reason behind Creation, which emanated from His singular Name, until Moses our Teacher, as it says, וָאֵרָא . . . וּשְׁמִי ה׳ לֹא נוֹדַעְתִּי לָהֶם, *I appeared . . . but My Name, HASHEM, I made not known to them (Exodus* 6:3).

הִתְהַלֵּךְ לְפָנַי — *Walk before Me.* Wherever you go (and turn) as it were, gaze at Me, to know My ways, to the full extent of your capacity, as we find, שִׁוִּיתִי ה׳ לְנֶגְדִּי תָמִיד, *I have set HASHEM before me always (Psalms* 16:8).

NOTES

assures him that He has heard his prayer. Hence the name Ishmael is an appropriate one to be chosen by Abram, indicated by the word בְּנוֹ, *his son,* and also for Hagar, indicated by the phrase אֲשֶׁר יָלְדָה הָגָר, *that Hagar bore him.*

XVII

1. וַיֵּרָא ה׳ — *HASHEM appeared.* Before Abram enters *Eretz Yisrael,* God speaks to him but only His voice is 'heard.' In the land of Canaan, God 'appears' as well. There is to a certain extent, 'visibility,' hence the word וַיֵּרָא is used. Not until Moses, the man chosen to receive and transmit the Torah, is there 'prophecy' and also 'open miracles' transcending nature. This is expressed through the four-letter Name, which transmits the idea of God as the essence of all existence and that nothing can exist without His will. This Name is revealed not to the Patriarchs, but to Moses when God says to him אֶהְיֶה אֲשֶׁר אֶהְיֶה, *I am that I am (Exodus* 3:14).

אֲנִי אֵל שַׁדַּי — *I am El-Shaddai.* The name שַׁדַּי, *Shaddai,* is used here for the first time in the Torah. Subsequently, it can be found in a number of other verses (28:3; 35:11; 43:14) as well. *Rashi* explains this Name of God as indicating *sufficiency* (from the word דַּי, *enough).* Its meaning varies according to the context of its usage. At times it is the sufficiency of His Divinity, at others of His Blessings and at others of His Mercy. The *Sforno* interprets it to mean the sufficiency of His Existence. Similar to the *Rambam's* approach in his writings, the *Sforno* interprets the name *Shaddai* to mean, 'He Who is self-sufficient, independent of all other beings.' As such, only God could create a world *ex nihilo,* יֵשׁ מֵאַיִן, *something from nothing.* This concept of שַׁדַּי, *Shaddai,* was made known to the patriarchs, as we see here and in the other verses cited. It is the Divine Name with its special connotations mentioned above which was not revealed to them, but to Moses.

ב־ג תָמִים: וְאֶתְּנָה בְרִיתִי בֵּינִי וּבֵינֶךָ וְאַרְבֶּה אוֹתְךָ בִּמְאֹד מְאֹד: וַיִּפֹּל אַבְרָם
ד עַל־פָּנָיו וַיְדַבֵּר אִתּוֹ אֱלֹהִים לֵאמֹר: אֲנִי הִנֵּה בְרִיתִי אִתָּךְ וְהָיִיתָ לְאַב
ה הֲמוֹן גּוֹיִם: וְלֹא־יִקָּרֵא עוֹד אֶת־שִׁמְךָ אַבְרָם וְהָיָה שִׁמְךָ אַבְרָהָם כִּי אַב־
ו הֲמוֹן גּוֹיִם נְתַתִּיךָ: וְהִפְרֵתִי אֹתְךָ בִּמְאֹד מְאֹד וּנְתַתִּיךָ לְגוֹיִם וּמְלָכִים מִמְּךָ
שביעי ז יֵצֵאוּ: וַהֲקִמֹתִי אֶת־בְּרִיתִי בֵּינִי וּבֵינֶךָ וּבֵין זַרְעֲךָ אַחֲרֶיךָ לְדֹרֹתָם לִבְרִית
ח עוֹלָם לִהְיוֹת לְךָ לֵאלֹהִים וּלְזַרְעֲךָ אַחֲרֶיךָ: וְנָתַתִּי לְךָ וּלְזַרְעֲךָ אַחֲרֶיךָ אֵת

וֶהְיֵה תָמִים — *And be perfect.* Seek to attain the perfection attainable to man, i.e., knowing Me through My ways and emulating Me, to the degree possible for you, for the actions of every being reflects his essence, as it says, הוֹדִעֵנִי נָא אֶת דְּרָכֶךָ וְאֵדָעֲךָ, *Show me Your ways, that I may know You (Exodus* 33:13). This, then, is man's ultimate perfection and God's purpose in Creation, as it says, נַעֲשֶׂה אָדָם בְּצַלְמֵנוּ כִּדְמוּתֵנוּ, *Let us make man in our image, after our likeness* (1:26).

2. וְאֶתְּנָה בְרִיתִי בֵּינִי וּבֵינֶךָ — *I will set My covenant between Me and you.* In this manner, I will establish a covenant with you, to be a God to you and your offspring after you, for you will teach them (the fundamentals of faith).

3. וַיִּפֹּל אַבְרָם עַל פָּנָיו — *Abram fell upon his face . . .* in acceptance of, and gratitude to God, for this covenant.

4. אֲנִי הִנֵּה בְרִיתִי אִתָּךְ — *As for Me, this is My covenant with you.* I will now do what I (already) said, to establish the covenant.

5. וְהָיָה שִׁמְךָ אַבְרָהָם — *Your name shall be Abraham . . .* starting now.

כִּי אַב הֲמוֹן גּוֹיִם נְתַתִּיךָ — *For I have made you the father of a multitude of nations.* The significance of this (new) name starts today, for I have already made you the father of a multitude of nations, therefore, *you shall no longer be called by your name Abram* at all; forever. This will not be so regarding the name of Israel, since the main purpose of the name Israel is (meant) for the distant future, as will be explained in its proper place (32:39 and 35:10).

7. לִהְיוֹת לְךָ לֵאלֹהִים וּלְזַרְעֲךָ אַחֲרֶיךָ — *To be a God to you and to your offspring after you.* I will associate My Name with yours without an intermediary, as I associate it with all that is eternal, as it says, כִּי כָּל אֲשֶׁר יַעֲשֶׂה הָאֱלֹהִים הוּא יִהְיֶה לְעוֹלָם, *For whatever God does, it shall be forever (Ecclesiastes* 3:14). Whatever is perishable

NOTES

וֶהְיֵה תָמִים — *And be perfect.* The Almighty's being and essence cannot possibly be grasped by man's finite mind. We *know* Him only as manifested through His ways. The verse quoted by the *Sforno* regarding Moses's request of God to show him His ways is to be understood thus: Moses is not asking God to literally show him His essence and being, rather to show him His ways so that he in turn can emulate God. In this manner he will know Him, to the extent that man can ever know God! To inquire, search and seek this knowledge of God is proper and commendable. To attain it is 'perfection,' and indeed, this is the ultimate purpose of man's creation.

5. כִּי אַב הֲמוֹן גּוֹיִם נְתַתִּיךָ — *For I have made you the father of a multitude of nations.* The order used in the commentary is in accordance with the *Sforno's* interpretation of the sequence. When God changes Abram's name to Abraham it takes effect immediately, for the significance of this new name, i.e., *father of a multitude of nations,* begins at once, since God has already set this process in motion. Therefore there is no hiatus, and it is prohibited to call him by his original name, Abram (see *Berachos* 13). That is also why the past tense is used — נְתַתִּיךָ, and וְהָיָה. This however is not the case with Jacob, whose name is changed to Israel by the angel and concurred with by

׀ אֶרֶץ מְגֻרֶיךָ אֵת כָּל־אֶרֶץ כְּנַעַן לַאֲחֻזַּת עוֹלָם וְהָיִיתִי לָהֶם לֵאלֹהִים׃
ט וַיֹּאמֶר אֱלֹהִים אֶל־אַבְרָהָם וְאַתָּה אֶת־בְּרִיתִי תִשְׁמֹר אַתָּה וְזַרְעֲךָ אַחֲרֶיךָ
י לְדֹרֹתָם׃ זֹאת בְּרִיתִי אֲשֶׁר תִּשְׁמְרוּ בֵּינִי וּבֵינֵיכֶם וּבֵין זַרְעֲךָ אַחֲרֶיךָ הִמּוֹל
יא לָכֶם כָּל־זָכָר׃ וּנְמַלְתֶּם אֵת בְּשַׂר עָרְלַתְכֶם וְהָיָה לְאוֹת בְּרִית בֵּינִי
יב וּבֵינֵיכֶם׃ וּבֶן־שְׁמֹנַת יָמִים יִמּוֹל לָכֶם כָּל־זָכָר לְדֹרֹתֵיכֶם יְלִיד בָּיִת
יג וּמִקְנַת־כֶּסֶף מִכֹּל בֶּן־נֵכָר אֲשֶׁר לֹא מִזַּרְעֲךָ הוּא׃ הִמּוֹל ׀ יִמּוֹל יְלִיד בֵּיתְךָ
יד וּמִקְנַת כַּסְפֶּךָ וְהָיְתָה בְרִיתִי בִּבְשַׂרְכֶם לִבְרִית עוֹלָם׃ וְעָרֵל ׀ זָכָר אֲשֶׁר

(subject to decay or destruction) is not God's direct work or action, but (functions) through an intermediary. Therefore, (God is saying) that with the establishment and keeping of the covenant, he (Abraham) and his offspring will forever be before Him as individuals (lit., 'as a man').

8. לַאֲחֻזַּת עוֹלָם — *As an everlasting possession* ... and I will be their God, so that you will be able to fulfill My will in it (the land) as we find, ... וַיִּתֵּן לָהֶם אַרְצוֹת גּוֹיִם בַּעֲבוּר יִשְׁמְרוּ חֻקָּיו, *And He gave them the lands of nations ... that they might keep His statutes (Psalms* 105:44,45). In this manner I will be your God, that you be everlasting as individuals (lit., 'as a man').

9. וְאַתָּה אֶת בְּרִיתִי תִשְׁמֹר — *And as for you, you shall keep My covenant.* Just as (v. 4), אֲנִי הִנֵּה בְרִיתִי אִתָּךְ, *As for Me, this is My covenant with you,* you (in turn) shall keep My covenant, otherwise the covenant will not be valid.

11. לְאוֹת בְּרִית — *The sign of the covenant* ... a perpetual reminder to walk in His ways, it being as it were the master's seal on his servant.

13. בִּבְשַׂרְכֶם — *In your flesh.* The word בָּשָׂר, *flesh,* is a euphemism in the holy tongue for the organ of procreation; similar to גִּדְלֵי בָשָׂר, *great of flesh* (*Ezekiel* 16:26); זָב מִבְּשָׂרוֹ, *an issue out of his flesh,* and אוֹ הֶחְתִּים בְּשָׂרוֹ מִזּוֹבוֹ, *or his flesh be stopped from his issue (Lev.* 15:2,3) and other examples. Since the sign of the covenant is (in the physical sense) in the organ whereby the species is perpetuated, it symbolizes the eternity associated with this covenant. (And) since this organ is the reproductive one, the sign impressed upon it symbolizes the continuity of the covenant among later generations.

NOTES

God. In that instance, both names will continue to be used. Only at the 'end of days' will 'Jacob' be discontinued and 'Israel' will supplant it (see *Sforno* 32:39 and 35:10).

7-8. לִהְיוֹת לְךָ לֵאלֹהִים ... וְהָיִיתִי לָהֶם לֵאלֹהִים — *To be a God to you ... And I shall be a God to them.* In these two verses the phrase *to be a God to you* (or *to them)* is repeated. The first refers to the covenant between the Almighty and Abraham's descendants; the second to the promise of the Land. In the first case God pledges Himself to הַשְׁגָּחָה פְּרָטִית, *individualized, direct involvement and supervision* of the people of Israel. As such, the Jewish people will be an everlasting one, for only that which is under the control and supervision of Divine intermediaries, as opposed to that under God's direct supervision, is subject to destruction. Abraham is also being assured that this special providence is not only a general one, but also (at times) a particular one — such as the association of God's Name with the patriarchs, i.e., *God of Abraham, God of Isaac and God of Jacob.* In the second verse, the phrase *and I will be a God to them* is to be understood as the purpose for which the Land is being given to the offspring of Abraham, namely to fulfill God's will and, by conducting themselves as a holy nation, become a light to the nations of the world. In this manner the people and the Land of Israel will be everlasting as well.

9. וְאַתָּה אֶת בְּרִיתִי תִשְׁמֹר — *And as for you, you*

לֹא־יִמּוֹל אֶת־בְּשַׂר עָרְלָתוֹ וְנִכְרְתָה הַנֶּפֶשׁ הַהִוא מֵעַמֶּיהָ אֶת־בְּרִיתִי
טו הֵפַר: וַיֹּאמֶר אֱלֹהִים אֶל־אַבְרָהָם שָׂרַי אִשְׁתְּךָ לֹא־תִקְרָא
טז אֶת־שְׁמָהּ שָׂרָי כִּי שָׂרָה שְׁמָהּ: וּבֵרַכְתִּי אֹתָהּ וְגַם נָתַתִּי מִמֶּנָּה לְךָ בֵּן
יז וּבֵרַכְתִּיהָ וְהָיְתָה לְגוֹיִם מַלְכֵי עַמִּים מִמֶּנָּה יִהְיוּ: וַיִּפֹּל אַבְרָהָם עַל־פָּנָיו
וַיִּצְחָק וַיֹּאמֶר בְּלִבּוֹ הַלְּבֶן מֵאָה־שָׁנָה יִוָּלֵד וְאִם־שָׂרָה הֲבַת־תִּשְׁעִים שָׁנָה
יח־יט תֵּלֵד: וַיֹּאמֶר אַבְרָהָם אֶל־הָאֱלֹהִים לוּ יִשְׁמָעֵאל יִחְיֶה לְפָנֶיךָ: וַיֹּאמֶר
אֱלֹהִים אֲבָל שָׂרָה אִשְׁתְּךָ יֹלֶדֶת לְךָ בֵּן וְקָרָאתָ אֶת־שְׁמוֹ יִצְחָק וַהֲקִמֹתִי
כ אֶת־בְּרִיתִי אִתּוֹ לִבְרִית עוֹלָם לְזַרְעוֹ אַחֲרָיו: וּלְיִשְׁמָעֵאל שְׁמַעְתִּיךָ הִנֵּה
׀ בֵּרַכְתִּי אֹתוֹ וְהִפְרֵיתִי אֹתוֹ וְהִרְבֵּיתִי אֹתוֹ בִּמְאֹד מְאֹד שְׁנֵים־עָשָׂר
כא נְשִׂיאִם יוֹלִיד וּנְתַתִּיו לְגוֹי גָּדוֹל: וְאֶת־בְּרִיתִי אָקִים אֶת־יִצְחָק אֲשֶׁר תֵּלֵד
כב לְךָ שָׂרָה לַמּוֹעֵד הַזֶּה בַּשָּׁנָה הָאַחֶרֶת: וַיְכַל לְדַבֵּר אִתּוֹ וַיַּעַל אֱלֹהִים מֵעַל
כג אַבְרָהָם: וַיִּקַּח אַבְרָהָם אֶת־יִשְׁמָעֵאל בְּנוֹ וְאֵת כָּל־יְלִידֵי בֵיתוֹ וְאֵת
כָּל־מִקְנַת כַּסְפּוֹ כָּל־זָכָר בְּאַנְשֵׁי בֵּית אַבְרָהָם וַיָּמָל אֶת־בְּשַׂר עָרְלָתָם
מפטיר כד בְּעֶצֶם הַיּוֹם הַזֶּה כַּאֲשֶׁר דִּבֶּר אִתּוֹ אֱלֹהִים: וְאַבְרָהָם בֶּן־תִּשְׁעִים וָתֵשַׁע
כה שָׁנָה בְּהִמֹּלוֹ בְּשַׂר עָרְלָתוֹ: וְיִשְׁמָעֵאל בְּנוֹ בֶּן־שְׁלֹשׁ עֶשְׂרֵה שָׁנָה בְּהִמֹּלוֹ
כו אֵת בְּשַׂר עָרְלָתוֹ: בְּעֶצֶם הַיּוֹם הַזֶּה נִמּוֹל אַבְרָהָם וְיִשְׁמָעֵאל בְּנוֹ:
כז וְכָל־אַנְשֵׁי בֵיתוֹ יְלִיד בָּיִת וּמִקְנַת־כֶּסֶף מֵאֵת בֶּן־נֵכָר נִמֹּלוּ אִתּוֹ:

---

16. וּבֵרַכְתִּיהָ — *I will bless her.* She will carry, give birth and rear her son without suffering, contrary to the curse pronounced over Eve, בְּעֶצֶב תֵּלְדִי בָנִים, *In pain you shall bring forth children* (3:16). Sarah will carry, give birth and bring up her son without suffering, as our Sages tell us, אֲשֶׁר פָּדָה אֶת אַבְרָהָם, *Who redeemed Abraham (Isaiah* 29:22), 'He was redeemed from the suffering of child rearing' *(Sanhedrin* 19b).

17. הַלְּבֶן מֵאָה שָׁנָה יִוָּלֵד — *Shall a child be born to a hundred-year-old man?* Although it is possible for a woman past her youth to conceive, it is usually from a young man, not an old one.

הֲבַת תִּשְׁעִים שָׁנָה תֵּלֵד — *Shall a ninety-year-old woman give birth?* ... from any man, even a young one.

22. וַיַּעַל אֱלֹהִים מֵעַל אַבְרָהָם — *God ascended from upon Abraham.* (This was) the reverse (of Cain, as it says), וַיֵּצֵא קַיִן מִלִּפְנֵי ה׳, *And Cain went out from the presence of* HASHEM (4:16).

23. בְּעֶצֶם הַיּוֹם הַזֶּה — *On that very day.* He did not postpone (it).

NOTES

shall keep My covenant. Every covenant, to be valid, must be a mutual agreement with both parties accepting responsibilities upon themselves. Verse 4 represents God's acceptance, while this verse represents Abraham's.

17. הַלְּבֶן מֵאָה שָׁנָה יִוָּלֵד — *Shall a child be born to a hundred-year-old man?* Abraham wonders how it is possible for him, an old man, and Sarah, an old woman, to have a child born to them. Each separately, with a younger mate, perhaps — but not the two of them together.

22. וַיַּעַל אֱלֹהִים מֵעַל אַבְרָהָם — *God ascended from upon Abraham.* Unlike Cain, who did not wait for God to ascend but left His presence, Abraham, showing honor to God,, waits until He has ascended and only then does Abraham leave.

פרשת וירא
Parashas Vayeira

יח א-ב וַיֵּרָא אֵלָיו יהוה בְּאֵלֹנֵי מַמְרֵא וְהוּא יֹשֵׁב פֶּתַח־הָאֹהֶל כְּחֹם הַיּוֹם: וַיִּשָּׂא
עֵינָיו וַיַּרְא וְהִנֵּה שְׁלֹשָׁה אֲנָשִׁים נִצָּבִים עָלָיו וַיַּרְא וַיָּרָץ לִקְרָאתָם מִפֶּתַח
ג הָאֹהֶל וַיִּשְׁתַּחוּ אָרְצָה: וַיֹּאמַר אֲדֹנָי אִם־נָא מָצָאתִי חֵן בְּעֵינֶיךָ אַל־נָא

XVIII

1. וַיֵּרָא אֵלָיו ה׳ בְּאֵלֹנֵי מַמְרֵא — *HASHEM appeared to him in the plains of Mamre* . . . because there Abraham and his household were circumcised, and there God's Divine presence revealed itself, to *stand* there (confirming) the covenant, as was the practice of all who entered a covenant. (This is) similar to אַתֶּם נִצָּבִים . . . לְעָבְרְךָ בִּבְרִית, *You are* standing . . . *to enter into the covenant (Deut.* 29:9,11), and . . . וַיִּכְרֹת לִפְנֵי ה׳ . . . וַיַּעֲמֹד כָּל הָעָם בַּבְּרִית, *And made a covenant before HASHEM . . . and all the people* stood *to the covenant (II Kings* 23:3). He *appeared* (however only to) Abraham, for he (Abraham) was more prepared than the others to see the visions. This was also the case (with Moses), וַיִּפְגְּשֵׁהוּ ה׳, *HASHEM met him (Exodus* 4:24), at which time God did not appear to speak with Moses but to be present, and accept the covenant (of circumcision) of his son, as it says: בֵּינִי וּבֵינֵיכֶם . . . לְדֹרֹתֵיכֶם, *Between Me and you . . . throughout your generations* (17:11,12). Possibly that is the reason for the custom of preparing a (special) chair at a circumcision.

2. וַיִּשָּׂא עֵינָיו — *He lifted his eyes* . . . with intent to observe.

נִצָּבִים עָלָיו — *Standing over him* . . . turning toward him, as though waiting to speak with him when he would be available, following the glorious vision. Whoever waits in the presence of another to speak to him is referred to as נִצָּבִים עָלָיו, *standing over him*, similar to לְהִתְאַפֵּק לְכֹל הַנִּצָּבִים עָלָיו, *Joseph could not refrain himself, before all them that stood over him* (45:1), and וְכָל הָעָם נִצָּב עָלֶיךָ, *and all the people stand over you (Exodus* 18:14).

וַיָּרָץ לִקְרָאתָם — *He ran toward them* . . . even before they approached to speak with him.

מִפֶּתַח הָאֹהֶל — *From the entrance of the tent.* He began to run from the entrance in their honor, for one's alacrity and eagerness to do something indicates the importance of that deed in his eyes, as we find, וַיְמַהֵר מֹשֶׁה וַיִּקֹּד אַרְצָה וַיִּשְׁתָּחוּ, *And Moses made haste and bowed toward the earth (Exodus* 34:8).

וַיִּשְׁתַּחוּ אָרְצָה — *And bowed toward the ground* . . . for their appearance was awesome, as it says, וּמַרְאֵהוּ כְּמַרְאֵה מַלְאַךְ הָאֱלֹהִים נוֹרָא מְאֹד, *And his appearance was like the countenance of an angel of God, very awesome (Judges* 13:6). (Abraham) thought they were the messengers of some king.

NOTES

XVIII

1. וַיֵּרָא אֵלָיו — *HASHEM appeared to him.* We do not find God appearing without a direct communication immediately following. In this verse (וַיֵּרָא), God 'appears' for some reason other than communication. *Rashi,* quoting the Talmud, tells us the purpose was to visit Abraham who was sick, recuperating from his circumcision. The *Sforno,* however, interprets this 'appearance' as being linked to the *covenant* of circumcision, where God as a party to the covenant comes to participate and confirm it, as it were. The custom of setting up a 'chair of Elijah' at every *bris* is to symbolize God's presence, through His representative, Elijah.

2. וַיָּרָץ . . . וַיִּשְׁתַּחוּ — *He ran . . . and bowed.* Unlike *Rashi,* who says that the three men appeared as Arabs (based on *Baba Metzia* 86), the *Sforno* feels that even when angels appear

ד תַּעֲבֹר מֵעַל עַבְדֶּךָ: יֻקַּח־נָא מְעַט־מַיִם וְרַחֲצוּ רַגְלֵיכֶם וְהִשָּׁעֲנוּ תַּחַת הָעֵץ:
ה וְאֶקְחָה פַת־לֶחֶם וְסַעֲדוּ לִבְּכֶם אַחַר תַּעֲבֹרוּ כִּי־עַל־כֵּן עֲבַרְתֶּם עַל־
ו עַבְדְּכֶם וַיֹּאמְרוּ כֵּן תַּעֲשֶׂה כַּאֲשֶׁר דִּבַּרְתָּ: וַיְמַהֵר אַבְרָהָם הָאֹהֱלָה אֶל־
ז שָׂרָה וַיֹּאמֶר מַהֲרִי שְׁלֹשׁ סְאִים קֶמַח סֹלֶת לוּשִׁי וַעֲשִׂי עֻגוֹת: וְאֶל־הַבָּקָר
רָץ אַבְרָהָם וַיִּקַּח בֶּן־בָּקָר רַךְ וָטוֹב וַיִּתֵּן אֶל־הַנַּעַר וַיְמַהֵר לַעֲשׂוֹת אֹתוֹ:
ח וַיִּקַּח חֶמְאָה וְחָלָב וּבֶן־הַבָּקָר אֲשֶׁר עָשָׂה וַיִּתֵּן לִפְנֵיהֶם וְהוּא־עֹמֵד עֲלֵיהֶם
ט תַּחַת הָעֵץ וַיֹּאכֵלוּ: וַיֹּאמְרוּ אֵלָיו אַיֵּה שָׂרָה אִשְׁתֶּךָ וַיֹּאמֶר הִנֵּה בָאֹהֶל:
י וַיֹּאמֶר שׁוֹב אָשׁוּב אֵלֶיךָ כָּעֵת חַיָּה וְהִנֵּה־בֵן לְשָׂרָה אִשְׁתֶּךָ וְשָׂרָה שֹׁמַעַת
יא פֶּתַח הָאֹהֶל וְהוּא אַחֲרָיו: וְאַבְרָהָם וְשָׂרָה זְקֵנִים בָּאִים בַּיָּמִים חָדַל לִהְיוֹת
יב לְשָׂרָה אֹרַח כַּנָּשִׁים: וַתִּצְחַק שָׂרָה בְּקִרְבָּהּ לֵאמֹר אַחֲרֵי בְלֹתִי הָיְתָה־לִּי

---

3. אַל נָא תַעֲבֹר — *Please pass not away.* You, the head of the messengers, do not hasten to pass away, as is the custom of every messenger who is in a hurry to bring a report back to the one who sent him.

5. כֵּן תַּעֲשֶׂה — *Do so.* But do not keep us beyond this; therefore (Abraham) runs and says (to Sarah) מַהֲרִי, *Hurry* (verse 6).

9. אַיֵּה שָׂרָה — *Where is Sarah?* The purpose of their mission was to inform Sarah (personally) so she might rejoice and thank God, for (in this manner) her pregnancy will be more perfect. Abraham had already been told this tiding by God (17:16). They inquired regarding Sarah *through* Abraham, as our Sages have said (advised us to do) (*Baba Metzia* 87a).

10. שׁוֹב אָשׁוּב אֵלֶיךָ — *I will surely return to you* . . . at the time of each and every circumcision.

וְהוּא אַחֲרָיו — *Which was behind him.* The entrance (to the tent) where Sarah was listening was behind the angel who was speaking, therefore he did not speak directly (to her) as did Elisha (*II Kings* 4:15).

12. וַתִּצְחַק שָׂרָה — *And Sarah laughed.* She thought that the angel's words were only akin to the blessing of a prophet, similar to the episode of Elisha (*II Kings* 4:16), not a prophecy sent by God, the Blessed One. She thought that since they were (both) old, even if a prophet should bless them, it was unattainable. Such a rejuvenation, given their old age, would be like the revival of the dead, which could only be accomplished through the command of God Himself, or through prayer which would find special favor with Him.

NOTES

as men their countenance is awe inspiring, and that is why Abraham ran to greet them and bowed down to them.

9. אַיֵּה שָׂרָה— *Where is Sarah?* The Talmud (*Baba Metzia* 87) tells us that one should not inquire after the health of a man's wife directly, except through her husband.

10. וְהוּא אַחֲרָיו – *Which was behind him.* Although one does not address himself directly to a married woman, as mentioned in the previous note, it is proper to do so if one is transmitting a promise from God, or giving a blessing. When Elisha spoke to the Shunamis promising her a child, he did so directly. The only reason the angel did not do so was because Sarah was standing in the entrance of the tent behind him.

12. וַתִּצְחַק שָׂרָה – *And Sarah laughed.* The unique power of prayer resulting in the birth of a child, mentioned by the *Sforno*, refers to the prayers of Rebecca and Hannah.

יג עֶדְנָה וַאדֹנִי זָקֵן: וַיֹּאמֶר יְהוָה אֶל־אַבְרָהָם לָמָּה זֶּה צָחֲקָה שָׂרָה לֵאמֹר
יד הַאַף אֻמְנָם אֵלֵד וַאֲנִי זָקַנְתִּי: הֲיִפָּלֵא מֵיְהוָה דָּבָר לַמּוֹעֵד אָשׁוּב אֵלֶיךָ
שני טו כָּעֵת חַיָּה וּלְשָׂרָה בֵן: וַתְּכַחֵשׁ שָׂרָה | לֵאמֹר לֹא צָחַקְתִּי כִּי | יָרֵאָה וַיֹּאמֶר
טז | לֹא כִּי צָחָקְתְּ: וַיָּקֻמוּ מִשָּׁם הָאֲנָשִׁים וַיַּשְׁקִפוּ עַל־פְּנֵי סְדֹם וְאַבְרָהָם הֹלֵךְ
יז עִמָּם לְשַׁלְּחָם: וַיהוָה אָמָר הַמְכַסֶּה אֲנִי מֵאַבְרָהָם אֲשֶׁר אֲנִי עֹשֶׂה:
יח-יט וְאַבְרָהָם הָיוֹ יִהְיֶה לְגוֹי גָּדוֹל וְעָצוּם וְנִבְרְכוּ־בוֹ כֹּל גּוֹיֵי הָאָרֶץ: כִּי יְדַעְתִּיו

---

14. הֲיִפָּלֵא מֵה׳ דָּבָר — *Is anything beyond* HASHEM*?* The angel did not make this statement as a blessing, but (he) brought tidings in the name (of God).

15. כִּי יָרֵאָה — *For she was frightened* . . . to say, 'I have sinned.' However, in her heart (inwardly) she repented.

וַיֹּאמֶר לֹא — *But he said, 'No.'* For he (Abraham) knew that, לֹא אִישׁ אֵל וִיכַזֵּב, *God is not a man, that He should lie (Numbers* 23:19) and he did not believe her, at all.

16-17. וַיַּשְׁקִפוּ — *And they gazed* . . . gazing for the purpose of bringing evil.

עַל פְּנֵי סְדֹם — *Down, toward Sodom.* In contrast to the house of Abraham, as the Prophet testifies, saying, הִנֵּה זֶה הָיָה עֲוֹן סְדֹם אֲחוֹתֵךְ, גָּאוֹן שִׂבְעַת לֶחֶם וְשַׁלְוַת הַשְׁקֵט הָיָה לָהּ וְלִבְנוֹתֶיהָ, וְיַד עָנִי וְאֶבְיוֹן לֹא הֶחֱזִיקָה, *Behold this was the iniquity of your sister Sodom, pride, fullness of bread and quiet ease was in her and her daughter; neither did she strengthen the hand of the poor and needy (Ezekiel* 16:49).

וְאַבְרָהָם הֹלֵךְ . . . וַה׳ אָמָר — *While Abraham walked . . . And* HASHEM *said.* (While) he was occupied with the precept *(mitzvah)* of acts of loving-kindness, i.e., accompanying his guests, God said (that) He would reveal Himself to him 'so that he will command his children,' as our Sages say, שְׂכַר מִצְוָה מִצְוָה, *The reward of one mitzvah is another mitzvah* (*Avos* 4:2).

הַמְכַסֶּה אֲנִי — *Shall I conceal?* It is proper that I should not conceal My attribute of goodness from Abraham, and inform him that if indeed there are a number of righteous men in the midst of the wicked ones, through whom there is hope the wicked may repent, I would tilt (the scale) toward loving-kindness and be forbearing, even toward the wicked, in the hope that they might repent. (God) *does not desire the death of the wicked* (based on *Ezekiel* 18:32); only if there is no hope for repentance will He exact justice.

18. וְאַבְרָהָם הָיוֹ יִהְיֶה — *Now that Abraham will surely be.* As one who shall be a standard for many nations, his teachings (admonition) will be most effective.

NOTES

15. וַיֹּאמֶר לֹא – *But he said, 'No.'* The commentators have different opinions regarding the word וַיֹּאמֶר, *He said.* Some feel it is God, Who is speaking to Sarah. The *Sforno*, however, interprets it as Abraham chiding his wife.

16-17. וְאַבְרָהָם הֹלֵךְ . . . וַה׳ אָמָר – *While Abraham walked . . . And* HASHEM *said.* These two verses are linked with the letter *vav* (וַה׳), being a וָי״ו הַדְּרִית — because Abraham performed the *mitzvah* of hospitality including the accompanying of his guests as they were leaving, God reveals His plan, and reason, for punishing Sodom so that Abraham will be able to teach his children the ways of God, that they might act in accordance with His will.

17. הַמְכַסֶּה אֲנִי – *Shall I conceal?* The phrase used here by the *Sforno* — I would tilt (the scales) toward (*chesed*) loving-kindness' is based upon *Rosh Hashanah*, 17. Our Sages tell us that there are times when the scales of

לְמַעַן אֲשֶׁר יְצַוֶּה אֶת־בָּנָיו וְאֶת־בֵּיתוֹ אַחֲרָיו וְשָׁמְרוּ דֶּרֶךְ יהוה לַעֲשׂוֹת
כ צְדָקָה וּמִשְׁפָּט לְמַעַן הָבִיא יהוה עַל־אַבְרָהָם אֵת אֲשֶׁר־דִּבֶּר עָלָיו׃ וַיֹּאמֶר
כא יהוה זַעֲקַת סְדֹם וַעֲמֹרָה כִּי־רָבָּה וְחַטָּאתָם כִּי כָבְדָה מְאֹד׃ אֵרְדָה־נָּא
כב וְאֶרְאֶה הַכְּצַעֲקָתָהּ הַבָּאָה אֵלַי עָשׂוּ ׀ כָּלָה וְאִם־לֹא אֵדָעָה׃ וַיִּפְנוּ מִשָּׁם

---

19. כִּי יְדַעְתִּיו — *For I have known him.* I admonish him with directness.

לְמַעַן אֲשֶׁר יְצַוֶּה אֶת בָּנָיו — *Because he commands his children.* All this (the blessings in the previous verse), God says He shall do — so that Abraham, observing the great loving-kindness (of God) even toward the wicked, and His justice against those who do not repent (will teach his children) . . .

וְשָׁמְרוּ . . . לַעֲשׂוֹת צְדָקָה וּמִשְׁפָּט לְמַעַן הָבִיא ה׳ עַל אַבְרָהָם אֵת אֲשֶׁר דִּבֶּר עָלָיו — *That they keep . . . doing charity and justice, in order that HASHEM might then bring upon Abraham that which He had spoken of him.* The ultimate purpose intended by the Almighty was to bring upon Abraham that which He had spoken, when He said, *'To be a God to you and to your offspring after you'* (17:7).

20. וַיֹּאמֶר ה׳ — *So HASHEM said.* (With this expression וַיֹּאמֶר) a higher degree of prophecy than the vision mentioned in verse 1, i.e., וַיֵּרָא אֵלָיו, *appeared to him,* begins.

21. אֵרְדָה נָּא — *I will descend.* I will delve into the ultimate consequences of their wickedness, which progresses from evil to evil, similar to, הָבָה נֵרְדָה וְנָבְלָה שָׁם שְׂפָתָם, *Come, let us go down and there confound their language* (11:7), as explained earlier.

וְאֶרְאֶה הַכְּצַעֲקָתָהּ — *And see, (whether) in accordance with its outcry.* I will demonstrate this (evil) concretely, when they openly reveal (their wickedness) by rising up against Lot's hospitality; then all will know (recognize) that this great punishment was not for naught.

עָשׂוּ כָּלָה — *They have all done.* They have all done (evil) and there is none among

NOTES

justice may be balanced, evil and good being equal. The Almighty, in His infinite compassion, tilts the scales in our favor.

19. וְשָׁמְרוּ . . . לַעֲשׂוֹת צְדָקָה וּמִשְׁפָּט — *That they keep . . . doing charity and justice.* The fate of Sodom is a dramatic forceful lesson for Abraham and his descendants. God decides to reveal to Abraham the reasoning behind this Divine decision so that he in turn can use it as an example when instructing his children the fundamentals of דַּרְכֵי ה׳, *the Ways of Hashem.* The *Sforno,* consistent with his commentary in the previous verses, explains that the expressions צְדָקָה, *righteousness,* and מִשְׁפָּט, *justice,* which are the two key teachings to be transmitted by Abraham, are reflected in the ways of God with Sodom. He was prepared to be benevolent, even with the wicked, but not to the extent of ignoring the demands of justice toward those who refuse to repent. The חֶסֶד the *Sforno* mentions is the equivalent of צְדָקָה, while the מִשְׁפָּט He metes out to Sodom is the same מִשְׁפָּט Abraham is to teach to his children. The Sodom episode demonstrates the vital need for both צְדָקָה and מִשְׁפָּט.

20. וַיֹּאמֶר ה׳ — *So HASHEM said.* Heretofore God only 'appears' to Abraham in a vision. For the first time the phrase וַיֹּאמֶר, *he said* — a more direct and higher level of prophecy — is used.

21. אֵרְדָה נָּא — *I will descend.* There is no need, obviously, for the Almighty to descend in order to see what is happening on earth. All is known to Him. The expression אֵרְדָה must therefore be understood as projection into the future — what will eventually come forth from their present evil behavior? To determine this, God tests the people of Sodom with the visit of the angels, giving them one last chance to repent. Unfortunately, they all fail the test.

עָשׂוּ כָּלָה — *They have all done.* The word כָּלָה

כג הָאֲנָשִׁים וַיֵּלְכוּ סְדֹמָה וְאַבְרָהָם עוֹדֶנּוּ עֹמֵד לִפְנֵי יהוה: וַיִּגַּשׁ אַבְרָהָם
כד וַיֹּאמַר הַאַף תִּסְפֶּה צַדִּיק עִם־רָשָׁע: אוּלַי יֵשׁ חֲמִשִּׁים צַדִּיקִם בְּתוֹךְ הָעִיר
הַאַף תִּסְפֶּה וְלֹא־תִשָּׂא לַמָּקוֹם לְמַעַן חֲמִשִּׁים הַצַּדִּיקִם אֲשֶׁר בְּקִרְבָּהּ:
כה חָלִלָה לְּךָ מֵעֲשֹׂת | כַּדָּבָר הַזֶּה לְהָמִית צַדִּיק עִם־רָשָׁע וְהָיָה כַצַּדִּיק

---

them to protest, similar to כָּלָה גָּרֵשׁ יְגָרֵשׁ, *He shall thrust all of you out* (*Exodus* 11:1), (the word כָּלָה) meaning, *all of you*. This was also demonstrated through the visit of the angels, where it is written, כָּל הָעָם מִקָּצֶה, *all the people from every quarter* (19:4), none being ashamed.

22. וַיִּפְנוּ מִשָּׁם הָאֲנָשִׁים — *And the men turned from there.* They turned from the house of kindness.

וְאַבְרָהָם עוֹדֶנּוּ עֹמֵד — *While Abraham was still standing.* Although the angels who were sent to destroy (Sodom) had already reached Sodom, Abraham still stood (in prayer) to beseech (God) for mercy on their behalf and seek merits (for them), as our Sages tell us, 'One must not desist from asking (God's) mercy, even when a sharp sword is on his neck' (*Berachos* 10a). We also find regarding those condemned to death, 'We bring him back (from the execution place) even four or five times, providing he presents a substantive defense' (*Sanhedrin* 42b).

23. הַאַף תִּסְפֶּה צַדִּיק עִם רָשָׁע — *Will You also stamp out the righteous with the wicked?* Since You said, *'The outcry of Sodom and Amorah has become great'* (verse 20), (the implication is) that You are judging the entire place according to the (actions) of the majority, not of the sinners alone.

24. הַאַף תִּסְפֶּה וְלֹא תִשָּׂא לַמָּקוֹם — *Would You still stamp it out rather than spare the place?* Even though You will stamp out and not spare the wicked (in the merit of) the righteous, it would be sacrilegious for You to bring death upon the righteous.

25. וְהָיָה כַצַּדִּיק כָּרָשָׁע — *And it would be like the righteous as the wicked . . .* subject to the (destructive) event, even though there be some righteous in the midst of the wicked.

NOTES

is translated by most commentators as *destruction.* They interpret the verse to mean, *if they are indeed guilty, then I will decree destruction.* The Sforno, however, translates כָּלָה as synonymous with כֻּלָּה, *all of it.* The verse accordingly means 'Have they *all* done this evil — or are there still some righteous among them?'

22. וַיִּפְנוּ מִשָּׁם הָאֲנָשִׁים – *And the men turned from there.* The word וַיִּפְנוּ, *they turned,* is not to be understood in the physical sense, for they were angels. Rather it means they considered and compared Abraham's home of kindness with the wickedness of Sodom, where the people could not abide Lot's willingness to extend hospitality to strangers.

וְאַבְרָהָם עוֹדֶנּוּ עֹמֵד – *While Abraham was still standing.* The verse explicitly states that the men had already gone to Sodom – וַיֵּלְכוּ סְדֹמָה — following which we are told that Abraham was still standing and praying. Though Heavenly sentence had been passed, there was still a remote chance it could be changed. Abraham therefore refuses to accept the finality of Sodom's destruction and pleads with God to rescind His decision, which He would have done if only there were a sufficient number of righteous men to make a difference. (See *Sforno's* commentary on 19:1.)

23. הַאַף תִּסְפֶּה צַדִּיק עִם רָשָׁע – *Will You also stamp out the righteous with the wicked.* Abraham's concern is that God seems to be judging them *collectively,* not individually. He argues (in verses 24-25) that even if God is not willing to save the wicked in the merit of the righteous, at least let not the righteous be swept along in the wake of destruction visited upon the wicked. God answers (verse 26) that

כו כָּרָשָׁע חָלִלָה לָּךְ הֲשֹׁפֵט כָּל־הָאָרֶץ לֹא יַעֲשֶׂה מִשְׁפָּט: וַיֹּאמֶר יהוה אִם־
אֶמְצָא בִסְדֹם חֲמִשִּׁים צַדִּיקִם בְּתוֹךְ הָעִיר וְנָשָׂאתִי לְכָל־הַמָּקוֹם בַּעֲבוּרָם:
כז וַיַּעַן אַבְרָהָם וַיֹּאמַר הִנֵּה־נָא הוֹאַלְתִּי לְדַבֵּר אֶל־אֲדֹנָי וְאָנֹכִי עָפָר וָאֵפֶר:
כח אוּלַי יַחְסְרוּן חֲמִשִּׁים הַצַּדִּיקִם חֲמִשָּׁה הֲתַשְׁחִית בַּחֲמִשָּׁה אֶת־כָּל־הָעִיר
כט וַיֹּאמֶר לֹא אַשְׁחִית אִם־אֶמְצָא שָׁם אַרְבָּעִים וַחֲמִשָּׁה: וַיֹּסֶף עוֹד לְדַבֵּר
אֵלָיו וַיֹּאמַר אוּלַי יִמָּצְאוּן שָׁם אַרְבָּעִים וַיֹּאמֶר לֹא אֶעֱשֶׂה בַּעֲבוּר
ל הָאַרְבָּעִים: וַיֹּאמֶר אַל־נָא יִחַר לַאדֹנָי וַאֲדַבֵּרָה אוּלַי יִמָּצְאוּן שָׁם שְׁלֹשִׁים
לא וַיֹּאמֶר לֹא אֶעֱשֶׂה אִם־אֶמְצָא שָׁם שְׁלֹשִׁים: וַיֹּאמֶר הִנֵּה־נָא הוֹאַלְתִּי

הַשֹּׁפֵט כָּל הָאָרֶץ — *Shall the Judge of all the earth.* Considering that You are the judge of all the earth, if You decide the fate of all by following the majority, You will, without a doubt, destroy all, since the majority of people are wicked!

26. אִם אֶמְצָא בִסְדֹם — *If I find in Sodom.* Now, when I test them through (the visit) of the angels whom I sent, if I find fifty righteous men who will protest against the wicked ones of Sodom, which is the major city of the area, as it says סְדֹם וּבְנוֹתֶיהָ, *Sodom and her suburbs (Ezekiel* 16:46) where the leaders of the people from all the cities of the area gather together (then . . .)

וְנָשָׂאתִי לְכָל הַמָּקוֹם — *Then I would spare the entire place.* Not only the righteous.

27. הִנֵּה נָא הוֹאַלְתִּי לְדַבֵּר — *Behold, now, I have taken upon me to speak* . . . to ask (You) regarding the doubts I have in my mind about the manner of God's justice.

וְאָנֹכִי עָפָר וָאֵפֶר — *Although I am but dust and ashes* . . . (and as such) I have still not been able to fathom the implications (meaning) of Your answer.

28. הֲתַשְׁחִית בַּחֲמִשָּׁה אֶת כָּל הָעִיר — *Would You destroy the entire city because of the five?* Tell me whether this number (ten) is an exact one, for if a city has less than ten (righteous men) it lacks 'a saving congregation,' and accordingly You will destroy the fifth city, which is the most guilty, lacking a saving congregation (and God) says . . .

לֹא אַשְׁחִית — *I will not destroy.* The fifth one.

30. לֹא אֶעֱשֶׂה — *I will not act.* I will do no evil at all to the three *least* guilty cities.

NOTES

He is prepared to spare the entire place, including the wicked who are the majority, providing there is a sufficient number of righteous men in their midst.

28. הֲתַשְׁחִית בַּחֲמִשָּׁה אֶת כָּל הָעִיר — *Would You destroy the entire city because of the five.* The expression עֵדָה מַצֶּלֶת, *a saving congregation,* is based upon the Sages' interpretation of the verses in *Numbers* 35:24,25 where the phrases וְשָׁפְטוּ הָעֵדָה, *and the congregation shall judge,* and וְהִצִּילוּ הָעֵדָה, *and the congregation shall deliver (save)* are used. This juxtaposition teaches us that wherever possible to do so within the law, we attempt to exonerate the accused. The *Sforno* applies this concept to the episode at hand. Ten righteous men represent a congregation, which is of sufficient weight to tilt the scales and save the community.

28-30. לֹא אַשְׁחִית . . . לֹא אֶעֱשֶׂה — *I will not destroy . . . I will not act.* According to the *Sforno,* the responses of God are to be understood in the following manner: In response to Abraham's question as to what the fate of the fifth city would be, God answers, '*I will not destroy it,* but I will still punish it' (v. 28). As for the three cities that are relatively less sinful, He answers, '*I will not act* (at all).' Here (v. 30) the word used is אֶעֱשֶׂה, *to do* or *act*, not אַשְׁחִית, *to destroy,* which accounts for the *Sforno's* subtle change of interpretation. When, however, the number of righteous men is reduced to a mere twenty or ten, God's

לְדַבֵּר אֶל־אֲדֹנָי אוּלַי יִמָּצְאוּן שָׁם עֶשְׂרִים וַיֹּאמֶר לֹא אַשְׁחִית בַּעֲבוּר
לב הָעֶשְׂרִים: וַיֹּאמֶר אַל־נָא יִחַר לַאדֹנָי וַאֲדַבְּרָה אַךְ־הַפַּעַם אוּלַי יִמָּצְאוּן
לג שָׁם עֲשָׂרָה וַיֹּאמֶר לֹא אַשְׁחִית בַּעֲבוּר הָעֲשָׂרָה: וַיֵּלֶךְ יהוה כַּאֲשֶׁר כִּלָּה
יט שלישי א לְדַבֵּר אֶל־אַבְרָהָם וְאַבְרָהָם שָׁב לִמְקֹמוֹ: וַיָּבֹאוּ שְׁנֵי הַמַּלְאָכִים סְדֹמָה
בָּעֶרֶב וְלוֹט יֹשֵׁב בְּשַׁעַר־סְדֹם וַיַּרְא־לוֹט וַיָּקָם לִקְרָאתָם וַיִּשְׁתַּחוּ אַפַּיִם
ב אָרְצָה: וַיֹּאמֶר הִנֶּה נָּא־אֲדֹנַי סוּרוּ נָא אֶל־בֵּית עַבְדְּכֶם וְלִינוּ וְרַחֲצוּ
רַגְלֵיכֶם וְהִשְׁכַּמְתֶּם וַהֲלַכְתֶּם לְדַרְכְּכֶם וַיֹּאמְרוּ לֹּא כִּי בָרְחוֹב נָלִין:

31-32. לֹא אַשְׁחִית בַּעֲבוּר הָעֶשְׂרִים ... הָעֲשָׂרָה ... — *I will not destroy on account of the twenty ... of the ten.* For if three (of the five) are destroyed, the remaining two cannot escape harm and damage as a result of the destruction of the neighboring towns, as it says, 'Babylon is cursed, her neighbors are (also) cursed' (*Berachos* 58a).

33. וַיֵּלֶךְ ה׳ — *And HASHEM departed.* Abraham waited there and did not interrupt his prophetic concentration until the Divine presence left; (this being) the reverse of, וַיֵּצֵא קַיִן מִלִּפְנֵי ה׳, *And Cain went out from the presence of HASHEM* (4:16).

וְאַבְרָהָם שָׁב — *And Abraham returned.* He returned from the place to which he had accompanied the angels, for it was there that God had spoken to him.

לִמְקֹמוֹ — *To his place.* To his house.

XIX

1. וַיָּבֹאוּ שְׁנֵי הַמַּלְאָכִים סְדֹמָה בָּעֶרֶב — *The two angels came to Sodom in the evening.* Although they arrived there without delay, as our Sages tell us, גַּבְרִיאֵל בִּשְׁתַּיִם מִיכָאֵל בְּאַחַת, *Gabriel (reaches his goal) in two flights, Michael in one* (*Berachos* 4b), and we are (also) told this above, *and they went to Sodom* (18:22), nonetheless, they did not *enter* Sodom until the evening, (delaying) until Abraham's intercession had been denied and the final (Divine) sentence passed.

וַיָּקָם לִקְרָאתָם — *And stood up to meet them* ... lest they spend the night in the streets, as was the custom in those cities where there was no hospitality extended, and (by so doing expose themselves) to harm by the wicked townspeople.

וַיִּשְׁתַּחוּ אַפַּיִם אָרְצָה — *And he bowed, face to the ground* ... for their countenance was, without a doubt, awe inspiring.

NOTES

mercy increases perforce, for as the *Sforno* explains, the one or two cities worthy of salvation will still be doomed if all the others are destroyed, since they cannot survive in an area of total destruction (verses 31-32).

33. לִמְקֹמוֹ – *To his place.* See note to 17:22. The word שָׁב, *returned*, denotes *from* a certain place, whereas לִמְקֹמוֹ, *to his place*, is to go *toward* a certain destination. The former word is therefore to be understood as departing from the place to which he had accompanied the angels and communicated with God, while the latter refers to his return home.

XIX

1. וַיָּבֹאוּ שְׁנֵי הַמַּלְאָכִים סְדֹמָה בָּעֶרֶב – *The two angels came to Sodom in the evening.* The *Sforno* quotes the Talmudic saying regarding the angels Gabriel and Michael, for they were two of the three who came to Abraham and subsequently went on to Sodom (*Yoma* 37). In the previous chapter (18:22) the *Sforno* established that the angels had already arrived at the gates of Sodom well before evening. He therefore explains the reason for their delaying their actual entrance to the city.

וַיָּקָם לִקְרָאתָם – *And stood up to meet them.* The *Sforno* in 28:11 describes the custom of wayfarers to spend the night in the village square. The reason Lot insists that they not do so in Sodom is because of the danger to which

ג וַיִּפְצַר־בָּם מְאֹד וַיָּסֻרוּ אֵלָיו וַיָּבֹאוּ אֶל־בֵּיתוֹ וַיַּעַשׂ לָהֶם מִשְׁתֶּה וּמַצּוֹת
ד אָפָה וַיֹּאכֵלוּ׃ טֶרֶם יִשְׁכָּבוּ וְאַנְשֵׁי הָעִיר אַנְשֵׁי סְדֹם נָסַבּוּ עַל־הַבַּיִת מִנַּעַר
ה וְעַד־זָקֵן כָּל־הָעָם מִקָּצֶה׃ וַיִּקְרְאוּ אֶל־לוֹט וַיֹּאמְרוּ לוֹ אַיֵּה הָאֲנָשִׁים
ו אֲשֶׁר־בָּאוּ אֵלֶיךָ הַלָּיְלָה הוֹצִיאֵם אֵלֵינוּ וְנֵדְעָה אֹתָם׃ וַיֵּצֵא אֲלֵהֶם לוֹט
ז-ח הַפֶּתְחָה וְהַדֶּלֶת סָגַר אַחֲרָיו׃ וַיֹּאמַר אַל־נָא אַחַי תָּרֵעוּ׃ הִנֵּה־נָא לִי שְׁתֵּי
בָנוֹת אֲשֶׁר לֹא־יָדְעוּ אִישׁ אוֹצִיאָה־נָּא אֶתְהֶן אֲלֵיכֶם וַעֲשׂוּ לָהֶן כַּטּוֹב
בְּעֵינֵיכֶם רַק לָאֲנָשִׁים הָאֵל אַל־תַּעֲשׂוּ דָבָר כִּי־עַל־כֵּן בָּאוּ בְּצֵל קֹרָתִי׃
ט וַיֹּאמְרוּ ׀ גֶּשׁ־הָלְאָה וַיֹּאמְרוּ הָאֶחָד בָּא־לָגוּר וַיִּשְׁפֹּט שָׁפוֹט עַתָּה נָרַע לְךָ
י מֵהֶם וַיִּפְצְרוּ בָאִישׁ בְּלוֹט מְאֹד וַיִּגְּשׁוּ לִשְׁבֹּר הַדָּלֶת׃ וַיִּשְׁלְחוּ הָאֲנָשִׁים
יא אֶת־יָדָם וַיָּבִיאוּ אֶת־לוֹט אֲלֵיהֶם הַבָּיְתָה וְאֶת־הַדֶּלֶת סָגָרוּ׃ וְאֶת־
הָאֲנָשִׁים אֲשֶׁר־פֶּתַח הַבַּיִת הִכּוּ בַּסַּנְוֵרִים מִקָּטֹן וְעַד־גָּדוֹל וַיִּלְאוּ לִמְצֹא
יב הַפָּתַח׃ וַיֹּאמְרוּ הָאֲנָשִׁים אֶל־לוֹט עֹד מִי־לְךָ פֹה חָתָן וּבָנֶיךָ וּבְנֹתֶיךָ וְכֹל

---

3. מִשְׁתֶּה — *A feast.* A feast centered on wine, of which he was fond, as later events prove. Abraham, however, did not prepare a feast (of wine) for them, doing so only on the day Isaac was weaned (21:8) with the participation of the leaders of that generation who were accustomed to drink (quantities of) wine on their joyous occasions, as our Sages tell us, קַמֵּי דְשָׁתָא חַמְרָא — חַמְרָא, *For one accustomed to drink wine — bring (him) wine* (*Sotah* 10a).

8. אוֹצִיאָה נָּא אֶתְהֶן אֲלֵיכֶם — *I shall bring them out to you.* He was certain that the men betrothed to his daughters would rise up (to defend their honor) and there would be tumult among them (thereby deterring the crowd).

9. גֶּשׁ הָלְאָה — *Stand back!* . . . from the opening and we will break down the door.

הָאֶחָד בָּא לָגוּר — *This one came to sojourn.* Is there anyone who would (dare) do such a thing?

10. וְאֶת הַדֶּלֶת סָגָרוּ — *And closed the door* . . . so that they will (be forced) to weary themselves in vain to locate the entrance, and thus their utter wickedness would be demonstrated.

11. וַיִּלְאוּ לִמְצֹא הַפָּתַח — *They wearied themselves in vain to find the entrance.* Although they were stricken with blindness, they exerted themselves to find the entrance so as to break down the door, as our Sages tell us: 'The wicked do not repent even at the entrance of *Gehinnom* (Hell)' (*Eruvin* 19a).

NOTES

they will be exposed, given the wickedness of the inhabitants.

3. מִשְׁתֶּה — *A feast.* The phrase מִשְׁתֶּה (from the root שתה, *drink)* is used only regarding Lot, but not when Abraham entertained them. The word connotes a 'feast' focused on wine. The *Sforno* is of the opinion that the Torah is hinting to the important role that wine will later play, in the episode of Lot and his daughters (verse 32).

8. אוֹצִיאָה נָּא אֶתְהֶן אֲלֵיכֶם — *I shall bring them out to you.* It is incomprehensible that a father would sacrifice his daughters to a mob, instead of defending their honor. Various answers are given by the commentators to resolve this difficulty. The *Sforno* gives his unique interpretation, that this was a strategic ploy to create a confrontation between his daughters' fiances and the mob, and in the ensuing confusion he would spirit away his guests.

10-11. וְאֶת הַדֶּלֶת סָגָרוּ . . . וַיִּלְאוּ לִמְצֹא הַפָּתַח — *And closed the door . . . they wearied themselves in vain to find the entrance.* The *Sforno*

יג אֲשֶׁר־לְךָ בָּעִיר הוֹצֵא מִן־הַמָּקוֹם: כִּי־מַשְׁחִתִים אֲנַחְנוּ אֶת־הַמָּקוֹם הַזֶּה
יד כִּי־גָדְלָה צַעֲקָתָם אֶת־פְּנֵי יהוה וַיְשַׁלְּחֵנוּ יהוה לְשַׁחֲתָהּ: וַיֵּצֵא לוֹט וַיְדַבֵּר ׀
אֶל־חֲתָנָיו ׀ לֹקְחֵי בְנֹתָיו וַיֹּאמֶר קוּמוּ צְּאוּ מִן־הַמָּקוֹם הַזֶּה כִּי־מַשְׁחִית
טו יהוה אֶת־הָעִיר וַיְהִי כִמְצַחֵק בְּעֵינֵי חֲתָנָיו: וּכְמוֹ הַשַּׁחַר עָלָה וַיָּאִיצוּ
הַמַּלְאָכִים בְּלוֹט לֵאמֹר קוּם קַח אֶת־אִשְׁתְּךָ וְאֶת־שְׁתֵּי בְנֹתֶיךָ הַנִּמְצָאֹת
טז פֶּן־תִּסָּפֶה בַּעֲוֹן הָעִיר: וַיִּתְמַהְמָהּ ׀ וַיַּחֲזִיקוּ הָאֲנָשִׁים בְּיָדוֹ וּבְיַד־אִשְׁתּוֹ וּבְיַד
יז שְׁתֵּי בְנֹתָיו בְּחֶמְלַת יהוה עָלָיו וַיֹּצִאֻהוּ וַיַּנִּחֻהוּ מִחוּץ לָעִיר: וַיְהִי כְהוֹצִיאָם
אֹתָם הַחוּצָה וַיֹּאמֶר הִמָּלֵט עַל־נַפְשֶׁךָ אַל־תַּבִּיט אַחֲרֶיךָ וְאַל־תַּעֲמֹד
יח בְּכָל־הַכִּכָּר הָהָרָה הִמָּלֵט פֶּן־תִּסָּפֶה: וַיֹּאמֶר לוֹט אֲלֵהֶם אַל־נָא אֲדֹנָי:
יט הִנֵּה־נָא מָצָא עַבְדְּךָ חֵן בְּעֵינֶיךָ וַתַּגְדֵּל חַסְדְּךָ אֲשֶׁר עָשִׂיתָ עִמָּדִי לְהַחֲיוֹת
כ אֶת־נַפְשִׁי וְאָנֹכִי לֹא אוּכַל לְהִמָּלֵט הָהָרָה פֶּן־תִּדְבָּקַנִי הָרָעָה וָמַתִּי: הִנֵּה־
נָא הָעִיר הַזֹּאת קְרֹבָה לָנוּס שָׁמָּה וְהִוא מִצְעָר אִמָּלְטָה נָּא שָׁמָּה הֲלֹא
רביעי כא מִצְעָר הִוא וּתְחִי נַפְשִׁי: וַיֹּאמֶר אֵלָיו הִנֵּה נָשָׂאתִי פָנֶיךָ גַּם לַדָּבָר הַזֶּה
כב לְבִלְתִּי הָפְכִּי אֶת־הָעִיר אֲשֶׁר דִּבַּרְתָּ: מַהֵר הִמָּלֵט שָׁמָּה כִּי לֹא אוּכַל
כג לַעֲשׂוֹת דָּבָר עַד־בֹּאֲךָ שָׁמָּה עַל־כֵּן קָרָא שֵׁם־הָעִיר צוֹעַר: הַשֶּׁמֶשׁ יָצָא
כד עַל־הָאָרֶץ וְלוֹט בָּא צֹעֲרָה: וַיהוה הִמְטִיר עַל־סְדֹם וְעַל־עֲמֹרָה גָּפְרִית

---

14. וַיֵּצֵא לוֹט — *So Lot went out* . . . after they failed (to find the entrance) and left.

15. וַיָּאִיצוּ — *(The angels) urged.* So that their misfortune (calamity) befall them (precisely) at sunrise, when their great deity (the sun) appears, as our Sages tell us, 'At the time when the sun rises and all the kings . . . bow down to the sun, the Holy One, Blessed is He, becomes angry immediately' (*Berachos* 7a).

16. בְּחֶמְלַת ה׳ עָלָיו — *In HASHEM's mercy on him.* Although he was saved in the merit of Abraham, as it states, *God remembered Abraham, so he sent Lot from amidst the upheaval* (verse 29), nonetheless, since he tarried and lingered after the angels warned him, he deserved to be swept away. However, (God) had mercy on him, because he was not motivated by a rebellious spirit or defiance, rather (this was) a result of lethargy and bewilderment.

17. אַל תַּבִּיט אַחֲרֶיךָ — *Do not look behind you.* The evil will spread to you as if it were following you, but will not harm you. However, if you stop to peer (behind you), it will (overtake you) and cleave to you, as indeed happened to his wife, as it says, *and she became a pillar of salt* (verse 26).

NOTES

established in the previous chapter (verse 21) that the angels came to Lot's house to test the reaction of the populace and to give them one last chance to repent. The closing of the door by the angels is meant to underscore the townspeople's wickedness and demonstrate how corrupted they were, that even when blinded, their passion does not subside. The saying of the Sages quoted by the *Sforno* is a play on words — the Sodomites stand at 'the entrance,' as do the wicked at 'the entrance' of Hell — and fail to repent.

16. בְּחֶמְלַת ה׳ עָלָיו – *In HASHEM's mercy on him.* The expression בְּחֶמְלַת ה׳, *in HASHEM's mercy*, is not to be understood as the *reason* for Lot's deliverance. That was due to the merit of Abraham, his uncle. God's mercy is necessary only to prevent punishment for Lot's procrastination.

כה וְאֵשׁ מֵאֵת יהוה מִן־הַשָּׁמָיִם: וַיַּהֲפֹךְ אֶת־הֶעָרִים הָאֵל וְאֵת כָּל־הַכִּכָּר וְאֵת
כו כָּל־יֹשְׁבֵי הֶעָרִים וְצֶמַח הָאֲדָמָה: וַתַּבֵּט אִשְׁתּוֹ מֵאַחֲרָיו וַתְּהִי נְצִיב מֶלַח:
כז־כח וַיַּשְׁכֵּם אַבְרָהָם בַּבֹּקֶר אֶל־הַמָּקוֹם אֲשֶׁר־עָמַד שָׁם אֶת־פְּנֵי יהוה: וַיַּשְׁקֵף
עַל־פְּנֵי סְדֹם וַעֲמֹרָה וְעַל־כָּל־פְּנֵי אֶרֶץ הַכִּכָּר וַיַּרְא וְהִנֵּה עָלָה קִיטֹר
כט הָאָרֶץ כְּקִיטֹר הַכִּבְשָׁן: וַיְהִי בְּשַׁחֵת אֱלֹהִים אֶת־עָרֵי הַכִּכָּר וַיִּזְכֹּר אֱלֹהִים
אֶת־אַבְרָהָם וַיְשַׁלַּח אֶת־לוֹט מִתּוֹךְ הַהֲפֵכָה בַּהֲפֹךְ אֶת־הֶעָרִים אֲשֶׁר־

---

24. מֵאֵת ה׳ מִן הַשָּׁמָיִם — *From HASHEM, out of heaven.* He did not cause clouds to form from the ends of the earth that would traverse the atmosphere, as is the natural phenomena with lightning and hail.

25. וַיַּהֲפֹךְ — *He overturned* (lit., *changed*). The nature of the land and its inhabitants *changed* to brimstone and fire, similar to הָפַךְ אֶת מֵימֵיהֶם לְדָם, *He changed their waters to blood (Psalms* 105:29). In their case, the dew which forms before sunrise changed from its natural state to one of salt, as it is written, גָּפְרִית וָמֶלַח שְׂרֵפָה כָל אַרְצָהּ, *The whole land thereof is brimstone and salt, with a burning (Deut.* 29:22), as is the case with all neutral moisture when mixed with burnt particles.

27. אֶל הַמָּקוֹם אֲשֶׁר עָמַד שָׁם אֶת פְּנֵי ה׳ — *To the place where he had stood before HASHEM* . . . to the place to which he had accompanied the angels (18:16), for it was there that the 'hand of *HASHEM*' had come to rest upon him. Since he had failed to find justification for them (Sodom) in law, he thought to plead for mercy on their behalf.

28. וַיַּשְׁקֵף — *He gazed* . . . a gaze of animosity because of their great wickedness.

וַיַּרְא וְהִנֵּה עָלָה קִיטֹר הָאָרֶץ — *And he saw, and behold, the smoke of the earth rose.* Therefore he realized there was no longer any reason to pray on their behalf.

29. מִתּוֹךְ הַהֲפֵכָה בַּהֲפֹךְ אֶת הֶעָרִים — *From amidst the upheaval when He overturned the cities.* Since (Lot) was saved in the merit of Abraham from the midst of the upheaval, even while God was overturning these cities before Lot had left the area; and he (on his own) would never have merited (such salvation) being that he did not flee *before* the catastrophe struck, due to his lethargy, as it says, וַיִּתְמַהְמָה, *Still he lingered* (verse 16), therefore he was afraid to dwell in Zoar, for he thought that its upheaval would only be delayed until he (Lot) departed from it, (also) in the merit of Abraham, but once he left, the upheaval would spread to Zoar (as well).

NOTES

24. מֵאֵת ה׳ מִן הַשָּׁמָיִם — *From HASHEM, out of heaven.* This phrase seems superfluous since we are told at the beginning of the verse that God caused sulphur and fire to rain upon Sodom and Amorah. The *Sforno* explains that the Torah is emphasizing that this was not a natural phenomena but a Divine punishment, *from HASHEM, out of heaven.*

29. מִתּוֹךְ הַהֲפֵכָה בַּהֲפֹךְ אֶת הֶעָרִים — *From amidst the upheaval when He overturned the cities.* Lot was convinced that Zoar was also marked for destruction. The only reason it was spared was due to his dwelling there and not because of his merit but the merit of Abraham, which is mentioned here in this verse, followed by the cryptic statement in the next verse *and Lot went up from Zoar.* The *Sforno* interprets the *order* of the two verses as explained above. Lot does not choose to dwell too long in such a precarious place, so he moves to the mountain, which he believes is safer, since the angel had indeed suggested it to him as a haven, when they first fled Sodom.

ל יָשַׁב בְּהֶן לוֹט׃ וַיַּעַל לוֹט מִצּוֹעַר וַיֵּשֶׁב בָּהָר וּשְׁתֵּי בְנֹתָיו עִמּוֹ כִּי יָרֵא
לא לָשֶׁבֶת בְּצוֹעַר וַיֵּשֶׁב בַּמְּעָרָה הוּא וּשְׁתֵּי בְנֹתָיו׃ וַתֹּאמֶר הַבְּכִירָה אֶל־
לב הַצְּעִירָה אָבִינוּ זָקֵן וְאִישׁ אֵין בָּאָרֶץ לָבוֹא עָלֵינוּ כְּדֶרֶךְ כָּל־הָאָרֶץ׃ לְכָה
לג נַשְׁקֶה אֶת־אָבִינוּ יַיִן וְנִשְׁכְּבָה עִמּוֹ וּנְחַיֶּה מֵאָבִינוּ זָרַע׃ וַתַּשְׁקֶיןָ אֶת־
אֲבִיהֶן יַיִן בַּלַּיְלָה הוּא וַתָּבֹא הַבְּכִירָה וַתִּשְׁכַּב אֶת־אָבִיהָ וְלֹא־יָדַע
לד בְּשִׁכְבָהּ וּבְקוּמָהּ׃ וַיְהִי מִמָּחֳרָת וַתֹּאמֶר הַבְּכִירָה אֶל־הַצְּעִירָה הֵן־שָׁכַבְתִּי
אֶמֶשׁ אֶת־אָבִי נַשְׁקֶנּוּ יַיִן גַּם־הַלַּיְלָה וּבֹאִי שִׁכְבִי עִמּוֹ וּנְחַיֶּה מֵאָבִינוּ זָרַע׃
לה וַתַּשְׁקֶיןָ גַּם בַּלַּיְלָה הַהוּא אֶת־אֲבִיהֶן יָיִן וַתָּקָם הַצְּעִירָה וַתִּשְׁכַּב עִמּוֹ
לו-לז וְלֹא־יָדַע בְּשִׁכְבָהּ וּבְקֻמָהּ׃ וַתַּהֲרֶיןָ שְׁתֵּי בְנוֹת־לוֹט מֵאֲבִיהֶן׃ וַתֵּלֶד
לח הַבְּכִירָה בֵּן וַתִּקְרָא שְׁמוֹ מוֹאָב הוּא אֲבִי־מוֹאָב עַד־הַיּוֹם׃ וְהַצְּעִירָה
גַם־הִוא יָלְדָה בֵּן וַתִּקְרָא שְׁמוֹ בֶּן־עַמִּי הוּא אֲבִי בְנֵי־עַמּוֹן עַד־
כ א הַיּוֹם׃ וַיִּסַּע מִשָּׁם אַבְרָהָם אַרְצָה הַנֶּגֶב וַיֵּשֶׁב בֵּין־קָדֵשׁ וּבֵין
ב שׁוּר וַיָּגָר בִּגְרָר׃ וַיֹּאמֶר אַבְרָהָם אֶל־שָׂרָה אִשְׁתּוֹ אֲחֹתִי הִוא וַיִּשְׁלַח

---

30. וַיֵּשֶׁב בָּהָר — *And settled on the mountain* . . . for he thought that the upheaval would spread throughout the area up to (but not including) the mountain, as the angel had indicated when he said, *flee to the mountain* (verse 17).

31. אָבִינוּ זָקֵן — *Our father is old* . . . and he will not exert himself to travel on to a different land.

וְאִישׁ אֵין בָּאָרֶץ לָבוֹא עָלֵינוּ — *And there is no man to marry us.* There is no man in this region worthy to marry us.

כְּדֶרֶךְ כָּל הָאָרֶץ — *In the manner of all the land* . . . for it was customary that a woman would only marry a (man) who was proper for her.

37-38. וַתִּקְרָא שְׁמוֹ מוֹאָב — *And she named him Moab* (lit., *from father*) . . .

וַתִּקְרָא שְׁמוֹ בֶּן עַמִּי — *And she named him Ben-Ami* (lit., *son of my people*) . . . to indicate that they had not conceived from one who was unworthy (improper).

הוּא אֲבִי מוֹאָב . . . הוּא אֲבִי בְנֵי עַמּוֹן — *He is the ancestor of the Moabites* . . . *he is the ancestor of the people of Ammon* . . . who inherited the land. Because the motivation of these women was acceptable, their offspring became two nations who were partially Abraham's heirs, as our Sages tell us, בְּכָל דְּרָכֶיךָ דָעֵהוּ, *In all your ways acknowledge Him (Proverbs* 3:6) — even for a matter of transgression (*Berachos* 63a).

XX

1. וַיֵּשֶׁב בֵּין קָדֵשׁ וּבֵין שׁוּר — *And settled between Kadesh and Shur.* (He settled) between two large cities to invoke *HASHEM,* the Eternal One, by Name, as he later did, *to strengthen the covenant with many* (based on *Daniel* 9:27).

NOTES

31-38. אָבִינוּ זָקֵן וְאִישׁ אֵין בָּאָרֶץ . . . הוּא אֲבִי מוֹאָב . . . הוּא אֲבִי בְנֵי עַמּוֹן — *Our father is old and there is no man to marry us . . . he is the ancestor of the Moabites . . . he is the ancestor of the people of Ammon.* Departing from *Rashi's* interpretation of this episode, the *Sforno* explains that: (a) the advanced age of their father precluded his journeying on to another community where suitable husbands might be found for them; (b) even under these

ג אֲבִימֶלֶךְ מֶלֶךְ גְּרָר וַיִּקַּח אֶת־שָׂרָה׃ וַיָּבֹא אֱלֹהִים אֶל־אֲבִימֶלֶךְ בַּחֲלוֹם
הַלָּיְלָה וַיֹּאמֶר לוֹ הִנְּךָ מֵת עַל־הָאִשָּׁה אֲשֶׁר־לָקַחְתָּ וְהִוא בְּעֻלַת בָּעַל׃
ד־ה וַאֲבִימֶלֶךְ לֹא קָרַב אֵלֶיהָ וַיֹּאמַר אֲדֹנָי הֲגוֹי גַּם־צַדִּיק תַּהֲרֹג׃ הֲלֹא הוּא
אָמַר־לִי אֲחֹתִי הִוא וְהִיא־גַם־הִוא אָמְרָה אָחִי הוּא בְּתָם־לְבָבִי וּבְנִקְיֹן
ו כַּפַּי עָשִׂיתִי זֹאת׃ וַיֹּאמֶר אֵלָיו הָאֱלֹהִים בַּחֲלֹם גַּם אָנֹכִי יָדַעְתִּי כִּי בְתָם־
לְבָבְךָ עָשִׂיתָ זֹּאת וָאֶחְשֹׂךְ גַּם־אָנֹכִי אוֹתְךָ מֵחֲטוֹ־לִי עַל־כֵּן לֹא־נְתַתִּיךָ
ז לִנְגֹּעַ אֵלֶיהָ׃ וְעַתָּה הָשֵׁב אֵשֶׁת־הָאִישׁ כִּי־נָבִיא הוּא וְיִתְפַּלֵּל בַּעַדְךָ וֶחְיֵה
ח וְאִם־אֵינְךָ מֵשִׁיב דַּע כִּי־מוֹת תָּמוּת אַתָּה וְכָל־אֲשֶׁר־לָךְ׃ וַיַּשְׁכֵּם אֲבִימֶלֶךְ
בַּבֹּקֶר וַיִּקְרָא לְכָל־עֲבָדָיו וַיְדַבֵּר אֶת־כָּל־הַדְּבָרִים הָאֵלֶּה בְּאָזְנֵיהֶם
ט וַיִּירְאוּ הָאֲנָשִׁים מְאֹד׃ וַיִּקְרָא אֲבִימֶלֶךְ לְאַבְרָהָם וַיֹּאמֶר לוֹ מֶה־עָשִׂיתָ

---

3. וַיָּבֹא אֱלֹהִים אֶל אֲבִימֶלֶךְ — *And God came to Abimelech.* (This expression, *came,)* is also used by Laban and Bilaam. The expressions וַיֵּרָא, *He appeared to him,* and מַרְאוֹת אֱלֹהִים, *visions of God,* are not mentioned, nor is דִּבּוּר, *speaking,* as we do find with the patriarchs and other prophets, as it says, בַּמַּרְאָה אֵלָיו אֶתְוַדָּע בַּחֲלוֹם אֲדַבֶּר בּוֹ, *I make Myself known to him in a vision; I speak to him in a dream* (*Numbers* 12:6). God did not *appear* to them (Abimelech, Laban and Bilaam) at all; only a voice came to them.

הִנְּךָ מֵת — *Behold you are to die.* You will fade away and die from this illness which has already commenced, for God had *completely restrained (every womb of Abimelech's household* — verse 18).

4. הֲגוֹי גַּם צַדִּיק תַּהֲרֹג — *Will You slay a people though it is righteous?* — Is it proper for You to destroy a people by slaying their king; (and) to slay the king who is righteous in this regard, having not sinned?

7. וְעַתָּה הָשֵׁב אֵשֶׁת הָאִישׁ — *But now, return the man's wife.* Before you are wiped out by this illness.

וֶחְיֵה — *And you will live.* You will be healed, similar to, עַד חֲיוֹתָם, *till they were whole* (*Joshua* 5:8).

אַתָּה וְכָל אֲשֶׁר לָךְ — *You and all that is yours* . . . the embryos in the wombs of your wife and your maidservants.

NOTES

extremely difficult circumstances they were concerned to conceive only from a man (or men) worthy to marry them; (c) their motivation was 'for the sake of heaven,' and though the act itself was immodest and unchaste, their reward is not denied them, and their children become the founders of two nations. Compare the term 'Abraham's heirs' to the *Sforno's* commentary on 11:32.

XX

3. וַיָּבֹא אֱלֹהִים אֶל אֲבִימֶלֶךְ – *And God came to Abimelech.* There are various levels of prophecy which the *Sforno* touched upon at the beginning of this *sidrah* (17:1). He feels it is important to emphasize that God's communication with those who were not righteous men, such as Abimelech, Laban and Bilaam, was only through the medium of 'a voice,' never on *any* level of prophecy, which was reserved exclusively for the patriarchs and other prophets.

4. הֲגוֹי גַּם צַדִּיק תַּהֲרֹג – *Will You slay a people though it is righteous?* (a) Although only Abimelech and his immediate household were afflicted (verse 17), still if the king is punished it affects all the people. (b) Abimelech does not claim to be a perfect man, without blemish. When he refers to himself as a צַדִּיק, *righteous one,* he only pleads innocence in this particular

לָּנוּ וּמֶה־חָטָאתִי לָךְ כִּי־הֵבֵאתָ עָלַי וְעַל־מַמְלַכְתִּי חֲטָאָה גְדֹלָה מַעֲשִׂים
י אֲשֶׁר לֹא־יֵעָשׂוּ עָשִׂיתָ עִמָּדִי: וַיֹּאמֶר אֲבִימֶלֶךְ אֶל־אַבְרָהָם מָה רָאִיתָ כִּי
יא עָשִׂיתָ אֶת־הַדָּבָר הַזֶּה: וַיֹּאמֶר אַבְרָהָם כִּי אָמַרְתִּי רַק אֵין־יִרְאַת אֱלֹהִים
יב בַּמָּקוֹם הַזֶּה וַהֲרָגוּנִי עַל־דְּבַר אִשְׁתִּי: וְגַם־אָמְנָה אֲחֹתִי בַת־אָבִי הִוא אַךְ
יג לֹא בַת־אִמִּי וַתְּהִי־לִי לְאִשָּׁה: וַיְהִי כַּאֲשֶׁר הִתְעוּ אֹתִי אֱלֹהִים מִבֵּית אָבִי
וָאֹמַר לָהּ זֶה חַסְדֵּךְ אֲשֶׁר תַּעֲשִׂי עִמָּדִי אֶל כָּל־הַמָּקוֹם אֲשֶׁר נָבוֹא שָׁמָּה
יד אִמְרִי־לִי אָחִי הוּא: וַיִּקַּח אֲבִימֶלֶךְ צֹאן וּבָקָר וַעֲבָדִים וּשְׁפָחֹת וַיִּתֵּן
טו לְאַבְרָהָם וַיָּשֶׁב לוֹ אֵת שָׂרָה אִשְׁתּוֹ: וַיֹּאמֶר אֲבִימֶלֶךְ הִנֵּה אַרְצִי לְפָנֶיךָ
טז בַּטּוֹב בְּעֵינֶיךָ שֵׁב: וּלְשָׂרָה אָמַר הִנֵּה נָתַתִּי אֶלֶף כֶּסֶף לְאָחִיךְ הִנֵּה
יז הוּא־לָךְ כְּסוּת עֵינַיִם לְכֹל אֲשֶׁר אִתָּךְ וְאֵת כֹּל וְנֹכָחַת: וַיִּתְפַּלֵּל אַבְרָהָם

---

9. מַעֲשִׂים אֲשֶׁר לֹא יֵעָשׂוּ — *Deeds that ought not to be done* ... to cause harm to a man you have not known before, and with whom you have no quarrel. All this will in no way benefit you, (therefore) it is most unusual to act thus.

11. רַק אֵין יִרְאַת אֱלֹהִים בַּמָּקוֹם הַזֶּה — *There is no fear of Elohim in this place.* There is no fear of the ruling authority, for the Philistine chieftains were not really kings (accepted or) feared by the people, as we see from Goliath who said, הֲלוֹא אָנֹכִי הַפְּלִשְׁתִּי, וְאַתֶּם עֲבָדִים לְשָׁאוּל, *Behold I am the Philistine, while you are slaves to Saul* (*I Samuel* 17:8).

12. וְגַם אָמְנָה — *And moreover.* And even you the king, who is the righteous one among them, sinned by taking this woman because I told you she was my sister. (By right) you should have inquired whether she was also my wife, for in truth she is (both) my 'sister' and my wife.

13. הִתְעוּ אֹתִי אֱלֹהִים — *When Elohim caused me to wander.* Because of the strange gods whom I abhorred, I was caused to leave my father's home for an unknown destination, not a specific chosen one. Therefore it is called תּוֹעֶה, *to wander.*

16. הִנֵּה נָתַתִּי אֶלֶף כֶּסֶף לְאָחִיךְ — *Behold I have given your brother a thousand pieces of silver* ... as a dowry, as was the custom when one married a man's daughter or sister.

הִנֵּה הוּא לָךְ כְּסוּת עֵינַיִם — *Let it be for you an eye-covering* ... a multicolored garment which women wore as an honored apparel. The dowry I give you demonstrates the honor (in which you are held) and that I did not take you as a courtesan or a concubine, but as a wife, and I would never have released you so quickly were it not that God was with you, and I had to return you!

לְכֹל אֲשֶׁר אִתָּךְ — *For all who are with you* ... in the eyes (presence) of all who are with you and the members of your household.

וְאֵת כֹּל וְנֹכָחַת — *And to all, you will be vindicated* ... in the eyes of all who heard

NOTES

case, since he was misled and is blameless.

11. רַק אֵין יִרְאַת אֱלֹהִים בַּמָּקוֹם הַזֶּה — *There is no fear of Elohim in this place.* The *Sforno,* unlike other commentators, interprets the word אֱלֹהִים as meaning, *ruler, judge* or *monarch,* not the Deity. He feels that Abraham's justification for his actions was not predicated on a religious base but a social-political one.

13. הִתְעוּ אֹתִי אֱלֹהִים — *When Elohim caused me to wander.* In this verse, the *Sforno*

אֶל־הָאֱלֹהִים וַיִּרְפָּא אֱלֹהִים אֶת־אֲבִימֶלֶךְ וְאֶת־אִשְׁתּוֹ וְאַמְהֹתָיו וַיֵּלֵדוּ׃
יח כִּי־עָצֹר עָצַר יהוה בְּעַד כָּל־רֶחֶם לְבֵית אֲבִימֶלֶךְ עַל־דְּבַר שָׂרָה אֵשֶׁת
כא א אַבְרָהָם׃ וַיהוָה פָּקַד אֶת־שָׂרָה כַּאֲשֶׁר אָמָר וַיַּעַשׂ יהוה
ב לְשָׂרָה כַּאֲשֶׁר דִּבֵּר׃ וַתַּהַר וַתֵּלֶד שָׂרָה לְאַבְרָהָם בֵּן לִזְקֻנָיו לַמּוֹעֵד אֲשֶׁר־
ג דִּבֶּר אֹתוֹ אֱלֹהִים׃ וַיִּקְרָא אַבְרָהָם אֶת־שֶׁם־בְּנוֹ הַנּוֹלַד־לוֹ אֲשֶׁר־יָלְדָה־לּוֹ

(of this episode), (as well) as in the eyes of all those present who might seek to disgrace you, as is the custom of women who chasten and disparage one another regarding sexual immorality.

18. כִּי עָצֹר עָצַר ה׳ בְּעַד כָּל רֶחֶם — *For HASHEM had completely restrained every womb* ... to destroy the embryos had Abimelech not repented. This is in accord with the warning given to him: *Be aware that you will surely die, you and all that is yours* (verse 7).

XXI

1. וַה׳ פָּקַד — *HASHEM had remembered (Sarah)* ... when Abraham prayed on Abimelech's behalf, then *HASHEM remembered Sarah*, as it says, וַה׳ שָׁב אֶת שְׁבוּת אִיּוֹב בְּהִתְפַּלְלוֹ בְּעַד רֵעֵהוּ, *And HASHEM changed the fortune of Job, when he prayed for his friends (Job* 42:10).

כַּאֲשֶׁר אָמָר — *As He had said* ... when He said *I will bless her* (17:16), meaning that the curse of Eve, i.e., (the difficulties associated with) pregnancy, childbirth and child raising, were all removed from her (Sarah) as it says, *I will greatly multiply your pain and travail* (3:16).

וַיַּעַשׂ ה׳ לְשָׂרָה כַּאֲשֶׁר דִּבֵּר — *And HASHEM did for Sarah as He had spoken* ... as He said, *'Indeed, I will give you a son through her'* (17:16). (This is) contrary to the usual occurrence when an older woman gives birth, for the majority (of such births) are females.

NOTES

interprets the name אֱלֹהִים as a deity in the non-sacred sense, referring to the false gods revered by Abraham's father. *Rashi*, and others, however, interpret it as meaning *God*.

16. הִנֵּה נָתַתִּי . . . וְאֵת כֹּל וְנֹכָחַת — *Behold I have given . . . and to all, you will be vindicated.* The flow of this verse, according to the *Sforno*, is: Since Abraham's greatest fear would be that people would say the king used Sarah and then discarded her, something must be done to defend her honor and dignity. To prove that she was taken by the king with the intent to wed her, a dowry is now offered, and to demonstrate her status, and the king's great respect for her, she is clothed in a garment reserved for women of high position. All this will hopefully prevent the spreading of malicious gossip which would damage Sarah's reputation.

XXI

1. וַה׳ פָּקַד — *HASHEM had remembered.* Similar to (18:16,17) the letter *vav* (וַה׳ פָּקַד) is a וי״ו הַדְרִית, linking the previous verses which tell us of Abraham's intercession on behalf of Abimelech, to Sarah's conception. The Talmudic dictum which *Rashi* quotes is echoed in the *Sforno*'s commentary as well, i.e., 'He who prays on behalf of his fellow, and is himself in need of the same help, is answered first' (*Baba Kama* 92). The Talmud proves this concept from our verses, whereas the *Sforno* strengthens it from the verse in *Job;* when Job prays for others, he himself is blessed.

כַּאֲשֶׁר אָמָר — *As He had said.* The two phrases used, כַּאֲשֶׁר אָמָר, *as He had said*, and כַּאֲשֶׁר דִּבֵּר, *as He had spoken*, are not redundant. The former refers to Sarah's special blessing from God relieving her from Eve's curse, which is true of all righteous women, as our Sages tell us in *Sotah* 14. The latter refers to her bearing a son rather than a daughter, which was contrary to the norm, as the *Sforno* explains. In both cases, Sarah is granted special favor and grace.

ד שָׂרָה יִצְחָק: וַיָּמָל אַבְרָהָם אֶת־יִצְחָק בְּנוֹ בֶּן־שְׁמֹנַת יָמִים כַּאֲשֶׁר צִוָּה אֹתוֹ
חמישי ה־ו אֱלֹהִים: וְאַבְרָהָם בֶּן־מְאַת שָׁנָה בְּהִוָּלֶד לוֹ אֵת יִצְחָק בְּנוֹ: וַתֹּאמֶר שָׂרָה
ז צְחֹק עָשָׂה לִי אֱלֹהִים כָּל־הַשֹּׁמֵעַ יִצְחַק־לִי: וַתֹּאמֶר מִי מִלֵּל לְאַבְרָהָם
ח הֵינִיקָה בָנִים שָׂרָה כִּי־יָלַדְתִּי בֵן לִזְקֻנָיו: וַיִּגְדַּל הַיֶּלֶד וַיִּגָּמַל וַיַּעַשׂ אַבְרָהָם
ט מִשְׁתֶּה גָדוֹל בְּיוֹם הִגָּמֵל אֶת־יִצְחָק: וַתֵּרֶא שָׂרָה אֶת־בֶּן־הָגָר הַמִּצְרִית
י אֲשֶׁר־יָלְדָה לְאַבְרָהָם מְצַחֵק: וַתֹּאמֶר לְאַבְרָהָם גָּרֵשׁ הָאָמָה הַזֹּאת וְאֶת־
יא בְּנָהּ כִּי לֹא יִירַשׁ בֶּן־הָאָמָה הַזֹּאת עִם־בְּנִי עִם־יִצְחָק: וַיֵּרַע הַדָּבָר מְאֹד

---

4. וַיָּמָל אַבְרָהָם אֶת יִצְחָק בְּנוֹ — *And Abraham circumcised his son Isaac . . .*

5. וְאַבְרָהָם בֶּן מְאַת שָׁנָה — *And Abraham was a hundred years old . . .* and yet he circumcised his son, and did not have tender concern for the infant of his old age.

6. צְחֹק עָשָׂה לִי אֱלֹהִים — *God has made laughter for me.* Although there is pain associated with the circumcision of the infant, God, the Blessed One, has given joy to my heart, therefore . . .

כָּל הַשֹּׁמֵעַ יִצְחַק לִי — *Whoever hears will laugh for me . . .* rejoicing for me, and will not be concerned for the pain of the circumcision.

9. אֶת בֶּן הָגָר הַמִּצְרִית — *The son of Hagar the Egyptian.* Sarah assumed that this scoffing was instigated by (Hagar) his mother, from whom he first heard it, as our Sages say, שׁוּתָא דִּינוּקָא בְּשׁוּקָא אוֹ דַאֲבוּהִי אוֹ דְאִמֵּיה, *The talk of a child in the marketplace is either that of his father or that of his mother (Succah* 56b).

מְצַחֵק — *Mocking . . .* scoffing at the feast made in Abraham's house (upon the weaning of Isaac), for he said, (Sarah) conceived from Abimelech. The reason he did not claim this at the time of Isaac's birth was because Ishmael heard it later from the 'scoffers of the time,' or perhaps even if he did mock at the time of (Isaac's) birth, Sarah was not aware of it since she was preoccupied at that time.

10. גָּרֵשׁ הָאָמָה הַזֹּאת וְאֶת בְּנָהּ — *Drive out this slavewoman with her son.* It was her advice which caused him to slander (me) so that her son should inherit all (from you), therefore drive (her out) because it is not right for him to even inherit a portion (of your estate).

כִּי לֹא יִירַשׁ בֶּן הָאָמָה — *For the son of this slavewoman shall not inherit . . .* inasmuch that he is not considered genealogically yours, for 'the child follows the status of the tainted (פָּגוּם) parent' (*Kiddushin* 66b).

NOTES

5. וְאַבְרָהָם בֶּן מְאַת שָׁנָה – *And Abraham was a hundred years old.* We already know how old Abraham was when Isaac was born, since we have already been told that he was ninety-nine when he himself was circumcised and Isaac was born a year later. The reason we are told that Abraham was one hundred years old when he circumcised his son is to emphasize his righteousness and great trust in Hashem, as the *Sforno* explains.

9. אֶת בֶּן הָגָר הַמִּצְרִית – *The son of Hagar the Egyptian.* Since we are not told that Ishmael mocked, but *the son of Hagar*, the implication must be that his behavior was influenced by his mother. She, of course, had an ulterior motive in questioning Abraham's paternity of Isaac, for then her son would be the sole heir of Abraham's considerable wealth.

10. גָּרֵשׁ הָאָמָה הַזֹּאת וְאֶת בְּנָהּ – *Drive out this slavewoman with her son.* The *Sforno's* interpretation explains why Sarah said בְּנָהּ, *her son,* implying, not yours, insofar as inheritance is concerned. Hagar questioned Abraham's paternity of Isaac; Sarah denied Hagar's son (Ishmael) the patrimony of Abraham. Halachically her argument was sound. Since Hagar

יב בְּעֵינֵ֣י אַבְרָהָ֑ם עַ֖ל אוֹדֹ֥ת בְּנֽוֹ׃ וַיֹּ֨אמֶר אֱלֹהִ֜ים אֶל־אַבְרָהָ֗ם אַל־יֵרַ֤ע בְּעֵינֶ֙יךָ֙
עַל־הַנַּ֣עַר וְעַל־אֲמָתֶ֔ךָ כֹּל֩ אֲשֶׁ֨ר תֹּאמַ֥ר אֵלֶ֛יךָ שָׂרָ֖ה שְׁמַ֣ע בְּקֹלָ֑הּ כִּ֣י
יג בְיִצְחָ֔ק יִקָּרֵ֥א לְךָ֖ זָֽרַע׃ וְגַ֥ם אֶת־בֶּן־הָאָמָ֖ה לְג֣וֹי אֲשִׂימֶ֑נּוּ כִּ֥י זַרְעֲךָ֖ הֽוּא׃
יד וַיַּשְׁכֵּ֣ם אַבְרָהָ֣ם ׀ בַּבֹּ֡קֶר וַיִּֽקַּֽח־לֶחֶם֩ וְחֵ֨מַת מַ֜יִם וַיִּתֵּ֣ן אֶל־הָ֠גָר שָׂ֧ם עַל־
טו שִׁכְמָ֛הּ וְאֶת־הַיֶּ֖לֶד וַֽיְשַׁלְּחֶ֑הָ וַתֵּ֣לֶךְ וַתֵּ֔תַע בְּמִדְבַּ֖ר בְּאֵ֥ר שָֽׁבַע׃ וַיִּכְל֥וּ הַמַּ֖יִם
טז מִן־הַחֵ֑מֶת וַתַּשְׁלֵ֣ךְ אֶת־הַיֶּ֔לֶד תַּ֖חַת אַחַ֥ד הַשִּׂיחִֽם׃ וַתֵּלֶךְ֩ וַתֵּ֨שֶׁב לָ֜הּ מִנֶּ֗גֶד
הַרְחֵק֙ כִּמְטַחֲוֵ֣י קֶ֔שֶׁת כִּ֣י אָֽמְרָ֔ה אַל־אֶרְאֶ֖ה בְּמ֣וֹת הַיָּ֑לֶד וַתֵּ֣שֶׁב מִנֶּ֔גֶד
יז וַתִּשָּׂ֥א אֶת־קֹלָ֖הּ וַתֵּֽבְךְּ׃ וַיִּשְׁמַ֣ע אֱלֹהִים֮ אֶת־ק֣וֹל הַנַּ֒עַר֒ וַיִּקְרָא֩ מַלְאַ֨ךְ
אֱלֹהִ֤ים ׀ אֶל־הָגָר֙ מִן־הַשָּׁמַ֔יִם וַיֹּ֥אמֶר לָ֖הּ מַה־לָּ֣ךְ הָגָ֑ר אַל־תִּ֣ירְאִ֔י כִּֽי־שָׁמַ֧ע

---

12. אַל יֵרַע בְּעֵינֶיךָ עַל הַנַּעַר וְעַל אֲמָתֶךָ כֹּל אֲשֶׁר תֹּאמַר אֵלֶיךָ שָׂרָה — *Be not distressed over the youth or your slavewoman: Whatever Sarah tells you.* Do not be distressed by her demands regarding the youth and the slavewoman, i.e., to drive them out with a sign of (their status) as slaves, as it says, *he placed them on her shoulder* (verse 14 — see explanation ahead).

שְׁמַע בְּקֹלָהּ — *Heed her voice* . . . for she is justified in telling you to do so.

כִּי בְיִצְחָק יִקָּרֵא לְךָ זָרַע — *Since through Isaac will offspring be considered yours* . . . and not through him (Ishmael).

13. וְגַם אֶת בֶּן הָאָמָה — *But, the son of the slavewoman as well.* Do not worry over driving out the son, for you are driving out *the son of the slavewoman,* not *your* son, nonetheless . . .

לְגוֹי אֲשִׂימֶנּוּ כִּי זַרְעֲךָ הוּא — *I will make him into a nation for he is your offspring* . . . but he himself is not worthy to be a nation.

14. שָׂם עַל שִׁכְמָהּ — *He placed them on her shoulder* . . . the 'skin of water'; as a sign that she is a bondwoman, similar to, וְהִתְעַנִּי תַּחַת יָדֶיהָ — *submit yourself to her domination* (16:9). However, this righteous man (Abraham) did not refrain from providing them with all their needs, as our Sages tell us, *God was with the youth* (verse 20) — this teaches us to amplify the verse to include his asses, camels and laborers (*Bereishis Rabbah* 53:15). Therefore, they lacked naught except for water when they strayed in the wilderness, and once they found water he dwelled in the wilderness according to his nature which was that of a פֶּרֶא אָדָם, *wild ass of a man.*

וְאֶת הַיֶּלֶד — *And the boy.* He also gave her the boy.

וַיְשַׁלְּחֶהָ — *And he saw her off.* In his great kindness he accompanied her, similar to, *while Abraham walked with them to see them off* (18:16).

NOTES

had not been set free by Sarah, her status of slavewoman establishes the status of her son as well, based upon the Talmudic decision in *Kiddushin* cited by the *Sforno.*

14. שָׂם עַל שִׁכְמָהּ – *He placed them on her shoulder.* Abraham placed the skin of water on Hagar's shoulder, not to burden her, for there were beasts of burden at her disposal as the *Midrash* cited by the *Sforno* indicates. This was done only as a symbolic act, to establish her continuing status as a slavewoman.

וְאֶת הַיֶּלֶד – *And the boy.* The expression וְאֶת הַיֶּלֶד, *and the boy,* is not to be understood as placing him on her shoulder as well. It simply means that he gave along the boy with her, to be in her care.

וַיְשַׁלְּחֶהָ – *And he saw her off* (lit., *sent her away*). The Hebrew word לְשַׁלֵּחַ, *to send*

יח אֱלֹהִים אֶל־קוֹל הַנַּעַר בַּאֲשֶׁר הוּא־שָׁם: קוּמִי שְׂאִי אֶת־הַנַּעַר וְהַחֲזִיקִי
יט אֶת־יָדֵךְ בּוֹ כִּי־לְגוֹי גָּדוֹל אֲשִׂימֶנּוּ: וַיִּפְקַח אֱלֹהִים אֶת־עֵינֶיהָ וַתֵּרֶא בְּאֵר
כ מָיִם וַתֵּלֶךְ וַתְּמַלֵּא אֶת־הַחֵמֶת מַיִם וַתַּשְׁקְ אֶת־הַנָּעַר: וַיְהִי אֱלֹהִים
כא אֶת־הַנַּעַר וַיִּגְדָּל וַיֵּשֶׁב בַּמִּדְבָּר וַיְהִי רֹבֶה קַשָּׁת: וַיֵּשֶׁב בְּמִדְבַּר פָּארָן
וַתִּקַּח־לוֹ אִמּוֹ אִשָּׁה מֵאֶרֶץ מִצְרָיִם:
ששי כב וַיְהִי בָּעֵת הַהִוא וַיֹּאמֶר אֲבִימֶלֶךְ וּפִיכֹל שַׂר־צְבָאוֹ אֶל־אַבְרָהָם לֵאמֹר
כג אֱלֹהִים עִמְּךָ בְּכֹל אֲשֶׁר־אַתָּה עֹשֶׂה: וְעַתָּה הִשָּׁבְעָה לִּי בֵאלֹהִים הֵנָּה
אִם־תִּשְׁקֹר לִי וּלְנִינִי וּלְנֶכְדִּי כַּחֶסֶד אֲשֶׁר־עָשִׂיתִי עִמְּךָ תַּעֲשֶׂה עִמָּדִי וְעִם־
כד־כה הָאָרֶץ אֲשֶׁר־גַּרְתָּה בָּהּ: וַיֹּאמֶר אַבְרָהָם אָנֹכִי אִשָּׁבֵעַ: וְהוֹכִחַ אַבְרָהָם אֶת־
כו אֲבִימֶלֶךְ עַל־אֹדוֹת בְּאֵר הַמַּיִם אֲשֶׁר גָּזְלוּ עַבְדֵי אֲבִימֶלֶךְ: וַיֹּאמֶר
אֲבִימֶלֶךְ לֹא יָדַעְתִּי מִי עָשָׂה אֶת־הַדָּבָר הַזֶּה וְגַם־אַתָּה לֹא־הִגַּדְתָּ לִּי וְגַם
כז אָנֹכִי לֹא שָׁמַעְתִּי בִּלְתִּי הַיּוֹם: וַיִּקַּח אַבְרָהָם צֹאן וּבָקָר וַיִּתֵּן לַאֲבִימֶלֶךְ
כח וַיִּכְרְתוּ שְׁנֵיהֶם בְּרִית: וַיַּצֵּב אַבְרָהָם אֶת־שֶׁבַע כִּבְשֹׂת הַצֹּאן לְבַדְּהֶן:
כט וַיֹּאמֶר אֲבִימֶלֶךְ אֶל־אַבְרָהָם מָה הֵנָּה שֶׁבַע כְּבָשֹׂת הָאֵלֶּה אֲשֶׁר הִצַּבְתָּ

---

19. וַיִּפְקַח אֱלֹהִים אֶת עֵינֶיהָ — *Then God opened her eyes.* He gave her understanding to perceive that water was in that place; for she was not blind before that.

22. אֱלֹהִים עִמְּךָ — *God is with you.* Therefore I fear you and desire a treaty with you, not because of your might or wealth.

23. כַּחֶסֶד אֲשֶׁר עָשִׂיתִי עִמְּךָ תַּעֲשֶׂה עִמָּדִי — *According to the kindness that I have done with you, do with me.* Do this kindness with me, and take an oath on behalf of your children.

24. אָנֹכִי אִשָּׁבֵעַ — *I will swear.* I will do this kindness and swear, but you did not do any kindness to me as you claim, for your servants stole (my well).

25. אֲשֶׁר גָּזְלוּ עַבְדֵי אֲבִימֶלֶךְ — *That Abimelech's servants stole.* He rebuked him, as king, for the violent robbery committed without shame in his land, and also for keeping wicked men in his household, which is not the way of the righteous, as it says, לֹא יֵשֵׁב בְּקֶרֶב בֵּיתִי עֹשֵׂה רְמִיָּה, *He that is deceitful shall not dwell within my house* (*Psalms* 101:7).

26. לֹא יָדַעְתִּי מִי עָשָׂה — *I do not know who did (this thing).* Even now that you tell me my servants committed this violence, I have no idea who (among them) could have done it, for there is no one among them I suspect (of such an act). Were there (one) who was suspect, he would not be a member of my household.

וְגַם אַתָּה לֹא הִגַּדְתָּ לִּי וְגַם אָנֹכִי לֹא שָׁמַעְתִּי — *Furthermore, you have never told me, and moreover, I myself have heard nothing of it.* Regarding your reproof that as king I should have relieved the oppressed, certainly the king can only react to one of two circumstances: either to the cry of the victim of violence, or to the outcry of the populace protesting such violence, and (in this case) you (the victim) never told me, and moreover I have heard no public outcry regarding this matter.

NOTES

away, at times has a different connotation. We see the word used when Abraham accompanied the angels וְאַבְרָהָם הֹלֵךְ עִמָּם לְשַׁלְּחָם, which certainly does not mean that he sent them away. Here also Abraham did not callously send Hagar and Ishmael away. The phrase

ל לְבַדָּנָה: וַיֹּאמֶר כִּי אֶת־שֶׁבַע כְּבָשֹׂת תִּקַּח מִיָּדִי בַּעֲבוּר תִּהְיֶה־לִּי לְעֵדָה
לא כִּי חָפַרְתִּי אֶת־הַבְּאֵר הַזֹּאת: עַל־כֵּן קָרָא לַמָּקוֹם הַהוּא בְּאֵר שָׁבַע כִּי
לב שָׁם נִשְׁבְּעוּ שְׁנֵיהֶם: וַיִּכְרְתוּ בְרִית בִּבְאֵר שָׁבַע וַיָּקָם אֲבִימֶלֶךְ וּפִיכֹל שַׂר־
לג צְבָאוֹ וַיָּשֻׁבוּ אֶל־אֶרֶץ פְּלִשְׁתִּים: וַיִּטַּע אֶשֶׁל בִּבְאֵר שָׁבַע וַיִּקְרָא־שָׁם
לד בְּשֵׁם יהוה אֵל עוֹלָם: וַיָּגָר אַבְרָהָם בְּאֶרֶץ פְּלִשְׁתִּים יָמִים רַבִּים:
כב שביעי א וַיְהִי אַחַר הַדְּבָרִים הָאֵלֶּה וְהָאֱלֹהִים נִסָּה אֶת־אַבְרָהָם וַיֹּאמֶר אֵלָיו

---

30. כִּי אֶת שֶׁבַע כְּבָשֹׂת תִּקַּח מִיָּדִי — *Because you are to take these seven ewes from me.* Similar to, שָׁלַף אִישׁ נַעֲלוֹ וְנָתַן לְרֵעֵהוּ וְזֹאת הַתְּעוּדָה, *one would draw off his shoe and give it to his friend (Ruth* 4:7) (as a symbolic act) testifying to the agreement of the parties and their acknowledgment of the matter (at hand).

בַּעֲבוּר תִּהְיֶה לִּי — *That it may serve me* . . . this covenant . . .

לְעֵדָה כִּי חָפַרְתִּי אֶת הַבְּאֵר הַזֹּאת — *as testimony* . . . of your acknowledgement *that I dug this well.*

32. וַיָּשֻׁבוּ אֶל אֶרֶץ פְּלִשְׁתִּים — *And they returned to the land of the Philistines.* They returned from Beer Sheba, which was not part of the land of the Philistines. They came there to speak to Abraham, who (in turn) had come there to oversee his herds. It was there that he gave them sheep, cattle and ewes to establish the covenant.

33. וַיִּקְרָא שָׁם בְּשֵׁם ה׳ אֵל עוֹלָם — *And there he proclaimed the name of* HASHEM, *God of eternity.* He proclaimed and made known to the populace that the Almighty is the God Who not only directs time, but preceded and created it, a concept contrary to that of early and later scholars of the nations.

XXII

1. נִסָּה אֶת אַבְרָהָם — *Tested Abraham.* (God's) intention was that he (Abraham) should translate his love and reverence (of God) from the potential to the actual. In this manner he would be similar to his Creator, Who is good to this world in

NOTES

וַיְשַׁלְּחֵהּ is interpreted by the *Sforno* as *he accompanied her,* similar to the expression used in 18:16.

30. כִּי אֶת שֶׁבַע כְּבָשֹׂת תִּקַּח מִיָּדִי – *Because you are to take these seven ewes from me.* The animals given by Abraham to Abimelech are not meant as a gift. That would not fit into the context of this event. Rather it is meant to be a means of exchange (חֲלִיפִין) whereby one party gives an item of value to the second party which consummates the transaction. This is done when property or goods are sold or given as a gift. It also was done to finalize an agreement or treaty, as in this case. The source of this *halachah* is found in the Book of Ruth, cited by the *Sforno,* where Boaz and his relative reach an understanding regarding Ruth and the land of Elimelech.

32. וַיָּשֻׁבוּ אֶל אֶרֶץ פְּלִשְׁתִּים – *And they returned to the land of the Philistines.* The word *returned* presents a difficulty to some commentators, who consider Beer Sheba to be a part of the land of the Philistines. The *Sforno* however considers this clear proof that Beer Sheba never was part of that land, but only bordered on it.

33. וַיִּקְרָא שָׁם בְּשֵׁם ה׳ אֵל עוֹלָם – *And there he proclaimed the name of* HASHEM, *God of eternity.* Most commentators understand the term אֵל עוֹלָם as *God of the Universe.* However, the *Sforno* translates it as *Eternal God.* Hence Abraham is teaching the populace the concept of God as the First Cause, Who is Eternal and existed before the creation of time. The *Sforno* is alluding to this idea in his commentary on this verse.

XXII

1. נִסָּה אֶת אַבְרָהָם – *Tested Abraham.* Since God foresees everything, and nothing is un-

ב אַבְרָהָם וַיֹּאמֶר הִנֵּנִי: וַיֹּאמֶר קַח־נָא אֶת־בִּנְךָ אֶת־יְחִידְךָ אֲשֶׁר־אָהַבְתָּ
אֶת־יִצְחָק וְלֶךְ־לְךָ אֶל־אֶרֶץ הַמֹּרִיָּה וְהַעֲלֵהוּ שָׁם לְעֹלָה עַל אַחַד הֶהָרִים
ג אֲשֶׁר אֹמַר אֵלֶיךָ: וַיַּשְׁכֵּם אַבְרָהָם בַּבֹּקֶר וַיַּחֲבֹשׁ אֶת־חֲמֹרוֹ וַיִּקַּח אֶת־שְׁנֵי
נְעָרָיו אִתּוֹ וְאֵת יִצְחָק בְּנוֹ וַיְבַקַּע עֲצֵי עֹלָה וַיָּקָם וַיֵּלֶךְ אֶל־הַמָּקוֹם
ד אֲשֶׁר־אָמַר־לוֹ הָאֱלֹהִים: בַּיּוֹם הַשְּׁלִישִׁי וַיִּשָּׂא אַבְרָהָם אֶת־עֵינָיו וַיַּרְא
ה אֶת־הַמָּקוֹם מֵרָחֹק: וַיֹּאמֶר אַבְרָהָם אֶל־נְעָרָיו שְׁבוּ־לָכֶם פֹּה עִם־הַחֲמוֹר
ו וַאֲנִי וְהַנַּעַר נֵלְכָה עַד־כֹּה וְנִשְׁתַּחֲוֶה וְנָשׁוּבָה אֲלֵיכֶם: וַיִּקַּח אַבְרָהָם
אֶת־עֲצֵי הָעֹלָה וַיָּשֶׂם עַל־יִצְחָק בְּנוֹ וַיִּקַּח בְּיָדוֹ אֶת־הָאֵשׁ וְאֶת־הַמַּאֲכֶלֶת
ז וַיֵּלְכוּ שְׁנֵיהֶם יַחְדָּו: וַיֹּאמֶר יִצְחָק אֶל־אַבְרָהָם אָבִיו וַיֹּאמֶר אָבִי וַיֹּאמֶר
ח הִנֶּנִּי בְנִי וַיֹּאמֶר הִנֵּה הָאֵשׁ וְהָעֵצִים וְאַיֵּה הַשֶּׂה לְעֹלָה: וַיֹּאמֶר אַבְרָהָם
ט אֱלֹהִים יִרְאֶה־לּוֹ הַשֶּׂה לְעֹלָה בְּנִי וַיֵּלְכוּ שְׁנֵיהֶם יַחְדָּו: וַיָּבֹאוּ אֶל־הַמָּקוֹם
אֲשֶׁר אָמַר־לוֹ הָאֱלֹהִים וַיִּבֶן שָׁם אַבְרָהָם אֶת־הַמִּזְבֵּחַ וַיַּעֲרֹךְ אֶת־הָעֵצִים
י וַיַּעֲקֹד אֶת־יִצְחָק בְּנוֹ וַיָּשֶׂם אֹתוֹ עַל־הַמִּזְבֵּחַ מִמַּעַל לָעֵצִים: וַיִּשְׁלַח
יא אַבְרָהָם אֶת־יָדוֹ וַיִּקַּח אֶת־הַמַּאֲכֶלֶת לִשְׁחֹט אֶת־בְּנוֹ: וַיִּקְרָא אֵלָיו מַלְאַךְ
יב יהוה מִן־הַשָּׁמַיִם וַיֹּאמֶר אַבְרָהָם | אַבְרָהָם וַיֹּאמֶר הִנֵּנִי: וַיֹּאמֶר
אַל־תִּשְׁלַח יָדְךָ אֶל־הַנַּעַר וְאַל־תַּעַשׂ לוֹ מְאוּמָה כִּי | עַתָּה יָדַעְתִּי כִּי־יְרֵא

---

actuality, for the purpose of man's existence is to imitate his Creator as far as possible, as the (Torah) testifies, in saying: נַעֲשֶׂה אָדָם בְּצַלְמֵנוּ כִּדְמוּתֵנוּ, *Let us make man in our image, after our likeness* (1:26).

3. וַיֵּלֶךְ אֶל הַמָּקוֹם — *And he went to the place* . . . to the Land of Moriah.

4. וַיִּשָּׂא אַבְרָהָם אֶת עֵינָיו וַיַּרְא אֶת הַמָּקוֹם — *Abraham looked up and perceived the place* . . . the place for the sacrifice on Mount Moriah.

מֵרָחֹק — *From afar.* By the will of God he was granted the ability to see clearly from afar, as we find (by Moses), וַיַּרְאֵהוּ ה׳ אֶת כָּל הָאָרֶץ, *HASHEM showed him all the land* (*Deut.* 34:1). He therefore understood that that particular place was to be the place of sacrifice.

5. שְׁבוּ לָכֶם פֹּה — *Stay here by yourselves* . . . so that they should not prevent him from, or interfere with him in, bringing this sacrifice.

12. עַתָּה יָדַעְתִּי — *Now I know.* I, the angel, now know God is justified in

NOTES

known to Him, there is no need for Him to test man to see whether he will meet the test. The concept of נִסָּיוֹן, *test*, has therefore given Torah commentators pause, and presented numerous difficulties, which they have answered with a variety of explanations. The *Sforno*, in this verse, offers a quite simple, but profound, explanation. God is not testing Abraham to determine whether he will sacrifice his son or not. Rather he is drawing forth the potential inner powers of faith and trust which are latent in Abraham, bringing them to the fore and translating them into actuality through the *Akeidah* (the binding of Isaac). In this manner, man also fulfills his purpose, which is to imitate his Creator, who manifests Himself in this world בְּפוֹעַל, *through the actual* (i.e., His works) and not only בְּכֹחַ, *in potential*.

3-4. וַיֵּלֶךְ אֶל הַמָּקוֹם . . . וַיַּרְא אֶת הַמָּקוֹם מֵרָחֹק — *And he went to the place . . . and perceived the place from afar.* The word מָקוֹם, *place*, is used in both verses. The first refers to the Land of Moriah; the second to the particular place on the mountain where the sacrifice is to be held.

יג אֱלֹהִים֙ אַתָּ֔ה וְלֹ֥א חָשַׂ֛כְתָּ אֶת־בִּנְךָ֥ אֶת־יְחִֽידְךָ֖ מִמֶּֽנִּי: וַיִּשָּׂ֨א אַבְרָהָ֜ם
אֶת־עֵינָ֗יו וַיַּרְא֙ וְהִנֵּה־אַ֔יִל אַחַ֕ר נֶֽאֱחַ֥ז בַּסְּבַ֖ךְ בְּקַרְנָ֑יו וַיֵּ֤לֶךְ אַבְרָהָם֙ וַיִּקַּ֣ח
יד אֶת־הָאַ֔יִל וַיַּֽעֲלֵ֥הוּ לְעֹלָ֖ה תַּ֣חַת בְּנֽוֹ: וַיִּקְרָ֧א אַבְרָהָ֛ם שֵֽׁם־הַמָּק֥וֹם הַה֖וּא
טו יהו֣ה ׀ יִרְאֶ֑ה אֲשֶׁר֙ יֵֽאָמֵ֣ר הַיּ֔וֹם בְּהַ֥ר יהו֖ה יֵֽרָאֶֽה: וַיִּקְרָ֛א מַלְאַ֥ךְ יהו֖ה
טז אֶל־אַבְרָהָ֑ם שֵׁנִ֖ית מִן־הַשָּׁמָֽיִם: וַיֹּ֕אמֶר בִּ֥י נִשְׁבַּ֖עְתִּי נְאֻם־יהו֑ה כִּ֗י יַ֚עַן אֲשֶׁ֣ר
יז עָשִׂ֙יתָ֙ אֶת־הַדָּבָ֣ר הַזֶּ֔ה וְלֹ֥א חָשַׂ֖כְתָּ אֶת־בִּנְךָ֥ אֶת־יְחִידֶֽךָ: כִּֽי־בָרֵ֣ךְ אֲבָרֶכְךָ֗

---

considering you greater than His angels, as our Sages say, 'The righteous are greater than the ministering angels' (*Sanhedrin* 93a).

מִמֶּנִּי — *Than I.* (I now know that) you fear God 'more than I,' an angel, and hence you are more worthy of elevated status than I, as our Sages state 'the righteous are greater, etc.' You (have proven) in actuality that you are God fearing. The Almighty had prior knowledge of your potential as a God-fearing (man), but an angel's actual knowledge can only be drawn from what is actual (not potential).

13. וְהִנֵּה אַיִל אַחַר נֶאֱחַז בַּסְּבַךְ — *Behold a ram, afterward, caught in the thicket.* Since he did not see a ram there before (the angel intervened) — only immediately afterward — caught in the thicket, he realized that the ram had been sent through the will of God and there was no fear of theft (attached to his taking it).

תַּחַת בְּנוֹ — *Instead of his son.* As exchange (for him) since he had committed himself to offer his son (as a sacrifice) in keeping with, וְדֹבֵר אֱמֶת בִּלְבָבוֹ, *And speaks truth in his heart (Psalms 15:2).*

14. אֲשֶׁר יֵאָמֵר הַיּוֹם — *As it is said this day.* That place which Israel referred to on the day the Torah was written, as being the mountain (on which) HASHEM is seen, (meaning) when He will reveal its location, as it says, וְהָיָה הַמָּקוֹם אֲשֶׁר יִבְחַר, *Then it shall come to pass that the place which (God) shall choose (Deut. 12:11),* (and this was in the time of David); that place, Abraham called ה' יִרְאֶה, *HASHEM yireh.*

16. בִּי נִשְׁבַּעְתִּי — *By Myself, I swear . . .* that I will bless you.

נְאֻם ה' כִּי יַעַן אֲשֶׁר עָשִׂיתָ — *Declared HASHEM, That since you have done (this thing).* I, God, say that since you have done this thing . . .

NOTES

The very fact that God granted Abraham (an old man) such unusual vision to be able to see the place from so far was a clear indication that this was indeed the place chosen by Him for the *Akeidah.*

12. עַתָּה יָדַעְתִּי . . . מִמֶּנִּי — *Now I know . . . than I.* The *Sforno* interprets this verse as recording the words of the angel, speaking on his own, and not as the messenger of God, speaking in His name. עַתָּה יָדַעְתִּי means *now I know* that man can be 'higher than the angels,' and superior מִמֶּנִּי, *than I,* in יִרְאַת ה', *the fear of* HASHEM. The word מִמֶּנִּי, according to the *Sforno,* is not linked to, *you have not withheld your son from Me* (the word *Me* referring to God); rather this word reverts back to *you are a God-fearing man.* The sense of the sentence

is: The angel states that he now realizes that Abraham is superior to him in the fear of *Hashem,* which he proved by not withholding his son from Him.

13. וְהִנֵּה אַיִל אַחַר נֶאֱחַז בַּסְּבַךְ — *Behold a ram, afterward, caught in the thicket.* The word אַחַר, *afterward,* refers to the sequence of events. Abraham did not see any ram there, until the angel commanded him to desist from sacrificing Isaac. Only *afterward* did he see the ram, and realized that it had been sent by God to be used as a sacrifice in place of Isaac. By sacrificing the ram, Abraham will fulfill his commitment to bring an offering.

14. אֲשֶׁר יֵאָמֵר הַיּוֹם — *As it is said this day.* The flow of the verse is to be understood thus,

וְהַרְבָּ֣ה אַרְבֶּ֣ה אֶֽת־זַרְעֲךָ֗ כְּכוֹכְבֵ֤י הַשָּׁמַ֨יִם֙ וְכַח֕וֹל אֲשֶׁ֖ר עַל־שְׂפַ֣ת הַיָּ֑ם וְיִרַ֣שׁ

יח זַרְעֲךָ֔ אֵ֖ת שַׁ֣עַר אֹֽיְבָֽיו: וְהִתְבָּרֲכ֣וּ בְזַרְעֲךָ֔ כֹּ֖ל גּוֹיֵ֣י הָאָ֑רֶץ עֵ֕קֶב אֲשֶׁ֥ר שָׁמַ֖עְתָּ

יט בְּקֹלִֽי: וַיָּ֤שָׁב אַבְרָהָם֙ אֶל־נְעָרָ֔יו וַיָּקֻ֛מוּ וַיֵּֽלְכ֥וּ יַחְדָּ֖ו אֶל־בְּאֵ֣ר שָׁ֑בַע וַיֵּ֥שֶׁב

אַבְרָהָ֖ם בִּבְאֵ֥ר שָֽׁבַע:

מפטיר כ וַיְהִ֗י אַֽחֲרֵי֙ הַדְּבָרִ֣ים הָאֵ֔לֶּה וַיֻּגַּ֥ד לְאַבְרָהָ֖ם לֵאמֹ֑ר הִ֠נֵּה יָֽלְדָ֙ה מִלְכָּ֥ה גַם־

כא הִ֛וא בָּנִ֖ים לְנָח֥וֹר אָחִֽיךָ: אֶת־ע֥וּץ בְּכֹר֖וֹ וְאֶת־בּ֣וּז אָחִ֑יו וְאֶת־קְמוּאֵ֖ל אֲבִ֥י

כב-כג אֲרָֽם: וְאֶת־כֶּ֤שֶׂד וְאֶת־חֲזוֹ֙ וְאֶת־פִּלְדָּ֔שׁ וְאֶת־יִדְלָ֖ף וְאֵ֥ת בְּתוּאֵֽל: וּבְתוּאֵ֖ל

כד יָלַ֣ד אֶת־רִבְקָ֑ה שְׁמֹנָ֥ה אֵ֨לֶּה֙ יָֽלְדָ֣ה מִלְכָּ֔ה לְנָח֖וֹר אֲחִ֥י אַבְרָהָֽם: וּפִֽילַגְשׁ֣וֹ

וּשְׁמָ֣הּ רְאוּמָ֑ה וַתֵּ֤לֶד גַּם־הִוא֙ אֶת־טֶ֣בַח וְאֶת־גַּ֔חַם וְאֶת־תַּ֖חַשׁ וְאֶת־מַֽעֲכָֽה:

---

17. כִּ֣י בָרֵ֤ךְ אֲבָרֶכְךָ֙ — *That I shall surely bless you.*

18. וְהִתְבָּרֲכ֣וּ בְזַרְעֲךָ֔ כֹּ֖ל גּוֹיֵ֣י הָאָ֑רֶץ — *And all the nations of the earth shall bless themselves by your offspring.* When the nations will all call upon God's Name to serve Him with one accord (based on *Zephaniah* 3:9), they will all seek blessings through your seed and endeavor to emulate them.

עֵ֕קֶב אֲשֶׁ֥ר שָׁמַ֖עְתָּ בְּקֹלִֽי — *Because you have listened to My voice.* Because שְׂכַ֣ר מִצְוָ֑ה מִצְוָ֑ה, *the reward of one mitzvah is another mitzvah* (*Avos* 4:2), therefore you will merit (through this willingness to sacrifice Isaac) that your children will be a 'banner for the nations,' teaching them to serve the Almighty, and this will be considered as a righteousness for you.

20. הִ֠נֵּה יָֽלְדָ֙ה מִלְכָּ֥ה — *Behold, Milcah too has borne children.* Behold, you already know that Milcah gave birth to children.

גַם־הִוא — *She also . . .* in addition to his (Nachor's) concubine.

23. וּבְתוּאֵ֖ל יָלַ֣ד אֶת־רִבְקָ֑ה — *And Bethuel begot Rebecca.* The reporter told (Abraham) that Bethuel, who was a son of the wife (of Nachor, not of his concubine) begot Rebecca. This tiding came to (tell Abraham) that he would be able to find a wife for his son in his father's house, and would not have to become associated (through marriage) with Canaan.

24. וּפִֽילַגְשׁ֣וֹ . . . וַתֵּ֤לֶד גַּם הִוא — *And his concubine . . . also bore children.* The reporter told (Abraham) that his (Nachor's) concubine gave birth to Maacah, who was also worthy to wed his son if he chose not to marry Rebecca, and it would not be necessary to (take a wife) from the seed of Canaan.

NOTES

according to the *Sforno*: Abraham called the name of the place HASHEM Yireh, God will see and seek out this place for the dwelling of His Shechinah (see *Onkelos*). This place is the one which the Torah alludes to as *the place which God shall choose.* This in turn did not happen until the time of David. And it is in this place that ה' יֵרָאֶה, HASHEM *is seen (always).*

פרשת חיי שרה
Parashas Chayei Sarah

כג א-ב וַיִּהְיוּ חַיֵּי שָׂרָה מֵאָה שָׁנָה וְעֶשְׂרִים שָׁנָה וְשֶׁבַע שָׁנִים שְׁנֵי חַיֵּי שָׂרָה: וַתָּמָת
שָׂרָה בְּקִרְיַת אַרְבַּע הִוא חֶבְרוֹן בְּאֶרֶץ כְּנָעַן וַיָּבֹא אַבְרָהָם לִסְפֹּד לְשָׂרָה
ג-ד וְלִבְכֹּתָהּ: וַיָּקָם אַבְרָהָם מֵעַל פְּנֵי מֵתוֹ וַיְדַבֵּר אֶל־בְּנֵי־חֵת לֵאמֹר: גֵּר־
וְתוֹשָׁב אָנֹכִי עִמָּכֶם תְּנוּ לִי אֲחֻזַּת־קֶבֶר עִמָּכֶם וְאֶקְבְּרָה מֵתִי מִלְּפָנָי:

XXIII

2. וַתָּמָת שָׂרָה — *And Sarah died.* After Rebecca — who is fit to replace Sarah — is born, and Abraham is notified, Sarah dies. As (our Sages tell us), 'One righteous person does not die before another is born, as it is written, וְזָרַח הַשֶּׁמֶשׁ וּבָא הַשָּׁמֶשׁ, *and the sun rises, and the sun sets (Ecclesiastes* 1:5)' *(Yoma* 38b).

לִסְפֹּד לְשָׂרָה — *To eulogize Sarah* . . . on her behalf and in her honor, as (our Sages) tell us, 'The eulogy is for the honor of the deceased' *(Sanhedrin* 46b).

3. מֵעַל פְּנֵי מֵתוֹ וַיְדַבֵּר אֶל בְּנֵי חֵת — *From the presence of his dead and spoke to the children of Heth.* The laws of mourning had not yet gone into effect; therefore he was permitted to leave his residence and speak to the children of Heth.

4. גֵּר וְתוֹשָׁב — *An alien and a resident.* Since I am a stranger I have no gravesite here, as it is written, וּמִי לְךָ פֹּה כִּי חָצַבְתָּ לְּךָ פֹּה קָבֶר, *Whom do you have here that you have hewed out a sepulcher here for yourself? (Isaiah* 22:16). The reason I wish to purchase one is because I reside among you and my intention is to establish myself here in your midst.

תְּנוּ לִי אֲחֻזַּת קֶבֶר — *Grant me an estate for a burial site.* Please agree to give me the right to have a possession of a grave as is written, *Unto Abraham for a possession of a burying place by the children of Heth* (v. 20).

NOTES

XXIII

2. וַתָּמָת שָׂרָה — *And Sarah died.* The *Sforno* links the conclusion of the previous *sidrah* (וַיֵּרָא) to the beginning of this *sidrah.* After Abraham is informed of the birth of Rebecca, the Torah relates that Sarah died. From heaven it is ordained that a righteous person leaves this earth only after another righteous one is born to take his or her place. Only after the new sun of Rebecca has risen does the sun of Sarah set.

לִסְפֹּד לְשָׂרָה — *To eulogize (for) Sarah.* The phraseology in this verse is a bit awkward and difficult to reconcile with the rules of Hebrew grammar. It should have been written לִסְפֹּד אֶת שָׂרָה, *to eulogize Sarah,* not לְשָׂרָה, *for Sarah.* The Torah, however, is teaching us that the opinion of those who contend that every eulogy is meant for the honor of the dead, and not for the living, is correct; hence לִסְפֹּד לְשָׂרָה, *for Sarah,* on her behalf, not in accordance with those who contend that the eulogy is for the honor of the living.

3. מֵעַל פְּנֵי מֵתוֹ וַיְדַבֵּר אֶל בְּנֵי חֵת — *From the presence of his dead and spoke to the children of Heth.* Upon the death of a relative for whom one is obligated to mourn, one's status is that of an *onen.* Only after burial does one become an *ovel.* Unlike an *ovel,* a mourner, who is prohibited to leave his house or engage in any business transaction, an *onen* is permitted to do so providing it is in conjunction with the needs and honor of the deceased. Therefore Abraham is permitted to approach the children of Heth and negotiate the purchase of a gravesite for his wife Sarah.

4. גֵּר וְתוֹשָׁב — *An alien and a resident.* The custom of the land and the culture of the Hittites was that strangers were not permitted to bury their dead in their midst, since this would be considered staking out a claim to that particular parcel of land, a right reserved only for residents. Abraham appreciated this obstacle confronting him and assured the children of Heth that he intended to change his status and take up permanent residence in this land. Indeed, he was not misleading them, for this land would some day become the permanent residence of his descendants. The

ה־ו וַיַּעֲנוּ בְנֵי־חֵת אֶת־אַבְרָהָם לֵאמֹר לוֹ: שְׁמָעֵנוּ ׀ אֲדֹנִי נְשִׂיא אֱלֹהִים אַתָּה
בְּתוֹכֵנוּ בְּמִבְחַר קְבָרֵינוּ קְבֹר אֶת־מֵתֶךָ אִישׁ מִמֶּנּוּ אֶת־קִבְרוֹ לֹא־יִכְלֶה
ז־ח מִמְּךָ מִקְּבֹר מֵתֶךָ: וַיָּקָם אַבְרָהָם וַיִּשְׁתַּחוּ לְעַם־הָאָרֶץ לִבְנֵי־חֵת: וַיְדַבֵּר
אִתָּם לֵאמֹר אִם־יֵשׁ אֶת־נַפְשְׁכֶם לִקְבֹּר אֶת־מֵתִי מִלְּפָנַי שְׁמָעוּנִי וּפִגְעוּ־
ט לִי בְּעֶפְרוֹן בֶּן־צֹחַר: וְיִתֶּן־לִי אֶת־מְעָרַת הַמַּכְפֵּלָה אֲשֶׁר־לוֹ אֲשֶׁר בִּקְצֵה
י שָׂדֵהוּ בְּכֶסֶף מָלֵא יִתְּנֶנָּה לִּי בְּתוֹכְכֶם לַאֲחֻזַּת־קָבֶר: וְעֶפְרוֹן יֹשֵׁב בְּתוֹךְ

---

6. בְּמִבְחַר קְבָרֵינוּ קְבֹר — *In the choicest of our burial places bury . . .* and do not wait until you have made your purchase, as (our Sages) have taught us, כָּל הַמֵּתִים כֻּלָּם הַמַּדְחֶה מִטָּתָם הֲרֵי זֶה מְשֻׁבָּח, *Regarding all deceased, he who hastens to inter them is praiseworthy* (*Moed Katan* 22a).

7. וַיִּשְׁתַּחוּ לְעַם הָאָרֶץ — *And he bowed to the people of the land . . .* to the assembled chiefs who represented the populace.

8. אִם יֵשׁ אֶת נַפְשְׁכֶם לִקְבֹּר — *If it is your will to bury.* If indeed you wish me to bury my dead quickly and not tarry as you indicated by saying, *In the choice of our sepulcher bury* (v. 6), then . . .

שְׁמָעוּנִי — *Hear me.* Assist me in the acquisition of a burying place.

וּפִגְעוּ לִי בְּעֶפְרוֹן — *and intercede for me with Ephron . . .* that he shall sell me (a parcel of his land) though it is unseemly for a distinguished person to sell any part of his patrimony, as Naboth states, חָלִילָה לִי מֵה׳ מִתִּתִּי אֶת נַחֲלַת אֲבֹתַי לָךְ, *a profanation to me from* HASHEM *from giving the inheritance of my fathers to you* (*I Kings* 21:3).

9. מְעָרַת הַמַּכְפֵּלָה — *The cave of Machpelah.* (It is located in) a place named Machpelah, as it is written, וַיָּקָם שְׂדֵה עֶפְרוֹן אֲשֶׁר בַּמַּכְפֵּלָה, *The field of Ephron which was in Machpelah* (v. 17).

אֲשֶׁר בִּקְצֵה שָׂדֵהוּ — *Which is on the edge of his field . . .* therefore the sale of it will not impair his estate.

בְּכֶסֶף מָלֵא — *For its full price.* I do not want him to reduce the price in your honor.

בְּתוֹכְכֶם — *In your midst.* (This means) in your presence. I do not ask for time but will pay immediately; and so he did, as it says, *and Abraham weighed to Ephron the silver, in the presence of the children of Heth* (vs. 16 and 18).

לַאֲחֻזַּת קָבֶר — *For a possession of a burying place.* Even though he (Ephron) may agree to sell me a portion of his estate, he may object to my using it for a burying site, therefore I want it understood that it is to be used for that purpose.

NOTES

children of Heth might not have grasped the subtle truth of Abraham's statement, and interpreted it their way. Abraham was telling the truth; they were the victims of self-deception.

6. בְּמִבְחַר קְבָרֵינוּ קְבֹר — *In the choicest of our burial places bury . . .* The Talmud teaches us that a deceased relative should be buried as quickly as possible. This was apparently the ancient custom of the Hittites as well, therefore they urged Abraham to bury his wife at once, even before he had concluded the purchase of the gravesite.

7. וַיִּשְׁתַּחוּ לְעַם הָאָרֶץ — *And he bowed to the people of the land . . .* Abraham did not bow down to *all* the people of the land. However, since he did so to the leaders, it is as though he bowed to the populace.

9. מְעָרַת הַמַּכְפֵּלָה . . . בְּכֶסֶף מָלֵא — *The cave of Machpelah . . . for its full price.* A careful examination of the verses will show that

בְּנֵי־חֵת וַיַּעַן עֶפְרוֹן הַחִתִּי אֶת־אַבְרָהָם בְּאָזְנֵי בְנֵי־חֵת לְכֹל בָּאֵי שַׁעַר־
יא עִירוֹ לֵאמֹר: לֹא־אֲדֹנִי שְׁמָעֵנִי הַשָּׂדֶה נָתַתִּי לָךְ וְהַמְּעָרָה אֲשֶׁר־בּוֹ לְךָ
יב נְתַתִּיהָ לְעֵינֵי בְנֵי־עַמִּי נְתַתִּיהָ לָּךְ קְבֹר מֵתֶךָ: וַיִּשְׁתַּחוּ אַבְרָהָם לִפְנֵי
יג עַם־הָאָרֶץ: וַיְדַבֵּר אֶל־עֶפְרוֹן בְּאָזְנֵי עַם־הָאָרֶץ לֵאמֹר אַךְ אִם־אַתָּה לוּ
יד שְׁמָעֵנִי נָתַתִּי כֶּסֶף הַשָּׂדֶה קַח מִמֶּנִּי וְאֶקְבְּרָה אֶת־מֵתִי שָׁמָּה: וַיַּעַן עֶפְרוֹן

---

11. לֹא אֲדֹנִי — *No, my lord.* It is not necessary for the leaders of the populace to intercede and entreat me.

שְׁמָעֵנִי — *Hear me.* Listen to me directly, there is no need for any intermediary.

הַשָּׂדֶה נָתַתִּי לָךְ — *I have given you the field.* As soon as you spoke I mentally gave it to you.

וְהַמְּעָרָה אֲשֶׁר בּוֹ — *And the cave that is in it . . .* so you need not go through the field of another to bury your dead.

לְעֵינֵי בְנֵי עַמִּי נְתַתִּיהָ לָּךְ קְבֹר מֵתֶךָ — *In the presence of the children of my people I give it to you; bury your dead.* In their presence do I give it to you for the explicit purpose of burying your dead, as you requested when you said, *'For a possession of a burying place.'*

12. וַיִּשְׁתַּחוּ אַבְרָהָם לִפְנֵי עַם הָאָרֶץ — *And Abraham bowed down before the people of the land.* He bowed down in gratitude to them to indicate that it was in their honor that Ephron agreed to accede to his request, as (our Sages) tell us, "If one knows that his father is highly regarded in a certain place he should not say, 'Hasten to serve me or release me for my sake,' but 'for my father's sake' " (*Kiddushin* 31b).

13. אַךְ אִם . . . נָתַתִּי כֶּסֶף הַשָּׂדֶה — *But if only you . . . I give you the price of the field.* I will do as you say and bury my dead in your field but only if I will (be permitted) to pay the price, otherwise I will not bury her there.

אַתָּה לוּ שְׁמָעֵנִי — *If only you would heed me.* Please listen to me.

קַח מִמֶּנִּי וְאֶקְבְּרָה — *Accept it from me that I may bury my dead there.* Only after you accept the silver will I bury her.

NOTES

Machpelah was the name of an area. In that area there was a field and in that field a cave was located. The phrase מְעָרַת הַמַּכְפֵּלָה does not mean, *the cave of Machpelah,* rather the cave situated in the field which was located in Machpelah.

בְּכֶסֶף מָלֵא — *For its full price.* Abraham had already demonstrated, following the Battle of the Kings, that he adamantly refused to accept anything from others, even when it was richly deserved. So here also he rejected the offer of Ephron to give him a grave and insisted upon paying immediately in full. He did so, wisely, in the presence of the populace who would serve as witness, with the clear understanding that this cave will be used for a burying place, so that Ephron will not be able to renege.

11. הַשָּׂדֶה נָתַתִּי לָךְ — *I have given you the field.* Even though Abraham has only requested the cave, Ephron includes the field as well, so that Abraham will have access to the cave without the need to acquire a right of way from another landowner.

12. וַיִּשְׁתַּחוּ אַבְרָהָם לִפְנֵי עַם הָאָרֶץ — *And Abraham bowed down before the people of the land.* Ephron was most generous and Abraham should have thanked *him,* not the children of Heth, but he bowed to them in gratitude, not to Ephron! The *Sforno* explains that Abraham was convinced that Ephron's magnanimity was motivated by his desire to impress his countrymen, hence he expressed his gratitude to them, rather than directly to Ephron.

טו אֶת־אַבְרָהָם לֵאמֹר לוֹ: אֲדֹנִי שְׁמָעֵנִי אֶרֶץ אַרְבַּע מֵאֹת שֶׁקֶל־כֶּסֶף בֵּינִי
טז וּבֵינְךָ מַה־הִוא וְאֶת־מֵתְךָ קְבֹר: וַיִּשְׁמַע אַבְרָהָם אֶל־עֶפְרוֹן וַיִּשְׁקֹל
אַבְרָהָם לְעֶפְרֹן אֶת־הַכֶּסֶף אֲשֶׁר דִּבֶּר בְּאָזְנֵי בְנֵי־חֵת אַרְבַּע מֵאוֹת שֶׁקֶל
שני יז כֶּסֶף עֹבֵר לַסֹּחֵר: וַיָּקָם | שְׂדֵה עֶפְרוֹן אֲשֶׁר בַּמַּכְפֵּלָה אֲשֶׁר לִפְנֵי מַמְרֵא
הַשָּׂדֶה וְהַמְּעָרָה אֲשֶׁר־בּוֹ וְכָל־הָעֵץ אֲשֶׁר בַּשָּׂדֶה אֲשֶׁר בְּכָל־גְּבֻלוֹ סָבִיב:
יח־יט לְאַבְרָהָם לְמִקְנָה לְעֵינֵי בְנֵי־חֵת בְּכֹל בָּאֵי שַׁעַר־עִירוֹ: וְאַחֲרֵי־כֵן קָבַר
אַבְרָהָם אֶת־שָׂרָה אִשְׁתּוֹ אֶל־מְעָרַת שְׂדֵה הַמַּכְפֵּלָה עַל־פְּנֵי מַמְרֵא הִוא
כ חֶבְרוֹן בְּאֶרֶץ כְּנָעַן: וַיָּקָם הַשָּׂדֶה וְהַמְּעָרָה אֲשֶׁר־בּוֹ לְאַבְרָהָם לַאֲחֻזַּת־
כד א קָבֶר מֵאֵת בְּנֵי־חֵת: וְאַבְרָהָם זָקֵן בָּא בַּיָּמִים וַיהוָה בֵּרַךְ
ב אֶת־אַבְרָהָם בַּכֹּל: וַיֹּאמֶר אַבְרָהָם אֶל־עַבְדּוֹ זְקַן בֵּיתוֹ הַמֹּשֵׁל בְּכָל־
ג אֲשֶׁר־לוֹ שִׂים־נָא יָדְךָ תַּחַת יְרֵכִי: וְאַשְׁבִּיעֲךָ בַּיהוה אֱלֹהֵי הַשָּׁמַיִם וֵאלֹהֵי

---

15. מַה הִוא — *What is it.* It is such a paltry sum that our word will suffice, and (even) prior to payment you can proceed to bury your dead.

16. וַיִּשְׁמַע אַבְרָהָם אֶל עֶפְרוֹן — *And Abraham heeded Ephron.* He accepted Ephron's valuation of the field.

וַיִּשְׁקֹל — *And weighed out* ... (i.e.,) he paid, as we find, כִּכַּר כֶּסֶף תִּשְׁקוֹל, *You shall pay* (lit., *weigh out*) *a talent of silver* (*I Kings* 20:39).

17-18. וַיָּקָם שְׂדֵה ... לְאַבְרָהָם לְמִקְנָה — *And the field was secured ... to Abraham as a purchase.* The deed of purchase was validated by its signatories.

20. וַיָּקָם הַשָּׂדֶה ... מֵאֵת בְּנֵי חֵת — *And the field was secured ... from the children of Heth.* The whole community agreed that it should be his for a burial place.

XXIV

1. וְאַבְרָהָם זָקֵן ... וַה׳ בֵּרַךְ אֶת אַבְרָהָם — *And Abraham was old ... and* HASHEM *had blessed Abraham.* The Torah explains the reasons which motivated Abraham to send his servant to another land to find a wife for his son, and why he had to adjure him with an oath. Firstly, since he was old he was concerned lest he die before a match was arranged for his son, and since he was convinced that there was no worthy wife for his son (in Canaan) he sent (Eliezer) to another land. Also, since Abraham was wealthy he feared that someone might bribe his servant to select an unfit wife for Isaac; hence he made him swear.

NOTES

13. See note on verse 9.

16. וַיִּשְׁמַע אַבְרָהָם אֶל עֶפְרוֹן — *And Abraham heeded Ephron.* Since Abraham refused to accept Ephron's offer to bury Sarah prior to payment, why does the Torah tell us that *he listened to Ephron?* The *Sforno* explains that this refers only to his acceptance of the price, not the *conditions* of the sale set forth by Ephron.

16-20. וַיִּשְׁקֹל ... וַיָּקָם הַשָּׂדֶה ... מֵאֵת בְּנֵי חֵת — *And weighed out ... and the field was secured ... from the children of Heth.* So that there be no question of the legality and validity of this sale, a number of steps were taken by Abraham. The silver was weighed and paid, the deed was validated and the entire community concurred that this cave might be used as a burial place.

XXIV

1-3. וְאַבְרָהָם זָקֵן ... וַה׳ בֵּרַךְ אֶת אַבְרָהָם — *And Abraham was old ... and* HASHEM *had blessed Abraham.* The *Sforno* reads into these verses three reasons for Abraham's decision to send

הָאָרֶץ אֲשֶׁר לֹא־תִקַּח אִשָּׁה לִבְנִי מִבְּנוֹת הַכְּנַעֲנִי אֲשֶׁר אָנֹכִי יוֹשֵׁב
ד בְּקִרְבּוֹ: כִּי אֶל־אַרְצִי וְאֶל־מוֹלַדְתִּי תֵּלֵךְ וְלָקַחְתָּ אִשָּׁה לִבְנִי לְיִצְחָק:
ה וַיֹּאמֶר אֵלָיו הָעֶבֶד אוּלַי לֹא־תֹאבֶה הָאִשָּׁה לָלֶכֶת אַחֲרַי אֶל־הָאָרֶץ
ו הַזֹּאת הֶהָשֵׁב אָשִׁיב אֶת־בִּנְךָ אֶל־הָאָרֶץ אֲשֶׁר־יָצָאתָ מִשָּׁם: וַיֹּאמֶר אֵלָיו
ז אַבְרָהָם הִשָּׁמֶר לְךָ פֶּן־תָּשִׁיב אֶת־בְּנִי שָׁמָּה: יהוה | אֱלֹהֵי הַשָּׁמַיִם אֲשֶׁר
לְקָחַנִי מִבֵּית אָבִי וּמֵאֶרֶץ מוֹלַדְתִּי וַאֲשֶׁר דִּבֶּר־לִי וַאֲשֶׁר נִשְׁבַּע־לִי לֵאמֹר
לְזַרְעֲךָ אֶתֵּן אֶת־הָאָרֶץ הַזֹּאת הוּא יִשְׁלַח מַלְאָכוֹ לְפָנֶיךָ וְלָקַחְתָּ אִשָּׁה
ח לִבְנִי מִשָּׁם: וְאִם־לֹא תֹאבֶה הָאִשָּׁה לָלֶכֶת אַחֲרֶיךָ וְנִקִּיתָ מִשְּׁבֻעָתִי זֹאת
ט רַק אֶת־בְּנִי לֹא תָשֵׁב שָׁמָּה: וַיָּשֶׂם הָעֶבֶד אֶת־יָדוֹ תַּחַת יֶרֶךְ אַבְרָהָם
שלישי י אֲדֹנָיו וַיִּשָּׁבַע לוֹ עַל־הַדָּבָר הַזֶּה: וַיִּקַּח הָעֶבֶד עֲשָׂרָה גְמַלִּים מִגְּמַלֵּי אֲדֹנָיו

---

3. אֱלֹהֵי הַשָּׁמַיִם וֵאלֹהֵי הָאָרֶץ — *God of heaven and God of earth.* Should you prove false to the oath, He will punish you in this world (*earth*) and in the next *(heaven).*

5. אֲשֶׁר יָצָאתָ מִשָּׁם — *To the land from which you departed* ... which you have rejected by your departure from there! Now if I swear to find a proper wife (and betroth her on behalf of Isaac) and she refuses to come back with me to Canaan, then Isaac will be obligated to fulfill all the duties of a husband, i.e., food, clothing, and marital duties, and be obligated to travel there. If not, he would betray the wife of his youth.

7. אֱלֹהֵי הַשָּׁמַיִם ... יִשְׁלַח מַלְאָכוֹ — *The God of heaven ... will send His angel.* May it be His will to send His angel from on High; since He took me forth from that land, and to Him all deeds are known, He will arrange matters so that my son need not return there.

וַאֲשֶׁר דִּבֶּר לִי — *And Who spoke to me* ... in addition to which He spoke to me, saying, כִּי בְיִצְחָק יִקָּרֵא לְךָ זָרַע, *Through Isaac will offspring be considered yours* (21:12).

וַאֲשֶׁר נִשְׁבַּע לִי — *And Who swore to me.* Since He swore to me He will not renege, and without a doubt He will assure (the success of this mission), that my son wed a woman fitting for him so as to bring into the world worthy children who are prepared to fulfill the oath given by God.

9. וַיִּשָּׁבַע לוֹ עַל הַדָּבָר הַזֶּה — *And swore to him regarding this matter.* He swore, including in his oath all the conditions made by Abraham.

10. וַיִּקַּח הָעֶבֶד עֲשָׂרָה גְמַלִּים מִגְּמַלֵּי אֲדֹנָיו וַיֵּלֶךְ — *And the servant took ten camels of his master, and departed.* He requested permission of his master to depart, after preparing the (ten) camels, and left.

NOTES

Eliezer to Haran to find a bride for his son and for the need to administer an oath to him: (a) he was old and time was running out (זָקֵן); (b) he was determined not to have Isaac marry one of the Canaanite women (מִבְּנוֹת הַכְּנַעֲנִי); and (c) because he was rich he was afraid that there will be unscrupulous people who will try to become part of his family through marriage, hence וְאַשְׁבִּיעֲךָ, *I adjure you.*

5. אֲשֶׁר יָצָאתָ מִשָּׁם — *To the land from which you departed.* Eliezer was sent not only to *find* a bride but also to betroth her on behalf of Isaac, acting as a שָׁלִיחַ, *agent*, hence, if she would refuse to accompany him back to Canaan after he betroths her, serious problems would arise.

7. אֱלֹהֵי הַשָּׁמַיִם — *The God of heaven.* In verse 3 the God of heaven and earth is invoked,

וַיֵּלֶךְ וְכָל־טוּב אֲדֹנָיו בְּיָדוֹ וַיָּקָם וַיֵּלֶךְ אֶל־אֲרַם נַהֲרַיִם אֶל־עִיר נָחוֹר׃
יא וַיַּבְרֵךְ הַגְּמַלִּים מִחוּץ לָעִיר אֶל־בְּאֵר הַמָּיִם לְעֵת עֶרֶב לְעֵת צֵאת
יב הַשֹּׁאֲבֹת׃ וַיֹּאמַר ׀ יהוה אֱלֹהֵי אֲדֹנִי אַבְרָהָם הַקְרֵה־נָא לְפָנַי הַיּוֹם וַעֲשֵׂה־
יג חֶסֶד עִם אֲדֹנִי אַבְרָהָם׃ הִנֵּה אָנֹכִי נִצָּב עַל־עֵין הַמָּיִם וּבְנוֹת אַנְשֵׁי הָעִיר
יד יֹצְאֹת לִשְׁאֹב מָיִם׃ וְהָיָה הַנַּעֲרָ אֲשֶׁר אֹמַר אֵלֶיהָ הַטִּי־נָא כַדֵּךְ וְאֶשְׁתֶּה
וְאָמְרָה שְׁתֵה וְגַם־גְּמַלֶּיךָ אַשְׁקֶה אֹתָהּ הֹכַחְתָּ לְעַבְדְּךָ לְיִצְחָק וּבָהּ אֵדַע
טו כִּי־עָשִׂיתָ חֶסֶד עִם־אֲדֹנִי׃ וַיְהִי־הוּא טֶרֶם כִּלָּה לְדַבֵּר וְהִנֵּה רִבְקָה יֹצֵאת

וְכָל טוּב אֲדֹנָיו בְּיָדוֹ — *With all the bounty of his master in his hand.* He took with him gold, silver and garments. There was no need to get permission to do so, since the affairs of Abraham's household were in his hands and his authority was unquestioned.

וַיָּקָם וַיֵּלֶךְ — *And he arose and departed* . . . on his journey.

14. וְהָיָה הַנַּעֲרָ אֲשֶׁר אֹמַר אֵלֶיהָ — *So let it be that the maiden to whom I shall say.* He did not make this a sign whereby he might recognize Isaac's destined wife, because that would be divination (נַחֵשׁ), rather he prayed that it might fall out so; and so it was with Jonathan the son of Saul (see *I Samuel* 14:8-12). As for the saying of our Sages, כָּל נַחַשׁ שֶׁאֵינוֹ כֶּאֱלִיעֶזֶר עֶבֶד אַבְרָהָם וִיהוֹנָתָן בֶּן שָׁאוּל אֵינוֹ נַחַשׁ, *An omen which is not as that pronounced by Abraham's servant Eliezer, or by Jonathan the son of Saul is not considered a divination (Chullin* 95b), their intent and meaning is: if the individual says it not as a prayer, but as divination, i.e., 'If thus and thus happens then I shall do this,' then he is guilty of divination (נַחֵשׁ).

וְגַם גְּמַלֶּיךָ אַשְׁקֶה — *And I will even water your camels.* One who asks should request less than he actually needs so as not to overly bother others, while the person responding should go beyond it and offer all, or more, than is needed.

אֹתָהּ הֹכַחְתָּ — *She has been instructed* (lit., *designated) by You.* You have taught her proper ethical understanding so that she is indeed worthy to be Isaac's wife.

15. טֶרֶם כִּלָּה — *Before he had finished speaking* . . . even before he finished, similar to, וְהָיָה טֶרֶם יִקְרָאוּ וַאֲנִי אֶעֱנֶה, *Before they call I will answer (Isaiah* 65:24).

NOTES

whereas here only the God of heaven. The reason, as given by the *Sforno,* is because Abraham is referring to the intervention of the Almighty from on High.

10. וַיִּקַּח הָעֶבֶד . . . וַיֵּלֶךְ . . . וַיָּקָם וַיֵּלֶךְ — *And the servant took . . . and departed . . . and he arose and departed.* The phrase וַיֵּלֶךְ, *he departed,* is used twice in this verse. The first means he asked permission to go; the second means he went.

14. וְהָיָה הַנַּעֲרָ אֲשֶׁר אֹמַר אֵלֶיהָ — *So let it be that the maiden to whom I shall say.* The Talmud *(Chullin* 95b) discusses the episodes of Eliezer and Jonathan son of Saul. In both cases it would seem that they are 'divining,' i.e., relying upon a sign to determine their ultimate action. Since this is prohibited, *Tosafos* asks how they allowed themselves to do so. He explains the reasoning used by Eliezer and Jonathan, but the *Sforno* answers this question quite simply. In both cases they are but praying that it might fall out so. It is interesting to note that the *Rambam* and *Raavad* also disagree as to how to interpret this passage in the Talmud. Again, the *Sforno's* interpretation would reconcile the difficulties they both encounter.

אֹתָהּ הֹכַחְתָּ — *She has been instructed by You.* The word הוֹכָחָה can mean *to prove, to appoint, to admonish,* or *to instruct.* The *Sforno* chooses the latter interpretation. If Rebecca should demonstrate unusual kind-

אֲשֶׁר יֻלְּדָה לִבְתוּאֵל בֶּן־מִלְכָּה אֵשֶׁת נָחוֹר אֲחִי אַבְרָהָם וְכַדָּהּ עַל־
טז שִׁכְמָהּ: וְהַנַּעֲרָ טֹבַת מַרְאֶה מְאֹד בְּתוּלָה וְאִישׁ לֹא יְדָעָהּ וַתֵּרֶד הָעַיְנָה
יז וַתְּמַלֵּא כַדָּהּ וַתָּעַל: וַיָּרָץ הָעֶבֶד לִקְרָאתָהּ וַיֹּאמֶר הַגְמִיאִינִי נָא מְעַט־מַיִם
יח־יט מִכַּדֵּךְ: וַתֹּאמֶר שְׁתֵה אֲדֹנִי וַתְּמַהֵר וַתֹּרֶד כַּדָּהּ עַל־יָדָהּ וַתַּשְׁקֵהוּ: וַתְּכַל
כ לְהַשְׁקֹתוֹ וַתֹּאמֶר גַּם לִגְמַלֶּיךָ אֶשְׁאָב עַד אִם־כִּלּוּ לִשְׁתֹּת: וַתְּמַהֵר וַתְּעַר
כַּדָּהּ אֶל־הַשֹּׁקֶת וַתָּרָץ עוֹד אֶל־הַבְּאֵר לִשְׁאֹב וַתִּשְׁאַב לְכָל־גְּמַלָּיו:
כא־כב וְהָאִישׁ מִשְׁתָּאֵה לָהּ מַחֲרִישׁ לָדַעַת הַהִצְלִיחַ יהוה דַּרְכּוֹ אִם־לֹא: וַיְהִי
כַּאֲשֶׁר כִּלּוּ הַגְּמַלִּים לִשְׁתּוֹת וַיִּקַּח הָאִישׁ נֶזֶם זָהָב בֶּקַע מִשְׁקָלוֹ וּשְׁנֵי
כג צְמִידִים עַל־יָדֶיהָ עֲשָׂרָה זָהָב מִשְׁקָלָם: וַיֹּאמֶר בַּת־מִי אַתְּ הַגִּידִי נָא לִי

אֲשֶׁר יֻלְּדָה לִבְתוּאֵל בֶּן מִלְכָּה — *Who was born to Bethuel the son of Milkah . . .* the son of the wife, not of Reumah the concubine (22:23,24).

16. טֹבַת מַרְאֶה — *Fair to look upon.* (She had a) beautiful complexion.

19. וַתְּכַל לְהַשְׁקֹתוֹ וַתֹּאמֶר — *When she finished giving him drink, she said.* She waited until he had finished drinking before speaking to him, as our Sages say, אֵין מְשִׂיחִין בִּסְעוּדָה שֶׁמָּא יַקְדִּים קָנֶה לַוֶּשֶׁט, *One should not converse at meals, lest the windpipe acts before the gullet* (*Taanis* 5b).

20. וַתְּמַהֵר — *So she hurried.* Haste in serving another is a sign of regard and respect.

וַתָּרָץ עוֹד אֶל הַבְּאֵר — *And ran again to the well . . .* the well in front of the fountain from whence the animals drink.

21. מִשְׁתָּאֵה — *Looked wonderingly.* He wondered at the alacrity with which she hastened to do this kindness.

מַחֲרִישׁ — *Maintaining silence.* He did not urge her to desist from exerting herself, as would have been proper.

לָדַעַת — *To learn . . .* to determine and judge from her act of kindness and haste to perform it.

הַהִצְלִיחַ ה׳ דַּרְכּוֹ אִם לֹא — *Whether God had made his journey successful . . .* whether she was motivated by natural kindness or by the hope of reward.

22. כַּאֲשֶׁר כִּלּוּ הַגְּמַלִּים לִשְׁתּוֹת — *And it was when the camels had finished drinking.* (Although this) took considerable time, still she did not ask for aught, doing it purely from a motivation of kindness.

וּשְׁנֵי צְמִידִים עַל יָדֶיהָ — *And two bracelets on her arms.* They proved to be a perfect fit (for her hands) similar to, וְעָשִׂיתָ עַל הַחֹשֶׁן שַׁרְשֹׁת גַּבְלֻת, *And you shall make upon*

NOTES

ness, then Eliezer attributes this virtue to a unique aspect of her character granted her by the Almighty, Who was also (כביכול) her instructor, since she had no other teacher from her family.

15. אֲשֶׁר יֻלְּדָה לִבְתוּאֵל — *Who was born to Bethuel.* Born to *Bethuel the son of Nahor* would have been more appropriate than *son of Milkah.* The answer must be that the Torah is stressing that Rebecca's father is the son of Nahor's wife, not his concubine.

22. וּשְׁנֵי צְמִידִים עַל יָדֶיהָ — *And two bracelets*

כד הֲיֵשׁ בֵּית־אָבִיךְ מָקוֹם לָנוּ לָלִין: וַתֹּאמֶר אֵלָיו בַּת־בְּתוּאֵל אָנֹכִי בֶּן־
כה מִלְכָּה אֲשֶׁר יָלְדָה לְנָחוֹר: וַתֹּאמֶר אֵלָיו גַּם־תֶּבֶן גַּם־מִסְפּוֹא רַב עִמָּנוּ גַּם־
רביעי כו־כז מָקוֹם לָלוּן: וַיִּקֹּד הָאִישׁ וַיִּשְׁתַּחוּ לַיהוָה: וַיֹּאמֶר בָּרוּךְ יהוה אֱלֹהֵי אֲדֹנִי
אַבְרָהָם אֲשֶׁר לֹא־עָזַב חַסְדּוֹ וַאֲמִתּוֹ מֵעִם אֲדֹנִי אָנֹכִי בַּדֶּרֶךְ נָחַנִי יהוה
כח־כט בֵּית אֲחֵי אֲדֹנִי: וַתָּרָץ הַנַּעֲרָ וַתַּגֵּד לְבֵית אִמָּהּ כַּדְּבָרִים הָאֵלֶּה: וּלְרִבְקָה
ל אָח וּשְׁמוֹ לָבָן וַיָּרָץ לָבָן אֶל־הָאִישׁ הַחוּצָה אֶל־הָעָיִן: וַיְהִי ׀ כִּרְאֹת
אֶת־הַנֶּזֶם וְאֶת־הַצְּמִדִים עַל־יְדֵי אֲחֹתוֹ וּכְשָׁמְעוֹ אֶת־דִּבְרֵי רִבְקָה אֲחֹתוֹ
לֵאמֹר כֹּה־דִבֶּר אֵלַי הָאִישׁ וַיָּבֹא אֶל־הָאִישׁ וְהִנֵּה עֹמֵד עַל־הַגְּמַלִּים
לא עַל־הָעָיִן: וַיֹּאמֶר בּוֹא בְּרוּךְ יהוה לָמָּה תַעֲמֹד בַּחוּץ וְאָנֹכִי פִּנִּיתִי הַבַּיִת

---

the breastplate plaited chains (Exodus 28:22), and וְעָשִׂיתָ עָלָיו זֵר זָהָב, *And make upon it a crown of gold (Exodus 25:11),* (meaning) a proper fit (for the חֹשֶׁן and אָרוֹן).

23. הֲיֵשׁ בֵּית אָבִיךְ מָקוֹם — *Is there room in your father's house . . .* available for guest lodging, as was then the custom.

לָלִין — *To lodge in . . .* where we may stable (our camels).

25. גַּם תֶּבֶן גַּם מִסְפּוֹא — *Even straw and feed.* Not only place to stable them but provender to feed them as well.

גַּם מָקוֹם לָלוּן — *And room to lodge in . . .* for you and your people.

29. וַיָּרָץ לָבָן אֶל הָאִישׁ — *And Laban ran out to the man.* He ran to see the wealthy visitor, not to offer him hospitality.

30. וַיְהִי כִּרְאֹת אֶת הַנֶּזֶם וְאֶת הַצְּמִדִים עַל יְדֵי אֲחֹתוֹ — *When he saw the nose ring and the bracelets on his sister's arm.* He did not wish to be ungrateful.

וּכְשָׁמְעוֹ אֶת דִּבְרֵי רִבְקָה אֲחֹתוֹ לֵאמֹר כֹּה דִבֶּר אֵלַי הָאִישׁ — *And when he heard the word of Rebecca his sister saying, thus spoke the man to me . . .* asking her, *'Is there room in thy father's house for us to lodge in?'* (v. 23).

וַיָּבֹא אֶל הָאִישׁ — *And he approached the man . . .* to invite him into his house.

וְהִנֵּה עֹמֵד עַל הַגְּמַלִּים — *Who was still standing by the camels . . .* to attend to their needs. He did not intend to lodge in Rebecca's father's house, unless invited by him.

31. לָמָּה תַעֲמֹד בַּחוּץ — *Why should you stand outside?* You only asked lodging for your camels, but why should you and your men remain outside?

וְאָנֹכִי פִּנִּיתִי הַבַּיִת — *I have cleared the house . . .* for you and your men.

NOTES

on her arms. As the *Ramban* points out, this verse lacks a verb, i.e., וַיִּתֵּן, *and he gave,* or וַיָּשֶׂם, *and he placed.* All it states is *two bracelets on her hands.* The answer perforce is that these bracelets were destined for her hands, fitting her wrists perfectly, indicating that this match of Rebecca and Isaac is also destined.

23-25. מָקוֹם לָלִין . . . מָקוֹם לָלוּן — *Room to lodge in . . . room to lodge in.* לָלִין, *to lodge in,* is written in the הִפְעִיל, as a transitive verb, whereas לָלוּן is a simple verb in the light קַל form. The former is applicable to the camels, while the latter is fitting for Eliezer and his men.

31. לָמָּה תַעֲמֹד בַּחוּץ — *Why should you stand outside?* The question poses a difficulty, for it is obvious that a person will not enter unless invited to do so. Therefore the interpretation must be, as the *Sforno* says, that Laban

לב וּמָק֖וֹם לַגְּמַלִּ֑ים וַיָּבֹ֤א הָאִישׁ֙ הַבַּ֔יְתָה וַיְפַתַּח֙ הַגְּמַלִּ֔ים וַיִּתֵּ֤ן תֶּ֙בֶן֙ וּמִסְפּוֹא֙

לג לַגְּמַלִּ֔ים וּמַ֕יִם לִרְחֹ֣ץ רַגְלָ֔יו וְרַגְלֵ֥י הָאֲנָשִׁ֖ים אֲשֶׁ֥ר אִתּֽוֹ: °וַיּיִשָֹ֤ם קֿ לְפָנָיו֙

לד לֶֽאֱכֹ֔ל וַיֹּ֕אמֶר לֹ֣א אֹכַ֔ל עַ֥ד אִם־דִּבַּ֖רְתִּי דְּבָרָ֑י וַיֹּ֖אמֶר דַּבֵּֽר: וַיֹּאמַ֑ר עֶ֥בֶד

לה אַבְרָהָ֖ם אָנֹֽכִי: וַֽיהֹוָ֞ה בֵּרַ֧ךְ אֶת־אֲדֹנִ֛י מְאֹ֖ד וַיִּגְדָּ֑ל וַיִּתֶּן־ל֞וֹ צֹ֤אן וּבָקָר֙ וְכֶ֣סֶף

לו וְזָהָ֗ב וַֽעֲבָדִם֙ וּשְׁפָחֹ֔ת וּגְמַלִּ֖ים וַֽחֲמֹרִֽים: וַתֵּ֡לֶד שָׂרָה֩ אֵ֨שֶׁת אֲדֹנִ֥י בֵן֙ לַֽאדֹנִ֔י

לז אַֽחֲרֵ֖י זִקְנָתָ֑הּ וַיִּתֶּן־ל֖וֹ אֶת־כָּל־אֲשֶׁר־לֽוֹ: וַיַּשְׁבִּעֵ֥נִי אֲדֹנִ֖י לֵאמֹ֑ר לֹֽא־תִקַּ֤ח

לח אִשָּׁה֙ לִבְנִ֔י מִבְּנוֹת֙ הַֽכְּנַֽעֲנִ֔י אֲשֶׁ֥ר אָֽנֹכִ֖י ישֵׁ֥ב בְּאַרְצֽוֹ: אִם־לֹ֧א אֶל־בֵּֽית־

לט אָבִ֛י תֵּלֵ֖ךְ וְאֶל־מִשְׁפַּחְתִּ֑י וְלָֽקַחְתָּ֥ אִשָּׁ֖ה לִבְנִֽי: וָֽאֹמַ֖ר אֶל־אֲדֹנִ֑י אֻלַ֥י לֹֽא־

מ תֵלֵ֥ךְ הָֽאִשָּׁ֖ה אַֽחֲרָֽי: וַיֹּ֖אמֶר אֵלָ֑י יְהֹוָ֞ה אֲשֶׁר־הִתְהַלַּ֣כְתִּי לְפָנָ֗יו יִשְׁלַ֣ח

מַלְאָכ֤וֹ אִתָּךְ֙ וְהִצְלִ֣יחַ דַּרְכֶּ֔ךָ וְלָֽקַחְתָּ֤ אִשָּׁה֙ לִבְנִ֔י מִמִּשְׁפַּחְתִּ֖י וּמִבֵּ֥ית אָבִֽי:

מא אָ֤ז תִּנָּקֶה֙ מֵאָ֣לָתִ֔י כִּ֥י תָב֖וֹא אֶל־מִשְׁפַּחְתִּ֑י וְאִם־לֹ֤א יִתְּנוּ֙ לָ֔ךְ וְהָיִ֥יתָ נָקִ֖י

מב מֵאָֽלָתִֽי: וָֽאָבֹ֥א הַיּ֖וֹם אֶל־הָעָ֑יִן וָֽאֹמַ֗ר יְהֹוָה֙ אֱלֹהֵי֙ אֲדֹנִ֣י אַבְרָהָ֔ם אִם־יֶשְׁךָ־

מג נָּא֙ מַצְלִ֣יחַ דַּרְכִּ֔י אֲשֶׁ֥ר אָֽנֹכִ֖י הֹלֵ֣ךְ עָלֶ֑יהָ: הִנֵּ֛ה אָֽנֹכִ֥י נִצָּ֖ב עַל־עֵ֣ין הַמָּ֑יִם

וְהָיָ֤ה הָֽעַלְמָה֙ הַיֹּצֵ֣את לִשְׁאֹ֔ב וְאָֽמַרְתִּ֣י אֵלֶ֔יהָ הַשְׁקִ֥ינִי־נָ֖א מְעַט־מַ֥יִם

מד מִכַּדֵּֽךְ: וְאָֽמְרָ֤ה אֵלַי֙ גַּם־אַתָּ֣ה שְׁתֵ֔ה וְגַ֥ם לִגְמַלֶּ֖יךָ אֶשְׁאָ֑ב הִ֣וא הָֽאִשָּׁ֔ה

מה אֲשֶׁר־הֹכִ֥יחַ יְהֹוָ֖ה לְבֶן־אֲדֹנִֽי: אֲנִי֩ טֶ֨רֶם אֲכַלֶּ֜ה לְדַבֵּ֣ר אֶל־לִבִּ֗י וְהִנֵּ֨ה רִבְקָ֤ה

יֹצֵאת֙ וְכַדָּ֣הּ עַל־שִׁכְמָ֔הּ וַתֵּ֥רֶד הָעַ֖יְנָה וַתִּשְׁאָ֑ב וָֽאֹמַ֥ר אֵלֶ֖יהָ הַשְׁקִ֥ינִי נָֽא:

מו וַתְּמַהֵ֗ר וַתּ֤וֹרֶד כַּדָּהּ֙ מֵֽעָלֶ֔יהָ וַתֹּ֣אמֶר שְׁתֵ֔ה וְגַם־גְּמַלֶּ֖יךָ אַשְׁקֶ֑ה וָאֵ֕שְׁתְּ וְגַ֥ם

מז הַגְּמַלִּ֖ים הִשְׁקָֽתָה: וָֽאֶשְׁאַ֣ל אֹתָ֗הּ וָֽאֹמַר֙ בַּת־מִ֣י אַ֔תְּ וַתֹּ֗אמֶר בַּת־בְּתוּאֵל֙

בֶּן־נָח֔וֹר אֲשֶׁ֥ר יָֽלְדָה־לּ֖וֹ מִלְכָּ֑ה וָֽאָשִׂ֤ם הַנֶּ֙זֶם֙ עַל־אַפָּ֔הּ וְהַצְּמִידִ֖ים עַל־יָדֶֽיהָ:

מח וָֽאֶקֹּ֥ד וָֽאֶשְׁתַּֽחֲוֶ֖ה לַֽיהֹוָ֑ה וָֽאֲבָרֵ֗ךְ אֶת־יְהֹוָה֙ אֱלֹהֵי֙ אֲדֹנִ֣י אַבְרָהָ֔ם אֲשֶׁר֙

וּמָק֖וֹם לַגְּמַלִּ֑ים — *And made room for the camels . . .* as well as for your camels.

35. בֵּרַ֧ךְ אֶת־אֲדֹנִ֥י מְאֹ֖ד — *Hath blessed my master greatly . . .* and without a doubt many in our country would be glad to marry into his family.

36. אַֽחֲרֵ֖י זִקְנָתָ֑הּ — *When she was old.* This made him (Isaac) all the more beloved.

37. וַיַּשְׁבִּעֵ֥נִי אֲדֹנִ֖י — *And my master made me take an oath.* I come to you because my master has rejected the families in Canaan in favor of those here, but not because there is a lack of potential wives in Canaan.

44. הִ֣וא הָֽאִשָּׁ֔ה אֲשֶׁר־הֹכִ֥יחַ — *She is the woman designated (by God).* As our Sages state, בַּת ק֥וֹל מַכְרֶ֥זֶת וְאוֹמֶ֥רֶת בַּת פְּלוֹנִ֥י לִפְלוֹנִ֥י, *A heavenly voice proclaims, 'The daughter of this man (is destined) for this man'* (Sotah 2a).

45. אֲנִי֩ טֶ֨רֶם אֲכַלֶּ֜ה לְדַבֵּ֣ר — *And before I had finished meditating.* This proved that she was destined by the Almighty (to be Isaac's wife).

NOTES

remonstrated with Eliezer, saying to him, 'Why did you only concern yourself with a place for your camels and not for yourself and your men?'

44. הִ֣וא הָֽאִשָּׁ֔ה אֲשֶׁר־הֹכִ֥יחַ — *She is the woman*

designated (by God). Here the *Sforno* interprets the phrase הוכיח in a different manner than he does in *posuk* 14. The reason may be because when Eliezer related the episode to Bethuel and Laban he wished to impress upon them that Rebecca is destined from heaven to

מט הִנְחַנִי בְּדֶרֶךְ אֱמֶת לָקַחַת אֶת־בַּת־אֲחִי אֲדֹנִי לִבְנוֹ׃ וְעַתָּה אִם־יֶשְׁכֶם
עֹשִׂים חֶסֶד וֶאֱמֶת אֶת־אֲדֹנִי הַגִּידוּ לִי וְאִם־לֹא הַגִּידוּ לִי וְאֶפְנֶה עַל־יָמִין
נ אוֹ עַל־שְׂמֹאל׃ וַיַּעַן לָבָן וּבְתוּאֵל וַיֹּאמְרוּ מֵיְהוָה יָצָא הַדָּבָר לֹא נוּכַל
נא דַּבֵּר אֵלֶיךָ רַע אוֹ־טוֹב׃ הִנֵּה־רִבְקָה לְפָנֶיךָ קַח וָלֵךְ וּתְהִי אִשָּׁה לְבֶן־
נב אֲדֹנֶיךָ כַּאֲשֶׁר דִּבֶּר יְהוָה׃ וַיְהִי כַּאֲשֶׁר שָׁמַע עֶבֶד אַבְרָהָם אֶת־דִּבְרֵיהֶם
חמישי נג וַיִּשְׁתַּחוּ אַרְצָה לַיהוָה׃ וַיּוֹצֵא הָעֶבֶד כְּלֵי־כֶסֶף וּכְלֵי זָהָב וּבְגָדִים וַיִּתֵּן
נד לְרִבְקָה וּמִגְדָּנֹת נָתַן לְאָחִיהָ וּלְאִמָּהּ׃ וַיֹּאכְלוּ וַיִּשְׁתּוּ הוּא וְהָאֲנָשִׁים אֲשֶׁר־
נה עִמּוֹ וַיָּלִינוּ וַיָּקוּמוּ בַבֹּקֶר וַיֹּאמֶר שַׁלְּחֻנִי לַאדֹנִי׃ וַיֹּאמֶר אָחִיהָ וְאִמָּהּ תֵּשֵׁב
נו הַנַּעֲרָ אִתָּנוּ יָמִים אוֹ עָשׂוֹר אַחַר תֵּלֵךְ׃ וַיֹּאמֶר אֲלֵהֶם אַל־תְּאַחֲרוּ אֹתִי
נז וַיהוָה הִצְלִיחַ דַּרְכִּי שַׁלְּחוּנִי וְאֵלְכָה לַאדֹנִי׃ וַיֹּאמְרוּ נִקְרָא לַנַּעֲרָ וְנִשְׁאֲלָה
נח אֶת־פִּיהָ׃ וַיִּקְרְאוּ לְרִבְקָה וַיֹּאמְרוּ אֵלֶיהָ הֲתֵלְכִי עִם־הָאִישׁ הַזֶּה וַתֹּאמֶר
נט אֵלֵךְ׃ וַיְשַׁלְּחוּ אֶת־רִבְקָה אֲחֹתָם וְאֶת־מֵנִקְתָּהּ וְאֶת־עֶבֶד אַבְרָהָם וְאֶת־
ס אֲנָשָׁיו׃ וַיְבָרְכוּ אֶת־רִבְקָה וַיֹּאמְרוּ לָהּ אֲחֹתֵנוּ אַתְּ הֲיִי לְאַלְפֵי רְבָבָה

---

49. אִם יֶשְׁכֶם עֹשִׂים חֶסֶד — *If you intend to do kindness.* If you are prepared to allow your daughter to go so far away, and forgo your preference that she wed a man closer to home, so as to fulfill the wish of my master . . .

וֶאֱמֶת — *And truthfulness* . . . while at the same time considering her *true* interests by bringing honor and position to your daughter, i.e., by bringing her into Abraham's house.

50. לֹא נוּכַל דַּבֵּר אֵלֶיךָ רַע אוֹ טוֹב — *We can say to you neither bad nor good.* It is God's decree which we can neither annul nor confirm, because it does not depend on us.

51. קַח וָלֵךְ — *Take her and go* . . . even without our permission.

כַּאֲשֶׁר דִּבֶּר ה׳ — *As the Lord has spoken* . . . Who decreed בַּת פְּלוֹנִי לִפְלוֹנִי, *the daughter of this man (is destined) for this man,* for has He not given a sign that this is His will?

55. יָמִים אוֹ עָשׂוֹר — *A year or ten months.* They asked for the delay in order to help Rebecca gradually accustom herself to the idea of leaving home for such a long journey, since such a radical change is difficult to accept.

57. וְנִשְׁאֲלָה אֶת פִּיהָ — *And inquire of her mouth* . . . whether she is capable of going immediately (in spite of the trauma of going so far away).

60. אַתְּ הֲיִי לְאַלְפֵי רְבָבָה וְיִירַשׁ זַרְעֵךְ — *May you be the mother of thousands, of ten thousands, and may your offspring inherit (the gates).* Be you acceptable and

NOTES

become the wife of Isaac, as we see in the very next verse.

49. אִם יֶשְׁכֶם עֹשִׂים חֶסֶד וֶאֱמֶת — *If you intend to do kindness and truthfulness.* חֶסֶד is a kindness, אֱמֶת is an act dictated by the reality of a situation. Eliezer pointed out to Bethuel and Laban that by agreeing to let Rebecca go to Abraham's house they would do both; a *kindness* to Abraham who was so anxious to see his son wed to the proper woman before he dies, while at the same time it was *truly* a benefit to her, and for their prestige, to have her become a part of this princely household.

60. אַתְּ הֲיִי לְאַלְפֵי רְבָבָה — *May you be the*

סא וְיִירַשׁ זַרְעֵךְ אֵת שַׁעַר שֹׂנְאָיו: וַתָּקָם רִבְקָה וְנַעֲרֹתֶיהָ וַתִּרְכַּבְנָה עַל־
סב הַגְּמַלִּים וַתֵּלַכְנָה אַחֲרֵי הָאִישׁ וַיִּקַּח הָעֶבֶד אֶת־רִבְקָה וַיֵּלַךְ: וְיִצְחָק בָּא
סג מִבּוֹא בְּאֵר לַחַי רֹאִי וְהוּא יוֹשֵׁב בְּאֶרֶץ הַנֶּגֶב: וַיֵּצֵא יִצְחָק לָשׂוּחַ בַּשָּׂדֶה
סד לִפְנוֹת עָרֶב וַיִּשָּׂא עֵינָיו וַיַּרְא וְהִנֵּה גְמַלִּים בָּאִים: וַתִּשָּׂא רִבְקָה אֶת־עֵינֶיהָ
סה וַתֵּרֶא אֶת־יִצְחָק וַתִּפֹּל מֵעַל הַגָּמָל: וַתֹּאמֶר אֶל־הָעֶבֶד מִי־הָאִישׁ הַלָּזֶה

---

cherished by your husband as a result of your good conduct, so that only through you will the blessing given by God to Abraham (*Your seed shall possess the gates of his enemies;* 22:17) be fulfilled, and not through another wife.

61. **וַיִּקַּח הָעֶבֶד אֶת רִבְקָה** — *The servant took Rebecca.* Eliezer, as the agent of Isaac (the husband), took her into his custody, from the agent of her father. In this manner she now becomes wedded to Isaac, hence she is now Eliezer's mistress and he is her servant.

62. **בָּא מִבּוֹא בְּאֵר לַחַי רֹאִי** — *Came from having gone to Be'er-Lahai-Ro'i . . .* to pray in the place where Hagar's prayer had been heard (16:14). But before he even prayed his prayer had already been answered and his wife was approaching, as we read, טֶרֶם יִקְרָאוּ וַאֲנִי אֶעֱנֶה, *Before they call I will answer (Isaiah* 65:24).

וְהוּא יוֹשֵׁב בְּאֶרֶץ הַנֶּגֶב — *For he dwelt in the land of the South.* Isaac was still living to the south of Be'er-Lahai-Ro'i (with his father) and did not establish his residence there at that time (until later, see 25:11).

63. **וַיֵּצֵא יִצְחָק לָשׂוּחַ בַּשָּׂדֶה** — *And Isaac went out to supplicate in the field.* He turned away from the public path so as not to be interrupted by wayfarers, and went into the field to pray, even though he had already prayed in Be'er-Lahai-Ro'i. But before he prayed he was answered, similar to, מִן הַיּוֹם הָרִאשׁוֹן אֲשֶׁר נָתַתָּ אֶת לִבְּךָ לְהָבִין וּלְהִתְעַנּוֹת . . . נִשְׁמְעוּ דְבָרֶיךָ, *From the first day that you set your heart to understand and humble yourself . . . your words were heard (Daniel* 10:12).

וְהִנֵּה גְמַלִּים בָּאִים — *And behold there were camels coming.* When he went forth to meditate (pray) his direction took him toward them (Eliezer and Rebecca), as it states הַהֹלֵךְ בַּשָּׂדֶה לִקְרָאתֵנוּ, *that walks in the field to meet us* (v. 65). When Isaac returned home from Be'er-Lehai-Ro'i he traveled from north to south; those who were coming from Haran to Abraham's house traveled from east to west. When Isaac turned away from the road, going north-south, he went eastward which brought him toward the caravan conveying Rebecca, who thought that he was coming to welcome her.

64. **וַתִּפֹּל מֵעַל הַגָּמָל** — *She inclined while upon the camel.* She bowed her head to Isaac from her seat on the camel, as a sign of respect. This is similar to the episode of Naaman, וַיִּפֹּל מֵעַל הַמֶּרְכָּבָה לִקְרָאתוֹ, *He alighted from the chariot to meet him (II Kings* 5:21).

NOTES

mother of thousands, of ten thousands. They were not giving her a blessing. They were rather urging her to conduct herself in such a manner that she be worthy of God's blessings!

61. **וַיִּקַּח הָעֶבֶד אֶת רִבְקָה** — *The servant took Rebecca.* The Torah refers to Eliezer as אִישׁ, *man,* the majority of the time, in relating the story of his efforts to arrange the match between Isaac and Rebecca. Still, in this verse the term אִישׁ suddenly changes to that of עֶבֶד — i.e., *and she followed the 'man,' and the*

הַהֹלֵךְ בַּשָּׂדֶה לִקְרָאתֵנוּ וַיֹּאמֶר הָעֶבֶד הוּא אֲדֹנִי וַתִּקַּח הַצָּעִיף וַתִּתְכָּס׃
סו־סז וַיְסַפֵּר הָעֶבֶד לְיִצְחָק אֵת כָּל־הַדְּבָרִים אֲשֶׁר עָשָׂה׃ וַיְבִאֶהָ יִצְחָק הָאֹהֱלָה
שָׂרָה אִמּוֹ וַיִּקַּח אֶת־רִבְקָה וַתְּהִי־לוֹ לְאִשָּׁה וַיֶּאֱהָבֶהָ וַיִּנָּחֵם יִצְחָק אַחֲרֵי
אִמּוֹ׃

כה ששי א־ב וַיֹּסֶף אַבְרָהָם וַיִּקַּח אִשָּׁה וּשְׁמָהּ קְטוּרָה׃ וַתֵּלֶד לוֹ אֶת־זִמְרָן וְאֶת־יָקְשָׁן
ג וְאֶת־מְדָן וְאֶת־מִדְיָן וְאֶת־יִשְׁבָּק וְאֶת־שׁוּחַ׃ וְיָקְשָׁן יָלַד אֶת־שְׁבָא וְאֶת־
ד דְּדָן וּבְנֵי דְדָן הָיוּ אַשּׁוּרִם וּלְטוּשִׁים וּלְאֻמִּים׃ וּבְנֵי מִדְיָן עֵיפָה וָעֵפֶר וַחֲנֹךְ
ה וַאֲבִידָע וְאֶלְדָּעָה כָּל־אֵלֶּה בְּנֵי קְטוּרָה׃ וַיִּתֵּן אַבְרָהָם אֶת־כָּל־אֲשֶׁר־לוֹ
ו לְיִצְחָק׃ וְלִבְנֵי הַפִּילַגְשִׁים אֲשֶׁר לְאַבְרָהָם נָתַן אַבְרָהָם מַתָּנֹת וַיְשַׁלְּחֵם
ז מֵעַל יִצְחָק בְּנוֹ בְּעוֹדֶנּוּ חַי קֵדְמָה אֶל־אֶרֶץ קֶדֶם׃ וְאֵלֶּה יְמֵי שְׁנֵי־חַיֵּי
ח אַבְרָהָם אֲשֶׁר־חָי מְאַת שָׁנָה וְשִׁבְעִים שָׁנָה וְחָמֵשׁ שָׁנִים׃ וַיִּגְוַע וַיָּמָת

---

65. וַתִּתְכָּס — *And covered herself* . . . because she was afraid to look (upon Isaac), as we find, וַיַּסְתֵּר מֹשֶׁה פָּנָיו, *And Moses hid his face* (*Exodus* 3:6).

67. וַיִּנָּחֵם יִצְחָק אַחֲרֵי אִמּוֹ — *And Isaac was comforted after his mother.* Until now he could not be comforted, for he had loved and respected his mother so much.

XXV

2. וַתֵּלֶד לוֹ אֶת זִמְרָן — *And she bore him Zimran.* She brought them up in his house, but they were not his children, similar to חֲמֵשֶׁת בְּנֵי מִיכַל . . . אֲשֶׁר יָלְדָה לְעַדְרִיאֵל, *The five sons of Michal, whom she bore to Adriel* (*II Samuel* 21:8), which also means she brought them up, but they were not her children. Abraham only begot two, Isaac and Ishmael, as it is recorded, בְּנֵי אַבְרָהָם יִצְחָק וְיִשְׁמָעֵאל, *The sons of Abraham — Isaac and Ishmael* (whereas Zimran et al. are recorded as בְּנֵי קְטוּרָה, *The children of Keturah — I Chronicles* 1:28, 32).

6. נָתַן אַבְרָהָם מַתָּנֹת — *Abraham gave gifts.* These were given not as an inheritance (but a gift) so that it be legal and binding (at once).

בְּעוֹדֶנּוּ חַי — *While he was still alive.* He did not rely upon a will or a disposition of property by testament.

NOTES

'servant' took Rebecca. The answer given by the *Sforno* is that until Rebecca is taken by Eliezer as Isaac's wife, his relationship to her is simply that of אִישׁ, *a man;* however, once he, as Isaac's agent, takes her into the domain of the husband she now becomes Eliezer's mistress (as the wife of his master) and his status vis-a-vis Rebecca is that of an עֶבֶד, *a servant.*

65. וַתִּתְכָּס — *And covered herself.* Isaac was an עוֹלָה תְמִימָה, *an offering to God without blemish.* His piety and sanctity of being was such that his appearance inspired awe and reverence in others. The impact made by him upon Rebecca was similar to that of God's appearance in the burning bush upon Moses.

XXV

2. וַתֵּלֶד לוֹ אֶת זִמְרָן — *And she bore him Zimran.* To prove that the word וַתֵּלֶד need not mean *she gave birth* but *she raised,* the *Sforno* cites the verse in *II Samuel* where five sons of Michal the daughter of Saul are mentioned, which perforce must be translated *to raise* since Michal had no children of her own.

6. נָתַן אַבְרָהָם מַתָּנֹת — *Abraham gave gifts.* The Mishnah in *Baba Basra* (12b) teaches us that if a man gives property to any of his children as a gift, in his lifetime, it is valid — providing he does not call it 'an inheritance.' This Abraham did with the children of the concubines.

ט אַבְרָהָם בְּשֵׂיבָה טוֹבָה זָקֵן וְשָׂבֵעַ וַיֵּאָסֶף אֶל־עַמָּיו: וַיִּקְבְּרוּ אֹתוֹ יִצְחָק
וְיִשְׁמָעֵאל בָּנָיו אֶל־מְעָרַת הַמַּכְפֵּלָה אֶל־שְׂדֵה עֶפְרֹן בֶּן־צֹחַר הַחִתִּי אֲשֶׁר
י עַל־פְּנֵי מַמְרֵא: הַשָּׂדֶה אֲשֶׁר־קָנָה אַבְרָהָם מֵאֵת בְּנֵי־חֵת שָׁמָּה קֻבַּר
יא אַבְרָהָם וְשָׂרָה אִשְׁתּוֹ: וַיְהִי אַחֲרֵי מוֹת אַבְרָהָם וַיְבָרֶךְ אֱלֹהִים אֶת־יִצְחָק
בְּנוֹ וַיֵּשֶׁב יִצְחָק עִם־בְּאֵר לַחַי רֹאִי:
שביעי יב וְאֵלֶּה תֹּלְדֹת יִשְׁמָעֵאל בֶּן־אַבְרָהָם אֲשֶׁר יָלְדָה הָגָר הַמִּצְרִית שִׁפְחַת
יג שָׂרָה לְאַבְרָהָם: וְאֵלֶּה שְׁמוֹת בְּנֵי יִשְׁמָעֵאל בִּשְׁמֹתָם לְתוֹלְדֹתָם בְּכֹר
יד-טו יִשְׁמָעֵאל נְבָיֹת וְקֵדָר וְאַדְבְּאֵל וּמִבְשָׂם: וּמִשְׁמָע וְדוּמָה וּמַשָּׂא: חֲדַד
מפטיר טז וְתֵימָא יְטוּר נָפִישׁ וָקֵדְמָה: אֵלֶּה הֵם בְּנֵי יִשְׁמָעֵאל וְאֵלֶּה שְׁמֹתָם
יז בְּחַצְרֵיהֶם וּבְטִירֹתָם שְׁנֵים־עָשָׂר נְשִׂיאִם לְאֻמֹּתָם: וְאֵלֶּה שְׁנֵי חַיֵּי
יִשְׁמָעֵאל מְאַת שָׁנָה וּשְׁלֹשִׁים שָׁנָה וְשֶׁבַע שָׁנִים וַיִּגְוַע וַיָּמָת וַיֵּאָסֶף
יח אֶל־עַמָּיו: וַיִּשְׁכְּנוּ מֵחֲוִילָה עַד־שׁוּר אֲשֶׁר עַל־פְּנֵי מִצְרַיִם בֹּאֲכָה אַשּׁוּרָה
עַל־פְּנֵי כָל־אֶחָיו נָפָל:

---

8. וְשָׂבֵעַ — *and content.* He saw all the desires of his heart fulfilled, and was satisfied with all he wished to see and do.

וַיֵּאָסֶף אֶל עַמָּיו — *And was gathered to his people.* He was gathered into the bond of eternal life together with the righteous of all generations who, being like him in that respect, were his people. The word עַמָּיו is in the plural, however, to indicate that even the righteous are on different levels, even though they all merit the eternal life, as our Sages teach us, שֶׁכָּל אֶחָד וְאֶחָד נִכְוָה מֵחֻפָּתוֹ שֶׁל חֲבֵירוֹ, *Each one will be burned by reason of his envy of the superior canopy of his fellow (Baba Basra* 75a).

NOTES

8. וַיֵּאָסֶף אֶל עַמָּיו — *And was gathered to his people.* The expression *to his people* is a bit difficult to understand. Who are *his people,* since it cannot mean his ancestors who were far from being righteous? The *Sforno* answers that in the generations preceding Abraham there *were* righteous men and in that respect they are called *his people,* even though they may not have reached Abraham's level of wisdom, piety and spirituality. Our Sages tell us that in the world to come, each righteous person will be given a canopy, where he shall 'dwell,' according to his rank. These canopies will not be equal, hence there will be envy among them. This lesson of the Talmud is brought by the *Sforno* to prove that there are different levels of the righteous, even in the bond of eternal life.

פרשת תולדות
Parashas Toldos

יט־כ וְאֵלֶּה תּוֹלְדֹת יִצְחָק בֶּן־אַבְרָהָם אַבְרָהָם הוֹלִיד אֶת־יִצְחָק׃ וַיְהִי יִצְחָק בֶּן־
אַרְבָּעִים שָׁנָה בְּקַחְתּוֹ אֶת־רִבְקָה בַּת־בְּתוּאֵל הָאֲרַמִּי מִפַּדַּן אֲרָם אֲחוֹת
כא לָבָן הָאֲרַמִּי לוֹ לְאִשָּׁה׃ וַיֶּעְתַּר יִצְחָק לַיהוה לְנֹכַח אִשְׁתּוֹ כִּי עֲקָרָה הִוא
כב וַיֵּעָתֶר לוֹ יהוה וַתַּהַר רִבְקָה אִשְׁתּוֹ׃ וַיִּתְרֹצֲצוּ הַבָּנִים בְּקִרְבָּהּ וַתֹּאמֶר
°גּוֹיִם ק׳ כג אִם־כֵּן לָמָּה זֶּה אָנֹכִי וַתֵּלֶךְ לִדְרֹשׁ אֶת־יהוה׃ וַיֹּאמֶר יהוה לָהּ שְׁנֵי °גיים

---

19. וְאֵלֶּה תּוֹלְדֹת יִצְחָק — *And these are the offspring of Isaac* . . . the events to which his days gave birth (i.e., the historical events of his life).

אַבְרָהָם הוֹלִיד אֶת יִצְחָק — *Abraham begot Isaac.* He (Isaac) alone is considered the seed of Abraham.

20. אֲחוֹת לָבָן הָאֲרַמִּי — *The sister of Laban the Aramean.* From her Esau was born. (He) resembled his mother's brother.

21. לְנֹכַח אִשְׁתּוֹ — *Opposite his wife (for his wife).* Even though he had been assured children, he prayed to God that it be from this worthy woman who stood opposite him.

22. וַתֹּאמֶר אִם כֵּן — *And she said, 'If so.'* Since they are struggling (within her) and there is the possibility that one will die, I will be in danger at the time of birth, as often happens when a dead infant is delivered.

לָמָּה זֶּה אָנֹכִי — *Why am I thus?* Why did my family so desire that the children of

NOTES

19. וְאֵלֶּה תּוֹלְדֹת יִצְחָק — *And these are the offspring of Isaac.* The *Sforno* departs from *Rashi's* interpretation of this verse. Whereas the word תּוֹלְדוֹת is explained by *Rashi* as referring to Jacob and Esau the offspring of Isaac, the *Sforno* translates it as meaning the 'life story' of Isaac, the events which represent the offspring of his activities, just as children are one's offspring.

אַבְרָהָם הוֹלִיד אֶת יִצְחָק — *Abraham begot Isaac.* This second part of the verse is explained by *Rashi* as refuting the canard that Isaac was not the child of Abraham but of Abimelech (based on the Talmud, *Baba Metzia* 87). The *Sforno* gives a simple answer to the question: why does the Torah have to state *Abraham begot Isaac,* since we are told that Isaac was the son of Abraham? This is meant to tell us that only Isaac is considered to be the true and worthy seed of Abraham, akin to, כִּי בְיִצְחָק יִקָּרֵא לְךָ זָרַע, *for in Isaac shall seed be called to you* (21:12), i.e., Isaac and not Ishmael, even though he is also the son of Abraham.

20. אֲחוֹת לָבָן הָאֲרַמִּי – *The sister of Laban the Aramean.* Here again *Sforno* differs from *Rashi.* Whereas *Rashi* explains that the reason the Torah tells us, once again, that Rebecca is the sister of Laban is to praise her piety even though she was raised in such an evil household, the *Sforno* interprets the phrase as explaining how two such *tzaddikim* as Isaac and Rebecca could have given birth to a son such as Esau. The answer is that her brother was Laban and our Rabbis teach us, 'Most sons are like their mother's brother' (*Baba Basra* 110b). This interpretation may well answer the question *Rashi* poses in 28:5 where the Torah tells us, . . . *and he went* . . . *to Laban the brother of Rebecca, the mother of Jacob and Esau. Rashi* comments, 'I do not know what this comes to teach us.' However using the *Sforno's* interpretation here the answer might well be that the Torah is telling us how it is possible for a woman like Rebecca to be the mother of both a Jacob and an Esau — because she had a brother Laban!

21. לְנֹכַח אִשְׁתּוֹ – *Opposite his wife (for his wife).* Isaac was assured of children after the *Akeidah,* his binding — (see *Perek* 22:17), hence his prayer cannot be to *have* children; the question is only through whom? He prays that it be from pious Rebecca.

22. וַתֹּאמֶר אִם כֵּן – *And she said, 'If so'.* She, in turn, although desirous to have Isaac's children, did not want to do so at the price of her own life. She had no objection to his

בְּבִטְנֵךְ וּשְׁנֵי לְאֻמִּים מִמֵּעַיִךְ יִפָּרֵדוּ וּלְאֹם מִלְאֹם יֶאֱמָץ וְרַב יַעֲבֹד צָעִיר׃
כד־כה וַיִּמְלְאוּ יָמֶיהָ לָלֶדֶת וְהִנֵּה תוֹמִם בְּבִטְנָהּ׃ וַיֵּצֵא הָרִאשׁוֹן אַדְמוֹנִי כֻּלּוֹ
כו כְּאַדֶּרֶת שֵׂעָר וַיִּקְרְאוּ שְׁמוֹ עֵשָׂו׃ וְאַחֲרֵי־כֵן יָצָא אָחִיו וְיָדוֹ אֹחֶזֶת בַּעֲקֵב
כז עֵשָׂו וַיִּקְרָא שְׁמוֹ יַעֲקֹב וְיִצְחָק בֶּן־שִׁשִּׁים שָׁנָה בְּלֶדֶת אֹתָם׃ וַיִּגְדְּלוּ
הַנְּעָרִים וַיְהִי עֵשָׂו אִישׁ יֹדֵעַ צַיִד אִישׁ שָׂדֶה וְיַעֲקֹב אִישׁ תָּם יֹשֵׁב אֹהָלִים׃

Isaac be born through me, as it is written, *Be thou the mother of thousands and tens of thousands* (24:60) and why did my husband pray that I bear his children?

23. שְׁנֵי גוֹיִם בְּבִטְנֵךְ — *Two nations are in your womb.* The cause of the struggling within you is because they are destined to be two nations with opposing ideas of religion.

וּשְׁנֵי לְאֻמִּים — *And two peoples.* They will also be two peoples who have opposing ideas of nationalism.

מִמֵּעַיִךְ יִפָּרֵדוּ — *Shall be separated from your insides.* Neither will die due to their struggling.

24. וְהִנֵּה תוֹמִם בְּבִטְנָהּ — *Behold, there were twins in her womb.* Those who were assisting with the birth recognized, even before the actual birth, that twins were being delivered, and when the first to be born proved to be covered as with a hairy mantle, they realized that his birth should have been more difficult and later than that of the smooth one, therefore they called his name עֵשָׂו (Esau) (as though to say) his brother did it by forcing him out first (עֵשָׂו related to עשוי, i.e., the efforts exerted by the other infant forced him out).

26. וַיִּקְרָא שְׁמוֹ יַעֲקֹב — *So he named him* (lit., *called his name) Jacob.* (From the root עקב, *the end*, i.e., he will remain at the end.) This was indicated by the fact that his hand held on to his brother's heel. Our Sages tell us that God gave him this name (Jacob) to show that he will survive after the destruction of all the nations, as it is written, כִּי אֶעֱשֶׂה כָלָה בְּכָל הַגּוֹיִם . . . וְאֹתְךָ לֹא אֶעֱשֶׂה כָלָה, *For I will make a full end of all the nations . . . but I will not make a full end of you (Jeremiah* 46:28).

27. אִישׁ שָׂדֶה — *A man of the field . . .* a man skilled in working the earth.

יֹשֵׁב אֹהָלִים — *Abiding in tents . . .* two kinds of tents, one the tent of a shepherd and the second a non-folding tent of meditation where he learned to know his Maker and to become sanctified in His glory.

NOTES

taking another wife, as did his father, and to build his family with her. This explains the phrase לָמָּה זֶּה אָנֹכִי, *why me* — let it be with another that G-d's promise be fulfilled.

23. שְׁנֵי גוֹיִם בְּבִטְנֵךְ – *Two nations are in your womb.* The Torah uses two terms — גּוֹיִם, *nations*, and לְאֻמִּים, *peoples.* The first refers to a community of faith, the second to a political, national entity.

26. וַיִּקְרָא שְׁמוֹ יַעֲקֹב – *So he named him* (lit., *called his name) Jacob.* The name 'Jacob' is given by the Almighty. That is why the word וַיִּקְרָא, *and he called*, is in the singular, as opposed to וַיִּקְרְאוּ, *and they called*, in the plural, regarding Esau. The root of the name is עָקֵב, which means *heel* but also means *the end*, referring to the end of time when Jacob will prevail. G-d Himself assures us that Jacob and his children will survive all other nations.

27. יֹשֵׁב אֹהָלִים – *Abiding in tents.* The word used is אֹהָלִים, *tents*, in the plural. A man normally resides in one tent, not two. *Rashi* explains that it refers to the tents of Shem and

כח-כט וַיֶּאֱהַב יִצְחָק אֶת־עֵשָׂו כִּי־צַיִד בְּפִיו וְרִבְקָה אֹהֶבֶת אֶת־יַעֲקֹב׃ וַיָּזֶד יַעֲקֹב
ל נָזִיד וַיָּבֹא עֵשָׂו מִן־הַשָּׂדֶה וְהוּא עָיֵף׃ וַיֹּאמֶר עֵשָׂו אֶל־יַעֲקֹב הַלְעִיטֵנִי נָא
לא מִן־הָאָדֹם הָאָדֹם הַזֶּה כִּי עָיֵף אָנֹכִי עַל־כֵּן קָרָא־שְׁמוֹ אֱדוֹם׃ וַיֹּאמֶר יַעֲקֹב
לב מִכְרָה כַיּוֹם אֶת־בְּכֹרָתְךָ לִי׃ וַיֹּאמֶר עֵשָׂו הִנֵּה אָנֹכִי הוֹלֵךְ לָמוּת וְלָמָּה־זֶּה
לג לִי בְּכֹרָה׃ וַיֹּאמֶר יַעֲקֹב הִשָּׁבְעָה לִּי כַּיּוֹם וַיִּשָּׁבַע לוֹ וַיִּמְכֹּר אֶת־בְּכֹרָתוֹ
לד לְיַעֲקֹב׃ וְיַעֲקֹב נָתַן לְעֵשָׂו לֶחֶם וּנְזִיד עֲדָשִׁים וַיֹּאכַל וַיֵּשְׁתְּ וַיָּקָם וַיֵּלַךְ וַיִּבֶז

---

28. וַיֶּאֱהַב יִצְחָק אֶת עֵשָׂו — *Now Isaac loved Esau ... also* Esau; even though he certainly knew that he was not as perfect as Jacob.

וְרִבְקָה אֹהֶבֶת אֶת יַעֲקֹב — *But Rebecca loved Jacob ...* for she recognized the wickedness of Esau.

30. עַל כֵּן קָרָא שְׁמוֹ אֱדוֹם — *Therefore was his name called Edom* (lit., *Red*). When they saw that Esau was totally committed to coarse meaningless labors not befitting civilized man, to the extent that he was incapable of even recognizing the lentils as such, (knowing only) their color (not their name), they called him אֱדוֹם. This word is to be understood as an imperative: 'Be red by the pottage you swallow.'

31. מִכְרָה כַיּוֹם — *Sell as this day.* As your time is wholly occupied with your labors (hunting) in such a manner that you are so tired you cannot even identify a pottage of lentils, then doubtless you will not be able to occupy yourself with the responsibilities of the birthright, to serve God as befits a firstborn.

32. הוֹלֵךְ לָמוּת — *I am going to die ...* through weariness and fatigue.

33. הִשָּׁבְעָה לִּי — *Swear to me.* Since the transaction involved nothing concrete it was necessary to swear, for there could be no *act* of purchase.

וַיִּמְכֹּר אֶת בְּכֹרָתוֹ — *And he sold his birthright ...* for the price agreed to, even though the Torah does not reveal it explicitly.

34. וְיַעֲקֹב נָתַן לְעֵשָׂו — *And Jacob gave Esau (bread and lentils).* The lentils, or the vessel in which they were cooked, was used as the means of exchange (חֲלִיפִין) as we find, שָׁלַף אִישׁ נַעֲלוֹ וְנָתַן לְרֵעֵהוּ, *One would draw off his shoe and give it to his friend (Ruth* 4:7).

NOTES

Eber, tents of study. The *Sforno* feels that this would be redundant, therefore he interprets it to mean that one was for Jacob's work as a shepherd while the second was for study and meditation.

30. עַל כֵּן קָרָא שְׁמוֹ אֱדוֹם – *Therefore was his name called Edom* (lit., *Red*). When Esau was born he was אַדְמוֹנִי, *red complexioned.* Hence the name אֱדוֹם was not a new appellation given to him now when he demanded to be fed *'this red food.'* The *Sforno* therefore interprets the phrase *therefore was his name called red* (אֱדוֹם) as meaning, 'be red by the pottage you swallow' and as a result everyone now called him אֱדוֹם, *Red.*

31. מִכְרָה כַיּוֹם – *Sell as this day.* The key word is כַיּוֹם, *as the day,* which the *Sforno* understands as *this* day. The experience of 'this day' demonstrates that Esau's interests in life are such as to preclude any serious desire for the spiritual service which the birthright demanded. Our Rabbis tell us that the lentils were prepared as a meal of condolence, for Abraham had died that day. The fact that Esau is so insensitive to this tragic event and is concerned only for his hunting and the satisfaction of his appetites underlines his unworthiness to be the *bechor* (firstborn).

33-34. הִשָּׁבְעָה לִּי ... וְיַעֲקֹב נָתַן לְעֵשָׂו — *Swear to me ... And Jacob gave Esau (bread and lentils).* According to *halachah* every transaction that entails transfer of ownership requires a *kinyan* (an act of purchase) which varies,

עֵשָׂו אֶת־הַבְּכֹרָה׃

כו א וַיְהִי רָעָב בָּאָרֶץ מִלְּבַד הָרָעָב הָרִאשׁוֹן אֲשֶׁר הָיָה בִּימֵי אַבְרָהָם וַיֵּלֶךְ
ב יִצְחָק אֶל־אֲבִימֶלֶךְ מֶלֶךְ־פְּלִשְׁתִּים גְּרָרָה׃ וַיֵּרָא אֵלָיו יהוה וַיֹּאמֶר אַל־
ג תֵּרֵד מִצְרָיְמָה שְׁכֹן בָּאָרֶץ אֲשֶׁר אֹמַר אֵלֶיךָ׃ גּוּר בָּאָרֶץ הַזֹּאת וְאֶהְיֶה
עִמְּךָ וַאֲבָרְכֶךָּ כִּי־לְךָ וּלְזַרְעֲךָ אֶתֵּן אֶת־כָּל־הָאֲרָצֹת הָאֵל וַהֲקִמֹתִי אֶת־

וַיִּבֶז עֵשָׂו אֶת הַבְּכֹרָה — *Thus Esau spurned the birthright.* In Esau's eyes the birthright was not worth the price Jacob set, even after the sale; hence the seller was not deceived for to him it had little value.

XXVI

1. אֲשֶׁר הָיָה בִּימֵי אַבְרָהָם — *That was in the days of Abraham.* From the time (of Abraham) until now, there had been no famine so severe as to compel the inhabitants of the land to leave, as Abraham did (in his time).

וַיֵּלֶךְ יִצְחָק אֶל אֲבִימֶלֶךְ — *And Isaac went to Abimelech* ... as a courtesy, to ask permission of him to leave his land due to the famine.

2. אַל תֵּרֵד מִצְרָיְמָה — *Do not descend to Egypt.* Do not let the lack of pasture persuade you to go there (i.e., Egypt), as we find (regarding the sons of Jacob), *for there is no pasture for your servants' flocks* (47:4).

שְׁכֹן בָּאָרֶץ אֲשֶׁר אֹמַר אֵלֶיךָ — *Dwell in the land that I shall indicate to you.* Set up shepherd's tents for your flocks and cattle in the place where I tell you to dwell (i.e., here in Gerar), for your flocks will also be successful here. (This assurance is given) since the reason he planned to leave was because of the lack of pasture.

3. גּוּר בָּאָרֶץ הַזֹּאת — *Reside in this land.* Reside in this land (of Canaan).

וְאֶהְיֶה עִמְּךָ וַאֲבָרְכֶךָּ — *And I will be with you and bless you.* Even though there is a

NOTES

depending upon the property being sold or given. To sell the birthright is to transfer rights and responsibilities which have value but no substance until one actually inherits. An oath, however, can be taken and is valid even for דָּבָר שֶׁלֹּא בָא לְעוֹלָם, *that which is not yet in this world.* For this reason Jacob asks Esau to swear. In addition, they also make a *sale of exchange* which is done with a סודר, *a handkerchief,* vessel or any article. The *Sforno,* therefore, suggests that this could have been the role played by the lentils themselves, or the container in which they were cooked, as the means of exchange. This would consummate the deal for which a specific price had been agreed to, willingly, by both parties, and not under duress of hunger and fatigue.

XXVI

1. אֲשֶׁר הָיָה בִּימֵי אַבְרָהָם וַיֵּלֶךְ יִצְחָק אֶל אֲבִימֶלֶךְ — *That was in the days of Abraham, and Isaac went to Abimelech.* There is no need to mention the famine in the days of Abraham, unless it is to underscore the severity of this famine, which was sufficiently serious and exceptional that it caused people to leave, as it had forced Abraham to go down to Egypt in his time. Isaac, who always looked upon his father as a role model, therefore planned to do the same. Since that was his intent, then the reason to go first to Abimelech was as a courtesy, to take leave of him.

2-3. שְׁכֹן בָּאָרֶץ אֲשֶׁר אֹמַר אֵלֶיךָ גּוּר בָּאָרֶץ הַזֹּאת — *Dwell in the land that I shall indicate to you. Reside in this land.* The two words used in these verses — שְׁכֹן and גּוּר — are interpreted by the *Sforno* as applicable to different categories. The first refers to *dwelling* in shepherd's tents (which is a temporary abode) while the second is the more permanent term, referring to one's residence.

3. וְאֶהְיֶה עִמְּךָ וַאֲבָרְכֶךָּ — *And I will be with you and bless you.* God's assurances to Isaac are

ד הַשְּׁבֻעָה אֲשֶׁר נִשְׁבַּעְתִּי לְאַבְרָהָם אָבִיךָ: וְהִרְבֵּיתִי אֶת־זַרְעֲךָ כְּכוֹכְבֵי
הַשָּׁמַיִם וְנָתַתִּי לְזַרְעֲךָ אֵת כָּל־הָאֲרָצֹת הָאֵל וְהִתְבָּרְכוּ בְזַרְעֲךָ כֹּל גּוֹיֵי
ה הָאָרֶץ: עֵקֶב אֲשֶׁר־שָׁמַע אַבְרָהָם בְּקֹלִי וַיִּשְׁמֹר מִשְׁמַרְתִּי מִצְוֹתַי חֻקּוֹתַי
שני ו־ז וְתוֹרֹתָי: וַיֵּשֶׁב יִצְחָק בִּגְרָר: וַיִּשְׁאֲלוּ אַנְשֵׁי הַמָּקוֹם לְאִשְׁתּוֹ וַיֹּאמֶר אֲחֹתִי

---

lack of pasture now in Canaan, I shall be with you and you will have no lack of pasture.

וַאֲבָרְכֶךָּ — *And bless you* . . . with money and cattle (here), but not outside the land (of Canaan).

כִּי לְךָ וּלְזַרְעֲךָ אֶתֵּן אֶת כָּל הָאֲרָצֹת הָאֵל וַהֲקִמֹתִי אֶת הַשְּׁבֻעָה — *For to you and your offspring will I give all these lands and establish the oath.* The reason I tell you to reside in this land whereby I will do good for you, is because I gave an oath to Abraham to grant him and his descendants this land, therefore by living here you will be a prince in their midst and take possession of it, so as to transmit it (through inheritance) to your children.

5. עֵקֶב אֲשֶׁר שָׁמַע אַבְרָהָם בְּקֹלִי — *Because Abraham hearkened to My voice* . . . to all that I commanded him.

וַיִּשְׁמֹר מִשְׁמַרְתִּי — *And safeguarded My charge.* He constantly kept My special charge which is to do kindness, as it says, כָּל אָרְחוֹת ה׳ חֶסֶד וֶאֱמֶת, *All the paths of God are mercy and truth* (*Psalms* 25:10), and to teach sinners the correct way. This he did when he *called upon the Name of God*. He also kept . . .

מִצְוֹתַי חֻקּוֹתַי וְתוֹרֹתָי — *My commandments, My statutes, and My laws* . . . which were commanded to the 'sons of Noah,' thereby practicing what he taught and acting as a model to others. We see here that the merit of others is invoked when (God) speaks to Isaac; also when He says, וְהִרְבֵּיתִי אֶת זַרְעֲךָ בַּעֲבוּר אַבְרָהָם עַבְדִּי, *I will multiply your seed for My servant Abraham* (v. 24). Not so with Jacob, and certainly not with Abraham. This, however, was *before* Isaac was inspired to call upon the Name of God, but after he did so it is written, וַאֲבִימֶלֶךְ הָלַךְ אֵלָיו מִגְּרָר,

NOTES

manifold. He promises pastureland for his cattle (וְאֶהְיֶה עִמְּךָ); wealth (וַאֲבָרְכֶךָּ) and the eventual possession of the land. So as not to forfeit his claim to the land, it is vital for Isaac to remain and establish his rights and strengthen his status as a prince in the midst of the populace.

5. עֵקֶב אֲשֶׁר שָׁמַע אַבְרָהָם בְּקֹלִי וַיִּשְׁמֹר מִשְׁמַרְתִּי מִצְוֹתַי חֻקּוֹתַי וְתוֹרֹתָי — *Because Abraham hearkened to My voice and safeguarded My charge, My commandments, My statutes, and My laws.* Multiple phrases are used in the verse, i.e., 'hearken,' 'safeguarding My charge,' My 'commandments,' 'statutes' and 'laws.' The commentators offer a number of interpretations to explain the variety of words depicting Abraham's observance and loyalty to the Almighty. The *Sforno* divides this verse into three parts: the specific commands given to Abraham by God (בְּקֹלִי); the seven Noahide commandments in general (מִצְוֹתַי חֻקּוֹתַי וְתוֹרֹתָי); and מִשְׁמַרְתִּי, *My charge.* The latter is interpreted by the *Sforno* as referring to God's special charge and unique responsibility, i.e., to exercise kindness and to instruct sinners how to return to the ways of truth. This was precisely what Abraham dedicated himself to, and as such he was *doing God's work* (as it were). This is the meaning of וַיִּשְׁמֹר מִשְׁמַרְתִּי, *Abraham kept and safeguarded My (God's) charge.*

מִצְוֹתַי חֻקּוֹתַי וְתוֹרֹתָי — *My commandments, My statutes, and My laws.* The *Sforno* makes a most important point in his commentary on this verse. Although זְכוּת אָבוֹת, *the merit of ancestors,* is a fundamental concept in our

הוּא כִּי יָרֵא לֵאמֹר אִשְׁתִּי פֶּן־יַהַרְגֻנִי אַנְשֵׁי הַמָּקוֹם עַל־רִבְקָה כִּי־טוֹבַת
ח מַרְאֶה הִוא: וַיְהִי כִּי־אָרְכוּ־לוֹ שָׁם הַיָּמִים וַיַּשְׁקֵף אֲבִימֶלֶךְ מֶלֶךְ פְּלִשְׁתִּים
ט בְּעַד הַחַלּוֹן וַיַּרְא וְהִנֵּה יִצְחָק מְצַחֵק אֵת רִבְקָה אִשְׁתּוֹ: וַיִּקְרָא אֲבִימֶלֶךְ
לְיִצְחָק וַיֹּאמֶר אַךְ הִנֵּה אִשְׁתְּךָ הִוא וְאֵיךְ אָמַרְתָּ אֲחֹתִי הִוא וַיֹּאמֶר אֵלָיו
י יִצְחָק כִּי אָמַרְתִּי פֶּן־אָמוּת עָלֶיהָ: וַיֹּאמֶר אֲבִימֶלֶךְ מַה־זֹּאת עָשִׂיתָ לָּנוּ
יא כִּמְעַט שָׁכַב אַחַד הָעָם אֶת־אִשְׁתֶּךָ וְהֵבֵאתָ עָלֵינוּ אָשָׁם: וַיְצַו אֲבִימֶלֶךְ
יב אֶת־כָּל־הָעָם לֵאמֹר הַנֹּגֵעַ בָּאִישׁ הַזֶּה וּבְאִשְׁתּוֹ מוֹת יוּמָת: וַיִּזְרַע יִצְחָק
שלישי יג בָּאָרֶץ הַהִוא וַיִּמְצָא בַּשָּׁנָה הַהִוא מֵאָה שְׁעָרִים וַיְבָרְכֵהוּ יהוה: וַיִּגְדַּל

Abimelech went to him from Gerar (v. 26), and said, רָאוֹ רָאִינוּ כִּי הָיָה ה׳ עִמָּךְ . . . אַתָּה עַתָּה בְּרוּךְ ה׳, *We saw that God is with you . . . you are now the blessed of God* (vs. 28-29), and he no longer experienced the hardships of envy and quarrels as he had previously. Jacob, however, never had to depend upon the merits of others, for from his youth he dwelled in the tents of Shem and Eber, studying and teaching knowledge (of God) to the people, who doubtless came (to these tents) to seek God.

10. כִּמְעַט שָׁכַב אַחַד הָעָם — *One of the people has nearly lain.* (אַחַד) refers to the king who is singular among his people; he never thought it was necessary to ask your opinion or desire regarding (Rebecca) for doubtless, considering his exalted position, you would be satisfied to have him marry your sister.

וְהֵבֵאתָ עָלֵינוּ אָשָׁם — *And you have brought guilt upon us* . . . and (by your concealment of her status) you almost brought guilt and punishment upon (all of) us. He said עָלֵינוּ, *all of us*, for when the leader of the generation (the king) is punished, great harm also befalls those who dwell under his protective (rule).

12. וַיִּזְרַע יִצְחָק בָּאָרֶץ הַהִוא — *Isaac sowed in that land.* As God had said to him, *'Reside in this land'* (verse 3).

מֵאָה שְׁעָרִים — *A hundredfold* . . . as He had promised, *'And I will be with you and bless you'* (ibid.).

וַיְבָרְכֵהוּ ה׳ — *And God blessed him* . . . with wealth, for he sold his produce at a high price. (And) according to what our Sages tell us that 'this computation was made for the sake of tithing' (*Bereishis Rabbah* 64), this in turn granted him a blessing, as it is written: הָבִיאוּ אֶת כָּל הַמַּעֲשֵׂר אֶל בֵּית הָאוֹצָר . . . וַהֲרִיקֹתִי לָכֶם בְּרָכָה עַד בְּלִי דָי, *Bring the whole tithe into the storehouse . . . and I will pour out a blessing to you that will be more than sufficient* (*Malachi* 3:10).

NOTES

faith, it is only invoked regarding Isaac, among the three patriarchs. Abraham, as the son of Terach, certainly had to develop his own merits, while Jacob had no need for the merit of fathers since he, like his grandfather, proclaimed the name of God and taught it to others. Isaac, however, practiced his faith in private and as such needed the merit of Abraham (as we see in this verse and verse 24) for his own preservation, and to insure his future. However once he *calls upon the Name of God*, he is worthy on his own to be blessed by God (verses 28-29).

12. וַיְבָרְכֵהוּ ה׳ — *And God blessed him.* The word וַיְבָרְכֵהוּ is in addition to the previous phrase, *and found, that year, a hundredfold;* hence it must mean an added blessing of money, not only the produce of the land. The amount recorded (a hundred) is used to denote that ten percent of this produce was given by Isaac to *tzedakah* (charity). The Torah, by

יד הָאִישׁ וַיֵּלֶךְ הָלוֹךְ וְגָדֵל עַד כִּי־גָדַל מְאֹד: וַיְהִי־לוֹ מִקְנֵה־צֹאן וּמִקְנֵה בָקָר
טו וַעֲבֻדָּה רַבָּה וַיְקַנְאוּ אֹתוֹ פְּלִשְׁתִּים: וְכָל־הַבְּאֵרֹת אֲשֶׁר חָפְרוּ עַבְדֵי אָבִיו
טז בִּימֵי אַבְרָהָם אָבִיו סִתְּמוּם פְּלִשְׁתִּים וַיְמַלְאוּם עָפָר: וַיֹּאמֶר אֲבִימֶלֶךְ אֶל־
יז יִצְחָק לֵךְ מֵעִמָּנוּ כִּי־עָצַמְתָּ מִמֶּנּוּ מְאֹד: וַיֵּלֶךְ מִשָּׁם יִצְחָק וַיִּחַן בְּנַחַל־גְּרָר
יח וַיֵּשֶׁב שָׁם: וַיָּשָׁב יִצְחָק וַיַּחְפֹּר | אֶת־בְּאֵרֹת הַמַּיִם אֲשֶׁר חָפְרוּ בִּימֵי
אַבְרָהָם אָבִיו וַיְסַתְּמוּם פְּלִשְׁתִּים אַחֲרֵי מוֹת אַבְרָהָם וַיִּקְרָא לָהֶן שֵׁמוֹת
יט כַּשֵּׁמֹת אֲשֶׁר־קָרָא לָהֶן אָבִיו: וַיַּחְפְּרוּ עַבְדֵי־יִצְחָק בַּנָּחַל וַיִּמְצְאוּ־שָׁם בְּאֵר
כ מַיִם חַיִּים: וַיָּרִיבוּ רֹעֵי גְרָר עִם־רֹעֵי יִצְחָק לֵאמֹר לָנוּ הַמָּיִם וַיִּקְרָא שֵׁם־
כא הַבְּאֵר עֵשֶׂק כִּי הִתְעַשְּׂקוּ עִמּוֹ: וַיַּחְפְּרוּ בְּאֵר אַחֶרֶת וַיָּרִיבוּ גַּם־עָלֶיהָ
כב וַיִּקְרָא שְׁמָהּ שִׂטְנָה: וַיַּעְתֵּק מִשָּׁם וַיַּחְפֹּר בְּאֵר אַחֶרֶת וְלֹא רָבוּ עָלֶיהָ
רביעי כג וַיִּקְרָא שְׁמָהּ רְחֹבוֹת וַיֹּאמֶר כִּי־עַתָּה הִרְחִיב יהוה לָנוּ וּפָרִינוּ בָאָרֶץ: וַיַּעַל
כד מִשָּׁם בְּאֵר שָׁבַע: וַיֵּרָא אֵלָיו יהוה בַּלַּיְלָה הַהוּא וַיֹּאמֶר אָנֹכִי אֱלֹהֵי
אַבְרָהָם אָבִיךָ אַל־תִּירָא כִּי־אִתְּךָ אָנֹכִי וּבֵרַכְתִּיךָ וְהִרְבֵּיתִי אֶת־זַרְעֲךָ
כה בַּעֲבוּר אַבְרָהָם עַבְדִּי: וַיִּבֶן שָׁם מִזְבֵּחַ וַיִּקְרָא בְּשֵׁם יהוה וַיֶּט־שָׁם אָהֳלוֹ
כו וַיִּכְרוּ־שָׁם עַבְדֵי־יִצְחָק בְּאֵר: וַאֲבִימֶלֶךְ הָלַךְ אֵלָיו מִגְּרָר וַאֲחֻזַּת מֵרֵעֵהוּ
כז וּפִיכֹל שַׂר־צְבָאוֹ: וַיֹּאמֶר אֲלֵהֶם יִצְחָק מַדּוּעַ בָּאתֶם אֵלָי וְאַתֶּם שְׂנֵאתֶם
כח אֹתִי וַתְּשַׁלְּחוּנִי מֵאִתְּכֶם: וַיֹּאמְרוּ רָאוֹ רָאִינוּ כִּי־הָיָה יהוה | עִמָּךְ וַנֹּאמֶר

---

14. וַעֲבֻדָּה רַבָּה — *And many enterprises* . . . lands ready to be tilled.

וַיְקַנְאוּ אֹתוֹ פְּלִשְׁתִּים — *And the Philistines envied him* . . . because in their fields the opposite was true; they planted much and produced little.

15. סִתְּמוּם פְּלִשְׁתִּים — *The Philistines stopped up.* Fearing to harm Isaac (in person) because of Abimelech's orders, they stopped up the wells, because of envy and animosity.

16. כִּי עָצַמְתָּ מִמֶּנּוּ — *You have become mightier than us.* Your (great) wealth will enable you to rise up against us.

20. הִתְעַשְּׂקוּ עִמּוֹ — *They involved themselves with him.* They endeavored to make Isaac abandon the well.

24. אַל תִּירָא — *Fear not* . . . that your property will be diminished through this strife.

וּבֵרַכְתִּיךָ — *And I will bless you* . . . with additional wealth.

25-26. וַיִּקְרָא בְּשֵׁם ה׳ . . . וַיִּכְרוּ שָׁם עַבְדֵי יִצְחָק בְּאֵר . . . וַאֲבִימֶלֶךְ הָלַךְ אֵלָיו — *And called upon the name of God . . . and there Isaac's servants dug a well . . . Then Abimelech went to him.* After he was inspired to 'call upon the name of God,' the servants of Isaac successfully dug a well without conflict and Abimelech came to him to make a covenant and no longer harmed him.

28. כִּי הָיָה ה׳ עִמָּךְ — *That God has been with you.* It is not out of fear of you that we make this covenant with you.

NOTES

telling us this, indicates that God's blessing was due to this praiseworthy behavior on his part.

24. וּבֵרַכְתִּיךָ – *And I will bless you.* Consistent with his interpretation of בְּרָכָה, *blessing,* in verse 12, the *Sforno* interprets the word

כט תְּהִי נָא אָלָה בֵּינוֹתֵינוּ בֵּינֵינוּ וּבֵינֶךָ וְנִכְרְתָה בְרִית עִמָּךְ: אִם־תַּעֲשֵׂה עִמָּנוּ
רָעָה כַּאֲשֶׁר לֹא נְגַעֲנוּךָ וְכַאֲשֶׁר עָשִׂינוּ עִמְּךָ רַק־טוֹב וַנְּשַׁלֵּחֲךָ בְּשָׁלוֹם
חמישי ל-לא אַתָּה עַתָּה בְּרוּךְ יהוה: וַיַּעַשׂ לָהֶם מִשְׁתֶּה וַיֹּאכְלוּ וַיִּשְׁתּוּ: וַיַּשְׁכִּימוּ בַבֹּקֶר
לב וַיִּשָּׁבְעוּ אִישׁ לְאָחִיו וַיְשַׁלְּחֵם יִצְחָק וַיֵּלְכוּ מֵאִתּוֹ בְּשָׁלוֹם: וַיְהִי | בַּיּוֹם הַהוּא
וַיָּבֹאוּ עַבְדֵי יִצְחָק וַיַּגִּדוּ לוֹ עַל־אֹדוֹת הַבְּאֵר אֲשֶׁר חָפָרוּ וַיֹּאמְרוּ לוֹ
לג מָצָאנוּ מָיִם: וַיִּקְרָא אֹתָהּ שִׁבְעָה עַל־כֵּן שֵׁם־הָעִיר בְּאֵר שֶׁבַע עַד הַיּוֹם
לד הַזֶּה: וַיְהִי עֵשָׂו בֶּן־אַרְבָּעִים שָׁנָה וַיִּקַּח אִשָּׁה אֶת־יְהוּדִית
לה בַּת־בְּאֵרִי הַחִתִּי וְאֶת־בָּשְׂמַת בַּת־אֵילֹן הַחִתִּי: וַתִּהְיֶיןָ מֹרַת רוּחַ לְיִצְחָק

---

29. אִם תַּעֲשֶׂה עִמָּנוּ רָעָה . . . אַתָּה עַתָּה — *If you dare do evil to us . . . Now, you . . .* that you will do us no harm, as we have not molested you.

33. וַיִּקְרָא אֹתָהּ שִׁבְעָה — *And he named it Shivah.* He called the well *shivah* because it was the 'seventh' place where he had dug a well; the three of Abraham which the Philistines stopped, as it says, וְכָל הַבְּאֵרֹת . . . סִתְּמוּם פְּלִשְׁתִּים, *All the wells . . . the Philistines had stopped* (verse 15), and the word כָּל, *all,* is never used for less than three; the three wells of Isaac: Esek, Sitnah and Rehoboth; and this was the seventh, which was called *Shivah.*

עַל כֵּן שֵׁם הָעִיר בְּאֵר שֶׁבַע — *Therefore the name of the city is Beer-Sheba.* (The word שֶׁבַע) with a סֶגוֹל (ֶ), indicates both שְׁבוּעָה, *the oath,* and the number שִׁבְעָה, *seven.* In the days of Abraham, however, the name of the city was בְּאֵר שָׁבַע, with a קָמָץ (ָ), indicating only the 'oath' (21:31).

34. וַיְהִי עֵשָׂו בֶּן אַרְבָּעִים שָׁנָה — *And Esau was forty years old.* Isaac did not concern himself with wedding him and his brother to appropriate wives.

וַיִּקַּח אִשָּׁה אֶת יְהוּדִית בַּת בְּאֵרִי הַחִתִּי — *And he took to wife Judith the daughter of Be'eri the Hittite.* Isaac did not protest against his marrying these Hittite women, as had his father (24:3).

35. וַתִּהְיֶיןָ מֹרַת רוּחַ — *And they cut short the spirit.* They were as a razor and knife which cut short the spirit in the lives of Isaac and Rebecca. The word מֹרַת is cognate to מוֹרָה, as we find, וּמוֹרָה לֹא יַעֲלֶה עַל רֹאשׁוֹ, *And no razor shall come upon his head* (*Judges* 13:5). Now, in spite of all this, Isaac did not recognize the great wickedness of Esau, nor did he protest against (these wives). As a result, (Isaac) failed by trying to bless Esau. From this (error) a mishap resulted whereby he (Isaac) gave a blessing and counsel (to Esau) and subsequently hatred increased among his sons, and Jacob was compelled to flee to another country.

NOTES

וּבֵרַכְתִּיךָ, *And I will bless you,* similarly — with additional wealth.

34. וַיְהִי עֵשָׂו בֶּן אַרְבָּעִים שָׁנָה וַיִּקַּח אִשָּׁה אֶת יְהוּדִית — *And Esau was forty years old and he took to wife Judith.* Abraham took the initiative and involved himself in finding a proper wife for his son. Unfortunately, Isaac, the private retiring person, did not, and consequently Esau, without parental restraint, married unsuitable wives, causing much distress to his parents.

35. וַתִּהְיֶיןָ מֹרַת רוּחַ — *And they cut short the spirit.* Two expressions are used by the *Sforno,* בְּרָכָה, *blessing,* and עֵצָה, *counsel.* The former refers to the blessings recorded in 27:39, i.e., *the fat of the earth* and *the dew of heaven,* while the latter refers to *by thy sword shall you live* (27:40).

כז
א וּלְרִבְקָה׃ וַיְהִי כִּי־זָקֵן יִצְחָק וַתִּכְהֶיןָ עֵינָיו מֵרְאֹת וַיִּקְרָא
ב אֶת־עֵשָׂו ׀ בְּנוֹ הַגָּדֹל וַיֹּאמֶר אֵלָיו בְּנִי וַיֹּאמֶר אֵלָיו הִנֵּנִי׃ וַיֹּאמֶר הִנֵּה־נָא
ג זָקַנְתִּי לֹא יָדַעְתִּי יוֹם מוֹתִי׃ וְעַתָּה שָׂא־נָא כֵלֶיךָ תֶּלְיְךָ וְקַשְׁתֶּךָ וְצֵא
ד הַשָּׂדֶה וְצוּדָה לִּי °צידה׃ וַעֲשֵׂה־לִי מַטְעַמִּים כַּאֲשֶׁר אָהַבְתִּי וְהָבִיאָה לִּי °צַיִד ק׳
ה וְאֹכֵלָה בַּעֲבוּר תְּבָרֶכְךָ נַפְשִׁי בְּטֶרֶם אָמוּת׃ וְרִבְקָה שֹׁמַעַת בְּדַבֵּר יִצְחָק
ו אֶל־עֵשָׂו בְּנוֹ וַיֵּלֶךְ עֵשָׂו הַשָּׂדֶה לָצוּד צַיִד לְהָבִיא׃ וְרִבְקָה אָמְרָה אֶל־

XXVII

1. וַתִּכְהֶיןָ עֵינָיו — *And his eyesight dimmed . . .* as happened to Eli who (also) did not restrain (the wickedness) of his sons, as it is written, וְלֹא כִהָה בָּם, *And he did not rebuke them (I Samuel* 3:13), and (as a result), וְעֵינָיו קָמָה וְלֹא יָכוֹל לִרְאוֹת, *His eyes were set and he could not see (* ibid. 4:15). Now this (dimness of sight) did not occur with Abraham or Jacob even when they were older than Isaac or Eli. Of Abraham it is written, וַיֹּסֶף אַבְרָהָם וַיִּקַּח אִשָּׁה, *And Abraham took another wife* (25:1), and as for Jacob, in spite of all his distress and (constant) weeping, it is written, וַיַּרְא יִשְׂרָאֵל אֶת בְּנֵי יוֹסֵף, *And Israel saw Joseph's sons* (48:8). Even though his sight was dim, as it says, וְעֵינֵי יִשְׂרָאֵל כָּבְדוּ מִזֹּקֶן, *The eyes of Israel were dim from old age* (48:10), this was (only) to the extent that he could not *identify* an individual image (but he could distinguish people).

2. לֹא יָדַעְתִּי יוֹם מוֹתִי — *I know not the day of my death.* A blessing is more effective when the one who gives the blessing is close to death, as we find by Jacob and Moses (as well), because the soul is separated from the physical (bonds) more so, at that time.

3. שָׂא נָא כֵלֶיךָ — *Now sharpen, please, your gear . . .* so that you not return empty-handed nor tarry.

4. וַעֲשֵׂה לִי מַטְעַמִּים — *And make me delicacies.* He asked for savory food that (Esau) should occupy himself with כִּבּוּד אָב, *filial honor,* (and be worthy) that the blessing be effective, for even though he did not recognize Esau's great wickedness, nonetheless he did not feel him worthy to receive the blessing that he had in mind to give him. Because of this, when he blessed Jacob later (before he left for Haran) he did not request him to bring savory food, but blessed him at once, saying וְאֵל שַׁדַּי יְבָרֵךְ אֹתְךָ, *And God Almighty bless you* (28:3), for he knew that he was worthy to be blessed.

NOTES

XXVII

1. וַתִּכְהֶיןָ עֵינָיו – *And his eyesight dimmed.* The *Sforno* links the physical dimming of one's eyes to the failure to perceive the behavior of one's children and their effect upon the family's future. The *Sforno* is also critical of Isaac's passivity when Esau marries Hittite women (26:34) and his lack of involvement in choosing wives for his sons, as his father had done for him. All this can be termed *the dimming of one's eyes.*

2. לֹא יָדַעְתִּי יוֹם מוֹתִי – *I know not the day of my death.* When a righteous person gives a blessing it is inspired from above. That is why the expression נַפְשִׁי, *my soul,* is used by Isaac (verse 4). The person's spiritual self is purer when unencumbered by his physical being. Thus, before one's death, when the body is weak, the soul is stronger, hence the blessing is more effective. This is why Isaac stresses the imminence of his death in this verse and Rebecca does so, in verse 7, where she also adds the words, לִפְנֵי מוֹתוֹ, *before he dies,* to stress the inspiration from on High when Isaac will give his blessing.

יַעֲקֹב בְּנָהּ לֵאמֹר הִנֵּה שָׁמַעְתִּי אֶת־אָבִיךָ מְדַבֵּר אֶל־עֵשָׂו אָחִיךָ לֵאמֹר:
ז הָבִיאָה לִּי צַיִד וַעֲשֵׂה־לִי מַטְעַמִּים וְאֹכֵלָה וַאֲבָרֶכְכָה לִפְנֵי יהוה לִפְנֵי
ח־ט מוֹתִי: וְעַתָּה בְנִי שְׁמַע בְּקֹלִי לַאֲשֶׁר אֲנִי מְצַוָּה אֹתָךְ: לֶךְ־נָא אֶל־הַצֹּאן
וְקַח־לִי מִשָּׁם שְׁנֵי גְּדָיֵי עִזִּים טֹבִים וְאֶעֱשֶׂה אֹתָם מַטְעַמִּים לְאָבִיךָ כַּאֲשֶׁר
י־יא אָהֵב: וְהֵבֵאתָ לְאָבִיךָ וְאָכָל בַּעֲבֻר אֲשֶׁר יְבָרֶכְךָ לִפְנֵי מוֹתוֹ: וַיֹּאמֶר יַעֲקֹב
יב אֶל־רִבְקָה אִמּוֹ הֵן עֵשָׂו אָחִי אִישׁ שָׂעִר וְאָנֹכִי אִישׁ חָלָק: אוּלַי יְמֻשֵּׁנִי אָבִי
יג וְהָיִיתִי בְעֵינָיו כִּמְתַעְתֵּעַ וְהֵבֵאתִי עָלַי קְלָלָה וְלֹא בְרָכָה: וַתֹּאמֶר לוֹ אִמּוֹ
יד עָלַי קִלְלָתְךָ בְּנִי אַךְ שְׁמַע בְּקֹלִי וְלֵךְ קַח־לִי: וַיֵּלֶךְ וַיִּקַּח וַיָּבֵא לְאִמּוֹ
טו וַתַּעַשׂ אִמּוֹ מַטְעַמִּים כַּאֲשֶׁר אָהֵב אָבִיו: וַתִּקַּח רִבְקָה אֶת־בִּגְדֵי עֵשָׂו בְּנָהּ
טז הַגָּדֹל הַחֲמֻדֹת אֲשֶׁר אִתָּהּ בַּבָּיִת וַתַּלְבֵּשׁ אֶת־יַעֲקֹב בְּנָהּ הַקָּטָן: וְאֵת
יז עֹרֹת גְּדָיֵי הָעִזִּים הִלְבִּישָׁה עַל־יָדָיו וְעַל חֶלְקַת צַוָּארָיו: וַתִּתֵּן אֶת־
יח הַמַּטְעַמִּים וְאֶת־הַלֶּחֶם אֲשֶׁר עָשָׂתָה בְּיַד יַעֲקֹב בְּנָהּ: וַיָּבֹא אֶל־אָבִיו
יט וַיֹּאמֶר אָבִי וַיֹּאמֶר הִנֶּנִּי מִי אַתָּה בְּנִי: וַיֹּאמֶר יַעֲקֹב אֶל־אָבִיו אָנֹכִי עֵשָׂו
בְּכֹרֶךָ עָשִׂיתִי כַּאֲשֶׁר דִּבַּרְתָּ אֵלָי קוּם־נָא שְׁבָה וְאָכְלָה מִצֵּידִי בַּעֲבוּר
כ תְּבָרֲכַנִּי נַפְשֶׁךָ: וַיֹּאמֶר יִצְחָק אֶל־בְּנוֹ מַה־זֶּה מִהַרְתָּ לִמְצֹא בְּנִי וַיֹּאמֶר כִּי
כא הִקְרָה יהוה אֱלֹהֶיךָ לְפָנָי: וַיֹּאמֶר יִצְחָק אֶל־יַעֲקֹב גְּשָׁה־נָּא וַאֲמֻשְׁךָ בְּנִי
כב הַאַתָּה זֶה בְּנִי עֵשָׂו אִם־לֹא: וַיִּגַּשׁ יַעֲקֹב אֶל־יִצְחָק אָבִיו וַיְמֻשֵּׁהוּ וַיֹּאמֶר
כג הַקֹּל קוֹל יַעֲקֹב וְהַיָּדַיִם יְדֵי עֵשָׂו: וְלֹא הִכִּירוֹ כִּי־הָיוּ יָדָיו כִּידֵי עֵשָׂו אָחִיו

---

12. וְלֹא בְרָכָה — *Rather than a blessing.* Even if he has reserved a blessing for me he will not bless me, if I deceive him.

13. עָלַי קִלְלָתְךָ — *Your curse be on me.* I will accept the curse in your place, as our Sages tell us regarding Solomon who accepted upon himself the curses of Yoab, and so it came to pass (*Sanhedrin* 48b).

22. וְהַיָּדַיִם יְדֵי עֵשָׂו — *The hands are the hands of Esau.* Doubtless, the skins were prepared in such a fashion that their hair was similar to that of a human, (still) there is a vast difference between the hair of a man and that of a kid, unless it is thoroughly prepared. Now, we are told that (Jacob's) hands were as the hands of his brother Esau, 'hairy.' Perhaps (this was so) because (Isaac's) sense of touch was weakened (as was his sight) similar to: אִם יִטְעַם עַבְדְּךָ אֶת אֲשֶׁר אֹכַל, *Can I, your servant, taste what I eat? (II Samuel* 19:36).

NOTES

13. עָלַי קִלְלָתְךָ – *Your curse be on me.* The Sages' interpretation of the episode cited by the *Sforno* clarifies the meaning of עָלַי קִלְלָתְךָ, *Your curse be on me,* which implies that one *can* transfer a curse. When Yoab killed Abner, David was appalled and cursed him. Before David died he commanded his son Solomon to avenge the blood of Abner and Amasa. When Solomon prepared to execute Yoab, our Sages tell us that Yoab argued that since he was cursed he should not be killed, and if Solomon insisted upon slaying him then the curse of David should be transferred to Solomon and the Davidic house. Solomon accepted the curse, Joab was executed, and indeed the curses of David were visited upon various generations of his descendants. Thus we see that Rebecca's willingness to accept any curse pronounced over her son is a valid transfer.

22. וְהַיָּדַיִם יְדֵי עֵשָׂו – *The hands are the hands of Esau.* To prove that in old age one's senses are dulled, the *Sforno* cites the incident recorded in *II Samuel* where Barzilai respect-

כד־כה שְׂעִרֹת וַיְבָרְכֵהוּ: וַיֹּאמֶר אַתָּה זֶה בְּנִי עֵשָׂו וַיֹּאמֶר אָנִי: וַיֹּאמֶר הַגִּשָׁה לִּי
וְאֹכְלָה מִצֵּיד בְּנִי לְמַעַן תְּבָרֶכְךָ נַפְשִׁי וַיַּגֶּשׁ־לוֹ וַיֹּאכַל וַיָּבֵא לוֹ יַיִן וַיֵּשְׁתְּ:
כו־כז וַיֹּאמֶר אֵלָיו יִצְחָק אָבִיו גְּשָׁה־נָּא וּשְׁקָה־לִּי בְּנִי: וַיִּגַּשׁ וַיִּשַּׁק־לוֹ וַיָּרַח אֶת־
רֵיחַ בְּגָדָיו וַיְבָרְכֵהוּ וַיֹּאמֶר רְאֵה רֵיחַ בְּנִי כְּרֵיחַ שָׂדֶה אֲשֶׁר בֵּרְכוֹ יהוה:
ששי כח־כט וְיִתֶּן־לְךָ הָאֱלֹהִים מִטַּל הַשָּׁמַיִם וּמִשְׁמַנֵּי הָאָרֶץ וְרֹב דָּגָן וְתִירֹשׁ: יַעַבְדוּךָ

---

23. שְׂעִרֹת וַיְבָרְכֵהוּ — *Hairy, and he blessed him.* Because he (first) suspected him that he deserved to be cursed, as (Jacob himself) said, *and I shall bring a curse upon me* (verse 12) (therefore he blessed him). As our Sages teach us, הַחוֹשֵׁד אֶת חֲבֵרוֹ בְּדָבָר שֶׁאֵין בּוֹ צָרִיךְ לְפַיְּיסוֹ וְלֹא עוֹד אֶלָּא שֶׁצָּרִיךְ לְבָרְכוֹ, *One who suspects another of a fault which he has not committed, must appease him; even more, he must bless him (Berachos* 31b). (This is) similar to Eli who suspected Hannah of being drunk.

27. וַיָּרַח אֶת רֵיחַ בְּגָדָיו — *And he smelled the fragrance of his garments* ... so as to expand his soul through the pleasure of the fragrance, as our Sages tell us, אֵיזֶהוּ דָּבָר שֶׁהַנְּשָׁמָה נֶהֱנֵית מִמֶּנּוּ וְאֵין הַגּוּף נֶהֱנֶה מִמֶּנּוּ הֱוֵי אוֹמֵר זֶה הָרֵיחַ, *What is it which gives enjoyment to the soul and not to the body? You must say that this refers to a fragrant aroma (Berachos* 43b).

וַיְבָרְכֵהוּ — *And blessed him.* This is similar to, וְהָיָה כְּנַגֵּן הַמְנַגֵּן וַתְּהִי עָלָיו יַד ה׳, *And it came to pass when the musician played, that the hand of* HASHEM *was upon him (II Kings* 3:15).

רְאֵה רֵיחַ בְּנִי — *See, the fragrance of my son.* You, my son, see and understand that this aroma is ...

כְּרֵיחַ שָׂדֶה אֲשֶׁר בֵּרְכוֹ ה׳ — *Like the fragrance of a field which God has blessed.* Besides the existence in fact (of a field) which provides food for all living creatures, God in His goodness added the pleasant aroma which gives pleasure and satisfies the spiritual and aesthetic needs (of man).

28. וְיִתֶּן לְךָ הָאֱלֹהִים — *And may God give you.* When you will consider (and appreciate) this attribute of His goodness, He will give you, as the Creator (הָאֱלֹהִים) a field blessed ...

NOTES

fully refused David's invitation to become a member of his household in Jerusalem, pleading that he was an old man and could no longer enjoy the physical pleasure of life, for he could not even enjoy food and drink, so he preferred to go home and live simply.

23. שְׂעִרֹת וַיְבָרְכֵהוּ — *Hairy, and he blessed him.* The blessing mentioned in this verse is not the one that follows in verses 28-29, but a separate one given as compensation for suspecting him of a misdeed which he had not committed. Since Isaac was in error (for indeed Jacob had deceived him) the text of this blessing is not revealed to us.

27. וַיָּרַח אֶת רֵיחַ בְּגָדָיו וַיְבָרְכֵהוּ — *And he smelled the fragrance of his garments and blessed him.* In order to bless from the depth of one's inner being it is necessary to be joyful and elevated in spirit. This sense of joy can be aroused through fragrance, which appeals to the soul of man, or through music, which elevated Elisha's spirit, enabling him to prophesy (*II Kings* chap. 3).

רְאֵה רֵיחַ בְּנִי — *See, the fragrance of my son.* The *Sforno* interprets the word רְאֵה, *see,* (the imperative form) as being directed by Isaac to Jacob. He urged him to be sensitive to the fragrance of the field, which should be appreciated as a blessing from God, i.e., satisfying man's inherent aesthetic needs. This aspect of God's goodness — often overlooked — if considered and appreciated, would cause God to give you the fat of the land and the dew of

עַמִּים וְיִשְׁתַּחֲוֻ לְךָ לְאֻמִּים הֱוֵה גְבִיר לְאַחֶיךָ וְיִשְׁתַּחֲוּוּ לְךָ בְּנֵי אִמֶּךָ אֹרְרֶיךָ
ל אָרוּר וּמְבָרְכֶיךָ בָּרוּךְ: וַיְהִי כַּאֲשֶׁר כִּלָּה יִצְחָק לְבָרֵךְ אֶת־יַעֲקֹב וַיְהִי אַךְ
לא יָצֹא יָצָא יַעֲקֹב מֵאֵת פְּנֵי יִצְחָק אָבִיו וְעֵשָׂו אָחִיו בָּא מִצֵּידוֹ: וַיַּעַשׂ גַּם־הוּא
מַטְעַמִּים וַיָּבֵא לְאָבִיו וַיֹּאמֶר לְאָבִיו יָקֻם אָבִי וְיֹאכַל מִצֵּיד בְּנוֹ בַּעֲבֻר
לב תְּבָרְכַנִּי נַפְשֶׁךָ: וַיֹּאמֶר לוֹ יִצְחָק אָבִיו מִי־אָתָּה וַיֹּאמֶר אֲנִי בִּנְךָ בְכֹרְךָ
לג עֵשָׂו: וַיֶּחֱרַד יִצְחָק חֲרָדָה גְּדֹלָה עַד־מְאֹד וַיֹּאמֶר מִי־אֵפוֹא הוּא הַצָּד־צַיִד

מִטַּל הַשָּׁמַיִם — *Of the dew of the heavens.* The dew of heaven will be sufficient (for your needs) gladdening all, for it will not interfere with the comings and goings (of people).

וְרֹב דָּגָן וְתִירֹשׁ — *And abundant grain and wine.* To be able to sustain others, as we find, וְהִלְוִיתָ גּוֹיִם רַבִּים וְאַתָּה לֹא תִלְוֶה, *And you will lend to many nations, but you will not borrow (Deut.* 28:12).

29. וְיִשְׁתַּחֲוּוּ לְךָ לְאֻמִּים — *And nations will bow down to you.* Even those who will not *serve* you will bow down to you, for you will be superior to the kings of the land.

הֱוֵה גְבִיר לְאַחֶיךָ — *Be a lord to your kinsmen.* (Isaac) felt it would be good and sufficient for Jacob to have *Eretz Yisrael* as his possession, and to live there with a measure of submissiveness, so as not to trouble himself with the demands of leadership (or occupy himself) with passing vanities, as indeed happened to his descendants later on, as it says, מְתָאֵב אָנֹכִי אֶת גְּאוֹן יַעֲקֹב, *I abhor the pride of Jacob (Amos* 6:8). It would (also) be better for him to be subjugated to his brother rather than to another people, as our Sages teach us, אוֹ בְּטוּלָךְ אוֹ בְּטוּלָא דְבַר עֵשָׂו, *Either in your shadow or in the shadow of the son of Esau (Gittin* 17a). Now since (Isaac) knew that *Eretz Yisrael* was fitting only for Jacob, he therefore omitted the blessings of Abraham and *Eretz Yisrael* in this blessing, which he thought was being given to Esau, and gave it (later) to Jacob, doing so knowingly (28:4).

אֹרְרֶיךָ אָרוּר — *Cursed be they who curse you . . .* for there are many who do curse kings and lords when their requests are not granted. It is for this reason that (the Torah) cautions us, אֱלֹהִים לֹא תְקַלֵּל, *You shall not curse the judges (Exodus* 22:27).

33. מִי אֵפוֹא הוּא — *If so, who is the one (who hunted game)?* If it is true that you are Esau, who then is he who brought me game? The word אֵפוֹא, spelled with an א at the end, means *if so,* but when אֵיפֹה has a ה at the end, then it means *where,* as we find, אֵיפֹה הֵם רֹעִים, *Where are they feeding the flock* (37:16)?

NOTES

the heavens. According to the *Sforno,* then, this verse is the prerequisite for the blessings which follow in verses 28-29.

29. הֱוֵה גְבִיר לְאַחֶיךָ — *Be a lord to your kinsmen.* Isaac was under the impression that he was blessing Esau, therefore he did not include בִּרְכַּת אַבְרָהָם, the blessings given by God to Abraham (see *Rashi* 28:4), nor did he mention the inheritance of *Eretz Yisrael.* These were reserved for Jacob, for Isaac knew full well that Esau was not worthy to receive these special, unique spiritual gifts. By the same token he also knew that for Jacob's own good he should be submissive rather than assertive or aggressive, if his mission and purpose in life would be accomplished and fulfilled. That is why he designated Esau as the 'lord' over his brother, which would be beneficial for both.

לד וַיָּבֵא לִי וָאֹכַל מִכֹּל בְּטֶרֶם תָּבוֹא וָאֲבָרְכֵהוּ גַּם־בָּרוּךְ יִהְיֶה: כִּשְׁמֹעַ עֵשָׂו
אֶת־דִּבְרֵי אָבִיו וַיִּצְעַק צְעָקָה גְּדֹלָה וּמָרָה עַד־מְאֹד וַיֹּאמֶר לְאָבִיו בָּרֲכֵנִי
לה-לו גַם־אָנִי אָבִי: וַיֹּאמֶר בָּא אָחִיךָ בְּמִרְמָה וַיִּקַּח בִּרְכָתֶךָ: וַיֹּאמֶר הֲכִי קָרָא
שְׁמוֹ יַעֲקֹב וַיַּעְקְבֵנִי זֶה פַעֲמַיִם אֶת־בְּכֹרָתִי לָקָח וְהִנֵּה עַתָּה לָקַח בִּרְכָתִי
לז וַיֹּאמַר הֲלֹא־אָצַלְתָּ לִּי בְּרָכָה: וַיַּעַן יִצְחָק וַיֹּאמֶר לְעֵשָׂו הֵן גְּבִיר שַׂמְתִּיו
לָךְ וְאֶת־כָּל־אֶחָיו נָתַתִּי לוֹ לַעֲבָדִים וְדָגָן וְתִירֹשׁ סְמַכְתִּיו וּלְכָה אֵפוֹא מָה
לח אֶעֱשֶׂה בְּנִי: וַיֹּאמֶר עֵשָׂו אֶל־אָבִיו הַבְרָכָה אַחַת הִוא־לְךָ אָבִי בָּרֲכֵנִי גַם־
לט אָנִי אָבִי וַיִּשָּׂא עֵשָׂו קֹלוֹ וַיֵּבְךְּ: וַיַּעַן יִצְחָק אָבִיו וַיֹּאמֶר אֵלָיו הִנֵּה מִשְׁמַנֵּי
מ הָאָרֶץ יִהְיֶה מוֹשָׁבֶךָ וּמִטַּל הַשָּׁמַיִם מֵעָל: וְעַל־חַרְבְּךָ תִחְיֶה וְאֶת־אָחִיךָ

גַּם בָּרוּךְ יִהְיֶה — *Indeed, he shall remain blessed.* If so, then he who brought me the game did so deceitfully; still he merited to be blessed, for I felt at the time I blessed him that it took effect, similar to what (our Sages tell us) regarding Rabbi Chanina when he prayed for the sick *(Berachos* 34b).

35. וַיִּקַּח בִּרְכָתֶךָ — *And took away your blessing . . .* that blessing which was fitting and proper for you, dealing as it did with things of this world and **חוּץ לָאָרֶץ**, *outside Eretz Yisrael,* for the blessing of Abraham is not worthy (or fitting) for you.

36. הֲכִי קָרָא שְׁמוֹ יַעֲקֹב וַיַּעְקְבֵנִי — *Is it because he was named Jacob that he outwitted me?* Did the fact that he was named Jacob influence him to deceive me, since **שְׁמָא גָּרִים**, *a name can influence one's character (Berachos* 7b)?

הֲלֹא אָצַלְתָּ לִּי בְּרָכָה — *Have you not reserved a blessing for me?* Even though you intended to bless me with the superior blessing, you did not intend for me to have everything while my brother be denied and deprived of all blessing.

37. וְאֶת כָּל אֶחָיו נָתַתִּי לוֹ לַעֲבָדִים — *And all his kin have I given him as servants . . .* the children of Ishmael, Keturah and the kings of the nations, as he said, יַעַבְדוּךָ עַמִּים, *Peoples will serve you* (verse 29).

וּלְכָה אֵפוֹא מָה אֶעֱשֶׂה — *What then shall I do for you? . . .* therefore what can I do for you; what blessing (can I give you) which will be of benefit to you?

39-40. הִנֵּה מִשְׁמַנֵּי הָאָרֶץ יִהְיֶה מוֹשָׁבֶךָ — *Behold, of the fat of the earth shall be your dwelling.* This blessing I can give to you that your dwelling be in a land of fat (plenty) combined with some subservience to your brother.

וּמִטַּל הַשָּׁמַיִם מֵעָל. וְעַל חַרְבְּךָ תִחְיֶה — *And of the dew of heaven from above. And by your sword shall you live.* You shall live from *the dew of heaven,* i.e., you will not have to work the land which requires rain; and you shall also live *by your sword,* as a warrior waging war at the behest of your brother, or others. From this it shall follow . . .

NOTES

33. גַּם בָּרוּךְ יִהְיֶה — *Indeed, he shall remain blessed.* The Mishnah *(Berachos* 34b) relates that Rabbi Chanina ben Dosa would pray for ill people and then state, 'This one will die, this one will live.' When asked how he knew this, he answered, 'If my prayer comes out fluently, I know it is accepted.' And so here Isaac felt that his prayer was effective, for Heaven inspired his words, hence how can he negate it?

39-40. וּמִטַּל הַשָּׁמַיִם מֵעָל. וְעַל חַרְבְּךָ תִחְיֶה — *And of the dew of heaven from above. And by your sword shall you live.* The *Sforno* inter-

מא תַּעֲבֹד וְהָיָה כַּאֲשֶׁר תָּרִיד וּפָרַקְתָּ עֻלּוֹ מֵעַל צַוָּארֶךָ: וַיִּשְׂטֹם עֵשָׂו אֶת־
יַעֲקֹב עַל־הַבְּרָכָה אֲשֶׁר בֵּרְכוֹ אָבִיו וַיֹּאמֶר עֵשָׂו בְּלִבּוֹ יִקְרְבוּ יְמֵי אֵבֶל
מב אָבִי וְאַהַרְגָה אֶת־יַעֲקֹב אָחִי: וַיֻּגַּד לְרִבְקָה אֶת־דִּבְרֵי עֵשָׂו בְּנָהּ הַגָּדֹל
וַתִּשְׁלַח וַתִּקְרָא לְיַעֲקֹב בְּנָהּ הַקָּטָן וַתֹּאמֶר אֵלָיו הִנֵּה עֵשָׂו אָחִיךָ מִתְנַחֵם
מג לְךָ לְהָרְגֶךָ: וְעַתָּה בְנִי שְׁמַע בְּקֹלִי וְקוּם בְּרַח־לְךָ אֶל־לָבָן אָחִי חָרָנָה:
מד־מה וְיָשַׁבְתָּ עִמּוֹ יָמִים אֲחָדִים עַד אֲשֶׁר־תָּשׁוּב חֲמַת אָחִיךָ: עַד־שׁוּב אַף־אָחִיךָ
מִמְּךָ וְשָׁכַח אֵת אֲשֶׁר־עָשִׂיתָ לּוֹ וְשָׁלַחְתִּי וּלְקַחְתִּיךָ מִשָּׁם לָמָה אֶשְׁכַּל
מו גַּם־שְׁנֵיכֶם יוֹם אֶחָד: וַתֹּאמֶר רִבְקָה אֶל־יִצְחָק קַצְתִּי בְחַיַּי מִפְּנֵי בְּנוֹת חֵת
אִם־לֹקֵחַ יַעֲקֹב אִשָּׁה מִבְּנוֹת־חֵת כָּאֵלֶּה מִבְּנוֹת הָאָרֶץ לָמָּה לִּי חַיִּים:

כח

א וַיִּקְרָא יִצְחָק אֶל־יַעֲקֹב וַיְבָרֶךְ אֹתוֹ וַיְצַוֵּהוּ וַיֹּאמֶר לוֹ לֹא־תִקַּח אִשָּׁה
ב מִבְּנוֹת כְּנָעַן: קוּם לֵךְ פַּדֶּנָה אֲרָם בֵּיתָה בְתוּאֵל אֲבִי אִמֶּךָ וְקַח־לְךָ מִשָּׁם
ג אִשָּׁה מִבְּנוֹת לָבָן אֲחִי אִמֶּךָ: וְאֵל שַׁדַּי יְבָרֵךְ אֹתְךָ וְיַפְרְךָ וְיַרְבֶּךָ וְהָיִיתָ
ד לִקְהַל עַמִּים: וְיִתֶּן־לְךָ אֶת־בִּרְכַּת אַבְרָהָם לְךָ וּלְזַרְעֲךָ אִתָּךְ לְרִשְׁתְּךָ

וְהָיָה כַּאֲשֶׁר תָּרִיד — *It shall come to pass that when you are aggrieved.* When you will cry out from the violence of your brother who will overly subjugate you . . .

וּפָרַקְתָּ עֻלּוֹ מֵעַל צַוָּארֶךָ — *You shall remove his yoke from your neck* . . . for you are learned in battle and thus qualified for kingship. However, if during your subjugation you will turn to tilling the soil and other such labors, you will never be free of subjugation to your brother or others.

XXVIII

3. וְאֵל שַׁדַּי יְבָרֵךְ אֹתְךָ — *And may God Almighty bless you* . . . with material wealth.

וְיַפְרְךָ — *And make you fruitful* . . . with children.

וְיַרְבֶּךָ — *And multiply you* . . . (with) position and power.

4. וְיִתֶּן לְךָ אֶת בִּרְכַּת אַבְרָהָם — *And give you the blessings of Abraham* . . . as (God) said, 'וֶהְיֵה בְּרָכָה, *And you shall be a blessing*' (12:2), which can (only) be by teaching the knowledge (of God) to the people, for in this manner God, the Blessed One, will be blessed.

לְךָ וּלְזַרְעֲךָ אִתָּךְ לְרִשְׁתְּךָ — *To you and to your seed with you that you may inherit the land* . . . for when your children teach the ways of righteousness they will be worthy to inherit (the land), and this is considered sanctification of God's name, rather than

NOTES

prets the phrase *shall you live* as applying both to the conclusion of verse 39 and the beginning of verse 40. Esau will live from the land, to some extent, but also from his role as warrior. Hence *shall you live* refers to *dew of the heaven* as well as to *by your sword*. Since he is subservient to his brother, however, he cannot initiate a war, but must do battle at his brother's behest. If Jacob's overlordship is, however, unduly harsh, Esau's cry of protest will be heard and Jacob's yoke will be cast off.

XXVIII

3. וְאֵל שַׁדַּי יְבָרֵךְ אֹתְךָ וְיַפְרְךָ וְיַרְבֶּךָ — *And may God Almighty bless you and make you fruitful and multiply you.* Three expressions (יְבָרֵךְ, יַפְרְךָ, יַרְבֶּךָ) are used by Isaac in this blessing. It is a threefold blessing, of material wealth, children and position amongst his fellow men.

4. וְיִתֶּן לְךָ אֶת בִּרְכַּת אַבְרָהָם — *And give you the blessings of Abraham.* In his commentary on

שביעי ה אֶת־אֶרֶץ מְגֻרֶיךָ אֲשֶׁר־נָתַן אֱלֹהִים לְאַבְרָהָם: וַיִּשְׁלַח יִצְחָק אֶת־יַעֲקֹב
וַיֵּלֶךְ פַּדֶּנָה אֲרָם אֶל־לָבָן בֶּן־בְּתוּאֵל הָאֲרַמִּי אֲחִי רִבְקָה אֵם יַעֲקֹב וְעֵשָׂו:
ו וַיַּרְא עֵשָׂו כִּי־בֵרַךְ יִצְחָק אֶת־יַעֲקֹב וְשִׁלַּח אֹתוֹ פַּדֶּנָה אֲרָם לָקַחַת־לוֹ
מִשָּׁם אִשָּׁה בְּבָרְכוֹ אֹתוֹ וַיְצַו עָלָיו לֵאמֹר לֹא־תִקַּח אִשָּׁה מִבְּנוֹת כְּנָעַן:
מפטיר ז־ח וַיִּשְׁמַע יַעֲקֹב אֶל־אָבִיו וְאֶל־אִמּוֹ וַיֵּלֶךְ פַּדֶּנָה אֲרָם: וַיַּרְא עֵשָׂו כִּי רָעוֹת
ט בְּנוֹת כְּנָעַן בְּעֵינֵי יִצְחָק אָבִיו: וַיֵּלֶךְ עֵשָׂו אֶל־יִשְׁמָעֵאל וַיִּקַּח אֶת־מָחֲלַת
| בַּת־יִשְׁמָעֵאל בֶּן־אַבְרָהָם אֲחוֹת נְבָיוֹת עַל־נָשָׁיו לוֹ לְאִשָּׁה:

---

the opposite, as we find, יִשְׂרָאֵל אֲשֶׁר בְּךָ אֶתְפָּאָר, *Israel in whom I will be glorified* (*Isaiah* 49:3), for this will bring about יִשְׂמַח ה׳ בְּמַעֲשָׂיו, *Let God rejoice in His works* (*Psalms* 104:31).

אֶרֶץ מְגֻרֶיךָ — *The land of your sojournings* ... the land of Canaan where you presently reside.

6. וַיַּרְא עֵשָׂו כִּי בֵרַךְ יִצְחָק — *Now Esau saw that Isaac had blessed.* Even though Esau sees that when Isaac blesses Jacob, he commands him not to marry a Canaanite woman which would negate his blessing, still he does not pay serious attention to this (stricture) except he does see ...

8. כִּי רָעוֹת בְּנוֹת כְּנָעַן בְּעֵינֵי יִצְחָק אָבִיו — *That the daughters of Canaan were evil in the eyes of Isaac his father* ... But he thought that this was because they opposed the will of his father, as it says, *and they cut short the spirit (of Isaac and Rebecca)* (26:35) so he (then) went to Ishmael (to marry his daughter). With this (the Torah) informs us that Isaac could have opposed Esau when he married the Canaanite women, had he but attended to it, as he does now when Rebecca alerts (and urges) him to (i.e., to warn) Jacob.

NOTES

the phrase וֶהְיֵה בְּרָכָה, *and you be a blessing* (12:2), the *Sforno* explains that the greatest blessing one can give to God is to teach mankind the knowledge of the Almighty, so that through their moral and ethical behavior they will cause Him to rejoice in His creation. This is the charge given by God to Abraham when he states, *'Be a blessing,'* i.e., give a בְּרָכָה. It is this same admonition which Isaac now gives to Jacob.

6-8. וַיַּרְא עֵשָׂו כִּי בֵרַךְ יִצְחָק ... כִּי רָעוֹת בְּנוֹת כְּנָעַן בְּעֵינֵי יִצְחָק אָבִיו — *Now Esau saw that Isaac had blessed ... that the daughters of Canaan were evil in the eyes of Isaac his father.* The word וַיַּרְא, *and he saw,* is used at the beginning of each of these two verses. The first refers to the blessing given to Jacob coupled with the admonition not to marry a Cananite woman, thus indicating Isaac's *preference* for a non-Canaanite wife. The second is Esau's realization that the Hittite women he married (26:31) caused his father's spirit to be cut short. Now the first does not deter him but the second does, and to appease his father he marries 'in the family' by taking Ishmael's daughter. We see then that Esau was sensitive to his father's approval or lack of same; hence the *Sforno* feels that the Torah is telling us that Isaac could have influenced and controlled Esau, had he but expressed his strong disapproval of Canaanite wives.

פרשת ויצא
Parashas Vayeitzei

י־יא וַיֵּצֵא יַעֲקֹב מִבְּאֵר שָׁבַע וַיֵּלֶךְ חָרָנָה: וַיִּפְגַּע בַּמָּקוֹם וַיָּלֶן שָׁם כִּי־בָא
יב הַשֶּׁמֶשׁ וַיִּקַּח מֵאַבְנֵי הַמָּקוֹם וַיָּשֶׂם מְרַאֲשֹׁתָיו וַיִּשְׁכַּב בַּמָּקוֹם הַהוּא: וַיַּחֲלֹם
וְהִנֵּה סֻלָּם מֻצָּב אַרְצָה וְרֹאשׁוֹ מַגִּיעַ הַשָּׁמָיְמָה וְהִנֵּה מַלְאֲכֵי אֱלֹהִים עֹלִים
יג וְיֹרְדִים בּוֹ: וְהִנֵּה יהוה נִצָּב עָלָיו וַיֹּאמַר אֲנִי יהוה אֱלֹהֵי אַבְרָהָם אָבִיךָ
יד וֵאלֹהֵי יִצְחָק הָאָרֶץ אֲשֶׁר אַתָּה שֹׁכֵב עָלֶיהָ לְךָ אֶתְּנֶנָּה וּלְזַרְעֶךָ: וְהָיָה
זַרְעֲךָ כַּעֲפַר הָאָרֶץ וּפָרַצְתָּ יָמָּה וָקֵדְמָה וְצָפֹנָה וָנֶגְבָּה וְנִבְרְכוּ בְךָ כָּל־

---

10. וַיֵּצֵא יַעֲקֹב . . . וַיֵּלֶךְ חָרָנָה — *And Jacob departed . . . and went toward Haran.* He went to reach Haran, but before he arrived there the events recorded here occurred.

11. וַיִּפְגַּע בַּמָּקוֹם — *And he encountered the place.* He came to a place which he had not planned on as a destination. The definite article *the place* denotes a place where travelers could spend the night. Such places were to be found in every town, usually on the road. Similarly, the angels say to Lot, 'We will spend the night בָרְחוֹב, *on the road* (19:2), and so in the episode of the concubine in Givah, רַק בָּרְחוֹב אַל תָּלַן, *but do not spend the night on the road* [where wayfarers customarily stay] (*Judges* 19:20).

מֵאַבְנֵי הַמָּקוֹם — *From the stones of the place* . . . which were prepared there for guests to eat or sit on.

12-13. וְהִנֵּה מַלְאֲכֵי אֱלֹהִים עֹלִים וְיֹרְדִים . . . וְהִנֵּה ה׳ נִצָּב עָלָיו — *And behold angels of God ascending and descending . . . And behold God stood over him.* For indeed as it shall come to pass at the end (of time), the heavenly representatives of the nations after having ascended will fall, but God, the Blessed One, Who stands (guard) eternally (over Israel), will not forsake His people, as it says, כִּי אֶעֱשֶׂה כָלָה בְּכָל הַגּוֹיִם . . . וְאֹתְךָ לֹא אֶעֱשֶׂה כָלָה, *For I will make a full end of all the nations . . . but I will not make a full end of you* (*Jeremiah* 46:28).

הָאָרֶץ אֲשֶׁר אַתָּה שֹׁכֵב עָלֶיהָ — *The ground upon which you are lying* . . . which is the center of the Land of Canaan.

לְךָ אֶתְּנֶנָּה — *To you will I give it.* You will be a 'mighty prince' in the midst of its inhabitants as were Abraham and Isaac.

14. וְהָיָה זַרְעֲךָ כַּעֲפַר הָאָרֶץ וּפָרַצְתָּ — *And your offspring shall be as the dust of the earth, and you shall spread abroad.* When your seed will be treated as the dust of the earth, as we read, וַתָּשִׂימִי כָאָרֶץ גֵּוךְ וְכַחוּץ לַעֹבְרִים, *And you laid your back as the*

NOTES

11. וַיִּפְגַּע בַּמָּקוֹם . . . מֵאַבְנֵי הַמָּקוֹם — *And he encountered the place . . . from the stones of the place.* The word פְּגִיעָה means to chance upon a place which one had not originally planned as his destination. Since according to the *Sforno* this place was one used frequently by travelers, the stones were not lying around aimlessly, but were part of the furnishings put there for the convenience of travelers. Jacob now took some of these stones to place under his head.

12-13. וְהִנֵּה מַלְאֲכֵי אֱלֹהִים עֹלִים וְיֹרְדִים . . . וְהִנֵּה ה׳ נִצָּב עָלָיו — *And behold angels of God ascending and descending . . . And behold God stood over him.* The *Sforno* follows the interpretation of the Midrash *Tanchuma* that the imagery of this dream is symbolic of the rise and fall of empires and of the Eternal One guarding His People who will, unlike all other nations, survive forever.

לְךָ אֶתְּנֶנָּה — *To you will I give it.* The expression *to you will I give it* cannot be meant as a promise, for this has already been given (28:4). Rather it is to be understood as an assurance of Jacob's standing and stature among the inhabitants of this land.

14. וְהָיָה זַרְעֲךָ כַּעֲפַר הָאָרֶץ וּפָרַצְתָּ . . . וְנִבְרְכוּ בְךָ כָּל מִשְׁפְּחֹת הָאֲדָמָה — *And your offspring shall be*

טו מִשְׁפְּחֹת הָאֲדָמָה וּבְזַרְעֶךָ: וְהִנֵּה אָנֹכִי עִמָּךְ וּשְׁמַרְתִּיךָ בְּכֹל אֲשֶׁר־תֵּלֵךְ
וַהֲשִׁבֹתִיךָ אֶל־הָאֲדָמָה הַזֹּאת כִּי לֹא אֶעֱזָבְךָ עַד אֲשֶׁר אִם־עָשִׂיתִי אֵת
טז אֲשֶׁר־דִּבַּרְתִּי לָךְ: וַיִּיקַץ יַעֲקֹב מִשְּׁנָתוֹ וַיֹּאמֶר אָכֵן יֵשׁ יהוה בַּמָּקוֹם הַזֶּה

ground, and as the street to them that go over (Isaiah 51:23), i.e., after they have reached the lowest depths, then shall they spread abroad, crossing over the boundaries of this land on which you lie, to every side.

יָמָּה וָקֵדְמָה וְצָפֹנָה וָנֶגְבָּה — *To the west, east, north and south* . . . as it is attested, וְקַרְקַר כָּל בְּנֵי שֵׁת, *and break down all the sons of Seth (Numbers* 24:17), for the salvation from God will come only after the present unprecedented degradation of Israel in exile, as our Sages state, 'If you see a generation subjected to suffering, engulfing it as a river, wait and observe (the salvation which is nigh), as it is written, כִּי יָבֹא כַנָּהָר צָר, *For distress will come as a river (Isaiah* 59:19), followed by, וּבָא לְצִיּוֹן גּוֹאֵל, *And a redeemer will come to Zion* (ibid. v. 20).

וְנִבְרְכוּ בְךָ כָּל מִשְׁפְּחֹת הָאֲדָמָה וּבְזַרְעֶךָ — *And in you shall all the families of the earth be blessed* . . . in the sense of, וְאַתֶּם כֹּהֲנֵי ה׳ תִּקָּרֵאוּ מְשָׁרְתֵי אֱלֹהֵינוּ יֵאָמֵר לָכֶם, *You shall be named priests of HASHEM, they shall call you the ministers of our God (Isaiah* 61:6).

15. כִּי לֹא אֶעֱזָבְךָ — *For I will not forsake you.* The assurance I have given to you, that after a lengthy exile you will spread abroad, crossing every boundary, and not be destroyed by the suffering and distress of your exile, is because during that exile I will not leave you, as it is written, לֹא מְאַסְתִּים וְלֹא גְעַלְתִּים, *I will not reject them, neither will I abhor them (Lev.* 26:44).

עַד אֲשֶׁר אִם עָשִׂיתִי — *Until I have done.* (I will not leave you) even before I will have done that which I have spoken to you, i.e., וּפָרַצְתָּ, *and you will spread abroad.* The word עַד, *until*, at times means בְּעוֹד, *while*, [i.e., while I have not yet done], as we find, עַד שֶׁהַמֶּלֶךְ בִּמְסִבּוֹ, *While the king was (still) at his table (Song of Songs* 1:12), and עַד לֹא עָשָׂה אֶרֶץ וְחוּצוֹת, *Before He had made the earth and the outside places (Proverbs* 8:26). However, once this great salvation will come, its nature will not only be the (negative) kindness of not leaving (them) but this kindness will abundantly grow to the point where (God) will walk in our midst, as it says, וְהִתְהַלַּכְתִּי בְּתוֹכְכֶם, *And I will walk among you (Lev.* 26:12).

16. אָכֵן יֵשׁ ה׳ בַּמָּקוֹם הַזֶּה — *Surely HASHEM is in this place.* Without a doubt this place is conducive to prophecy, for I have seen such a vision without even preparing myself for prophecy. A change of place and climate can affect man's intellectual

NOTES

as the dust of the earth, and you shall spread abroad . . . and in you shall all the families of the earth be blessed. Here again the expression *as the dust of the earth* cannot be meant as a promise of Israel's great numbers since it was already pledged. Therefore, it is to be understood as a *condition* for Jacob's seed to be 'spread abroad.' Only after they have come to a state of degradation, trampled upon as the dust of the earth, will their salvation come. The *Sforno's* interpretation of וְנִבְרְכוּ, *And in you shall be blessed*, is consistent with his commentary on verse 4. See note there.

15. כִּי לֹא אֶעֱזָבְךָ — *For I will not forsake you.* This expression is not to be understood as part of God's assurance, i.e., a continuation of the promise made in the previous verses (13-14) or the first part of this verse. Rather it is the key to their survival. They will continue to exist in exile because of God's special providence. This unique protection of the Almighty granted to

יז וְאָנֹכִי לֹא יָדָעְתִּי׃ וַיִּירָא וַיֹּאמַר מַה־נּוֹרָא הַמָּקוֹם הַזֶּה אֵין זֶה כִּי אִם־בֵּית
יח אֱלֹהִים וְזֶה שַׁעַר הַשָּׁמָיִם׃ וַיַּשְׁכֵּם יַעֲקֹב בַּבֹּקֶר וַיִּקַּח אֶת־הָאֶבֶן אֲשֶׁר־שָׂם
יט מְרַאֲשֹׁתָיו וַיָּשֶׂם אֹתָהּ מַצֵּבָה וַיִּצֹק שֶׁמֶן עַל־רֹאשָׁהּ׃ וַיִּקְרָא אֶת־שֵׁם־
כ הַמָּקוֹם הַהוּא בֵּית־אֵל וְאוּלָם לוּז שֵׁם־הָעִיר לָרִאשֹׁנָה׃ וַיִּדַּר יַעֲקֹב נֶדֶר

---

capacities, faculties, and spirit, as (our Sages) tell us, אֲוִירָא שֶׁל אֶרֶץ יִשְׂרָאֵל מַחְכִּים, *The atmosphere of Eretz Yisrael makes one wise* (*Baba Basra* 158b).

וְאָנֹכִי לֹא יָדָעְתִּי — *And I did not know.* Had I known it I would have prepared myself to reach the degree of prophecy (to which such a place is conducive), but I did not.

17. וַיִּירָא — *And he was afraid.* Because of his error.

אֵין זֶה — *This is none other.* The place I saw in the vision where the ladder was standing is none other . . .

כִּי אִם בֵּית אֱלֹהִים — *Than the house of God . . .* the place of the Holy Temple, as our Sages tell us, 'Jacob called it a house' (*Pesachim* 88a).

וְזֶה שַׁעַר הַשָּׁמָיִם — *And this is the gate of heaven.* And this ladder that I saw teaches that from this place where the ladder was, God, Who stood upon it, will hear the prayers of the petitioners, and their prayers will ascend to His holy abode in heaven.

18. וַיָּשֶׂם אֹתָהּ מַצֵּבָה — *And he set it up as a pillar.* He sanctified it by setting it aside to *eventually* be a מַצֵּבָה, when he would dedicate it as such upon his return, as the verse states, *And Jacob set up a pillar in the place where He spoke with him, a pillar of stone, and he poured a libation upon it* (35:14).

NOTES

Israel is undeserved — it is a *chesed,* but ultimately it will be earned, at which time God will dwell in their midst.

16-17. אָכֵן יֵשׁ ה׳ בַּמָּקוֹם הַזֶּה . . . וַיִּירָא — *Surely* HASHEM *is in this place . . . and he was afraid.* Prophecy is usually experienced by those who have prepared themselves for it. However, not only must it be the right person but the right place as well. According to our Sages, once the Jewish people established themselves in *Eretz Yisrael,* prophecy can only occur in the Holy Land. The power and efficacy of this place where Jacob lay down to sleep (the place where Isaac was brought as a sacrifice and where the Holy Temple is destined to be built) was already so great, that he beheld a vision even though he had not prepared himself spiritually. This indicated the sacred nature of this place. Had he known and prepared himself, this prophecy would have been even greater and more intense. Jacob considered this lack of knowledge a blemish on his character and he faulted himself for it. Hence he was afraid.

17. כִּי אִם בֵּית אֱלֹהִים – *Than the house of God.* Our Sages tell us that each of the three אָבוֹת, *Patriarchs,* called this place of prayer by different names. Abraham called it הַר, *a mountain,* as we find by the *Akeidah.* Isaac called it שָׂדֶה, *a field,* as we find, *And Isaac went out to meditate in the field* (24:63). Jacob called it בַּיִת, *a house,* as we find here. To Abraham, prayer demanded an extraordinary elevation of the spirit akin to climbing to the mountain top. It also required removing oneself from the mundane so as to reach the heights. Isaac, however, was inspired to commune with the Almighty in the broad, open field, which expanded his heart and mind. Still he also sought out a special place, away from the ordinary and the confined enclosure of his dwelling place. It was Jacob who taught that to concentrate the mind and heart of the worshiper it is better to pray in the confines of a house. He also taught that man can pray to the Almighty in any house, thereby creating a House of God through the medium of his prayer.

18. וַיָּשֶׂם אֹתָהּ מַצֵּבָה — *And he set it up as a pillar.* If Jacob had completed the consecration of this stone as a pillar (מַצֵּבָה), the word used should not have been וַיָּשֶׂם, *and he placed,* but וַיַּצֵּב, *and he established.* The *Sforno* therefore explains that Jacob now performed a prelimi-

לֵאמֹר אִם־יִהְיֶה אֱלֹהִים עִמָּדִי וּשְׁמָרַנִי בַּדֶּרֶךְ הַזֶּה אֲשֶׁר אָנֹכִי הוֹלֵךְ וְנָתַן־
כא לִי לֶחֶם לֶאֱכֹל וּבֶגֶד לִלְבֹּשׁ: וְשַׁבְתִּי בְשָׁלוֹם אֶל־בֵּית אָבִי וְהָיָה יהוה לִי
כב לֵאלֹהִים: וְהָאֶבֶן הַזֹּאת אֲשֶׁר־שַׂמְתִּי מַצֵּבָה יִהְיֶה בֵּית אֱלֹהִים וְכֹל אֲשֶׁר
כט שני א תִּתֶּן־לִי עַשֵּׂר אֲעַשְּׂרֶנּוּ לָךְ: וַיִּשָּׂא יַעֲקֹב רַגְלָיו וַיֵּלֶךְ אַרְצָה בְנֵי־קֶדֶם:

---

20. אִם יִהְיֶה אֱלֹהִים עִמָּדִי — *If God will be with me.* If He will remove from me all oppression and obstacles which bring men to transgress the will of his Maker, as our Sages say, שְׁלֹשָׁה דְבָרִים מַעֲבִירִים אֶת הָאָדָם עַל דַּעְתּוֹ וְעַל דַּעַת קוֹנוֹ . . . גּוֹיִם וְרוּחַ רָעָה וְדִקְדּוּקֵי עֲנִיּוּת, *Three things deprive a man of his senses and a knowledge of his Creator . . . viz. idolaters, an evil spirit and oppressive poverty (Eruvin* 41b).

וּשְׁמָרַנִי — *And will keep me . . .* guard me from the evil of the pagans who rise up against me and force me (to transgress).

וְנָתַן לִי לֶחֶם לֶאֱכֹל — *And will give me bread to eat . . .* so that a state of poverty will not bring me to rebel against my own will, the will of my Maker.

21. וְשַׁבְתִּי בְשָׁלוֹם — *And come back in peace.* (Unharmed by) the illnesses which cause a man to transgress. This is the meaning of רוּחַ רָעָה, *an evil spirit,* which our Sages mentioned.

וְהָיָה ה׳ לִי לֵאלֹהִים — *Then shall HASHEM be my God.* Then shall *HASHEM* be my judge if I will not serve Him with all my strength. The letter ו here (וְהָיָה) means *behold* (וְהִנֵּה), i.e., I hereby accept upon myself that *HASHEM,* the compassionate God, will then be to as me אֱלֹהִים, conducting Himself with the attribute of justice.

XXIX

1. וַיִּשָּׂא יַעֲקֹב רַגְלָיו — *So Jacob lifted his feet.* When a person sets out to go willingly to a chosen destination, we may rightly say of him that he 'carries his feet.' But if he is forced to leave because of difficulties we may properly say of him that 'his feet carry him,' similar to, יֹבִלוּהָ רַגְלֶיהָ, *Whose feet carried her* (from afar to sojourn) (*Isaiah* 23:7).

NOTES

nary act of sanctification (הֶקְדֵּשׁ) by anointing the stone with oil, a method used to sanctify the vessels of the Sanctuary. The actual erection of this stone and its use as a מַצֵּבָה would be later, upon his return. Then, Jacob would consecrate it through the libation (נֶסֶךְ).

20-21. אִם יִהְיֶה אֱלֹהִים עִמָּדִי . . . וְהָיָה ה׳ לִי לֵאלֹהִים — *If God will be with me . . . then shall HASHEM be my God.* Jacob made a vow. His words in these verses are to be understood as part of the vow, not as conditions. Jacob however, was aware that difficult conditions of life — such as oppression, poverty and illness — could impair his ability to keep the vow. He prayed that these should not befall him and lead him away from God. If this prayer would be answered then Jacob would be prepared to be judged by God as אֱלֹהִים, denoting justice, if he failed to serve Him with all his might. Until his return, however, he could only hope that God would treat him as ה׳, denoting mercy and compassion.

XXIX

1. וַיִּשָּׂא יַעֲקֹב רַגְלָיו — *So Jacob lifted his feet.* Jacob had just seen a vision of angels, experienced the nearness of the Almighty and received the assurance of God's protection — small wonder that his spirit was elevated. Thus he set out on his journey with confidence and hope. To indicate this the Torah states that Jacob *lifted his feet.* Far from being an awkward, archaic phrase it reveals Jacob's attitude, as the *Sforno* explains. Cheerfully and confidently Jacob *carried his feet,* for he was master of his destiny, capable of making his own decisions, with the assistance of God.

ב וַיַּרְא וְהִנֵּה בְאֵר בַּשָּׂדֶה וְהִנֵּה־שָׁם שְׁלֹשָׁה עֶדְרֵי־צֹאן רֹבְצִים עָלֶיהָ כִּי מִן־
ג הַבְּאֵר הַהִוא יַשְׁקוּ הָעֲדָרִים וְהָאֶבֶן גְּדֹלָה עַל־פִּי הַבְּאֵר׃ וְנֶאֶסְפוּ־שָׁמָּה
כָל־הָעֲדָרִים וְגָלֲלוּ אֶת־הָאֶבֶן מֵעַל פִּי הַבְּאֵר וְהִשְׁקוּ אֶת־הַצֹּאן וְהֵשִׁיבוּ
ד אֶת־הָאֶבֶן עַל־פִּי הַבְּאֵר לִמְקֹמָהּ׃ וַיֹּאמֶר לָהֶם יַעֲקֹב אַחַי מֵאַיִן אַתֶּם
ה וַיֹּאמְרוּ מֵחָרָן אֲנָחְנוּ׃ וַיֹּאמֶר לָהֶם הַיְדַעְתֶּם אֶת־לָבָן בֶּן־נָחוֹר וַיֹּאמְרוּ
ו יָדָעְנוּ׃ וַיֹּאמֶר לָהֶם הֲשָׁלוֹם לוֹ וַיֹּאמְרוּ שָׁלוֹם וְהִנֵּה רָחֵל בִּתּוֹ בָּאָה עִם־
ז הַצֹּאן׃ וַיֹּאמֶר הֵן עוֹד הַיּוֹם גָּדוֹל לֹא־עֵת הֵאָסֵף הַמִּקְנֶה הַשְׁקוּ הַצֹּאן וּלְכוּ
ח רְעוּ׃ וַיֹּאמְרוּ לֹא נוּכַל עַד אֲשֶׁר יֵאָסְפוּ כָּל־הָעֲדָרִים וְגָלֲלוּ אֶת־הָאֶבֶן
ט מֵעַל פִּי הַבְּאֵר וְהִשְׁקִינוּ הַצֹּאן׃ עוֹדֶנּוּ מְדַבֵּר עִמָּם וְרָחֵל ׀ בָּאָה עִם־הַצֹּאן
י אֲשֶׁר לְאָבִיהָ כִּי רֹעָה הִוא׃ וַיְהִי כַּאֲשֶׁר רָאָה יַעֲקֹב אֶת־רָחֵל בַּת־לָבָן
אֲחִי אִמּוֹ וְאֶת־צֹאן לָבָן אֲחִי אִמּוֹ וַיִּגַּשׁ יַעֲקֹב וַיָּגֶל אֶת־הָאֶבֶן מֵעַל פִּי
יא הַבְּאֵר וַיַּשְׁקְ אֶת־צֹאן לָבָן אֲחִי אִמּוֹ׃ וַיִּשַּׁק יַעֲקֹב לְרָחֵל וַיִּשָּׂא אֶת־קֹלוֹ
יב וַיֵּבְךְּ׃ וַיַּגֵּד יַעֲקֹב לְרָחֵל כִּי אֲחִי אָבִיהָ הוּא וְכִי בֶן־רִבְקָה הוּא וַתָּרָץ וַתַּגֵּד

---

6. הֲשָׁלוֹם לוֹ — *Is it well with him?* He attempted to find out (Laban's) circumstances before visiting him, since a guest's behavior with his host is determined by his (host's) circumstances.

7. הֵן עוֹד הַיּוֹם גָּדוֹל — *Look, the day is yet great.* A righteous man objects to a wrong being done even to strangers, as it is said, תּוֹעֲבַת צַדִּיקִים אִישׁ עָוֶל, *An unjust man is an abomination to the righteous (Proverbs 29:27).*

9. כִּי רֹעָה הִוא — *For she was a shepherdess.* She was skilled in the art of tending (sheep).

10. כַּאֲשֶׁר רָאָה יַעֲקֹב אֶת רָחֵל — *And it was when Jacob saw Rachel ...* but not before, so as not to deprive others, for he feared that if he did so sooner (i.e., roll off the stone) the shepherds would water the three flocks and not wait to help others.

11. וַיִּשָּׂא אֶת קֹלוֹ וַיֵּבְךְּ — *And he raised his voice and cried ...* at the thought of his not having merited to marry her in his youth, for he would then have had children born to him as a young man.

12. כִּי אֲחִי אָבִיהָ הוּא — *That he was her father's relative ...* to assure her that he had not acted improperly (immodestly) by kissing her.

NOTES

7. הֵן עוֹד הַיּוֹם גָּדוֹל — *Look, the day is yet great.* There is an imperative for every person to protest wrongdoing and attempt to correct it, unafraid of being accused of meddling. This episode of Jacob establishes a precedent for Moses many years later, when he is similarly confronted with the unfair actions of the shepherds against the daughters of Jethro. A righteous man cannot abide to witness injustice in silence.

9. כִּי רֹעָה הִוא — *For she was a shepherdess.* Under normal circumstances it would be immodest for a young girl to tend the flocks. She did so only because she was unusually skilled in the art of shepherding.

11. וַיִּשָּׂא אֶת קֹלוֹ וַיֵּבְךְּ — *And he raised his voice and cried.* Jacob was seventy-seven years old when he first met Rachel. He left home at the age of sixty-three and then spent fourteen years studying at the Academy of Shem and Eber. He realized that it is far better for children to have a young, energetic father. Had he met her earlier, by now he would have had grown children. He wept for those lost years. And that is also the reason for his impatience recorded in verse 21, as interpreted by the *Sforno*.

12. The *halachah* forbids such intimacy even

יג לְאָבִיהָ: וַיְהִי כִשְׁמֹעַ לָבָן אֶת־שֵׁמַע ׀ יַעֲקֹב בֶּן־אֲחֹתוֹ וַיָּרָץ לִקְרָאתוֹ
וַיְחַבֶּק־לוֹ וַיְנַשֶּׁק־לוֹ וַיְבִיאֵהוּ אֶל־בֵּיתוֹ וַיְסַפֵּר לְלָבָן אֵת כָּל־הַדְּבָרִים
יד הָאֵלֶּה: וַיֹּאמֶר לוֹ לָבָן אַךְ עַצְמִי וּבְשָׂרִי אָתָּה וַיֵּשֶׁב עִמּוֹ חֹדֶשׁ יָמִים:
טו וַיֹּאמֶר לָבָן לְיַעֲקֹב הֲכִי־אָחִי אַתָּה וַעֲבַדְתַּנִי חִנָּם הַגִּידָה לִּי מַה־
טז־יז מַשְׂכֻּרְתֶּךָ: וּלְלָבָן שְׁתֵּי בָנוֹת שֵׁם הַגְּדֹלָה לֵאָה וְשֵׁם הַקְּטַנָּה רָחֵל: וְעֵינֵי
שלישי יח לֵאָה רַכּוֹת וְרָחֵל הָיְתָה יְפַת־תֹּאַר וִיפַת מַרְאֶה: וַיֶּאֱהַב יַעֲקֹב אֶת־רָחֵל
יט וַיֹּאמֶר אֶעֱבָדְךָ שֶׁבַע שָׁנִים בְּרָחֵל בִּתְּךָ הַקְּטַנָּה: וַיֹּאמֶר לָבָן טוֹב תִּתִּי

וְכִי בֶן רִבְקָה הוּא — *And that he was Rebecca's son.* He mentioned Rebecca, although Rachel did not know her, so that she might inform her father.

13. אֶת שֵׁמַע יַעֲקֹב — *The news of Jacob* . . . that he alone had rolled away the stone.

וַיְסַפֵּר לְלָבָן — *He recounted to Laban* . . . that he had not come to him for a livelihood, but to escape from his brother and live with him (Laban), at the behest of his mother.

14. אַךְ עַצְמִי וּבְשָׂרִי אָתָּה — *Nevertheless, you are my flesh and blood.* Although you can earn your living as a shepherd elsewhere or in some other occupation, since you are *my flesh and blood* you should stay in my house.

וַיֵּשֶׁב עִמּוֹ — *And he stayed with him* . . . working for him as a shepherd, as we find in, שְׁבָה עִמָּדִי, *Remain with me* (v. 19); and in, וַיּוֹאֶל מֹשֶׁה לָשֶׁבֶת אֶת הָאִישׁ, *And Moses was willing to stay with the man (Exodus* 2:21). That is why (Laban) later says to him, 'וַעֲבַדְתַּנִי חִנָּם, *Should you serve me for nothing?*' (v. 15).

17. יְפַת תֹּאַר — *Beautiful of form* . . . beautiful features (image) similar to, וּבַמְּחוּגָה יְתָאֳרֵהוּ, *and marks it out with a compass (Isaiah* 44:13).

וִיפַת מַרְאֶה — *And beautiful of appearance* . . . beautiful complexion and radiant appearance; one's natural coloring which appeals to the (beholder's) sense of sight.

18. אֶעֱבָדְךָ שֶׁבַע שָׁנִים בְּרָחֵל — *I will work for you seven years for Rachel.* Without a doubt, this righteous man (Jacob) would not have wed and had children unless he had the wherewithal to support (his wife), specifically her food and clothing, as our Sages state, נוֹשֵׂא אָדָם כַּמָּה נָשִׁים וְהוּא דְאִית לֵיה לְמֵיזְנִינְהוּ, *A man may marry many wives (in addition to his first) provided he possesses the means to support them (Yevamos* 68a). Laban, in turn, who was a man of means, would not have allowed his daughters to marry a man who could not provide for them. We must therefore say that when (Jacob) said, *'For with my staff I crossed this Jordan'* (32:11) he meant that he had neither flocks nor a way to earn a living. The work he did for

NOTES

with members of one's family unless they are very young children, except between parent and child (*Even HaEzer* 21:6). *Ramban* points out that Rachel was still too young to arouse one's passion. Moreover, as the Sforno states in verse 18, Jacob had to wait seven years until she would reach marriageable age. This fact, coupled with the fact that he was 'her father's relative' prompted his action.

14. וַיֵּשֶׁב עִמּוֹ – *And he stayed with him.* The expression וַיֵּשֶׁב is not to be understood as 'dwelling with his uncle as a guest.' Jacob worked for Laban from the outset. He was never a guest enjoying Laban's hospitality.

18. אֶעֱבָדְךָ שֶׁבַע שָׁנִים בְּרָחֵל – *I will work for you seven years for Rachel.* The *Sforno* is convinced that Jacob would never have asked for Rachel's hand in marriage, nor would Laban have consented, if he was impoverished. That is why he interprets the verse as meaning a lack of substantial assets, but still with sufficient means to wed and support a

כ אֹתָהּ לָךְ מִתִּתִּי אֹתָהּ לְאִישׁ אַחֵר שְׁבָה עִמָּדִי: וַיַּעֲבֹד יַעֲקֹב בְּרָחֵל שֶׁבַע
כא שָׁנִים וַיִּהְיוּ בְעֵינָיו כְּיָמִים אֲחָדִים בְּאַהֲבָתוֹ אֹתָהּ: וַיֹּאמֶר יַעֲקֹב אֶל־לָבָן
כב הָבָה אֶת־אִשְׁתִּי כִּי מָלְאוּ יָמָי וְאָבוֹאָה אֵלֶיהָ: וַיֶּאֱסֹף לָבָן אֶת־כָּל־אַנְשֵׁי
כג הַמָּקוֹם וַיַּעַשׂ מִשְׁתֶּה: וַיְהִי בָעֶרֶב וַיִּקַּח אֶת־לֵאָה בִתּוֹ וַיָּבֵא אֹתָהּ אֵלָיו
כד־כה וַיָּבֹא אֵלֶיהָ: וַיִּתֵּן לָבָן לָהּ אֶת־זִלְפָּה שִׁפְחָתוֹ לְלֵאָה בִתּוֹ שִׁפְחָה: וַיְהִי
בַבֹּקֶר וְהִנֵּה־הִוא לֵאָה וַיֹּאמֶר אֶל־לָבָן מַה־זֹּאת עָשִׂיתָ לִּי הֲלֹא בְרָחֵל
כו עָבַדְתִּי עִמָּךְ וְלָמָּה רִמִּיתָנִי: וַיֹּאמֶר לָבָן לֹא־יֵעָשֶׂה כֵן בִּמְקוֹמֵנוּ לָתֵת
כז הַצְּעִירָה לִפְנֵי הַבְּכִירָה: מַלֵּא שְׁבֻעַ זֹאת וְנִתְּנָה לְךָ גַּם־אֶת־זֹאת בַּעֲבֹדָה
כח אֲשֶׁר תַּעֲבֹד עִמָּדִי עוֹד שֶׁבַע־שָׁנִים אֲחֵרוֹת: וַיַּעַשׂ יַעֲקֹב כֵּן וַיְמַלֵּא שְׁבֻעַ
כט זֹאת וַיִּתֶּן־לוֹ אֶת־רָחֵל בִּתּוֹ לוֹ לְאִשָּׁה: וַיִּתֵּן לָבָן לְרָחֵל בִּתּוֹ אֶת־בִּלְהָה
ל שִׁפְחָתוֹ לָהּ לְשִׁפְחָה: וַיָּבֹא גַּם אֶל־רָחֵל וַיֶּאֱהַב גַּם־אֶת־רָחֵל מִלֵּאָה

Rachel was in the form of a dowry to the father of the daughter as it says, אִם מָאֵן יְמָאֵן אָבִיהָ לְתִתָּהּ לוֹ כֶּסֶף יִשְׁקוֹל כְּמֹהַר הַבְּתוּלֹת, *If her father refuses to give her to him, he shall pay money according to the dowry of virgins* (*Exodus* 22:16). And what they meant later by saying, 'כִּי מְכָרָנוּ, *For he has sold us*' (31:15), was because in their humility they believed that the dowry was more than they were worth.

בִּתְּךָ הַקְּטַנָּה — *Your younger daughter.* During these seven years (Rachel) would reach marriageable age and in the interim (Laban) would be able to find a husband for the older daughter (Leah).

20. וַיִּהְיוּ בְעֵינָיו כְּיָמִים אֲחָדִים — *And they seemed to him a few days . . .* because he thought that he should have given an even bigger dowry for her.

בְּאַהֲבָתוֹ אֹתָהּ — *Because of his love for her . . .* for 'love upsets the rule of normal conduct' (*Sanhedrin* 105b).

21. וְאָבוֹאָה אֵלֶיהָ — *And I will consort with her.* Let us proceed immediately with the marriage, not only the betrothal, for he desired to acquire 'the Godly heritage of children.'

26. לֹא יֵעָשֶׂה כֵן בִּמְקוֹמֵנוּ — *Such is not done in our place.* The people here would not allow me to keep my word.

27. וְנִתְּנָה לְךָ — *And we will give her to you.* Then the people (of the place) will also agree.

30. וַיֶּאֱהַב גַּם אֶת רָחֵל מִלֵּאָה — *And he also loved Rachel more than Leah . . .* not only because of the intimacy of marriage but because she was Rachel; (i.e.,) her deeds

NOTES

wife. The years of labor are not for this purpose, rather for the purpose of giving a dowry to his prospective father-in-law.

20. וַיִּהְיוּ בְעֵינָיו . . . בְּאַהֲבָתוֹ אֹתָהּ — *And they seemed to him . . . because of his love for her.* Jacob's love for Rachel, and his estimation of her value, was such that he felt the dowry he was giving (through the seven years of labor) was far too little. The *Sforno*, however, comments that since love affects man's objectivity, perhaps Jacob's willingness to pay this price was in reality a bit extravagant.

21. וְאָבוֹאָה אֵלֶיהָ — *And I will consort with her.* Based on, *Children are a heritage of* HASHEM (*Psalms* 127:3).

30. וַיֶּאֱהַב גַּם אֶת רָחֵל — *And he also loved Rachel more than Leah.* The word גַּם, *also*, is to

לא וַיַּעֲבֹד עִמּוֹ עוֹד שֶׁבַע־שָׁנִים אֲחֵרוֹת׃ וַיַּרְא יהוה כִּי־שְׂנוּאָה לֵאָה וַיִּפְתַּח
לב אֶת־רַחְמָהּ וְרָחֵל עֲקָרָה׃ וַתַּהַר לֵאָה וַתֵּלֶד בֵּן וַתִּקְרָא שְׁמוֹ רְאוּבֵן כִּי
לג אָמְרָה כִּי־רָאָה יהוה בְּעָנְיִי כִּי עַתָּה יֶאֱהָבַנִי אִישִׁי׃ וַתַּהַר עוֹד וַתֵּלֶד בֵּן
וַתֹּאמֶר כִּי־שָׁמַע יהוה כִּי־שְׂנוּאָה אָנֹכִי וַיִּתֶּן־לִי גַּם־אֶת־זֶה וַתִּקְרָא שְׁמוֹ
לד שִׁמְעוֹן׃ וַתַּהַר עוֹד וַתֵּלֶד בֵּן וַתֹּאמֶר עַתָּה הַפַּעַם יִלָּוֶה אִישִׁי אֵלַי כִּי־
לה יָלַדְתִּי לוֹ שְׁלֹשָׁה בָנִים עַל־כֵּן קָרָא־שְׁמוֹ לֵוִי׃ וַתַּהַר עוֹד וַתֵּלֶד בֵּן וַתֹּאמֶר
ל א הַפַּעַם אוֹדֶה אֶת־יהוה עַל־כֵּן קָרְאָה שְׁמוֹ יְהוּדָה וַתַּעֲמֹד מִלֶּדֶת׃ וַתֵּרֶא
רָחֵל כִּי לֹא יָלְדָה לְיַעֲקֹב וַתְּקַנֵּא רָחֵל בַּאֲחֹתָהּ וַתֹּאמֶר אֶל־יַעֲקֹב הָבָה־

---

which stemmed from her personality. Even though Leah was his first wife, and it is common for a man to find greater contentment with her, as our Sages tell us, 'A man finds contentment only with his first wife' (*Yevamos* 63b).

31. כִּי שְׂנוּאָה לֵאָה — *That Leah was unloved.* (Jacob did not love Leah because) after a while he recognized (certain) signs of barrenness in her, as it says, *So He (God)opened her womb,* and he (Jacob) thought that because of this (condition) she had agreed to deceive him.

וְרָחֵל עֲקָרָה — *But Rachel remained barren.* She was by nature barren, and remained so until God opened her womb.

32. בְּעָנְיִי — *In my affliction.* Because my husband suspected me of willfully deceiving him, therefore God, may He be blessed, granted me children as vindication, similar to a *sotah* (a woman suspected of infidelity unjustly, who when cleared conceives — see *Numbers* 5:28).

33. כִּי שְׂנוּאָה אָנֹכִי — *That I am unloved . . .* and as compensation for this unfounded suspicion He has granted me this (son) also.

34. הַפַּעַם יִלָּוֶה — *This time (my husband) will become attached (to me).* For I have established that I am capable of having many children, as our Sages teach us, בִּתְלָתָא זִימְנֵי הָוְיָא חֲזָקָה, *A chazakah (presumption) is established when it occurs three times* (*Yevamos* 64b).

35. עַל כֵּן קָרְאָה שְׁמוֹ יְהוּדָה — *Therefore she named him Judah.* This name contains the letters of the honored name of God as well as those of 'thankfulness' (praise). It appears that these were names of the ancients, as we find before this, יְהוּדִית בַּת בְּאֵרִי, *Judith the daughter of Be'eri* (26:34), and we also find, שְׁמוּאֵל בֶּן עַמִּיהוּד, *Samuel the son of Amihud* (*Numbers* 34:20), antedating Samuel the prophet. (Apparently) they chose these earlier names which fit events (at the time of their children's birth).

NOTES

be understood thus: 'He loved' Rachel as his wife, but he 'also' loved her for her personal traits and qualities — i.e., for being Rachel.

32. בְּעָנְיִי — *In my affliction.* The name רְאוּבֵן is a bit difficult to understand. Leah said, *God has seen my affliction,* which accounts for the first part of the name, i.e., רְאוּ (from רָאָה), but the concluding part בֵּן can only be explained by accepting the *Sforno's* interpretation. Since Leah was unjustly suspected by Jacob of collusion with her father, she was similar to a *sotah,* hence worthy to be granted a child (בֵּן) as compensation. The name רְאוּבֵן is now quite understandable. By 'seeing' my suffering, a 'son' was born to me.

ב לִי בָנִים וְאִם־אַיִן מֵתָה אָנֹכִי׃ וַיִּחַר־אַף יַעֲקֹב בְּרָחֵל וַיֹּאמֶר הֲתַחַת
ג אֱלֹהִים אָנֹכִי אֲשֶׁר־מָנַע מִמֵּךְ פְּרִי־בָטֶן׃ וַתֹּאמֶר הִנֵּה אֲמָתִי בִלְהָה בֹּא
ד אֵלֶיהָ וְתֵלֵד עַל־בִּרְכַּי וְאִבָּנֶה גַם־אָנֹכִי מִמֶּנָּה׃ וַתִּתֶּן־לוֹ אֶת־בִּלְהָה
ה שִׁפְחָתָהּ לְאִשָּׁה וַיָּבֹא אֵלֶיהָ יַעֲקֹב׃ וַתַּהַר בִּלְהָה וַתֵּלֶד לְיַעֲקֹב בֵּן׃
ו וַתֹּאמֶר רָחֵל דָּנַנִּי אֱלֹהִים וְגַם שָׁמַע בְּקֹלִי וַיִּתֶּן־לִי בֵּן עַל־כֵּן קָרְאָה שְׁמוֹ

XXX

1. מֵתָה אָנֹכִי — *(Otherwise) I am dead . . .* similar to, הֵן אֲנִי עֵץ יָבֵשׁ, *Behold, I am a dry tree (Isaiah* 56:3).

2. וַיִּחַר אַף יַעֲקֹב — *Jacob's anger flared up . . .* for saying, 'הָבָה לִי בָנִים, *Give me children,'* implying that he had the power to do so. In his zeal for the honor of God he disregarded his love for her.

אֲשֶׁר מָנַע מִמֵּךְ — *Who has withheld from you.* (God) has created you barren. He (Jacob) recognized in her the signs of a woman incapable of conception (אַילוֹנִית).

3. בֹּא אֵלֶיהָ — *Consort with her.* This is what I meant when I said, *'Give me children.'* I never thought that you possess the key to (open) a barren woman.

וְאִבָּנֶה גַם אָנֹכִי מִמֶּנָּה — *And I too may be built from her . . .* similar to my sister.

מִמֶּנָּה — *From her.* My jealousy of my co-wife may stimulate the nature of my reproductive system [so that it will function normally].

6. דָּנַנִּי אֱלֹהִים — *God has judged me.* God was righteous in His judgment by not granting me a pregnancy . . .

וְגַם שָׁמַע בְּקֹלִי — *He also heard my voice.* But nevertheless He accepted my prayer.

וַיִּתֶּן לִי בֵּן — *And has given me a son.* (He will be) חוּטְרָא לִיַדָא וּמָרָא לִקְבוּרָה, *A staff in my hand and a spade for my burial (Kesubos* 64a), since he was born on my knees (see 50:23). The wives (Rachel and Leah) by these statements (adopting the children of the maidservants as their own) agreed to set them (Bilhah and Zilpah) free. Since these children were accepted as sons, they would not have a status of slaves, since their mothers were no longer maidservants, otherwise it would have been a case of, הָאִשָּׁה וִילָדֶיהָ תִּהְיֶה לַאדֹנֶיהָ, *The wife and her children shall be her*

NOTES

XXX

1. מֵתָה אָנֹכִי – *(Otherwise) I am dead.* When Rachel said מֵתָה אָנֹכִי, *I am dead,* her remark is to be understood in the same sense as that of the eunuch who said 'Behold, I am a dry tree,' for just as he is unable to have children and is compared to a dry tree which has no life, so one who is childless may be regarded as dead. This is the intent of Rachel's remark. If she was childless, it is as though she was dead. (See *Nedarim* 64b, 'Four may be regarded as dead: the leper, the blind, he who is childless and he who is impoverished').

2. וַיִּחַר אַף יַעֲקֹב – *Jacob's anger flared up.* Jacob was angry with Rachel for saying *'Give me,'* not *'Pray for me.'* The latter request would have been proper; the former was not, since it implied that Jacob had the power to grant that which only God can give. Normally, the great love Jacob had for Rachel would have made him more patient, and he would have controlled his anger. His great zeal for God's honor, however, caused him to set aside his feelings of love for Rachel, for his love of God was greater.

3. מִמֶּנָּה – *From her.* The word מִמֶּנָּה, *from her,* is translated literally by the *Sforno.* From Bilhah's ability to conceive and give birth to a child whom I will raise, the functioning of my reproductive system will hopefully be aroused.

6. וַיִּתֶּן לִי בֵּן – *And has given me a son.* Our Sages use this expression 'a staff, etc.' in the

ז־ח דָּן: וַתַּהַר עוֹד וַתֵּלֶד בִּלְהָה שִׁפְחַת רָחֵל בֵּן שֵׁנִי לְיַעֲקֹב: וַתֹּאמֶר רָחֵל
נַפְתּוּלֵי אֱלֹהִים | נִפְתַּלְתִּי עִם־אֲחֹתִי גַּם־יָכֹלְתִּי וַתִּקְרָא שְׁמוֹ נַפְתָּלִי:
ט וַתֵּרֶא לֵאָה כִּי עָמְדָה מִלֶּדֶת וַתִּקַּח אֶת־זִלְפָּה שִׁפְחָתָהּ וַתִּתֵּן אֹתָהּ
°בָּא גָד י־יא לְיַעֲקֹב לְאִשָּׁה: וַתֵּלֶד זִלְפָּה שִׁפְחַת לֵאָה לְיַעֲקֹב בֵּן: וַתֹּאמֶר לֵאָה °בגד

master's (Exodus 21:4). For this reason they no longer subjugated (their maidservants) as Sarah did with Hagar, with Abraham's consent, when he said, הִנֵּה שִׁפְחָתֵךְ בְּיָדֵךְ, *Behold your maid is in your hand* (16:6). Therefore, all (the sons) are considered to be 'the children of Jacob' to inherit him, and all are worthy to be remembered before God, (inscribed) on the *Ephod* and *Choshen* (breastplate), for each of them is considered to be the legitimate descendant of Jacob. This is not so regarding Ishmael, as it says, כִּי בְיִצְחָק יִקָּרֵא לְךָ זָרַע, *Since through Isaac will offspring be considered yours* (21:12).

8. נַפְתּוּלֵי אֱלֹהִים נִפְתַּלְתִּי — *With Godly bonds have I been bound.* (נַפְתּוּלֵי) From the expression, צָמִיד פָּתִיל, *tightly bound (Numbers* 19:15). With Godly and sacred cleaving did I cleave to my husband.

עִם אֲחֹתִי — *With my sister* . . . this I did together with my sister, since we both gave our handmaids (to Jacob) to facilitate the birth of the (twelve) tribes. Leah, perforce, had already given Zilpah to Jacob *before* the birth of Naphtali, for in seven years eight tribes were born — six sons to Leah and two to Zilpah. Now if we figure nine months for each pregnancy, it totals seventy-two months, which equals six years, besides the nine months for Dan who preceded (Zilpah's children), totaling eight tribes. From all this we must conclude that Leah gave Zilpah to Jacob (as a wife) prior to Naphtali's birth, otherwise seven years would not suffice for all, unless we assume that every pregnancy was only seven months, and that immediately after each birth they conceived again, (implying) that they did not observe any restrictions regulating post-natal impurity.

גַּם יָכֹלְתִּי — *I have also prevailed.* I have attained my intentions by giving my maidservant to my husband.

11. בָּא גָד (בְּגָד) — *Good luck has come.* He has come by chance, for had I not ceased

NOTES

following sense. By having a son, one is assured of support in old age (if necessary) and someone to attend to his burial when the time comes. The *Sforno* applies this saying to Rachel's gratification at the birth of Dan, whom she intended to raise *on her knees.*

The *Sforno* draws a fine, and vital, distinction between the children born to Jacob through Bilhah and Zilpah and the son that Hagar bore to Abraham. In the former case, the mothers were set free; hence the status of their sons is the same as the sons of their former mistresses. Hagar was not set free by Sarah. As a result, her son Ishmael was the son of a maidservant and was not considered genealogically equal to his half-brother Isaac.

8. עִם אֲחֹתִי – *With my sister.* The phrase עִם אֲחֹתִי, *with my sister,* is interpreted by the *Sforno* in consonance with his translation of נַפְתּוּלֵי as meaning *bound,* i.e., bound together with her sister Leah in their common endeavor to assist Jacob in bringing twelve tribes into the world. Toward that end, Leah had already given Zilpah to her husband as a wife, prior to Naphtali's birth. The *Sforno* proves this sequence of events by showing that only in this manner could eight tribes be born in seven years. He rejects the unlikely theory (held by some commentators) that a number of these pregnancies were of seven month duration, as well as the equally unlikely theory of conception following immediately after each birth, which would have negated the observance of the laws of purity governing marital relations after childbirth.

11. בָּא גָד – *Good luck has come.* The explana-

יב־יג וַתִּקְרָא אֶת־שְׁמוֹ גָּד: וַתֵּלֶד זִלְפָּה שִׁפְחַת לֵאָה בֵּן שֵׁנִי לְיַעֲקֹב: וַתֹּאמֶר
רביעי יד לֵאָה בְּאָשְׁרִי כִּי אִשְּׁרוּנִי בָּנוֹת וַתִּקְרָא אֶת־שְׁמוֹ אָשֵׁר: וַיֵּלֶךְ רְאוּבֵן בִּימֵי
קְצִיר־חִטִּים וַיִּמְצָא דוּדָאִים בַּשָּׂדֶה וַיָּבֵא אֹתָם אֶל־לֵאָה אִמּוֹ וַתֹּאמֶר
טו רָחֵל אֶל־לֵאָה תְּנִי־נָא לִי מִדּוּדָאֵי בְּנֵךְ: וַתֹּאמֶר לָהּ הַמְעַט קַחְתֵּךְ
אֶת־אִישִׁי וְלָקַחַת גַּם אֶת־דּוּדָאֵי בְּנִי וַתֹּאמֶר רָחֵל לָכֵן יִשְׁכַּב עִמָּךְ
טז הַלַּיְלָה תַּחַת דּוּדָאֵי בְנֵךְ: וַיָּבֹא יַעֲקֹב מִן־הַשָּׂדֶה בָּעֶרֶב וַתֵּצֵא לֵאָה
לִקְרָאתוֹ וַתֹּאמֶר אֵלַי תָּבוֹא כִּי שָׂכֹר שְׂכַרְתִּיךָ בְּדוּדָאֵי בְּנִי וַיִּשְׁכַּב עִמָּהּ

---

to bear (children) I had no intention to bring him into the world (through my maidservant). בָּגָד is written as one word, implying 'failure,' because she *failed* to bear, after she had done so heretofore. (בָּגָד is derived from) אַחַי בָּגְדוּ כְמוֹ נָחַל, *My brethren have dealt deceitfully as a brook (Job* 6:15).

13. בְּאָשְׁרִי — *In my good fortune.* This son represents another instance of my good fortune, for he also is considered as my son.

14. וַיֵּלֶךְ רְאוּבֵן — *Reuben went out . . .* when he perceived that his mother (Leah) was painfully distressed by the cessation of her childbearing.

וַיִּמְצָא דוּדָאִים — *He found duda'im (mandrakes) . . .* a most fragrant plant which (supposedly) promotes fertility, similar to garlic which our Sages suggested be eaten Friday nights by men (since they increase fertility). The *duda'im* were similar, and even superior, since it also increased the love of (husband and wife) as it is written, שָׁם אֶתֵּן אֶת דֹּדַי לָךְ, הַדּוּדָאִים נָתְנוּ רֵיחַ, *There I will give my love to you; the mandrakes yield fragrance (Song of Songs* 7:13,14). We are being told (in this story) that even though Reuben at this time was at most four or five years old, he possessed mature judgment (and sensitivity).

15. הַמְעַט קַחְתֵּךְ אֶת אִישִׁי — *Is it a small matter that you have taken away my husband.* You should never have consented to become my rival-wife, as it says, וְאִשָּׁה אֶל אֲחֹתָהּ לֹא תִקָּח לִצְרֹר, *You shall not take a woman to her sister to be a rival-wife (Leviticus* 18:18).

וְלָקַחַת גַּם אֶת דּוּדָאֵי בְּנִי — *And now to take even my son's duda'im . . .* to increase his love for you and hatred for me!

לָכֵן יִשְׁכַּב עִמָּךְ הַלַּיְלָה — *Therefore, he shall lie with you tonight.* Hence, the effectiveness and magical power of these *duda'im* (for me) will be preceded by your (spending the night with Jacob) and so no harm will come to you, by giving me the *duda'im* now; and, as for the future, what is to prevent anyone from finding some for me, since, as our Sages tell us (*Sanhedrin* 99b), these were brought from (הֶפְקֵר) ownerless property (see *Rashi* on verse 14).

16. אֵלַי תָּבוֹא כִּי שָׂכֹר שְׂכַרְתִּיךָ — *It is to me that you must come for I have surely hired you.* You will not be guilty of any wrongdoing by depriving my sister her

NOTES

tion of the verse from *Job*, quoted by the *Sforno*, is that there are brooks (wadis) which flow abundantly in the rainy season but dry up completely during the summer. Job complains that similarly there are friends whose sympathy at first flows, then ceases (fails) completely. The Hebrew word for *failure* in that verse is בָּגְדוּ although it can also be

יז בַּלַּיְלָה הוּא: וַיִּשְׁמַע אֱלֹהִים אֶל־לֵאָה וַתַּהַר וַתֵּלֶד לְיַעֲקֹב בֵּן חֲמִישִׁי:
יח וַתֹּאמֶר לֵאָה נָתַן אֱלֹהִים שְׂכָרִי אֲשֶׁר־נָתַתִּי שִׁפְחָתִי לְאִישִׁי וַתִּקְרָא שְׁמוֹ
יט-כ יִשָּׂשכָר: וַתַּהַר עוֹד לֵאָה וַתֵּלֶד בֵּן־שִׁשִּׁי לְיַעֲקֹב: וַתֹּאמֶר לֵאָה זְבָדַנִי
אֱלֹהִים ׀ אֹתִי זֶבֶד טוֹב הַפַּעַם יִזְבְּלֵנִי אִישִׁי כִּי־יָלַדְתִּי לוֹ שִׁשָּׁה בָנִים

---

conjugal rights since she has willingly consented (to relinquish her right). This incident may appear immodest to those who brazenly misinterpret (Torah) but it reveals to us that the Patriarchs viewed marital intimacy as innocently as did Adam and Eve before they sinned, for there was no thought or intent of physical gratification at all; they were solely motivated to produce offspring, to serve and honor God. This incident also tells us that the motive of the Matriarchs was acceptable to God, the Blessed One, when they tried (to build the house of Israel) by bringing in co-wives (Bilhah and Zilpah) and the incident of the *duda'im* (as well). Because of their (pure deeds) their prayers were accepted, for it is proper for the *tzaddik* to utilize every possible natural means to attain his goal, combined with prayer, as our Sages tell us, הַקָּדוֹשׁ בָּרוּךְ הוּא מִתְאַוֶּה לִתְפִלָּתָם שֶׁל צַדִּיקִים, *the Holy One, Blessed is He, desires the prayers of the righteous (Yevamos* 64a).

וַיִּשְׁכַּב עִמָּהּ בַּלַּיְלָה הוּא — *So he lay with her that night* ... with his full knowledge and consent, cognizant of Leah's zest and pure motives.

17. וַיִּשְׁמַע אֱלֹהִים אֶל לֵאָה — *And God hearkened to Leah* ... for she had preceded her prayer with (her own) efforts, as she said ...

18. נָתַן אֱלֹהִים שְׂכָרִי אֲשֶׁר נָתַתִּי שִׁפְחָתִי לְאִישִׁי — *God has granted my reward because I gave my maidservant to my husband.* This was my first effort, when I brought this rival-wife into my house.

20. זְבָדַנִי אֱלֹהִים אֹתִי — *God has endowed me.* He has granted me a (generous) portion and rewarded me for my second effort, i.e., with the *duda'im*, for, שְׂכַר מִצְוָה מִצְוָה, *The reward of a mitzvah is a mitzvah (Avos* 4:2).

זֶבֶד טוֹב — *A good endowment* ... for I (now) have a goodly portion, because I did not have any intention for physical pleasure. (I acted) only for His honor.

NOTES

associated with *treachery*. Hence the name given by Leah to Zilpah's child, גָּד, from בָּא גָד, has a twofold meaning. Written as two words it can mean *Good luck has come*. Written as one (בְּגָד) it is linked to the same word in *Job* (6:15) meaning *failed* and *betrayed*, as the *Sforno* explains.

16. וַיִּשְׁכַּב עִמָּהּ בַּלַּיְלָה הוּא — *So he lay with her that night*. The word הוּא at the end of this verse is seemingly superfluous. Our Sages interpreted it as referring to the Almighty's involvement in the conception of Issachar. The *Sforno* interprets it as referring to Jacob, revealing to us that he did not cohabit with Leah because of her arrangement with Rachel, but of his own free will. A positive attitude of both husband and wife is vital to happy and fulfilling marital relations, in the view of the Torah.

17-20. נָתַן אֱלֹהִים שְׂכָרִי אֲשֶׁר נָתַתִּי שִׁפְחָתִי לְאִישִׁי ... זְבָדַנִי אֱלֹהִים — *God has granted my reward because I gave my maidservant to my husband ... God has endowed me.* The *Sforno* explains that two additional sons were born to Leah as reward for the two efforts she expended — giving Zilpah to her husband as a co-wife and the incident of the *duda'im*. The first child (Issachar) is a reward for the first good deed, while Zebulun is in recognition of the *duda'im*. It is possible that this is so not only because of the sequence of these two events, but also to remove the immediacy of Leah's hiring Jacob with her *duda'im* from the conception of Issachar. Even though the motivation was pure, as mentioned in verse 16, for the sake of modesty it is preferable to let time

כא-כב וַתִּקְרָא אֶת־שְׁמוֹ זְבֻלוּן: וְאַחַר יָלְדָה בַּת וַתִּקְרָא אֶת־שְׁמָהּ דִּינָה: וַיִּזְכֹּר
כג אֱלֹהִים אֶת־רָחֵל וַיִּשְׁמַע אֵלֶיהָ אֱלֹהִים וַיִּפְתַּח אֶת־רַחְמָהּ: וַתַּהַר וַתֵּלֶד
כד בֵּן וַתֹּאמֶר אָסַף אֱלֹהִים אֶת־חֶרְפָּתִי: וַתִּקְרָא אֶת־שְׁמוֹ יוֹסֵף לֵאמֹר יֹסֵף
כה יהוה לִי בֵּן אַחֵר: וַיְהִי כַּאֲשֶׁר יָלְדָה רָחֵל אֶת־יוֹסֵף וַיֹּאמֶר יַעֲקֹב אֶל־לָבָן
כו שַׁלְּחֵנִי וְאֵלְכָה אֶל־מְקוֹמִי וּלְאַרְצִי: תְּנָה אֶת־נָשַׁי וְאֶת־יְלָדַי אֲשֶׁר
עָבַדְתִּי אֹתְךָ בָּהֵן וְאֵלֵכָה כִּי אַתָּה יָדַעְתָּ אֶת־עֲבֹדָתִי אֲשֶׁר עֲבַדְתִּיךָ:
כז וַיֹּאמֶר אֵלָיו לָבָן אִם־נָא מָצָאתִי חֵן בְּעֵינֶיךָ נִחַשְׁתִּי וַיְבָרְכֵנִי יהוה בִּגְלָלֶךָ:
חמישי כח-כט וַיֹּאמַר נָקְבָה שְׂכָרְךָ עָלַי וְאֶתֵּנָה: וַיֹּאמֶר אֵלָיו אַתָּה יָדַעְתָּ אֵת אֲשֶׁר
ל עֲבַדְתִּיךָ וְאֵת אֲשֶׁר־הָיָה מִקְנְךָ אִתִּי: כִּי מְעַט אֲשֶׁר־הָיָה לְךָ לְפָנַי וַיִּפְרֹץ

---

22. וַיִּזְכֹּר אֱלֹהִים אֶת רָחֵל — *God remembered Rachel* . . . her efforts to conceive by bringing her handmaiden into the house as a rival-wife and the incident of the *duda'im.*

וַיִּשְׁמַע אֵלֶיהָ אֱלֹהִים — *And God hearkened to her* . . . to her prayers, after she had made both efforts.

23. אֶת חֶרְפָּתִי — *My disgrace* . . . that God had accepted her sister's prayer and not hers.

24. יֹסֵף ה׳ לִי בֵּן אַחֵר — *May* HASHEM *add on for me another son* . . . (as a reward) for my second effort (i.e., the *duda'im),* as He did for my sister.

25. שַׁלְּחֵנִי וְאֵלְכָה — *Grant me leave that I may go.* Even though (Jacob) had no flocks or cattle at that time, having come only with his staff, still he had sufficient to provide his wives and children with bread, clothing and provision for the road. Otherwise, a wise righteous man (such as Jacob) would never have set out (on this journey) to die from hunger, nor would Laban, who was a rich man, respected in his city, have allowed him to leave with his daughters and family to die in hunger, thirst and deprivation, far from home. Now, Laban implores him (Jacob) to remain for his *own* benefit, as it is said וַיְבָרְכֵנִי ה׳ בִּגְלָלֶךָ, HASHEM *has blessed me on account of you* (verse 27).

27. אִם נָא מָצָאתִי חֵן בְּעֵינֶיךָ — *If I have found favor in your eyes.* If you love me to the degree that our kinship would warrant, you would not leave me, for I have learned by divination that my house has been blessed on account of you, with cattle and other possessions, as our Sages say, תֵּיכֶף לְתַלְמִיד חָכָם בְּרָכָה, *A blessing follows immediately on the (entertaining) of a scholar (Berachos* 42a).

וַיְבָרְכֵנִי ה׳ בִּגְלָלֶךָ — HASHEM *has blessed me on account of you.* And I am also cognizant of the fact that I have realized from my cattle much money and wealth to an abnormal extent, and I know that this is on account of you.

29. אַתָּה יָדַעְתָּ אֵת אֲשֶׁר עֲבַדְתִּיךָ — *You know how I have served you.* Do not attribute the increase in your flocks to divination and good luck, rather attribute it to my (hard) committed labors, performed by skill and much effort in tending the sheep.

NOTES

elapse before Leah is rewarded with a child for the *duda'im* episode.

23. אֶת חֶרְפָּתִי – *My disgrace.* The righteous Rachel's greatest disgrace is not her barren-

לא לָרֹב וַיְבָרֶךְ יהוה אֹתְךָ לְרַגְלִי וְעַתָּה מָתַי אֶעֱשֶׂה גַם־אָנֹכִי לְבֵיתִי: וַיֹּאמֶר
מָה אֶתֶּן־לָךְ וַיֹּאמֶר יַעֲקֹב לֹא־תִתֶּן־לִי מְאוּמָה אִם־תַּעֲשֶׂה־לִּי הַדָּבָר הַזֶּה
לב אָשׁוּבָה אֶרְעֶה צֹאנְךָ אֶשְׁמֹר: אֶעֱבֹר בְּכָל־צֹאנְךָ הַיּוֹם הָסֵר מִשָּׁם כָּל־שֶׂה
| נָקֹד וְטָלוּא וְכָל־שֶׂה־חוּם בַּכְּשָׂבִים וְטָלוּא וְנָקֹד בָּעִזִּים וְהָיָה שְׂכָרִי:
לג וְעָנְתָה־בִּי צִדְקָתִי בְּיוֹם מָחָר כִּי־תָבוֹא עַל־שְׂכָרִי לְפָנֶיךָ כֹּל אֲשֶׁר־אֵינֶנּוּ
לד נָקֹד וְטָלוּא בָּעִזִּים וְחוּם בַּכְּשָׂבִים גָּנוּב הוּא אִתִּי: וַיֹּאמֶר לָבָן הֵן לוּ יְהִי
לה כִדְבָרֶךָ: וַיָּסַר בַּיּוֹם הַהוּא אֶת־הַתְּיָשִׁים הָעֲקֻדִּים וְהַטְּלֻאִים וְאֵת כָּל־

וְאֵת אֲשֶׁר הָיָה מִקְנְךָ אִתִּי — *And what your cattle were with me.* There were among them broken and sick ones. I bound the broken ones and healed the sick, as befits an expert shepherd.

30. וַיְבָרֶךְ ה׳ אֹתְךָ לְרַגְלִי — *HASHEM has blessed you with my coming.* However, when you said that God blessed you with my coming, that is without a doubt true.

וְעַתָּה — *And now* . . . since God, the Blessed One, blessed you on my account.

מָתַי אֶעֱשֶׂה גַם אָנֹכִי — *When will I also do something (for my own house)?* When will I (be able) to do something which will bring blessing to my house, just as you have benefited through me; and for that the normal compensation of shepherds will not suffice.

31. מָה אֶתֶּן לָךְ — *What shall I give you?* . . . to compensate for what you expect to get.

לֹא תִתֶּן לִי מְאוּמָה — *You shall give me nothing* . . . because if God will favor me (with His blessing) what you have will not be diminished, as our Sages say, **אֵין אָדָם נוֹגֵעַ בַּמּוּכָן לַחֲבֵרוֹ**, *No man can touch what is prepared for his fellow* (*Yoma* 38b).

32. הָסֵר מִשָּׁם כָּל שֶׂה — *Remove from there every (speckled and spotted) sheep* . . . the young ones (lambs and kids), not the mature ones, so that they will reproduce (some) offspring that are similarly (speckled and spotted) which will then belong to me.

33. וְעָנְתָה בִּי צִדְקָתִי . . . כִּי תָבוֹא עַל שְׂכָרִי לְפָנֶיךָ — *Let my integrity testify for me* . . . *When you will come regarding my wage from you.* When you will come to inspect the additions to my flock, their number will testify to the integrity of my labor, for the Almighty will abnormally increase my share as compensation for my labors.

34. לוּ יְהִי כִדְבָרֶךָ — *If only it would remain as you say.* If only you would be appeased (satisfied) with your statement.

35. וַיָּסַר בַּיּוֹם הַהוּא אֶת הַתְּיָשִׁים — *So he removed on that very day the he-goats.* After (agreeing) and saying, 'יְהִי כִדְבָרֶךָ, *let it be as you say*,' he reneged and

NOTES

ness, but that her prayers are not deemed worthy of acceptance by God, while her sister's are!

29. אַתָּה יָדַעְתָּ אֵת אֲשֶׁר עֲבַדְתִּיךָ . . . וַיְבָרֶךְ ה׳ אֹתְךָ לְרַגְלִי – *You know how I have served you* . . . *HASHEM has blessed you with my coming.* Jacob does not deny that Laban's household has been blessed by God on his account, but he also wants Laban to know that he has labored excessively and skillfully over the years. The *Sforno* constantly stresses the importance of combining one's own efforts with God's blessing and assistance.

33. וְעָנְתָה בִּי צִדְקָתִי . . . כִּי תָבוֹא עַל שְׂכָרִי לְפָנֶיךָ – *Let my integrity testify for me* . . . *when you will come regarding my wage from you.* There

הָֽעִזִּים֙ הַנְּקֻדּ֣וֹת וְהַטְּלֻאֹ֔ת כֹּ֚ל אֲשֶׁר־לָבָן֙ בּ֔וֹ וְכָל־ח֖וּם בַּכְּשָׂבִ֑ים וַיִּתֵּ֖ן בְּיַד־
לו בָּנָֽיו׃ וַיָּ֗שֶׂם דֶּ֚רֶךְ שְׁלֹ֣שֶׁת יָמִ֔ים בֵּינ֖וֹ וּבֵ֣ין יַעֲקֹ֑ב וְיַעֲקֹ֗ב רֹעֶ֛ה אֶת־צֹ֥אן לָבָ֖ן
לז הַנּוֹתָרֹֽת׃ וַיִּֽקַּֽח־ל֣וֹ יַעֲקֹ֗ב מַקַּ֥ל לִבְנֶ֛ה לַ֖ח וְל֣וּז וְעַרְמ֑וֹן וַיְפַצֵּ֤ל בָּהֵן֙ פְּצָל֣וֹת
לח לְבָנ֔וֹת מַחְשֹׂף֙ הַלָּבָ֔ן אֲשֶׁ֖ר עַל־הַמַּקְלֽוֹת׃ וַיַּצֵּ֗ג אֶת־הַמַּקְלוֹת֙ אֲשֶׁ֣ר פִּצֵּ֔ל
בָּרְהָטִ֖ים בְּשִֽׁקֲת֣וֹת הַמָּ֑יִם אֲשֶׁ֨ר תָּבֹ֤אןָ הַצֹּאן֙ לִשְׁתּ֔וֹת לְנֹ֣כַח הַצֹּ֔אן וַיֵּחַ֖מְנָה
לט בְּבֹאָ֥ן לִשְׁתּֽוֹת׃ וַיֶּחֱמ֥וּ הַצֹּ֖אן אֶל־הַמַּקְל֑וֹת וַתֵּלַ֣דְןָ הַצֹּ֔אן עֲקֻדִּ֥ים נְקֻדִּ֖ים
מ וּטְלֻאִֽים׃ וְהַכְּשָׂבִים֮ הִפְרִ֣יד יַעֲקֹב֒ וַ֠יִּתֵּן פְּנֵ֨י הַצֹּ֧אן אֶל־עָקֹ֛ד וְכָל־ח֖וּם בְּצֹ֣אן
מא לָבָ֑ן וַיָּֽשֶׁת־ל֤וֹ עֲדָרִים֙ לְבַדּ֔וֹ וְלֹ֥א שָׁתָ֖ם עַל־צֹ֥אן לָבָֽן׃ וְהָיָ֗ה בְּכָל־יַחֵם֮ הַצֹּ֣אן
הַֽמְקֻשָּׁרוֹת֒ וְשָׂ֨ם יַעֲקֹ֧ב אֶת־הַמַּקְל֛וֹת לְעֵינֵ֥י הַצֹּ֖אן בָּרְהָטִ֑ים לְיַחְמֵ֖נָּה
מב בַּמַּקְלֽוֹת׃ וּבְהַעֲטִ֥יף הַצֹּ֖אן לֹ֣א יָשִׂ֑ים וְהָיָ֤ה הָעֲטֻפִים֙ לְלָבָ֔ן וְהַקְּשֻׁרִ֖ים
מג לְיַעֲקֹֽב׃ וַיִּפְרֹ֥ץ הָאִ֖ישׁ מְאֹ֣ד מְאֹ֑ד וַֽיְהִי־לוֹ֙ צֹ֣אן רַבּ֔וֹת וּשְׁפָחוֹת֙ וַעֲבָדִ֔ים
לא א וּגְמַלִּ֖ים וַחֲמֹרִֽים׃ וַיִּשְׁמַ֗ע אֶת־דִּבְרֵ֤י בְנֵֽי־לָבָן֙ לֵאמֹ֔ר לָקַ֣ח יַעֲקֹ֔ב אֵ֖ת
ב כָּל־אֲשֶׁ֣ר לְאָבִ֑ינוּ וּמֵאֲשֶׁ֣ר לְאָבִ֔ינוּ עָשָׂ֕ה אֵ֥ת כָּל־הַכָּבֹ֖ד הַזֶּֽה׃ וַיַּ֥רְא יַעֲקֹ֖ב
ג אֶת־פְּנֵ֣י לָבָ֑ן וְהִנֵּ֥ה אֵינֶ֛נּוּ עִמּ֖וֹ כִּתְמ֥וֹל שִׁלְשֽׁוֹם׃ וַיֹּ֤אמֶר יהוה אֶל־יַעֲקֹ֔ב שׁ֛וּב

removed on that very day both the young and mature ones.

38. לְנֹכַח הַצֹּאן — *Facing the sheep.* He set up the rods in front of the sheep so that they should look at this phenomena and picture it in their mind when they conceive, for the picture impressed upon the imagination at that time is a determining factor in the appearance (nature) of the offspring.

40. אֶל עָקֹד וְכָל חוּם בְּצֹאן לָבָן — *The ringed ones and all the brownish ones.* After (Laban) changed his wages, and kept the spotted and brown ones in his own flock.

42. וּבְהַעֲטִיף הַצֹּאן לֹא יָשִׂים — *When the sheep were late-bearing he would not place* ... so that Laban should not think that (Jacob) had deceived him in some manner.

43. וַיִּפְרֹץ הָאִישׁ — *The man became exceedingly prosperous.* He exceeded the limitations of prosperity which would be normal for those occupied with shepherding.

XXXI

1. וַיִּשְׁמַע אֶת דִּבְרֵי בְנֵי לָבָן — *Then he heard the words of Laban's sons* ... slanderous remarks against him, caused by their jealousy of him.

2. וַיַּרְא יַעֲקֹב אֶת פְּנֵי — *And Jacob saw the countenance (of Laban).* He perceived that (Laban) had accepted the slander (of his sons).

3. וַיֹּאמֶר ה׳ אֶל יַעֲקֹב שׁוּב — *And HASHEM said to Jacob, Return.* The Torah tells us the three reasons why Jacob fled and did not ask permission of Laban, such behavior being unseemly for a man such as (Jacob). He felt that since Laban had

NOTES

are commentators, including *Rashi,* who interpret the phrase כִּי תָבוֹא as *when* it *comes,* referring to *my integrity* (צִדְקָתִי). Not so the *Sforno,* who interprets it as referring to Laban — *when you will come* to investigate my flocks, you will see how God has blessed me due to my integrity.

XXXI

1-3. וַיִּשְׁמַע . . . וַיַּרְא . . . וַיֹּאמֶר ה׳ אֶל יַעֲקֹב — *Then he heard . . . and saw . . . and HASHEM said to Jacob.* Jacob *hears* the slanderous remarks of

ד אֶל־אֶרֶץ אֲבוֹתֶיךָ וּלְמוֹלַדְתֶּךָ וְאֶהְיֶה עִמָּךְ׃ וַיִּשְׁלַח יַעֲקֹב וַיִּקְרָא לְרָחֵל
ה וּלְלֵאָה הַשָּׂדֶה אֶל־צֹאנוֹ׃ וַיֹּאמֶר לָהֶן רֹאֶה אָנֹכִי אֶת־פְּנֵי אֲבִיכֶן כִּי־אֵינֶנּוּ
ו אֵלַי כִּתְמֹל שִׁלְשֹׁם וֵאלֹהֵי אָבִי הָיָה עִמָּדִי׃ וְאַתֵּנָה יְדַעְתֶּן כִּי בְּכָל־כֹּחִי
ז עָבַדְתִּי אֶת־אֲבִיכֶן׃ וַאֲבִיכֶן הֵתֶל בִּי וְהֶחֱלִף אֶת־מַשְׂכֻּרְתִּי עֲשֶׂרֶת מֹנִים
ח וְלֹא־נְתָנוֹ אֱלֹהִים לְהָרַע עִמָּדִי׃ אִם־כֹּה יֹאמַר נְקֻדִּים יִהְיֶה שְׂכָרֶךָ וְיָלְדוּ
כָל־הַצֹּאן נְקֻדִּים וְאִם־כֹּה יֹאמַר עֲקֻדִּים יִהְיֶה שְׂכָרֶךָ וְיָלְדוּ כָל־הַצֹּאן
ט־י עֲקֻדִּים׃ וַיַּצֵּל אֱלֹהִים אֶת־מִקְנֵה אֲבִיכֶם וַיִּתֶּן־לִי׃ וַיְהִי בְּעֵת יַחֵם הַצֹּאן
וָאֶשָּׂא עֵינַי וָאֵרֶא בַּחֲלוֹם וְהִנֵּה הָעַתֻּדִים הָעֹלִים עַל־הַצֹּאן עֲקֻדִּים נְקֻדִּים
יא־יב וּבְרֻדִּים׃ וַיֹּאמֶר אֵלַי מַלְאַךְ הָאֱלֹהִים בַּחֲלוֹם יַעֲקֹב וָאֹמַר הִנֵּנִי׃ וַיֹּאמֶר
שָׂא־נָא עֵינֶיךָ וּרְאֵה כָּל־הָעַתֻּדִים הָעֹלִים עַל־הַצֹּאן עֲקֻדִּים נְקֻדִּים
יג וּבְרֻדִּים כִּי רָאִיתִי אֵת כָּל־אֲשֶׁר לָבָן עֹשֶׂה לָּךְ׃ אָנֹכִי הָאֵל בֵּית־אֵל אֲשֶׁר
מָשַׁחְתָּ שָּׁם מַצֵּבָה אֲשֶׁר נָדַרְתָּ לִּי שָׁם נֶדֶר עַתָּה קוּם צֵא מִן־הָאָרֶץ הַזֹּאת
יד וְשׁוּב אֶל־אֶרֶץ מוֹלַדְתֶּךָ׃ וַתַּעַן רָחֵל וְלֵאָה וַתֹּאמַרְנָה לוֹ הַעוֹד לָנוּ חֵלֶק
טו וְנַחֲלָה בְּבֵית אָבִינוּ׃ הֲלוֹא נָכְרִיּוֹת נֶחְשַׁבְנוּ לוֹ כִּי מְכָרָנוּ וַיֹּאכַל גַּם־אָכוֹל
טז אֶת־כַּסְפֵּנוּ׃ כִּי כָל־הָעֹשֶׁר אֲשֶׁר הִצִּיל אֱלֹהִים מֵאָבִינוּ לָנוּ הוּא וּלְבָנֵינוּ
ששי יז וְעַתָּה כֹּל אֲשֶׁר אָמַר אֱלֹהִים אֵלֶיךָ עֲשֵׂה׃ וַיָּקָם יַעֲקֹב וַיִּשָּׂא אֶת־בָּנָיו
יח וְאֶת־נָשָׁיו עַל־הַגְּמַלִּים׃ וַיִּנְהַג אֶת־כָּל־מִקְנֵהוּ וְאֶת־כָּל־רְכֻשׁוֹ אֲשֶׁר רָכָשׁ

---

accepted (his sons') slander, then if he would know of his departure he would steal (all from him), as it says, פֶּן תִּגְזֹל אֶת בְּנוֹתֶיךָ, *Perhaps you might steal your daughters (from me)* (v. 31).

וְאֶהְיֶה עִמָּךְ — *And I will be with you* . . . that no harm befall you during the journey.

5. כִּי אֵינֶנּוּ אֵלַי כִּתְמֹל שִׁלְשֹׁם — *Is not toward me as yesterday and the day before* . . . for he thinks that I have (appropriated) what is his.

וֵאלֹהֵי אָבִי הָיָה עִמָּדִי — *But the God of my father was with me.* God alone has given me what I possess and I have stolen nothing from Laban.

14. הַעוֹד לָנוּ — *Have we then still (a share . . .).* How can you even think that it would be difficult for us to leave our father?

16. כִּי כָל הָעֹשֶׁר — *But all the wealth.* Similar to, כִּי צָחָקְתְּ, *But you laughed* (18:15). We have no hope of inheriting from our father. However, all the wealth which God has taken away from him, that alone is ours and our children's.

וְעַתָּה — *So now* . . . after you have seen that he has accepted the slander against you, and there is (valid) suspicion that he will steal (all) from you.

כֹּל אֲשֶׁר אָמַר אֱלֹהִים — *Whatever God has said to you* . . . that alone must you do. Proceed and go, you do not need (his) permission.

NOTES

Laban's sons (Jacob's brothers-in-law); he *sees* the changed countenance of Laban (his father-in-law) and also hears the word of God to return to *Eretz Yisrael.* These are the three reasons for Jacob's precipitous departure.

16. וְעַתָּה כֹּל אֲשֶׁר אָמַר אֱלֹהִים – *So now, whatever God has said to you.* First Jacob's wives — Laban's daughters — argue that logically there is every reason to leave. But even if these reasons were not valid, God's

מִקְנֵה קִנְיָנוֹ אֲשֶׁר רָכַשׁ בְּפַדַּן אֲרָם לָבוֹא אֶל־יִצְחָק אָבִיו אַרְצָה כְּנָעַן׃
יט־כ וְלָבָן הָלַךְ לִגְזֹז אֶת־צֹאנוֹ וַתִּגְנֹב רָחֵל אֶת־הַתְּרָפִים אֲשֶׁר לְאָבִיהָ׃ וַיִּגְנֹב
כא יַעֲקֹב אֶת־לֵב לָבָן הָאֲרַמִּי עַל־בְּלִי הִגִּיד לוֹ כִּי בֹרֵחַ הוּא׃ וַיִּבְרַח הוּא
כב וְכָל־אֲשֶׁר־לוֹ וַיָּקָם וַיַּעֲבֹר אֶת־הַנָּהָר וַיָּשֶׂם אֶת־פָּנָיו הַר הַגִּלְעָד׃ וַיֻּגַּד
כג לְלָבָן בַּיּוֹם הַשְּׁלִישִׁי כִּי בָרַח יַעֲקֹב׃ וַיִּקַּח אֶת־אֶחָיו עִמּוֹ וַיִּרְדֹּף אַחֲרָיו
כד דֶּרֶךְ שִׁבְעַת יָמִים וַיַּדְבֵּק אֹתוֹ בְּהַר הַגִּלְעָד׃ וַיָּבֹא אֱלֹהִים אֶל־לָבָן הָאֲרַמִּי
בַּחֲלֹם הַלָּיְלָה וַיֹּאמֶר לוֹ הִשָּׁמֶר לְךָ פֶּן־תְּדַבֵּר עִם־יַעֲקֹב מִטּוֹב עַד־רָע׃
כה וַיַּשֵּׂג לָבָן אֶת־יַעֲקֹב וְיַעֲקֹב תָּקַע אֶת־אָהֳלוֹ בָּהָר וְלָבָן תָּקַע אֶת־אֶחָיו
כו בְּהַר הַגִּלְעָד׃ וַיֹּאמֶר לָבָן לְיַעֲקֹב מֶה עָשִׂיתָ וַתִּגְנֹב אֶת־לְבָבִי וַתְּנַהֵג
כז אֶת־בְּנֹתַי כִּשְׁבֻיוֹת חָרֶב׃ לָמָּה נַחְבֵּאתָ לִבְרֹחַ וַתִּגְנֹב אֹתִי וְלֹא־הִגַּדְתָּ לִּי
כח וָאֲשַׁלֵּחֲךָ בְּשִׂמְחָה וּבְשִׁרִים בְּתֹף וּבְכִנּוֹר׃ וְלֹא נְטַשְׁתַּנִי לְנַשֵּׁק לְבָנַי

---

20. וַיִּגְנֹב יַעֲקֹב אֶת לֵב לָבָן — *Jacob deceived Laban.* He did not reveal how he felt regarding Laban's acceptance of the slanderous remarks made against him, nor that he realized that Laban was no longer well disposed toward him as before.

הָאֲרַמִּי — *The Aramean.* He (Jacob) did thus because he was Laban the Aramean, a cheat (*ramai,* רַמַּאי, a play on the word אֲרַמִּי). If Laban had suspected that Jacob knew anything about (the slander and Laban's change of heart) he would have 'counted the steps' of Jacob who would have found no way to flee.

עַל בְּלִי הִגִּיד לוֹ — *Besides not telling him.* Similar to, עַל עֹלַת הַתָּמִיד, *Besides the continual burnt offering (Numbers* 28:10). Jacob acted as though he did not sense the enmity of Laban, *besides* concealing his desire to leave. All this was not unethical but done under duress, because . . .

כִּי בֹרֵחַ הוּא — *That he was fleeing.* He was worried that Laban would steal all from him with the help of his townspeople, as he said later when he defended himself to Laban.

21. וַיִּבְרַח — *He fled.* The word בְּרִיחָה, *fleeing,* is used to indicate flight from a place in anticipation of future danger, and in cases where there is no pursuer. The term נִסָּה, *to run away*, is used when one flees from a place due to a clear and present danger, or from a pursuer.

24. פֶּן תְּדַבֵּר עִם יַעֲקֹב — *Lest you speak with Jacob.* Even speech is forbidden to you.

מִטּוֹב עַד רָע — *Either good or bad.* Do not persuade him to return by giving him hope that you will be good to him, and do not exaggerate the evil that you will do to him (if he refuses to return).

NOTES

command must be obeyed. Hence, do not delay; proceed and go!

20. עַל בְּלִי הִגִּיד לוֹ — *Besides not telling him.* The word עַל in this context does not mean *on,* but *in addition to,* as it does regarding the daily offering and the additional *Shabbos* sacrifice. Jacob, in addition to concealing his determination to leave, also acts as though his relationship with Laban is unchanged.

24. מִטּוֹב עַד רָע — *Either good or bad.* The expression מִטּוֹב עַד רָע, *good or bad,* cannot refer to the content of Laban's remarks to Jacob, since we see that he *did* incorporate both elements in his speech to his son-in-law. The *Sforno* therefore interprets this to mean that Laban is prohibited from making

כט וְלִבְנֹתָי עַתָּה הִסְכַּלְתָּ עֲשׂוֹ: יֶשׁ־לְאֵל יָדִי לַעֲשׂוֹת עִמָּכֶם רָע וֵאלֹהֵי
אֲבִיכֶם אֶמֶשׁ ׀ אָמַר אֵלַי לֵאמֹר הִשָּׁמֶר לְךָ מִדַּבֵּר עִם־יַעֲקֹב מִטּוֹב
ל עַד־רָע: וְעַתָּה הָלֹךְ הָלַכְתָּ כִּי־נִכְסֹף נִכְסַפְתָּה לְבֵית אָבִיךָ לָמָּה גָנַבְתָּ
לא אֶת־אֱלֹהָי: וַיַּעַן יַעֲקֹב וַיֹּאמֶר לְלָבָן כִּי יָרֵאתִי כִּי אָמַרְתִּי פֶּן־תִּגְזֹל
לב אֶת־בְּנוֹתֶיךָ מֵעִמִּי: עִם אֲשֶׁר תִּמְצָא אֶת־אֱלֹהֶיךָ לֹא יִחְיֶה נֶגֶד אַחֵינוּ
לג הַכֶּר־לְךָ מָה עִמָּדִי וְקַח־לָךְ וְלֹא־יָדַע יַעֲקֹב כִּי רָחֵל גְּנָבָתַם: וַיָּבֹא לָבָן
בְּאֹהֶל־יַעֲקֹב ׀ וּבְאֹהֶל לֵאָה וּבְאֹהֶל שְׁתֵּי הָאֲמָהֹת וְלֹא מָצָא וַיֵּצֵא מֵאֹהֶל
לד לֵאָה וַיָּבֹא בְּאֹהֶל רָחֵל: וְרָחֵל לָקְחָה אֶת־הַתְּרָפִים וַתְּשִׂמֵם בְּכַר הַגָּמָל
לה וַתֵּשֶׁב עֲלֵיהֶם וַיְמַשֵּׁשׁ לָבָן אֶת־כָּל־הָאֹהֶל וְלֹא מָצָא: וַתֹּאמֶר אֶל־אָבִיהָ
אַל־יִחַר בְּעֵינֵי אֲדֹנִי כִּי לוֹא אוּכַל לָקוּם מִפָּנֶיךָ כִּי־דֶרֶךְ נָשִׁים לִי וַיְחַפֵּשׂ
לו וְלֹא מָצָא אֶת־הַתְּרָפִים: וַיִּחַר לְיַעֲקֹב וַיָּרֶב בְּלָבָן וַיַּעַן יַעֲקֹב וַיֹּאמֶר לְלָבָן

---

29. וֵאלֹהֵי אֲבִיכֶם — *But the God of your father.* Not in your merit (but in that of the God of your *father),* for you departed without my permission and deceived me in doing so.

30. הָלֹךְ הָלַכְתָּ כִּי נִכְסֹף נִכְסַפְתָּה — *You have left because you longed greatly for your father's house.* Granted that you went in this fashion because of your great desire to return to your father's house, come what may ...

לָמָּה גָנַבְתָּ אֶת אֱלֹהָי — *But why did you steal my gods?* For this there is no excuse. Your great desire for your father's house cannot justify your stealing my gods.

31. פֶּן תִּגְזֹל אֶת בְּנוֹתֶיךָ — *Perhaps you might steal your daughters ...* for when you claim that you did not give your daughters to me to have me take them away from you (you will use that as an excuse) to steal them, the children and my possessions from me, as (indeed) he later said, 'הַבָּנוֹת בְּנֹתַי וְהַבָּנִים בָּנַי וְהַצֹּאן צֹאנִי, *The daughters are my daughters, the children are my children and the flock is my flock'* (verse 43). Now, all this you could have done with the help of your townspeople if I remained (in Charan) but you will not be able to do so (as readily), once I have left your country.

32. לֹא יִחְיֶה — *He shall not live.* (Jacob) was convinced that one of his servants had stolen it to worship it (in secret) thereby lapsing back into idolatry. This in turn would condemn him to death.

הַכֶּר לְךָ מָה עִמָּדִי — *Ascertain for yourself what is with me ...* that belongs to you and take it, once you recognize (it is yours).

וְלֹא יָדַע יַעֲקֹב — *And Jacob did not know ...* for if he had known he would never have had the audacity to deny it, nor would he have said, 'לֹא יִחְיֶה, *He shall not live.'*

36. וַיִּחַר לְיַעֲקֹב וַיָּרֶב בְּלָבָן — *Then Jacob became angered and strove with Laban.* Once nothing was found, Jacob thought that the תְּרָפִים, *terafim,* had never been

NOTES

promises or threats to Jacob. This admonition Laban does obey.

32. לֹא יִחְיֶה — *He shall not live.* The servants in Jacob's household would not have been permitted to accompany him to *Eretz Yisrael* unless they had rejected idolatry, thereby qualifying as גֵּרֵי תוֹשָׁב, *non-Jews who* (agree to observe the seven Noahide laws and) *are permitted to dwell in our midst.* However, if such a person lapsed back into idolatry, the laws regarding idolaters apply, and he is now

לז מַה־פִּשְׁעִי מַה חַטָּאתִי כִּי דָלַקְתָּ אַחֲרָי: כִּי־מִשַּׁשְׁתָּ אֶת־כָּל־כֵּלַי מַה־
לח מָּצָאתָ מִכֹּל כְּלֵי־בֵיתֶךָ שִׂים כֹּה נֶגֶד אַחַי וְאַחֶיךָ וְיוֹכִיחוּ בֵּין שְׁנֵינוּ: זֶה
עֶשְׂרִים שָׁנָה אָנֹכִי עִמָּךְ רְחֵלֶיךָ וְעִזֶּיךָ לֹא שִׁכֵּלוּ וְאֵילֵי צֹאנְךָ לֹא אָכָלְתִּי:
לט טְרֵפָה לֹא־הֵבֵאתִי אֵלֶיךָ אָנֹכִי אֲחַטֶּנָּה מִיָּדִי תְּבַקְשֶׁנָּה גְּנֻבְתִי יוֹם וּגְנֻבְתִי
מ־מא לָיְלָה: הָיִיתִי בַיּוֹם אֲכָלַנִי חֹרֶב וְקֶרַח בַּלָּיְלָה וַתִּדַּד שְׁנָתִי מֵעֵינָי: זֶה־לִּי
עֶשְׂרִים שָׁנָה בְּבֵיתֶךָ עֲבַדְתִּיךָ אַרְבַּע־עֶשְׂרֵה שָׁנָה בִּשְׁתֵּי בְנֹתֶיךָ וְשֵׁשׁ
מב שָׁנִים בְּצֹאנֶךָ וַתַּחֲלֵף אֶת־מַשְׂכֻּרְתִּי עֲשֶׂרֶת מֹנִים: לוּלֵי אֱלֹהֵי אָבִי אֱלֹהֵי
אַבְרָהָם וּפַחַד יִצְחָק הָיָה לִי כִּי עַתָּה רֵיקָם שִׁלַּחְתָּנִי אֶת־עָנְיִי וְאֶת־יְגִיעַ
שביעי מג כַּפַּי רָאָה אֱלֹהִים וַיּוֹכַח אָמֶשׁ: וַיַּעַן לָבָן וַיֹּאמֶר אֶל־יַעֲקֹב הַבָּנוֹת בְּנֹתַי
וְהַבָּנִים בָּנַי וְהַצֹּאן צֹאנִי וְכֹל אֲשֶׁר־אַתָּה רֹאֶה לִי־הוּא וְלִבְנֹתַי מָה־אֶעֱשֶׂה

---

stolen, and that Laban had used this accusation as a pretext to enable him to make a general search, because he suspected (Jacob) of stealing something from him.

מָה פִּשְׁעִי מַה חַטָּאתִי — *What is my transgression? What is my sin?* What wrongdoing have you found me guilty of in the past, that you suspect me now of being a robber?

38. רְחֵלֶיךָ וְעִזֶּיךָ לֹא שִׁכֵּלוּ — *Your ewes and she-goats never miscarried.* The opposite (of theft) is what you have found in my behavior; not only did I serve you faithfully as befits the righteous, but I also benefited you by my efforts to prevent any miscarriages (among your animals).

וְאֵילֵי צֹאנְךָ לֹא אָכָלְתִּי — *Nor did I eat rams of your flock* . . . as other shepherds allow themselves to do.

39. לֹא הֵבֵאתִי אֵלֶיךָ אָנֹכִי אֲחַטֶּנָּה — *I did not bring to you, I myself would bear the loss.* (I never brought to you) any animal mangled due to my sinful negligence; but I only brought to you those mangled through (non-preventable accidents) and even so . . .

מִיָּדִי תְּבַקְשֶׁנָּה — *From me you would exact it* . . . (unjustly) contrary to the law.

41. וַתַּחֲלֵף אֶת מַשְׂכֻּרְתִּי — *And you changed my wage* . . . which is contrary to what you say; it is you (not I) who changed my wage.

43. וְהַצֹּאן צֹאנִי — *And the flock is my flock.* Even if I changed your wage, or sent you away empty-handed, I would not have been taking away anything from you since everything belongs to me; and whatever you possess is through fraud, not by right.

וְלִבְנֹתַי — *Yet to my daughters* . . . and it should go to my daughters as their dowry.

מָה אֶעֱשֶׂה לָאֵלֶּה — *What could I do to them?* Even though I could (rightfully) take away everything from you, what could I (then) do to provide for them in the future?

NOTES

punishable by death for the transgression of stealing.

36-39. וַיִּחַר לְיַעֲקֹב וַיָּרֶב בְּלָבָן . . . לֹא הֵבֵאתִי אֵלֶיךָ — *Then Jacob become angered and strove with Laban . . . I did not bring to you.* Jacob is incensed that Laban accuses him of theft, given his record and past performance. He never rationalized, as did other shepherds, that he was justified in taking some animals for his personal use, nor did he ever attempt to evade compensating Laban for any negligence. In-

מד לָאֵלֶּה הַיּוֹם אוֹ לִבְנֵיהֶן אֲשֶׁר יָלָדוּ: וְעַתָּה לְכָה נִכְרְתָה בְרִית אֲנִי וָאָתָּה
מה־מו וְהָיָה לְעֵד בֵּינִי וּבֵינֶךָ: וַיִּקַּח יַעֲקֹב אָבֶן וַיְרִימֶהָ מַצֵּבָה: וַיֹּאמֶר יַעֲקֹב לְאֶחָיו
מז לִקְטוּ אֲבָנִים וַיִּקְחוּ אֲבָנִים וַיַּעֲשׂוּ־גָל וַיֹּאכְלוּ שָׁם עַל־הַגָּל: וַיִּקְרָא־לוֹ לָבָן
מח יְגַר שָׂהֲדוּתָא וְיַעֲקֹב קָרָא לוֹ גַּלְעֵד: וַיֹּאמֶר לָבָן הַגַּל הַזֶּה עֵד בֵּינִי וּבֵינְךָ
מט הַיּוֹם עַל־כֵּן קָרָא־שְׁמוֹ גַּלְעֵד: וְהַמִּצְפָּה אֲשֶׁר אָמַר יִצֶף יהוה בֵּינִי וּבֵינֶךָ
נ כִּי נִסָּתֵר אִישׁ מֵרֵעֵהוּ: אִם־תְּעַנֶּה אֶת־בְּנֹתַי וְאִם־תִּקַּח נָשִׁים עַל־בְּנֹתַי
נא אֵין אִישׁ עִמָּנוּ רְאֵה אֱלֹהִים עֵד בֵּינִי וּבֵינֶךָ: וַיֹּאמֶר לָבָן לְיַעֲקֹב הִנֵּה | הַגַּל
נב הַזֶּה וְהִנֵּה הַמַּצֵּבָה אֲשֶׁר יָרִיתִי בֵּינִי וּבֵינֶךָ: עֵד הַגַּל הַזֶּה וְעֵדָה הַמַּצֵּבָה
אִם־אָנִי לֹא־אֶעֱבֹר אֵלֶיךָ אֶת־הַגַּל הַזֶּה וְאִם־אַתָּה לֹא־תַעֲבֹר אֵלַי
נג אֶת־הַגַּל הַזֶּה וְאֶת־הַמַּצֵּבָה הַזֹּאת לְרָעָה: אֱלֹהֵי אַבְרָהָם וֵאלֹהֵי נָחוֹר
נד יִשְׁפְּטוּ בֵינֵינוּ אֱלֹהֵי אֲבִיהֶם וַיִּשָּׁבַע יַעֲקֹב בְּפַחַד אָבִיו יִצְחָק: וַיִּזְבַּח יַעֲקֹב

---

44. וְעַתָּה — *And now.* Considering that I do not want to harm you.

לְכָה נִכְרְתָה בְרִית — *Come, let us make a covenant* ... that you, in turn, will not harm me.

45. וַיְרִימֶהָ מַצֵּבָה — *And raised it up as a monument* ... to symbolize that the matter would stand permanently.

47. וְיַעֲקֹב קָרָא לוֹ גַּלְעֵד — *But Jacob called it Gal-ed.* He had not abandoned his (Hebrew) language.

48. וַיֹּאמֶר לָבָן הַגַּל הַזֶּה עֵד — *And Laban declared, 'This mound is a witness.'* He subordinated himself to Jacob by agreeing to call it by the Hebrew name. He declared that it be a witness of what he was about to say.

49. וְהַמִּצְפָּה — *And as for the Mitzpah* ... and let the adjoining place, Mitzpah (lit., 'watchtower'), also be a witness, reminding us what will (now) be said.

אֲשֶׁר אָמַר — *Because he said.* The reason he said that the Mitzpah should also testify to his statement, was because Laban said to Jacob ...

יִצֶף ה׳ בֵּינִי וּבֵינֶךָ — *May* HASHEM *keep watch between me and you* ... and be our Judge and Referee.

50. רְאֵה אֱלֹהִים עֵד — *But see, God is a witness.* Behold, if you will betray me, you trespass against Him, and He will punish you, similar to, וּמָעֲלָה מַעַל בַּה׳ וְכִחֵשׁ בַּעֲמִיתוֹ, *And commit a trespass against God and deal falsely with his neighbor (Lev.* 5:21). As our Sages say, (if one deals falsely) *he offends God, (Who is the invisible) Witness among them.* (See *Rashi,* quoting *Sifra,* in *Lev.* 5:21.)

53. אֱלֹהֵי אֲבִיהֶם — *The god of their father.* Laban argued that (Jacob) should not refuse to accept as judge the god of Nahor together with the God of Abraham, since the god of Nahor was also the deity of Terach, who was the father of both Nahor and Abraham.

וַיִּשָּׁבַע יַעֲקֹב בְּפַחַד אָבִיו יִצְחָק — *And Jacob swore by the Dread of his father Isaac* ... for Isaac was not the son of Terach. (Jacob) swears that only the God of Isaac shall

NOTES

deed, he even paid for losses caused by accidents which were non-preventable (אוֹנֶס).

49. וְהַמִּצְפָּה — *And as for the Mitzpah.* The name Mitzpah is not being given now. It was

לב מפטיר א זָבַח בָּהָר וַיִּקְרָא לְאֶחָיו לֶאֱכָל־לָחֶם וַיֹּאכְלוּ לֶחֶם וַיָּלִינוּ בָּהָר: וַיַּשְׁכֵּם לָבָן
בַּבֹּקֶר וַיְנַשֵּׁק לְבָנָיו וְלִבְנוֹתָיו וַיְבָרֶךְ אֶתְהֶם וַיֵּלֶךְ וַיָּשָׁב לָבָן לִמְקֹמוֹ:
ב־ג וְיַעֲקֹב הָלַךְ לְדַרְכּוֹ וַיִּפְגְּעוּ־בוֹ מַלְאֲכֵי אֱלֹהִים: וַיֹּאמֶר יַעֲקֹב כַּאֲשֶׁר רָאָם
מַחֲנֵה אֱלֹהִים זֶה וַיִּקְרָא שֵׁם־הַמָּקוֹם הַהוּא מַחֲנָיִם:

---

judge them if there is any betrayal.

54. וַיִּקְרָא לְאֶחָיו — *And summoned his kinsmen* ... (the kinsmen) of Laban, but there was no need to summon Laban, since he was, at that time, as a father to the House of Jacob.

XXXII

1. וַיְבָרֶךְ אֶתְהֶם — *And blessed them.* (Our Sages) have said, 'Even the blessing of a common man should not be treated lightly' (*Megillah* 15a); the Torah tells us of Laban's blessing to his daughters to teach us that a father's blessing is, without a doubt, given with all his soul, and is worthy to be accepted (effective) reflecting as it does the 'image of God' within the (father) who blesses, similar to, בַּעֲבוּר תְּבָרֶכְךָ נַפְשִׁי, *That my soul may bless you* (27:4).

3. מַחֲנֵה אֱלֹהִים זֶה — *This is a Godly camp.* Without a doubt my camp, met by the camp of angels, is a camp of God, as we find, *and he called the place* אֵל בֵּית אֵל, (lit., *the God of Beth El) because there, God was revealed to him* (35:7).

מַחֲנָיִם — *Machanaim (two camps)* ... two Godly camps — one of angels, the other his (Jacob's), in keeping with the (grammatical) rule that when the plural suffix יִם is preceded by a *patach* (_), and the word is accented on the second to last syllable, it means *two*, e.g., פַּעֲמַיִם, *two times* (from פַּעַם); שְׁבוּעַיִם, *two weeks* (from שָׁבוּעַ); שְׁנָתַיִם, *two years* (from שָׁנָה); etc. (Similarly מַחֲנַיִם, *two camps*, from מַחֲנֶה.)

NOTES

an ancient name, but Laban is calling upon this *watch-place* (or tower) to keep watch over their agreement, since fortuitously the name Mitzpah connotes *watching over*, from צפה, *to observe.*

54. וַיִּקְרָא לְאֶחָיו – *And summoned his kinsmen.* It was only necessary to summon to this farewell feast those who were not part of Jacob's family. Therefore the *Sforno* interprets אֶחָיו, *his kinsmen,* to mean the kinsmen of Laban who had accompanied him. However, just as Jacob does not summon his own sons, so he does not find it necessary to summon Laban, who is still considered the head of the household.

XXXII

1. וַיְבָרֶךְ אֶתְהֶם – *And blessed them.* The phrase צֶלֶם אֱלֹהִים, *in the image of God* (1:27), is explained by the *Sforno* as meaning that man has the potential to understand God and perfect himself to the extent of reaching a level of Godliness and immortality. This power is hidden in his נֶפֶשׁ *(soul),* and when this force is released its impact is powerful. When a father blesses his children, the blessing emanates from the depth of his soul and therefore it is extremely effective. This is true whether it be an Isaac or a Laban.

3. מַחֲנֵה אֱלֹהִים זֶה ... מַחֲנָיִם – *This is a Godly camp ... Machanaim (two camps).* The statement *this is a Godly camp* does not refer to the angels' camp but to the camp of Jacob, which is deemed worthy to be met by angels. Wherever God reveals Himself, either directly or through angels, it is a *holy place,* as we see from the name Beth El (House of God) which the Torah explains by stating *because there God was revealed.* We have now established that both camps — Jacob's and the angels — are Godly, hence it is proper to call the place Machanaim — *two camps* — for both are similar in nature and character.

פרשת וישלח
Parashas Vayishlach

ד וַיִּשְׁלַח יַעֲקֹב מַלְאָכִים לְפָנָיו אֶל־עֵשָׂו אָחִיו אַרְצָה שֵׂעִיר שְׂדֵה אֱדוֹם:
ה וַיְצַו אֹתָם לֵאמֹר כֹּה תֹאמְרוּן לַאדֹנִי לְעֵשָׂו כֹּה אָמַר עַבְדְּךָ יַעֲקֹב
ו עִם־לָבָן גַּרְתִּי וָאֵחַר עַד־עָתָּה: וַיְהִי־לִי שׁוֹר וַחֲמוֹר צֹאן וְעֶבֶד וְשִׁפְחָה
ז וָאֶשְׁלְחָה לְהַגִּיד לַאדֹנִי לִמְצֹא־חֵן בְּעֵינֶיךָ: וַיָּשֻׁבוּ הַמַּלְאָכִים אֶל־יַעֲקֹב
לֵאמֹר בָּאנוּ אֶל־אָחִיךָ אֶל־עֵשָׂו וְגַם הֹלֵךְ לִקְרָאתְךָ וְאַרְבַּע־מֵאוֹת אִישׁ
ח עִמּוֹ: וַיִּירָא יַעֲקֹב מְאֹד וַיֵּצֶר לוֹ וַיַּחַץ אֶת־הָעָם אֲשֶׁר־אִתּוֹ וְאֶת־הַצֹּאן
ט וְאֶת־הַבָּקָר וְהַגְּמַלִּים לִשְׁנֵי מַחֲנוֹת: וַיֹּאמֶר אִם־יָבוֹא עֵשָׂו אֶל־הַמַּחֲנֶה
י הָאַחַת וְהִכָּהוּ וְהָיָה הַמַּחֲנֶה הַנִּשְׁאָר לִפְלֵיטָה: וַיֹּאמֶר יַעֲקֹב אֱלֹהֵי אָבִי
אַבְרָהָם וֵאלֹהֵי אָבִי יִצְחָק יהוה הָאֹמֵר אֵלַי שׁוּב לְאַרְצְךָ וּלְמוֹלַדְתְּךָ

---

4. וַיִּשְׁלַח יַעֲקֹב מַלְאָכִים — *And Jacob sent angels ...* to learn his brother's plans and his intentions.

אַרְצָה שֵׂעִיר שְׂדֵה אֱדוֹם — *To the land of Seir, the field of Edom ...* to the region called Seir and to the locale called Edom where Esau dwelled, for at that time Esau had as yet not conquered the entire area from the Hori who were the inhabitants of the land.

5. וָאֵחַר עַד עָתָּה — *And have lingered until now.* That is why I did not come to pay my respects (lit., 'bow down') sooner.

6. לִמְצֹא חֵן בְּעֵינֶיךָ — *To gain favor in your eyes.* I am confident that you will be pleased to hear of my wealth and honored position, and that I will find favor by telling you this.

7. וְגַם הֹלֵךְ לִקְרָאתְךָ — *And moreover he is heading toward you.* Not only was he not impressed or pleased when we told him of your good fortune, but he is also coming toward you.

וְאַרְבַּע מֵאוֹת אִישׁ עִמּוֹ — *And four hundred men are with him ...* and his intent must be to attack you as we find, וַיֵּצֵא אֱדוֹם לִקְרָאתוֹ בְּעַם כָּבֵד, *and Edom came out against him with many people* (*Numbers* 20:20).

9. וְהָיָה הַמַּחֲנֶה הַנִּשְׁאָר לִפְלֵיטָה — *Then the camp which is left will survive.* While (the enemy) is descending upon the first camp to pillage, the second will escape with their weapons — or at least will be able to flee.

10. אֱלֹהֵי אָבִי אַבְרָהָם — *O God of my father Abraham.* He began (his prayer) by reciting praises of God's kindness, and he also mentions the merit of his fathers (Abraham and Isaac) similar to the order of prayer instituted by the Men of the Great Assembly at the beginning of *Shemoneh Esrei* (the *Amidah*).

NOTES

4. אַרְצָה שֵׂעִיר שְׂדֵה אֱדוֹם — *To the land of Seir, the field of Edom.* The expression *the land of Seir, the field of Edom,* is not redundant. Although later on the two are the same, at this particular time the Hori were still in control of Seir, while Esau only ruled over a small section of that land, which was called Edom.

7. וְאַרְבַּע מֵאוֹת אִישׁ עִמּוֹ — *And four hundred men are with him.* It is interesting that the *Sforno* should bring as proof to his interpretation an incident that happened so many years later when Moses was leading Israel close by the land of Edom. He feels that Edom did not change his practice of confronting and attacking his brother — i.e., Esau did not change his spots.

10. אֱלֹהֵי אָבִי אַבְרָהָם — *O God of my father Abraham.* Jacob petitioned God to help him in

יא וְאֵיטִיבָה עִמָּךְ׃ קָטֹנְתִּי מִכֹּל הַחֲסָדִים וּמִכָּל־הָאֱמֶת אֲשֶׁר עָשִׂיתָ אֶת־
עַבְדֶּךָ כִּי בְמַקְלִי עָבַרְתִּי אֶת־הַיַּרְדֵּן הַזֶּה וְעַתָּה הָיִיתִי לִשְׁנֵי מַחֲנוֹת׃
יב הַצִּילֵנִי נָא מִיַּד אָחִי מִיַּד עֵשָׂו כִּי־יָרֵא אָנֹכִי אֹתוֹ פֶּן־יָבוֹא וְהִכַּנִי אֵם
יג עַל־בָּנִים׃ וְאַתָּה אָמַרְתָּ הֵיטֵב אֵיטִיב עִמָּךְ וְשַׂמְתִּי אֶת־זַרְעֲךָ כְּחוֹל הַיָּם
שני יד אֲשֶׁר לֹא־יִסָּפֵר מֵרֹב׃ וַיָּלֶן שָׁם בַּלַּיְלָה הַהוּא וַיִּקַּח מִן־הַבָּא בְיָדוֹ מִנְחָה
טו לְעֵשָׂו אָחִיו׃ עִזִּים מָאתַיִם וּתְיָשִׁים עֶשְׂרִים רְחֵלִים מָאתַיִם וְאֵילִים
טז עֶשְׂרִים׃ גְּמַלִּים מֵינִיקוֹת וּבְנֵיהֶם שְׁלֹשִׁים פָּרוֹת אַרְבָּעִים וּפָרִים עֲשָׂרָה
יז אֲתֹנֹת עֶשְׂרִים וַעְיָרִם עֲשָׂרָה׃ וַיִּתֵּן בְּיַד־עֲבָדָיו עֵדֶר עֵדֶר לְבַדּוֹ וַיֹּאמֶר
יח אֶל־עֲבָדָיו עִבְרוּ לְפָנַי וְרֶוַח תָּשִׂימוּ בֵּין עֵדֶר וּבֵין עֵדֶר׃ וַיְצַו אֶת־הָרִאשׁוֹן

---

11. קָטֹנְתִּי מִכֹּל הַחֲסָדִים וּמִכָּל הָאֱמֶת — *I have been diminished by all the kindnesses and by all the truth.* I was not worthy to be the recipient of all the kindness (shown to me), nor of the good fortune which is mine. In truth, it is because of the merit of my fathers, and because of them You conducted Yourself toward me beyond the requirement of the law (i.e., with *chesed* — undeserved blessing). Now, therefore, do I ask that You save me in the same manner, as it is said, כְּגֹדֶל חַסְדֶּךָ וְכַאֲשֶׁר נָשָׂאתָה לָעָם הַזֶּה, *(Pardon the iniquity of this people) according to the greatness of Your loving-kindness, and as You have forgiven this people, etc. (Numbers* 14:19).

12. וְהִכַּנִי אֵם עַל בָּנִים — *And strike me down mother and children.* By killing the mother and the children he will smite *me,* even if I personally escape.

13. וְאַתָּה אָמַרְתָּ הֵיטֵב אֵיטִיב עִמָּךְ — *And You have said, 'I will surely do good with you'* . . . and if this comes to pass it will negate the promise to do good with me, as well as the promise of . . .

וְשַׂמְתִּי אֶת זַרְעֲךָ — *And I will make your offspring.* For if my family is exterminated, this will negate the promise made to multiply my offspring; and even if I am unworthy, save me for the sake of Your Name, as we find, אִם עֲוֹנֵינוּ עָנוּ בָנוּ ה׳ עֲשֵׂה לְמַעַן שְׁמֶךָ, *Though our iniquities testify against us,* HASHEM, *do for Your Name's sake (Jeremiah* 14:7).

17. עֵדֶר עֵדֶר לְבַדּוֹ — *Each drove separately* . . . so that (Esau) might see that there was the proper proportion of males and females in each species so that they may yield maximum productivity, as he says, *'Take my blessing'* (33:11), for the gift was so constituted that there would surely be a blessing (of natural increase).

וְרֶוַח תָּשִׂימוּ בֵּין עֵדֶר וּבֵין עֵדֶר — *And leave a space between drove and drove* . . . so

NOTES

this difficult hour. The order of prayer ordained by the Men of the Great Assembly is to invoke the merits of our ancestors, mention the *chesed* of the Almighty, and only then to submit our requests. This order is followed by our father Jacob and could well be the source for the order of our *tefillos.*

11. קָטֹנְתִּי מִכֹּל הַחֲסָדִים וּמִכָּל הָאֱמֶת — *I have been diminished by all the kindnesses and by all the truth.* What God has done for Jacob may be undeserved, hence it is called *chesed,* but what is done in the merit of his fathers is *truth,* and is justified. What he asked for now was to be saved from the clutches of Esau even if it would be but an act of mercy on the part of the Almighty, for since this attribute of mercy was already demonstrated in the past, Jacob felt justified in asking for it once again. To prove that this is proper, the *Sforno* quotes the verse in *Numbers.*

17. עֵדֶר עֵדֶר לְבַדּוֹ — *Each drove separately.* When Jacob urged Esau to accept his offering

לֵאמֹר כִּי יִפְגָשְׁךָ עֵשָׂו אָחִי וּשְׁאֵלְךָ לֵאמֹר לְמִי־אַתָּה וְאָנָה תֵלֵךְ וּלְמִי
יט אֵלֶּה לְפָנֶיךָ: וְאָמַרְתָּ לְעַבְדְּךָ לְיַעֲקֹב מִנְחָה הִוא שְׁלוּחָה לַאדֹנִי לְעֵשָׂו
כ וְהִנֵּה גַם־הוּא אַחֲרֵינוּ: וַיְצַו גַּם אֶת־הַשֵּׁנִי גַּם אֶת־הַשְּׁלִישִׁי גַּם אֶת־כָּל־
הַהֹלְכִים אַחֲרֵי הָעֲדָרִים לֵאמֹר כַּדָּבָר הַזֶּה תְּדַבְּרוּן אֶל־עֵשָׂו בְּמֹצַאֲכֶם
כא אֹתוֹ: וַאֲמַרְתֶּם גַּם הִנֵּה עַבְדְּךָ יַעֲקֹב אַחֲרֵינוּ כִּי־אָמַר אֲכַפְּרָה פָנָיו בַּמִּנְחָה
כב הַהֹלֶכֶת לְפָנָי וְאַחֲרֵי־כֵן אֶרְאֶה פָנָיו אוּלַי יִשָּׂא פָנָי: וַתַּעֲבֹר הַמִּנְחָה עַל־

---

that the animals should not wander from drove to drove, preventing the observer from appreciating how wisely the offering was selected and the blessing it would bring.

19. וְאָמַרְתָּ לְעַבְדְּךָ לְיַעֲקֹב — *You shall say, 'They are your servant Jacob's.'* He instructed the messenger not to acknowledge that he recognizes Esau nor that he is being sent to him (en route), lest Esau think that Jacob is aware of his approach and is sending him this gift due to fear. Rather the messenger should act as though he is being sent to the land of Seir, unaware [that the man marching on Jacob's camp] is Esau.

20. כַּדָּבָר הַזֶּה תְּדַבְּרוּן אֶל עֵשָׂו — *In this manner shall you speak to Esau.* He instructed each messenger what to say to Esau. They were to tell him that all these droves were Jacob's, sent as a gift to his older brother.

21. וַאֲמַרְתֶּם גַּם הִנֵּה עַבְדְּךָ יַעֲקֹב אַחֲרֵינוּ — *And you shall say, 'Moreover, behold, your servant Jacob is behind us.'* Each messenger was told to give a specific answer, but all were told to tell Esau that Jacob was following them. In this manner Esau would find their answers consistent, namely, that Jacob was coming after them to Seir to greet his brother.

כִּי אָמַר אֲכַפְּרָה פָנָיו בַּמִּנְחָה — *For he said, 'I will appease him with the tribute.'* He instructed his servants to say these words in order to lessen Esau's anger through these words of submission coupled with the tribute.

אֶרְאֶה פָנָיו — *I will face him.* (This is) the accepted manner of appearing before lords, as we find, יֵרָאֶה כָּל זְכוּרְךָ אֶת פְּנֵי הָאָדֹן, *All your males shall appear before the Lord*

NOTES

he did not say, *'Take my gift'*, rather, *'my blessing,'* which indicates the nature and ultimate purpose of the gift. In the case of animals — goats, sheep and camels — blessing is measured by the growth of the flocks and herds through reproduction.

19. וְאָמַרְתָּ לְעַבְדְּךָ לְיַעֲקֹב — *You shall say, 'They are your servant Jacob's.'* Although Jacob was prepared to appease Esau by means of this generous gift he wisely did not want him to believe that he was afraid of him, for a perception of weakness would have increased Jacob's vulnerability. That is why Jacob preferred that Esau believe the gift was being sent to him in his homeland as a gesture of friendship, motivated by a spirit of brotherhood, and not due to fear of an approaching army — which would transform the gift into a bribe.

20. כַּדָּבָר הַזֶּה תְּדַבְּרוּן אֶל עֵשָׂו — *In this manner shall you speak to Esau.* Jacob acknowledged that Esau was the *bechor*, the firstborn son, even though the birthright was sold to him. That is why Jacob referred to Esau as אֲדֹנִי, *my lord* (33:8), and to himself as עַבְדְּךָ, *your servant* (33:6). At this moment, Jacob was willing to forgo his own claim to the birthright, so as to save his family.

21. כִּי אָמַר אֲכַפְּרָה פָנָיו בַּמִּנְחָה — *For he said, 'I will appease him with the tribute.'* Whereas others interpret the phrase, *For he said ...*, as an *unspoken* explanation of Jacob's motives, the *Sforno* is of the opinion that these words

כג פָּנָיו וְהוּא לָן בַּלַּיְלָה־הַהוּא בַּמַּחֲנֶה: וַיָּקָם ׀ בַּלַּיְלָה הוּא וַיִּקַּח אֶת־שְׁתֵּי
נָשָׁיו וְאֶת־שְׁתֵּי שִׁפְחֹתָיו וְאֶת־אַחַד עָשָׂר יְלָדָיו וַיַּעֲבֹר אֵת מַעֲבַר יַבֹּק:
כד־כה וַיִּקָּחֵם וַיַּעֲבִרֵם אֶת־הַנָּחַל וַיַּעֲבֵר אֶת־אֲשֶׁר־לוֹ: וַיִּוָּתֵר יַעֲקֹב לְבַדּוֹ וַיֵּאָבֵק
כו אִישׁ עִמּוֹ עַד עֲלוֹת הַשָּׁחַר: וַיַּרְא כִּי לֹא יָכֹל לוֹ וַיִּגַּע בְּכַף־יְרֵכוֹ וַתֵּקַע

(*Exodus* 34:23); (also) וְלֹא יֵרָאוּ פָנַי רֵיקָם, *And none shall appear before Me empty-handed* (*Exodus* 23:15). So (Jacob) says to Esau, *I have seen your face as one sees the face of the Divine* (33:10). It is the custom to greet one's superiors by appearing before them personally bearing gifts.

22. וַתַּעֲבֹר הַמִּנְחָה עַל פָּנָיו — *So the tribute passed before him* . . . to check and make sure that all was in the proper order, so as to insure the desired end.

24. וַיַּעֲבֵר אֶת אֲשֶׁר לוֹ — *And he sent over all his possessions.* He instructed everyone to precede him in crossing over the ford, as we find, וַיַּעֲבוֹר אֶת הַכּוּשִׁי, *And went ahead of the Cushite* (*II Samuel* 18:23).

25. וַיִּוָּתֵר יַעֲקֹב לְבַדּוֹ — *And Jacob was left alone.* He was the last to leave the camp in order to direct everyone to take along all his possessions so that nothing be left behind.

וַיֵּאָבֵק אִישׁ עִמּוֹ — *And there wrestled a man with him.* Without a doubt this was the work of an angel sent by God, as we find, יְרֵה וַיּוֹר, *'Shoot!' And he shot.* (*II Kings* 13:17). (The purpose of this encounter) was to demonstrate that God will save Jacob and his children (in all their confrontations) with Esau and even though there will be material loss at times, ultimately there will be salvation and blessing, with mastery both in heaven above and here on earth.

26. לֹא יָכֹל לוֹ — *He perceived he could not overcome him* . . . because Jacob cleaved fully and constantly to God in thought and speech.

וַיִּגַּע — *He touched.* (The angel) told him the sins which the future leaders of Israel would commit. His (resultant) concern stopped his concentration on God, enabling the angel to touch the hollow of his thigh as they wrestled.

NOTES

were part of the message; they were to tell Esau that Jacob said, 'I will appease him,' for this would have a desired effect upon Esau and impress upon him Jacob's sincerity.

25. וַיֵּאָבֵק אִישׁ עִמּוֹ — *And there wrestled a man with him.* (a) Even though the word אִישׁ, *man*, is used, it refers to an angel sent by God. However, if so, what is God's purpose? The *Sforno* explains that this encounter is symbolic of the constant conflict between the forces of Israel and Esau, which will harm and damage Israel over the centuries, but in the end Israel will prevail, not only here on earth but in heaven above. In a mystical manner, the representatives of every nation contend with each other in heaven and the outcome above affects the destiny of these nations on earth. This explains the expression used later — *you have striven with the Divine and man*, the phrase *God* referring to שָׂרוֹ שֶׁל עֵשָׂו, *the heavenly lord of Esau.* This concept is alluded to by the *Sforno* in his commentary on verse 29 when he quotes *Isaiah* 24:21.

(b) The verse from *II Kings* 13:17 cited by the *Sforno* speaks of Elisha commanding King Yoash to shoot an arrow through the window, while the prophet rests his hand on the hand of the king. The arrow is called 'the arrow of salvation.' From this episode proof is being brought that a simple, prosaic act can have profound historic meaning. And so here, the man (angel) who wrestled with Jacob is symbolic of significant truths regarding Israel and Esau.

26. לֹא יָכֹל לוֹ — *He perceived he could not overcome him.* The *Sforno* uses the expression

כז כַּף־יֶרֶךְ יַעֲקֹב בְּהֵאָבְקוֹ עִמּוֹ: וַיֹּאמֶר שַׁלְּחֵנִי כִּי עָלָה הַשָּׁחַר וַיֹּאמֶר לֹא
כח־כט אֲשַׁלֵּחֲךָ כִּי אִם־בֵּרַכְתָּנִי: וַיֹּאמֶר אֵלָיו מַה־שְּׁמֶךָ וַיֹּאמֶר יַעֲקֹב: וַיֹּאמֶר לֹא
יַעֲקֹב יֵאָמֵר עוֹד שִׁמְךָ כִּי אִם־יִשְׂרָאֵל כִּי־שָׂרִיתָ עִם־אֱלֹהִים וְעִם־אֲנָשִׁים
ל וַתּוּכָל: וַיִּשְׁאַל יַעֲקֹב וַיֹּאמֶר הַגִּידָה־נָּא שְׁמֶךָ וַיֹּאמֶר לָמָּה זֶּה תִּשְׁאַל
שלישי לא לִשְׁמִי וַיְבָרֶךְ אֹתוֹ שָׁם: וַיִּקְרָא יַעֲקֹב שֵׁם הַמָּקוֹם פְּנִיאֵל כִּי־רָאִיתִי אֱלֹהִים
לב פָּנִים אֶל־פָּנִים וַתִּנָּצֵל נַפְשִׁי: וַיִּזְרַח־לוֹ הַשֶּׁמֶשׁ כַּאֲשֶׁר עָבַר אֶת־פְּנוּאֵל
לג וְהוּא צֹלֵעַ עַל־יְרֵכוֹ: עַל־כֵּן לֹא־יֹאכְלוּ בְנֵי־יִשְׂרָאֵל אֶת־גִּיד הַנָּשֶׁה אֲשֶׁר

---

27. לֹא אֲשַׁלֵּחֲךָ — *I will not let you go* . . . for 'the righteous are greater than the angels' *(Sanhedrin* 92a).

29. לֹא יַעֲקֹב יֵאָמֵר עוֹד שִׁמְךָ — *No longer will it be said that your name is Jacob* . . . at the 'end of days.' You will survive all the nations and therefore the significance of the name 'Jacob' will be fulfilled since it implies existence 'at the end.' Hence the name Jacob is no longer necessary to indicate that you will be there at the 'end' of all the nations.

כִּי אִם יִשְׂרָאֵל כִּי שָׂרִיתָ — *But Israel, for you have striven.* You will then be called Israel to show that 'you have striven with the Divine and man,' as we find, יִפְקֹד ה׳ עַל צְבָא הַמָּרוֹם בַּמָּרוֹם וְעַל מַלְכֵי הָאֲדָמָה עַל הָאֲדָמָה, *HASHEM will punish the host of the high heaven, on high, and the kings of the earth upon the earth (Isaiah* 24:21).

30. הַגִּידָה נָּא שְׁמֶךָ — *Tell me, if you please, your name* . . . which indicates your essence and your mission, that I might know why you were sent to confront me, so I will be able to repent and pray (to rectify the sin which caused you to come and confront me).

לָמָּה זֶּה תִּשְׁאַל לִשְׁמִי — *Why then do you inquire of My name?* Our spiritual essence, clothed in human form, cannot be defined in human terminology, as it says, וְהוּא פֶלְאִי, *It is hidden (Judges* 13:18) and as for the mission, that is according to the will of God.

32. וַיִּזְרַח לוֹ הַשֶּׁמֶשׁ כַּאֲשֶׁר עָבַר אֶת פְּנוּאֵל וְהוּא צֹלֵעַ — *And the sun rose upon him after he passed over Penuel and he limped.* After he passed Penuel limping, the sun rose and its rays healed him, as it will come to pass in the future, as it says, וְזָרְחָה לָכֶם יִרְאֵי שְׁמִי שֶׁמֶשׁ צְדָקָה וּמַרְפֵּא בִּכְנָפֶיהָ, *But to you who fear My name, the sun of righteousness will rise with healing in its wings (Malachi* 3:20).

33. עַל כֵּן לֹא יֹאכְלוּ בְּנֵי יִשְׂרָאֵל — *Therefore the children of Israel eat not* . . . to demonstrate that the injury inflicted on the hollow of his thigh is unessential to us.

NOTES

פָּסַק הַדִּבּוּק, *his cleaving to God was severed.* Since Jacob's strength was derived from his connection to the Almighty 'in thought and speech,' when this link was cut, Jacob was vulnerable. We find a similar situation with David and the Angel of Death *(Shabbos* 30b). As long as David was immersed in Torah study the Angel of Death had no power over him; once David paused in his study the Angel of Death was able to conquer him.

30. הַגִּידָה נָּא שְׁמֶךָ — *Tell me, if you please, your name.* Jacob asked the angel to reveal *his name,* which means his mission, for then he would be able to understand why God had sent this adversary. He was not simply curious. Only by knowing what his transgression was, would he be able to do *teshuvah,* to repent.

33. עַל כֵּן לֹא יֹאכְלוּ בְּנֵי יִשְׂרָאֵל — *Therefore the children of Israel eat not.* The prohibition to eat the גִּיד הַנָּשֶׁה, *the sinew of the thigh-vein,* is not in memory of this event, but to demon-

לג
א עַל־כַּף הַיָּרֵךְ עַד הַיּוֹם הַזֶּה כִּי נָגַע בְּכַף־יֶרֶךְ יַעֲקֹב בְּגִיד הַנָּשֶׁה: וַיִּשָּׂא
יַעֲקֹב עֵינָיו וַיַּרְא וְהִנֵּה עֵשָׂו בָּא וְעִמּוֹ אַרְבַּע מֵאוֹת אִישׁ וַיַּחַץ אֶת־הַיְלָדִים
ב עַל־לֵאָה וְעַל־רָחֵל וְעַל שְׁתֵּי הַשְּׁפָחוֹת: וַיָּשֶׂם אֶת־הַשְּׁפָחוֹת וְאֶת־יַלְדֵיהֶן
ג רִאשֹׁנָה וְאֶת־לֵאָה וִילָדֶיהָ אַחֲרֹנִים וְאֶת־רָחֵל וְאֶת־יוֹסֵף אַחֲרֹנִים: וְהוּא
ד עָבַר לִפְנֵיהֶם וַיִּשְׁתַּחוּ אַרְצָה שֶׁבַע פְּעָמִים עַד־גִּשְׁתּוֹ עַד־אָחִיו: וַיָּרָץ עֵשָׂו
ה לִקְרָאתוֹ וַיְחַבְּקֵהוּ וַיִּפֹּל עַל־צַוָּארָו וַיִּשָּׁקֵהוּ וַיִּבְכּוּ: וַיִּשָּׂא אֶת־עֵינָיו וַיַּרְא
אֶת־הַנָּשִׁים וְאֶת־הַיְלָדִים וַיֹּאמֶר מִי־אֵלֶּה לָּךְ וַיֹּאמַר הַיְלָדִים אֲשֶׁר־חָנַן
רביעי ו־ז אֱלֹהִים אֶת־עַבְדֶּךָ: וַתִּגַּשְׁןָ הַשְּׁפָחוֹת הֵנָּה וְיַלְדֵיהֶן וַתִּשְׁתַּחֲוֶיןָ: וַתִּגַּשׁ גַּם־
ח לֵאָה וִילָדֶיהָ וַיִּשְׁתַּחֲווּ וְאַחַר נִגַּשׁ יוֹסֵף וְרָחֵל וַיִּשְׁתַּחֲווּ: וַיֹּאמֶר מִי לְךָ כָּל־
ט הַמַּחֲנֶה הַזֶּה אֲשֶׁר פָּגָשְׁתִּי וַיֹּאמֶר לִמְצֹא־חֵן בְּעֵינֵי אֲדֹנִי: וַיֹּאמֶר עֵשָׂו יֶשׁ־
י לִי רָב אָחִי יְהִי לְךָ אֲשֶׁר־לָךְ: וַיֹּאמֶר יַעֲקֹב אַל־נָא אִם־נָא מָצָאתִי חֵן

XXXIII

1. וְעִמּוֹ אַרְבַּע מֵאוֹת אִישׁ — *Accompanied by four hundred men.* The gift had not appeased him.

4. וַיָּרָץ עֵשָׂו לִקְרָאתוֹ — *Esau ran toward him.* He quickly changed his mind due to Jacob's obeisances. This (episode) reflects our relationship with Esau in exile, who feels, *'Who shall bring me down to the ground?'* (see *Obadiah* 1:3). It teaches us that we will be saved from the sword of (Esau's) pride through submission and gifts, as our Sages tell us regarding Achiyah Hashiloni who 'cursed' Israel, comparing them to a reed *(Taanis* 20a) which bends in the wind. Had the zealots *(biryoni)* guarding the city followed this policy in the time of the Second Temple, our Holy Temple would not have been destroyed, as Rabban Yochanan ben Zakkai testifies, when he says, בִּרְיוֹנֵי דְאִית בָּן לָא שַׁבְקִינָן, *The biryoni among us did not let me (Gittin* 56b).

5. מִי אֵלֶּה לָּךְ — *Who are these to you?* He asked: 'Are they your children, your servants, or members of your household?'

8. מִי לְךָ כָּל הַמַּחֲנֶה — *What did you intend by that whole camp?* The camp that said to me, *'It is a gift sent to my lord'* (32:19), was it meant as a mark of honor, or as an act of kindness thinking that I might be in need of it?

9. יֶשׁ לִי רָב — *I have plenty* . . . and need naught.

אָחִי יְהִי לְךָ אֲשֶׁר לָךְ — *My brother, let what you have remain yours.* Since you are my brother, you need not honor me with this gift.

NOTES

strate for all time that the damage inflicted upon Jacob by the angel is of no account to us and we eschew it completely to indicate that it is of no importance to us.

XXXIII

4. וַיָּרָץ עֵשָׂו לִקְרָאתוֹ — *Esau ran toward him.* Although Esau's original intention was to attack his brother, Jacob's submission and gift altered Esau's plans and appeased him. The *Sforno,* citing various selections from the Talmud, interprets this episode as a model lesson for the Jewish people in exile. Although courage and a willingness to do battle is praiseworthy, it is only so in the proper time and circumstances. In general, Israel in exile among the nations will find far greater security if like a reed she will bend with the wind and resist false heroics, which will in most cases accomplish nothing. The 'curse' of Achiyah was in reality a blessing, and Rabban Yochanan ben Zakkai accomplished far more with his strategy than the *biryoni* did with theirs. He was able to salvage Yavneh and its

בְּעֵינֶיךָ וְלָקַחְתָּ מִנְחָתִי מִיָּדִי כִּי עַל־כֵּן רָאִיתִי פָנֶיךָ כִּרְאֹת פְּנֵי אֱלֹהִים
יא וַתִּרְצֵנִי׃ קַח־נָא אֶת־בִּרְכָתִי אֲשֶׁר הֻבָאת לָךְ כִּי־חַנַּנִי אֱלֹהִים וְכִי
יב־יג יֶשׁ־לִי־כֹל וַיִּפְצַר־בּוֹ וַיִּקָּח׃ וַיֹּאמֶר נִסְעָה וְנֵלֵכָה וְאֵלְכָה לְנֶגְדֶּךָ׃ וַיֹּאמֶר
אֵלָיו אֲדֹנִי יֹדֵעַ כִּי־הַיְלָדִים רַכִּים וְהַצֹּאן וְהַבָּקָר עָלוֹת עָלָי וּדְפָקוּם יוֹם
יד אֶחָד וָמֵתוּ כָּל־הַצֹּאן׃ יַעֲבָר־נָא אֲדֹנִי לִפְנֵי עַבְדּוֹ וַאֲנִי אֶתְנַהֲלָה לְאִטִּי
לְרֶגֶל הַמְּלָאכָה אֲשֶׁר־לְפָנַי וּלְרֶגֶל הַיְלָדִים עַד אֲשֶׁר־אָבֹא אֶל־אֲדֹנִי
טו שֵׂעִירָה׃ וַיֹּאמֶר עֵשָׂו אַצִּיגָה־נָּא עִמְּךָ מִן־הָעָם אֲשֶׁר אִתִּי וַיֹּאמֶר לָמָּה
טז־יז זֶּה אֶמְצָא־חֵן בְּעֵינֵי אֲדֹנִי׃ וַיָּשָׁב בַּיּוֹם הַהוּא עֵשָׂו לְדַרְכּוֹ שֵׂעִירָה׃ וְיַעֲקֹב
נָסַע סֻכֹּתָה וַיִּבֶן לוֹ בָּיִת וּלְמִקְנֵהוּ עָשָׂה סֻכֹּת עַל־כֵּן קָרָא שֵׁם־הַמָּקוֹם
יח סֻכּוֹת׃ וַיָּבֹא יַעֲקֹב שָׁלֵם עִיר שְׁכֶם אֲשֶׁר בְּאֶרֶץ כְּנַעַן בְּבֹאוֹ

---

10. כִּרְאֹת פְּנֵי אֱלֹהִים — *Like seeing the face of a Divine being.* (Accept it) because it is customary to bring a tribute to a lord (an honored man), as it is written, וְלֹא יֵרָאוּ פָנַי רֵיקָם, *And do not appear before Me empty-handed (Exodus* 23:15).

וַתִּרְצֵנִי — *And you were appeased by me.* For you received me graciously, similar to, הֲיִרְצְךָ אוֹ הֲיִשָּׂא פָנֶיךָ, *Will he be pleased with you, or will he forgive you? (Malachi* 1:8). And for this reason, also, it is proper that I greet you with a gift.

11. וַיִּפְצַר בּוֹ — *He urged him* ... to accept it, (knowing that) bribery blinds (the recipient).

וַיִּקָּח — *And he accepted.* The reverse of Elisha, as it says, וַיִּפְצַר בּוֹ לָקַחַת, וַיְמָאֵן, *He urged him to take it, but he refused (II Kings* 5:16).

12. נִסְעָה וְנֵלֵכָה — *Travel on, and let us go.* (Let us go) to Seir, as those who brought the gift said, *'Moreover, behold your servant Jacob is behind us'* (32:21).

13. כִּי הַיְלָדִים רַכִּים וְהַצֹּאן וְהַבָּקָר עָלוֹת עָלָי — *The children are tender and the nursing flocks and herds are upon me.* They are my responsibility.

וּדְפָקוּם — *If they will be driven hard* ... in your honor, not to delay you on the road.

18. וַיָּבֹא יַעֲקֹב שָׁלֵם עִיר שְׁכֶם — *Jacob arrived intact at the city of Shechem* ... as soon as he arrived in peace in the Land of Canaan, as he had said, *'And (if) I return*

NOTES

Academy, and would perhaps have saved the Temple as well if the *biryoni* had not thwarted his policy of moderation and conciliation.

9. אָחִי יְהִי לְךָ אֲשֶׁר לָךְ — *My brother, let what you have remain yours.* The *Sforno* connects the word אָחִי, *my brother,* with the latter part of the verse rather than the first. It is not meant to be a title or salutation, it is rather an explanation: 'Since we are brothers there is no need for you to honor me with such an extravagant gift.'

11. וַיִּפְצַר בּוֹ — *He urged him.* Jacob was not deterred by Esau's protestations. He knew full well that Esau really wanted to keep the gift, and he also appreciated that it would, like any bribe, reduce his enmity and appease him.

12. נִסְעָה וְנֵלֵכָה — *Travel on, and let us go.* In 32:21 the *Sforno* explained that Jacob told the messengers to imply to Esau that the gift was being sent to Esau *in Seir,* and Jacob would follow them there. Hence, Esau now wanted to hold him to his word.

13. עָלָי — *Are upon me.* The word עָלָי, *are upon me,* is linked by the *Sforno* to both the children and the animals. They are *my* responsibility and weigh heavily upon me, hence I must be prudent and ask you to be understanding.

18. וַיָּבֹא יַעֲקֹב שָׁלֵם עִיר שְׁכֶם . . . בְּבֹאוֹ מִפַּדַּן אֲרָם — *Jacob arrived intact at the city of Shechem*

יט מִפַּדַּן אֲרָם וַיִּחַן אֶת־פְּנֵי הָעִיר: וַיִּקֶן אֶת־חֶלְקַת הַשָּׂדֶה אֲשֶׁר נָטָה־שָׁם
כ אָהֳלוֹ מִיַּד בְּנֵי־חֲמוֹר אֲבִי שְׁכֶם בְּמֵאָה קְשִׂיטָה: וַיַּצֶּב־שָׁם מִזְבֵּחַ
לד חמישי א וַיִּקְרָא־לוֹ אֵל אֱלֹהֵי יִשְׂרָאֵל: וַתֵּצֵא דִינָה בַּת־לֵאָה אֲשֶׁר
ב יָלְדָה לְיַעֲקֹב לִרְאוֹת בִּבְנוֹת הָאָרֶץ: וַיַּרְא אֹתָהּ שְׁכֶם בֶּן־חֲמוֹר הַחִוִּי
ג נְשִׂיא הָאָרֶץ וַיִּקַּח אֹתָהּ וַיִּשְׁכַּב אֹתָהּ וַיְעַנֶּהָ: וַתִּדְבַּק נַפְשׁוֹ בְּדִינָה
ד בַּת־יַעֲקֹב וַיֶּאֱהַב אֶת־הַנַּעֲרָ וַיְדַבֵּר עַל־לֵב הַנַּעֲרָ: וַיֹּאמֶר שְׁכֶם אֶל־חֲמוֹר
ה אָבִיו לֵאמֹר קַח־לִי אֶת־הַיַּלְדָּה הַזֹּאת לְאִשָּׁה: וְיַעֲקֹב שָׁמַע כִּי טִמֵּא

---

in peace' (28:21). He did not wait (to build an altar) until he reached his father's home.

בְּבֹאוֹ מִפַּדַּן אֲרָם — *Upon arriving from Padan Aram.* While he was still on the way to his father's house, even though he had not yet arrived there, he began to fulfill his vow and built an altar, as he had said, *'And HASHEM will be a God to me'* (28:21).

19-20. וַיִּקֶן אֶת חֶלְקַת הַשָּׂדֶה . . . וַיַּצֶּב שָׁם מִזְבֵּחַ — *He bought the parcel of land . . . He set up an altar . . .* as it is said, אֵיךְ נָשִׁיר אֶת שִׁיר ה׳ עַל אַדְמַת נֵכָר, *How shall we sing the song of HASHEM in a foreign land (Psalms* 137:4)*?*

וַיִּקְרָא לוֹ אֵל אֱלֹהֵי יִשְׂרָאֵל — *And proclaimed it, 'God is the God of Israel.'* In his prayers he invoked God as God (of Israel), in keeping with his statement, וְהָיָה ה׳ לִי לֵאלֹהִים, *And HASHEM will be a God to me* (28:21), i.e., when (Jacob) will become 'Israel,' and the nations will be unable to 'deprive him of his senses and of a knowledge of his Creator' as mentioned in his vow (28:20).

XXXIV

3. וַתִּדְבַּק נַפְשׁוֹ בְּדִינָה — *And his soul cleaved to Dinah.* The effect in the case of Amnon and Tamar was the reverse, once he violated her.

בַּת יַעֲקֹב — *Daughter of Jacob . . .* because she was the daughter of Jacob, who was a man honored by all, as it later says, *for he wanted Jacob's daughter* (verse 19).

NOTES

. . . upon arriving from Padan Aram. The *Sforno* interprets the word שָׁלֵם as שָׁלוֹם *(in peace* rather than *intact),* linking it to the condition of his vow, 'וְשַׁבְתִּי בְשָׁלוֹם, *and if I return in peace'* (28:21). Once this had been fulfilled, he immediately kept his promise upon his arrival in Shechem and built an altar. This is also indicated by the words בְּבֹאוֹ מִפַּדַּן אֲרָם, *'upon' arriving from Padan Aram,* i.e., as soon as he arrived in Canaan, even before he had completed the next part of his vow; i.e., אֶל בֵּית אָבִי, *to my father's house.*

19-20. וַיִּקֶן אֶת חֶלְקַת הַשָּׂדֶה . . . וַיַּצֶּב שָׁם מִזְבֵּחַ וַיִּקְרָא לוֹ אֵל אֱלֹהֵי יִשְׂרָאֵל — *He bought the parcel of land . . . He set up an altar and proclaimed it, 'God is the God of Israel.'* The *Sforno* connects these two verses. Jacob bought a portion of land in *Eretz Yisrael* and only then, שָׁם, *there,* not outside of the land, did he build an altar to God, for 'how can he sing the song of HASHEM outside of *Eretz Yisrael?'* Jacob had stated that if God would help him to remain loyal to Him, and not allow the exigencies of exile to undermine his faith, he would then accept God as his Judge *(Elohim),* and forgo God's mercy as HASHEM. This he now did by calling God, *Elohim,* but also connecting this name to *his* new name — Israel (אֱלֹהֵי יִשְׂרָאֵל) — since this name implied that he was now capable of confronting any and all challenges, and prevailing.

XXXIV

3. וַתִּדְבַּק נַפְשׁוֹ בְּדִינָה — *And his soul cleaved to Dinah.* Once passion was spent, Amnon's love for Tamar changed to שִׂנְאָה, *hatred (II Samuel* 13:14,15). Not so Shechem, who became deeply attached to Dinah *after* he had taken and violated her.

ו אֶת־דִּינָה בִתּוֹ וּבָנָיו הָיוּ אֶת־מִקְנֵהוּ בַּשָּׂדֶה וְהֶחֱרִשׁ יַעֲקֹב עַד־בֹּאָם׃ וַיֵּצֵא
ז חֲמוֹר אֲבִי־שְׁכֶם אֶל־יַעֲקֹב לְדַבֵּר אִתּוֹ׃ וּבְנֵי יַעֲקֹב בָּאוּ מִן־הַשָּׂדֶה
כְּשָׁמְעָם וַיִּתְעַצְּבוּ הָאֲנָשִׁים וַיִּחַר לָהֶם מְאֹד כִּי נְבָלָה עָשָׂה בְיִשְׂרָאֵל
ח לִשְׁכַּב אֶת־בַּת־יַעֲקֹב וְכֵן לֹא יֵעָשֶׂה׃ וַיְדַבֵּר חֲמוֹר אִתָּם לֵאמֹר שְׁכֶם בְּנִי
ט חָשְׁקָה נַפְשׁוֹ בְּבִתְּכֶם תְּנוּ נָא אֹתָהּ לוֹ לְאִשָּׁה׃ וְהִתְחַתְּנוּ אֹתָנוּ בְּנֹתֵיכֶם
י תִּתְּנוּ־לָנוּ וְאֶת־בְּנֹתֵינוּ תִּקְחוּ לָכֶם׃ וְאִתָּנוּ תֵּשֵׁבוּ וְהָאָרֶץ תִּהְיֶה לִפְנֵיכֶם
יא שְׁבוּ וּסְחָרוּהָ וְהֵאָחֲזוּ בָּהּ׃ וַיֹּאמֶר שְׁכֶם אֶל־אָבִיהָ וְאֶל־אַחֶיהָ אֶמְצָא־חֵן
יב בְּעֵינֵיכֶם וַאֲשֶׁר תֹּאמְרוּ אֵלַי אֶתֵּן׃ הַרְבּוּ עָלַי מְאֹד מֹהַר וּמַתָּן וְאֶתְּנָה
יג כַּאֲשֶׁר תֹּאמְרוּ אֵלָי וּתְנוּ־לִי אֶת־הַנַּעֲרָ לְאִשָּׁה׃ וַיַּעֲנוּ בְנֵי־יַעֲקֹב אֶת־
שְׁכֶם וְאֶת־חֲמוֹר אָבִיו בְּמִרְמָה וַיְדַבֵּרוּ אֲשֶׁר טִמֵּא אֵת דִּינָה אֲחֹתָם׃

---

5. וְהֶחֱרִשׁ יַעֲקֹב עַד בֹּאָם — *So Jacob kept silent until their arrival.* He avoided any confrontation until his sons' arrival. Thus, they would be alerted (before the confrontation began, and would be able) to guard themselves against their antagonists.

6. וַיֵּצֵא חֲמוֹר — *Chamor went out.* Observing (Jacob's) silence, he grew worried that he was plotting against him.

7. וַיִּתְעַצְּבוּ הָאֲנָשִׁים וַיִּחַר לָהֶם מְאֹד — *The men were distressed and very angry.* Their distress was due to the outrage which had been perpetrated in Israel. Even though this was not considered a shame among the heathen nations, it was a shameful act in Israel. (Furthermore . . .)

וְכֵן לֹא יֵעָשֶׂה — *Such a thing was not done.* It was most uncommon to violate the daughter of a person of renown, therefore they were extremely angered that it had happened to them.

10. וּסְחָרוּהָ — *And trade in it.* Normally strangers were not allowed to trade, as we find, בַּר מָתָא אַבַּר מָתָא אַחֲרִיתָא מָצֵי מְעַכֵּב, *A local person can prevent an outsider (from trading or doing business)* (*Baba Basra* 21a).

12. הַרְבּוּ עָלַי מְאֹד מֹהַר — *Inflate exceedingly upon me the dowry* . . . as compensation for my guilt and transgression against you.

13. בְּמִרְמָה — *Cleverly.* The request that they should circumcise themselves was made either in the belief that they would refuse, or that they would be unable to convince their townspeople to do so.

וַיְדַבְּרוּ אֲשֶׁר טִמֵּא אֵת דִּינָה — *And they spoke, after he had defiled Dinah.* They answered that the offer of extravagant gifts made by Shechem and his father was

NOTES

7. וַיִּתְעַצְּבוּ הָאֲנָשִׁים וַיִּחַר לָהֶם מְאֹד — *The men were distressed and very angry.* Two expressions are used to describe the emotions of the brothers — *distress* and *anger.* The former is a reaction to the moral outrage which was peculiar to them as Israelites. The latter is because even among the heathens respect was shown to a girl who is the daughter of an important personage. This lack of elemental respect for the status and position of their father and family incensed them.

13. וַיְדַבְּרוּ אֲשֶׁר טִמֵּא אֵת דִּינָה — *And they spoke, after he had defiled Dinah.* According to the Midrash these words, *because he had defiled their sister Dinah,* were interjected by

יד וַיֹּאמְר֣וּ אֲלֵיהֶ֗ם לֹ֤א נוּכַל֙ לַעֲשׂוֹת֙ הַדָּבָ֣ר הַזֶּ֔ה לָתֵת֙ אֶת־אֲחֹתֵ֔נוּ לְאִ֖ישׁ
טו אֲשֶׁר־ל֣וֹ עׇרְלָ֑ה כִּֽי־חֶרְפָּ֥ה הִ֖וא לָֽנוּ: אַ֣ךְ־בְּזֹ֣את נֵא֣וֹת לָכֶ֔ם אִ֚ם תִּהְי֣וּ כָמֹ֔נוּ
טז לְהִמֹּ֥ל לָכֶ֖ם כׇּל־זָכָֽר: וְנָתַ֤נּוּ אֶת־בְּנֹתֵ֙ינוּ֙ לָכֶ֔ם וְאֶת־בְּנֹתֵיכֶ֖ם נִֽקַּֽח־לָ֑נוּ
יז וְיָשַׁ֣בְנוּ אִתְּכֶ֔ם וְהָיִ֖ינוּ לְעַ֣ם אֶחָֽד: וְאִם־לֹ֧א תִשְׁמְע֛וּ אֵלֵ֖ינוּ לְהִמּ֑וֹל וְלָקַ֥חְנוּ
יח אֶת־בִּתֵּ֖נוּ וְהָלָֽכְנוּ: וַיִּֽיטְב֥וּ דִבְרֵיהֶ֖ם בְּעֵינֵ֣י חֲמ֑וֹר וּבְעֵינֵ֖י שְׁכֶ֥ם בֶּן־חֲמֽוֹר:
יט וְלֹֽא־אֵחַ֤ר הַנַּ֙עַר֙ לַעֲשׂ֣וֹת הַדָּבָ֔ר כִּ֥י חָפֵ֖ץ בְּבַֽת־יַעֲקֹ֑ב וְה֣וּא נִכְבָּ֔ד מִכֹּ֖ל בֵּ֥ית
כ אָבִֽיו: וַיָּבֹ֥א חֲמ֛וֹר וּשְׁכֶ֥ם בְּנ֖וֹ אֶל־שַׁ֣עַר עִירָ֑ם וַֽיְדַבְּר֛וּ אֶל־אַנְשֵׁ֥י עִירָ֖ם
כא לֵאמֹֽר: הָאֲנָשִׁ֨ים הָאֵ֤לֶּה שְֽׁלֵמִ֥ים הֵ֨ם אִתָּ֜נוּ וְיֵשְׁב֣וּ בָאָ֗רֶץ וְיִסְחֲר֣וּ אֹתָ֔הּ
וְהָאָ֛רֶץ הִנֵּ֥ה רַֽחֲבַת־יָדַ֖יִם לִפְנֵיהֶ֑ם אֶת־בְּנֹתָם֙ נִֽקַּֽח־לָ֣נוּ לְנָשִׁ֔ים וְאֶת־בְּנֹתֵ֖ינוּ
כב נִתֵּ֥ן לָהֶֽם: אַךְ־בְּ֠זֹ֠את יֵאֹ֨תוּ לָ֤נוּ הָאֲנָשִׁים֙ לָשֶׁ֣בֶת אִתָּ֔נוּ לִֽהְי֖וֹת לְעַ֣ם אֶחָ֑ד
כג בְּהִמּ֥וֹל לָ֙נוּ֙ כׇּל־זָכָ֔ר כַּאֲשֶׁ֖ר הֵ֥ם נִמֹּלִֽים: מִקְנֵהֶ֤ם וְקִנְיָנָם֙ וְכׇל־בְּהֶמְתָּ֔ם הֲל֣וֹא
כד לָ֥נוּ הֵ֑ם אַ֚ךְ נֵא֣וֹתָה לָהֶ֔ם וְיֵשְׁב֖וּ אִתָּֽנוּ: וַיִּשְׁמְע֣וּ אֶל־חֲמ֗וֹר וְאֶל־שְׁכֶ֣ם בְּנ֔וֹ
כה כׇּל־יֹצְאֵ֖י שַׁ֣עַר עִיר֑וֹ וַיִּמֹּ֙לוּ֙ כׇּל־זָכָ֔ר כׇּל־יֹצְאֵ֖י שַׁ֥עַר עִירֽוֹ: וַיְהִי֩ בַיּ֨וֹם
הַשְּׁלִישִׁ֜י בִּֽהְיוֹתָ֣ם כֹּֽאֲבִ֗ים וַיִּקְח֣וּ שְׁנֵֽי־בְנֵי־יַ֠עֲקֹ֠ב שִׁמְע֨וֹן וְלֵוִ֜י אֲחֵ֤י דִינָה֙ אִ֣ישׁ
כו חַרְבּ֔וֹ וַיָּבֹ֥אוּ עַל־הָעִ֖יר בֶּ֑טַח וַיַּֽהַרְג֖וּ כׇּל־זָכָֽר: וְאֶת־חֲמוֹר֙ וְאֶת־שְׁכֶ֣ם בְּנ֔וֹ
כז הָרְג֖וּ לְפִי־חָ֑רֶב וַיִּקְח֛וּ אֶת־דִּינָ֥ה מִבֵּ֥ית שְׁכֶ֖ם וַיֵּצֵֽאוּ: בְּנֵ֣י יַעֲקֹ֗ב בָּ֚אוּ

---

inappropriate inasmuch as he had already defiled her, for it would appear as a harlot's hire.

14. כִּי חֶרְפָּה הִוא לָנוּ — *For that would be a disgrace among us . . .* for it would imply that there is no fitting man among the circumcised who would marry her.

17. וְלָקַחְנוּ אֶת בִּתֵּנוּ — *We will take our daughter.* Though she is still in your house, we will take her from you.

וְהָלָכְנוּ — *And go.* With all our wealth, from which you will derive no benefit.

19. וְהוּא נִכְבָּד — *He was the most respected.* Even so, he did not delay doing the thing (circumcision), for he wanted Jacob's daughter.

21. שְׁלֵמִים הֵם אִתָּנוּ — *These people are peaceable with us.* They are peaceable toward us and do not wish to avenge their humiliation.

25. וַיַּהַרְגוּ כָּל זָכָר — *They killed every male.* For they had circumcised themselves only in the hope of gaining their livestock and possessions, as Chamor and Shechem had said to them (verse 23).

26. וְאֶת חֲמוֹר וְאֶת שְׁכֶם בְּנוֹ הָרְגוּ — *And Chamor and Shechem his son they killed.* They searched and located them.

NOTES

the Divine Spirit parenthetically, to justify their 'clever' proposal. The *Sforno*, however, interprets these words as having been said by Jacob's sons to Chamor and Shechem. What good is your offer of gifts and dowry since the deed is already done? The word אֲשֶׁר is to be understood here as אַחֲרֵי (*after* he had defiled)

similar to, כַּאֲשֶׁר עָבַר אֶת פְּנוּאֵל, *'after' he had passed over Penuel* (32:32).

25. וַיַּהַרְגוּ כָּל זָכָר — *They killed every male.* Their motive was impure. The only way Chamor and Shechem convinced them to do this act was by promising them that all the

כח עַל־הַחֲלָלִים וַיָּבֹזּוּ הָעִיר אֲשֶׁר טִמְּאוּ אֲחוֹתָם: אֶת־צֹאנָם וְאֶת־בְּקָרָם
כט וְאֶת־חֲמֹרֵיהֶם וְאֵת אֲשֶׁר־בָּעִיר וְאֶת־אֲשֶׁר בַּשָּׂדֶה לָקָחוּ: וְאֶת־כָּל־חֵילָם
ל וְאֶת־כָּל־טַפָּם וְאֶת־נְשֵׁיהֶם שָׁבוּ וַיָּבֹזּוּ וְאֵת כָּל־אֲשֶׁר בַּבָּיִת: וַיֹּאמֶר יַעֲקֹב
אֶל־שִׁמְעוֹן וְאֶל־לֵוִי עֲכַרְתֶּם אֹתִי לְהַבְאִישֵׁנִי בְּיֹשֵׁב הָאָרֶץ בַּכְּנַעֲנִי
לא וּבַפְּרִזִּי וַאֲנִי מְתֵי מִסְפָּר וְנֶאֶסְפוּ עָלַי וְהִכּוּנִי וְנִשְׁמַדְתִּי אֲנִי וּבֵיתִי: וַיֹּאמְרוּ
הַכְזוֹנָה יַעֲשֶׂה אֶת־אֲחוֹתֵנוּ:
לה א וַיֹּאמֶר אֱלֹהִים אֶל־יַעֲקֹב קוּם עֲלֵה בֵית־אֵל וְשֶׁב־שָׁם וַעֲשֵׂה־שָׁם מִזְבֵּחַ
ב לָאֵל הַנִּרְאֶה אֵלֶיךָ בְּבָרְחֲךָ מִפְּנֵי עֵשָׂו אָחִיךָ: וַיֹּאמֶר יַעֲקֹב אֶל־בֵּיתוֹ וְאֶל

27. הָעִיר אֲשֶׁר טִמְּאוּ אֲחוֹתָם — *The city which had defiled their sister.* For Shechem would never have committed (this evil) if it had not been considered non-abhorrent (acceptable) to them and common practice for the lords to take any girl they desired without her consent, as wives or concubines, as we find, וַיִּקְחוּ לָהֶם נָשִׁים מִכֹּל אֲשֶׁר בָּחָרוּ, *And they took for themselves women, whoever they chose* (6:2).

30. לְהַבְאִישֵׁנִי — *Making me odious.* They will say we broke our word after they became circumcised.

31. הַכְזוֹנָה יַעֲשֶׂה אֶת אֲחוֹתֵנוּ — *Should he treat our sister as a harlot?* Is she a harlot who is not worthy to have her humiliation avenged, that the people of the land (treat her) in this manner? She is our sister, not a harlot, and we were right to avenge her humiliation. When the inhabitants of the land will consider all this they will not be inclined to attack us.

XXXV

1. וְשֶׁב שָׁם — *And remain there* . . . to attune your mind spiritually before you build the altar, as our Sages tell us, 'The pious men of old used to wait an hour before praying in order to concentrate their thoughts upon their Father in Heaven' (*Berachos* 30b).

וַעֲשֵׂה שָׁם מִזְבֵּחַ לָאֵל הַנִּרְאֶה אֵלֶיךָ בְּבָרְחֲךָ — *And make an altar there to God, Who appeared to you when you fled* . . . to give thanks (to God) for having fulfilled the promise made there. This is akin to the Sages' statement, (מְבָרֵךְ) בָּרוּךְ שֶׁעָשָׂה לִי נֵס בַּמָּקוֹם הַזֶּה, *He utters the benediction: 'Blessed is He Who wrought a miracle for me in this place'* (*Berachos* 54a).

NOTES

wealth of the Israelites would *be ours* (לָנוּ הֵם) (verse 23). Their greed eventually led to their downfall.

27. הָעִיר אֲשֶׁר טִמְּאוּ אֲחוֹתָם — *The city which had defiled their sister.* Shechem alone — not the city — had defiled Dinah! Why is the entire city to blame? The Torah tells us that they, *the city*, were all guilty, for they all accepted and condoned the immoral behavior of their lords.

31. הַכְזוֹנָה יַעֲשֶׂה אֶת אֲחוֹתֵנוּ — *Should he treat our sister as a harlot?* The brothers strongly affirmed the innocence of their sister. Shechem's act was a dastardly outrageous one and, as her brothers, they were justified in punishing him and his townspeople who were not innocents, having condoned this kind of behavior in their midst. As for the danger they exposed themselves to, they were convinced that after due deliberation and thought the inhabitants of the land would understand their need to avenge their sister's honor and would not harm them.

XXXV

1. וְשֶׁב שָׁם — *And remain there.* The com-

כָּל־אֲשֶׁר עִמּוֹ הָסִרוּ אֶת־אֱלֹהֵי הַנֵּכָר אֲשֶׁר בְּתֹכְכֶם וְהִטַּהֲרוּ וְהַחֲלִיפוּ
ג שִׂמְלֹתֵיכֶם: וְנָקוּמָה וְנַעֲלֶה בֵּית־אֵל וְאֶעֱשֶׂה־שָּׁם מִזְבֵּחַ לָאֵל הָעֹנֶה אֹתִי
ד בְּיוֹם צָרָתִי וַיְהִי עִמָּדִי בַּדֶּרֶךְ אֲשֶׁר הָלָכְתִּי: וַיִּתְּנוּ אֶל־יַעֲקֹב אֵת כָּל־
אֱלֹהֵי הַנֵּכָר אֲשֶׁר בְּיָדָם וְאֶת־הַנְּזָמִים אֲשֶׁר בְּאָזְנֵיהֶם וַיִּטְמֹן אֹתָם יַעֲקֹב
ה תַּחַת הָאֵלָה אֲשֶׁר עִם־שְׁכֶם: וַיִּסָּעוּ וַיְהִי | חִתַּת אֱלֹהִים עַל־הֶעָרִים אֲשֶׁר
ו סְבִיבוֹתֵיהֶם וְלֹא רָדְפוּ אַחֲרֵי בְּנֵי יַעֲקֹב: וַיָּבֹא יַעֲקֹב לוּזָה אֲשֶׁר בְּאֶרֶץ
ז כְּנַעַן הִוא בֵּית־אֵל הוּא וְכָל־הָעָם אֲשֶׁר־עִמּוֹ: וַיִּבֶן שָׁם מִזְבֵּחַ וַיִּקְרָא
ח לַמָּקוֹם אֵל בֵּית־אֵל כִּי שָׁם נִגְלוּ אֵלָיו הָאֱלֹהִים בְּבָרְחוֹ מִפְּנֵי אָחִיו: וַתָּמָת
דְּבֹרָה מֵינֶקֶת רִבְקָה וַתִּקָּבֵר מִתַּחַת לְבֵית־אֵל תַּחַת הָאַלּוֹן וַיִּקְרָא שְׁמוֹ
אַלּוֹן בָּכוּת:

---

2. הָסִרוּ אֶת אֱלֹהֵי הַנֵּכָר — *Discard the alien gods . . .* which you took from Shechem. Even though the women of Shechem who worshiped them had renounced (nullified) them, and it was now permitted to derive benefit from them, as our Sages state, 'A gentile can annul an idol, even if forced to do so' (*Avodah Zarah* 43a), nonetheless, remove them from your midst now that we are going to Beth El, so that any thought of idolatry be removed from your minds.

4. וַיִּטְמֹן אֹתָם יַעֲקֹב — *And Jacob buried them.* But he did not destroy them since they had been nullified and (halachically) it was permitted to derive benefit from them.

5. וַיִּסָּעוּ וַיְהִי חִתַּת אֱלֹהִים — *They set out, and there fell a Godly terror (on the cities).* When they left Shechem which was a fortified city they were in danger of being attacked along the way by the people of the surrounding cities, therefore it was necessary for God's terror to fall upon their enemies.

7. וַיִּקְרָא לַמָּקוֹם — *And named the place . . .* the inn where he lodged on his way to Haran, as it says, וַיִּפְגַּע בַּמָּקוֹם, *he encountered the place* (28:11, see the *Sforno's* comment there).

אֵל בֵּית אֵל — *El Bethel . . .* the sanctuary of Beth El.

8. אַלּוֹן בָּכוּת — *Alon Bachus.* This caused the manifestation of the *Shechinah* (Divine Presence) to cease, as our Sages state, שֶׁאֵין הַשְּׁכִינָה שׁוֹרָה לֹא מִתּוֹךְ עַצְבוּת, *The Shechinah cannot rest amidst gloom (Shabbos* 30b).

NOTES

mandment of God to Jacob should have read simply, 'Go to Beth El and build an altar.' The phrase וְשֶׁב שָׁם, *and remain (settle down) there*, seems superfluous. Indeed the *Ramban* (initially) says that he does not know the significance of this command. The *Sforno* interprets it as a period of preparation, of contemplation, before one proceeds to pray or perform a religious act, such as the building of an altar.

2. הָסִרוּ אֶת אֱלֹהֵי הַנֵּכָר — *Discard the alien gods.* The *Sforno* mentions the *women of Shechem* because the males had all been killed.

4. וַיִּטְמֹן אֹתָם יַעֲקֹב — *And Jacob buried them.* The Talmud in tractate *Avodah Zarah* (43b and 51b) requires one to pulverize or scatter idols to the wind, or cast them into the sea. The reason Jacob only *buried* them is because strictly speaking even this was unnecessary, since these idols had been nullified and it was permitted to benefit from them. Nonetheless, Jacob buried them for he did not want his children and household to have any contact whatsoever with these idols.

ט-י וַיֵּרָא אֱלֹהִים אֶל־יַעֲקֹב עוֹד בְּבֹאוֹ מִפַּדַּן אֲרָם וַיְבָרֶךְ אֹתוֹ: וַיֹּאמֶר־לוֹ
אֱלֹהִים שִׁמְךָ יַעֲקֹב לֹא־יִקָּרֵא שִׁמְךָ עוֹד יַעֲקֹב כִּי אִם־יִשְׂרָאֵל יִהְיֶה שְׁמֶךָ
יא וַיִּקְרָא אֶת־שְׁמוֹ יִשְׂרָאֵל: וַיֹּאמֶר לוֹ אֱלֹהִים אֲנִי אֵל שַׁדַּי פְּרֵה וּרְבֵה גּוֹי

---

9. וַיֵּרָא אֱלֹהִים — *And God appeared* . . . after the period of weeping had ended.

אֶל יַעֲקֹב עוֹד — *To Jacob again* . . . as He had appeared to him there when he went to Haran, as it says, *Who appeared to you when you fled* (v. 1).

בְּבֹאוֹ מִפַּדַּן אֲרָם — *When he came from Padan Aram.* But in Padan Aram God did not appear to him, though He did speak to him through an angel, as it states, *And an angel of God said to me in a dream* (31:11).

10. שִׁמְךָ יַעֲקֹב — *Your name is Jacob.* I now confirm this name (Jacob) indicating that you alone will survive the destruction of all other nations in the end of days, as it is said, כִּי אֶעֱשֶׂה כָלָה בְּכָל הַגּוֹיִם . . . וְאֹתְךָ לֹא אֶעֱשֶׂה כָלָה, *For I will make full end of all the nations . . . but I will not make a full end of you (Jer.* 46:28).

לֹא יִקָּרֵא שִׁמְךָ עוֹד יַעֲקֹב — *You shall not always be named Jacob.* When the implication of the name *Jacob* will be fulfilled, i.e., that you alone (of the nations) will remain at the end of days, as it says, הֶן עָם לְבָדָד יִשְׁכֹּן, *Lo, it is a people that shall dwell alone (Numbers* 23:9), then there will no longer be any need for this name, *Jacob.*

כִּי אִם יִשְׂרָאֵל יִהְיֶה שְׁמֶךָ — *But Israel shall be your name* . . . for you will rule over the remnants of the nations, as it says, וְקַרְקַר כָּל בְּנֵי שֵׁת, *and break down all the sons of Seth (Numbers* 24:17).

וַיִּקְרָא אֶת שְׁמוֹ יִשְׂרָאֵל — *Thus, He named him Israel.* He blessed him that the implication of the name *Israel,* sovereignty, should commence (to a degree) *immediately,* to the extent that he might be able to withstand his enemies even in lands which are not his (i.e., in exile), as our Sages state, 'Wherever they went, they became lords over their masters' (*Sanhedrin* 104a).

11. אֲנִי אֵל שַׁדַּי — *I am El Shaddai.* I swear by My Name, similar to, וְאָמַרְתִּי חַי אָנֹכִי לְעֹלָם, *And I say: As I live forever (Deut.* 32:40). This is the only place we find that God swore in His Name to Jacob.

פְּרֵה וּרְבֵה — *Be fruitful and multiply.* Do not be concerned that your children will be destroyed by the nations, nor that they will be unworthy. Therefore, do not cease

NOTES

9. בְּבֹאוֹ מִפַּדַּן אֲרָם — *When he came from Padan Aram.* The verse quoted by the *Sforno* (31:11) states specifically *angel of God.* We must assume that 31:3 which states, וַיֹּאמֶר ה׳ אֶל יַעֲקֹב, *And* HASHEM *said to Jacob,* also means through the medium of an angel, since God does not appear outside of *Eretz Yisrael.* The *Radak* interprets 31:3 in like manner.

10. שִׁמְךָ יַעֲקֹב — *Your name is Jacob.* Compare the *Sforno's* commentary to 25:26 and 32:29.

וַיִּקְרָא אֶת שְׁמוֹ יִשְׂרָאֵל — *Thus, He named him Israel.* The last two words of the previous verse are וַיְבָרֶךְ אֹתוֹ, *and He blessed him.* The *Sforno* apparently interprets this blessing as allowing Jacob to profit from his new name Israel *immediately,* so that he might benefit from this name even before the end of days, i.e., while still in *galus* (exile).

11. אֲנִי אֵל שַׁדַּי — *I am El Shaddai. Rashi* interprets this introductory statement, אֲנִי אֵל שַׁדַּי, *I am El Shaddai,* as implying, 'I am *sufficient* to bless, for the blessings are Mine.'

ששי יב וּקְהַל גּוֹיִם יִהְיֶה מִמֶּךָּ וּמְלָכִים מֵחֲלָצֶיךָ יֵצֵאוּ: וְאֶת־הָאָרֶץ אֲשֶׁר נָתַתִּי
יג לְאַבְרָהָם וּלְיִצְחָק לְךָ אֶתְּנֶנָּה וּלְזַרְעֲךָ אַחֲרֶיךָ אֶתֵּן אֶת־הָאָרֶץ: וַיַּעַל
יד מֵעָלָיו אֱלֹהִים בַּמָּקוֹם אֲשֶׁר־דִּבֶּר אִתּוֹ: וַיַּצֵּב יַעֲקֹב מַצֵּבָה בַּמָּקוֹם אֲשֶׁר־
טו דִּבֶּר אִתּוֹ מַצֶּבֶת אָבֶן וַיַּסֵּךְ עָלֶיהָ נֶסֶךְ וַיִּצֹק עָלֶיהָ שָׁמֶן: וַיִּקְרָא יַעֲקֹב

---

from being fruitful and multiplying, as opposed to the advice of Rabbi Ishmael who said, 'From the day that the evil kingdom came to power . . . we ought by rights to accept upon ourselves not to marry and beget children, and the seed of Abraham our father would come to an end by itself (*Baba Basra* 60b). (All) this is said because, 'I am *El Shaddai*, who does not need a prepared recipient. I shall do what I have said, regardless, even without a recipient prepared (for my blessing).'

וּמְלָכִים מֵחֲלָצֶיךָ יֵצֵאוּ — *And kings shall issue forth from your loins* . . . men, fit to be kings. There will be no need to appoint strangers as (Israel's) kings, as Edom did, i.e., Samlah of Masrekah, Saul of Rechovos and others (36:36,37).

12. וּלְזַרְעֲךָ אַחֲרֶיךָ אֶתֵּן אֶת הָאָרֶץ — *And to your offspring after you I will give the land.* In the end of days I will give your offspring the entire earth, not only *Eretz Yisrael*, as it says, *You will spread powerfully westward, eastward, northward and southward* (28:14); and as it is said, וְקַרְקַר כָּל בְּנֵי שֵׁת, *and break down all the sons of Seth (Numbers* 24:17).

13. בַּמָּקוֹם אֲשֶׁר דִּבֶּר אִתּוֹ — *In the place where He had spoken to him* . . . when he left (home) to go to Haran, in the same inn that (God's) word was spoken; there *God appeared* (verse 9) and there He ascended, therefore (Jacob) set up a pillar in that self-same place.

14. וַיַּסֵּךְ עָלֶיהָ נֶסֶךְ — *And he poured a libation upon it* . . . thereby completing the fulfillment of his oath, as he said, *'Then this stone which I have set up as a pillar shall become a House of God'* (28:22), for in this manner he prepared this place for the House of God. This is similar to David, when the angel appeared to him in the threshing floor of Aravnah (Arnan) the Jebusite (see *II Chronicles* 21:15-26).

NOTES

The *Sforno*, however, explains this expression as denoting a Divine oath. This will explain *Exodus* 33:1 — *The land which I swore to Abraham, to Isaac and to Jacob*. This was the oath given to Jacob.

פְּרֵה וּרְבֵה — *Be fruitful and multiply*. According to the *Sforno, be fruitful and multiply* is not to be understood as a commandment, but as an exhortation and reassurance. He also is cognizant of the deeper meaning of this Divine Name, as indicating 'I am sufficient' (שַׁדַּי = שֶׁאֲנִי דַּי). He interprets this to mean that God can give a blessing even without a proper recipient, for in His hand there is sufficient power to always give. Apparently the *Sforno* now interprets the phrase אֲנִי אֵל שַׁדַּי akin to *Rashi*, and also gives the added interpretation of 'blessing' to the phrase פְּרֵה וּרְבֵה, *Be fruitful and multiply*.

12. וּלְזַרְעֲךָ אַחֲרֶיךָ אֶתֵּן אֶת הָאָרֶץ — *And to your offspring after you I will give the land.* The word הָאָרֶץ, *The land*, at the beginning of the verse refers to *Eretz Yisrael*. The same word at the end of the verse is not redundant. There it refers to the earth.

13-14. בַּמָּקוֹם אֲשֶׁר דִּבֶּר אִתּוֹ . . . וַיַּסֵּךְ עָלֶיהָ נֶסֶךְ — *In the place where He had spoken to him . . . and he poured a libation upon it. Rashi* states that he does not know what the phrase, *In the place where He had spoken to him*, is meant to teach us. The *Sforno* interprets it to mean that God speaks to Jacob now, on his return, at the very site where He had spoken to him when he left home for Haran. When Jacob poured the libation on the pillar, he was completing the consecration of the מַצֵּבָה which he had begun so many years earlier. And since, according to the *Sforno, this place*, i.e., Beth

טז אֶת־שֵׁם הַמָּקוֹם אֲשֶׁר דִּבֶּר אִתּוֹ שָׁם אֱלֹהִים בֵּית־אֵל: וַיִּסְעוּ מִבֵּית אֵל
יז וַיְהִי־עוֹד כִּבְרַת־הָאָרֶץ לָבוֹא אֶפְרָתָה וַתֵּלֶד רָחֵל וַתְּקַשׁ בְּלִדְתָּהּ: וַיְהִי
בְהַקְשֹׁתָהּ בְּלִדְתָּהּ וַתֹּאמֶר לָהּ הַמְיַלֶּדֶת אַל־תִּירְאִי כִּי־גַם־זֶה לָךְ בֵּן:
יח וַיְהִי בְּצֵאת נַפְשָׁהּ כִּי מֵתָה וַתִּקְרָא שְׁמוֹ בֶּן־אוֹנִי וְאָבִיו קָרָא־לוֹ בִנְיָמִין:
יט־כ וַתָּמָת רָחֵל וַתִּקָּבֵר בְּדֶרֶךְ אֶפְרָתָה הִוא בֵּית לָחֶם: וַיַּצֵּב יַעֲקֹב מַצֵּבָה
כא עַל־קְבֻרָתָהּ הִוא מַצֶּבֶת קְבֻרַת־רָחֵל עַד־הַיּוֹם: וַיִּסַּע יִשְׂרָאֵל וַיֵּט אָהֳלֹה
כב מֵהָלְאָה לְמִגְדַּל־עֵדֶר: וַיְהִי בִּשְׁכֹּן יִשְׂרָאֵל בָּאָרֶץ הַהִוא וַיֵּלֶךְ רְאוּבֵן
וַיִּשְׁכַּב אֶת־בִּלְהָה פִּילֶגֶשׁ אָבִיו וַיִּשְׁמַע יִשְׂרָאֵל
כג וַיִּהְיוּ בְנֵי־יַעֲקֹב שְׁנֵים עָשָׂר: בְּנֵי לֵאָה בְּכוֹר יַעֲקֹב רְאוּבֵן וְשִׁמְעוֹן וְלֵוִי
כד־כה וִיהוּדָה וְיִשָּׂשכָר וּזְבֻלוּן: בְּנֵי רָחֵל יוֹסֵף וּבִנְיָמִן: וּבְנֵי בִלְהָה שִׁפְחַת רָחֵל דָּן
כו וְנַפְתָּלִי: וּבְנֵי זִלְפָּה שִׁפְחַת לֵאָה גָּד וְאָשֵׁר אֵלֶּה בְּנֵי יַעֲקֹב אֲשֶׁר יֻלַּד־לוֹ
כז בְּפַדַּן אֲרָם: וַיָּבֹא יַעֲקֹב אֶל־יִצְחָק אָבִיו מַמְרֵא קִרְיַת הָאַרְבַּע הִוא חֶבְרוֹן
כח אֲשֶׁר־גָּר־שָׁם אַבְרָהָם וְיִצְחָק: וַיִּהְיוּ יְמֵי יִצְחָק מְאַת שָׁנָה וּשְׁמֹנִים שָׁנָה:

---

17. אַל תִּירְאִי — *Have no fear* . . . that your hard labor indicates it will be a girl, as our Sages tell us, חֶבְלֵי נְקֵבָה מְרוּבִּים מִשֶּׁל זָכָר, *The travail (of childbirth) is much greater when a girl (is born) than when a boy (is born)* (*Niddah* 31a).

כִּי גַם זֶה לָךְ בֵּן — *For this one, too, is a son for you.* Even though the pains are great, it is still a boy.

20. מַצֵּבָה עַל קְבֻרָתָהּ — *A monument over her grave.* Since her grave was on a public thoroughfare, he feared it might be disturbed or plundered.

22. וַיִּשְׁמַע יִשְׂרָאֵל וַיִּהְיוּ בְנֵי יַעֲקֹב שְׁנֵים עָשָׂר — *And Israel heard, and the sons of Jacob were twelve.* Though he was aware (of Reuben's deed) he did not remove him from the roster of his sons, for he was certain that (Reuben) had repented immediately. (As a result) he was not omitted from the roster of the sons of Jacob, who were destined to remain at the end of days and survive all the other nations.

23. בְּכוֹר יַעֲקֹב רְאוּבֵן — *Jacob's firstborn, Reuben.* Because he had repented, and repentance reaches God's Throne of Glory, he did not forfeit his birthright according to the law of heaven. He was not deprived (of his birthright as firstborn) until Jacob took it away from him in accordance with the law of man. This is similar to one who is deservant of excommunication but is not considered excommunicated until a leading scholar pronounces him as such, as our Sages teach us, 'What is the source for שַׁמְתָּא, *excommunication?* It is written, אוֹרוּ מֵרוֹז, *Curse Meroz (Judges* 5:23), (providing) this is concurred with by a prominent person, as it is written: אָמַר מַלְאַךְ ה׳, *Said the angel of God* (ibid.)' (*Moed Katan* 16a). And the latter authorities also concur with this decision.

27. אֲשֶׁר גָּר שָׁם אַבְרָהָם וְיִצְחָק — *Where Abraham and Isaac dwelled.* The mention of the dwelling of the righteous in (a particular place) is of benefit to their children,

NOTES

El-Luz and Mt. Moriah, were merged into one at this time, this consecration was a preparation for the House of God (the Temple) which would one day be constructed on *this place.*

23. בְּכוֹר יַעֲקֹב רְאוּבֵן – *Jacob's firstborn, Reuben.* The Talmud in tractate *Shabbos* (55b) explains that Reuben had defended his mother Leah's honor. Upon the death of Rachel, Jacob

כט וַיִּגְוַע יִצְחָק וַיָּמָת וַיֵּאָסֶף אֶל־עַמָּיו זָקֵן וּשְׂבַע יָמִים וַיִּקְבְּרוּ אֹתוֹ עֵשָׂו
וְיַעֲקֹב בָּנָיו:

לו

א־ב וְאֵלֶּה תֹּלְדוֹת עֵשָׂו הוּא אֱדוֹם: עֵשָׂו לָקַח אֶת־נָשָׁיו מִבְּנוֹת כְּנָעַן אֶת־עָדָה
ג בַּת־אֵילוֹן הַחִתִּי וְאֶת־אָהֳלִיבָמָה בַּת־עֲנָה בַּת־צִבְעוֹן הַחִוִּי: וְאֶת־בָּשְׂמַת
ד בַּת־יִשְׁמָעֵאל אֲחוֹת נְבָיוֹת: וַתֵּלֶד עָדָה לְעֵשָׂו אֶת־אֱלִיפָז וּבָשְׂמַת יָלְדָה
ה אֶת־רְעוּאֵל: וְאָהֳלִיבָמָה יָלְדָה אֶת־°יעיש וְאֶת־יַעְלָם וְאֶת־קֹרַח אֵלֶּה בְּנֵי °יְעוּשׁ
ו עֵשָׂו אֲשֶׁר יֻלְּדוּ־לוֹ בְּאֶרֶץ כְּנָעַן: וַיִּקַּח עֵשָׂו אֶת־נָשָׁיו וְאֶת־בָּנָיו
וְאֶת־בְּנֹתָיו וְאֶת־כָּל־נַפְשׁוֹת בֵּיתוֹ וְאֶת־מִקְנֵהוּ וְאֶת־כָּל־בְּהֶמְתּוֹ וְאֵת
כָּל־קִנְיָנוֹ אֲשֶׁר רָכַשׁ בְּאֶרֶץ כְּנָעַן וַיֵּלֶךְ אֶל־אֶרֶץ מִפְּנֵי יַעֲקֹב אָחִיו:

---

for it creates an attitude of affection and good will among the inhabitants of that place. The reverse is true of the wicked of whom it is said, הָכִינוּ לְבָנָיו מַטְבֵּחַ בַּעֲוֹן אֲבוֹתָם בַּל יָקֻמוּ וְיָרְשׁוּ אָרֶץ, *Prepare slaughter for his children, for the iniquity of their fathers, that they rise not up and possess the earth* (*Isaiah* 14:21).

XXXVI

1. וְאֵלֶּה תֹּלְדוֹת — *And these are the chronicles.* These are the chronicles and happenings (of Esau) similar to, מַה יֵּלֶד יוֹם, *What a day may bring forth* (*Proverbs* 27:1).

עֵשָׂו הוּא אֱדוֹם — *Esau, who is Edom.* He was always (a person of) acquisitive greed consumed with desire, as we find on the day he (sold his birthright and) was called Edom. Since he was exhausted from his evil deeds he was not able to recognize the lentils to call them by name (only by color, אָדוֹם, red).

2. וְאֶת אָהֳלִיבָמָה בַּת עֲנָה — *Oholibamah daughter of Anah.* She was descended from the children of Seir, the Horites (see verse 20). It was through her that Esau went (to dwell) in the land of Seir, as it says, *So Esau settled on Mount Seir* (verse 8). His children later destroyed the Hori, as it is written, כַּאֲשֶׁר עָשָׂה לִבְנֵי עֵשָׂו הַיֹּשְׁבִים בְּשֵׂעִיר אֲשֶׁר הִשְׁמִיד אֶת הַחֹרִי מִפְּנֵיהֶם, *As He did for the children of Esau, that dwell in Seir, when He destroyed the Hori from before them* (*Deut.* 2:22). Therefore (the Torah) continues and says . . .

NOTES

had taken up residence in the tent of Bilhah, and Reuben strongly felt that this was improper, and so he 'arose and transposed her couch.' For this rash act, according to heavenly law (דִּינֵי שָׁמַיִם), he was not guilty of any overt transgression. His father, however, had the authority and right, according to temporal law (דִּינֵי אָדָם), to impose a ban upon him for this action. Jacob did so on his death bed, when he referred to the incident, and removed the birthright from Reuben (see 49:4). Hence, in our verse, the Torah correctly states that Reuben was the firstborn in accordance with heavenly law, but nonetheless, Jacob was justified when he punished him later in accordance with the 'law of man.' The *Sforno* quotes the passage from tractate *Moed Katan* to prove that a prominent scholar (in our case, Jacob) has the power to pronounce a ban, and Reuben's demotion is considered to be, in a sense, a ban.

XXXVI

1. וְאֵלֶּה תֹּלְדוֹת — *And these are the chronicles.* The phrase תּוֹלְדוֹת has a variety of meanings, i.e., descendants, genealogies, chronicles, etc. In our verse the *Sforno* chooses the latter interpretation, as he does in 25:19 and 37:2.

עֵשָׂו הוּא אֱדוֹם — *Esau, who is Edom.* Regarding the name *Edom*, see the *Sforno's* commentary to 25:30.

ז כִּי־הָיָה רְכוּשָׁם רָב מִשֶּׁבֶת יַחְדָּו וְלֹא יָכְלָה אֶרֶץ מְגוּרֵיהֶם לָשֵׂאת אֹתָם
ח-ט מִפְּנֵי מִקְנֵיהֶם: וַיֵּשֶׁב עֵשָׂו בְּהַר שֵׂעִיר עֵשָׂו הוּא אֱדוֹם: וְאֵלֶּה תֹּלְדוֹת עֵשָׂו
י אֲבִי אֱדוֹם בְּהַר שֵׂעִיר: אֵלֶּה שְׁמוֹת בְּנֵי־עֵשָׂו אֱלִיפַז בֶּן־עָדָה אֵשֶׁת עֵשָׂו
יא רְעוּאֵל בֶּן־בָּשְׂמַת אֵשֶׁת עֵשָׂו: וַיִּהְיוּ בְּנֵי אֱלִיפָז תֵּימָן אוֹמָר צְפוֹ וְגַעְתָּם
יב וּקְנַז: וְתִמְנַע | הָיְתָה פִילֶגֶשׁ לֶאֱלִיפַז בֶּן־עֵשָׂו וַתֵּלֶד לֶאֱלִיפַז אֶת־עֲמָלֵק
יג אֵלֶּה בְּנֵי עָדָה אֵשֶׁת עֵשָׂו: וְאֵלֶּה בְּנֵי רְעוּאֵל נַחַת וָזֶרַח שַׁמָּה וּמִזָּה אֵלֶּה
יד הָיוּ בְּנֵי בָשְׂמַת אֵשֶׁת עֵשָׂו: וְאֵלֶּה הָיוּ בְּנֵי אָהֳלִיבָמָה בַת־עֲנָה בַּת־צִבְעוֹן
°יְעוּשׁ טו אֵשֶׁת עֵשָׂו וַתֵּלֶד לְעֵשָׂו אֶת־°יעיש וְאֶת־יַעְלָם וְאֶת־קֹרַח: אֵלֶּה אַלּוּפֵי
בְנֵי־עֵשָׂו בְּנֵי אֱלִיפַז בְּכוֹר עֵשָׂו אַלּוּף תֵּימָן אַלּוּף אוֹמָר אַלּוּף צְפוֹ אַלּוּף
טז קְנַז: אַלּוּף־קֹרַח אַלּוּף גַּעְתָּם אַלּוּף עֲמָלֵק אֵלֶּה אַלּוּפֵי אֱלִיפַז בְּאֶרֶץ
יז אֱדוֹם אֵלֶּה בְּנֵי עָדָה: וְאֵלֶּה בְּנֵי רְעוּאֵל בֶּן־עֵשָׂו אַלּוּף נַחַת אַלּוּף זֶרַח
אַלּוּף שַׁמָּה אַלּוּף מִזָּה אֵלֶּה אַלּוּפֵי רְעוּאֵל בְּאֶרֶץ אֱדוֹם אֵלֶּה בְּנֵי בָשְׂמַת
יח אֵשֶׁת עֵשָׂו: וְאֵלֶּה בְּנֵי אָהֳלִיבָמָה אֵשֶׁת עֵשָׂו אַלּוּף יְעוּשׁ אַלּוּף יַעְלָם
יט אַלּוּף קֹרַח אֵלֶּה אַלּוּפֵי אָהֳלִיבָמָה בַּת־עֲנָה אֵשֶׁת עֵשָׂו: אֵלֶּה בְנֵי־עֵשָׂו
שביעי כ וְאֵלֶּה אַלּוּפֵיהֶם הוּא אֱדוֹם: אֵלֶּה בְנֵי־שֵׂעִיר הַחֹרִי יֹשְׁבֵי
כא הָאָרֶץ לוֹטָן וְשׁוֹבָל וְצִבְעוֹן וַעֲנָה: וְדִשׁוֹן וְאֵצֶר וְדִישָׁן אֵלֶּה אַלּוּפֵי הַחֹרִי
כב בְּנֵי שֵׂעִיר בְּאֶרֶץ אֱדוֹם: וַיִּהְיוּ בְנֵי־לוֹטָן חֹרִי וְהֵימָם וַאֲחוֹת לוֹטָן תִּמְנָע:
כג-כד וְאֵלֶּה בְּנֵי שׁוֹבָל עַלְוָן וּמָנַחַת וְעֵיבָל שְׁפוֹ וְאוֹנָם: וְאֵלֶּה בְנֵי־צִבְעוֹן וְאַיָּה
וַעֲנָה הוּא עֲנָה אֲשֶׁר מָצָא אֶת־הַיֵּמִם בַּמִּדְבָּר בִּרְעֹתוֹ אֶת־הַחֲמֹרִים
כה-כו לְצִבְעוֹן אָבִיו: וְאֵלֶּה בְנֵי־עֲנָה דִּשֹׁן וְאָהֳלִיבָמָה בַּת־עֲנָה: וְאֵלֶּה בְּנֵי דִישָׁן
כז-כח חֶמְדָּן וְאֶשְׁבָּן וְיִתְרָן וּכְרָן: אֵלֶּה בְּנֵי־אֵצֶר בִּלְהָן וְזַעֲוָן וַעֲקָן: אֵלֶּה בְנֵי־דִישָׁן
כט עוּץ וַאֲרָן: אֵלֶּה אַלּוּפֵי הַחֹרִי אַלּוּף לוֹטָן אַלּוּף שׁוֹבָל אַלּוּף צִבְעוֹן אַלּוּף
ל עֲנָה: אַלּוּף דִּשֹׁן אַלּוּף אֵצֶר אַלּוּף דִּישָׁן אֵלֶּה אַלּוּפֵי הַחֹרִי לְאַלֻּפֵיהֶם
בְּאֶרֶץ שֵׂעִיר:

---

9. וְאֵלֶּה תֹּלְדוֹת עֵשָׂו אֲבִי אֱדוֹם בְּהַר שֵׂעִיר — *And these are the progeny of Esau, ancestor of Edom, on Mount Seir ...* (proceeding) to enumerate the chiefs, for his sons later conquered the land (of Seir); Timna became the concubine of Eliphaz and the descendants of Esau (born in Seir) became chiefs.

12. וְתִמְנַע הָיְתָה פִּילֶגֶשׁ — *And Timna was a concubine.* Eliphaz was among the conquerors of the land (of Seir) and he took Timna, who was a sister of the (Hori) chieftains, as his concubine.

20. אֵלֶּה בְנֵי שֵׂעִיר הַחֹרִי — *These are the sons of Seir, the Hori.* (The Torah) records the names of these mighty men of repute to tell us that even so, the children of Esau were able to destroy them, for this was the will of the Almighty, as it says, כַּאֲשֶׁר עָשָׂה לִבְנֵי עֵשָׂו הַיֹּשְׁבִים בְּשֵׂעִיר, *As He did for the children of Esau that dwell in Seir* (*Deut.* 2:22).

NOTES

2-20. וְאֵת אָהֳלִיבָמָה בַּת עֲנָה ... אֵלֶּה בְנֵי שֵׂעִיר — *Oholibamah daughter of Anah ... These are the sons of Seir.* The *Sforno* traces the conquests of Esau as follows: He first moved to the

לא וְאֵלֶּה הַמְּלָכִים אֲשֶׁר מָלְכוּ בְּאֶרֶץ אֱדוֹם לִפְנֵי מְלָךְ־מֶלֶךְ לִבְנֵי יִשְׂרָאֵל:
לב־לג וַיִּמְלֹךְ בֶּאֱדוֹם בֶּלַע בֶּן־בְּעוֹר וְשֵׁם עִירוֹ דִּנְהָבָה: וַיָּמָת בָּלַע וַיִּמְלֹךְ תַּחְתָּיו
לד יוֹבָב בֶּן־זֶרַח מִבָּצְרָה: וַיָּמָת יוֹבָב וַיִּמְלֹךְ תַּחְתָּיו חֻשָׁם מֵאֶרֶץ הַתֵּימָנִי:
לה וַיָּמָת חֻשָׁם וַיִּמְלֹךְ תַּחְתָּיו הֲדַד בֶּן־בְּדַד הַמַּכֶּה אֶת־מִדְיָן בִּשְׂדֵה מוֹאָב
לו־לז וְשֵׁם עִירוֹ עֲוִית: וַיָּמָת הֲדָד וַיִּמְלֹךְ תַּחְתָּיו שַׂמְלָה מִמַּשְׂרֵקָה: וַיָּמָת שַׂמְלָה
לח וַיִּמְלֹךְ תַּחְתָּיו שָׁאוּל מֵרְחֹבוֹת הַנָּהָר: וַיָּמָת שָׁאוּל וַיִּמְלֹךְ תַּחְתָּיו בַּעַל חָנָן
לט בֶּן־עַכְבּוֹר: וַיָּמָת בַּעַל חָנָן בֶּן־עַכְבּוֹר וַיִּמְלֹךְ תַּחְתָּיו הֲדַר וְשֵׁם עִירוֹ פָּעוּ
מפטיר מ וְשֵׁם אִשְׁתּוֹ מְהֵיטַבְאֵל בַּת־מַטְרֵד בַּת מֵי זָהָב: וְאֵלֶּה שְׁמוֹת אַלּוּפֵי עֵשָׂו
לְמִשְׁפְּחֹתָם לִמְקֹמֹתָם בִּשְׁמֹתָם אַלּוּף תִּמְנָע אַלּוּף עַלְוָה אַלּוּף יְתֵת:
מא־מב אַלּוּף אָהֳלִיבָמָה אַלּוּף אֵלָה אַלּוּף פִּינֹן: אַלּוּף קְנַז אַלּוּף תֵּימָן אַלּוּף
מג מִבְצָר: אַלּוּף מַגְדִּיאֵל אַלּוּף עִירָם אֵלֶּה ׀ אַלּוּפֵי אֱדוֹם לְמֹשְׁבֹתָם בְּאֶרֶץ
אֲחֻזָּתָם הוּא עֵשָׂו אֲבִי אֱדוֹם:

---

31. וְאֵלֶּה הַמְּלָכִים — *Now these are the kings.* We are being told that they were constrained to appoint strangers as kings, for there were none among them worthy to reign; (also) they were unable to establish a dynasty (lit., a king, the son of a king).

לִפְנֵי מְלָךְ מֶלֶךְ — *Before a king reigned (over the children of Israel).* Before Moses reigned over (Israel) at the behest of God, the Blessed One, as it says, וַיְצַוֵּם אֶל בְּנֵי יִשְׂרָאֵל, *And gave them (Moses and Aaron) a charge to the children of Israel (Exodus* 6:13); similar to, וְצִוְּךָ לְנָגִיד, *And He will appoint you as ruler (over Israel) (I Samuel* 25:30). However, once a king reigned (over Israel), the kingdom of Esau ceased, and there were only chiefs, in keeping with, וּלְאֹם מִלְאֹם יֶאֱמָץ, *And one people shall be stronger than the other* (25:23).

40. וְאֵלֶּה שְׁמוֹת אַלּוּפֵי עֵשָׂו לְמִשְׁפְּחֹתָם לִמְקֹמֹתָם בִּשְׁמֹתָם — *And these are the names of the chiefs of Esau by their families, by their regions, by their names. By their regions, by their names,* implies that they were not sufficiently important (distinguished) to be called by their names, only by their regions.

NOTES

region of Seir, apparently after his marriage to Oholibamah who came from Seir, since she was the daughter of Anah the Hori (see verse 20). There he established himself in a small area called Edom, while the Hori controlled the major area called Seir (see the *Sforno* to 32:4). The sons of Esau eventually destroyed the Hori, in spite of the latter's great strength and might, as indicated in verse 20 according to the *Sforno's* commentary. And with God's help (recorded in *Deut.* 2) the descendants of Esau took over Seir.

31. וְאֵלֶּה הַמְּלָכִים — *Now these are the kings.* See the *Sforno* on 35:11.

לִפְנֵי מְלָךְ מֶלֶךְ — *Before a king reigned (over the children of Israel).* The *Sforno* interprets the word צִוָּה as meaning *to appoint as a leader,* when used in a context such as the verse in *Exodus* 6:14 regarding Moses and Aaron; the verse in *Numbers* 27:23 regarding Joshua; and the verse in *I Samuel* 25:30 regarding David. The *Sforno* quotes the phrase וּלְאֹם מִלְאֹם (25:23), to explain why once Moses became a king over Israel, Esau no longer had kings reigning, only chieftains. *Rashi* on that verse states, 'When one rises the other falls,' i.e., Jacob and Esau cannot reign simultaneously. Since Moses was considered a king, Esau could no longer have a king ruling over his people.

פרשת וישב
Parasha Vayeishev

לז א-ב וַיֵּשֶׁב יַעֲקֹב בְּאֶרֶץ מְגוּרֵי אָבִיו בְּאֶרֶץ כְּנָעַן: אֵלֶּה | תֹּלְדוֹת יַעֲקֹב יוֹסֵף
בֶּן־שְׁבַע־עֶשְׂרֵה שָׁנָה הָיָה רֹעֶה אֶת־אֶחָיו בַּצֹּאן וְהוּא נַעַר אֶת־בְּנֵי בִלְהָה
וְאֶת־בְּנֵי זִלְפָּה נְשֵׁי אָבִיו וַיָּבֵא יוֹסֵף אֶת־דִּבָּתָם רָעָה אֶל־אֲבִיהֶם:
ג וְיִשְׂרָאֵל אָהַב אֶת־יוֹסֵף מִכָּל־בָּנָיו כִּי־בֶן־זְקֻנִים הוּא לוֹ וְעָשָׂה לוֹ כְּתֹנֶת

XXXVII

1. וַיֵּשֶׁב יַעֲקֹב בְּאֶרֶץ מְגוּרֵי אָבִיו בְּאֶרֶץ כְּנָעַן — *And Jacob dwelt in the land of his father's sojournings, in the Land of Canaan.* He dwelt in that portion of the Land of Canaan where his father lived, as we find, *where Abraham and Isaac lived* (35:27).

2. אֵלֶּה תֹּלְדוֹת יַעֲקֹב — *These are the generations of Jacob.* These are the events which happened to him after he dwelt there (in Canaan). The events which occurred to him when he first left his father's house foreshadow our history during the first exile, while the events which occurred to him after he returned to his father's (home) foreshadow our history during the Second Temple and our subsequent exile — and redemption at the end of time.

הָיָה רֹעֶה אֶת אֶחָיו בַּצֹּאן — *Tending the sheep with his brethren.* He guided and instructed them in the technique of raising and tending sheep.

וְהוּא נַעַר — *He was a lad.* Because he was only a lad, he sinned by telling tales about his brothers, for he was inexperienced and could not foresee where this would lead; even though he was very intelligent and soon thereafter counseled the elders of Egypt, as we read, וּזְקֵנָיו יְחַכֵּם, *And teach his elders wisdom* (*Psalms* 105:22). This bears out what our Sages tell us, וְלֹא בְּדַרְדְּקֵי עֵצָה, *There is no counsel in the young* (*Shabbos* 89b).

וַיָּבֵא יוֹסֵף אֶת דִּבָּתָם רָעָה — *And Joseph brought evil report of them.* He accused them (his brothers) of neglecting the flocks and not caring for them properly; all this at a time when this enterprise represented the major source of their income and wealth.

3. וְעָשָׂה לוֹ כְּתֹנֶת פַּסִּים — *And he made him a coat of many colors* . . . as a sign that he will be the leader in the house and in the field, as we find, וְהִלְבַּשְׁתִּיו כֻּתָּנְתֶּךָ, *And I will clothe him with your robe* (*Isaiah* 22:21), and as our Sages have said, 'The

NOTES

XXXVII

1. וַיֵּשֶׁב יַעֲקֹב בְּאֶרֶץ מְגוּרֵי אָבִיו בְּאֶרֶץ כְּנָעַן — *And Jacob dwelt in the land of his father's sojournings, in the Land of Canaan.* The Land of Canaan was comparatively large and the section where Jacob's father lived was also sizeable, hence אֶרֶץ כְּנָעַן and מְגוּרֵי אָבִיו does not necessarily mean that Jacob actually resided in the community of his fathers. The *Sforno* however interprets it so, based on 35:27. In his commentary there the *Sforno* points out that it is advantageous for a son and/or grandson of a prominent man to reside in his father's and grandfather's community where they have established a good name and were beloved to the people.

2. אֵלֶּה תֹּלְדוֹת יַעֲקֹב — *These are the generations of Jacob.* This is in keeping with the saying of our Sages, 'Everything that happened to Jacob happened later to his children.'

וְהוּא נַעַר — *He was a lad.* — The *Sforno*, reflecting the attitude of our Sages, states that intelligence, and even wisdom, are independent of maturity, while the ability to offer counsel comes with the experience of age. Joseph possessed the former but lacked the latter.

וַיָּבֵא יוֹסֵף אֶת דִּבָּתָם רָעָה — *And Joseph brought evil report of them.* Unlike other commentators, the *Sforno* feels that the word דִּבָּה does not mean *evil tidings* in this case, rather informing and complaining.

3. וְעָשָׂה לוֹ כְּתֹנֶת פַּסִּים — *And he made him a coat of many colors.* The coat of many colors,

ד פַּסִּים: וַיִּרְא֣וּ אֶחָ֗יו כִּֽי־אֹת֞וֹ אָהַ֤ב אֲבִיהֶם֙ מִכָּל־אֶחָ֔יו וַֽיִּשְׂנְא֖וּ אֹת֑וֹ וְלֹ֥א
ה יָכְל֖וּ דַּבְּר֥וֹ לְשָׁלֹֽם: וַיַּחֲלֹ֤ם יוֹסֵף֙ חֲל֔וֹם וַיַּגֵּ֖ד לְאֶחָ֑יו וַיּוֹסִ֥פוּ ע֖וֹד שְׂנֹ֥א אֹתֽוֹ:
ו־ז וַיֹּ֖אמֶר אֲלֵיהֶ֑ם שִׁמְעוּ־נָ֕א הַחֲל֥וֹם הַזֶּ֖ה אֲשֶׁ֥ר חָלָֽמְתִּי׃ וְהִנֵּ֗ה אֲנַ֜חְנוּ
מְאַלְּמִ֤ים אֲלֻמִּים֙ בְּת֣וֹךְ הַשָּׂדֶ֔ה וְהִנֵּ֛ה קָ֥מָה אֲלֻמָּתִ֖י וְגַם־נִצָּ֑בָה וְהִנֵּ֤ה
ח תְסֻבֶּ֨ינָה֙ אֲלֻמֹּ֣תֵיכֶ֔ם וַתִּֽשְׁתַּחֲוֶ֖יןָ לַאֲלֻמָּתִֽי׃ וַיֹּ֤אמְרוּ לוֹ֙ אֶחָ֔יו הֲמָלֹ֤ךְ תִּמְלֹךְ֙
עָלֵ֔ינוּ אִם־מָשׁ֥וֹל תִּמְשֹׁ֖ל בָּ֑נוּ וַיּוֹסִ֤פוּ עוֹד֙ שְׂנֹ֣א אֹת֔וֹ עַל־חֲלֹמֹתָ֖יו וְעַל־
ט דְּבָרָֽיו׃ וַיַּחֲלֹ֥ם עוֹד֙ חֲל֣וֹם אַחֵ֔ר וַיְסַפֵּ֥ר אֹת֖וֹ לְאֶחָ֑יו וַיֹּ֗אמֶר הִנֵּ֨ה חָלַ֤מְתִּי
י חֲלוֹם֙ ע֔וֹד וְהִנֵּ֧ה הַשֶּׁ֣מֶשׁ וְהַיָּרֵ֗חַ וְאַחַ֤ד עָשָׂר֙ כּֽוֹכָבִ֔ים מִֽשְׁתַּחֲוִ֖ים לִֽי׃ וַיְסַפֵּ֣ר

---

brothers are content that the eldest brother wear the finest clothes so that he be respected' (*Baba Kamma* 11b).

4. וַיִּרְא֣וּ אֶחָיו כִּי אֹתוֹ אָהַב אֲבִיהֶם — *And when his brothers saw that their father loved him.* Jacob erred in differentiating between his sons, in a manner that revealed to the brothers the love he felt (for Joseph) in his heart.

וְלֹא יָכְלוּ דַּבְּרוֹ לְשָׁלֹם — *And would not speak peaceably with him.* Even though the brothers found it necessary to speak with (Joseph) with regard to the household and flocks, since Joseph was in charge of them, at the direction of his father. (Nevertheless) they could not speak peaceably with him in friendship, as is customary among brothers.

5. וַיַּגֵּד לְאֶחָיו — *And he told it to his brothers.* In this, too, he acted with the inexperience of youth.

6. שִׁמְעוּ נָא הַחֲלוֹם הַזֶּה — *Hear, I pray you, this dream.* Not only did he tell them the dream but asked them to listen attentively and understand its significance. In this manner he added to their animosity as indicated in their response, '*Shall you indeed reign over us?*' (verse 8).

7. וְגַם נִצָּבָה — *And also stood upright.* This indicated that his rule would endure for a long time, as it did in fact, for eighty years, longer than the reign of any (Jewish) ruler recorded in the holy Scriptures.

8. עַל חֲלֹמֹתָיו — *For his dreams ...* the detailed manner in which he related it, in a spirit of eager anticipation for its fulfillment.

וְעַל דְּבָרָיו — *And for his words ...* when he said to them, '*Hear, I pray you*' (verse 6), urging them to pay heed and grasp the significance of the dream.

NOTES

in itself, would not have upset the brothers. They could have had the same finery, if they so chose. It was what this cloak *represented* that angered them, namely the status and position of Joseph, their younger brother.

7. וְגַם נִצָּבָה — *And also stood upright.* The word נִצָּב has a special implication, that which stands firmly and well established. Since the phrase used by Joseph is not עוֹמֵד but נִצָּב, it has special significance.

8. עַל חֲלֹמֹתָיו וְעַל דְּבָרָיו — *For his dreams and for his words.* The verse uses two phrases — *his dreams* and *his words*. The Hebrew word חֲלֹמֹתָיו is in the plural form — but Joseph only told them one dream! The answer given by the *Sforno* is that even though the dream was one, the details given by Joseph were elaborate. They objected not only to his expansive telling of the dream but also the manner (*his words*) where he insisted that they pay close attention to its implications.

אֶל־אָבִיו֙ וְאֶל־אֶחָיו֒ וַיִּגְעַר־בּ֣וֹ אָבִ֔יו וַיֹּ֣אמֶר ל֔וֹ מָ֛ה הַחֲל֥וֹם הַזֶּ֖ה אֲשֶׁ֣ר
יא חָלָ֑מְתָּ הֲב֣וֹא נָב֗וֹא אֲנִי֙ וְאִמְּךָ֣ וְאַחֶ֔יךָ לְהִשְׁתַּחֲוֺ֥ת לְךָ֖ אָֽרְצָה׃ וַיְקַנְאוּ־ב֖וֹ
שני יב אֶחָ֑יו וְאָבִ֖יו שָׁמַ֥ר אֶת־הַדָּבָֽר׃ וַיֵּלְכ֖וּ אֶחָ֑יו לִרְע֛וֹת אֶת־צֹ֥אן אֲבִיהֶ֖ם בִּשְׁכֶֽם׃
יג וַיֹּ֨אמֶר יִשְׂרָאֵ֜ל אֶל־יוֹסֵ֗ף הֲל֤וֹא אַחֶ֙יךָ֙ רֹעִ֣ים בִּשְׁכֶ֔ם לְכָ֖ה וְאֶשְׁלָחֲךָ֣ אֲלֵיהֶ֑ם
יד וַיֹּ֥אמֶר ל֖וֹ הִנֵּֽנִי׃ וַיֹּ֣אמֶר ל֗וֹ לֶךְ־נָ֨א רְאֵ֜ה אֶת־שְׁל֤וֹם אַחֶ֙יךָ֙ וְאֶת־שְׁל֣וֹם
טו הַצֹּ֔אן וַהֲשִׁבֵ֖נִי דָּבָ֑ר וַיִּשְׁלָחֵ֙הוּ֙ מֵעֵ֣מֶק חֶבְר֔וֹן וַיָּבֹ֖א שְׁכֶֽמָה׃ וַיִּמְצָאֵ֣הוּ אִ֔ישׁ
טז וְהִנֵּ֥ה תֹעֶ֖ה בַּשָּׂדֶ֑ה וַיִּשְׁאָלֵ֧הוּ הָאִ֛ישׁ לֵאמֹ֖ר מַה־תְּבַקֵּֽשׁ׃ וַיֹּ֕אמֶר אֶת־אַחַ֖י
יז אָנֹכִ֣י מְבַקֵּ֑שׁ הַגִּֽידָה־נָּ֣א לִ֔י אֵיפֹ֖ה הֵ֥ם רֹעִֽים׃ וַיֹּ֤אמֶר הָאִישׁ֙ נָסְע֣וּ מִזֶּ֔ה כִּ֤י
יח שָׁמַ֙עְתִּי֙ אֹֽמְרִ֔ים נֵלְכָ֖ה דֹּתָ֑יְנָה וַיֵּ֤לֶךְ יוֹסֵף֙ אַחַ֣ר אֶחָ֔יו וַיִּמְצָאֵ֖ם בְּדֹתָֽן׃ וַיִּרְא֥וּ

---

10. מָה הַחֲלוֹם הַזֶּה — *What is this dream?* It is your evil thoughts (which) cause you to dream of ruling over us; your thoughts came while on your bed.

11. וַיְקַנְאוּ בוֹ אֶחָיו — *And his brothers envied him.* They believed that only because he was held in high esteem by his father, did (Joseph) dare to tell such a dream to his father.

וְאָבִיו שָׁמַר — *But his father kept it in mind.* He was convinced that it was a true dream and he looked forward to its realization, as our Sages tell us, 'One is jealous of all, except his son and his student' *(Sanhedrin* 105b).

13. הֲלוֹא אַחֶיךָ רֹעִים בִּשְׁכֶם — *Behold, your brothers are tending the flock in Shechem* ... and it is not too far to go there.

14. לֶךְ נָא רְאֵה — *Go now, please, and see.* Observe and judge (whether all is well) and do whatever is needed to be corrected, for had (Jacob) wanted only a report he could have sent one of his servants.

וַיִּשְׁלָחֵהוּ מֵעֵמֶק חֶבְרוֹן — *And he sent him from the vale of Hebron.* (Jacob) accompanied him to the vale.

15. תֹעֶה בַּשָּׂדֶה — *Wandering in the field* ... walking hither and yon to find their pasture land.

מַה תְּבַקֵּשׁ — *What do you seek?* ... that you do not follow a single, straight path.

16. אֵיפֹה הֵם רֹעִים — *Where they are tending the flock?* ... in which part of this area.

17. נָסְעוּ מִזֶּה — *They have departed from here.* Without a doubt they have left this pasture land and there is no reason to continue your search in any part of this area.

כִּי שָׁמַעְתִּי אֹמְרִים — *For I heard them say.* The reason I say that they have departed is not that I saw them leave, but because I heard them say, 'נֵלְכָה דֹּתָיְנָה, *Let us go to Dothan.'*

אַחַר אֶחָיו — *After his brothers.* Even though he did not find them in Shechem, as his father had said, nonetheless he still exerted himself to find them so as to fulfill his father's will and desire.

NOTES

10. מָה הַחֲלוֹם הַזֶּה — *What is this dream?* The expression, 'your thoughts came while on your bed,' is borrowed from *Daniel* 2:29. It is the basis of our Sages' saying, 'A person dreams at night that which he thinks about during the day' *(Berachos* 55b).

17. אַחַר אֶחָיו — *After his brothers.* By going

יט אֹתוֹ מֵרָחֹק וּבְטֶרֶם יִקְרַב אֲלֵיהֶם וַיִּתְנַכְּלוּ אֹתוֹ לַהֲמִיתוֹ: וַיֹּאמְרוּ אִישׁ
כ אֶל־אָחִיו הִנֵּה בַּעַל הַחֲלֹמוֹת הַלָּזֶה בָּא: וְעַתָּה | לְכוּ וְנַהַרְגֵהוּ וְנַשְׁלִכֵהוּ
בְּאַחַד הַבֹּרוֹת וְאָמַרְנוּ חַיָּה רָעָה אֲכָלָתְהוּ וְנִרְאֶה מַה־יִּהְיוּ חֲלֹמֹתָיו:

---

18. וַיִּתְנַכְּלוּ אֹתוֹ לַהֲמִיתוֹ — *They were conspired against by him, that he slay (them).* The root נכל (*to beguile*) means to use one's wiles for an evil end, as we find, אֲשֶׁר נִכְּלוּ לָכֶם, *wherewith they have beguiled you (Numbers* 25:18). The brothers considered Joseph to be a נוֹכֵל (one who uses deceit and wiles to harm) even to the point of death. They reasoned, 'He has not come in our interest, but only to find fault or transgression which he can report to our father so that he will curse us, or for which we will be punished by God; then he alone would remain blessed.' The grammatical (Hebrew) form הִתְפָּעֵל (a reflective verb) is applicable to thought and imagination (as well as action, i.e., that which has an impact upon one's designs and plans) as we find, אַתָּה מִתְנַקֵּשׁ בְּנַפְשִׁי, *You are setting a trap to harm my soul (I Samuel* 28:9). (The word) לַהֲמִיתוֹ, *to slay him,* means that he (Joseph) wishes to slay his brothers, as we find לַעֲשֹׂתְכֶם אֹתָם, *that* you *might do them (Deut.* 4:14), or לְעָבְרְךָ בִּבְרִית, *that* you *should enter into the covenant (Deut.* 29:11). We are then being told (by the Torah) that the brothers were convinced that Joseph was beguiling and deceiving them with the interest of destroying them in this world or in the world to come (or both), hence they felt justified in slaying (or selling) him to prevent him from slaying them, וְהַתּוֹרָה אָמְרָה הַבָּא לְהָרְגְךָ הַשְׁכֵּם לְהָרְגוֹ, *as the Torah teaches us, 'He who comes to kill you, arise to slay him (Sanhedrin 72a).*

(This we say) for they were all righteous men — so much so that their names are inscribed as a memorial before God (on the breastplate and *ephod* of the High Priest) — how then is it conceivable that they would kill or sell Joseph (without good reason) and subsequently not even regret their act? For even though they later say, *'We are guilty concerning our brother'* (42:21), they are not lamenting the sale or their intended slaying of him, only their cruelty and callousness in turning a deaf ear to his pleas.

19. הִנֵּה בַּעַל הַחֲלֹמוֹת — *Behold, this dreamer comes.* He intentionally told us his dreams to provoke us to take revenge on him, so as to make us sin against God or our father (or both), that we might perish.

20. וְעַתָּה לְכוּ — *Come now therefore.* They encouraged one another to prepare to kill him.

וְאָמַרְנוּ חַיָּה רָעָה אֲכָלָתְהוּ — *And we will say an evil beast has devoured him . . .* lest (our father) become angry and curse us.

וְנִרְאֶה מַה יִּהְיוּ חֲלֹמֹתָיו — *And we shall see what will become of his dreams.* The dreams he told us which foretold that he would be a ruler over us will now be proven false and they will be as naught, discredited and unfulfilled.

NOTES

to Shechem Joseph has fulfilled the commandment of כִּבּוּד אָב (respect for his father). He continues on, because he is anxious to fulfill this *mitzvah* in spirit as well as to the letter.

18. וַיִּתְנַכְּלוּ אֹתוֹ לַהֲמִיתוֹ — *They were conspired against by him, that he slay (them).* The *Sforno* interprets the three words, וַיִּתְנַכְּלוּ אֹתוֹ לַהֲמִיתוֹ, not in the traditional sense of *they conspired against him to slay him,* but the reverse, Joseph was conspiring to destroy them. Departing from his usual concise, succinct style, he expands on this theory by explaining the use of the הִתְפָּעֵל form (וַיִּתְנַכְּלוּ)

כא־כב וַיִּשְׁמַע רְאוּבֵן וַיַּצִּלֵהוּ מִיָּדָם וַיֹּאמֶר לֹא נַכֶּנּוּ נָפֶשׁ: וַיֹּאמֶר אֲלֵהֶם ׀ רְאוּבֵן
אַל־תִּשְׁפְּכוּ־דָם הַשְׁלִיכוּ אֹתוֹ אֶל־הַבּוֹר הַזֶּה אֲשֶׁר בַּמִּדְבָּר וְיָד אַל־
שלישי כג תִּשְׁלְחוּ־בוֹ לְמַעַן הַצִּיל אֹתוֹ מִיָּדָם לַהֲשִׁיבוֹ אֶל־אָבִיו: וַיְהִי כַּאֲשֶׁר־בָּא
יוֹסֵף אֶל־אֶחָיו וַיַּפְשִׁיטוּ אֶת־יוֹסֵף אֶת־כֻּתָּנְתּוֹ אֶת־כְּתֹנֶת הַפַּסִּים אֲשֶׁר
כד־כה עָלָיו: וַיִּקָּחֻהוּ וַיַּשְׁלִכוּ אֹתוֹ הַבֹּרָה וְהַבּוֹר רֵק אֵין בּוֹ מָיִם: וַיֵּשְׁבוּ לֶאֱכָל־
לֶחֶם וַיִּשְׂאוּ עֵינֵיהֶם וַיִּרְאוּ וְהִנֵּה אֹרְחַת יִשְׁמְעֵאלִים בָּאָה מִגִּלְעָד וּגְמַלֵּיהֶם
כו נֹשְׂאִים נְכֹאת וּצְרִי וָלֹט הוֹלְכִים לְהוֹרִיד מִצְרָיְמָה: וַיֹּאמֶר יְהוּדָה אֶל־

---

21. וַיַּצִּלֵהוּ מִיָּדָם — *And delivered him out of their hand* ... by preventing them from taking a rash irremediable step, which even the righteous man can be guilty of at times, as we find by Reuben and Bilhah, as (Jacob) says, פַּחַז כַּמַּיִם, *unstable (or hasty) as water* (49:4).

22. וְיָד אַל תִּשְׁלְחוּ בוֹ — *But lay no hand upon him.* To actually commit an act of cruelty, as it is written, מֵרְשָׁעִים יֵצֵא רֶשַׁע וְיָדִי לֹא תִהְיֶה בָּךְ, *Out of the wicked comes forth wickedness; but my hand shall not be upon you (I Samuel* 24:13).

לְמַעַן הַצִּיל אֹתוֹ — *That he might deliver him* ... to bring him up later (from the pit).

25. וַיֵּשְׁבוּ לֶאֱכָל לֶחֶם — *And they sat down to eat bread.* In their eyes they had done no wrong, nor committed any sin, which would have deterred them from sitting down to eat a meal, for a righteous person who feels he has done wrong refrains from eating, as we find when the Israelites slew the tribe of Benjamin, as it is written, וַיֵּשְׁבוּ שָׁם עַד הָעֶרֶב לִפְנֵי הָאֱלֹהִים וַיִּשְׂאוּ קוֹלָם וַיִּבְכּוּ בְּכִי גָדוֹל, וַיֹּאמְרוּ לָמָה ה׳ אֱלֹהֵי יִשְׂרָאֵל הָיְתָה זֹּאת בְּיִשְׂרָאֵל, *And they sat there till the evening, before God, and lifted up their voices and wept exceedingly. And they said, 'O HASHEM, God of Israel, why is this come to pass in Israel?' (Judges* 21:2,3). Similarly we find by Darius, when he cast Daniel into the lions' den, as it is written, וּבָת טְוָת וְדַחֲוָן לָא הַנְעֵל קָדָמוֹהִי, *And (he) passed the night fasting, neither were diversions brought before him (Daniel* 6:19). The reason the brothers felt no remorse is because they considered Joseph to be a 'pursuer' and the pursued is permitted to save himself, even if he must kill the pursuer, if there is no alternative.

הוֹלְכִים לְהוֹרִיד מִצְרָיְמָה — *Going to carry it down to Egypt.* They (the Ishmaelites) were the camel drivers, but not the owners of the merchandise, therefore their job was only to transport the merchandise (to Egypt) thereby concluding their task.

NOTES

and also shows that the word לַהֲמִיתוֹ need not mean *to kill him,* Joseph being the object, but can also mean that he will slay them. This interpretation the *Sforno* feels is correct since the brothers were righteous men, and it is inconceivable that they would plot to kill Joseph, unless it was in self-defense. Obviously, the fear of the brothers that Joseph intended to harm them was unfounded.

22. וְיָד אַל תִּשְׁלְחוּ בוֹ — *But lay no hand upon him.* An overt act of violence is far graver than a passive one — such as casting him into the pit — even though he will be exposed to danger. The parallel brought by the *Sforno* is from the episode of David and Saul, where Saul was vulnerable and David could easily have slain him but desisted, for he did not want to do so in an overt manner. If evil is destined to befall a person, let it come through a רָשָׁע, *an evil man,* not through a צַדִּיק, *a righteous person.*

25. הוֹלְכִים לְהוֹרִיד מִצְרָיְמָה — *Going to carry it down to Egypt.* The story of the sale of Joseph recorded in the Torah is a bit confusing. What is the role of the Ishmaelites and what is that of the Midianites? The *Sforno* explains that the Ishmaelites were only the camel drivers (the teamsters) while the Midianites were the

כז אָחִיו מַה־בֶּצַע כִּי נַהֲרֹג אֶת־אָחִינוּ וְכִסִּינוּ אֶת־דָּמוֹ: לְכוּ וְנִמְכְּרֶנּוּ
לַיִּשְׁמְעֵאלִים וְיָדֵנוּ אַל־תְּהִי־בוֹ כִּי־אָחִינוּ בְשָׂרֵנוּ הוּא וַיִּשְׁמְעוּ אֶחָיו:
כח וַיַּעַבְרוּ אֲנָשִׁים מִדְיָנִים סֹחֲרִים וַיִּמְשְׁכוּ וַיַּעֲלוּ אֶת־יוֹסֵף מִן־הַבּוֹר וַיִּמְכְּרוּ
כט אֶת־יוֹסֵף לַיִּשְׁמְעֵאלִים בְּעֶשְׂרִים כָּסֶף וַיָּבִיאוּ אֶת־יוֹסֵף מִצְרָיְמָה: וַיָּשָׁב
ל רְאוּבֵן אֶל־הַבּוֹר וְהִנֵּה אֵין־יוֹסֵף בַּבּוֹר וַיִּקְרַע אֶת־בְּגָדָיו: וַיָּשָׁב אֶל־אֶחָיו
לא וַיֹּאמַר הַיֶּלֶד אֵינֶנּוּ וַאֲנִי אָנָה אֲנִי־בָא: וַיִּקְחוּ אֶת־כְּתֹנֶת יוֹסֵף וַיִּשְׁחֲטוּ
לב שְׂעִיר עִזִּים וַיִּטְבְּלוּ אֶת־הַכֻּתֹּנֶת בַּדָּם: וַיְשַׁלְּחוּ אֶת־כְּתֹנֶת הַפַּסִּים וַיָּבִיאוּ
אֶל־אֲבִיהֶם וַיֹּאמְרוּ זֹאת מָצָאנוּ הַכֶּר־נָא הַכְּתֹנֶת בִּנְךָ הִוא אִם־לֹא:
לג-לד וַיַּכִּירָהּ וַיֹּאמֶר כְּתֹנֶת בְּנִי חַיָּה רָעָה אֲכָלָתְהוּ טָרֹף טֹרַף יוֹסֵף: וַיִּקְרַע יַעֲקֹב
לה שִׂמְלֹתָיו וַיָּשֶׂם שַׂק בְּמָתְנָיו וַיִּתְאַבֵּל עַל־בְּנוֹ יָמִים רַבִּים: וַיָּקֻמוּ כָל־בָּנָיו

---

26. מַה בֶּצַע — *What profit is it?* What will we accomplish? Revenge must serve one of two ends (to satisfy one's desire to punish the wrongdoer or to serve as an example and deterrent). As for the satisfaction of revenge if we kill our own brother, it will recoil upon our own heads, for our hearts will grieve over his death and our cruelty towards him; and if we intend it to be a warning to other potential enemies not to harm us, how will it be so, seeing that we intend to conceal his death (and none will know)?

וְכִסִּינוּ אֶת דָּמוֹ — *And we will conceal his blood . . .* for our own honor and out of fear of our father.

27. לְכוּ וְנִמְכְּרֶנּוּ — *Come and let us sell him.* By so doing we will punish him measure for measure; because he wanted to rule over us, now he will become a slave.

28. מִדְיָנִים סֹחֲרִים — *Midianite merchantmen . . .* the owners of the merchandise, being transported by the Ishmaelite camel drivers.

וַיִּמְכְּרוּ אֶת יוֹסֵף לַיִּשְׁמְעֵאלִים — *And sold Joseph to the Ishmaelites.* They sold him to the Ishmaelites (who, however, only acted as) intermediaries for the Midianites. They did not wish to deal directly with the merchantmen who came to sojourn in many towns and might recognize them, but dealt with the Ishmaelites who never remained in the towns (for any length of time), but merely passed through them. With them (the Ishmaelites) they (the brothers) concluded their deal. The purchasers were in reality the Midianites, as it says, *And the Midianites sold him to Egypt* (verse 36). A parallel occurred during the period of the Second Temple when Jews sold their own fellow Jews to the Romans during the time of the Hasmonean Kings; this caused the exile, just as the sale of Joseph by his brothers caused the exile of our forefathers to Egypt, as our Sages tell us (*Shabbos* 10b).

32. וַיְשַׁלְּחוּ אֶת כְּתֹנֶת הַפַּסִּים — *And they (sent) the coat of many colors.* They gashed (tore) it with a spear to make it appear torn by wild beasts.

34. וַיָּשֶׂם שַׂק בְּמָתְנָיו — *And put sackcloth upon his loins.* (He made a belt from) a

NOTES

merchants. The purchasers of Joseph were the Midianites, who subsequently sold him to Potiphar, while the Ishmaelites were only the intermediaries through whom the initial sale was made. The reason for this indirect transaction is explained by the *Sforno* in his commentary on verse 28.

32. וַיְשַׁלְּחוּ אֶת כְּתֹנֶת הַפַּסִּים — *And they (sent) the coat of many colors.* In Hebrew, שָׁלַח

וְכָל־בְּנֹתָיו לְנַחֲמוֹ וַיְמָאֵן לְהִתְנַחֵם וַיֹּאמֶר כִּי־אֵרֵד אֶל־בְּנִי אָבֵל שְׁאֹלָה
לו וַיֵּבְךְּ אֹתוֹ אָבִיו: וְהַמְּדָנִים מָכְרוּ אֹתוֹ אֶל־מִצְרָיִם לְפוֹטִיפַר סְרִיס פַּרְעֹה
שַׂר הַטַּבָּחִים:
לח רביעי א וַיְהִי בָּעֵת הַהִוא וַיֵּרֶד יְהוּדָה מֵאֵת אֶחָיו וַיֵּט עַד־אִישׁ עֲדֻלָּמִי וּשְׁמוֹ חִירָה:
ב־ג וַיַּרְא־שָׁם יְהוּדָה בַּת־אִישׁ כְּנַעֲנִי וּשְׁמוֹ שׁוּעַ וַיִּקָּחֶהָ וַיָּבֹא אֵלֶיהָ: וַתַּהַר
ד וַתֵּלֶד בֵּן וַיִּקְרָא אֶת־שְׁמוֹ עֵר: וַתַּהַר עוֹד וַתֵּלֶד בֵּן וַתִּקְרָא אֶת־שְׁמוֹ אוֹנָן:
ה וַתֹּסֶף עוֹד וַתֵּלֶד בֵּן וַתִּקְרָא אֶת־שְׁמוֹ שֵׁלָה וְהָיָה בִכְזִיב בְּלִדְתָּהּ אֹתוֹ:

---

strip of the woven material called שַׂק, *sackcloth* (usually made from goats' hair) which because of its thickness was used to make שַׂקִּים, *sacks.* (This was a common sign of mourning).

35. וַיְמָאֵן לְהִתְנַחֵם — *He refused to be comforted.* He refused to listen to words of comfort, for he did not want to remove (the sense and feeling of) worry from his heart.

וַיֹּאמֶר כִּי אֵרֵד אֶל בְּנִי אָבֵל שְׁאֹלָה — *He said, 'I will go down to the grave, to my son, mourning.'* He assumed lifelong mourning, because he blamed himself for having caused the calamity, since he was the one who sent Joseph to his brothers.

וַיֵּבְךְּ אֹתוֹ אָבִיו — *And his father wept for him.* Isaac wept that Jacob had assumed lifelong mourning, which would have the effect of keeping the Divine presence (*Shechinah*) away from him.

XXXVIII

1. וַיְהִי בָּעֵת הַהִוא — *And it came to pass at that time.* At the time Joseph was sold to Egypt due to Judah's counsel, (advising to) sell him and not (advising) to return him, thus bereaving his father, Judah was requited according to the fruits of his action (by) having two sons who would die (prematurely), and (thus) he would remain bereaved of both.

5. וְהָיָה בִכְזִיב — *And he was at Chezib.* She called him Shelah, a word denoting deceit and disappointment, as we find, לֹא תַשְׁלֶה, *Do not deceive me* (II *Kings* 4:28) which is an unbecoming name. She did so because her husband was absent (in Chezib) when he was born, hence she was disappointed. (Judah) would not have agreed to such an unseemly name, had he been present.

NOTES

means a sword. The phrase וַיְשַׁלְּחוּ is therefore translated by the *Sforno* not as *sent*, but *gashed* or *cut*, to make it appear that a wild beast had torn the coat while attacking Joseph. See *Da'as Zekeinim* on this verse.

35. וַיְמָאֵן לְהִתְנַחֵם — *He refused to be comforted.* Jacob did not want to be comforted. By continuing to mourn and grieve for his son he kept alive the hope that Joseph was still alive, for it is ordained that a deceased person is ultimately forgotten (the intensity of the memory fades) and one can find comfort. That is why Jacob did not cease to grieve. *Rashi* gives a similar explanation.

וַיֵּבְךְּ אֹתוֹ אָבִיו — *And his father wept for him.* Isaac cried for his son Jacob, not only because of his personal loss, but because by continually mourning he was denied the opportunity and privilege of receiving the blessing of the Divine presence (שְׁכִינָה) which can only dwell where there is joy and happiness.

XXXVIII

1. וַיְהִי בָּעֵת הַהִוא — *And it came to pass at that time.* This chapter is linked to the concluding verse of the previous one, *And the Midianites sold him, etc.* Although this episode seems to interrupt the natural sequence, which is picked up later (chap. 39), it is placed here to

ו־ז וַיִּקַּח יְהוּדָה אִשָּׁה לְעֵר בְּכוֹרוֹ וּשְׁמָהּ תָּמָר: וַיְהִי עֵר בְּכוֹר יְהוּדָה רַע בְּעֵינֵי
ח יהוה וַיְמִתֵהוּ יהוה: וַיֹּאמֶר יְהוּדָה לְאוֹנָן בֹּא אֶל־אֵשֶׁת אָחִיךָ וְיַבֵּם אֹתָהּ
ט וְהָקֵם זֶרַע לְאָחִיךָ: וַיֵּדַע אוֹנָן כִּי לֹּא לוֹ יִהְיֶה הַזָּרַע וְהָיָה אִם־בָּא
י אֶל־אֵשֶׁת אָחִיו וְשִׁחֵת אַרְצָה לְבִלְתִּי נְתָן־זֶרַע לְאָחִיו: וַיֵּרַע בְּעֵינֵי יהוה
יא אֲשֶׁר עָשָׂה וַיָּמֶת גַּם־אֹתוֹ: וַיֹּאמֶר יְהוּדָה לְתָמָר כַּלָּתוֹ שְׁבִי אַלְמָנָה
בֵית־אָבִיךְ עַד־יִגְדַּל שֵׁלָה בְנִי כִּי אָמַר פֶּן־יָמוּת גַּם־הוּא כְּאֶחָיו וַתֵּלֶךְ
יב תָּמָר וַתֵּשֶׁב בֵּית אָבִיהָ: וַיִּרְבּוּ הַיָּמִים וַתָּמָת בַּת־שׁוּעַ אֵשֶׁת־יְהוּדָה וַיִּנָּחֶם
יג יְהוּדָה וַיַּעַל עַל־גֹּזְזֵי צֹאנוֹ הוּא וְחִירָה רֵעֵהוּ הָעֲדֻלָּמִי תִּמְנָתָה: וַיֻּגַּד לְתָמָר

---

7. וַיְהִי עֵר . . . רַע בְּעֵינֵי ה׳ – *And Er . . . was wicked in the sight of* H*ASHEM* . . . but not in the eyes of his fellow men.

9. כִּי לֹא לוֹ יִהְיֶה הַזָּרַע – *That the seed would not be his.* He knew that he would not gain exclusive credit for this *mitzvah,* since his (deceased) brother had wed her, and he (Onan) is only completing the *mitzvah* (of fathering a child).

לְבִלְתִּי נְתָן זֶרַע לְאָחִיו – *Lest he should give seed to his brother* . . . so that his (deceased) brother should not realize, through him, the desired goal of his marriage.

11. שְׁבִי אַלְמָנָה – *Remain a widow.* Wait for a period of time, continuing your role as a widow, as we find, יָמִים רַבִּים תֵּשְׁבִי לִי, *You shall sit solitary for me many days* (*Hoshea* 3:3).

פֶּן יָמוּת גַּם הוּא כְּאֶחָיו – *Lest he also die as his brothers* . . . lest he sin because of her beauty as his brother had done, and would die.

12. וַתָּמָת בַּת שׁוּעַ – *The daughter of Shua died.* Judah should have brought in his daughter-in-law to run his household in place of his wife, as Abraham had done, as it says, *And Isaac brought her into the tent of Sarah his mother* (24:67). Tamar, therefore, abandoned hope of ever remaining part of Judah's family.

NOTES

teach us the great lesson of 'measure for measure'; how consequences come forth from man's deeds. The sale of Joseph and the following tragic events in Judah's life are connected, as the *Sforno* so well explains, through the common theme of losing one's children.

5. וְהָיָה בִכְזִיב – *And he was at Chezib.* The Torah tells us that Judah was away when Shelah was born. This seemingly gratuitous information is to explain how such an improper name was given to his son. It reflected his wife's feelings of frustration when she gave birth while her husband was away from her. The proof brought by the *Sforno* in support of his interpretation is from the story of the Shunamis and Elisha, where she bitterly remonstrates with the prophet for first granting her a child, only to have him taken from her.

7. וַיְהִי עֵר . . . רַע בְּעֵינֵי ה׳ – *And Er . . . was wicked in the sight of* H*ASHEM*. The transgression of Er was a totally private one, known only to God. Hence it did not affect his standing and reputation amongst his fellow men.

9. כִּי לֹא לוֹ יִהְיֶה הַזָּרַע – *That the seed would not be his.* Onan was obviously a most selfish man. He could not bring himself to fulfill the *mitzvah* of 'establishing a name for his brother,' since the *zechus* (merit) would not be exclusively his.

11. שְׁבִי אַלְמָנָה – *Remain a widow.* The custom was for a widow who was not yet prepared to remarry to live in seclusion. The expression *to sit* as a widow is used here and in *Hoshea* to indicate that her state of widowhood shall remain unchanged for a given period.

12. וַתָּמָת בַּת שׁוּעַ – *The daughter of Shua died.* The Hebrew term עֲקֶרֶת הַבַּיִת, *mainstay of the house,* is given to the woman (wife, daughter

יד לֵאמֹר הִנֵּה חָמִיךְ עֹלֶה תִמְנָתָה לָגֹז צֹאנוֹ: וַתָּסַר בִּגְדֵי אַלְמְנוּתָהּ מֵעָלֶיהָ
וַתְּכַס בַּצָּעִיף וַתִּתְעַלָּף וַתֵּשֶׁב בְּפֶתַח עֵינַיִם אֲשֶׁר עַל־דֶּרֶךְ תִּמְנָתָה כִּי
טו רָאֲתָה כִּי־גָדַל שֵׁלָה וְהִוא לֹא־נִתְּנָה לוֹ לְאִשָּׁה: וַיִּרְאֶהָ יְהוּדָה וַיַּחְשְׁבֶהָ
טז לְזוֹנָה כִּי כִסְּתָה פָּנֶיהָ: וַיֵּט אֵלֶיהָ אֶל־הַדֶּרֶךְ וַיֹּאמֶר הָבָה נָּא אָבוֹא אֵלַיִךְ
יז כִּי לֹא יָדַע כִּי כַלָּתוֹ הִוא וַתֹּאמֶר מַה־תִּתֶּן־לִּי כִּי תָבוֹא אֵלָי: וַיֹּאמֶר
אָנֹכִי אֲשַׁלַּח גְּדִי־עִזִּים מִן־הַצֹּאן וַתֹּאמֶר אִם־תִּתֵּן עֵרָבוֹן עַד שָׁלְחֶךָ:
יח וַיֹּאמֶר מָה הָעֵרָבוֹן אֲשֶׁר אֶתֶּן־לָּךְ וַתֹּאמֶר חֹתָמְךָ וּפְתִילֶךָ וּמַטְּךָ אֲשֶׁר
יט בְּיָדֶךָ וַיִּתֶּן־לָהּ וַיָּבֹא אֵלֶיהָ וַתַּהַר לוֹ: וַתָּקָם וַתֵּלֶךְ וַתָּסַר צְעִיפָהּ מֵעָלֶיהָ
כ וַתִּלְבַּשׁ בִּגְדֵי אַלְמְנוּתָהּ: וַיִּשְׁלַח יְהוּדָה אֶת־גְּדִי הָעִזִּים בְּיַד רֵעֵהוּ
כא הָעֲדֻלָּמִי לָקַחַת הָעֵרָבוֹן מִיַּד הָאִשָּׁה וְלֹא מְצָאָהּ: וַיִּשְׁאַל אֶת־אַנְשֵׁי
מְקֹמָהּ לֵאמֹר אַיֵּה הַקְּדֵשָׁה הִוא בָעֵינַיִם עַל־הַדָּרֶךְ וַיֹּאמְרוּ לֹא־הָיְתָה

---

14. בְּפֶתַח עֵינַיִם – *At the fork in the road ...* where two roads begin, for a road is called עַיִן, as we find עַל הָעַיִן בְּדֶרֶךְ שׁוּר *By the road on the way to Shur* (16:7).

אֲשֶׁר עַל דֶּרֶךְ תִּמְנָתָה – *Which is on the way to Timnas.* It would then be impossible for Judah not to meet her as he returned from Timnas.

כִּי רָאֲתָה כִּי גָדַל שֵׁלָה – *For she saw that Shelah was grown up.* She reasoned that if Judah would see her without her widow's garments and ask her why she had removed them, she would tell him that the time had come to do so, since (Judah) had told her to wear them until Shelah grew up (verse 11) and now he had grown up.

16. כִּי לֹא יָדַע כִּי כַלָּתוֹ הִוא – *For he knew not that she was his daughter-in-law.* Even after he turned aside to her he did not recognize her, for had he recognized her he would have arranged for her to marry his son (Shelah). God's divine plan, however, was that she conceive from Judah, for he was more worthy than Shelah to father the ancestor of the *Mashiach* (Messiah).

מַה תִּתֶּן לִי – *What will you give me?* She began to speak so that he might recognize her (by her voice). She undoubtedly did not want any gift, her only desire being to have a child from (the house of) Judah. She therefore accepted the pledge, not for personal use but as proof; had he given her a gift she would not have accepted it. (The reason she accepted the pledge is) because she had no (other) proof to vindicate herself.

17. אִם תִּתֵּן עֵרָבוֹן – *If you will give me a pledge.* If you do so then I will do as you asked, *'Come, I pray, let me come in unto you'* (verse 16).

18. וּפְתִילֶךָ – *Your cord ...* that which is connected close to your body, i.e., your belt (girdle). She chose these items (signet, cord and staff) which symbolize power and authority as we find, אֱזָר נָא כְגֶבֶר חֲלָצֶיךָ, *Gird up now your loins like a man (Job* 38:3). She did this in order to contemplate the elevated stature of Judah and have a child with his (qualities).

19. וַתִּלְבַּשׁ בִּגְדֵי אַלְמְנוּתָהּ – *Then she put on the garments of her widowhood.* Because she had no further desire to marry, now that she was with child (from Judah).

NOTES

or daughter-in-law) who is in charge of the household. Tamar hoped to assume that role by becoming Shelah's wife after Judah's wife died. When this did not occur she began to

כב בָּזֶה קְדֵשָׁה: וַיָּשָׁב אֶל־יְהוּדָה וַיֹּאמֶר לֹא מְצָאתִיהָ וְגַם אַנְשֵׁי הַמָּקוֹם
כג אָמְרוּ לֹא־הָיְתָה בָזֶה קְדֵשָׁה: וַיֹּאמֶר יְהוּדָה תִּקַּח־לָהּ פֶּן נִהְיֶה לָבוּז הִנֵּה
כד שָׁלַחְתִּי הַגְּדִי הַזֶּה וְאַתָּה לֹא מְצָאתָהּ: וַיְהִי | כְּמִשְׁלֹשׁ חֳדָשִׁים וַיֻּגַּד
לִיהוּדָה לֵאמֹר זָנְתָה תָּמָר כַּלָּתֶךָ וְגַם הִנֵּה הָרָה לִזְנוּנִים וַיֹּאמֶר יְהוּדָה
כה הוֹצִיאוּהָ וְתִשָּׂרֵף: הִוא מוּצֵאת וְהִיא שָׁלְחָה אֶל־חָמִיהָ לֵאמֹר לְאִישׁ
אֲשֶׁר־אֵלֶּה לּוֹ אָנֹכִי הָרָה וַתֹּאמֶר הַכֶּר־נָא לְמִי הַחֹתֶמֶת וְהַפְּתִילִים
כו וְהַמַּטֶּה הָאֵלֶּה: וַיַּכֵּר יְהוּדָה וַיֹּאמֶר צָדְקָה מִמֶּנִּי כִּי־עַל־כֵּן לֹא־נְתַתִּיהָ
כז לְשֵׁלָה בְנִי וְלֹא־יָסַף עוֹד לְדַעְתָּהּ: וַיְהִי בְּעֵת לִדְתָּהּ וְהִנֵּה תְאוֹמִים

---

22. וְגַם אַנְשֵׁי הַמָּקוֹם אָמְרוּ – *And the people of that place also said* ... as though mocking you and shaming your honor.

23. הִנֵּה שָׁלַחְתִּי – *Behold I have sent.* I kept my word and did not break my promise.

24. וְגַם הִנֵּה הָרָה – *And behold she is with child.* And she has not (even) tried to prevent or conceal this shameful affront to your honor, as it is said (by our Sages), 'A woman playing the harlot turns over (or uses an absorbent) to prevent conception' *(Yevamos* 35a).

25. הִיא מוּצֵאת וְהִיא שָׁלְחָה – *When she was brought forth, she sent (to her father-in-law).* She did not despair of defending and saving herself even as she was being taken out to be burnt, for her heart was strong as a lion.

לְאִישׁ אֲשֶׁר אֵלֶּה לוֹ – *By the man whose these are (am I with child).* Even though she was in mortal danger she would not shame him, as our Sages tell us, 'It is better for a man that he should cast himself into a fiery furnace rather than that he should put his fellow to shame in public. Whence do we know this? From Tamar' *(Berachos* 43b).

26. צָדְקָה מִמֶּנִּי – *She is more righteous than I.* Even though she deceived me and I never recognized her, because I sent (her) the kid, nevertheless she was right to do what she did for it was for a (positive and) good purpose, acceptable by God. (Her purpose was) to have children (from him) not for personal (gain or) satisfaction, since we see that she returned immediately to her widow's status. (She was) more righteous than I was in keeping my word, since my intentions were (to maintain) my personal honor and to acquire my pledge, a false and deficient goal. (This is) as our Sages teach us, גְּדוֹלָה עֲבֵרָה לִשְׁמָהּ מִמִּצְוָה שֶׁלֹּא לִשְׁמָהּ, *A transgression performed with good intentions is better than a precept performed with evil intention (Nazir* 23b).

27. וְהִנֵּה תְאוֹמִים בְּבִטְנָהּ – *Behold twins were in her womb.* Before they were born it

NOTES

devise an alternate plan to fulfill her desire to bring the Messiah into the world.

26. צָדְקָה מִמֶּנִּי —*She is more righteous than I.* This expression implies that there were two actions, one by Tamar and one by Judah, which were to be weighed and judged to determine which was the more righteous. Judah was fair enough to recognize that a person's intent and motivation is more important than one's action. A seemingly improper, even immoral act, if done for the sake of heaven, is superior to a *mitzvah* performed to assuage one's guilt feeling and satisfy one's ego. Tamar's motive was pure. Judah's was not.

27. וְהִנֵּה תְאוֹמִים בְּבִטְנָהּ – *Behold twins were in*

כח בְּבִטְנָהּ: וַיְהִי בְלִדְתָּהּ וַיִּתֶּן־יָד וַתִּקַּח הַמְיַלֶּדֶת וַתִּקְשֹׁר עַל־יָדוֹ שָׁנִי לֵאמֹר
כט זֶה יָצָא רִאשֹׁנָה: וַיְהִי | כְּמֵשִׁיב יָדוֹ וְהִנֵּה יָצָא אָחִיו וַתֹּאמֶר מַה־פָּרַצְתָּ
ל עָלֶיךָ פָּרֶץ וַיִּקְרָא שְׁמוֹ פָּרֶץ: וְאַחַר יָצָא אָחִיו אֲשֶׁר עַל־יָדוֹ הַשָּׁנִי וַיִּקְרָא
לט חמישי א שְׁמוֹ זָרַח: וְיוֹסֵף הוּרַד מִצְרָיְמָה וַיִּקְנֵהוּ פּוֹטִיפַר סְרִיס פַּרְעֹה
ב שַׂר הַטַּבָּחִים אִישׁ מִצְרִי מִיַּד הַיִּשְׁמְעֵאלִים אֲשֶׁר הוֹרִדֻהוּ שָׁמָּה: וַיְהִי יהוה
ג אֶת־יוֹסֵף וַיְהִי אִישׁ מַצְלִיחַ וַיְהִי בְּבֵית אֲדֹנָיו הַמִּצְרִי: וַיַּרְא אֲדֹנָיו כִּי יהוה
ד אִתּוֹ וְכֹל אֲשֶׁר־הוּא עֹשֶׂה יהוה מַצְלִיחַ בְּיָדוֹ: וַיִּמְצָא יוֹסֵף חֵן בְּעֵינָיו
ה וַיְשָׁרֶת אֹתוֹ וַיַּפְקִדֵהוּ עַל־בֵּיתוֹ וְכָל־יֶשׁ־לוֹ נָתַן בְּיָדוֹ: וַיְהִי מֵאָז הִפְקִיד

---

was perceived that they were twins; therefore the midwife tied a scarlet thread (on his hand) so as to identify the firstborn.

29. וַיְהִי כְּמֵשִׁיב יָדוֹ – *And it came to pass, as he drew back his hand.* It was as though *he drew back his hand*, but it was not actually so, for it was not of his own volition but rather as a result of his brother pushing past him (that the first child) was forced back (entirely).

XXXIX

1. וְיוֹסֵף הוּרַד – *And Joseph was brought down.* At the same time that Judah departed from his brethren, and the events recorded above unfolded, Joseph was brought down (to Egypt).

מִיַּד הַיִּשְׁמְעֵאלִים – *Of the hand of the Ishmaelites* ... the owners of the camels which bore the caravan, and acted as agents for the sale (on behalf of the Midianite merchants).

2. וַיְהִי ה׳ אֶת יוֹסֵף – *And God was with Joseph* ... to save him from his enemies.

וַיְהִי אִישׁ מַצְלִיחַ – *And he was a prosperous man* ... attaining whatever was required of him.

וַיְהִי בְּבֵית אֲדֹנָיו הַמִּצְרִי – *And he was in the house of his master the Egyptian* ... prepared to serve him in his private chamber. The expression (here) of הָיָה (i.e., the word וַיְהִי from the root היה, *to be)* is to be understood as עָמַד, *standing* or *being (prepared)*, as we find, וְהָיָה שָׁם, *that it may be* (i.e., *stand) there (Deut.* 31:26); also, וַיִּהְיוּ שָׁם כַּאֲשֶׁר צִוַּנִי ה׳, *that they are there* (i.e., *they stand) as God commanded me* (ibid. 10:5).

4. וַיְשָׁרֶת אֹתוֹ – *And he ministered unto him* ... in personal matters.

NOTES

her womb. The word בְּבִטְנָהּ, *in her womb*, indicates that this was known while they were still in the womb, i.e., before birth. Compare this to Rebecca in 25:24.

XXXIX

1. וְיוֹסֵף הוּרַד – *And Joseph was brought down.* The Torah does not say, וַיּוֹרִדוּ אֶת יוֹסֵף, *And they took Joseph down*, which would have been the proper way to begin a new story. Rather it says, וְיוֹסֵף הוּרַד, the letter ו׳ in this case being a ו׳ הַדְּדִית – used not only to link (in the usual sense of 'and') but to emphasize that two events took place at the same time. In our story the two events were Judah's departing from his brethren, who rejected him because of his role in selling Joseph, and Joseph's going down to Egypt.

2. וַיְהִי ה׳ אֶת יוֹסֵף וַיְהִי אִישׁ מַצְלִיחַ – *And God was with Joseph and he was a prosperous man.* The word וַיְהִי is repeated to teach us that Joseph was protected by God from his enemies and also blessed by God with success in all his endeavors.

4. וַיְשָׁרֶת אֹתוֹ – *And he ministered to him.*

אֹתוֹ בְּבֵיתוֹ וְעַל כָּל־אֲשֶׁר יֶשׁ־לוֹ וַיְבָרֶךְ יהוה אֶת־בֵּית הַמִּצְרִי בִּגְלַל יוֹסֵף
ו וַיְהִי בִּרְכַּת יהוה בְּכָל־אֲשֶׁר יֶשׁ־לוֹ בַּבַּיִת וּבַשָּׂדֶה: וַיַּעֲזֹב כָּל־אֲשֶׁר־לוֹ
בְּיַד־יוֹסֵף וְלֹא־יָדַע אִתּוֹ מְאוּמָה כִּי אִם־הַלֶּחֶם אֲשֶׁר־הוּא אוֹכֵל וַיְהִי יוֹסֵף
ששי ז יְפֵה־תֹאַר וִיפֵה מַרְאֶה: וַיְהִי אַחַר הַדְּבָרִים הָאֵלֶּה וַתִּשָּׂא אֵשֶׁת־אֲדֹנָיו
ח אֶת־עֵינֶיהָ אֶל־יוֹסֵף וַתֹּאמֶר שִׁכְבָה עִמִּי: וַיְמָאֵן | וַיֹּאמֶר אֶל־אֵשֶׁת אֲדֹנָיו
ט הֵן אֲדֹנִי לֹא־יָדַע אִתִּי מַה־בַּבָּיִת וְכֹל אֲשֶׁר־יֶשׁ־לוֹ נָתַן בְּיָדִי: אֵינֶנּוּ גָדוֹל
בַּבַּיִת הַזֶּה מִמֶּנִּי וְלֹא־חָשַׂךְ מִמֶּנִּי מְאוּמָה כִּי אִם־אוֹתָךְ בַּאֲשֶׁר אַתְּ־
י אִשְׁתּוֹ וְאֵיךְ אֶעֱשֶׂה הָרָעָה הַגְּדֹלָה הַזֹּאת וְחָטָאתִי לֵאלֹהִים: וַיְהִי כְּדַבְּרָהּ
יא אֶל־יוֹסֵף יוֹם | יוֹם וְלֹא־שָׁמַע אֵלֶיהָ לִשְׁכַּב אֶצְלָהּ לִהְיוֹת עִמָּהּ: וַיְהִי
כְּהַיּוֹם הַזֶּה וַיָּבֹא הַבַּיְתָה לַעֲשׂוֹת מְלַאכְתּוֹ וְאֵין אִישׁ מֵאַנְשֵׁי הַבַּיִת שָׁם
יב בַּבָּיִת: וַתִּתְפְּשֵׂהוּ בְּבִגְדוֹ לֵאמֹר שִׁכְבָה עִמִּי וַיַּעֲזֹב בִּגְדוֹ בְּיָדָהּ וַיָּנָס וַיֵּצֵא
יג־יד הַחוּצָה: וַיְהִי כִּרְאוֹתָהּ כִּי־עָזַב בִּגְדוֹ בְּיָדָהּ וַיָּנָס הַחוּצָה: וַתִּקְרָא לְאַנְשֵׁי

---

6. וַיַּעֲזֹב כָּל אֲשֶׁר לוֹ – *And he left all that he had* ... without demanding an accounting.

וַיְהִי יוֹסֵף יְפֵה תֹאַר וִיפֵה מַרְאֶה – *And Joseph was of beautiful form, and fair to look upon* ... after he was (entrusted with all of Potiphar's household possessions), in contrast to his early period of servitude when he had to do menial hard labor, as it says, הֲסִירוֹתִי מִסֵּבֶל שִׁכְמוֹ, *I removed his shoulder from the burden (Psalms 81:7).*

7. וַתִּשָּׂא אֵשֶׁת אֲדֹנָיו – *His master's wife cast her eyes* ... because of his great beauty, as mentioned (in the previous verse).

9. כִּי אִם אוֹתָךְ בַּאֲשֶׁר אַתְּ אִשְׁתּוֹ – *But you, because you are his wife.* Only you, his wife, has he kept back from me.

הָרָעָה הַגְּדֹלָה הַזֹּאת – *This great wickedness.* (How can I do this) to repay evil for good.

10. לִהְיוֹת עִמָּהּ – *To be with her* ... alone (in the privacy of her chamber).

11. כְּהַיּוֹם הַזֶּה – *On a certain day* ... when she set her eyes (on him) and desired him.

וַיָּבֹא הַבַּיְתָה – *When he went into the house.* He entered *his* room, not knowing that she was there.

שָׁם בַּבָּיִת – *There within* ... in that room.

12. וַיָּנָס – *And fled* ... from the room, fearing that his evil inclination might prevail.

וַיֵּצֵא הַחוּצָה – *He went out.* Once outside the room he resumed his normal gait so as not to arouse curiosity and to deflect the question, 'Why are you fleeing; who is

NOTES

When Joseph first came into the house of Potiphar, he was a lowly slave of the Hebrew race, loathed by the Egyptians. During that period his physical appearance must have been most unattractive. Only after his elevation to that of trusted steward does he have the wherewithal to eat properly and dress decently. Ironically, this good fortune is what precipitates his problems with Potiphar's wife and his subsequent imprisonment.

11. וַיָּבֹא הַבַּיְתָה – *When he went into the house.* The word בַּיִת in this verse does not mean *house* but *room.*

בֵּיתָהּ וַתֹּאמֶר לָהֶם לֵאמֹר רְאוּ הֵבִיא לָנוּ אִישׁ עִבְרִי לְצַחֶק בָּנוּ בָּא אֵלַי
טו לִשְׁכַּב עִמִּי וָאֶקְרָא בְּקוֹל גָּדוֹל: וַיְהִי כְשָׁמְעוֹ כִּי־הֲרִימֹתִי קוֹלִי וָאֶקְרָא
טז וַיַּעֲזֹב בִּגְדוֹ אֶצְלִי וַיָּנָס וַיֵּצֵא הַחוּצָה: וַתַּנַּח בִּגְדוֹ אֶצְלָהּ עַד־בּוֹא אֲדֹנָיו
יז אֶל־בֵּיתוֹ: וַתְּדַבֵּר אֵלָיו כַּדְּבָרִים הָאֵלֶּה לֵאמֹר בָּא־אֵלַי הָעֶבֶד הָעִבְרִי
יח אֲשֶׁר־הֵבֵאתָ לָּנוּ לְצַחֶק בִּי: וַיְהִי כַּהֲרִימִי קוֹלִי וָאֶקְרָא וַיַּעֲזֹב בִּגְדוֹ אֶצְלִי
יט וַיָּנָס הַחוּצָה: וַיְהִי כִשְׁמֹעַ אֲדֹנָיו אֶת־דִּבְרֵי אִשְׁתּוֹ אֲשֶׁר דִּבְּרָה אֵלָיו לֵאמֹר
כ כַּדְּבָרִים הָאֵלֶּה עָשָׂה לִי עַבְדֶּךָ וַיִּחַר אַפּוֹ: וַיִּקַּח אֲדֹנֵי יוֹסֵף אֹתוֹ וַיִּתְּנֵהוּ
°אֲסִירֵי ק׳ אֶל־בֵּית הַסֹּהַר מְקוֹם אֲשֶׁר־°אסורי הַמֶּלֶךְ אֲסוּרִים וַיְהִי־שָׁם בְּבֵית הַסֹּהַר:
כא־כב וַיְהִי יהוה אֶת־יוֹסֵף וַיֵּט אֵלָיו חָסֶד וַיִּתֵּן חִנּוֹ בְּעֵינֵי שַׂר בֵּית־הַסֹּהַר: וַיִּתֵּן
שַׂר בֵּית־הַסֹּהַר בְּיַד־יוֹסֵף אֵת כָּל־הָאֲסִירִם אֲשֶׁר בְּבֵית הַסֹּהַר וְאֵת כָּל־
כג אֲשֶׁר עֹשִׂים שָׁם הוּא הָיָה עֹשֶׂה: אֵין | שַׂר בֵּית־הַסֹּהַר רֹאֶה אֶת־כָּל־
מְאוּמָה בְּיָדוֹ בַּאֲשֶׁר יהוה אִתּוֹ וַאֲשֶׁר־הוּא עֹשֶׂה יהוה מַצְלִיחַ:
מ שביעי א וַיְהִי אַחַר הַדְּבָרִים הָאֵלֶּה חָטְאוּ מַשְׁקֵה מֶלֶךְ־מִצְרַיִם וְהָאֹפֶה לַאֲדֹנֵיהֶם
ב לְמֶלֶךְ מִצְרָיִם: וַיִּקְצֹף פַּרְעֹה עַל שְׁנֵי סָרִיסָיו עַל שַׂר הַמַּשְׁקִים וְעַל שַׂר

---

pursuing you?' But she, seeing him flee, thought that he was still running and on being queried would tell all that had transpired — therefore ...

14. וַתִּקְרָא לְאַנְשֵׁי בֵיתָהּ – *She called to the men of her house* ... to protect herself. However, when she realized that once outside (Joseph) did not run, and that her household had also seen this, she was compelled to tell the truth, i.e., *He fled, and went out* (verse 15). Nevertheless, when she related the story to her husband who was not present at the time (verse 18), she said, 'וַיָּנָס הַחוּצָה, *he fled out*,' (after leaving the room he kept running), so as to avoid his pursuers. This she did to substantiate her false story (that she was victimized by Joseph).

לְצַחֶק בָּנוּ – *To mock us* ... with his lewd and immoral ways, which in turn brought him to attempt to lie with me.

19. וַיִּחַר אַפּוֹ – *His wrath was kindled.* He was angry because she complained about his bringing a Hebrew into the house, not because of her accusations which he disbelieved. Nonetheless, he put Joseph in prison to demonstrate publicly that he did believe his wife (so as to defend her honor and reputation). Even in prison (Potiphar) utilized the services of Joseph, as we read: *And the captain of the guard (Potiphar) charged Joseph to be with them* (40:4).

XL

1. חָטְאוּ מַשְׁקֵה מֶלֶךְ מִצְרַיִם וְהָאֹפֶה – *The butler of the King of Egypt and his baker offended him* ... the subordinates of the chief of the butlers and of the bakers.

2. וַיִּקְצֹף פַּרְעֹה עַל שְׁנֵי סָרִיסָיו – *And Pharaoh was wroth against his two officers* ... for not properly overseeing their subordinates.

NOTES

12-14. וַיָּנָס וַיֵּצֵא הַחוּצָה ... וַתִּקְרָא לְאַנְשֵׁי בֵיתָהּ – *And fled, he went out ... She called to the men of her house.* The *Sforno,* noting the subtle change in the language of these verses, gives this interpretation to the episode: When the Torah tells us of Joseph's actions it states **וַיֵּצֵא הַחוּצָה**, *he went out*, rather than **וַיָּנָס**, *he fled*, indicating that once he fled the room he purposely walked normally so as not to raise a hue and cry. Potiphar's wife, when she called

ג הָאוֹפִים: וַיִּתֵּן אֹתָם בְּמִשְׁמַר בֵּית שַׂר הַטַּבָּחִים אֶל־בֵּית הַסֹּהַר מְקוֹם
ד אֲשֶׁר יוֹסֵף אָסוּר שָׁם: וַיִּפְקֹד שַׂר הַטַּבָּחִים אֶת־יוֹסֵף אִתָּם וַיְשָׁרֶת אֹתָם
ה וַיִּהְיוּ יָמִים בְּמִשְׁמָר: וַיַּחַלְמוּ חֲלוֹם שְׁנֵיהֶם אִישׁ חֲלֹמוֹ בְּלַיְלָה אֶחָד אִישׁ
כְּפִתְרוֹן חֲלֹמוֹ הַמַּשְׁקֶה וְהָאֹפֶה אֲשֶׁר לְמֶלֶךְ מִצְרַיִם אֲשֶׁר אֲסוּרִים בְּבֵית
ו־ז הַסֹּהַר: וַיָּבֹא אֲלֵיהֶם יוֹסֵף בַּבֹּקֶר וַיַּרְא אֹתָם וְהִנָּם זֹעֲפִים: וַיִּשְׁאַל
אֶת־סְרִיסֵי פַרְעֹה אֲשֶׁר אִתּוֹ בְמִשְׁמַר בֵּית אֲדֹנָיו לֵאמֹר מַדּוּעַ פְּנֵיכֶם
ח רָעִים הַיּוֹם: וַיֹּאמְרוּ אֵלָיו חֲלוֹם חָלַמְנוּ וּפֹתֵר אֵין אֹתוֹ וַיֹּאמֶר אֲלֵהֶם יוֹסֵף
ט הֲלוֹא לֵאלֹהִים פִּתְרֹנִים סַפְּרוּ־נָא לִי: וַיְסַפֵּר שַׂר־הַמַּשְׁקִים אֶת־חֲלֹמוֹ
י לְיוֹסֵף וַיֹּאמֶר לוֹ בַּחֲלוֹמִי וְהִנֵּה־גֶפֶן לְפָנָי: וּבַגֶּפֶן שְׁלֹשָׁה שָׂרִיגִם וְהִוא
יא כְפֹרַחַת עָלְתָה נִצָּהּ הִבְשִׁילוּ אַשְׁכְּלֹתֶיהָ עֲנָבִים: וְכוֹס פַּרְעֹה בְּיָדִי וָאֶקַּח
אֶת־הָעֲנָבִים וָאֶשְׂחַט אֹתָם אֶל־כּוֹס פַּרְעֹה וָאֶתֵּן אֶת־הַכּוֹס עַל־כַּף פַּרְעֹה:
יב־יג וַיֹּאמֶר לוֹ יוֹסֵף זֶה פִּתְרֹנוֹ שְׁלֹשֶׁת הַשָּׂרִגִים שְׁלֹשֶׁת יָמִים הֵם: בְּעוֹד ׀
שְׁלֹשֶׁת יָמִים יִשָּׂא פַרְעֹה אֶת־רֹאשֶׁךָ וַהֲשִׁיבְךָ עַל־כַּנֶּךָ וְנָתַתָּ כוֹס־פַּרְעֹה
יד בְּיָדוֹ כַּמִּשְׁפָּט הָרִאשׁוֹן אֲשֶׁר הָיִיתָ מַשְׁקֵהוּ: כִּי אִם־זְכַרְתַּנִי אִתְּךָ כַּאֲשֶׁר

---

5. הַמַּשְׁקֶה וְהָאֹפֶה ... אֲשֶׁר אֲסוּרִים – *The butler and the baker ... who were imprisoned.* They dreamed as a butler and baker would, not as chiefs in positions of authority, for since they were incarcerated they were humbled and did not think as officers normally would.

7. סְרִיסֵי פַרְעֹה אֲשֶׁר אִתּוֹ בְמִשְׁמַר בֵּית אֲדֹנָיו – *Pharaoh's officers that were with him in the ward of his master's house.* Only because his master had appointed him to minister to their needs, as it states, *And the captain of the guard charged Joseph to be with them* (v.4), did he (have the temerity) to ask them why they were so sad.

8. הֲלוֹא לֵאלֹהִים פִּתְרֹנִים – *Do not interpretations belong to God?* Man has wisdom in interpreting dreams because he is formed in the image of God; therefore I may have it, too, even though I am a slave languishing in prison. Hence you may be wrong in saying, *'And there is none who can interpret it.'*

13. כַּמִּשְׁפָּט הָרִאשׁוֹן – *After the former manner* ... before you became the chief of the butlers.

אֲשֶׁר הָיִיתָ מַשְׁקֵהוּ – *When you were his butler* ... you yourself (directly). This (Pharaoh) will do to indicate to you that he is appeased, and looks upon you again with favor.

14. כִּי אִם זְכַרְתַּנִי אִתְּךָ – *But have me in your remembrance* ... for the king will so cherish you, that if you will but remember (and mention me) ...

NOTES

her servants to tell them what happened, began with וַיָּנָס, *he fled,* but quickly changed it to וַיֵּצֵא הַחוּצָה, since they saw what happened. When she related the story to her husband, however, she used the phrase וַיָּנָס הַחוּצָה, *he fled outside;* the word וַיֵּצֵא no longer appears, for she wanted her charge and accusation to be buttressed by the guilty action and panicked flight of Joseph.

XL

1-13. חָטְאוּ מַשְׁקֵה מֶלֶךְ מִצְרַיִם וְהָאֹפֶה ... כַּמִּשְׁפָּט הָרִאשׁוֹן – *The butler of the King of Egypt and his baker offended him ... after the former manner.* The *Sforno* examines these verses

יִיטַב לָךְ וְעָשִׂיתָ־נָּא עִמָּדִי חָסֶד וְהִזְכַּרְתַּנִי אֶל־פַּרְעֹה וְהוֹצֵאתַנִי מִן־הַבַּיִת
טו הַזֶּה: כִּי־גֻנֹּב גֻּנַּבְתִּי מֵאֶרֶץ הָעִבְרִים וְגַם־פֹּה לֹא־עָשִׂיתִי מְאוּמָה כִּי־שָׂמוּ
טז אֹתִי בַּבּוֹר: וַיַּרְא שַׂר־הָאֹפִים כִּי טוֹב פָּתָר וַיֹּאמֶר אֶל־יוֹסֵף אַף־אֲנִי
יז בַּחֲלוֹמִי וְהִנֵּה שְׁלֹשָׁה סַלֵּי חֹרִי עַל־רֹאשִׁי: וּבַסַּל הָעֶלְיוֹן מִכֹּל מַאֲכַל
יח פַּרְעֹה מַעֲשֵׂה אֹפֶה וְהָעוֹף אֹכֵל אֹתָם מִן־הַסַּל מֵעַל רֹאשִׁי: וַיַּעַן יוֹסֵף
יט וַיֹּאמֶר זֶה פִּתְרֹנוֹ שְׁלֹשֶׁת הַסַּלִּים שְׁלֹשֶׁת יָמִים הֵם: בְּעוֹד ׀ שְׁלֹשֶׁת יָמִים
יִשָּׂא פַרְעֹה אֶת־רֹאשְׁךָ מֵעָלֶיךָ וְתָלָה אוֹתְךָ עַל־עֵץ וְאָכַל הָעוֹף
מפטיר כ אֶת־בְּשָׂרְךָ מֵעָלֶיךָ: וַיְהִי ׀ בַּיּוֹם הַשְּׁלִישִׁי יוֹם הֻלֶּדֶת אֶת־פַּרְעֹה וַיַּעַשׂ
מִשְׁתֶּה לְכָל־עֲבָדָיו וַיִּשָּׂא אֶת־רֹאשׁ ׀ שַׂר הַמַּשְׁקִים וְאֶת־רֹאשׁ שַׂר
כא הָאֹפִים בְּתוֹךְ עֲבָדָיו: וַיָּשֶׁב אֶת־שַׂר הַמַּשְׁקִים עַל־מַשְׁקֵהוּ וַיִּתֵּן הַכּוֹס
כב-כג עַל־כַּף פַּרְעֹה: וְאֵת שַׂר הָאֹפִים תָּלָה כַּאֲשֶׁר פָּתַר לָהֶם יוֹסֵף: וְלֹא־זָכַר
שַׂר־הַמַּשְׁקִים אֶת־יוֹסֵף וַיִּשְׁכָּחֵהוּ:

כַּאֲשֶׁר יִיטַב לָךְ – *When it shall be well with you* . . . at an appropriate time . . .

וְהִזְכַּרְתַּנִי אֶל פַּרְעֹה – *And make mention of me to Pharaoh* . . . he knows me from the time I was in the house of the captain of the guards.

וְהוֹצֵאתַנִי – *And bring me out* . . . then surely you will win my release.

15. כִּי גֻנֹּב גֻּנַּבְתִּי . . . וְגַם פֹּה לֹא עָשִׂיתִי מְאוּמָה – *For indeed I was stolen . . . and here also have I done nothing.* You will assuredly procure my release for it can be proven that neither my state of slavery nor my imprisonment was justified.

16. כִּי טוֹב פָּתָר – *That the interpretation was good* . . . and he hoped that Joseph would also interpret his dream for good, because the fulfillment of a dream depends on how it is interpreted, as our Sages tell us *(Berachos* 55b), and as the Torah later states, *As Joseph had interpreted to them* (verse 22).

NOTES

carefully and finds that at times the words מַשְׁקֶה, *butler*, and אֹפֶה, *baker*, are used; at others שַׂר הַמַּשְׁקִים, *chief butler*, and שַׂר הָאוֹפִים, *chief baker*, as well as the phrase סְרִיסֵי פַרְעֹה, *Pharaoh's officers*. He determines that the phrase מַשְׁקֶה or אֹפֶה means the vassal who does the actual act of *pouring the wine* or *baking;* the expression שַׂר הַמַּשְׁקִים or שַׂר הָאוֹפִים means chief butler or baker and סָרִיס is an officer of the king, implying a position of honor and respect. The initial offense was committed by the functionaries, not the chiefs; nevertheless the chiefs were held responsible. Hence in verse 1, the phrases used are מַשְׁקֶה and אֹפֶה, whereas in verse 2 it is סָרִיסָיו and שַׂר. In verse 5, even though we are speaking of the chiefs, the phrases used are מַשְׁקֶה and אֹפֶה, for the reason given in the *Sforno's* commentary. In verse 7, סְרִיסֵי is used again to emphasize that were it not for the fact that Joseph had been given the responsibility by Potiphar to watch over them, he would never have had the temerity to speak so familiarly with them, or to ask them such a personal question. In verse 13, the phrase כַּמִּשְׁפָּט הָרִאשׁוֹן, *after the former manner*, must mean that the chief butler, after being rehabilitated, would once again assume his original task of actually pouring the wine and serving it to Pharaoh.

16. כִּי טוֹב פָּתָר — *That the interpretation was good.* The expression, *as Joseph had interpreted*, implies that this was the cause for the eventual fate of the butler and baker. This then is the biblical source of our Sages' saying 'All dreams follow the mouth,' i.e., 'The fulfillment of all dreams depends upon their interpretation' (*Berachos* 55b).

פרשת מקץ
Parashas Mikeitz

מא א-ב וַיְהִ֕י מִקֵּ֖ץ שְׁנָתַ֣יִם יָמִ֑ים וּפַרְעֹ֣ה חֹלֵ֔ם וְהִנֵּ֖ה עֹמֵ֥ד עַל־הַיְאֹֽר׃ וְהִנֵּ֣ה מִן־הַיְאֹ֗ר
ג עֹלֹת֙ שֶׁ֣בַע פָּר֔וֹת יְפ֥וֹת מַרְאֶ֖ה וּבְרִיאֹ֣ת בָּשָׂ֑ר וַתִּרְעֶ֖ינָה בָּאָֽחוּ׃ וְהִנֵּ֞ה שֶׁ֧בַע
פָּר֣וֹת אֲחֵר֗וֹת עֹל֤וֹת אַחֲרֵיהֶן֙ מִן־הַיְאֹ֔ר רָע֥וֹת מַרְאֶ֖ה וְדַקּ֣וֹת בָּשָׂ֑ר
ד וַֽתַּעֲמֹ֛דְנָה אֵ֥צֶל הַפָּר֖וֹת עַל־שְׂפַ֥ת הַיְאֹֽר׃ וַתֹּאכַ֣לְנָה הַפָּר֗וֹת רָע֤וֹת הַמַּרְאֶה֙
ה וְדַקֹּ֣ת הַבָּשָׂ֔ר אֵ֚ת שֶׁ֣בַע הַפָּר֔וֹת יְפֹ֥ת הַמַּרְאֶ֖ה וְהַבְּרִיאֹ֑ת וַיִּיקַ֖ץ פַּרְעֹֽה׃ וַיִּישָׁ֕ן
ו וַֽיַּחֲלֹ֖ם שֵׁנִ֑ית וְהִנֵּ֣ה ׀ שֶׁ֣בַע שִׁבֳּלִ֗ים עֹל֛וֹת בְּקָנֶ֥ה אֶחָ֖ד בְּרִיא֥וֹת וְטֹבֽוֹת׃ וְהִנֵּה֙
ז שֶׁ֣בַע שִׁבֳּלִ֔ים דַּקּ֖וֹת וּשְׁדוּפֹ֣ת קָדִ֑ים צֹמְח֖וֹת אַחֲרֵיהֶֽן׃ וַתִּבְלַ֙עְנָה֙ הַשִּׁבֳּלִ֣ים
הַדַּקּ֔וֹת אֵ֚ת שֶׁ֣בַע הַשִּׁבֳּלִ֔ים הַבְּרִיא֖וֹת וְהַמְּלֵא֑וֹת וַיִּיקַ֥ץ פַּרְעֹ֖ה וְהִנֵּ֥ה חֲלֽוֹם׃
ח וַיְהִ֤י בַבֹּ֙קֶר֙ וַתִּפָּ֣עֶם רוּח֔וֹ וַיִּשְׁלַ֛ח וַיִּקְרָ֥א אֶת־כָּל־חַרְטֻמֵּ֥י מִצְרַ֖יִם וְאֶת־כָּל־

XLI

1. וַיְהִי מִקֵּץ . . . וּפַרְעֹה חֹלֵם — *And it came to pass at the end of . . . that Pharaoh dreamed.* Among other dreams he had, which were without significance, he dreamed this also, that he was standing by the river, as our Sages say, כְּשֵׁם שֶׁאִי אֶפְשָׁר לְבַר בְּלֹא תֶּבֶן, כָּךְ אִי אֶפְשָׁר לַחֲלוֹם בְּלֹא דְּבָרִים בְּטֵלִים, *Just as wheat cannot do without straw so there cannot be a dream without nonsense (Berachos* 55b).

3. וַתַּעֲמֹדְנָה אֵצֶל הַפָּרוֹת — *And stood by the (other) cows.* They stood by them (for some time) before eating, symbolizing that for a period there would be both famine and plenty, as we find, *There was famine in all lands, but in all the land of Egypt there was plenty* (verse 54).

7. וְהִנֵּה חֲלוֹם — *And, behold, it was a dream.* He felt it was all one dream, for when he dreamed the second dream he knew it was a continuation of the first, and so he explains later, when he says, '*And I saw in my dream*' (verse 22) (i.e., he said *dream*, not *dreams).*

NOTES

XLI

1. וּפַרְעֹה חֹלֵם וְהִנֵּה עֹמֵד — *Pharaoh was dreaming and behold he was standing.* The verse does not state וַיַּחֲלוֹם פַּרְעֹה, *and Pharaoh dreamed,* rather וּפַרְעֹה חוֹלֵם, *and Pharaoh was dreaming,* meaning that among his other dreams was this dream of the cattle and the corn. As our Sages teach us, only a very small percentage of our dreams are significant, and this is a very good example of a dream coming for the specific purpose of revealing future events. This is especially true when a dream does not reflect a person's thoughts and experiences of the day but occurs unexpectedly and suddenly. The word הִנֵּה, *behold,* appears twice; once in verse 1 regarding Pharaoh standing by the river and again in verse 2 regarding the cows. This word indicates suddenness, and tells us that Pharaoh was taken unawares since he had not been thinking of the river, and certainly not of the bizarre appearance of the kine. Hence he is convinced that the dream is pregnant with meaning. This thought is repeated by the *Sforno* again in verse 19, where he interprets the words *such as I never saw* to mean that Pharaoh had not seen such kine that day, which would have explained why he dreamed of them that night. It does not mean that he never saw such lean-fleshed kine before, as this phrase is usually explained.

3. וַתַּעֲמֹדְנָה אֵצֶל הַפָּרוֹת — *And stood by the (other) cows.* The fat-fleshed and lean-fleshed cattle standing side by side indicated that there would be a period of time when there would be both plenty and famine. This, the *Sforno* explains (based upon verse 54), refers to the time when the seven good years had concluded and the seven bad years had just begun. All other lands would feel the effects of the famine, while Egypt would still be insulated from hunger, as a result of its preparations during the good years.

ט חַכָמֶיהָ וַיְסַפֵּר פַּרְעֹה לָהֶם אֶת־חֲלֹמוֹ וְאֵין־פּוֹתֵר אוֹתָם לְפַרְעֹה: וַיְדַבֵּר
י שַׂר הַמַּשְׁקִים אֶת־פַּרְעֹה לֵאמֹר אֶת־חֲטָאַי אֲנִי מַזְכִּיר הַיּוֹם: פַּרְעֹה קָצַף
עַל־עֲבָדָיו וַיִּתֵּן אֹתִי בְּמִשְׁמַר בֵּית שַׂר הַטַּבָּחִים אֹתִי וְאֵת שַׂר הָאֹפִים:
יא-יב וַנַּחַלְמָה חֲלוֹם בְּלַיְלָה אֶחָד אֲנִי וָהוּא אִישׁ כְּפִתְרוֹן חֲלֹמוֹ חָלָמְנוּ: וְשָׁם
אִתָּנוּ נַעַר עִבְרִי עֶבֶד לְשַׂר הַטַּבָּחִים וַנְּסַפֶּר־לוֹ וַיִּפְתָּר־לָנוּ אֶת־חֲלֹמֹתֵינוּ
יג אִישׁ כַּחֲלֹמוֹ פָּתָר: וַיְהִי כַּאֲשֶׁר פָּתַר־לָנוּ כֵּן הָיָה אֹתִי הֵשִׁיב עַל־כַּנִּי וְאֹתוֹ
יד תָלָה: וַיִּשְׁלַח פַּרְעֹה וַיִּקְרָא אֶת־יוֹסֵף וַיְרִיצֻהוּ מִן־הַבּוֹר וַיְגַלַּח וַיְחַלֵּף
שני טו שִׂמְלֹתָיו וַיָּבֹא אֶל־פַּרְעֹה: וַיֹּאמֶר פַּרְעֹה אֶל־יוֹסֵף חֲלוֹם חָלַמְתִּי וּפֹתֵר
טז אֵין אֹתוֹ וַאֲנִי שָׁמַעְתִּי עָלֶיךָ לֵאמֹר תִּשְׁמַע חֲלוֹם לִפְתֹּר אֹתוֹ: וַיַּעַן יוֹסֵף

---

8. וְאֵין פּוֹתֵר אוֹתָם – *There was none that could interpret them.* Because they (the magicians and wise men) thought that these were two (distinct and separate) dreams, therefore they erred in their interpretation. (The reason they were misled was because) the first part consisted of active, physical causes, i.e., the cattle that plough and the river that waters, whereas the second consisted of ultimate form and purpose, i.e., the ears of corn.

9. אֶת חֲטָאַי אֲנִי מַזְכִּיר – *I make mention of my faults.* I do not complain that you imprisoned me, for it was due to my own fault.

14. וַיְרִיצֻהוּ מִן הַבּוֹר – *They brought him hastily out of the dungeon.* The Divine salvation always come hastily (unexpectedly), as it is written, כִּי קְרוֹבָה יְשׁוּעָתִי לָבוֹא, *For my salvation is near to come (Isaiah* 56:1), and also, לוּ עַמִּי שֹׁמֵעַ לִי ... כִּמְעַט אוֹיְבֵיהֶם אַכְנִיעַ, *Oh, that My people would hearken unto me ... I would soon subdue their enemies (Psalms* 81:14-15). And so it came to pass in the Egyptian bondage, as it says, כִּי גֹרְשׁוּ מִמִּצְרַיִם, *because they were thrust out of Egypt (Exodus* 12:39), as our Sages have told us, 'Their dough had no time to rise, for the King of Kings, the Almighty, revealed Himself to them and redeemed them' (*Passover Haggadah*). And so it shall be in the future, as it is written, וּפִתְאֹם יָבוֹא אֶל הֵיכָלוֹ הָאָדוֹן אֲשֶׁר אַתֶּם מְבַקְשִׁים, *And the Lord Whom you seek, will suddenly come to His Temple (Malachi* 3:1).

וַיְחַלֵּף שִׂמְלֹתָיו – *And changed his clothes ...* for it is not fitting to come to the gate of the King's palace wearing sackcloth. (Compare to *Esther* 4:2.)

15. תִּשְׁמַע חֲלוֹם לִפְתֹּר אֹתוֹ – *When you hear a dream you can interpret it.* You have a talent for interpretation, and understand the true meaning of a dream, interpreting it wisely, not merely guessing the truth by chance.

NOTES

7-8. וְהִנֵּה חֲלוֹם ... וְאֵין פּוֹתֵר – *And, behold, it was a dream ... there was none that could interpret them.* Pharaoh knew that the two dreams were one. Joseph realized this after hearing the dreams, and his initial response to Pharaoh was, 'The dream of Pharaoh is one.' The necromancers and wise men failed to grasp this, for they were convinced that the two dreams were separate and distinct, since the first one dealt with the forces of productivity, the cause, i.e., the cattle that plough and the river that waters the plantings, while the second dealt with the result, i.e., the growing corn, which is the purpose and goal of the labor of the kine and the contribution of the water. This thought is repeated later by the *Sforno* in verse 24.

14. וַיְרִיצֻהוּ מִן הַבּוֹר – *They brought him hastily out of the dungeon.* The sudden release

יז אֶת־פַּרְעֹה לֵאמֹר בִּלְעָדָי אֱלֹהִים יַעֲנֶה אֶת־שְׁלוֹם פַּרְעֹה: וַיְדַבֵּר פַּרְעֹה
יח אֶל־יוֹסֵף בַּחֲלֹמִי הִנְנִי עֹמֵד עַל־שְׂפַת הַיְאֹר: וְהִנֵּה מִן־הַיְאֹר עֹלֹת שֶׁבַע
יט פָּרוֹת בְּרִיאוֹת בָּשָׂר וִיפֹת תֹּאַר וַתִּרְעֶינָה בָּאָחוּ: וְהִנֵּה שֶׁבַע פָּרוֹת אֲחֵרוֹת
עֹלוֹת אַחֲרֵיהֶן דַּלּוֹת וְרָעוֹת תֹּאַר מְאֹד וְרַקּוֹת בָּשָׂר לֹא־רָאִיתִי כָהֵנָּה
כ בְּכָל־אֶרֶץ מִצְרַיִם לָרֹעַ: וַתֹּאכַלְנָה הַפָּרוֹת הָרַקּוֹת וְהָרָעוֹת אֵת שֶׁבַע
כא הַפָּרוֹת הָרִאשֹׁנוֹת הַבְּרִיאֹת: וַתָּבֹאנָה אֶל־קִרְבֶּנָה וְלֹא נוֹדַע כִּי־בָאוּ אֶל־
כב קִרְבֶּנָה וּמַרְאֵיהֶן רַע כַּאֲשֶׁר בַּתְּחִלָּה וָאִיקָץ: וָאֵרֶא בַּחֲלֹמִי וְהִנֵּה ׀ שֶׁבַע
כג שִׁבֳּלִים עֹלֹת בְּקָנֶה אֶחָד מְלֵאֹת וְטֹבוֹת: וְהִנֵּה שֶׁבַע שִׁבֳּלִים צְנֻמוֹת דַּקּוֹת
כד שְׁדֻפוֹת קָדִים צֹמְחוֹת אַחֲרֵיהֶם: וַתִּבְלַעְןָ הַשִּׁבֳּלִים הַדַּקֹּת אֵת שֶׁבַע
כה הַשִּׁבֳּלִים הַטֹּבוֹת וָאֹמַר אֶל־הַחַרְטֻמִּים וְאֵין מַגִּיד לִי: וַיֹּאמֶר יוֹסֵף אֶל־
פַּרְעֹה חֲלוֹם פַּרְעֹה אֶחָד הוּא אֵת אֲשֶׁר הָאֱלֹהִים עֹשֶׂה הִגִּיד לְפַרְעֹה:

---

16. בִּלְעָדָי – *It is not in me.* Even though you say, 'None can interpret it,' as though I alone have this special talent, nonetheless I think that there are others besides me who can do so.

אֱלֹהִים יַעֲנֶה – *It is God who will respond.* He will cause me (teach me) to answer properly.

אֶת שְׁלוֹם פַּרְעֹה – *With Pharaoh's welfare* . . . an answer (interpretation) which will benefit Pharaoh, for 'all dreams follow the mouth' *(Berachos* 55b).

19. לֹא רָאִיתִי כָהֵנָּה – *Such as I never saw.* Hence this cannot be a case of, *Your thoughts came upon your bed (Daniel* 2:29; see note to 37:10).

21. וְלֹא נוֹדַע כִּי בָאוּ אֶל קִרְבֶּנָה – *It could not be known that they had eaten them.* (This is) similar to, וַאֲכַלְתֶּם וְלֹא תִשְׂבָּעוּ, *And you shall eat and not be satisfied (Lev.* 26:26). As our Sages tell us, אֵינוֹ דּוֹמֶה מִי שֶׁיֵּשׁ לוֹ פַּת בְּסַלּוֹ לְמִי שֶׁאֵין לוֹ פַּת בְּסַלּוֹ, *You cannot compare one who has bread in his basket with one who has no bread in his basket (Yoma* 74b).

24. וְאֵין מַגִּיד לִי – *But there was none to tell me.* He saw that they all thought there were two separate dreams, and interpreted accordingly, while he recognized that the two were one, as he said, *'And I saw in my dream'* (verse 22).

25. חֲלוֹם פַּרְעֹה אֶחָד הוּא – *The dream of Pharaoh is one* . . . and that is why the interpreters have erred.

אֵת אֲשֶׁר הָאֱלֹהִים עֹשֶׂה הִגִּיד לְפַרְעֹה – *What God is about to do, He has declared to Pharaoh* . . . therefore the necromancers did not know or understand it, for it is unknown to the spirits (who commune with the necromancers). But it has been declared to Pharaoh alone.

NOTES

of Joseph from the dungeon and his meteoric rise to greatness is a portent of the future destiny of *Klal Yisrael.* 'The story of our ancestors is a sign for the children.'

21. וְלֹא נוֹדַע כִּי בָאוּ אֶל קִרְבֶּנָה — *It could not be known that they had eaten them.* The verse quoted by the *Sforno* appears in the תּוֹכֵחָה, *the admonition.* The quote from tractate *Yoma* explains why one can eat and still not be satisfied. This occurs when he has food only for today and knows not where his bread will come from tomorrow, for just as a man who is blessed with bread feels so secure that he is

כו שֶׁבַע פָּרֹת הַטֹּבֹת שֶׁבַע שָׁנִים הֵנָּה וְשֶׁבַע הַשִּׁבֳּלִים הַטֹּבֹת שֶׁבַע שָׁנִים
כז הֵנָּה חֲלוֹם אֶחָד הוּא: וְשֶׁבַע הַפָּרוֹת הָרַקּוֹת וְהָרָעֹת הָעֹלֹת אַחֲרֵיהֶן שֶׁבַע
שָׁנִים הֵנָּה וְשֶׁבַע הַשִּׁבֳּלִים הָרֵקוֹת שְׁדֻפוֹת הַקָּדִים יִהְיוּ שֶׁבַע שְׁנֵי רָעָב:
כח הוּא הַדָּבָר אֲשֶׁר דִּבַּרְתִּי אֶל־פַּרְעֹה אֲשֶׁר הָאֱלֹהִים עֹשֶׂה הֶרְאָה אֶת־
כט־ל פַּרְעֹה: הִנֵּה שֶׁבַע שָׁנִים בָּאוֹת שָׂבָע גָּדוֹל בְּכָל־אֶרֶץ מִצְרָיִם: וְקָמוּ שֶׁבַע
שְׁנֵי רָעָב אַחֲרֵיהֶן וְנִשְׁכַּח כָּל־הַשָּׂבָע בְּאֶרֶץ מִצְרָיִם וְכִלָּה הָרָעָב אֶת־
לא הָאָרֶץ: וְלֹא־יִוָּדַע הַשָּׂבָע בָּאָרֶץ מִפְּנֵי הָרָעָב הַהוּא אַחֲרֵי־כֵן כִּי־כָבֵד הוּא
לב מְאֹד: וְעַל הִשָּׁנוֹת הַחֲלוֹם אֶל־פַּרְעֹה פַּעֲמָיִם כִּי־נָכוֹן הַדָּבָר מֵעִם הָאֱלֹהִים
לג וּמְמַהֵר הָאֱלֹהִים לַעֲשֹׂתוֹ: וְעַתָּה יֵרֶא פַרְעֹה אִישׁ נָבוֹן וְחָכָם וִישִׁיתֵהוּ
לד עַל־אֶרֶץ מִצְרָיִם: יַעֲשֶׂה פַרְעֹה וְיַפְקֵד פְּקִדִים עַל־הָאָרֶץ וְחִמֵּשׁ אֶת־אֶרֶץ
לה מִצְרַיִם בְּשֶׁבַע שְׁנֵי הַשָּׂבָע: וְיִקְבְּצוּ אֶת־כָּל־אֹכֶל הַשָּׁנִים הַטֹּבֹת הַבָּאֹת
לו הָאֵלֶּה וְיִצְבְּרוּ־בָר תַּחַת יַד־פַּרְעֹה אֹכֶל בֶּעָרִים וְשָׁמָרוּ: וְהָיָה הָאֹכֶל
לְפִקָּדוֹן לָאָרֶץ לְשֶׁבַע שְׁנֵי הָרָעָב אֲשֶׁר תִּהְיֶיןָ בְּאֶרֶץ מִצְרָיִם וְלֹא־תִכָּרֵת

---

28. הוּא הַדָּבָר – *That is the thing* ... the (impending) famine which has been told to you, so that the people shall not be decimated by the famine.

הֶרְאָה אֶת פַּרְעֹה – *He has shown to Pharaoh* ... the years of plenty (as well), to tell (you) how to save your people during the famine years.

33. וְעַתָּה יֵרֶא פַּרְעֹה – *Now therefore let Pharaoh seek out*. Since God informed you that there will be a famine to enable you to save your people, and He (even) showed you the (years of) plenty, informing you *how* you may save (them), it is proper that you do so and not sin against Him.

אִישׁ נָבוֹן וְחָכָם – *A man discerning and wise* ... one who can plan, execute and administer a governmental project efficiently, that the king shall have no damage.

34. יַעֲשֶׂה פַרְעֹה וְיַפְקֵד – *Let Pharaoh do this and appoint*. And let this discerning man appoint overseers for each city who will accept his authority, so that there be a unified program and not a divided, fragmented one, as we find, וְקַמְתָּ וְעָלִיתָ אֶל הַמָּקוֹם, *And you shall arise and go up to the place* (*Deut*. 17:8).

NOTES

never hungry, so one who is unsure cannot even enjoy what he has now. This is symbolized here by the lean-fleshed kine being unaffected after eating the fat-fleshed cattle.

25-28. אֶת אֲשֶׁר הָאֱלֹהִים עֹשֶׂה הִגִּיד לְפַרְעֹה ... הֶרְאָה אֶת פַּרְעֹה – *What God is about to do, He has declared to Pharaoh ... He has shown to Pharaoh*. The word הִגִּיד, *declared*, is used in one verse and הֶרְאָה, *shown*, in the other. The former refers to the foretelling of the famine, while the latter is instructing Pharaoh what action to take to save his people. God is 'telling' and 'showing,' revealing and teaching. Therefore when Joseph, in verse 33, told Pharaoh to appoint an administrator, he was not advising him, for that would be presumptuous. He was merely continuing to interpret the dream which he had been invited to do.

33. אִישׁ נָבוֹן וְחָכָם – *A man discerning and wise*. (a) The dual expression נָבוֹן, *discerning*, and חָכָם, *wise*, was used advisedly by Joseph, for this man must be both theoretician and manager. (b) The expression 'that the king shall have no damage' is borrowed from *Daniel* 6:3.

34. יַעֲשֶׂה פַרְעֹה וְיַפְקֵד – *Let Pharaoh do this and appoint*. The verse from *Deuteronomy* quoted by the *Sforno* speaks of the Supreme

לז-לח הָאָרֶץ בָּרָעָב: וַיִּיטַב הַדָּבָר בְּעֵינֵי פַרְעֹה וּבְעֵינֵי כָּל־עֲבָדָיו: וַיֹּאמֶר פַּרְעֹה
שלישי לט אֶל־עֲבָדָיו הֲנִמְצָא כָזֶה אִישׁ אֲשֶׁר רוּחַ אֱלֹהִים בּוֹ: וַיֹּאמֶר פַּרְעֹה אֶל־יוֹסֵף
מ אַחֲרֵי הוֹדִיעַ אֱלֹהִים אוֹתְךָ אֶת־כָּל־זֹאת אֵין־נָבוֹן וְחָכָם כָּמוֹךָ: אַתָּה
מא תִּהְיֶה עַל־בֵּיתִי וְעַל־פִּיךָ יִשַּׁק כָּל־עַמִּי רַק הַכִּסֵּא אֶגְדַּל מִמֶּךָּ: וַיֹּאמֶר
מב פַּרְעֹה אֶל־יוֹסֵף רְאֵה נָתַתִּי אֹתְךָ עַל כָּל־אֶרֶץ מִצְרָיִם: וַיָּסַר פַּרְעֹה אֶת־
טַבַּעְתּוֹ מֵעַל יָדוֹ וַיִּתֵּן אֹתָהּ עַל־יַד יוֹסֵף וַיַּלְבֵּשׁ אֹתוֹ בִּגְדֵי־שֵׁשׁ וַיָּשֶׂם
מג רְבִד הַזָּהָב עַל־צַוָּארוֹ: וַיַּרְכֵּב אֹתוֹ בְּמִרְכֶּבֶת הַמִּשְׁנֶה אֲשֶׁר־לוֹ וַיִּקְרְאוּ
מד לְפָנָיו אַבְרֵךְ וְנָתוֹן אֹתוֹ עַל כָּל־אֶרֶץ מִצְרָיִם: וַיֹּאמֶר פַּרְעֹה אֶל־יוֹסֵף אֲנִי
פַרְעֹה וּבִלְעָדֶיךָ לֹא־יָרִים אִישׁ אֶת־יָדוֹ וְאֶת־רַגְלוֹ בְּכָל־אֶרֶץ מִצְרָיִם:
מה וַיִּקְרָא פַרְעֹה שֵׁם־יוֹסֵף צָפְנַת פַּעְנֵחַ וַיִּתֶּן־לוֹ אֶת־אָסְנַת בַּת־פּוֹטִי פֶרַע
מו כֹּהֵן אֹן לְאִשָּׁה וַיֵּצֵא יוֹסֵף עַל־אֶרֶץ מִצְרָיִם: וְיוֹסֵף בֶּן־שְׁלֹשִׁים שָׁנָה בְּעָמְדוֹ
לִפְנֵי פַּרְעֹה מֶלֶךְ־מִצְרָיִם וַיֵּצֵא יוֹסֵף מִלִּפְנֵי פַרְעֹה וַיַּעֲבֹר בְּכָל־אֶרֶץ
מז-מח מִצְרָיִם: וַתַּעַשׂ הָאָרֶץ בְּשֶׁבַע שְׁנֵי הַשָּׂבָע לִקְמָצִים: וַיִּקְבֹּץ אֶת־כָּל־אֹכֶל ׀
שֶׁבַע שָׁנִים אֲשֶׁר הָיוּ בְּאֶרֶץ מִצְרַיִם וַיִּתֶּן־אֹכֶל בֶּעָרִים אֹכֶל שְׂדֵה־הָעִיר
מט אֲשֶׁר סְבִיבֹתֶיהָ נָתַן בְּתוֹכָהּ: וַיִּצְבֹּר יוֹסֵף בָּר כְּחוֹל הַיָּם הַרְבֵּה מְאֹד עַד
נ כִּי־חָדַל לִסְפֹּר כִּי־אֵין מִסְפָּר: וּלְיוֹסֵף יֻלַּד שְׁנֵי בָנִים בְּטֶרֶם תָּבוֹא שְׁנַת

---

37. וַיִּיטַב הַדָּבָר — *And the thing was good* . . . Joseph's advice and (suggested) plan.

41. רְאֵה נָתַתִּי אֹתְךָ עַל כָּל אֶרֶץ מִצְרָיִם — *See, I have set you over all the land of Egypt.* See that you do your best, for I have entrusted you with a great responsibility.

43. וַיִּקְרְאוּ לְפָנָיו אַבְרֵךְ — *And they cried before him, 'Avrech'* . . . similar to הַבְרֵךְ, *let all bend the knee*, as it is customary to cry out to the people when the king passes by.

וְנָתוֹן אֹתוֹ עַל כָּל אֶרֶץ מִצְרָיִם — *And he set him over all the land of Egypt.* They all accepted his authority as is customary when a new king is coronated.

45. וַיֵּצֵא יוֹסֵף עַל אֶרֶץ מִצְרָיִם — *And Joseph went out over the land of Egypt.* He left the presence of Pharaoh in an authoritative and stately manner, indicating that he was the governor of all Egypt.

46. וַיַּעֲבֹר בְּכָל אֶרֶץ מִצְרָיִם — *And went throughout the land of Egypt* . . . to attend to its affairs and make all necessary arrangements, as we find by Samuel, וְסָבַב בֵּית אֵל . . . וְהַמִּצְפָּה, *(He would set forth) and go to Bethel . . . and Mitzpah (I Samuel* 7:16).

47. לִקְמָצִים — *In heaps.* Every ear of corn produced a handful.

49. כִּי אֵין מִסְפָּר — *For it was without number.* The quantities were beyond human calculation.

NOTES

Court in Jerusalem, be it the priests, the Levites, the king or the Sanhedrin, who are the final arbiters. And here too, there must be one central authority, else there will be anarchy and chaos.

37. וַיִּיטַב הַדָּבָר — *And the thing was good.* The phrase וַיִּיטַב הַדָּבָר, *And the thing was good*, does not refer to Joseph's interpretation of the dream. An interpretation is either accepted or not. It is not a matter of judgment and taste.

נא הָרָעָב אֲשֶׁר יָלְדָה־לּוֹ אָסְנַת בַּת־פּוֹטִי פֶרַע כֹּהֵן אוֹן׃ וַיִּקְרָא יוֹסֵף אֶת־שֵׁם
נב הַבְּכוֹר מְנַשֶּׁה כִּי־נַשַּׁנִי אֱלֹהִים אֶת־כָּל־עֲמָלִי וְאֵת כָּל־בֵּית אָבִי׃ וְאֵת
רביעי נג שֵׁם הַשֵּׁנִי קָרָא אֶפְרָיִם כִּי־הִפְרַנִי אֱלֹהִים בְּאֶרֶץ עָנְיִי׃ וַתִּכְלֶינָה שֶׁבַע שְׁנֵי
נד הַשָּׂבָע אֲשֶׁר הָיָה בְּאֶרֶץ מִצְרָיִם׃ וַתְּחִלֶּינָה שֶׁבַע שְׁנֵי הָרָעָב לָבוֹא כַּאֲשֶׁר
נה אָמַר יוֹסֵף וַיְהִי רָעָב בְּכָל־הָאֲרָצוֹת וּבְכָל־אֶרֶץ מִצְרַיִם הָיָה לָחֶם׃ וַתִּרְעַב
כָּל־אֶרֶץ מִצְרַיִם וַיִּצְעַק הָעָם אֶל־פַּרְעֹה לַלָּחֶם וַיֹּאמֶר פַּרְעֹה לְכָל־מִצְרַיִם
נו לְכוּ אֶל־יוֹסֵף אֲשֶׁר־יֹאמַר לָכֶם תַּעֲשׂוּ׃ וְהָרָעָב הָיָה עַל כָּל־פְּנֵי הָאָרֶץ
וַיִּפְתַּח יוֹסֵף אֶת־כָּל־אֲשֶׁר בָּהֶם וַיִּשְׁבֹּר לְמִצְרַיִם וַיֶּחֱזַק הָרָעָב בְּאֶרֶץ
נז מִצְרָיִם׃ וְכָל־הָאָרֶץ בָּאוּ מִצְרַיְמָה לִשְׁבֹּר אֶל־יוֹסֵף כִּי־חָזַק הָרָעָב
מב א בְּכָל־הָאָרֶץ׃ וַיַּרְא יַעֲקֹב כִּי יֶשׁ־שֶׁבֶר בְּמִצְרָיִם וַיֹּאמֶר יַעֲקֹב לְבָנָיו לָמָּה
ב תִּתְרָאוּ׃ וַיֹּאמֶר הִנֵּה שָׁמַעְתִּי כִּי יֶשׁ־שֶׁבֶר בְּמִצְרָיִם רְדוּ־שָׁמָּה וְשִׁבְרוּ־לָנוּ
ג מִשָּׁם וְנִחְיֶה וְלֹא נָמוּת׃ וַיֵּרְדוּ אֲחֵי־יוֹסֵף עֲשָׂרָה לִשְׁבֹּר בָּר מִמִּצְרָיִם׃

---

51. כִּי נַשַּׁנִי אֱלֹהִים — *For God has made me forget* ... as it shall be regarding the future, as it is written, כִּי נִשְׁכְּחוּ הַצָּרוֹת הָרִאשֹׁנוֹת, *Because the former troubles are forgotten (Isaiah* 65:16).

56. וַיִּפְתַּח יוֹסֵף אֶת כָּל אֲשֶׁר בָּהֶם — *And Joseph opened all the storehouses* ... to show them that there was enough to feed all of them.

וַיֶּחֱזַק הָרָעָב — *And the famine was sore* ... in all kinds of food, besides bread.

XLII

1. לָמָּה תִּתְרָאוּ — *Why do you look upon one another?* Why do you look at each other, each waiting for the other to go? As our Sages say: קִדְרָא דְבֵי שֻׁתְּפֵי לָא חֲמִימָא וְלָא קְרִירָא, *A partners' pot is neither hot or cold (Eruvin* 3a), and נִתְרָאֶה פָנִים, *Let us look one another in the face* (*II Kings* 14:8), i.e., let us meet with one another.

2. וְנִחְיֶה — *That we may live* ... not in plenty, but that we may have enough to keep us alive, and thus ...

וְלֹא נָמוּת — *And not die.* From hunger.

3. וַיֵּרְדוּ אֲחֵי יוֹסֵף עֲשָׂרָה — *And Joseph's ten brothers went down.* The Egyptian

NOTES

Therefore the *Sforno* comments, 'advice and plan,' regarding the appointment of a governor, especially since it presents the opportunity for a new important government position.

51. כִּי נַשַּׁנִי אֱלֹהִים — *For God has made me forget.* Joseph certainly did not forget his father Jacob and all that he had taught him. Indeed, the image of his father had prevented him from sinning with Potiphar's wife. Rather it must be understood in the manner that the quote from *Isaiah* implies: the memory of his travail and suffering had faded and was not as keen and painful as it once had been. This is also a portent for the future destiny of the Jewish people. They will also eventually forget the troubles of the past when they will be redeemed.

56. וַיִּפְתַּח יוֹסֵף — *And Joseph opened.* Joseph showed the people that there was plenty of food in the storehouses so as to prevent panic and food riots.

XLII

1. לָמָּה תִּתְרָאוּ — *Why do you look upon one another?* The reason that the partners' pot is 'neither hot nor cold' is because each depends on the other to light the fire and keep it

ד וְאֶת־בִּנְיָמִין֙ אֲחִ֣י יוֹסֵ֔ף לֹא־שָׁלַ֥ח יַעֲקֹ֖ב אֶת־אֶחָ֑יו כִּ֣י אָמַ֔ר פֶּן־יִקְרָאֶ֖נּוּ
ה אָסֽוֹן׃ וַיָּבֹ֙אוּ֙ בְּנֵ֣י יִשְׂרָאֵ֔ל לִשְׁבֹּ֖ר בְּת֣וֹךְ הַבָּאִ֑ים כִּֽי־הָיָ֥ה הָרָעָ֖ב בְּאֶ֥רֶץ כְּנָֽעַן׃
ו וְיוֹסֵ֗ף ה֚וּא הַשַּׁלִּ֣יט עַל־הָאָ֔רֶץ ה֥וּא הַמַּשְׁבִּ֖יר לְכָל־עַ֣ם הָאָ֑רֶץ וַיָּבֹ֙אוּ֙ אֲחֵ֣י
ז יוֹסֵ֔ף וַיִּשְׁתַּֽחֲווּ־ל֥וֹ אַפַּ֖יִם אָֽרְצָה׃ וַיַּ֥רְא יוֹסֵ֛ף אֶת־אֶחָ֖יו וַיַּכִּרֵ֑ם וַיִּתְנַכֵּ֨ר
אֲלֵיהֶ֜ם וַיְדַבֵּ֧ר אִתָּ֣ם קָשׁ֗וֹת וַיֹּ֤אמֶר אֲלֵהֶם֙ מֵאַ֣יִן בָּאתֶ֔ם וַיֹּ֣אמְר֔וּ מֵאֶ֥רֶץ
ח-ט כְּנַ֖עַן לִשְׁבָּר־אֹֽכֶל׃ וַיַּכֵּ֥ר יוֹסֵ֖ף אֶת־אֶחָ֑יו וְהֵ֖ם לֹ֥א הִכִּרֻֽהוּ׃ וַיִּזְכֹּ֣ר יוֹסֵ֔ף אֵ֚ת
הַחֲלֹמ֔וֹת אֲשֶׁ֥ר חָלַ֖ם לָהֶ֑ם וַיֹּ֤אמֶר אֲלֵהֶם֙ מְרַגְּלִ֣ים אַתֶּ֔ם לִרְא֛וֹת אֶת־עֶרְוַ֥ת

---

authorities sold only to private households and not large quantities to individuals who might trade in the corn, as is customary in time of famine.

5. בְּתוֹךְ הַבָּאִים — *Among those that came.* They traveled in large companies as protection against bandits who would be particularly numerous because of the famine.

6. הוּא הַשַּׁלִּיט עַל הָאָרֶץ הוּא הַמַּשְׁבִּיר — *He was the governor over the land; it was he that sold.* Though he was the governor, he himself attended to the sales, not trusting his servants, for it involved large sums of money which belonged to Pharaoh, as it is written, *And Joseph brought the money into Pharaoh's house* (47:14); therefore he arranged that nothing should be sold without his seal or signature.

וַיָּבֹאוּ אֲחֵי יוֹסֵף וַיִּשְׁתַּחֲווּ לוֹ — *And Joseph's brothers came and bowed down to him.* Since Joseph was both governor and seller (of the corn) the brothers had to deal directly with him, and not through his servants.

7. וַיַּכִּרֵם — *And he knew them.* He recognized them (at first) as his brothers collectively, but not individually.

וַיִּתְנַכֵּר אֲלֵיהֶם — *But made himself strange with them.* He changed his manner, and did not speak humbly, as was his usual manner.

קָשׁוֹת — *(And spoke) roughly . . .* lest they recognize him by his voice.

8. וַיַּכֵּר יוֹסֵף אֶת אֶחָיו — *And Joseph knew his brethren.* Afterward (he recognized them) individually.

9. וַיִּזְכֹּר יוֹסֵף אֵת הַחֲלֹמוֹת אֲשֶׁר חָלַם לָהֶם — *And Joseph remembered the dreams which he dreamed of them.* He remembered his dreams of them, that in the dream

NOTES

burning. Jacob chided his sons for failing to do anything about obtaining food from Egypt, each depending upon the other.

3. וַיֵּרְדוּ אֲחֵי יוֹסֵף עֲשָׂרָה — *And Joseph's ten brothers went down.* Were it not for the restrictions placed upon the purchase of corn by Egypt, limiting a certain amount per person, there would be no reason for all ten brothers to come.

6. הוּא הַשַּׁלִּיט . . . הוּא הַמַּשְׁבִּיר — *He was the governor . . . it was he that sold.* The terms שַׁלִּיט and מַשְׁבִּיר refer to two separate and different roles, one was governor while the other was in charge of selling the provisions. Normally Joseph would have delegated the latter to his servants. The reason he did not do so was because he was concerned for the integrity of the coffers of Pharaoh. This dual role played by Joseph explains how his brothers came face to face with him, for under normal circumstances they would have dealt with an underling and would never have met their brother.

9. וַיִּזְכֹּר יוֹסֵף אֵת הַחֲלֹמוֹת — *And Joseph remembered the dreams.* Joseph did not reveal

י־יא הָאָרֶץ בָּאתֶם: וַיֹּאמְרוּ אֵלָיו לֹא אֲדֹנִי וַעֲבָדֶיךָ בָּאוּ לִשְׁבָּר־אֹכֶל: כֻּלָּנוּ
יב בְּנֵי אִישׁ־אֶחָד נָחְנוּ כֵּנִים אֲנַחְנוּ לֹא־הָיוּ עֲבָדֶיךָ מְרַגְּלִים: וַיֹּאמֶר אֲלֵהֶם
יג לֹא כִּי־עֶרְוַת הָאָרֶץ בָּאתֶם לִרְאוֹת: וַיֹּאמְרוּ שְׁנֵים עָשָׂר עֲבָדֶיךָ אַחִים ׀
אֲנַחְנוּ בְּנֵי אִישׁ־אֶחָד בְּאֶרֶץ כְּנָעַן וְהִנֵּה הַקָּטֹן אֶת־אָבִינוּ הַיּוֹם וְהָאֶחָד
יד אֵינֶנּוּ: וַיֹּאמֶר אֲלֵהֶם יוֹסֵף הוּא אֲשֶׁר דִּבַּרְתִּי אֲלֵכֶם לֵאמֹר מְרַגְּלִים אַתֶּם:

---

of the sheaves all bowed (to him) and that his sheaf stood upright, not falling. He therefore wanted them all to come and recognize him in order to fulfill, וְגַם נִצָּבָה, *and it stood* (37:7). (He did this) in order that he be a symbol of the future redeemer, as we find, יְרֵה וַיּוֹר, *'Shoot!' And he shot* (*II Kings* 13:17), as it says, וְנִקְבְּצוּ בְּנֵי יְהוּדָה וּבְנֵי יִשְׂרָאֵל יַחְדָּו וְשָׂמוּ לָהֶם רֹאשׁ אֶחָד, *And the children of Judah and the children of Israel shall be gathered together and they shall appoint themselves one head* (*Hosea* 2:2), and that (the symbolism of) וְגַם נִצָּבָה be fulfilled, as it says, מַלְכוּ דִּי לְעָלְמִין לָא תִתְחַבַּל, *A kingdom which shall never be destroyed* (*Daniel* 2:44).

לִרְאוֹת אֶת עֶרְוַת הָאָרֶץ בָּאתֶם — *To see the nakedness of the land did you come . . .* to determine the quantity of our food stores if it be sufficient for our needs. You did not come simply to purchase for it is not customary for so many (ten) to come as one group.

11. כֻּלָּנוּ בְּנֵי אִישׁ אֶחָד נָחְנוּ — *We are all one man's sons.* If we are spies, spying on behalf of a foreign power, no king would choose ten men from one family! We are together, because we are indeed brothers.

כֵּנִים אֲנַחְנוּ — *We are upright men . . .* in all our endeavors.

לֹא הָיוּ עֲבָדֶיךָ מְרַגְּלִים — *Your servants are no spies.* We never were, and there is no reason to suspect us now, of being spies.

12. לֹא — *Nay.* It is not true that you are brothers.

כִּי עֶרְוַת הָאָרֶץ בָּאתֶם לִרְאוֹת — *But to see the nakedness of the land have you come.* You plotted to claim you are brothers, so as to mask your (true intentions) to see the nakedness of the land.

13. שְׁנֵים עָשָׂר עֲבָדֶיךָ אַחִים אֲנַחְנוּ בְּנֵי אִישׁ אֶחָד בְּאֶרֶץ כְּנָעַן — *We, your servants, are twelve brothers, the sons of one man in the Land of Canaan.* What we say can be ascertained, for our father lives in Canaan, and it can be verified by him and our neighbors that we were twelve sons, but one is missing and the youngest is home attending to the household. All these details can be established as true, to your satisfaction.

14. הוּא אֲשֶׁר דִּבַּרְתִּי אֲלֵכֶם — *That is that which I spoke to you.* The one that you say is *not,* and you do not explain what happened to him, has probably gone back to reveal the information that you gathered or (perhaps) you plotted (all this) in order to spy, as I have said.

NOTES

himself immediately to his brothers for a variety of reasons, one of them being his conviction that the fulfillment of his dreams in their entirety was necessary to establish a precedent for the future complete and lasting redemption of Israel. He represented the model for the אַחֲרִית הַיָּמִים, *the end of days,* when Israel will be unified under one leader, never to

טו בְּזֹאת תִּבָּחֵנוּ חֵי פַרְעֹה אִם־תֵּצְאוּ מִזֶּה כִּי אִם־בְּבוֹא אֲחִיכֶם הַקָּטֹן הֵנָּה:
טז שִׁלְחוּ מִכֶּם אֶחָד וְיִקַּח אֶת־אֲחִיכֶם וְאַתֶּם הֵאָסְרוּ וְיִבָּחֲנוּ דִּבְרֵיכֶם הַאֱמֶת
יז אִתְּכֶם וְאִם־לֹא חֵי פַרְעֹה כִּי מְרַגְּלִים אַתֶּם: וַיֶּאֱסֹף אֹתָם אֶל־מִשְׁמָר
יח שְׁלֹשֶׁת יָמִים: וַיֹּאמֶר אֲלֵהֶם יוֹסֵף בַּיּוֹם הַשְּׁלִישִׁי זֹאת עֲשׂוּ וִחְיוּ אֶת־
חמישי יט הָאֱלֹהִים אֲנִי יָרֵא: אִם־כֵּנִים אַתֶּם אֲחִיכֶם אֶחָד יֵאָסֵר בְּבֵית מִשְׁמַרְכֶם
כ וְאַתֶּם לְכוּ הָבִיאוּ שֶׁבֶר רַעֲבוֹן בָּתֵּיכֶם: וְאֶת־אֲחִיכֶם הַקָּטֹן תָּבִיאוּ אֵלַי
כא וְיֵאָמְנוּ דִבְרֵיכֶם וְלֹא תָמוּתוּ וַיַּעֲשׂוּ־כֵן: וַיֹּאמְרוּ אִישׁ אֶל־אָחִיו אֲבָל
אֲשֵׁמִים | אֲנַחְנוּ עַל־אָחִינוּ אֲשֶׁר רָאִינוּ צָרַת נַפְשׁוֹ בְּהִתְחַנְנוֹ אֵלֵינוּ וְלֹא
כב שָׁמָעְנוּ עַל־כֵּן בָּאָה אֵלֵינוּ הַצָּרָה הַזֹּאת: וַיַּעַן רְאוּבֵן אֹתָם לֵאמֹר הֲלוֹא
אָמַרְתִּי אֲלֵיכֶם | לֵאמֹר אַל־תֶּחֶטְאוּ בַיֶּלֶד וְלֹא שְׁמַעְתֶּם וְגַם־דָּמוֹ הִנֵּה
כג־כד נִדְרָשׁ: וְהֵם לֹא יָדְעוּ כִּי שֹׁמֵעַ יוֹסֵף כִּי הַמֵּלִיץ בֵּינֹתָם: וַיִּסֹּב מֵעֲלֵיהֶם וַיֵּבְךְּ
וַיָּשָׁב אֲלֵהֶם וַיְדַבֵּר אֲלֵהֶם וַיִּקַּח מֵאִתָּם אֶת־שִׁמְעוֹן וַיֶּאֱסֹר אֹתוֹ לְעֵינֵיהֶם:

---

15. בְּזֹאת תִּבָּחֵנוּ — *Hereby, you shall be proved.* If you are not brothers, the younger one will not risk coming with you and thereby place himself unnecessarily (lit., 'falsely') at risk of death which now faces you (lit., 'together with you').

18. אֶת הָאֱלֹהִים אֲנִי יָרֵא — *For I fear God* ... therefore, I will allow you to take home the provisions that you need.

20. וְלֹא תָמוּתוּ — *And you shall not die* ... for even in Canaan I can have you put to death if you do not return.

21. בְּהִתְחַנְנוֹ אֵלֵינוּ וְלֹא שָׁמָעְנוּ — *When he besought us and we would not hear.* Because we were so callous toward our brother, and we should have had more compassion, even though we considered him a רוֹדֵף, *pursuer.* Now this ruler is treating us cruelly just as we did our brother (measure for measure).

22. הֲלוֹא אָמַרְתִּי אֲלֵיכֶם לֵאמֹר אַל תֶּחֶטְאוּ בַיֶּלֶד — *Didn't I speak and say to you, 'Don't sin against the boy'?* He had no intention to kill you when he did what he did, even though you thought so. What he did was due to his childish immaturity, not done with (malice).

וְגַם דָּמוֹ הִנֵּה נִדְרָשׁ — *Therefore also behold, his blood is required.* Not only is the cruelty shown to him being repaid to you now, but *his blood* as well, for you slew him as well, even though he was innocent, since he must have died by now through (the) hard labor (imposed on him).

24. וַיֵּבְךְּ — *And he wept* ... because of their distress.

NOTES

be dispersed or destroyed (as the verses from *Hosea* and *Daniel* prophesy). Therefore Benjamin had to come down as well, to complete the number of eleven as shown in the dream of the sheaves, and eventually his father Jacob as well, to fulfill the second dream.

21-28. בְּהִתְחַנְנוֹ אֵלֵינוּ ... מַה זֹּאת עָשָׂה אֱלֹהִים לָנוּ — *When he besought us ... What is this that God has done to us?* The brothers did not regret the sale of Joseph for they felt justified in their decision, based upon their conviction that he was a רוֹדֵף, *pursuer,* who according to *Halachah* can even be killed in self-defense. If anything, they felt that they were lenient with him by selling him rather than executing him as they had originally decided to do before being dissuaded by Judah. They did however

כה וַיְצַו יוֹסֵף וַיְמַלְא֣וּ אֶת־כְּלֵיהֶם֮ בָּר֒ וּלְהָשִׁיב כַּסְפֵּיהֶם֙ אִ֣ישׁ אֶל־שַׂקּ֔וֹ וְלָתֵ֥ת

כו לָהֶ֛ם צֵדָ֖ה לַדָּ֑רֶךְ וַיַּ֥עַשׂ לָהֶ֖ם כֵּֽן: וַיִּשְׂא֥וּ אֶת־שִׁבְרָ֖ם עַל־חֲמֹרֵיהֶ֑ם וַיֵּלְכ֖וּ

כז מִשָּֽׁם: וַיִּפְתַּ֨ח הָאֶחָ֜ד אֶת־שַׂקּ֗וֹ לָתֵ֥ת מִסְפּ֛וֹא לַחֲמֹר֖וֹ בַּמָּל֑וֹן וַיַּרְא֙ אֶת־

כח כַּסְפּ֔וֹ וְהִנֵּה־ה֖וּא בְּפִ֣י אַמְתַּחְתּֽוֹ: וַיֹּ֣אמֶר אֶל־אֶחָיו֩ הוּשַׁ֨ב כַּסְפִּ֜י וְגַ֨ם הִנֵּ֤ה

בְאַמְתַּחְתִּי֙ וַיֵּצֵ֣א לִבָּ֔ם וַיֶּחֶרְד֞וּ אִ֣ישׁ אֶל־אָחִ֣יו לֵאמֹ֔ר מַה־זֹּ֛את עָשָׂ֥ה

כט אֱלֹהִ֖ים לָֽנוּ: וַיָּבֹ֛אוּ אֶל־יַעֲקֹ֥ב אֲבִיהֶ֖ם אַ֣רְצָה כְּנָ֑עַן וַיַּגִּ֣ידוּ ל֔וֹ אֵ֥ת כָּל־הַקֹּרֹ֖ת

ל אֹתָ֖ם לֵאמֹֽר: דִּ֠בֶּר הָאִ֨ישׁ אֲדֹנֵ֥י הָאָ֛רֶץ אִתָּ֖נוּ קָשׁ֑וֹת וַיִּתֵּ֣ן אֹתָ֔נוּ כִּֽמְרַגְּלִ֖ים

לא-לב אֶת־הָאָֽרֶץ: וַנֹּ֥אמֶר אֵלָ֖יו כֵּנִ֣ים אֲנָ֑חְנוּ לֹ֥א הָיִ֖ינוּ מְרַגְּלִֽים: שְׁנֵים־עָשָׂ֧ר

אֲנַ֛חְנוּ אַחִ֖ים בְּנֵ֣י אָבִ֑ינוּ הָאֶחָ֣ד אֵינֶ֔נּוּ וְהַקָּטֹ֥ן הַיּ֛וֹם אֶת־אָבִ֖ינוּ בְּאֶ֥רֶץ כְּנָֽעַן:

לג וַיֹּ֣אמֶר אֵלֵ֗ינוּ הָאִישׁ֙ אֲדֹנֵ֣י הָאָ֔רֶץ בְּזֹ֣את אֵדַ֔ע כִּ֥י כֵנִ֖ים אַתֶּ֑ם אֲחִיכֶ֤ם הָֽאֶחָד֙

לד הַנִּ֣יחוּ אִתִּ֔י וְאֶת־רַעֲב֥וֹן בָּתֵּיכֶ֖ם קְח֣וּ וָלֵֽכוּ: וְ֠הָבִ֠יאוּ אֶת־אֲחִיכֶ֣ם הַקָּטֹן֮ אֵלַי֒

וְאֵ֣דְעָ֔ה כִּ֣י לֹ֤א מְרַגְּלִים֙ אַתֶּ֔ם כִּ֥י כֵנִ֖ים אַתֶּ֑ם אֶת־אֲחִיכֶם֙ אֶתֵּ֣ן לָכֶ֔ם

לה וְאֶת־הָאָ֖רֶץ תִּסְחָֽרוּ: וַיְהִ֗י הֵ֚ם מְרִיקִ֣ים שַׂקֵּיהֶ֔ם וְהִנֵּה־אִ֥ישׁ צְרוֹר־כַּסְפּ֖וֹ

לו בְּשַׂקּ֑וֹ וַיִּרְא֞וּ אֶת־צְרֹר֧וֹת כַּסְפֵּיהֶ֛ם הֵ֥מָּה וַאֲבִיהֶ֖ם וַיִּירָֽאוּ: וַיֹּ֣אמֶר אֲלֵהֶם֮

יַעֲקֹ֣ב אֲבִיהֶם֒ אֹתִ֖י שִׁכַּלְתֶּ֑ם יוֹסֵ֣ף אֵינֶ֗נּוּ וְשִׁמְע֤וֹן אֵינֶ֙נּוּ֙ וְאֶת־בִּנְיָמִ֣ן תִּקָּ֔חוּ

לז עָלַ֖י הָי֥וּ כֻלָּֽנָה: וַיֹּ֤אמֶר רְאוּבֵן֙ אֶל־אָבִ֣יו לֵאמֹ֔ר אֶת־שְׁנֵ֤י בָנַי֙ תָּמִ֔ית

לח אִם־לֹ֥א אֲבִיאֶ֖נּוּ אֵלֶ֑יךָ תְּנָ֤ה אֹתוֹ֙ עַל־יָדִ֔י וַאֲנִ֖י אֲשִׁיבֶ֣נּוּ אֵלֶ֑יךָ: וַיֹּ֖אמֶר

---

25. וּלְהָשִׁיב כַּסְפֵּיהֶם — *And to restore their silver coins* (lit., *their monies*). The plural form (of the word כֶּסֶף which can mean either silver or money) does not apply to money but to (silver) coins.

28. מַה־זֹּאת עָשָׂה אֱלֹהִים לָנוּ — *What is this that God has done to us?* . . . that He has caused this man, who claims to fear God, to use this pretext to enslave us, as it is written later, *and to take us for slaves* (43:18). This has come to pass to repay us, measure for measure, for selling our brother; even though we did it not because of wickedness, but because we believed him to be a רוֹדֵף, *pursuer*, and worthy even to be put to death, which we refrained from doing as a חֶסֶד, *kindness*, since he is our brother.

36. עָלַי הָיוּ כֻלָּנָה — *Upon me have all these things come.* Such things have happened to my children, but to none of yours. The reason must undoubtedly be on account of your quarrels. (Therefore I regard) you as the cause of my bereavement.

37. אֶת שְׁנֵי בָנַי תָּמִית — *You shall slay my two sons.* Curse my two sons that they should die if I do not bring him (Benjamin) back to you, as we find the curse of Rav to Shmuel, יְהֵא רַעֲוָא . . . דְּלָא לוֹקְמוּ לֵיהּ בְּנֵי, וְכֵן הֲוָה, 'May no sons arise from him.' And thus it was (*Shabbos* 108a).

NOTES

admit their callousness and cruelty in turning a deaf ear to Joseph's pleas, and therefore felt that their present plight and distress was a punishment from God for this transgression.

37. אֶת שְׁנֵי בָנַי תָּמִית — *You shall slay my two sons.* The *Sforno*, like many other commentators, wishes to avoid the literal meaning of תָּמִית, *to slay;* therefore he chooses to translate

לֹא־יֵרֵד בְּנִי עִמָּכֶם כִּי־אָחִיו מֵת וְהוּא לְבַדּוֹ נִשְׁאָר וּקְרָאָהוּ אָסוֹן בַּדֶּרֶךְ
מג א אֲשֶׁר תֵּלְכוּ־בָהּ וְהוֹרַדְתֶּם אֶת־שֵׂיבָתִי בְּיָגוֹן שְׁאוֹלָה: וְהָרָעָב כָּבֵד בָּאָרֶץ:
ב וַיְהִי כַּאֲשֶׁר כִּלּוּ לֶאֱכֹל אֶת־הַשֶּׁבֶר אֲשֶׁר הֵבִיאוּ מִמִּצְרָיִם וַיֹּאמֶר אֲלֵיהֶם
ג אֲבִיהֶם שֻׁבוּ שִׁבְרוּ־לָנוּ מְעַט־אֹכֶל: וַיֹּאמֶר אֵלָיו יְהוּדָה לֵאמֹר הָעֵד הֵעִד
ד בָּנוּ הָאִישׁ לֵאמֹר לֹא־תִרְאוּ פָנַי בִּלְתִּי אֲחִיכֶם אִתְּכֶם: אִם־יֶשְׁךָ מְשַׁלֵּחַ
ה אֶת־אָחִינוּ אִתָּנוּ נֵרְדָה וְנִשְׁבְּרָה לְךָ אֹכֶל: וְאִם־אֵינְךָ מְשַׁלֵּחַ לֹא נֵרֵד
ו כִּי־הָאִישׁ אָמַר אֵלֵינוּ לֹא־תִרְאוּ פָנַי בִּלְתִּי אֲחִיכֶם אִתְּכֶם: וַיֹּאמֶר
ז יִשְׂרָאֵל לָמָה הֲרֵעֹתֶם לִי לְהַגִּיד לָאִישׁ הַעוֹד לָכֶם אָח: וַיֹּאמְרוּ שָׁאוֹל
שָׁאַל־הָאִישׁ לָנוּ וּלְמוֹלַדְתֵּנוּ לֵאמֹר הַעוֹד אֲבִיכֶם חַי הֲיֵשׁ לָכֶם אָח
וַנַּגֶּד־לוֹ עַל־פִּי הַדְּבָרִים הָאֵלֶּה הֲיָדוֹעַ נֵדַע כִּי יֹאמַר הוֹרִידוּ אֶת־אֲחִיכֶם:
ח וַיֹּאמֶר יְהוּדָה אֶל־יִשְׂרָאֵל אָבִיו שִׁלְחָה הַנַּעַר אִתִּי וְנָקוּמָה וְנֵלֵכָה וְנִחְיֶה
ט וְלֹא נָמוּת גַּם־אֲנַחְנוּ גַם־אַתָּה גַּם־טַפֵּנוּ: אָנֹכִי אֶעֶרְבֶנּוּ מִיָּדִי תְּבַקְשֶׁנּוּ
י אִם־לֹא הֲבִיאֹתִיו אֵלֶיךָ וְהִצַּגְתִּיו לְפָנֶיךָ וְחָטָאתִי לְךָ כָּל־הַיָּמִים: כִּי לוּלֵא
יא הִתְמַהְמָהְנוּ כִּי־עַתָּה שַׁבְנוּ זֶה פַעֲמָיִם: וַיֹּאמֶר אֲלֵהֶם יִשְׂרָאֵל אֲבִיהֶם

---

38. לֹא יֵרֵד בְּנִי — *My son shall not go down.* He is the only one left of his mother who was the cornerstone of the house.

XLIII

2. שֻׁבוּ שִׁבְרוּ לָנוּ — *Go again, bring us (a little food).* (Jacob) disbelieved their story and thought that they only wanted an opportunity to kill Benjamin as they had Joseph, as he said to them, 'אֹתִי שִׁכַּלְתֶּם, *You have bereaved me*' (42:36).

8. וְנִחְיֶה — *That we may live.* With food.

וְלֹא נָמוּת — *And not die* . . . in accordance with the words of the master of the land (Egypt) who said to us, *So shall your words be verified and you shall not die* (42:20).

10. כִּי לוּלֵא הִתְמַהְמָהְנוּ — *For had we not lingered.* The reason I accepted upon myself everlasting blame (lit., 'eternal sin') if I didn't bring him back is because it is clear to me that had we not lingered from the time we told you the words of the man or from the time the (supply of) grain ended (and returned with Benjamin earlier . . .)

NOTES

it as *curse.*

38. לֹא יֵרֵד בְּנִי — *My son shall not go down.* The phrase בְּנִי, *my son,* applied by Jacob to Benjamin is explained as referring to the only son left him from his beloved wife Rachel.

XLIII

2. שֻׁבוּ שִׁבְרוּ לָנוּ — *Go again, bring us (a little food).* By using the expression שֻׁבוּ, *return,* Jacob is stressing and reiterating that only those who went the first time should now return — without Benjamin, for he does not trust them when it comes to the children of Rachel.

8. וְנִחְיֶה וְלֹא נָמוּת — *That we may live and not die.* Once Judah said וְנִחְיֶה, *that we may live,* it is not necessary to add וְלֹא נָמוּת, *and not die.* The reason he added these words was to remind his father that the ruler of Egypt had warned them that if they failed to return with their youngest brother, he would pursue and find them even in Canaan and have them punished. See the *Sforno* to 42:20.

10. כִּי לוּלֵא הִתְמַהְמָהְנוּ כִּי עַתָּה שַׁבְנוּ זֶה פַעֲמָיִם — *For had we not lingered surely we had now returned a second time.* Judah would never have jeopardized his share in the World to

אִם־כֵּן | אֵפוֹא זֹאת עֲשׂוּ קְחוּ מִזִּמְרַת הָאָרֶץ בִּכְלֵיכֶם וְהוֹרִידוּ לָאִישׁ
מִנְחָה מְעַט צֳרִי וּמְעַט דְּבַשׁ נְכֹאת וָלֹט בָּטְנִים וּשְׁקֵדִים: וְכֶסֶף מִשְׁנֶה קְחוּ יב
בְיֶדְכֶם וְאֶת־הַכֶּסֶף הַמּוּשָׁב בְּפִי אַמְתְּחֹתֵיכֶם תָּשִׁיבוּ בְיֶדְכֶם אוּלַי מִשְׁגֶּה
הוּא: וְאֶת־אֲחִיכֶם קָחוּ וְקוּמוּ שׁוּבוּ אֶל־הָאִישׁ: וְאֵל שַׁדַּי יִתֵּן לָכֶם רַחֲמִים יג־יד
לִפְנֵי הָאִישׁ וְשִׁלַּח לָכֶם אֶת־אֲחִיכֶם אַחֵר וְאֶת־בִּנְיָמִין וַאֲנִי כַּאֲשֶׁר
שָׁכֹלְתִּי שָׁכָלְתִּי: וַיִּקְחוּ הָאֲנָשִׁים אֶת־הַמִּנְחָה הַזֹּאת וּמִשְׁנֶה־כֶּסֶף לָקְחוּ טו
בְיָדָם וְאֶת־בִּנְיָמִן וַיָּקֻמוּ וַיֵּרְדוּ מִצְרַיִם וַיַּעַמְדוּ לִפְנֵי יוֹסֵף: וַיַּרְא יוֹסֵף אִתָּם טז ששי

כִּי עַתָּה שַׁבְנוּ זֶה פַעֲמָיִם — *Surely we had now returned a second time* . . . for the ruler would have done no harm or deterred us, once he knew the truth (regarding the money) since he is a God-fearing man.

11. אִם כֵּן — *If it be so* . . . as you say that this man who contends with you is a God-fearing man.

אֵפוֹא — *So now (do this).* Perforce this is the proper thing to do.

קְחוּ מִזִּמְרַת הָאָרֶץ . . . מְעַט צֳרִי — *Take of the choice fruits . . . a little balm.* True, if one brings a gift to a greedy man, it must be of great quantity to satisfy his excessive desire, as was the manner of gift sent by Jacob to Esau. However, when a gift is brought to a generous, high-placed person who wants for naught, it is better to bring a smaller gift of high quality, a choice, rare item which he will appreciate. This was the kind of gift suggested by Jacob.

וְהוֹרִידוּ לָאִישׁ מִנְחָה — *Carry down a present to the man.* Before you present yourselves to him (make your offering), and you will determine from the manner in which he receives it whether he is favorably disposed toward you or not, as it is written, לוּ חָפֵץ ה׳ לַהֲמִיתֵנוּ, לֹא לָקַח מִיָּדֵנוּ עֹלָה וּמִנְחָה, *If HASHEM desired to kill us, He would not have received a burnt-offering or meal-offering at our hand (Judges* 13:23).

13. וְקוּמוּ שׁוּבוּ אֶל הָאִישׁ — *And arise, go again unto the man.* For in any event you will appease him to some extent by sending him this gift as it says, אֶבֶן חֵן הַשֹּׁחַד בְּעֵינֵי בְעָלָיו, אֶל כָּל אֲשֶׁר יִפְנֶה יַשְׂכִּיל, *A gift is as a precious stone in the eyes of him that has it, wherever he turns, he prospers (Proverbs* 17:8).

15. וַיַּעַמְדוּ לִפְנֵי יוֹסֵף — *And they stood before Joseph* . . . before they had presented the gift to him, hence they were afraid when *they were brought into Joseph's house* (see verse 18).

NOTES

Come unless he was convinced that he could bring Benjamin back to his father unharmed. This certainty was based on his conviction that the individual they were dealing with was a God-fearing man, and once he knew the full story regarding the money, he would not detain them. The *Sforno* explains: 'Had we not lingered' but had returned immediately after relating the story to you or as soon as our food ran out, then 'we would have returned twice,' literally. Judah was not exaggerating when he says פַּעֲמָיִם, *twice.* They would have made one trip shortly upon their first return and a second when their provisions began to run low.

11-15. וְהוֹרִידוּ לָאִישׁ מִנְחָה . . . וַיַּעַמְדוּ לִפְנֵי יוֹסֵף — *Carry down a present to the man . . . And they stood before Joseph.* Jacob, in his perceptive wisdom of human behavior, advised his sons to send the gift to the ruler *prior* to their personal appearance, as he had done with

אֶת־בִּנְיָמִין וַיֹּאמֶר לַאֲשֶׁר עַל־בֵּיתוֹ הָבֵא אֶת־הָאֲנָשִׁים הַבָּיְתָה וּטְבֹחַ
יז טֶבַח וְהָכֵן כִּי אִתִּי יֹאכְלוּ הָאֲנָשִׁים בַּצָּהֳרָיִם: וַיַּעַשׂ הָאִישׁ כַּאֲשֶׁר אָמַר
יח יוֹסֵף וַיָּבֵא הָאִישׁ אֶת־הָאֲנָשִׁים בֵּיתָה יוֹסֵף: וַיִּירְאוּ הָאֲנָשִׁים כִּי הוּבְאוּ
בֵּית יוֹסֵף וַיֹּאמְרוּ עַל־דְּבַר הַכֶּסֶף הַשָּׁב בְּאַמְתְּחֹתֵינוּ בַּתְּחִלָּה אֲנַחְנוּ
מוּבָאִים לְהִתְגֹּלֵל עָלֵינוּ וּלְהִתְנַפֵּל עָלֵינוּ וְלָקַחַת אֹתָנוּ לַעֲבָדִים וְאֶת־
יט חֲמֹרֵינוּ: וַיִּגְּשׁוּ אֶל־הָאִישׁ אֲשֶׁר עַל־בֵּית יוֹסֵף וַיְדַבְּרוּ אֵלָיו פֶּתַח הַבָּיִת:
כ־כא וַיֹּאמְרוּ בִּי אֲדֹנִי יָרֹד יָרַדְנוּ בַּתְּחִלָּה לִשְׁבָּר־אֹכֶל: וַיְהִי כִּי־בָאנוּ
אֶל־הַמָּלוֹן וַנִּפְתְּחָה אֶת־אַמְתְּחֹתֵינוּ וְהִנֵּה כֶסֶף־אִישׁ בְּפִי אַמְתַּחְתּוֹ כַּסְפֵּנוּ
כב בְּמִשְׁקָלוֹ וַנָּשֶׁב אֹתוֹ בְּיָדֵנוּ: וְכֶסֶף אַחֵר הוֹרַדְנוּ בְיָדֵנוּ לִשְׁבָּר־אֹכֶל לֹא
כג יָדַעְנוּ מִי־שָׂם כַּסְפֵּנוּ בְּאַמְתְּחֹתֵינוּ: וַיֹּאמֶר שָׁלוֹם לָכֶם אַל־תִּירָאוּ
אֱלֹהֵיכֶם וֵאלֹהֵי אֲבִיכֶם נָתַן לָכֶם מַטְמוֹן בְּאַמְתְּחֹתֵיכֶם כַּסְפְּכֶם בָּא אֵלָי
כד וַיּוֹצֵא אֲלֵהֶם אֶת־שִׁמְעוֹן: וַיָּבֵא הָאִישׁ אֶת־הָאֲנָשִׁים בֵּיתָה יוֹסֵף וַיִּתֶּן־מַיִם
כה וַיִּרְחֲצוּ רַגְלֵיהֶם וַיִּתֵּן מִסְפּוֹא לַחֲמֹרֵיהֶם: וַיָּכִינוּ אֶת־הַמִּנְחָה עַד־בּוֹא יוֹסֵף
כו בַּצָּהֳרָיִם כִּי שָׁמְעוּ כִּי־שָׁם יֹאכְלוּ לָחֶם: וַיָּבֹא יוֹסֵף הַבַּיְתָה וַיָּבִיאוּ לוֹ
כז אֶת־הַמִּנְחָה אֲשֶׁר־בְּיָדָם הַבָּיְתָה וַיִּשְׁתַּחֲווּ־לוֹ אָרְצָה: וַיִּשְׁאַל לָהֶם לְשָׁלוֹם
כח וַיֹּאמֶר הֲשָׁלוֹם אֲבִיכֶם הַזָּקֵן אֲשֶׁר אֲמַרְתֶּם הַעוֹדֶנּוּ חָי: וַיֹּאמְרוּ שָׁלוֹם

---

16. וַיֹּאמֶר לַאֲשֶׁר עַל בֵּיתוֹ — *He said to the steward of his house.* He did not want to speak to his brothers until all who were standing before him left, for he needed time (and privacy) for a lengthy discussion with them.

הָבֵא אֶת הָאֲנָשִׁים הַבָּיְתָה — *Bring the men into the house* . . . into the living quarters. They were as yet in the king's gate, or in the hall of justice.

כִּי אִתִּי יֹאכְלוּ — *For (the men) shall dine with me.* This was meant as a test. Joseph wished to see how they behaved with Benjamin, and whether they would display envy when he gave him larger portions than the rest.

21. כַּסְפֵּנוּ בְּמִשְׁקָלוֹ — *Our silver coins in full weight* . . . the same coins (with which we had paid); therefore we cannot think that other money had gotten into our sacks by mistake.

27. לְשָׁלוֹם — *Of their welfare* (lit., *peace*). Are you 'at peace' regarding your physical health? Good health depends upon the harmony of opposing drives; this (peace) occurs when one drive does not overpower another.

אֲבִיכֶם הַזָּקֵן אֲשֶׁר אֲמַרְתֶּם — *(Is) your old father of whom you spoke (well)?* The health of an old person is precarious, as our Sages state, *The lips of older people slacken and their ears become hard of hearing (Shabbos* 152a).

NOTES

Esau. They failed to do so, and 'stand before Joseph' *before* the presentation of the gift; hence when they were summoned to his chambers they were afraid.

27. לְשָׁלוֹם — *Of their welfare* (lit., *peace*). The *Sforno*, a physician, was aware that good health depends upon proper metabolism, which in turn means that the bodily functions are in perfect balance and harmony. Thus he explains the Torah's use of the word שָׁלוֹם, *peace*, in connection with the health of a person. If there is no conflict or tension within one's physical and mental being, one is 'at

כט לְעַבְדְּךָ לְאָבִינוּ עוֹדֶנּוּ חָי וַיִּקְּדוּ וַיִּשְׁתַּחֲוּ׃ וַיִּשָּׂא עֵינָיו וַיַּרְא אֶת־בִּנְיָמִין
אָחִיו בֶּן־אִמּוֹ וַיֹּאמֶר הֲזֶה אֲחִיכֶם הַקָּטֹן אֲשֶׁר אֲמַרְתֶּם אֵלָי וַיֹּאמַר
שביעי ל אֱלֹהִים יָחְנְךָ בְּנִי׃ וַיְמַהֵר יוֹסֵף כִּי־נִכְמְרוּ רַחֲמָיו אֶל־אָחִיו וַיְבַקֵּשׁ לִבְכּוֹת
לא וַיָּבֹא הַחַדְרָה וַיֵּבְךְּ שָׁמָּה׃ וַיִּרְחַץ פָּנָיו וַיֵּצֵא וַיִּתְאַפַּק וַיֹּאמֶר שִׂימוּ לָחֶם׃
לב וַיָּשִׂימוּ לוֹ לְבַדּוֹ וְלָהֶם לְבַדָּם וְלַמִּצְרִים הָאֹכְלִים אִתּוֹ לְבַדָּם כִּי לֹא יוּכְלוּן
לג הַמִּצְרִים לֶאֱכֹל אֶת־הָעִבְרִים לֶחֶם כִּי־תוֹעֵבָה הִוא לְמִצְרָיִם׃ וַיֵּשְׁבוּ לְפָנָיו
לד הַבְּכֹר כִּבְכֹרָתוֹ וְהַצָּעִיר כִּצְעִרָתוֹ וַיִּתְמְהוּ הָאֲנָשִׁים אִישׁ אֶל־רֵעֵהוּ׃ וַיִּשָּׂא
מַשְׂאֹת מֵאֵת פָּנָיו אֲלֵהֶם וַתֵּרֶב מַשְׂאַת בִּנְיָמִן מִמַּשְׂאֹת כֻּלָּם חָמֵשׁ יָדוֹת
מד א וַיִּשְׁתּוּ וַיִּשְׁכְּרוּ עִמּוֹ׃ וַיְצַו אֶת־אֲשֶׁר עַל־בֵּיתוֹ לֵאמֹר מַלֵּא אֶת־אַמְתְּחֹת

---

28. שָׁלוֹם לְעַבְדְּךָ לְאָבִינוּ עוֹדֶנּוּ חָי — *Your servant, our father, is well, he is yet alive.* He is also well (as we are), i.e., at peace, and not 'the peace of the dead' for he still lives.

וַיִּקְּדוּ וַיִּשְׁתַּחֲווּ — *And they bowed and made obeisance* ... in recognition of his inquiry regarding their welfare (and their father's).

29. אֱלֹהִים יָחְנְךָ בְּנִי — *God be gracious unto you, my son* ... since you are the only one left of your mother, as it is written, *and he alone is left of his mother* (44:20), may God give you grace that your brothers, and also others, befriend you.

30. וַיֵּבְךְּ שָׁמָּה — *And he wept there.* He considered the grief of his father and brothers.

32. וַיָּשִׂימוּ לוֹ לְבַדּוֹ — *And they served for him separately* ... that his brothers should not sense that he was (also) a Hebrew.

כִּי לֹא יוּכְלוּן הַמִּצְרִים — *Because the Egyptians may not* (*eat bread with the Hebrews*) ... therefore he did not eat with his brothers, nor did he or his brothers eat with the Egyptians.

34. וַתֵּרֶב מַשְׂאַת בִּנְיָמִן — *And Benjamin's portion was greater.* (Joseph did this) to see whether they would be jealous.

חָמֵשׁ יָדוֹת — *Five times as much.* For each portion he sent to two of them, as was the custom, he sent a similar one to Benjamin, to demonstrate his greater importance.

וַיִּשְׁכְּרוּ עִמּוֹ — *And they became intoxicated with him.* They were not accustomed to the great variety and volume of wine served at the royal table, and did not take heed not to drink all they wanted with the first goblet, as would be proper for those dining with princes, as it says, כִּי תֵשֵׁב לִלְחוֹם אֶת מוֹשֵׁל, בִּין תָּבִין אֶת אֲשֶׁר לְפָנֶיךָ, *When you sit to eat with a ruler, consider well that which is before you* (*Proverbs* 23:1).

NOTES

peace' with himself, i.e., he enjoys good health.

30. וַיֵּבְךְּ שָׁמָּה — *And he wept there.* Both here and in 42:24 Joseph wept and in both cases the *Sforno* stresses that it was not because of self-pity but because he felt for his brothers and father. Small wonder that Joseph is referred to by our Sages as a צַדִּיק, *righteous man.*

34. וַיִּשְׁכְּרוּ עִמּוֹ — *And they became intoxicated with him.* The Torah would not tell us something derogatory about the sons of Jacob, 'the tribes of God.' Therefore when we are told

הָאֲנָשִׁים אֹכֶל כַּאֲשֶׁר יוּכְלוּן שְׂאֵת וְשִׂים כֶּסֶף־אִישׁ בְּפִי אַמְתַּחְתּוֹ:
ב וְאֶת־גְּבִיעִי גְּבִיעַ הַכֶּסֶף תָּשִׂים בְּפִי אַמְתַּחַת הַקָּטֹן וְאֵת כֶּסֶף שִׁבְרוֹ וַיַּעַשׂ
ג־ד כִּדְבַר יוֹסֵף אֲשֶׁר דִּבֵּר: הַבֹּקֶר אוֹר וְהָאֲנָשִׁים שֻׁלְּחוּ הֵמָּה וַחֲמֹרֵיהֶם: הֵם
יָצְאוּ אֶת־הָעִיר לֹא הִרְחִיקוּ וְיוֹסֵף אָמַר לַאֲשֶׁר עַל־בֵּיתוֹ קוּם רְדֹף אַחֲרֵי
ה הָאֲנָשִׁים וְהִשַּׂגְתָּם וְאָמַרְתָּ אֲלֵהֶם לָמָּה שִׁלַּמְתֶּם רָעָה תַּחַת טוֹבָה: הֲלוֹא
ו זֶה אֲשֶׁר יִשְׁתֶּה אֲדֹנִי בּוֹ וְהוּא נַחֵשׁ יְנַחֵשׁ בּוֹ הֲרֵעֹתֶם אֲשֶׁר עֲשִׂיתֶם: וַיַּשִּׂגֵם
ז וַיְדַבֵּר אֲלֵהֶם אֶת־הַדְּבָרִים הָאֵלֶּה: וַיֹּאמְרוּ אֵלָיו לָמָּה יְדַבֵּר אֲדֹנִי
ח כַּדְּבָרִים הָאֵלֶּה חָלִילָה לַעֲבָדֶיךָ מֵעֲשׂוֹת כַּדָּבָר הַזֶּה: הֵן כֶּסֶף אֲשֶׁר
מָצָאנוּ בְּפִי אַמְתְּחֹתֵינוּ הֱשִׁיבֹנוּ אֵלֶיךָ מֵאֶרֶץ כְּנָעַן וְאֵיךְ נִגְנֹב מִבֵּית
ט אֲדֹנֶיךָ כֶּסֶף אוֹ זָהָב: אֲשֶׁר יִמָּצֵא אִתּוֹ מֵעֲבָדֶיךָ וָמֵת וְגַם־אֲנַחְנוּ נִהְיֶה
י לַאדֹנִי לַעֲבָדִים: וַיֹּאמֶר גַּם־עַתָּה כְדִבְרֵיכֶם כֶּן־הוּא אֲשֶׁר יִמָּצֵא אִתּוֹ

XLIV

1. וְשִׂים כֶּסֶף אִישׁ בְּפִי אַמְתַּחְתּוֹ — *And put every man's money in his sack's mouth ...* with their knowledge. Tell them this is reparation for their harsh treatment (on their first trip).

2. תָּשִׂים בְּפִי אַמְתַּחַת הַקָּטֹן — *Put it in the mouth of the youngest's sack.* His purpose was to see how they would commit themselves to save him.

5. הֲלוֹא זֶה אֲשֶׁר יִשְׁתֶּה אֲדֹנִי בּוֹ — *Is this not that in which my lord drinks?* He spoke to them on the assumption that they were aware of everything.

7. לָמָּה יְדַבֵּר אֲדֹנִי כַּדְּבָרִים הָאֵלֶּה — *Why does my lord say such things? ...* as though you suspect all of us.

10. גַּם עַתָּה כְדִבְרֵיכֶם כֶּן הוּא — *Now also let it be according to your words.* Even though justice demands exactly as you have stated, seeing that we are dealing with (the theft of) the king's goblet who rewarded you with only good by returning your money, nonetheless ...

NOTES

וַיִּשְׁכְּרוּ, *they became intoxicated,* the *Sforno* comments that we are being taught a lesson to be careful of our conduct when we find ourselves in a new and strange setting and to conduct ourselves with prudence.

XLIV

1. וְשִׂים כֶּסֶף אִישׁ — *And put every man's money.* It must have been with their knowledge, for when they searched the sacks and found the goblet they also found the money, yet no one was concerned. The reason must therefore be that this time the money was returned as a gesture of appeasement for their initial distress.

2. תָּשִׂים בְּפִי אַמְתַּחַת הַקָּטֹן — *Put it in the mouth of the youngest's sack.* Joseph continually tested his brothers to determine their relationship with Benjamin. Had they learned a lesson in brotherly love from the episode of his sale into slavery and the subsequent grief and distress of their father? First he tested their jealousy — or lack of it — with the portions of food at his table. Now he wanted to know if they were prepared to deliver Benjamin from becoming a bondsman. *Teshuvah,* repentance, is measured by a man's behavior when he is given an opportunity to rectify his past sins by not repeating them under similar circumstances. They were jealous of Joseph — had this shortcoming been corrected? They sold him into slavery — would they now be willing to sacrifice all to save his brother from a similar fate?

5. הֲלוֹא זֶה אֲשֶׁר יִשְׁתֶּה אֲדֹנִי בּוֹ — *Is this not that in which my lord drinks?* The only word used

יא יִהְיֶה־לִּי עָבֶד וְאַתֶּם תִּהְיוּ נְקִיִּם: וַיְמַהֲרוּ וַיּוֹרִדוּ אִישׁ אֶת־אַמְתַּחְתּוֹ אָרְצָה
יב וַיִּפְתְּחוּ אִישׁ אַמְתַּחְתּוֹ: וַיְחַפֵּשׂ בַּגָּדוֹל הֵחֵל וּבַקָּטֹן כִּלָּה וַיִּמָּצֵא הַגָּבִיעַ
יג בְּאַמְתַּחַת בִּנְיָמִן: וַיִּקְרְעוּ שִׂמְלֹתָם וַיַּעֲמֹס אִישׁ עַל־חֲמֹרוֹ וַיָּשֻׁבוּ הָעִירָה:
מפטיר יד וַיָּבֹא יְהוּדָה וְאֶחָיו בֵּיתָה יוֹסֵף וְהוּא עוֹדֶנּוּ שָׁם וַיִּפְּלוּ לְפָנָיו אָרְצָה:
טו וַיֹּאמֶר לָהֶם יוֹסֵף מָה־הַמַּעֲשֶׂה הַזֶּה אֲשֶׁר עֲשִׂיתֶם הֲלוֹא יְדַעְתֶּם כִּי־נַחֵשׁ
טז יְנַחֵשׁ אִישׁ אֲשֶׁר כָּמֹנִי: וַיֹּאמֶר יְהוּדָה מַה־נֹּאמַר לַאדֹנִי מַה־נְּדַבֵּר וּמַה־
נִּצְטַדָּק הָאֱלֹהִים מָצָא אֶת־עֲוֺן עֲבָדֶיךָ הִנֶּנּוּ עֲבָדִים לַאדֹנִי גַּם־אֲנַחְנוּ גַּם
יז אֲשֶׁר־נִמְצָא הַגָּבִיעַ בְּיָדוֹ: וַיֹּאמֶר חָלִילָה לִּי מֵעֲשׂוֹת זֹאת הָאִישׁ אֲשֶׁר
נִמְצָא הַגָּבִיעַ בְּיָדוֹ הוּא יִהְיֶה־לִּי עָבֶד וְאַתֶּם עֲלוּ לְשָׁלוֹם אֶל־אֲבִיכֶם:

אֲשֶׁר יִמָּצֵא אִתּוֹ יִהְיֶה לִּי עָבֶד — *He with whom it is found shall be my slave* . . . and not all of you; nor shall he die, as the law would require.

וְאַתֶּם תִּהְיוּ נְקִיִּם — *And you shall be blameless* . . . (undeserving) of bondage or any other punishment.

15. מָה הַמַּעֲשֶׂה הַזֶּה — *What deed is this.* It was both wicked and foolish, for you should have known that it could not succeed.

16. מַה נֹּאמַר לַאדֹנִי — *What shall we say unto my lord?* . . . in answer to your question, *'What deed is this?'* For . . .

מַה נְּדַבֵּר — *What shall we speak?* . . . to refute (the accusation) and deny our involvement, even though we are innocent.

וּמַה נִּצְטַדָּק — *How shall we justify ourselves?* . . . and prove that this is all a trumped-up charge.

הָאֱלֹהִים מָצָא אֶת עֲוֺן עֲבָדֶיךָ — *God has found out the iniquity of your servants.* We are not being punished for this 'sin' for we are innocent. However, we sinned years ago in an entirely different matter and God has chosen to punish us through you, in the sense of, מֵרְשָׁעִים יֵצֵא רֶשַׁע, *From the wicked comes forth wickedness (I Samuel* 24:13). And as we find in the story of Lulainus and Pappas who said to Trajan, 'We have deserved of the Omnipresent that we should die . . . and He has many agents of death, leopards and lions who can attack and kill us, but He has chosen to punish us by your hand, and at some future time He will exact punishment of you for our blood' (*Taanis* 18b).

17. חָלִילָה לִּי מֵעֲשׂוֹת זֹאת — *Far be it from me that I should do so.* I do not wish to be the means of your being punished for a former sin, in the sense of, מֵרְשָׁעִים יֵצֵא

NOTES

is זֶה, *this*, not גָּבִיעַ, *goblet*, which indicates that when the steward spoke to the brothers he assumed that they knew to what זֶה referred.

16. מַה נֹּאמַר לַאדֹנִי מַה נְּדַבֵּר וּמַה נִּצְטַדָּק — *What shall we say unto my lord? What shall we speak? How shall we justify ourselves?* Three expressions are used – נֹּאמַר, *say;* נְדַבֵּר, *speak;* and נִצְטַדָּק, *justify.* The *Sforno* explains Judah's statement thus: There is really nothing for us to say, nor is it of any use to 'speak,' i.e., to argue our case, for any proof of our innocence will be rejected, since we have been pre-judged.

16-17. הָאֱלֹהִים מָצָא אֶת עֲוֺן עֲבָדֶיךָ . . . חָלִילָה לִּי מֵעֲשׂוֹת זֹאת — *God has found out the iniquity of your servants . . . Far be it from me that I*

רֶשַׁע, וְיָדִי לֹא תִהְיֶה בָּךְ, *From the wicked comes forth wickedness, but my hand shall not be upon you (I Samuel* 24:13). I will only punish and take as a slave the miscreant who sinned against me now.

NOTES

should do so. Judah put Joseph into the position of being used by God as the instrument of their punishment for an old heinous crime. Joseph, in turn, rejected this role since it implied that he was wicked. Rather he insisted that was is dealing only with the present transgression and punishing the guilty party leniently.

פרשת ויגש
Parashas Vayigash

יח וַיִּגַּשׁ אֵלָיו יְהוּדָה וַיֹּאמֶר בִּי אֲדֹנִי יְדַבֶּר־נָא עַבְדְּךָ דָבָר בְּאָזְנֵי אֲדֹנִי וְאַל־
יט יִחַר אַפְּךָ בְּעַבְדֶּךָ כִּי כָמוֹךָ כְּפַרְעֹה׃ אֲדֹנִי שָׁאַל אֶת־עֲבָדָיו לֵאמֹר הֲיֵשׁ־
כ לָכֶם אָב אוֹ־אָח׃ וַנֹּאמֶר אֶל־אֲדֹנִי יֶשׁ־לָנוּ אָב זָקֵן וְיֶלֶד זְקֻנִים קָטָן וְאָחִיו
כא מֵת וַיִּוָּתֵר הוּא לְבַדּוֹ לְאִמּוֹ וְאָבִיו אֲהֵבוֹ׃ וַתֹּאמֶר אֶל־עֲבָדֶיךָ הוֹרִדֻהוּ אֵלָי
כב וְאָשִׂימָה עֵינִי עָלָיו׃ וַנֹּאמֶר אֶל־אֲדֹנִי לֹא־יוּכַל הַנַּעַר לַעֲזֹב אֶת־אָבִיו
כג וְעָזַב אֶת־אָבִיו וָמֵת׃ וַתֹּאמֶר אֶל־עֲבָדֶיךָ אִם־לֹא יֵרֵד אֲחִיכֶם הַקָּטֹן

XLIV

18. יְדַבֶּר נָא עַבְדְּךָ דָבָר — *Let your servant, I pray, speak a word.* Since you said, *'Far be it from me that I should do so'* (v. 17), for you do not want damage or harm to come through you — even for the guilty — let me tell you the harm which you will inflict if you do this thing.

וְאַל יִחַר אַפְּךָ — *And let not your anger burn ...* when I tell you that you are the cause of all this trouble.

כִּי כָמוֹךָ כְּפַרְעֹה — *For you are even as Pharaoh.* The harsh words I address to you are not meant as disrespect, for in my eyes you are as important and distinguished as Pharaoh, who is the king.

20. וְאָבִיו אֲהֵבוֹ — *And his father loves him ...* more than the rest, and that is why he did not let him accompany us at first. For this reason he was not with us at that time; not as you thought, that our youngest brother was sent back to reveal the information gathered (see 42:14).

21. וְאָשִׂימָה עֵינִי עָלָיו — *That I may keep an eye* (lit., *set my eyes) upon him ...* and there is no reason for his father to worry about sending him (for I will look after him).

22. לֹא יוּכַל הַנַּעַר לַעֲזֹב אֶת אָבִיו — *The lad cannot leave his father ...* for if he is separated from his father he (Benjamin) will miss him so deeply that he will pine away and become ill, or even die.

וְעָזַב אֶת אָבִיו וָמֵת — *For if he should leave his father, he will die ...* and consequently his father will, without question, die (as well).

23. אִם לֹא יֵרֵד — *If he would not come down.* Even though you heard our logical reasoned pleas, you decreed that we must perforce bring him down.

NOTES

20. וְאָבִיו אֲהֵבוֹ — *And his father loves him ...* When the brothers argued with Joseph regarding his accusation that they were spies, Joseph triumphantly cried out, 'הוּא אֲשֶׁר דִּבַּרְתִּי אֲלֵכֶם, *That is it that I spoke unto you'* (42:14), which the *Sforno* interprets to mean that he claimed that the 'missing one' or the 'twelfth one' came and went to report their findings. Judah alluded to this now, saying that their youngest brother was not allowed to accompany them due to his father's great love for him and fear for his safety, not for subversive reasons.

22. וְעָזַב אֶת אָבִיו וָמֵת — *For if he should leave his father, he will die.* The word וָמֵת, *he would die,* at the conclusion of this verse is ambiguous. It can refer to Benjamin or to Jacob, and indeed the commentators differ as to who the subject is *(Rashi* and *Rashbam).* The *Sforno's* interpretation clarifies the verse: the first part refers to Benjamin and the second to Jacob. The word וָמֵת, *he will die,* could therefore refer to both; Benjamin would long for his father and pine away and die, causing his father in turn to die from grief.

23. אִם לֹא יֵרֵד — *If he would not come down.* You insisted, and that is why I say that you are the cause of this trouble which you

כד אִתְּכֶם לֹא תֹסִפוּן לִרְאוֹת פָּנָי: וַיְהִי כִּי עָלִינוּ אֶל־עַבְדְּךָ אָבִי וַנַּגֶּד־לוֹ אֵת
כה-כו דִּבְרֵי אֲדֹנִי: וַיֹּאמֶר אָבִינוּ שֻׁבוּ שִׁבְרוּ־לָנוּ מְעַט־אֹכֶל: וַנֹּאמֶר לֹא נוּכַל
לָרֶדֶת אִם־יֵשׁ אָחִינוּ הַקָּטֹן אִתָּנוּ וְיָרַדְנוּ כִּי־לֹא נוּכַל לִרְאוֹת פְּנֵי הָאִישׁ
כז וְאָחִינוּ הַקָּטֹן אֵינֶנּוּ אִתָּנוּ: וַיֹּאמֶר עַבְדְּךָ אָבִי אֵלֵינוּ אַתֶּם יְדַעְתֶּם כִּי שְׁנַיִם
כח יָלְדָה־לִּי אִשְׁתִּי: וַיֵּצֵא הָאֶחָד מֵאִתִּי וָאֹמַר אַךְ טָרֹף טֹרָף וְלֹא רְאִיתִיו
כט עַד־הֵנָּה: וּלְקַחְתֶּם גַּם־אֶת־זֶה מֵעִם פָּנַי וְקָרָהוּ אָסוֹן וְהוֹרַדְתֶּם אֶת־שֵׂיבָתִי
ל בְּרָעָה שְׁאֹלָה: וְעַתָּה כְּבֹאִי אֶל־עַבְדְּךָ אָבִי וְהַנַּעַר אֵינֶנּוּ אִתָּנוּ וְנַפְשׁוֹ
שני לא קְשׁוּרָה בְנַפְשׁוֹ: וְהָיָה כִּרְאוֹתוֹ כִּי־אֵין הַנַּעַר וָמֵת וְהוֹרִידוּ עֲבָדֶיךָ אֶת־
לב שֵׂיבַת עַבְדְּךָ אָבִינוּ בְּיָגוֹן שְׁאֹלָה: כִּי עַבְדְּךָ עָרַב אֶת־הַנַּעַר מֵעִם אָבִי
לג לֵאמֹר אִם־לֹא אֲבִיאֶנּוּ אֵלֶיךָ וְחָטָאתִי לְאָבִי כָּל־הַיָּמִים: וְעַתָּה יֵשֶׁב־נָא
לד עַבְדְּךָ תַּחַת הַנַּעַר עֶבֶד לַאדֹנִי וְהַנַּעַר יַעַל עִם־אֶחָיו: כִּי־אֵיךְ אֶעֱלֶה
מה א אֶל־אָבִי וְהַנַּעַר אֵינֶנּוּ אִתִּי פֶּן אֶרְאֶה בָרָע אֲשֶׁר יִמְצָא אֶת־אָבִי: וְלֹא־

---

24. וַנַּגֶּד לוֹ אֵת דִּבְרֵי אֲדֹנִי — *We told him the words of my lord.* In spite of this he (Jacob) refused to send him (Benjamin) at that time.

25. שֻׁבוּ שִׁבְרוּ לָנוּ — *Go again, buy us (a little food).* Pressured by the famine, we forced him (Jacob) to send (Benjamin), even though he warned us that if we did not bring him back, we would be the cause of his death in sorrow.

30-31. וְעַתָּה כְּבֹאִי . . . וְהוֹרִידוּ עֲבָדֶיךָ — *Now therefore when I come . . . And your servants will bring down (our father with sorrow).* Since he warned us so strongly, he will disregard all that happened here, and it will be as if we had deliberately brought this misfortune upon him; similar to, בְּטֶרֶם תָּבוֹא הִשְׁמַעְתִּיךָ, פֶּן תֹּאמַר עָצְבִּי עָשָׂם, *Before it came to pass I announced it to you, lest you should say, 'My idol has done them' (Isaiah* 48:5).

32. כִּי עַבְדְּךָ עָרַב — *For your servant became surety.* He will die at once when he doesn't see (Benjamin returning with me), without even inquiring what happened to him, because since (I) became surety for him and did not bring him back, he will think that he is definitely dead, and that is why I could not fulfill my vow (to him).

33. וְעַתָּה יֵשֶׁב נָא עַבְדְּךָ תַּחַת הַנַּעַר — *Now therefore, let your servant, I pray, stay instead of the lad.* I beseech you to allow me to take his place, so that I can keep my promise and not sin against my father forever.

34. כִּי אֵיךְ אֶעֱלֶה — *For how shall I go up (to my father).* Even though I know he will be pained by my absence, it is preferable to my witnessing his death (over the loss of Benjamin).

NOTES

claimed was not your intent (see *Sforno* verse 18).

30-31. וְעַתָּה כְּבֹאִי . . . וְהוֹרִידוּ עֲבָדֶיךָ — *Now therefore when I come . . . And your servants will bring down (our father with sorrow).* The proof brought from *Isaiah* is that when a person is forewarned, he cannot attribute what happens to some other cause or reason, save that which he has been warned about.

32. כִּי עַבְדְּךָ עָרַב — *For your servant became surety.* Judah argued that before they would have an opportunity to reassure Jacob that Benjamin was still alive, Jacob would die, convinced that if Benjamin were alive Judah

יָכֹל יוֹסֵף לְהִתְאַפֵּק לְכֹל הַנִּצָּבִים עָלָיו וַיִּקְרָא הוֹצִיאוּ כָל־אִישׁ מֵעָלָי
ב וְלֹא־עָמַד אִישׁ אִתּוֹ בְּהִתְוַדַּע יוֹסֵף אֶל־אֶחָיו: וַיִּתֵּן אֶת־קֹלוֹ בִּבְכִי
ג וַיִּשְׁמְעוּ מִצְרַיִם וַיִּשְׁמַע בֵּית פַּרְעֹה: וַיֹּאמֶר יוֹסֵף אֶל־אֶחָיו אֲנִי יוֹסֵף הַעוֹד
ד אָבִי חָי וְלֹא־יָכְלוּ אֶחָיו לַעֲנוֹת אֹתוֹ כִּי נִבְהֲלוּ מִפָּנָיו: וַיֹּאמֶר יוֹסֵף אֶל־
אֶחָיו גְּשׁוּ־נָא אֵלַי וַיִּגָּשׁוּ וַיֹּאמֶר אֲנִי יוֹסֵף אֲחִיכֶם אֲשֶׁר־מְכַרְתֶּם אֹתִי
ה מִצְרָיְמָה: וְעַתָּה | אַל־תֵּעָצְבוּ וְאַל־יִחַר בְּעֵינֵיכֶם כִּי־מְכַרְתֶּם אֹתִי הֵנָּה כִּי
ו לְמִחְיָה שְׁלָחַנִי אֱלֹהִים לִפְנֵיכֶם: כִּי־זֶה שְׁנָתַיִם הָרָעָב בְּקֶרֶב הָאָרֶץ וְעוֹד
ז חָמֵשׁ שָׁנִים אֲשֶׁר אֵין־חָרִישׁ וְקָצִיר: וַיִּשְׁלָחֵנִי אֱלֹהִים לִפְנֵיכֶם לָשׂוּם לָכֶם
שלישי ח שְׁאֵרִית בָּאָרֶץ וּלְהַחֲיוֹת לָכֶם לִפְלֵיטָה גְּדֹלָה: וְעַתָּה לֹא־אַתֶּם שְׁלַחְתֶּם
אֹתִי הֵנָּה כִּי הָאֱלֹהִים וַיְשִׂימֵנִי לְאָב לְפַרְעֹה וּלְאָדוֹן לְכָל־בֵּיתוֹ וּמֹשֵׁל
ט בְּכָל־אֶרֶץ מִצְרָיִם: מַהֲרוּ וַעֲלוּ אֶל־אָבִי וַאֲמַרְתֶּם אֵלָיו כֹּה אָמַר בִּנְךָ יוֹסֵף
י שָׂמַנִי אֱלֹהִים לְאָדוֹן לְכָל־מִצְרָיִם רְדָה אֵלַי אַל־תַּעֲמֹד: וְיָשַׁבְתָּ בְאֶרֶץ־
גֹּשֶׁן וְהָיִיתָ קָרוֹב אֵלַי אַתָּה וּבָנֶיךָ וּבְנֵי בָנֶיךָ וְצֹאנְךָ וּבְקָרְךָ וְכָל־אֲשֶׁר־לָךְ:

XLV

1. לְהִתְאַפֵּק לְכֹל הַנִּצָּבִים עָלָיו — *Could not refrain himself before all those that stood by him* . . . to adequately control himself so as to be able to attend to all who were standing before him.

3. הַעוֹד אָבִי חָי — *Does my father yet live.* Is it possible that he has survived his sorrow and worry over me?

4. גְּשׁוּ נָא אֵלַי — *Come near to me* . . . so that those who hear my weeping will not hear about my sale.

אֲשֶׁר מְכַרְתֶּם — *Whom you sold.* That I am aware of the incident is proof that I am Joseph, since no one else knew that I was your brother, including those who purchased me.

8. וְעַתָּה לֹא אַתֶּם שְׁלַחְתֶּם — *So now it was not you who sent me.* Now that you realize the Divine plan and purpose behind all this, a design which could not have been achieved without the earlier causes (of our conflicts), (then) undoubtedly those earlier causes were also the will of God (Who willed it so) in order to achieve (His) goal.

לְאָב לְפַרְעֹה — *A father to Pharaoh* . . . an advisor to the king.

וּלְאָדוֹן לְכָל בֵּיתוֹ — *And lord of all his house* . . . appointed over his house.

וּמֹשֵׁל בְּכָל אֶרֶץ מִצְרָיִם — *And ruler over all the land of Egypt* . . . to conduct matters of state.

9. מַהֲרוּ — *Hasten* . . . so that he (Jacob) spend no more time grieving.

NOTES

would have found a way to bring him back.

XLV

1. לְהִתְאַפֵּק לְכֹל הַנִּצָּבִים עָלָיו — *Could not refrain himself before all those that stood by him.* Joseph was so emotionally distraught by the anguished plea of Judah that he was incapable of continuing his audiences that day and therefore asked all to leave. The words לְכֹל הַנִּצָּבִים, *all those that stood,* is interpreted

יא וְכִלְכַּלְתִּי אֹתְךָ שָׁם כִּי־עוֹד חָמֵשׁ שָׁנִים רָעָב פֶּן־תִּוָּרֵשׁ אַתָּה וּבֵיתְךָ וְכָל־
יב אֲשֶׁר־לָךְ: וְהִנֵּה עֵינֵיכֶם רֹאוֹת וְעֵינֵי אָחִי בִנְיָמִין כִּי־פִי הַמְדַבֵּר אֲלֵיכֶם:
יג וְהִגַּדְתֶּם לְאָבִי אֶת־כָּל־כְּבוֹדִי בְּמִצְרַיִם וְאֵת כָּל־אֲשֶׁר רְאִיתֶם וּמִהַרְתֶּם
יד וְהוֹרַדְתֶּם אֶת־אָבִי הֵנָּה: וַיִּפֹּל עַל־צַוְּארֵי בִנְיָמִן־אָחִיו וַיֵּבְךְּ וּבִנְיָמִן בָּכָה
טו עַל־צַוָּארָיו: וַיְנַשֵּׁק לְכָל־אֶחָיו וַיֵּבְךְּ עֲלֵהֶם וְאַחֲרֵי כֵן דִּבְּרוּ אֶחָיו אִתּוֹ:
טז וְהַקֹּל נִשְׁמַע בֵּית פַּרְעֹה לֵאמֹר בָּאוּ אֲחֵי יוֹסֵף וַיִּיטַב בְּעֵינֵי פַרְעֹה וּבְעֵינֵי
יז עֲבָדָיו: וַיֹּאמֶר פַּרְעֹה אֶל־יוֹסֵף אֱמֹר אֶל־אַחֶיךָ זֹאת עֲשׂוּ טַעֲנוּ אֶת־
יח בְּעִירְכֶם וּלְכוּ־בֹאוּ אַרְצָה כְּנָעַן: וּקְחוּ אֶת־אֲבִיכֶם וְאֶת־בָּתֵּיכֶם וּבֹאוּ אֵלָי
רביעי יט וְאֶתְּנָה לָכֶם אֶת־טוּב אֶרֶץ מִצְרַיִם וְאִכְלוּ אֶת־חֵלֶב הָאָרֶץ: וְאַתָּה צֻוֵּיתָה

---

11. פֶּן תִּוָּרֵשׁ — *Lest you come to poverty* . . . due to lack of pasture for the flocks, as indeed they later said, *'For there is no pasture for the flocks'* (47:4).

12. וְעֵינֵי אָחִי בִנְיָמִין — *And the eyes of my brother Benjamin* . . . who had no knowledge of my sale.

כִּי פִי הַמְדַבֵּר אֲלֵיכֶם — *That it is my mouth that speaks to you* . . . without an interpreter (as hitherto). Now consider, that at my sale there was no one who spoke our language (Hebrew) save us, for the purchasers were Ishmaelites and Midianites.

13. וּמִהַרְתֶּם וְהוֹרַדְתֶּם אֶת אָבִי הֵנָּה — *And you shall hasten and bring down my father here* . . . so that he may rejoice to see all this.

16. וַיִּיטַב בְּעֵינֵי פַרְעֹה — *And it pleased Pharaoh well.* Pharaoh thinks that now Joseph's care over (Egypt) will not be as that of a stranger but that of a citizen, dwelling in the land with his family and he would care (for them) wholeheartedly, (thus) benefiting the land and its people.

17. אֱמֹר אֶל אַחֶיךָ זֹאת עֲשׂוּ — *Say to your brethren, 'This do.'* (You should tell them) that this is your intent and desire that they take your father and families (and come down to Egypt).

19. וְאַתָּה צֻוֵּיתָה — *Now you are commanded.* And tell them also that you have been so commanded (by me).

NOTES

by the *Sforno* as referring to those who had appointments with Joseph, either for matters of state or their personal affairs.

4-12. אֲשֶׁר מְכַרְתֶּם . . . כִּי פִי הַמְדַבֵּר אֲלֵיכֶם — *Whom you sold . . . That it is my mouth that speaks to you.* Joseph realized that he must convince his brothers of his identity. His knowledge of the sale would not have been sufficient proof since it could have been related to him by another. That is why he stressed two points. One is the fact that no one involved in the sale knew that he was their brother, and secondly, even the possibility of overhearing them speak of Joseph as their brother would not reveal his identity, since only they spoke the Hebrew language. All this the *Sforno* reads into the phrases, אֲחִיכֶם אֲשֶׁר מְכַרְתֶּם, *your brother whom you sold,* and כִּי פִי הַמְדַבֵּר אֲלֵיכֶם, *that it is my mouth that speaks to you,* in Hebrew (as *Rashi* states).

13. וּמִהַרְתֶּם וְהוֹרַדְתֶּם אֶת אָבִי הֵנָּה — *And you shall hasten and bring down my father here.* Even though he will hear the story from you, 'one cannot compare hearing to seeing,' therefore hasten to bring him down.

16. וַיִּיטַב בְּעֵינֵי פַרְעֹה — *And it pleased Pharaoh well.* Pharaoh was pleased, not because of the reunion of the brothers, but because once his family would join him Joseph would feel that

זֹאת עֲשׂוּ קְחוּ־לָכֶם מֵאֶרֶץ מִצְרַיִם עֲגָלוֹת לְטַפְּכֶם וְלִנְשֵׁיכֶם וּנְשָׂאתֶם
כ אֶת־אֲבִיכֶם וּבָאתֶם׃ וְעֵינְכֶם אַל־תָּחֹס עַל־כְּלֵיכֶם כִּי־טוּב כָּל־אֶרֶץ
כא מִצְרַיִם לָכֶם הוּא׃ וַיַּעֲשׂוּ־כֵן בְּנֵי יִשְׂרָאֵל וַיִּתֵּן לָהֶם יוֹסֵף עֲגָלוֹת עַל־פִּי
כב פַּרְעֹה וַיִּתֵּן לָהֶם צֵדָה לַדָּרֶךְ׃ לְכֻלָּם נָתַן לָאִישׁ חֲלִפוֹת שְׂמָלֹת וּלְבִנְיָמִן
כג נָתַן שְׁלֹשׁ מֵאוֹת כֶּסֶף וְחָמֵשׁ חֲלִפֹת שְׂמָלֹת׃ וּלְאָבִיו שָׁלַח כְּזֹאת עֲשָׂרָה
חֲמֹרִים נֹשְׂאִים מִטּוּב מִצְרָיִם וְעֶשֶׂר אֲתֹנֹת נֹשְׂאֹת בָּר וָלֶחֶם וּמָזוֹן לְאָבִיו
כד־כה לַדָּרֶךְ׃ וַיְשַׁלַּח אֶת־אֶחָיו וַיֵּלֵכוּ וַיֹּאמֶר אֲלֵהֶם אַל־תִּרְגְּזוּ בַּדָּרֶךְ׃ וַיַּעֲלוּ
כו מִמִּצְרָיִם וַיָּבֹאוּ אֶרֶץ כְּנַעַן אֶל־יַעֲקֹב אֲבִיהֶם׃ וַיַּגִּדוּ לוֹ לֵאמֹר עוֹד יוֹסֵף חַי
כז וְכִי־הוּא מֹשֵׁל בְּכָל־אֶרֶץ מִצְרָיִם וַיָּפָג לִבּוֹ כִּי לֹא־הֶאֱמִין לָהֶם׃ וַיְדַבְּרוּ

זאת עֲשׂוּ — *This do* — so that you realize this objective, and your father not refuse to come . . .

קחוּ לָכֶם מֵאֶרֶץ מִצְרַיִם עֲגָלוֹת — *Take your wagons out of Egypt.* When Jacob will see the wagons prepared to transport them, he will have no excuse to refuse. This indeed was shown to be so later, where it says, *And he saw the wagons which Joseph had sent to carry him . . . And Israel said, 'I will go and see him'* (vs. 27-28).

20. וְעֵינְכֶם אַל תָּחֹס עַל כְּלֵיכֶם — *Also regard not your stuff.* Do not delay on that account, because the ultimate loss would be greater in the value of the cattle sacrificed by your delay.

23. וּלְאָבִיו שָׁלַח כְּזֹאת — *And to his father he sent in like manner* . . . the same as Benjamin's gift, and in addition ten asses and ten she-asses. When there is a listing of many items, the letter *vav* appears at the end, similar to, יִשָׂשכָר זְבוּלֻן וּבִנְיָמִן, *Issachar, Zebulun and Benjamin (Exodus* 1:2).

24. וַיְשַׁלַּח אֶת אֶחָיו — *So he dismissed* (lit., *sent) his brothers.* He dismissed them and gave them permission, similar to, שַׁלְּחֵנִי כִּי עָלָה הַשָּׁחַר, *Let me go for the day breaks* (32:27), (also) שַׁלְּחוּנִי וְאֵלְכָה לַאדֹנִי, *Send me away so that I may go to my master* (24:56).

26. וַיָּפָג לִבּוֹ — *And his heart fainted.* He fainted, his pulse rate dropped and his heartbeat slowed as happens when one faints. (This occurred) due to his concern caused by their mentioning Joseph.

כִּי לֹא הֶאֱמִין לָהֶם — *For he believed them not.* Therefore *the spirit of Jacob revived,* and his heartbeat did not fail when he later believed them, as happens (from) the shock of sudden joy which can even cause death, (because) the deceleration of his

NOTES

he was an integral part of Egypt. His loyalty to Pharaoh and commitment to the welfare of the land would therefore become strengthened and enhanced.

23. וּלְאָבִיו שָׁלַח כְּזֹאת — *And to his father he sent in like manner.* The prefix ו׳ of וּלְאָבִיו, *'and' to his father,* connects this word to the end of the previous sentence, i.e., Joseph gave Benjamin three hundred shekels and five garments, which he also sent to his father — in addition to which he sent his father the gifts enumerated in this verse.

24. וַיְשַׁלַּח אֶת אֶחָיו — *So he dismissed* (lit., *sent) his brothers.* The word וַיְשַׁלַּח normally is translated *and he sent.* In the context of this sentence, as is true in those verses quoted by the *Sforno,* it means granting permission to take one's leave.

אֵלָיו אֵת כָּל־דִּבְרֵי יוֹסֵף אֲשֶׁר דִּבֶּר אֲלֵהֶם וַיַּרְא אֶת־הָעֲגָלוֹת אֲשֶׁר־
חמישי כח שָׁלַח יוֹסֵף לָשֵׂאת אֹתוֹ וַתְּחִי רוּחַ יַעֲקֹב אֲבִיהֶם: וַיֹּאמֶר יִשְׂרָאֵל רַב עוֹד־
מו א יוֹסֵף בְּנִי חָי אֵלְכָה וְאֶרְאֶנּוּ בְּטֶרֶם אָמוּת: וַיִּסַּע יִשְׂרָאֵל וְכָל־אֲשֶׁר־לוֹ
ב וַיָּבֹא בְּאֵרָה שָּׁבַע וַיִּזְבַּח זְבָחִים לֵאלֹהֵי אָבִיו יִצְחָק: וַיֹּאמֶר אֱלֹהִים ׀
ג לְיִשְׂרָאֵל בְּמַרְאֹת הַלַּיְלָה וַיֹּאמֶר יַעֲקֹב ׀ יַעֲקֹב וַיֹּאמֶר הִנֵּנִי: וַיֹּאמֶר אָנֹכִי

---

heart caused by his original concern, when he disbelieved them, (counterbalanced) its acceleration later (when he did believe them).

27. וַיְדַבְּרוּ אֵלָיו אֵת כָּל דִּבְרֵי יוֹסֵף — *And they told him all the words of Joseph.* (The words in v. 6) *And there are yet five years in which there will be neither plowing nor harvest,* so that the glad tiding was tempered by worry and concern.

וַתְּחִי רוּחַ יַעֲקֹב — *The spirit of Jacob revived.* He was healed from his fainting spell by gradually mitigating the joy with worry.

28. רַב . . . אֵלְכָה וְאֶרְאֶנּוּ — *It is enough . . . I will go and see him . . .* (only to see him), not to settle there as he requests.

XLVI

1. לֵאלֹהֵי אָבִיו יִצְחָק — *To the God of his father Isaac . . .* Who had said to Isaac, *'Go not down into Egypt'* (26:2).

2. וַיֹּאמֶר אֱלֹהִים לְיִשְׂרָאֵל — *And God said to Israel.* He spoke thus to him because he was 'Israel,' whose descendants would one day rule over their enemies.

NOTES

26-27. וַיָּפָג לִבּוֹ כִּי לֹא הֶאֱמִין לָהֶם . . . וַתְּחִי רוּחַ יַעֲקֹב — *And his heart fainted, for he believed them not . . . The spirit of Jacob revived.* Careful examination of these two verses reveal what brings the *Sforno* to his unique interpretation. Jacob did not believe his sons, yet he fainted. After they convinced him, he revived. In the middle of these expressions — he 'didn't believe' and 'his spirit revived' — the brothers told their father *all* the words of Joseph. The *Sforno* feels that the sequence here is all important and occurred for Jacob's physical welfare. Extreme happiness and joy can be harmful, especially when one is taken unaware. To mingle concern with great *simchah* is beneficial, and to precede the inevitable acceleration of the heart with deceleration is prophylactic. Hence his fainting first prevented the shock of joy from harming him, and the information of five years more of famine tempered the intensity of the joy as well.

28. רַב . . . אֵלְכָה וְאֶרְאֶנּוּ — *It is enough . . . I will go and see him.* The word רַב is difficult to understand, and is explained in various ways by the commentators. The *Sforno* gives a simple interpretation. Jacob agreed *only* to go see his son, but did not agree to settle in Egypt. Hence the word רַב means: it is enough and sufficient that I go to see him.

XLVI

1. לֵאלֹהֵי אָבִיו יִצְחָק — *To the God of his father Isaac.* The question is obvious. Why didn't Jacob offer sacrifices to the God of his grandfather Abraham as well as his father Isaac? The commentators give a variety of answers. The *Sforno* ties together verses 1 and 3, explaining that since Jacob was mindful of Isaac's prohibition by God to leave Israel for Egypt, he had to be reassured by God that he was permitted to do so, and to placate his father, he brought a sacrifice to the *God of his father Isaac.*

2-5. וַיֹּאמֶר אֱלֹהִים לְיִשְׂרָאֵל . . . וַיִּשְׂאוּ בְנֵי יִשְׂרָאֵל — *And God said to Israel . . . And the sons of Israel carried.* These verses (2 and 5) present a strange mixture of the two names — Israel and Jacob. God spoke to *Israel,* but called him *Jacob* (v. 2). *Jacob* rose up from Beer Sheba, but the children of *Israel* carried their father *Jacob* (v. 5). The Sforno explains: *Israel* implies the power to confront one's enemies and prevail.

הָאֵל אֱלֹהֵי אָבִיךָ אַל־תִּירָא מֵרְדָה מִצְרַיְמָה כִּי־לְגוֹי גָּדוֹל אֲשִׂימְךָ שָׁם׃
ד אָנֹכִי אֵרֵד עִמְּךָ מִצְרַיְמָה וְאָנֹכִי אַעַלְךָ גַם־עָלֹה וְיוֹסֵף יָשִׁית יָדוֹ עַל־
ה עֵינֶיךָ׃ וַיָּקָם יַעֲקֹב מִבְּאֵר שָׁבַע וַיִּשְׂאוּ בְנֵי־יִשְׂרָאֵל אֶת־יַעֲקֹב אֲבִיהֶם
ו וְאֶת־טַפָּם וְאֶת־נְשֵׁיהֶם בָּעֲגָלוֹת אֲשֶׁר־שָׁלַח פַּרְעֹה לָשֵׂאת אֹתוֹ׃ וַיִּקְחוּ
אֶת־מִקְנֵיהֶם וְאֶת־רְכוּשָׁם אֲשֶׁר רָכְשׁוּ בְּאֶרֶץ כְּנַעַן וַיָּבֹאוּ מִצְרָיְמָה יַעֲקֹב
ז וְכָל־זַרְעוֹ אִתּוֹ׃ בָּנָיו וּבְנֵי בָנָיו אִתּוֹ בְּנֹתָיו וּבְנוֹת בָּנָיו וְכָל־זַרְעוֹ הֵבִיא

---

3. אָנֹכִי הָאֵל אֱלֹהֵי אָבִיךָ — *I am God, the God of your father.* I, Who told your father, *Go not down into Egypt* (26:2), tell you . . .

אַל תִּירָא מֵרְדָה מִצְרַיְמָה, כִּי לְגוֹי גָּדוֹל אֲשִׂימְךָ שָׁם — *Fear not to go down into Egypt, for I will make of you a great nation there.* If you remain here your children will intermarry and become absorbed by the Caananites, but in Egypt they will not be able to do so, *because the Egyptians may not eat bread with the Hebrews* (43:32); therefore they will be a separate, distinct people, as our Sages state, "The verse, וַיְהִי שָׁם לְגוֹי, *'And he became there a nation'* (*Deut.* 26:5), teaches us that they were distinctive there" (*Sifri*).

4. אַעַלְךָ גַם עָלֹה — *And I will also surely bring you up.* After I bring you up from there, I will raise you even higher than you were before going down there, as it is written, וּלְהַעֲלֹתוֹ מִן הָאָרֶץ הַהִוא אֶל אֶרֶץ טוֹבָה, *And to bring them up out of that land unto a good land* (*Exodus* 3:8).

יָשִׁית יָדוֹ עַל עֵינֶיךָ — *Shall put his hand upon your eyes.* You will not have to concern yourself with your affairs, for Joseph will look after everything you need, and you will not find it necessary to deal with the Egyptians who are unworthy of your company.

5. וַיִּשְׂאוּ בְנֵי יִשְׂרָאֵל — *And the sons of Israel carried.* From now on they would have to be the people of *the sons of Israel*, striving with God and with men who rise against them, as they now go into a strange land.

אֶת יַעֲקֹב אֲבִיהֶם — *Jacob their father.* Going to a joy which would not be followed by any sorrow, following all the troubles of his life, teaches us what will occur at the end of days (when *Mashiach*, the Messiah, will come), as it is written, רָנּוּ לְיַעֲקֹב שִׂמְחָה, *Sing with gladness for Jacob* (*Jeremiah* 31:6).

NOTES

Jacob represents both submission and ultimate victory over adversity, since עָקֵב means *heel* or the *end* (of time). Hence the names are used with great care. God spoke to *Israel*, to reassure him of his ability to deal with his adversaries as he went into exile, even though he would be enslaved there (i.e., Jacob). The sons had to appreciate their role as champions of Israel, strong and resolute, as they accompanied their father to Egypt, even though he was a *Jacob* in *Eretz Yisrael* — a luxury which he could afford in exile! And finally, the *Sforno* explains the use of the name Jacob (v. 5) to indicate that just as the joy of reuniting father and son would be complete — untouched by subsequent sorrow — so shall it be at the end of time for his descendants.

4. אַעַלְךָ גַם עָלֹה — *And I will also surely bring you up.* The word עָלֹה, *to bring up*, is repeated twice (אַעַלְךָ – עָלֹה) to teach us that first the children of Israel would be 'brought up' from Egypt at the time of their deliverance, and secondly they would be brought up to *Eretz Yisrael*, which is a spiritual as well as a physical elevation.

5. אֶת יַעֲקֹב אֲבִיהֶם — *Jacob their father.* The verse in *Jeremiah* also uses the terms 'Jacob'

ח אִתּוֹ מִצְרָיְמָה׃ וְאֵלֶּה שְׁמוֹת בְּנֵי־יִשְׂרָאֵל הַבָּאִים מִצְרַיְמָה
ט־י יַעֲקֹב וּבָנָיו בְּכֹר יַעֲקֹב רְאוּבֵן׃ וּבְנֵי רְאוּבֵן חֲנוֹךְ וּפַלּוּא וְחֶצְרֹן וְכַרְמִי׃ וּבְנֵי
יא שִׁמְעוֹן יְמוּאֵל וְיָמִין וְאֹהַד וְיָכִין וְצֹחַר וְשָׁאוּל בֶּן־הַכְּנַעֲנִית׃ וּבְנֵי לֵוִי גֵּרְשׁוֹן
יב קְהָת וּמְרָרִי׃ וּבְנֵי יְהוּדָה עֵר וְאוֹנָן וְשֵׁלָה וָפֶרֶץ וָזָרַח וַיָּמָת עֵר וְאוֹנָן בְּאֶרֶץ
יג כְּנַעַן וַיִּהְיוּ בְנֵי־פֶרֶץ חֶצְרֹן וְחָמוּל׃ וּבְנֵי יִשָּׂשכָר תּוֹלָע וּפֻוָּה וְיוֹב וְשִׁמְרֹן׃
יד־טו וּבְנֵי זְבֻלוּן סֶרֶד וְאֵלוֹן וְיַחְלְאֵל׃ אֵלֶּה ׀ בְּנֵי לֵאָה אֲשֶׁר יָלְדָה לְיַעֲקֹב בְּפַדַּן
טז אֲרָם וְאֵת דִּינָה בִתּוֹ כָּל־נֶפֶשׁ בָּנָיו וּבְנוֹתָיו שְׁלֹשִׁים וְשָׁלֹשׁ׃ וּבְנֵי גָד צִפְיוֹן
יז וְחַגִּי שׁוּנִי וְאֶצְבֹּן עֵרִי וַאֲרוֹדִי וְאַרְאֵלִי׃ וּבְנֵי אָשֵׁר יִמְנָה וְיִשְׁוָה וְיִשְׁוִי
יח וּבְרִיעָה וְשֶׂרַח אֲחֹתָם וּבְנֵי בְרִיעָה חֶבֶר וּמַלְכִּיאֵל׃ אֵלֶּה בְּנֵי זִלְפָּה אֲשֶׁר־
יט נָתַן לָבָן לְלֵאָה בִתּוֹ וַתֵּלֶד אֶת־אֵלֶּה לְיַעֲקֹב שֵׁשׁ עֶשְׂרֵה נָפֶשׁ׃ בְּנֵי רָחֵל
כ אֵשֶׁת יַעֲקֹב יוֹסֵף וּבִנְיָמִן׃ וַיִּוָּלֵד לְיוֹסֵף בְּאֶרֶץ מִצְרַיִם אֲשֶׁר יָלְדָה־לּוֹ
כא אָסְנַת בַּת־פּוֹטִי פֶרַע כֹּהֵן אֹן אֶת־מְנַשֶּׁה וְאֶת־אֶפְרָיִם׃ וּבְנֵי בִנְיָמִן בֶּלַע
כב וָבֶכֶר וְאַשְׁבֵּל גֵּרָא וְנַעֲמָן אֵחִי וָרֹאשׁ מֻפִּים וְחֻפִּים וָאָרְדְּ׃ אֵלֶּה בְּנֵי רָחֵל
כג־כד אֲשֶׁר יֻלַּד לְיַעֲקֹב כָּל־נֶפֶשׁ אַרְבָּעָה עָשָׂר׃ וּבְנֵי־דָן חֻשִׁים׃ וּבְנֵי נַפְתָּלִי
כה יַחְצְאֵל וְגוּנִי וְיֵצֶר וְשִׁלֵּם׃ אֵלֶּה בְּנֵי בִלְהָה אֲשֶׁר־נָתַן לָבָן לְרָחֵל בִּתּוֹ
כו וַתֵּלֶד אֶת־אֵלֶּה לְיַעֲקֹב כָּל־נֶפֶשׁ שִׁבְעָה׃ כָּל־הַנֶּפֶשׁ הַבָּאָה לְיַעֲקֹב
כז מִצְרַיְמָה יֹצְאֵי יְרֵכוֹ מִלְּבַד נְשֵׁי בְנֵי־יַעֲקֹב כָּל־נֶפֶשׁ שִׁשִּׁים וָשֵׁשׁ׃ וּבְנֵי יוֹסֵף
אֲשֶׁר־יֻלַּד־לוֹ בְמִצְרַיִם נֶפֶשׁ שְׁנָיִם כָּל־הַנֶּפֶשׁ לְבֵית־יַעֲקֹב הַבָּאָה מִצְרַיְמָה
ששי כח שִׁבְעִים׃ וְאֶת־יְהוּדָה שָׁלַח לְפָנָיו אֶל־יוֹסֵף לְהוֹרֹת לְפָנָיו
כט גֹּשְׁנָה וַיָּבֹאוּ אַרְצָה גֹּשֶׁן׃ וַיֶּאְסֹר יוֹסֵף מֶרְכַּבְתּוֹ וַיַּעַל לִקְרַאת־יִשְׂרָאֵל

---

8. וְאֵלֶּה שְׁמוֹת . . . יַעֲקֹב וּבָנָיו — *And these are the names . . . Jacob and his sons.* (Only Jacob and his sons) were worthy to be mentioned by name, as it is written, וְנָשָׂא אַהֲרֹן אֶת שְׁמוֹתָם לִפְנֵי ה׳, *And Aaron shall bear their names before HASHEM* (*Exodus* 28:12), but the rest of the seventy, although righteous, did not reach their height (stature).

19. בְּנֵי רָחֵל אֵשֶׁת יַעֲקֹב — *The sons of Rachel, Jacob's wife* . . . because she was the prime focus of his intentions and from her were born . . .

יוֹסֵף וּבִנְיָמִן — *Joseph and Benjamin* . . . who were the outstanding ones among the tribes, as our Sages tell us, רָאוּי הָיָה יוֹסֵף שֶׁיֵּצְאוּ מִמֶּנּוּ שְׁנֵים עָשָׂר שְׁבָטִים כְּיַעֲקֹב, *Joseph was worthy to have twelve tribes issue forth from him, as they did from Jacob* (*Sotah* 36b), and as they (also) tell us that Benjamin died (only) בְּעֶטְיוֹ שֶׁל נָחָשׁ, *through the serpent's machinations* (*Shabbos* 55b) (not on account of his sins), and so it is written, לִפְנֵי אֶפְרַיִם וּבִנְיָמִן וּמְנַשֶּׁה עוֹרְרָה אֶת גְּבוּרָתֶךָ, *Before Ephraim and Benjamin and Menasseh stir up Your might (and come to save us)* (*Psalms* 80:3).

28. לְהוֹרֹת לְפָנָיו גֹּשְׁנָה — *To show the way before him unto Goshen* . . . so that Judah should prepare and establish a home in Goshen before the arrival of Jacob.

NOTES

and 'Israel' (the conclusion of that sentence refers to שְׁאֵרִית יִשְׂרָאֵל, *the remnant of Israel*). The song of gladness, however, is for Jacob, which alludes to the 'heel,' i.e., the end of time.

ל אָבִיו גֹּשְׁנָה וַיֵּרָא אֵלָיו וַיִּפֹּל עַל־צַוָּארָיו וַיֵּבְךְּ עַל־צַוָּארָיו עוֹד: וַיֹּאמֶר
יִשְׂרָאֵל אֶל־יוֹסֵף אָמוּתָה הַפָּעַם אַחֲרֵי רְאוֹתִי אֶת־פָּנֶיךָ כִּי עוֹדְךָ חָי:
לא וַיֹּאמֶר יוֹסֵף אֶל־אֶחָיו וְאֶל־בֵּית אָבִיו אֶעֱלֶה וְאַגִּידָה לְפַרְעֹה וְאֹמְרָה
לב אֵלָיו אַחַי וּבֵית־אָבִי אֲשֶׁר בְּאֶרֶץ־כְּנַעַן בָּאוּ אֵלָי: וְהָאֲנָשִׁים רֹעֵי צֹאן כִּי־
לג אַנְשֵׁי מִקְנֶה הָיוּ וְצֹאנָם וּבְקָרָם וְכָל־אֲשֶׁר לָהֶם הֵבִיאוּ: וְהָיָה כִּי־יִקְרָא
לד לָכֶם פַּרְעֹה וְאָמַר מַה־מַּעֲשֵׂיכֶם: וַאֲמַרְתֶּם אַנְשֵׁי מִקְנֶה הָיוּ עֲבָדֶיךָ
מִנְּעוּרֵינוּ וְעַד־עַתָּה גַּם־אֲנַחְנוּ גַּם־אֲבֹתֵינוּ בַּעֲבוּר תֵּשְׁבוּ בְּאֶרֶץ גֹּשֶׁן כִּי־
מז א תוֹעֲבַת מִצְרַיִם כָּל־רֹעֵה צֹאן: וַיָּבֹא יוֹסֵף וַיַּגֵּד לְפַרְעֹה וַיֹּאמֶר אָבִי וְאַחַי
ב וְצֹאנָם וּבְקָרָם וְכָל־אֲשֶׁר לָהֶם בָּאוּ מֵאֶרֶץ כְּנָעַן וְהִנָּם בְּאֶרֶץ גֹּשֶׁן: וּמִקְצֵה
ג אֶחָיו לָקַח חֲמִשָּׁה אֲנָשִׁים וַיַּצִּגֵם לִפְנֵי פַרְעֹה: וַיֹּאמֶר פַּרְעֹה אֶל־אֶחָיו מַה־
מַּעֲשֵׂיכֶם וַיֹּאמְרוּ אֶל־פַּרְעֹה רֹעֵה צֹאן עֲבָדֶיךָ גַּם־אֲנַחְנוּ גַּם־אֲבוֹתֵינוּ:
ד וַיֹּאמְרוּ אֶל־פַּרְעֹה לָגוּר בָּאָרֶץ בָּאנוּ כִּי־אֵין מִרְעֶה לַצֹּאן אֲשֶׁר לַעֲבָדֶיךָ
ה כִּי־כָבֵד הָרָעָב בְּאֶרֶץ כְּנָעַן וְעַתָּה יֵשְׁבוּ־נָא עֲבָדֶיךָ בְּאֶרֶץ גֹּשֶׁן: וַיֹּאמֶר
ו פַּרְעֹה אֶל־יוֹסֵף לֵאמֹר אָבִיךָ וְאַחֶיךָ בָּאוּ אֵלֶיךָ: אֶרֶץ מִצְרַיִם לְפָנֶיךָ הִוא
בְּמֵיטַב הָאָרֶץ הוֹשֵׁב אֶת־אָבִיךָ וְאֶת־אַחֶיךָ יֵשְׁבוּ בְּאֶרֶץ גֹּשֶׁן וְאִם־יָדַעְתָּ
ז וְיֶשׁ־בָּם אַנְשֵׁי־חַיִל וְשַׂמְתָּם שָׂרֵי מִקְנֶה עַל־אֲשֶׁר־לִי: וַיָּבֵא יוֹסֵף אֶת־

---

29. וַיֵּרָא אֵלָיו — *And he appeared before him* . . . from the midst of (the many) servants surrounding him, and he did not wait until his father (would) come to him in his chariot.

30. אָמוּתָה הַפָּעַם — *Now let me die.* I had other troubles in my life; salvation came, only to be followed by more sorrows. Now that this salvation has come, and I have seen your face, may it be God's will that I may die in this salvation before any fresh sorrow comes upon me.

31. אֶעֱלֶה וְאַגִּידָה — *I will go up and tell Pharaoh* . . . that your occupation is that of shepherds. I will not, however, ask of him to give you the land of Goshen (to live in and tend your flocks) so that he will believe (you) when you tell him what your occupation is. (In this way) he will not assume that you told him this in order that he give you that land.

XLVII

2. וּמִקְצֵה אֶחָיו לָקַח — *And from among his brothers he took* . . . so that Pharaoh should know from their words and manner that their exclusive occupation is the tending of sheep.

NOTES

Following this joy there will be no sorrow, just as the joy of Jacob's reunion with Joseph was not marred by subsequent sorrow.

XLVII

2. וּמִקְצֵה אֶחָיו לָקַח — *And from among his brothers he took.* Joseph was concerned lest Pharaoh believe that his brothers had various talents which the king would attempt to tap and use. Although he was able as viceroy to withstand the test and retain his faith and way of life, he was not sure that his brothers had the same strength of character. Far better that they retain their semi-isolated lifestyle as shepherds, living in Goshen. That is why he presented his brothers to Pharaoh in a manner

ח יַעֲקֹב אָבִיו וַיַּעֲמִדֵהוּ לִפְנֵי פַרְעֹה וַיְבָרֶךְ יַעֲקֹב אֶת־פַּרְעֹה׃ וַיֹּאמֶר פַּרְעֹה
ט אֶל־יַעֲקֹב כַּמָּה יְמֵי שְׁנֵי חַיֶּיךָ׃ וַיֹּאמֶר יַעֲקֹב אֶל־פַּרְעֹה יְמֵי שְׁנֵי מְגוּרַי
שְׁלֹשִׁים וּמְאַת שָׁנָה מְעַט וְרָעִים הָיוּ יְמֵי שְׁנֵי חַיַּי וְלֹא הִשִּׂיגוּ אֶת־יְמֵי שְׁנֵי
י חַיֵּי אֲבֹתַי בִּימֵי מְגוּרֵיהֶם׃ וַיְבָרֶךְ יַעֲקֹב אֶת־פַּרְעֹה וַיֵּצֵא מִלִּפְנֵי פַרְעֹה׃
שביעי יא וַיּוֹשֵׁב יוֹסֵף אֶת־אָבִיו וְאֶת־אֶחָיו וַיִּתֵּן לָהֶם אֲחֻזָּה בְּאֶרֶץ מִצְרַיִם בְּמֵיטַב
יב הָאָרֶץ בְּאֶרֶץ רַעְמְסֵס כַּאֲשֶׁר צִוָּה פַרְעֹה׃ וַיְכַלְכֵּל יוֹסֵף אֶת־אָבִיו
יג וְאֶת־אֶחָיו וְאֵת כָּל־בֵּית אָבִיו לֶחֶם לְפִי הַטָּף׃ וְלֶחֶם אֵין בְּכָל־הָאָרֶץ
יד כִּי־כָבֵד הָרָעָב מְאֹד וַתֵּלַהּ אֶרֶץ מִצְרַיִם וְאֶרֶץ כְּנַעַן מִפְּנֵי הָרָעָב׃ וַיְלַקֵּט
יוֹסֵף אֶת־כָּל־הַכֶּסֶף הַנִּמְצָא בְאֶרֶץ־מִצְרַיִם וּבְאֶרֶץ כְּנַעַן בַּשֶּׁבֶר אֲשֶׁר־הֵם
טו שֹׁבְרִים וַיָּבֵא יוֹסֵף אֶת־הַכֶּסֶף בֵּיתָה פַרְעֹה׃ וַיִּתֹּם הַכֶּסֶף מֵאֶרֶץ מִצְרַיִם

---

7. וַיְבָרֶךְ יַעֲקב — *And Jacob blessed (Pharaoh).* But he did not bow down to him as he entered nor as he left.

8. כַּמָּה יְמֵי שְׁנֵי חַיֶּיךָ — *How many are the days of the years of your life?* This was asked wonderingly, such old age as Jacob reached being rare in Egypt. And (since) Jacob looked older than his years (the wonder was even greater).

9. מְעַט וְרָעִים הָיוּ יְמֵי שְׁנֵי חַיַּי — *Few and evil have been the days of the years of my life.* In response to your question, 'How many are the days, etc.', the days of these years are 'few and evil,' filled with worries of livelihood and many troubles. In that sense these cannot even be called שְׁנֵי חַיִּים, *years of life.* However in regard to יְמֵי שְׁנֵי מְגוּרַי, *the days of the years of my sojourning,* they are one hundred and thirty.

וְלֹא הִשִּׂיגוּ אֶת יְמֵי שְׁנֵי חַיֵּי אֲבֹתַי בִּימֵי מְגוּרֵיהֶם — *And they have not attained unto the days of the years of the life of my fathers in the days of their sojournings.* Although my fathers were also strangers in foreign lands, they enjoyed a longer trouble-free period of actual 'living' than I have. And (also) the years of my life have not reached the years of my fathers' lives in the days in their sojournings.

12. לֶחֶם לְפִי הַטָּף — *Bread, according to the want of (their) little ones ...* only according to their essential needs. Although Joseph could have provided them with much more (it would not be fitting to do so), as our Sages state, "When the community is in trouble let not a man say, 'I will go to my house and I will eat and drink and all will be well with me' " *(Taanis* 11a).

14. וַיָּבֵא יוֹסֵף אֶת הַכֶּסֶף בֵּיתָה פַּרְעֹה — *And Joseph brought the money into Pharaoh's house.* He did not permit himself anything, despite the justification he could have found (being the one upon whom the) entire burden (of sustaining the country) fell.

NOTES

that would convince the king that they are 'only' simple shepherds.

8. כַּמָּה יְמֵי שְׁנֵי חַיֶּיךָ — *How many are the days of the years of your life?* Because of his many trials and tribulations, Jacob appeared older than his years. Egyptians were not accustomed to seeing very old people, for apparently their lifespan was comparatively brief. The word כַּמָּה is interpreted by some not as *how many,* but as a term of exclamation and wonder.

9. מְעַט וְרָעִים הָיוּ יְמֵי שְׁנֵי חַיַּי — *Few and evil have been the days of the years of my life.* Jacob differentiated between the quantitative and qualitative years of his life. The total period of his sojourn on earth was one hundred and thirty years. Those years, how-

וּמֵאֶרֶץ כְּנָעַן וַיָּבֹאוּ כָל־מִצְרַיִם אֶל־יוֹסֵף לֵאמֹר הָבָה־לָּנוּ לֶחֶם וְלָמָּה
טז נָמוּת נֶגְדֶּךָ כִּי אָפֵס כָּסֶף׃ וַיֹּאמֶר יוֹסֵף הָבוּ מִקְנֵיכֶם וְאֶתְּנָה לָכֶם בְּמִקְנֵיכֶם
יז אִם־אָפֵס כָּסֶף׃ וַיָּבִיאוּ אֶת־מִקְנֵיהֶם אֶל־יוֹסֵף וַיִּתֵּן לָהֶם יוֹסֵף לֶחֶם
בַּסּוּסִים וּבְמִקְנֵה הַצֹּאן וּבְמִקְנֵה הַבָּקָר וּבַחֲמֹרִים וַיְנַהֲלֵם בַּלֶּחֶם בְּכָל־
יח מִקְנֵהֶם בַּשָּׁנָה הַהִוא׃ וַתִּתֹּם הַשָּׁנָה הַהִוא וַיָּבֹאוּ אֵלָיו בַּשָּׁנָה הַשֵּׁנִית
וַיֹּאמְרוּ לוֹ לֹא־נְכַחֵד מֵאֲדֹנִי כִּי אִם־תַּם הַכֶּסֶף וּמִקְנֵה הַבְּהֵמָה אֶל־אֲדֹנִי
יט לֹא נִשְׁאַר לִפְנֵי אֲדֹנִי בִּלְתִּי אִם־גְּוִיָּתֵנוּ וְאַדְמָתֵנוּ׃ לָמָּה נָמוּת לְעֵינֶיךָ גַּם־
אֲנַחְנוּ גַּם־אַדְמָתֵנוּ קְנֵה־אֹתָנוּ וְאֶת־אַדְמָתֵנוּ בַּלָּחֶם וְנִהְיֶה אֲנַחְנוּ
וְאַדְמָתֵנוּ עֲבָדִים לְפַרְעֹה וְתֶן־זֶרַע וְנִחְיֶה וְלֹא נָמוּת וְהָאֲדָמָה לֹא תֵשָׁם׃
כ וַיִּקֶן יוֹסֵף אֶת־כָּל־אַדְמַת מִצְרַיִם לְפַרְעֹה כִּי־מָכְרוּ מִצְרַיִם אִישׁ שָׂדֵהוּ כִּי־
כא חָזַק עֲלֵהֶם הָרָעָב וַתְּהִי הָאָרֶץ לְפַרְעֹה׃ וְאֶת־הָעָם הֶעֱבִיר אֹתוֹ לֶעָרִים

---

17. וַיְנַהֲלֵם בַּלֶּחֶם — *He fed them with bread.* He gently led them, similar to, עָלוֹת יְנַהֵל, *And gently lead the lambkin (Isaiah* 40:11), i.e., he gave them bread in small quantities, so as not to overeat, since it is not proper to do so in a time of famine, as (our Sages) say, "He who starves himself in years of famine escapes unnatural death" *(Taanis* 11a). As the learned men of medicine have taught us, overeating after a period of hunger leads to fatal illnesses.

בַּשָּׁנָה הַהִוא — *For that year* ... after the money ran out, which was the sixth year of the famine.

18. בַּשָּׁנָה הַשֵּׁנִית — *The second year* ... the second year after the money gave out which was the seventh year of the famine.

לֹא נְכַחֵד מֵאֲדֹנִי — *We will not hide from my lord* ... that we still have cattle.

19. לָמָּה נָמוּת לְעֵינֶיךָ — *Wherefore should we die before your eyes?* For even if it be true, that our money is all spent and our cattle are by now all yours, it would not be right for you to allow us to die from hunger.

21. הֶעֱבִיר אֹתוֹ לֶעָרִים — *He removed them city by city.* (Joseph) brought them with him to each parcel of land (so as to take legal possession on behalf of Pharaoh of the אַדְמַת מִצְרַיִם, *the land of Egypt* — v. 20) in their presence, with their acquiescence. He had them state explicitly, 'לֵךְ חֲזֵק וּקְנֵי, *go and perform an act of acquisition.'*

NOTES

ever, in which he experienced pleasure and contentment, were but few.

17-18. בַּשָּׁנָה הַהִוא ... בַּשָּׁנָה הַשֵּׁנִית — *For that year ... The second year.* Unlike *Rashi* who interprets the phrase *that year* as referring to the first year of the famine and interprets *the second year* literally, the *Sforno* is of the opinion that the Torah is not *resuming* the story of the famine in verse 13, but *continuing* it, hence *that year* refers to the sixth year of the famine, when the money ran out, and the *second year* means the second year after the money was spent, which was the seventh of the famine. The reason for *Rashi's* interpretation is based on the statement of our Sages that the famine ceased when Jacob arrived in Egypt. Hence the first and second years must refer to the first two of the seven, for the last five were suspended thanks to Jacob.

19. לָמָּה נָמוּת לְעֵינֶיךָ — *Wherefore should we die before your eyes?* The argument of the people was that even though it was true that they no longer had any money or cattle, and therefore they could no longer purchase bread

כב מִקְצֵה גְבוּל־מִצְרַיִם וְעַד־קָצֵהוּ: רַק אַדְמַת הַכֹּהֲנִים לֹא קָנָה כִּי חֹק
לַכֹּהֲנִים מֵאֵת פַּרְעֹה וְאָכְלוּ אֶת־חֻקָּם אֲשֶׁר נָתַן לָהֶם פַּרְעֹה עַל־כֵּן לֹא
כג מָכְרוּ אֶת־אַדְמָתָם: וַיֹּאמֶר יוֹסֵף אֶל־הָעָם הֵן קָנִיתִי אֶתְכֶם הַיּוֹם וְאֶת־
כד אַדְמַתְכֶם לְפַרְעֹה הֵא־לָכֶם זֶרַע וּזְרַעְתֶּם אֶת־הָאֲדָמָה: וְהָיָה בַּתְּבוּאֹת
וּנְתַתֶּם חֲמִישִׁית לְפַרְעֹה וְאַרְבַּע הַיָּדֹת יִהְיֶה לָכֶם לְזֶרַע הַשָּׂדֶה וּלְאָכְלְכֶם
מפטיר כה וְלַאֲשֶׁר בְּבָתֵּיכֶם וְלֶאֱכֹל לְטַפְּכֶם: וַיֹּאמְרוּ הֶחֱיִתָנוּ נִמְצָא־חֵן בְּעֵינֵי אֲדֹנִי
כו וְהָיִינוּ עֲבָדִים לְפַרְעֹה: וַיָּשֶׂם אֹתָהּ יוֹסֵף לְחֹק עַד־הַיּוֹם הַזֶּה עַל־אַדְמַת
מִצְרַיִם לְפַרְעֹה לַחֹמֶשׁ רַק אַדְמַת הַכֹּהֲנִים לְבַדָּם לֹא הָיְתָה לְפַרְעֹה:
כז וַיֵּשֶׁב יִשְׂרָאֵל בְּאֶרֶץ מִצְרַיִם בְּאֶרֶץ גֹּשֶׁן וַיֵּאָחֲזוּ בָהּ וַיִּפְרוּ וַיִּרְבּוּ מְאֹד:

---

23. הֵן קָנִיתִי אֶתְכֶם הַיּוֹם וְאֶת אַדְמַתְכֶם לְפַרְעֹה — *Behold I have bought you this day and your land for Pharaoh* ... and therefore you are his bondmen and as such obligated to work the land. He in turn is responsible for your food and for seed to sow the land. Thus, according to law, all the produce will belong to Pharaoh.

הֵא לָכֶם זֶרַע וּזְרַעְתֶּם — *Here is seed for you, and you shall sow.* You are his bondmen, work ...

אֶת הָאֲדָמָה — *The land* ... which belongs to him (Pharaoh).

24. וְהָיָה בַּתְּבוּאֹת — *And it shall come to pass at the ingathering* ... which is also his.

וּנְתַתֶּם חֲמִישִׁית לְפַרְעֹה — *You shall give a fifth to Pharaoh* ... because it is due to him, after he will have given you all that he is obligated to give.

וְאַרְבַּע הַיָּדֹת יִהְיֶה לָכֶם לְזֶרַע הַשָּׂדֶה — *And four parts shall be your own for seed of the field* ... which he is obligated to give to you as owner of the field.

וּלְאָכְלְכֶם — *And for your food* ... which he is also obligated to give to you. And so the law remained, that a fifth belongs to Pharaoh.

26. וַיָּשֶׂם אֹתָהּ יוֹסֵף לְחֹק — *And Joseph made it a statute.* After Joseph convinced (the populace) that this law was just, and not a new extortionist tax, it was entered into the legal code of Egypt.

NOTES

or seed, nonetheless they pleaded with Joseph that since he was aware of their circumstances, how could he permit them to perish?

21. הֶעֱבִיר אֹתוֹ לֶעָרִים — *He removed them city by city.* The *Sforno* explains why it was necessary to bring the people with him in order to take possession of the land on behalf of Pharaoh. According to law, the transfer of land is executed by having the owner state publicly and openly to the purchaser, 'לֵךְ חֲזַק וּקְנֵי, *Go and perform an act of acquisition,*' and thereby you will take legal possession of this land. Joseph was determined that there be no irregularities in this transfer, or any question of illegality; hence he insisted that they go with him from city to city to finalize the sale.

23-24. הֵן קָנִיתִי אֶתְכֶם הַיּוֹם ... וּנְתַתֶּם חֲמִישִׁית לְפַרְעֹה וְאַרְבַּע הַיָּדֹת יִהְיֶה לָכֶם — *Behold I have bought you this day ... You shall give a fifth to Pharaoh and four parts shall be your own.* Joseph clearly and explicitly explained to the people the consequences of their transferral of land to Pharaoh. From this time forward, Pharaoh was to be the legal owner not only of their land, but of themselves as well. They were obligated to work the fields on his behalf as he in turn was obligated to provide them with seed. They were entitled to four-fifths of

NOTES

the produce while Pharaoh would receive one-fifth.

26. וַיָּשֶׂם אֹתָהּ יוֹסֵף לְחֹק – *And Joseph made it a statute.* Joseph was not only careful to arrange the transferral of the land properly, as well as the sharecropper agreement between the people and Pharaoh, but he was also anxious that the people realize the voluntary nature of this transaction and arrangement. He felt that it was important not to perceive this plan as a harshly imposed exorbitant tax. Only then did he enter this arrangement into the legal code of Egypt.

פרשת ויחי
Parasha Vayechi

כח וַיְחִי יַעֲקֹב בְּאֶרֶץ מִצְרַיִם שְׁבַע עֶשְׂרֵה שָׁנָה וַיְהִי יְמֵי־יַעֲקֹב שְׁנֵי חַיָּיו שֶׁבַע
כט שָׁנִים וְאַרְבָּעִים וּמְאַת שָׁנָה׃ וַיִּקְרְבוּ יְמֵי־יִשְׂרָאֵל לָמוּת וַיִּקְרָא ׀ לִבְנוֹ
לְיוֹסֵף וַיֹּאמֶר לוֹ אִם־נָא מָצָאתִי חֵן בְּעֵינֶיךָ שִׂים־נָא יָדְךָ תַּחַת יְרֵכִי
ל וְעָשִׂיתָ עִמָּדִי חֶסֶד וֶאֱמֶת אַל־נָא תִקְבְּרֵנִי בְּמִצְרָיִם׃ וְשָׁכַבְתִּי עִם־אֲבֹתַי
וּנְשָׂאתַנִי מִמִּצְרַיִם וּקְבַרְתַּנִי בִּקְבֻרָתָם וַיֹּאמַר אָנֹכִי אֶעֱשֶׂה כִדְבָרֶךָ׃
לא וַיֹּאמֶר הִשָּׁבְעָה לִי וַיִּשָּׁבַע לוֹ וַיִּשְׁתַּחוּ יִשְׂרָאֵל עַל־רֹאשׁ הַמִּטָּה׃

---

29. אַל נָא תִקְבְּרֵנִי בְּמִצְרָיִם — *Please do not bury me in Egypt.* Even in a coffin, similar to, *and he was put in a coffin in Egypt* (50:26), for if you will do so, even temporarily, they will not allow you to carry (my body) for (burial) in the cave (of Machpelah), for they will say that this (placing in the coffin) is sufficient considering that this was their custom.

30. וְשָׁכַבְתִּי עִם אֲבֹתַי — *When I will lie with my fathers.* The meaning of this phrase is the placing of the deceased on a bier for the purpose of eulogy. This phrase is therefore used in the Book of *Kings* regarding all kings, be they righteous or wicked, who died on their beds.

וּנְשָׂאתַנִי מִמִּצְרַיִם — *And you shall carry me out of Egypt.* If you will do this you will be permitted to carry me out of Egypt, for once the days of eulogy are completed the grief will subside, as we find, *And when the days of weeping for him were past* (50:4), and they will not prevent my body from being carried elsewhere.

אָנֹכִי אֶעֱשֶׂה כִדְבָרֶךָ — *I will do as you have said.* As far as I am concerned, I will do as you say with all my power.

31. הִשָּׁבְעָה לִי — *Swear unto me . . .* so that you will have a valid, strong excuse (to do as I ask) in case Pharaoh decides to forbid it.

וַיִּשְׁתַּחוּ יִשְׂרָאֵל — *And Israel bowed down . . .* in gratitude to God, that he was privileged to have this wish granted by his son, similar to, *And it came to pass when Abraham's servant heard their words, he bowed down to the earth unto God* (24:52).

NOTES

29. אַל נָא תִקְבְּרֵנִי בְּמִצְרָיִם — *Please do not bury me in Egypt.* Since the custom of the Egyptians was to inter royalty in a coffin and not to bury them in the ground, Jacob was afraid that once he would be placed in a coffin, the Egyptians, who considered him as king, would consider this act as one of permanent burial and not permit Joseph to transport his father to the Land of Canaan. He therefore asked his son not to place him into a coffin at all, but to transport his body directly to the Cave of Machpelah. Thus the phrase *do not bury me in Egypt* does not refer to interment in the earth of Egypt but to his being placed in a coffin in accordance with Egyptian custom.

30. וְשָׁכַבְתִּי עִם אֲבֹתַי — *When I will lie with my fathers.* The expression used by Jacob וְשָׁכַבְתִּי עִם אֲבֹתַי, *when I will lie with my fathers,* is interpreted by the *Sforno* as referring to the custom called אֲשְׁכָּבָה, when the deceased would lie in state for a period of time, be eulogized and then interred. A similar expression is found in Scripture regarding the kings of Israel, וַיִּשְׁכַּב עִם אֲבֹתָיו, *and he did lie (slept) with his fathers (I Kings* 2:10) which also refers to אֲשְׁכָּבָה. There is, however, another explanation for the expression *and he slept with his fathers,* meaning that one's soul returns to the abode of his ancestors in *Gan Eden* (Paradise). The former interpretation is applicable to all kings, be they righteous or wicked, while the latter only applies to righteous ones. In general the custom of lying in state was only practiced when the king died on his bed, not if he fell in battle or was assassinated.

31. הִשָּׁבְעָה לִי — *Swear unto me.* Jacob certainly trusted Joseph and his word was

מח א וַיְהִי אַחֲרֵי הַדְּבָרִים הָאֵלֶּה וַיֹּאמֶר לְיוֹסֵף הִנֵּה אָבִיךָ חֹלֶה וַיִּקַּח אֶת־שְׁנֵי
ב בָנָיו עִמּוֹ אֶת־מְנַשֶּׁה וְאֶת־אֶפְרָיִם: וַיַּגֵּד לְיַעֲקֹב וַיֹּאמֶר הִנֵּה בִּנְךָ יוֹסֵף בָּא
ג אֵלֶיךָ וַיִּתְחַזֵּק יִשְׂרָאֵל וַיֵּשֶׁב עַל־הַמִּטָּה: וַיֹּאמֶר יַעֲקֹב אֶל־יוֹסֵף אֵל שַׁדַּי
ד נִרְאָה־אֵלַי בְּלוּז בְּאֶרֶץ כְּנָעַן וַיְבָרֶךְ אֹתִי: וַיֹּאמֶר אֵלַי הִנְנִי מַפְרְךָ
וְהִרְבִּיתִךָ וּנְתַתִּיךָ לִקְהַל עַמִּים וְנָתַתִּי אֶת־הָאָרֶץ הַזֹּאת לְזַרְעֲךָ אַחֲרֶיךָ
ה אֲחֻזַּת עוֹלָם: וְעַתָּה שְׁנֵי־בָנֶיךָ הַנּוֹלָדִים לְךָ בְּאֶרֶץ מִצְרַיִם עַד־בֹּאִי אֵלֶיךָ
ו מִצְרַיְמָה לִי־הֵם אֶפְרַיִם וּמְנַשֶּׁה כִּרְאוּבֵן וְשִׁמְעוֹן יִהְיוּ־לִי: וּמוֹלַדְתְּךָ אֲשֶׁר־
ז הוֹלַדְתָּ אַחֲרֵיהֶם לְךָ יִהְיוּ עַל שֵׁם אֲחֵיהֶם יִקָּרְאוּ בְּנַחֲלָתָם: וַאֲנִי | בְּבֹאִי

XLVIII

2. וַיֵּשֶׁב עַל הַמִּטָּה — *And sat upon the bed* ... to pay homage to Joseph's royal position, to the extent of his physical ability; we find the reverse (by Mordechai who refused to pay homage to Haman), וְלֹא קָם וְלֹא זָע מִמֶּנּוּ, *He stood not up nor moved for him (Esther* 5:9).

4. וּנְתַתִּיךָ לִקְהַל עַמִּים וְנָתַתִּי אֶת הָאָרֶץ — *I will make of you a company of peoples; and will give this Land (to your seed).* At the time this promise was made by God (35:11), all the tribes, save Benjamin, had been born, and since the promise of *the Land whereon you lie, to you will I give it, and to your seed* (28:13) was already made (when I left for Haran) the promise made (in Luz, upon my return) regarding a קְהַל עַמִּים, *a company of people,* had to refer to the inheritance of the Land. This in turn could only mean you and your sons, for you were all given to me together.

5. וְעַתָּה שְׁנֵי בָנֶיךָ הַנּוֹלָדִים לְךָ . . . לִי הֵם — *And now your two sons who were born unto you (in Egypt) . . . are mine.* For they alone were given to me, together with you, as we read, *I had not thought to see your face, and lo, God has let me see your seed also* (verse 11).

6. וּמוֹלַדְתְּךָ אֲשֶׁר הוֹלַדְתָּ אַחֲרֵיהֶם — *And your issue which you begot after them* . . . namely, your grandchildren, who are properly called מוֹלַדְתְּךָ, *your issue.*

לְךָ יִהְיוּ — *Shall be yours.* They will be called 'the house of Joseph' and be blessed with your blessings.

עַל שֵׁם אֲחֵיהֶם יִקָּרְאוּ בְּנַחֲלָתָם — *They shall be called after the name of their brethren in their inheritance.* The children of Menasseh will be called, each one like his brother, after the name of Menasseh to inherit with them in his share (of the Land)

NOTES

sufficient without any need to swear. The oath was given only for the purpose of being used by him in case Pharaoh would try to create difficulties. Indeed this proved to be of great importance, as we see later, *And Pharaoh said, 'Go up and bury your father, as he made you swear'* (50:6).

וַיִּשְׁתַּחוּ יִשְׂרָאֵל — *And Israel bowed down.* Unlike other commentators who interpret the object of the phrase *and Israel bowed down* as referring to Joseph, the *Sforno* rejects this as being unfitting and interprets it to mean, 'to God,' bringing proof from Eliezer the servant of Abraham.

XLVIII

4-5. וּנְתַתִּיךָ לִקְהַל עַמִּים . . . הַנּוֹלָדִים לְךָ . . . לִי הֵם — *I will make of you a company of peoples . . . who were born unto you . . . are mine.* The terminology used by God when He speaks to Jacob upon his return from Paddan Aram is, *I am God Almighty . . . a nation and a company of nations shall be from you . . . and the Land . . . to you I will give it and to your seed* (35:11,12). The phrase *nation* refers to Ben-

מִפַּדָּן מֵתָה עָלַי רָחֵל בְּאֶרֶץ כְּנַעַן בַּדֶּרֶךְ בְּעוֹד כִּבְרַת־אֶרֶץ לָבֹא אֶפְרָתָה
ח וָאֶקְבְּרֶהָ שָּׁם בְּדֶרֶךְ אֶפְרָת הִוא בֵּית לָחֶם: וַיַּרְא יִשְׂרָאֵל אֶת־בְּנֵי יוֹסֵף
ט וַיֹּאמֶר מִי־אֵלֶּה: וַיֹּאמֶר יוֹסֵף אֶל־אָבִיו בָּנַי הֵם אֲשֶׁר־נָתַן־לִי אֱלֹהִים בָּזֶה

and so also each son of Ephraim will be considered (lit., 'called') as his brother after the name of Ephraim to inherit together the share (in the Land) of Ephraim.

7. וַאֲנִי — *And as for me.* Do not think that when God said to me, *'I will make of you a company of peoples,'* the intent was that I would have more children, but my sins denied me (this privilege); this is not so, for . . .

בְּבֹאִי מִפַּדָּן — *When I came from Paddan . . .* and God appeared to me at that time.

מֵתָה עָלַי רָחֵל — *Rachel died unto me.* As our Sages say, אֵין אִשָּׁה מֵתָה אֶלָּא לְבַעְלָהּ, *The death of a woman is felt only by her husband (Sanhedrin* 22b).

בַּדֶּרֶךְ בְּעוֹד כִּבְרַת אֶרֶץ לָבֹא אֶפְרָתָה — *On the way, when there was still some way to come to Ephras . . .* immediately, when I traveled from that place where God spoke to me and was still en route, before I came to Bethlehem.

וָאֶקְבְּרֶהָ שָּׁם בְּדֶרֶךְ אֶפְרָת — *And I buried her there in the way to Ephras.* So intense was my grief that I had not the strength even to carry her to the cemetery in Bethlehem. From that moment on, all physical desire left me, and I no longer cohabited (with my wives).

8. וַיַּרְא יִשְׂרָאֵל אֶת בְּנֵי יוֹסֵף — *And Israel beheld Joseph's sons.* (His sight was good enough) to distinguish people but not to identify them.

9. בָּנַי הֵם אֲשֶׁר נָתַן לִי אֱלֹהִים בָּזֶה — *They are my sons whom God has given me here.* They are my sons, not my grandsons. They are those sons which God had given me while I was here alone (before your arrival, thereby meeting your condition of) *who were born unto you in Egypt before I came to you* (verse 5); (hence they are included in) your statement of לִי הֵם, *are mine.*

NOTES

jamin, while the phrase *company of nations* alludes to Menasseh and Ephraim as Jacob understands it, for since Joseph was presumed dead by Jacob and now he is 'returned to life' together with his sons as one, Jacob considers them as *his*, hence entitled to inherit equal portions in the land.

6. לְךָ יִהְיוּ עַל שֵׁם אֲחֵיהֶם יִקָּרְאוּ — *Shall be yours; they shall be called after the name of their brethren.* The wording in this verse presents certain difficulties. First Jacob says to Joseph, לְךָ יִהְיוּ, *shall be yours,* then he says they shall be called *after the name of their brethren.* The *Sforno* interprets the phrase וּמוֹלַדְתְּךָ, *and your issue,* as referring to his grandchildren, who will be called *the house of Joseph,* which explains *shall be yours,* but insofar as inheritance of the land is concerned they will only share in the portion already allocated to Menasseh and Ephraim.

7. מֵתָה עָלַי רָחֵל . . . וָאֶקְבְּרֶהָ שָּׁם — *Rachel died unto me . . . And I buried her there.* Jacob presents his case to Joseph so as to reassure him that the double portion granted to him is in keeping with God's promise regarding *a company of peoples.* He asserts that it could not have alluded to Jacob's own children, still unborn, since that particular revelation of God was followed immediately by the death of Rachel, which affected Jacob so profoundly that he no longer had marital relations; hence the *company of peoples* could only be fulfilled through one of his sons, namely, Joseph.

9. בָּנַי הֵם אֲשֶׁר נָתַן לִי אֱלֹהִים בָּזֶה — *They are my sons whom God has given me here.* Jacob had differentiated between those children born to Joseph before he came to Egypt, as well as any grandchildren of Joseph born afterwards. They would not be eligible to be considered as one of the tribes of Israel — as are Menasseh

שני י וַיֹּאמַר קָחֶם־נָא אֵלַי וַאֲבָרְכֵם׃ וְעֵינֵי יִשְׂרָאֵל כָּבְדוּ מִזֹּקֶן לֹא יוּכַל לִרְאוֹת
יא וַיַּגֵּשׁ אֹתָם אֵלָיו וַיִּשַּׁק לָהֶם וַיְחַבֵּק לָהֶם׃ וַיֹּאמֶר יִשְׂרָאֵל אֶל־יוֹסֵף רְאֹה
יב פָנֶיךָ לֹא פִלָּלְתִּי וְהִנֵּה הֶרְאָה אֹתִי אֱלֹהִים גַּם אֶת־זַרְעֶךָ׃ וַיּוֹצֵא יוֹסֵף
יג אֹתָם מֵעִם בִּרְכָּיו וַיִּשְׁתַּחוּ לְאַפָּיו אָרְצָה׃ וַיִּקַּח יוֹסֵף אֶת־שְׁנֵיהֶם אֶת־
אֶפְרַיִם בִּימִינוֹ מִשְּׂמֹאל יִשְׂרָאֵל וְאֶת־מְנַשֶּׁה בִשְׂמֹאלוֹ מִימִין יִשְׂרָאֵל וַיַּגֵּשׁ
יד אֵלָיו׃ וַיִּשְׁלַח יִשְׂרָאֵל אֶת־יְמִינוֹ וַיָּשֶׁת עַל־רֹאשׁ אֶפְרַיִם וְהוּא הַצָּעִיר
טו וְאֶת־שְׂמֹאלוֹ עַל־רֹאשׁ מְנַשֶּׁה שִׂכֵּל אֶת־יָדָיו כִּי מְנַשֶּׁה הַבְּכוֹר׃ וַיְבָרֶךְ
אֶת־יוֹסֵף וַיֹּאמַר הָאֱלֹהִים אֲשֶׁר הִתְהַלְּכוּ אֲבֹתַי לְפָנָיו אַבְרָהָם וְיִצְחָק

---

10. לֹא יוּכַל לִרְאוֹת — *So that he could not see.* He could not see them clearly, which was an impediment for his blessing to be effective; similar to, אֲשֶׁר תִּרְאֶנּוּ מִשָּׁם, *From whence you may see them* (*Numbers* 23:13), and to, וַיַּרְאֵהוּ ה׳ אֶת כָּל הָאָרֶץ, *And God showed him all the Land* (*Deut.* 34:1), so that (Moses) might bless it. Also we find by Elisha, וַיִּפֶן אַחֲרָיו וַיִּרְאֵם, *He looked behind him and saw them* (*II Kings* 2:24).

וַיִּשַּׁק לָהֶם וַיְחַבֵּק לָהֶם — *And he kissed them and embraced them* . . . so that his soul might cleave to them and his blessing take effect.

11. גַּם אֶת זַרְעֶךָ — *Your seed also* . . . and regarding them it is said קְהַל עַמִּים, *a company of peoples* (verse 4). Now this (blessing) was given in conjunction with the inheritance of the land, as it states above וַיְבָרֶךְ אוֹתִי, *(God) blessed me* (verse 3), therefore it is fitting that that blessing be given to them (and to Joseph) so (Jacob) blessed both Joseph and his sons (see verses 15-16).

12. מֵעִם בִּרְכָּיו — *From between his knees* . . . the knees of his father who was embracing them.

14. שִׂכֵּל אֶת יָדָיו — *Guiding his hands wittingly.* He detected (their identity) through the sense of feeling, though he could not see.

15. וַיְבָרֶךְ אֶת יוֹסֵף — *And he blessed Joseph.* For this blessing (i.e., Joseph's) he did not have to see, kiss or embrace him. The Torah does not tell us what the blessing was.

וַיֹּאמַר — *And he said* . . . after he blessed Joseph.

הָאֱלֹהִים אֲשֶׁר הִתְהַלְּכוּ אֲבֹתַי לְפָנָיו — *'The God before Whom my forefathers walked.'* O God, in the merit of my forefathers who walked before You (bless them).

NOTES

and Ephraim. Therefore when Jacob asks who these young men are, Joseph stresses that they are indeed his sons and qualify to receive a special blessing.

10. לֹא יוּכַל לִרְאוֹת — *So that he could not see.* The phrase *he could not see* in this verse cannot refer to his inability to recognize them, since their identity had already been established in the previous verse. Therefore the *Sforno* interprets it to mean that Jacob could not 'connect' and relate to them through seeing, so he had to feel and touch them in order to have the blessing flow from him to the lads.

11. גַּם אֶת זַרְעֶךָ — *Your seed also.* See commentary and notes on verse 4.

15. . . . וַיְבָרֶךְ אֶת יוֹסֵף וַיֹּאמַר הָאֱלֹהִים — *And he blessed Joseph and he said, 'The God*. . . Since Jacob was linked to his son Joseph over the years with a profound and abiding love, there was no need, as there was with his grandchildren, to make physical contact with him before he blessed him. The *Sforno* is of the opinion that the phrase וַיְבָרֶךְ אֶת יוֹסֵף, *and he*

טז הָאֱלֹהִים הָרֹעֶה אֹתִי מֵעוֹדִי עַד־הַיּוֹם הַזֶּה: הַמַּלְאָךְ הַגֹּאֵל אֹתִי מִכָּל־רָע
יְבָרֵךְ אֶת־הַנְּעָרִים וְיִקָּרֵא בָהֶם שְׁמִי וְשֵׁם אֲבֹתַי אַבְרָהָם וְיִצְחָק וְיִדְגּוּ לָרֹב
שלישי יז בְּקֶרֶב הָאָרֶץ: וַיַּרְא יוֹסֵף כִּי־יָשִׁית אָבִיו יַד־יְמִינוֹ עַל־רֹאשׁ אֶפְרַיִם וַיֵּרַע
בְּעֵינָיו וַיִּתְמֹךְ יַד־אָבִיו לְהָסִיר אֹתָהּ מֵעַל רֹאשׁ־אֶפְרַיִם עַל־רֹאשׁ מְנַשֶּׁה:
יח וַיֹּאמֶר יוֹסֵף אֶל־אָבִיו לֹא־כֵן אָבִי כִּי־זֶה הַבְּכֹר שִׂים יְמִינְךָ עַל־רֹאשׁוֹ:
יט וַיְמָאֵן אָבִיו וַיֹּאמֶר יָדַעְתִּי בְנִי יָדַעְתִּי גַּם־הוּא יִהְיֶה־לְּעָם וְגַם־הוּא יִגְדָּל
כ וְאוּלָם אָחִיו הַקָּטֹן יִגְדַּל מִמֶּנּוּ וְזַרְעוֹ יִהְיֶה מְלֹא־הַגּוֹיִם: וַיְבָרְכֵם בַּיּוֹם הַהוּא
לֵאמוֹר בְּךָ יְבָרֵךְ יִשְׂרָאֵל לֵאמֹר יְשִׂמְךָ אֱלֹהִים כְּאֶפְרַיִם וְכִמְנַשֶּׁה וַיָּשֶׂם

הָאֱלֹהִים הָרֹעֶה אֹתִי — *The God Who has been my shepherd.* You, Who always showed me kindness (bless them).

16. הַמַּלְאָךְ הַגֹּאֵל אֹתִי מִכָּל רָע יְבָרֵךְ — *The angel who has redeemed me from all evil, bless (the lads).* (O God,) do order *the angel who has redeemed me* to bless the lads, if they do not deserve to be blessed directly by You, without an intermediary.

וְיִקָּרֵא בָהֶם שְׁמִי וְשֵׁם אֲבֹתַי אַבְרָהָם וְיִצְחָק — *And let my name be named in them and the name of my forefathers Abraham and Isaac ...* but not Terach or Nachor, because righteous men are not called by their fathers' names when these are wicked, nor vice versa, as our Sages say, 'A wicked man is called the son of a wicked man, even if he is actually the son of a righteous man' *(Sanhedrin* 52a), so that (this רָשָׁע) not be called by his righteous father's name but be traced back to some wicked forebear. Hence his blessing was a prayer that they might be prepared to serve the Almighty so that they will be worthy to be called after Abraham and Isaac, in keeping with (the expression), יַחֵד לְבָבִי לְיִרְאָה שְׁמֶךָ, *Make one my heart, to fear Your name (Psalms* 86:11).

18. כִּי זֶה הַבְּכֹר שִׂים יְמִינְךָ עַל רֹאשׁוֹ — *For this is the firstborn; put your right hand upon his head.* Placing one's hand upon (the head) of the recipient of a blessing (or a charge) concentrates the thoughts and intent of the 'giver' to the recipient, similar to, וַיִּסְמֹךְ אֶת יָדָיו עָלָיו, *And he laid his hands upon him (Numbers* 27:23). The power of the right hand is greater than the left, and it is (also) more effective to place the right hand on the right side, more so than the left hand on the left side.

NOTES

blessed Joseph, is not connected to the וַיֹּאמַר, *and he said,* which follows, rather this word (וַיֹּאמַר) introduces the following phrase, *O God, etc.* The two expressions used by Jacob, i.e., *The God before Whom my forefathers walked* and *The God Who has been my shepherd,* are not redundant. The first is a request to consider the merits of his forefathers, therefore it is an earned reward he is asking for, whereas the second is in reference to himself which he acknowledges, with due modesty, is unearned, for God was his shepherd only out of kindness.

16. הַמַּלְאָךְ הַגֹּאֵל אֹתִי ... וְיִקָּרֵא בָהֶם שְׁמִי וְשֵׁם אֲבֹתַי — *The angel who has redeemed me ... And let my name be named in them and the name of my forefathers.* First Jacob asks God to bless his grandchildren *directly,* and if that be excessive, let it be through his guardian angel. Jacob prays that Ephraim and Menasseh be worthy, through their own piety, to be called after Abraham and Isaac. Even though our Sages have taught us that 'fear of Heaven' cannot be granted by God, but must be formed and developed by the person on his own, nevertheless one *can* pray that the Almighty should assist him to withstand temptation and cleave to Him. To support this concept the *Sforno* correctly quotes David who also asks the assistance of God in bringing him to the level of יִרְאָה, *reverence* for God.

כא אֶת־אֶפְרַיִם לִפְנֵי מְנַשֶּׁה: וַיֹּאמֶר יִשְׂרָאֵל אֶל־יוֹסֵף הִנֵּה אָנֹכִי מֵת וְהָיָה
כב אֱלֹהִים עִמָּכֶם וְהֵשִׁיב אֶתְכֶם אֶל־אֶרֶץ אֲבֹתֵיכֶם: וַאֲנִי נָתַתִּי לְךָ שְׁכֶם
אַחַד עַל־אַחֶיךָ אֲשֶׁר לָקַחְתִּי מִיַּד הָאֱמֹרִי בְּחַרְבִּי וּבְקַשְׁתִּי:
מט רביעי א וַיִּקְרָא יַעֲקֹב אֶל־בָּנָיו וַיֹּאמֶר הֵאָסְפוּ וְאַגִּידָה לָכֶם אֵת אֲשֶׁר־יִקְרָא
ב אֶתְכֶם בְּאַחֲרִית הַיָּמִים: הִקָּבְצוּ וְשִׁמְעוּ בְּנֵי יַעֲקֹב וְשִׁמְעוּ אֶל־יִשְׂרָאֵל

---

21. הִנֵּה אָנֹכִי מֵת — *Behold I die.* I instruct you at the time of death, thereby confirming the gift I give to you.

וְהֵשִׁיב אֶתְכֶם אֶל אֶרֶץ — *And (He) will bring you back unto the Land . . .* and there my gift will become a reality (fulfilled).

22. וַאֲנִי נָתַתִּי לְךָ שְׁכֶם אַחַד עַל אַחֶיךָ אֲשֶׁר לָקַחְתִּי מִיַּד הָאֱמֹרִי — *I have given to you Shechem above your brethren, which I took out of the hand of the Amorite.* Do not think that I have (improperly) transferred the inheritance of all your brothers by giving you Shechem, for what I give (I am entitled to) since I took it from those who conducted themselves wickedly, akin to the Amorite. (Or) I took it from Esau who 'says' much but does little beneficial, hence I bought the birthright from him, for had I not, your brothers would not have so large an inheritance in the Land (of Israel).

בְּחַרְבִּי וּבְקַשְׁתִּי — *With my sword and with my bow . . .* my wisdom and discernment which are referred to as the sword and bow of the righteous, as it is written: חֲגוֹר חַרְבְּךָ עַל יָרֵךְ גִּבּוֹר, *Gird your sword upon your thigh, O mighty one (Psalms* 45:4), which is explained by our Sages as referring to דִּבְרֵי תוֹרָה, *the words of Torah (Shabbos* 63a). The opposite is true (of the wicked), as it is written, שִׁנֵּיהֶם חֲנִית וְחִצִּים וּלְשׁוֹנָם חֶרֶב חַדָּה, *Whose teeth are spears and arrows, and their tongue a sharp sword (Psalms* 57:5), and also, וַיַּדְרְכוּ אֶת לְשׁוֹנָם קַשְׁתָּם שֶׁקֶר, *And they bend their tongue, their bow of falsehood (Jeremiah* 9:2).

XLIX

1. בְּאַחֲרִית הַיָּמִים — *In the end of days.* 'The end of days' (refers to) the Messianic era which will mark the decline and fall of those nations who are enemies of God. (This

NOTES

21. הִנֵּה אָנֹכִי מֵת — *Behold I die.* The *halachah* is that a person on his death bed (שְׁכִיב מְרַע) can effect a legal transfer by making a statement without the need for an act of selling or giving; nor must it be put in writing. That is why Jacob stresses that he is about to die, and as a שְׁכִיב מְרַע his gift of Shechem to Joseph is valid.

22. מִיַּד הָאֱמֹרִי בְּחַרְבִּי וּבְקַשְׁתִּי — *Which I took out of the hand of the Amorite with my sword and with my bow.* The *Sforno* gives two different interpretations to the word אֱמֹרִי. One is that it refers to Shechem and Chamor who conducted themselves in the devious manner of the Amorite. The second is that it refers to Esau, who used words to ensnare and mislead his father and others. The word אֱמֹרִי is related to אמר, *say.* Jacob, according to this latter interpretation, argues that Joseph's brothers should have no grievance against their father for giving a double portion to Joseph (whom he considers his בְּכוֹר, *firstborn),* for had Jacob not bought the birthright from Esau there would be far less land to divide between themselves. The point made here by the *Sforno* is that the words *sword* and *bow* are similes for wisdom, discernment and planning. The righteous man uses these gifts, which are developed through Torah, for positive ends, while the wicked person uses these same talents for evil ends.

XLIX

1. בְּאַחֲרִית הַיָּמִים — *In the end of days.* The *Sforno,* as do other commentators, interprets

ג־ד אֲבִיכֶם: רְאוּבֵן בְּכֹרִי אַתָּה כֹּחִי וְרֵאשִׁית אוֹנִי יֶתֶר שְׂאֵת וְיֶתֶר עָז: פַּחַז
כַּמַּיִם אַל־תּוֹתַר כִּי עָלִיתָ מִשְׁכְּבֵי אָבִיךָ אָז חִלַּלְתָּ יְצוּעִי עָלָה:
ה־ו שִׁמְעוֹן וְלֵוִי אַחִים כְּלֵי חָמָס מְכֵרֹתֵיהֶם: בְּסֹדָם אַל־תָּבֹא נַפְשִׁי בִּקְהָלָם

---

will come to pass) when their measure (of evil) will be filled to overflowing, as it is said, כִּי אֶעֱשֶׂה כָלָה בְּכָל הַגּוֹיִם . . . וְאֹתְךָ לֹא אֶעֱשֶׂה כָלָה, *For I will make a full end of all the nations . . . but I will not make a full end of you (Jeremiah* 46:28). This is also what Balaam means when he says, בְּאַחֲרִית הַיָּמִים, *at the end of days (Numbers* 24:14). Proof can be found in what he later states, וְקַרְקַר כָּל בְּנֵי שֵׁת, *And break down all the sons of Seth* (ibid. v. 17). The prophets also refer to the Messianic Era when they use this phrase, וְהָיָה בְּאַחֲרִית הַיָּמִים יִהְיֶה הַר בֵּית ה׳ נָכוֹן בְּרֹאשׁ הֶהָרִים, *In the end of days it shall come to pass that the mountain of God's house shall be established as the top of the mountain (Micah* 4:1). And it is of this (same era) that Jacob speaks when he later says (verses 10-11), *Until Shiloh comes and unto him the obedience of the people be; binding his foal unto the vine.*

2. וְשִׁמְעוּ אֶל יִשְׂרָאֵל אֲבִיכֶם — *And hearken unto Israel your father.* Accept the way which he has taught you all his life. Thereby you will be true 'sons of Israel' and he in turn will be your father; you will strive with God and man (and prevail) and not forfeit the good (reward) which will be yours in the future.

4. פַּחַז כַּמַּיִם אַל תּוֹתַר — *Unstable as water, therefore you will not have (this) excellency.* You (Reuben, who are) unstable as water, will not be exalted over your brothers with an 'excellency of dignity,' i.e., priesthood and בְּכוֹרָה (the rights and privileges of the firstborn) even though you are רֵאשִׁית אוֹנִי, *the first fruits of my strength,* and entitled to these rights, as it says, . . . כִּי הוּא רֵאשִׁית אֹנוֹ, *for he is the first fruits of his strength, the right of the firstborn is his (Deut.* 21:17). Nor will you be exalted with 'excellency of power,' i.e., kingship, which is designated by (this term) 'strength' as our Sages state, אֵין עוֹז אֶלָּא מַלְכוּת, *When the verse states 'strength,' it refers only to 'kingship' (Bereishis Rabbah* 99:6). Kingship would also have been fitting for the firstborn, as it is written, וְאֶת הַמַּמְלָכָה נָתַן לִיהוֹרָם כִּי הוּא הַבְּכוֹר, *And the kingship he gave to Yehoram for he was the firstborn (II Chronicles* 21:3).

אָז חִלַּלְתָּ יְצוּעִי עָלָה — *Then you defiled it; he went up to my couch.* You defiled (desecrated) the honor of your father (or) the honor of the *Shechinah* (Divine Presence) which was wont to ascend my bed, and therefore your honor will be defiled and you will descend from your original status.

5. שִׁמְעוֹן וְלֵוִי אַחִים — *Simeon and Levi are brothers.* The honors which Reuben was entitled to (but forfeited) should have been theirs (Simeon and Levi) as next in seniority, however . . .

NOTES

the words אַחֲרִית הַיָּמִים, *the end of days,* as referring to the time of *Mashiach,* the Messiah. His proof from Balaam's words are to be understood in the sense that mankind is called 'sons of Seth' since they are descended from Seth, after the death of Cain and Abel, and *Mashiach* will rule over all mankind. The phrases used by Jacob in verses 10 and 11 also refer to *Mashiach,* who will come riding on a foal (ass) as a symbol of peace, and not a horse which is associated with war.

2. וְשִׁמְעוּ אֶל יִשְׂרָאֵל אֲבִיכֶם – *And hearken unto Israel your father.* The phrase, *hearken to Israel,* is not a repetition of, *hear you sons of Jacob.* The first phrase is to be understood in the literal sense, but the second one refers to the mission and purpose of 'Israel,' to strive

ז אַל־תֵּחַד כְּבֹדִי כִּי בְאַפָּם הָרְגוּ אִישׁ וּבִרְצֹנָם עִקְּרוּ־שׁוֹר: אָרוּר אַפָּם כִּי עָז
וְעֶבְרָתָם כִּי קָשָׁתָה אֲחַלְּקֵם בְּיַעֲקֹב וַאֲפִיצֵם בְּיִשְׂרָאֵל:
ח-ט יְהוּדָה אַתָּה יוֹדוּךָ אַחֶיךָ יָדְךָ בְּעֹרֶף אֹיְבֶיךָ יִשְׁתַּחֲווּ לְךָ בְּנֵי אָבִיךָ: גּוּר
אַרְיֵה יְהוּדָה מִטֶּרֶף בְּנִי עָלִיתָ כָּרַע רָבַץ כְּאַרְיֵה וּכְלָבִיא מִי יְקִימֶנּוּ:

כְּלֵי חָמָס מְכֵרֹתֵיהֶם — *Weapons of violence (are) their kinship* . . . and it is not fitting for a king, who בְּמִשְׁפָּט יַעֲמִיד אָרֶץ, *with justice establishes the land (Proverbs* 29:4) (to use instruments of violence); therefore it is not fitting that the kingship be theirs.

7. אָרוּר אַפָּם — *Cursed be their anger.* Their anger will (perforce) be lessened through their lowly state and hard life, caused by the fact that they will be divided and scattered.

The priesthood, however, still remained with the firstborn until it was given to the Levites (in the merit of their loyalty to God) as it is written, בָּעֵת הַהִוא הִבְדִּיל ה׳ אֶת שֵׁבֶט הַלֵּוִי, *At that time the Lord separated the tribe of Levi (Deut.* 10:8).

8. יְהוּדָה אַתָּה יוֹדוּךָ אַחֶיךָ — *Judah, your brothers shall praise you.* You are worthy of kingship for one cannot find a blemish in you to disqualify you, as is the case with your (older) brothers; therefore (your brothers) shall accept you as king, because they shall praise you as worthy of ruling.

יָדְךָ בְּעֹרֶף אֹיְבֶיךָ — *Your hand shall be on the neck of your enemies.* They shall flee before you, similar to, וְנָתַתִּי אֶת כָּל אֹיְבֶיךָ אֵלֶיךָ עֹרֶף, *And I will make all your enemies turn their backs unto you (Exodus* 23:27).

יִשְׁתַּחֲווּ לְךָ בְּנֵי אָבִיךָ — *Your father's sons shall bow down before you.* You will reign over your father's sons but not over the nations, *until Shiloh comes* (verse 10), at which time you will rule not only over your father's sons but the nations as well, as it is written, *and unto him shall be the obedience of the peoples* (ibid.).

9. גּוּר אַרְיֵה יְהוּדָה — *Judah is a lion's whelp.* Though presently Judah is not yet a lion, for he is not yet a king, still he is like a גּוּר אַרְיֵה, *young lion,* ruling over his brothers, and ultimately will be a king, nonetheless . . .

מִטֶּרֶף בְּנִי עָלִיתָ — *From the prey, my son, you are gone up.* You, my son Joseph, are gone up from the prey, i.e., (Judah was) not prepared to kill you in his anger, even though he (also) hated you, because . . .

NOTES

with God and man, and to prevail.

5. שִׁמְעוֹן וְלֵוִי אַחִים – *Simeon and Levi are brothers.* The key word is אַחִים, *brothers.* As the brothers of Reuben, next to him in age, they should have succeeded to his rights and privileges, but were also found wanting — especially insofar as Jewish kingship is concerned. A king of Israel rules with justice and by right, not might and violence. Simeon and Levi's temperaments were such that they could not fit this required role.

7. אָרוּר אַפָּם – *Cursed be their anger.* Jacob does not curse his sons. The word אָרוּר in this case means *diminishment* or *reduction,* just as בְּרָכָה, *blessing,* denotes *increase* and *growth* (compare to 4:11). Their anger will be kept under control due to their difficult circumstances. The tribe of Simeon was destined to become itinerant teachers while the Levites had no portion in the Land and were dependent upon the gifts granted to them by the Torah.

8. יִשְׁתַּחֲווּ לְךָ בְּנֵי אָבִיךָ — *Your father's sons shall bow down before you.* Here again the *Sforno* weaves the theme of *Mashiach* into the blessings of Jacob. At the beginning of Israel's sojourn in *Eretz Yisrael,* the descendants of Judah will reign over their own people. At the 'end of time,' however, *Mashiach* will rule over the nations as well.

י לֹא־יָסוּר שֵׁבֶט מִיהוּדָה וּמְחֹקֵק מִבֵּין רַגְלָיו עַד כִּי־יָבֹא שִׁילֹה וְלוֹ יִקְּהַת
יא עַמִּים: אֹסְרִי לַגֶּפֶן עִירֹה וְלַשֹּׂרֵקָה בְּנִי אֲתֹנוֹ כִּבֵּס בַּיַּיִן לְבֻשׁוֹ וּבְדַם־עֲנָבִים

כָּרַע רָבַץ כְּאַרְיֵה — *He stooped down, he crouched as a lion.* He was like a lion that crouches but doesn't leap; he did not order his brothers to kill you.

וּכְלָבִיא מִי יְקִימֶנּוּ — *And as a lioness, who shall rise him up?* In the future, there will be a period when he shall crouch as a lioness in his homeland, none daring to frighten him away.

10. לֹא יָסוּר שֵׁבֶט מִיהוּדָה — *The scepter shall not depart from Judah* . . . as long as there is kingship in Israel, as it says, וּכְלָבִיא מִי יְקִימֶנּוּ (verse 9). The scepter of kingship will not be removed from Judah in favor of another tribe of Israel, as it is written: וְחַסְדִּי לֹא יָסוּר מִמֶּנּוּ כַּאֲשֶׁר הֲסִרֹתִי מֵעִם שָׁאוּל אֲשֶׁר הֲסִרֹתִי מִלְּפָנֶיךָ, *But My mercy shall not depart from him, as I took it from Saul, whom I put away before you (II Samuel* 7:15). However, when Judah fell, (conquered) by other nations (even though the scepter *was* removed) this is not called הֲסָרָה, *removal,* for this (word) is only (applicable to the) moving of an item (or power) from place to place (within a similar area or category). When, however, something is totally lost and no longer exists, the term הֲסָרָה cannot be used. (Since, at the time of the *churban,* destruction,) the scepter did not pass to another tribe of Israel, but was totally wrested from (Judah by the enemy, the prophecy of Jacob was not refuted).

וּמְחֹקֵק מִבֵּין רַגְלָיו — *Nor the ruler's staff from between his feet.* The judge who sits on the chair (throne) will be his descendant, and between (at) his feet will be the scribe, as was their custom.

עַד כִּי יָבֹא שִׁילֹה — *Until Shiloh does come.* The word *Shiloh* is derived from two roots: שול which means *sole,* and שלה which denotes שָׁלוֹם, *peace,* hence Shiloh means *peace at the end.* The prophecy (of Jacob) that Judah will be ruler and judge *only* among his brothers will be so *until Shiloh comes* (i.e., *Mashiach*) . . .

וְלוֹ יִקְּהַת עַמִּים — *And unto him shall be the obedience of the peoples.* But when *Mashiach* appears, and there will be שָׁלוֹם בַּסּוֹף, *peace at the end,* then his shall be the weakening of peoples, יִקְּהַת, similar to אִם קֵהָה הַבַּרְזֶל, *If the iron be blunt (Ecclesiastes* 10:10). Those who remain, weakened after the destruction of their kingdom, will be obedient (and subjugated) to Shiloh *(Mashiach)* as it says: וְקַרְקַר כָּל בְּנֵי שֵׁת, *And break down all the sons of Seth (Numbers* 24:17).

11. אֹסְרִי לַגֶּפֶן עִירֹה וְלַשֹּׂרֵקָה בְּנִי אֲתֹנוֹ כִּבֵּס בַּיַּיִן לְבֻשׁוֹ — *Binding his foal unto the vine*

NOTES

9. גּוּר אַרְיֵה יְהוּדָה . . . כָּרַע רָבַץ כְּאַרְיֵה — *Judah is a lion's whelp . . . He stooped down, he crouched as a lion.* The final decision regarding Joseph's fate rested with Judah, who was acknowledged by his brothers as their leader. In this respect he was like a lion's whelp. It was not until later, in *Eretz Yisrael,* that he was destined to become a lion (i.e., a king). Nonetheless, even though he had the power to dispose of Joseph he declared, *'What profit is it, if we slay our brother?'* (37:26). So he is compared to a lion that crouches but does not leap.

10. וְלוֹ יִקְּהַת עַמִּים — *And unto him shall be the obedience of the peoples.* The *Sforno,* like the *Ramban* on this verse, connects the word יִקְּהַת, *obedience,* with the root meaning *to weaken,* thus the interpretation is 'and his (*Mashiach's* — Shiloh's) shall be the weakening of peoples,' i.e., the remnant of the nations who will survive the heavenly wrath and destruction will be subjugated by him. As in verse 1 the *Sforno* cites the words of Balaam to support this interpretation; the children of Seth (mankind) will be 'broken down' by *Mashiach.*

יב סוּתֹה: חַכְלִילִי עֵינַיִם מִיָּיִן וּלְבֶן־שִׁנַּיִם מֵחָלָב:
יג זְבוּלֻן לְחוֹף יַמִּים יִשְׁכֹּן וְהוּא לְחוֹף אֳנִיֹּת וְיַרְכָתוֹ עַל־צִידֹן:

---

and his ass's colt unto the choice vine, he washes his garment in wine. The signs of the *Mashiach* are:

(a) He will appear on an עַיִר בֶּן אֲתֹנוֹת, *a colt, the foal of an ass* (*Zechariah* 9:9), as the prophet says. He will not ride on a horse which is ready for battle (see *Proverbs* 21:31 — *a horse prepared for the day of battle)* because the war of the nations and the destruction of their kingdoms will have already been completed through the Almighty, and he *(Mashiach)* will be the king of peace.

(b) He will *bind the foal to a vine,* which is symbolic of his kingdom of peace dwelling in the midst of Israel, who are compared to the vine, as our Sages tell us, אוּמָּה זוּ לְגֶפֶן נִמְשְׁלָה, *This nation (Israel) is compared to a vine* (*Chullin* 92a), and so the prophet also testifies: כִּי כֶרֶם ה׳ צְבָאוֹת בֵּית יִשְׂרָאֵל, *For the vineyard of* H*ASHEM*, *Lord of Hosts, is the house of Israel* (*Isaiah* 5:7).

(c) The third of the signs (by which he will be recognized) is the tying of his ass to the choice vine, which means that he will cause his face to shine with favor upon the righteous ones of that generation — not upon the entire vineyard.

(d) The fourth of the signs will be his ability to *wash his garment* in blood, for his arrival will be preceded by the slaughter (of the nations), as we find, מַדּוּעַ אָדֹם לִלְבוּשֶׁךָ, *Wherefore is your apparel red?* (*Isaiah* 63:2), and, יָדִין בַּגּוֹיִם מָלֵא גְוִיּוֹת, *He will judge among the nations, He fills it with dead bodies* (*Psalms* 110:6).

12. חַכְלִילִי עֵינַיִם מִיָּיִן — *His eyes shall be red with wine.* The fifth sign will be the unusual abundance (of food) in the world, as it says: יְהִי פִסַּת בַּר בָּאָרֶץ בְּרֹאשׁ הָרִים יִרְעַשׁ כַּלְּבָנוֹן פִּרְיוֹ, *May he be as a rich cornfield in the land upon the top of the mountains, may his fruit rustle like Lebanon* (*Psalms* 72:16), and as our Sages tell us, '*Eretz Yisrael* is destined to bring forth cakes and woolen robes' (*Shabbos* 30b).

13. זְבוּלֻן לְחוֹף יַמִּים יִשְׁכֹּן — *Zebulun shall dwell at the shore of the sea* . . . in his Land, he dwelt at the shore for that was his inheritance. Zebulun is mentioned before Issachar (even though he is younger) because he occupied himself with commerce while Issachar studied Torah and one cannot study Torah unless his material wants are satisfied, as our Sages teach us, אִם אֵין קֶמַח אֵין תּוֹרָה, *Without flour there can be no Torah* (*Avos* 3:17). By Zebulun aiding Issachar the merit belongs to both. That is also why Moses in his blessing states: שְׂמַח זְבוּלֻן בְּצֵאתֶךָ וְיִשָּׂשכָר בְּאֹהָלֶיךָ, *Rejoice, Zebulun in your going out, and Issachar in your tents* (*Deut.* 33:18). This is also the Torah's purpose in commanding that gifts be given

NOTES

11-12. אֹסְרִי לַגֶּפֶן עִירֹה . . . כִּבֵּס בַּיַּיִן לְבֻשׁוֹ . . . חַכְלִילִי עֵינַיִם מִיָּיִן — *Binding his foal unto the vine . . . He washes his garment in wine . . . His eyes shall be red with wine.* Consistent with his interpretation of Shiloh as *Mashiach*, the *Sforno* interprets these verses as a series of signs by which he will be recognized. These include: the method by which he will appear; his dwelling in the midst of Israel with special favor shown to the righteous among them; the violent upheaval and destruction which will precede his arrival; and the blessing of material abundance which will follow upon his coming. The *Sforno* stresses that *Mashiach* is not a man of war, but of peace. The battles and annihilation will take place among the nations as part of a Divine plan, *preceding* the appearance of שִׁילֹה who is the embodiment of 'peace at the end,' as this name indicates.

13. זְבוּלֻן לְחוֹף יַמִּים יִשְׁכֹּן — *Zebulun shall dwell at the shore of the sea.* The *Sforno's* development of this verse mirrors the teachings of our Sages, that a partnership exists between the

יד-טו יִשָּׂשכָר חֲמֹר גָּרֶם רֹבֵץ בֵּין הַמִּשְׁפְּתָיִם: וַיַּרְא מְנֻחָה כִּי טוֹב וְאֶת־הָאָרֶץ
טז כִּי נָעֵמָה וַיֵּט שִׁכְמוֹ לִסְבֹּל וַיְהִי לְמַס־עֹבֵד: דָּן יָדִין עַמּוֹ

(by Israel) to the Priests and Levites, so that all shall support the scholars and teachers of Torah, i.e., the Priests and Levites, as it says יוֹרוּ מִשְׁפָּטֶיךָ לְיַעֲקֹב, *They shall teach Jacob your law (Deut.* 33:10), and thereby merit, together with them, eternal life, as our Sages teach us, כָּל יִשְׂרָאֵל יֵשׁ לָהֶם חֵלֶק לְעוֹלָם הַבָּא, *All Israel have a portion in the world to come (Sanhedrin* 90a).

וְהוּא לְחוֹף אֳנִיֹּת — *And he shall be a shore for ships.* (This refers to Zebulun when he travels abroad), going to other shores to trade in various merchandise such as small fishes, purple (goods) and milk glass, which are found in the sea and sand, as the verse testifies, כִּי שֶׁפַע יַמִּים יִינָקוּ וּשְׂפֻנֵי טְמוּנֵי חוֹל, *For they shall suck the abundance of the seas, and the hidden treasures of the sand (Deut.* 33:19).

14. יִשָּׂשכָר חֲמֹר — *Issachar is a (large-boned) ass* . . . unsuited for war, as our Sages say: אִי סַפְרָא לָא סַיְיפָא, *If one is a scholar, he is not a robber* (lit., *a man of the sword) (Avodah Zarah* 17b)

גָּרֶם — *Large-boned.* Strong and firm-boned, as a result of which . . .

רֹבֵץ בֵּין הַמִּשְׁפְּתָיִם — *Crouching down between the sheepfolds.* When he takes his rest he does so while his burdens are still upon him (overflowing his flanks), for they are not removed until the task is done; now this can only be done by an ass that is extremely strong. In a similar fashion will Issachar carry the burdens of Torah study, worldly occupation and communal administration, as is fitting for a wise man who has attained perfection, intellectually and ethically.

15. וַיַּרְא מְנֻחָה כִּי טוֹב — *He saw a resting place that it was good.* He saw that peace of mind and fulfillment can be found in perfecting one's mental and spiritual potential, which is the ultimate good, as is written, וּמִצְאוּ מַרְגּוֹעַ לְנַפְשְׁכֶם, *And you shall find rest for your souls (Jeremiah* 6:16).

וְאֶת הָאָרֶץ כִּי נָעֵמָה — *And the land that it was pleasant.* He also saw that his portion of land (in *Eretz Yisrael*) was capable of sustaining him without difficulty and furnishing a livelihood without discomfort.

וַיֵּט שִׁכְמוֹ לִסְבֹּל — *And he bowed his shoulder to bear* . . . the double burden of Torah study and communal responsibility, as our Sages teach us, 'A Torah scholar

NOTES

Torah scholar and the supporter of Torah. Both shall be equally rewarded, but the supporter is given precedence over the scholar since we see that Jacob blessed Zebulun before Issachar, even though the former was younger.

14. יִשָּׂשכָר חֲמֹר גָּרֶם רֹבֵץ בֵּין הַמִּשְׁפְּתָיִם — *Issachar is a large-boned ass, crouching down between the sheepfolds.* Compare to verse 11 where the *Sforno* posits that the horse symbolizes war, while the ass represents peace — which is the reason that *Mashiach* will arrive riding on 'the foal of an ass.' Here Issachar is also compared to חֲמוֹר, *an ass,* symbolizing peace, contentment and tranquility — the characteristics of the Torah scholar. The *Sforno's* philosophy, expressed in much of his writings, is that the אִישׁ שָׁלֵם — *complete man* — in the view of Torah, is one who combines Torah scholarship with דֶּרֶךְ אֶרֶץ, worldly occupation; מִדּוֹת, ethical excellence and the acceptance of communal responsibility. All these virtues Issachar possesses.

15. וַיַּרְא מְנֻחָה כִּי טוֹב וְאֶת הָאָרֶץ כִּי נָעֵמָה — *He saw a resting place that it was good, and the land that it was pleasant.* Careful review of this verse will clarify the profound interpretation of the *Sforno.* מְנוּחָה, *rest* and *tranquility,*

יז כְּאַחַד שִׁבְטֵי יִשְׂרָאֵל: יְהִי־דָן נָחָשׁ עֲלֵי־דֶרֶךְ שְׁפִיפֹן עֲלֵי־אֹרַח הַנֹּשֵׁךְ
חמישי יח־יט עִקְּבֵי־סוּס וַיִּפֹּל רֹכְבוֹ אָחוֹר: לִישׁוּעָתְךָ קִוִּיתִי יהוה: גָּד גְּדוּד
כ יְגוּדֶנּוּ וְהוּא יָגֻד עָקֵב: מֵאָשֵׁר שְׁמֵנָה לַחְמוֹ וְהוּא יִתֵּן מַעֲדַנֵּי־
כא־כב מֶלֶךְ: נַפְתָּלִי אַיָּלָה שְׁלֻחָה הַנֹּתֵן אִמְרֵי־שָׁפֶר: בֵּן פֹּרָת יוֹסֵף

---

dwelling in a community should accept upon himself the responsibility of community affairs' (*Moed Katan* 6a).

וַיְהִי לְמַס עֹבֵד — *And became a servant under taskwork* . . . (whereupon) the rest of the community, which engaged only in worldly occupation (accepted to work for him and relieve him of that burden), as our Sages tell us, 'His townspeople are commanded to do his work' (*Yoma* 72b).

17. יְהִי דָן נָחָשׁ — *Dan shall be a serpent* . . . a species of snake called צִפְעוֹנִי, *adder*, or חוּרְמוֹן, *chormon*, as called by Arab naturalists, which is most deadly — for one such serpent can kill many victims. Thus did Samson destroy many of his enemies swiftly by himself.

שְׁפִיפֹן — *A horned snake* . . . a long, thin snake, as our Sages tell us, כְּחוּט הַשַּׂעֲרָה הוּא וּשְׁפִיפוֹן שְׁמוֹ, *(Long and thin) like a single hair, and it is called sh'fifon* (*Yerushalmi Terumos* 8:5), and of this snake the experts tell us that he hides among the trees and attacks (his prey) like an arrow; so did Samson, who fought alone (without any army and suddenly attacked) whereupon he disappeared.

19. גָּד גְּדוּד יְגוּדֶנּוּ — *Gad, a troop shall troop upon him.* After telling us that Dan will fight like a serpent, (biting the horse's heels) and causing the horse and rider to fall, he now (foresees) that Gad will do battle by cutting down the rider and his horse, as we find, וְטָרַף זְרוֹעַ אַף קָדְקֹד, *And tears the arm, even the crown of the head* (*Deut.* 33:20).

וְהוּא יָגֻד עָקֵב — *And he shall cut down (their) heel.* When he cuts down the horse and rider it shall be from the rear, for (his enemy) will be fleeing from him, as we find, וְנָתַתִּי אֶת כָּל אֹיְבֶיךָ אֵלֶיךָ עֹרֶף, *And I will make all your enemies turn their backs unto you* (*Exodus* 23:27) (compare to verse 8).

22. בֵּן פֹּרָת יוֹסֵף — *Joseph is a fruitful vine.* Behold, Joseph is the son of a fruitful vine, the branch of a flowing vine which casts a protecting shade as does the vine, as it says: כָּסּוּ הָרִים צִלָּהּ, *The mountains were covered with the shadow of it* (*Psalms* 80:11). So did (Joseph) protect his father and brothers in Egypt.

NOTES

is not to be understood in the negative sense i.e., inaction and non-exertion. The *Midrash* tells us that מְנוּחָה זוּ תּוֹרָה, *true tranquility results from the study of Torah.* This is the מְנוּחָה of the soul, and this is the real meaning of שָׁלוֹם, *peace*, which concludes the priestly blessing, i.e., וְיָשֵׂם לְךָ שָׁלוֹם, *and grant you peace*, which the *Sforno* explains as 'the tranquility of peace that is eternity' (*Numbers* 6:26). This is the way of life chosen by Issachar — pursuit of Torah coupled with communal responsibility.

As for his basic needs, even though Zebulun assisted him, Issachar apparently still tended to much of his own material requirements. The portion of land allocated to Issachar in *Eretz Yisrael* was fertile and productive, and hence did not require arduous labor. Still, in order to free Issachar from time-consuming worldly pursuits, the community of laymen lent him their assistance, a custom followed to this very day.

19. וְהוּא יָגֻד עָקֵב – *And he shall cut down (their) heel.* The verb גד means to cut, as we

כג בֵּן פֹּרָת עֲלֵי־עָיִן בָּנוֹת צָעֲדָה עֲלֵי־שׁוּר: וַיְמָרְרֻהוּ וָרֹבּוּ וַיִּשְׂטְמֻהוּ בַּעֲלֵי
כד חִצִּים: וַתֵּשֶׁב בְּאֵיתָן קַשְׁתּוֹ וַיָּפֹזּוּ זְרֹעֵי יָדָיו מִידֵי אֲבִיר יַעֲקֹב מִשָּׁם

בֵּן פֹּרָת עֲלֵי עָיִן בָּנוֹת — *A fruitful vine by a fountain, whose branches* (lit., *daughters*). He was like the bough of a fruitful vine growing by a fountain, from which many branches grow . . .

צָעֲדָה עֲלֵי שׁוּר — *Run over the wall.* That vine which ran over the wall near the fountain (grew) in a manner in which beforehand it was not visible on the other side and (therefore its existence) was unknown to those who lived there; so did Joseph and his sons suddenly make themselves known to Jacob and the brothers, as it is written: רְאֹה פָנֶיךָ לֹא פִלָּלְתִּי וְהִנֵּה הֶרְאָה אֹתִי אֱלֹהִים גַּם אֶת זַרְעֶךָ, *I had not thought to see your face; and lo, God has let me see your seed also* (48:11).

23. וַיִּשְׂטְמֻהוּ בַּעֲלֵי חִצִּים — *The archers dealt bitterly with him.* Slanderers, as it is written, חֵץ שָׁחוּט לְשׁוֹנָם, *Their tongue is a sharpened arrow (Jeremiah 9:7)*, among them being the chief butler (who when recalling Joseph to Pharaoh) says (slightingly), נַעַר עִבְרִי עֶבֶד, *a young man, a Hebrew, a slave* (41:12), as well as a number of Pharaoh's servants who disparaged Joseph by protesting, עֶבֶד שֶׁקָּנָה אוֹתוֹ רַבּוֹ בְּעֶשְׂרִים כֶּסֶף תַּמְלִיכֵהוּ עָלֵינוּ, *How can you appoint as your viceroy a slave, purchased by his master for twenty pieces of silver? (Sotah* 36b).

24. וַתֵּשֶׁב בְּאֵיתָן קַשְׁתּוֹ — *But his bow abode firm.* However his was a bow from which arrows were shot accurately to refute these slanderers, i.e., Pharaoh, who said (firmly) to his servants, הֲנִמְצָא כָזֶה אִישׁ אֲשֶׁר רוּחַ אֱלֹהִים בּוֹ, *Can we find such a one as this, a man in whom the spirit of God is?* (41:38), and אֵין נָבוֹן וְחָכָם כָּמוֹךָ, *There is none so discreet and wise as you* (41:39).

וַיָּפֹזּוּ זְרֹעֵי יָדָיו — *And the arms of his hands were made supple . . .* when Pharaoh placed his ring on (Joseph's) finger.

מִידֵי אֲבִיר יַעֲקֹב — *By the hands of the Mighty One of Jacob.* This salvation and success was yours thanks to the intervention of the Mighty One of Jacob (God), Who insures the survival of His children among the nations unto the very end, as the name יַעֲקֹב, *Jacob*, implies, that his children will survive to the (end of time). So, also, He is the One Who saved you from the arrows of your enemies who dealt so bitterly with you.

מִשָּׁם — *From there . . .* and it is ever from this source of God's goodness . . .

NOTES

see in, לֹא תִתְגֹּדְדוּ, *You shall not cut yourselves (Deuteronomy* 14:1*)*. The *Sforno's* interpretation is based on this premise.

22. בֵּן פֹּרָת עֲלֵי עָיִן בָּנוֹת — *A fruitful vine by a fountain, whose branches . . .* The *Sforno* links the word בָּנוֹת, *branches* (lit., *daughter*) to the phrase above, i.e., *a fruitful vine by a fountain*, rather than with the subsequent one, i.e., 'run over the wall.' In this manner the imagery is quite clear and reasonable. The vine grows on one side of the wall producing new branches (Joseph and his sons), then suddenly appears on the other side becoming visible to others (Jacob and the brothers).

23. וַיִּשְׂטְמֻהוּ בַּעֲלֵי חִצִּים — *The archers dealt bitterly with him.* The *Sforno*, as do other commentators, rejects the interpretation that this refers to Joseph's brothers, for as the *Radak* states, 'Jacob would never denigrate his sons thus.' Therefore the word *archers* must refer to the chief butler and Pharaoh's servants.

24. וַתֵּשֶׁב בְּאֵיתָן קַשְׁתּוֹ – *But his bow abode firm.* The bow is Joseph's, the arrows are Pharaoh's. True, Pharaoh is the one who defends him, but were it not for Joseph's

כה רֹעֶה אֶבֶן יִשְׂרָאֵל: מֵאֵל אָבִיךָ וְיַעְזְרֶךָּ וְאֵת שַׁדַּי וִיבָרְכֶךָּ בִּרְכֹת שָׁמַיִם
כו מֵעָל בִּרְכֹת תְּהוֹם רֹבֶצֶת תָּחַת בִּרְכֹת שָׁדַיִם וָרָחַם: בִּרְכֹת אָבִיךָ גָּבְרוּ

רֹעֶה אֶבֶן יִשְׂרָאֵל — *The shepherd, the Stone of Israel.* He shepherds the remnant of Israel and insures their survival among the nations, be it as precious or non-precious stones, which (both) last many a year, similar to, הִתְגְּזֶרֶת אֶבֶן דִּי לָא בִידַיִן וּמְחָת לְצַלְמָא עַל רַגְלוֹהִי, *That a stone was cut out without hands, which smote the image upon its feet (Daniel* 2:34), referring to Israel who strive with God and man, as our Sages state, 'Wherever they go they become princes to their masters' (*Sanhedrin* 104b).

25. מֵאֵל אָבִיךָ — *Even by the God of your father.* This (good fortune) befell you because He is the God of your father, Who assured me that after my seed will have fallen to the lowest level, they will be elevated, as it is written, וְהָיָה זַרְעֲךָ כַּעֲפַר הָאָרֶץ וּפָרַצְתָּ, *And your seed shall be as the dust of the earth, and you shall spread abroad* (28:14).

וְיַעְזְרֶךָּ — *Who shall help you . . .* that you shall fall no more.

וְאֵת שַׁדַּי — *And by the Almighty.* And from God Almighty, Who said to me, '*I am God Almighty, be fruitful and multiply; a nation and a company of nations shall be of you*' (35:11).

וִיבָרְכֶךָּ — *Who shall bless you . . .* Himself, without an intermediary. Unlike Menasseh and Ephraim who were blessed through הַמַּלְאָךְ הַגֹּאֵל, *The redeeming angel* (48:16), and Esau who was blessed by Isaac or (Israel) blessed by Moses; all these were blessed by man. (You however will be) blessed by the Almighty, in keeping with Isaac's statement to Jacob, וְאֵל שַׁדַּי יְבָרֵךְ אֹתְךָ, *And God Almighty bless you* (28:3), and as was true of Israel before the sin of the spies when Moses said to them, וִיבָרֵךְ אֶתְכֶם כַּאֲשֶׁר דִּבֶּר לָכֶם, *And may He bless you as He has promised you (Deut.* 1:11).

בִּרְכֹת שָׁמַיִם מֵעָל — *With blessings of heaven above . . .* that the days of your life be complete.

בִּרְכֹת תְּהוֹם רֹבֶצֶת תָּחַת — *Blessings of the deep that crouches beneath . . .* the blessing of food and wealth.

בִּרְכֹת שָׁדַיִם וָרָחַם — *Blessings of the breasts and of the womb . . .* the blessing of children, the opposite of רֶחֶם מַשְׁכִּיל וְשָׁדַיִם צֹמְקִים, *A miscarrying womb and dry breasts (Hoshea* 9:14).

26. בִּרְכֹת אָבִיךָ — *The blessings of your father.* And may He bless you with the

NOTES

talents and wisdom, represented by the bow, Pharaoh's defense, represented by the arrows, could not be effective.

מִידֵי אֲבִיר יַעֲקֹב מִשָּׁם רֹעֶה אֶבֶן יִשְׂרָאֵל — *By the hands of the Mighty One of Jacob, from there the shepherd, the Stone of Israel.* As we find in other instances, the names 'Jacob' and 'Israel' are used in the same verse. In this particular case the reason given by the *Sforno* is that Jacob is used when the Torah speaks of the survival of his children and Israel is used when the reference is to their status and position. The 'Mighty One of Jacob' insures our survival to the end of time, whereas the 'stone of Israel' insures our prestige and honor among the nations even if we are not on the highest spiritual level, hence, non-precious stones . . .

25. מֵאֵל אָבִיךָ . . . וְאֵת שַׁדַּי — *Even by the God of your father . . . And by the Almighty.* God is called by two names in this blessing. He is *the God of your father* and *the Almighty.* The former, as the latter, refers to specific promises

עַל־בִּרְכֹת הוֹרַי עַד־תַּאֲוַת גִּבְעֹת עוֹלָם תִּהְיֶיןָ לְרֹאשׁ יוֹסֵף וּלְקָדְקֹד נְזִיר אֶחָיו׃

blessing He gave to (me), 'וּפָרַצְתָּ יָמָּה וָקֵדְמָה וְצָפֹנָה וָנֶגְבָּה', *You shalt spread abroad to the west, and to the east, and to the north and to the south'* (28:14), which is a boundless, unlimited possession; and it is said, וְנִבְרְכוּ בְךָ כָּל מִשְׁפְּחֹת הָאֲדָמָה, *And in you shall all the families of the earth be blessed* (ibid.). This assures the future of Israel, of the שְׂרִידִים אֲשֶׁר ה׳ קֹרֵא, *The remnant called by God (Joel* 3:5), as it is said, כָּעֵת יֵאָמֵר לְיַעֲקֹב וּלְיִשְׂרָאֵל מַה פָּעַל אֵל, *Now it is said of Jacob and Israel, what has God wrought? (Numbers* 23:23), and it is written: וְאַתֶּם כֹּהֲנֵי ה׳ תִּקָּרֵאוּ, *You shall be named the priests of the Lord (Isaiah* 61:6); also אֲשֶׁר יַחֲזִיקוּ עֲשָׂרָה אֲנָשִׁים מִכֹּל לְשֹׁנוֹת הַגּוֹיִם . . . בִּכְנַף אִישׁ יְהוּדִי לֵאמֹר, נֵלְכָה עִמָּכֶם כִּי שָׁמַעְנוּ אֱלֹהִים עִמָּכֶם, *Ten men, out of all the languages of the nations shall . . . take hold of the skirt of a Jew saying, 'We will go with you, for we have heard that God is with you' (Zechariah* 8:23).

גָּבְרוּ עַל בִּרְכֹת הוֹרַי — *Are mighty beyond the blessings of my progenitors.* I gave you (*my* blessings from God) for they are more mighty than those given by God to Abraham and Isaac.

עַד תַּאֲוַת גִּבְעֹת עוֹלָם — *Unto the utmost bound of the everlasting hills.* The blessing given to me will spread to the outermost boundaries of the earth, to both poles of the axis. These he calls *everlasting hills* because they are the farthest points from the center of the earth, i.e., as hills. This is the blessing of וּפָרַצְתָּ . . . וְנִבְרְכוּ בְךָ, *You shall spread, . . . in you shall be blessed* (28:14), a blessing which insures everlasting happiness and success for all mankind (through the people of Israel).

תִּהְיֶיןָ לְרֹאשׁ יוֹסֵף — *They shall be on the head of Joseph.* These blessings shall come from on High upon the head of Joseph without any intermediary. Moses also expresses this thought (regarding Joseph) when he says וּרְצוֹן שֹׁכְנִי סְנֶה, *And the good will of Him that dwelt in the bush,* i.e., God on High (Whose) blessings come from on High, followed by, תָּבוֹאתָה לְרֹאשׁ יוֹסֵף, *come upon the head of Joseph (Deut.* 33:16).

וּלְקָדְקֹד נְזִיר אֶחָיו — *And on the crown of the head of the prince among his brethren.* Since he was deemed worthy to be the prince among all his brothers, he is therefore also worthy to have God's blessings granted to him directly, without any intermediary. This is also true of his descendants whose superiority (among their brethren) brings them to positions of leadership, including מַלְכוּת, *kingship,* as it states, כְּדַבֵּר אֶפְרַיִם רְתֵת נָשָׂא הוּא בְּיִשְׂרָאֵל, *When Ephraim spoke there was trembling, He exalted himself in Israel (Hoshea* 13:1).

From Joseph came the first Judge (Joshua) and the king of the northern kingdom

NOTES

made when using these names. It was as 'the God of your father (Jacob)' that He promised to elevate my descendants after they fall, at which time they will never fall again (akin to נָפְלָה וְלֹא תֹסִיף, see *Isaiah* 24:20); and it was 'the Almighty' that gave me the blessing of *a nation and company of nations,* which I have given in turn to you. Also, He will bless you (Joseph) directly without an intermediary, as befits one who is a צַדִּיק, *righteous man.*

26. בִּרְכֹת אָבִיךָ — *The blessings of your father.* The blessing given by God to Jacob was unique in the sense that he was promised that ultimately his children would spread and disseminate the word of God throughout the world. The expression וּפָרַצְתָּ, *You shalt spread abroad,* is not meant as geographic expansion but the spreading of Judaism's spiritual teachings to all mankind. Hence we are called 'priests of HASHEM,' for it is the duty of the כֹּהֵן,

ששי כז-כח בִּנְיָמִין֙ זְאֵ֣ב יִטְרָ֔ף בַּבֹּ֖קֶר יֹ֣אכַל עַ֑ד וְלָעֶ֖רֶב יְחַלֵּ֥ק שָׁלָֽל׃ כָּל־אֵ֛לֶּה שִׁבְטֵ֥י
יִשְׂרָאֵ֖ל שְׁנֵ֣ים עָשָׂ֑ר וְ֠זֹאת אֲשֶׁר־דִּבֶּ֨ר לָהֶ֤ם אֲבִיהֶם֙ וַיְבָ֣רֶךְ אוֹתָ֔ם אִ֛ישׁ אֲשֶׁ֥ר
כט כְּבִרְכָת֖וֹ בֵּרַ֥ךְ אֹתָֽם׃ וַיְצַ֣ו אוֹתָ֗ם וַיֹּ֤אמֶר אֲלֵהֶם֙ אֲנִי֙ נֶאֱסָ֣ף אֶל־עַמִּ֔י קִבְר֥וּ

after the break away from the Davidic royal house (Jeroboam).

27. זְאֵב יִטְרָף — *A wolf that ravens.* The wolf attacks his prey at dawn or twilight when there is a minimum of light, as it is written, וְחַדּוּ מִזְּאֵבֵי עֶרֶב, *And more fierce than the wolves of the desert (Habbakuk* 1:8). So it shall be with Benjamin. The first king of Israel will be Saul (who is a descendant of Benjamin), when the sun of Jewish kingship first rises, and again at the conclusion of Jewish rulership in the days of Mordechai and Esther (who were also descended from Benjamin). Even though they were followed by the kingdom of the Second Temple, that period was comparatively brief, and included many years of subjugation as well.

28. כָּל אֵלֶּה שִׁבְטֵי יִשְׂרָאֵל שְׁנֵים עָשָׂר — *All these are the twelve tribes of Israel.* These who were mentioned and blessed by Jacob are the twelve authentic tribes; they are written on the breastplate and *ephod* as a remembrance before God; they were present at the time of the covenant at Mount Gerizim and Mount Ebal. For these twelve, Moses set up twelve pillars and Joshua twelve stones in the Jordan and at Gilgal, as did Elijah when he built the altar. Menasseh and Ephraim are not included in the number of the tribes, except in the dividing of the land, where Levi is excluded (and Joseph's portion is doubled on behalf of Menasseh and Ephraim).

וַיְבָרֶךְ אוֹתָם — *And he blessed them . . .* (an added blessing) to those already recorded above.

אִישׁ אֲשֶׁר כְּבִרְכָתוֹ בֵּרַךְ אֹתָם — *Every one according to his blessings he blessed them* — each according to his particular requirement; for Judah in the area of kingship, for Issachar regarding Torah, and for Levi pertaining to the *Avodah* (Sanctuary service).

NOTES

priest, to teach the Torah. This special blessing was not given to Abraham or Isaac, only to Jacob. He stresses in his blessing to Joseph that he is transferring this unique blessing to him and his children, since he is the prince among his own brothers, and even in later generations the first judge will be Joshua and the first king of the Northern Kingdom will be Jeroboam, both descendants of Ephraim. Because of this special merit, Joseph also is worthy that God bless him directly and not through an intermediary. Although Jacob has stated this in the previous verse he reiterates it here.

27. זְאֵב יִטְרָף — *A wolf that ravens.* To answer the obvious question as to how one can compare the leadership of Mordechai to the twilight of Jewish kingship in view of the ensuing period of the Second Temple (at which time there were periods during which they ruled, independent of foreign powers), the *Sforno* explains that since this period of Jewish history was brief and burdened with foreign rule, it is not considered as a period of authentic Jewish power and greatness.

28. כָּל אֵלֶּה שִׁבְטֵי יִשְׂרָאֵל שְׁנֵים עָשָׂר . . . וַיְבָרֶךְ אוֹתָם — *All these are the twelve tribes of Israel . . . And he blessed them.* The *Sforno* answers the question, 'Why state *the twelve tribes of Israel;* isn't it self evident?' Prior to these blessings given by Jacob to his sons, he stated, *'Ephraim and Menasseh even as Reuben and Simeon shall be mine.'* That being the case, who are the twelve tribes? Or are there now thirteen? The Sages tell us that only in regard to inheritance of *Eretz Yisrael* will Ephraim and Menasseh be reckoned as tribes, not insofar as any other privileges are concerned. Hence, when Jacob blesses his own sons, including Levi who has no share in *Eretz Yisrael*, the Torah stresses *these are the twelve tribes*, excluding Ephraim and Menasseh, who are not included in the twelve. The same is true later in Jewish history, when they stood at Mt. Grizim and Mt. Ebal, and at Gilgal, where

ל אֹתִי אֶל־אֲבֹתָי אֶל־הַמְּעָרָה אֲשֶׁר בִּשְׂדֵה עֶפְרוֹן הַחִתִּי: בַּמְּעָרָה אֲשֶׁר
בִּשְׂדֵה הַמַּכְפֵּלָה אֲשֶׁר־עַל־פְּנֵי מַמְרֵא בְּאֶרֶץ כְּנָעַן אֲשֶׁר קָנָה אַבְרָהָם
לא אֶת־הַשָּׂדֶה מֵאֵת עֶפְרֹן הַחִתִּי לַאֲחֻזַּת־קָבֶר: שָׁמָּה קָבְרוּ אֶת־אַבְרָהָם
וְאֵת שָׂרָה אִשְׁתּוֹ שָׁמָּה קָבְרוּ אֶת־יִצְחָק וְאֵת רִבְקָה אִשְׁתּוֹ וְשָׁמָּה קָבַרְתִּי
לב-לג אֶת־לֵאָה: מִקְנֵה הַשָּׂדֶה וְהַמְּעָרָה אֲשֶׁר־בּוֹ מֵאֵת בְּנֵי־חֵת: וַיְכַל יַעֲקֹב
נ א לְצַוֺּת אֶת־בָּנָיו וַיֶּאֱסֹף רַגְלָיו אֶל־הַמִּטָּה וַיִּגְוַע וַיֵּאָסֶף אֶל־עַמָּיו: וַיִּפֹּל יוֹסֵף
ב עַל־פְּנֵי אָבִיו וַיֵּבְךְּ עָלָיו וַיִּשַּׁק־לוֹ: וַיְצַו יוֹסֵף אֶת־עֲבָדָיו אֶת־הָרֹפְאִים
ג לַחֲנֹט אֶת־אָבִיו וַיַּחַנְטוּ הָרֹפְאִים אֶת־יִשְׂרָאֵל: וַיִּמְלְאוּ־לוֹ אַרְבָּעִים יוֹם כִּי
ד כֵּן יִמְלְאוּ יְמֵי הַחֲנֻטִים וַיִּבְכּוּ אֹתוֹ מִצְרַיִם שִׁבְעִים יוֹם: וַיַּעַבְרוּ יְמֵי בְכִיתוֹ
וַיְדַבֵּר יוֹסֵף אֶל־בֵּית פַּרְעֹה לֵאמֹר אִם־נָא מָצָאתִי חֵן בְּעֵינֵיכֶם דַּבְּרוּ־נָא
ה בְּאָזְנֵי פַרְעֹה לֵאמֹר: אָבִי הִשְׁבִּיעַנִי לֵאמֹר הִנֵּה אָנֹכִי מֵת בְּקִבְרִי אֲשֶׁר
כָּרִיתִי לִי בְּאֶרֶץ כְּנַעַן שָׁמָּה תִּקְבְּרֵנִי וְעַתָּה אֶעֱלֶה־נָּא וְאֶקְבְּרָה אֶת־אָבִי
ו-ז וְאָשׁוּבָה: וַיֹּאמֶר פַּרְעֹה עֲלֵה וּקְבֹר אֶת־אָבִיךָ כַּאֲשֶׁר הִשְׁבִּיעֶךָ: וַיַּעַל יוֹסֵף
לִקְבֹּר אֶת־אָבִיו וַיַּעֲלוּ אִתּוֹ כָּל־עַבְדֵי פַרְעֹה זִקְנֵי בֵיתוֹ וְכֹל זִקְנֵי אֶרֶץ־

---

30. אֲשֶׁר קָנָה אַבְרָהָם ... מֵאֵת עֶפְרֹן — *Which Abraham bought ... from Ephron.* Since they lived in another land for many years, Jacob told them the details regarding the purchase by Abraham from Ephron, and that his ancestors were already buried there, so that no one can challenge their rights.

L

2-3. וַיַּחַנְטוּ ... יִשְׂרָאֵל ... וַיִּבְכּוּ אֹתוֹ מִצְרַיִם — *They embalmed ... Israel ... The Egyptians wept for him.* They did so not only in Joseph's honor, or because they had been so ordered, but because he was 'Israel,' a worthy leader (in his own right); hence (they wept) as an act of homage.

4. וַיְדַבֵּר יוֹסֵף אֶל בֵּית פַּרְעֹה — *Joseph spoke unto the house of Pharaoh ...* because one is not allowed to enter the palace of the king while in mourning (lit., 'in sackcloth').

7. וַיַּעֲלוּ אִתּוֹ — *And with him went up ...* of their own accord (not having been ordered by Joseph).

NOTES

they entered into a covenant with God. The tribes are twelve in number, 'no more, no less.'

The expression וַיְבָרֶךְ אוֹתָם, *And he blessed them,* is not repetitious, nor is it necessary to add, *Every one according to his blessings,* unless the Torah is adding the thought, as explained by the *Sforno,* that there were special blessings *added* by Jacob which fit the particular needs of those sons who were to play important roles of leadership, scholarship and service to God.

L

2-3. וַיַּחַנְטוּ ... אֶת יִשְׂרָאֵל ... וַיִּבְכּוּ אֹתוֹ — *They embalmed ... Israel ... wept for him.* The *Sforno* links the usage of the name Israel, rather than Jacob, to the mourning of the Egyptians. 'Israel' denotes prestige and leadership qualities, virtues that the Egyptians recognized and appreciated in Jacob, and that is why their weeping was genuine.

4. וַיְדַבֵּר יוֹסֵף אֶל בֵּית פַּרְעֹה — *Joseph spoke unto the house of Pharaoh.* The phrase בֵּית פַּרְעֹה, *the house of Pharaoh,* implies that Joseph communicated with officials of the government, not directly with Pharaoh. This is strange; since Joseph certainly had access to the king himself, why use intermediaries for

ח מִצְרָיִם: וְכֹל בֵּית יוֹסֵף וְאֶחָיו וּבֵית אָבִיו רַק טַפָּם וְצֹאנָם וּבְקָרָם עָזְבוּ
ט־י בְּאֶרֶץ גֹּשֶׁן: וַיַּעַל עִמּוֹ גַּם־רֶכֶב גַּם־פָּרָשִׁים וַיְהִי הַמַּחֲנֶה כָּבֵד מְאֹד: וַיָּבֹאוּ
עַד־גֹּרֶן הָאָטָד אֲשֶׁר בְּעֵבֶר הַיַּרְדֵּן וַיִּסְפְּדוּ־שָׁם מִסְפֵּד גָּדוֹל וְכָבֵד מְאֹד
יא וַיַּעַשׂ לְאָבִיו אֵבֶל שִׁבְעַת יָמִים: וַיַּרְא יוֹשֵׁב הָאָרֶץ הַכְּנַעֲנִי אֶת־הָאֵבֶל
בְּגֹרֶן הָאָטָד וַיֹּאמְרוּ אֵבֶל־כָּבֵד זֶה לְמִצְרָיִם עַל־כֵּן קָרָא שְׁמָהּ אָבֵל
יב־יג מִצְרַיִם אֲשֶׁר בְּעֵבֶר הַיַּרְדֵּן: וַיַּעֲשׂוּ בָנָיו לוֹ כֵּן כַּאֲשֶׁר צִוָּם: וַיִּשְׂאוּ אֹתוֹ
בָנָיו אַרְצָה כְּנַעַן וַיִּקְבְּרוּ אֹתוֹ בִּמְעָרַת שְׂדֵה הַמַּכְפֵּלָה אֲשֶׁר קָנָה אַבְרָהָם
יד אֶת־הַשָּׂדֶה לַאֲחֻזַּת־קֶבֶר מֵאֵת עֶפְרֹן הַחִתִּי עַל־פְּנֵי מַמְרֵא: וַיָּשָׁב יוֹסֵף
מִצְרַיְמָה הוּא וְאֶחָיו וְכָל־הָעֹלִים אִתּוֹ לִקְבֹּר אֶת־אָבִיו אַחֲרֵי קָבְרוֹ
טו אֶת־אָבִיו: וַיִּרְאוּ אֲחֵי־יוֹסֵף כִּי־מֵת אֲבִיהֶם וַיֹּאמְרוּ לוּ יִשְׂטְמֵנוּ יוֹסֵף וְהָשֵׁב
טז יָשִׁיב לָנוּ אֵת כָּל־הָרָעָה אֲשֶׁר גָּמַלְנוּ אֹתוֹ: וַיְצַוּוּ אֶל־יוֹסֵף לֵאמֹר אָבִיךָ
יז צִוָּה לִפְנֵי מוֹתוֹ לֵאמֹר: כֹּה־תֹאמְרוּ לְיוֹסֵף אָנָּא שָׂא נָא פֶּשַׁע אַחֶיךָ
וְחַטָּאתָם כִּי־רָעָה גְמָלוּךָ וְעַתָּה שָׂא נָא לְפֶשַׁע עַבְדֵי אֱלֹהֵי אָבִיךָ וַיֵּבְךְּ
יח יוֹסֵף בְּדַבְּרָם אֵלָיו: וַיֵּלְכוּ גַּם־אֶחָיו וַיִּפְּלוּ לְפָנָיו וַיֹּאמְרוּ הִנֶּנּוּ לְךָ לַעֲבָדִים:

זִקְנֵי בֵיתוֹ וְכֹל זִקְנֵי אֶרֶץ מִצְרָיִם — *The elders of his house and the elders of the land of Egypt.* Because Jacob had been esteemed as a wise man in the eyes of the wise men of that generation. (*Elders* means 'wise men') as it is written: וּזְקֵנָיו יְחַכֵּם, *And teach his elders wisdom* (*Psalms* 105:22).

9. גַּם רֶכֶב גַּם פָּרָשִׁים — *Also chariots and horsemen ...* because the military chiefs regarded Jacob as a great warrior.

16. וַיְצַוּוּ אֶל יוֹסֵף — *And they (sent a message) to Joseph.* They sent (a message) through the servants of Jacob, or others, *regarding* Joseph, as we find, וַיְצַוֵּם אֶל בְּנֵי יִשְׂרָאֵל, *And gave them a charge unto the children of Israel* (*Exodus* 6:13).

לֵאמֹר אָבִיךָ צִוָּה — *Saying, 'Your father did command.'* He commanded us that we should say to you these words if we are concerned and apprehensive (lest you punish us), *but not in his name,* for he would never suspect you of doing us any harm.

לִפְנֵי מוֹתוֹ — *Before his death.* (Since this happened right before he died) we had no opportunity to tell you about it until now.

17. וַיֵּבְךְּ יוֹסֵף — *And Joseph wept ...* when reminded of his father, and his love and confidence in him (that he would do no evil).

NOTES

such an important request? The answer must be that he could not enter the palace while in a state of mourning, since his clothes were probably rent and his appearance unkempt.

7-9. זִקְנֵי בֵיתוֹ וְכֹל זִקְנֵי אֶרֶץ מִצְרָיִם ... גַּם רֶכֶב גַּם פָּרָשִׁים — *The elders of his house and the elders of the land of Egypt ... Also chariots and horsemen.* Jacob was held in high regard for his great wisdom as well as for his military prowess. Hence both the wise men and the military chiefs paid him homage.

16. וַיְצַוּוּ אֶל יוֹסֵף — *And they (sent a message) to Joseph.* The word וַיְצַוּוּ, *and they commanded,* cannot be understood literally, for how could the brothers command Joseph? The meaning must therefore be they instructed messengers to speak to Joseph; the word אֶל in this case does not mean *to* but *regarding* Joseph.

17. וַיֵּבְךְּ יוֹסֵף — *And Joseph wept.* The

יט־כ וַיֹּאמֶר אֲלֵהֶם יוֹסֵף אַל־תִּירָאוּ כִּי הֲתַחַת אֱלֹהִים אָנִי׃ וְאַתֶּם חֲשַׁבְתֶּם
עָלַי רָעָה אֱלֹהִים חֲשָׁבָהּ לְטֹבָה לְמַעַן עֲשֹׂה כַּיּוֹם הַזֶּה לְהַחֲיֹת עַם־רָב׃
שביעי כא וְעַתָּה אַל־תִּירָאוּ אָנֹכִי אֲכַלְכֵּל אֶתְכֶם וְאֶת־טַפְּכֶם וַיְנַחֵם אוֹתָם וַיְדַבֵּר
כב עַל־לִבָּם׃ וַיֵּשֶׁב יוֹסֵף בְּמִצְרַיִם הוּא וּבֵית אָבִיו וַיְחִי יוֹסֵף מֵאָה וָעֶשֶׂר
מפטיר כג שָׁנִים׃ וַיַּרְא יוֹסֵף לְאֶפְרַיִם בְּנֵי שִׁלֵּשִׁים גַּם בְּנֵי מָכִיר בֶּן־מְנַשֶּׁה יֻלְּדוּ
כד עַל־בִּרְכֵּי יוֹסֵף׃ וַיֹּאמֶר יוֹסֵף אֶל־אֶחָיו אָנֹכִי מֵת וֵאלֹהִים פָּקֹד יִפְקֹד
אֶתְכֶם וְהֶעֱלָה אֶתְכֶם מִן־הָאָרֶץ הַזֹּאת אֶל־הָאָרֶץ אֲשֶׁר נִשְׁבַּע לְאַבְרָהָם
כה לְיִצְחָק וּלְיַעֲקֹב׃ וַיַּשְׁבַּע יוֹסֵף אֶת־בְּנֵי יִשְׂרָאֵל לֵאמֹר פָּקֹד יִפְקֹד אֱלֹהִים
כו אֶתְכֶם וְהַעֲלִתֶם אֶת־עַצְמֹתַי מִזֶּה׃ וַיָּמָת יוֹסֵף בֶּן־מֵאָה וָעֶשֶׂר שָׁנִים
וַיַּחַנְטוּ אֹתוֹ וַיִּישֶׂם בָּאָרוֹן בְּמִצְרָיִם׃

---

19. הֲתַחַת אֱלֹהִים אָנִי — *Am I in the place of God?* It is not for me to judge you, or to judge God's decrees. How can I punish His agents, for certainly you were God's agents, as we read, לֹא אַתֶּם שְׁלַחְתֶּם אֹתִי הֵנָּה כִּי הָאֱלֹהִים, *It was not you who sent me hither, but God* (45:8). This would be akin to בֵּית דִּין הַמְבַטֵּל דִּבְרֵי בֵּית דִּין חֲבֵירוֹ, *A court setting aside the decision of another court* (*Eduyos* 1:5).

20. וְאַתֶּם חֲשַׁבְתֶּם עָלַי רָעָה — *You meant evil against me.* Your act was in error, because you considered me to be a רוֹדֵף, *pursuer*, and had it been so, your act would have been justified.

אֱלֹהִים חֲשָׁבָהּ לְטֹבָה — *God meant it for good.* He utilized this error for a good purpose.

26. וַיַּחַנְטוּ אֹתוֹ וַיִּישֶׂם בָּאָרוֹן — *And they embalmed him and he was put in a coffin.* His bones were placed in the same coffin in which he was embalmed. He was never buried in the earth, hence the coffin was known to future generations. Moses was able therefore to take it with him, as it is written, וַיִּקַּח מֹשֶׁה אֶת עַצְמוֹת יוֹסֵף, *And Moses took the bones of Joseph* (*Ex.* 13:19).

NOTES

Midrash explains Joseph's weeping differently; he was distraught that his father suspected him of hatred toward his brothers. The *Sforno* rejects this interpretation and explains the weeping as tears of joy and relief that his father was confident he would not take revenge on his brothers.

19. הֲתַחַת אֱלֹהִים אָנִי — *Am I in the place of God?* God's decision and decree is comparable to the *p'sak* (decision) of a religious court. The law is that a court cannot override the decision of the first court unless they are greater in number and wisdom. No man dare arrogate such authority to himself vis-a-vis the Almighty! Therefore Joseph reassures his brothers that he would never punish them for an act which God utilized for the fulfillment of His divine plan.

26. וַיַּחַנְטוּ אֹתוֹ וַיִּישֶׂם בָּאָרוֹן — *And they embalmed him and he was put in a coffin.* The word בָּאָרוֹן, *in a coffin*, is vowelized with a קָמָץ (ָ) under the ב, not a שְׁוָא (ְ). This transforms it into a definite article, *the coffin.* This indicates that Joseph's bones were placed in the same coffin in which he was embalmed, and this coffin was known to future generations. This in turn enabled Moses to locate it at the time of the Exodus.

ספר שמות
Sh'mos/Exodus

Sforno's Introduction

In this second book it is related how the seed of Israel became enslaved in Egypt because of their violation of the covenant of the Patriarchs. As the Prophet Ezekiel states, וַיַּמְרוּ בִי וְלֹא אָבוּ לִשְׁמֹעַ אֵלַי, אִישׁ אֶת שִׁקּוּצֵי עֵינֵיהֶם לֹא הִשְׁלִיכוּ, וְאֶת גִּלּוּלֵי מִצְרַיִם לֹא עָזָבוּ, וָאֹמַר לִשְׁפֹּךְ חֲמָתִי עֲלֵיהֶם, לְכַלּוֹת אַפִּי בָּהֶם בְּתוֹךְ אֶרֶץ מִצְרָיִם, *And they rebelled against Me and chose not to listen to Me; they, each one (of them), did not cast away the detestable things of their eyes nor did they forsake the idols of Egypt; then I said I would pour out My fury upon them to spend My anger upon them in the land of Egypt* (*Ezekiel* 20:8). Thus were they enslaved with hard labor until a small number repented, prayed to God and a messenger did save them.[1]

The book then proceeds to relate how initially, when God chose to honor the Israelites, He spoke to them face to face and thus they were granted crowns of spiritual glory at Mount Horeb. They did, however, rebel against God and (were forced) to remove their crowns (*Exodus* 33:6), and the Divine Presence departed from them.[2]

The book then continues to tell us how in spite of all this God did not refrain from correcting their ways so that His presence (*Shechinah*) might dwell once again in their midst. He commanded that a Sanctuary be built, vessels be fashioned, and priests be invested in their sacred service; thus did the *Shechinah* return to their midst after their seemingly complete spiritual impairment and state of despair. Thus does this second book conclude.[3]

---

1. In the history of the Jewish people naught *occurs*, there are no accidental events — everything is the result of God's decrees and decisions, determining the destiny of Israel. The bondage in Egypt was not the result of political developments or military considerations; it was due to the straying of Israel from the path of righteousness and holiness as lived by the Patriarchs. Their subsequent liberation resulted from their repentance, which encompassed only a small percentage of the total Jewish people; as our Sages have taught us that only one-fifth were redeemed and left Egypt. The messenger refers to Moses.

2. This refers to the events immediately following the episode of the Golden Calf. The unique level of spiritual greatness realized by the Jews at the time of receiving the Torah was dissipated and God no longer appeared to Moses in the Camp of Israel — only outside the Camp. This indicated His displeasure with the Jews and demonstrated their fall from grace.

3. The second Tablets of Law represented a fresh opportunity granted to the Jews whereby they could regain once again their former spiritual status. This renewed elevated status was to be captured and concentrated in the *Mishkan* (Sanctuary) where God would cause His Divine Presence to dwell. Though Israel had fallen they were shown the way to return, and after transgression and rejection, fulfillment and hope became theirs once again.

פרשת שמות
Parashas Sh'mos

א

א וְאֵ֗לֶּה שְׁמוֹת֙ בְּנֵ֣י יִשְׂרָאֵ֔ל הַבָּאִ֖ים מִצְרָ֑יְמָה אֵ֣ת יַעֲקֹ֔ב אִ֥ישׁ וּבֵית֖וֹ בָּֽאוּ׃
ב־ד רְאוּבֵ֣ן שִׁמְע֔וֹן לֵוִ֖י וִיהוּדָֽה׃ יִשָּׂשכָ֥ר זְבוּלֻ֖ן וּבִנְיָמִֽן׃ דָּ֥ן וְנַפְתָּלִ֖י גָּ֥ד וְאָשֵֽׁר׃
ה־ו וַֽיְהִ֗י כָּל־נֶ֛פֶשׁ יֹצְאֵ֥י יֶֽרֶךְ־יַעֲקֹ֖ב שִׁבְעִ֣ים נָ֑פֶשׁ וְיוֹסֵ֖ף הָיָ֥ה בְמִצְרָֽיִם׃ וַיָּ֤מָת
ז יוֹסֵף֙ וְכָל־אֶחָ֔יו וְכֹ֖ל הַדּ֥וֹר הַהֽוּא׃ וּבְנֵ֣י יִשְׂרָאֵ֗ל פָּר֧וּ וַֽיִּשְׁרְצ֛וּ וַיִּרְבּ֥וּ וַיַּֽעַצְמ֖וּ
בִּמְאֹ֣ד מְאֹ֑ד וַתִּמָּלֵ֥א הָאָ֖רֶץ אֹתָֽם׃
ח־ט וַיָּ֥קָם מֶֽלֶךְ־חָדָ֖שׁ עַל־מִצְרָ֑יִם אֲשֶׁ֥ר לֹֽא־יָדַ֖ע אֶת־יוֹסֵֽף׃ וַיֹּ֖אמֶר אֶל־עַמּ֑וֹ

I

1. וְאֵלֶּה שְׁמוֹת — *These are the names.* Those who are mentioned here were worthy to be named for each was worthy of his name which indicates and reflects the stature and character of that man. These men were a beacon of light throughout their lifetime so that their generation did not become degraded. However, after their demise, even the righteous among their children were not equally important and worthy in the eyes of God and man.

6. וְכֹל הַדּוֹר הַהוּא — *And all that generation.* All seventy souls; that generation did not become (totally) degraded or demeaned all the days of their life.

7. פָּרוּ וַיִּשְׁרְצוּ — *Were fruitful and increased abundantly.* After the death of the original seventy souls, their descendants deviated from the ways of their fathers and followed the ways of creeping creatures, for they pursue a path leading to the pit. (And therefore . . .)

8. וַיָּקָם מֶלֶךְ חָדָשׁ . . . אֲשֶׁר לֹא יָדַע אֶת יוֹסֵף — *There arose a new king . . . who knew not Joseph.* Although there certainly was a record of Joseph's accomplishments in the annals of the kings, especially regarding the law of the 'Fifth' (*Gen.* 47:26) promulgated by him, nonetheless, the new king could not conceive that Joseph could have been a member of this same people so that Israel should be worthy of consideration on his account.

NOTES

I

1. וְאֵלֶּה שְׁמוֹת — *These are the names.* A man's name is important; it is an indication of his stature, an index to his very essence and character. This is reflected in the fact that the Torah considers him of sufficient worth to be recorded and mentioned. We find a similar approach in the *Sforno* in *Genesis* (46:8) and *Numbers* (1:2) where he also stresses the honored and valued role that names play in our Torah. Only certain names are carried by Aaron on his vestments before God. Those who are elevated from their brethren are alone considered worthy to have their names recorded. וָאֵדָעֲךָ בְּשֵׁם, *and I know you by name* (*Exodus* 33:17), is a sign of favor.

6. וְכֹל הַדּוֹר הַהוּא — *And all that generation.* Although all the seventy souls are not considered important enough to be listed individually again here (the seventy are enumerated in *Genesis* 46:8-27), nonetheless a spirit of piety and sanctity permeated all of them and they remained steadfast in their unique way of life, unaffected by the alien environment.

7. פָּרוּ וַיִּשְׁרְצוּ — *Were fruitful and increased abundantly.* The text reads שרצים שרצים, — the first is to be vowelized שְׁרָצִים, *creeping creatures,* the second שָׂרְצִים, *who run*. The *Sforno* allows himself a play on words, those who behave as creeping creatures pursue a path which leads hastily to the pit.

The expression used by the *Sforno,* שָׂרְצִים לִבְאֵר שַׁחַת, *for they pursue a path leading to the pit,* is taken from tractate *Berachos* 28b.

8. וַיָּקָם מֶלֶךְ חָדָשׁ . . . אֲשֶׁר לֹא יָדַע אֶת יוֹסֵף — *There arose a new king . . . who knew not Joseph.* It is nigh impossible for any king of Egypt to have forgotten Joseph, or even to *act*

י הִנֵּה עַם בְּנֵי יִשְׂרָאֵל רַב וְעָצוּם מִמֶּנּוּ: הָבָה נִתְחַכְּמָה לוֹ פֶּן־יִרְבֶּה וְהָיָה כִּי־
תִקְרֶאנָה מִלְחָמָה וְנוֹסַף גַּם־הוּא עַל־שֹׂנְאֵינוּ וְנִלְחַם־בָּנוּ וְעָלָה מִן־הָאָרֶץ:
יא וַיָּשִׂימוּ עָלָיו שָׂרֵי מִסִּים לְמַעַן עַנֹּתוֹ בְּסִבְלֹתָם וַיִּבֶן עָרֵי מִסְכְּנוֹת לְפַרְעֹה
יב אֶת־פִּתֹם וְאֶת־רַעַמְסֵס: וְכַאֲשֶׁר יְעַנּוּ אֹתוֹ כֵּן יִרְבֶּה וְכֵן יִפְרֹץ וַיָּקֻצוּ מִפְּנֵי

---

10. הָבָה נִתְחַכְּמָה לוֹ — *Come let us deal wisely with them.* To deal with them in a devious manner.

וְעָלָה מִן הָאָרֶץ — *And get them up out of the land.* By their own volition; so it will not be necessary to drive them out by force, without reason, for this course would cause us to be a derision among our enemies. And this we shall do . . .

פֶּן יִרְבֶּה וְהָיָה כִּי תִקְרֶאנָה מִלְחָמָה — *Lest they multiply and it come to pass when there befalls us any war.* When the evils and hardships of war befall us — (this abbreviated expression is) similar to וַתְּכַל דָּוִד הַמֶּלֶךְ, *and (the soul of) King David failed with longing (II Samuel* 13:39) (the word *soul* is understood and not specifically stated) . . .

וְנוֹסַף גַּם הוּא עַל שֹׂנְאֵינוּ — *They also will join themselves to our enemies.* Since they are separated from us (and different from us) in that they are circumcised, speak a different language and follow Hebrew customs in a manner that, לֹא יוּכְלוּן הַמִּצְרִים לֶאֱכֹל אֶת הָעִבְרִים לֶחֶם, *the Egyptians might not eat bread with the Hebrews (Genesis* 43:32), then they are without a doubt our enemies and their enmity will be revealed during the (strain and) duress of wartime.

11. לְמַעַן עַנֹּתוֹ — *To afflict them.* So that they (the Jews) shall voluntarily leave our land for another.

וַיִּבֶן עָרֵי מִסְכְּנוֹת — *And they built store-cities.* But they accepted upon themselves the task of building these cities.

NOTES

unknowing. Such deceit is unthinkable and would be unwise politically, since the law of granting one-fifth of all produce to Pharaoh was instituted by Joseph. The *Sforno*, consistent with his principle that evil befell the Jews due to their sinfulness, explains that this Pharaoh could not conceive that such a noble soul — Joseph — and such a base people — Israel — could be related. Hence gratitude and appreciation were uncalled for.

10. הָבָה נִתְחַכְּמָה לוֹ . . . וְעָלָה מִן הָאָרֶץ — *Come let us deal wisely with them . . . and get them up out of the land.* The original intention of the Egyptians was not to enslave the Hebrews but to make conditions unbearable for them, thereby compelling them to leave voluntarily. The Egyptians were sensitive to the opinion of other nations, hence they attempted in devious ways to rid themselves of this potential 'fifth column' for they were convinced that a people so alien and strange as the Jews would certainly be disloyal in a time of national crisis.

The *Sforno* changes the sequence of the verse in his commentary. In the text, the phrase וְעָלָה מִן הָאָרֶץ, *and get them up out of the land*, appears after פֶּן יִרְבֶּה, *lest they multiply*, and וְנוֹסַף גַּם הוּא עַל שֹׂנְאֵינוּ, *they also will join themselves to our enemies.* The *Sforno*, however, comments on the former phrase before the latter phrases. The reason is because the *Sforno* wishes to explain the goal and purpose of Pharaoh's decree before stating the motivation. The goal was to force the Israelites to leave the land of their own volition, thereby ridding Egypt of an element which Pharaoh considered a threat to his kingdom. After interpreting the verse of *get them up out of the land*, he then explains the fear and apprehension which motivated Pharaoh's actions. These are reflected in the phrases of *lest they multiply*, and *they also will join themselves to our enemies.*

יג־יד בְּנֵ֥י יִשְׂרָאֵֽל׃ וַיַּעֲבִ֧דוּ מִצְרַ֛יִם אֶת־בְּנֵ֥י יִשְׂרָאֵ֖ל בְּפָֽרֶךְ׃ וַיְמָרְר֨וּ אֶת־חַיֵּיהֶ֜ם
בַּעֲבֹדָ֣ה קָשָׁ֗ה בְּחֹ֙מֶר֙ וּבִלְבֵנִ֔ים וּבְכָל־עֲבֹדָ֖ה בַּשָּׂדֶ֑ה אֵ֚ת כָּל־עֲבֹ֣דָתָ֔ם
טו אֲשֶׁר־עָבְד֥וּ בָהֶ֖ם בְּפָֽרֶךְ׃ וַיֹּ֙אמֶר֙ מֶ֣לֶךְ מִצְרַ֔יִם לַֽמְיַלְּדֹ֖ת הָֽעִבְרִיֹּ֑ת אֲשֶׁ֨ר שֵׁ֤ם
טז הָֽאַחַת֙ שִׁפְרָ֔ה וְשֵׁ֥ם הַשֵּׁנִ֖ית פּוּעָֽה׃ וַיֹּ֗אמֶר בְּיַלֶּדְכֶן֙ אֶת־הָֽעִבְרִיּ֔וֹת וּרְאִיתֶ֖ן
יז עַל־הָאָבְנָ֑יִם אִם־בֵּ֥ן הוּא֙ וַהֲמִתֶּ֣ן אֹת֔וֹ וְאִם־בַּ֥ת הִ֖וא וָחָֽיָה׃ וַתִּירֶ֤אןָ
הַֽמְיַלְּדֹת֙ אֶת־הָ֣אֱלֹהִ֔ים וְלֹ֣א עָשׂ֔וּ כַּאֲשֶׁ֛ר דִּבֶּ֥ר אֲלֵיהֶ֖ן מֶ֣לֶךְ מִצְרָ֑יִם וַתְּחַיֶּ֖יןָ
שני יח אֶת־הַיְלָדִֽים׃ וַיִּקְרָ֤א מֶֽלֶךְ־מִצְרַ֙יִם֙ לַֽמְיַלְּדֹ֔ת וַיֹּ֣אמֶר לָהֶ֔ן מַדּ֥וּעַ עֲשִׂיתֶ֖ן
יט הַדָּבָ֣ר הַזֶּ֑ה וַתְּחַיֶּ֖יןָ אֶת־הַיְלָדִֽים׃ וַתֹּאמַ֤רְןָ הַֽמְיַלְּדֹת֙ אֶל־פַּרְעֹ֔ה כִּ֣י לֹ֤א

---

13. וַיַּעֲבִדוּ מִצְרַיִם — *And the Egyptians made (the children of Israel) to serve.* When (the Egyptians) observed how the Jews degraded themselves and were willing to occupy themselves with such base labor they made them into slaves. All this resulted, for as the Jews continued to add חַטָּאת עַל חַטָּאת, *sin upon sin*, so they were deprived of reason and progressed מֵרָעָה אֶל רָעָה, *from evil to evil.*

14. וַיְמָרְרוּ אֶת חַיֵּיהֶם — *And they made their lives bitter.* As the Jews continued to sin in beliefs and practices, as the Prophet testifies: וַיַּמְרוּ בִי וְלֹא אָבוּ לִשְׁמֹעַ אֵלַי, אִישׁ אֶת שִׁקּוּצֵי עֵינֵיהֶם לֹא הִשְׁלִיכוּ, וְאֶת גִּלּוּלֵי מִצְרַיִם לֹא עָזָבוּ, וָאֹמַר לִשְׁפֹּךְ חֲמָתִי עֲלֵיהֶם, לְכַלּוֹת אַפִּי בָּהֶם בְּתוֹךְ אֶרֶץ מִצְרָיִם, *But they rebelled against Me and would not hearken unto Me; they did not every man cast away the detestable things of their eyes, neither did they forsake the idols of Egypt; then I said I would pour out My fury upon them, to spend My anger upon them, in the midst of the land of Egypt* (*Ezekiel* 20:8), so did the hand of the oppressor increase in severity.

15. לַמְיַלְּדֹת הָעִבְרִיֹּת — *To the Hebrew midwives.* Certainly among such a large population there were more than two midwives. These, however, were the trusted ones in the capital city of Egypt, and after they betrayed the trust placed in them personally by the king, he no longer felt he could rely upon midwives in other places.

18. מַדּוּעַ עֲשִׂיתֶן — *Why have you done (this thing)?* You betrayed me, for when I made my request you did not refuse me and I trusted you to destroy the children, but my hope was frustrated.

וַתְּחַיֶּיןָ אֶת הַיְלָדִים — *And you have saved the children alive.* Not only did you fail to do as I commanded to destroy the infants, but you also counseled them (the women in childbirth) so as to preserve (the children).

NOTES

11-13. לְמַעַן עַנֹּתוֹ . . . וַיַּעֲבִדוּ מִצְרַיִם — *To afflict them ... And the Egyptians made (the children of Israel) to serve.* Ironically, the Jews accepted upon themselves as a civic duty the building of these cities and voluntarily subjected themselves. This subjection resulted in their total subjugation. How did they permit themselves such folly? The *Sforno* answers that the transgressions of man cause reason to flee and wisdom to depart from him.

The expression *sin upon sin* is based on *Isaiah* 30:1; and *from evil to evil*, on *Jeremiah* 9:2.

14. וַיְמָרְרוּ אֶת חַיֵּיהֶם — *And they made their lives bitter.* God has many messengers — and the severity of oppression reflects the seriousness of Israel's spiritual decline. The *Sforno* interprets the sentence in *Ezekiel* as referring to the period when the Jews were in Egypt and departed from God's ways, thereby bringing upon themselves Divine wrath and punishment. *In the land of Egypt* does not refer to the

כַּנָּשִׁים הַמִּצְרִיֹּת הָעִבְרִיֹּת כִּי־חָיוֹת הֵנָּה בְּטֶרֶם תָּבוֹא אֲלֵהֶן הַמְיַלֶּדֶת
כ־כא וְיָלָדוּ: וַיֵּיטֶב אֱלֹהִים לַמְיַלְּדֹת וַיִּרֶב הָעָם וַיַּעַצְמוּ מְאֹד: וַיְהִי כִּי־יָרְאוּ
כב הַמְיַלְּדֹת אֶת־הָאֱלֹהִים וַיַּעַשׂ לָהֶם בָּתִּים: וַיְצַו פַּרְעֹה לְכָל־עַמּוֹ לֵאמֹר
כָּל־הַבֵּן הַיִּלּוֹד הַיְאֹרָה תַּשְׁלִיכֻהוּ וְכָל־הַבַּת תְּחַיּוּן:
ב א־ב וַיֵּלֶךְ אִישׁ מִבֵּית לֵוִי וַיִּקַּח אֶת־בַּת־לֵוִי: וַתַּהַר הָאִשָּׁה וַתֵּלֶד בֵּן וַתֵּרֶא
ג אֹתוֹ כִּי־טוֹב הוּא וַתִּצְפְּנֵהוּ שְׁלֹשָׁה יְרָחִים: וְלֹא־יָכְלָה עוֹד הַצְּפִינוֹ וַתִּקַּח־
לוֹ תֵּבַת גֹּמֶא וַתַּחְמְרָה בַחֵמָר וּבַזָּפֶת וַתָּשֶׂם בָּהּ אֶת־הַיֶּלֶד וַתָּשֶׂם בַּסּוּף
ד־ה עַל־שְׂפַת הַיְאֹר: וַתֵּתַצַּב אֲחֹתוֹ מֵרָחֹק לְדֵעָה מַה־יֵּעָשֶׂה לוֹ: וַתֵּרֶד בַּת־

---

19. כִּי חָיוֹת הֵנָּה — *For they are lively.* (The Jewish women are) skilled in childbirth and if we should attempt to act improperly through deed or word, they will immediately be aware of our intent and no longer will our services be solicited, and 'it would not profit the king' to kill only one or two.

II

2. כִּי טוֹב הוּא — *That he was fair* (lit., *good*). 'Fair,' as we find, כִּי טֹבֹת הֵנָּה, *they were fair (Genesis* 6:2). She saw that he was unusually beautiful and she felt that this must be for some specific purpose of his Maker, for beauty of form indicates physical superiority and perfection of one's imaginative powers.

3. וַתָּשֶׂם בַּסּוּף — *And she placed it in the bulrushes.* A place where the passersby would not be likely to observe her when she placed the basket there. Nonetheless, she chose a place in the reeds so as to transfer the royal decree of casting the child in the river, to that of placing him into the reeds at the banks of the river.

4. לְדֵעָה מַה יֵּעָשֶׂה לוֹ — *To know what would be done to him.* She thought that some Egyptian would claim him as a foundling, for there were many foundlings in the land, without a doubt, since the land was filled with lewdness and immorality, as the Prophet testifies, וְזִרְמַת סוּסִים זִרְמָתָם, *their issue is like the issue of horses (Ezekiel* 23:20).

NOTES

Israelites' *subsequent* wickedness in pursuing Egyptian ways years later, as is understood by other commentaries.

19. כִּי חָיוֹת הֵנָּה — *For they are lively.* The midwives argued that it would be far better for them to bide their time and gain the confidence of the other women. Then they would be able to comply with Pharaoh's request in a more successful manner.

II

2. כִּי טוֹב הוּא — *That he was a fair child.* The word טוֹב in the context of the sentence does not mean *good,* but *fair.* The *Sforno* cites as proof the expression used in *Genesis* regarding the beautiful women who were coveted by the *B'nai Elohim,* where the word טֹבֹת is also used in the context of that episode, where it cannot mean *good,* but *fair.*

3. וַתָּשֶׂם בַּסּוּף — *And she placed it in the bulrushes.* Although a decree is issued by a temporal ruler, it is our belief that without the tacit acquiescence of God it would not have been decreed. Hence we must not defy it outright. We can, however, circumvent the decree, and this Yocheved did by placing the basket at the edge of the river in the reeds — thereby not actually defying the decree but observing, as it were, the spirit although not the letter of the law. The *Sforno,* in this manner, answers the obvious question: Why set the infant in such a comparatively hazardous place rather than a more secure one? But then the decree would have been flaunted outright — now it is partially observed. The Abarbanel gives a similar interpretation.

פַּרְעֹה לִרְחֹץ עַל־הַיְאֹר וְנַעֲרֹתֶיהָ הֹלְכֹת עַל־יַד הַיְאֹר וַתֵּרֶא אֶת־הַתֵּבָה
ו בְּתוֹךְ הַסּוּף וַתִּשְׁלַח אֶת־אֲמָתָהּ וַתִּקָּחֶהָ: וַתִּפְתַּח וַתִּרְאֵהוּ אֶת־הַיֶּלֶד
ז וְהִנֵּה־נַעַר בֹּכֶה וַתַּחְמֹל עָלָיו וַתֹּאמֶר מִיַּלְדֵי הָעִבְרִים זֶה: וַתֹּאמֶר אֲחֹתוֹ

---

5. לִרְחֹץ עַל הַיְאֹר — *To bathe in the river.* In a royal room close to and overlooking the river, for without a doubt, since כְּבוּדָּה בַת מֶלֶךְ פְּנִימָה, *the king's daughter is all glorious within* (*Psalms* 45:14), she would not go down to the (open) river.

וְנַעֲרֹתֶיהָ הֹלְכֹת עַל יַד הַיְאֹר — *And her maidens* (i.e., her ladies-in-waiting) *walked along the riverside.* Therefore, she did not send one of them to fetch the basket since they were not with her.

וַתִּשְׁלַח אֶת אֲמָתָהּ — *And she sent her handmaiden (to fetch it).* The handmaiden who was attending her at her bath. All this happened by the will of God so that one of her ladies-in-waiting should not be sent to fetch (the child), since she might decide to cast the child into the river (of her own volition).

6. וַתִּפְתַּח וַתִּרְאֵהוּ — *And she opened it and saw (the child).* She saw that he was exceptionally beautiful and goodly.

אֶת הַיֶּלֶד וְהִנֵּה נַעַר בֹּכֶה — *The child and behold a lad wept.* She saw that although he was a child, a lad was crying. A child, from birth until growth and development is called יֶלֶד, as we find regarding Rehoboam, הַיְלָדִים אֲשֶׁר גָּדְלוּ אִתּוֹ, *the young men that were grown up with him* (*I Kings* 12:10); and also, יְלָדִים אֲשֶׁר אֵין בָּהֶם כָּל מאום, *youths in whom were no blemish* (*Daniel* 1:4), regarding Daniel and his friends. As soon as the young boy begins to awaken, develop and pursue activities leading to a specific goal, incomplete and unfinished as these actions may be, he is called נַעַר. For this reason every servant is called a lad or young boy (נַעַר), for the majority of his actions are imperfect in attaining the intended goal of his master. Now she (the daughter of Pharaoh) observed that although he was a *child*, recently born, nonetheless, *a lad wept*, i.e., his actions were, in a wondrous manner, far more advanced than any child his age.

וַתַּחְמֹל עָלָיו — *And she had compassion on him.* (She felt pity) that a child so fair, with such potential for perfection, be cast into the river.

וַתֹּאמֶר מִיַּלְדֵי הָעִבְרִים זֶה — *And she said, 'This is one of the Hebrew children.'* This cannot be a foundling born illegitimately who would be prepared to betray his benefactor, as it is said, יַלְדֵי פֶשַׁע זֶרַע שָׁקֶר, *children of transgression, seed of falsehood* (*Isaiah* 57:4).

NOTES

5. וַתִּשְׁלַח אֶת אֲמָתָהּ — *And she sent her handmaiden (to fetch it).* A lady-in-waiting is likely to use her own discretion and cast away the child without first consulting the princess. A mere handmaiden would never make her own decision but would always obey her mistress. The Divine pattern of God's intervention and concern is apparent in this initial episode of Moses's life.

6. וַתִּפְתַּח וַתִּרְאֵהוּ . . . וַתֹּאמֶר מִיַּלְדֵי הָעִבְרִים זֶה — *And she opened it and saw (the child) . . . and she said, 'This is one of the Hebrew children.'* The unusual physical appearance of the child causes Pharaoh's daughter to be attracted to him. She is motivated in her subsequent actions not only by pity, but by the consideration that he will be a welcome and valuable addition to the royal court. This reasoning could only be valid if he were not an illegitimate child, born from an act of immorality, for then his loyalty would ever be

אֶל־בַּת־פַּרְעֹה הַאֵלֵךְ וְקָרָאתִי לָךְ אִשָּׁה מֵינֶקֶת מִן הָעִבְרִיֹּת וְתֵינִק לָךְ
ח אֶת־הַיָּלֶד: וַתֹּאמֶר־לָהּ בַּת־פַּרְעֹה לֵכִי וַתֵּלֶךְ הָעַלְמָה וַתִּקְרָא אֶת־אֵם
ט הַיָּלֶד: וַתֹּאמֶר לָהּ בַּת־פַּרְעֹה הֵילִיכִי אֶת־הַיֶּלֶד הַזֶּה וְהֵינִקִהוּ לִי וַאֲנִי
י אֶתֵּן אֶת־שְׂכָרֵךְ וַתִּקַּח הָאִשָּׁה הַיֶּלֶד וַתְּנִיקֵהוּ: וַיִּגְדַּל הַיֶּלֶד וַתְּבִאֵהוּ
לְבַת־פַּרְעֹה וַיְהִי־לָהּ לְבֵן וַתִּקְרָא שְׁמוֹ מֹשֶׁה וַתֹּאמֶר כִּי מִן־הַמַּיִם
שלישי יא מְשִׁיתִהוּ: וַיְהִי | בַּיָּמִים הָהֵם וַיִּגְדַּל מֹשֶׁה וַיֵּצֵא אֶל־אֶחָיו וַיַּרְא בְּסִבְלֹתָם
יב וַיַּרְא אִישׁ מִצְרִי מַכֶּה אִישׁ־עִבְרִי מֵאֶחָיו: וַיִּפֶן כֹּה וָכֹה וַיַּרְא כִּי אֵין אִישׁ
יג וַיַּךְ אֶת־הַמִּצְרִי וַיִּטְמְנֵהוּ בַּחוֹל: וַיֵּצֵא בַּיּוֹם הַשֵּׁנִי וְהִנֵּה שְׁנֵי־אֲנָשִׁים עִבְרִים
יד נִצִּים וַיֹּאמֶר לָרָשָׁע לָמָּה תַכֶּה רֵעֶךָ: וַיֹּאמֶר מִי שָׂמְךָ לְאִישׁ שַׂר וְשֹׁפֵט

---

7. מֵינֶקֶת מִן הָעִבְרִיֹּת — *A nurse of the Hebrew women.* So that the milk he nurses will be more befitting to his nature.

וְתֵינִק לָךְ אֶת הַיָּלֶד — *That she may nurse the child for you.* (He will be prepared) to serve you since his appearance and attributes are such that he is surely prepared to לִפְנֵי מְלָכִים יִתְיַצָּב, *stand before Kings (Proverbs* 22:29).

10. וַתִּקְרָא שְׁמוֹ מֹשֶׁה — *And she called his name Moses.* He who rescues and draws forth others from trouble (and danger).

וַתֹּאמֶר כִּי מִן הַמַּיִם מְשִׁיתִהוּ — *And she said, 'Because I drew him out of the water.'* The reason I called him Moses is to indicate that he will save others. True, (at this moment) *I have drawn him from the water* where he was put, but this was all ordained by the *decree of the watchers* (based on *Daniel* 4:14) so that he (in turn) shall rescue others.

11. וַיַּרְא בְּסִבְלֹתָם — *And looked on their burdens.* He turned his attention to the sufferings of his brothers.

וַיַּרְא אִישׁ מִצְרִי מַכֶּה אִישׁ עִבְרִי מֵאֶחָיו — *And he saw an Egyptian smiting a Hebrew, one of his brethren.* And because of his sense of brotherhood he was aroused to avenge him.

13. וַיֹּאמֶר לָרָשָׁע — *And he said to the wicked one.* Because they were both his brothers he did not smite the guilty one but rather admonished him.

NOTES

suspect, as we see from the verse in *Isaiah* which the *Sforno* quotes.

7. וְתֵינִק לָךְ אֶת הַיָּלֶד — *That she may nurse the child for you.* Since the Torah uses the phrase *for you,* it indicates that the retaining of a Hebrew woman to nurse the child would accrue to the benefit of Pharaoh's daughter, for in this manner the child's health would be more readily insured so he would be fit to be a member of the royal court.

10. וַתִּקְרָא שְׁמוֹ מֹשֶׁה — *And she called his name Moses.* The name given by Pharaoh's daughter to the rescued child should have been מָשׁוּי, *Mashui,* implying one who is drawn forth, rather than מֹשֶׁה, *Moshe,* implying one who draws forth. The explanation is that he was called by a name reflecting his eventual role as *a rescuer,* a role played by Moses over a prolonged period, as opposed to *a rescued one,* which was a brief and isolated, although important, event in his life.

11. וַיַּרְא אִישׁ מִצְרִי מַכֶּה אִישׁ עִבְרִי מֵאֶחָיו — *And he saw an Egyptian smiting a Hebrew, one of his brethren.* When a brother was attacked by a stranger Moses reacted with alacrity to defend and punish. When two Israelites were involved he admonished (v. 13). When it was two strangers he neither punished nor admonished but defended the weak and oppressed (v.

עָלֵינוּ הֲלְהָרְגֵנִי אַתָּה אֹמֵר כַּאֲשֶׁר הָרַגְתָּ אֶת־הַמִּצְרִי וַיִּירָא מֹשֶׁה וַיֹּאמַר
טו אָכֵן נוֹדַע הַדָּבָר: וַיִּשְׁמַע פַּרְעֹה אֶת־הַדָּבָר הַזֶּה וַיְבַקֵּשׁ לַהֲרֹג אֶת־מֹשֶׁה
טז וַיִּבְרַח מֹשֶׁה מִפְּנֵי פַרְעֹה וַיֵּשֶׁב בְּאֶרֶץ־מִדְיָן וַיֵּשֶׁב עַל־הַבְּאֵר: וּלְכֹהֵן מִדְיָן
שֶׁבַע בָּנוֹת וַתָּבֹאנָה וַתִּדְלֶנָה וַתְּמַלֶּאנָה אֶת־הָרְהָטִים לְהַשְׁקוֹת צֹאן
יז אֲבִיהֶן: וַיָּבֹאוּ הָרֹעִים וַיְגָרְשׁוּם וַיָּקָם מֹשֶׁה וַיּוֹשִׁעָן וַיַּשְׁקְ אֶת־צֹאנָם:
יח־יט וַתָּבֹאנָה אֶל־רְעוּאֵל אֲבִיהֶן וַיֹּאמֶר מַדּוּעַ מִהַרְתֶּן בֹּא הַיּוֹם: וַתֹּאמַרְןָ אִישׁ
כ מִצְרִי הִצִּילָנוּ מִיַּד הָרֹעִים וְגַם־דָּלֹה דָלָה לָנוּ וַיַּשְׁקְ אֶת־הַצֹּאן: וַיֹּאמֶר
כא אֶל־בְּנֹתָיו וְאַיּוֹ לָמָּה זֶּה עֲזַבְתֶּן אֶת־הָאִישׁ קִרְאֶן לוֹ וְיֹאכַל לָחֶם: וַיּוֹאֶל
כב מֹשֶׁה לָשֶׁבֶת אֶת־הָאִישׁ וַיִּתֵּן אֶת־צִפֹּרָה בִתּוֹ לְמֹשֶׁה: וַתֵּלֶד בֵּן וַיִּקְרָא

---

14. הֲלְהָרְגֵנִי אַתָּה אֹמֵר — *Do you intend to kill me?* You are (apparently) seeking an excuse to kill me (as you did the Egyptian).

וַיִּירָא מֹשֶׁה — *And Moses feared.* He therefore sought to protect himself, and fled.

וַיֹּאמַר אָכֵן נוֹדַע הַדָּבָר — *And he said, 'Surely the matter is known.'* Since the informer made these remarks publicly he did not kill him, for it would serve no purpose once he had informed.

15. וַיֵּשֶׁב בְּאֶרֶץ מִדְיָן — *And he dwelled in the land of Midian.* He chose to dwell for a time in Midian.

וַיֵּשֶׁב עַל הַבְּאֵר — *And he sat down by a well.* As he was passing through the land he chanced to stop at a well, as we find written, וַיִּפְגַּע בַּמָּקוֹם, *And he lighted upon the place (Genesis* 28:11), a certain place, as explained above.

17. וַיָּקָם מֹשֶׁה וַיּוֹשִׁעָן — *Moses arose and helped them.* Since both parties were strangers (non-Hebrews) he did not seek revenge nor did he bother to correct their conduct by admonishment; he only arose to save the oppressed from their oppressors.

20. לָמָּה זֶּה עֲזַבְתֶּן — *Why is it that you have left (the man)?* Since he is a guest and a kind man, it would have been proper to deal kindly with him and extend our hospitality to him.

21. לָשֶׁבֶת אֶת הָאִישׁ — *To dwell with the man.* To be a shepherd, similar to שְׁבָה עִמָּדִי, *dwell with me (Genesis* 29:19).

NOTES

17). These three episodes are recorded by the Torah to teach us what one's reaction should be to events which may seem similar but are not, for it all depends on the identity of those involved and the circumstances.

14. וַיֹּאמַר אָכֵן נוֹדַע הַדָּבָר — *And he said, 'Surely the matter is known.'* This explains the term, *the matter is known*, which is the reason for Moses's failure to react with the same degree of firm resolve as demonstrated in the previous episode. One's emotions must be controlled so as to resort to violence only if it will accomplish a reasonable end, not just to spend one's anger and frustration. Were it not for the futility of disposing of the informer, Moses would have been justified in killing him, for the law is: *One is permitted to slay an informer before he informs (Rambam,* חובל ומזיק י׳ י״א).

15. וַיֵּשֶׁב בְּאֶרֶץ מִדְיָן וַיֵּשֶׁב עַל הַבְּאֵר — *And he dwelt in the land of Midian and he sat down by a well.* The first phrase וַיֵּשֶׁב, *and he dwelled*, is by choice, but the second one is through providence. Man is granted freedom of choice and action, but when there is need for Divine intervention in the course of human history, seemingly human events are guided by God. To rest at that particular well was ordained, as was the case with Jacob when

אֶת־שְׁמוֹ גֵּרְשֹׁם כִּי אָמַר גֵּר הָיִיתִי בְּאֶרֶץ נָכְרִיָּה:
כג וַיְהִי בַיָּמִים הָרַבִּים הָהֵם וַיָּמָת מֶלֶךְ מִצְרַיִם וַיֵּאָנְחוּ בְנֵי־יִשְׂרָאֵל מִן־
כד הָעֲבֹדָה וַיִּזְעָקוּ וַתַּעַל שַׁוְעָתָם אֶל־הָאֱלֹהִים מִן־הָעֲבֹדָה: וַיִּשְׁמַע אֱלֹהִים
אֶת־נַאֲקָתָם וַיִּזְכֹּר אֱלֹהִים אֶת־בְּרִיתוֹ אֶת־אַבְרָהָם אֶת־יִצְחָק וְאֶת־

---

22. גֵּר הָיִיתִי בְּאֶרֶץ נָכְרִיָּה — *I have been a stranger in a strange land.* A stranger in a land which is not the land of my birth.

23. בַיָּמִים הָרַבִּים הָהֵם — *In the course of those many days.* From the time Moses fled Egypt, as a young man, until Gershom was born, at which time he (Moses) was close to eighty, for Eliezer was born when Moses was en route to fulfill God's mission (*Exodus* 4:24), at which time Moses was eighty years old.

וַיָּמָת מֶלֶךְ מִצְרַיִם — *The king of Egypt died.* The king who was pursuing Moses died. He (Moses) therefore named his (second) son Eliezer for (only) then was he assured that he had been saved from the sword of Pharaoh.

וַיִּזְעָקוּ — *And they cried.* They cried with pained hearts because of their labors, similar to, הֵילִילִי שַׁעַר, זַעֲקִי עִיר, *Howl, O gate; cry, O city* (*Isaiah* 14:31).

וַתַּעַל שַׁוְעָתָם אֶל הָאֱלֹהִים מִן הָעֲבֹדָה — *And their cry came up to God from the bondage.* Not because of their repentance and prayers, but because God reacts zealously to the cruelty of oppressors, as we read, וְגַם רָאִיתִי אֶת הַלַּחַץ, *and I have also seen the oppression* (3:9).

24. וַיִּשְׁמַע אֱלֹהִים אֶת נַאֲקָתָם — *And God heard their groaning.* The prayer of the few righteous who prayed, as it is said, וַנִּצְעַק אֶל ה׳ וַיִּשְׁמַע קֹלֵנוּ, *and we cried unto* HASHEM, *and He heard our voice* (*Numbers* 20:16).

וַיִּזְכֹּר אֱלֹהִים אֶת בְּרִיתוֹ — *And God remembered His covenant.* As He said, וַהֲקִמֹתִי אֶת בְּרִיתִי בֵּינִי וּבֵינֶךָ וּבֵין זַרְעֲךָ אַחֲרֶיךָ ... לִהְיוֹת לְךָ לֵאלֹהִים וּלְזַרְעֲךָ אַחֲרֶיךָ, *and I will establish My covenant between Me and you and your seed after you (throughout their generations for an everlasting covenant) to be a God unto you and unto your seed after you* (*Genesis* 17:7). And this (God) does whenever we call upon Him, as it is testified to further, וְגַם אֲנִי שָׁמַעְתִּי אֶת נַאֲקַת בְּנֵי יִשְׂרָאֵל ... וָאֶזְכֹּר אֶת בְּרִיתִי, *And I have heard the groaning of the children of Israel ... and I have remembered My covenant* (6:5).

NOTES

he was fleeing from Esau.

21. לָשֶׁבֶת אֶת הָאִישׁ — *To dwell with the man.* The invitation extended by Jethro is not simply to dwell with him, but to assist him with his flocks, as was the case with Laban and Jacob, where the same phrase is used.

22. גֵּר הָיִיתִי בְּאֶרֶץ נָכְרִיָּה — *I have been a stranger in a strange land.* In Egypt, Moses was a stranger, yet he did live in the land of his birth. In Midian, he is both a stranger and one who lives in a land which is not his native land.

23. בַיָּמִים הָרַבִּים הָהֵם וַיָּמָת מֶלֶךְ מִצְרַיִם — *In the course of those many days the king of Egypt died.* Moses called his first son Gershom and his second Eliezer, which means *God has saved me.* The reason he did not show his gratitude to God immediately, by naming his firstborn Eliezer, is because he could not be certain of his complete salvation until the death of the king that was pursuing him, and this occurred after the birth of his first child.

וַיִּזְעָקוּ וַתַּעַל שַׁוְעָתָם אֶל הָאֱלֹהִים מִן הָעֲבֹדָה — *And they cried, and their cry came up to God from the bondage.* The Israelites did not cry out to God because they regretted their transgressions and repented their sins, which was the

ג רביעי כה־א יַעֲקֹב׃ וַיַּרְא אֱלֹהִים אֶת־בְּנֵי יִשְׂרָאֵל וַיֵּדַע אֱלֹהִים׃ וּמֹשֶׁה
הָיָה רֹעֶה אֶת־צֹאן יִתְרוֹ חֹתְנוֹ כֹּהֵן מִדְיָן וַיִּנְהַג אֶת־הַצֹּאן אַחַר הַמִּדְבָּר
ב וַיָּבֹא אֶל־הַר הָאֱלֹהִים חֹרֵבָה׃ וַיֵּרָא מַלְאַךְ יהוה אֵלָיו בְּלַבַּת־אֵשׁ מִתּוֹךְ

---

25. וַיַּרְא אֱלֹהִים אֶת בְּנֵי יִשְׂרָאֵל — *And God saw the children of Israel.* He extended His providence and no longer hid His face from them, similar to, כִּי רָאִיתִי אֶת עַמִּי, כִּי בָּאָה צַעֲקָתוֹ אֵלָי, *I have seen the pain of My people, for their cries have come to Me* (*I Samuel* 9:16); and as is proven later when He says, רָאֹה רָאִיתִי אֶת עֳנִי עַמִּי אֲשֶׁר בְּמִצְרָיִם, *I have surely seen the affliction of My people that are in Egypt* (3:7).

וַיֵּדַע אֱלֹהִים — *And God knew.* He recognized the anguish of their hearts and that their prayers and cries were heartfelt, as we are later told, כִּי יָדַעְתִּי אֶת מַכְאֹבָיו, *for I know their pains* (3:7), the reverse of וַיְפַתּוּהוּ בְּפִיהֶם . . . וְלִבָּם לֹא נָכוֹן עִמּוֹ, *And they beguiled Him with their mouth . . . but their heart was not steadfast with Him* (*Psalms* 78:36-37).

III

1. וַיָּבֹא אֶל הַר הָאֱלֹהִים חֹרֵבָה — *And he came to the mountain of God, to Horeb.* He came alone, to seclude himself and pray (to God), similar to, וַיָּבֹא עַד חֶבְרוֹן, *and he came to Hebron* (*Numbers* 13:22).

2. וַיֵּרָא מַלְאַךְ ה׳ אֵלָיו — *And an angel of God appeared to him.* In a vision of prophecy. However, when angels appear in human form, not for the purpose of prophecy, as we find in the case of Abraham, Lot and Balaam, the phrase is not וַיֵּרָא, *he appeared*, but וַיַּרְא, *he saw;* as we find, וַיַּרְא וְהִנֵּה שְׁלֹשָׁה אֲנָשִׁים, *and behold, he saw three men* (*Genesis* 18:2); וַיַּרְא לוֹט, *and Lot saw* (*Genesis* 19:1); וַיַּרְא אֶת מַלְאַךְ ה׳ נִצָּב בַּדֶּרֶךְ, *and he (Balaam) saw the angel of God standing in the way* (*Numbers* 22:31).

NOTES

real cause of their suffering. They cried, not due to any noble motivation, but simply because of their unbearable state of slavery. Nonetheless, God listened and reached a decision, to begin the process of liberation and salvation. The Israelites might cry out *from the bondage* which was incomplete, yet God determined to act because of their debilitating and destructive oppression. *From the bondage* is the cause of God's action, although the prayers of the Jews were sparse and their repentance, though stirring within them, was as yet non-existent.

25. וַיַּרְא אֱלֹהִים אֶת בְּנֵי יִשְׂרָאֵל וַיֵּדַע אֱלֹהִים — *And God saw the children of Israel and God knew.* The Almighty is all-seeing and naught escapes Him. This does not mean, however, that God's attention and concern is ever present with His people. There are times when His face is hidden — when His providence is removed and at such moments in history Israel is abandoned to the mercies of others and the vicissitudes and forces of nature and man. At this moment God *sees* Israel anew, His *hashgachah* (concern and supervision) is reactivated, and He *knows* that the initial cries of anguish have blossomed into sincere heartfelt prayer.

III

1. . . . וַיָּבֹא — *And he came . . .* The verse first tells us that Moses led the sheep into the wilderness (וַיִּנְהַג אֶת הַצֹּאן), then the word וַיָּבֹא is used, apparently introducing another action on his part. The *Sforno* therefore interprets this to mean that Moses used the solitude of the wilderness to commune with God. Proof is brought from Caleb who came (the same word וַיָּבֹא is used) to Hebron to seek guidance and pray at the gravesite of the Patriarchs, as our Sages tell us in tractate *Sotah* 34b.

2. וַיֵּרָא מַלְאַךְ ה׳ אֵלָיו — *And an angel of God appeared to him.* In the three cases cited the angel of God appears, in human form, and

ג הַסְּנֶה וַיַּרְא וְהִנֵּה הַסְּנֶה בֹּעֵר בָּאֵשׁ וְהַסְּנֶה אֵינֶנּוּ אֻכָּל: וַיֹּאמֶר מֹשֶׁה
ד אָסֻרָה־נָּא וְאֶרְאֶה אֶת־הַמַּרְאֶה הַגָּדֹל הַזֶּה מַדּוּעַ לֹא־יִבְעַר הַסְּנֶה: וַיַּרְא

וַיַּרְא וְהִנֵּה הַסְּנֶה בֹּעֵר בָּאֵשׁ — *And he looked and behold the bush is burning with fire.* בֹּעֵר means *burning.* This (vision) was a prophecy (clothed) in an enigma. The angel was in the midst of the bush and the fire was burning around the angel symbolizing that the righteous Israelites, who are as Godly angels, were caught up in the midst of the bush, (which represented) the Egyptian people, who were as briers and thorns. The bush would burn with the anguished fire of the ten plagues but they would not be consumed in that distress, as indicated in the phrase, *and the bush is not consumed,* (meaning) it was not destroyed by the fire burning within it.

The prophetic power of Moses at this stage was not the same as it would become later — as is indicated in the phrase, כִּי יָרֵא מֵהַבִּיט אֶל הָאֱלֹהִים, *For he feared to look at God* (verse 6) as opposed to וּתְמֻנַת ה׳ יַבִּיט, *The image of God he did perceive* (*Numbers* 12:8). However, from the day of the giving of the Torah and onward, when God revealed Himself to all Israel, face to face, although they could not tolerate (this exalted experience), as it is written, לֹא אֹסִף עוֹד לִשְׁמֹעַ אֶת קוֹל ה׳ אֱלֹהָי, *Let me not hear again the voice of* HASHEM, *my God* (*Deut.* 18:16). (Moses) alone remained on that high level, as it is written, שׁוּבוּ לָכֶם לְאָהֳלֵיכֶם וְאַתָּה פֹּה עֲמֹד עִמָּדִי, *Return, you (the nation), to your tents; but as for you (Moses), stand here with Me* (*Deut.* 5:27-28); and as is written, וַיַּעֲמֹד הָעָם מֵרָחֹק וּמֹשֶׁה נִגַּשׁ, *And the people stood from afar but Moses approached* (*Exodus* 20:18). (From that moment) the prophecy of Moses was פָּנִים אֶל פָּנִים, *face to face* (*Exodus* 33:11), and וּמַרְאֶה וְלֹא בְחִידֹת, *manifestly, and not in dark speeches* (*Numbers* 12:8).

3. אָסֻרָה נָּא וְאֶרְאֶה — *I will turn aside now and see.* I will consider and see.

מַדּוּעַ לֹא יִבְעַר הַסְּנֶה — *Why the bush does not burn.* Why are the Egyptians not destroyed by the plagues; similar to, וְדָלְקוּ בָהֶם וַאֲכָלוּם, *And they shall kindle in them and devour them* (*Obadiah* 1:18).

NOTES

since his coming is not to *reveal* the will or wish of God but rather to *fulfill* some mission or purpose, he is *seen* rather than *appears.* In the case of Abraham the angels came to assist him in fulfilling the *mitzvah* of hospitality and to tell him of the impending birth of Isaac; Lot was visited so as to be rescued; and Balaam saw the angel blocking his path. When, however, the angel of God is sent for the purpose of prophecy — as in this case — the correct phrase is *he appeared* rather than *he saw.*

וַיַּרְא וְהִנֵּה הַסְּנֶה בֹּעֵר בָּאֵשׁ — *And he looked and behold the bush is burning with fire.* The *Sforno* makes two points here: (a) He interprets the symbolism of the bush in the following manner: The angel represents the righteous of Israel, caught up, as it were, in the midst of the burning bush, which symbolizes Egypt. The bush, which is not consumed, though enveloped in flames, is symbolic of Egypt ravaged by the ten plagues but not destroyed — for that is not the purpose of God's punishment, as is further developed in verse 7. (b) Prophecy through the medium of images and visions wrapped in enigmas and riddles is not the method God would use later in communicating with Moses. At this stage of Moses's calling, however, he was not yet prepared for direct, clear communication with the Almighty. From the moment of Sinai, however, when revelation occurred on the highest level of human experience, Moses alone remained on that exalted plane to which all were elevated momentarily. From that moment on he spoke to God — *face to face* — through a clear and vivid lens, and not through clouded visions and mysterious riddles.

בֹּעֵר — *Burned.* The root בער can either mean *removal* or *burn.* The *Sforno* stresses that the

יְהוָה כִּי סָר לִרְאוֹת וַיִּקְרָא אֵלָיו אֱלֹהִים מִתּוֹךְ הַסְּנֶה וַיֹּאמֶר מֹשֶׁה מֹשֶׁה
ה וַיֹּאמֶר הִנֵּנִי: וַיֹּאמֶר אַל־תִּקְרַב הֲלֹם שַׁל־נְעָלֶיךָ מֵעַל רַגְלֶיךָ כִּי הַמָּקוֹם
ו אֲשֶׁר אַתָּה עוֹמֵד עָלָיו אַדְמַת־קֹדֶשׁ הוּא: וַיֹּאמֶר אָנֹכִי אֱלֹהֵי אָבִיךָ אֱלֹהֵי
אַבְרָהָם אֱלֹהֵי יִצְחָק וֵאלֹהֵי יַעֲקֹב וַיַּסְתֵּר מֹשֶׁה פָּנָיו כִּי יָרֵא מֵהַבִּיט אֶל־
ז הָאֱלֹהִים: וַיֹּאמֶר יהוה רָאֹה רָאִיתִי אֶת־עֳנִי עַמִּי אֲשֶׁר בְּמִצְרָיִם וְאֶת־
ח צַעֲקָתָם שָׁמַעְתִּי מִפְּנֵי נֹגְשָׂיו כִּי יָדַעְתִּי אֶת־מַכְאֹבָיו: וָאֵרֵד לְהַצִּילוֹ ׀ מִיַּד
מִצְרַיִם וּלְהַעֲלֹתוֹ מִן־הָאָרֶץ הַהִוא אֶל־אֶרֶץ טוֹבָה וּרְחָבָה אֶל־אֶרֶץ זָבַת
חָלָב וּדְבָשׁ אֶל־מְקוֹם הַכְּנַעֲנִי וְהַחִתִּי וְהָאֱמֹרִי וְהַפְּרִזִּי וְהַחִוִּי וְהַיְבוּסִי:

---

4. וַיַּרְא ה׳ כִּי סָר לִרְאוֹת — *And* H*ASHEM saw that he turned aside to see.* To (study and) discern the matter.

וַיִּקְרָא אֵלָיו אֱלֹהִים — *And God called to him.* To inform him — as our Sages tell us, הַבָּא לְטַהֵר מְסַיְּעִין אוֹתוֹ, *he who comes to be purified will be assisted from on High (Sabbath* 104a), and as we find, וּמֹשֶׁה עָלָה אֶל הָאֱלֹהִים וַיִּקְרָא אֵלָיו ה׳ מִן הָהָר, *Moses went up to God, and* H*ASHEM called to him from the mountain (Exodus* 19:3).

5. שַׁל נְעָלֶיךָ — *Take off your shoes.* Even in this place where you now stand.

7. רָאֹה רָאִיתִי אֶת עֳנִי עַמִּי — *I have surely seen the affliction of My people.* The righteous ones of this generation who sigh and bemoan the sins of their generation and their sufferings and who pray (to God). The angel of God who revealed himself in the bush symbolizes them.

The (double phrase) רָאֹה רָאִיתִי is meant as *'indeed' I have seen.* Whenever a phrase is repeated (as it is here), and as we find in the expression עָלֹה נַעֲלֶה, *ascend we shall ascend (Numbers* 13:30); or יָכוֹל נוּכַל, *able we will be able* (ibid.); or יָדַעְתִּי בְנִי יָדַעְתִּי, *I know, my son, I know (Genesis* 48:19); it is similar to (use of the word) אָמְנָם indicating that it is true in spite of evidence or claims to the contrary.

(The sense of the verse is:) Even though I have seen the affliction of My people in Egypt, demonstrated by the angel in the bush, and although I intend to punish their oppressors, as indicated by the fire in the bush, nonetheless they will not be utterly destroyed by the plagues, as indicated by the bush not being consumed. For the purpose of the plagues is not to destroy Egypt so that the Israelites can replace them, but to save the Israelites from their hand and establish them in another place. And this is the reason for . . .

8. וָאֵרֵד לְהַצִּילוֹ . . . וּלְהַעֲלֹתוֹ מִן הָאָרֶץ הַהִוא אֶל אֶרֶץ טוֹבָה — *And I have come down to save them from the land of Egypt to bring them up from this land to a good Land* . . . i.e., I have revealed myself in this vision to save them and bring them up, not to destroy the Egyptians.

זָבַת חָלָב וּדְבָשׁ — *(A Land) flowing with milk and honey.* (With) many cattle, plentiful food, pleasant and nutritious, as it is written, אֱכָל בְּנִי דְבַשׁ כִּי טוֹב וְנֹפֶת מָתוֹק, *My son, eat your honey for it is good and the honeycomb is sweet (Proverbs* 24:13).

NOTES

phrase בֹּעֵר in this instance must mean *is burning,* since *the bush is not* (totally) *consumed.*

4. וַיַּרְא ה׳ כִּי סָר לִרְאוֹת — *And* H*ASHEM saw that he turned aside to see.* Man must take the first step in seeking out God. He must initiate,

ט וְעַתָּה הִנֵּה צַעֲקַת בְּנֵי־יִשְׂרָאֵל בָּאָה אֵלָי וְגַם־רָאִיתִי אֶת־הַלַּחַץ אֲשֶׁר
י מִצְרַיִם לֹחֲצִים אֹתָם׃ וְעַתָּה לְכָה וְאֶשְׁלָחֲךָ אֶל־פַּרְעֹה וְהוֹצֵא אֶת־עַמִּי
יא בְנֵי־יִשְׂרָאֵל מִמִּצְרָיִם׃ וַיֹּאמֶר מֹשֶׁה אֶל־הָאֱלֹהִים מִי אָנֹכִי כִּי אֵלֵךְ אֶל־
יב פַּרְעֹה וְכִי אוֹצִיא אֶת־בְּנֵי יִשְׂרָאֵל מִמִּצְרָיִם׃ וַיֹּאמֶר כִּי־אֶהְיֶה עִמָּךְ וְזֶה־
לְּךָ הָאוֹת כִּי אָנֹכִי שְׁלַחְתִּיךָ בְּהוֹצִיאֲךָ אֶת־הָעָם מִמִּצְרַיִם תַּעַבְדוּן אֶת־

---

9. וְעַתָּה — *And now.* Since all this is true (this always being the meaning of the word וְעַתָּה, *now),* the sense is: since this is true, that I know their hurt and the anguish of their heart . . .

הִנֵּה צַעֲקַת בְּנֵי יִשְׂרָאֵל בָּאָה אֵלָי — *The cry of the children of Israel has come unto Me.* I have accepted their prayers for they have called to Me sincerely and not in the sense of, וַיְפַתּוּהוּ בְּפִיהֶם, *And they beguiled Him with their mouth (Psalms* 78:36).

וְגַם רָאִיתִי אֶת הַלַּחַץ — *Moreover I have seen the oppression.* And because the oppression is so great the oppressors are worthy of punishment; similar to, וְקֶצֶף גָּדוֹל אֲנִי קֹצֵף עַל הַגּוֹיִם הַשַּׁאֲנַנִּים אֲשֶׁר אֲנִי קָצַפְתִּי מְּעָט וְהֵמָּה עָזְרוּ לְרָעָה, *And I am very displeased with the nations that are at ease; for I was but a little displeased and they helped for evil (Zechariah* 1:15).

10. וְעַתָּה לְכָה וְאֶשְׁלָחֲךָ — *And now therefore come and I will send you (to Pharaoh).* To warn them before I punish them.

11. מִי אָנֹכִי כִּי אֵלֵךְ — *Who am I that I should go?* How will my warning carry weight?

וְכִי אוֹצִיא אֶת בְּנֵי יִשְׂרָאֵל — *And that I should bring forth the children of Israel?* . . . that I shall be worthy to take forth Israel since they are at present unworthy (of liberation).

12. כִּי אֶהְיֶה עִמָּךְ וְזֶה לְּךָ הָאוֹת — *I will be with you and this shall be the sign.* You shall decree a thing and it shall be established for you wherever you will turn, and all will recognize that I sent you and will respect you and your words, as we find, גַּם הָאִישׁ מֹשֶׁה גָּדוֹל מְאֹד בְּאֶרֶץ מִצְרַיִם, *The man Moses was very great in the land of Egypt* (11:3).

NOTES

i.e., begin, then God will meet him. Only when Moses turned to observe and witness, did God call to him. At the time of the giving of the Torah, it was only after Moses went up to God that the Almighty called to him — here again man had to make the first move.

9. וְעַתָּה — *And now.* The *Sforno* explains the meaning of the word וְעַתָּה, *and now,* as indicating something that is true — the reality of a given situation or condition. The sense of the verse according to him is: the reality of Israel's state and their bitter condition is known to Me and I am fully aware of their pain and suffering. However, My plan of action is not to punish the oppressor, but to save the Israelites and lead them forth from Egypt to another land (as the *Sforno* explained in verse 7).

וְגַם רָאִיתִי אֶת הַלַּחַץ — *Moreover I have seen the oppression.* The *Sforno* explains why the Egyptians were worthy of punishment though they were but the instruments of God in fulfilling the Divine plan revealed to Abraham when He said, *they will serve them and be afflicted by them (Genesis* 15:13). Their guilt lies in their excessive cruelty.

12. כִּי אֶהְיֶה עִמָּךְ וְזֶה לְּךָ הָאוֹת — *I will be with you and this shall be the sign.* God here answers Moses's first reservation, i.e., 'What weight can my warning carry?' by reassuring him that his prestige and stature will grow and be recognized in time.

יג הָאֱלֹהִים עַל הָהָר הַזֶּה: וַיֹּאמֶר מֹשֶׁה אֶל־הָאֱלֹהִים הִנֵּה אָנֹכִי בָא אֶל־בְּנֵי
יִשְׂרָאֵל וְאָמַרְתִּי לָהֶם אֱלֹהֵי אֲבוֹתֵיכֶם שְׁלָחַנִי אֲלֵיכֶם וְאָמְרוּ־לִי מַה־שְּׁמוֹ
יד מָה אֹמַר אֲלֵהֶם: וַיֹּאמֶר אֱלֹהִים אֶל־מֹשֶׁה אֶהְיֶה אֲשֶׁר אֶהְיֶה וַיֹּאמֶר כֹּה
טו תֹאמַר לִבְנֵי יִשְׂרָאֵל אֶהְיֶה שְׁלָחַנִי אֲלֵיכֶם: וַיֹּאמֶר עוֹד אֱלֹהִים אֶל־מֹשֶׁה
כֹּה־תֹאמַר אֶל־בְּנֵי יִשְׂרָאֵל יהוה אֱלֹהֵי אֲבֹתֵיכֶם אֱלֹהֵי אַבְרָהָם אֱלֹהֵי

בְּהוֹצִיאֲךָ אֶת הָעָם מִמִּצְרַיִם תַּעַבְדוּן אֶת הָאֱלֹהִים עַל הָהָר הַזֶּה — *When you will bring forth the people out of Egypt, you shall serve God upon this mountain.* Although they are not worthy, they are prepared to serve 'God on the mountain,' when you will 'bring them forth' from among these transgressors.

13. וְאָמְרוּ לִי מַה שְּׁמוֹ — *And they shall say to me, 'What is His Name?'* A name reveals one's personal form (i.e., disposition), and the form is the cause of the unique function of that person. Therefore what they will say is: By which function emanating from Him, by which He can be called by name, did He send you to deliver us?

14. אֶהְיֶה אֲשֶׁר אֶהְיֶה — *I am that I am.* He Whose existence is constant and consistent, and Whose essence is His existence. From this (concept we are obliged to believe that) God loves (all) existence and detests all waste (loss or nihility) which is opposed to *what is,* as He says, כִּי לֹא אֶחְפֹּץ בְּמוֹת הַמֵּת, *For I do not desire the death of him who dies (Ezekiel* 18:32). And this impels (us to believe that) He loves justice and righteousness, for their objective is existence, while detesting injustice and brutality which cause destruction, loss and waste. Therefore He abhors the violence and brutality of the Egyptians directed against you.

15. וַיֹּאמֶר עוֹד אֱלֹהִים אֶל מֹשֶׁה כֹּה תֹאמַר אֶל בְּנֵי יִשְׂרָאֵל — *And God again said unto Moses, 'Thus shall you say to the Children of Israel.'* To the wise men of the generation.

ה' אֱלֹהֵי אֲבֹתֵיכֶם — *HASHEM, the God of your Fathers.* (Both as the God) Whose unique function is indicated by the special name (used to send Moses) and also as the God of your Fathers Who entered into a covenant with them and their children.

NOTES

בְּהוֹצִיאֲךָ אֶת הָעָם מִמִּצְרַיִם תַּעַבְדוּן אֶת הָאֱלֹהִים עַל הָהָר הַזֶּה — *When you will bring forth the people out of Egypt, you shall serve God upon this mountain.* Moses was concerned, for since he felt incapable of liberating the Israelites by virtue of his own powers of leadership and personal powers, he could succeed only by virtue of the Jews' great merits, which he knew were woefully inadequate. He was therefore understandably dubious and pessimistic. God reassured him that one must not judge a people as they *are,* especially when imprisoned in an environment that militates against their spiritual development. What is all-important is their willingness to listen, to learn and to serve if only granted the opportunity. Moses was assured by God that though unworthy they were not unprepared to hearken and obey. It was for this unrealized potential that they would be brought forth.

14. אֶהְיֶה אֲשֶׁר אֶהְיֶה — *I am that I am.* In response to Moses's question, 'What is God's name?' the answer is given by defining and describing the essential attribute by which God is known, for a name is that which sums up the essence and being of a person or object. That God 'is' and 'will be' denotes not only an element of timelessness but also a God, a Being that 'is' in the sense of affirming and ratifying all that gives life, being and existence; in other words, all that serves a constructive end. Those forces which are destructive, that corrupt and destroy life and 'being,' are opposed

חמישי טו יִצְחָק וֵאלֹהֵי יַעֲקֹב שְׁלָחַנִי אֲלֵיכֶם זֶה־שְּׁמִי לְעֹלָם וְזֶה זִכְרִי לְדֹר דֹּר: לֵךְ
וְאָסַפְתָּ אֶת־זִקְנֵי יִשְׂרָאֵל וְאָמַרְתָּ אֲלֵהֶם יהוה אֱלֹהֵי אֲבֹתֵיכֶם נִרְאָה אֵלַי
אֱלֹהֵי אַבְרָהָם יִצְחָק וְיַעֲקֹב לֵאמֹר פָּקֹד פָּקַדְתִּי אֶתְכֶם וְאֶת־הֶעָשׂוּי לָכֶם
יז בְּמִצְרָיִם: וָאֹמַר אַעֲלֶה אֶתְכֶם מֵעֳנִי מִצְרַיִם אֶל־אֶרֶץ הַכְּנַעֲנִי וְהַחִתִּי
יח וְהָאֱמֹרִי וְהַפְּרִזִּי וְהַחִוִּי וְהַיְבוּסִי אֶל־אֶרֶץ זָבַת חָלָב וּדְבָשׁ: וְשָׁמְעוּ לְקֹלֶךָ
וּבָאתָ אַתָּה וְזִקְנֵי יִשְׂרָאֵל אֶל־מֶלֶךְ מִצְרַיִם וַאֲמַרְתֶּם אֵלָיו יהוה אֱלֹהֵי
הָעִבְרִיִּים נִקְרָה עָלֵינוּ וְעַתָּה נֵלֲכָה־נָּא דֶּרֶךְ שְׁלֹשֶׁת יָמִים בַּמִּדְבָּר וְנִזְבְּחָה
יט לַיהוה אֱלֹהֵינוּ: וַאֲנִי יָדַעְתִּי כִּי לֹא־יִתֵּן אֶתְכֶם מֶלֶךְ מִצְרַיִם לַהֲלֹךְ וְלֹא
כ בְּיָד חֲזָקָה: וְשָׁלַחְתִּי אֶת־יָדִי וְהִכֵּיתִי אֶת־מִצְרַיִם בְּכֹל נִפְלְאֹתַי אֲשֶׁר

זֶה שְׁמִי לְעֹלָם — *This is My Name forever.* The special (unique) Name Which is the original Name that manifests My being, eternity and (role of) originator — that is . . .

זִכְרִי לְדֹר דֹּר — *My memorial for every generation.* This is what the wise men of every generation have grasped, new and old alike, that there must perforce be an eternal unchanging 'first cause.'

16. פָּקֹד פָּקַדְתִּי אֶתְכֶם — *I have surely remembered you* . . . as descendants of the Patriarchs.

וְאֶת הֶעָשׂוּי לָכֶם בְּמִצְרָיִם — *And that which is done to you in Egypt.* Because (God) despises the cruelty and violence (demonstrated by the Egyptians).

18. וְשָׁמְעוּ לְקֹלֶךָ — *And they shall hearken to your voice.* All that you will command them.

אֱלֹהֵי הָעִבְרִיִּים — *The God of the Hebrews.* The God of those who adhere to the beliefs of Eber.

נִקְרָה עָלֵינוּ — *Has met with us.* At a time when it was not our intent to receive prophecy nor were we requesting aught from Him, (He met with us) and commanded us to sacrifice to fulfill His will.

19. כִּי לֹא יִתֵּן אֶתְכֶם מֶלֶךְ מִצְרַיִם לַהֲלֹךְ — *The king of Egypt will not give you leave to go.* He will not agree to do so.

וְלֹא בְּיָד חֲזָקָה — *Except by a mighty hand.* And I shall so ordain that he will not permit you to leave when My hand will be strengthened against him, for when each plague will cease I will harden his heart so that he will be unafraid of additional plagues.

20. וְהִכֵּיתִי אֶת מִצְרַיִם בְּכֹל נִפְלְאֹתָי — *And I will smite Egypt with all My wonders.* In

NOTES

to God and He to them, hence His fury is directed against the Egyptians who have unleashed forces of destruction and loss.

15. זֶה שְּׁמִי לְעֹלָם . . . זִכְרִי לְדֹר דֹּר — *This is My Name forever . . . my memorial for every generation.* 'To be remembered' means not to be forgotten or ignored. At no time in the history of mankind was God ever unknown or denied completely; hence His Name (being known) is ever His remembrance — *This is My Name forever,* because it is *My memorial for every generation.*

18. אֱלֹהֵי הָעִבְרִיִּים נִקְרָא עָלֵינוּ — *The God of the Hebrews has met with us.* The Israelites did

כא אֶעֱשֶׂה בְּקִרְבּוֹ וְאַחֲרֵי־כֵן יְשַׁלַּח אֶתְכֶם: וְנָתַתִּי אֶת־חֵן הָעָם־הַזֶּה בְּעֵינֵי
כב מִצְרָיִם וְהָיָה כִּי תֵלֵכוּן לֹא תֵלְכוּ רֵיקָם: וְשָׁאֲלָה אִשָּׁה מִשְּׁכֶנְתָּהּ וּמִגָּרַת
בֵּיתָהּ כְּלֵי־כֶסֶף וּכְלֵי זָהָב וּשְׂמָלֹת וְשַׂמְתֶּם עַל־בְּנֵיכֶם וְעַל־בְּנֹתֵיכֶם
ד א וְנִצַּלְתֶּם אֶת־מִצְרָיִם: וַיַּעַן מֹשֶׁה וַיֹּאמֶר וְהֵן לֹא־יַאֲמִינוּ לִי וְלֹא יִשְׁמְעוּ
°מַה־זֶּה ק׳ ב בְּקֹלִי כִּי יֹאמְרוּ לֹא־נִרְאָה אֵלֶיךָ יהוה: וַיֹּאמֶר אֵלָיו יהוה °מזה בְּיָדֶךָ
ג וַיֹּאמֶר מַטֶּה: וַיֹּאמֶר הַשְׁלִיכֵהוּ אַרְצָה וַיַּשְׁלִכֵהוּ אַרְצָה וַיְהִי לְנָחָשׁ וַיָּנָס

---

a manner that all who hear will wonder (and marvel), and many will see and fear and perhaps some will repent.

22. וְנִצַּלְתֶּם אֶת מִצְרָיִם — *And you shall empty Egypt.* Although you will receive everything from them as a loan, and be obligated to return (these articles to them), all this however will be corrected later according to law by their pursuing you to do battle against you and plunder your possessions. When they (the Egyptians) perished in battle, for God did battle for (Israel), then legally all the booty of the pursuer belonged to the pursued, measure for measure, as is the custom in every war.

IV

1. וְהֵן לֹא יַאֲמִינוּ לִי וְלֹא יִשְׁמְעוּ בְּקֹלִי — *They will not believe me nor listen to my voice.* When they realize that the king of Egypt will not permit them to leave.

כִּי יֹאמְרוּ לֹא נִרְאָה אֵלֶיךָ ה׳ — *For they will say, 'HASHEM did not appear to you.'* For כִּי הוּא אָמַר וַיֶּהִי, *He says and it becomes* (*Psalms* 33:9).

2. מַזֶּה בְיָדֶךָ — *What is this in your hand?* A rod is inanimate whereas a hand is alive, but I (God) Who can destroy and bring to life, will cause the (living) hand to be as dead through leprosy, and grant life to the inanimate rod.

NOTES

not force the issue. God's appearance is neither contrived nor 'coerced,' it is entirely the will and volition of God; hence, they were not to be accused of initiating this troublesome demand. It was the command of the Almighty and they must obey.

20. וְהִכֵּיתִי אֶת מִצְרַיִם בְּכֹל נִפְלְאֹתָי — *And I will smite Egypt with all My wonders.* A 'wonder' is an act which arouses wonder in the beholder. Its purpose is not to impress the witness but to awaken and arouse him to react. It is not meant to evoke admiration, but awe and reverence which will bring man to repentance.

22. וְנִצַּלְתֶּם אֶת מִצְרָיִם — *And you shall empty Egypt.* The Jews were told to 'borrow' items of value from their Egyptian neighbors, which certainly obligated them to return them to their owners. How then can we justify their appropriation of these valuables? The answer is given in the final portion of the verse: The Egyptians, by pursuing the Israelites, intent upon destruction and plunder, would relinquish their rights of ownership, for now all would become the prize of war; and to the victor belong the spoils.

IV

1. וְהֵן לֹא יַאֲמִינוּ לִי וְלֹא יִשְׁמְעוּ בְּקֹלִי — *They will not believe me nor listen to my voice.* Moses did not mean that they would question the omnipotence of the Almighty when Pharaoh would refuse to send them forth. He meant that they would refuse to believe that he is God's true messenger, since they know that God decrees and it 'is,' whereas in this instance the will of God was frustrated and unfulfilled.

2. מַזֶּה בְיָדֶךָ — *What is this in your hand?* The *Sforno* interprets this question as God revealing His intention to show a double sign and wonder, one with his hand and one with what the hand is holding, i.e., the rod. They are coupled because the opposing nature of the two signs — the living hand perishing and the inanimate rod becoming alive — manifest God's power to grant life and take it away.

ד מֹשֶׁה מִפָּנָיו: וַיֹּאמֶר יהוה אֶל־מֹשֶׁה שְׁלַח יָדְךָ וֶאֱחֹז בִּזְנָבוֹ וַיִּשְׁלַח יָדוֹ
ה וַיַּחֲזֶק בּוֹ וַיְהִי לְמַטֶּה בְּכַפּוֹ: לְמַעַן יַאֲמִינוּ כִּי־נִרְאָה אֵלֶיךָ יהוה אֱלֹהֵי
ו אֲבֹתָם אֱלֹהֵי אַבְרָהָם אֱלֹהֵי יִצְחָק וֵאלֹהֵי יַעֲקֹב: וַיֹּאמֶר יהוה לוֹ עוֹד
הָבֵא־נָא יָדְךָ בְּחֵיקֶךָ וַיָּבֵא יָדוֹ בְּחֵיקוֹ וַיּוֹצִאָהּ וְהִנֵּה יָדוֹ מְצֹרַעַת כַּשָּׁלֶג:
ז וַיֹּאמֶר הָשֵׁב יָדְךָ אֶל־חֵיקֶךָ וַיָּשֶׁב יָדוֹ אֶל־חֵיקוֹ וַיּוֹצִאָהּ מֵחֵיקוֹ וְהִנֵּה־שָׁבָה
ח כִּבְשָׂרוֹ: וְהָיָה אִם־לֹא יַאֲמִינוּ לָךְ וְלֹא יִשְׁמְעוּ לְקֹל הָאֹת הָרִאשׁוֹן וְהֶאֱמִינוּ
ט לְקֹל הָאֹת הָאַחֲרוֹן: וְהָיָה אִם־לֹא יַאֲמִינוּ גַּם לִשְׁנֵי הָאֹתוֹת הָאֵלֶּה וְלֹא
יִשְׁמְעוּן לְקֹלֶךָ וְלָקַחְתָּ מִמֵּימֵי הַיְאֹר וְשָׁפַכְתָּ הַיַּבָּשָׁה וְהָיוּ הַמַּיִם אֲשֶׁר
י תִּקַּח מִן־הַיְאֹר וְהָיוּ לְדָם בַּיַּבָּשֶׁת: וַיֹּאמֶר מֹשֶׁה אֶל־יהוה בִּי אֲדֹנָי לֹא

---

3. וַיָּנָס מֹשֶׁה מִפָּנָיו — *And Moses fled from it.* For this snake was a real one which pursued him, whereas the serpents made by Pharaoh's magicians through their secret arts had no real movement although they appeared as serpents. Sorcery cannot produce any authentic natural creatures, as our Sages taught us: 'By God! They cannot create a camel (or any other creature)' (*Sanhedrin* 67b). Therefore (God) says, וְהַמַּטֶּה אֲשֶׁר נֶהְפַּךְ לְנָחָשׁ, *And the rod which was turned into a snake* (7:15) and not לְתַנִּין, *into a serpent.*

8. וְהֶאֱמִינוּ לְקֹל הָאֹת הָאַחֲרוֹן — *And they will believe the voice of the latter sign.* For it is far more unnatural to heal a particular limb of leprosy, which is strong (and white) as snow and undoubtedly akin to the death of that limb.

9. וְלָקַחְתָּ מִמֵּימֵי הַיְאֹר — *You shall take of the water of the river.* For a (primary) element (i.e., water) to be totally transformed into a composition without (benefit of) an intermediary is unimaginable.

10. לֹא אִישׁ דְּבָרִים אָנֹכִי — *I am not a man of words.* (I am) unskilled in the ways of eloquence and ordered speech, so as to speak (properly) before a king.

NOTES

This is a most appropriate introduction to the drama of punishment and liberation that is about to unfold.

3. וַיָּנָס מֹשֶׁה מִפָּנָיו — *And Moses fled from it.* An examination of the phrases in 7:10 and 7:15 will reveal that in the presence of the magicians and wise men, Aaron transformed his rod לְתַנִּין, *into a serpent*, whereas when Moses was sent to warn Pharaoh regarding the first plague, the rod is referred to as that which turned into a נָחָשׁ, *a snake*! To resolve this incongruity the *Sforno* explains that in this episode the snake was real — hence Moses *fled;* whereas in the case of the sorcerers it was an illusion (and even if Aaron did create a נָחָשׁ the sorcerers felt it was only a תַּנִּין, and hence were unafraid) which also explains the lack of fear and fleeing there!

The quotation from *Sanhedrin* cited by the *Sforno* is to be understood thus: It is easier to 'create' something large through sorcery than something very small, like a gnat. The Talmud therefore uses a camel as an example of the impotence of sorcerers, who can create illusions but never reality.

8. וְהֶאֱמִינוּ לְקֹל הָאֹת הָאַחֲרוֹן — *And they will believe the voice of the latter sign.* To heal is more impressive than turning a rod into a serpent. Therefore the impact and impression of the second sign will convince those who were unmoved by the first. This is an appropriate appreciation of healing powers by *Sforno*, who was a physician.

9. וְלָקַחְתָּ מִמֵּימֵי הַיְאֹר — *You shall take of the water of the river.* Water, from the river, is a basic element of nature, while blood is composed of more than one part. To transform the former into the latter without any act or process is so unimaginable that it will certainly impress everyone, including those who were skeptical of the first two signs.

אִ֣ישׁ דְּבָרִ֜ים אָנֹ֗כִי גַּ֤ם מִתְּמוֹל֙ גַּ֣ם מִשִּׁלְשֹׁ֔ם גַּ֛ם מֵאָ֥ז דַּבֶּרְךָ֖ אֶל־עַבְדֶּ֑ךָ כִּ֧י
יא כְבַד־פֶּ֛ה וּכְבַ֥ד לָשׁ֖וֹן אָנֹֽכִי׃ וַיֹּ֨אמֶר יהוה אֵלָ֗יו מִ֣י שָׂ֣ם פֶּה֮ לָֽאָדָם֒ א֚וֹ
יב מִֽי־יָשׂ֣וּם אִלֵּ֔ם א֣וֹ חֵרֵ֔שׁ א֥וֹ פִקֵּ֖חַ א֣וֹ עִוֵּ֑ר הֲלֹ֥א אָנֹכִ֖י יהוה׃ וְעַתָּ֖ה לֵ֑ךְ וְאָנֹכִי֙
יג אֶֽהְיֶ֣ה עִם־פִּ֔יךָ וְהוֹרֵיתִ֖יךָ אֲשֶׁ֥ר תְּדַבֵּֽר׃ וַיֹּ֖אמֶר בִּ֣י אֲדֹנָ֑י שְֽׁלַֽח־נָ֖א בְּיַד־
יד תִּשְׁלָֽח׃ וַיִּֽחַר־אַ֨ף יהוה בְּמֹשֶׁ֗ה וַיֹּ֙אמֶר֙ הֲלֹ֨א אַהֲרֹ֤ן אָחִ֙יךָ֙ הַלֵּוִ֔י יָדַ֕עְתִּי כִּֽי־
טו דַבֵּ֥ר יְדַבֵּ֖ר ה֑וּא וְגַ֤ם הִנֵּה־הוּא֙ יֹצֵ֣א לִקְרָאתֶ֔ךָ וְרָאֲךָ֖ וְשָׂמַ֥ח בְּלִבּֽוֹ׃ וְדִבַּרְתָּ֣

גַּם מִתְּמוֹל — *Neither yesterday* ... when I was a stranger in a strange land ...

גַּם מִשִּׁלְשֹׁם — *Nor heretofore* ... when I was in Pharaoh's palace.

גַּם מֵאָז דַּבֶּרְךָ אֶל עַבְדֶּךָ — *Nor since You have spoken to Your servant.* And even when my intellect and power of speech were exposed to the light of God, I did not attain the gift of learned speech.

כִּי כְבַד פֶּה וּכְבַד לָשׁוֹן אָנֹכִי — *For I am slow of speech and tongue.* This is so because my vessels of speech are unprepared, therefore I am incapable of learning how לָדַעַת לָעוּת אֶת יָעֵף דָּבָר, *to sustain with words him that is weary (Isaiah* 50:4).

11. מִי שָׂם פֶּה לָאָדָם — *Who has made man's mouth?* Who has given the natural preparation in the nature of man?

12. וְאָנֹכִי אֶהְיֶה עִם פִּיךָ — *I will be with your mouth* ... to prepare the vessels of speech.

וְהוֹרֵיתִיךָ — *And teach you* ... a skilled לְשׁוֹן לִמּוּדִים, *learned tongue (Isaiah* 50:4).

13. שְׁלַח נָא בְּיַד תִּשְׁלָח — *Send please by the hand of an agent* ... through one who is (better) prepared to accomplish Your mission, and not a man such as I who will need Your (constant) support and guidance so that (in reality) You will be the one Who speaks.

14. הֲלֹא אַהֲרֹן אָחִיךָ הַלֵּוִי — *Is there not Aaron your brother, the Levite?* If the purpose was to send a man prepared to speak, then your brother Aaron, who is a Levite and without a doubt a wise person as are all his Levite brothers (would have been chosen).

יָדַעְתִּי כִּי דַבֵּר יְדַבֵּר הוּא — *I know that he can speak well* ... that he is, unassisted, an eloquent and skilled speaker.

וְגַם הִנֵּה הוּא יֹצֵא לִקְרָאתֶךָ — *And behold he comes to greet you.* Though he comes to greet you and honor you because of your superior position (status) nonetheless he will doubtless rejoice and be your spokesman with a full heart.

NOTES

10. כִּי כְבַד פֶּה וּכְבַד לָשׁוֹן אָנֹכִי — *For I am slow of speech and tongue.* Though God grants blessing one must have the capacity to receive. Moses claimed that he had no vessel of an articulate tongue with which to receive God's blessing. God's answer to him was that the power to receive would also be granted to him (v. 11).

13-14. שְׁלַח נָא בְּיַד תִּשְׁלָח ... הֲלֹא אַהֲרֹן אָחִיךָ הַלֵּוִי יָדַעְתִּי כִּי דַבֵּר יְדַבֵּר הוּא וְגַם הִנֵּה הוּא יֹצֵא לִקְרָאתֶךָ — *Send please by the hand of an agent ... Is there not Aaron your brother, the Levite? I know that he can speak well. And behold he comes to greet you.* Moses' error lay in his assumption that the messenger had to have the skill and ability to fulfill this mission on his own, once direction and guidance had been given. The Almighty told him otherwise. That Aaron was capable and available was known to Him as well. If in spite of this Moses was called, it was precisely because God chose to

אֵלָיו וְשַׂמְתָּ אֶת־הַדְּבָרִים בְּפִיו וְאָנֹכִי אֶהְיֶה עִם־פִּיךָ וְעִם־פִּיהוּ וְהוֹרֵיתִי
טז אֶתְכֶם אֵת אֲשֶׁר תַּעֲשׂוּן׃ וְדִבֶּר־הוּא לְךָ אֶל־הָעָם וְהָיָה הוּא יִהְיֶה־לְּךָ
לְפֶה וְאַתָּה תִּהְיֶה־לּוֹ לֵאלֹהִים׃ וְאֶת־הַמַּטֶּה הַזֶּה תִּקַּח בְּיָדֶךָ אֲשֶׁר
יז תַּעֲשֶׂה־בּוֹ אֶת־הָאֹתֹת׃
ששי יח וַיֵּלֶךְ מֹשֶׁה וַיָּשָׁב ׀ אֶל־יֶתֶר חֹתְנוֹ וַיֹּאמֶר לוֹ אֵלְכָה נָּא וְאָשׁוּבָה אֶל־אַחַי
אֲשֶׁר־בְּמִצְרַיִם וְאֶרְאֶה הַעוֹדָם חַיִּים וַיֹּאמֶר יִתְרוֹ לְמֹשֶׁה לֵךְ לְשָׁלוֹם׃
יט וַיֹּאמֶר יהוה אֶל־מֹשֶׁה בְּמִדְיָן לֵךְ שֻׁב מִצְרָיִם כִּי־מֵתוּ כָּל־הָאֲנָשִׁים
כ הַמְבַקְשִׁים אֶת־נַפְשֶׁךָ׃ וַיִּקַּח מֹשֶׁה אֶת־אִשְׁתּוֹ וְאֶת־בָּנָיו וַיַּרְכִּבֵם עַל־
כא הַחֲמֹר וַיָּשָׁב אַרְצָה מִצְרָיִם וַיִּקַּח מֹשֶׁה אֶת־מַטֵּה הָאֱלֹהִים בְּיָדוֹ׃ וַיֹּאמֶר
יהוה אֶל־מֹשֶׁה בְּלֶכְתְּךָ לָשׁוּב מִצְרַיְמָה רְאֵה כָּל־הַמֹּפְתִים אֲשֶׁר־שַׂמְתִּי

---

15. וְשַׂמְתָּ אֶת הַדְּבָרִים בְּפִיו וְאָנֹכִי אֶהְיֶה עִם פִּיךָ וְעִם פִּיהוּ — *And put the words in his mouth and I will be with your mouth and with his mouth.* Even though you will place the words in his mouth, that will not be sufficient. I must be with you so that your words will enter Pharaoh's heart so that he do you no harm nor drive you forth from his presence.

16. לֵאלֹהִים — *In God's stead.* To perform wonders at your behest.

17. וְאֶת הַמַּטֶּה הַזֶּה — *And this rod.* Although it is not taken from a significant tree I have hallowed it for you as a sign.

תִּקַּח בְּיָדֶךָ — *Take in your hand.* As the scepter of a ruler, for I have apppointed you to change the course of nature at your behest.

אֲשֶׁר תַּעֲשֶׂה בּוֹ אֶת הָאֹתֹת — *Wherewith you shall do the signs.* You will command the natural forces, in accordance with My behest, for this is your assignment and appointment.

18. אֵלְכָה נָּא וְאָשׁוּבָה — *Let me go and return.* In the interim my wife and sons will remain with you.

לֵךְ לְשָׁלוֹם — *Go in peace.* For I will do so.

19. כִּי מֵתוּ כָּל הָאֲנָשִׁים — *For all the men are dead.* The king and his servants who sought to kill you, as explained above when it says, וַיָּמָת מֶלֶךְ מִצְרַיִם, *And the king of Egypt died* (2:23).

20. וַיַּרְכִּבֵם עַל הַחֲמֹר — *And he seated them upon an ass . . .* to bring them from the wilderness to his father-in-law's home in Midian.

וַיָּשָׁב אַרְצָה מִצְרָיִם — *And he returned to Egypt . . .* he alone, after he had sent them away.

21. בְּלֶכְתְּךָ לָשׁוּב מִצְרַיְמָה — *When you go to return to Egypt.* Whenever I will send you from your tent to Egypt, for his tent was pitched outside the city, as we read,

NOTES

use him as His instrument, and was not concerned with one's natural talents of speech. However, Moses's reluctance was so real that Aaron had to be co-opted to the leadership that was originally meant for Moses alone.

20. וַיָּשָׁב אַרְצָה מִצְרָיִם — *And he returned to Egypt.* As the *Sforno* points out in this verse — as does *Rashi* — the Torah does not always present events in chronological order (אֵין מוּקְדָּם וּמְאוּחָר בַּתּוֹרָה).

בְּיָדֶךָ וַעֲשִׂיתָם לִפְנֵי פַרְעֹה וַאֲנִי אֲחַזֵּק אֶת־לִבּוֹ וְלֹא יְשַׁלַּח אֶת־הָעָם:
כב־כג וְאָמַרְתָּ אֶל־פַּרְעֹה כֹּה אָמַר יהוה בְּנִי בְכֹרִי יִשְׂרָאֵל: וָאֹמַר אֵלֶיךָ שַׁלַּח
כד אֶת־בְּנִי וְיַעַבְדֵנִי וַתְּמָאֵן לְשַׁלְּחוֹ הִנֵּה אָנֹכִי הֹרֵג אֶת־בִּנְךָ בְּכֹרֶךָ: וַיְהִי

כְּצֵאתִי אֶת הָעִיר אֶפְרֹשׂ כַּפַּי, *When I go forth from the city, I will lift up my hands* (9:29), and I will command you to return to Egypt to speak to Pharaoh.

רְאֵה כָּל הַמֹּפְתִים אֲשֶׁר שַׂמְתִּי בְיָדֶךָ — *See all the wonders.* Examine each time all the wonders that will be placed in your hands, to perform them in the manner and order which I shall command you.

וַעֲשִׂיתָם לִפְנֵי פַרְעֹה — *And do them before Pharaoh.* You will succeed to do them before Pharaoh providing you change nothing, for if one sins regarding the commandments of his Creator by adding or subtracting, he impairs the intent and it will fail, as was the case with the *waters of strife* (*Numbers* 20), and so we are instructed regarding fulfillment of the *mitzvos*, לֹא תוֹסִפוּ וְלֹא תִגְרְעוּ, *You shall not add nor subtract* (*Deut.* 4:2).

וַאֲנִי אֲחַזֵּק אֶת לִבּוֹ — *And I will harden his heart.* The inability of Pharaoh to withstand the plagues would have doubtless caused him to send forth the people, (but) not because of his submission to God, the Blessed One, and (a desire) to do His will. Therefore God hardens his heart so as to strengthen him to be able to accept the plagues and not send them forth.

22. בְּנִי בְכֹרִי יִשְׂרָאֵל — *Israel, My firstborn son.* Even though at the end of days אֶהְפֹּךְ אֶל עַמִּים שָׂפָה בְרוּרָה, לִקְרֹא כֻלָּם בְּשֵׁם ה׳ וּלְעָבְדוֹ שְׁכֶם אֶחָד, *I (God) will turn to the peoples a pure language that they may all call unto the Name of* HASHEM *to serve Him with one consent* (*Zephaniah* 3:9), nonetheless Israel will be honored above them all for he is My son, who serves (Me) as a son motivated by love, not as a slave who labors (motivated) by the love of money or the fear of punishment. He is My firstborn because he was the first to serve Me when all other people strayed from Me, as it says, כִּי כָּל הָעַמִּים יֵלְכוּ אִישׁ בְּשֵׁם אֱלֹהָיו, וַאֲנַחְנוּ נֵלֵךְ בְּשֵׁם ה׳ אֱלֹהֵינוּ לְעוֹלָם וָעֶד, *Let all the nations walk each one in the name of his god, but we will walk in the name of* HASHEM, *our God, forever* (*Micah* 4:5).

23. הִנֵּה אָנֹכִי הֹרֵג אֶת בִּנְךָ בְּכֹרֶךָ — *Behold I will slay your son, your firstborn.* In keeping with the Divine judgment of 'measure for measure,' as it says, וּכְאֹרַח אִישׁ יַמְצִאֶנּוּ, *And cause every man to find according to his ways* (*Job* 34:11). Indeed only

NOTES

21. בְּלֶכְתְּךָ לָשׁוּב ... רְאֵה כָּל הַמֹּפְתִים — *When you go to return ... see all the wonders.* The phrases *to return* and *all the wonders* are the key to the *Sforno's* interpretation of this sentence. God is not referring to his present return to Egypt, but to those periods of return during his future sojourn *outside* the city. The expression *see 'all' the wonders* is explained as a word of caution to Moses to follow carefully the exact order of the mission entrusted to him.

וַאֲנִי אֲחַזֵּק אֶת לִבּוֹ — *And I will harden his heart.* Were Pharaoh to have submitted to God's will because he could not withstand the pressure of the plagues, it would have defeated God's purpose in visiting these plagues upon Egypt. The purpose was to bring Pharaoh to a recognition of God's might and kingship of the world, thereby causing him to submit willingly to God's rulership, not under duress. It is for this reason that God hardens his heart.

22. בְּנִי בְכֹרִי יִשְׂרָאֵל — *Israel, My firstborn son.* All people are considered the children of God. Israel, however, is worthy to be called His

כה בַדֶּרֶךְ בַּמָּלוֹן וַיִּפְגְּשֵׁהוּ יהוה וַיְבַקֵּשׁ הֲמִיתוֹ: וַתִּקַּח צִפֹּרָה צֹר וַתִּכְרֹת
כו אֶת־עָרְלַת בְּנָהּ וַתַּגַּע לְרַגְלָיו וַתֹּאמֶר כִּי חֲתַן־דָּמִים אַתָּה לִי: וַיִּרֶף מִמֶּנּוּ

the plague of the firstborn, of all the plagues, was visited upon Pharaoh as a punishment. The other plagues were meant to serve as signs and wonders for the purpose of bringing them to repentance, for (God) does not desire the death of any man. He did not close the door to true repentance, at all. Had they but had the wisdom to return to God, the Blessed One, from (a source) of love for His goodness or reverence for His greatness (they would have been spared), as our Sages state, 'Transgressions are considered as merits' (*Yoma* 86b), or at the very least if they would have repented as servants, motivated by a fear of punishment. However, the plague of the firstborn and the drowning of Pharaoh and his army in the sea were Divine judgments — measure for measure.

24. וַיְהִי בַדֶּרֶךְ בַּמָּלוֹן — *And it came to pass on the way, at the lodging place.* On his way from the wilderness to Midian with his wife and sons. This episode took place after the completion of God's instructions to him regarding his mission.

וַיִּפְגְּשֵׁהוּ ה׳ — *And HASHEM met him.* This happened because it was the day of his son's circumcision, at which time the Divine Presence *(Shechinah)* comes to be present at the *bris*, as we find, נִמֹּלוּ אִתּוֹ . . . וַיֵּרָא אֵלָיו ה׳, *They were circumcised with him . . . And God appeared to him (Genesis* 17:27-18:1). Perhaps this is the reason for the custom to prepare a chair of honor at a *bris*.

וַיְבַקֵּשׁ הֲמִיתוֹ — *And he sought to slay him.* The angel of the covenant, who sanctifies the infant being circumcised to serve God. He wanted to kill Moses for his laxity (in performing this *mitzvah).*

25. וַתֹּאמֶר כִּי חֲתַן דָּמִים אַתָּה לִי — *And she said, 'A bridegroom of blood are you to me.'* I did this because when you wed me and became my bridegroom, you made a condition that we would circumcise our children and draw forth the blood of the covenant. All this she said in defense of Moses, to (the angel) who wanted to slay him.

26. וַיִּרֶף מִמֶּנּוּ — *He let him alone . . .* but did not release him completely.

NOTES

firstborn for two reasons: (a) they serve God from a motivation of love, not for any reward nor out of fear of punishment; and (b) when none recognized God, they did, and when all others forsook Him, Israel remained steadfast in their loyalty.

23. הִנֵּה אָנֹכִי הֹרֵג אֶת בִּנְךָ בְּכֹרֶךָ — *Behold I will slay your son, your firstborn.* The Egyptians decreed that all Jewish males be cast into the river. They were also responsible for the suffering and death of countless Jews, the firstborn of God. The retribution of drowning in the Red Sea and the plague of the firstborn are direct punishments, *measure for measure,* unlike the earlier plagues that were visited upon the Egyptians to awaken their reverence, in the hope that they might repent.

24. וַיִּפְגְּשֵׁהוּ ה׳ וַיְבַקֵּשׁ הֲמִיתוֹ — *And HASHEM met him, and he sought to slay him. — And he sought to slay him (Moses)* refers not to God Who came to the circumcision, but to the angel of the covenant who sought to slay Moses for his laxity in delaying the performance of the *mitzvah*. Regarding God's presence at a circumcision, see the *Sforno* to *Genesis* 18:1 and the notes.

25. וַתֹּאמֶר כִּי חֲתַן דָּמִים אַתָּה לִי — *And she said, 'A bridegroom of blood are you to me.'* Zipporah is defending Moses before the avenging angel. She explains that her groom (Moses) had insisted upon her agreement to circumcise their children. This was important since she was the daughter of Jethro, the Midianite priest, and the concept of drawing

אָז אָמְרָה חֲתַן דָּמִים לַמּוּלֹת:
כז וַיֹּאמֶר יהוה אֶל־אַהֲרֹן לֵךְ לִקְרַאת מֹשֶׁה הַמִּדְבָּרָה וַיֵּלֶךְ וַיִּפְגְּשֵׁהוּ בְּהַר
כח הָאֱלֹהִים וַיִּשַּׁק־לוֹ: וַיַּגֵּד מֹשֶׁה לְאַהֲרֹן אֵת כָּל־דִּבְרֵי יהוה אֲשֶׁר שְׁלָחוֹ
כט וְאֵת כָּל־הָאֹתֹת אֲשֶׁר צִוָּהוּ: וַיֵּלֶךְ מֹשֶׁה וְאַהֲרֹן וַיַּאַסְפוּ אֶת־כָּל־זִקְנֵי בְּנֵי
ל יִשְׂרָאֵל: וַיְדַבֵּר אַהֲרֹן אֵת כָּל־הַדְּבָרִים אֲשֶׁר־דִּבֶּר יהוה אֶל־מֹשֶׁה וַיַּעַשׂ
לא הָאֹתֹת לְעֵינֵי הָעָם: וַיַּאֲמֵן הָעָם וַיִּשְׁמְעוּ כִּי־פָקַד יהוה אֶת־בְּנֵי יִשְׂרָאֵל וְכִי
ה שביעי א רָאָה אֶת־עָנְיָם וַיִּקְּדוּ וַיִּשְׁתַּחֲווּ: וְאַחַר בָּאוּ מֹשֶׁה וְאַהֲרֹן וַיֹּאמְרוּ אֶל־פַּרְעֹה
ב כֹּה־אָמַר יהוה אֱלֹהֵי יִשְׂרָאֵל שַׁלַּח אֶת־עַמִּי וְיָחֹגּוּ לִי בַּמִּדְבָּר: וַיֹּאמֶר
פַּרְעֹה מִי יהוה אֲשֶׁר אֶשְׁמַע בְּקֹלוֹ לְשַׁלַּח אֶת־יִשְׂרָאֵל לֹא יָדַעְתִּי אֶת־

אָז אָמְרָה חֲתַן דָּמִים לַמּוּלֹת — *Then she said, 'A bridegroom of blood' regarding the circumcision.* When you were my groom you said that we would draw the blood of the circumcision twice, i.e., the cutting of the foreskin and the exposing (of the glans).

27. לֵךְ לִקְרַאת מֹשֶׁה הַמִּדְבָּרָה — *Go into the wilderness to meet Moses . . .* as a disciple goes forth to greet his teacher, as it says, וְאַתָּה תִּהְיֶה לּוֹ לֵאלֹהִים, *And you shall be to him in God's stead* (4:16).

וַיִּפְגְּשֵׁהוּ בְּהַר הָאֱלֹהִים — *And he met him at the mountain of God . . .* when he returned from Midian to go to Egypt.

וַיִּשַּׁק לוֹ — *And he kissed him . . .* as one kisses a holy object, similar to, וַיִּשָּׁקֵהוּ, וַיֹּאמֶר הֲלוֹא כִּי מְשָׁחֲךָ ה׳ עַל נַחֲלָתוֹ לְנָגִיד, *And he (Samuel) kissed him (Saul) and said, 'Behold HASHEM has anointed you to be a prince over His inheritance'* (I Samuel 10:1).

V

2. לֹא יָדַעְתִּי אֶת ה׳ — *I know not HASHEM.* I do not know any Being that can bring another into being יֵשׁ מֵאַיִן, *ex nihilo* (from naught)..

NOTES

forth blood as a sign of the covenant was totally strange to her. The fact that Moses made this condition with her indicates that he was committed to this *mitzvah.* Therefore the *angel of the covenant* should spare Moses for his laxity in circumcising Eliezer, being that it was not due to a rejection of the covenant.

26. וַיִּרֶף מִמֶּנּוּ — *He let him alone.* The root רפה means to *weaken* one's hold, but not to release completely. The reason was because cutting the foreskin is not sufficient to fulfill the *mitzvah* until the glans is totally exposed (פְּרִיעָה). The angel, therefore, is not completely satisfied with Zipporah's cutting the foreskin (verse 25) until she reminded Moses to shed the blood doubly (לַמּוּלֹת), i.e., cutting (חֲתִיכָה) and exposing (פְּרִיעָה), for thus had he told her when they were first married. This basic law is established in the Talmud (*Sabbath* 137b): מָל וְלֹא פָרַע . . . כְּאִלּוּ לֹא מָל, *If one circumcises but does not expose (the glans), it is as though he did not circumcise.*

חֲתַן דָּמִים לַמּוּלֹת — *'A bridegroom of blood' regarding the circumcision.* This interpretation explains the plural מוּלֹת, *circumcisions.*

27. לֵךְ לִקְרַאת מֹשֶׁה הַמִּדְבָּרָה . . . וַיִּשַּׁק לוֹ — *Go into the wilderness to meet Moses . . . And he kissed him.* Aaron was older than Moses, still God told him to go and greet his younger brother. The *Sforno* explains that this was because Aaron's relationship to Moses was that of a disciple to a teacher, who must pay him respect. Consequently the kiss bestowed by Aaron upon Moses was not only one of a brother to a brother, but was also meant as a

ג יְהוָה וְגַם אֶת־יִשְׂרָאֵל לֹא אֲשַׁלֵּחַ: וַיֹּאמְרוּ אֱלֹהֵי הָעִבְרִים נִקְרָא עָלֵינוּ
נֵלְכָה־נָּא דֶּרֶךְ שְׁלֹשֶׁת יָמִים בַּמִּדְבָּר וְנִזְבְּחָה לַיהוָה אֱלֹהֵינוּ פֶּן־יִפְגָּעֵנוּ
ד בַּדֶּבֶר אוֹ בֶחָרֶב: וַיֹּאמֶר אֲלֵהֶם מֶלֶךְ מִצְרַיִם לָמָּה מֹשֶׁה וְאַהֲרֹן תַּפְרִיעוּ
ה אֶת־הָעָם מִמַּעֲשָׂיו לְכוּ לְסִבְלֹתֵיכֶם: וַיֹּאמֶר פַּרְעֹה הֵן־רַבִּים עַתָּה עַם
ו הָאָרֶץ וְהִשְׁבַּתֶּם אֹתָם מִסִּבְלֹתָם: וַיְצַו פַּרְעֹה בַּיּוֹם הַהוּא אֶת־הַנֹּגְשִׂים
ז בָּעָם וְאֶת־שֹׁטְרָיו לֵאמֹר: לֹא תֹאסִפוּן לָתֵת תֶּבֶן לָעָם לִלְבֹּן הַלְּבֵנִים
ח כִּתְמוֹל שִׁלְשֹׁם הֵם יֵלְכוּ וְקֹשְׁשׁוּ לָהֶם תֶּבֶן: וְאֶת־מַתְכֹּנֶת הַלְּבֵנִים אֲשֶׁר
הֵם עֹשִׂים תְּמוֹל שִׁלְשֹׁם תָּשִׂימוּ עֲלֵיהֶם לֹא תִגְרְעוּ מִמֶּנּוּ כִּי־נִרְפִּים הֵם
ט עַל־כֵּן הֵם צֹעֲקִים לֵאמֹר נֵלְכָה נִזְבְּחָה לֵאלֹהֵינוּ: תִּכְבַּד הָעֲבֹדָה עַל־
י הָאֲנָשִׁים וְיַעֲשׂוּ־בָהּ וְאַל־יִשְׁעוּ בְּדִבְרֵי־שָׁקֶר: וַיֵּצְאוּ נֹגְשֵׂי הָעָם וְשֹׁטְרָיו
יא וַיֹּאמְרוּ אֶל־הָעָם לֵאמֹר כֹּה אָמַר פַּרְעֹה אֵינֶנִּי נֹתֵן לָכֶם תֶּבֶן: אַתֶּם לְכוּ
יב קְחוּ לָכֶם תֶּבֶן מֵאֲשֶׁר תִּמְצָאוּ כִּי אֵין נִגְרָע מֵעֲבֹדַתְכֶם דָּבָר: וַיָּפֶץ הָעָם
יג בְּכָל־אֶרֶץ מִצְרָיִם לְקֹשֵׁשׁ קַשׁ לַתֶּבֶן: וְהַנֹּגְשִׂים אָצִים לֵאמֹר כַּלּוּ מַעֲשֵׂיכֶם
יד דְּבַר־יוֹם בְּיוֹמוֹ כַּאֲשֶׁר בִּהְיוֹת הַתֶּבֶן: וַיֻּכּוּ שֹׁטְרֵי בְּנֵי יִשְׂרָאֵל אֲשֶׁר־שָׂמוּ
עֲלֵהֶם נֹגְשֵׂי פַרְעֹה לֵאמֹר מַדּוּעַ לֹא כִלִּיתֶם חָקְכֶם לִלְבֹּן כִּתְמוֹל שִׁלְשֹׁם
טו גַּם־תְּמוֹל גַּם־הַיּוֹם: וַיָּבֹאוּ שֹׁטְרֵי בְּנֵי יִשְׂרָאֵל וַיִּצְעֲקוּ אֶל־פַּרְעֹה לֵאמֹר
טז לָמָּה תַעֲשֶׂה כֹה לַעֲבָדֶיךָ: תֶּבֶן אֵין נִתָּן לַעֲבָדֶיךָ וּלְבֵנִים אֹמְרִים לָנוּ עֲשׂוּ
יז וְהִנֵּה עֲבָדֶיךָ מֻכִּים וְחָטָאת עַמֶּךָ: וַיֹּאמֶר נִרְפִּים אַתֶּם נִרְפִּים עַל־כֵּן אַתֶּם

וְגַם אֶת יִשְׂרָאֵל לֹא אֲשַׁלֵּחַ — *And moreover I will not let Israel go.* And even if this be so, that there is such a Being, I will not send forth Israel on this account.

3. אֱלֹהֵי הָעִבְרִים — *The God of the Hebrews.* In answer to your question, 'Who is He (God)?,' He is the God of the Hebrews, who are well known as those who adhere to the beliefs of Eber. And regarding your statement that you will not send them forth, it would be far better to listen to Him ...

פֶּן יִפְגָּעֵנוּ — *Lest he fall upon us* ... us and you (both will be affected).

5. הֵן רַבִּים עַתָּה עַם הָאָרֶץ — *Behold the people are now many.* For the intelligent ones will certainly not listen to you.

16. וְהִנֵּה עֲבָדֶיךָ מֻכִּים — *And behold your servants are beaten.* Behold, we the beaten ones, and the sinners who beat us, are all your people, therefore you should be concerned for both.

17. נִרְפִּים אַתֶּם נִרְפִּים — *You are idle.* You, the idle and lazy ones, are lax in your labors, therefore I have increased the work so as to stimulate you.

NOTES

gesture of respect, i.e., akin to kissing a sacred object.

V

2. לֹא יָדַעְתִּי אֶת ה׳ — *I know not* HASHEM. In 3:14 it was established that God's name is derived from the concept of being and creating. Moses and Aaron doubtless explained this to Pharaoh who exclaimed that he could not recognize the existence of such a power.

5. הֵן רַבִּים עַתָּה עַם הָאָרֶץ — *Behold the people are now many.* Pharaoh lamented that the intelligent ones were few, while the *people of the land*, a euphemism for the ignorant ones, were many, and they would unfortunately

יח אֹמְרִ֔ים נֵלְכָ֖ה נִזְבְּחָ֣ה לַֽיהוָֹה׃ וְעַתָּה֙ לְכ֣וּ עִבְד֔וּ וְתֶ֖בֶן לֹֽא־יִנָּתֵ֣ן לָכֶ֑ם וְתֹ֥כֶן
יט לְבֵנִ֖ים תִּתֵּֽנּוּ׃ וַיִּרְא֞וּ שֹֽׁטְרֵ֧י בְנֵֽי־יִשְׂרָאֵ֛ל אֹתָ֖ם בְּרָ֣ע לֵאמֹ֑ר לֹֽא־תִגְרְע֥וּ
כ מִלִּבְנֵיכֶ֖ם דְּבַר־י֥וֹם בְּיוֹמֽוֹ׃ וַיִּפְגְּעוּ֙ אֶת־מֹשֶׁ֣ה וְאֶֽת־אַהֲרֹ֔ן נִצָּבִ֖ים לִקְרָאתָ֑ם
כא בְּצֵאתָ֖ם מֵאֵ֣ת פַּרְעֹֽה׃ וַיֹּאמְר֣וּ אֲלֵהֶ֔ם יֵ֧רֶא יְהוָ֛ה עֲלֵיכֶ֖ם וְיִשְׁפֹּ֑ט אֲשֶׁ֧ר
הִבְאַשְׁתֶּ֣ם אֶת־רֵיחֵ֗נוּ בְּעֵינֵ֤י פַרְעֹה֙ וּבְעֵינֵ֣י עֲבָדָ֔יו לָֽתֶת־חֶ֥רֶב בְּיָדָ֖ם
כב לְהָרְגֵֽנוּ׃ וַיָּ֧שָׁב מֹשֶׁ֛ה אֶל־יְהוָ֖ה וַיֹּאמַ֑ר אֲדֹנָ֗י לָמָ֤ה הֲרֵעֹ֙תָה֙ לָעָ֣ם הַזֶּ֔ה לָ֥מָּה
כג זֶּ֖ה שְׁלַחְתָּֽנִי׃ וּמֵאָ֞ז בָּ֤אתִי אֶל־פַּרְעֹה֙ לְדַבֵּ֣ר בִּשְׁמֶ֔ךָ הֵרַ֖ע לָעָ֣ם הַזֶּ֑ה וְהַצֵּ֥ל
א לֹֽא־הִצַּ֖לְתָּ אֶת־עַמֶּֽךָ׃ וַיֹּ֤אמֶר יְהוָה֙ אֶל־מֹשֶׁ֔ה עַתָּ֣ה תִרְאֶ֔ה אֲשֶׁ֥ר אֶֽעֱשֶׂ֖ה
לְפַרְעֹ֑ה כִּ֣י בְיָ֤ד חֲזָקָה֙ יְשַׁלְּחֵ֔ם וּבְיָ֣ד חֲזָקָ֔ה יְגָרְשֵׁ֖ם מֵֽאַרְצֽוֹ׃

מפטיר

ו

עַל כֵּן אַתֶּם אֹמְרִים נֵלְכָה נִזְבְּחָה — *Therefore you say, 'Let us go and sacrifice.'* This proves that you are idle, else why insist upon going to sacrifice if not to avoid your labors?

22. לָמָה זֶּה שְׁלַחְתָּנִי — *Why have You sent me?* If they deserve to be punished, why has it been done through me?

23. וְהַצֵּל לֹא הִצַּלְתָּ — *Neither have You delivered . . .* the Jewish officers who are beaten.

VI

1. עַתָּה תִרְאֶה — *Now you shall see.* Now that you have seen the iniquity of Pharaoh, who is determined to keep Israel (under him) with his rod of anger, (so shall) you see . . .

כִּי בְיָד חֲזָקָה יְשַׁלְּחֵם — *By a strong hand shall he let them go.* He will strive with all his might to send them forth, pressured by the evil and sorrow (which will befall him).

וּבְיָד חֲזָקָה יְגָרְשֵׁם מֵאַרְצוֹ — *And by a strong hand he will drive them out of his land.* Whereas now Pharaoh has caused the Israelites to be dispersed throughout the land of Egypt (5:12), he will (later) strive to drive them out of his land so that not even one will remain.

NOTES

listen to Moses, thereby causing idleness and unrest.

22. לָמָה זֶּה שְׁלַחְתָּנִי — *Why have You sent me?* Our Sages teach us, 'Merits are brought through meritorious ones and punishment through guilty ones' (*Sanhedrin* 8a, *Sabbath* 32a). Therefore Moses lamented that he was chosen as the instrument of God to bring pain and suffering.

23. וְהַצֵּל לֹא הִצַּלְתָּ — *Neither have You delivered.* God had already told Moses that Pharaoh would not allow the Israelites to leave Egypt (3:19). Therefore Moses could not very well be upset that his demands for their liberation had been rejected by Pharaoh. What disturbed him was that as a result of his demands the Israelite officers were being beaten. For this reason he confronted God with the complaint that He had not delivered these righteous men from the hands of their oppressors.

פרשת וארא
Parashas Va'eira

ב־ג וַיְדַבֵּר אֱלֹהִים אֶל־מֹשֶׁה וַיֹּאמֶר אֵלָיו אֲנִי יהוה: וָאֵרָא אֶל־אַבְרָהָם אֶל־
ד יִצְחָק וְאֶל־יַעֲקֹב בְּאֵל שַׁדָּי וּשְׁמִי יהוה לֹא נוֹדַעְתִּי לָהֶם: וְגַם הֲקִמֹתִי אֶת־
בְּרִיתִי אִתָּם לָתֵת לָהֶם אֶת־אֶרֶץ כְּנָעַן אֵת אֶרֶץ מְגֻרֵיהֶם אֲשֶׁר־גָּרוּ בָהּ:

---

2. אֲנִי ה׳ — *I am HASHEM.* Not only the Creator, but He Who preserves existence, for existence has no substance or continuity except for that which emanates from Me, as it says, וְאַתָּה מְחַיֶּה אֶת כֻּלָּם, *And you preserve them all (Nehemiah* 9:6). From all this it follows that nothing can exist without His will.

3. וָאֵרָא — *And I appeared.* In a vision, which precedes (is lower than) prophecy, similar to, וַיֵּרָא אֵלָיו ה׳, *And HASHEM appeared to him (Genesis* 18:1).

בְּאֵל שַׁדָּי — *As God Almighty.* Which indicates Creator of all existence, as explained in *Lech Lecha* (*Genesis* 17:1) . . .

וּשְׁמִי ה׳ לֹא נוֹדַעְתִּי לָהֶם — *But My Name HASHEM I made not known to them.* The letter ב in the phrase בְּאֵל שַׁדָּי, *as God Almighty,* is to be incorporated in the word וּשְׁמִי, *and My Name.* (The phrase would then read,) וּבִשְׁמִי ה׳ לֹא נוֹדַעְתִּי לָהֶם, *But in My Name HASHEM I did not become known to them,* i.e., in that vision I did not make any changes in the laws of nature for them pertaining to any aspect which is unchanging. Therefore it is proper that I inform their descendants, since they did not receive (this information) from their fathers, so that I might establish them to Me as a people, and thus I will redeem them.

4. וְגַם הֲקִמֹתִי אֶת בְּרִיתִי — *And I have also established My covenant.* A second cause of their redemption is the covenant which I entered into with their fathers.

NOTES

2. אֲנִי ה׳ — *I am HASHEM.* The Almighty is called by a variety of names, each depicting an attribute of the Divine. When Moses asks Him to reveal His name (3:13), the cryptic answer given is, *'I am that I am'* (3:14). The *Sforno* there explains this four-letter Name (הֲוָיָ״ה) as reflecting God's love of that which *is* and *exists,* since He is the Creator. In this verse, the statement אֲנִי ה׳, *I am HASHEM,* is explained by the *Sforno* as referring to God not only as Creator but also as the force which ensures the ongoing existence of all He originally created. Without this power emanating from Him naught would continue to exist. This statement is an introduction to that which is expanded upon in the next verse.

3. וָאֵרָא — *And I appeared.* See notes on *Genesis* 18:1 for clarification of the various levels of prophecy.

בְּאֵל שַׁדָּי — *As God Almighty.* See commentary of the *Sforno* and the explanatory notes on *Genesis* 17:1 regarding the name אֵל שַׁדָּי, *God Almighty.*

The name שַׁדָּי, *Almighty,* is derived from the expression *it is sufficient,* denoting that God set limitations on His creation in nature. In accordance with His will boundaries were established. This attribute of God was known to the Patriarchs and they in turn transmitted this knowledge to their children. However, the readiness of God to transform nature and involve Himself in the destiny of nations was never revealed to them. This manifestation of God's 'finger in history,' to use Rabbi S. R. Hirsch's felicitous term, and the changing of nature's laws, is expressed in the four-letter name *HASHEM* (הֲוָיָ״ה). This attribute would now be demonstrated through the signs and wonders in Egypt, on behalf of the Children of Israel, and since this aspect of God was not known heretofore, God must now instruct Moses to teach it to Israel. It is through this manifestation of God as *HASHEM* that they will become His people and be delivered.

3-5. וּשְׁמִי ה׳ לֹא נוֹדַעְתִּי לָהֶם . . . וְגַם הֲקִמֹתִי אֶת בְּרִיתִי . . . וְגַם אֲנִי שָׁמַעְתִּי — *But My Name HASHEM I made not known to them . . . And I have also established My covenant . . . And I have, moreover, heard.* The *Sforno* interprets verses 3-5 as representing three reasons for God's redemption of Israel: (a) to reveal His

ה וְגַם ׀ אֲנִי שָׁמַעְתִּי אֶת־נַאֲקַת בְּנֵי יִשְׂרָאֵל אֲשֶׁר מִצְרַיִם מַעֲבִדִים אֹתָם
ו וָאֶזְכֹּר אֶת־בְּרִיתִי: לָכֵן אֱמֹר לִבְנֵי־יִשְׂרָאֵל אֲנִי יהוה וְהוֹצֵאתִי אֶתְכֶם
מִתַּחַת סִבְלֹת מִצְרַיִם וְהִצַּלְתִּי אֶתְכֶם מֵעֲבֹדָתָם וְגָאַלְתִּי אֶתְכֶם בִּזְרוֹעַ
ז נְטוּיָה וּבִשְׁפָטִים גְּדֹלִים: וְלָקַחְתִּי אֶתְכֶם לִי לְעָם וְהָיִיתִי לָכֶם לֵאלֹהִים
וִידַעְתֶּם כִּי אֲנִי יהוה אֱלֹהֵיכֶם הַמּוֹצִיא אֶתְכֶם מִתַּחַת סִבְלוֹת מִצְרָיִם:

---

5. וְגַם אֲנִי שָׁמַעְתִּי — *And I have, moreover, heard.* The third cause of their redemption is that I have heard their groaning and prayers in their distress.

וָאֶזְכֹּר אֶת בְּרִיתִי — *And I have remembered My covenant.* And because of (all) this, they are worthy that I remember My covenant for them, similar to: וַיַּרְא בַּצַּר לָהֶם בְּשָׁמְעוֹ אֶת רִנָּתָם, וַיִּזְכֹּר לָהֶם בְּרִיתוֹ, *He looked upon their distress, when He heard their cry; and He remembered for them His covenant (Psalms* 106:44-45).

6. לָכֵן אֱמֹר לִבְנֵי יִשְׂרָאֵל אֲנִי יהוה — *Therefore, say to the Children of Israel, 'I am* H*ASHEM*.' For the (aforementioned) three reasons, *say to the Children of Israel* that I, Who grant existence to all that exists, shall with this power bring them out by partially modifying nature.

וְהוֹצֵאתִי אֶתְכֶם מִתַּחַת סִבְלֹת מִצְרַיִם — *And I will bring you out from under the burdens of the Egyptians.* As soon as the plagues begin the bondage will subside.

וְהִצַּלְתִּי אֶתְכֶם — *And I will deliver you . . .* on the day you pass over the frontier at Raamses.

וְגָאַלְתִּי אֶתְכֶם — *And I will redeem you . . .* when the Egyptians drown in the sea, as (the Torah) testifies, וַיּוֹשַׁע ה' בַּיּוֹם הַהוּא, *And* H*ASHEM saved Israel that day* (14:30), for after the demise of their oppressors they were no longer (in the category of) runaway slaves.

7. וְלָקַחְתִּי אֶתְכֶם לִי לְעָם — *And I will take you to Me for a people.* When you (will) stand at Mount Sinai.

וִידַעְתֶּם — *And you shall know.* Consider and recognize that all this will come to pass, similar to, וִידַעְתֶּם הַיּוֹם, כִּי לֹא אֶת בְּנֵיכֶם, *For you shall know this day, that it is not with your children . . . (Deut.* 11:2).

כִּי אֲנִי ה' אֱלֹהֵיכֶם הַמּוֹצִיא — *That I am* H*ASHEM, your God, Who brought you out.* Since I am your God Who watches over you in a particular sense, and I am (the One) Who is involved in bringing you out, (then) without a doubt I will do all that I have said (promised).

NOTES

control of nature's forces and concern for the destiny of His people; (b) to fulfill the covenant made with the Patriarchs; and (c) to respond to the prayers and cries of the Children of Israel.

6-8. וְהוֹצֵאתִי אֶתְכֶם . . . וְהִצַּלְתִּי אֶתְכֶם . . . וְגָאַלְתִּי אֶתְכֶם . . . וְלָקַחְתִּי אֶתְכֶם . . . וְהֵבֵאתִי אֶתְכֶם — *And I will bring you out . . . and I will deliver you . . . and I will redeem you . . . and I will take you . . . and I will bring you . . .* Israel's deliverance and redemption shall come in separate phases. They will first find relief from their hard labor (וְהוֹצֵאתִי, *And I will bring you out*), then they will be delivered (וְהִצַּלְתִּי) when they cross the frontier of Egypt. The third phase is *redemption* (וְגָאַלְתִּי) when the Egyptians drown in the sea. At Mount Sinai, when the Torah will be given, Israel will be *taken as a people* (וְלָקַחְתִּי). The final step will be when God brings them

ח וְהֵבֵאתִ֤י אֶתְכֶם֙ אֶל־הָאָ֔רֶץ אֲשֶׁ֤ר נָשָׂ֙אתִי֙ אֶת־יָדִ֔י לָתֵ֣ת אֹתָ֔הּ לְאַבְרָהָ֥ם
ט לְיִצְחָ֖ק וּֽלְיַעֲקֹ֑ב וְנָתַתִּ֨י אֹתָ֥הּ לָכֶ֛ם מוֹרָשָׁ֖ה אֲנִ֥י יהוה׃ וַיְדַבֵּ֥ר מֹשֶׁ֛ה כֵּ֖ן אֶל־
בְּנֵ֣י יִשְׂרָאֵ֑ל וְלֹ֤א שָֽׁמְעוּ֙ אֶל־מֹשֶׁ֔ה מִקֹּ֣צֶר ר֔וּחַ וּמֵעֲבֹדָ֖ה קָשָֽׁה׃
י־יא וַיְדַבֵּ֥ר יהוה אֶל־מֹשֶׁ֥ה לֵּאמֹֽר׃ בֹּ֣א דַבֵּ֔ר אֶל־פַּרְעֹ֖ה מֶ֣לֶךְ מִצְרָ֑יִם וִֽישַׁלַּ֥ח
יב אֶת־בְּנֵֽי־יִשְׂרָאֵ֖ל מֵאַרְצֽוֹ׃ וַיְדַבֵּ֣ר מֹשֶׁ֔ה לִפְנֵ֥י יהוה לֵאמֹ֑ר הֵ֤ן בְּנֵֽי־יִשְׂרָאֵל֙
לֹא־שָׁמְע֣וּ אֵלַ֔י וְאֵיךְ֙ יִשְׁמָעֵ֣נִי פַרְעֹ֔ה וַאֲנִ֖י עֲרַ֥ל שְׂפָתָֽיִם׃
יג וַיְדַבֵּ֣ר יהוה֮ אֶל־מֹשֶׁ֣ה וְאֶֽל־אַהֲרֹן֒ וַיְצַוֵּם֙ אֶל־בְּנֵ֣י יִשְׂרָאֵ֔ל וְאֶל־פַּרְעֹ֖ה מֶ֣לֶךְ

---

8. וְהֵבֵאתִי אֶתְכֶם אֶל הָאָרֶץ — *And I will bring you into the Land.* When you will consider (examine closely) all this, you will (then) be worthy that I bring you to the Land and give it to you.

9. וְלֹא שָׁמְעוּ אֶל מֹשֶׁה — *But they did not listen to Moses.* To consider all this in a manner which would (have caused them) to trust the salvation of God, the Blessed One, which would have been counted to them for righteousness, as it was for Abraham *(Genesis* 15:6). Therefore, the promise of *and I will give it to 'you'* (v. 8) was not fulfilled, but (instead) was given to their children.

מִקֹּצֶר רוּחַ — *From impatience of spirit.* For their spirit prevented them from having faith in God, and they did not concentrate their mind (lit., 'heart') to understand (the words of Moses).

וּמֵעֲבֹדָה קָשָׁה — *And from hard labor.* Were it not for the hard labor they would have considered and attended to the words of Moses and understood from his arguments that they should trust God.

12. הֵן בְּנֵי יִשְׂרָאֵל לֹא שָׁמְעוּ אֵלַי — *Behold the children of Israel have not listened to me.* For he thought that (their refusal) was because they saw that from the time he came to speak to Pharaoh their condition had worsened and the messenger had not saved them. How much more so will Pharaoh, who does as he pleases and has even increased (the intensity of their labors), refuse to listen!

וַאֲנִי עֲרַל שְׂפָתָיִם — *And I am of 'uncircumcised' lips.* For he thought that Aaron was only to be his associate (spokesman) for the initial message when they spoke to the people (of Israel).

13. וַיְצַוֵּם — *And He charged them.* He appointed them as leaders, similar to, וַיִּסְמֹךְ אֶת יָדָיו עָלָיו וַיְצַוֵּהוּ, *he (Moses) laid his hands upon him (Joshua) and charged him (Numbers* 27:23), and וְצִוְּךָ לְנָגִיד, *has appointed you as a prince (I Samuel* 25:30), and other such examples.

NOTES

to the Land (וְהֵבֵאתִי). Only when they will appreciate and recognize God's role in their history and destiny will they be worthy to be brought to the Promised Land.

9. וְלֹא שָׁמְעוּ אֶל מֹשֶׁה — *But they did not listen to Moses.* Had Israel listened to Moses, this demonstration of faith would have been considered as a great merit and they would have been given the Land of Israel as promised in the previous verse. Since they failed to do so, they would not receive the Land; their children, however, would.

12. וַאֲנִי עֲרַל שְׂפָתָיִם — *And I am of 'uncircumcised' lips.* Moses, from the very start, protested that he could not speak clearly and God had therefore appointed Aaron as his spokesman (4:16). Seemingly this statement of Moses, *I am of uncircumcised lips,* is repeti-

שני יד מִצְרַיִם לְהוֹצִיא אֶת־בְּנֵי־יִשְׂרָאֵל מֵאֶרֶץ מִצְרָיִם: אֵלֶּה רָאשֵׁי
בֵית־אֲבֹתָם בְּנֵי רְאוּבֵן בְּכֹר יִשְׂרָאֵל חֲנוֹךְ וּפַלּוּא חֶצְרֹן וְכַרְמִי אֵלֶּה
טו מִשְׁפְּחֹת רְאוּבֵן: וּבְנֵי שִׁמְעוֹן יְמוּאֵל וְיָמִין וְאֹהַד וְיָכִין וְצֹחַר וְשָׁאוּל בֶּן־

אֶל בְּנֵי יִשְׂרָאֵל — *Over* (lit., *to*) *the Children of Israel.* Over the Children of Israel, similar to אֶל הֶהָרִים לֹא אָכָל, *And has not eaten upon the mountain* (*Ezekiel* 18:6).

וְאֶל פַּרְעֹה מֶלֶךְ מִצְרַיִם לְהוֹצִיא — *And over Pharaoh, king of Egypt, to bring out.* He appointed them as leaders over Pharaoh, the king of Egypt, regarding the bringing out of Israel from Egypt, in such a manner that Israel and also Pharaoh would perforce listen to Moses and Aaron who were appointed over them by God, the Blessed One.

14. אֵלֶּה רָאשֵׁי בֵית אֲבֹתָם — *These are the heads of their fathers' houses.* It was proper (justified) that these men be appointed leaders over Israel for they were the most distinguished (honored) of the entire nation. For (even though) . . .

רְאוּבֵן בְּכֹר יִשְׂרָאֵל — *Reuben was the firstborn of Israel.* Except for his own children, who were included among the (original) seventy souls and who were now dead, none of their offspring were worthy to be mentioned by name, as it is explained when the verse states, וַיָּמָת יוֹסֵף וְכָל אֶחָיו, *And Joseph and all his brothers died . . .* (1:6). And so it was regarding the children of Simeon. Levi, however, outlived them all and was able to rear his grandchildren (teaching them) to understand and (in turn) to teach (others), and so it was with Kehath and Amram, in such a manner that Moses, Aaron and Miriam came forth from them.

NOTES

tious. The *Sforno* therefore explains that Moses was under the impression that Aaron had only been appointed to speak to the Children of Israel, not to Pharaoh. In this fashion the following verse also becomes clearer.

13. אֶל בְּנֵי יִשְׂרָאֵל — *Over the children of Israel.* The word אֶל is to be understood not as *to* but *over* or *upon,* as we see in the verse from *Ezekiel* cited by the *Sforno.*

וְאֶל פַּרְעֹה מֶלֶךְ מִצְרַיִם לְהוֹצִיא — *And over Pharaoh, king of Egypt, to bring out.* God now appointed both Moses and Aaron as leaders over *both* Israel and Pharaoh, to the extent that regarding the deliverance of the Israelites, Pharaoh would be subservient to them. Hence, eventually he would listen to them, as would the Israelites.

14. אֵלֶּה רָאשֵׁי בֵית אֲבֹתָם — *These are the heads of their fathers' houses. Rashi* gives two reasons for inserting this genealogical table at this point, breaking the continuity of the narrative, which does not resume until verse 27. The flow of these verses is to be understood as follows: God appointed Moses and Aaron as leaders, though they are the descendants of Jacob's third son. Why were Reuben and Simeon denied leadership? The *Sforno* explains that although Reuben was the firstborn, only his four sons were worthy to be mentioned by name in the Torah, but none of the next generation. The same was true of Simeon. This indicates that the following generations were not on the same high level of importance and distinction as the previous generation. Levi's offspring however are mentioned by name through the fourth generation. The years of Levi, his son Kehath, and his grandson Amram are also recorded. The reason is to emphasize that the longevity of these men enabled them to educate and influence their grandsons, as well as their sons. The choice fruit of these spiritual plantings were Moses and Aaron. This is the significance of the expression in verse 26, הוּא אַהֲרֹן וּמֹשֶׁה, *These are that Aaron and Moses,* as well as verse 27, *These are they who spoke to Pharaoh . . . these are Moses and Aaron.* They are the end result of the many years of education and guidance contributed by Levi, Kehath and Amram, and they are worthy to be chosen as leaders and spokesmen.

טז הַכְּנַעֲנִית אֵלֶּה מִשְׁפְּחֹת שִׁמְעוֹן: וְאֵלֶּה שְׁמוֹת בְּנֵי־לֵוִי לְתֹלְדֹתָם גֵּרְשׁוֹן
יז וּקְהָת וּמְרָרִי וּשְׁנֵי חַיֵּי לֵוִי שֶׁבַע וּשְׁלֹשִׁים וּמְאַת שָׁנָה: בְּנֵי גֵרְשׁוֹן לִבְנִי
יח וְשִׁמְעִי לְמִשְׁפְּחֹתָם: וּבְנֵי קְהָת עַמְרָם וְיִצְהָר וְחֶבְרוֹן וְעֻזִּיאֵל וּשְׁנֵי חַיֵּי קְהָת
יט שָׁלֹשׁ וּשְׁלֹשִׁים וּמְאַת שָׁנָה: וּבְנֵי מְרָרִי מַחְלִי וּמוּשִׁי אֵלֶּה מִשְׁפְּחֹת הַלֵּוִי
כ לְתֹלְדֹתָם: וַיִּקַּח עַמְרָם אֶת־יוֹכֶבֶד דֹּדָתוֹ לוֹ לְאִשָּׁה וַתֵּלֶד לוֹ אֶת־אַהֲרֹן
כא וְאֶת־מֹשֶׁה וּשְׁנֵי חַיֵּי עַמְרָם שֶׁבַע וּשְׁלֹשִׁים וּמְאַת שָׁנָה: וּבְנֵי יִצְהָר קֹרַח
כב־כג וָנֶפֶג וָזִכְרִי: וּבְנֵי עֻזִּיאֵל מִישָׁאֵל וְאֶלְצָפָן וְסִתְרִי: וַיִּקַּח אַהֲרֹן אֶת־אֱלִישֶׁבַע
בַּת־עַמִּינָדָב אֲחוֹת נַחְשׁוֹן לוֹ לְאִשָּׁה וַתֵּלֶד לוֹ אֶת־נָדָב וְאֶת־אֲבִיהוּא
כד אֶת־אֶלְעָזָר וְאֶת־אִיתָמָר: וּבְנֵי קֹרַח אַסִּיר וְאֶלְקָנָה וַאֲבִיאָסָף אֵלֶּה
כה מִשְׁפְּחֹת הַקָּרְחִי: וְאֶלְעָזָר בֶּן־אַהֲרֹן לָקַח־לוֹ מִבְּנוֹת פּוּטִיאֵל לוֹ לְאִשָּׁה
כו וַתֵּלֶד לוֹ אֶת־פִּינְחָס אֵלֶּה רָאשֵׁי אֲבוֹת הַלְוִיִּם לְמִשְׁפְּחֹתָם: הוּא אַהֲרֹן
וּמֹשֶׁה אֲשֶׁר אָמַר יהוה לָהֶם הוֹצִיאוּ אֶת־בְּנֵי יִשְׂרָאֵל מֵאֶרֶץ מִצְרַיִם
כז עַל־צִבְאֹתָם: הֵם הַמְדַבְּרִים אֶל־פַּרְעֹה מֶלֶךְ־מִצְרַיִם לְהוֹצִיא אֶת־בְּנֵי־
כח יִשְׂרָאֵל מִמִּצְרָיִם הוּא מֹשֶׁה וְאַהֲרֹן: וַיְהִי בְּיוֹם דִּבֶּר יהוה אֶל־מֹשֶׁה בְּאֶרֶץ
שלישי כט מִצְרָיִם: וַיְדַבֵּר יהוה אֶל־מֹשֶׁה לֵּאמֹר אֲנִי יהוה דַּבֵּר

---

23. וַיִּקַּח אַהֲרֹן ... אֲחוֹת נַחְשׁוֹן — *And Aaron took ... the daughter of Nachshon.* Who was the most important man of his generation, (thereby) giving birth to leaders of the generation, who were later chosen as priests; Elazar in turn took ...

25. מִבְּנוֹת פּוּטִיאֵל — *Of the daughters of Putiel* ... who was also important in his generation, and gave birth to ...

פִּינְחָס — *Pinchas* ... who merited the *covenant of peace (Numbers* 25:12).

אֵלֶּה רָאשֵׁי אֲבוֹת הַלְוִיִּם — *These are the heads of the fathers' houses of the Levites.* (Therefore) in this manner the aforementioned Moses and Aaron were *the heads of the fathers' houses of the Levites.*

26. הוּא אַהֲרֹן וּמֹשֶׁה — *These are that Aaron and Moses.* These were the most honored of the houses of their fathers, (therefore) they are the men who properly are the most worthy that God say to them ...

הוֹצִיאוּ אֶת בְּנֵי יִשְׂרָאֵל — *Bring out the Children of Israel* ... for they are deserving to have their words listened to by the Children of Israel.

עַל צִבְאֹתָם — *According to their hosts* ... the entire community together with its component sections.

27. הֵם הַמְדַבְּרִים — *These are they who spoke.* They were worthy to speak to Pharaoh and to be hearkened to by him.

28. וַיְהִי בְּיוֹם דִּבֶּר ה׳ אֶל מֹשֶׁה — *And it came to pass on the day when* HASHEM *spoke to Moses.* When God spoke to Moses and told him to speak to Pharaoh (v. 11), and Moses responded that Pharaoh would not listen to him, (whereupon) He appointed him and Aaron as leaders over Israel and Pharaoh, as mentioned above (v. 13); (the Torah now) explains that the intent was not to equate them (i.e., Moses and Aaron), but that ...

ל אֶל־פַּרְעֹה מֶלֶךְ מִצְרָיִם אֵת כָּל־אֲשֶׁר אֲנִי דֹּבֵר אֵלֶיךָ: וַיֹּאמֶר מֹשֶׁה לִפְנֵי
יהוה הֵן אֲנִי עֲרַל שְׂפָתַיִם וְאֵיךְ יִשְׁמַע אֵלַי פַּרְעֹה:
ז א וַיֹּאמֶר יהוה אֶל־מֹשֶׁה רְאֵה נְתַתִּיךָ אֱלֹהִים לְפַרְעֹה וְאַהֲרֹן אָחִיךָ יִהְיֶה
ב נְבִיאֶךָ: אַתָּה תְדַבֵּר אֵת כָּל־אֲשֶׁר אֲצַוֶּךָּ וְאַהֲרֹן אָחִיךָ יְדַבֵּר אֶל־פַּרְעֹה
ג וְשִׁלַּח אֶת־בְּנֵי־יִשְׂרָאֵל מֵאַרְצוֹ: וַאֲנִי אַקְשֶׁה אֶת־לֵב פַּרְעֹה וְהִרְבֵּיתִי

VII

1. נְתַתִּיךָ אֱלֹהִים לְפַרְעֹה וְאַהֲרֹן אָחִיךָ יִהְיֶה נְבִיאֶךָ — *I have set you in God's stead to Pharaoh, and Aaron your brother shall be your prophet.* Moses will be as *Elohim* to Pharaoh, and Aaron will serve as an interpreter and expounder.

3. וַאֲנִי אַקְשֶׁה — *And I will harden.* Being that God desires the repentance of the wicked and not their death, as it says, חַי אָנִי, נְאֻם אֲדֹנָי אֱלֹהִים אִם אֶחְפֹּץ בְּמוֹת הָרָשָׁע, כִּי אִם בְּשׁוּב הָרָשָׁע מִדַּרְכּוֹ וְחָיָה, *As I live, says my Lord, HASHEM/ELOHIM, I do not desire the death of the wicked, but that the wicked turn from his way and live* (*Ezekiel* 33:11). Therefore, the signs and wonders will be increased for the purpose of bringing the Egyptians to repentance, by demonstrating to them His greatness and kindness, through the signs and wonders, as it says, *For this cause I have made you stand to show you My power* (9:16). (Another reason was) so Israel would see and (be brought to) reverence, as it says, *That I might show My signs in their midst . . . that you may tell . . .* (10:1,2).

Without a doubt, were it not for the hardening of Pharaoh's heart he would have sent forth Israel, not because of repentance or submission to God, the Blessed One, (nor because) he regretted his rebellion, recognizing God's greatness and goodness — but because he could no longer abide the anguish of the plagues, as his (own) servants said, *Do you not know that Egypt is lost?* (10:7). Now this would not have been repentance. However, if Pharaoh would have (truly) wished to submit to God, the Blessed One, and return to Him in full repentance, there would have been no (Divine) deterrent at all. Now, God states, *and I will harden Pharaoh's heart,* granting him the strength to withstand the plagues, hence he will not send forth Israel because he fears the plagues, *but that I might show My signs in their midst* (10:1), through which they will perceive My greatness and goodness and repent to a degree, in sincerity. (And also) לְמַעַן תְּסַפֵּר, *that you may tell* (10:2), i.e., *you* Israel who see their anguish, (may tell) בְּאָזְנֵי בִנְךָ, *in the ears of your son* (ibid.), to tell (everyone) that all these things does God work with man (based on *Job* 33:29) so as to bring (man) to repentance, which will occur if they examine their deeds when misfortune befalls them.

NOTES

VII

3. וַאֲנִי אַקְשֶׁה — *And I will harden.* The hardening of Pharaoh's heart is for the purpose of counteracting the pressure of the plagues. Normally, one would crumble under the onslaught of such constant plagues and agree to whatever he was asked to do. This, however, was not God's intent, for then the submission would not be sincere nor would the Egyptians truly repent. By giving them strength to resist (hardening their hearts) their freedom of will was unimpaired; hence if they repented their evil ways, it would be a voluntary act. This, the *Sforno* explains, was the intent of the multiplicity of plagues (compare to 4:21).

Another reason for the many plagues was to impress the Israelites with God's might and His love for them, thereby bringing them to a

ד אֶת־אֹתֹתַי וְאֶת־מוֹפְתַי בְּאֶרֶץ מִצְרָיִם: וְלֹא־יִשְׁמַע אֲלֵכֶם פַּרְעֹה וְנָתַתִּי
אֶת־יָדִי בְּמִצְרָיִם וְהוֹצֵאתִי אֶת־צִבְאֹתַי אֶת־עַמִּי בְנֵי־יִשְׂרָאֵל מֵאֶרֶץ
ה מִצְרַיִם בִּשְׁפָטִים גְּדֹלִים: וְיָדְעוּ מִצְרַיִם כִּי־אֲנִי יהוה בִּנְטֹתִי אֶת־יָדִי
ו עַל־מִצְרָיִם וְהוֹצֵאתִי אֶת־בְּנֵי־יִשְׂרָאֵל מִתּוֹכָם: וַיַּעַשׂ מֹשֶׁה וְאַהֲרֹן כַּאֲשֶׁר
ז צִוָּה יהוה אֹתָם כֵּן עָשׂוּ: וּמֹשֶׁה בֶּן־שְׁמֹנִים שָׁנָה וְאַהֲרֹן בֶּן־שָׁלֹשׁ וּשְׁמֹנִים
שָׁנָה בְּדַבְּרָם אֶל־פַּרְעֹה:
רביעי ח־ט וַיֹּאמֶר יהוה אֶל־מֹשֶׁה וְאֶל־אַהֲרֹן לֵאמֹר: כִּי יְדַבֵּר אֲלֵכֶם פַּרְעֹה לֵאמֹר
תְּנוּ לָכֶם מוֹפֵת וְאָמַרְתָּ אֶל־אַהֲרֹן קַח אֶת־מַטְּךָ וְהַשְׁלֵךְ לִפְנֵי־פַרְעֹה יְהִי

---

4. וְלֹא יִשְׁמַע אֲלֵכֶם פַּרְעֹה — *But Pharaoh will not listen to you.* Neither before nor after the hardening (of his heart) even though he will see (witness) the increasing number of (lit., 'many') signs and wonders, I will therefore bring judgments upon them, namely the plague of the firstborn and the drowning of Egypt in the Sea of Reeds. These two alone were in the category of punishment, measure for measure. The other plagues, however, were signs and wonders for the purpose of bringing them back (to God) through repentance, as it says: *In this you shall know that I am* HASHEM (v. 17); *To the end that you may know that I am* HASHEM *in the midst of the earth* (8:18); *That you may know that the earth is* HASHEM*'s* (9:29); *That I might show these My signs in the midst of them . . . that you may tell . . . that you may know* (10:1-2), you i.e., Israel and Egypt. Even when they were drowned the intent was to do it in such a way that the Egyptian survivors recognize and know Him, as it says, *and the Egyptians shall know that I am* HASHEM (v. 5).

6. וַיַּעַשׂ מֹשֶׁה וְאַהֲרֹן כַּאֲשֶׁר צִוָּה ה׳ אֹתָם — *And Moses and Aaron did as* HASHEM *commanded them.* Every directive (given to them) was observed in accordance with the commandment and its order, i.e., Moses first spoke as the messenger of God, the Blessed One, after which Aaron interpreted.

כֵּן עָשׂוּ — *So they did.* They neither added nor detracted.

7. וּמֹשֶׁה בֶּן שְׁמֹנִים שָׁנָה — *And Moses was eighty years old.* In spite of their advanced age they rose up with enthusiasm to (fulfill) the will of their Maker. Indeed, he who had reached the age of eighty, even in those days, had already passed the days of 'gray hair' (old age) and reached (those of) 'strength,' as (Moses) attests to in his prayer, saying, יְמֵי שְׁנוֹתֵינוּ בָהֶם שִׁבְעִים שָׁנָה, וְאִם בִּגְבוּרֹת שְׁמוֹנִים שָׁנָה, *The days of our years are seventy years, or even by reason of strength, eighty years* (*Psalms* 90:10).

9. תְּנוּ לָכֶם מוֹפֵת — *Show a wonder for them.* A מוֹפֵת, *wonder,* comes to demonstrate

NOTES

state of awareness and reverence of God which in turn would motivate them to relate these wonders and God's providence to future generations (see 10:1-2).

4. וְלֹא יִשְׁמַע אֲלֵכֶם פַּרְעֹה — *But Pharaoh will not listen to you.* As explained in 4:23, all the plagues were meant to serve as a spur to repentance, not as punishment, except for the tenth one and the drowning of the Egyptians in the sea. Even then, the survival of some Egyptians was for the purpose of recognizing the true God, which is the first step to repentance.

7. וּמֹשֶׁה בֶּן שְׁמֹנִים שָׁנָה — *And Moses was eighty years old.* The terms שֵׂיבָה, *old age,* and גְּבוּרָה, *strength,* are used in *Pirkei Avos* 5:20:

י לְתַנִּין: וַיָּבֹא מֹשֶׁה וְאַהֲרֹן֙ אֶל־פַּרְעֹ֔ה וַיַּעֲשׂוּ־כֵ֔ן כַּאֲשֶׁ֖ר צִוָּ֣ה יהו֑ה וַיַּשְׁלֵ֨ךְ

יא אַהֲרֹ֜ן אֶת־מַטֵּ֗הוּ לִפְנֵ֥י פַרְעֹ֛ה וְלִפְנֵ֥י עֲבָדָ֖יו וַיְהִ֥י לְתַנִּֽין: וַיִּקְרָא֙ גַּם־פַּרְעֹ֔ה

יב לַחֲכָמִ֖ים וְלַֽמְכַשְּׁפִ֑ים וַיַּעֲשׂ֨וּ גַם־הֵ֜ם חַרְטֻמֵּ֥י מִצְרַ֛יִם בְּלַהֲטֵיהֶ֖ם כֵּֽן: וַיַּשְׁלִ֙יכוּ֙

יג אִ֣ישׁ מַטֵּ֔הוּ וַיִּהְי֖וּ לְתַנִּינִ֑ם וַיִּבְלַ֥ע מַטֵּֽה־אַהֲרֹ֖ן אֶת־מַטֹּתָֽם: וַיֶּחֱזַק֙ לֵ֣ב פַּרְעֹ֔ה

יד וְלֹ֥א שָׁמַ֖ע אֲלֵהֶ֑ם כַּאֲשֶׁ֖ר דִּבֶּ֥ר יהוֹֽה: וַיֹּ֤אמֶר יהו֙ה אֶל־מֹשֶׁ֔ה

טו כָּבֵ֖ד לֵ֣ב פַּרְעֹ֑ה מֵאֵ֖ן לְשַׁלַּ֣ח הָעָֽם: לֵ֣ךְ אֶל־פַּרְעֹ֞ה בַּבֹּ֗קֶר הִנֵּה֙ יֹצֵ֣א הַמַּ֔יְמָה

וְנִצַּבְתָּ֥ לִקְרָאת֖וֹ עַל־שְׂפַ֣ת הַיְאֹ֑ר וְהַמַּטֶּ֛ה אֲשֶׁר־נֶהְפַּ֥ךְ לְנָחָ֖שׁ תִּקַּ֥ח בְּיָדֶֽךָ:

טז וְאָמַרְתָּ֣ אֵלָ֗יו יהו֞ה אֱלֹהֵ֤י הָעִבְרִים֙ שְׁלָחַ֣נִי אֵלֶ֣יךָ לֵאמֹ֔ר שַׁלַּח֙ אֶת־עַמִּ֔י

יז וְיַֽעַבְדֻ֖נִי בַּמִּדְבָּ֑ר וְהִנֵּ֥ה לֹא־שָׁמַ֖עְתָּ עַד־כֹּֽה: כֹּ֚ה אָמַ֣ר יהו֔ה בְּזֹ֣את תֵּדַ֔ע כִּ֖י

אֲנִ֣י יהו֑ה הִנֵּ֣ה אָנֹכִ֣י מַכֶּ֣ה ׀ בַּמַּטֶּ֣ה אֲשֶׁר־בְּיָדִ֗י עַל־הַמַּ֛יִם אֲשֶׁ֥ר בַּיְאֹ֖ר

---

the greatness of the sender, that it is proper to hearken to His voice. A אוֹת, *sign*, however, testifies to the authenticity of the messenger. That is why Moses performed 'signs' in the presence of Israel, who did not doubt the greatness and ability of the Sender but questioned whether the messenger was authentic. Pharaoh, however, had (serious) doubts regarding the Sender — and even denied (His existence), as he said, לֹא יָדַעְתִּי אֶת ה', *I know not HASHEM* (5:2). (That is why) he asks for a 'wonder,' to authenticate the greatness of the Sender, in a manner which will demonstrate that He is worthy to be listened to. It is not unprecedented for the same object to be used as a sign and a wonder for different people.

12. וַיִּהְיוּ לְתַנִּינִם — *And they became serpents.* With the appearance of serpents, but inert, without movement.

וַיִּבְלַע מַטֵּה אַהֲרֹן אֶת מַטֹּתָם — *And Aaron's rod swallowed up their rods.* To show that only God, the Blessed One, can grant living spirit (lit., 'soul and spirit') whereas the sorcerers had no power to grant movement to their serpents.

14. כָּבֵד לֵב פַּרְעֹה — *Pharaoh's heart is stubborn.* Even though he has seen the difference between Your wonder and the deed of his sorcerers.

15. נֶהְפַּךְ לְנָחָשׁ — *Which turned to a snake.* In its movements (and actions) as well, as it says, וַיִּבְלַע, *and it swallowed* (v. 12); and above also, *And Moses fled from it* (4:3).

17. בְּזֹאת תֵּדַע כִּי אֲנִי ה' — *In this you shall know that I am HASHEM.* For I shall change the nature of a permanent (unchanging) thing in its totality, namely the river.

NOTES

Seventy to old age and eighty to strength.

9. תְּנוּ לָכֶם מוֹפֵת — *Show a wonder for them.* When the *Sforno* states, 'for the same object to be used as a sign and a wonder,' he is referring to the rod which was used as a 'sign' for Israel (4:30) and a 'wonder' for Pharaoh.

12. וַיִּהְיוּ לְתַנִּינִם — *And they became serpents.* See 4:3, the *Sforno*'s commentary.

17. בְּזֹאת תֵּדַע כִּי אֲנִי ה' — *In this you shall know that I am HASHEM.* The phrase בְּזֹאת, *in this*, implies that the transformation of the river into blood will be more effective in impressing the Egyptians than the wonder of the rod turning into a snake. Therefore the *Sforno* explains that to change the nature of an unchanging, permanent part of nature (בִּלְתִּי נִפְסָד), is a far greater feat than changing a rod (which is a perishable object) into a snake.

יח וְנֶהְפְּכוּ לְדָם: וְהַדָּגָה אֲשֶׁר־בַּיְאֹר תָּמוּת וּבָאַשׁ הַיְאֹר וְנִלְאוּ מִצְרַיִם
יט לִשְׁתּוֹת מַיִם מִן־הַיְאֹר: וַיֹּאמֶר יהוה אֶל־מֹשֶׁה אֱמֹר
אֶל־אַהֲרֹן קַח מַטְּךָ וּנְטֵה־יָדְךָ עַל־מֵימֵי מִצְרַיִם עַל־נַהֲרֹתָם ׀ עַל־יְאֹרֵיהֶם
וְעַל־אַגְמֵיהֶם וְעַל כָּל־מִקְוֵה מֵימֵיהֶם וְיִהְיוּ־דָם וְהָיָה דָם בְּכָל־אֶרֶץ מִצְרַיִם
כ וּבָעֵצִים וּבָאֲבָנִים: וַיַּעֲשׂוּ־כֵן מֹשֶׁה וְאַהֲרֹן כַּאֲשֶׁר ׀ צִוָּה יהוה וַיָּרֶם בַּמַּטֶּה
וַיַּךְ אֶת־הַמַּיִם אֲשֶׁר בַּיְאֹר לְעֵינֵי פַרְעֹה וּלְעֵינֵי עֲבָדָיו וַיֵּהָפְכוּ כָּל־הַמַּיִם
כא אֲשֶׁר־בַּיְאֹר לְדָם: וְהַדָּגָה אֲשֶׁר־בַּיְאֹר מֵתָה וַיִּבְאַשׁ הַיְאֹר וְלֹא־יָכְלוּ
כב מִצְרַיִם לִשְׁתּוֹת מַיִם מִן־הַיְאֹר וַיְהִי הַדָּם בְּכָל־אֶרֶץ מִצְרָיִם: וַיַּעֲשׂוּ־כֵן
חַרְטֻמֵּי מִצְרַיִם בְּלָטֵיהֶם וַיֶּחֱזַק לֵב־פַּרְעֹה וְלֹא־שָׁמַע אֲלֵהֶם כַּאֲשֶׁר דִּבֶּר
כג־כד יהוה: וַיִּפֶן פַּרְעֹה וַיָּבֹא אֶל־בֵּיתוֹ וְלֹא־שָׁת לִבּוֹ גַּם־לָזֹאת: וַיַּחְפְּרוּ
כָל־מִצְרַיִם סְבִיבֹת הַיְאֹר מַיִם לִשְׁתּוֹת כִּי לֹא יָכְלוּ לִשְׁתֹּת מִמֵּימֵי הַיְאֹר:
כה וַיִּמָּלֵא שִׁבְעַת יָמִים אַחֲרֵי הַכּוֹת־יהוה אֶת־הַיְאֹר:
כו וַיֹּאמֶר יהוה אֶל־מֹשֶׁה בֹּא אֶל־פַּרְעֹה וְאָמַרְתָּ אֵלָיו כֹּה אָמַר יהוה שַׁלַּח
כז אֶת־עַמִּי וְיַעַבְדֻנִי: וְאִם־מָאֵן אַתָּה לְשַׁלֵּחַ הִנֵּה אָנֹכִי נֹגֵף אֶת־כָּל־גְּבוּלְךָ
כח בַּצְפַרְדְּעִים: וְשָׁרַץ הַיְאֹר צְפַרְדְּעִים וְעָלוּ וּבָאוּ בְּבֵיתֶךָ וּבַחֲדַר מִשְׁכָּבְךָ
כט וְעַל־מִטָּתֶךָ וּבְבֵית עֲבָדֶיךָ וּבְעַמֶּךָ וּבְתַנּוּרֶיךָ וּבְמִשְׁאֲרוֹתֶיךָ: וּבְכָה וּבְעַמְּךָ
ח א וּבְכָל־עֲבָדֶיךָ יַעֲלוּ הַצְפַרְדְּעִים: וַיֹּאמֶר יהוה אֶל־מֹשֶׁה אֱמֹר אֶל־אַהֲרֹן
נְטֵה אֶת־יָדְךָ בְּמַטֶּךָ עַל־הַנְּהָרֹת עַל־הַיְאֹרִים וְעַל־הָאֲגַמִּים וְהַעַל אֶת־
ב הַצְפַרְדְּעִים עַל־אֶרֶץ מִצְרָיִם: וַיֵּט אַהֲרֹן אֶת־יָדוֹ עַל מֵימֵי מִצְרָיִם וַתַּעַל
ג הַצְּפַרְדֵּעַ וַתְּכַס אֶת־אֶרֶץ מִצְרָיִם: וַיַּעֲשׂוּ־כֵן הַחַרְטֻמִּים בְּלָטֵיהֶם וַיַּעֲלוּ
ד אֶת־הַצְפַרְדְּעִים עַל־אֶרֶץ מִצְרָיִם: וַיִּקְרָא פַרְעֹה לְמֹשֶׁה וּלְאַהֲרֹן וַיֹּאמֶר

---

18. וְהַדָּגָה אֲשֶׁר בַּיְאֹר תָּמוּת — *And the fish that are in the river shall die.* There will be no form (essence) of water (combined) with the appearance of blood, rather it shall become the essence (form) as well as the appearance of blood; hence the fish will die.

וְנִלְאוּ מִצְרַיִם — *And the Egyptians will weary themselves . . .* digging around the river (in an attempt) to find water to drink, as it says, וַיַּחְפְּרוּ כָל מִצְרַיִם סְבִיבוֹת הַיְאוֹר, *And all the Egyptians dug round about the river* (v. 24).

23. וְלֹא שָׁת לִבּוֹ גַּם לָזֹאת — *Nor did he lay even this to his heart . . .* to understand the difference in this occurrence between the Divine act to that of the sorcerers.' The act of God, the Blessed One, was a change in the nature of the river, which is (normally) unchanging, into the authentic nature of blood, causing the death of the fish. The act of the sorcerers (on the other hand) was a change in that (portion) which is impermanent (i.e., a portion of the water), and perhaps (it was only) conjuring.

VIII

3. וַיַּעֲלוּ אֶת הַצְפַרְדְּעִים — *And brought up crocodiles.* However, these (crocodiles)

NOTES

18. וְהַדָּגָה אֲשֶׁר בַּיְאֹר תָּמוּת — *And the fish that are in the river shall die.* The transformation of the water into blood was real, not an illusion, as we find in the story of Elishah and

הַעְתִּירוּ אֶל־יְהוָה וְיָסֵר הַצְפַרְדְּעִים מִמֶּנִּי וּמֵעַמִּי וַאֲשַׁלְּחָה אֶת־הָעָם
ה וְיִזְבְּחוּ לַיהוָה: וַיֹּאמֶר מֹשֶׁה לְפַרְעֹה הִתְפָּאֵר עָלַי לְמָתַי | אַעְתִּיר לְךָ
וְלַעֲבָדֶיךָ וּלְעַמְּךָ לְהַכְרִית הַצְפַרְדְּעִים מִמְּךָ וּמִבָּתֶּיךָ רַק בַּיְאֹר תִּשָּׁאַרְנָה:
ו וַיֹּאמֶר לְמָחָר וַיֹּאמֶר כִּדְבָרְךָ לְמַעַן תֵּדַע כִּי־אֵין כַּיהוָה אֱלֹהֵינוּ:

---

could not reproduce, for the (sorcerers) are incapable of producing a (living) authentically moving creature.

4. הַעְתִּירוּ אֶל ה׳ — *Entreat HASHEM.* For in this (case) he did take it to his heart and saw the superiority of God's act in comparison to the act of the sorcerers.

5. לְמָתַי אַעְתִּיר לְךָ — *Against what time shall I entreat for you.* So that you may recognize the great difference between the act of the sorcerers (as compared to) the act of God, as he says *against what time,* and also *and remain in the river only.* For indeed an act of sorcery lasts for a (specific) limited time after which nature returns to its strength, as soon as the sorcery ceases, for then the deterrent to the course of nature is removed, as our Sages say, 'Why are they (magic or sorcery) called כְּשָׁפִים? For they deny the heavenly court' (*Sanhedrin* 67b). However, God, the Blessed One, commands nature to cease, change or function partially or fully, in a time (period) that He sets, and it will never disobey His word.

6. כִּדְבָרְךָ — *According to your word.* As you said, *'Take away the crocodiles from me and from my people'* (v. 4), but you did not request that they be totally destroyed.

לְמַעַן תֵּדַע כִּי אֵין כַּה׳ אֱלֹהֵינוּ — *That you may know there is none like HASHEM our God.* For there is no other power that can create a change in nature, except for a (limited) set time. Now these crocodiles in the river were a result of a change in the nature of the river, considering that they were crocodiles, different than all other

NOTES

the Moabites (*II Kings* 3:22), where the sun shining on the water made it appear כַּדָּם, *as blood.* Here, however, the fish died, for the blood was real, unlike the sleight of hand of the sorcerers.

VIII

3. וַיַּעֲלוּ אֶת הַצְפַרְדְּעִים — *And brought up the crocodiles.* Unlike most commentators, the *Sforno* is of the opinion that the צְפַרְדְּעִים were not frogs but crocodiles. See the *Sforno* to verse 6.

4. הַעְתִּירוּ אֶל ה׳ — *Entreat HASHEM.* In the previous chapter the *Sforno* discusses the difference between Aaron's snake and the magician's serpents, as well as that of the Divine plague of blood and the sorcerer's sleight of hand which seemingly duplicated this feat (see 7:12,14,15 and 23). Still Pharaoh was not moved to ask Moses and Aaron to entreat God on his behalf until this second plague. The reason is that the differentiation of the former signs were subtle and not as apparent. Here, however, we are dealing with living creatures (as opposed to the inanimate rod and water), and Pharaoh perceived that the crocodiles were not the same.

5. לְמָתַי אַעְתִּיר לְךָ — *Against what time shall I entreat for you.* Although Moses was challenging Pharaoh to set a specific time for the crocodiles to be removed, he was not doing so to impress Pharaoh with his powers or even those of the Almighty. The purpose was to teach Pharaoh the basic difference between God's control over nature, which is His creation, and the illusions created by the sorcerers. Even though they had the ability to temporarily suspend nature's course, only *Hashem* can command its *positive* order or institute changes which are permanent, or temporary, in accordance with His will. This is the reason Moses told Pharaoh to set the time, to underscore this fundamental lesson.

6. כִּדְבָרְךָ לְמַעַן תֵּדַע ... — *According to your word that you may know ...* There is a subtle change in Pharaoh's request and Moses's

חמישי ז וְסָרוּ הַצְפַרְדְּעִים מִמְּךָ וּמִבָּתֶּיךָ וּמֵעֲבָדֶיךָ וּמֵעַמֶּךָ רַק בַּיְאֹר תִּשָּׁאַרְנָה׃
ח וַיֵּצֵא מֹשֶׁה וְאַהֲרֹן מֵעִם פַּרְעֹה וַיִּצְעַק מֹשֶׁה אֶל־יהוה עַל־דְּבַר הַצְפַרְדְּעִים
ט אֲשֶׁר־שָׂם לְפַרְעֹה׃ וַיַּעַשׂ יהוה כִּדְבַר מֹשֶׁה וַיָּמֻתוּ הַצְפַרְדְּעִים מִן־הַבָּתִּים
י־יא מִן־הַחֲצֵרֹת וּמִן־הַשָּׂדֹת׃ וַיִּצְבְּרוּ אֹתָם חֳמָרִם חֳמָרִם וַתִּבְאַשׁ הָאָרֶץ׃ וַיַּרְא
פַּרְעֹה כִּי הָיְתָה הָרְוָחָה וְהַכְבֵּד אֶת־לִבּוֹ וְלֹא שָׁמַע אֲלֵהֶם כַּאֲשֶׁר דִּבֶּר
יב יהוה׃ וַיֹּאמֶר יהוה אֶל־מֹשֶׁה אֱמֹר אֶל־אַהֲרֹן נְטֵה אֶת־
יג מַטְּךָ וְהַךְ אֶת־עֲפַר הָאָרֶץ וְהָיָה לְכִנִּם בְּכָל־אֶרֶץ מִצְרָיִם׃ וַיַּעֲשׂוּ־כֵן וַיֵּט

---

creatures in that they move their upper jaw and ingest without defecating. Behold God the Blessed One will destroy those (that are in) your houses only (but the others will remain in the river).

7. וְסָרוּ הַצְפַרְדְּעִים — *And the crocodiles shall depart.* Not only will He destroy these but He will also decree that the remaining (ones) no longer come up to your houses.

מִמְּךָ וּמִבָּתֶּיךָ — *From you and from your houses.* However, not from the entire land, for indeed they will perish on the land and smell.

רַק בַּיְאֹר תִּשָּׁאַרְנָה — *They shall remain in the river only.* For generations, and will not come up on the land.

8. וַיִּצְעַק מֹשֶׁה אֶל ה׳ עַל דְּבַר הַצְפַרְדְּעִים אֲשֶׁר שָׂם לְפַרְעֹה — *And Moses cried to HASHEM concerning the crocodiles which He had brought upon Pharaoh.* That He remove those crocodiles alone, *which He had brought upon Pharaoh,* that they remain in the river. For this (request) it was necessary to cry out in prayer, (since as the Sages teach) 'From Heaven, a half is not granted' (*Sanhedrin* 64a).

11. כִּי הָיְתָה הָרְוָחָה — *That there was respite.* Although the evil was not completely removed, for the stench remained in the land, and the crocodiles — which cause injury to this very day — remained in the river.

וְהַכְבֵּד אֶת לִבּוֹ — *He hardened his heart.* He strengthened (his resolve), overcoming his natural fear of the remaining crocodiles, (and he was prepared) to withstand the bad stench, so as not to listen to the voice of God, the Blessed One.

12. וְהַךְ אֶת עֲפַר הָאָרֶץ — *And smite the dust of the earth.* No warning was given to Pharaoh before this plague, nor the boils, nor darkness. The reason is that the nine plagues of דצ״ך, עד״ש, בא״ח *(blood, crocodiles, gnats; mixture, murrain, boils; hail,*

NOTES

initial response. Pharaoh asks that the crocodiles be *removed* (v. 4), whereas Moses speaks of their *destruction* (v. 5). However, in this verse, Moses states כִּדְבָרְךָ, *according to your word,* i.e., as you originally requested, *removal* not *destruction.* Hence, although some will be destroyed, others will remain in the river. The *Sforno* is of the opinion that crocodiles only now took up their habitation in the Nile at the command of *Hashem.*

8. וַיִּצְעַק מֹשֶׁה אֶל ה׳ — *And Moses cried to HASHEM.* When man prays he cannot qualify his petition, asking that it only be answered partially. This is the meaning of the saying of our Sages cited by the *Sforno.* Moses was confronted with this dilemma, since he was asking that only certain crocodiles be removed and brought back to the river. That is why he had to *cry out,* not just *entreat.*

12. וְהַךְ אֶת עֲפַר הָאָרֶץ — *And smite the dust of the earth.* A careful study of the first nine plagues will reveal that Pharaoh is given fair

אַהֲרֹן אֶת־יָדוֹ בְמַטֵּהוּ וַיַּךְ אֶת־עֲפַר הָאָרֶץ וַתְּהִי הַכִּנָּם בָּאָדָם וּבַבְּהֵמָה
יד כָּל־עֲפַר הָאָרֶץ הָיָה כִנִּים בְּכָל־אֶרֶץ מִצְרָיִם: וַיַּעֲשׂוּ־כֵן הַחַרְטֻמִּים
בְּלָטֵיהֶם לְהוֹצִיא אֶת־הַכִּנִּים וְלֹא יָכֹלוּ וַתְּהִי הַכִּנָּם בָּאָדָם וּבַבְּהֵמָה:
טו וַיֹּאמְרוּ הַחַרְטֻמִּם אֶל־פַּרְעֹה אֶצְבַּע אֱלֹהִים הִוא וַיֶּחֱזַק לֵב־פַּרְעֹה וְלֹא־
טז שָׁמַע אֲלֵהֶם כַּאֲשֶׁר דִּבֶּר יהוה: וַיֹּאמֶר יהוה אֶל־מֹשֶׁה
הַשְׁכֵּם בַּבֹּקֶר וְהִתְיַצֵּב לִפְנֵי פַרְעֹה הִנֵּה יוֹצֵא הַמָּיְמָה וְאָמַרְתָּ אֵלָיו כֹּה
יז אָמַר יהוה שַׁלַּח עַמִּי וְיַעַבְדֻנִי: כִּי אִם־אֵינְךָ מְשַׁלֵּחַ אֶת־עַמִּי הִנְנִי מַשְׁלִיחַ
בְּךָ וּבַעֲבָדֶיךָ וּבְעַמְּךָ וּבְבָתֶּיךָ אֶת־הֶעָרֹב וּמָלְאוּ בָּתֵּי מִצְרַיִם אֶת־הֶעָרֹב
יח וְגַם הָאֲדָמָה אֲשֶׁר־הֵם עָלֶיהָ: וְהִפְלֵיתִי בַיּוֹם הַהוּא אֶת־אֶרֶץ גֹּשֶׁן אֲשֶׁר
עַמִּי עֹמֵד עָלֶיהָ לְבִלְתִּי הֱיוֹת־שָׁם עָרֹב לְמַעַן תֵּדַע כִּי אֲנִי יהוה בְּקֶרֶב
ששי יט-כ הָאָרֶץ: וְשַׂמְתִּי פְדֻת בֵּין עַמִּי וּבֵין עַמֶּךָ לְמָחָר יִהְיֶה הָאֹת הַזֶּה: וַיַּעַשׂ יהוה
כֵּן וַיָּבֹא עָרֹב כָּבֵד בֵּיתָה פַרְעֹה וּבֵית עֲבָדָיו וּבְכָל־אֶרֶץ מִצְרַיִם תִּשָּׁחֵת
כא הָאָרֶץ מִפְּנֵי הֶעָרֹב: וַיִּקְרָא פַרְעֹה אֶל־מֹשֶׁה וּלְאַהֲרֹן וַיֹּאמֶר לְכוּ זִבְחוּ
כב לֵאלֹהֵיכֶם בָּאָרֶץ: וַיֹּאמֶר מֹשֶׁה לֹא נָכוֹן לַעֲשׂוֹת כֵּן כִּי תּוֹעֲבַת מִצְרַיִם
נִזְבַּח לַיהוה אֱלֹהֵינוּ הֵן נִזְבַּח אֶת־תּוֹעֲבַת מִצְרַיִם לְעֵינֵיהֶם וְלֹא יִסְקְלֻנוּ:
כג דֶּרֶךְ שְׁלֹשֶׁת יָמִים נֵלֵךְ בַּמִּדְבָּר וְזָבַחְנוּ לַיהוה אֱלֹהֵינוּ כַּאֲשֶׁר יֹאמַר אֵלֵינוּ:
כד וַיֹּאמֶר פַּרְעֹה אָנֹכִי אֲשַׁלַּח אֶתְכֶם וּזְבַחְתֶּם לַיהוה אֱלֹהֵיכֶם בַּמִּדְבָּר רַק
כה הַרְחֵק לֹא־תַרְחִיקוּ לָלֶכֶת הַעְתִּירוּ בַּעֲדִי: וַיֹּאמֶר מֹשֶׁה הִנֵּה אָנֹכִי יוֹצֵא
מֵעִמָּךְ וְהַעְתַּרְתִּי אֶל־יהוה וְסָר הֶעָרֹב מִפַּרְעֹה מֵעֲבָדָיו וּמֵעַמּוֹ מָחָר רַק

---

locusts, darkness) alone were meant to be signs and wonders, (not so) the plague of the firstborn which was not meant to be a sign or wonder, but was a punishment, as explained above (4:23 and 7:4). Now the blood, crocodiles and gnats were signs in the two 'heavy' elements (water and dust); mixture, murrain and boils were signs in living creatures; while hail, locusts and darkness were signs in the air (atmosphere). The first two in each (category) were (preceded) by a warning, while the third sign was sent without a warning, as it says, הֶן כָּל אֵלֶּה יִפְעַל אֵל, פַּעֲמַיִם שָׁלוֹשׁ עִם גָּבֶר, *All these things does God work, twice, yes thrice with a man (Job* 33:29).

14. וְלֹא יָכֹלוּ — *But they could not.* For it was impossible for them to bring into being anything which truly moved (alive).

17. וְגַם הָאֲדָמָה אֲשֶׁר הֵם עָלֶיהָ — *And also the ground on which they are.* The very ground on which the houses (of the Egyptians) stood would teem with serpents and other creatures which breed in the deep earth, in such a manner that they will not feel secure at night even in a locked house.

19. וְשַׂמְתִּי פְדֻת בֵּין עַמִּי וּבֵין עַמֶּךָ — *And I will put a division between my people and your people.* Even if some of *my people* come to the place where the mixtures are they will not be harmed; only *your people* will be harmed, in that self-same place.

NOTES

warning before each of the plagues except for numbers three, six and nine. A warning is very important when the purpose of the plague is to encourage repentance and not for punishment. This difficulty is answered by the *Sforno,* based on the verse in *Job,* that the

כו אַל־יֹסֵף פַּרְעֹה הָתֵל לְבִלְתִּי שַׁלַּח אֶת־הָעָם לִזְבֹּחַ לַיהוָה׃ וַיֵּצֵא מֹשֶׁה
כז מֵעִם פַּרְעֹה וַיֶּעְתַּר אֶל־יהוה׃ וַיַּעַשׂ יהוה כִּדְבַר מֹשֶׁה וַיָּסַר הֶעָרֹב מִפַּרְעֹה
כח מֵעֲבָדָיו וּמֵעַמּוֹ לֹא נִשְׁאַר אֶחָד׃ וַיַּכְבֵּד פַּרְעֹה אֶת־לִבּוֹ גַּם בַּפַּעַם הַזֹּאת
וְלֹא שִׁלַּח אֶת־הָעָם׃

ט

א וַיֹּאמֶר יהוה אֶל־מֹשֶׁה בֹּא אֶל־פַּרְעֹה וְדִבַּרְתָּ אֵלָיו כֹּה־אָמַר יהוה אֱלֹהֵי
ב הָעִבְרִים שַׁלַּח אֶת־עַמִּי וְיַעַבְדֻנִי׃ כִּי אִם־מָאֵן אַתָּה לְשַׁלֵּחַ וְעוֹדְךָ מַחֲזִיק
ג בָּם׃ הִנֵּה יַד־יהוה הוֹיָה בְּמִקְנְךָ אֲשֶׁר בַּשָּׂדֶה בַּסּוּסִים בַּחֲמֹרִים בַּגְּמַלִּים
ד בַּבָּקָר וּבַצֹּאן דֶּבֶר כָּבֵד מְאֹד׃ וְהִפְלָה יהוה בֵּין מִקְנֵה יִשְׂרָאֵל וּבֵין
ה מִקְנֵה מִצְרָיִם וְלֹא יָמוּת מִכָּל־לִבְנֵי יִשְׂרָאֵל דָּבָר׃ וַיָּשֶׂם יהוה מוֹעֵד לֵאמֹר
ו מָחָר יַעֲשֶׂה יהוה הַדָּבָר הַזֶּה בָּאָרֶץ׃ וַיַּעַשׂ יהוה אֶת־הַדָּבָר הַזֶּה מִמָּחֳרָת
ז וַיָּמָת כֹּל מִקְנֵה מִצְרָיִם וּמִמִּקְנֵה בְנֵי־יִשְׂרָאֵל לֹא־מֵת אֶחָד׃ וַיִּשְׁלַח פַּרְעֹה
וְהִנֵּה לֹא־מֵת מִמִּקְנֵה יִשְׂרָאֵל עַד־אֶחָד וַיִּכְבַּד לֵב פַּרְעֹה וְלֹא שִׁלַּח
אֶת־הָעָם׃
ח וַיֹּאמֶר יהוה אֶל־מֹשֶׁה וְאֶל־אַהֲרֹן קְחוּ לָכֶם מְלֹא חָפְנֵיכֶם פִּיחַ כִּבְשָׁן

---

26. וַיֶּעְתַּר — *And entreated.* To remove the mixture at the time established (by Moses) and in the manner he designated to Pharaoh, as it says, *The mixture will depart* (v. 25), i.e., not to extirpate and cause to die, as it was with the crocodiles. This is indicated by the (expression), *And HASHEM did according to the word of Moses* (v. 27) regarding (both) the manner of removal and the time.

28. גַּם בַּפַּעַם הַזֹּאת — *This time also.* As he did by the (plague) of the crocodiles, even though he should have feared the mixture, who *did not die* but were only removed and could easily have been returned by God.

IX

7. וְהִנֵּה לֹא מֵת מִמִּקְנֵה יִשְׂרָאֵל עַד אֶחָד — *And behold there was not so much as one of the cattle of the Israelites dead.* Although this was a clear wonder, which could not be attributed to anyone (or anything) except God, the Blessed One, for there is none that can assure life, except He.

NOTES

concept of הַתְרָאָה, *warning,* is called for only the first two times but not the third. Hence by dividing the plagues into three divisions there is no reason to warn whenever it is the third plague of that section. This explains the lack of warning for the third, sixth and ninth plagues.

28. גַּם בַּפַּעַם הַזֹּאת — *This time also.* The expression *this time also* must refer to a previous *similar* case. The *Sforno* connects this verse to verse 11, explaining in both instances that Pharaoh hardened his heart even though the crocodiles and the mixture of wild beasts still existed and could quickly invade his land again.

IX

7. וְהִנֵּה לֹא מֵת מִמִּקְנֵה יִשְׂרָאֵל עַד אֶחָד — *And behold there was not so much as one of the cattle of the Israelites dead.* The interpretation of the *Sforno* is to be understood as follows. Even if the murrain would not kill the cattle of the Israelites, nonetheless there could be other causes of death. The fact that not even one of the cattle of the Israelites died, of any cause, can only be attributed to the One Who controls life and death.

ט וּזְרָקוֹ מֹשֶׁה הַשָּׁמַיְמָה לְעֵינֵי פַרְעֹה: וְהָיָה לְאָבָק עַל כָּל־אֶרֶץ מִצְרָיִם וְהָיָה
י עַל־הָאָדָם וְעַל־הַבְּהֵמָה לִשְׁחִין פֹּרֵחַ אֲבַעְבֻּעֹת בְּכָל־אֶרֶץ מִצְרָיִם: וַיִּקְחוּ
אֶת־פִּיחַ הַכִּבְשָׁן וַיַּעַמְדוּ לִפְנֵי פַרְעֹה וַיִּזְרֹק אֹתוֹ מֹשֶׁה הַשָּׁמָיְמָה וַיְהִי שְׁחִין
יא אֲבַעְבֻּעֹת פֹּרֵחַ בָּאָדָם וּבַבְּהֵמָה: וְלֹא־יָכְלוּ הַחַרְטֻמִּים לַעֲמֹד לִפְנֵי מֹשֶׁה
יב מִפְּנֵי הַשְּׁחִין כִּי־הָיָה הַשְּׁחִין בַּחֲרְטֻמִּם וּבְכָל־מִצְרָיִם: וַיְחַזֵּק יהוה אֶת־לֵב
יג פַּרְעֹה וְלֹא שָׁמַע אֲלֵהֶם כַּאֲשֶׁר דִּבֶּר יהוה אֶל־מֹשֶׁה: וַיֹּאמֶר
יהוה אֶל־מֹשֶׁה הַשְׁכֵּם בַּבֹּקֶר וְהִתְיַצֵּב לִפְנֵי פַרְעֹה וְאָמַרְתָּ אֵלָיו כֹּה־אָמַר
יד יהוה אֱלֹהֵי הָעִבְרִים שַׁלַּח אֶת־עַמִּי וְיַעַבְדֻנִי: כִּי | בַּפַּעַם הַזֹּאת אֲנִי שֹׁלֵחַ
אֶת־כָּל־מַגֵּפֹתַי אֶל־לִבְּךָ וּבַעֲבָדֶיךָ וּבְעַמֶּךָ בַּעֲבוּר תֵּדַע כִּי אֵין כָּמֹנִי
טו בְּכָל־הָאָרֶץ: כִּי עַתָּה שָׁלַחְתִּי אֶת־יָדִי וָאַךְ אוֹתְךָ וְאֶת־עַמְּךָ בַּדָּבֶר

---

8. לְעֵינֵי פַרְעֹה — *In the sight of Pharaoh.* So that he may see that this plague was not caused by contamination of the air's quality or by the position of the heavenly bodies, (both of) which can at times bring about (such) a natural epidemic.

12. וַיְחַזֵּק ה׳ — *And HASHEM hardened.* For otherwise he doubtless would not have been able to withstand (this plague), similar to Job, וְגַע אֶל עַצְמוֹ וְאֶל בְּשָׂרוֹ, *And touch his bone and flesh* (*Job* 2:5).

14. כִּי בַּפַּעַם הַזֹּאת — *For this time.* (This refers to) the third category of plagues affecting the air (atmosphere).

אֲנִי שֹׁלֵחַ אֶת כָּל מַגֵּפֹתַי אֶל לִבְּךָ וּבַעֲבָדֶיךָ וּבְעַמֶּךָ — *I will send all My plagues upon your person* (lit., *your heart*), *your servants and upon your people.* Each one of these plagues (i.e., hail, locust, darkness) which I will visit upon you will have a lasting effect (lit., 'will remain in your hearts') even after they have been removed, for even later the prolonged damage will be felt. (In the case of hail and locust) there will be damage to vegetation and all food; and there will be physical illness (as an aftermath) from the plague of darkness which spoiled the climactic condition without a doubt. Also since *no man rose from his place*, doubtless serious illness resulted. The previous plagues, however, once they were removed left no protracted damage.

בַּעֲבוּר תֵּדַע כִּי אֵין כָּמֹנִי בְּכָל הָאָרֶץ — *That you may know that there is none like Me in all the earth.* When you will observe My power even in the atmosphere enveloping (the earth). However, His power in the upper regions was demonstrated to them at the Sea of Reeds through the angel of God, the pillar of cloud and the pillar of fire, for the existence of all these are supernatural.

NOTES

12. וַיְחַזֵּק ה׳ — *And HASHEM hardened.* The previous plagues, severe as they may have been, did not affect the physical being of Pharaoh and his servants. This plague of boils did, and as such should have brought Pharaoh to the point of surrender. That is why God had to harden Pharaoh's heart, for otherwise he could not have withstood this particular plague. The quotation from *Job* refers to Satan's statement that even righteous Job, if afflicted in his body, would rebel against God.

14. כִּי בַּפַּעַם הַזֹּאת . . . אֶל לִבְּךָ — *For this time . . . upon your person.* The expression *this time* does not refer to the seventh plague (hail) alone but to the third category, for they have a common characteristic, namely the lasting effect they will leave on the people and the

טז וַתִּכָּחֵד מִן־הָאָרֶץ: וְאוּלָם בַּעֲבוּר זֹאת הֶעֱמַדְתִּיךָ בַּעֲבוּר הַרְאֹתְךָ אֶת־
שביעי יז כֹּחִי וּלְמַעַן סַפֵּר שְׁמִי בְּכָל־הָאָרֶץ: עוֹדְךָ מִסְתּוֹלֵל בְּעַמִּי לְבִלְתִּי שַׁלְּחָם:
יח הִנְנִי מַמְטִיר כָּעֵת מָחָר בָּרָד כָּבֵד מְאֹד אֲשֶׁר לֹא־הָיָה כָמֹהוּ בְּמִצְרַיִם
יט לְמִן־הַיּוֹם הִוָּסְדָה וְעַד־עָתָּה: וְעַתָּה שְׁלַח הָעֵז אֶת־מִקְנְךָ וְאֵת כָּל־אֲשֶׁר
לְךָ בַּשָּׂדֶה כָּל־הָאָדָם וְהַבְּהֵמָה אֲשֶׁר־יִמָּצֵא בַשָּׂדֶה וְלֹא יֵאָסֵף הַבַּיְתָה
כ וְיָרַד עֲלֵהֶם הַבָּרָד וָמֵתוּ: הַיָּרֵא אֶת־דְּבַר יהוה מֵעַבְדֵי פַּרְעֹה הֵנִיס
כא אֶת־עֲבָדָיו וְאֶת־מִקְנֵהוּ אֶל־הַבָּתִּים: וַאֲשֶׁר לֹא־שָׂם לִבּוֹ אֶל־דְּבַר יהוה
וַיַּעֲזֹב אֶת־עֲבָדָיו וְאֶת־מִקְנֵהוּ בַּשָּׂדֶה:
כב וַיֹּאמֶר יהוה אֶל־מֹשֶׁה נְטֵה אֶת־יָדְךָ עַל־הַשָּׁמַיִם וִיהִי בָרָד בְּכָל־אֶרֶץ
כג מִצְרָיִם עַל־הָאָדָם וְעַל־הַבְּהֵמָה וְעַל כָּל־עֵשֶׂב הַשָּׂדֶה בְּאֶרֶץ מִצְרָיִם: וַיֵּט
מֹשֶׁה אֶת־מַטֵּהוּ עַל־הַשָּׁמַיִם וַיהוה נָתַן קֹלֹת וּבָרָד וַתִּהֲלַךְ אֵשׁ אָרְצָה

---

16. בַּעֲבוּר הַרְאֹתְךָ אֶת כֹּחִי — *So that I might show you My power* . . . that you might repent, for כִּי לֹא אֶחְפֹּץ בְּמוֹת הַמֵּת, *I do not desire the death of him who dies* (*Ezekiel* 18:32).

וּלְמַעַן סַפֵּר שְׁמִי — *And that My Name may be declared* . . . thereby turning many away from sin.

19. וְעַתָּה שְׁלַח הָעֵז אֶת מִקְנְךָ — *Now therefore send, hasten in your cattle* . . . so that your servants, who are with the cattle, will be saved, as our Sages say, חָבִיב אָדָם שֶׁנִּבְרָא בְּצֶלֶם, *Precious is man who was created in (God's) image* (*Avos* 3:18).

20. הַיָּרֵא אֶת דְּבַר ה׳ . . . הֵנִיס — *He that feared the word of* HASHEM . . . *made flee.* The reason I cautioned, *'Send and hasten'* (v. 19), is because I saw that at the plague of murrain, *he that feared the word of* HASHEM *(did) make flee.*

21. וַאֲשֶׁר לֹא שָׂם לִבּוֹ — *And he that regarded not.* But (he who regarded not) sinned.

וַיַּעֲזֹב אֶת עֲבָדָיו — *And left his servants* . . . In a manner that his sin caused him loss; therefore I am now warning so that the men in the field will not die.

23. וַתִּהֲלַךְ אֵשׁ אָרְצָה — *And fire ran down onto the earth.* The enflamed air came down to the earth through the forceful thrust (lit., 'movement') of the hail which pressed upon it as it descended.

NOTES

produce which is their sustenance. The expression אֶל לִבְּךָ literally means *to your heart.* The *Sforno* feels that this expression is chosen deliberately to indicate that these three plagues were directed to the very heart of man's economic and physical condition.

19. וְעַתָּה שְׁלַח הָעֵז אֶת מִקְנְךָ — *Now therefore send, hasten in your cattle.* Pharaoh had demonstrated, during the plague of murrain, that he had no pity on the cattle of his people. Now, however, since the hail could kill human beings as well, he is cautioned to take proper steps to protect human lives, in the hope that even Pharaoh will respect the value of man who was created in the Divine Image.

20-21. הַיָּרֵא אֶת דְּבַר ה׳ . . . הֵנִיס . . . וַאֲשֶׁר לֹא שָׂם לִבּוֹ — *He that feared the word of* HASHEM . . . *made flee* ... *And he that regarded not.* Obviously there were those who took in their cattle during the plague of murrain thereby saving them. These were the Egyptians who feared the word of God. Otherwise there would be no cattle remaining following that plague. The sense of these verses is therefore as follows: Since I saw that there were those who believed the warning at the time of the murrain, I therefore am cautioning you now, before the hail, to do likewise especially since human life is now at stake.

23. וַתִּהֲלַךְ אֵשׁ אָרְצָה — *And fire ran down onto*

כד וַיַּמְטֵר יְהוָה בָּרָד עַל־אֶרֶץ מִצְרָיִם: וַיְהִי בָרָד וְאֵשׁ מִתְלַקַּחַת בְּתוֹךְ הַבָּרָד
כה כָּבֵד מְאֹד אֲשֶׁר לֹא־הָיָה כָמֹהוּ בְּכָל־אֶרֶץ מִצְרַיִם מֵאָז הָיְתָה לְגוֹי: וַיַּךְ
הַבָּרָד בְּכָל־אֶרֶץ מִצְרַיִם אֵת כָּל־אֲשֶׁר בַּשָּׂדֶה מֵאָדָם וְעַד־בְּהֵמָה וְאֵת
כו כָּל־עֵשֶׂב הַשָּׂדֶה הִכָּה הַבָּרָד וְאֶת־כָּל־עֵץ הַשָּׂדֶה שִׁבֵּר: רַק בְּאֶרֶץ גֹּשֶׁן
כז אֲשֶׁר־שָׁם בְּנֵי יִשְׂרָאֵל לֹא הָיָה בָּרָד: וַיִּשְׁלַח פַּרְעֹה וַיִּקְרָא לְמֹשֶׁה וּלְאַהֲרֹן
כח וַיֹּאמֶר אֲלֵהֶם חָטָאתִי הַפָּעַם יְהוָה הַצַּדִּיק וַאֲנִי וְעַמִּי הָרְשָׁעִים: הַעְתִּירוּ
אֶל־יְהוָה וְרַב מִהְיֹת קֹלֹת אֱלֹהִים וּבָרָד וַאֲשַׁלְּחָה אֶתְכֶם וְלֹא תֹסִפוּן
כט לַעֲמֹד: וַיֹּאמֶר אֵלָיו מֹשֶׁה כְּצֵאתִי אֶת־הָעִיר אֶפְרֹשׂ אֶת־כַּפַּי אֶל־יְהוָה
ל הַקֹּלוֹת יֶחְדָּלוּן וְהַבָּרָד לֹא יִהְיֶה־עוֹד לְמַעַן תֵּדַע כִּי לַיהוָה הָאָרֶץ: וְאַתָּה
לא וַעֲבָדֶיךָ יָדַעְתִּי כִּי טֶרֶם תִּירְאוּן מִפְּנֵי יְהוָה אֱלֹהִים: וְהַפִּשְׁתָּה וְהַשְּׂעֹרָה
לב נֻכָּתָה כִּי הַשְּׂעֹרָה אָבִיב וְהַפִּשְׁתָּה גִּבְעֹל: וְהַחִטָּה וְהַכֻּסֶּמֶת לֹא נֻכּוּ כִּי

24. וְאֵשׁ מִתְלַקַּחַת בְּתוֹךְ הַבָּרָד — *And fire flashing up midst the hail.* The forceful thrust of the hail enflamed the atmosphere, causing thunder. The forceful movement was so great (intense) that it damaged the soft (pliable) as well as the hard (growths), as it says, *and the hail smote every herb of the field and broke every tree of the field* (v. 25).

29. כְּצֵאתִי אֶת הָעִיר — *As I go out of the city.* Even though you said, *'And let there be enough of these mighty thunderings and hail'* (v. 28), all this will not cease until I go out of the city.

הַקֹּלוֹת יֶחְדָּלוּן וְהַבָּרָד לֹא יִהְיֶה עוֹד לְמַעַן תֵּדַע כִּי לַה׳ הָאָרֶץ — *The thunders shall cease, neither shall there by any more hail, that you may know that the earth is* HASHEM*'s.* All this will occur simultaneously, as in a minute, which is contrary to the laws of nature. This will happen *that you may know . . .*, not because I think that you have repented, for indeed . . .

30. יָדַעְתִּי כִּי טֶרֶם תִּירְאוּן — *I know that you will not yet fear.* You still do not fear *(God).*

31. וְהַפִּשְׁתָּה וְהַשְּׂעֹרָה נֻכָּתָה — *And the flax and the barley were smitten.* Even though the flax and barley were smitten, which was a heavy loss for Egypt, as it says, ובֹשׁוּ עֹבְדֵי פִּשְׁתִּים, *And the workers of flax will be shamed (Isaiah* 19:9).

32. וְהַחִטָּה וְהַכֻּסֶּמֶת — *But the wheat and the spelt.* Come and see how great was the wickedness of Pharaoh and his servants, for even though the wheat and spelt were not smitten, and Moses prayed, and Pharaoh observed that the evil (decree) ceased through his prayers, for otherwise even the residue would have been destroyed,

NOTES

the earth. Normally fire goes upward. In the case of the plague of hail, however, the fiery air was forced downward by the impact of the strong hail.

24. וְאֵשׁ מִתְלַקַּחַת בְּתוֹךְ הַבָּרָד — *And fire flashing up midst the hail.* Under normal circumstances the hail would not have damaged the soft, pliable plantings. However, in this case, the hail's force was so great that it affected both the hard and the soft, the pliable no different than the inflexible.

32. וְהַחִטָּה וְהַכֻּסֶּמֶת — *But the wheat and the spelt.* The *Sforno's* explanation answers the question of some commentators (the *Ramban* among them) as to the need for this verse. It comes to underscore the obdurate stand of

מפטיר לג אֲפִילֹת הֵנָּה: וַיֵּצֵא מֹשֶׁה מֵעִם פַּרְעֹה אֶת־הָעִיר וַיִּפְרֹשׂ כַּפָּיו אֶל־יהוה
לד וַיַּחְדְּלוּ הַקֹּלוֹת וְהַבָּרָד וּמָטָר לֹא־נִתַּךְ אָרְצָה: וַיַּרְא פַּרְעֹה כִּי־חָדַל הַמָּטָר
לה וְהַבָּרָד וְהַקֹּלֹת וַיֹּסֶף לַחֲטֹא וַיַּכְבֵּד לִבּוֹ הוּא וַעֲבָדָיו: וַיֶּחֱזַק לֵב פַּרְעֹה וְלֹא
שִׁלַּח אֶת־בְּנֵי יִשְׂרָאֵל כַּאֲשֶׁר דִּבֶּר יהוה בְּיַד־מֹשֶׁה:

---

nonetheless Pharaoh and his servants continued to sin and willfully hardened their hearts.

35. וַיֶּחֱזַק לֵב פַּרְעֹה — *And the heart of Pharaoh was hardened.* Not by himself but *as* HASHEM *had spoken by Moses,* before Aaron was associated with him, when he said, '*And I know that the king of Egypt will not permit you to go*' (3:19), meaning, he will not give you leave to go willingly, *except by a mighty hand* (ibid.). (Now) I do not want him to do so (motivated by) fear of My mighty hand (as a result of which) he will be unable to withstand (the pressures). And thus God acted; after (Pharaoh) continued to sin willfully and he himself hardened his heart contrary to his own nature, but (he was still) unsure whether he could (continue) to withstand, *then* (God) strengthened his heart in the manner that He had spoken to Moses, and (thereby) Pharaoh convinced himself that he would no longer be smitten.

NOTES

Pharaoh who, in spite of the efficacy of Moses's prayers which salvaged the wheat and spelt, still continued to sin and refused to send forth the Israelites.

35. וַיֶּחֱזַק לֵב פַּרְעֹה — *And the heart of Pharaoh was hardened.* In the previous verse we are told that Pharaoh himself hardened his heart. Seemingly, this verse which speaks of God hardening his heart is either redundant or unnecessary, since Pharaoh was resisting God on his own! The *Sforno* explains that from the very beginning God had told Moses that Pharaoh's refusal to comply with the command of God would be buttressed by God Himself, for He did not want Pharaoh to succumb to the pressure of the plagues, but to repent of his own volition. This interpretation of the *Sforno* is repeated a number of times (see 3:19, 4:21 and 7:3). In our verse, the *Sforno* once again tells us that the hardening of Pharaoh's heart on his own (v. 34) was in danger of eroding, so God strengthened his resolve, as He had said He would do when He first spoke to Moses. All this is for the purpose of permitting Pharaoh to repent voluntarily and sincerely — being that the first nine plagues were visited upon Egypt for the sole purpose of bringing them to repentance.

פרשת בא

Parashas Bo

י א וַיֹּאמֶר יהוה אֶל־מֹשֶׁה בֹּא אֶל־פַּרְעֹה כִּי־אֲנִי הִכְבַּדְתִּי אֶת־לִבּוֹ וְאֶת־לֵב
ב עֲבָדָיו לְמַעַן שִׁתִי אֹתֹתַי אֵלֶּה בְּקִרְבּוֹ׃ וּלְמַעַן תְּסַפֵּר בְּאָזְנֵי בִנְךָ וּבֶן־בִּנְךָ
אֵת אֲשֶׁר הִתְעַלַּלְתִּי בְּמִצְרַיִם וְאֶת־אֹתֹתַי אֲשֶׁר־שַׂמְתִּי בָם וִידַעְתֶּם כִּי־
ג אֲנִי יהוה׃ וַיָּבֹא מֹשֶׁה וְאַהֲרֹן אֶל־פַּרְעֹה וַיֹּאמְרוּ אֵלָיו כֹּה־אָמַר יהוה
ד אֱלֹהֵי הָעִבְרִים עַד־מָתַי מֵאַנְתָּ לֵעָנֹת מִפָּנָי שַׁלַּח עַמִּי וְיַעַבְדֻנִי׃ כִּי אִם־

X

1. כִּי אֲנִי הִכְבַּדְתִּי — *For I have hardened.* Although Moses had said, *'I know that as yet you do not fear'* (9:30), he thought that even though he (Pharaoh) did not humble himself before God, the Blessed One, (motivated) by reverence of His greatness, nonetheless he will listen because he would not be able to withstand the evil of the plagues. The reason he (Moses) thought so was because he saw that as a result of the plague (of hail) he said, ה׳ הַצַּדִּיק, *HASHEM is righteous* (9:27). However, when he saw that following all this he (still) did not hearken, Moses felt that the warnings were in vain, for even though he could not tolerate (the plagues), he would not listen. Therefore, God, the Blessed One, says to him, 'Even though presently he himself also hardened his heart (9:34), (but) behold I already *hardened his heart* at the plague of boils. All this is (for the purpose) of increasing the signs in the midst of Egypt, so that some of them might repent, and (secondly) that Israel may tell (the story) to (future) generations and recognize My greatness and goodness.' Therefore the warning is suitable even though Pharaoh will not listen.

לְמַעַן שִׁתִי אֹתֹתַי אֵלֶּה בְּקִרְבּוֹ — *That I might show these signs in their midst.* So that through them, the people will recognize My greatness and repent of their wickedness.

2. וּלְמַעַן תְּסַפֵּר — *And that you may tell.* So that the generations of Israel shall know all these (events).

וִידַעְתֶּם — *That you may know.* You, your generations and the Egyptians.

3. עַד מָתַי מֵאַנְתָּ — *How long will you refuse?* Since you have not humbled yourself

NOTES

X

1. כִּי אֲנִי הִכְבַּדְתִּי — *For I have hardened.* The difficulty of this verse is obvious. If God has hardened Pharaoh's heart, then what is the purpose of sending Moses to him? The *Sforno* resolves this difficulty by reviewing God's actions, Pharaoh's responses, and Moses's own statements during the previous two plagues, i.e., boils and hail. When Pharaoh said, *'God is right,'* during the plague of hail, Moses was convinced that the pressure of the plagues had finally broken down his resistance. However, when Pharaoh stubbornly continued to refuse to humble himself before God, Moses was frustrated and felt that any future warnings would be futile. God, however, reassured Moses that there is a purpose in coming to Pharaoh, for even though He had hardened Pharaoh's heart *before* the plague of hail, i.e., during that of boils which enabled Pharaoh to withstand the pressure of this last plague (i.e., hail), nonetheless there are two reasons for bringing additional plagues as signs and warnings. One is in the hope that some of Pharaoh's subjects will repent, even if he does not. The second is so that Israel will tell their children and children's children of God's greatness and goodness.

2. וִידַעְתֶּם — *That you may know.* The *Sforno* interprets the word *you* in the phrase *that you may know* as referring not only to the Israelites but to those sensitive Egyptians, who will be impressed and moved to repentance, as well.

3. עַד מָתַי מֵאַנְתָּ — *How long will you refuse?* No one plague had proven to be of sufficient

ה מָאֵן אַתָּה לְשַׁלֵּחַ אֶת־עַמִּי הִנְנִי מֵבִיא מָחָר אַרְבֶּה בִּגְבֻלֶךָ: וְכִסָּה אֶת־עֵין
הָאָרֶץ וְלֹא יוּכַל לִרְאֹת אֶת־הָאָרֶץ וְאָכַל | אֶת־יֶתֶר הַפְּלֵטָה הַנִּשְׁאֶרֶת
ו לָכֶם מִן־הַבָּרָד וְאָכַל אֶת־כָּל־הָעֵץ הַצֹּמֵחַ לָכֶם מִן־הַשָּׂדֶה: וּמָלְאוּ בָתֶּיךָ
וּבָתֵּי כָל־עֲבָדֶיךָ וּבָתֵּי כָל־מִצְרַיִם אֲשֶׁר לֹא־רָאוּ אֲבֹתֶיךָ וַאֲבוֹת אֲבֹתֶיךָ
ז מִיּוֹם הֱיוֹתָם עַל־הָאֲדָמָה עַד הַיּוֹם הַזֶּה וַיִּפֶן וַיֵּצֵא מֵעִם פַּרְעֹה: וַיֹּאמְרוּ
עַבְדֵי פַרְעֹה אֵלָיו עַד־מָתַי יִהְיֶה זֶה לָנוּ לְמוֹקֵשׁ שַׁלַּח אֶת־הָאֲנָשִׁים
ח וְיַעַבְדוּ אֶת־יהוה אֱלֹהֵיהֶם הֲטֶרֶם תֵּדַע כִּי אָבְדָה מִצְרָיִם: וַיּוּשַׁב אֶת־
מֹשֶׁה וְאֶת־אַהֲרֹן אֶל־פַּרְעֹה וַיֹּאמֶר אֲלֵהֶם לְכוּ עִבְדוּ אֶת־יהוה אֱלֹהֵיכֶם
ט מִי וָמִי הַהֹלְכִים: וַיֹּאמֶר מֹשֶׁה בִּנְעָרֵינוּ וּבִזְקֵנֵינוּ נֵלֵךְ בְּבָנֵינוּ וּבִבְנוֹתֵנוּ
י בְּצֹאנֵנוּ וּבִבְקָרֵנוּ נֵלֵךְ כִּי חַג־יהוה לָנוּ: וַיֹּאמֶר אֲלֵהֶם יְהִי כֵן יהוה עִמָּכֶם
יא כַּאֲשֶׁר אֲשַׁלַּח אֶתְכֶם וְאֶת־טַפְּכֶם רְאוּ כִּי רָעָה נֶגֶד פְּנֵיכֶם: לֹא כֵן לְכוּ־נָא
הַגְּבָרִים וְעִבְדוּ אֶת־יהוה כִּי אֹתָהּ אַתֶּם מְבַקְשִׁים וַיְגָרֶשׁ אֹתָם מֵאֵת פְּנֵי
שני יב פַרְעֹה: וַיֹּאמֶר יהוה אֶל־מֹשֶׁה נְטֵה יָדְךָ עַל־אֶרֶץ מִצְרַיִם
בָּאַרְבֶּה וְיַעַל עַל־אֶרֶץ מִצְרָיִם וְיֹאכַל אֶת־כָּל־עֵשֶׂב הָאָרֶץ אֵת כָּל־אֲשֶׁר
יג הִשְׁאִיר הַבָּרָד: וַיֵּט מֹשֶׁה אֶת־מַטֵּהוּ עַל־אֶרֶץ מִצְרַיִם וַיהוה נִהַג רוּחַ־קָדִים
בָּאָרֶץ כָּל־הַיּוֹם הַהוּא וְכָל־הַלָּיְלָה הַבֹּקֶר הָיָה וְרוּחַ הַקָּדִים נָשָׂא אֶת־

---

now, even after observing My mastery (lit., 'ability') over the enveloping atmosphere (surrounding the earth, without which) you cannot live even for a moment, there is no hope that you will repent impelled by the force of any great plague; but perhaps you *will* repent from the force of their constancy over a long period. Therefore, it is proper to ask, 'Until what time will the constancy of your refusal (match) the ongoing constancy of the plagues?'

5. וְאָכַל אֶת כָּל הָעֵץ — *And shall eat every tree* . . . i.e., destroy it, similar to וְהָיָה לֶאֱכֹל, *and they shall be devoured (Deut.* 31:17), and כִּי אָכַל אֶת יַעֲקֹב, *for they have devoured Jacob (Psalms* 79:7).

10. כַּאֲשֶׁר אֲשַׁלַּח אֶתְכֶם וְאֶת טַפְּכֶם — *As I will let you go and your little ones.* How much more so the cattle.

רְאוּ כִּי רָעָה נֶגֶד פְּנֵיכֶם — *See that evil is before your face.* See that with your actions you are headed to an evil (end) which you will (certainly) reach, similar to הוֹלֵךְ לָמוּת, *I am going to die (Genesis* 25:32), and רַגְלֶיהָ יֹרְדוֹת מָוֶת, *Her feet go down to death (Proverbs* 5:5), as our Sages say, 'And they run to the destructive pit' (*Berachos* 28b).

12. עַל אֶרֶץ מִצְרַיִם בָּאַרְבֶּה — *Over the land of Egypt for the locusts.* Toward the direction of the locusts which is south, as though commanding the locusts to come, similar to, וְנָשָׂא נֵס לַגּוֹיִם מֵרָחוֹק, וְשָׁרַק לוֹ מִקְצֵה הָאָרֶץ, וְהִנֵּה מְהֵרָה קַל יָבוֹא, *And He will lift up a banner to the nations from afar, and will whistle to them from the ends of the earth and behold they shall come with speed swiftly (Isaiah* 5:26).

NOTES

strength to break Pharaoh's will. The cumulative effect of all the plagues, and their incessant impact will, however, take its toll. The only question is when. This is the question posed to Pharaoh by Moses and Aaron, *'How long will you refuse?'* The implication being that at some point God's endurance will outlast Pharaoh's persistence.

יד הָאַרְבֶּה: וַיַּעַל הָאַרְבֶּה עַל כָּל־אֶרֶץ מִצְרַיִם וַיָּנַח בְּכֹל גְּבוּל מִצְרָיִם כָּבֵד
טו מְאֹד לְפָנָיו לֹא־הָיָה כֵן אַרְבֶּה כָּמֹהוּ וְאַחֲרָיו לֹא יִהְיֶה־כֵּן: וַיְכַס אֶת־עֵין
כָּל־הָאָרֶץ וַתֶּחְשַׁךְ הָאָרֶץ וַיֹּאכַל אֶת־כָּל־עֵשֶׂב הָאָרֶץ וְאֵת כָּל־פְּרִי הָעֵץ
אֲשֶׁר הוֹתִיר הַבָּרָד וְלֹא־נוֹתַר כָּל־יֶרֶק בָּעֵץ וּבְעֵשֶׂב הַשָּׂדֶה בְּכָל־אֶרֶץ
טז מִצְרָיִם: וַיְמַהֵר פַּרְעֹה לִקְרֹא לְמֹשֶׁה וּלְאַהֲרֹן וַיֹּאמֶר חָטָאתִי לַיהוָה
יז אֱלֹהֵיכֶם וְלָכֶם: וְעַתָּה שָׂא נָא חַטָּאתִי אַךְ הַפַּעַם וְהַעְתִּירוּ לַיהוָה אֱלֹהֵיכֶם
יח-יט וְיָסֵר מֵעָלַי רַק אֶת־הַמָּוֶת הַזֶּה: וַיֵּצֵא מֵעִם פַּרְעֹה וַיֶּעְתַּר אֶל־יהוָה: וַיַּהֲפֹךְ
יהוָה רוּחַ־יָם חָזָק מְאֹד וַיִּשָּׂא אֶת־הָאַרְבֶּה וַיִּתְקָעֵהוּ יָמָּה סּוּף לֹא נִשְׁאַר
כ אַרְבֶּה אֶחָד בְּכֹל גְּבוּל מִצְרָיִם: וַיְחַזֵּק יהוָה אֶת־לֵב פַּרְעֹה וְלֹא שִׁלַּח
אֶת־בְּנֵי יִשְׂרָאֵל:
כא וַיֹּאמֶר יהוָה אֶל־מֹשֶׁה נְטֵה יָדְךָ עַל־הַשָּׁמַיִם וִיהִי חֹשֶׁךְ עַל־אֶרֶץ מִצְרָיִם
כב וְיָמֵשׁ חֹשֶׁךְ: וַיֵּט מֹשֶׁה אֶת־יָדוֹ עַל־הַשָּׁמָיִם וַיְהִי חֹשֶׁךְ־אֲפֵלָה בְּכָל־אֶרֶץ
כג מִצְרַיִם שְׁלֹשֶׁת יָמִים: לֹא־רָאוּ אִישׁ אֶת־אָחִיו וְלֹא־קָמוּ אִישׁ מִתַּחְתָּיו
שלישי כד שְׁלֹשֶׁת יָמִים וּלְכָל־בְּנֵי יִשְׂרָאֵל הָיָה אוֹר בְּמוֹשְׁבֹתָם: וַיִּקְרָא פַרְעֹה
אֶל־מֹשֶׁה וַיֹּאמֶר לְכוּ עִבְדוּ אֶת־יהוָה רַק צֹאנְכֶם וּבְקַרְכֶם יֻצָּג גַּם־טַפְּכֶם
כה יֵלֵךְ עִמָּכֶם: וַיֹּאמֶר מֹשֶׁה גַּם־אַתָּה תִּתֵּן בְּיָדֵנוּ זְבָחִים וְעֹלֹת וְעָשִׂינוּ לַיהוָה
כו אֱלֹהֵינוּ: וְגַם־מִקְנֵנוּ יֵלֵךְ עִמָּנוּ לֹא תִשָּׁאֵר פַּרְסָה כִּי מִמֶּנּוּ נִקַּח לַעֲבֹד
אֶת־יהוָה אֱלֹהֵינוּ וַאֲנַחְנוּ לֹא־נֵדַע מַה־נַּעֲבֹד אֶת־יהוָה עַד־בֹּאֵנוּ שָׁמָּה:
כז-כח וַיְחַזֵּק יהוָה אֶת־לֵב פַּרְעֹה וְלֹא אָבָה לְשַׁלְּחָם: וַיֹּאמֶר־לוֹ פַרְעֹה לֵךְ מֵעָלָי
כט הִשָּׁמֶר לְךָ אַל־תֹּסֶף רְאוֹת פָּנַי כִּי בְּיוֹם רְאֹתְךָ פָנַי תָּמוּת: וַיֹּאמֶר מֹשֶׁה

---

16. וַיְמַהֵר פַּרְעֹה — *And Pharaoh made haste.* Before the locust could consume the roots of the wheat and spelt and the rest of the herbage.

21. נְטֵה יָדְךָ עַל הַשָּׁמַיִם — *Stretch out your hand toward heaven.* To that part of the atmosphere which is called heaven (שָׁמַיִם), as explained in *Genesis* (1:7).

וְיָמֵשׁ חֹשֶׁךְ — *And darkness will depart.* And the natural (normal) darkness of night will be removed. For indeed the darkness of night is atmosphere prepared to receive light. It is only dark due to the absence of light. This darkness, however, will be a substance that cannot receive light because of its great density (thickness), not because of the absence of light, and since it is not prepared to receive (light), therefore . . .

23. לֹא רָאוּ אִישׁ אֶת אָחִיו — *They saw not one another.* For the light of a candle and torch was not sufficient (to illuminate this darkness).

NOTES

16. וַיְמַהֵר פַּרְעֹה — *And Pharaoh made haste.* The *Sforno* says, 'the roots of the wheat' because the produce itself was already consumed by the locusts. The only thing remaining were the roots.

21. נְטֵה יָדְךָ עַל הַשָּׁמַיִם — *Stretch out your hand toward heaven.* For the definition of שָׁמַיִם *(heaven)* see the *Sforno* on *Genesis* 1:7,8 and the explanatory notes there.

וְיָמֵשׁ חֹשֶׁךְ — *And darkness will depart.* The verb וְיָמֵשׁ is usually interpreted as meaning a darkness that was so intense and substantive it could be *felt*. The *Sforno*, however, interprets it as the *hiphil* of the root מוש, *to depart*, or *remove*. The meaning of the phrase is thus: the usual normal darkness of the night would

כֵּן דִּבַּרְתָּ לֹא־אֹסִף עוֹד רְאוֹת פָּנֶיךָ׃

יא א וַיֹּאמֶר יהוה אֶל־מֹשֶׁה עוֹד נֶגַע אֶחָד אָבִיא עַל־פַּרְעֹה וְעַל־מִצְרַיִם אַחֲרֵי־
ב כֵן יְשַׁלַּח אֶתְכֶם מִזֶּה כְּשַׁלְּחוֹ כָּלָה גָּרֵשׁ יְגָרֵשׁ אֶתְכֶם מִזֶּה׃ דַּבֶּר־נָא בְּאָזְנֵי
הָעָם וְיִשְׁאֲלוּ אִישׁ ׀ מֵאֵת רֵעֵהוּ וְאִשָּׁה מֵאֵת רְעוּתָהּ כְּלֵי־כֶסֶף וּכְלֵי זָהָב׃
ג וַיִּתֵּן יהוה אֶת־חֵן הָעָם בְּעֵינֵי מִצְרָיִם גַּם ׀ הָאִישׁ מֹשֶׁה גָּדוֹל מְאֹד בְּאֶרֶץ
רביעי ד מִצְרַיִם בְּעֵינֵי עַבְדֵי־פַרְעֹה וּבְעֵינֵי הָעָם׃ וַיֹּאמֶר מֹשֶׁה

---

29. לֹא אֹסִף עוֹד רְאוֹת פָּנֶיךָ — *I will see your face no more.* For you shall die, similar to, לֹא תוֹסִפוּ לִרְאֹתָם עוֹד עַד עוֹלָם, *You shall see them again no more forever* (14:13). When he summoned Moses and Aaron that night he did so only through his servants, as it says, וְיָרְדוּ כָל עֲבָדֶיךָ אֵלֶּה אֵלַי, *And all these, your servants, shall come down to me* (11:8).

XI

1. יְשַׁלַּח אֶתְכֶם מִזֶּה כְּשַׁלְּחוֹ — *He shall send you forth from here as he sent you forth (previously).* In the same manner that he willingly sent you and Aaron away, with his *rod of anger*, as it says, וַיְגָרֶשׁ אֹתָם מֵאֵת פְּנֵי פַרְעֹה, *and they were driven out from Pharaoh's presence* (10:11), in a similar manner he will now be forced to send you forth in anguish.

כָּלָה גָּרֵשׁ יְגָרֵשׁ אֶתְכֶם — *He shall surely thrust all of you out.* But the (previous) time he drove only the two of you out and it was only from his presence, now however he will drive all of you out of the entire place (i.e., Egypt). Indeed this is the measure of God's justice, that when a man stubbornly refuses to comply with the wishes of His Maker, he will (ultimately) do what he fled from doing, in distress and sorrow, against his will, as it says, תַּחַת אֲשֶׁר לֹא עָבַדְתָּ . . . וְעָבַדְתָּ אֶת אֹיְבֶיךָ, *because you did not serve HASHEM . . . therefore shall you serve your enemy (Deut.* 28:47,48), (and also) אִם לֹא כַּאֲשֶׁר דִּבַּרְתֶּם בְּאָזְנָי כֵּן אֶעֱשֶׂה לָכֶם, *As you have spoken in My ears, so will I do to you (Numbers* 14:28). As our Sages say: 'He who abolishes (nullifies) the Torah when he is rich, will eventually do so in poverty' (*Avos* 4:10).

2. דַּבֶּר נָא בְּאָזְנֵי הָעָם וְיִשְׁאֲלוּ — *Speak, I pray you, in the ears of the people and let them ask (borrow).* They (i.e., the Jews) should not worry lest they (i.e., the Egyptians) will be induced to pursue them because of the monetary (loss), for that (in itself) will be their salvation.

3. גַּם הָאִישׁ מֹשֶׁה גָּדוֹל מְאֹד — *Moreover, the man Moses was very great.* And in his honor they increased (the amount) loaned.

NOTES

depart and be replaced by a dense unique darkness which no light could penetrate.

XI

1. יְשַׁלַּח אֶתְכֶם מִזֶּה כְּשַׁלְּחוֹ כָּלָה גָּרֵשׁ — *He shall send you forth from here as he sent you forth (previously), he shall surely thrust.* The *Sforno* explains the word כְּשַׁלְּחוֹ, *as he sent*, as referring back to the time when Pharaoh drove Moses and Aaron out of his court. The phrase גָּרֵשׁ, *to cast* or *thrust out*, is used here, as well as in 10:11, indicating a parallel between these two cases. The sense of this verse then is as follows. On a previous occasion Pharaoh drove Moses and Aaron out of his presence by his own volition. Now he would thrust out all the Israelites from his land under Divine compulsion. The word כָּלָה, *everyone*, is connected to the concluding part of the verse, i.e., all will be thrust out.

The *Sforno* draws an important moral lesson from this verse. What man fails to do of his free will, he will eventually be forced by God to do under adverse circumstances.

ה כֹּה אָמַר יהוה כַּחֲצֹת הַלַּיְלָה אֲנִי יוֹצֵא בְּתוֹךְ מִצְרָיִם: וּמֵת כָּל־בְּכוֹר
בְּאֶרֶץ מִצְרַיִם מִבְּכוֹר פַּרְעֹה הַיֹּשֵׁב עַל־כִּסְאוֹ עַד בְּכוֹר הַשִּׁפְחָה אֲשֶׁר
ו אַחַר הָרֵחָיִם וְכֹל בְּכוֹר בְּהֵמָה: וְהָיְתָה צְעָקָה גְדֹלָה בְּכָל־אֶרֶץ מִצְרָיִם
ז אֲשֶׁר כָּמֹהוּ לֹא נִהְיָתָה וְכָמֹהוּ לֹא תֹסִף: וּלְכֹל | בְּנֵי יִשְׂרָאֵל לֹא
יֶחֱרַץ־כֶּלֶב לְשֹׁנוֹ לְמֵאִישׁ וְעַד־בְּהֵמָה לְמַעַן תֵּדְעוּן אֲשֶׁר יַפְלֶה יהוה בֵּין
ח מִצְרַיִם וּבֵין יִשְׂרָאֵל: וְיָרְדוּ כָל־עֲבָדֶיךָ אֵלֶּה אֵלַי וְהִשְׁתַּחֲווּ־לִי לֵאמֹר צֵא
אַתָּה וְכָל־הָעָם אֲשֶׁר־בְּרַגְלֶיךָ וְאַחֲרֵי־כֵן אֵצֵא וַיֵּצֵא מֵעִם־פַּרְעֹה בָּחֳרִי־
ט אָף: וַיֹּאמֶר יהוה אֶל־מֹשֶׁה לֹא־יִשְׁמַע אֲלֵיכֶם פַּרְעֹה
י לְמַעַן רְבוֹת מוֹפְתַי בְּאֶרֶץ מִצְרָיִם: וּמֹשֶׁה וְאַהֲרֹן עָשׂוּ אֶת־כָּל־הַמֹּפְתִים

5. מִבְּכוֹר פַּרְעֹה . . . עַד בְּכוֹר הַשִּׁפְחָה — *From the firstborn of Pharaoh even unto the firstborn of the maidservant.* From the most honored to the most base of all. (The expression used later however) מִבְּכֹר פַּרְעֹה . . . עַד בְּכוֹר הַשְּׁבִי, *From the firstborn of Pharaoh . . . to the firstborn of the captive* (12:29) implies from the most guilty in this matter (of slavery and hard labor) to the least guilty of all.

6. אֲשֶׁר כָּמֹהוּ לֹא נִהְיָתָה — *Such as there has been none like it.* That in such a night there was never such a cry, for considering that it was not a night of battle with enemy soldiers (invading) when indeed there is a great cry in the city, as we find, קוֹל צְעָקָה מִשַּׁעַר הַדָּגִים וִילָלָה מִן הַמִּשְׁנֶה וְשֶׁבֶר גָּדוֹל מֵהַגְּבָעוֹת, *The noise of a cry from the fish gate, and a wailing from the second quarter and a great crashing from the hills* (*Zephaniah* 1:10). But on a night such as this, when Egypt was at peace, there never was, nor would there be, a cry such as this.

8. וְאַחֲרֵי כֵן אֵצֵא — *And after that I will go out.* I will not leave immediately when you ask me to go out, only *after that;* for I will wait until morning.

9. וַיֹּאמֶר ה' אֶל מֹשֶׁה לֹא יִשְׁמַע אֲלֵיכֶם פַּרְעֹה — *And HASHEM said to Moses, 'Pharaoh will not listen to you.'* Being that God, the Blessed One, said to Moses that the reason for the hardening of Pharaoh's heart was because God hardened his (Pharaoh's) spirit in order to increase His wonders so that the Egyptians and Israel would (come) to recognize His greatness and goodness, as it says, וִידַעְתֶּם כִּי אֲנִי ה', *That you may know that I am HASHEM* (10:2). And being that Moses and Aaron together occupied themselves in performing these wonders, so as to implement (lit., 'complete') this intent (of God), therefore, now that God, the Blessed One, has decreed to punish Egypt and save Israel from that punishment, even though some of them were to an

NOTES

5. מִבְּכוֹר פַּרְעֹה . . . עַד בְּכוֹר הַשִּׁפְחָה — *From the firstborn of Pharaoh even unto the firstborn of the maidservant.* The parallel passage in 12:29 alters the latter part of the verse from *firstborn of the maidservant* to *firstborn of the captive.* The reason for this variation is explained by the *Sforno* in his interpretation of this verse.

6. אֲשֶׁר כָּמֹהוּ לֹא נִהְיָתָה — *Such as there has been none like it.* The Torah does not exaggerate. Certainly there can be circumstances which would cause an outcry equal to this one. However, during a time of peace as opposed to war, such a great cry never was and never will be.

9. לֹא יִשְׁמַע אֲלֵיכֶם פַּרְעֹה — *Pharaoh will not listen to you.* The *Sforno* explains the reason for inserting verses 9 and 10 here, which repeat the reason for hardening Pharaoh's heart and also couples Aaron with Moses regarding the performance of the wonders. This concluding verse of chapter 11 explains the reason for including Aaron in the opening

הָאֵלֶּה לִפְנֵי פַרְעֹה וַיְחַזֵּק יהוה אֶת־לֵב פַּרְעֹה וְלֹא־שִׁלַּח אֶת־בְּנֵי־יִשְׂרָאֵל
יב א מֵאַרְצוֹ׃ וַיֹּאמֶר יהוה אֶל־מֹשֶׁה וְאֶל־אַהֲרֹן בְּאֶרֶץ מִצְרַיִם
ב לֵאמֹר׃ הַחֹדֶשׁ הַזֶּה לָכֶם רֹאשׁ חֳדָשִׁים רִאשׁוֹן הוּא לָכֶם לְחָדְשֵׁי הַשָּׁנָה׃
ג דַּבְּרוּ אֶל־כָּל־עֲדַת יִשְׂרָאֵל לֵאמֹר בֶּעָשֹׂר לַחֹדֶשׁ הַזֶּה וְיִקְחוּ לָהֶם אִישׁ
ד שֶׂה לְבֵית־אָבֹת שֶׂה לַבָּיִת׃ וְאִם־יִמְעַט הַבַּיִת מִהְיוֹת מִשֶּׂה וְלָקַח הוּא
וּשְׁכֵנוֹ הַקָּרֹב אֶל־בֵּיתוֹ בְּמִכְסַת נְפָשֹׁת אִישׁ לְפִי אָכְלוֹ תָּכֹסּוּ עַל־הַשֶּׂה׃
ה־ו שֶׂה תָמִים זָכָר בֶּן־שָׁנָה יִהְיֶה לָכֶם מִן־הַכְּבָשִׂים וּמִן־הָעִזִּים תִּקָּחוּ׃ וְהָיָה

---

extent worthy (of punishment), and (also) to destroy the Egyptian gods so that the punishment could come to pass — and all this through the *Pesach* sacrifice, as it says: וְעָבַרְתִּי . . . וְהִכֵּיתִי . . . אֶעֱשֶׂה שְׁפָטִים . . . וּפָסַחְתִּי, *And I will go through . . . and will smite . . . and execute judgment . . . and I will pass over* (12:12,13). He wanted this commandment (i.e., which follows *this month,* etc. — 12:2) to be (given) through Moses and Aaron together, for just as they both attempted to bring Egypt to repentance and teach the children of Israel, so shall they both merit to bring into reality the fruit of their efforts.

XII

2. הַחֹדֶשׁ הַזֶּה לָכֶם רֹאשׁ חֳדָשִׁים — *This month shall be to you the beginning of months.* Henceforth the months (of the year) shall be yours, to do with them as you will. During the bondage, however, your days (time) did not belong to you but (were used) to work for others and fulfill their will, therefore . . .

רִאשׁוֹן הוּא לָכֶם לְחָדְשֵׁי הַשָּׁנָה — *It shall be the first month of the year to you.* For in (this month) your existence as a people of (free) choice began.

4. וּשְׁכֵנוֹ הַקָּרֹב אֶל בֵּיתוֹ — *And the neighbor closest to his house.* Even though there may be many Egyptians residing between the house of a Hebrew and the house of his friend, (nonetheless) that Hebrew is called his neighbor, for he is the nearest of all the Hebrews.

NOTES

verses of the next chapter. Since Aaron was involved with his brother in performing the wonders, whose purpose was to teach and inspire, it is only fair and proper that he also be included as the moment of redemption arrives. *Let the one who guards the fig tree eat of its fruit (Proverbs 27:18).*

XII

2. הַחֹדֶשׁ הַזֶּה לָכֶם . . . רִאשׁוֹן הוּא לָכֶם — *This month shall be to you . . . It shall be the first . . . to you.* The word לָכֶם, *to you,* appears twice in this verse. The *Sforno* interprets the sense of the verse in a manner which explains the reason for this repetition. A slave has no time which he can call his own. He has no freedom of choice for he is totally subservient to his master who decides how his time shall be used and thereby controls his days and months. Therefore freedom would grant the Hebrew slaves mastery over their days and months, and they themselves would decide how to utilize their time. Hence, *this month is 'to you.'* It also represents the first month of a new era for the nation of Israel (indeed a new existence), which is also categorized as being *to you.* Therefore the word לָכֶם is repeated.

4. וּשְׁכֵנוֹ הַקָּרֹב אֶל בֵּיתוֹ — *And the neighbor closest to his house.* Normally the term *neighbor* refers to one who lives adjacent to, or in close proximity of, another resident or person. In this particular instance, however, the word קָרוֹב, *close,* qualifies the word שָׁכֵן, *neighbor.* Only a fellow Hebrew, who is a קָרוֹב, in the sense of being *close* to you in belief and practice, is a neighbor that can join with you in the *Pesach* sacrifice.

לָכֶם֙ לְמִשְׁמֶ֔רֶת עַ֠ד אַרְבָּעָ֨ה עָשָׂ֥ר י֛וֹם לַחֹ֥דֶשׁ הַזֶּ֖ה וְשָׁחֲט֣וּ אֹת֑וֹ כֹּ֛ל קְהַ֥ל

ז עֲדַת־יִשְׂרָאֵ֖ל בֵּ֣ין הָעַרְבָּֽיִם: וְלָֽקְחוּ֙ מִן־הַדָּ֔ם וְנָ֥תְנ֛וּ עַל־שְׁתֵּ֥י הַמְּזוּזֹ֖ת וְעַל־

ח הַמַּשְׁק֑וֹף עַ֚ל הַבָּ֣תִּ֔ים אֲשֶׁר־יֹֽאכְל֥וּ אֹת֖וֹ בָּהֶֽם: וְאָֽכְל֥וּ אֶת־הַבָּשָׂ֖ר בַּלַּ֣יְלָה

ט הַזֶּ֑ה צְלִי־אֵ֣שׁ וּמַצּ֔וֹת עַל־מְרֹרִ֖ים יֹֽאכְלֻֽהוּ: אַל־תֹּֽאכְל֤וּ מִמֶּ֨נּוּ֙ נָ֔א וּבָשֵׁ֥ל

י מְבֻשָּׁ֖ל בַּמָּ֑יִם כִּ֣י אִם־צְלִי־אֵ֔שׁ רֹאשׁ֥וֹ עַל־כְּרָעָ֖יו וְעַל־קִרְבּֽוֹ: וְלֹא־תוֹתִ֥ירוּ

יא מִמֶּ֖נּוּ עַד־בֹּ֑קֶר וְהַנֹּתָ֥ר מִמֶּ֛נּוּ עַד־בֹּ֖קֶר בָּאֵ֥שׁ תִּשְׂרֹֽפוּ: וְכָ֘כָה֮ תֹּֽאכְל֣וּ אֹתוֹ֒

מָתְנֵיכֶ֣ם חֲגֻרִ֔ים נַֽעֲלֵיכֶם֙ בְּרַגְלֵיכֶ֔ם וּמַקֶּלְכֶ֖ם בְּיֶדְכֶ֑ם וַֽאֲכַלְתֶּ֤ם אֹתוֹ֙ בְּחִפָּז֔וֹן

יב פֶּ֥סַח ה֖וּא לַֽיהוָֽה: וְעָֽבַרְתִּ֣י בְאֶֽרֶץ־מִצְרַ֘יִם֮ בַּלַּ֣יְלָה הַזֶּה֒ וְהִכֵּיתִ֤י כָל־בְּכוֹר֙

בְּאֶ֣רֶץ מִצְרַ֔יִם מֵֽאָדָ֖ם וְעַד־בְּהֵמָ֑ה וּבְכָל־אֱלֹהֵ֥י מִצְרַ֛יִם אֶֽעֱשֶׂ֥ה שְׁפָטִ֖ים אֲנִ֥י

יג יְהוָֽה: וְהָיָה֩ הַדָּ֨ם לָכֶ֜ם לְאֹ֗ת עַ֤ל הַבָּתִּים֙ אֲשֶׁ֣ר אַתֶּ֣ם שָׁ֔ם וְרָאִ֨יתִי֙ אֶת־הַדָּ֔ם

---

11. מָתְנֵיכֶם חֲגֻרִים — *With your loins girded.* Prepared to travel, similar to וַיְשַׁנֵּס מָתְנָיו, *And he girded his loins* (I Kings 18:46), to demonstrate implicit trust in God, the Blessed One, preparing themselves for the road while they were still in prison.

12. וְעָבַרְתִּי — *I will go through . . .* to level a path for My anger, (something) which no messenger could do.

וְהִכֵּיתִי כָל בְּכוֹר — *And will smite all the firstborn.* I will differentiate between (lit., 'examine') the 'drop' of a firstborn and the 'drop' of one who is not a firstborn.

וּבְכָל אֱלֹהֵי מִצְרַיִם אֶעֱשֶׂה שְׁפָטִים — *And against all the gods of Egypt I will execute judgment.* I will cast down the 'princes on high' who now guide their (destiny) so that this punishment shall come to pass more (fully).

אֲנִי ה׳ — *I am* HASHEM. And all this cannot come to pass except through HASHEM, as it says, אֲנִי ה׳ — אֲנִי הוּא וְלֹא אַחֵר, *I am* HASHEM — *I am He and no other* (Pesach Haggadah). With this (statement, i.e., *I am* HASHEM) the reason is given for all the above, explaining why it was necessary for God Himself to do all the aforementioned, which He did not do with Sennacherib and others.

NOTES

12. וְעָבַרְתִּי . . . וְהִכֵּיתִי כָל בְּכוֹר — *I will go through . . . And will smite all the firstborn.* The *Sforno* in his commentary on this verse explains why it was necessary for God Himself to smite the Egyptian firstborn, unlike other similar historic events when the enemy was also smitten, such as the time Sennacherib's army beleaguered Jerusalem. At that time a messenger sufficed while here, as the *Haggadah* stresses, *I and no other.* In Psalms 78, David describes the many miracles and acts of salvation enacted by God when the Israelites were in Egypt and after their deliverance. When he describes the plague of the firstborn he uses the expression: *He leveled* (יְפַלֵּס) *a path for His wrath* (v. 50). This refers to an exact, undeviating punishment which targets only those who are destined to die while guarding and protecting others. Our Rabbis have taught us that 'Once the de-

stroyer is given permission to destroy he does not differentiate between the innocent and the guilty.' Therefore, to protect the Jewish firstborn, and even those Egyptians who were not really firstborn, it was imperative that God Himself exact this punishment. The word פֶּלֶס also means to balance, which is most appropriate in this context, for only God Himself could so perfectly and exactly focus this plague on those who were the chosen targets, while sparing the others.

וּבְכָל אֱלֹהֵי מִצְרַיִם אֶעֱשֶׂה שְׁפָטִים — *And against all the gods of Egypt I will execute judgment.* Our Sages teach us that every nation has a heavenly representative on high who guides the destiny of his people, in some mysterious manner. Before that nation can be punished, its heavenly prince or lord must first be cast down. This is what the *Sforno* referrs to in his

יד וּפָסַחְתִּי עֲלֵכֶם וְלֹא־יִהְיֶה בָכֶם נֶגֶף לְמַשְׁחִית בְּהַכֹּתִי בְּאֶרֶץ מִצְרָיִם: וְהָיָה
הַיּוֹם הַזֶּה לָכֶם לְזִכָּרוֹן וְחַגֹּתֶם אֹתוֹ חַג לַיהוָה לְדֹרֹתֵיכֶם חֻקַּת עוֹלָם
טו תְּחָגֻּהוּ: שִׁבְעַת יָמִים מַצּוֹת תֹּאכֵלוּ אַךְ בַּיּוֹם הָרִאשׁוֹן תַּשְׁבִּיתוּ שְּׂאֹר
מִבָּתֵּיכֶם כִּי | כָּל־אֹכֵל חָמֵץ וְנִכְרְתָה הַנֶּפֶשׁ הַהִוא מִיִּשְׂרָאֵל מִיּוֹם הָרִאשֹׁן
טז עַד־יוֹם הַשְּׁבִעִי: וּבַיּוֹם הָרִאשׁוֹן מִקְרָא־קֹדֶשׁ וּבַיּוֹם הַשְּׁבִיעִי מִקְרָא־קֹדֶשׁ
יִהְיֶה לָכֶם כָּל־מְלָאכָה לֹא־יֵעָשֶׂה בָהֶם אַךְ אֲשֶׁר יֵאָכֵל לְכָל־נֶפֶשׁ הוּא
יז לְבַדּוֹ יֵעָשֶׂה לָכֶם: וּשְׁמַרְתֶּם אֶת־הַמַּצּוֹת כִּי בְּעֶצֶם הַיּוֹם הַזֶּה הוֹצֵאתִי
אֶת־צִבְאוֹתֵיכֶם מֵאֶרֶץ מִצְרָיִם וּשְׁמַרְתֶּם אֶת־הַיּוֹם הַזֶּה לְדֹרֹתֵיכֶם חֻקַּת
יח עוֹלָם: בָּרִאשֹׁן בְּאַרְבָּעָה עָשָׂר יוֹם לַחֹדֶשׁ בָּעֶרֶב תֹּאכְלוּ מַצֹּת עַד יוֹם
יט הָאֶחָד וְעֶשְׂרִים לַחֹדֶשׁ בָּעָרֶב: שִׁבְעַת יָמִים שְׂאֹר לֹא יִמָּצֵא בְּבָתֵּיכֶם כִּי |

---

13. וְלֹא יִהְיֶה בָכֶם נֶגֶף לְמַשְׁחִית — *And there shall be no plague upon you to destroy you.* The plague will not affect you as a result of the destruction which I (will) visit upon Egypt.

בְּהַכֹּתִי — *When I smite.* For in addition to the plague of the firstborn, He sent upon the people as a whole, עֶבְרָה וָזַעַם וְצָרָה מִשְׁלַחַת מַלְאֲכֵי רָעִים, *wrath, fury and anguish, a delegation of evil angels (Psalms* 78:49). Without the *skipping over* of Israel which God did in His mercy, they would not have been saved from the distress of the rest of Egypt, similar to, פֶּן תִּסָּפֶה בַּעֲוֹן הָעִיר, *lest you be swept away in the iniquity of the city (Genesis* 19:15). He (therefore) commanded them to place the blood as a sign so that they might be saved, all this for לְמַעַן שְׁמִי לְבִלְתִּי הֵחֵל, *the sake of My Name so it be not profaned* (based on *Ezekiel* 20:9) as it is said, וָאֹמַר לָךְ בְּדָמַיִךְ חֲיִי, *And I said to you, in your blood live (Ezekiel* 16:6).

17. וּשְׁמַרְתֶּם אֶת הַמַּצּוֹת — *You shall watch the matzos* (or, *observe the feast of matzos).* Which symbolizes the haste (by which it was made) without waiting for it to leaven.

כִּי בְּעֶצֶם הַיּוֹם הַזֶּה — *For in this selfsame day.* In this (one) day everyone was gathered (assembled) together, a (feat) which normally should have taken several days and nights.

הוֹצֵאתִי אֶת צִבְאוֹתֵיכֶם — *I brought forth your hosts.* Each group, as they were constituted, all together.

NOTES

commentary.

13. וְלֹא יִהְיֶה בָכֶם נֶגֶף לְמַשְׁחִית בְּהַכֹּתִי — *And there shall be no plague upon you to destroy you when I smite.* Since God Himself would exact the punishment of the firstborn on this night, what danger could the Israelites be exposed to that they had to be confined to their houses and reassured that no plague will destroy them? The *Sforno* answers that in addition to the plague of the firstborn many other punishments were visited upon the Egyptians, as enumerated in *Psalms* 78. Exposure to these plagues would have endangered even the Israelites, akin to 'woe to the wicked, woe to his neighbor' (*Succah* 56b); hence the need to remain indoors where the sign of the blood on the lintel and doorposts would guard them. From the *Sforno's* commentary on verse 23 we see that it was a messenger, not God Himself, who inflicted these additional punishments, therefore it was necessary for the Israelites to exercise caution, as explained above. The *Sforno* also implies that the Israelites, relying on their own merits, would not have been worthy to be saved but God rescued them for His Name's sake, as we find from time to time in Scriptures. Hence the

כָּל־אֹכֵל מַחְמֶצֶת וְנִכְרְתָה הַנֶּפֶשׁ הַהִוא מֵעֲדַת יִשְׂרָאֵל בַּגֵּר וּבְאֶזְרַח
כ הָאָרֶץ׃ כָּל־מַחְמֶצֶת לֹא תֹאכֵלוּ בְּכֹל מוֹשְׁבֹתֵיכֶם תֹּאכְלוּ מַצּוֹת׃
חמישי כא וַיִּקְרָא מֹשֶׁה לְכָל־זִקְנֵי יִשְׂרָאֵל וַיֹּאמֶר אֲלֵהֶם מִשְׁכוּ וּקְחוּ לָכֶם צֹאן
כב לְמִשְׁפְּחֹתֵיכֶם וְשַׁחֲטוּ הַפָּסַח׃ וּלְקַחְתֶּם אֲגֻדַּת אֵזוֹב וּטְבַלְתֶּם בַּדָּם
אֲשֶׁר־בַּסַּף וְהִגַּעְתֶּם אֶל־הַמַּשְׁקוֹף וְאֶל־שְׁתֵּי הַמְּזוּזֹת מִן־הַדָּם אֲשֶׁר בַּסָּף
כג וְאַתֶּם לֹא תֵצְאוּ אִישׁ מִפֶּתַח־בֵּיתוֹ עַד־בֹּקֶר׃ וְעָבַר יהוה לִנְגֹּף אֶת־

---

22. מִן הַדָּם אֲשֶׁר בַּסַּף — *From the blood that is in the basin.* For each sprinkling there shall be a dipping, as God commanded when He said, עַל שְׁתֵּי הַמְּזוּזוֹת, *On the two doorposts* (verse 7), which is (to be done) first, followed by עַל הַמַּשְׁקוֹף, *on the lintel.* Now, this is only possible if there are three (separate) sprinklings, to indicate the three *yudin* (i.e., three letters 'י), as our Sages tell us, 'The world to come was created with a *yud*' (*Menachos* 29b). This was also so before the sin of Adam and on the day of the giving of the Torah until the (Golden) Calf was made, כִּי בְּיָהּ ה' צוּר עוֹלָמִים, *For HASHEM, God is an eternal Rock* (*Isaiah* 26:4), i.e., everlasting, for the (letter) *yud* indicates 'eternal expansion.' The upper *yud* indicates the existence of the One in His world, (ruling over) the (other) two eternal worlds.

וְאַתֶּם לֹא תֵצְאוּ — *And none of you shall go out.* For the house will be marked by the blood; (therefore) וְאַתֶּם לֹא תֵצְאוּ, *and you shall not go out*, and only in this manner *He will pass over*, similar to, וְהִתְוִיתָ תָּו, *And set a mark* (*Ezekiel* 9:4).

23. לִנְגֹּף — *To smite* . . . the Egyptian people with עֶבְרָה וָזַעַם וְצָרָה מִשְׁלַחַת מַלְאֲכֵי רָעִים, *wrath, fury and anguish and a delegation of evil messengers* (*Psalms* 78:49), for the (expression) נֶגֶף, *plague*, is used for every plague including those that are not fatal, as it says, וְנָגְפוּ אִשָּׁה הָרָה . . . וְלֹא יִהְיֶה אָסוֹן, *and hurt* (וְנָגְפוּ) *a woman with child . . . and yet no harm follow* (21:22).

NOTES

verse in *Ezekiel* could also mean, בְּדָמַיִךְ, *the blood placed by you* on your doorposts and lintel were effective because of חַיַי, *My life*, i.e., My Name.

22. מִן הַדָּם אֲשֶׁר בַּסַּף — *From the blood that is in the basin.* The *Zohar* states that the three dots of blood placed by the Israelites on the lintel and the two doorposts are similar to three *yudin* which represent God's Name. In the Middle Ages God's name in holy books, including *Siddurim*, was represented by three *yudin*, not two, as the custom is today. The three *yudin* used centuries ago represented three Divine Names. There are those who say that the three *yudin* represent the first letters of the priestly benediction (יְבָרֶכְךָ, יָאֵר, יִשָּׂא). *Rashi* in tractate *Menachos* 29b quotes the *Sefer Yetzirah* which states that at the time of Creation three drops were sprinkled from a letter of God's Name which in turn became water, fire and air. Three drops, as mentioned above, are similar to three dots or three *yudin*. Based upon all of the above we can understand the significance of the three *yudin* mentioned by the *Sforno* in this verse.

The *Sforno* also links these three *yudin* to three worlds that are or could have been everlasting: (a) the world to come; (b) this world from the time of creation to the time of the original sin; and (c) the world of Torah which began with the revelation at Sinai and lasted until the sin of the Golden Calf. The *yud* on the lintel represents God and the world to come. The drops on the doorpost represent what was and could have been eternal worlds. If Adam had not sinned this world would have enjoyed נִצְחִיוּת, *eternity*, and had the Jews not sinned with the Golden Calf, the new world of Torah would have likewise been an everlasting one. These three perfect worlds are each represented by the letter *yud*, which is a simple, perfect dot and reflects 'eternal expansion,' as the *Sforno* puts it. The Talmud (*Menachos* 29b) explains that the letter *yud* was chosen to create the world to come because it is the smallest letter of the alphabet, and by the same token the truly righteous men

מִצְרַ֗יִם וְרָאָ֤ה אֶת־הַדָּם֙ עַל־הַמַּשְׁק֔וֹף וְעַ֖ל שְׁתֵּ֣י הַמְּזוּזֹ֑ת וּפָסַ֤ח יְהוָה֙ עַל־
כד הַפֶּ֔תַח וְלֹ֤א יִתֵּן֙ הַמַּשְׁחִ֔ית לָבֹ֥א אֶל־בָּתֵּיכֶ֖ם לִנְגֹּֽף׃ וּשְׁמַרְתֶּ֖ם אֶת־הַדָּבָ֣ר
כה הַזֶּ֑ה לְחָק־לְךָ֥ וּלְבָנֶ֖יךָ עַד־עוֹלָֽם׃ וְהָיָ֞ה כִּֽי־תָבֹ֣אוּ אֶל־הָאָ֗רֶץ אֲשֶׁ֨ר יִתֵּ֧ן יְהוָ֛ה
כו לָכֶ֖ם כַּאֲשֶׁ֣ר דִּבֵּ֑ר וּשְׁמַרְתֶּ֖ם אֶת־הָעֲבֹדָ֥ה הַזֹּֽאת׃ וְהָיָ֕ה כִּֽי־יֹאמְר֥וּ אֲלֵיכֶ֖ם
כז בְּנֵיכֶ֑ם מָ֛ה הָעֲבֹדָ֥ה הַזֹּ֖את לָכֶֽם׃ וַאֲמַרְתֶּ֡ם זֶֽבַח־פֶּ֨סַח ה֜וּא לַֽיהוָ֗ה אֲשֶׁ֨ר פָּ֜סַח
עַל־בָּתֵּ֤י בְנֵֽי־יִשְׂרָאֵל֙ בְּמִצְרַ֔יִם בְּנָגְפּ֥וֹ אֶת־מִצְרַ֖יִם וְאֶת־בָּתֵּ֣ינוּ הִצִּ֑יל וַיִּקֹּ֥ד
כח הָעָ֖ם וַיִּשְׁתַּחֲוֽוּ׃ וַיֵּלְכ֥וּ וַיַּעֲשׂ֖וּ בְּנֵ֣י יִשְׂרָאֵ֑ל כַּאֲשֶׁ֨ר צִוָּ֧ה יְהוָ֛ה אֶת־מֹשֶׁ֥ה
ששי כט וְאַהֲרֹ֖ן כֵּ֥ן עָשֽׂוּ׃ וַיְהִ֣י ׀ בַּחֲצִ֣י הַלַּ֗יְלָה וַֽיהוָה֮ הִכָּ֣ה כָל־בְּכוֹר֒
בְּאֶ֣רֶץ מִצְרַ֔יִם מִבְּכֹ֤ר פַּרְעֹה֙ הַיֹּשֵׁ֣ב עַל־כִּסְא֔וֹ עַ֚ד בְּכ֣וֹר הַשְּׁבִ֔י אֲשֶׁ֖ר בְּבֵ֣ית
ל הַבּ֑וֹר וְכֹ֖ל בְּכ֥וֹר בְּהֵמָֽה׃ וַיָּ֨קָם פַּרְעֹ֜ה לַ֗יְלָה ה֤וּא וְכָל־עֲבָדָיו֙ וְכָל־מִצְרַ֔יִם
לא וַתְּהִ֛י צְעָקָ֥ה גְדֹלָ֖ה בְּמִצְרָ֑יִם כִּֽי־אֵ֣ין בַּ֔יִת אֲשֶׁ֥ר אֵֽין־שָׁ֖ם מֵֽת׃ וַיִּקְרָא֩ לְמֹשֶׁ֨ה
וּֽלְאַהֲרֹ֜ן לַ֗יְלָה וַיֹּ֙אמֶר֙ ק֤וּמוּ צְּאוּ֙ מִתּ֣וֹךְ עַמִּ֔י גַּם־אַתֶּ֖ם גַּם־בְּנֵ֣י יִשְׂרָאֵ֑ל וּלְכ֛וּ

הַמַּשְׁחִית — *The destroyer* ... (who) destroys the Egyptian people, through *anger, fury,* etc.

26. מָה הָעֲבֹדָה הַזֹּאת לָכֶם — *What is this service to you?* ... (since) it is not on a day of holy convocation, as are other sacrifices, nor is it in the time frame of other sacrifices, which are brought after the morning daily sacrifice and before the evening daily sacrifice. (Also) why shouldn't one offering suffice for all Israel, as is the case with other communal sacrifices?

27. זֶבַח פֶּסַח הוּא לַה׳ — *It is the sacrifice of HASHEM's Pesach.* This sacrifice is brought (to mark) the future passing over on the following midnight, and since one is not permitted to sacrifice at night we must offer it at a time which continues into the following night (i.e., toward evening). And each one must bring this sacrifice, for the miracle occurred with each individual as such, not to the community as a whole.

29. וַה׳ הִכָּה — *And HASHEM smote.* That is, Israel occupied themselves with the commandment of the *Pesach,* while God Himself, at the same time, smote the firstborn Egyptians, so as to redeem them (i.e., Israel).

NOTES

in the world to come are few in numbers, as well as being humble in their demeanor, as suggested by the top of the *yud* which turns down a little.

26-27. מָה הָעֲבֹדָה הַזֹּאת לָכֶם ... זֶבַח פֶּסַח הוּא לַה׳ — *What is this service to you ... It is the sacrifice of HASHEM's Pesach.* Three inquiries are included in the question *'What is this service to you?'* (a) A sacrifice is usually brought on a day of holy convocation (מִקְרָא קֹדֶשׁ), see *Leviticus* 23:5; (b) no sacrifice is brought before or after the daily offering; and (c) a communal sacrifice can fulfill everyone's obligation. The *Pesach* sacrifice therefore puzzles the son who observes that each Israelite brings his own (or at least is a partner to the lamb); it is brought on the *eve* of the holiday, i.e., the fourteenth of Nissan, and it is brought toward evening, *after* the daily sacrifice. The three answers given in verse 27 are that since the miracle affected every individual Israelite it is proper that each one bring a sacrifice; and since the miracle of Passover occurred at night, were it not for the prohibition to bring sacrifices at night the *Pesach* would have been brought the night of the fifteenth of Nissan. We therefore bring it as close as possible to that time, which is toward the evening of the fourteenth, after the evening daily sacrifice.

29. וַה׳ הִכָּה — *And HASHEM smote.* The letter ו׳ is to be understood as a parallelism. The Israelites were occupied with the fulfillment of

לב עִבְדוּ אֶת־יְהוָה כְּדַבֶּרְכֶם: גַּם־צֹאנְכֶם גַּם־בְּקַרְכֶם קְחוּ כַּאֲשֶׁר דִּבַּרְתֶּם
לג וָלֵכוּ וּבֵרַכְתֶּם גַּם־אֹתִי: וַתֶּחֱזַק מִצְרַיִם עַל־הָעָם לְמַהֵר לְשַׁלְּחָם מִן־הָאָרֶץ
לד כִּי אָמְרוּ כֻּלָּנוּ מֵתִים: וַיִּשָּׂא הָעָם אֶת־בְּצֵקוֹ טֶרֶם יֶחְמָץ מִשְׁאֲרֹתָם צְרֻרֹת
לה בְּשִׂמְלֹתָם עַל־שִׁכְמָם: וּבְנֵי־יִשְׂרָאֵל עָשׂוּ כִּדְבַר מֹשֶׁה וַיִּשְׁאֲלוּ מִמִּצְרַיִם
לו כְּלֵי־כֶסֶף וּכְלֵי זָהָב וּשְׂמָלֹת: וַיהוָה נָתַן אֶת־חֵן הָעָם בְּעֵינֵי מִצְרַיִם
וַיַּשְׁאִלוּם וַיְנַצְּלוּ אֶת־מִצְרָיִם:
לז וַיִּסְעוּ בְנֵי־יִשְׂרָאֵל מֵרַעְמְסֵס סֻכֹּתָה כְּשֵׁשׁ־מֵאוֹת אֶלֶף רַגְלִי הַגְּבָרִים לְבַד
לח־לט מִטָּף: וְגַם־עֵרֶב רַב עָלָה אִתָּם וְצֹאן וּבָקָר מִקְנֶה כָּבֵד מְאֹד: וַיֹּאפוּ
אֶת־הַבָּצֵק אֲשֶׁר הוֹצִיאוּ מִמִּצְרַיִם עֻגֹת מַצּוֹת כִּי לֹא חָמֵץ כִּי־גֹרְשׁוּ
מ מִמִּצְרַיִם וְלֹא יָכְלוּ לְהִתְמַהְמֵהַּ וְגַם־צֵדָה לֹא־עָשׂוּ לָהֶם: וּמוֹשַׁב בְּנֵי
מא יִשְׂרָאֵל אֲשֶׁר יָשְׁבוּ בְּמִצְרָיִם שְׁלֹשִׁים שָׁנָה וְאַרְבַּע מֵאוֹת שָׁנָה: וַיְהִי מִקֵּץ
שְׁלֹשִׁים שָׁנָה וְאַרְבַּע מֵאוֹת שָׁנָה וַיְהִי בְּעֶצֶם הַיּוֹם הַזֶּה יָצְאוּ כָּל־צִבְאוֹת
מב יְהוָה מֵאֶרֶץ מִצְרָיִם: לֵיל שִׁמֻּרִים הוּא לַיהוָה לְהוֹצִיאָם מֵאֶרֶץ מִצְרָיִם
הוּא־הַלַּיְלָה הַזֶּה לַיהוָה שִׁמֻּרִים לְכָל־בְּנֵי יִשְׂרָאֵל לְדֹרֹתָם:

---

38. וְצֹאן וּבָקָר — *And flocks and herds* . . . belonging to the mixed multitude that went up with them to dwell among them with all their possessions.

39. כִּי לֹא חָמֵץ — *For it was not leavened* . . . for it had not leavened, due to the brief time period which elapsed from the time they departed Raamses, which is in the land of Egypt, until they reached Succos, which is outside its boundary, as our Sages say, 'For the dough of our forefathers did not have time to become leavened until the King of Kings, the Holy One, Blessed is He, appeared and redeemed them' *(Pesach Haggadah)*. For indeed when they were in Succos, beyond the boundary of Egypt, the pillars of cloud and fire revealed themselves, וַה׳ הֹלֵךְ לִפְנֵיהֶם, *and* H*ASHEM went before them* (see 13:21).

40. אֲשֶׁר יָשְׁבוּ בְּמִצְרָיִם שְׁלֹשִׁים שָׁנָה וְאַרְבַּע מֵאוֹת שָׁנָה — *That they dwelled in Egypt was four hundred and thirty years.* The completion of 430 years (is reckoned) from the time Abraham our father was delivered from Ur Casdim to enter into the Covenant of the Parts, as it says, אֲנִי ה׳ אֲשֶׁר הוֹצֵאתִיךָ מֵאוּר כַּשְׂדִּים, *I am* H*ASHEM Who brought you forth from Ur Casdim (Genesis* 15:7). This is stated in the *Seder Olam* (ch. 1), 'Abraham our father was seventy years old at the Covenant of the Parts.'

42. לֵיל שִׁמֻּרִים הוּא לַה׳ לְהוֹצִיאָם — *It was a night of watching to* H*ASHEM for bringing them out.* He looked forward to bringing them out, כִּי לֹא עִנָּה מִלִּבּוֹ, *He does*

NOTES

God's commandment while God was occupied with punishing the Egyptians — both at the same time. The latter act can be considered a reward for the former one.

39. כִּי לֹא חָמֵץ — *For it was not leavened.* The heavenly presence, manifested in the pillars of cloud and fire, were not revealed in the unclean land of Egypt. Only when the Israelites crossed the border did they appear.

40. אֲשֶׁר יָשְׁבוּ בְּמִצְרָיִם שְׁלֹשִׁים שָׁנָה וְאַרְבַּע מֵאוֹת שָׁנָה — *That they dwelled in Egypt was four hundred and thirty years.* The number of years recorded in the Torah (430) during which Israel dwelled in Egypt must be calculated, according to the *Sforno* and other commentators, from the time that Abraham

מג וַיֹּאמֶר יהוה אֶל־מֹשֶׁה וְאַהֲרֹן זֹאת חֻקַּת הַפָּסַח כָּל־בֶּן־נֵכָר לֹא־יֹאכַל בּוֹ׃
מד־מה וְכָל־עֶבֶד אִישׁ מִקְנַת־כָּסֶף וּמַלְתָּה אֹתוֹ אָז יֹאכַל בּוֹ׃ תּוֹשָׁב וְשָׂכִיר
מו לֹא־יֹאכַל בּוֹ׃ בְּבַיִת אֶחָד יֵאָכֵל לֹא־תוֹצִיא מִן־הַבַּיִת מִן־הַבָּשָׂר חוּצָה
מז־מח וְעֶצֶם לֹא תִשְׁבְּרוּ־בוֹ׃ כָּל־עֲדַת יִשְׂרָאֵל יַעֲשׂוּ אֹתוֹ׃ וְכִי־יָגוּר אִתְּךָ גֵּר
וְעָשָׂה פֶסַח לַיהוה הִמּוֹל לוֹ כָל־זָכָר וְאָז יִקְרַב לַעֲשֹׂתוֹ וְהָיָה כְּאֶזְרַח
מט הָאָרֶץ וְכָל־עָרֵל לֹא־יֹאכַל בּוֹ׃ תּוֹרָה אַחַת יִהְיֶה לָאֶזְרָח וְלַגֵּר הַגָּר
נ בְּתוֹכְכֶם׃ וַיַּעֲשׂוּ כָּל־בְּנֵי יִשְׂרָאֵל כַּאֲשֶׁר צִוָּה יהוה אֶת־מֹשֶׁה וְאֶת־אַהֲרֹן
נא כֵּן עָשׂוּ׃ וַיְהִי בְּעֶצֶם הַיּוֹם הַזֶּה הוֹצִיא יהוה אֶת־בְּנֵי
יִשְׂרָאֵל מֵאֶרֶץ מִצְרַיִם עַל־צִבְאֹתָם׃
יג שביעי א־ב וַיְדַבֵּר יהוה אֶל־מֹשֶׁה לֵּאמֹר׃ קַדֶּשׁ־לִי כָל־בְּכוֹר פֶּטֶר כָּל־רֶחֶם בִּבְנֵי

---

not willingly afflict (*Lamentations* 3:33), but He did not find Israel ready or worthy for redemption until that night, and it was for this He watched and waited, for He desires kindness as our Sages say, 'The Holy One, Blessed is He, calculated the end' (*Pesach Haggadah*).

הוּא הַלַּיְלָה הַזֶּה לַה׳ שִׁמֻּרִים — *This same night is a night of watching unto* HASHEM. And just as He watched and looked forward to the redemption of Israel all the days of their exile in Egypt, so He watches and waits for the future redemption of Israel, as it says, וְלָכֵן יְחַכֶּה ה׳ לַחֲנַנְכֶם, *And therefore* HASHEM *will wait that He may be gracious to you* (*Isaiah* 30:18).

לְכָל בְּנֵי יִשְׂרָאֵל לְדֹרֹתָם — *For all the children of Israel throughout their generations.* As we are told, 'In Nissan they were redeemed, and in Nissan they will eventually be redeemed' (*Rosh Hashanah* 11a).

43. זֹאת חֻקַּת הַפָּסַח — *This is the ordinance of the Passover.* For (future) generations, regarding those who may partake and regarding the proper place. However, the commandments enumerated above, except for these two, do not apply to future generations, as our Sages state, 'The *Pesach* of generations does not require sprinkling on the lintel and the two doorposts, nor is it eaten in haste' (*Pesachim* 96a).

XIII

2. קַדֶּשׁ לִי כָל בְּכוֹר — *Sanctify unto Me all the firstborn.* They are all obligated to be redeemed similar to all other consecrated objects, in order that they be permitted to do secular work, for without redemption they are prohibited to occupy themselves with secular work, similar to, לֹא תַעֲבֹד בִּבְכֹר שׁוֹרֶךָ, *You shall do no work with the*

NOTES

was seventy years old and entered into a covenant with God.

42. הוּא הַלַּיְלָה הַזֶּה לַה׳ שִׁמֻּרִים — *This same night is a night of watching unto* HASHEM. The expression, הוּא הַלַּיְלָה הַזֶּה, *This same night*, is a cryptic one. What does it refer to? (See *Rashi*.) The *Sforno* explains that it is the promise of our future redemption which will also occur in Nissan. This also explains the concluding part of the verse, *throughout their generations.*

43. זֹאת חֻקַּת הַפָּסַח — *This is the ordinance of the Passover.* The word זאת, *this*, usually is meant to exclude. In this case it also comes to emphasize that only certain laws of the Egyptian Pesach will apply in the future — not all.

ג יִשְׂרָאֵל בָּאָדָם וּבַבְּהֵמָה לִי הוּא: וַיֹּאמֶר מֹשֶׁה אֶל־הָעָם זָכוֹר אֶת־הַיּוֹם
הַזֶּה אֲשֶׁר יְצָאתֶם מִמִּצְרַיִם מִבֵּית עֲבָדִים כִּי בְּחֹזֶק יָד הוֹצִיא יהוה
ד־ה אֶתְכֶם מִזֶּה וְלֹא יֵאָכֵל חָמֵץ: הַיּוֹם אַתֶּם יֹצְאִים בְּחֹדֶשׁ הָאָבִיב: וְהָיָה
כִּי־יְבִיאֲךָ יהוה אֶל־אֶרֶץ הַכְּנַעֲנִי וְהַחִתִּי וְהָאֱמֹרִי וְהַחִוִּי וְהַיְבוּסִי אֲשֶׁר
נִשְׁבַּע לַאֲבֹתֶיךָ לָתֶת לָךְ אֶרֶץ זָבַת חָלָב וּדְבָשׁ וְעָבַדְתָּ אֶת־הָעֲבֹדָה
ו הַזֹּאת בַּחֹדֶשׁ הַזֶּה: שִׁבְעַת יָמִים תֹּאכַל מַצֹּת וּבַיּוֹם הַשְּׁבִיעִי חַג לַיהוה:
ז מַצּוֹת יֵאָכֵל אֵת שִׁבְעַת הַיָּמִים וְלֹא־יֵרָאֶה לְךָ חָמֵץ וְלֹא־יֵרָאֶה לְךָ שְׂאֹר
ח בְּכָל־גְּבֻלֶךָ: וְהִגַּדְתָּ לְבִנְךָ בַּיּוֹם הַהוּא לֵאמֹר בַּעֲבוּר זֶה עָשָׂה יהוה לִי
ט בְּצֵאתִי מִמִּצְרָיִם: וְהָיָה לְךָ לְאוֹת עַל־יָדְךָ וּלְזִכָּרוֹן בֵּין עֵינֶיךָ לְמַעַן תִּהְיֶה
י תּוֹרַת יהוה בְּפִיךָ כִּי בְּיָד חֲזָקָה הוֹצִאֲךָ יהוה מִמִּצְרָיִם: וְשָׁמַרְתָּ אֶת־
הַחֻקָּה הַזֹּאת לְמוֹעֲדָהּ מִיָּמִים יָמִימָה:
יא וְהָיָה כִּי־יְבִאֲךָ יהוה אֶל־אֶרֶץ הַכְּנַעֲנִי כַּאֲשֶׁר נִשְׁבַּע לְךָ וְלַאֲבֹתֶיךָ וּנְתָנָהּ
יב לָךְ: וְהַעֲבַרְתָּ כָל־פֶּטֶר־רֶחֶם לַיהוה וְכָל־פֶּטֶר | שֶׁגֶר בְּהֵמָה אֲשֶׁר יִהְיֶה לְךָ
יג הַזְּכָרִים לַיהוה: וְכָל־פֶּטֶר חֲמֹר תִּפְדֶּה בְשֶׂה וְאִם־לֹא תִפְדֶּה וַעֲרַפְתּוֹ וְכֹל

---

firstborn of your ox (*Deut.* 15:19). Their redemption is according to the valuation of a one-month-old (as set) in the chapter of *Arachin* (valuations) (*Leviticus* 27:6), being that (one month) is the time for his redemption, as it says, וּפְדוּיָו מִבֶּן חֹדֶשׁ תִּפְדֶּה, *And their redemption money from a month old shall you redeem them* (*Numbers* 18:16).

4. הַיּוֹם אַתֶּם יֹצְאִים בְּחֹדֶשׁ הָאָבִיב — *This day you go forth in the month Aviv.* This year it happened that the lunar month of your exodus is the month of *Aviv*; therefore observe this day, and (when necessary) intercalate the year in such a manner that you always make this festival in the month of *Aviv*.

9. כִּי בְּיָד חֲזָקָה הוֹצִאֲךָ — *For with a strong hand (HASHEM) brought you out* . . . when He changed the nature of the (normally) immutable (laws of nature), as it is said regarding the dividing of the waters of the Jordan, לְמַעַן דַּעַת כָּל עַמֵּי הָאָרֶץ אֶת יַד ה׳ כִּי חֲזָקָה הִיא, *So that all the people of the earth shall know that the hand of HASHEM is mighty* (*Joshua* 4:24).

NOTES

XIII

2. קַדֶּשׁ לִי כָל בְּכוֹר — *Sanctify unto Me all the firstborn.* Sanctity implies the exclusive right of use and labor by הֶקְדֵּשׁ, *the sacred domain.* Release can only be through redemption. The Torah establishes here the special sacred status of every Jewish firstborn because of their salvation and rescue by God when He smote the firstborn of the Egyptians and spared them. Although the amount of redemption money is not specified here, it is set at five *shekalim* in *Numbers* 18:16. (See the *Sforno's* commentary in verse 15 regarding the firstborn of Israel.)

4. הַיּוֹם אַתֶּם יֹצְאִים בְּחֹדֶשׁ הָאָבִיב — *This day you go forth in the month Aviv. Aviv* signifies the first ripening of the barley ears. The Torah stresses the word הַיּוֹם, *this day,* to indicate the importance of Pesach coinciding with the season of 'ripe ears.' The previous verse says, זָכוֹר, *remember this day,* while the verse in *Deuteronomy* (16:1) states שָׁמוֹר, *observe* or *guard,* the month of *Aviv*. Since ours is a lunar year, eleven days shorter than the solar year, it necessitates adjustment which is accomplished by inserting an extra month (*Adar Sheni*) seven times in every cycle of nineteen years. By doing so we both *remember* and *observe* the month of *Aviv* when God took us forth

מפטיר יד בְּכוֹר אָדָם בְּבָנֶיךָ תִּפְדֶּה: וְהָיָה כִּי־יִשְׁאָלְךָ בִנְךָ מָחָר לֵאמֹר מַה־זֹּאת
טו וְאָמַרְתָּ אֵלָיו בְּחֹזֶק יָד הוֹצִיאָנוּ יהוה מִמִּצְרַיִם מִבֵּית עֲבָדִים: וַיְהִי כִּי־
הִקְשָׁה פַרְעֹה לְשַׁלְּחֵנוּ וַיַּהֲרֹג יהוה כָּל־בְּכוֹר בְּאֶרֶץ מִצְרַיִם מִבְּכֹר אָדָם

---

14. מַה זֹּאת — *What is this?* (What is the reason for) the redemption of the firstborn of an ass, considering that it is an unclean animal and no sanctity of body can devolve on it? Also, (what is the reason for) breaking its neck if it is not redeemed?

בְּחֹזֶק יָד הוֹצִיאָנוּ ה׳ מִמִּצְרָיִם — *By strength of hand HASHEM brought us out from Egypt.* By the strong hand of the Egyptians, God brought us out, as it says, וַתֶּחֱזַק מִצְרַיִם עַל הָעָם, *And the Egyptians were urgent (strongly insistent) upon the people* (12:33) in such a manner that we could not carry our possessions on wagons, as was the Egyptian custom, (and) therefore we were forced to carry it on asses. Now, a miracle occurred and (these) asses were suddenly able to do so, therefore a certain sanctity devolved upon them, hence they became worthy of redemption.

15. וַיְהִי כִּי הִקְשָׁה פַרְעֹה — *And it came to pass when Pharaoh stubbornly (refused to let us go).* And since Pharaoh strongly (refused) to send us forth, and he is likened to an ass, as it says, אֲשֶׁר בְּשַׂר חֲמוֹרִים בְּשָׂרָם, *Whose flesh is as the flesh of asses (Ezekiel* 23:20). Now he could have redeemed himself and his people by sending out Israel, who are compared to a lamb, as it says, שֶׂה פְזוּרָה יִשְׂרָאֵל, *Israel is a scattered sheep (Jeremiah* 50:17), and also it says, וְאַתֵּנָה צֹאנִי, *You are my sheep (Ezekiel* 34:17).

וַיַּהֲרֹג ה׳ — *And HASHEM slew.* God slew those compared to the ass when they did not redeem themselves through the lamb.

כָּל בְּכוֹר בְּאֶרֶץ מִצְרַיִם — *All the firstborn in the land of Egypt.* And the firstborn of the Israelites were (also) worthy to be smitten with them, similar to, פֶּן תִּסָּפֶה בַּעֲוֹן הָעִיר, *Lest you be swept away in the iniquity of the city (Genesis* 19:15), but He saved them by sanctifying them to Himself in such a manner that the Israelite firstborn men were as Nazirites, or even higher, designated to serve God, the Blessed One, and prohibited to do common work ... *therefore I sacrifice the firstborns*

NOTES

from Egypt. This is what the *Sforno* refers to in his commentary on this verse.

9. כִּי בְּיָד חֲזָקָה הוֹצִאֲךָ — *For with a strong hand (HASHEM) brought you out.* The phrase יָד חֲזָקָה, *strong hand,* used in relationship to God implies a change in the laws of nature, as we see from the verse in *Joshua.*

14. מַה זֹּאת ... בְּחֹזֶק יָד הוֹצִיאָנוּ ה׳ מִמִּצְרָיִם — *What is this? ... By strength of hand HASHEM brought us out from Egypt.* The *Sforno,* departing from the usual interpretation which attributes this question *(What is this?)* to the simple son, explains it as a legitimate, even learned, question. Since we never find the concept of קְדוּשַּׁת הַגּוּף, *sanctity of body,* applied to an unclean animal, why is there a degree of sanctity attached to the ass which is an unclean animal? The answer given by the Torah, בְּחֹזֶק יָד, *by a strong hand,* is interpreted by the *Sforno* as referring to the firm, insistent pressure by Egypt on the Israelites to leave quickly, thereby necessitating them to carry their considerable possessions on the backs of asses which normally could never accommodate such huge burdens. Since, miraculously, they were able to accomplish this feat, their species took on a degree of sanctity, hence the requirement to redeem or dispose of the firstborn. (Similarly, the *Sforno* explains the question in verse 12:26, traditionally attributed to the wicked son, as also being a most incisive and proper one. See above.)

15. וַיְהִי כִּי הִקְשָׁה פַרְעֹה — *And it came to pass when Pharaoh stubbornly (refused to let us*

וְעַד־בְּכוֹר בְּהֵמָה עַל־כֵּן אֲנִי זֹבֵחַ לַיהוָה כָּל־פֶּטֶר רֶחֶם הַזְּכָרִים וְכָל־בְּכוֹר
טז בָּנַי אֶפְדֶּה׃ וְהָיָה לְאוֹת עַל־יָדְכָה וּלְטוֹטָפֹת בֵּין עֵינֶיךָ כִּי בְּחֹזֶק יָד
הוֹצִיאָנוּ יהוה מִמִּצְרָיִם׃

---

among the animals but all the firstborn of my sons I redeem, so that they may be permitted to do secular work.

NOTES

go). The *Sforno* continues his interpretation of these verses to be understood as an answer to the question *'What is this?'* i.e., what is the significance of the ass and the lamb? He explains the symbolism thus: Pharaoh is compared to the ass while Israel is likened to the lamb. Pharaoh could have redeemed himself by sending forth the lamb (Israel), but since he failed to do so, Egypt's 'neck' was broken.

פרשת בשלח
Parashas Beshalach

יז וַיְהִי בְּשַׁלַּח פַּרְעֹה אֶת־הָעָם וְלֹא־נָחָם אֱלֹהִים דֶּרֶךְ אֶרֶץ פְּלִשְׁתִּים כִּי
קָרוֹב הוּא כִּי ׀ אָמַר אֱלֹהִים פֶּן־יִנָּחֵם הָעָם בִּרְאֹתָם מִלְחָמָה וְשָׁבוּ
יח מִצְרָיְמָה: וַיַּסֵּב אֱלֹהִים ׀ אֶת־הָעָם דֶּרֶךְ הַמִּדְבָּר יַם־סוּף וַחֲמֻשִׁים עָלוּ
יט בְנֵי־יִשְׂרָאֵל מֵאֶרֶץ מִצְרָיִם: וַיִּקַּח מֹשֶׁה אֶת־עַצְמוֹת יוֹסֵף עִמּוֹ כִּי הַשְׁבֵּעַ

---

17. וְלֹא נָחָם אֱלֹהִים דֶּרֶךְ אֶרֶץ פְּלִשְׁתִּים — *God did not lead them by the way of the land of the Philistines.* Even though the Divine intention was to lead Israel to Mount Sinai to receive the Torah and from there to *Eretz Yisrael*, as it says, וְלָקַחְתִּי אֶתְכֶם לִי לְעָם . . . וְהֵבֵאתִי אֶתְכֶם אֶל הָאָרֶץ, *And I will take you to Me for a people . . . and I will bring you to the Land* (6:7,8), nonetheless the *present* intention was to lead them to the Sea of Reeds (although) it was not the way to either of these (i.e., Mount Sinai or the Land of Israel). The purpose was to drown Pharaoh and his army there, similar to, וּמָשַׁכְתִּי אֵלֶיךָ אֶל נַחַל קִישׁוֹן אֶת סִיסְרָא, *And I will draw out to you to the wadi of Kishon, Sisera (Judges* 4:7).

Now the straightest and shortest route from Egypt to the Sea of Reeds was *by the way of the land of the Philistines* but God, the Blessed One, did not want to lead them on that way . . .

כִּי קָרוֹב הוּא — *Because it was near.* And since that road was near to Egypt many travelers frequented it coming and going from and to Egypt, hence . . .

בִּרְאֹתָם מִלְחָמָה — *When they see war.* When they (the Israelites) will hear (from these travelers) the news of Pharaoh's preparations to pursue them together with his army, they will without a doubt, due to their fear of war, regret and return to Egypt. Therefore He led them about by a way where no other man traveled.

18. דֶּרֶךְ הַמִּדְבָּר יַם סוּף — *By the way of the wilderness by the Sea of Reeds.* So they would travel by way of the wilderness, since no informers from Egypt would come (on that road); hence they will not be aware of Pharaoh's pursuit of them until he overtakes them, as it says; וַיִּשְׂאוּ בְנֵי יִשְׂרָאֵל אֶת עֵינֵיהֶם וְהִנֵּה מִצְרַיִם נֹסֵעַ אַחֲרֵיהֶם, *And the Children of Israel lifted up their eyes and behold the Egyptians were marching after them* (14:10), by which time they (no longer) could make amends by returning, for Pharaoh and his army would not accept them.

וַחֲמֻשִׁים עָלוּ בְנֵי יִשְׂרָאֵל — *And the children of Israel went up armed.* All this had to be done, even though they were (well) armed, for with all their weapons they lacked the courage to fight with the Egyptians and escape, for they were inexperienced in all this (i.e., warfare).

19. וַיִּקַּח מֹשֶׁה אֶת עַצְמוֹת יוֹסֵף עִמּוֹ — *And Moses took the bones of Joseph with him* . . . for he (Moses) was then the leader of the generation . . .

NOTES

17-18. וְלֹא נָחָם אֱלֹהִים דֶּרֶךְ אֶרֶץ פְּלִשְׁתִּים כִּי קָרוֹב הוּא . . . בִּרְאֹתָם מִלְחָמָה . . . דֶּרֶךְ הַמִּדְבָּר יַם סוּף — *God did not lead them by the way of the land of the Philistines because it was near . . . When they see war . . . By the way of the wilderness by the Sea of Reeds.* Since God's intention was to entice Pharaoh to pursue the Israelites so that judgment might be executed upon him and the Egyptians at the Sea of Reeds, and that the miracle of the dividing of the waters take place, it would have been logical to lead the Israelites on a direct route to the sea through the land of the Philistines. The reason this was not done was because if a well-frequented route were used, travelers would have informed the Israelites of Pharaoh's pursuit,

הִשְׁבִּיעַ אֶת־בְּנֵי יִשְׂרָאֵל לֵאמֹר פָּקֹד יִפְקֹד אֱלֹהִים אֶתְכֶם וְהַעֲלִיתֶם
כ־כא אֶת־עַצְמֹתַי מִזֶּה אִתְּכֶם: וַיִּסְעוּ מִסֻּכֹּת וַיַּחֲנוּ בְאֵתָם בִּקְצֵה הַמִּדְבָּר: וַיהוָה
הֹלֵךְ לִפְנֵיהֶם יוֹמָם בְּעַמּוּד עָנָן לַנְחֹתָם הַדֶּרֶךְ וְלַיְלָה בְּעַמּוּד אֵשׁ לְהָאִיר
כב לָהֶם לָלֶכֶת יוֹמָם וָלָיְלָה: לֹא־יָמִישׁ עַמּוּד הֶעָנָן יוֹמָם וְעַמּוּד הָאֵשׁ לָיְלָה
לִפְנֵי הָעָם:
יד א־ב וַיְדַבֵּר יהוָה אֶל־מֹשֶׁה לֵּאמֹר: דַּבֵּר אֶל־בְּנֵי יִשְׂרָאֵל וְיָשֻׁבוּ וְיַחֲנוּ לִפְנֵי פִּי
ג הַחִירֹת בֵּין מִגְדֹּל וּבֵין הַיָּם לִפְנֵי בַּעַל צְפֹן נִכְחוֹ תַחֲנוּ עַל־הַיָּם: וְאָמַר
ד פַּרְעֹה לִבְנֵי יִשְׂרָאֵל נְבֻכִים הֵם בָּאָרֶץ סָגַר עֲלֵיהֶם הַמִּדְבָּר: וְחִזַּקְתִּי
אֶת־לֵב־פַּרְעֹה וְרָדַף אַחֲרֵיהֶם וְאִכָּבְדָה בְּפַרְעֹה וּבְכָל־חֵילוֹ וְיָדְעוּ מִצְרַיִם
ה כִּי־אֲנִי יהוָה וַיַּעֲשׂוּ־כֵן: וַיֻּגַּד לְמֶלֶךְ מִצְרַיִם כִּי בָרַח הָעָם וַיֵּהָפֵךְ לְבַב
פַּרְעֹה וַעֲבָדָיו אֶל־הָעָם וַיֹּאמְרוּ מַה־זֹּאת עָשִׂינוּ כִּי־שִׁלַּחְנוּ אֶת־יִשְׂרָאֵל

כִּי הַשְׁבֵּעַ הִשְׁבִּיעַ אֶת בְּנֵי יִשְׂרָאֵל — *For he had strictly sworn the children of Israel* ... and the obligation of the people (lit., 'generation') rests on its leader.

21. וַה׳ הֹלֵךְ לִפְנֵיהֶם — *And* HASHEM *went before them* ... from the time they reached Succos which was across the border of Egypt, and entered the wilderness.

XIV

3. סָגַר עֲלֵיהֶם הַמִּדְבָּר — *The wilderness has shut them in.* Baal-Zephon has closed in the wilderness on them.

5. כִּי בָרַח הָעָם — *That the people had fled.* For they did not proceed in a direct route into the wilderness, as they had (originally) indicated when they said, דֶּרֶךְ שְׁלֹשֶׁת יָמִים נֵלֵךְ בַּמִּדְבָּר, *We will go three days journey into the wilderness* (8:23), but turned back, akin to runaways who are confused, unsure of their direction.

וַיֵּהָפֵךְ לְבַב פַּרְעֹה — *And the heart of Pharaoh changed.* He thought that Baal-Zephon could withstand God, the Blessed One.

מַה זֹּאת עָשִׂינוּ כִּי שִׁלַּחְנוּ — *What is this we have done that we have sent forth?* We did not beseech Baal-Zephon who would have helped us and spared us the need to send (them forth).

NOTES

which in turn would have resulted in panic and an attempt to return to Egypt. By traveling along an unfrequented route the Israelites first became aware of Pharaoh's pursuit at a time when it was impossible for them to return. Their only option was to march forward, into the sea.

19. וַיִּקַּח מֹשֶׁה אֶת עַצְמוֹת יוֹסֵף עִמּוֹ — *And Moses took the bones of Joseph with him.* Since Joseph had strictly sworn the Children of Israel to bring his coffin to *Eretz Yisrael*, why then did Moses alone feel the obligation to honor this pledge? The *Sforno's* answer is that the leader of a people must accept the responsibility for his generation's obligation.

21. וַה׳ הֹלֵךְ לִפְנֵיהֶם — *And* HASHEM *went before them.* The *Sforno* in 12:39 established that God did not reveal Himself to the Israelites in the unclean land of Egypt. Not until they came to Succos, which was across the border, did the pillars of cloud and fire appear. Similarly, in this verse he stresses that *HASHEM went before them* only when they had crossed the border of Egypt at Succos.

XIV

3-5. סָגַר עֲלֵיהֶם הַמִּדְבָּר ... וַיֵּהָפֵךְ לְבַב פַּרְעֹה — *The wilderness has shut them in ... And the heart of Pharaoh changed.* The *Mechilta* states that only Baal-Zephon of all the Egyptian

ו־ז מֵעֲבְדֵנוּ: וַיֶּאְסֹר אֶת־רִכְבּוֹ וְאֶת־עַמּוֹ לָקַח עִמּוֹ: וַיִּקַּח שֵׁשׁ־מֵאוֹת רֶכֶב
ח בָּחוּר וְכֹל רֶכֶב מִצְרָיִם וְשָׁלִשִׁם עַל־כֻּלּוֹ: וַיְחַזֵּק יהוה אֶת־לֵב פַּרְעֹה מֶלֶךְ
שני ט מִצְרַיִם וַיִּרְדֹּף אַחֲרֵי בְּנֵי יִשְׂרָאֵל וּבְנֵי יִשְׂרָאֵל יֹצְאִים בְּיָד רָמָה: וַיִּרְדְּפוּ
מִצְרַיִם אַחֲרֵיהֶם וַיַּשִּׂיגוּ אוֹתָם חֹנִים עַל־הַיָּם כָּל־סוּס רֶכֶב פַּרְעֹה וּפָרָשָׁיו
י וְחֵילוֹ עַל־פִּי הַחִירֹת לִפְנֵי בַּעַל צְפֹן: וּפַרְעֹה הִקְרִיב וַיִּשְׂאוּ בְנֵי־יִשְׂרָאֵל
אֶת־עֵינֵיהֶם וְהִנֵּה מִצְרַיִם ׀ נֹסֵעַ אַחֲרֵיהֶם וַיִּירְאוּ מְאֹד וַיִּצְעֲקוּ בְנֵי־יִשְׂרָאֵל
יא אֶל־יהוה: וַיֹּאמְרוּ אֶל־מֹשֶׁה הֲמִבְּלִי אֵין־קְבָרִים בְּמִצְרַיִם לְקַחְתָּנוּ לָמוּת
יב בַּמִּדְבָּר מַה־זֹּאת עָשִׂיתָ לָּנוּ לְהוֹצִיאָנוּ מִמִּצְרָיִם: הֲלֹא־זֶה הַדָּבָר אֲשֶׁר
דִּבַּרְנוּ אֵלֶיךָ בְמִצְרַיִם לֵאמֹר חֲדַל מִמֶּנּוּ וְנַעַבְדָה אֶת־מִצְרַיִם כִּי טוֹב לָנוּ

---

6. וְאֶת עַמּוֹ לָקַח עִמּוֹ — *And took his people with him* . . . his choice horsemen and his army.

7. וְכֹל רֶכֶב מִצְרָיִם — *And all the chariots of Egypt* . . . the multitude.

וְשָׁלִשִׁם עַל כֻּלּוֹ — *And captains over all of them.* Also over the multitude who were not included among his people and army, did he appoint captains learned in warfare, for indeed the strength of an army depends on the skill and strategy of its commanders.

8. וּבְנֵי יִשְׂרָאֵל יֹצְאִים בְּיָד רָמָה — *And the children of Israel went out with a high hand.* Similar to יָדֵינוּ רָמָה, *our hand is exalted (Deut.* 32:27). They strove to vanquish Pharaoh and his army who were not as numerous as they; however, this demonstrated their lack of military knowledge, for indeed they should have feared them, for though less in number they (the professional Egyptian army) were (superior) in military skill, and more to be feared than all the multitude of Egyptians who later traveled after them.

9. וַיִּרְדְּפוּ מִצְרַיִם אַחֲרֵיהֶם — *And the Egyptians pursued after them.* After those who went out with a high hand.

10. וּפַרְעֹה הִקְרִיב — *And Pharaoh drew close.* The assembled multitude of all the chariots of Egypt.

11. לְקַחְתָּנוּ לָמוּת בַּמִּדְבָּר — *You have taken us to die in the wilderness.* For even if Pharaoh and his army do not wage war against us, still they will stand before us to bar our way in obtaining any food, so we will die in the wilderness from hunger, (and) thirst and in nakedness, deprived of everything.

NOTES

idols was left intact and not destroyed by God (see 12:12). This was done to mislead Pharaoh into thinking that Baal-Zephon could measure up to God. This explains Pharaoh's delusion, as explained by the *Sforno* in verse 5, and his regret for not having beseeched this idol earlier.

6-7. וְאֶת עַמּוֹ לָקַח עִמּוֹ . . . וְכֹל רֶכֶב מִצְרַיִם וְשָׁלִשִׁם עַל כֻּלּוֹ — *And took his people with him . . . And all the chariots of Egypt, and captains over all of them.* The *Sforno* divides the Egyptian host into three categories: Pharaoh; his choice professional military men; and the Egyptian masses in their chariots. The latter, however, were untrained and needed the guidance and direction of skilled captains. This same division is alluded to by Moses in his song, which the *Sforno* (15:1, 6,8) refers to as the first, second and third 'battles of Hashem.'

8. וּבְנֵי יִשְׂרָאֵל יֹצְאִים בְּיָד רָמָה — *And the children of Israel went out with a high hand.* The *Sforno* demonstrates his respect for the

יג עֲבֹד אֶת־מִצְרַיִם מִמֻּתֵנוּ בַּמִּדְבָּר׃ וַיֹּאמֶר מֹשֶׁה אֶל־הָעָם אַל־תִּירָאוּ
הִתְיַצְּבוּ וּרְאוּ אֶת־יְשׁוּעַת יהוה אֲשֶׁר־יַעֲשֶׂה לָכֶם הַיּוֹם כִּי אֲשֶׁר רְאִיתֶם
יד אֶת־מִצְרַיִם הַיּוֹם לֹא תֹסִפוּ לִרְאֹתָם עוֹד עַד־עוֹלָם׃ יהוה יִלָּחֵם לָכֶם
וְאַתֶּם תַּחֲרִשׁוּן׃
שלישי טו־טז וַיֹּאמֶר יהוה אֶל־מֹשֶׁה מַה־תִּצְעַק אֵלָי דַּבֵּר אֶל־בְּנֵי־יִשְׂרָאֵל וְיִסָּעוּ׃ וְאַתָּה
הָרֵם אֶת־מַטְּךָ וּנְטֵה אֶת־יָדְךָ עַל־הַיָּם וּבְקָעֵהוּ וְיָבֹאוּ בְנֵי־יִשְׂרָאֵל בְּתוֹךְ
יז הַיָּם בַּיַּבָּשָׁה׃ וַאֲנִי הִנְנִי מְחַזֵּק אֶת־לֵב מִצְרַיִם וְיָבֹאוּ אַחֲרֵיהֶם וְאִכָּבְדָה
יח בְּפַרְעֹה וּבְכָל־חֵילוֹ בְּרִכְבּוֹ וּבְפָרָשָׁיו׃ וְיָדְעוּ מִצְרַיִם כִּי־אֲנִי יהוה בְּהִכָּבְדִי

---

15. מַה תִּצְעַק אֵלָי — *Why do you cry out to Me?* For he was certainly included in וַיִּצְעֲקוּ בְנֵי יִשְׂרָאֵל אֶל ה׳, *and the Children of Israel cried out to HASHEM* (v. 10). However, the cry of Moses was not motivated by fear of Pharaoh and his army, for he had already told Israel of the fall and death of the Egyptians, as it says, לֹא תֹסִפוּ לִרְאֹתָם עוֹד עַד עוֹלָם, *You shall never again see them forever* (v. 13), and ה׳ יִלָּחֵם לָכֶם, *HASHEM will fight for you* (v. 14). His cry was caused by the arrogance of the Jewish leaders who said, הֲמִבְּלִי אֵין קְבָרִים, *Are there not graves (in Egypt)* (v. 11). He thought that because of this (defiance of him) the (people) would not listen to him to enter the sea. Therefore God says to him, *'Why do you cry out to Me?'* regarding this matter, for indeed you are distrustful of worthy ones.

דַּבֵּר אֶל בְּנֵי יִשְׂרָאֵל וְיִסָּעוּ — *Speak to the Children of Israel, and they will go forward.* They will not disobey you.

16. הָרֵם אֶת מַטְּךָ — *Lift up your rod* ... to the east wind that it should dry the sea.

וּנְטֵה אֶת יָדְךָ עַל הַיָּם — *And stretch out your hand over the sea* ... that the waters shall divide to one side and the other, similar to Elijah *(II Kings* 2:8).

18. וְיָדְעוּ מִצְרַיִם — *And the Egyptians shall know* ... those who remained in Egypt and who will return (repent) to Me, כִּי לֹא אֶחְפֹּץ בְּמוֹת הַמֵּת, *for I have no desire for the death of him who dies (Ezekiel* 18:32).

NOTES

superiority of military skills over that of sheer numbers in his interpretation of this verse, as he does in the previous verse as well.

15. מַה תִּצְעַק אֵלָי דַּבֵּר אֶל בְּנֵי יִשְׂרָאֵל וְיִסָּעוּ — *Why do you cry out to Me? Speak to the Children of Israel, and they will go forward.* In verse 10 we are told that the Children of Israel cried out to *Hashem*, but Moses is not mentioned. Indeed he reassures them and allays their fears. Still in this verse God says to Moses, 'Why do *you* cry out to Me?' The *Sforno* interprets the cry of Moses, which is implied in God's retort, as being far different than that of the Israelites. They are afraid of Pharaoh, while Moses is afraid that the people will not obey him to enter the sea, having been influenced and dissuaded by their leaders. God must therefore reassure him that they will follow. The expression וְיִסָּעוּ does not mean *and let them go forward*, as some commentators would have it, but *they 'will' go forward.*

16. וּנְטֵה אֶת יָדְךָ עַל הַיָּם — *And stretch out your hand over the sea.* The *Sforno* uses the expression הֵנָּה וָהֵנָּה, *to one side and to the other*, based upon an expression used in the episode of Elijah and Elisha when they approached the Jordan river and Elijah took his mantle, rolled it up and struck the water whereupon *it divided to one side and the other.*

18. וְיָדְעוּ מִצְרַיִם — *And the Egyptians shall know.* Since all the Egyptians who pursued the Israelites perished, the only ones who could *know that I am HASHEM* were those who remained behind. They would be so impressed by the miracle, they would repent and recognize God.

יט בְּפַרְעֹה בְּרִכְבּוֹ וּבְפָרָשָׁיו: וַיִּסַּע מַלְאַךְ הָאֱלֹהִים הַהֹלֵךְ לִפְנֵי מַחֲנֵה יִשְׂרָאֵל
כ וַיֵּלֶךְ מֵאַחֲרֵיהֶם וַיִּסַּע עַמּוּד הֶעָנָן מִפְּנֵיהֶם וַיַּעֲמֹד מֵאַחֲרֵיהֶם: וַיָּבֹא בֵּין ׀
מַחֲנֵה מִצְרַיִם וּבֵין מַחֲנֵה יִשְׂרָאֵל וַיְהִי הֶעָנָן וְהַחֹשֶׁךְ וַיָּאֶר אֶת־הַלָּיְלָה
כא וְלֹא־קָרַב זֶה אֶל־זֶה כָּל־הַלָּיְלָה: וַיֵּט מֹשֶׁה אֶת־יָדוֹ עַל־הַיָּם וַיּוֹלֶךְ יהוה ׀
אֶת־הַיָּם בְּרוּחַ קָדִים עַזָּה כָּל־הַלַּיְלָה וַיָּשֶׂם אֶת־הַיָּם לֶחָרָבָה וַיִּבָּקְעוּ
כב הַמָּיִם: וַיָּבֹאוּ בְנֵי־יִשְׂרָאֵל בְּתוֹךְ הַיָּם בַּיַּבָּשָׁה וְהַמַּיִם לָהֶם חוֹמָה מִימִינָם
כג וּמִשְּׂמֹאלָם: וַיִּרְדְּפוּ מִצְרַיִם וַיָּבֹאוּ אַחֲרֵיהֶם כֹּל סוּס פַּרְעֹה רִכְבּוֹ וּפָרָשָׁיו
כד אֶל־תּוֹךְ הַיָּם: וַיְהִי בְּאַשְׁמֹרֶת הַבֹּקֶר וַיַּשְׁקֵף יהוה אֶל־מַחֲנֵה מִצְרַיִם בְּעַמּוּד
כה אֵשׁ וְעָנָן וַיָּהָם אֵת מַחֲנֵה מִצְרָיִם: וַיָּסַר אֵת אֹפַן מַרְכְּבֹתָיו וַיְנַהֲגֵהוּ בִּכְבֵדֻת

---

19. הַהֹלֵךְ לִפְנֵי מַחֲנֵה יִשְׂרָאֵל — *Who went before the camp of Israel* ... in the pillar of fire.

וַיֵּלֶךְ מֵאַחֲרֵיהֶם — *And went behind them* ... to soften the deep (bed of the sea) which had hardened (lit., 'frozen') before the Israelites when they crossed over, thereby transforming the sea bed into mud when the Egyptians passed through in pursuit. It was unnecessary at this time for the pillar of cloud before Israel to lead the way, for the path made by the splitting of the sea directed them.

וַיַּעֲמֹד מֵאַחֲרֵיהֶם — *And stood behind them* ... behind the Israelites and behind the pillar of fire.

20. וַיָּבֹא — *And it came.* The angel came between the camp of Egypt and the camp of Israel to guide the two pillars.

וַיְהִי הֶעָנָן וְהַחֹשֶׁךְ — *And there was the cloud and the darkness.* The dark of night together with the cloud was behind Israel and the pillar of fire.

וַיָּאֶר אֶת הַלָּיְלָה — *And he gave light to the night.* (This refers to) the angel in the pillar of fire, for he removed the dark of night and there was no cloud separating between them (i.e., the Israelites) and the illuminating fire as there was on the Egyptian side.

וְלֹא קָרַב זֶה אֶל זֶה — *And the one did not come near the other.* For those who walk in darkness must perforce do so slowly not knowing what obstacles (lie before them).

21. וַיָּשֶׂם אֶת הַיָּם לֶחָרָבָה — *And made the sea into dry land.* The east wind hardened (lit., 'froze') the mud of the sea floor.

וַיִּבָּקְעוּ הַמָּיִם — *And the waters were divided* ... by the stretching forth of Moses's hand at the command of his Creator.

22. בַּיַּבָּשָׁה — *Upon the dry ground.* For the deeps were congealed by the east wind and they covered over the hardened mud.

24. וַיַּשְׁקֵף ה׳ אֶל מַחֲנֵה מִצְרַיִם בְּעַמּוּד אֵשׁ וְעָנָן — *And* HASHEM *looked to the camp of Egypt through the pillar of fire and the cloud.* The two pillars that were going in the middle expanse between the camp of Egypt and the camp of Israel were brought close to the Egyptian camp.

וַיָּהָם — *And brought disease.* Through many kinds of ailments, similar to the Philistines. וַתְּהִי יַד ה׳ בָּעִיר מְהוּמָה גְּדוֹלָה מְאֹד, וַיַּךְ אֶת אַנְשֵׁי הָעִיר מִקָּטֹן וְעַד גָּדוֹל וַיִּשָּׂתְרוּ

וַיֹּאמֶר מִצְרַיִם אָנוּסָה מִפְּנֵי יִשְׂרָאֵל כִּי יהוה נִלְחָם לָהֶם בְּמִצְרָיִם׃
רביעי כו וַיֹּאמֶר יהוה אֶל־מֹשֶׁה נְטֵה אֶת־יָדְךָ עַל־הַיָּם וְיָשֻׁבוּ הַמַּיִם עַל־מִצְרַיִם
כז עַל־רִכְבּוֹ וְעַל־פָּרָשָׁיו׃ וַיֵּט מֹשֶׁה אֶת־יָדוֹ עַל־הַיָּם וַיָּשָׁב הַיָּם לִפְנוֹת בֹּקֶר
כח לְאֵיתָנוֹ וּמִצְרַיִם נָסִים לִקְרָאתוֹ וַיְנַעֵר יהוה אֶת־מִצְרַיִם בְּתוֹךְ הַיָּם׃ וַיָּשֻׁבוּ

לָהֶם בַּטְחֹרִים, *The hand of* HASHEM *was against the city with great epidemic* (מְהוּמָה) *and He smote the people of the city, both small and big, and they were struck with swellings (I Samuel* 5:9). These ailments are (what is meant by) מַדְוֵי מִצְרַיִם הָרָעִים, *the evil diseases of Egypt (Deut.* 7:15), and that is הַיָּד הַגְּדֹלָה אֲשֶׁר עָשָׂה ה׳ בְּמִצְרַיִם, *the great hand which* HASHEM *placed upon the Egyptians* (v. 31), which Israel saw and feared, as it says, אֲשֶׁר יָגֹרְתָּ מִפְּנֵיהֶם, *which you were in dread of (Deut.* 28:60). However, the plagues which are detailed in the Torah did not include any ailment except for boils, and indeed the Torah mentions (specifies) the boils (visited) upon Egypt and also mentions the *diseases of Egypt.*

25. וַיָּסַר אֵת אֹפַן — *And He took off the wheels* . . . through the pillar of fire.

בִּכְבֵדֻת — *Heavily* . . . because of the mud.

כִּי ה׳ נִלְחָם לָהֶם — *For* HASHEM *is fighting for them.* And if we flee He will no longer fight with us.

27. לְאֵיתָנוֹ — *To its strength* . . . with the return of the waves to the divided path, which had not occurred since it divided.

וּמִצְרַיִם נָסִים לִקְרָאתוֹ — *And the Egyptians fled towards it.* From the beginning of the morning watch, God's hand was upon them to confuse them and it was then they said, אָנוּסָה, *Let us flee,* and they fled till the morning by the way of the divided path, and at the time of the morning's appearance the sea returned to its strength carrying the waves to the (former) divided section which the Egyptians had then reached and thus they found themselves fleeing *toward* the water.

וַיְנַעֵר ה׳ אֶת מִצְרַיִם — *And* HASHEM *shook out the Egyptians* . . . the king and his people. He threw them out of the chariots to the floor of the sea, similar to, חָצְנִי נָעַרְתִּי, *Also I shook out my lap (Nehemiah* 5:13), and הִתְנַעֲרִי מֵעָפָר, *Shake yourself from the dust (Isaiah* 52:2).

28. וַיָּשֻׁבוּ הַמַּיִם — *And the waters returned* . . . by the accretion of the waves to the place of division.

NOTES

24. וַיָּהָם — *And brought disease.* The expression וַיָּהָם, translated by many as *and brought confusion,* is interpreted by the *Sforno* as the bringing upon them of many kinds of ailments. Since the plagues visited upon the Egyptians in their land were not in the form of ailments, except for שְׁחִין, *boils,* we must conclude that the *evil diseases* mentioned in *Deut.* 7:15 refer to those brought upon them at the Sea of Reeds. This theory is buttressed by the verse in *Deut.* 28:60 where the Almighty refers to the *diseases of Egypt* and the fear of the Israelites, in the chapter of the תּוֹכָחָה, *admonition.* He draws a parallel to the fear of the Israelites mentioned in verse 31 (וַיִּירְאוּ הָעָם). What was the cause of this fear considering that they had crossed over the sea safely? The answer must be that they dreaded the diseases inflicted on the Egyptians at the sea, lest it affect them as well. Indeed the expression וְדָבְקוּ בָּךְ, *and cleave unto you,* is used in the verse cited above (*Deut.* 28:60).

הַמַּיִם וַיְכַסּוּ אֶת־הָרֶכֶב וְאֶת־הַפָּרָשִׁים לְכֹל חֵיל פַּרְעֹה הַבָּאִים אַחֲרֵיהֶם
כט בַּיָּם לֹא־נִשְׁאַר בָּהֶם עַד־אֶחָד: וּבְנֵי יִשְׂרָאֵל הָלְכוּ בַיַּבָּשָׁה בְּתוֹךְ הַיָּם
ל וְהַמַּיִם לָהֶם חֹמָה מִימִינָם וּמִשְּׂמֹאלָם: וַיּוֹשַׁע יהוה בַּיּוֹם הַהוּא אֶת־יִשְׂרָאֵל
לא מִיַּד מִצְרָיִם וַיַּרְא יִשְׂרָאֵל אֶת־מִצְרַיִם מֵת עַל־שְׂפַת הַיָּם: וַיַּרְא יִשְׂרָאֵל
אֶת־הַיָּד הַגְּדֹלָה אֲשֶׁר עָשָׂה יהוה בְּמִצְרַיִם וַיִּירְאוּ הָעָם אֶת־יהוה וַיַּאֲמִינוּ
בַּיהוה וּבְמֹשֶׁה עַבְדּוֹ:

טו
א אָז יָשִׁיר־מֹשֶׁה וּבְנֵי יִשְׂרָאֵל אֶת־הַשִּׁירָה הַזֹּאת לַיהוה וַיֹּאמְרוּ
לֵאמֹר אָשִׁירָה לַיהוה כִּי־גָאֹה גָּאָה סוּס

וַיְכַסּוּ אֶת הָרֶכֶב — *And covered the chariots* ... after the people who were in them were shaken out.

וְאֶת הַפָּרָשִׁים — *And the horsemen* ... the riders on the horses.

לְכֹל חֵיל פַּרְעֹה הַבָּאִים אַחֲרֵיהֶם — *And all the hosts of Pharaoh that came after them* ... the multitude of the Egyptian chariots and their riders who followed the horsemen into battle.

29. וּבְנֵי יִשְׂרָאֵל הָלְכוּ בַיַּבָּשָׁה — *And the Children of Israel walked on dry land* ... while the Egyptians were drowning in the sea, since the sea did not return to its strength on the side where the Israelites were.

30. וַיּוֹשַׁע ה׳ בַּיּוֹם הַהוּא אֶת יִשְׂרָאֵל — *And* HASHEM *saved Israel that day* ... through the death of those who oppressed them by bondage. They now became free men, for until their death (i.e., of their masters) the Israelites were considered runaway slaves.

31. הַיָּד הַגְּדֹלָה אֲשֶׁר עָשָׂה ה׳ בְּמִצְרַיִם — *The great work* (lit., *hand*) *which* HASHEM *did upon the Egyptians.* (These are) מַדְוֵי מִצְרַיִם הָרָעִים, *the evil diseases of Egypt* (*Deut.* 7:15) with which they were smitten on the sea.

וַיִּירְאוּ הָעָם — *And the people feared.* As it says, אֲשֶׁר יָגֹרְתָּ מִפְּנֵיהֶם, *which you were in dread of* (*Deut.* 28:60).

XV

1. אָז יָשִׁיר מֹשֶׁה — *Then Moses sang.* He determined (lit., 'agreed') to sing.

כִּי גָאֹה גָּאָה — *For being exalted is He exalted.* To Him alone is the exaltation, (for)

NOTES

29. וּבְנֵי יִשְׂרָאֵל הָלְכוּ בַיַּבָּשָׁה — *And the Children of Israel walked on dry land.* The prefix ו of וּבְנֵי יִשְׂרָאֵל, *'and' the Children of Israel,* is a ו׳ הַדְדִית, *reciprocal vav,* i.e., at the same moment that the Egyptians were drowning, the children of Israel were walking on dry land.

30. וַיּוֹשַׁע ה׳ בַּיּוֹם הַהוּא אֶת יִשְׂרָאֵל — *And* HASHEM *saved Israel that day.* A runaway slave is still considered to be in the possession of his master. He cannot be considered 'saved' from him unless his master is no longer alive. The term וַיּוֹשַׁע, *He saved,* or יְשׁוּעָה, *salvation,* is not used until now, even though the Israelites had fled Egypt. The reason given by the *Sforno* is because only when they see *the Egyptians dead on the seashore* are they truly saved.

31. הַיָּד הַגְּדֹלָה אֲשֶׁר עָשָׂה ה׳ בְּמִצְרַיִם וַיִּירְאוּ הָעָם — *The great hand which* HASHEM *did upon the Egyptians, and the people feared.* See notes on verse 24.

ב וְרֹכְבוֹ רָמָה בַיָּם: עָזִּי וְזִמְרָת יָהּ וַיְהִי־לִי
לִישׁוּעָה זֶה אֵלִי וְאַנְוֵהוּ אֱלֹהֵי

---

to Him (we) attribute the good which exists, not to Pharaoh, הַתַּנִּים הַגָּדוֹל ... אָמַר לִי יְאֹרִי וַאֲנִי עֲשִׂיתִנִי, *the great crocodile ... who has said, 'My river is my own and I have made it for myself' (Ezekiel* 29:3).

סוּס וְרֹכְבוֹ רָמָה בַיָּם — *The horse and his rider He threw into the sea ...* Pharaoh's horse and his rider, as it says, וְנִעֵר פַּרְעֹה וְחֵילוֹ בְיַם סוּף, *He overthrew Pharaoh and his army in the Sea of Reeds (Psalms* 136:15).

2. עָזִּי וְזִמְרָת יָהּ — *The strength and (praiseful) song of God.* The strength and song of the Holy One, Blessed is He (is reflected in), *He threw into the sea,* i.e., the horse and its rider (Pharaoh) thereby demonstrating His strength, that He is the King over all kings. Therefore, it is fitting that He be praised by the rescued through the sound of song, rejoicing that they are servants of the eternal King.

וַיְהִי לִי לִישׁוּעָה — *And He is become my salvation.* He who threw the enemy into the sea is my salvation, as it says: וְנוֹדְעָה יַד ה׳ אֶת עֲבָדָיו וְזָעַם אֶת אֹיְבָיו, *And the hand of* HASHEM *shall be known to His servants and His indignation toward His enemies (Isaiah* 66:14).

זֶה אֵלִי — *This is my God.* His is to be the everlasting and First Cause Who perforce is the causal (force) and from Whom flows the continuing, ongoing existence of all which is impermanent and transitory (lit., 'perishable').

וְאַנְוֵהוּ — *And I will build a dwelling for Him.* I will build a habitation (the Holy Temple) for Him to dwell therein, and there I shall pray to Him alone and serve Him as is proper to (He) Who bestows good or evil, as it says, וְיִתְפַּלֵּל אֵלָיו, וְיֹאמַר הַצִּילֵנִי, כִּי אֵלִי אָתָּה, *And prays to Him and says, deliver me for You are my God (Isaiah* 44:17), for indeed the intent of (all) service and prayer is to find favor.

אֱלֹהֵי אָבִי — *The God of my fathers ...* the God of Jacob who proclaimed by saying, אֵל אֱלֹהֵי יִשְׂרָאֵל, *El Elohai Israel* (God, the God of Israel) *(Genesis* 33:20), that He is awesome in His greatness and providence, which are the attributes of mercy and justice.

NOTES

XV

1. כִּי גָאֹה גָּאָה סוּס וְרֹכְבוֹ רָמָה בַיָּם — *For being exalted He is exalted, the horse and his rider He threw into the sea.* The *Sforno* interprets the song of praise to God as first being in recognition of His triumph over Pharaoh the king; secondly over the army and its captains; and finally over the multitude of Egypt and their chariots. Therefore he interprets the phrase *the horse and his rider* as referring to Pharaoh. The reason it is necessary to stress this victory over Pharaoh is because he had boastfully claimed to be a deity who possessed great power and was the great king to whom even other kings were subservient. The downfall of Pharaoh and the great miracle of the dividing of the waters established the supremacy of *HASHEM* and refuted the absurd claims of the king of Egypt. As the *Sforno* explains in the next verse, through His strength manifested at the Sea of Reeds, God demonstrated that He, and He alone, is the King of kings.

2. זֶה אֵלִי ... אֱלֹהֵי אָבִי — *This is my God ... the God of my fathers.* Consistent with his commentary in *Genesis* 1:1, the *Sforno* interprets the name אֵל as signifying the Eternal, everlasting One Who grants existence to all things. This power has now been demonstrated by God and as such Moses calls Him אֵלִי, *My God,* and states his readiness to worship Him alone. The Name of God (אֵל) denotes the attribute of

ג אָבִי וַאֲרֹמְמֶנְהוּ׃ יְהוָה אִישׁ מִלְחָמָה יְהוָה
ד שְׁמוֹ׃ מַרְכְּבֹת פַּרְעֹה וְחֵילוֹ יָרָה בַיָּם וּמִבְחַר
ה שָׁלִשָׁיו טֻבְּעוּ בְיַם־סוּף׃ תְּהֹמֹת יְכַסְיֻמוּ יָרְדוּ בִמְצוֹלֹת כְּמוֹ־
ו אָבֶן׃ יְמִינְךָ יְהוָה נֶאְדָּרִי בַּכֹּחַ יְמִינְךָ
ז יְהוָה תִּרְעַץ אוֹיֵב׃ וּבְרֹב גְּאוֹנְךָ תַּהֲרֹס
ח קָמֶיךָ תְּשַׁלַּח חֲרֹנְךָ יֹאכְלֵמוֹ כַּקַּשׁ׃ וּבְרוּחַ

וַאֲרֹמְמֶנְהוּ — *And I will elevate Him* ... by bowing down (to Him) and humbling (myself) and by proclaiming to all that the intended purpose (of mankind) is to do His will, which (represents) the most exemplary of all purposes, being that מְרוֹמָם עַל כָּל בְּרָכָה וּתְהִלָּה, *He is exalted above all blessing and praise* (*Nehemiah* 9:5), similar to לַמְּדֵנִי לַעֲשׂוֹת רְצוֹנֶךָ כִּי אַתָּה אֱלֹהָי, *Teach me to do Your will for You are my God* (*Psalms* 143:10).

3. ה׳ אִישׁ מִלְחָמָה ה׳ שְׁמוֹ — *HASHEM is a man of war; HASHEM is His Name.* Even though He is a *man of war*, decimating the wicked with the attribute of justice, nonetheless *HASHEM is His Name*, (indicating) the attribute of mercy, for by this (action) He grants being and existence to His world by *removing the thorns from the vineyard* (*Baba Metzia* 83b), since they (the wicked) destroy the world.

4. מַרְכְּבֹת פַּרְעֹה וְחֵילוֹ — *Pharaoh's chariots and his host.* After telling of the loss of the horse and its rider, i.e., Pharaoh and his horse, for which they gave thanks to God, the Blessed One, they now tell of His battle against the army of Pharaoh and his chosen captains, who were the principal elements of the entire army.

6. יְמִינְךָ ה׳ נֶאְדָּרִי בַּכֹּחַ — *Your right hand, HASHEM, is glorious in power* ... not the right (hand) of Pharaoh's host and choice captains who rely on the arm of flesh. This thanks is given to God, the Blessed One, for this second phase of battle.

יְמִינְךָ ה׳ תִּרְעַץ אוֹיֵב — *Your right hand, HASHEM, dashes the enemy to pieces.* May it be Thy will that it shall be so in the future that You dash in pieces every enemy of Israel, similar to כֵּן יֹאבְדוּ כָל אוֹיְבֶיךָ ה׳, *So let all Your enemies perish, HASHEM* (*Judges* 5:31).

NOTES

mercy, while אֱלֹהִים represents the attribute of justice. Both Names are used by Moses (אֵלִי־אֱלֹהֵי), therefore the *Sforno* interprets אָבִי, *my father*, as referring to Jacob since he also proclaimed God as both אֵל and אֱלֹהֵי, for he recognized God's attributes of mercy and justice, accepting both in perfect faith and love. Perhaps this is why Jacob is the symbol of אֱמֶת, *truth*, for this attribute represents חֶסֶד שֶׁבִּגְבוּרָה, *kindness in strength*, which combines mercy and justice.

3. ה׳ אִישׁ מִלְחָמָה ה׳ שְׁמוֹ — *HASHEM is a man of war; HASHEM is His Name.* The Name HASHEM (also) represents the attribute of mercy. To use this Name associated with war may seem incongruous. The *Sforno*, however, explains that it is for the benefit of mankind that the wicked are destroyed, just as the clearing away of weeds and thorns benefits the field and its productivity. Hence although He is a *man of war*, His Name is *HASHEM*, the Merciful One.

6. יְמִינְךָ ה׳ נֶאְדָּרִי בַּכֹּחַ — *Your right hand, HASHEM, is glorious in power.* As mentioned above (verses 1 and 14:6,7), Pharaoh's downfall represents the first battle while the destruction of the army and its choice captains is called the second phase of battle by the *Sforno*.

יְמִינְךָ ה׳ תִּרְעַץ אוֹיֵב — *Your right hand, HASHEM, dashes the enemy into pieces.* The *Sforno* interprets the phrase *Your right hand*, etc., as a prayer that God should always destroy the

אַפֶּיךָ נֶעֶרְמוּ מַיִם   נִצְּבוּ כְמוֹ־נֵד
ט נֹזְלִים   קָפְאוּ תְהֹמֹת בְּלֶב־יָם: אָמַר
אוֹיֵב אֶרְדֹּף אַשִּׂיג   אֲחַלֵּק שָׁלָל תִּמְלָאֵמוֹ
י נַפְשִׁי   אָרִיק חַרְבִּי תּוֹרִישֵׁמוֹ יָדִי: נָשַׁפְתָּ
בְרוּחֲךָ כִּסָּמוֹ יָם   צָלְלוּ כַּעוֹפֶרֶת בְּמַיִם
יא אַדִּירִים: מִי־כָמֹכָה בָּאֵלִם יהוה   מִי
כָּמֹכָה נֶאְדָּר בַּקֹּדֶשׁ   נוֹרָא תְהִלֹּת עֹשֵׂה

---

8. וּבְרוּחַ אַפֶּיךָ נֶעֶרְמוּ מַיִם — *And with the blast of Your nostrils the waters were piled up.* Now they tell of the third battle engaged in by God, the Blessed One, against the multitude of Egypt. And he says: Behold with the blast of Your nostrils the waters were divided and the waters became a pile and heap.

קָפְאוּ תְהֹמֹת — *The deeps were congealed.* (This means) the ground of the sea (became solid) in a manner which (allowed) the Israelites to cross over.

9. אָמַר אוֹיֵב אֶרְדֹּף — *The enemy said, 'I will chase . . . after them into the sea.'*

אַשִּׂיג אֲחַלֵּק שָׁלָל — *I will overtake, I will divide the spoil.* These were the multitude, all the chariots of Egypt who only came to rob the money of the Israelites.

10. נָשַׁפְתָּ בְרוּחֲךָ — *You blew with Your wind.* The same wind which congealed the sea bed so that a path for the redeemed was created (now is) blown to cover over the pursuers and destroy them.

אַדִּירִים — *Mighty (ones).* (The) princes and leaders of the people sank as lead in the water, (and) among them were שָׁלִשִׁים עַל כֻּלּוֹ, *the captains over all of them* (14:7), whom Pharaoh had appointed over all the Egyptian chariots.

11. מִי כָמֹכָה בָּאֵלִם ה׳ — *Who is like unto You, HASHEM?* He gave praise to God, the Blessed One, for this third battle against the multitude of Egyptian chariots, saying, 'Who is like unto You among the mighty who can change the nature of that which is permanent (unchanging) in its nature?'

נֶאְדָּר בַּקֹּדֶשׁ — *Glorious in holiness.* Behold, the holy that is absolute is that which never withers (nor loses its essence) as our Sages say, 'The righteous whom the Holy One, Blessed is He, will resurrect will not return to dust, as it is written, . . . הַנִּשְׁאָר בִּירוּשָׁלַיִם קָדוֹשׁ יֵאָמֶר לוֹ, *He that remains . . . in Jerusalem shall be called holy (Isaiah* 4:3), as the holy exists forever, etc.' (*Sanhedrin* 92a). Now, he says, there is none like God, the Blessed One, recognized as the mighty (one) King over all holy and eternal forces, therefore for Him alone it is proper to change the nature of all the permanent (unchanging) existing elements, since the eternal aspect of all that is everlasting cannot be without Him, Blessed is He.

NOTES

enemies of Israel. He interprets the phrase עַד יַעֲבֹר in verse 15, תִּפֹּל עֲלֵיהֶם and יֹאחֲזֵמוֹ רָעַד in verse 16, and ה׳ יִמְלֹךְ וכו׳ in verse 18 in a similar fashion, i.e., as a prayer for the future.

8. וּבְרוּחַ אַפֶּיךָ . . . — *And with the blast of Your nostrils* . . . See notes on verse 6.

10. אַדִּירִים — *Mighty (ones).* Unlike some commentators who interpret the word אַדִּירִים, *mighty,* as an adjective describing the noun *water,* the *Sforno* explains it to mean the mighty leaders who sank as lead in the waters.

11. מִי כָמֹכָה בָּאֵלִם ה׳ . . . נֶאְדָּר בַּקֹּדֶשׁ — *Who is*

יב־יג פֶּלֶא׃ נָטִיתָ יְמִינְךָ תִּבְלָעֵמוֹ אָרֶץ׃ נָחִיתָ
בְחַסְדְּךָ עַם־זוּ גָּאָלְתָּ נֵהַלְתָּ בְעָזְּךָ אֶל־נְוֵה
יד קָדְשֶׁךָ׃ שָׁמְעוּ עַמִּים יִרְגָּזוּן חִיל
טו אָחַז יֹשְׁבֵי פְּלָשֶׁת׃ אָז נִבְהֲלוּ אַלּוּפֵי
אֱדוֹם אֵילֵי מוֹאָב יֹאחֲזֵמוֹ רָעַד נָמֹגוּ

נוֹרָא תְהִלֹּת — *Fearful in praises.* And he who recognizes the greatness of His praises will fear Him for Himself, not because he fears any punishment coming from Him.

עֹשֵׂה פֶלֶא — *Doing wonders.* Doing (wonders) which are (acknowledged to) transcend natural phenomena, such as the pillar of cloud and pillar of fire.

13. נָחִיתָ בְחַסְדְּךָ עַם זוּ גָּאָלְתָּ — *In loving-kindness You led this people that You redeemed.* From the time You redeemed them, which was when You took them forth from the borders of Egypt and they came to Succos, You began to show them the way, as it says, וַיִּסְעוּ מִסֻּכֹּת . . . וַה׳ הֹלֵךְ לִפְנֵיהֶם, *And they traveled from Succos . . . and HASHEM went before them* (13:20,21).

נֵהַלְתָּ בְעָזְּךָ — *You guided them in Your strength.* You guided them *gently* (see *Genesis* 33:14) on the dry land in the midst of the sea, as it says, מוֹלִיכָם בַּתְּהֹמוֹת, כַּסּוּס בַּמִּדְבָּר לֹא יִכָּשֵׁלוּ, *He Who led them through the deep, like a horse in the wilderness, that they should not stumble (Isaiah* 63:13).

אֶל נְוֵה קָדְשֶׁךָ — *To Your holy habitation.* On a direct (lit., 'correct') way to come *to Your holy habitation* there to sanctify them in Your service.

15. אָז נִבְהֲלוּ אַלּוּפֵי אֱדוֹם אֵילֵי מוֹאָב — *Then the chiefs of Edom were frightened; (may trembling take hold of) the mighty men of Moab.* When they observed all these miracles, even though they knew that Israel would not wage war against them, nonetheless they were frightened by what they saw.

יֹאחֲזֵמוֹ רָעַד — *May trembling take hold of them.* May it be Your will that they be seized by trembling so that they not rise up against us.

NOTES

like unto You, HASHEM . . . glorious in holiness. The *Sforno's* belief, similar to that of the *Rambam,* is that this world and everything in nature is everlasting and unchanging. Hence the dividing of the waters represents a radical change in nature, which manifests the might of God, Who alone can execute such a phenomena in a בִּלְתִּי נִפְסָד, *permanent unchanging,* part of nature. God alone can do so for He is eternal, the ultimate in holiness, which represents the absolute in permanence and the everlasting, and He is the Creator, granting existence to all, hence He can do with His creation as He wills. (There are those Sages who feel that every change in nature was ordained from the beginning of Creation and as such the permanence of nature's character was never affected.)

13. נֵהַלְתָּ בְעָזְּךָ — *You guided them in Your strength.* The expression לְנַהֵל, *to lead,* is interpreted by the *Sforno* as meaning *to lead gently,* based upon *Genesis* 33:14 where Jacob says, אֶתְנַהֲלָה לְאִטִּי, *I will journey on gently.* Therefore in our verse the phrase נֵהַלְתָּ בְעָזְּךָ means *You guided them 'gently' in Your strength.* Similarly, the *Sforno* interprets the phrase in *Genesis* 47:17, וַיְנַהֲלֵם בַּלֶּחֶם, as *he gently led them with bread,* i.e., Joseph gave them bread in small quantities as was proper in a time of famine.

15. אָז נִבְהֲלוּ אַלּוּפֵי אֱדוֹם אֵילֵי מוֹאָב — *Then were the chiefs of Edom frightened; (may trembling take hold of) the mighty men of Moab.* Israel was prohibited to wage war against Edom and Moab (see *Deut.* 2:5 and 9).

יֹאחֲזֵמוֹ רָעַד — *May trembling take hold of.* See notes to verse 6.

טז כֹּל יֹשְׁבֵי כְנָעַן׃ תִּפֹּל עֲלֵיהֶם אֵימָתָה
וָפַחַד בִּגְדֹל זְרוֹעֲךָ יִדְּמוּ כָּאָבֶן עַד־
יַעֲבֹר עַמְּךָ יהוה עַד־יַעֲבֹר עַם־זוּ
יז קָנִיתָ׃ תְּבִאֵמוֹ וְתִטָּעֵמוֹ בְּהַר נַחֲלָתְךָ מָכוֹן
לְשִׁבְתְּךָ פָּעַלְתָּ יהוה מִקְּדָּשׁ אֲדֹנָי כּוֹנְנוּ
יח־יט יָדֶיךָ׃ יהוה ׀ יִמְלֹךְ לְעֹלָם וָעֶד׃ כִּי

נָמֹגוּ כֹּל יֹשְׁבֵי כְנָעַן — *All the inhabitants of Canaan melted away.* For indeed the inhabitants of Canaan, when they heard of all these (events), without a doubt (their resolve) melted, for they knew the (Israelites) would go up against them and drive them out (of the land), as it says, וַנִּשְׁמַע וַיִּמַּס לְבָבֵנוּ וְלֹא קָמָה עוֹד רוּחַ בְּאִישׁ מִפְּנֵיכֶם, *And we heard, and our hearts melted, nor did there remain any more courage in any man because of you (Joshua* 2:11).

16. תִּפֹּל עֲלֵיהֶם אֵימָתָה וָפַחַד בִּגְדֹל זְרוֹעֲךָ — *May terror and dread fall upon them by the greatness of Your arm.* May it be Your will that *terror and dread fall upon them* in a manner which will (cause) them to flee from our presence (motivated) by fear of Your arm, similar to, אָנוּסָה מִפְּנֵי יִשְׂרָאֵל כִּי ה׳ נִלְחָם, *Let us flee from before Israel, for HASHEM fights for them* (14:25).

עַד יַעֲבֹר עַמְּךָ ה׳ — *Till Your people pass over.* And also may it be Your will that they will not rise up against us, when we go up to do battle with them, until we have crossed over the rivers Arnon and Jordan, for to do battle at the river crossing is difficult and we will need a great miracle, one we may not be worthy of (receiving).

17. תְּבִאֵמוֹ וְתִטָּעֵמוֹ — *Bring them in and plant them* ... that they not be exiled therefrom.

בְּהַר נַחֲלָתְךָ — *In the mountain of Your inheritance* ... the mountain of the Temple of which it is said, בְּהַר ה׳ יֵרָאֶה, *On the mountain where HASHEM is seen (Genesis* 22:14).

מָכוֹן לְשִׁבְתְּךָ פָּעַלְתָּ ה׳ — *The place which You have made to dwell in* ... as it says, פֹּה אֵשֵׁב כִּי אִוִּתִיהָ, *here will I dwell for I have desired it (Psalms* 132:14).

מִקְּדָּשׁ ה׳ כּוֹנְנוּ יָדֶיךָ — *The Sanctuary, HASHEM, which Your hands established* ... as it says, וְעָשׂוּ לִי מִקְדָּשׁ ... כְּכֹל אֲשֶׁר אֲנִי מַרְאֶה אוֹתְךָ, *Let them make Me a sanctuary ... according to all that I show you* (25:8,9), and David (also) said, הַכֹּל בִּכְתָב, מִיַּד ה׳ עָלַי הִשְׂכִּיל, כֹּל מַלְאֲכוֹת הַתַּבְנִית, *All is in writing, by the hand of HASHEM Who instructed me, all the works of this plan (I Chronicles* 28:19).

18. ה׳ יִמְלֹךְ לְעֹלָם וָעֶד — *HASHEM shall reign forever and ever.* May it be (Heaven's) will that He alone shall reign forever and ever — וְאֵין עִמּוֹ אֵל נֵכָר, *and no strange god be with Him (Deut.* 32:12).

NOTES

17. תְּבִאֵמוֹ וְתִטָּעֵמוֹ — *Bring them in and plant them. Bring them in and plant them* is interpreted by the *Sforno* as a prayer uttered by Moses that Israel become firmly planted in the Land; similar to a tree or plant which takes root and cannot easily be uprooted, so may Israel not be exiled from its Land. Although God Himself did not construct the Temple, still the expression *which Your hands established* is valid since the Almighty prepared the

בָא סוּס פַּרְעֹה בְּרִכְבּוֹ וּבְפָרָשָׁיו בַּיָּם וַיָּשֶׁב יהוה עֲלֵהֶם אֶת־מֵי הַיָּם וּבְנֵי
יִשְׂרָאֵל הָלְכוּ בַיַּבָּשָׁה בְּתוֹךְ הַיָּם:
כ וַתִּקַּח מִרְיָם הַנְּבִיאָה אֲחוֹת אַהֲרֹן אֶת־הַתֹּף בְּיָדָהּ וַתֵּצֶאןָ כָל־הַנָּשִׁים
כא אַחֲרֶיהָ בְּתֻפִּים וּבִמְחֹלֹת: וַתַּעַן לָהֶם מִרְיָם שִׁירוּ לַיהוה כִּי־גָאֹה גָּאָה סוּס
כב וְרֹכְבוֹ רָמָה בַיָּם: וַיַּסַּע מֹשֶׁה אֶת־יִשְׂרָאֵל מִיַּם־סוּף וַיֵּצְאוּ
כג אֶל־מִדְבַּר־שׁוּר וַיֵּלְכוּ שְׁלֹשֶׁת־יָמִים בַּמִּדְבָּר וְלֹא־מָצְאוּ מָיִם: וַיָּבֹאוּ
מָרָתָה וְלֹא יָכְלוּ לִשְׁתֹּת מַיִם מִמָּרָה כִּי מָרִים הֵם עַל־כֵּן קָרָא־שְׁמָהּ מָרָה:
כד־כה וַיִּלֹּנוּ הָעָם עַל־מֹשֶׁה לֵּאמֹר מַה־נִּשְׁתֶּה: וַיִּצְעַק אֶל־יהוה וַיּוֹרֵהוּ יהוה עֵץ
כו וַיַּשְׁלֵךְ אֶל־הַמַּיִם וַיִּמְתְּקוּ הַמָּיִם שָׁם שָׂם לוֹ חֹק וּמִשְׁפָּט וְשָׁם נִסָּהוּ: וַיֹּאמֶר
אִם־שָׁמוֹעַ תִּשְׁמַע לְקוֹל ׀ יהוה אֱלֹהֶיךָ וְהַיָּשָׁר בְּעֵינָיו תַּעֲשֶׂה וְהַאֲזַנְתָּ
לְמִצְוֹתָיו וְשָׁמַרְתָּ כָּל־חֻקָּיו כָּל־הַמַּחֲלָה אֲשֶׁר־שַׂמְתִּי בְמִצְרַיִם לֹא־אָשִׂים
חמישי כז עָלֶיךָ כִּי אֲנִי יהוה רֹפְאֶךָ: וַיָּבֹאוּ אֵילִמָה וְשָׁם שְׁתֵּים עֶשְׂרֵה

---

19. כִּי בָא סוּס פַּרְעֹה — *For the horses of Pharaoh went.* The אָז יָשִׁיר, *then sang,* etc., occurred *when Pharaoh's horses went in with his chariots and horsemen into the sea,* and God, the Blessed One, drowned them while the Children of Israel were still walking *on the dry land in the midst of the sea.* Before they came out they began to sing.

25. וְשָׁם נִסָּהוּ — *And there He tested them ...* whether they would accept the statute and ordinance which He had set for them, and not revert to their deviation. This test was (given) for indeed He said to Israel ...

26. אִם שָׁמוֹעַ תִּשְׁמַע לְקוֹל ה׳ אֱלֹהֶיךָ — *If you will listen to the voice of* HASHEM, *your God* ... to accept upon yourselves the statute which He set before you, and from now onward, *do that which is right in His eyes and give ear,* etc., only then shall you escape *the diseases of Egypt.* However, if now you accept, (but) later you will betray (your pledge), then He shall doubtless visit upon you thus and thus. This is similar to what our Sages say, "A proselyte who comes to convert (to Judaism) ... is told, 'Be advised that until now if you ate forbidden fat you would not be punished with כָּרֵת, *extirpation;* if you violated the Sabbath you would not be punished with stoning. Now, however, if you eat forbidden fat you will be punished with כָּרֵת, etc.' " *(Yebamoth* 47a).

כִּי אֲנִי ה׳ רֹפְאֶךָ — *For I am* HASHEM *Who heals you.* The reason you will be punished if you accept, but later betray (your promise), is because all My commandments are meant to heal your soul from the illness of false and corrupt desires and ideas, so you

NOTES

plans and instructed them how to build it. The words כּוֹנְנוּ, *established,* and תַּבְנִית, *plan* are closely related.

19. כִּי בָא סוּס פַּרְעֹה — *For the horses of Pharaoh went.* This concluding verse of the Song is understood by the *Sforno* (as well as the *Ramban)* as setting the time frame of the song which Moses and the Children of Israel sang. When Pharaoh's horse and his chariots and horsemen came into the sea and were drowned there, at that same time the Israelites were walking on dry land (see 14:19), and it was then (before they went out) that they began to sing.

26. אִם שָׁמוֹעַ תִּשְׁמַע לְקוֹל ה׳ אֱלֹהֶיךָ ... כִּי אֲנִי ה׳ רֹפְאֶךָ — *If you will listen to the voice of* HASHEM, *your God ... for I am* HASHEM *Who heals you.* The Jewish people, chosen by God

טז

א עֵינֹת מַיִם וְשִׁבְעִים תְּמָרִים וַיַּחֲנוּ־שָׁם עַל־הַמָּיִם: וַיִּסְעוּ מֵאֵילִם וַיָּבֹאוּ
כָּל־עֲדַת בְּנֵי־יִשְׂרָאֵל אֶל־מִדְבַּר־סִין אֲשֶׁר בֵּין־אֵילִם וּבֵין סִינָי בַּחֲמִשָּׁה
ב עָשָׂר יוֹם לַחֹדֶשׁ הַשֵּׁנִי לְצֵאתָם מֵאֶרֶץ מִצְרָיִם: °וילינו כָּל־עֲדַת בְּנֵי־ °וַיִּלּוֹנוּ ק׳
ג יִשְׂרָאֵל עַל־מֹשֶׁה וְעַל־אַהֲרֹן בַּמִּדְבָּר: וַיֹּאמְרוּ אֲלֵהֶם בְּנֵי יִשְׂרָאֵל מִי־יִתֵּן
מוּתֵנוּ בְיַד־יהוה בְּאֶרֶץ מִצְרַיִם בְּשִׁבְתֵּנוּ עַל־סִיר הַבָּשָׂר בְּאָכְלֵנוּ לֶחֶם
לָשֹׂבַע כִּי־הוֹצֵאתֶם אֹתָנוּ אֶל־הַמִּדְבָּר הַזֶּה לְהָמִית אֶת־כָּל־הַקָּהָל הַזֶּה

---

shall become holy to your God, as it says, וָאַבְדִּל אֶתְכֶם מִן הָעַמִּים לִהְיוֹת לִי, *I have set you apart from the peoples, that you should be Mine* (*Leviticus* 20:26). But if you deal treacherously, you will become ill and profane your soul, and it is fitting that one who *profanes the holiness of* HASHEM *which he loved* (based on *Malachi* 2:11) be punished.

27. וְשָׁם שְׁתֵּים עֶשְׂרֵה עֵינֹת מַיִם — *And there were twelve springs of water there.* And despite all this . . .

XVI

1. וַיִּסְעוּ מֵאֵילִם . . . אֶל מִדְבַּר סִין — *And they journeyed from Elim . . . to the wilderness of Sin;* similar to, לֶכְתֵּךְ אַחֲרַי בַּמִּדְבָּר, *When you went after Me in the wilderness* (*Jeremiah* 2:2).

3. מִי יִתֵּן מוּתֵנוּ . . . בְּשִׁבְתֵּנוּ עַל סִיר הַבָּשָׂר — *Would that we had died . . . when we sat by the pot of flesh.* If God, the Blessed One, desired our death it would have been better for us (had He) slain us there (in Egypt) where we were satiated; similar to, טוֹבִים הָיוּ חַלְלֵי חֶרֶב מֵחַלְלֵי רָעָב, *those slain with the sword are better than those slain with hunger* (*Lamentations* 4:9).

NOTES

and delivered from Egypt, have been granted God's special protection and providence. This status carries with it responsibilities on their part. Their acceptance to listen and obey was for all time. If they betray the trust placed in them by God they must suffer the consequences of their sins. Their punishment, however, will not necessarily be one imposed on them in a physical manner. Deviation from the commandments will result in an illness of the spirit and a debilitation of the soul. God, as a good doctor, urges them to guard their uniqueness and to recognize that they have been set apart from other nations for the purpose of serving God. By so doing they will guarantee their spiritual health and well being. This is the sense of the *Sforno's* commentary on this vital verse.

27. וְשָׁם שְׁתֵּים עֶשְׂרֵה עֵינֹת מַיִם — *And there were twelve springs of water there.* The *Sforno* links this verse to the following one (16:1), explaining that the Israelites demonstrated great faith and trust in the Almighty by leaving the springs of water in Elim and following Moses into the wilderness at God's behest. Jeremiah calls this an act of *chesed,* loving-kindness, demonstrated by Israel to their God.

XVI

3. מִי יִתֵּן מוּתֵנוּ . . . בְּשִׁבְתֵּנוּ עַל סִיר הַבָּשָׂר — *Would that we had died . . . when we sat by the pot of flesh.* If they are going to die regardless, then why complain to Moses and God for taking them out of Egypt? The *Sforno,* basing himself on the verse in *Lamentations,* explains that although one may be destined to die, there are different degrees of suffering connected with the manner of one's death. Hunger is far worse than execution, therefore they would have preferred death at the hands of the Egyptians to their slow starvation in the wilderness.

ד בָּעֶרֶב: וַיֹּאמֶר יהוה אֶל־מֹשֶׁה הִנְנִי מַמְטִיר לָכֶם לֶחֶם מִן־
הַשָּׁמָיִם וְיָצָא הָעָם וְלָקְטוּ דְּבַר־יוֹם בְּיוֹמוֹ לְמַעַן אֲנַסֶּנּוּ הֲיֵלֵךְ בְּתוֹרָתִי אִם־
ה לֹא: וְהָיָה בַּיּוֹם הַשִּׁשִּׁי וְהֵכִינוּ אֵת אֲשֶׁר־יָבִיאוּ וְהָיָה מִשְׁנֶה עַל אֲשֶׁר־
ו יִלְקְטוּ יוֹם | יוֹם: וַיֹּאמֶר מֹשֶׁה וְאַהֲרֹן אֶל־כָּל־בְּנֵי יִשְׂרָאֵל עֶרֶב וִידַעְתֶּם כִּי
ז יהוה הוֹצִיא אֶתְכֶם מֵאֶרֶץ מִצְרָיִם: וּבֹקֶר וּרְאִיתֶם אֶת־כְּבוֹד יהוה בְּשָׁמְעוֹ

---

4. מַמְטִיר לָכֶם לֶחֶם . . . לְמַעַן אֲנַסֶּנּוּ הֲיֵלֵךְ בְּתוֹרָתִי — *(I) will cause to rain bread . . . that I may test them, whether they will walk in My Torah.* When they will have food without toil (lit., 'pain') as our Sages say, לֹא נִתְּנָה תוֹרָה לִדְרוֹשׁ אֶלָּא לְאוֹכְלֵי הַמָּן, *The (power of) interpretation of Torah was granted only to those who eat the manna (Mechilta).*

5. וְהֵכִינוּ אֵת אֲשֶׁר יָבִיאוּ וְהָיָה מִשְׁנֶה — *And they shall prepare that which they bring in, and it shall be twice as much.* After they have prepared it (i.e., cooked it) it will (still) be double, for it will not diminish with cooking. (The reason) it says *prepare* is to alert them that they should eagerly get ready the delight of Sabbath (by preparing) savory food and that all their alacrity in this area shall be from the eve of the Sabbath.

6. עֶרֶב וִידַעְתֶּם — *At evening, and you shall know.* May it be the will (of Heaven) that (God's) promise to me to give you food will be in such a manner that He will give you your evening requirements at evening time, so that you may know that God, the Blessed One, has delivered you *totally* from the land of Egypt (including) their customs (as well). There you sat at the pots of flesh without a set time for meals, like animals; as our Sages say, 'At first, Israel was compared to chickens that peck (constantly) in the rubbish, until Moses came and set (specific) times for meals' (*Yoma* 75b).

7. וּבֹקֶר — *And in the morning.* You will have your morning food.

וּרְאִיתֶם אֶת כְּבוֹד ה׳ — *Then you shall see the glory of HASHEM.* And so may it be the will (of Heaven) that you shall see the glory of *HASHEM* when He comes to establish

NOTES

4. מַמְטִיר לָכֶם לֶחֶם — *I will cause to rain bread.* The word לֶחֶם usually means *bread.* In this instance, however, it is to be interpreted as *food,* which included both the manna and the flesh of the quails.

4. לְמַעַן אֲנַסֶּנּוּ הֲיֵלֵךְ בְּתוֹרָתִי — *That I may test them, whether they will walk in My Torah.* The test mentioned in this verse is to be understood as one which challenged them to spend their time, effort and energy in the toil of Torah, since their material needs were being met by the Almighty.

5. וְהֵכִינוּ אֵת אֲשֶׁר יָבִיאוּ וְהָיָה מִשְׁנֶה — *And they shall prepare that which they bring in, and it shall be twice as much.* The *Sforno's* interpretation explains the sequence of this verse. *After* they prepare the manna there shall remain the full measure gathered, which on Sabbath eve was double the normal amount. He also explains why the word וְהֵכִינוּ, *prepare,* is used instead of וּבִשְּׁלוּ, *cook.* This teaches us the importance and significance of preparing for the Sabbath, as our Sages stress in the Talmud (*Sabbath* 117b; *Kiddushin* 41a; *Beitzah* 16a).

6. עֶרֶב וִידַעְתֶּם — *At evening, and you shall know.* The *Sforno* teaches us a most interesting and basic *halachah* regulating man's consumption of food. Established, set times for the intake of food differentiates the human from animals and fowl. By so doing man emphasizes that there are many more important pursuits in life than eating, or satisfying one's physical hunger.

7. וּרְאִיתֶם אֶת כְּבוֹד ה׳ — *Then you shall see the glory of HASHEM.* The *Sforno* implies that if

°תַּלִּינוּ ק׳ ח אֶת־תְּלֻנֹּתֵיכֶם עַל־יְהוָה וְנַחְנוּ מָה כִּי °תלונו עָלֵינוּ: וַיֹּאמֶר מֹשֶׁה בְּתֵת
יְהוָה לָכֶם בָּעֶרֶב בָּשָׂר לֶאֱכֹל וְלֶחֶם בַּבֹּקֶר לִשְׂבֹּעַ בִּשְׁמֹעַ יְהוָה אֶת־
תְּלֻנֹּתֵיכֶם אֲשֶׁר־אַתֶּם מַלִּינִם עָלָיו וְנַחְנוּ מָה לֹא־עָלֵינוּ תְלֻנֹּתֵיכֶם כִּי עַל־
ט יְהוָה: וַיֹּאמֶר מֹשֶׁה אֶל־אַהֲרֹן אֱמֹר אֶל־כָּל־עֲדַת בְּנֵי יִשְׂרָאֵל קִרְבוּ לִפְנֵי
י יְהוָה כִּי שָׁמַע אֵת תְּלֻנֹּתֵיכֶם: וַיְהִי כְּדַבֵּר אַהֲרֹן אֶל־כָּל־עֲדַת בְּנֵי־יִשְׂרָאֵל
וַיִּפְנוּ אֶל־הַמִּדְבָּר וְהִנֵּה כְּבוֹד יְהוָה נִרְאָה בֶּעָנָן:
ששי יא־יב וַיְדַבֵּר יְהוָה אֶל־מֹשֶׁה לֵּאמֹר: שָׁמַעְתִּי אֶת־תְּלוּנֹּת בְּנֵי יִשְׂרָאֵל דַּבֵּר
אֲלֵהֶם לֵאמֹר בֵּין הָעַרְבַּיִם תֹּאכְלוּ בָשָׂר וּבַבֹּקֶר תִּשְׂבְּעוּ־לָחֶם וִידַעְתֶּם כִּי

---

these times (for food) in order that you will know that your murmurings are directed toward Him, and therefore He will appear to remove them from Himself.

8. וַיֹּאמֶר מֹשֶׁה בְּתֵת ה׳ לָכֶם — *And Moses said, 'When HASHEM shall give you.'* Moses said, 'When we prayed that *HASHEM* give you food in the evening so that you may know that God, the Blessed One, took you forth (from Egypt), we intended that He give you *in the evening flesh to eat,* but not (to the degree of) satiation as is the custom of the Egyptians who have no other interest than (to satisfy) their physical (needs). And (our intent also was) that in the morning He give you bread, (but) only to satisfy (your hunger) sufficient to fill you.'

בִּשְׁמֹעַ ה׳ אֶת תְּלֻנֹּתֵיכֶם — *That HASHEM hears your murmurings.* (Moses continued) 'And as for our prayer that you shall see the glory of HASHEM, our intention is that He grant you this (flesh and bread) in a manner that He show you that your murmurings are (directed) to Him, and that He has heard your murmurings.'

9. אֱמֹר אֶל כָּל עֲדַת — *Say unto all the congregation . . .* once he knew that his prayer was accepted, similar to Rabbi Chanina when he would pray on behalf of the sick — or even more so.

קִרְבוּ לִפְנֵי ה׳ — *Come near before HASHEM . . .* Who went before them in the pillar of cloud.

10. וַיִּפְנוּ אֶל הַמִּדְבָּר — *And they turned toward the wilderness . . .* for the (pillar of) cloud was traveling in the direction of the wilderness as they journeyed.

NOTES

man is sensitive to the fact that his sustenance comes from God, then he merits to see *the glory of HASHEM* every time he sits down to his morning and evening meal. This may well be the source of the Torah *hashkafah* (perspective) which views the Jewish table as an altar and the consuming of food (if done properly) as a form of עֲבוֹדָה, *service of Hashem.*

8. וַיֹּאמֶר מֹשֶׁה בְּתֵת ה׳ לָכֶם — *And Moses said, 'When HASHEM shall give you.'* The sense of the verse, according to the *Sforno,* is: Although we interceded with God on your behalf to obtain meat and bread, we want you to understand how we, as opposed to others, view these blessings from God. While the Egyptians live to eat, we eat to live. Hence, even when we eat bread it is only for the purpose of satisfying our hunger.

Bread is a necessity while meat is a luxury. Therefore the word used regarding bread is לִשְׂבֹּעַ, *to the full,* but regarding meat the Torah states לֶאֱכֹל, *to eat,* implying that it should be partaken of sparingly. *Rashi* makes the same comment, based on the Talmud (*Chullin* 84a).

9. אֱמֹר אֶל כָּל עֲדַת — *Say unto all the congregation.* Moses, as a prophet and *tzaddik,* could sense whether his prayer had been accepted by God. Only after sensing its acceptance would he say to the people, with

יג אֲנִי יְהוָה אֱלֹהֵיכֶם: וַיְהִי בָעֶרֶב וַתַּעַל הַשְּׂלָו וַתְּכַס אֶת־הַמַּחֲנֶה וּבַבֹּקֶר
יד הָיְתָה שִׁכְבַת הַטַּל סָבִיב לַמַּחֲנֶה: וַתַּעַל שִׁכְבַת הַטָּל וְהִנֵּה עַל־פְּנֵי
טו הַמִּדְבָּר דַּק מְחֻסְפָּס דַּק כַּכְּפֹר עַל־הָאָרֶץ: וַיִּרְאוּ בְנֵי־יִשְׂרָאֵל וַיֹּאמְרוּ אִישׁ
אֶל־אָחִיו מָן הוּא כִּי לֹא יָדְעוּ מַה־הוּא וַיֹּאמֶר מֹשֶׁה אֲלֵהֶם הוּא הַלֶּחֶם
טז אֲשֶׁר נָתַן יְהוָה לָכֶם לְאָכְלָה: זֶה הַדָּבָר אֲשֶׁר צִוָּה יְהוָה לִקְטוּ מִמֶּנּוּ אִישׁ
לְפִי אָכְלוֹ עֹמֶר לַגֻּלְגֹּלֶת מִסְפַּר נַפְשֹׁתֵיכֶם אִישׁ לַאֲשֶׁר בְּאָהֳלוֹ תִּקָּחוּ:
יז־יח וַיַּעֲשׂוּ־כֵן בְּנֵי יִשְׂרָאֵל וַיִּלְקְטוּ הַמַּרְבֶּה וְהַמַּמְעִיט: וַיָּמֹדּוּ בָעֹמֶר וְלֹא
יט הֶעְדִּיף הַמַּרְבֶּה וְהַמַּמְעִיט לֹא הֶחְסִיר אִישׁ לְפִי־אָכְלוֹ לָקָטוּ: וַיֹּאמֶר מֹשֶׁה
כ אֲלֵהֶם אִישׁ אַל־יוֹתֵר מִמֶּנּוּ עַד־בֹּקֶר: וְלֹא־שָׁמְעוּ אֶל־מֹשֶׁה וַיּוֹתִרוּ
כא אֲנָשִׁים מִמֶּנּוּ עַד־בֹּקֶר וַיָּרֻם תּוֹלָעִים וַיִּבְאַשׁ וַיִּקְצֹף עֲלֵהֶם מֹשֶׁה: וַיִּלְקְטוּ

---

14. וְהִנֵּה עַל פְּנֵי הַמִּדְבָּר דַּק — *And behold upon the face of the wilderness a fine ...* a thing (plant) whose berry was fine, as it says, כִּזְרַע גַּד הוּא, *like coriander seed (Numbers 11:7).*

דַּק כַּכְּפֹר — *Fine as the frost.* As it lay (on the ground), it was also fine, i.e., one berry did not lie on (another) berry.

16. זֶה הַדָּבָר אֲשֶׁר צִוָּה ה׳ — *This is the thing which HASHEM has commanded ...* when He said, וּבַבֹּקֶר תִּשְׂבְּעוּ לָחֶם, *And in the morning you shall be filled with bread* (v. 12).

לִקְטוּ מִמֶּנּוּ — *Gather of it ...* every one as he desires, be it much or little.

אִישׁ לְפִי אָכְלוֹ עֹמֶר לַגֻּלְגֹּלֶת מִסְפַּר נַפְשֹׁתֵיכֶם אִישׁ לַאֲשֶׁר בְּאָהֳלוֹ תִּקָּחוּ — *Every man according to his eating, an omer a head, according to the number of your persons, each man for them that are in his tent, shall you take.* Regardless of how much you gather, whether a lot or a little, it shall always be for each one *according to his eating,* i.e., satisfying him who is accustomed to eat a lot, and not too much for him who is accustomed to eat a little. Also, whatever is gathered, be it much or a small amount, it will be (exactly) *an omer a head,* not more or less. Also, he who gathers for all his household will (find) an *omer* for each one, according to the number of persons in his tent.

20. וַיִּקְצֹף עֲלֵהֶם מֹשֶׁה — *And Moses was angry with them.* For indeed this did not occur (i.e., the manna did not spoil) because it was more than they needed, but it was done (i.e., some manna was kept overnight) intentionally, to test (God or Moses).

NOTES

surety, that God had heard their request. The *Sforno* draws a parallel to the incident related in the Talmud *(Berachos* 34b) where Rabbi Chanina could tell from the fluency of his prayer on behalf of a sick person — or the lack of it — whether the patient would recover or not.

14. דַּק ... דַּק כַּכְּפֹר — *Fine ... fine as the frost.* The *Sforno's* interpretation explains the repetition of the word דַּק, *fine.* One refers to the composition of the berry, the second to its positioning on the ground.

16. אִישׁ לְפִי אָכְלוֹ עֹמֶר לַגֻּלְגֹּלֶת מִסְפַּר נַפְשֹׁתֵיכֶם אִישׁ לַאֲשֶׁר בְּאָהֳלוֹ תִּקָּחוּ — *Every man according to his eating, an omer a head, according to the number of your persons, each man for them that are in his tent, shall you take.* The *Sforno* explains the three expressions used in this verse: לְפִי אָכְלוֹ, *according to his eating;* עֹמֶר לַגֻּלְגֹּלֶת, *an omer a head;* and מִסְפַּר נַפְשֹׁתֵיכֶם, *the number of your persons.* The amount of manna will be determined by the number of

כב אֹתוֹ בַּבֹּקֶר בַּבֹּקֶר אִישׁ כְּפִי אָכְלוֹ וְחַם הַשֶּׁמֶשׁ וְנָמָס: וַיְהִי | בַּיּוֹם הַשִּׁשִּׁי
לָקְטוּ לֶחֶם מִשְׁנֶה שְׁנֵי הָעֹמֶר לָאֶחָד וַיָּבֹאוּ כָּל־נְשִׂיאֵי הָעֵדָה וַיַּגִּידוּ
כג לְמֹשֶׁה: וַיֹּאמֶר אֲלֵהֶם הוּא אֲשֶׁר דִּבֶּר יהוה שַׁבָּתוֹן שַׁבַּת־קֹדֶשׁ לַיהוה
מָחָר אֵת אֲשֶׁר־תֹּאפוּ אֵפוּ וְאֵת אֲשֶׁר־תְּבַשְּׁלוּ בַּשֵּׁלוּ וְאֵת כָּל־הָעֹדֵף
כד הַנִּיחוּ לָכֶם לְמִשְׁמֶרֶת עַד־הַבֹּקֶר: וַיַּנִּיחוּ אֹתוֹ עַד־הַבֹּקֶר כַּאֲשֶׁר צִוָּה מֹשֶׁה
כה וְלֹא הִבְאִישׁ וְרִמָּה לֹא־הָיְתָה בּוֹ: וַיֹּאמֶר מֹשֶׁה אִכְלֻהוּ הַיּוֹם כִּי־שַׁבָּת
כו הַיּוֹם לַיהוה הַיּוֹם לֹא תִמְצָאֻהוּ בַּשָּׂדֶה: שֵׁשֶׁת יָמִים תִּלְקְטֻהוּ וּבַיּוֹם
כז הַשְּׁבִיעִי שַׁבָּת לֹא יִהְיֶה־בּוֹ: וַיְהִי בַּיּוֹם הַשְּׁבִיעִי יָצְאוּ מִן־הָעָם לִלְקֹט

---

21. בַּבֹּקֶר בַּבֹּקֶר — *Morning by morning.* Every morning, similar to, כְּדַבְּרָהּ אֶל יוֹסֵף יוֹם יוֹם, *as she spoke to Joseph day by day* (*Genesis* 39:10), and בַּבֹּקֶר בַּבֹּקֶר בְּהֵיטִיבוֹ אֶת הַנֵּרֹת, *Morning by morning when he dresses the lamps* (30:7).

וְחַם הַשֶּׁמֶשׁ וְנָמָס — *As the sun waxed hot it melted.* Therefore, they would gather it in the morning, so it should not melt in the heat of the sun.

23. אֵת אֲשֶׁר תֹּאפוּ אֵפוּ — *Bake that which you will bake.* That portion which you wish to bake in the oven, as it says, וְעָשׂוּ אֹתוֹ עֻגוֹת, *and make cakes of it* (*Numbers* 11:8), bake it now, on the eve of the Sabbath.

וְאֵת אֲשֶׁר תְּבַשְּׁלוּ בַּשֵּׁלוּ — *And cook that which you will cook . . .* similar to, וּבִשְּׁלוּ בַּפָּרוּר, *and cooked it in pots* (ibid.); cook it now (on the eve of the Sabbath).

25. אִכְלֻהוּ הַיּוֹם — *Eat it today.* At set times of this day.

כִּי שַׁבָּת הַיּוֹם לַה׳ — *For today is a Sabbath to HASHEM.* This entire day is Sabbath to God, and you are permitted to eat the manna left over from yesterday, this entire day. However, it will not be permitted after the Sabbath.

הַיּוֹם לֹא תִמְצָאֻהוּ בַּשָּׂדֶה — *Today you shall not find it in the field.* On every Sabbath day, as today, *you shall not find it.*

27. יָצְאוּ מִן הָעָם — *There went out some of the people . . .* from the camp to a distant place, thinking they would find the (manna) there, for they (lit., 'their spirits') did not believe God.

לִלְקֹט — *To gather.* Now this would have without a doubt been in violation of Sabbath (laws) were they to gather anything from its place of growth, as our Sages state, 'He who tears the cuscuta from thorns and thistles is guilty of עוֹקֵר, *tearing loose, detaching'* (*Sabbath* 107b).

NOTES

members in one's household; it will always be an exact amount per person and will satisfy everyone's hunger.

25. אִכְלֻהוּ הַיּוֹם כִּי שַׁבָּת הַיּוֹם לַה׳ הַיּוֹם לֹא תִמְצָאֻהוּ בַּשָּׂדֶה — *Eat it today, for today is a Sabbath to HASHEM; today you shall not find it in the field.* The word הַיּוֹם *(today)* is mentioned three times in this verse to teach us three things. One, that although the entire amount of manna was in one's hands from the eve of the Sabbath it should not be consumed at once but apportioned for specific meals. Second, that the food prepared on the eve of the Sabbath can be used the entire day of the Sabbath but not the next day. Third, that this order is to be followed every week on the Sabbath.

27. לִלְקֹט — *To gather.* The plucking or picking of מְחוּבָּר, *that which is attached to its natural source,* is prohibited on the Sabbath. The manna on the ground was considered

כח וְלֹא מָצָאוּ: וַיֹּאמֶר יְהוָה אֶל־מֹשֶׁה עַד־אָנָה מֵאַנְתֶּם לִשְׁמֹר
כט מִצְוֹתַי וְתוֹרֹתָי: רְאוּ כִּי־יְהוָה נָתַן לָכֶם הַשַּׁבָּת עַל־כֵּן הוּא נֹתֵן לָכֶם בַּיּוֹם
הַשִּׁשִּׁי לֶחֶם יוֹמָיִם שְׁבוּ ׀ אִישׁ תַּחְתָּיו אַל־יֵצֵא אִישׁ מִמְּקֹמוֹ בַּיּוֹם הַשְּׁבִיעִי:
ל-לא וַיִּשְׁבְּתוּ הָעָם בַּיּוֹם הַשְּׁבִעִי: וַיִּקְרְאוּ בֵית־יִשְׂרָאֵל אֶת־שְׁמוֹ מָן וְהוּא כְּזֶרַע
לב גַּד לָבָן וְטַעְמוֹ כְּצַפִּיחִת בִּדְבָשׁ: וַיֹּאמֶר מֹשֶׁה זֶה הַדָּבָר אֲשֶׁר צִוָּה יְהוָה
מְלֹא הָעֹמֶר מִמֶּנּוּ לְמִשְׁמֶרֶת לְדֹרֹתֵיכֶם לְמַעַן ׀ יִרְאוּ אֶת־הַלֶּחֶם אֲשֶׁר
לג הֶאֱכַלְתִּי אֶתְכֶם בַּמִּדְבָּר בְּהוֹצִיאִי אֶתְכֶם מֵאֶרֶץ מִצְרָיִם: וַיֹּאמֶר מֹשֶׁה
אֶל־אַהֲרֹן קַח צִנְצֶנֶת אַחַת וְתֶן־שָׁמָּה מְלֹא־הָעֹמֶר מָן וְהַנַּח אֹתוֹ לִפְנֵי
לד יְהוָה לְמִשְׁמֶרֶת לְדֹרֹתֵיכֶם: כַּאֲשֶׁר צִוָּה יְהוָה אֶל־מֹשֶׁה וַיַּנִּיחֵהוּ אַהֲרֹן לִפְנֵי

---

28. עַד אָנָה מֵאַנְתֶּם לִשְׁמֹר — *How long will you refuse to keep?* Behold the sin of (not) keeping is all inclusive (i.e., you are *all* responsible), for even though you did not go with them to gather, you caused them to do so by not instructing them in the laws of Sabbath and its affairs. You only said, 'שֵׁשֶׁת יָמִים תִּלְקְטֻהוּ, *Six days you shall gather it*' (v. 26) and not seven. In this they disobeyed you. You said, 'וּבַיּוֹם הַשְּׁבִיעִי שַׁבָּת לֹא יִהְיֶה בּוֹ,' *'But on the seventh day is the Sabbath, in it there shall be none'* (ibid.), and they did not believe you. But you did not teach them My commandments, that included in (the list of prohibited) work is the gathering of the manna, (and) that he who does so is guilty of תּוֹלֵשׁ, *plucking or tearing,* and (also) the (law of) bringing (carrying) from domain to domain, which is also among the prohibited labors (of Sabbath).

וְתוֹרֹתָי — *And My laws* ... the subject of Sabbath, its reasons and the reward and punishment (connected to it), for without a doubt all who know this will be careful to rest (properly) on the Sabbath.

29. רְאוּ — *See.* Consider.

כִּי ה׳ נָתַן לָכֶם הַשַּׁבָּת — *That HASHEM has given you the Sabbath.* And this is not only a commandment but a gift which was not given to any other (people) but you, as our Sages say, מַתָּנָה טוֹבָה יֵשׁ לִי בְּבֵית גְּנָזַי וְשַׁבָּת שְׁמָהּ, וַאֲנִי מְבַקֵּשׁ לִיתְּנָהּ לְיִשְׂרָאֵל, *(God said) 'I have a good gift in My treasure house, its name is Sabbath, and I wish to give it to Israel' (Sabbath* 10b). Also in the order of our prayers, וְלֹא נְתַתּוֹ ... לְגוֹיֵי הָאֲרָצוֹת ... וְגַם בִּמְנוּחָתוֹ לֹא יִשְׁכְּנוּ עֲרֵלִים, *And You ... did not give it to the nations of the earth ... and in its tranquility the uncircumcised do not rest (Amidah* for *Shacharis),* as it says, וְשָׁמְרוּ בְנֵי יִשְׂרָאֵל אֶת הַשַּׁבָּת לַעֲשׂוֹת אֶת הַשַּׁבָּת לְדֹרֹתָם, *The Children of Israel shall keep Sabbath to observe Sabbath throughout their generations* (31:16), and (through this observance) they will acquire the יוֹם שֶׁכֻּלּוֹ שַׁבָּת, *day that is entirely Sabbath (Tamid* 33b).

NOTES

attached, and as such had they found it and taken it, they would have transgressed the law of labor on the Sabbath, since removing it from its source would be considered עוֹקֵר, *detaching* or *uprooting,* or תּוֹלֵשׁ, *plucking* or *tearing.*

28. עַד אָנָה מֵאַנְתֶּם לִשְׁמֹר ... וְתוֹרֹתָי — *How long will you refuse to keep ... and My laws.* The Almighty included Moses in this chastisement. He did so because He held him responsible for not properly instructing the Israelites regarding the *halachos* (laws) of the Sabbath and also for not stressing sufficiently the importance and significance of the Sabbath, the unique role it plays in the eyes of Heaven

לה הָעֵדֻת לְמִשְׁמָרֶת: וּבְנֵי יִשְׂרָאֵל אָכְלוּ אֶת־הַמָּן אַרְבָּעִים שָׁנָה עַד־בֹּאָם
לו אֶל־אֶרֶץ נוֹשָׁבֶת אֶת־הַמָּן אָכְלוּ עַד־בֹּאָם אֶל־קְצֵה אֶרֶץ כְּנָעַן: וְהָעֹמֶר
עֲשִׂרִית הָאֵיפָה הוּא:
יז שביעי א וַיִּסְעוּ כָּל־עֲדַת בְּנֵי־יִשְׂרָאֵל מִמִּדְבַּר־סִין לְמַסְעֵיהֶם עַל־פִּי יְהוָה וַיַּחֲנוּ
ב בִּרְפִידִים וְאֵין מַיִם לִשְׁתֹּת הָעָם: וַיָּרֶב הָעָם עִם־מֹשֶׁה וַיֹּאמְרוּ תְּנוּ־לָנוּ
מַיִם וְנִשְׁתֶּה וַיֹּאמֶר לָהֶם מֹשֶׁה מַה־תְּרִיבוּן עִמָּדִי מַה־תְּנַסּוּן אֶת־יְהוָה:

---

35. אָכְלוּ אֶת הַמָּן — *They ate the manna* ... in place of bread made of wheat or other (grain), as it says, בִּלְתִּי אֶל הַמָּן עֵינֵינוּ, *We have naught but this manna to look to (Numbers* 11:6).

עַד בֹּאָם אֶל אֶרֶץ נוֹשָׁבֶת — *Until they came to a land inhabited* ... to the land of Sichon and Og where they also ate the bread of the land.

אֶת הַמָּן אָכְלוּ עַד בֹּאָם אֶל קְצֵה אֶרֶץ כְּנָעַן — *They ate the manna until they came to the borders of the land of Canaan.* Together with the bread of the land, they (also) ate the manna after coming to the land of Sichon and Og, until they crossed over the Jordan, as it says, וַיֹּאכְלוּ מֵעֲבוּר הָאָרֶץ מִמָּחֳרַת הַפֶּסַח . . . וַיִּשְׁבֹּת הַמָּן מִמָּחֳרָת, *And they ate of the corn of the Land on the morrow of the Pesach ... and the manna ceased on the morrow (Joshua* 5:11,12).

XVII

1. לִשְׁתֹּת הָעָם — *For the people to drink.* For the people to drink, similar to לְשֶׁבֶת אַבְרָם, *that Abram had dwelled (Genesis* 16:3).

2. מַה תְּרִיבוּן עִמָּדִי — *Why do you strive with me?* You certainly know that I am but commanded (by God) and perform (His will).

מַה תְּנַסּוּן אֶת ה׳ — *Why do you test HASHEM?* And if your strife with me is for the purpose of testing Him Who sent me, why do you do so for your own evil, for this

NOTES

and the reward and punishment attached to it. Had he done so the Israelites would have treated it with greater care and respect. This idea is also continued in the next verse.

35. אָכְלוּ אֶת הַמָּן . . . אֶת הַמָּן אָכְלוּ עַד בֹּאָם אֶל קְצֵה אֶרֶץ כְּנָעַן — *They ate the manna ... They ate the manna until they came to the borders of the land of Canaan.* The *Sforno's* interpretation of this verse reconciles a number of difficulties. Until when did they eat the manna and exactly when did they supplement it with other produce of the land? Also the verse repeats the phrase אָכְלוּ, *they ate,* regarding the manna but changes the order — first אָכְלוּ אֶת הַמָּן, *they ate the manna,* then אֶת הַמָּן אָכְלוּ, *the manna they ate.* The *Sforno* explains that during their wandering in the wilderness they ate the manna exclusively. When they came to the territory of Sichon and Og they *also* ate of the bread of the land. This combined diet continued until they crossed the Jordan when the manna ceased and they began to eat exclusively the produce of *Eretz Yisrael,* once חָדָשׁ, *new grain,* was permitted after the sixteenth day of Nissan.

XVII

1. לִשְׁתֹּת הָעָם — *For the people to drink.* The expression לִשְׁתֹּת הָעָם if translated literally would mean, *to drink the people,* which of course cannot be the intent of this phrase. The *Sforno* therefore explains that it is to be translated *for the people to drink,* similar to the expression in *Genesis,* לְשֶׁבֶת אַבְרָם, which is not to be translated literally but *that Abram had dwelled.*

2. מַה תְּרִיבוּן עִמָּדִי — *Why do you strive with me?* The verse is divided into two parts thereby obviating the question of redundancy. The sense of the verse is: Why argue with me

ג וַיִּצְמָא שָׁם הָעָם לַמַּיִם וַיָּלֶן הָעָם עַל־מֹשֶׁה וַיֹּאמֶר לָמָּה זֶּה הֶעֱלִיתָנוּ
ד מִמִּצְרַיִם לְהָמִית אֹתִי וְאֶת־בָּנַי וְאֶת־מִקְנַי בַּצָּמָא: וַיִּצְעַק מֹשֶׁה אֶל־יְהוָה
ה לֵאמֹר מָה אֶעֱשֶׂה לָעָם הַזֶּה עוֹד מְעַט וּסְקָלֻנִי: וַיֹּאמֶר יְהוָה אֶל־מֹשֶׁה
עֲבֹר לִפְנֵי הָעָם וְקַח אִתְּךָ מִזִּקְנֵי יִשְׂרָאֵל וּמַטְּךָ אֲשֶׁר הִכִּיתָ בּוֹ אֶת־הַיְאֹר
ו קַח בְּיָדְךָ וְהָלָכְתָּ: הִנְנִי עֹמֵד לְפָנֶיךָ שָּׁם ׀ עַל־הַצּוּר בְּחֹרֵב וְהִכִּיתָ בַצּוּר
ז וְיָצְאוּ מִמֶּנּוּ מַיִם וְשָׁתָה הָעָם וַיַּעַשׂ כֵּן מֹשֶׁה לְעֵינֵי זִקְנֵי יִשְׂרָאֵל: וַיִּקְרָא
שֵׁם הַמָּקוֹם מַסָּה וּמְרִיבָה עַל־רִיב ׀ בְּנֵי יִשְׂרָאֵל וְעַל נַסֹּתָם אֶת־יְהוָה
לֵאמֹר הֲיֵשׁ יְהוָה בְּקִרְבֵּנוּ אִם־אָיִן:
ח-ט וַיָּבֹא עֲמָלֵק וַיִּלָּחֶם עִם־יִשְׂרָאֵל בִּרְפִידִם: וַיֹּאמֶר מֹשֶׁה אֶל־יְהוֹשֻׁעַ בְּחַר־
לָנוּ אֲנָשִׁים וְצֵא הִלָּחֵם בַּעֲמָלֵק מָחָר אָנֹכִי נִצָּב עַל־רֹאשׁ הַגִּבְעָה וּמַטֵּה
י הָאֱלֹהִים בְּיָדִי: וַיַּעַשׂ יְהוֹשֻׁעַ כַּאֲשֶׁר אָמַר־לוֹ מֹשֶׁה לְהִלָּחֵם בַּעֲמָלֵק וּמֹשֶׁה

---

testing is fraught with great danger, for if He is angered He will show His deeds to destroy you, and this test will result in dire consequences for you, as He says, 'בְּחָנוּנִי, גַּם רָאוּ פָעֳלִי, *They tested me, even though they saw My deeds' (Psalms* 95:9), that is, (bringing) misfortune upon them.

5. עֲבֹר לִפְנֵי הָעָם — *Pass before the people.* And their murmurings will cease when they will see how you are exerting yourself to supply their need.

וּמַטְּךָ אֲשֶׁר הִכִּיתָ בּוֹ אֶת הַיְאֹר — *And your rod with which you smote the river.* And with that smiting the Egyptians wearied themselves to (find water to) drink. Now it will have the opposite effect.

וְהָלָכְתָּ — *And go* . . . from the camp to the rock.

6. וְהִכִּיתָ בַצּוּר . . . וְשָׁתָה הָעָם — *And you shall smite the rock . . . that the people may drink.* Thus they will appreciate (lit., 'recognize') that the functions of the rod are not part of its nature, for natural (actions) are always consistent. Rather, its actions are according to (God's) will, which can accomplish contrasting (opposite) actions.

8. וַיָּבֹא עֲמָלֵק — *Then Amalek came* . . . on hearing of their strife and thirst, as it says, וְאַתָּה עָיֵף וְיָגֵעַ, *When you were faint and weary (Deut.* 25:18), similar to לֹא מַיִם עָיֵף תַּשְׁקֶה, *You have not given water to the weary to drink (Job* 22:7), and בְּאֶרֶץ עֲיֵפָה, *in a weary land (Isaiah* 32:2).

9. וּמַטֵּה הָאֱלֹהִים בְּיָדִי — *With the rod of God in my hand* . . . to signal to the people

NOTES

since I am but a messenger? And if you mean to challenge God, then I warn you that you are exposing yourselves to grave punishment.

5. עֲבֹר לִפְנֵי הָעָם — *Pass before the people.* The *Sforno* is explaining why God tells Moses to *pass before the people.* What will he accomplish by doing so? The answer is that he will demonstrate his active concern and involvement on their behalf, and in this manner reassure them.

8. וַיָּבֹא עֲמָלֵק — *Then Amalek came.* The verses cited by the *Sforno* from *Job* and *Isaiah* are to prove that the expression *weary* denotes a lack of water, be it regarding people or land. Hence the reason given for Amalek's attack, *you were faint and weary,* indicates that there is a link between the opening episode of this chapter which relates Israel's contention regarding the lack of water, and the concluding event which relates the attack of Amalek.

9. וּמַטֵּה הָאֱלֹהִים בְּיָדִי — *With the rod of God in my hand.* Since the battle between Israel and

יא אַהֲרֹן וְחוּר עָלוּ רֹאשׁ הַגִּבְעָה: וְהָיָה כַּאֲשֶׁר יָרִים מֹשֶׁה יָדוֹ וְגָבַר יִשְׂרָאֵל
יב וְכַאֲשֶׁר יָנִיחַ יָדוֹ וְגָבַר עֲמָלֵק: וִידֵי מֹשֶׁה כְּבֵדִים וַיִּקְחוּ־אֶבֶן וַיָּשִׂימוּ תַחְתָּיו
וַיֵּשֶׁב עָלֶיהָ וְאַהֲרֹן וְחוּר תָּמְכוּ בְיָדָיו מִזֶּה אֶחָד וּמִזֶּה אֶחָד וַיְהִי יָדָיו
יג אֱמוּנָה עַד־בֹּא הַשָּׁמֶשׁ: וַיַּחֲלֹשׁ יְהוֹשֻׁעַ אֶת־עֲמָלֵק וְאֶת־עַמּוֹ לְפִי־חָרֶב:
מפטיר יד וַיֹּאמֶר יהוה אֶל־מֹשֶׁה כְּתֹב זֹאת זִכָּרוֹן בַּסֵּפֶר וְשִׂים בְּאָזְנֵי יְהוֹשֻׁעַ כִּי־מָחֹה
טו אֶמְחֶה אֶת־זֵכֶר עֲמָלֵק מִתַּחַת הַשָּׁמָיִם: וַיִּבֶן מֹשֶׁה מִזְבֵּחַ וַיִּקְרָא שְׁמוֹ יהוה
טז | נִסִּי: וַיֹּאמֶר כִּי־יָד עַל־כֵּס יָהּ מִלְחָמָה לַיהוה בַּעֲמָלֵק מִדֹּר דֹּר:

---

the time of his prayer so that they could direct their hearts and join him in prayer (as well), similar to the Alexandrian (Jews) in Egypt, who would wave scarves (in the synagogue, as signals) (*Succah* 51b).

13. אֶת עֲמָלֵק וְאֶת עַמּוֹ — *Amalek and his people* . . . who were gathered together from another people to do battle (alongside Amalek).

14. כְּתֹב זֹאת זִכָּרוֹן בַּסֵּפֶר — *Write this for a memorial in the book.* The section of זָכוֹר, *Zachor* (*Deut.* 25:17-19).

וְשִׂים בְּאָזְנֵי יְהוֹשֻׁעַ — *And place it in the ears of Joshua.* And place a memorial in the ears of Joshua. And this Moses did by building the altar through his prayer at that time and by stating, כִּי יָד עַל כֵּס יָהּ, *The hand upon the throne of* YAH (i.e., HASHEM) (v. 16).

מָחֹה אֶמְחֶה אֶת זֵכֶר עֲמָלֵק — *I will utterly blot out the remembrance of Amalek.* I will destroy their livestock as well, as it says, וְהַחֲרַמְתֶּם אֶת כָּל אֲשֶׁר לוֹ . . . מִשּׁוֹר וְעַד שֶׂה וכו׳, *And utterly destroy all that they have . . . ox and sheep . . .* (*I Samuel* 15:3).

15. וַיִּקְרָא שְׁמוֹ — *And called His Name.* (He) called (in) the Name of the Holy One, Blessed is He, in his prayer, similar to קָרָאתִי שִׁמְךָ ה׳, *I called upon Your Name,* HASHEM (*Lamentations* 3:54).

ה׳ נִסִּי — HASHEM *Nissi.* HASHEM is my exalted (banner), similar to, נָתַתָּה לִּירֵאֶיךָ נֵּס לְהִתְנוֹסֵס, *You have given a banner to raise high, to those who fear You* (*Psalms* 60:6); i.e., God will raise me up and elevate me over those who rise up (against us),

NOTES

Amalek was one waged in a normal natural manner, and not a miraculous one, what need was there for the rod of God? The *Sforno* explains that it was used as a signal to Israel, letting them know when Moses prayed so that they could join with him. He compares this to the great synagogue in Alexandria which was immense and the only way the people knew that the reader had reached a point which required their response was to have a scarf waved to the congregation as a signal.

13. אֶת עֲמָלֵק וְאֶת עַמּוֹ — *Amalek and his people.* The phrase *his people* indicates soldiers who were not part of the Amalekites. These were foreign mercenaries in Amalek's army.

14. כְּתֹב זֹאת זִכָּרוֹן בַּסֵּפֶר וְשִׂים בְּאָזְנֵי יְהוֹשֻׁעַ — *Write this for a memorial in the book and place it in the ears of Joshua.* The *Sforno* is of the opinion that the first and second section of this verse are to be understood as separate statements. *Write this for a memorial in the book* refers to *Parshas Zachor* found in the book of *Deuteronomy* (see tractate *Megillah* 7a). The command to *place it in the ears of Joshua* refers to the deeds and words of Moses at this time, i.e., the building of the altar and his prayer.

15. וַיִּקְרָא שְׁמוֹ ה׳ נִסִּי — *And called His Name* HASHEM *Nissi. Tosafos* in *Megillah* 18a is of the opinion that the verse means, *And he called the altar,* HASHEM*-is-my-banner.*

similar to, בְּשִׁמְךָ נָבוּס קָמֵינוּ, *through Your Name we will tread upon those who rise up against us* (*Psalms* 44:6), and וּבִשְׁמִי תָּרוּם קַרְנוֹ, *And in My Name shall his horn be exalted* (ibid. 89:25).

16. וַיֹּאמֶר כִּי יָד עַל כֵּס יָהּ — *And he said, 'The hand upon the throne of* YAH (i.e., HASHEM). (Moses) said: 'The reason for this prayer of mine is because God, the Blessed One, has sworn that He will wage *war with Amalek from generation to generation,* therefore we are obligated to fight this battle in every generation.' (This is) as our Sages say, 'Israel was given three commandments when they entered the Land: to appoint a king; to destroy the seed of Amalek; and to build the Holy Temple' (*Sanhedrin* 20b). Therefore I pray that He shall be my banner and raise me up over the enemy.

NOTES

16. כִּי יָד עַל כֵּס יָהּ — *The hand upon the throne of* YAH (i.e., HASHEM). Israel was given the mission to wage war against Amalek and destroy them. God took an oath at this moment in history to wipe out Amalek *through* the Jewish people. Hence it is our obligation, but we can only succeed with the help of the Almighty. Therefore Moses asked that *HASHEM* be our banner, raising us on high over Amalek.

פרשת יתרו

Parashas Yisro

יח

א וַיִּשְׁמַ֞ע יִתְר֣וֹ כֹהֵ֤ן מִדְיָן֙ חֹתֵ֣ן מֹשֶׁ֔ה אֵת֩ כָּל־אֲשֶׁ֨ר עָשָׂ֤ה אֱלֹהִים֙ לְמֹשֶׁ֔ה
ב וּלְיִשְׂרָאֵ֖ל עַמּ֑וֹ כִּֽי־הוֹצִ֧יא יְהוָֹ֛ה אֶת־יִשְׂרָאֵ֖ל מִמִּצְרָֽיִם: וַיִּקַּ֗ח יִתְר֣וֹ חֹתֵ֣ן
ג מֹשֶׁ֔ה אֶת־צִפֹּרָ֖ה אֵ֣שֶׁת מֹשֶׁ֑ה אַחַ֖ר שִׁלּוּחֶֽיהָ: וְאֵ֖ת שְׁנֵ֣י בָנֶ֑יהָ אֲשֶׁ֨ר שֵׁ֤ם
ד הָֽאֶחָד֙ גֵּֽרְשֹׁ֔ם כִּ֣י אָמַ֔ר גֵּ֣ר הָיִ֔יתִי בְּאֶ֖רֶץ נָכְרִיָּֽה: וְשֵׁ֤ם הָֽאֶחָד֙ אֱלִיעֶ֔זֶר
ה כִּֽי־אֱלֹהֵ֤י אָבִי֙ בְּעֶזְרִ֔י וַיַּצִּלֵ֖נִי מֵחֶ֥רֶב פַּרְעֹֽה: וַיָּבֹ֞א יִתְר֨וֹ חֹתֵ֤ן מֹשֶׁה֙ וּבָנָ֣יו

XVIII

1. וַיִּשְׁמַע יִתְרוֹ — *And Jethro heard.* The expression שְׁמִיעָה, *to hear*, is used regarding an event which is not occurring at the time that event is being related. If we are told of a current event then the phrase רְאִיָה, *to see*, is used, be it far (away) or nearby, as we find, וַיַּרְא יַעֲקֹב כִּי יֶשׁ שֶׁבֶר בְּמִצְרָיִם, *Now Jacob saw that there was corn in Egypt* (*Genesis* 42:1), (or) וַיַּרְא בָּלָק, *And Balak saw* (*Numbers* 22:2), (or) וְרָאוּ כָּל עַמֵּי הָאָרֶץ, *And all the people of the earth shall see* (*Deut.* 28:10). Now, since the exodus of Israel from Egypt was then a current event, our Sages therefore say, 'What did (Jethro) hear? The dividing of the waters of the Sea of Reeds and the war with Amalek' (*Zevachim* 116a), for these two events had already transpired. However, if we interpret כִּי הוֹצִיא ה' אֶת יִשְׂרָאֵל, (which literally means) *that HASHEM had brought Israel out*, as meaning כַּאֲשֶׁר הוֹצִיא, *'when' He brought them out*, then we may say that (Jethro) heard all that God, the Blessed One, had done when He took Israel out of Egypt, namely, the great plagues, signs and wonders, etc. Therefore he was moved to go himself to the wilderness and he did not send Moses' wife and children to him through an emissary, similar to the king of Babylonia who sent ambassadors to inquire of the wonder which was done in the land (*II Chronicles* 32:31), for he (himself) desired to seek out God.

2. אַחַר שִׁלּוּחֶיהָ — *After he had sent her* . . . after he (Jethro) had sent her to ascertain the place of his (Moses') encampment, and he was informed that they would not encamp until they reached *the Mount of God* where they would serve Him, as stated, תַּעַבְדוּן אֶת הָאֱלֹהִים עַל הָהָר הַזֶּה, *You shall serve God upon this mountain* (3:12). Therefore Jethro delayed his arrival until Moses and his people would be there.

4. וַיַּצִּלֵנִי מֵחֶרֶב פַּרְעֹה — *And delivered me from the sword of Pharaoh* . . . at the time

NOTES

XVIII

1. וַיִּשְׁמַע יִתְרוֹ — *And Jethro heard.* (a) To reconcile the difficulty presented by the expression וַיִּשְׁמַע, *and he heard*, which is used in the Torah only regarding something which has already happened, our Sages explain that it refers to two events which had already transpired, namely the dividing of the waters and Amalek's attack. The *Sforno*, however, chooses to explain the verse differently by interpreting the phrase כִּי הוֹצִיא, which indicates the ongoing journey of the Israelites, as כַּאֲשֶׁר הוֹצִיא, *when He brought out*, indicating the past events which occurred at the time of Israel's deliverance.

(b) The *Sforno* also makes a second point

regarding the difference between Jethro and the response of the Babylonian king at the time of Chizkiyahu the king of Judah. When Sennacherib, the king of Assyria, beleaguered Jerusalem only to have God smite Sennacherib's army, the king of Babylonia sent emissaries to inquire regarding this great wonder. He did not, however, come personally. Jethro, on the other hand, came himself, for he was not motivated by curiosity or by a wish to congratulate his son-in-law, but by a sincere desire to seek out God and convert to the Jewish faith.

2. אַחַר שִׁלּוּחֶיהָ — *After he had sent her.* Unlike other commentators who interpret the phrase שִׁלּוּחֶיהָ as meaning the *sending away*

ו וְאִשְׁתּוֹ אֶל־מֹשֶׁה אֶל־הַמִּדְבָּר אֲשֶׁר־הוּא חֹנֶה שָׁם הַר הָאֱלֹהִים: וַיֹּאמֶר
ז אֶל־מֹשֶׁה אֲנִי חֹתֶנְךָ יִתְרוֹ בָּא אֵלֶיךָ וְאִשְׁתְּךָ וּשְׁנֵי בָנֶיהָ עִמָּהּ: וַיֵּצֵא מֹשֶׁה
לִקְרַאת חֹתְנוֹ וַיִּשְׁתַּחוּ וַיִּשַּׁק־לוֹ וַיִּשְׁאֲלוּ אִישׁ־לְרֵעֵהוּ לְשָׁלוֹם וַיָּבֹאוּ
ח הָאֹהֱלָה: וַיְסַפֵּר מֹשֶׁה לְחֹתְנוֹ אֵת כָּל־אֲשֶׁר עָשָׂה יהוה לְפַרְעֹה וּלְמִצְרַיִם

---

of Eliezer's birth the king of Egypt, who was pursuing Moses, had died, as it says, וַיְהִי בַיָּמִים הָרַבִּים הָהֵם וַיָּמָת מֶלֶךְ מִצְרַיִם, *And it came to pass in the course of those many days that the king of Egypt died* (2:23), hence he was (now) confident that he had been saved from Pharaoh's sword, for until his (i.e., Pharaoh's) death Moses could not feel safe from his sword wherever he might be found by Pharaoh, similar to, אִם יֶשׁ גּוֹי וּמַמְלָכָה אֲשֶׁר לֹא שָׁלַח אֲדֹנִי שָׁם . . . וְהִשְׁבִּיעַ אֶת הַמַּמְלָכָה וְאֶת הַגּוֹי, *there is no nation or kingdom where my lord has not sent to seek you . . . and he made the kingdom and nation swear (I Kings* 18:10).

6. אֲנִי חֹתֶנְךָ יִתְרוֹ — *I, your father-in-law Jethro.* He announced his coming beforehand as an ethical act so that (Moses) could prepare a place for them to dwell, as our Sages say, אַל תִּכְנֵס לְבֵיתְךָ פִּתְאוֹם, כָּל שֶׁכֵּן לְבֵית חֲבֵרְךָ, *Do not enter your home suddenly (unannounced), how much more so the home of your friend (Pesachim* 112a).

7. וַיֵּצֵא מֹשֶׁה — *And Moses went out.* He did not refrain, because of his high position, to go out to meet the one who had helped him (lit., 'done him a favor') in his time of distress, similar to, וְאֶת מַאֲמַר מָרְדֳּכַי אֶסְתֵּר עֹשָׂה, *For Esther carried out the bidding of Mordecai (Esther* 2:20), and also the (behavior) of Joseph with his brothers when he was a ruler. The reverse (i.e., ingratitude) is (also) found: וְלֹא זָכַר שַׂר הַמַּשְׁקִים אֶת יוֹסֵף, *And the wine steward did not remember Joseph (Genesis* 40:23).

8. אֵת כָּל אֲשֶׁר עָשָׂה ה׳ לְפַרְעֹה וּלְמִצְרַיִם עַל אוֹדֹת יִשְׂרָאֵל — *All that HASHEM had done to Pharaoh and to the Egyptians for Israel's sake . . .* as one who renders vengeance to the adversaries of his people, similar to, אָשִׁיב נָקָם לְצָרָי, *I will render vengeance to My adversaries (Deut.* 32:41). This was done by smiting their bodies at the sea as it says, יְשַׁלַּח בָּם חֲרוֹן אַפּוֹ עֶבְרָה וָזַעַם וְצָרָה מִשְׁלַחַת מַלְאֲכֵי רָעִים, *He cast upon them the fierceness of His anger, wrath and indignation and trouble, a delegation of evil messengers (Psalms* 78:49); He thereby demonstrated that He had chosen Israel as His treasure from among all the nations.

NOTES

of Zipporah by Moses, the *Sforno* explains it to mean the sending of Zipporah by her father to ascertain the plans of Moses and the Israelites so that he would be able to determine the most appropriate time and place for his visit.

4. וַיַּצִּלֵנִי מֵחֶרֶב פַּרְעֹה — *And delivered me from the sword of Pharaoh.* Eliezer is the second son born to Moses and Zipporah. The question is obvious. Why did Moses delay giving thanks to God for delivering him from the sword of Pharaoh and not give this name to his firstborn? The *Sforno's* answer is that not until the death of Pharaoh could Moses feel safe *from the sword of Pharaoh,* for when his first son was born Pharaoh was still alive.

7. וַיֵּצֵא מֹשֶׁה — *And Moses went out.* Moses, Esther and Joseph are all considered as royalty. None of them, however, stood on ceremony when the time came to welcome, greet or comply with the wishes of those who had either dealt kindly with them or whose relationship with them demanded respect and regard.

8. אֵת כָּל אֲשֶׁר עָשָׂה ה׳ לְפַרְעֹה וּלְמִצְרַיִם עַל אוֹדֹת יִשְׂרָאֵל — *All that HASHEM had done to Pharaoh and to the Egyptians for Israel's sake.* Moses stressed in his report to his father-in-law that God's actions were not only motivated by His

עַל אוֹדֹת יִשְׂרָאֵל אֵת כָּל־הַתְּלָאָה אֲשֶׁר מְצָאָתַם בַּדֶּרֶךְ וַיַּצִּלֵם יהוה:
ט וַיִּחַדְּ יִתְרוֹ עַל כָּל־הַטּוֹבָה אֲשֶׁר־עָשָׂה יהוה לְיִשְׂרָאֵל אֲשֶׁר הִצִּילוֹ מִיַּד
י מִצְרָיִם: וַיֹּאמֶר יִתְרוֹ בָּרוּךְ יהוה אֲשֶׁר הִצִּיל אֶתְכֶם מִיַּד מִצְרַיִם וּמִיַּד
יא פַּרְעֹה אֲשֶׁר הִצִּיל אֶת־הָעָם מִתַּחַת יַד־מִצְרָיִם: עַתָּה יָדַעְתִּי כִּי־גָדוֹל יהוה
יב מִכָּל־הָאֱלֹהִים כִּי בַדָּבָר אֲשֶׁר זָדוּ עֲלֵיהֶם: וַיִּקַּח יִתְרוֹ חֹתֵן מֹשֶׁה עֹלָה

אֵת כָּל הַתְּלָאָה אֲשֶׁר מְצָאָתַם בַּדֶּרֶךְ — *All the travail that had come upon them by the way* . . . through hunger, thirst and the war against Amalek.

וַיַּצִּלֵם ה׳ — *And how* HASHEM *saved them.* Thereby He displayed His special Providence toward them. The cause of this perforce being their beliefs and deeds (which were) predisposed to serve Him with one accord.

9. וַיִּחַדְּ יִתְרוֹ עַל כָּל הַטּוֹבָה — *And Jethro rejoiced for all the goodness.* He did not rejoice over the destruction of Egypt, as would befit one who is zealous for the honor of His maker, similar to, יִשְׂמַח צַדִּיק כִּי חָזָה נָקָם, *The righteous shall rejoice when he sees vengeance (Psalms* 58:11). He rejoiced for the good that befell Israel as would one who feels compassion for the tears of the oppressed.

10. אֲשֶׁר הִצִּיל אֶתְכֶם — *Who delivered you* . . . Moses and Aaron.

מִיַּד מִצְרַיִם — *Out of the hand of the Egyptians* . . . when you did smite them.

וּמִיַּד פַּרְעֹה — *And out of the hand of Pharaoh* . . . when you came to warn him.

אֲשֶׁר הִצִּיל אֶת הָעָם — *Who had delivered the people* . . . who were in servitude.

11. כִּי בַדָּבָר אֲשֶׁר זָדוּ עֲלֵיהֶם — *For that they dealt presumptuously against them.* For He delivered the people by the same means that the Egyptians had planned against Israel, similar to, וְכִי יָזִד אִישׁ עַל רֵעֵהוּ, *And if a man comes presumptuously* (יָזִד) *upon his neighbor* (21:14). This came to pass when He killed their firstborn just as the Egyptians killed the Israelite sons; He drowned them in the sea just as they drowned the children in the river. He killed the firstborn as a parallel to (lit., 'opposed to'), בְּנִי בְכֹרִי יִשְׂרָאֵל . . . וַתְּמָאֵן לְשַׁלְּחוֹ, *Israel My son, My firstborn . . . and you have refused to let him go* (4:22-23). And He (also) hardened their hearts after they refused to listen of their own free will. Thus He displayed His greatness (and superiority) over all the gods (powers) for he (Jethro) could not find any nation whose deity (i.e.,

NOTES

abhorrence of Egypt's wickedness toward, and enslavement of, Israel in general, but also because of Israel's special status and God's love for them. What was done was *for Israel's sake,* not just to punish evil but to avenge the honor of His chosen children. Israel in turn was worthy of this special concern because they sincerely accepted God's sovereignty.

9. וַיִּחַדְּ יִתְרוֹ עַל כָּל הַטּוֹבָה — *And Jethro rejoiced for all the goodness.* Although the *Sforno* does not mention the comment of our Sages in *Sanhedrin* 94a (quoted here by *Rashi)* that Jethro felt pain for the punishment of his Egyptian brethren (hinted at in the choice of the word וַיִּחַדְּ), nonetheless it is inferred in his interpretation as well.

10. אֲשֶׁר הִצִּיל אֶתְכֶם מִיַּד מִצְרַיִם וּמִיַּד פַּרְעֹה אֲשֶׁר הִצִּיל אֶת הָעָם — *Who delivered you out of the hand of the Egyptians and out of the hand of Pharaoh, Who had delivered the people.* The *Sforno* interprets each part of this verse as applying to different subjects. Moses and Aaron had to confront Pharaoh and needed special Divine protection to enter and leave the palace unharmed. They also could have been held responsible by the people for their plight and attacked by them in their anger and anguish. The concluding section of the verse is self-explanatory, referring to Israel's bondage and their deliverance from slavery.

11. כִּי בַדָּבָר אֲשֶׁר זָדוּ עֲלֵיהֶם — *For that they dealt presumptuously against them.* The an-

וּזְבָחִים לֵאלֹהִים וַיָּבֹא אַהֲרֹן וְכֹל ׀ זִקְנֵי יִשְׂרָאֵל לֶאֱכָל־לֶחֶם עִם־חֹתֵן
שני יג מֹשֶׁה לִפְנֵי הָאֱלֹהִים: וַיְהִי מִמָּחֳרָת וַיֵּשֶׁב מֹשֶׁה לִשְׁפֹּט אֶת־הָעָם וַיַּעֲמֹד
יד הָעָם עַל־מֹשֶׁה מִן־הַבֹּקֶר עַד־הָעָרֶב: וַיַּרְא חֹתֵן מֹשֶׁה אֵת כָּל־אֲשֶׁר־הוּא
עֹשֶׂה לָעָם וַיֹּאמֶר מָה־הַדָּבָר הַזֶּה אֲשֶׁר אַתָּה עֹשֶׂה לָעָם מַדּוּעַ אַתָּה יוֹשֵׁב
טו לְבַדֶּךָ וְכָל־הָעָם נִצָּב עָלֶיךָ מִן־בֹּקֶר עַד־עָרֶב: וַיֹּאמֶר מֹשֶׁה לְחֹתְנוֹ כִּי־
טז יָבֹא אֵלַי הָעָם לִדְרֹשׁ אֱלֹהִים: כִּי־יִהְיֶה לָהֶם דָּבָר בָּא אֵלַי וְשָׁפַטְתִּי בֵּין

---

heavenly representative) could totally repay (punish) measure for measure, (although) he did think that he (the deity) could do so in one area which was specifically (exclusively) his.

12. עֹלָה וּזְבָחִים לֵאלֹהִים — *A burnt offering and sacrifices to God* ... as a token of his acceptance of the Divine Sovereignty, similar to Naaman when he said: כִּי לוֹא יַעֲשֶׂה עוֹד עַבְדְּךָ עֹלָה וָזֶבַח לֵאלֹהִים אֲחֵרִים כִּי אִם לַה׳, *For your servant will henceforth offer neither burnt offering nor sacrifice to other gods, but to* H*ASHEM* (*II Kings* 5:17).

לֶאֱכָל לֶחֶם עִם חֹתֵן מֹשֶׁה — *To eat bread with Moses' father-in-law* ... to rejoice with him on the occasion of his entering under 'God's wings,' similar to, יִשְׂמַח יִשְׂרָאֵל בְּעֹשָׂיו, *Let Israel rejoice in Him Who made him* (*Psalms* 149:2).

לִפְנֵי הָאֱלֹהִים — *Before God.* (This means) before the altar on which these sacrifices were offered — either the altar which Moses built when Amalek was defeated (17:15) or a different altar whose construction is not mentioned (in the Torah). The eating of the sacrifice before the altar is similar to the eating (of sacrifices) behind the curtains (of the Sanctuary).

14. מַדּוּעַ אַתָּה יוֹשֵׁב לְבַדֶּךָ — *Why do you sit alone* ... (occupied with) public affairs?

וְכָל הָעָם — *And all the people* ... who need (you) for whatever reason, to submit their case before you, have to wait from morning to evening.

15. לִדְרֹשׁ אֱלֹהִים — *To inquire of God.* The princes and leaders of the generation who come regarding public business and order must come to me to inquire of God for *according to* H*ASHEM they encamp* (and execute their tasks).

16. כִּי יִהְיֶה לָהֶם דָּבָר — *When they have a matter.* And when these heads who come to me regarding public business have a dispute.

NOTES

cient pagans believed that a particular god had special power in a given area. When Jethro realized that *HASHEM* had punished the Egyptians in a variety of ways, each matching the criminal action taken against the Israelites — for example, the drowning in the Sea of Reeds, as punishment for drowning Jewish infants and the slaying of the firstborn as punishment for slaying Jewish children, who are called God's firstborn — he appreciated the supremacy of *HASHEM*, whose powers are unlimited and whose ability to mete out punishment *measure for measure* proves His omnipotence.

12. עֹלָה וּזְבָחִים לֵאלֹהִים ... לִפְנֵי הָאֱלֹהִים — *A burnt offering and sacrifices to God ... before God*. The Torah is emphatic in its insistence upon monotheism which only permits the offering of sacrifices to God alone, *He that sacrifices to the gods, save unto* H*ASHEM only, will be utterly destroyed* (22:19). Therefore the act of bringing sacrifices to God — an act performed by both Jethro and Naaman — is a manifestation of one's willingness to accept Him as one's exclusive Deity. Such a commitment deserves to be celebrated at a feast in which the leadership and Jethro participate, partaking of the sacrifice in front of the altar, which the Torah calls *before God*.

15. לִדְרֹשׁ אֱלֹהִים — *To inquire of God.* The

יז אִישׁ וּבֵין רֵעֵהוּ וְהוֹדַעְתִּי אֶת־חֻקֵּי הָאֱלֹהִים וְאֶת־תּוֹרֹתָיו: וַיֹּאמֶר חֹתֵן
יח מֹשֶׁה אֵלָיו לֹא־טוֹב הַדָּבָר אֲשֶׁר אַתָּה עֹשֶׂה: נָבֹל תִּבֹּל גַּם־אַתָּה גַּם־הָעָם
יט הַזֶּה אֲשֶׁר עִמָּךְ כִּי־כָבֵד מִמְּךָ הַדָּבָר לֹא־תוּכַל עֲשֹׂהוּ לְבַדֶּךָ: עַתָּה שְׁמַע
בְּקֹלִי אִיעָצְךָ וִיהִי אֱלֹהִים עִמָּךְ הֱיֵה אַתָּה לָעָם מוּל הָאֱלֹהִים וְהֵבֵאתָ
כ אַתָּה אֶת־הַדְּבָרִים אֶל־הָאֱלֹהִים: וְהִזְהַרְתָּה אֶתְהֶם אֶת־הַחֻקִּים וְאֶת־
הַתּוֹרֹת וְהוֹדַעְתָּ לָהֶם אֶת־הַדֶּרֶךְ יֵלְכוּ בָהּ וְאֶת־הַמַּעֲשֶׂה אֲשֶׁר יַעֲשׂוּן:
כא וְאַתָּה תֶחֱזֶה מִכָּל־הָעָם אַנְשֵׁי־חַיִל יִרְאֵי אֱלֹהִים אַנְשֵׁי אֱמֶת שֹׂנְאֵי בָצַע

בָּא אֵלַי וְשָׁפַטְתִּי בֵּין אִישׁ וּבֵין רֵעֵהוּ — *Come to me and I judge between a man and his neighbor.* Between these leaders (lit., 'great men') of the generation who come to me regarding public business.

וְהוֹדַעְתִּי אֶת חֻקֵּי הָאֱלֹהִים וְאֶת תּוֹרֹתָיו — *And I inform them the statutes of God and His laws.* (I inform) those leaders so that they might know, as it says, וַיָּשֻׁבוּ אֵלָיו אַהֲרֹן וְכָל הַנְּשִׂאִים בָּעֵדָה . . . וְאַחֲרֵי כֵן נִגְּשׁוּ כָּל בְּנֵי יִשְׂרָאֵל, *And Aaron and all the rulers of the congregation returned to him ... and afterward all the Children of Israel drew close* (34:31-32); as our Sages tell us, כֵּיצַד סֵדֶר מִשְׁנָה, *How was the order of instruction (Erubin* 54b). Now, because of these three reasons the people were forced to wait from morning to evening, (waiting) until the leaders leave so I can then turn to them and judge the poor people.

18. גַּם הָעָם הַזֶּה אֲשֶׁר עִמָּךְ — *And this people that is with you* . . . your court.

לֹא תוּכַל עֲשֹׂהוּ לְבַדֶּךָ — *You are not able to do it alone* . . . to hear all the business of the leaders, and to listen (also) to all who need speak to you regarding those matters which they cannot (resolve) without you.

19. הֱיֵה אַתָּה לָעָם מוּל הָאֱלֹהִים — *You be for the people before God* . . . to teach them the commandments and judgments which He commands, as an interpreter (intermediary) between them and God, the Blessed One.

וְהֵבֵאתָ אַתָּה אֶת הַדְּבָרִים אֶל הָאֱלֹהִים — *And you will bring these matters to God* . . . (the matters) which (you yourself) have not heard, such as, עִמְדוּ וְאֶשְׁמְעָה, *Stay, that I may hear (Numbers* 9:8), (also) וַיַּקְרֵב מֹשֶׁה אֶת מִשְׁפָּטָן לִפְנֵי ה׳, *and Moses brought their cause before* HASHEM (ibid. 27:5).

21. וְאַתָּה תֶחֱזֶה מִכָּל הָעָם — *And you shall provide out of all the people.* You shall choose and appoint; (however) in these three areas (i.e., public affairs, dispute among the leaders, and teaching Torah to the leaders) you yourself will have to (be

NOTES

three areas which occupied Moses, according to the *Sforno,* were public business (v. 15); disputes between the leaders regarding public policy (v.16); and teaching them God's laws and statutes (v. 16). The order of instruction (סֵדֶר הַמִּשְׁנָה) mentioned by the *Sforno* refers to tractate *Eruvin* 54b where our Sages describe how Moses would learn Torah from the Almighty, then teach it to Aaron, then Aaron's sons, then the elders and finally the people. Jethro suggested that lower and higher courts be established so as to lighten Moses' load while at the same time expediting the dispensing of justice.

19. וְהֵבֵאתָ אַתָּה אֶת הַדְּבָרִים אֶל הָאֱלֹהִים — *And you will bring these matters to God.* Jethro, wisely, appreciated that there might be matters which even Moses had not learned from God, in which case he would have to submit the question to Him, as happened in the case of those who were unclean and could not

כב וְשַׂמְתָּ עֲלֵהֶם שָׂרֵי אֲלָפִים שָׂרֵי מֵאוֹת שָׂרֵי חֲמִשִּׁים וְשָׂרֵי עֲשָׂרֹת׃ וְשָׁפְטוּ
אֶת־הָעָם בְּכָל־עֵת וְהָיָה כָּל־הַדָּבָר הַגָּדֹל יָבִיאוּ אֵלֶיךָ וְכָל־הַדָּבָר הַקָּטֹן
כג יִשְׁפְּטוּ־הֵם וְהָקֵל מֵעָלֶיךָ וְנָשְׂאוּ אִתָּךְ׃ אִם אֶת־הַדָּבָר הַזֶּה תַּעֲשֶׂה וְצִוְּךָ
שלישי כד אֱלֹהִים וְיָכָלְתָּ עֲמֹד וְגַם כָּל־הָעָם הַזֶּה עַל־מְקֹמוֹ יָבֹא בְשָׁלוֹם׃ וַיִּשְׁמַע
כה מֹשֶׁה לְקוֹל חֹתְנוֹ וַיַּעַשׂ כֹּל אֲשֶׁר אָמָר׃ וַיִּבְחַר מֹשֶׁה אַנְשֵׁי־חַיִל מִכָּל־
יִשְׂרָאֵל וַיִּתֵּן אֹתָם רָאשִׁים עַל־הָעָם שָׂרֵי אֲלָפִים שָׂרֵי מֵאוֹת שָׂרֵי חֲמִשִּׁים
כו וְשָׂרֵי עֲשָׂרֹת׃ וְשָׁפְטוּ אֶת־הָעָם בְּכָל־עֵת אֶת־הַדָּבָר הַקָּשֶׁה יְבִיאוּן

---

involved), and no one else will do. But regarding private legal decisions the rulers of thousands, the rulers of hundreds, etc., will suffice. Indeed when there will be four levels (of judges), one higher than the other, then the lesser one will judge first and if (the litigant) protests the court's decision he can appeal to a higher one, and (if necessary) from the second to the third and from the third to the fourth. In this manner there will be fewer coming to you for adjudication.

22. וְהָקֵל מֵעָלֶיךָ — *So it shall be made easier for you.* (There will be) many disputes which it will not be necessary to bring to you.

וְנָשְׂאוּ אִתָּךְ — *And bear the burden with you.* In that which you will have to do they will assist you, for example in teaching knowledge to the people after they have heard it from you, as mentioned in סֵדֶר מִשְׁנָה, *the order of study* (*Erubin* 54b).

23. עַל מְקֹמוֹ יָבֹא בְשָׁלוֹם — *Shall go to their place in peace.* After the law will be clarified in so many courts of law every litigant will know that the decision is true and he will not continue to contend, as our Sages say, 'When one leaves a court which has taken away his cloak, let him go forth singing on his way' (*Sanhedrin* 7a).

25. וַיִּבְחַר מֹשֶׁה אַנְשֵׁי חַיִל — *And Moses chose able men.* After seeking and not finding men who possessed all the qualities mentioned by Jethro (v. 21), he chose able men, well versed (in law) and diligent in determining the veracity of a matter and bringing it to a definite conclusion. (These were chosen over) those who feared God but were not able men, as our Sages say, 'Even if a scholar is vengeful and bears malice like a serpent, gird him on your loins; whereas even if an *am haaretz* (an ignoramus) is pious, do not dwell in his vicinity' (*Shabbos* 63a).

NOTES

bring the *Pesach* lamb on time (*Numbers* 9:8); and also in the case of the inheritance of Zelaphchad who died leaving only daughters and no sons to inherit him (ibid. 27:5).

23. עַל מְקֹמוֹ יָבֹא בְשָׁלוֹם — *Shall go to their place in peace.* The partners to a dispute can only find peace of mind if they are satisfied that justice has been done and that there has been no miscarriage of justice due to negligence or ignorance on the part of the court. The system devised by Jethro would hopefully satisfy the parties that the decision rendered was a fair and just one.

25. וַיִּבְחַר מֹשֶׁה אַנְשֵׁי חַיִל — *And Moses chose able men.* Jethro mentioned four qualifications as the criteria for choosing judges — *able men, who fear God, men of truth, who hate bribes* (18:21). Unfortunately Moses could not find any who met *all* of these qualifications. He therefore chose those who possessed the most important quality of all — ability. As the *Sforno* explains, it is vital that a judge be well versed in law, astute and capable of making a decision. These are the most important qualities a judge must possess. The saying of our Sages, cited by the *Sforno*, is most apt, since he interprets *able men* as meaning scholars who are knowledgeable and of strong character, though lacking some of the other qualities

כז אֶל־מֹשֶׁה וְכָל־הַדָּבָר הַקָּטֹן יִשְׁפּוּטוּ הֵם׃ וַיְשַׁלַּח מֹשֶׁה אֶת־חֹתְנוֹ וַיֵּלֶךְ לוֹ
אֶל־אַרְצוֹ׃
יט רביעי א בַּחֹדֶשׁ הַשְּׁלִישִׁי לְצֵאת בְּנֵי־יִשְׂרָאֵל מֵאֶרֶץ מִצְרָיִם בַּיּוֹם הַזֶּה בָּאוּ מִדְבַּר
ב סִינָי׃ וַיִּסְעוּ מֵרְפִידִים וַיָּבֹאוּ מִדְבַּר סִינַי וַיַּחֲנוּ בַּמִּדְבָּר וַיִּחַן־שָׁם יִשְׂרָאֵל
ג נֶגֶד הָהָר׃ וּמֹשֶׁה עָלָה אֶל־הָאֱלֹהִים וַיִּקְרָא אֵלָיו יהוה מִן־הָהָר לֵאמֹר כֹּה
ד תֹאמַר לְבֵית יַעֲקֹב וְתַגֵּיד לִבְנֵי יִשְׂרָאֵל׃ אַתֶּם רְאִיתֶם אֲשֶׁר עָשִׂיתִי

---

27. וַיְשַׁלַּח מֹשֶׁה אֶת חֹתְנוֹ — *And Moses sent away his father-in-law.* He did not want to accompany Israel to the Land, as he said, לֹא אֵלֵךְ כִּי אִם אֶל אַרְצִי וְאֶל מוֹלַדְתִּי אֵלֵךְ, *I will not go (with you), but I will depart to my own land and go to my birthplace (Numbers* 10:30). Perhaps this was due to his advanced age, as we find in the case of Barzilai who said, יָשָׁב נָא עַבְדְּךָ וְאָמֻת בְּעִירִי עִם קֶבֶר אָבִי וְאִמִּי, *Let your servant, I pray you, turn back that I may die in my own city and be buried in the grave of my father and mother (II Samuel* 19:38). The children of Jethro, however, did without a doubt go with Israel to the Land, as it says, וּבְנֵי קֵינִי חֹתֵן מֹשֶׁה עָלוּ מֵעִיר הַתְּמָרִים אֶת בְּנֵי יְהוּדָה, *And the children of Keni, the father-in-law of Moses, went up from the city of palm trees with the children of Judah (Judges* 1:16), and regarding them Balaam said, אֵיתָן מוֹשָׁבֶךָ, *Firm be your dwelling place (Numbers* 24:21).

XIX

1. בַּיּוֹם הַזֶּה — *The same day* . . . the first day of the month.

2. וַיִּסְעוּ מֵרְפִידִים וַיָּבֹאוּ מִדְבַּר סִינַי — *And they traveled from Rephidim and came to the wilderness of Sinai.* Their traveling from Rephidim was directed at their coming to the wilderness of Sinai where the Mount of God was located, because they knew that there they would worship (serve) Him, as it says, תַּעַבְדוּן אֶת הָאֱלֹהִים עַל הָהָר הַזֶּה, *You shall serve God upon this mountain* (3:12).

3. וּמֹשֶׁה עָלָה אֶל הָאֱלֹהִים — *And Moses went up to God.* The (verse) tells us that while Israel attended (lit., 'set their face') to matters of encampment and its needs, Moses went up to prepare himself for the prophetic (spirit).

4. אַתֶּם רְאִיתֶם אֲשֶׁר עָשִׂיתִי לְמִצְרָיִם — *You have seen what I did to the Egyptians.* (You have seen) how I urged them to repent of their wickedness for I do not desire the death (of the wicked); but when they stiffened their neck, I was constrained to multiply my signs and wonders in their midst and to destroy them.

NOTES

mentioned by Jethro.

XIX

2. וַיִּסְעוּ מֵרְפִידִים וַיָּבֹאוּ מִדְבַּר סִינַי — *And they traveled from Rephidim and came to the wilderness of Sinai.* We have already been told in verse 1 that *they came into the wilderness of Sinai;* why then is it necessary to repeat it again? The *Sforno's* answer is that the Torah is stressing that they traveled from Rephidim for the express purpose of reaching this destination, which was the Mount of God in the Sinai wilderness.

3. וּמֹשֶׁה עָלָה אֶל הָאֱלֹהִים — *And Moses went up to God.* The expression עָלָה, *went up,* is of special significance when used in the context of this verse. The *Rambam* in his *Guide* (1:10) states that the expression *to ascend* used here regarding Moses going up to God is to be understood thus, 'When one directs his thoughts toward an exalted sublime object he is said *to have ascended.*' As for our verse he states, 'In addition to the fact that he ascended to the top of the mountain upon which the light of HASHEM had descended,' Moses also *ascended* in the sense explained above. This is

ה לְמִצְרָיִם וָאֶשָּׂא אֶתְכֶם עַל־כַּנְפֵי נְשָׁרִים וָאָבִא אֶתְכֶם אֵלָי: וְעַתָּה
אִם־שָׁמוֹעַ תִּשְׁמְעוּ בְּקֹלִי וּשְׁמַרְתֶּם אֶת־בְּרִיתִי וִהְיִיתֶם לִי סְגֻלָּה
ו מִכָּל־הָעַמִּים כִּי־לִי כָּל־הָאָרֶץ: וְאַתֶּם תִּהְיוּ־לִי מַמְלֶכֶת כֹּהֲנִים וְגוֹי קָדוֹשׁ

וָאֶשָּׂא אֶתְכֶם עַל כַּנְפֵי נְשָׁרִים — *And I carried you on eagles' wings* ... on a road that no other person had traversed, like the eagle who takes his young ones high in the air where no other bird can fly. This was (done) to separate you from all the nations, and their pursuits, to be unto Me.

וָאָבִא אֶתְכֶם אֵלָי — *And brought you to Myself* ... to the Mount of God which is predisposed to prophecy.

5. וְעַתָּה אִם שָׁמוֹעַ תִּשְׁמְעוּ בְּקֹלִי — *Now, therefore, if you will indeed hearken to My voice* ... to accept upon yourselves Torah and commandments.

וּשְׁמַרְתֶּם אֶת בְּרִיתִי — *And keep My covenant.* The covenant which I will make when you accept (the Torah) — (meaning) the covenant entered into after they said, נַעֲשֶׂה וְנִשְׁמָע, *We will do and we will listen* (24:7), as it says, הִנֵּה דַם הַבְּרִית אֲשֶׁר כָּרַת ה׳ עִמָּכֶם עַל כָּל הַדְּבָרִים הָאֵלֶּה, *Behold the blood of the covenant which HASHEM had made with you in agreement with all these words* (24:8) — that I will not have to deal with you as I did with Egypt.

וִהְיִיתֶם לִי סְגֻלָּה מִכָּל הָעַמִּים — *You shall be My own treasure from among all peoples.* Although the entire human race is more precious to Me than all other inferior creatures (lit., 'existent ones'), for he alone (i.e., man) among them represents My intention (purpose), as our Sages say, חָבִיב אָדָם שֶׁנִּבְרָא בְּצֶלֶם, *Precious is man who was created in the Image (Avos* 3:14), still you shall be to Me a treasure beyond all of them.

כִּי לִי כָּל הָאָרֶץ — *For all the earth is Mine.* And the difference between you and them is one of degree, for indeed *all the earth is Mine,* and the righteous of all people are without a doubt dear to Me.

6. וְאַתֶּם תִּהְיוּ לִי מַמְלֶכֶת כֹּהֲנִים — *And you shall be to Me a kingdom of priests.* In this fashion you will be the treasure of them all by being a *kingdom of priests* to

NOTES

the meaning of the *Sforno's* commentary when he states, 'Moses went up to prepare himself for the prophetic spirit.'

4. אֲשֶׁר עָשִׂיתִי לְמִצְרָיִם וָאֶשָּׂא אֶתְכֶם . . . — *What I did to the Egyptians, and I carried you ...* God does not say, *'What I did for you.'* Therefore the *Sforno* interprets the statement *what I did to the Egyptians* as referring not to the plagues and punishment but the attempt by the Almighty to encourage them to repent.

וָאֶשָּׂא אֶתְכֶם עַל כַּנְפֵי נְשָׁרִים — *And I carried you on eagles' wings.* Unlike other commentators the *Sforno* does not interpret this statement as a protective act of God on behalf of Israel. Rather he interprets it to mean that God elevated Israel to a level unique among nations, taking them to a place inaccessible to all others, i.e., separating them from other nations and taking them unto Himself.

5. וּשְׁמַרְתֶּם אֶת בְּרִיתִי — *And keep My covenant.* There is a difference of opinion between the commentators as to which covenant the verse refers. The *Sforno,* as do others, submits that it refers to the covenant which was to be entered into *after* the revelation.

וִהְיִיתֶם לִי סְגֻלָּה מִכָּל הָעַמִּים — *You shall be My own treasure from among all peoples.* The *Sforno* interprets the words of the Almighty as implying that God's love is granted to all of mankind but Israel is His special treasure. This does not mean, however, that only they are

חמישי ז אֵלֶּה הַדְּבָרִים אֲשֶׁר תְּדַבֵּר אֶל־בְּנֵי יִשְׂרָאֵל: וַיָּבֹא מֹשֶׁה וַיִּקְרָא לְזִקְנֵי
ח הָעָם וַיָּשֶׂם לִפְנֵיהֶם אֵת כָּל־הַדְּבָרִים הָאֵלֶּה אֲשֶׁר צִוָּהוּ יהוה: וַיַּעֲנוּ
כָל־הָעָם יַחְדָּו וַיֹּאמְרוּ כֹּל אֲשֶׁר־דִּבֶּר יהוה נַעֲשֶׂה וַיָּשֶׁב מֹשֶׁה אֶת־דִּבְרֵי
ט הָעָם אֶל־יהוה: וַיֹּאמֶר יהוה אֶל־מֹשֶׁה הִנֵּה אָנֹכִי בָּא אֵלֶיךָ בְּעַב הֶעָנָן

understand and teach the entire human race that all shall call in the Name of *HASHEM* and serve Him *in one accord*, as shall (indeed) be the (role) of Israel in the future, as it says, וְאַתֶּם כֹּהֲנֵי ה׳ תִּקָּרֵאוּ, *But you shall be named priests of HASHEM (Isaiah* 61:6), and as it says, כִּי מִצִּיּוֹן תֵּצֵא תוֹרָה, *For out of Zion shall Torah go forth* (ibid. 2:3).

וְגוֹי קָדוֹשׁ — *And a holy nation.* A (nation) that shall never perish but exist forever among men, as it shall be in future time, as it says, וְהָיָה הַנִּשְׁאָר בְּצִיּוֹן וְהַנּוֹתָר בִּירוּשָׁלַיִם קָדוֹשׁ יֵאָמֶר, *And it shall come to pass that he who is left in Zion and he that remains in Jerusalem shall be called holy (Isaiah* 4:3), and our Sages say, מה קדוש לעולם קיים אף הם לעולם קיימים, *As the holy remains forever so shall they remain forever (Sanhedrin* 92a). Now this was indeed the intent of God, the Blessed One, when He gave the Torah, to grant them all the future good, had they not corrupted their ways through the (Golden) Calf as it says, וַיִּתְנַצְּלוּ בְנֵי יִשְׂרָאֵל אֶת עֶדְיָם מֵהַר חוֹרֵב, *And the Children of Israel stripped themselves of their ornaments from Mount Horeb onward* (33:6).

8. וַיָּשֶׁב מֹשֶׁה אֶת דִּבְרֵי הָעָם — *And Moses reported the words of the people.* He reported what he understood from their words, to Him Who had sent him; namely, he understood from their response that they would only do what God commanded (i.e., כֹּל אֲשֶׁר דִּבֶּר ה׳ נַעֲשֶׂה, *All that HASHEM has spoken we will do).*

9. בְּעַב הֶעָנָן — *In a thick cloud.* Although all the prophecies of Moses from the time of the giving of the Torah and beyond were through a 'clear, bright lens' (and not through a 'cloudy lens'), as it says, וּתְמֻנַת ה׳ יַבִּיט, *and the similitude of HASHEM he beholds (Numbers* 12:8); nonetheless, this particular prophecy was in a thick cloud.

NOTES

precious to Him, rather that relatively speaking Israel is more precious in the eyes of God. This interpretation explains the meaning of the end of the verse *for all the earth is mine.* Every human being was created in the Image of God.

6. וְאַתֶּם תִּהְיוּ לִי מַמְלֶכֶת כֹּהֲנִים וְגוֹי קָדוֹשׁ — *And you shall be to Me a kingdom of priests and a holy nation.* Although all mankind is precious in the eyes of God, Israel is unique and special in two ways. First is their mission to teach mankind to recognize and serve God, as Abraham their father did from the very outset of his mission. This is the meaning of מַמְלֶכֶת כֹּהֲנִים, *a kingdom of priests,* for it is the responsibility of a priest to teach. The second difference between Israel and other people is that they are destined to be an eternal people. This characteristic of immortality is rooted in their being a holy nation, for our Sages have taught us that sanctity is the element which insures נִצְחִיּוּת, *everlasting existence.* (Compare to 15:11 — the *Sforno's* commentary on נֶאְדָּר בַּקֹּדֶשׁ.)

8-9. וַיָּשֶׁב מֹשֶׁה אֶת דִּבְרֵי הָעָם ... בַּעֲבוּר יִשְׁמַע הָעָם ... וְגַם בְּךָ יַאֲמִינוּ לְעוֹלָם וַיַּגֵּד מֹשֶׁה ... — *And Moses reported the words of the people ... that the people may hear ... and may also believe you forever; And Moses told ...* The *Rambam* in his *Guide* (2:45) writes of eleven degrees of prophecy. He stresses that 'prophecy occurs in a vision or in a dream;' however Moses was the exception to whom God spoke 'face to face,' which the *Rambam* explains as 'one presence to another presence without an intermediary' (1:37). Although the Torah tells us that this level of face to face was reached by Israel at Sinai *(Deut.* 5:4), the

בַּעֲב֞וּר יִשְׁמַ֤ע הָעָם֙ בְּדַבְּרִ֣י עִמָּ֔ךְ וְגַם־בְּךָ֖ יַאֲמִ֣ינוּ לְעוֹלָ֑ם וַיַּגֵּ֥ד מֹשֶׁ֛ה אֶת־
י דִּבְרֵ֥י הָעָ֖ם אֶל־יְהוָֽה׃ וַיֹּ֨אמֶר יְהוָ֤ה אֶל־מֹשֶׁה֙ לֵ֣ךְ אֶל־הָעָ֔ם וְקִדַּשְׁתָּ֥ם הַיּ֖וֹם

בַּעֲבוּר יִשְׁמַע הָעָם ... וְגַם בְּךָ יַאֲמִינוּ לְעוֹלָם — *That the people may hear ... and may also believe you forever.* They will believe the possibility that your prophecy can be *face to face,* for indeed I will speak to them *face to face,* without (any medium) of a dream, as it says, פָּנִים בְּפָנִים דִּבֶּר ה׳ עִמָּכֶם, *Face to face God spoke to you (Deut.* 5:4), implying that man can prophecy while in command of his senses, which they thought was impossible. *Now* they will also believe that your prophecy can be in such a manner, as it says, וְדִבֶּר ה׳ אֶל מֹשֶׁה פָּנִים אֶל פָּנִים, *And HASHEM spoke to Moses face to face* (33:11). Therefore it says, הַיּוֹם הַזֶּה רָאִינוּ כִּי יְדַבֵּר אֱלֹהִים אֶת הָאָדָם וָחָי, *We have seen this day that God does speak with man and he lives (Deut.* 5:21); for they never doubted the possibility of prophecy (as such), knowing that the patriarchs, Moses, Aaron and Miriam had already prophesied, but until now no prophecy of any prophet was other than in a vision or dream as God, the Blessed One, explained, saying, בַּמַּרְאָה אֵלָיו אֶתְוַדָּע בַּחֲלוֹם אֲדַבֶּר בּוֹ, *I make Myself known to him in a vision, I do speak to him in a dream (Numbers* 12:6). However, the prophecy of Moses occurred while he still used his senses, and this they doubted, were it not that they themselves also prophesied in this manner, and thereby they will believe the words of Moses; and no other prophet will be able to rise up against them, for their (i.e., other prophets') prophecy will (never) be on this level.

וַיַּגֵּד מֹשֶׁה אֶת דִּבְרֵי הָעָם אֶל ה׳ — *And Moses told the words of the people to HASHEM.* When he heard the ordinance of his Maker (instituted) so that (the people) would believe in the kind of prophecy which was his, he sensed the doubts of the people (and therefore) told their words (to God), thinking that the reason they said, כֹּל אֲשֶׁר

NOTES

Rambam explains that only the voice of God reached Israel but not His speech (articulation) which only reached Moses (2:33). The *Sforno* does not elaborate to the extent that the *Rambam* does on this entire subject of prophecy, but he does establish the following points which are reflected in these two verses. The people of Israel always believed that there was communication between God and man. This was a part of their tradition from the time of the Patriarchs. However, they believed that this unique experience only occurred in a dream or vision where the prophet's senses were suspended and he went into a trance, transcending his physical being. Therefore they could not grasp the fact that God spoke to Moses in a different fashion, i.e., face to face, where man could be in full command of his senses, totally aware, comparable to *a man speaking to his friend (Exodus* 33:11). The only way to convince them that this was indeed the unique nature of God's communication with Moses was to have *them* experience this same level of prophecy themselves. This occurred at the time of the revelation at Sinai, thereby bringing them to an unequivocal faith in Moses (וְגַם בְּךָ יַאֲמִינוּ לְעוֹלָם). This also precluded the possibility of any other prophet (who could never reach this degree of prophecy) questioning the authenticity of the Torah given through Moses. However, until God granted this historic gift of prophecy to the people, and as yet their faith in Moses had not been fully established, their acceptance was also qualified. Hence they say *'All that God has spoken we will do,'* implying that if these commandments were to be given through an angel (i.e., on a lower level of prophecy), they would not accept them, for they feared that they would be vulnerable to His wrath if they deviated even slightly, as we see from the verse (23:21) quoted by the *Sforno.* This explains the meaning of verse 8 as well as the conclusion of verse 9, where we are told of Moses' report to God of the people's response. The sense of these verses would then be that Moses *reports the words of the people* (v. 8) and Moses *tells the words of the people* (v. 9) prior to God's statement, *Lo, I came to you,* etc. (the first part of v. 9). God is telling Moses that by exposing the people themselves to the highest degree of prophecy they *will* believe.

יא וּמָחָר וְכִבְּסוּ שִׂמְלֹתָם: וְהָיוּ נְכֹנִים לַיּוֹם הַשְּׁלִישִׁי כִּי ׀ בַּיּוֹם הַשְּׁלִשִׁי יֵרֵד
יב יְהוָה לְעֵינֵי כָל־הָעָם עַל־הַר סִינָי: וְהִגְבַּלְתָּ אֶת־הָעָם סָבִיב לֵאמֹר הִשָּׁמְרוּ
יג לָכֶם עֲלוֹת בָּהָר וּנְגֹעַ בְּקָצֵהוּ כָּל־הַנֹּגֵעַ בָּהָר מוֹת יוּמָת: לֹא־תִגַּע בּוֹ יָד
כִּי־סָקוֹל יִסָּקֵל אוֹ־יָרֹה יִיָּרֶה אִם־בְּהֵמָה אִם־אִישׁ לֹא יִחְיֶה בִּמְשֹׁךְ הַיֹּבֵל
יד הֵמָּה יַעֲלוּ בָהָר: וַיֵּרֶד מֹשֶׁה מִן־הָהָר אֶל־הָעָם וַיְקַדֵּשׁ אֶת־הָעָם וַיְכַבְּסוּ
טו שִׂמְלֹתָם: וַיֹּאמֶר אֶל־הָעָם הֱיוּ נְכֹנִים לִשְׁלֹשֶׁת יָמִים אַל־תִּגְּשׁוּ אֶל־אִשָּׁה:
טז וַיְהִי בַיּוֹם הַשְּׁלִישִׁי בִּהְיֹת הַבֹּקֶר וַיְהִי קֹלֹת וּבְרָקִים וְעָנָן כָּבֵד עַל־הָהָר

דִּבֶּר ה׳ נַעֲשֶׂה, *All that HASHEM has said we will do*, but did not say, כֵּן נַעֲשֶׂה, *so we shall do* (i.e., without mentioning God) was because they were doubtful whether Moses' prophecy was (actually) the words of *HASHEM* or (received) from an angel, and if they were to accept upon themselves the words of an angel, he would examine carefully (their deeds) even (if they deviated) by a single hair and not forgive (the slightest deviation), as it says, כִּי לֹא יִשָּׂא לְפִשְׁעֲכֶם, *for he will not pardon your transgressions* (23:21), therefore they said that they would only do (fulfill) the words of *HASHEM* alone.

11. וְהָיוּ נְכֹנִים — *And be ready* ... that your body be pure also, and ready for prophecy, not only the soul, since the level of this imminent prophecy will be *face to face*, while still in command of their senses. That is why a woman was prohibited to Moses from the time he reached that level, since all his prophecies from the time of the giving of the Torah and forward were *face to face*, as it says: לֵךְ אֱמֹר לָהֶם שׁוּבוּ לָכֶם לְאָהֳלֵיכֶם וְאַתָּה פֹּה עֲמֹד עִמָּדִי, *Go say to them return to your tents, but as for you stand before Me* (*Deut.* 5:27,28), as our Sages have explained (*Shabbos* 87a).

12. הַנֹּגֵעַ בָּהָר מוֹת יוּמָת — *Whoever touches the mountain shall surely be put to death. Lest they break through to HASHEM to gaze and many of them perish* (v. 21), and thereby mitigate the joy of God, the Blessed One, by defiling the place with their dead bodies. This will also impose a state of mourning on their relatives and (as a result) the Divine presence will not dwell upon them.

16. וַיְהִי קֹלֹת וּבְרָקִים — *And there was thunder and lightning* ... similar to ... וְהִנֵּה וְרוּחַ גְּדוֹלָה וְחָזָק ... וְאַחַר הָרוּחַ רַעַשׁ ... וְאַחַר הָרַעַשׁ אֵשׁ, *And behold ... and a great and strong wind ... and after the wind an earthquake ... and after the earthquake a fire* (*I Kings* 19:11,12), and so the (verse) testifies, saying, אֶרֶץ רָעָשָׁה אַף שָׁמַיִם נָטְפוּ, *the earth shook, the heavens also dripped* (*Psalms* 68:9).

NOTES

11. וְהָיוּ נְכֹנִים — *And be ready.* Whereas all prophecies are through a vision or a dream, as mentioned above, the level of this prophecy at Sinai, as well as all of those experienced by Moses henceforth, were *face to face*, meaning that they were in full control of their feelings and senses, wide awake and aware, hence their *physical being* had to be holy and pure. This explains why they had to prepare themselves by sanctifying themselves and washing their garments. Now just as they had to abstain from marital relations during this preparatory period so Moses had to continue this discipline even later since God would appear to him periodically without prior warning.

12. הַנֹּגֵעַ בָּהָר מוֹת יוּמָת — *Whoever touches the mountain shall surely be put to death.* Prophecy can only be experienced in a state of joy. We see that Elisha was unable to receive God's spirit until the minstrel played. Based on this the *Sforno* explains the importance of cautioning the people to distance themselves from the mountain, not only for the purpose of self-preservation, but also to prevent the exclusion of many Israelites from this great

יז וְקֹל שֹׁפָר חָזָק מְאֹד וַיֶּחֱרַד כָּל־הָעָם אֲשֶׁר בַּמַּחֲנֶה׃ וַיּוֹצֵא מֹשֶׁה אֶת־הָעָם
יח לִקְרַאת הָאֱלֹהִים מִן־הַמַּחֲנֶה וַיִּתְיַצְּבוּ בְּתַחְתִּית הָהָר׃ וְהַר סִינַי עָשַׁן כֻּלּוֹ
מִפְּנֵי אֲשֶׁר יָרַד עָלָיו יהוה בָּאֵשׁ וַיַּעַל עֲשָׁנוֹ כְּעֶשֶׁן הַכִּבְשָׁן וַיֶּחֱרַד כָּל־הָהָר
יט מְאֹד׃ וַיְהִי קוֹל הַשֹּׁפָר הוֹלֵךְ וְחָזֵק מְאֹד מֹשֶׁה יְדַבֵּר וְהָאֱלֹהִים יַעֲנֶנּוּ בְקוֹל׃
ששי כ וַיֵּרֶד יהוה עַל־הַר סִינַי אֶל־רֹאשׁ הָהָר וַיִּקְרָא יהוה לְמֹשֶׁה אֶל־רֹאשׁ הָהָר
כא וַיַּעַל מֹשֶׁה׃ וַיֹּאמֶר יהוה אֶל־מֹשֶׁה רֵד הָעֵד בָּעָם פֶּן־יֶהֶרְסוּ אֶל־יהוה
כב לִרְאוֹת וְנָפַל מִמֶּנּוּ רָב׃ וְגַם הַכֹּהֲנִים הַנִּגָּשִׁים אֶל־יהוה יִתְקַדָּשׁוּ פֶּן־יִפְרֹץ
כג בָּהֶם יהוה׃ וַיֹּאמֶר מֹשֶׁה אֶל־יהוה לֹא־יוּכַל הָעָם לַעֲלֹת אֶל־הַר סִינָי כִּי־
כד אַתָּה הַעֵדֹתָה בָּנוּ לֵאמֹר הַגְבֵּל אֶת־הָהָר וְקִדַּשְׁתּוֹ׃ וַיֹּאמֶר אֵלָיו יהוה לֶךְ־
רֵד וְעָלִיתָ אַתָּה וְאַהֲרֹן עִמָּךְ וְהַכֹּהֲנִים וְהָעָם אַל־יֶהֶרְסוּ לַעֲלֹת אֶל־יהוה
כ כה־א פֶּן־יִפְרָץ־בָּם׃ וַיֵּרֶד מֹשֶׁה אֶל־הָעָם וַיֹּאמֶר אֲלֵהֶם׃ וַיְדַבֵּר

---

17. לִקְרַאת הָאֱלֹהִים — *To meet God* ... toward the heavenly household, who preceded the Holy One, Blessed is He, as it says later, וַיֵּרֶד ה׳ עַל הַר סִינַי, *And HASHEM came down on Mount Sinai* (v. 20).

21. רֵד הָעֵד בָּעָם פֶּן יֶהֶרְסוּ — *Go down, charge the people, lest they break through* ... when I speak with them, (for) perhaps they will think that since they have ascended to the level of prophecy of *face to face*, as you have, they are then (also) permitted to ascend to your division (i.e., class).

23. וְקִדַּשְׁתּוֹ — *And sanctify it.* When You said to them, אִם בְּהֵמָה אִם אִישׁ לֹא יִחְיֶה, *Whether it be beast or man it shall not live* (v. 13), similar to אַדְמַת קֹדֶשׁ הוּא, *it is holy ground* (3:5).

24. לֶךְ רֵד — *Go, get you down* ... now, while I speak, be together with them at the bottom of the mountain.

וְעָלִיתָ אַתָּה וְאַהֲרֹן — *And you shall come up, you and Aaron* ... after the completion of the Ten Commandments and the chapter of *Mishpatim* (the Ordinances), as it says: וְאֶל מֹשֶׁה אָמַר עֲלֵה אֶל ה׳ אַתָּה וְאַהֲרֹן, *And to Moses He said, come up to HASHEM, you and Aaron* (24:1).

25. וַיֹּאמֶר אֲלֵהֶם — *And told them* ... the warning and the punishment (if they transgress), i.e., פֶּן יֶהֶרְסוּ . . . וְנָפַל מִמֶּנּוּ רָב, *Lest they break through ... many of them shall perish* (v. 21).

XX

1. וַיְדַבֵּר אֱלֹהִים — *And God spoke.* After Moses' cautioning and warning, God spoke all these words to them, as it says, אֶת הַדְּבָרִים הָאֵלֶּה דִּבֶּר ה׳ אֶל כָּל קְהַלְכֶם בָּהָר, *These words HASHEM spoke to all your assembly in the mount (Deut.* 5:19).

NOTES

opportunity of experiencing the prophetic spirit as a result of their grief at the death of relatives, which would deny them the privilege of prophecy.

17. לִקְרַאת הָאֱלֹהִים — *To meet God.* The royal entourage precedes the arrival of the king. The 'heavenly household' (פַּמַלְיָא שֶׁל מַעְלָה) was the entourage of angels who came first, heralding the imminent arrival of God.

24. לֶךְ רֵד וְעָלִיתָ — *Go, get you down, and you shall come up.* Moses originally thought he was to be on the mountain when God spoke.

ב אֱלֹהִים אֵת כָּל־הַדְּבָרִים הָאֵלֶּה לֵאמֹר: אָנֹכִי יְהוָה
ג אֱלֹהֶיךָ אֲשֶׁר הוֹצֵאתִיךָ מֵאֶרֶץ מִצְרַיִם מִבֵּית עֲבָדִים: לֹא־יִהְיֶה לְךָ
ד אֱלֹהִים אֲחֵרִים עַל־פָּנָי: לֹא־תַעֲשֶׂה לְךָ פֶסֶל וְכָל־תְּמוּנָה אֲשֶׁר בַּשָּׁמַיִם

---

2. אָנֹכִי ה׳ אֱלֹהֶיךָ — *I am* HASHEM *your God.* I alone am HASHEM who grants existence; (I am) the Prime Cause known to you through tradition (lit., 'receiving') and (logical) proof; and I confirm that you have accepted upon yourself (My sovereignty), to be your God, with (no need) for a mediator, therefore to Me alone shall you pray, and Me (alone) shall you serve (worship) without any mediator.

אֲשֶׁר הוֹצֵאתִיךָ מֵאֶרֶץ מִצְרַיִם — *Who brought you out of the land of Egypt* . . . through actions which were contrary to the (normal) laws of all 'means,' i.e., of nature and the constellations (of heaven). This (He did) when you accepted (His omnipotence) by stating, זֶה אֵלִי וְאַנְוֵהוּ, *This is my God and I will glorify Him* (15:2).

מִבֵּית עֲבָדִים — *Out of the house of bondage* . . . to remove all impediments (lit., 'coercion') which (otherwise) would have prevented you from performing the commandments (of God) properly.

3. לֹא יִהְיֶה לְךָ אֱלֹהִים אֲחֵרִים — *You shall have no other gods.* Even though you accept My sovereignty, you shall serve none except Me, (even) as one serves the ministers (lit., 'servant') of the king, akin to, אֶת ה׳ הָיוּ יְרֵאִים וְאֶת אֱלֹהֵיהֶם הָיוּ עֹבְדִים, *They feared* HASHEM *and served their own gods (II Kings* 17:33).

עַל פָּנָי — *Before Me* . . . for it is not permitted to show honor to (the king's) servants in his presence, and I am omnipresent, hence all places are equally (before Me).

4. לֹא תַעֲשֶׂה לְךָ פֶסֶל — *You shall not make a graven image* . . . even if not intended for idolatry (lit., 'to be worshiped').

NOTES

According to the *Midrash* he wanted to be there, closer to God. God, however, told him to go down and be with the people when He proclaimed the Ten Commandments and the chapter of *Mishpatim*. Only after this was completed would Moses ascend the mountain once again.

XX

2. אָנֹכִי ה׳ אֱלֹהֶיךָ — *I am* HASHEM *your God.* The first three words of the Ten Commandments are considered by the *Sforno* to be of prime importance, each signifying a fundamental attribute of the Almighty:

אָנֹכִי, *I*, emphasizes the oneness of God. He alone is the Master of the universe.

ה׳, HASHEM, denotes the concept taught by God to Moses when He said *I am that I am* (3:14). The *Sforno* comments on that verse that the implication of this name (the Tetragrammaton) is that God not only grants existence to all living things but also that He loves existence (life) and detests cruelty which destroys human existence. This idea was now pronounced by God at the beginning of the Ten Commandments.

אֱלֹהֶיךָ, *Your God*, stresses the direct avenue of communication between God and His people without any need for intermediaries.

אֲשֶׁר הוֹצֵאתִיךָ מֵאֶרֶץ מִצְרַיִם — *Who brought you out of the land of Egypt.* Many commentators ask why God states, *'Who took you out of Egypt'* rather than, *'Who created heaven and earth.'* The *Sforno* explains that since the exodus from Egypt necessitated radical changes in nature, these phenomena proved God's omnipotence and also His role as Prime Cause and the Source of all existence. As such He demands of Israel that they accept Him alone as their God to the exclusion of all other deities, hence *you shall have no other gods.* Also their liberation from *the house of bondage* freed them to serve God and perform His commandments without the impediment of another master who would make demands on their time, energy and loyalty.

3. לֹא יִהְיֶה לְךָ אֱלֹהִים אֲחֵרִים עַל פָּנָי — *You shall*

ה מִמַּ֫עַל וַאֲשֶׁר֙ בָּאָ֔רֶץ מִתָּ֑חַת וַאֲשֶׁ֥ר בַּמַּ֖יִם מִתַּ֥חַת לָאָֽרֶץ׃ לֹֽא־תִשְׁתַּחֲוֶ֥ה
לָהֶ֖ם וְלֹ֣א תָעָבְדֵ֑ם כִּ֣י אָנֹכִ֞י יְהוָ֤ה אֱלֹהֶ֙יךָ֙ אֵ֣ל קַנָּ֔א פֹּ֠קֵד עֲוֺ֨ן אָבֹ֧ת עַל־בָּנִ֛ים
ו עַל־שִׁלֵּשִׁ֥ים וְעַל־רִבֵּעִ֖ים לְשֹׂנְאָֽי׃ וְעֹ֤שֶׂה חֶ֙סֶד֙ לַאֲלָפִ֔ים לְאֹהֲבַ֖י וּלְשֹׁמְרֵ֥י

---

5. **לֹא תִשְׁתַּחֲוֶה לָהֶם** — *You shall not bow down to them* ... to the objects found in the heavens and the earth.

אֵל קַנָּא — *A jealous God.* I resent that one who worships Me should worship another as well, for there is no (ground) for comparison between Me and another (object), therefore it is proper to be jealous for My honor, that it (not) be given to another who (or which) is unworthy.

פֹּקֵד עֲוֺן אָבֹת — *Remembering the iniquity of fathers.* The reason I practice forbearance to such an extent with some wicked (people) in this world is because I wait until their measure is full (and it is time) to destroy them even in this world; now I *remember* (or *visit*) *the iniquity of fathers* who have sinned ...

עַל בָּנִים — *Upon the children.* (This is only so with those) who retain the (evil) deeds of their fathers, and add the כָּל יֵצֶר מַחְשְׁבֹת לִבּוֹ, *imagination of the thoughts of their heart (Genesis* 6:5), proceeding from evil to evil in every generation, as happened with Jeroboam.

עַל שִׁלֵּשִׁים — *Unto the third generation* ... if they are more wicked than their fathers, as happened with the seed of Omri.

וְעַל רִבֵּעִים — *And unto the fourth generation.* This was the case with the offspring of Jehu, (who) did not add to the (wickedness) of their fathers, but who did reach the level of sin which had become the possession of (each) generation, (hence) there was no hope of repentance and they were liable for destruction, similar to כִּי לֹא שָׁלֵם עֲוֺן הָאֱמֹרִי, *for the iniquity of the Amorite is not yet full (Genesis* 15:16).

6. **וְעֹשֶׂה חֶסֶד לַאֲלָפִים** — *And showing mercy to the thousandth generation.* At times the cause for the extended (period) wherein I show kindness to thousands is because of the merit of a pious (lit., 'one who loved Me') ancestor, and in his merit I show mercy to his offspring (for a number of generations).

NOTES

have no other gods before Me. The *Sforno* explains the second commandment in this sense: the acceptance of the sovereignty of a king precludes the worship of any of his ministers. This is especially true in the presence of the king, and since God is omnipresent it would always be in His presence.

5. **פֹּקֵד עֲוֺן אָבֹת עַל בָּנִים עַל שִׁלֵּשִׁים וְעַל רִבֵּעִים** — *Remembering the iniquity of fathers upon the children, unto the third generation and unto the fourth generation.* The *Sforno* cites as examples, in his interpretation of this verse, Jeroboam, Omri and Jehu. The former's punishment came in the second generation visited upon his son Nadav *(I Kings* 15:26). In the case of Omri the third generation was punished, i.e., in the reign of his grandson Jehoram son of Ahab, the royal house of Ahab was wiped out by Jehu *(II Kings* 9). As for Jehu himself, four generations of kings ruled until they in turn were deposed; Jehu, Jehoachaz, Joash and Jeroboam. When the latter's son Zechariah served as king for only six months he was killed. Thus the statement that God visits the sins on the children, if they pursue the same path of wickedness as their forebears, is indeed *on children* (second generation), third and fourth generations. In each instance, punishment is executed only when God determines that the measure is full and there is no hope for repentance.

ז מִצְוֺתָֽי׃ לֹ֥א תִשָּׂ֛א אֶת־שֵֽׁם־יהוָ֥ה אֱלֹהֶ֖יךָ לַשָּׁ֑וְא כִּ֣י
לֹ֤א יְנַקֶּה֙ יהוָ֔ה אֵ֛ת אֲשֶׁר־יִשָּׂ֥א אֶת־שְׁמ֖וֹ לַשָּֽׁוְא׃
ח־ט זָכ֛וֹר אֶת־י֥וֹם הַשַּׁבָּ֖ת לְקַדְּשֽׁוֹ׃ שֵׁ֤שֶׁת יָמִים֙ תַּֽעֲבֹ֔ד וְעָשִׂ֖יתָ כָּל־מְלַאכְתֶּֽךָ׃

7. לֹא תִשָּׂא — *You shall not take the Name.* (This refers to) שְׁבוּעַת הָאָלָה, *the oath of cursing,* similar to, וְנָשָׁא בוֹ אָלָה לְהַאֲלֹתוֹ, *And an oath be laid upon him to cause him to swear (I Kings* 8:31).

לַשָּׁוְא — *In vain.* There is no doubt that the curse and oath (is valid and) will take effect upon the one who swears in this fashion.

כִּי לֹא יְנַקֶּה ה׳ אֵת אֲשֶׁר יִשָּׂא אֶת שְׁמוֹ לַשָּׁוְא — *For* H*ASHEM will not hold him guiltless that takes His Name in vain* . . . for naught and when it is unnecessary. Even if one swears truthfully, God will not hold him guiltless from the curse and oath, how much more so if he swears falsely, for it is a dishonor (to God) if a man takes His Name except to substantiate a truth which otherwise could not be confirmed. However, an oath in His Name which is (utterly) false, i.e., if one states with an oath, 'This is true, as God, the Blessed One, is true,' behold he is an atheist and has desecrated His Name, for it is as though he said that God, the Blessed One, is not true, as it says: וְלֹא תִשָּׁבְעוּ בִשְׁמִי לַשָּׁקֶר וְחִלַּלְתָּ אֶת שֵׁם אֱלֹהֶיךָ, *And you shall not swear by My Name falsely, so that you profane the Name of your God (Lev.* 19:12).

8. זָכוֹר אֶת יוֹם הַשַּׁבָּת — *Remember the Sabbath day.* Be mindful and remember the Sabbath day constantly in all your dealings during the days of work, similar to, זָכוֹר אֵת אֲשֶׁר עָשָׂה לְךָ עֲמָלֵק, *Remember what Amalek did to you (Deut.* 25:17); שָׁמוֹר אֶת חֹדֶשׁ הָאָבִיב, *Observe (guard) the month of Aviv (Deut.* 16:1).

לְקַדְּשׁוֹ — *To keep it holy.* This you shall do so that you be able to sanctify it. He cautions that a person should so order his affairs during the days of work in a manner that his mind be completely free of them on the Sabbath day.

9. שֵׁשֶׁת יָמִים תַּעֲבֹד — *Six days shall you labor.* In the works of earthly affairs (lit., 'life of the hour') which are, without a doubt, (akin) to the labor of a slave, for the majority of these matters are those of man's sufferings (engendered) on behalf of עוֹלָם שֶׁאֵינוֹ שֶׁלּוֹ, *a world that is not his.*

וְעָשִׂיתָ כָּל מְלַאכְתֶּךָ — *And do all your work.* Necessary for your basic needs.

NOTES

7. לֹא תִשָּׂא . . . לַשָּׁוְא . . . שְׁמוֹ לַשָּׁוְא — *You shall not take the Name . . . in vain . . . His Name in vain.* The word תִשָּׂא is ambiguous. To what is the commandment referring? By drawing a parallel to a similar word in *Kings,* וְנָשָׁא בוֹ, which specifies an *oath,* we learn that the phrase תִשָּׂא here also is speaking of swearing in God's Name. The first לַשָּׁוְא, *in vain,* refers to one who swears falsely, whereas the second refers to an unnecessary oath. The *Sforno* differentiates between one who swears falsely *in the Name of* H*ASHEM* and one who links the truth of his testimony *directly* to the very essence of God's truth, for then he desecrates and profanes God. This explains the reason for the Torah's apparent repetition of this warning in *Leviticus.* The two are identical and we see this from the added words there, *profane the Name of God.*

8. זָכוֹר אֶת יוֹם הַשַּׁבָּת לְקַדְּשׁוֹ — *Remember the Sabbath day to keep it holy.* The interpretation of the *Sforno* is based on the fact that זָכוֹר, *remember,* is an infinitive verb and as such is not limited in time. Therefore it implies that one should keep the Sabbath in mind during the week. The two verses cited are meant to demonstrate that the use of an infinitive verb is commonly used to indicate that one is exhorted to remember or observe continuously. The phrase *to keep it holy,* in turn, urges us to order our affairs during the week in such

י וְיוֹם הַשְּׁבִיעִי שַׁבָּת לַיהוָה אֱלֹהֶיךָ לֹא־תַעֲשֶׂה כָל־מְלָאכָה אַתָּה ׀ וּבִנְךָ
יא וּבִתֶּךָ עַבְדְּךָ וַאֲמָתְךָ וּבְהֶמְתֶּךָ וְגֵרְךָ אֲשֶׁר בִּשְׁעָרֶיךָ: כִּי שֵׁשֶׁת־יָמִים עָשָׂה
יְהוָה אֶת־הַשָּׁמַיִם וְאֶת־הָאָרֶץ אֶת־הַיָּם וְאֶת־כָּל־אֲשֶׁר־בָּם וַיָּנַח בַּיּוֹם
יב הַשְּׁבִיעִי עַל־כֵּן בֵּרַךְ יְהוָה אֶת־יוֹם הַשַּׁבָּת וַיְקַדְּשֵׁהוּ: כַּבֵּד
אֶת־אָבִיךָ וְאֶת־אִמֶּךָ לְמַעַן יַאֲרִכוּן יָמֶיךָ עַל הָאֲדָמָה אֲשֶׁר־יְהוָה אֱלֹהֶיךָ

---

10. שַׁבָּת לַה׳ אֱלֹהֶיךָ — *A Sabbath unto HASHEM, your God* . . . (totally dedicated) to God; to study and teach, to observe and do, and to take delight in it sufficient to serve and honor the Blessed One, similar to (the saying of our Sages), 'Wine and the aroma of spices made me bright' *(Yoma* 76b).

אַתָּה וּבִנְךָ וּבִתֶּךָ — *(Neither) you, nor your son, nor your daughter.* (This refers to) minor children who work at the behest of their father.

11. כִּי שֵׁשֶׁת יָמִים עָשָׂה ה׳ — *For in six days HASHEM made.* And the purpose of these (six days of Creation) was for man to be similar to his Creator as much as possible, which is in contemplation, study and freely chosen deeds, (all of which) will find favor in His presence.

וַיָּנַח בַּיּוֹם הַשְּׁבִיעִי — *And He rested on the seventh day.* For in it, all that was necessary to fulfill (God's) purpose and bring it to its goal was completed, and in (this) completion there is rest (tranquility).

עַל כֵּן בֵּרַךְ ה׳ אֶת יוֹם הַשַּׁבָּת — *Therefore HASHEM blessed the Sabbath day.* (He blessed it by granting man) a נְשָׁמָה יְתֵרָה, *added soul,* which is an expanded preparatory (spirit) for the service of God, the Blessed One.

וַיְקַדְּשֵׁהוּ — *And hallowed it* . . . that it be totally for God.

12. לְמַעַן יַאֲרִכוּן יָמֶיךָ — *That your days may be long.* These five commandments, if observed, will prolong your days, causing that your days be long (eternal life), i.e., without any natural or physical end, for the (concept) of width does not apply to these (days), as our Sages say, עוֹלָם שֶׁכֻּלּוֹ אָרוּךְ, *A world which is entirely 'long' (lasting) (Kiddushin* 39b). For indeed these five commandments deal entirely with the honor of God, the Blessed One, and he who honors Him (by observing them) will inherit everlasting life. They are: that we (recognize) and know Him as the One Who brought into being (something) from nothing (*ex nihilo*); that He alone shall

NOTES

a manner that our mind be completely free of them on the Sabbath.

10. שַׁבָּת לַה׳ אֱלֹהֶיךָ — *A Sabbath unto HASHEM, your God.* The *Sforno* uses the expression כֻּלּוֹ לַה׳, *totally dedicated to God,* twice in his commentary: first in this verse on the phrase לַה׳ אֱלֹהֶיךָ, *unto HASHEM your God,* and again in verse 11 on the phrase וַיְקַדְּשֵׁהוּ *(and hallowed it).* This presents a difficulty considering that the Talmud *(Pesachim* 68b) states, 'All agree that on the Sabbath one should satisfy his physical needs' (i.e., eating, drinking, etc.). This would seem to contradict the *Sforno's* interpretation of these two phrases as implying exclusive involvement in spiritual and intellectual pursuits. One might answer, however, that since the prophet tells us to *'Call the Sabbath a delight* (עֹנֶג)*, the holy day of HASHEM honorable* (מְכֻבָּד)*' (Isaiah* 58:13), therefore, when one engages in physical pleasures on the Sabbath motivated by the commandment to honor the Sabbath day, this is also considered as being לַה׳, *for HASHEM!*

12. לְמַעַן יַאֲרִכוּן יָמֶיךָ עַל הָאֲדָמָה — *That your days may be long upon the land.* The *Sforno* applies this promise *(that your days be long)* to the first five commandments, and following the interpretation of the Sages, explains that the length of days refers to the world to come where the term 'long-lasting' is applicable.

יג נֹתֵ֥ן לָֽךְ׃ לֹ֖א תִּרְצָֽח לֹ֖א
תִּנְאָ֑ף לֹ֖א תִּגְנֹ֑ב לֹֽא־
יד תַעֲנֶ֥ה בְרֵעֲךָ֖ עֵ֥ד שָֽׁקֶר׃ לֹ֖א
תַחְמֹ֖ד בֵּ֣ית רֵעֶ֑ךָ לֹֽא־

---

be your God and we will serve no other (deity), (and) we will not rebel against Him in thought, in speech, or deed, and we shall honor Him for He is our Father, our Maker.

עַל הָאֲדָמָה — *Upon the land.* By observing them (the first five commandments) you shall merit that the length of days which I have promised (lit., 'said') shall be attained when dwelling on the Land, i.e., you will not be exiled from it. However, the other five commandments, and they are: that we do not harm (lit., 'injure') any man physically (lit., 'his body'), his honor or his property, in deed, speech or thought, (all these) are warnings which protect (us) from punishment in this world and the world to come.

13. לֹא תִנְאָף — *You shall not commit adultery.* (This refers) primarily to a married woman, for it is the most common (offense) among sinners, but it also includes every prohibited intercourse.

לֹא תִגְנֹב — *You shall not steal.* This includes kidnapping, stealing property, stealing man's mind (i.e., deception), although the main warning applies to kidnapping, דָּבָר הַלָּמֵד מֵעִנְיָנוֹ, *an interpretation which is deduced from the text,* as our Sages say (*Sanhedrin* 86a).

לֹא תַעֲנֶה בְרֵעֲךָ עֵד שָׁקֶר — *Do not bear false witness against your neighbor.* Included in this (commandment) are tale-bearing and slander, although the main (warning) applies to testifying (falsely) in court.

14. לֹא תַחְמֹד — *You shall not covet.* You should consider everything (which is not yours) as something totally unattainable, for that which is unattainable (beyond one's reach) man's nature will not covet at all, similar to, וְלֹא יַחְמֹד אִישׁ אֶת אַרְצְךָ,

NOTES

Length implies eternity, whereas *width* is expansion, a concept applicable only to this world. The commandment to honor one's father and mother applies to God as well, Who is our Father. The commandments of אָנֹכִי, *I am HASHEM your God,* and לֹא יִהְיֶה, *You shall have no other,* are addressed to man's mind and thoughts (מַחְשָׁבָה); that of לֹא תִשָּׂא, *Thou shalt not take,* involves man's speech (דִּבּוּר) while לֹא תַעֲשֶׂה, *You shall not make,* and זָכוֹר, *Remember the Sabbath day,* involve deeds. By observing these commandments we honor God and are deserving of His blessing and protection on the soil of *Eretz Yisrael.*

The other five commandments deal with man's relationship to his fellow man. The prohibition against murder, adultery and robbery are בְּמַעֲשֶׂה, *acts in deed;* the admonition not to bear false witness entails דִּבּוּר, *speech,* while the commandment not to covet involves מַחְשָׁבָה, *thought.* Thus the first and second parts of the Ten Commandments complement one another.

13. לֹא תִנְאָף — *You shall not commit adultery.* Although the prohibition of adultery applies primarily to a relationship with a married woman, this commandment forbids all illicit relations between the sexes.

לֹא תִגְנֹב — *You shall not steal.* Our Sages, mindful of the verse in *Leviticus* 19:11, *You shall not steal,* explain that this verse in *Exodus* refers to kidnapping while the one in *Leviticus* refers to property. Their reasoning is based on the context of our chapter. Since the crimes of murder and adultery that immediately precede this commandment are punishable with death by a court, likewise that of stealing (לֹא תִגְנֹב) must involve a death penalty, hence it must be the act of stealing another person, i.e., kidnapping, since stealing property is not punishable by death.

תַחְמֹד אֵשֶׁת רֵעֶךָ וְעַבְדּוֹ וַאֲמָתוֹ וְשׁוֹרוֹ וַחֲמֹרוֹ וְכֹל אֲשֶׁר לְרֵעֶךָ׃
שביעי טו וְכָל־הָעָם רֹאִים אֶת־הַקּוֹלֹת וְאֶת־הַלַּפִּידִם וְאֵת קוֹל הַשֹּׁפָר וְאֶת־הָהָר
טז עָשֵׁן וַיַּרְא הָעָם וַיָּנֻעוּ וַיַּעַמְדוּ מֵרָחֹק׃ וַיֹּאמְרוּ אֶל־מֹשֶׁה דַּבֵּר־אַתָּה עִמָּנוּ
יז וְנִשְׁמָעָה וְאַל־יְדַבֵּר עִמָּנוּ אֱלֹהִים פֶּן־נָמוּת׃ וַיֹּאמֶר מֹשֶׁה אֶל־הָעָם
אַל־תִּירָאוּ כִּי לְבַעֲבוּר נַסּוֹת אֶתְכֶם בָּא הָאֱלֹהִים וּבַעֲבוּר תִּהְיֶה יִרְאָתוֹ
יח עַל־פְּנֵיכֶם לְבִלְתִּי תֶחֱטָאוּ׃ וַיַּעֲמֹד הָעָם מֵרָחֹק וּמֹשֶׁה נִגַּשׁ אֶל־הָעֲרָפֶל

---

neither shall any man covet your land (34:24), for covetousness causes (one) to steal, as we find by Achan, וָאֶחְמְדֵם וָאֶקָּחֵם, *then I coveted them and took them (Joshua* 7:21).

15. רֹאִים אֶת הַקּוֹלֹת — *Perceived the thunderings.* Comparable to וְלִבִּי רָאָה, *my heart has seen (Ecclesiastes* 1:16). They looked attentively at (considered) the thunderings and (realized) that they could not bear them, as it says, לֹא אֹסֵף לִשְׁמֹעַ אֶת קוֹל ה׳ אֱלֹהָי וְאֶת הָאֵשׁ הַגְּדֹלָה הַזֹּאת לֹא אֶרְאֶה עוֹד וְלֹא אָמוּת, *Let me not hear again the voice of HASHEM my God, neither let me see this great fire anymore, that I die not (Deut.* 18:16).

וַיַּרְא הָעָם — *And the people saw.* They considered what to do.

וַיָּנֻעוּ — *They reeled.* One who moves involuntarily to a place beyond his present one is called נָע, similar to וַיְנִעֵם בַּמִּדְבָּר, *and He made them wander to and fro in the wilderness (Numbers* 32:13); נוֹעַ תָּנוּעַ אֶרֶץ כַּשִּׁכּוֹר, *The earth shall reel to and fro like a drunkard (Isaiah* 24:20). As a result of this fear they involuntarily retreated from the area (where they stood) to a place beyond (them).

17. לְבַעֲבוּר נַסּוֹת אֶתְכֶם — *To test you.* To accustom (familiarize) you to the prophecy which you have merited 'face to face,' similar to the case of Elijah whose prophecy (at that moment) was experienced while (he was) in command of his senses, as it says, וַיָּלֶט פָּנָיו בְּאַדַּרְתּוֹ וַיֵּצֵא וַיַּעֲמֹד פֶּתַח הַמְּעָרָה, *He wrapped his face in his mantle and went out and stood in the entrance of the cave (I Kings* 19:13), although it may not have been through a bright lens as was the case with Moses, our teacher, of whom it is said, אֲשֶׁר יְדָעוֹ ה׳ פָּנִים אֶל פָּנִים, *Whom HASHEM knew face to face (Deut.* 34:10).

בָּא הָאֱלֹהִים — *God is come . . .* (i.e.,) the heavenly household, as said above, לִקְרַאת הָאֱלֹהִים, *to meet God* (19:17).

NOTES

14. לֹא תַחְמֹד — *You shall not covet.* The *Sforno* interprets the commandment, *You shall not covet*, which seemingly is an unrealistic demand made on frail man who is subject to desires and jealousies, to mean: what is another's should be considered as totally beyond your ken, utterly unavailable, akin to a princess beheld by a peasant, as other commentators put it. His proof from the verse which speaks of Israel going on their pilgrimage to Jerusalem during the festivals (34:24) is a most telling one. He interprets this assurance of God as meaning that the non-Jews will consider *Eretz Yisrael* as totally beyond their reach, a Land which they can never aspire to own!

17. לְבַעֲבוּר נַסּוֹת אֶתְכֶם — *To test you.* The parallel drawn by the *Sforno* to Elijah refers to the time when Elijah had vanquished the prophets of Baal on Mt. Carmel only to find himself fleeing from the wrath of Jezebel into the wilderness. At that moment of despair God spoke to him in *a still small voice.* This revelation was on a higher level than any previous appearance or communication by God to Elijah. Even this great prophet could not gaze upon God's glory and had to cover his face. For all Israel to have reached this level at Sinai was indeed proof of their readiness to receive God. This unique encounter left a lasting imprint of יִרְאַת ה׳, *reverence of HASHEM*, upon them.

מפטיר יט אֲשֶׁר־שָׁם הָאֱלֹהִים: וַיֹּאמֶר יהוה אֶל־מֹשֶׁה כֹּה תֹאמַר
כ אֶל־בְּנֵי יִשְׂרָאֵל אַתֶּם רְאִיתֶם כִּי מִן־הַשָּׁמַיִם דִּבַּרְתִּי עִמָּכֶם: לֹא תַעֲשׂוּן
כא אִתִּי אֱלֹהֵי כֶסֶף וֵאלֹהֵי זָהָב לֹא תַעֲשׂוּ לָכֶם: מִזְבַּח אֲדָמָה תַּעֲשֶׂה־לִּי
וְזָבַחְתָּ עָלָיו אֶת־עֹלֹתֶיךָ וְאֶת־שְׁלָמֶיךָ אֶת־צֹאנְךָ וְאֶת־בְּקָרֶךָ בְּכָל־
כב הַמָּקוֹם אֲשֶׁר אַזְכִּיר אֶת־שְׁמִי אָבוֹא אֵלֶיךָ וּבֵרַכְתִּיךָ: וְאִם־מִזְבַּח אֲבָנִים
תַּעֲשֶׂה־לִּי לֹא־תִבְנֶה אֶתְהֶן גָּזִית כִּי חַרְבְּךָ הֵנַפְתָּ עָלֶיהָ וַתְּחַלְלֶהָ:
כג וְלֹא־תַעֲלֶה בְמַעֲלֹת עַל־מִזְבְּחִי אֲשֶׁר לֹא־תִגָּלֶה עֶרְוָתְךָ עָלָיו:

וּבַעֲבוּר תִּהְיֶה יִרְאָתוֹ עַל פְּנֵיכֶם — *And that His fear may be before you.* (This is) similar to the reason given by Rabbi Yehoshua to the Caesar when he said, 'You say that you cannot look (directly at the sun) which is but one of the servants standing before the Holy One, Blessed is He; how much more so the Divine Presence!' (*Chullin* 60a).

19. אַתֶּם רְאִיתֶם כִּי מִן הַשָּׁמַיִם דִּבַּרְתִּי עִמָּכֶם — *You have seen that I have talked with you from heaven,* similar to הַמַּגְבִּיהִי לָשָׁבֶת . . . הַמַּשְׁפִּילִי לִרְאוֹת, *Who is enthroned on high . . . Who lowers Himself to see* (*Psalms* 113:5,6).

20. לֹא תַעֲשׂוּן אִתִּי אֱלֹהֵי כֶסֶף — *You shall not make with Me gods of silver.* Now since you saw that you need no intermediary to come close to Me, do not make *with Me* such (silver gods to serve as) intermediaries.

21. מִזְבַּח אֲדָמָה תַּעֲשֶׂה לִּי — *An altar of earth shall you make to Me.* It is also not necessary to make Temples of silver and gold and precious stones in order to bring Me close to you, but it is sufficient (to build) *an altar of earth.*

בְּכָל הַמָּקוֹם אֲשֶׁר אַזְכִּיר אֶת שְׁמִי — *In every place where I cause My Name to be mentioned.* (This means) which I shall choose as a meeting house to worship Me, similar to הַזְכִּירוּ כִּי נִשְׂגָּב שְׁמוֹ, *make mention that His Name is exalted* (*Isaiah* 12:4).

אָבוֹא אֵלֶיךָ וּבֵרַכְתִּיךָ — *I will come to you and bless you.* You will not have to attract My providence through the medium of gold, silver or other (precious metals and stones), for indeed I *will come to you and bless you.*

22. לֹא תִבְנֶה אֶתְהֶן גָּזִית — *You shall not build it of hewn stone . . .* to beautify it.

23. וְלֹא תַעֲלֶה בְמַעֲלֹת — *Neither shall you go up by steps.* Although I will not impose upon you to fashion adornments to (bring Me to) dwell in your midst, nonetheless be careful not to treat My altar lightly (with levity).

NOTES

19. אַתֶּם רְאִיתֶם כִּי מִן הַשָּׁמַיִם דִּבַּרְתִּי עִמָּכֶם — *You have seen that I have talked with you from heaven.* In this verse God says that He spoke to Israel from heaven. In 10:20, the Torah tells us that *HASHEM descended onto Mt. Sinai.* This seeming contradiction is what the *Sforno* is addressing in his quotation from *Psalms.* Since God's presence is everywhere, and He is *the place of the world,* the concept of God *being* in a place is in itself a misleading one. He is above and below at the same time.

20-23. לֹא תַעֲשׂוּן אִתִּי אֱלֹהֵי כֶסֶף . . . מִזְבַּח אֲדָמָה תַּעֲשֶׂה לִּי . . . וְלֹא תַעֲלֶה בְמַעֲלֹת — *You shall not make with Me gods of silver . . . An altar of earth shall you make to Me . . . Neither shall you go up by steps.* The thrust of these verses, as the *Sforno* sees it, is that God does not demand, or desire, any elaborate, ornate expensive expressions of reverence on the part of His people. However, this does not mean that we are to take our obligations to, and service of, God lightly, which is the reason for the prohibition of installing steps to ascend the altar. By installing a ramp instead, the priest's garments will not be disturbed and he will not expose himself while ascending. God may be content with a simple unadorned altar but His honor, and our respect and reverence, are of paramount importance.

פרשת משפטים
Parashas Mishpatim

כא א־ב וְאֵלֶּה הַמִּשְׁפָּטִים אֲשֶׁר תָּשִׂים לִפְנֵיהֶם: כִּי תִקְנֶה עֶבֶד עִבְרִי שֵׁשׁ שָׁנִים
ג יַעֲבֹד וּבַשְּׁבִעִת יֵצֵא לַחָפְשִׁי חִנָּם: אִם־בְּגַפּוֹ יָבֹא בְּגַפּוֹ יֵצֵא אִם־בַּעַל אִשָּׁה
ד הוּא וְיָצְאָה אִשְׁתּוֹ עִמּוֹ: אִם־אֲדֹנָיו יִתֶּן־לוֹ אִשָּׁה וְיָלְדָה־לוֹ בָנִים אוֹ בָנוֹת
ה הָאִשָּׁה וִילָדֶיהָ תִּהְיֶה לַאדֹנֶיהָ וְהוּא יֵצֵא בְגַפּוֹ: וְאִם־אָמֹר יֹאמַר הָעֶבֶד
ו אָהַבְתִּי אֶת־אֲדֹנִי אֶת־אִשְׁתִּי וְאֶת־בָּנָי לֹא אֵצֵא חָפְשִׁי: וְהִגִּישׁוֹ אֲדֹנָיו
אֶל־הָאֱלֹהִים וְהִגִּישׁוֹ אֶל־הַדֶּלֶת אוֹ אֶל־הַמְּזוּזָה וְרָצַע אֲדֹנָיו אֶת־אָזְנוֹ
ז בַּמַּרְצֵעַ וַעֲבָדוֹ לְעֹלָם: וְכִי־יִמְכֹּר אִישׁ אֶת־בִּתּוֹ לְאָמָה לֹא
ח תֵצֵא כְּצֵאת הָעֲבָדִים: אִם־רָעָה בְּעֵינֵי אֲדֹנֶיהָ אֲשֶׁר־°לֹא יְעָדָהּ וְהֶפְדָּהּ °לוֹ ק׳

XXI

1. וְאֵלֶּה הַמִּשְׁפָּטִים — *And these are the ordinances.* Behold, that in the previous chapter, the commandment (lit., 'warning'), לֹא תַחְמֹד . . . וְכֹל אֲשֶׁר לְרֵעֶךָ, *You shall not covet ... nor anything that is your neighbor's* (20:14) appears; (therefore) *and these are the ordinances* (follows), for through them men will know what is meant by *anything that is your neighbor's.*

אֲשֶׁר תָּשִׂים לִפְנֵיהֶם — *Which you shall set before them.* These do not consist of positive and negative commandments as the warnings of the previous chapter (did), rather when the occasion arises to judge, the legal decision shall be (determined) in the manner (set forth here).

7. לֹא תֵצֵא כְּצֵאת הָעֲבָדִים — *She shall not go out as the menservants do.* It is improper for a decent (lit., 'kosher') man to purchase a Jewish girl as a bondwoman without her consent. Rather this purchase shall be with the view of marriage to himself or his son, and the purchase money will be considered as given to her father to wed her, since he is entitled to it, as our Sages have stated (*Kesubos* 46b).

8. אִם רָעָה בְּעֵינֵי אֲדֹנֶיהָ — *If she please not her master.* Even so, if she does not please him, he should not marry her, lest he come to despise her. Rather her father and master should attempt to let her be redeemed.

NOTES

XXI

1. וְאֵלֶּה הַמִּשְׁפָּטִים — *And these are the ordinances.* The law determines legal ownership. Without civil laws which define the parameters of possession one has no way of identifying the true ownership of any item or object. Hence, the prohibition against coveting that which belongs to my neighbor can only be properly understood and observed if I know what is legally his. That is why the concluding commandment of the Ten Commandments is followed by the chapter of מִשְׁפָּטִים, *Ordinances,* and the corpus of civil law. With this interpretation the *Sforno* explains the use of the prefix ו׳, *and,* in the first word of this chapter, וְאֵלֶּה, *and these,* for it links the end of *Yisro* with the beginning of *Mishpatim.*

אֲשֶׁר תָּשִׂים לִפְנֵיהֶם — *Which you shall set before them.* The *Sforno* explains the choice of the phrase אֲשֶׁר תָּשִׂים, *which you shall set,* as opposed to a seemingly more appropriate one such as תֹּאמַר, *state,* תְּדַבֵּר, *speak,* or תְּצַוֶּה, *command.* These phrases would be fitting if this chapter spoke of positive or negative commandments. This, however, is not the case, for the Torah is not dealing here with obligatory injunctions. Rather we are being instructed how to deal justly with certain situations as they arise, hence the expression to *set before them* is a suitable one.

7-8. לֹא תֵצֵא כְּצֵאת הָעֲבָדִים . . . אִם רָעָה בְּעֵינֵי אֲדֹנֶיהָ . . . לְעַם נָכְרִי — *She shall not go out as the menservants do ... If she please not her master ... to a strange people.* The sense of these verses according to the *Sforno* is as follows. We consider it unseemly for a Jewish man to purchase a daughter of Israel as a bondwoman. It is improper, immodest and degrading. Therefore the money paid by him

ט לְעַם נָכְרִי לֹא־יִמְשֹׁל לְמָכְרָהּ בְּבִגְדוֹ־בָהּ: וְאִם־לִבְנוֹ יִיעָדֶנָּה כְּמִשְׁפַּט
י הַבָּנוֹת יַעֲשֶׂה־לָּהּ: אִם־אַחֶרֶת יִקַּח־לוֹ שְׁאֵרָהּ כְּסוּתָהּ וְעֹנָתָהּ לֹא יִגְרָע:
יא־יב וְאִם־שְׁלָשׁ־אֵלֶּה לֹא יַעֲשֶׂה לָהּ וְיָצְאָה חִנָּם אֵין כָּסֶף: מַכֵּה אִישׁ
יג וָמֵת מוֹת יוּמָת: וַאֲשֶׁר לֹא צָדָה וְהָאֱלֹהִים אִנָּה לְיָדוֹ וְשַׂמְתִּי לְךָ מָקוֹם
יד אֲשֶׁר יָנוּס שָׁמָּה: וְכִי־יָזִד אִישׁ עַל־רֵעֵהוּ לְהָרְגוֹ בְעָרְמָה
טו מֵעִם מִזְבְּחִי תִּקָּחֶנּוּ לָמוּת: וּמַכֵּה אָבִיו וְאִמּוֹ מוֹת

לְעַם נָכְרִי לֹא יִמְשֹׁל לְמָכְרָהּ בְּבִגְדוֹ בָהּ — *To sell her to a strange people he shall have no power, seeing he has dealt deceitfully with her.* Her father dealt deceitfully with his daughter by selling her, as it says, הֲלוֹא נָכְרִיּוֹת נֶחְשַׁבְנוּ לוֹ כִּי מְכָרָנוּ, *Are we not accounted by him strangers? For he has sold us (Genesis* 31:15). After he (the father) has seen the actions (of the purchaser) which are alien to an Israelite, who bought a Jewish daughter not for the purpose of marriage, then he (her father) no longer has the power to sell her later to another person who (might) act as alien as did (the first one).

9. כְּמִשְׁפַּט הַבָּנוֹת יַעֲשֶׂה לָּהּ — *He shall deal with her after the manner of daughters.* (The subject is) his son. The (duties) are food, raiment and conjugal rights, even though he (the son) did not purchase her or betroth her.

10. לֹא יִגְרָע — *He shall not diminish.* He is not permitted to take other wives unless he can meet their needs in a manner that he not diminish that to which his first wife is entitled.

13. וְהָאֱלֹהִים אִנָּה לְיָדוֹ — *But God caused it to come to his hand.* He was not guilty of negligence that this should have been caused (through him), but, מְגַלְגְּלִין חוֹבָה עַל יְדֵי חַיָּב, *punishment is brought about through a person of guilt (Sabbath* 32a), as it says, וְגַם רָשָׁע לְיוֹם רָעָה, *Even the wicked for the day of evil (Proverbs* 16:4).

וְשַׂמְתִּי לְךָ מָקוֹם אֲשֶׁר יָנוּס — *And I will appoint a place for you where he may flee . . .* to atone for his iniquity in exile.

14. מֵעִם מִזְבְּחִי — *From My altar.* (This is so) even though the entire camp of the Levites was a place of refuge in the wilderness.

NOTES

to the father should be considered as being כֶּסֶף קִדּוּשִׁין, *betrothal money*, and she then becomes his wife or his son's. To do otherwise is alien to Jewish norms and is therefore called נָכְרִי, *strange*, by the Torah. Once she has been spurned by the purchaser and wronged by her father, the Torah prohibits a repetition of this injustice (v. 8).

9. כְּמִשְׁפַּט הַבָּנוֹת יַעֲשֶׂה לָּהּ — *He shall deal with her after the manner of daughters.* Our Sages derive the laws of marital obligations from this verse, which are included in the *Kesubah* (marriage contract) to this very day. They are — support, clothing and conjugal rights.

10. לֹא יִגְרָע — *He shall not diminish.* The *Sforno* reflects the statement of our Sages (*Yevamos* 65a), 'A man may marry a number of women, providing he can attend to their needs.' (Compare the *Sforno's* comments to *Genesis* 29:18.)

13. וְהָאֱלֹהִים אִנָּה לְיָדוֹ — *But God caused it to come to his hand.* The first part of the verse from *Proverbs* reads: *HASHEM has made everything for His own purpose.* The Almighty uses many people as His messengers to exact justice. The Talmud in *Makkos* 10b (cited by *Rashi* on this verse) explains the expression, *caused it to come to his hand*, thus: Two people had committed murder in the past, one willfully, the other accidentally, but no witnesses were present. God brings them together at a given place and the latter falls upon the former, killing him accidentally in the presence of witnesses. In this manner the murderer is 'executed' while the accidental killer goes

טז־יז יוּמָת׃ וְגֹנֵב אִישׁ וּמְכָרוֹ וְנִמְצָא בְיָדוֹ מוֹת יוּמָת׃ וּמְקַלֵּל
יח אָבִיו וְאִמּוֹ מוֹת יוּמָת׃ וְכִי־יְרִיבֻן אֲנָשִׁים וְהִכָּה־אִישׁ אֶת־רֵעֵהוּ
יט בְּאֶבֶן אוֹ בְאֶגְרֹף וְלֹא יָמוּת וְנָפַל לְמִשְׁכָּב׃ אִם־יָקוּם וְהִתְהַלֵּךְ בַּחוּץ
שני כ עַל־מִשְׁעַנְתּוֹ וְנִקָּה הַמַּכֶּה רַק שִׁבְתּוֹ יִתֵּן וְרַפֹּא יְרַפֵּא׃ וְכִי־
כא יַכֶּה אִישׁ אֶת־עַבְדּוֹ אוֹ אֶת־אֲמָתוֹ בַּשֵּׁבֶט וּמֵת תַּחַת יָדוֹ נָקֹם יִנָּקֵם׃ אַךְ
כב אִם־יוֹם אוֹ יוֹמַיִם יַעֲמֹד לֹא יֻקַּם כִּי כַסְפּוֹ הוּא׃ וְכִי־יִנָּצוּ
אֲנָשִׁים וְנָגְפוּ אִשָּׁה הָרָה וְיָצְאוּ יְלָדֶיהָ וְלֹא יִהְיֶה אָסוֹן עָנוֹשׁ יֵעָנֵשׁ כַּאֲשֶׁר
כג יָשִׁית עָלָיו בַּעַל הָאִשָּׁה וְנָתַן בִּפְלִלִים׃ וְאִם־אָסוֹן יִהְיֶה וְנָתַתָּה נֶפֶשׁ תַּחַת
כד־כה נָפֶשׁ׃ עַיִן תַּחַת עַיִן שֵׁן תַּחַת שֵׁן יָד תַּחַת יָד רֶגֶל תַּחַת רָגֶל׃ כְּוִיָּה תַּחַת
כו כְּוִיָּה פֶּצַע תַּחַת פָּצַע חַבּוּרָה תַּחַת חַבּוּרָה׃ וְכִי־יַכֶּה אִישׁ

תִּקָּחֶנּוּ לָמוּת — *You shall take him, that he may die.* (This is) similar to, הַמְעָרַת פָּרִצִים הָיָה הַבַּיִת הַזֶּה, *Has this house become a den of robbers? (Jeremiah* 7:11).

20. נָקֹם יִנָּקֵם — *He shall surely be avenged.* The blood of the slave (shall be avenged), for the master is not permitted to smite (him) with such cruel blows, even though he does have the right to smite him to correct him, as it says: בִּדְבָרִים לֹא יִוָּסֶר עָבֶד, *A slave will not be corrected by words* (*Proverbs* 29:19).

21. כִּי כַסְפּוֹ הוּא — *For he is his money.* And he has the right to discipline him, and at times the slave defies him causing the master to become so angered that he smites him excessively, as it says, אַךְ מְרִי יְבַקֶּשׁ רָע, *An evil man seeks only to be insolent (Proverbs* 17:11).

24. עַיִן תַּחַת עַיִן — *An eye for an eye.* This would have been the fitting (punishment) according to the strict law of measure for measure, but we have received a tradition that he should pay money, because our conjecture may be at fault (lit., 'lacking'), and we may unwisely exceed the exact measure (in punishing) the guilty (one).

NOTES

into exile, which is his atonement and his punishment.

14. מֵעִם מִזְבְּחִי תִּקָּחֶנּוּ לָמוּת — *From My altar you shall take him, that he may die.* The *Sforno* explains the use of the word מִזְבְּחִי *(My altar)* in the sense of '*even* from the altar' you shall take the killer, for he will not find sanctuary by entering the sacred precincts of the Sanctuary or Temple, even if he grasps the *horns of the altar,* as we find by Joab *(I Kings* 2:28). The verse quoted by the *Sforno (Jeremiah* 7:11) is preceded by the words, *and come and stand before Me in this house . . . and say, 'We are delivered.'* The evildoers attempted to find sanctuary and deliverance from their transgressions by coming to the Temple, abusing its sanctity and perverting it to camouflage their wickedness. The prophet warned them that God would not permit His house to become a refuge for robbers and other sinners.

20. נָקֹם יִנָּקֵם — *He shall surely be avenged.* The Talmud *(Kesubos* 77a) applies this verse in *Proverbs* to every person, not only to a slave. Words alone do not suffice at all times to convince a person, and one must occasionally resort to physical persuasion.

24. עַיִן תַּחַת עַיִן — *An eye for an eye.* Our Sages have taught us that *an eye for an eye* means monetary compensation *(Baba Kama* 83b). The *Rambam (Mishneh Torah,* Laws of Injuries 1:3) states that the person who blinded the eye of another is *worthy* to have his eye blinded as well (measure for measure), but tradition teaches us not to do so. The reason given in the Talmud cited above is because this kind of punishment would not always be equitable and the Torah teaches us, מִשְׁפַּט אֶחָד יִהְיֶה לָכֶם, *You shall have one manner of law (Leviticus* 24:22). The *Sforno's* interpretation reflects all this.

אֶת־עֵין עַבְדּוֹ אוֹ־אֶת־עֵין אֲמָתוֹ וְשִׁחֲתָהּ לַחָפְשִׁי יְשַׁלְּחֶנּוּ תַּחַת עֵינוֹ:
כז וְאִם־שֵׁן עַבְדּוֹ אוֹ־שֵׁן אֲמָתוֹ יַפִּיל לַחָפְשִׁי יְשַׁלְּחֶנּוּ תַּחַת שִׁנּוֹ:
כח וְכִי־יִגַּח שׁוֹר אֶת־אִישׁ אוֹ אֶת־אִשָּׁה וָמֵת סָקוֹל יִסָּקֵל הַשּׁוֹר וְלֹא יֵאָכֵל
כט אֶת־בְּשָׂרוֹ וּבַעַל הַשּׁוֹר נָקִי: וְאִם שׁוֹר נַגָּח הוּא מִתְּמֹל שִׁלְשֹׁם וְהוּעַד
בִּבְעָלָיו וְלֹא יִשְׁמְרֶנּוּ וְהֵמִית אִישׁ אוֹ אִשָּׁה הַשּׁוֹר יִסָּקֵל וְגַם־בְּעָלָיו יוּמָת:
ל-לא אִם־כֹּפֶר יוּשַׁת עָלָיו וְנָתַן פִּדְיֹן נַפְשׁוֹ כְּכֹל אֲשֶׁר־יוּשַׁת עָלָיו: אוֹ־בֵן יִגָּח
לב אוֹ־בַת יִגָּח כַּמִּשְׁפָּט הַזֶּה יֵעָשֶׂה לּוֹ: אִם־עֶבֶד יִגַּח הַשּׁוֹר אוֹ אָמָה כֶּסֶף ׀
לג שְׁלֹשִׁים שְׁקָלִים יִתֵּן לַאדֹנָיו וְהַשּׁוֹר יִסָּקֵל: וְכִי־יִפְתַּח
לד אִישׁ בּוֹר אוֹ כִּי־יִכְרֶה אִישׁ בֹּר וְלֹא יְכַסֶּנּוּ וְנָפַל־שָׁמָּה שּׁוֹר אוֹ חֲמוֹר: בַּעַל
לה הַבּוֹר יְשַׁלֵּם כֶּסֶף יָשִׁיב לִבְעָלָיו וְהַמֵּת יִהְיֶה־לּוֹ: וְכִי־
יִגֹּף שׁוֹר־אִישׁ אֶת־שׁוֹר רֵעֵהוּ וָמֵת וּמָכְרוּ אֶת־הַשּׁוֹר הַחַי וְחָצוּ אֶת־כַּסְפּוֹ
לו וְגַם אֶת־הַמֵּת יֶחֱצוּן: אוֹ נוֹדַע כִּי שׁוֹר נַגָּח הוּא מִתְּמוֹל שִׁלְשֹׁם וְלֹא
לז יִשְׁמְרֶנּוּ בְּעָלָיו שַׁלֵּם יְשַׁלֵּם שׁוֹר תַּחַת הַשּׁוֹר וְהַמֵּת יִהְיֶה־לּוֹ: כִּי יִגְנֹב־אִישׁ
שׁוֹר אוֹ־שֶׂה וּטְבָחוֹ אוֹ מְכָרוֹ חֲמִשָּׁה בָקָר יְשַׁלֵּם תַּחַת הַשּׁוֹר וְאַרְבַּע־צֹאן
כב א תַּחַת הַשֶּׂה: אִם־בַּמַּחְתֶּרֶת יִמָּצֵא הַגַּנָּב וְהֻכָּה וָמֵת אֵין לוֹ דָּמִים:
ב אִם־זָרְחָה הַשֶּׁמֶשׁ עָלָיו דָּמִים לוֹ שַׁלֵּם יְשַׁלֵּם אִם־אֵין לוֹ וְנִמְכַּר בִּגְנֵבָתוֹ:
ג אִם־הִמָּצֵא תִמָּצֵא בְיָדוֹ הַגְּנֵבָה מִשּׁוֹר עַד־חֲמוֹר עַד־שֶׂה חַיִּים שְׁנַיִם

29. וְגַם בְּעָלָיו יוּמָת — *And its owner also shall be put to death.* If there are no witnesses (whose evidence would) make him liable to pay a ransom (כֹּפֶר), he is (then) guilty according to the law of Heaven.

30. אִם כֹּפֶר יוּשַׁת עָלָיו — *If there be laid on him a ransom.* If witnesses testify in such a manner that the judges will impose a ransom on him.

32. כֶּסֶף שְׁלֹשִׁים שְׁקָלִים — *Thirty shekels of silver.* Which is the evaluation (redemption money) of a female *(Leviticus* 27:4), for a slave is similar to a woman in respect to the performance of *mitzvos,* as we find in tractate *Chagigah* in the first chapter (4a).

XXII

2. וְנִמְכַּר בִּגְנֵבָתוֹ — *Then he shall be sold for his theft.* Were it not for this (punishment) the majority of impoverished people would (resort) to thievery, (reasoning that) if they destroy or consume what they have stolen there is no way

NOTES

29-30. וְגַם בְּעָלָיו יוּמָת ... אִם כֹּפֶר יוּשַׁת עָלָיו — *And its owner also shall be put to death ... If there be laid on him a ransom.* The *Sforno* is in agreement with *Rashi,* based upon the Talmud *(Sanhedrin* 15b and 33), that one is not put to death when his ox kills. He is, however, morally responsible and therefore liable to Heavenly capital punishment. The *Sforno,* however, deviates from *Rashi* regarding the word אִם in the phrase אִם כֹּפֶר יוּשַׁת עָלָיו. Whereas *Rashi* interprets אִם in this case as meaning אֲשֶׁר, *which,* and not *if,* similar to his interpretation of אִם in 22:24, the *Sforno* explains it as meaning *if,* i.e., if there are witnesses then a ransom is imposed. The *Sforno* is consistent in his translation of אִם, for in 22:24, אִם כֶּסֶף תַּלְוֶה, *If you lend money,* he also explains how the word אִם can be translated as a supposition *(if)* and not an obligation. See his interpretation there.

32. כֶּסֶף שְׁלֹשִׁים שְׁקָלִים — *Thirty shekels of silver.* The *Sforno* explains the Torah's yardstick for a person's value. It is based on one's

שלישי ד יְשַׁלֵּם׃ כִּי יַבְעֶר־אִישׁ שָׂדֶה אוֹ־כֶרֶם וְשִׁלַּח אֶת־בְּעִירֹה וּבִעֵר
ה בִּשְׂדֵה אַחֵר מֵיטַב שָׂדֵהוּ וּמֵיטַב כַּרְמוֹ יְשַׁלֵּם׃ כִּי־תֵצֵא אֵשׁ
וּמָצְאָה קֹצִים וְנֶאֱכַל גָּדִישׁ אוֹ הַקָּמָה אוֹ הַשָּׂדֶה שַׁלֵּם יְשַׁלֵּם הַמַּבְעִר
ו אֶת־הַבְּעֵרָה׃ כִּי־יִתֵּן אִישׁ אֶל־רֵעֵהוּ כֶּסֶף אוֹ־כֵלִים לִשְׁמֹר
ז וְגֻנַּב מִבֵּית הָאִישׁ אִם־יִמָּצֵא הַגַּנָּב יְשַׁלֵּם שְׁנָיִם׃ אִם־לֹא יִמָּצֵא הַגַּנָּב
ח וְנִקְרַב בַּעַל־הַבַּיִת אֶל־הָאֱלֹהִים אִם־לֹא שָׁלַח יָדוֹ בִּמְלֶאכֶת רֵעֵהוּ׃ עַל־
כָּל־דְּבַר־פֶּשַׁע עַל־שׁוֹר עַל־חֲמוֹר עַל־שֶׂה עַל־שַׂלְמָה עַל־כָּל־אֲבֵדָה

---

to force restitution, since they are unable to pay. In this fashion וַתִּמָּלֵא הָאָרֶץ חָמָס, *the earth will become filled with violence* (*Genesis* 6:11).

4. כִּי יַבְעֶר אִישׁ שָׂדֶה אוֹ כֶרֶם — *If a man cause a field or vineyard to be eaten* . . . i.e., in his own (field).

וּבִעֵר בִּשְׂדֵה אַחֵר — *And it feed in another man's field* . . . even though the animal strayed on its own into the field of another.

מֵיטַב שָׂדֵהוּ וּמֵיטַב כַּרְמוֹ יְשַׁלֵּם — *Of the best of his own field and of the best of his own vineyard shall he pay* . . . for (the damage of) שֵׁן וָעַיִן, *tooth and foot*, are considered as forewarned (מוּעָד) when inflicted in the domain of the injured (wronged) party.

6. כֶּסֶף אוֹ כֵלִים — *Money or vessels.* A rich man will (normally) guard these two things (immovable objects) without payment.

7. אִם לֹא שָׁלַח יָדוֹ — *If he has not sent forth his hand.* For if he did *send forth* (his hand) he is liable, even for accidental damages.

NOTES

mitzvah obligations. Hence the compensation for a slave and the evaluation of a woman are the same, since their *mitzvah* obligations are equal.

XXII

4. כִּי יַבְעֶר אִישׁ שָׂדֶה . . . וּבִעֵר בִּשְׂדֵה אַחֵר מֵיטַב שָׂדֵהוּ . . . יְשַׁלֵּם — *If a man cause a field to be eaten . . . and it feed in another man's field, of the best of his own field . . . shall he pay.* The *Sforno* interprets the first part of this verse as meaning that the owner of the animal originally put his animal in his *own* field to graze, however he did not properly guard it and prevent it from wandering into the adjacent fields of his neighbor; therefore he is liable to pay for damages incurred. This act of straying into another's property is a normal, common one and should have been anticipated by the owner of the animal even if there was no precedent. This is what we mean by the phrase מוּעָד, i.e., he is considered as being forewarned.

6. כֶּסֶף אוֹ כֵלִים — *Money or vessels.* There are four categories of שׁוֹמְרִים, *watchmen:* (1) One who does so without compensation (as a favor); (2) one who is paid; (3) one who leases and (4) a borrower. Verses 6 through 13 discuss the various laws pertaining to these watchmen. The Torah does not specify which verses apply to category (1) and (2); however, our Sages teach us that verses 6-8 apply to one who watches as a favor whereas verses 9-12 refer to one who receives compensation for his efforts. The *Sforno* explains logically how our Sages reached this opinion. The former verses deal with inanimate objects which are easily guarded, hence it refers to one who watches without compensation. The *Sforno* adds that we are probably speaking of a well-to-do person who must guard his own possessions; therefore it is no great bother to include his friend's as well. Verse 9, however, speaks of livestock, which demands time and effort; therefore it logically refers to a watchman who is paid, and performs this service as part of his livelihood. (See the *Sforno's* commentary there.) *Tosafos* in tractate *Baba Metzia* (41b) uses the same reasoning as does the *Sforno* in his commentary on these verses.

7. אִם לֹא שָׁלַח יָדוֹ — *If he has not sent forth his hand.* If the watchman uses the item in his safekeeping for his own purpose, since he does so without permission he is considered to be a גַּזְלָן, *robber*, and as such is liable for any and

אֲשֶׁר יֹאמַר כִּי־הוּא זֶה עַד הָאֱלֹהִים יָבֹא דְּבַר־שְׁנֵיהֶם אֲשֶׁר יַרְשִׁיעֻן
ט אֱלֹהִים יְשַׁלֵּם שְׁנַיִם לְרֵעֵהוּ׃ כִּי־יִתֵּן אִישׁ אֶל־רֵעֵהוּ חֲמוֹר
אוֹ־שׁוֹר אוֹ־שֶׂה וְכָל־בְּהֵמָה לִשְׁמֹר וּמֵת אוֹ־נִשְׁבַּר אוֹ־נִשְׁבָּה אֵין רֹאֶה׃
י שְׁבֻעַת יהוה תִּהְיֶה בֵּין שְׁנֵיהֶם אִם־לֹא שָׁלַח יָדוֹ בִּמְלֶאכֶת רֵעֵהוּ וְלָקַח
יא-יב בְּעָלָיו וְלֹא יְשַׁלֵּם׃ וְאִם־גָּנֹב יִגָּנֵב מֵעִמּוֹ יְשַׁלֵּם לִבְעָלָיו׃ אִם־טָרֹף יִטָּרֵף
יְבִאֵהוּ עֵד הַטְּרֵפָה לֹא יְשַׁלֵּם׃
יג וְכִי־יִשְׁאַל אִישׁ מֵעִם רֵעֵהוּ וְנִשְׁבַּר אוֹ־מֵת בְּעָלָיו אֵין־עִמּוֹ שַׁלֵּם יְשַׁלֵּם׃

---

8. עַד הָאֱלֹהִים יָבֹא דְּבַר שְׁנֵיהֶם — *The cause of both parties shall come before the judges.* The plaintiff and defendant (must come before the judges for the purpose) of taking an oath, be they depositor and bailee (or) lender and borrower, (providing that the bailee or borrower) admitted partially.

אֲשֶׁר יֹאמַר כִּי הוּא זֶה — *Whereof one says, 'This is it.'* (This oath) also applies when the defendant says, 'This is true, but not the rest of your claim'; and this is called 'confessing to a partial claim' (מוֹדֶה בְּמִקְצָת).

אֲשֶׁר יַרְשִׁיעֻן אֱלֹהִים יְשַׁלֵּם שְׁנַיִם — *He whom the judges condemn shall pay double.* But if the judges condemn him (i.e., the bailee) of being a thief, for he claimed falsely that the object was stolen, then he must pay double, as does a thief.

9. חֲמוֹר אוֹ שׁוֹר אוֹ שֶׂה — *An ass, or an ox or a sheep.* These are normally watched over by poorer people for compensation.

12. יְבִאֵהוּ עֵד — *Let him bring it for witness.* It has already been said that wherever (the Torah) says עֵד, *witness* (in the singular), it means two *(Sotah* 2a). The sense (of the verse) is therefore, *If it be torn in pieces* by a wild (lit., 'evil') beast, which usually is an event seen by others, for אֲשֶׁר יִקָּרֵא עָלָיו מְלֹא רֹעִים, *a multitude of shepherds is called out against him (Isaiah* 31:4), hence let him bring the torn animal and a pair of witnesses to testify that this animal was torn by accident.

הַטְּרֵפָה לֹא יְשַׁלֵּם — *He shall not make good that which was torn* . . . by accident. But if beasts ate it due to his lack of guarding, then he must pay, as our Sages say, 'One wolf is not considered an accident . . . two dogs are not considered accidental' *(Baba Metzia* 93b), and certainly a cat or marten or similar animals (where his intervention) could have saved (them).

NOTES

every damage, even if it is accidental.

8. עַד הָאֱלֹהִים יָבֹא דְּבַר שְׁנֵיהֶם — *The cause of both parties shall come before the judges.* The Torah stresses דְּבַר שְׁנֵיהֶם, *the cause of 'both' parties,* and the *Sforno* explains 'plaintiff and defendant.' This reflects the admonition of the *Mechilta* (23:1) that a judge should not accept the testimony of one party in the absence of the other party. Both must be present.

אֲשֶׁר יֹאמַר כִּי הוּא זֶה — *Whereof one says, 'This is it.'* Our Sages interpret the expression *Whereof one says,* 'כִּי הוּא זֶה, *This is it,'* as meaning a partial confession by the defendant. Only under such circumstances do we impose an oath upon the defendant. The *Sforno's* commentary explains how this principle of מוֹדֶה בְּמִקְצָת can reasonably be understood from the verse itself, 'This is true (i.e., *part* of your claim) but not the rest of it.'

12. יְבִאֵהוּ עֵד — *Let him bring it for witness.* The *Sforno* links this verse to verse 9. There the Torah states, אֵין רֹאֶה, *no man seeing it,* implying that the accident happened in a private place where there were no witnesses, hence the watchman must swear. In our case, however, the watchman was among other shepherds, for the Torah speaks not of death or hurt (as it does in verse 9) but of an attack by a beast which perforce is out in the open, therefore witnesses were available.

יד־טו אִם־בְּעָלָיו עִמּוֹ לֹא יְשַׁלֵּם אִם־שָׂכִיר הוּא בָּא בִּשְׂכָרוֹ: וְכִי־יְפַתֶּה
טז אִישׁ בְּתוּלָה אֲשֶׁר לֹא־אֹרָשָׂה וְשָׁכַב עִמָּהּ מָהֹר יִמְהָרֶנָּה לּוֹ לְאִשָּׁה: אִם־
יז מָאֵן יְמָאֵן אָבִיהָ לְתִתָּהּ לוֹ כֶּסֶף יִשְׁקֹל כְּמֹהַר הַבְּתוּלֹת: מְכַשֵּׁפָה
יח־יט לֹא תְחַיֶּה: כָּל־שֹׁכֵב עִם־בְּהֵמָה מוֹת יוּמָת: זֹבֵחַ לָאֱלֹהִים יָחֳרָם
כ בִּלְתִּי לַיהוָה לְבַדּוֹ: וְגֵר לֹא־תוֹנֶה וְלֹא תִלְחָצֶנּוּ כִּי־גֵרִים הֱיִיתֶם בְּאֶרֶץ
כא־כב מִצְרָיִם: כָּל־אַלְמָנָה וְיָתוֹם לֹא תְעַנּוּן: אִם־עַנֵּה תְעַנֶּה אֹתוֹ כִּי אִם־צָעֹק

---

14. אם בְּעָלָיו עִמּוֹ — *If the owner is with him.* (If he is with him) in his work at the time of his borrowing.

לֹא יְשַׁלֵּם — *He shall not pay.* One who lends under such circumstances, which (reflects) a close relationship, intends to give a gift on the understanding of the return of same (מַתָּנָה עַל מְנַת לְהַחֲזִיר). Now since no condition was made he is not obligated to return it unless it still exists (i.e., it is in his possession). Even according to the opinion (of the Sage) who states that a gift given on condition of return obligates (the recipient) to compensate (even) for accidental loss, (that) is only because the proviso of *on condition* cancels out the gift, if the condition is not fulfilled. However, in our case, where it is a gift with the understanding of return, (but) with no condition (attached) which can nullify the gift if it is not returned, then as long as it is in the hands of the recipient (borrower) it is his, even if he does later return it, (therefore) he will not be held liable for aught that occurs even through negligence. Hence the transmitted (law) there *(Baba Metzia* 95a) that when the owner is with the borrower (lit., 'guard') he is guiltless, even if negligent.

19. זֹבֵחַ לָאֱלֹהִים — *He that sacrifices to the gods.* To all the gods together, even though his intention is to include God, the Blessed One, as well.

יָחֳרָם — *Shall be destroyed ...* (including) soul and body, for they (i.e., the gods) are accursed and (it is) prohibited to derive any benefit at all from them. To the extent that one accepts them as deities he (himself) becomes accursed as they are, as it says, וְהָיִיתָ חֵרֶם כָּמֹהוּ, *And be accursed like unto it (Deut.* 7:26).

בִּלְתִּי לַה׳ לְבַדּוֹ — *Save unto* HASHEM *only ...* without the partnership of other gods.

21-22. לֹא תְעַנּוּן ... אִם עַנֵּה תְעַנֶּה אֹתוֹ — *You shall not afflict ... If you do afflict him.* (This law applies only) if when you afflict the orphan your intent is simply to afflict him, however, if you afflict him to instruct him and for his own good then it is an act of kindness.

NOTES

14. אִם בְּעָלָיו עִמּוֹ לֹא יְשַׁלֵּם — *If the owner is with him he shall not pay.* The *Sforno* explains why the law exempts a borrower from payment for loss incurred by his negligence, if the lender is *with it,* i.e., employed by the borrower or is present and witnesses the accident. He suggests that the presence of the lender in the home or field of the borrower indicates a close friendship between them to such an extent that the status of the borrowed object is that of a gift, except that it is understood that it will be returned. As such, any mishap which occurs while it is in the possession of the borrower, who is in reality the recipient of a gift, does not obligate him to pay.

19. זֹבֵחַ לָאֱלֹהִים — *He that sacrifices to the gods.* See the *Sforno's* commentary on 34:23.

21-22. לֹא תְעַנּוּן ... אִם עַנֵּה תְעַנֶּה אֹתוֹ — *You shall not afflict ... If you do afflict him.* The *Sforno* explains that the first part of verse 22 qualifies the prohibition of לֹא תְעַנּוּן, *you shall not oppress* (v. 21). You transgress only if your motivation is to oppress the orphan, but if it is pure, i.e., to discipline and instruct him for his own good, it is proper.

כג יִצְעַק אֵלַי שָׁמֹעַ אֶשְׁמַע צַעֲקָתוֹ׃ וְחָרָה אַפִּי וְהָרַגְתִּי אֶתְכֶם בֶּחָרֶב וְהָיוּ
נְשֵׁיכֶם אַלְמָנוֹת וּבְנֵיכֶם יְתֹמִים׃
כד אִם־כֶּסֶף ׀ תַּלְוֶה אֶת־עַמִּי אֶת־הֶעָנִי עִמָּךְ לֹא־תִהְיֶה לוֹ כְּנֹשֶׁה לֹא־
כה תְשִׂימוּן עָלָיו נֶשֶׁךְ׃ אִם־חָבֹל תַּחְבֹּל שַׂלְמַת רֵעֶךָ עַד־בֹּא הַשֶּׁמֶשׁ תְּשִׁיבֶנּוּ
כו לוֹ׃ כִּי הִוא כְסוּתֹה לְבַדָּהּ הִוא שִׂמְלָתוֹ לְעֹרוֹ בַּמֶּה יִשְׁכָּב וְהָיָה כִּי־יִצְעַק
רביעי כז אֵלַי וְשָׁמַעְתִּי כִּי־חַנּוּן אָנִי׃ אֱלֹהִים לֹא תְקַלֵּל וְנָשִׂיא בְעַמְּךָ

22-23. שָׁמֹעַ אֶשְׁמַע צַעֲקָתוֹ. וְחָרָה אַפִּי — *I will surely hear his cry. And My wrath shall be kindled.* I will have compassion on the one who cries and be angry with the oppressor, similar to Israel in Egypt. And the punishment shall be measure for measure — he who willfully afflicts the widow and orphan shall cause the affliction of his own wife and children.

24. אִם כֶּסֶף תַּלְוֶה — *If you lend money.* If (the verse) which says: אֶפֶס כִּי לֹא יִהְיֶה בְּךָ אֶבְיוֹן, *Nevertheless there shall be no needy among you (Deut.* 15:4), will not be fulfilled in Israel, but (the verse) כִּי לֹא יֶחְדַּל אֶבְיוֹן, *For the poor shall never cease* (ibid. 11), will come to pass, then it will occur that you will lend.

26. וְשָׁמַעְתִּי כִּי חַנּוּן אָנִי — *I will hear for I am gracious.* Even though he is (not justified) to cry out that you (are guilty) of wrongdoing, considering that he does owe you (the money), nonetheless when he cries out to Me regarding his impoverished state which has caused his nakedness (resulting from) your action which deprived him of his garment, hence I will (feel constrained) to grant him some of the substance which I would normally have granted you, above and beyond your needs, for the purpose of lending and supporting (lit., 'feeding') others.

27. אֱלֹהִים לֹא תְקַלֵּל — *You shall not blaspheme the judges.* Even if you think that the judge has miscarried justice do not curse him, for no person can find fault with himself.

וְנָשִׂיא בְעַמְּךָ לֹא תָאֹר — *And do not curse a ruler among your people.* For, indeed, the curse of a king and the evil which befalls him will in most cases cause great evil and

NOTES

22-23. שָׁמֹעַ אֶשְׁמַע צַעֲקָתוֹ. וְחָרָה אַפִּי — *I will surely hear his cry. And My wrath shall be kindled.* The comparison to Israel in Egypt drawn by the *Sforno* can be appreciated by consulting his commentary on 2:23 and 3:9.

24. אִם כֶּסֶף תַּלְוֶה — *If you lend money. Rashi* quotes the sage Rabbi Ishmael who states that although אִם usually means *if* and indicates an option, this אִם is not optional but mandatory, i.e., one is obligated to lend money to a person in need. The *Sforno,* however, teaches us how this verse can be translated literally. *If* (אִם) the promise that there will be no needy among us is not fulfilled and instead God's statement that *the poor shall never cease* comes to pass, then when you lend money do not take interest or press him unduly for repayment.

26. וְשָׁמַעְתִּי כִּי חַנּוּן אָנִי — *I will hear for I am gracious.* In verse 22, regarding the cry of the widow or orphan, God also says He will hear (אֶשְׁמַע), as it states here (וְשָׁמַעְתִּי), but the added phrase כִּי חַנּוּן אָנִי, *for I am gracious,* does not appear there. The reason is that in the case of the widow and orphan their cry is totally justified, hence the punishment of the oppressor is also based on justice, not compassion. Here, however, considering that the debtor owes the creditor and legally the latter is entitled to keep the pledge, there is no reason for God to listen to his complaint. Nonetheless, God does hearken to the cry of the poor man who has no cloak with which to cover himself, for God is gracious and merciful. The consequence of this act will be that God will transfer some of the creditor's blessing to the debtor.

27. וְנָשִׂיא בְעַמְּךָ לֹא תָאֹר — *And do not curse a ruler among your people.* The *Sforno* interprets

כח־כט לֹא תָאֹר: מְלֵאָתְךָ וְדִמְעֲךָ לֹא תְאַחֵר בְּכוֹר בָּנֶיךָ תִּתֶּן־לִי: כֵּן־תַּעֲשֶׂה
לְשֹׁרְךָ לְצֹאנֶךָ שִׁבְעַת יָמִים יִהְיֶה עִם־אִמּוֹ בַּיּוֹם הַשְּׁמִינִי תִּתְּנוֹ־לִי:
ל וְאַנְשֵׁי־קֹדֶשׁ תִּהְיוּן לִי וּבָשָׂר בַּשָּׂדֶה טְרֵפָה לֹא תֹאכֵלוּ לַכֶּלֶב תַּשְׁלִכוּן

---

harm to the community, as it says: יְרָא אֶת ה׳ בְּנִי וָמֶלֶךְ עִם שׁוֹנִים אַל תִּתְעָרָב, *My son, fear HASHEM and the king, and do not meddle with those who seek change (Proverbs* 24:21).

28. מְלֵאָתְךָ — *The fullness (of your harvest).* (This refers to) the offering of the corn, similar to מְלֵאֹת וְטֹבוֹת, *full and good (Genesis* 41:22).

וְדִמְעֲךָ — *And the outflow (of your presses).* (This is) the offerings of the wine and oil which flow.

בְּכוֹר בָּנֶיךָ תִּתֶּן לִי — *The firstborn of your sons you shall give to Me* . . . for all sacred service; (i.e.,) the service of the Sanctuary and the study of Torah, as the priests later functioned, as it says, כִּי שִׂפְתֵי כֹהֵן יִשְׁמְרוּ דַעַת וְתוֹרָה יְבַקְשׁוּ מִפִּיהוּ, *For the priest's lips should keep knowledge and they should seek Torah from his mouth (Malachi* 2:7).

29. כֵּן תַּעֲשֶׂה לְשֹׁרְךָ לְצֹאנֶךָ — *Likewise you shall do with your oxen and your sheep* . . . that you give to Me the firstborn once he no longer has the status of a נֵפֶל, *non-viable birth,* as our Sages say, 'Any human being who lives thirty days is not a non-viable . . . an animal which lives eight days is not a non-viable' *(Shabbos* 135b).

30. וְאַנְשֵׁי קֹדֶשׁ תִּהְיוּן לִי — *And you shall be holy men to Me.* In this manner you will be holy men, if you separate the firstborn sons and the gifts (of firstborn animals) to My service; (for then) the firstborn will teach knowledge to the people, and וְהִתְקַדִּשְׁתֶּם וִהְיִיתֶם קְדֹשִׁים, *you will sanctify yourselves and you will be holy (Lev.* 11:44).

וּבָשָׂר בַּשָּׂדֶה טְרֵפָה — *And flesh that is torn off in the field* . . . even טְרֵפָה, *torn flesh,* which does not defile at all.

NOTES

the phrase בְּעַמְּךָ to mean *among your people* in the sense of *affecting* the people. Undermining the authority of the ruler is harmful to the welfare of the community at large.

28. בְּכוֹר בָּנֶיךָ תִּתֶּן לִי — *The firstborn of your sons you shall give to Me.* Before the sin of the Golden Calf, the firstborn sons were designated to serve in the Sanctuary and teach Torah to the people. After the Jews transgressed but the Levites remained steadfast in their loyalty to God, the Levites replaced the firstborn in this role. The expression לִי, *to Me,* is used here in conjunction with the firstborn and is also used in conjunction with the Levites, וְהָיוּ לִי הַלְוִיִּם, *And the Levites shall be Mine (Numbers* 8:14). In both cases it means to serve.

30. וְאַנְשֵׁי קֹדֶשׁ תִּהְיוּן לִי — *And you shall be holy men to Me.* The *Sforno* explains the connection between the giving of the firstborn to God and the admonition to Israel to be holy men to Him. To attain holiness it is necessary to know God's commandments and study His Torah. Our Sages tell us that an ignorant man cannot be a pious man *(Avos* 2:5). Therefore, the people of Israel need teachers if they are to attain a level of holiness. Toward that end the firstborn were charged with the task of teaching the people knowledge of God, as the prophet proclaims.

וּבָשָׂר בַּשָּׂדֶה טְרֵפָה — *And flesh that is torn off in the field.* In addition to knowledge there must be performance of *mitzvos,* such as abstaining from prohibited food and defilement, if one is to attain holiness. Although an animal that is a טְרֵפָה, *torn,* does not defile, nonetheless its flesh is prohibited; therefore God admonishes us not to eat it, for the eating of prohibited foods is a deterrent to holiness.

כג
א אֹתוֹ: לֹא תִשָּׂא שֵׁמַע שָׁוְא אַל־תָּשֶׁת יָדְךָ עִם־רָשָׁע לִהְיֹת עֵד
ב חָמָס: לֹא־תִהְיֶה אַחֲרֵי־רַבִּים לְרָעֹת וְלֹא־תַעֲנֶה עַל־רִב לִנְטֹת אַחֲרֵי
ג-ד רַבִּים לְהַטֹּת: וְדָל לֹא תֶהְדַּר בְּרִיבוֹ: כִּי תִפְגַּע שׁוֹר אֹיִבְךָ אוֹ
ה חֲמֹרוֹ תֹּעֶה הָשֵׁב תְּשִׁיבֶנּוּ לוֹ: כִּי־תִרְאֶה חֲמוֹר שֹׂנַאֲךָ
חמישי ו רֹבֵץ תַּחַת מַשָּׂאוֹ וְחָדַלְתָּ מֵעֲזֹב לוֹ עָזֹב תַּעֲזֹב עִמּוֹ: לֹא

XXIII

1. אַל תָּשֶׁת יָדְךָ עִם רָשָׁע — *Do not put your hand with a wicked (one)* . . . to be a co-signatory on a document with him, as (our Sages) say regarding the men of Jerusalem that they did not sign on a document unless they knew who their co-signatory was *(Sanhedrin* 23a).

לִהְיֹת עֵד חָמָס — *To be an unrighteous witness.* (If you do so,) then you will be (but) a single witness, since a wicked person is not fit to testify, and (as a result) the judge will withdraw all the money from the defendant through your testimony alone, which is contrary to law.

2. לֹא תִהְיֶה אַחֲרֵי רַבִּים לְרָעֹת — *You shall not follow a multitude to do evil* . . . (i.e.,) to tilt the scale toward guilt, in a capital case, where we do not judge (condemn) him by the majority of one judge alone.

וְלֹא תַעֲנֶה עַל רִב — *Do not respond regarding a controversy* . . . when your fellow judges ask your opinion.

לִנְטֹת אַחֲרֵי רַבִּים — *To lean toward the multitude.* Let not your answer be that it is fitting to tend toward the majority, if (for example) ten find (the defendant) innocent and eleven guilty.

לְהַטֹּת — *To bend* (the verdict). That through your word (lit., 'mouth') the verdict will be decided toward guilt for then there will be twelve (voting) guilty. Instead voice your opinion and reasoning, and let it not suffice for you to say that it is proper to lean toward the opinion of the majority, without any reason other than that they outnumber those (who say) innocent, and (by your vote) a guilty verdict will be determined by a plurality of two.

NOTES

XXIII

1. לִהְיֹת עֵד חָמָס — *To be an unrighteous witness.* Whereas many commentators interpret the prohibition stated in this verse as meaning the support of a fictitious claim through false testimony, the *Sforno* is of the opinion that the Torah is not addressing itself to one who is himself a wicked person, rather to one who testifies truthfully, as does his fellow witness, who is a רָשָׁע, *a wicked person,* in the sense of being unqualified to serve as a witness. By so doing the honest witness becomes a party to the miscarrying of justice since his testimony stands alone and no case may be decided by one witness.

2. לֹא תִהְיֶה אַחֲרֵי רַבִּים לְרָעֹת וְלֹא תַעֲנֶה . . . לִנְטֹת אַחֲרֵי רַבִּים לְהַטֹּת — *You shall not follow a multitude to do evil. Do not respond . . . to lean toward the multitude so as to bend* (the verdict). The *Sforno* explains each section of this verse by interpreting its thrust as follows: Given the fact that a capital case cannot be decided by a majority of one *(Sanhedrin* 2a), the verse speaks of a case where one judge is undecided and is inclined to cast his vote on the side of the majority, because they are a majority, and not because he is convinced of the merit of their decision. By so doing he will tilt the scales of justice, for now there will be a majority of two. However, he will have failed to meet his responsibility since his decision is not based on reasoning and judgment but by a desire to concur with the majority of his colleagues.

ז תַטֶּה מִשְׁפַּט אֶבְיֹנְךָ בְּרִיבוֹ: מִדְּבַר־שֶׁקֶר תִּרְחָק וְנָקִי וְצַדִּיק אַל־תַּהֲרֹג כִּי
ח לֹא־אַצְדִּיק רָשָׁע: וְשֹׁחַד לֹא תִקָּח כִּי הַשֹּׁחַד יְעַוֵּר פִּקְחִים וִיסַלֵּף דִּבְרֵי
ט צַדִּיקִים: וְגֵר לֹא תִלְחָץ וְאַתֶּם יְדַעְתֶּם אֶת־נֶפֶשׁ הַגֵּר כִּי־גֵרִים הֱיִיתֶם
י בְּאֶרֶץ מִצְרָיִם: וְשֵׁשׁ שָׁנִים תִּזְרַע אֶת־אַרְצֶךָ וְאָסַפְתָּ אֶת־תְּבוּאָתָהּ:
יא וְהַשְּׁבִיעִת תִּשְׁמְטֶנָּה וּנְטַשְׁתָּהּ וְאָכְלוּ אֶבְיֹנֵי עַמֶּךָ וְיִתְרָם תֹּאכַל חַיַּת
יב הַשָּׂדֶה כֵּן־תַּעֲשֶׂה לְכַרְמְךָ לְזֵיתֶךָ: שֵׁשֶׁת יָמִים תַּעֲשֶׂה מַעֲשֶׂיךָ וּבַיּוֹם
יג הַשְּׁבִיעִי תִּשְׁבֹּת לְמַעַן יָנוּחַ שׁוֹרְךָ וַחֲמֹרֶךָ וְיִנָּפֵשׁ בֶּן־אֲמָתְךָ וְהַגֵּר: וּבְכֹל

---

6. לֹא תַטֶּה מִשְׁפַּט אֶבְיֹנְךָ בְּרִיבוֹ — *You shall not bend the judgment of your poor in his cause.* Do not be soft toward this one and harsh toward the (other) one at the time of judgment, while the litigants are presenting their claims. Likewise, do not (allow) one to stand and one to sit, or similar (disparate) situations.

7. מִדְּבַר שֶׁקֶר תִּרְחָק — *Keep far away from a false matter ...* from every word or thing which can cause falsehood, as our Sages say, וֶהֱוֵי זָהִיר בִּדְבָרֶיךָ שֶׁמָּא מִתּוֹכָם יִלְמְדוּ לְשַׁקֵּר, *Be careful of your words, lest by them (your words) they will be led* (lit., *learn) to lie (Avos* 1:9).

11. תִּשְׁמְטֶנָּה — *You shall cause release.* (This refers to) release from debts (lit., 'monies'), as it says, וְזֶה דְּבַר הַשְּׁמִטָּה שָׁמוֹט כָּל בַּעַל מַשֵּׁה יָדוֹ אֲשֶׁר יַשֶּׁה בְּרֵעֵהוּ, *And this is the manner of release, every creditor shall release that which he lent (Deut.* 15:2).

וּנְטַשְׁתָּהּ וְאָכְלוּ אֶבְיֹנֵי עַמֶּךָ — *Abandon it, that the poor of your people may eat.* Through the *shemittah* (release) of the soil, the poor will also be able to eat.

וְיִתְרָם — *And what they leave ...* (i.e.,) what is left (behind) by the poor.

תֹּאכַל חַיַּת הַשָּׂדֶה — *The beast of the field shall eat.* Nevertheless, the poor have priority, as our Sages say, food fit for human consumption may not be fed to dogs *(Taanis* 20b).

12. תִּשְׁבֹּת — *You shall rest ...* even from activities (lit., *things)* which are not (technically) labor, but they are burdensome (troublesome) and of a secular (lit., 'weekday') nature, as it says, וְכִבַּדְתּוֹ מֵעֲשׂוֹת דְּרָכֶיךָ מִמְּצוֹא חֶפְצְךָ וְדַבֵּר דָּבָר, *And shall honor it not doing your own ways, nor pursuing your own business, nor speaking vain matters (Isaiah* 58:13).

NOTES

6. לֹא תַטֶּה מִשְׁפַּט אֶבְיֹנְךָ בְּרִיבוֹ — *You shall not bend the judgment of your poor in his cause.* This interpretation of the *Sforno* is based upon the Talmud, *Kesubos* 46a and *Shevuos* 30a.

7. מִדְּבַר שֶׁקֶר תִּרְחָק — *Keep far away from a false matter.* As in verse 1, the *Sforno* feels that the Torah is not addressing itself to an outright perjurer or liar. There is no need for the Torah to prohibit lying, which is self-understood. Rather this is a prohibition of causing or prompting a witness to lie through an injudicious word. That accounts for the phraseology of this verse. It does not say 'Do not lie,' but, *'Keep far away from a false matter.*

11. תִּשְׁמְטֶנָּה וּנְטַשְׁתָּהּ — *You shall cause release. Abandon it.* Two words are used in this verse, תִּשְׁמְטֶנָּה and וּנְטַשְׁתָּהּ. The *Sforno* explains that the first verb denotes the release from debts at the end of the *Shemittah* (Sabbatical) year, while the second prohibits agricultural labor and also permits others to enjoy the produce of the land, since private ownership is not recognized during the *Shemittah* year.

12. תִּשְׁבֹּת — *You shall rest.* The Talmud in tractate *Shabbos* (138a) tells us that even an act which is permitted on the Sabbath should not be done exactly as it is done on a weekday, in order to emphasize that the Sabbath has sanctity, unlike the other days of the week.

אֲשֶׁר־אָמַרְתִּי אֲלֵיכֶם תִּשָּׁמֵרוּ וְשֵׁם אֱלֹהִים אֲחֵרִים לֹא תַזְכִּירוּ לֹא יִשָּׁמַע
יד־טו עַל־פִּיךָ: שָׁלֹשׁ רְגָלִים תָּחֹג לִי בַּשָּׁנָה: אֶת־חַג הַמַּצּוֹת תִּשְׁמֹר שִׁבְעַת

לְמַעַן יָנוּחַ שׁוֹרְךָ וַחֲמֹרֶךָ — *That your ox and your ass may rest . . .* when you also will rest from such work.

וְיִנָּפֵשׁ בֶּן אֲמָתְךָ וְהַגֵּר — *And the son of your handmaid and the stranger may be refreshed.* And consequently your handmaid and the stranger will also be refreshed, the opposite of your condition in Egypt where you were enslaved and had no rest, as it says, תִּכְבַּד הָעֲבֹדָה עַל הָאֲנָשִׁים, *Let heavier work be laid on the men* (5:9). In this manner you will remember the exodus from Egypt, as it says in the (Ten) Commandments of *Mishneh Torah (Deuteronomy)*, וְזָכַרְתָּ כִּי עֶבֶד הָיִיתָ, *And you shall remember that you were a servant (Deut.* 5:15).

13. וּבְכֹל אֲשֶׁר אָמַרְתִּי אֲלֵיכֶם תִּשָּׁמֵרוּ וְשֵׁם אֱלֹהִים אֲחֵרִים לֹא תַזְכִּירוּ — *And all the things I have said to you take heed; and make no mention of other gods.* All other prohibitions which I have commanded, you must take heed not to transgress, but it does not suffice regarding the prohibition against idolatry for one to (merely) refrain from transgressing; you must take care not to (even) mention its name.

לֹא יִשָּׁמַע עַל פִּיךָ — *Neither let it be heard out of your mouth.* It should not be mentioned, with your approval, even by others.

14. תָּחֹג לִי — *Keep a feast to Me.* (This is) similar to יִשְׂמַח יִשְׂרָאֵל בְּעֹשָׂיו, *Let Israel rejoice in his Maker (Psalms* 149:2), (which is) the opposite of וַיַּרְא אֶת הָעֵגֶל וּמְחֹלֹת, *and he saw the calf and the dancing* (32:19).

NOTES

The verse from *Isaiah,* quoted by the *Sforno,* is interpreted by our Sages in tractate *Shabbos* (113a) as teaching us that our Sabbath garments should be distinctive and unlike our weekday clothes; that the way we walk on the Sabbath should be different than our gait during the week; and that our manner of speech on the Sabbath should also be different than it is on a weekday.

לְמַעַן יָנוּחַ שׁוֹרְךָ וַחֲמֹרֶךָ וְיִנָּפֵשׁ בֶּן אֲמָתְךָ וְהַגֵּר — *That your ox and your ass may rest, and the son of your handmaid and the stranger may be refreshed.* The *Sforno* links the master's abstention from work to his animals and servants. When he ceases from labor so do they. He also links the resting of one's servants to our deliverance from Egypt as we see from the Ten Commandments recorded in *Deuteronomy.* In the version of the Ten Commandments in *Exodus,* the reason given for the Sabbath is to recognize that God created the world in six days and rested on the seventh day. In *Deuteronomy* the reason given is to remember that we were slaves in Egypt. As the *Sforno* points out in his commentary there, the animal is enjoined from working, thereby freeing the servant from his labors, and the reason is to remind us that God took us forth from Egypt, where we were slaves. This explains the sense of the *Sforno's* explanation here as well.

13. וּבְכֹל אֲשֶׁר אָמַרְתִּי אֲלֵיכֶם תִּשָּׁמֵרוּ וְשֵׁם אֱלֹהִים אֲחֵרִים לֹא תַזְכִּירוּ לֹא יִשָּׁמַע עַל פִּיךָ — *And all the things I have said to you take heed; and make no mention of other gods; neither let it be heard out of your mouth.* The portion of *Mishpatim* (Ordinances) consists of ordinances, laws and prohibitions culminating with this verse. The following verse deals with the three festivals followed in turn by narratives. The significance of positioning this prohibition at the conclusion of *Mishpatim* is to emphasize that whereas all other prohibitions are broken only when one does an action, the prohibition against idolatry is transgressed merely by mentioning the name of the idol and extends to the causing of others to mention the idol's name. According to the Talmudic Sage known as the father of Samuel *(Sanhedrin* 63b), this prohibits one from entering into partnership with a heathen, since a business dispute might ensue which would necessitate the taking of an oath by your partner, thereby causing the heathen to swear in the name of his god.

14. תָּחֹג לִי — *Keep a feast to Me.* This verse is the introduction to the observance of the three

יָמִים תֹּאכַל מַצּוֹת כַּאֲשֶׁר צִוִּיתִךָ לְמוֹעֵד חֹדֶשׁ הָאָבִיב כִּי־בוֹ יָצָאתָ
טז מִמִּצְרָיִם וְלֹא־יֵרָאוּ פָנַי רֵיקָם: וְחַג הַקָּצִיר בִּכּוּרֵי מַעֲשֶׂיךָ אֲשֶׁר תִּזְרַע
יז בַּשָּׂדֶה וְחַג הָאָסִף בְּצֵאת הַשָּׁנָה בְּאָסְפְּךָ אֶת־מַעֲשֶׂיךָ מִן־הַשָּׂדֶה: שָׁלֹשׁ
יח פְּעָמִים בַּשָּׁנָה יֵרָאֶה כָּל־זְכוּרְךָ אֶל־פְּנֵי הָאָדֹן ׀ יהוה: לֹא־תִזְבַּח עַל־חָמֵץ
יט דַּם־זִבְחִי וְלֹא־יָלִין חֵלֶב־חַגִּי עַד־בֹּקֶר: רֵאשִׁית בִּכּוּרֵי אַדְמָתְךָ תָּבִיא

---

15. אֶת חַג הַמַּצּוֹת תִּשְׁמֹר — *The Festival of Matzos you shall keep.* (This is) similar to שָׁמוֹר אֶת חֹדֶשׁ הָאָבִיב וְעָשִׂיתָ פֶּסַח, *Observe the month of Aviv and keep the Pesach* (*Deut.* 16:1), as it states here, *at the time appointed in the month of Aviv.* Take care that (*Pesach*) be in the month of *Aviv*, by intercalating years and months, as we find in our tradition (*Rosh Hashanah* 21a).

16. בְּצֵאת הַשָּׁנָה — *At the end of the year.* When all of the produce has been gathered.

17. שָׁלֹשׁ פְּעָמִים בַּשָּׁנָה יֵרָאֶה כָּל זְכוּרְךָ — *Three times in the year all your males shall appear* . . . to give thanks for their freedom, for the ripening of the fruit, the harvest and the ingathering, because all comes from Him.

אֶל פְּנֵי הָאָדֹן ה׳ — *Before the Lord* HASHEM. The (term) אָדֹן, *Lord,* indicates He Who conducts the affairs of all perishable (transitory) things. Therefore the (verse) says that He is the Lord of each one who appears before Him, and by appearing before Him they are akin to a servant who welcomes his master. Also He is the Lord of the soil as it says, כִּי לִי הָאָרֶץ כִּי גֵרִים וְתוֹשָׁבִים אַתֶּם עִמָּדִי, *for the land is Mine; for you are strangers and settlers with Me* (*Leviticus* 25:23), hence it is fitting that you thank Me for the ripening, the harvest, and the ingathering of the growth of the Land, therefore . . .

19. רֵאשִׁית בִּכּוּרֵי אַדְמָתְךָ — *The choicest first fruits of your Land.* The choicest of the first fruit, similar to וְרֵאשִׁית שְׁמָנִים יִמְשָׁחוּ, *and anoint themselves with chief* (רֵאשִׁית) *ointments* (*Amos* 6:6), and נְקֻבֵי רֵאשִׁית הַגּוֹיִם, *Who are named chief* (רֵאשִׁית) *of the nations* (ibid. 6:1). And these are the first fruit of the seven species, as we learn from tradition (*Bikkurim* 1:3).

NOTES

festivals. The *Sforno* is of the opinion that it introduces the theme and sets the tone of these holidays. He stresses the word לִי, *to Me,* indicating *to Me alone,* to counteract the tendency at that time in history for people to associate deities with one another and worship a variety of gods. The name אָדֹן, *Lord and Master*, used in verse 17 also is meant to stress our relationship to God as our exclusive master, and as such we come to pay Him — and Him alone — homage three times a year. *Ibn Ezra* gives a similar explanation.

15. אֶת חַג הַמַּצּוֹת תִּשְׁמֹר — *The Festival of Matzos you shall keep.* The *Sforno* explains that the phrase תִּשְׁמֹר, *keep,* is not meant as an admonition to keep the laws of *Pesach,* such as *chametz* and *matzah,* but should be understood as cautioning the court to be careful to arrange the calendar so as to insure that the holiday of *Pesach* shall fall in the time of *Aviv,* i.e., the season of ripe ears, which is springtime.

16. בְּצֵאת הַשָּׁנָה — *At the end of the year. The end of the year* means the end of the agricultural year.

17-19. שָׁלֹשׁ פְּעָמִים בַּשָּׁנָה יֵרָאֶה כָּל זְכוּרְךָ אֶל פְּנֵי הָאָדֹן ה׳ . . . רֵאשִׁית בִּכּוּרֵי אַדְמָתְךָ . . . לֹא תְבַשֵּׁל גְּדִי בַּחֲלֵב אִמּוֹ — *Three times in the year all your males shall appear before the Lord* HASHEM . . . *The choicest first fruits of your Land . . . you shall not boil a kid in its mother's milk.* See note on verse 14. The *Sforno* explains the close relationship between God and the earth's blessings which is acknowledged by Israel at these three festivals that are linked to the Land, marking as they do the various seasons

בֵּית יהוה אֱלֹהֶיךָ לֹא־תְבַשֵּׁל גְּדִי בַּחֲלֵב אִמּוֹ:
ששי כ הִנֵּה אָנֹכִי שֹׁלֵחַ מַלְאָךְ לְפָנֶיךָ לִשְׁמָרְךָ בַּדָּרֶךְ וְלַהֲבִיאֲךָ אֶל־הַמָּקוֹם אֲשֶׁר
כא הֲכִנֹתִי: הִשָּׁמֶר מִפָּנָיו וּשְׁמַע בְּקֹלוֹ אַל־תַּמֵּר בּוֹ כִּי לֹא יִשָּׂא לְפִשְׁעֲכֶם כִּי
כב שְׁמִי בְּקִרְבּוֹ: כִּי אִם־שָׁמוֹעַ תִּשְׁמַע בְּקֹלוֹ וְעָשִׂיתָ כֹּל אֲשֶׁר אֲדַבֵּר וְאָיַבְתִּי
כג אֶת־אֹיְבֶיךָ וְצַרְתִּי אֶת־צֹרְרֶיךָ: כִּי־יֵלֵךְ מַלְאָכִי לְפָנֶיךָ וֶהֱבִיאֲךָ אֶל־
כד הָאֱמֹרִי וְהַחִתִּי וְהַפְּרִזִּי וְהַכְּנַעֲנִי הַחִוִּי וְהַיְבוּסִי וְהִכְחַדְתִּיו: לֹא־תִשְׁתַּחֲוֶה

לֹא תְבַשֵּׁל גְּדִי בַּחֲלֵב אִמּוֹ — *You shall not boil a kid in its mother's milk.* You shall not engage in such actions so as to increase your fruit, as was the way of idolaters. Rather, *the choicest first fruit of your Land you shall bring,* as it says, וְרֵאשִׁית כָּל בִּכּוּרֵי כֹל וְכָל תְּרוּמַת כֹּל ... לְהָנִיחַ בְּרָכָה אֶל בֵּיתֶךָ, *The first of all the first fruits of all things, and every offering ... to cause a blessing to rest in your house (Ezekiel* 44:30).

21. הִשָּׁמֶר מִפָּנָיו — *Take heed of him.* Do not profane his honor; similar to the (angel who appeared) to Joshua (and commanded him), שַׁל נַעַלְךָ מֵעַל רַגְלֶךָ, *Take your shoe off your foot (Joshua* 5:15).

וּשְׁמַע בְּקֹלוֹ — *And listen to his voice ...* to go in his footsteps, as opposed to what they said, 'אָנָה אֲנַחְנוּ עֹלִים, *Whither are we going up?' (Deut.* 1:28).

אַל תַּמֵּר בּוֹ כִּי לֹא יִשָּׂא לְפִשְׁעֲכֶם — *Be not rebellious against him; for he will not pardon your transgressions.* (Even) if (but) one man will sin (the) many will be punished as was the case with Achan, as it says, הֲלוֹא עָכָן בֶּן זֶרַח מָעַל מַעַל בַּחֵרֶם וְעַל כָּל עֲדַת יִשְׂרָאֵל הָיָה קָצֶף וְהוּא אִישׁ אֶחָד לֹא גָוַע בַּעֲוֹנוֹ, *Did not Achan the son of Zerach commit a trespass in regard to the devoted property, and wrath fell on all the congregation of Israel, and that man did not perish alone in his iniquity? (Joshua* 22:20).

כִּי שְׁמִי בְּקִרְבּוֹ — *For My Name is in him.* And he does not have the power to pardon (the desecration of) My honor.

22. כִּי אִם שָׁמוֹעַ תִּשְׁמַע בְּקֹלוֹ ... וְאָיַבְתִּי אֶת אֹיְבֶיךָ — *But if you shall indeed hearken to his voice ... I will be an enemy to your enemies.* And I will have no pity on them, in keeping with My attribute of goodness, as opposed to, וַאֲנִי לֹא אָחוּס עַל נִינְוֵה, *'And should I not have pity on Nineveh?' (Jonah* 4:11).

23. כִּי יֵלֵךְ מַלְאָכִי לְפָנֶיךָ — *For My angel shall go before you.* He will not forgive the transgressions of the enemy.

NOTES

of the year and the cycle of ripening harvest and ingathering. It therefore follows logically that in verse 19 Israel is urged to offer their first, choicest fruit to God, demonstrating their gratitude to Him and acknowledging that the blessings of the Land come from Him alone. This realization in turn will deter them from engaging in heathen practices, such as the boiling of a kid in its mother's milk, which were followed by the idolaters to propitiate their gods in the hope of increasing their fruit. This explains the continuity of verse 19 and its connection to verse 17. See the *Sforno's* commentary on 34:18 where this thought is developed by him.

21. אַל תַּמֵּר בּוֹ כִּי לֹא יִשָּׂא לְפִשְׁעֲכֶם — *Be not rebellious against him; for he will not pardon your transgressions.* The reason for the angel's inability to forgive Israel if they transgress is because God's Name is in him. Since the angel's very being and essence emanates from God, to defy him is to rebel against God, and the angel has no power to pardon the desecration of God's honor. Now just as the angel cannot pardon the transgressions of Israel, he also cannot forgive those of Israel's enemies. This is the meaning of verse 23, as the *Sforno* explains in his commentary on that verse.

לֵאלֹהֵיהֶם וְלֹא תָעָבְדֵם וְלֹא תַעֲשֶׂה כְּמַעֲשֵׂיהֶם כִּי הָרֵס תְּהָרְסֵם וְשַׁבֵּר
כה תְּשַׁבֵּר מַצֵּבֹתֵיהֶם: וַעֲבַדְתֶּם אֵת יהוה אֱלֹהֵיכֶם וּבֵרַךְ אֶת־לַחְמְךָ וְאֶת־
שביעי כו מֵימֶיךָ וַהֲסִרֹתִי מַחֲלָה מִקִּרְבֶּךָ: לֹא תִהְיֶה מְשַׁכֵּלָה
כז וַעֲקָרָה בְּאַרְצֶךָ אֶת־מִסְפַּר יָמֶיךָ אֲמַלֵּא: אֶת־אֵימָתִי אֲשַׁלַּח לְפָנֶיךָ
וְהַמֹּתִי אֶת־כָּל־הָעָם אֲשֶׁר תָּבֹא בָּהֶם וְנָתַתִּי אֶת־כָּל־אֹיְבֶיךָ אֵלֶיךָ עֹרֶף:

---

24. לֹא תִשְׁתַּחֲוֶה לֵאלֹהֵיהֶם — *You shall not bow down to their gods.* Do not act as Amazyahu did after he conquered Seir — וַיָּבֵא אֶת אֱלֹהֵי בְּנֵי שֵׂעִיר . . . וְלִפְנֵיהֶם יִשְׁתַּחֲוֶה, *And he brought the gods of the children of Seir . . . and prostrated himself before them (II Chronicles* 25:14). Perhaps he wanted to appease them that they should not be angry with him for having killed their worshipers.

25. וַעֲבַדְתֶּם אֵת ה׳ אֱלֹהֵיכֶם — *And you shall serve* HASHEM, *your God.* And in this manner (i.e., by overthrowing their gods) you shall serve Him, for after the nations and their idols will be destroyed, (as well as) the places where they did worship, you will no longer have anyone to instigate and seduce you away from My service.

וּבֵרַךְ אֶת לַחְמְךָ — *And He will bless your bread.* It will nourish you and the abundance (thereof) will not be the cause of (any) ailments.

וַהֲסִרֹתִי מַחֲלָה מִקִּרְבֶּךָ — *And I will take sickness away from your midst.* (This refers to sickness) caused by the climate or the order (of the planets).

26. לֹא תִהְיֶה מְשַׁכֵּלָה וַעֲקָרָה — *None shall miscarry or be barren.* In this manner you will be able to teach your children.

אֶת מִסְפַּר יָמֶיךָ אֲמַלֵּא — *The number of your days I will fulfill.* You will live to the (full) measure of oil which is in your *lamp of God* (the soul of man), i.e., the vitality (or *natural force)* rooted (in man) from birth. The reverse of this mostly occurs when man dies from (various) illnesses before his basic vitality has ceased. This occurs due to wrong choices (made in life) or due to fate (lit., 'the order of the planets') and the elements (lit., 'foundations'). Now when a man's number of days are fulfilled he will in most cases see children born to his children and will be able to teach them, as it says, וְהוֹדַעְתָּם לְבָנֶיךָ וְלִבְנֵי בָנֶיךָ, *Make them known to your children and children's children (Deut.* 4:9). (In this fashion) the affairs of (new) generations will be remedied in the lifetime of their elders, as we are told happened with Levi, Kehath and Amram (see *Sforno* on 6:14).

27. וְהַמֹּתִי — *And will discomfit . . .* as it happened with the Egyptians (who said), 'אָנוּסָה מִפְּנֵי יִשְׂרָאֵל כִּי ה׳ נִלְחָם לָהֶם, *Let us flee from Israel, for* HASHEM *fights for them'* (14:25).

וְנָתַתִּי אֶת כָּל אֹיְבֶיךָ אֵלֶיךָ עֹרֶף — *And I will make all your enemies turn their backs to you.* Because of the terror and tumult which (God) designated when He said, *'I will*

NOTES

24. לֹא תִשְׁתַּחֲוֶה לֵאלֹהֵיהֶם — *You shall not bow down to their gods.* The allure of, and respect for, עֲבוֹדָה זָרָה, *idol worship,* was so strong and pervasive in ancient times that even after victory Amazyahu feared the consequence of his conquest and the retribution of the gods of Seir! The *Sforno* cites this incident to explain the imperative need for Israel to utterly eradicate the gods of the nations, to *overthrow them and break them in pieces.* Otherwise Israel will be vulnerable to the instigation and seduction of the idolaters, as the *Sforno* states in the next verse.

26. אֶת מִסְפַּר יָמֶיךָ אֲמַלֵּא — *The number of your days I will fulfill.* The *Sforno's* choice of

כח וְשִׁלַּחְתִּי אֶת־הַצִּרְעָה לְפָנֶיךָ וְגֵרְשָׁה אֶת־הַחִוִּי אֶת־הַכְּנַעֲנִי וְאֶת־הַחִתִּי
כט מִלְּפָנֶיךָ: לֹא אֲגָרְשֶׁנּוּ מִפָּנֶיךָ בְּשָׁנָה אֶחָת פֶּן־תִּהְיֶה הָאָרֶץ שְׁמָמָה וְרַבָּה
ל עָלֶיךָ חַיַּת הַשָּׂדֶה: מְעַט מְעַט אֲגָרְשֶׁנּוּ מִפָּנֶיךָ עַד אֲשֶׁר תִּפְרֶה וְנָחַלְתָּ
לא אֶת־הָאָרֶץ: וְשַׁתִּי אֶת־גְּבֻלְךָ מִיַּם־סוּף וְעַד־יָם פְּלִשְׁתִּים וּמִמִּדְבָּר
לב עַד־הַנָּהָר כִּי ׀ אֶתֵּן בְּיֶדְכֶם אֵת יֹשְׁבֵי הָאָרֶץ וְגֵרַשְׁתָּמוֹ מִפָּנֶיךָ: לֹא־תִכְרֹת
לג לָהֶם וְלֵאלֹהֵיהֶם בְּרִית: לֹא יֵשְׁבוּ בְּאַרְצְךָ פֶּן־יַחֲטִיאוּ אֹתְךָ לִי כִּי תַעֲבֹד
אֶת־אֱלֹהֵיהֶם כִּי־יִהְיֶה לְךָ לְמוֹקֵשׁ:
כד א וְאֶל־מֹשֶׁה אָמַר עֲלֵה אֶל־יהוה אַתָּה וְאַהֲרֹן נָדָב וַאֲבִיהוּא וְשִׁבְעִים מִזִּקְנֵי

---

send My terror before you' (beginning of this verse).

31. כִּי אֶתֵּן בְּיֶדְכֶם אֵת יֹשְׁבֵי הָאָרֶץ וְגֵרַשְׁתָּמוֹ — *For I will deliver the inhabitants of the Land into your hand and you shall drive them out.* The matter is in your hand, and you must not be indolent (neglectful) regarding it, as Joshua testified to them (Israel) saying, עַד אָנָה אַתֶּם מִתְרַפִּים לָבוֹא לָרֶשֶׁת אֶת הָאָרֶץ אֲשֶׁר נָתַן לָכֶם ה׳ אֱלֹהֵי אֲבוֹתֵיכֶם, *How long will you be remiss in going to possess the Land which HASHEM, the God of your fathers, has given to you?' (Joshua* 18:3).

33. לֹא יֵשְׁבוּ בְּאַרְצְךָ — *They shall not dwell in your Land.* In that portion of the Land which you will conquer and dwell in, they shall not dwell. (However) they did the opposite as the verse testifies saying, וַיֵּשֶׁב הַכְּנַעֲנִי בְּקִרְבּוֹ בְּגָזֶר ... וַיֵּשֶׁב ... בְּקֶרֶב הַכְּנַעֲנִי יֹשְׁבֵי הָאָרֶץ, *but the Canaanites dwelt in Gezer among them . . . But dwelt . . . among the Canaanites the inhabitants of the land (Judges* 1:29,32).

כִּי יִהְיֶה לְךָ לְמוֹקֵשׁ — *For they will be a snare unto you.* They will cause you to serve their gods.

XXIV

1. וְאֶל מֹשֶׁה אָמַר עֲלֵה — *And to Moses He said, 'Come up.'* After He concluded saying, "כֹּה תֹאמַר אֶל בְּנֵי יִשְׂרָאֵל אַתֶּם רְאִיתֶם, *Thus shall you say to the Children of Israel, 'You have seen' "* (20:19), and (after God) explained to them that they needed no intermediary to reach Him (see 20:20), and (also) that an earthen altar is sufficient (20:21), together with the observance of His commandments which He explained in the (Ten) Commandments and the chapter of *Mishpatim,* (now) all this was said and commanded to the congregation of Israel; (but) *to Moses He said, 'Come up,'* as He had ordained before the giving of the Torah, as He said, לֵךְ רֵד וְעָלִיתָ אַתָּה וְאַהֲרֹן עִמָּךְ, *Go, get you down and you shall come up, you and Aaron with you* (19:24).

NOTES

language to describe man's source of life as oil to the lamp is based on, *the soul of man is the lamp of HASHEM (Proverbs* 20:27). The expression 'natural force' or vitality is taken from *Deuteronomy* 34:7, *his natural force did not abate,* regarding Moses. The *Sforno* already developed the idea of long life affording one the opportunity to influence later generations in his commentary on 6:14. See the note there.

31. כִּי אֶתֵּן בְּיֶדְכֶם אֵת יֹשְׁבֵי הָאָרֶץ וְגֵרַשְׁתָּמוֹ — *For I will deliver the inhabitants of the Land into your hand and you shall drive them out.* God will do His part but you must do yours. He will give the inhabitants of the Land into Israel's hand but they must in turn drive them out. The matter is in their hand to act and they must not squander that opportunity.

XXIV

1. וְאֶל מֹשֶׁה אָמַר עֲלֵה — *And to Moses He said, 'Come up.'* The commentators disagree as to the time this chapter was spoken to Moses. The *Sforno* explains that it belongs to the order and sequence of events as recorded in these chapters. The narrative is now resuming what was said by God before He gave the

ב יִשְׂרָאֵל וְהִשְׁתַּחֲוִיתֶם מֵרָחֹק: וְנִגַּשׁ מֹשֶׁה לְבַדּוֹ אֶל־יהוה וְהֵם לֹא יִגָּשׁוּ
ג וְהָעָם לֹא יַעֲלוּ עִמּוֹ: וַיָּבֹא מֹשֶׁה וַיְסַפֵּר לָעָם אֵת כָּל־דִּבְרֵי יהוה וְאֵת
כָּל־הַמִּשְׁפָּטִים וַיַּעַן כָּל־הָעָם קוֹל אֶחָד וַיֹּאמְרוּ כָּל־הַדְּבָרִים אֲשֶׁר־דִּבֶּר
ד יהוה נַעֲשֶׂה: וַיִּכְתֹּב מֹשֶׁה אֵת כָּל־דִּבְרֵי יהוה וַיַּשְׁכֵּם בַּבֹּקֶר וַיִּבֶן מִזְבֵּחַ
ה תַּחַת הָהָר וּשְׁתֵּים עֶשְׂרֵה מַצֵּבָה לִשְׁנֵים עָשָׂר שִׁבְטֵי יִשְׂרָאֵל: וַיִּשְׁלַח
אֶת־נַעֲרֵי בְּנֵי יִשְׂרָאֵל וַיַּעֲלוּ עֹלֹת וַיִּזְבְּחוּ זְבָחִים שְׁלָמִים לַיהוה פָּרִים:
ו־ז וַיִּקַּח מֹשֶׁה חֲצִי הַדָּם וַיָּשֶׂם בָּאַגָּנֹת וַחֲצִי הַדָּם זָרַק עַל־הַמִּזְבֵּחַ: וַיִּקַּח סֵפֶר
הַבְּרִית וַיִּקְרָא בְּאָזְנֵי הָעָם וַיֹּאמְרוּ כֹּל אֲשֶׁר־דִּבֶּר יהוה נַעֲשֶׂה וְנִשְׁמָע:
ח וַיִּקַּח מֹשֶׁה אֶת־הַדָּם וַיִּזְרֹק עַל־הָעָם וַיֹּאמֶר הִנֵּה דַם־הַבְּרִית אֲשֶׁר כָּרַת
ט יהוה עִמָּכֶם עַל כָּל־הַדְּבָרִים הָאֵלֶּה: וַיַּעַל מֹשֶׁה וְאַהֲרֹן נָדָב וַאֲבִיהוּא
י וְשִׁבְעִים מִזִּקְנֵי יִשְׂרָאֵל: וַיִּרְאוּ אֵת אֱלֹהֵי יִשְׂרָאֵל וְתַחַת רַגְלָיו כְּמַעֲשֵׂה

---

3. וַיָּבֹא מֹשֶׁה וַיְסַפֵּר לָעָם אֵת כָּל דִּבְרֵי ה׳ — *And Moses came and told the people all the words of* HASHEM. From the beginning of כֹּה תֹאמַר, *Thus shall you say* (19:3), until וְאֵלֶּה הַמִּשְׁפָּטִים, *And these are the ordinances* (21:1).

וְאֵת כָּל הַמִּשְׁפָּטִים — *And all the ordinances.* From the beginning of וְאֵלֶּה הַמִּשְׁפָּטִים, *And these are the ordinances* (21:1) until וְאֶל מֹשֶׁה אָמַר, *And to Moses He said* (v. 1).

6. וַחֲצִי הַדָּם זָרַק עַל הַמִּזְבֵּחַ — *And half of the blood he dashed against the altar.* He considered the altar as the emissary of God, the Blessed One, (for the purpose of) entering into the covenant, therefore it received half the blood. The other half was sprinkled on the people who were entering into the covenant.

7. סֵפֶר הַבְּרִית — *The book of the covenant.* The book in which he had written the words of HASHEM, and the ordinances, based upon which they would enter into the covenant, as it states above, וַיִּכְתֹּב מֹשֶׁה, *And Moses wrote* (v. 4).

וַיִּקְרָא בְּאָזְנֵי הָעָם — *And read in the hearing of the people . . .* so that they would know what they were accepting upon themselves, and not be misled.

נַעֲשֶׂה וְנִשְׁמָע — *We will do, and we will listen.* We *will do* toward the end (purpose) of *listening* to His voice, akin to servants who serve the master without a motivation to receive reward, similar to, עֹשֵׂי דְבָרוֹ לִשְׁמֹעַ בְּקוֹל דְּבָרוֹ, *Who perform His bidding, hearkening to the voice of His word (Psalms* 103:20).

9. וַיַּעַל מֹשֶׁה וְאַהֲרֹן — *And Moses and Aaron went up.* After he fulfilled the commandment of God, the Blessed One, who said, 'כֹּה תֹאמַר אֶל בְּנֵי יִשְׂרָאֵל, *Thus shall you say to the Children of Israel'* (20:19), he then fulfilled what was later commanded to him, when (God) said, 'עֲלֵה אֶל ה׳ אַתָּה וְאַהֲרֹן, *Come up to* HASHEM, *you and Aaron'* (v. 1).

10. וְתַחַת רַגְלָיו — *And under His feet . . .* upon the earth, which is the lowest of all, as it says, וְהָאָרֶץ הֲדֹם רַגְלָי, *And the earth is My footstool (Isaiah* 66:1).

NOTES

Torah. The time had now come to implement that original plan.

6. וַחֲצִי הַדָּם זָרַק עַל הַמִּזְבֵּחַ — *And half of the blood he dashed against the altar.* It was customary to sprinkle the blood of the sacrifice, brought to mark the entering into a covenant, on the two parties to that covenant. In this case the altar represents God and, Israel of course, the party of the second part.

7. נַעֲשֶׂה וְנִשְׁמָע — *We will do, and we will*

יא לִבְנַת הַסַּפִּיר וּכְעֶצֶם הַשָּׁמַיִם לָטֹהַר: וְאֶל־אֲצִילֵי בְּנֵי יִשְׂרָאֵל לֹא שָׁלַח
יב יָדוֹ וַיֶּחֱזוּ אֶת־הָאֱלֹהִים וַיֹּאכְלוּ וַיִּשְׁתּוּ: וַיֹּאמֶר יהוה

כְּמַעֲשֵׂה לִבְנַת הַסַּפִּיר — *A work of the whiteness of sapphire stone.* An object lacking all the forms of intelligence and prepared to receive them, similar to the white sapphire which is deficient of all color. This (refers to) the substance of man's intelligent (soul) which lacks all knowledge but is prepared to receive it through free inquiry (contemplation directed by his choice).

וּכְעֶצֶם הַשָּׁמַיִם לָטֹהַר — *And like the very substance of heaven's clarity.* And they apprehended that this substance (i.e., man's soul) was separated from the matter of man and more pure than it, just as the substance of heaven, which is the spirit (soul) of the wheel, when uncombined with the material of the wheel or its body at all (is) purer and clearer than it. (Thus) this substance is as that of the heaven and its spirit (soul), insofar as purity and clearness from the material is concerned.

11. וְאֶל אֲצִילֵי בְּנֵי יִשְׂרָאֵל לֹא שָׁלַח יָדוֹ — *And upon the nobles of the Children of Israel He did not send forth His hand* ... to suspend their senses so that they might prophesy, as is the case with other prophets when *the hand of* HASHEM is upon them, as it says of Ezekiel, וַתִּפֹּל עָלַי שָׁם יַד ה׳, *the hand of* HASHEM *fell there upon me* (*Ezekiel* 8:1), for then the functioning of one's senses ceases, as it occurred to Saul when he prophesied, as it says, וַיִּפְשַׁט גַּם הוּא בְּגָדָיו וַיִּתְנַבֵּא גַּם הוּא לִפְנֵי שְׁמוּאֵל וַיִּפֹּל עָרֹם כָּל הַיּוֹם הַהוּא וְכָל הַלָּיְלָה, *And he also stripped off his clothes and he himself also prophesied before Samuel, and lay down naked all that day and all that night* (*I Samuel* 19:24). However, to these nobles He did not send forth His hand to suspend their senses in order for them to apprehend (grasp) what they then saw.

וַיֶּחֱזוּ אֶת הָאֱלֹהִים — *And they beheld God* ... in a prophetic vision.

וַיֹּאכְלוּ וַיִּשְׁתּוּ — *And they ate and drank.* They made a feast afterward, without changing their senses, and this they did to rejoice in their (spiritual) attainment.

NOTES

listen. The *Sforno* is paraphrasing the Mishnah in *Avos* 1:3, 'Be not like servants who serve their master with the thought of reward; rather be like servants who serve their master without thought of reward.'

10. כְּמַעֲשֵׂה לִבְנַת הַסַּפִּיר וּכְעֶצֶם הַשָּׁמַיִם לָטֹהַר — *A work of the whiteness of sapphire stone and like the very substance of heaven's clarity.* The *Rambam* in his *Guide* (I:28) explains that the word *whiteness* in this verse signifies 'transparency and not a white color.' He explains that 'a transparent body receives all colors in succession because it lacks a color of its own.' We can now understand the commentary here of the *Sforno.* The *object* referred to here is man's spirit of the intellect which begins as a clear substance lacking knowledge, just as the sapphire lacks color. Therefore it is prepared to *receive,* just as a transparent body can receive all colors. Hence Moses, Aaron and the elders of Israel apprehended God through a prophet's vision. They also comprehended that their intellect and soul was superior and purer than their material being just as the essence (soul) of heaven is purer and more clear than the matter of heaven. This is the meaning of the latter part of the verse, *and like the very substance of heaven's clarity,* i.e., their 'human intellectual spirit' (נֶפֶשׁ אֱנוֹשִׁית שִׂכְלִית) was separate from man's physical nature and superior to it, similar to נֶפֶשׁ הַגַּלְגַּל, *the spirit of the wheel,* which is separate from the wheel's material. This the verse calls *the substance of heaven's clarity.*

11. וְאֶל אֲצִילֵי בְּנֵי יִשְׂרָאֵל לֹא שָׁלַח יָדוֹ וַיֶּחֱזוּ אֶת הָאֱלֹהִים וַיֹּאכְלוּ וַיִּשְׁתּוּ — *And upon the nobles of the Children of Israel He did not send forth His hand, and they beheld God and they ate and drank.* The *Sforno* established in 19:9 that Israel reached an unusual level of prophecy at Sinai. Whereas all prophetic visions involve a suspension of man's senses, the highest form of prophecy such as that of Moses and of the

אֶל־מֹשֶׁה עֲלֵה אֵלַי הָהָרָה וֶהְיֵה־שָׁם וְאֶתְּנָה לְךָ אֶת־לֻחֹת הָאֶבֶן וְהַתּוֹרָה
יג וְהַמִּצְוָה אֲשֶׁר כָּתַבְתִּי לְהוֹרֹתָם: וַיָּקָם מֹשֶׁה וִיהוֹשֻׁעַ מְשָׁרְתוֹ וַיַּעַל מֹשֶׁה

---

12. עֲלֵה אֵלַי הָהָרָה — *Come up to Me onto the mount.* To the top of the mountain. After he had come nearer than the others who came up with him, as it says, וְנִגַּשׁ מֹשֶׁה לְבַדּוֹ, *And Moses alone shall come near* (v. 2), he still did not ascend to the top of the mountain. The elders (however) did apprehend the great vision at that site (position). (Now) He says to Moses to go up to the top of the mountain where the *appearance of the glory of HASHEM* was (present), as it is written: וּמַרְאֵה כְּבוֹד ה׳ כְּאֵשׁ אֹכֶלֶת בְּרֹאשׁ הָהָר, *And the appearance of the glory of HASHEM was like a devouring fire on the top of the mountain* (v. 17). This also (occurred) at the giving of the Torah, where it says, וַיִּקְרָא ה׳ לְמֹשֶׁה אֶל רֹאשׁ הָהָר, *And HASHEM called Moses to the top of the mountain* (19:20).

וֶהְיֵה שָׁם — *And be there.* Remain there for a long period of time, similar to, וַיִּהְיוּ שָׁם כַּאֲשֶׁר צִוַּנִי ה׳, *And there they are, as HASHEM commanded me (Deut.* 10:5).

וְהַתּוֹרָה — *And the Torah.* The theoretical part of it.

וְהַמִּצְוָה — *And the commandment.* The practical, active part of it.

אֲשֶׁר כָּתַבְתִּי — *Which I have written.* Had they not sinned with the (Golden) Calf, the entire Torah would have been given to them, written (lit., 'signed') by the Creator, the Blessed One, similar to the tablets, as (the verse) testifies, saying, וְאָתָה מֵרִבְבֹת קֹדֶשׁ מִימִינוֹ אֵשׁ דָּת לָמוֹ, *And He came from the myriads holy, at His right hand was a fiery law unto them (Deut.* 33:2). Once they sinned with the Calf they did not merit it, but (instead) Moses wrote it at His behest as it says later, כְּתָב לְךָ אֶת הַדְּבָרִים הָאֵלֶּה, *Write you these words* (34:27). Our teacher Moses brought (down) the tablets only (for the purpose) of breaking them in view (of the people), so as to break their straying hearts, that they might return and repent.

לְהוֹרֹתָם — *That you may teach them.* I will give them to you so that you may teach them, for although all is written, as our Sages say, 'Is there anything in the Prophets or Writings which is not intimated by Moses in the Torah?' *(Taanis* 9a), and as some of our Sages say, רוֹב בִּכְתָב, וּמִעוּט בְּעַל פֶּה, *The major part is written, (only) a minor part is oral (Gittin* 60b), (yet) behold that the allusions (implications) which are found in it, be it theoretical or in deed, cannot be understood by the majority of Israel save through a righteous teacher. Therefore the opinion of the other Sages who say, רוֹב בְּעַל פֶּה וּמִעוּט בִּכְתָב, *The major part (of Torah) is oral, and a minor part written* (ibid.), is also correct.

NOTES

Children of Israel at Sinai did not. The nobles in the episode related here were also able to experience a prophetic vision (וַיֶּחֱזוּ אֶת הָאֱלֹהִים) without taking leave of their physical senses. This explains the concluding part of the verse which states, *they ate and drank.* The Torah tells us that since their physical senses were not affected there was no need for a transition from the spiritual to the physical. Immediately after *beholding God,* they were able to *eat and drink!*

12. אֲשֶׁר כָּתַבְתִּי — *Which I have written.* Since it is not recorded that God wrote down the תּוֹרָה וּמִצְוָה, *law and commandment, Rashi* explains that these are implicit in the Ten Commandments which He did write, thereby clarifying the statement *which I have written.* The *Sforno,* however, interprets this phrase in the sense that *everything* was written originally in heaven and would have been given to Israel in its totality were it not for the sin of the Golden Calf. Ultimately the Torah was written by Moses at God's behest.

לְהוֹרֹתָם — *That you may teach them.* The

יד אֶל־הַר הָאֱלֹהִים: וְאֶל־הַזְּקֵנִים אָמַר שְׁבוּ־לָנוּ בָזֶה עַד אֲשֶׁר־נָשׁוּב אֲלֵיכֶם
טו וְהִנֵּה אַהֲרֹן וְחוּר עִמָּכֶם מִי־בַעַל דְּבָרִים יִגַּשׁ אֲלֵהֶם: וַיַּעַל מֹשֶׁה אֶל־הָהָר
מפטיר טז וַיְכַס הֶעָנָן אֶת־הָהָר: וַיִּשְׁכֹּן כְּבוֹד־יהוה עַל־הַר סִינַי וַיְכַסֵּהוּ הֶעָנָן שֵׁשֶׁת
יז יָמִים וַיִּקְרָא אֶל־מֹשֶׁה בַּיּוֹם הַשְּׁבִיעִי מִתּוֹךְ הֶעָנָן: וּמַרְאֵה כְּבוֹד יהוה
יח כְּאֵשׁ אֹכֶלֶת בְּרֹאשׁ הָהָר לְעֵינֵי בְּנֵי יִשְׂרָאֵל: וַיָּבֹא מֹשֶׁה בְּתוֹךְ הֶעָנָן וַיַּעַל
אֶל־הָהָר וַיְהִי מֹשֶׁה בָּהָר אַרְבָּעִים יוֹם וְאַרְבָּעִים לָיְלָה:

---

14. וְאֶל הַזְּקֵנִים אָמַר — *And to the elders he said . . .* when he left them, to go up to the top of the mount, as God, the Blessed One, had commanded him, saying, 'עֲלֵה אֵלַי הָהָרָה, *Come up to Me unto the mount*' (v. 12).

18. וַיְהִי מֹשֶׁה בָּהָר — *And Moses was in the mount.* Every time he went up there, from this time forward, (he was there) forty days and forty nights equal to the days of the forming of an embryo, (thereby) acquiring there a more honored (elevated) existence, (making him) worthy to listen (learn) from the mouth of the Teacher, (an experience) which no other person attained, as the (Torah) testifies, saying, כִּי קָרַן עוֹר פָּנָיו בְּדַבְּרוֹ אִתּוֹ, *the skin of his face sent forth beams while He talked with him* (34:29). (Now) their sin impaired this (lofty spiritual level) at the end of the first forty days, when they were worthy to grasp (attain) it, as it says, לֶךְ רֵד כִּי שִׁחֵת עַמְּךָ, *Go, get you down for your people have dealt corruptly* (32:7). During the 'middle' (forty days) which according to tradition were (marked) by (Divine) anger, they did not merit to enjoy the rays of glory, which were attained during the 'last' forty days, during which time (Moses) was commanded regarding the work of the Sanctuary, as it is explained (in the verse) saying, וְאֶל הָאָרֹן תִּתֵּן אֶת הָעֵדֻת אֲשֶׁר אֶתֵּן אֵלֶיךָ, *And in the Ark you shall put the testimony that I shall give you* (25:21). Now this was not realized with the first tablets which never rested in any ark, only the broken pieces without the 'testimony,' as our Sages say, לוּחוֹת נִשְׁבְּרוּ וְאוֹתִיּוֹת פּוֹרְחוֹת, *the tablets broke and the letters flew away* (*Pesachim* 87b). This itself is explained when He said, 'וְעָשׂוּ לִי מִקְדָּשׁ וְשָׁכַנְתִּי בְּתוֹכָם, *They shall make Me a Sanctuary that I may dwell in their midst*' (25:8), (that is) not as He had designated prior to this, when He said, 'מִזְבַּח אֲדָמָה תַּעֲשֶׂה לִּי . . . בְּכָל הַמָּקוֹם אֲשֶׁר אַזְכִּיר אֶת שְׁמִי אָבוֹא אֵלֶיךָ, *An altar of earth you shall make for Me . . . in every place where I cause My Name to be mentioned I will come to you*' (20:21). Now however they will need priests, which

NOTES

word לְהוֹרֹתָם *(to teach them)* implies that Torah was taught orally by Moses to Israel. The *Sforno* explains that although the written Torah (תּוֹרָה שֶׁבִּכְתָב) is precisely that, written, still one cannot possibly understand it without exposition by a righteous teacher. The Talmudic selection *(Gittin* 60b) which he cites is of particular interest. Rabbi Elazar is of the opinion that the major part of Torah was given in writing, basing his opinion on a verse in *Hoshea* (8:12). Rabbi Yochanan insists that the major part of Torah was transmitted orally, basing his opinion on *Exodus* (34:27). The *Sforno* reconciles the two opinions suggesting that indeed the written Torah *contains* the major elements of God's laws but it can only be understood through the interpretation, explanation and exposition of a master teacher.

18. וַיְהִי מֹשֶׁה בָּהָר — *And Moses was in the mount.* The *Sforno* interprets the phrase *And Moses was in the mount* as referring to each of the three forty-day periods which he spent with God. The first was from the seventh (or sixth) of Sivan until the 17th of Tammuz, when he descended and broke the tablets of law. The second was from the 19th of Tammuz, until Rosh Chodesh Elul. The third was from Rosh Chodesh Elul until Yom

is explained when He says, 'וְאַתָּה הַקְרֵב אֵלֶיךָ אֶת אַהֲרֹן אָחִיךָ', *And you (shall) bring near to you Aaron your brother'* (28:1). Behold that the tribe of Levi was not chosen to serve until *after* the incident of the Calf, as is proven by the verse, בָּעֵת הַהִוא הִבְדִּיל ה' אֶת שֵׁבֶט הַלֵּוִי ... לְשָׁרְתוֹ וּלְבָרֵךְ בִּשְׁמוֹ, *At that time* HASHEM *separated the tribe of Levi ... to serve Him and to bless in His Name (Deut.* 10:8).

Therefore (the Torah now) says that every time Moses went up to the mount he remained there forty days and forty nights, and the time he attained this end purpose was the last time of them all, when he was commanded regarding the work of the Sanctuary. Now after (the Torah) completes (the story of) the work of the Sanctuary, the priestly vestments, the incense and the oil of anointment, (then) it explains that at the end of the first (forty days) God, the Blessed One, gave (us) the first tablets, and He, the Blessed One, did not cause any delay, for כִּי לֹא עִנָּה מִלִּבּוֹ, *He did not willingly afflict (Lamentations* 3:33), rather it was Israel that corrupted their affairs as it says, כִּי שִׁחֵת עַמְּךָ, *your people have dealt corruptly* (32:7). During the 'middle' (forty days) according to the tradition of our Rabbis, of blessed memory, the chapter, רְאֵה אַתָּה אֹמֵר אֵלַי, *See, You say to me*, etc. (33:12), and פְּסָל לְךָ, *Hew thee out*, etc. (34:1) (took place). And in the 'third' (forty days) the entire event related in (34:28), וַיְהִי שָׁם עִם ה' אַרְבָּעִים יוֹם וְאַרְבָּעִים לַיְלָה ... וַיִּכְתֹּב עַל הַלֻּחֹת, *And he was there with* HASHEM *forty days and forty nights ... and he wrote upon the tablets* (occurred) and he descended with the rays of glory (shining from his face) and commanded them regarding the work of the Sanctuary.

NOTES

Kippur. The first and third were periods of grace, but the second was one of disfavor and anger because of the Golden Calf. Now the episode of the calf occurred at the end of the first forty-day period, hence it is strange that two *sidros* (portions), *Terumah* and *Tetzaveh*, separate the last verse of *Mishpatim*, which relates the ascent of Moses to the mountain, and the *sidrah* of *Ki Sissa* which relates the story of the Calf and the breaking of the tablets. The *Sforno* resolves this difficulty in his commentary on this verse. He first explains the significance of the number forty as representing the time it takes for an embryo to develop. Each time Moses spent this period of time with God he was reborn, as it were. The special privilege he enjoyed of studying Torah with God Himself resulted in the *rays of light* which shone forth from his face and this in turn would have radiated out to the people upon his descent, had they not sinned. After the forty days and nights of entreating God to forgive Israel for the sin of the calf, Moses ascended the mountain to spend the third, and last, period during which he was given the second tablets and told to build a Sanctuary. Now since he was told to place the tablets in the Ark, this proves that the commandment to construct the Sanctuary (which included the Ark) had to be during the last forty-day period since the first tablets were broken and only later were the שִׁבְרֵי לוּחוֹת, *broken fragments*, placed in the Ark alongside the second (whole) tablets, for which the Ark was made. Another proof that the order to build the Sanctuary was given after the sin of the Calf is the fact that whereas originally God said that He would come to the people *wherever they mentioned His Name*, i.e., without need of a special place or any intermediary, now however there was need for a Sanctuary, and for the tribe of Levi to serve as intermediary as a consequence of the sin. All this being the case, the *sidros* dealing with the Sanctuary, the priesthood, etc. (namely תְּרוּמָה and תְּצַוֶּה), follow *Mishpatim* which concludes with the *last* forty days and nights to complete the story, after which the Torah tells us (in כִּי תִשָּׂא) why there was a need for the second tablets, the Sanctuary and the priesthood.

פרשת תרומה
Parashas Terumah

כה א־ב וַיְדַבֵּר יהוה אֶל־מֹשֶׁה לֵּאמֹר: דַּבֵּר אֶל־בְּנֵי יִשְׂרָאֵל וְיִקְחוּ־לִי תְּרוּמָה
ג מֵאֵת כָּל־אִישׁ אֲשֶׁר יִדְּבֶנּוּ לִבּוֹ תִּקְחוּ אֶת־תְּרוּמָתִי: וְזֹאת הַתְּרוּמָה אֲשֶׁר
ד תִּקְחוּ מֵאִתָּם זָהָב וָכֶסֶף וּנְחֹשֶׁת: וּתְכֵלֶת וְאַרְגָּמָן וְתוֹלַעַת שָׁנִי וְשֵׁשׁ וְעִזִּים:
ה־ו וְעֹרֹת אֵילִם מְאָדָּמִים וְעֹרֹת תְּחָשִׁים וַעֲצֵי שִׁטִּים: שֶׁמֶן לַמָּאֹר בְּשָׂמִים
ז לְשֶׁמֶן הַמִּשְׁחָה וְלִקְטֹרֶת הַסַּמִּים: אַבְנֵי־שֹׁהַם וְאַבְנֵי מִלֻּאִים לָאֵפֹד וְלַחֹשֶׁן:
ח־ט וְעָשׂוּ לִי מִקְדָּשׁ וְשָׁכַנְתִּי בְּתוֹכָם: כְּכֹל אֲשֶׁר אֲנִי מַרְאֶה אוֹתְךָ אֵת תַּבְנִית

XXV

2. דַּבֵּר אֶל בְּנֵי יִשְׂרָאֵל וְיִקְחוּ לִי תְּרוּמָה — *Speak to the Children of Israel that they take for Me an offering.* Tell the Israelites that I want officers to collect offerings for Me. Moses did so when he descended the mountain, as it says, וְאַחֲרֵי כֵן נִגְּשׁוּ כָּל בְּנֵי יִשְׂרָאֵל וַיְצַוֵּם אֵת כָּל אֲשֶׁר דִּבֶּר ה׳ אִתּוֹ בְּהַר סִינָי, *And afterward all the Children of Israel drew close and he commanded them all that* H*ASHEM had spoken with him on Mount Sinai* (34:32), and afterward, וַיֹּאמֶר מֹשֶׁה אֶל כָּל עֲדַת בְּנֵי יִשְׂרָאֵל, *And Moses spoke to all the congregation of the Children of Israel* (i.e., the *Sanhedrin*), 'קְחוּ מֵאִתְּכֶם תְּרוּמָה, *Take from among you an offering*' (35:4,5). In this manner he commanded them to collect (for the Sanctuary) but Israel did not wait for the *Sanhedrin* to collect but immediately left Moses' presence and brought more than enough (36:5). Therefore naught remained for the princes, who had thought to collect, to do except (to bring) the (precious) stones and the oil which the Israelites had not yet brought.

מֵאֵת כָּל אִישׁ — *Of every man.* He commanded that they should not collect forcibly, similar to the placing of a lien for (matters of) *tzedakah* (charity) (*Baba Basra* 8b). Rather they are to collect only from voluntary contributors.

3. וְזֹאת הַתְּרוּמָה — *And this is the offering.* He commanded that they should not accept any items of monetary value such as fruit, pearls or precious stones which were not the stones (required for the) *ephod* and *choshen* (breastplate). But they should accept offerings which could themselves be used for the work of the Sanctuary, which are the thirteen items specified (in the following verses).

8-9. וְשָׁכַנְתִּי בְּתוֹכָם . . . כְּכֹל אֲשֶׁר אֲנִי מַרְאֶה אוֹתְךָ — *That I may dwell among them . . . According to all that I show you.* I will dwell among them to accept their prayer and worship, in the same manner that *I show you* My Divine Presence on the mountain

NOTES

XXV

2. דַּבֵּר אֶל בְּנֵי יִשְׂרָאֵל וְיִקְחוּ לִי תְּרוּמָה — *Speak to the children of Israel that they take for Me an offering.* This chapter relates what God commanded Moses regarding the Sanctuary and the offerings brought for its construction, while he was still with God on the mountaintop. The implementation of this commandment regarding the contributions took place when Moses descended, as recorded in 34:32 and 35:4. The *Sforno* indicates that the two phrases בְּנֵי יִשְׂרָאֵל, *Children of Israel* (34:32), and עֲדַת בְּנֵי יִשְׂרָאֵל, *the congregation of the Children of Israel* (35:4), are meant to differentiate between the people and their leaders — whom he refers to as the *Sanhedrin.* He also interprets the expression *speak to the Children of Israel* in the sense of informing them that they will be asked by the officers to contribute to the Sanctuary, while the leaders were to be told to appoint officers for this purpose, which is the meaning of *that they take for Me an offering.* The people, however, did not wait and brought their gifts with alacrity. As a result the leaders had no need to appoint officers to collect and the only thing remaining for them to do was to bring the precious stones and the oil.

3. וְזֹאת הַתְּרוּמָה — *And this is the offering.* Moses was given three commandments: (a) to have officers appointed to collect the offerings; (b) to do so on a purely voluntary basis —

י הַמִּשְׁכָּן וְאֵת תַּבְנִית כָּל־כֵּלָיו וְכֵן תַּעֲשׂוּ׃ וְעָשׂוּ אֲרוֹן עֲצֵי
יא שִׁטִּים אַמָּתַיִם וָחֵצִי אָרְכּוֹ וְאַמָּה וָחֵצִי רָחְבּוֹ וְאַמָּה וָחֵצִי קֹמָתוֹ׃ וְצִפִּיתָ
יב אֹתוֹ זָהָב טָהוֹר מִבַּיִת וּמִחוּץ תְּצַפֶּנּוּ וְעָשִׂיתָ עָלָיו זֵר זָהָב סָבִיב׃ וְיָצַקְתָּ לּוֹ

(and this will be) on the Ark cover between the two Cherubim with the תַּבְנִית הַמִּשְׁכָּן, *pattern of the Sanctuary,* and with the pattern of all its furnishings (vessels). For indeed the pattern of the Sanctuary indicates the Cherubim who are (as the) שְׂרָפִים עֹמְדִים מִמַּעַל לוֹ, *Serafim who stood above Him (Isaiah* 6:2), which is beheld by the Prophets, some in the Holy and some in the Holy of Holies. (Now) they (the Cherubim) are on two sets (of the curtains) coupled together by clasps, to become as one in the service of their Creator. And so it is proper that it be in Israel; all the holy ones shall be coupled (linked) to the multitude to instruct and teach them. In the Holy of Holies the Toraḥ (tablets of law) was placed in a receptacle (lit., 'body') overlaid with gold within and without (and) as our Sages say, regarding this: כָּל תַּלְמִיד חָכָם שֶׁאֵין תּוֹכוֹ כְּבָו אֵינוֹ תַּלְמִיד חָכָם, *A Torah scholar whose inner being is not as his outer one is not considered a Torah scholar (Yoma* 72b). On that receptacle (lit., 'body') which is the Ark a cover was placed, which was all gold indicating the *image of God,* which is not coupled with it at all. And so the Cherubim with פְּנֵיהֶם אִישׁ אֶל אָחִיו, *their faces one to another* (v. 20), symbolize the transmitting and receiving of the powers of understanding which comes through looking into the Torah, as it says, אֶל הַכַּפֹּרֶת יִהְיוּ פְּנֵי הַכְּרֻבִים, *toward the Ark cover shall the faces of the Cherubim be* (ibid.), and thus they spread their wings on high, as it says, אֹרַח חַיִּים לְמַעְלָה לְמַשְׂכִּיל, *the way of life for the wise leads upward (Proverbs* 15:24), and thus God will bethink Himself of us, as it says: וְאֶל זֶה אַבִּיט, *but to this man will I look (Isaiah* 66:2).

וְכֵן תַּעֲשׂוּ — *And so shall you make it . . .* you (yourself), so that I shall dwell in your midst to speak with you and receive the prayers and service of Israel, not as it was before the (Golden) Calf, as it says, בְּכָל הַמָּקוֹם . . . אָבוֹא אֵלֶיךָ, *in every place . . . I will come to you* (20:21).

NOTES

there was to be no coercion; and (c) to collect only the thirteen items enumerated in verses 3-7.

8-9. וְשָׁכַנְתִּי בְּתוֹכָם . . . כְּכֹל אֲשֶׁר אֲנִי מַרְאֶה אוֹתְךָ — *That I may dwell among them . . . According to all that I show you.* The sense of the *Sforno's* interpretation of these verses is as follows: Cherubim are found in two places in the Sanctuary — over the Ark cover and woven into the curtains which comprised the walls of the Sanctuary. The former was located in the Holy of Holies while the latter was only designated as 'Holy.' Now the Jewish people are called a holy people (19:6), while the Torah scholars and men of the spirit are considered 'Holy of Holies.' The curtains clasped together symbolize the need for Torah scholars to be connected to the multitude and instruct them in God's ways. On an even higher level, symbolized by the Cherubim in the Holy of Holies, there will be the select few who will transmit and receive the profound wisdom and mysteries of God by plumbing the depths of Torah. This is indicated by the Cherubim facing one another while at the same time looking down at the Ark which contains the testimony of law. God in turn will turn His attention and concern to them. (See the note on verse 20 for further elaboration.) The *Sforno* refers to the Ark as גּוּף, *body,* for it symbolizes the physical being of the Torah scholar. Just as the Ark was made of acacia wood and gold — actually three boxes, two of gold and one of wood, fitted into one another — so the body of a holy person, although physical, must be pure on the outside and the inside. The Ark cover, however, was totally made of gold for it represents the *image of God* (and in man, the soul), hence it was not attached to the Ark but separate from it. The concluding words of verse 9, *and so shall you*

אַרְבַּע טַבְּעֹת זָהָב וְנָתַתָּה עַל אַרְבַּע פַּעֲמֹתָיו וּשְׁתֵּי טַבָּעֹת עַל־צַלְעוֹ
יג הָאֶחָת וּשְׁתֵּי טַבָּעֹת עַל־צַלְעוֹ הַשֵּׁנִית: וְעָשִׂיתָ בַדֵּי עֲצֵי שִׁטִּים וְצִפִּיתָ
יד אֹתָם זָהָב: וְהֵבֵאתָ אֶת־הַבַּדִּים בַּטַּבָּעֹת עַל צַלְעֹת הָאָרֹן לָשֵׂאת
טו־טז אֶת־הָאָרֹן בָּהֶם: בְּטַבְּעֹת הָאָרֹן יִהְיוּ הַבַּדִּים לֹא יָסֻרוּ מִמֶּנּוּ: וְנָתַתָּ
שני יז אֶל־הָאָרֹן אֵת הָעֵדֻת אֲשֶׁר אֶתֵּן אֵלֶיךָ: וְעָשִׂיתָ כַפֹּרֶת זָהָב טָהוֹר אַמָּתַיִם
יח וָחֵצִי אָרְכָּהּ וְאַמָּה וָחֵצִי רָחְבָּהּ: וְעָשִׂיתָ שְׁנַיִם כְּרֻבִים זָהָב מִקְשָׁה תַּעֲשֶׂה
יט אֹתָם מִשְּׁנֵי קְצוֹת הַכַּפֹּרֶת: וַעֲשֵׂה כְּרוּב אֶחָד מִקָּצָה מִזֶּה וּכְרוּב־אֶחָד
כ מִקָּצָה מִזֶּה מִן־הַכַּפֹּרֶת תַּעֲשׂוּ אֶת־הַכְּרֻבִים עַל־שְׁנֵי קְצוֹתָיו: וְהָיוּ
הַכְּרֻבִים פֹּרְשֵׂי כְנָפַיִם לְמַעְלָה סֹכְכִים בְּכַנְפֵיהֶם עַל־הַכַּפֹּרֶת וּפְנֵיהֶם אִישׁ

---

12. פַּעֲמֹתָיו — *Feet* . . . the corners of its bottom rim.

וּשְׁתֵּי טַבָּעֹת עַל צַלְעוֹ הָאֶחָת — *And two rings shall be on the one side of it.* The long side (length) is called צֶלַע. He therefore commanded that the four (rings) should be placed on the four corners of the bottom (rim) and He also commanded that it not be placed on the narrow side (the breadth) but on the long side called צְלָעוֹת, two of them on one side and two of them on the second.

16. וְנָתַתָּ אֶל הָאָרֹן — *And you shall put into the Ark.* He had to explain its purpose since this was a furnishing which was not fit for any sacrificial service.

20. וְהָיוּ הַכְּרֻבִים פֹּרְשֵׂי כְנָפַיִם — *And the Cherubim shall spread out their wings.* The prophets have already explained that in their prophetic visions angels appeared to them in the form of Cherubim, with the face of a human and with wings. All this (comes to) teach the nature of the intellects separated from matter (i.e., angels) whose entire movement is in an upward direction, toward God — to understand and know Him. Each of these 'intellects separated from matter' according to its ability. Now by the statement, וְהָיוּ הַכְּרֻבִים פֹּרְשֵׂי כְנָפַיִם, *And the Cherubim shall spread out their wings,* we are being taught that the human intellect is one that (also) has the potential to reach a second (level) of perfection, which can be attained through principles (of truth and apprehension) and the removal of (one's physical) matter, so as to understand and know one's Creator to the extent possible, by examining (lit.,

NOTES

make it, is interpreted by the *Sforno* as implying a rebuke. Until the sin of the Golden Calf there was no need for a Sanctuary, since God was prepared to come wherever Israel would cause *His Name to be mentioned.* However, after the sin it was necessary to designate a specific, limited place for the Divine Presence to dwell.

12. וּשְׁתֵּי טַבָּעֹת עַל צַלְעוֹ הָאֶחָת — *And two rings shall be on the one side of it.* The *Sforno* disagrees with *Rashi* (and other commentators) regarding the positioning of the rings on the Ark. He is of the opinion that they were to be placed at the corners of the bottom rim — not at the top near the Ark cover, and they were to be placed along the length, not the width, for the word צֶלַע, used here by the Torah as opposed to צַד, means length.

16. וְנָתַתָּ אֶל הָאָרֹן — *And you shall put into the Ark.* Pagan worship was well known to the Israelites, hence they could relate to various furnishings and vessels of the Sanctuary since there were counterparts among the heathens. The Ark, however, was completely new and unique. What was the purpose of this box? This is what the *Sforno* means when he states that it was necessary to explain the purpose of the Ark, being that it did not fit any service known to them in that culture and time period.

20. וְהָיוּ הַכְּרֻבִים פֹּרְשֵׂי כְנָפַיִם — *And the Cherubim shall spread out their wings.* The *Sforno* in his commentary on verses 8-9 explains the symbolism of the Cherubim and their lesson for man insofar as our responsibility to understand God's ways through Torah and to

כא אֶל־אָחִיו אֶל־הַכַּפֹּרֶת יִהְיוּ פְּנֵי הַכְּרֻבִים: וְנָתַתָּ אֶת־הַכַּפֹּרֶת עַל־הָאָרֹן

'gazing at') the wonders in the Torah which clearly show His wondrous acts and merciful ways. For indeed the essence and form of a thing is made known to us through its deeds (actions) and this occurs to human understanding when one grasps (lit., 'understands') the existence of the Creator as much as he possibly can (through His ways), as it says, הוֹדִעֵנִי נָא אֶת דְּרָכֶךָ וְאֵדָעֲךָ לְמַעַן אֶמְצָא חֵן בְּעֵינֶיךָ, *Show me now Your ways that I may know You to the end that I may find grace in Your eyes* (33:13). (This the verse indicates by) saying that the Cherubim shall *spread out their wings on high.* Now (our Sages) have said (*Yoma* 54a) that the Cherubim were male and female, indicating the action of delivering (or giving) the general principles (of truth and apprehension) removed (from the physical) which is akin to the action of the male who conveys, (as well as) indicating receiving these (principles) which are removed from (the mundane), akin to the function of the female. And the (verse also) says, וּפְנֵיהֶם אִישׁ אֶל אָחִיו, *with their faces one to another,* for the process of giving these general principles and disseminating them (require one) to consider and concentrate toward the action of receiving these general principles that are removed from matter, (since) through them one attains the intended perfection. And it (then) says, אֶל הַכַּפֹּרֶת יִהְיוּ פְּנֵי הַכְּרֻבִים, *toward the Ark cover shall the faces of the Cherubim be.*

21. וְנָתַתָּ אֶת הַכַּפֹּרֶת עַל הָאָרֹן מִלְמָעְלָה וְאֶל הָאָרֹן תִּתֵּן אֶת הָעֵדֻת אֲשֶׁר אֶתֵּן אֵלֶיךָ — *And you shall put the Ark cover on the Ark above and in the Ark you shall put the testimony that I will give you.* For indeed the application (lit., 'gazing') of the intellect and the giving (delivering) of the general principles from which matter has been removed, as well as the receiving (of same), said receiving (being such) that it

NOTES

transmit this knowledge to others as well. In this verse he elaborates on the significance of the Cherubim and interprets the imagery of *two,* rather than one, and what is meant by their wings being *spread out on high.* The *Rambam* in his *Guide* (I:49) says, 'The angels are not endowed with bodies but are intellects separate from matter.' Based on this concept the *Sforno* explains that man, as well, can attain a higher understanding of God if he also could to a certain extent transcend his physical being and *remove his matter* as it were, thereby also becoming separate from matter, i.e., pure intellect, although still less than an angel. The *Rambam* explains the imagery of the wings thus: The act of flying represents the ability to soar to the heights as well as swiftness of movement. All this requires wings and it is in this sense that the concept of wings is linked to angels and to the Cherubim in particular. This explains the *Sforno's* opening comment that Cherubim have *the face of a human and wings.* A human being can also aspire to develop his spiritual and intellectual potential so as to soar to greater heights of apprehension and understanding of God. Now this can only be realized by examining God's ways, as we see from Moses that to *know God* can only be through the medium of knowing His ways, i.e., understanding the way of God as manifested through His attributive qualifications, as the *Rambam* puts it in the *Guide* (I:54): 'The apprehension of God's actions is an apprehension of His attributes with respect to which He is known' (ibid.). These actions are called מִדּוֹת, *characteristics,* by our Sages, hence the י"ג מִדּוֹת, *thirteen characteristics,* which are revealed to Moses. To know God's ways through His actions can only be achieved through His Torah which is why the Cherubim gaze at the Ark cover, to teach man this truth, which is the key to wisdom, for in the Torah are recorded 'His wondrous acts and merciful ways' as the *Sforno* states.

The *Sforno* also emphasizes that the statement of the Sages regarding the two Cherubim as being male and female is meant to teach us the importance of two forces in grasping God's ways and transmitting this understanding to others. The male represents the power of giving, delivering, conveying

כב מִלְמָ֑עְלָה וְאֶל־הָ֣אָרֹ֔ן תִּתֵּ֖ן אֶת־הָ֣עֵדֻ֔ת אֲשֶׁ֥ר אֶתֵּ֖ן אֵלֶֽיךָ׃ וְנוֹעַדְתִּ֣י לְךָ֮ שָׁם֒
וְדִבַּרְתִּ֨י אִתְּךָ֜ מֵעַ֣ל הַכַּפֹּ֗רֶת מִבֵּין֙ שְׁנֵ֣י הַכְּרֻבִ֔ים אֲשֶׁ֖ר עַל־אֲר֣וֹן הָעֵדֻ֑ת אֵ֣ת
כָּל־אֲשֶׁ֧ר אֲצַוֶּ֛ה אוֹתְךָ֖ אֶל־בְּנֵ֥י יִשְׂרָאֵֽל׃
כג וְעָשִׂ֥יתָ שֻׁלְחָ֖ן עֲצֵ֣י שִׁטִּ֑ים אַמָּתַ֤יִם אָרְכּוֹ֙ וְאַמָּ֣ה רָחְבּ֔וֹ וְאַמָּ֥ה וָחֵ֖צִי קֹמָתֽוֹ׃

becomes his possession; behold, all this can (only) be through the medium of analysis and active preparation. Therefore all this can (only) be attained by examining (studying) the testimony which is in the Ark upon which is the Ark cover, for indeed in the testimony, which is the Ten Commandments, are found the general principles (of Torah), the theoretical and active (deeds) portions (parts), and so He designated . . .

22. וְנוֹעַדְתִּי לְךָ שָׁם וְדִבַּרְתִּי אִתְּךָ — *And there I shall meet with you and I will speak with you.* For through this the Divine Presence came to rest (among them) and will dwell in every place where the wise men of the generation are found, whose purpose is to understand and know Him, as it is attested to by saying, וְשָׁכַנְתִּי בְּתוֹכָם כְּכֹל אֲשֶׁר אֲנִי מַרְאֶה אוֹתְךָ, *That I may dwell among them according to all that I show you,* to which He adds and says, וְכֵן תַּעֲשׂוּ, *and so shall you make it* (verses 8-9). As our Sages have testified that it happened to them when they were expounding the 'Work of the Chariot' as the Sages say, 'You are expounding the Work of the Chariot and the Divine Presence (שְׁכִינָה) is with us and the ministering angels accompany us, etc.' (*Chagigah* 14b).

23. וְעָשִׂיתָ שֻׁלְחָן — *And you shall make a table.* After (telling us) the work of the Ark, which was in the likeness of a throne for the Divine Presence, as it says, וְנוֹעַדְתִּי לְךָ שָׁם, *And there I will meet with you* (v. 22), (he) now commands regarding the table and menorah, in accordance with the custom of princes, as we find with the Shunamis when she said, וְנָשִׂים לוֹ שָׁם מִטָּה וְשֻׁלְחָן וְכִסֵּא וּמְנוֹרָה, *and let us set for him there a bed, table, chair and candlestick* (*II Kings* 4:10). Since the crown of the table represents the crown of kingship, as our Sages say (*Yoma* 72b), (and) the king's responsibilities (lit., 'affairs') in conducting matters of state are twofold; one being in

NOTES

while the female receives, just as it is in the physical union which results in a new life. So the ultimate truth and wisdom of Torah is drawn forth from the Torah and absorbed by the recipient. Hence the imagery is complete — the Cherubim face one another, spread out their wings and face the Ark cover.

21. וְנָתַתָּ אֶת הַכַּפֹּרֶת עַל הָאָרֹן מִלְמָעְלָה וְאֶל הָאָרֹן תִּתֵּן אֶת הָעֵדֻת אֲשֶׁר אֶתֵּן אֵלֶיךָ — *And you shall put the Ark cover on the Ark above and in the Ark you shall put the testimony that I will give you.* The *Sforno*, reflecting the opinion of the *Rambam*, explains that man can only hope to attain a true understanding of God and Torah through intellectual, in-depth analysis of God's existence and His ways, and preparation to accept His will and translate it into action. This in turn can only be realized through the study of Torah which will refine his character and grant him clarity of thought, resulting in purity of action. All this the Cherubim symbolize facing the Ark cover — כַּפֹּרֶת — which is on top of the Ark housing the Ten Commandments. The Ten Commandments, in turn, represent the totality of Torah — the theoretical-analytical as well as the action-deed aspect of Torah, as the *Sforno* explains in his commentary to chapter 20.

22. וְנוֹעַדְתִּי לְךָ שָׁם וְדִבַּרְתִּי אִתְּךָ — *And there I shall meet with you and I will speak with you.* The result of all that is described in the previous verses is that the Divine Presence (שְׁכִינָה) will come to rest in the Sanctuary between the Cherubim above the Ark cover. The *Sforno* carries this idea over to the study of the מַעֲשֵׂה מֶרְכָּבָה, *Work of the Chariot*, by a select group of wise men who attained the heights of Torah knowledge and were worthy of pursuing this esoteric wisdom. He proves this from the selection cited from the Talmud

כד־כה וְצִפִּיתָ אֹתוֹ זָהָב טָהוֹר וְעָשִׂיתָ לּוֹ זֵר זָהָב סָבִיב: וְעָשִׂיתָ לּוֹ מִסְגֶּרֶת טֹפַח
כו סָבִיב וְעָשִׂיתָ זֵר־זָהָב לְמִסְגַּרְתּוֹ סָבִיב: וְעָשִׂיתָ לּוֹ אַרְבַּע טַבְּעֹת זָהָב וְנָתַתָּ
כז אֶת־הַטַּבָּעֹת עַל אַרְבַּע הַפֵּאֹת אֲשֶׁר לְאַרְבַּע רַגְלָיו: לְעֻמַּת הַמִּסְגֶּרֶת
כח תִּהְיֶיןָ הַטַּבָּעֹת לְבָתִּים לְבַדִּים לָשֵׂאת אֶת־הַשֻּׁלְחָן: וְעָשִׂיתָ אֶת־הַבַּדִּים
כט עֲצֵי שִׁטִּים וְצִפִּיתָ אֹתָם זָהָב וְנִשָּׂא־בָם אֶת־הַשֻּׁלְחָן: וְעָשִׂיתָ קְּעָרֹתָיו
ל וְכַפֹּתָיו וּקְשׂוֹתָיו וּמְנַקִּיֹּתָיו אֲשֶׁר יֻסַּךְ בָּהֵן זָהָב טָהוֹר תַּעֲשֶׂה אֹתָם: וְנָתַתָּ
עַל־הַשֻּׁלְחָן לֶחֶם פָּנִים לְפָנַי תָּמִיד:

לא וְעָשִׂיתָ מְנֹרַת זָהָב טָהוֹר מִקְשָׁה תֵּיעָשֶׂה הַמְּנוֹרָה יְרֵכָהּ וְקָנָהּ גְּבִיעֶיהָ
לב כַּפְתֹּרֶיהָ וּפְרָחֶיהָ מִמֶּנָּה יִהְיוּ: וְשִׁשָּׁה קָנִים יֹצְאִים מִצִּדֶּיהָ שְׁלֹשָׁה ׀ קְנֵי
לג מְנֹרָה מִצִּדָּהּ הָאֶחָד וּשְׁלֹשָׁה קְנֵי מְנֹרָה מִצִּדָּהּ הַשֵּׁנִי: שְׁלֹשָׁה גְבִעִים
מְשֻׁקָּדִים בַּקָּנֶה הָאֶחָד כַּפְתֹּר וָפֶרַח וּשְׁלֹשָׁה גְבִעִים מְשֻׁקָּדִים בַּקָּנֶה הָאֶחָד
לד כַּפְתֹּר וָפָרַח כֵּן לְשֵׁשֶׁת הַקָּנִים הַיֹּצְאִים מִן־הַמְּנֹרָה: וּבַמְּנֹרָה אַרְבָּעָה
לה גְבִעִים מְשֻׁקָּדִים כַּפְתֹּרֶיהָ וּפְרָחֶיהָ: וְכַפְתֹּר תַּחַת שְׁנֵי הַקָּנִים מִמֶּנָּה
וְכַפְתֹּר תַּחַת שְׁנֵי הַקָּנִים מִמֶּנָּה וְכַפְתֹּר תַּחַת־שְׁנֵי הַקָּנִים מִמֶּנָּה לְשֵׁשֶׁת

---

the area of justice and the affairs of state, (while) the second is to defend the state from all enemies and oppressors, as it says, וּשְׁפָטָנוּ מַלְכֵּנוּ וְיָצָא לְפָנֵינוּ וְנִלְחַם אֶת מִלְחֲמֹתֵינוּ, *that our king may judge us and go out before us and fight our battles (I Samuel* 8:20), (therefore) two crowns were placed on the table, one for the table itself indicating the livelihood and order of the state and its affairs and the second for the border (rim) indicating a (protective) border for it (the state) against all harm and to *still the enemy and avenger (Psalms* 8:3).

29. קְעָרֹתָיו וְכַפֹּתָיו — *The pans and spoons thereof.* Which were well known at that time, used (in conjunction) with the table of kings.

31. וְעָשִׂיתָ מְנֹרַת זָהָב טָהוֹר — *And you shall make a menorah of pure gold.* After ordering the two crowns, which are the crown of Torah through the Ark and the crown of kingship through the table, He now orders (arranges) the menorah all beaten out of one piece, and the light of its candles (are also) one, as He says . . .

NOTES

(Chagigah 14b) where Rabban Yochanan ben Zakkai says that the Divine Presence was present at the time Rabbi Elazar ben Arach expounded on the 'Work of the Chariot,' for through his mastery of the truth of Torah he was able to bring God into their midst, similar to God's 'meeting' with Moses and speaking to him in the Sanctuary. The expression וְכֵן תַּעֲשׂוּ, *and so you shall do* (v. 9), is interpreted by the *Sforno* as encouraging those who have the capacity to pursue the knowledge of God to do so, as did the Sages of the Talmud mentioned above.

23. וְעָשִׂיתָ שֻׁלְחָן — *And you shall make a table.* The word זֵר, *crown,* appears twice in conjunction with the table — in verse 24 and verse 25. *Rashi* is of the opinion that there was only one crown and that verse 25 clarifies verse 24. The *Sforno,* however, interprets these verses literally and explains that one crown was for the table itself whereas the second one was for the border or rim, indicating the twofold responsibility of the king, domestic tranquility and national security. That the table represents kingship is based upon the Talmud *(Yoma* 72b) where our Sages tell us that there were three crowns in the furnishings of the Sanctuary — on the Ark, on the table and on the golden altar. The crown of the golden altar represents the crown of priesthood; the table represents שֻׁלְחַן מְלָכִים, *the royal table* (and its crown is thus the crown of kingship); while the crown on the Ark represents the crown of Torah.

31-37. וְעָשִׂיתָ מְנֹרַת זָהָב טָהוֹר . . . וְהֵאִיר עַל עֵבֶר פָּנֶיהָ — *And you shall make a menorah of pure*

לו הַקָּנִים הַיֹּצְאִים מִן־הַמְּנֹרָה: כַּפְתֹּרֵיהֶם וּקְנֹתָם מִמֶּנָּה יִהְיוּ כֻּלָּהּ מִקְשָׁה
לז אַחַת זָהָב טָהוֹר: וְעָשִׂיתָ אֶת־נֵרֹתֶיהָ שִׁבְעָה וְהֶעֱלָה אֶת־נֵרֹתֶיהָ וְהֵאִיר
לח־לט עַל־עֵבֶר פָּנֶיהָ: וּמַלְקָחֶיהָ וּמַחְתֹּתֶיהָ זָהָב טָהוֹר: כִּכַּר זָהָב טָהוֹר יַעֲשֶׂה
מ אֹתָהּ אֵת כָּל־הַכֵּלִים הָאֵלֶּה: וּרְאֵה וַעֲשֵׂה בְּתַבְנִיתָם אֲשֶׁר־אַתָּה מָרְאֶה
כו שלישי א בָּהָר: וְאֶת־הַמִּשְׁכָּן תַּעֲשֶׂה עֶשֶׂר יְרִיעֹת שֵׁשׁ מָשְׁזָר וּתְכֵלֶת
ב וְאַרְגָּמָן וְתֹלַעַת שָׁנִי כְּרֻבִים מַעֲשֵׂה חֹשֵׁב תַּעֲשֶׂה אֹתָם: אֹרֶךְ | הַיְרִיעָה
הָאַחַת שְׁמֹנֶה וְעֶשְׂרִים בָּאַמָּה וְרֹחַב אַרְבַּע בָּאַמָּה הַיְרִיעָה הָאֶחָת מִדָּה
ג אַחַת לְכָל־הַיְרִיעֹת: חֲמֵשׁ הַיְרִיעֹת תִּהְיֶיןָ חֹבְרֹת אִשָּׁה אֶל־אֲחֹתָהּ וְחָמֵשׁ

---

37. וְהֵאִיר עַל עֵבֶר פָּנֶיהָ — *To give light over against it.* The light of the right candles (wicks) and left candles will be directed toward the center, and it is proper that it be so; that the light of the intellect in the part of (Torah) which is theory (analysis) and also the light in the active part (of Torah, i.e., deeds) turn and face the Divine light, to serve Him in one accord, for then all will illuminate as designated regarding the menorah, when He said: בְּהַעֲלֹתְךָ אֶת הַנֵּרֹת אֶל מוּל פְּנֵי הַמְּנוֹרָה יָאִירוּ שִׁבְעַת הַנֵּרוֹת . . . וְזֶה מַעֲשֵׂה הַמְּנֹרָה מִקְשָׁה, *When you light the lamps the seven lamps shall give light over against the central candlestick ... and this was the work of the candlestick, (it should be) beaten (out of one piece) (Numbers* 8:2, 4). When all the light is directed *to one* — (similar to the fact that the menorah was) beaten out of one solid piece (piece of gold) — which teaches us (the lesson of) unity, then the light will be seen as shining from the great light.

XXVI

1. וְאֶת הַמִּשְׁכָּן תַּעֲשֶׂה — *And you shall make the mishkan.* He called the curtains by the name *mishkan* (sanctuary or tabernacle) because within them were the chair (i.e., Ark), table and menorah for the Divine Presence to dwell. They (the curtains) were made with Cherubim similar to שְׂרָפִים עֹמְדִים מִמַּעַל לוֹ, *Seraphim stood above Him (Isaiah* 6:2), and to, וְכָל צְבָא הַשָּׁמַיִם עֹמֵד עָלָיו מִימִינוֹ וּמִשְּׂמֹאלוֹ, *all the hosts of heaven standing by Him on His right and on His left (I Kings* 22:19), seen by the prophets in visions of prophecy.

3. חָמֵשׁ הַיְרִיעֹת תִּהְיֶיןָ חֹבְרֹת — *Five curtains shall be coupled together.* The work of each one of them should be directed (matched) to that of its mate in the work of

NOTES

gold ... To give light over against it. The commentary of the *Sforno* here and his commentary on *Numbers* 8:2,4 complement one another and clarify his explanation of the menorah and the arrangement of its wicks, as well as the significance of the candlestick being beaten out of one piece of gold. The central theme of the menorah is unity — the unity of Israel and of course, that of God. There are three lights on either side of the central candlestick which represent the different parts of Torah (the theoretical and the practical) as well as the two segments of Israel, i.e., those who occupy themselves exclusively with the spiritual and those who involve themselves with the temporal, as the *Sforno* explains in *Numbers* 8:2. By bending the wicks, from the left and right to the center which represents the Divine light, we are taught that all segments of Israel and all areas of Torah are to be united together and directed to a common purpose, i.e., to serve the Almighty with one accord. This is also the significance of the menorah itself being hammered out of one piece. In this manner the light of Torah and of Israel shall shine forth, emanating from the one great source of light — Almighty God.

XXVI

1. וְאֶת הַמִּשְׁכָּן תַּעֲשֶׂה — *And you shall make the mishkan.* The *Sforno* explains why the curtains are called *mishkan,* a term normally

ד יְרִיעֹת חֹבְרֹת אִשָּׁה אֶל־אֲחֹתָהּ: וְעָשִׂיתָ לֻלְאֹת תְּכֵלֶת עַל שְׂפַת הַיְרִיעָה
הָאֶחָת מִקָּצָה בַּחֹבָרֶת וְכֵן תַּעֲשֶׂה בִּשְׂפַת הַיְרִיעָה הַקִּיצוֹנָה בַּמַּחְבֶּרֶת
ה הַשֵּׁנִית: חֲמִשִּׁים לֻלָאֹת תַּעֲשֶׂה בַּיְרִיעָה הָאֶחָת וַחֲמִשִּׁים לֻלָאֹת תַּעֲשֶׂה
בִּקְצֵה הַיְרִיעָה אֲשֶׁר בַּמַּחְבֶּרֶת הַשֵּׁנִית מַקְבִּילֹת הַלֻּלָאֹת אִשָּׁה אֶל־
ו אֲחֹתָהּ: וְעָשִׂיתָ חֲמִשִּׁים קַרְסֵי זָהָב וְחִבַּרְתָּ אֶת־הַיְרִיעֹת אִשָּׁה אֶל־אֲחֹתָהּ
ז בַּקְּרָסִים וְהָיָה הַמִּשְׁכָּן אֶחָד: וְעָשִׂיתָ יְרִיעֹת עִזִּים לְאֹהֶל עַל־הַמִּשְׁכָּן
ח עַשְׁתֵּי־עֶשְׂרֵה יְרִיעֹת תַּעֲשֶׂה אֹתָם: אֹרֶךְ | הַיְרִיעָה הָאַחַת שְׁלֹשִׁים בָּאַמָּה
וְרֹחַב אַרְבַּע בָּאַמָּה הַיְרִיעָה הָאֶחָת מִדָּה אַחַת לְעַשְׁתֵּי עֶשְׂרֵה יְרִיעֹת:
ט וְחִבַּרְתָּ אֶת־חֲמֵשׁ הַיְרִיעֹת לְבָד וְאֶת־שֵׁשׁ הַיְרִיעֹת לְבָד וְכָפַלְתָּ אֶת־

---

their images (pictures). (All) this is (meant) to separate between the curtains of the Holy and the curtains of the Holy of Holies, for although all the work of the (woven images of the) Cherubim indicate (symbolize) 'intellects separated from matter' (i.e., angels), *given from one shepherd* (based on *Koheles* 11:11), nonetheless they are not on an equal level.

6. וְהָיָה הַמִּשְׁכָּן אֶחָד — *And the mishkan shall be one.* For although the various levels are not equal (in importance) nonetheless they are (all) arranged in one order to do the will of their Creator, as it says, וְקָרָא זֶה אֶל זֶה וְאָמַר קָדוֹשׁ, *And one cried to the other and said, 'Holy, etc. (Isaiah* 6:3).

7. לְאֹהֶל עַל הַמִּשְׁכָּן — *For a tent over the mishkan.* For the *mishkan* (itself) was not meant to serve as a tent but (for the purpose) that the Cherubim should envelope the chair, table and candlestick.

9. וְחִבַּרְתָּ אֶת חֲמֵשׁ הַיְרִיעֹת לְבָד — *And you shall couple five curtains by themselves.* For in the (curtains known as the) tent there is also a difference between the level of some and the level of others, similar to the movers of the spheres who are called אֹהֶל, *tent*, as it says, לַשֶּׁמֶשׁ שָׂם אֹהֶל בָּהֶם, *In them He has set a tent for the sun (Psalms* 19:5).

NOTES

reserved for the Sanctuary. Since they veil off the area in which the Ark (chair), table and candlestick are housed, they are referred to by this name.

The *Sforno* uses the term *chair* for the Ark, as he explained above (25:23), because it represents the throne of the Divine Presence since God comes and speaks from between the Cherubim over the Ark cover.

3. חֲמֵשׁ הַיְרִיעֹת תִּהְיֶיןָ חֹבְרֹת — *Five curtains shall be coupled together.* The word *coupled* does not only mean sewn together by a needle, as *Rashi* comments, but also to align the figures of the Cherubim, which were as the figures of a lion and eagle, with one another on the two sections. The *Sforno*, in keeping with his interpretation of the Cherubim as representing categories of angels, explains that the curtains enclosing the Holy are not equal in sanctity to those enclosing the Holy of Holies, even though these angels all emanate from the one God. As he points out in verse 6, they are not equal in rank yet they all serve God as one unit.

7. לְאֹהֶל עַל הַמִּשְׁכָּן — *For a tent over the mishkan.* Although the *mishkan* curtains could be considered אֹהֶל, *a tent*, nevertheless, the Torah uses this term only in conjunction with the goats'-hair curtains. The *Sforno* explains that since the curtains of linen and wool had the Cherubim woven into them their purpose was not to serve as a *tent* to protect the vessels and furnishings; hence the term *a tent* is reserved for the curtains which covered them.

9. וְחִבַּרְתָּ אֶת חֲמֵשׁ הַיְרִיעֹת לְבָד — *And you shall couple five curtains by themselves.* Whenever two sections are coupled together it indicates that although similar they are not the same. The goats'-hair curtains, although not as sacred as the inner curtains which have the design of Cherubim on them, nonetheless also represent Divine levels which are diverse,

י הַיְרִיעָה הַשִּׁשִּׁית אֶל־מוּל פְּנֵי הָאֹהֶל׃ וְעָשִׂיתָ חֲמִשִּׁים לֻלָאֹת עַל שְׂפַת
הַיְרִיעָה הָאֶחָת הַקִּיצֹנָה בַּחֹבָרֶת וַחֲמִשִּׁים לֻלָאֹת עַל שְׂפַת הַיְרִיעָה
יא הַחֹבֶרֶת הַשֵּׁנִית׃ וְעָשִׂיתָ קַרְסֵי נְחֹשֶׁת חֲמִשִּׁים וְהֵבֵאתָ אֶת־הַקְּרָסִים
יב בַּלֻּלָאֹת וְחִבַּרְתָּ אֶת־הָאֹהֶל וְהָיָה אֶחָד׃ וְסֶרַח הָעֹדֵף בִּירִיעֹת הָאֹהֶל חֲצִי
יג הַיְרִיעָה הָעֹדֶפֶת תִּסְרַח עַל אֲחֹרֵי הַמִּשְׁכָּן׃ וְהָאַמָּה מִזֶּה וְהָאַמָּה מִזֶּה
בָּעֹדֵף בְּאֹרֶךְ יְרִיעֹת הָאֹהֶל יִהְיֶה סָרוּחַ עַל־צִדֵּי הַמִּשְׁכָּן מִזֶּה וּמִזֶּה
יד לְכַסֹּתוֹ׃ וְעָשִׂיתָ מִכְסֶה לָאֹהֶל עֹרֹת אֵילִם מְאָדָּמִים וּמִכְסֵה עֹרֹת תְּחָשִׁים
מִלְמָעְלָה׃
רביעי טו־טז וְעָשִׂיתָ אֶת־הַקְּרָשִׁים לַמִּשְׁכָּן עֲצֵי שִׁטִּים עֹמְדִים׃ עֶשֶׂר אַמּוֹת אֹרֶךְ הַקָּרֶשׁ
יז וְאַמָּה וַחֲצִי הָאַמָּה רֹחַב הַקֶּרֶשׁ הָאֶחָד׃ שְׁתֵּי יָדוֹת לַקֶּרֶשׁ הָאֶחָד מְשֻׁלָּבֹת
יח אִשָּׁה אֶל־אֲחֹתָהּ כֵּן תַּעֲשֶׂה לְכֹל קַרְשֵׁי הַמִּשְׁכָּן׃ וְעָשִׂיתָ אֶת־הַקְּרָשִׁים
יט לַמִּשְׁכָּן עֶשְׂרִים קֶרֶשׁ לִפְאַת נֶגְבָּה תֵימָנָה׃ וְאַרְבָּעִים אַדְנֵי־כֶסֶף תַּעֲשֶׂה
תַּחַת עֶשְׂרִים הַקָּרֶשׁ שְׁנֵי אֲדָנִים תַּחַת־הַקֶּרֶשׁ הָאֶחָד לִשְׁתֵּי יְדֹתָיו וּשְׁנֵי
כ אֲדָנִים תַּחַת־הַקֶּרֶשׁ הָאֶחָד לִשְׁתֵּי יְדֹתָיו׃ וּלְצֶלַע הַמִּשְׁכָּן הַשֵּׁנִית לִפְאַת
כא צָפוֹן עֶשְׂרִים קָרֶשׁ׃ וְאַרְבָּעִים אַדְנֵיהֶם כָּסֶף שְׁנֵי אֲדָנִים תַּחַת הַקֶּרֶשׁ
כב הָאֶחָד וּשְׁנֵי אֲדָנִים תַּחַת הַקֶּרֶשׁ הָאֶחָד׃ וּלְיַרְכְּתֵי הַמִּשְׁכָּן יָמָּה תַּעֲשֶׂה
כג־כד שִׁשָּׁה קְרָשִׁים׃ וּשְׁנֵי קְרָשִׁים תַּעֲשֶׂה לִמְקֻצְעֹת הַמִּשְׁכָּן בַּיַּרְכָתָיִם׃ וְיִהְיוּ
תֹאֲמִם מִלְּמַטָּה וְיַחְדָּו יִהְיוּ תַמִּים עַל־רֹאשׁוֹ אֶל־הַטַּבַּעַת הָאֶחָת כֵּן יִהְיֶה
כה לִשְׁנֵיהֶם לִשְׁנֵי הַמִּקְצֹעֹת יִהְיוּ׃ וְהָיוּ שְׁמֹנָה קְרָשִׁים וְאַדְנֵיהֶם כֶּסֶף שִׁשָּׁה
עָשָׂר אֲדָנִים שְׁנֵי אֲדָנִים תַּחַת הַקֶּרֶשׁ הָאֶחָד וּשְׁנֵי אֲדָנִים תַּחַת הַקָּרֶשׁ
כו הָאֶחָד׃ וְעָשִׂיתָ בְרִיחִם עֲצֵי שִׁטִּים חֲמִשָּׁה לְקַרְשֵׁי צֶלַע־הַמִּשְׁכָּן הָאֶחָד׃
כז וַחֲמִשָּׁה בְרִיחִם לְקַרְשֵׁי צֶלַע־הַמִּשְׁכָּן הַשֵּׁנִית וַחֲמִשָּׁה בְרִיחִם לְקַרְשֵׁי צֶלַע
כח הַמִּשְׁכָּן לַיַּרְכָתַיִם יָמָּה׃ וְהַבְּרִיחַ הַתִּיכֹן בְּתוֹךְ הַקְּרָשִׁים מַבְרִחַ מִן־הַקָּצֶה
כט אֶל־הַקָּצֶה׃ וְאֶת־הַקְּרָשִׁים תְּצַפֶּה זָהָב וְאֶת־טַבְּעֹתֵיהֶם תַּעֲשֶׂה זָהָב בָּתִּים

---

15. עֲצֵי שִׁטִּים עֹמְדִים — *Acacia wood standing up.* (They should be standing vertically and) not lying (horizontally) one on the other as building planks.

24. אֶל הַטַּבַּעַת הָאֶחָת — *Unto one ring.* To that ring which was in the thickness of the corner board, which was even (parallel) in its placement to the width of the side boards. In that thickness there was one ring above lined up to the rings of the side boards on top, and one ring on the thickness below lined up to the rings of the side boards beneath. The bars entered the rings set in the thickness of the corner board and the side boards above and below, thereby joining together the west wall with the north and south (walls).

29. וְאֶת טַבְּעֹתֵיהֶם — *And their rings.* For all regular bars are inserted into rings

NOTES

hence they were made in sections and coupled together.

24. אֶל הַטַּבַּעַת הָאֶחָת — *Unto one ring.* The *Sforno* explains that the side sections of the *Mishkan,* i.e., the north and south sides, were joined together by inserting the bars into the rings set on the northwest and southwest corner. These were inserted into the incisions made in the thickness of the north and south boards respectively and the top of the board which was in the west row adjacent to it.

29. וְאֶת טַבְּעֹתֵיהֶם — *And their rings.* Although

ל לַבְּרִיחִם וְצִפִּיתָ אֶת־הַבְּרִיחִם זָהָב׃ וַהֲקֵמֹתָ אֶת־הַמִּשְׁכָּן כְּמִשְׁפָּטוֹ אֲשֶׁר
חמישי לא הָרְאֵיתָ בָּהָר׃ וְעָשִׂיתָ פָרֹכֶת תְּכֵלֶת וְאַרְגָּמָן וְתוֹלַעַת שָׁנִי
לב וְשֵׁשׁ מָשְׁזָר מַעֲשֵׂה חֹשֵׁב יַעֲשֶׂה אֹתָהּ כְּרֻבִים׃ וְנָתַתָּה אֹתָהּ עַל־אַרְבָּעָה
לג עַמּוּדֵי שִׁטִּים מְצֻפִּים זָהָב וָוֵיהֶם זָהָב עַל־אַרְבָּעָה אַדְנֵי־כָסֶף׃ וְנָתַתָּה אֶת־
הַפָּרֹכֶת תַּחַת הַקְּרָסִים וְהֵבֵאתָ שָׁמָּה מִבֵּית לַפָּרֹכֶת אֵת אֲרוֹן הָעֵדוּת
לד וְהִבְדִּילָה הַפָּרֹכֶת לָכֶם בֵּין הַקֹּדֶשׁ וּבֵין קֹדֶשׁ הַקֳּדָשִׁים׃ וְנָתַתָּ אֶת־הַכַּפֹּרֶת
לה עַל אֲרוֹן הָעֵדֻת בְּקֹדֶשׁ הַקֳּדָשִׁים׃ וְשַׂמְתָּ אֶת־הַשֻּׁלְחָן מִחוּץ לַפָּרֹכֶת וְאֶת־
הַמְּנֹרָה נֹכַח הַשֻּׁלְחָן עַל צֶלַע הַמִּשְׁכָּן תֵּימָנָה וְהַשֻּׁלְחָן תִּתֵּן עַל־צֶלַע צָפוֹן׃
לו וְעָשִׂיתָ מָסָךְ לְפֶתַח הָאֹהֶל תְּכֵלֶת וְאַרְגָּמָן וְתוֹלַעַת שָׁנִי וְשֵׁשׁ מָשְׁזָר
לז מַעֲשֵׂה רֹקֵם׃ וְעָשִׂיתָ לַמָּסָךְ חֲמִשָּׁה עַמּוּדֵי שִׁטִּים וְצִפִּיתָ אֹתָם זָהָב וָוֵיהֶם
כז ששי א זָהָב וְיָצַקְתָּ לָהֶם חֲמִשָּׁה אַדְנֵי נְחֹשֶׁת׃ וְעָשִׂיתָ אֶת־
הַמִּזְבֵּחַ עֲצֵי שִׁטִּים חָמֵשׁ אַמּוֹת אֹרֶךְ וְחָמֵשׁ אַמּוֹת רֹחַב רָבוּעַ יִהְיֶה הַמִּזְבֵּחַ
ב וְשָׁלֹשׁ אַמּוֹת קֹמָתוֹ׃ וְעָשִׂיתָ קַרְנֹתָיו עַל אַרְבַּע פִּנֹּתָיו מִמֶּנּוּ תִּהְיֶיןָ
ג קַרְנֹתָיו וְצִפִּיתָ אֹתוֹ נְחֹשֶׁת׃ וְעָשִׂיתָ סִּירֹתָיו לְדַשְּׁנוֹ וְיָעָיו וּמִזְרְקֹתָיו
ד וּמִזְלְגֹתָיו וּמַחְתֹּתָיו לְכָל־כֵּלָיו תַּעֲשֶׂה נְחֹשֶׁת׃ וְעָשִׂיתָ לּוֹ מִכְבָּר מַעֲשֵׂה
רֶשֶׁת נְחֹשֶׁת וְעָשִׂיתָ עַל־הָרֶשֶׁת אַרְבַּע טַבְּעֹת נְחֹשֶׁת עַל אַרְבַּע קְצוֹתָיו׃
ה וְנָתַתָּה אֹתָהּ תַּחַת כַּרְכֹּב הַמִּזְבֵּחַ מִלְּמָטָּה וְהָיְתָה הָרֶשֶׁת עַד חֲצִי הַמִּזְבֵּחַ׃

---

unless the opposite is stated, as it is explained regarding the middle bar, as it says, בְּתוֹךְ הַקְּרָשִׁים, *in the midst of the boards* (v. 28), that it should be inserted in the thickness of the boards, not in the rings.

35. וְשַׂמְתָּ אֶת הַשֻּׁלְחָן מִחוּץ לַפָּרֹכֶת — *And you shall set the table outside* (i.e., *in front*) *of the curtain.* After he arranged the seat inside, he arranged the table and menorah in front of it beyond the curtain, (for) they are put there to honor the One Who sits on the chair. The menorah is placed to the right and the table to the left, as it says, אֹרֶךְ יָמִים בִּימִינָהּ בִּשְׂמֹאולָהּ עֹשֶׁר וְכָבוֹד, *Length of days is in her right hand and in her left hand are riches and honor (Proverbs* 3:16).

XXVII

2. קַרְנֹתָיו — *The horns of it* ... (well) known (as part of) every altar, and the same (is true) when he says, *its shovels and its basins* (v. 3).

5. כַּרְכֹּב הַמִּזְבֵּחַ — *The ledge of the altar.* Which is customary for all wooden vessels, as our Sages say, 'The following wooden articles are regarded as unfinished, whatever still requires to be smoothed ... or trimmed wood (כַּרְכֹּב)' (*Chullin* 25a).

NOTES

the Torah did not mention the rings before, but since the bars have already been described, and the ordinary bar is one that is inserted in rings, it is appropriate to use the possessive form *'their' rings.*

35. וְשַׂמְתָּ אֶת הַשֻּׁלְחָן מִחוּץ לַפָּרֹכֶת — *And you shall set the table outside (i.e., in front) of the curtain.* The menorah's light represents Torah, and the table represents riches. Following the idea expressed in the verse quoted from *Proverbs,* he who pursues Torah will merit long life for *it is our life and the length of our days* while he who lives a proper, decent life of *mitzvos* and supports Torah will be granted riches and honor. Hence the menorah is placed on the right and the table on the left, in keeping with the wording of the verse in *Proverbs.*

XXVII

2. קַרְנֹתָיו — *The horns of it.* The verse assumes that one knows what is meant by the *horns, shovels* and *basins* of an altar since they were

ו-ז וְעָשִׂיתָ בַדִּים לַמִּזְבֵּחַ בַּדֵּי עֲצֵי שִׁטִּים וְצִפִּיתָ אֹתָם נְחֹשֶׁת׃ וְהוּבָא אֶת־
ח בַּדָּיו בַּטַּבָּעֹת וְהָיוּ הַבַּדִּים עַל־שְׁתֵּי צַלְעֹת הַמִּזְבֵּחַ בִּשְׂאֵת אֹתוֹ׃ נְבוּב
שביעי ט לֻחֹת תַּעֲשֶׂה אֹתוֹ כַּאֲשֶׁר הֶרְאָה אֹתְךָ בָּהָר כֵּן יַעֲשׂוּ׃ וְעָשִׂיתָ
אֵת חֲצַר הַמִּשְׁכָּן לִפְאַת נֶגֶב־תֵּימָנָה קְלָעִים לֶחָצֵר שֵׁשׁ מָשְׁזָר מֵאָה
י בָאַמָּה אֹרֶךְ לַפֵּאָה הָאֶחָת׃ וְעַמֻּדָיו עֶשְׂרִים וְאַדְנֵיהֶם עֶשְׂרִים נְחֹשֶׁת וָוֵי
יא הָעַמֻּדִים וַחֲשֻׁקֵיהֶם כָּסֶף׃ וְכֵן לִפְאַת צָפוֹן בָּאֹרֶךְ קְלָעִים מֵאָה אֹרֶךְ וְעַמֻּדָו
יב עֶשְׂרִים וְאַדְנֵיהֶם עֶשְׂרִים נְחֹשֶׁת וָוֵי הָעַמֻּדִים וַחֲשֻׁקֵיהֶם כָּסֶף׃ וְרֹחַב הֶחָצֵר
יג לִפְאַת־יָם קְלָעִים חֲמִשִּׁים אַמָּה עַמֻּדֵיהֶם עֲשָׂרָה וְאַדְנֵיהֶם עֲשָׂרָה׃ וְרֹחַב
יד הֶחָצֵר לִפְאַת קֵדְמָה מִזְרָחָה חֲמִשִּׁים אַמָּה׃ וַחֲמֵשׁ עֶשְׂרֵה אַמָּה קְלָעִים
טו לַכָּתֵף עַמֻּדֵיהֶם שְׁלֹשָׁה וְאַדְנֵיהֶם שְׁלֹשָׁה׃ וְלַכָּתֵף הַשֵּׁנִית חֲמֵשׁ עֶשְׂרֵה
טז קְלָעִים עַמֻּדֵיהֶם שְׁלֹשָׁה וְאַדְנֵיהֶם שְׁלֹשָׁה׃ וּלְשַׁעַר הֶחָצֵר מָסָךְ ׀ עֶשְׂרִים
אַמָּה תְּכֵלֶת וְאַרְגָּמָן וְתוֹלַעַת שָׁנִי וְשֵׁשׁ מָשְׁזָר מַעֲשֵׂה רֹקֵם עַמֻּדֵיהֶם
מפטיר יז אַרְבָּעָה וְאַדְנֵיהֶם אַרְבָּעָה׃ כָּל־עַמּוּדֵי הֶחָצֵר סָבִיב מְחֻשָּׁקִים כֶּסֶף וָוֵיהֶם
יח כָּסֶף וְאַדְנֵיהֶם נְחֹשֶׁת׃ אֹרֶךְ הֶחָצֵר מֵאָה בָאַמָּה וְרֹחַב ׀ חֲמִשִּׁים בַּחֲמִשִּׁים
יט וְקֹמָה חָמֵשׁ אַמּוֹת שֵׁשׁ מָשְׁזָר וְאַדְנֵיהֶם נְחֹשֶׁת׃ לְכֹל כְּלֵי הַמִּשְׁכָּן בְּכֹל
עֲבֹדָתוֹ וְכָל־יְתֵדֹתָיו וְכָל־יִתְדֹת הֶחָצֵר נְחֹשֶׁת׃

---

8. נְבוּב לֻחֹת — *Hollow (with) planks...* similar to a box which has no bottom or cover.

כַּאֲשֶׁר הֶרְאָה אֹתְךָ בָּהָר — *As it was shown to you in the mount.* That the hollow space is to be filled with earth when they encamp, and on that earth אֵשׁ תָּמִיד תּוּקַד, *fire shall be kept burning continually (Leviticus 6:6).*

9-10. מֵאָה בָאַמָּה . . . וְעַמֻּדָיו עֶשְׂרִים — *A hundred cubits . . . and its pillars twenty.* The space between them including the pillar was five (cubits). However, the twenty pillars on the north and the twenty pillars on the south did not start one across the other on a straight line. Rather the beginning of one side extended the equivalent of one space from the beginning of the opposite side, and the eastern and western pillars began the equivalent of one space away from the extended corner.

וַחֲשֻׁקֵיהֶם — *And their fillets.* Circles which encircled the pillar in its middle for beauty.

19. לְכֹל כְּלֵי הַמִּשְׁכָּן בְּכֹל עֲבֹדָתוֹ — *All the instruments of the Mishkan in all its service.* The tools needed for its service, such as hammers and mallets and other (such tools) which were needed when it was dismantled and erected.

NOTES

commonly used by others in their religious services.

9-10. מֵאָה בָאַמָּה . . . וְעַמֻּדָיו עֶשְׂרִים — *A hundred cubits ... and its pillars twenty.* The *Sforno* interprets the plan of the Tabernacle courtyard as follows: The last pillar on the west side, in the southwest corner, also served as the first support of the curtains on the south side and the first pillar on the south side was distanced five cubits from that corner. The last pillar at the southeast corner also served the curtains on the east side, therefore the first of the three pillars on the east side was drawn in five cubits from that corner. The pillar in the northeast corner served the north-side curtains as well so that the first of the twenty pillars on the north began five cubits in from the northeast corner, finishing at the northwest corner, where the first pillar of the west side began five cubits southward from that corner.

19. לְכֹל כְּלֵי הַמִּשְׁכָּן בְּכֹל עֲבֹדָתוֹ — *All the instruments of the Mishkan in all its service.* The expression *all the instruments* implies instruments which were not mentioned above. Hence it must refer to tools needed to erect and dismantle the *Mishkan* in their travels.

פרשת תצוה

Parashas Tetzaveh

כ וְאַתָּה תְּצַוֶּה ׀ אֶת־בְּנֵי יִשְׂרָאֵל וְיִקְחוּ אֵלֶיךָ שֶׁמֶן זַיִת זָךְ כָּתִית לַמָּאוֹר
כא לְהַעֲלֹת נֵר תָּמִיד: בְּאֹהֶל מוֹעֵד מִחוּץ לַפָּרֹכֶת אֲשֶׁר עַל־הָעֵדֻת יַעֲרֹךְ
אֹתוֹ אַהֲרֹן וּבָנָיו מֵעֶרֶב עַד־בֹּקֶר לִפְנֵי יהוה חֻקַּת עוֹלָם לְדֹרֹתָם מֵאֵת בְּנֵי
כח א יִשְׂרָאֵל: וְאַתָּה הַקְרֵב אֵלֶיךָ אֶת־אַהֲרֹן אָחִיךָ וְאֶת־בָּנָיו
אִתּוֹ מִתּוֹךְ בְּנֵי יִשְׂרָאֵל לְכַהֲנוֹ־לִי אַהֲרֹן נָדָב וַאֲבִיהוּא אֶלְעָזָר וְאִיתָמָר
ב־ג בְּנֵי אַהֲרֹן: וְעָשִׂיתָ בִגְדֵי־קֹדֶשׁ לְאַהֲרֹן אָחִיךָ לְכָבוֹד וּלְתִפְאָרֶת: וְאַתָּה
תְּדַבֵּר אֶל־כָּל־חַכְמֵי־לֵב אֲשֶׁר מִלֵּאתִיו רוּחַ חָכְמָה וְעָשׂוּ אֶת־בִּגְדֵי אַהֲרֹן

---

20. וְאַתָּה תְּצַוֶּה — *And you shall command.* Behold that until now when it states וְעָשִׂיתָ, *and you shall do,* it is to be understood that it should be done through others, i.e., that he (Moses) should command the artisans to do (certain tasks). Therefore regarding these three commandments which God commanded, He said, 'וְאַתָּה, *and you,*' to tell him (Moses) that he should do it himself. He shall command Israel regarding the making of the oil; he shall bring near to himself (appoint) Aaron and his sons; and he shall speak to all the wise-hearted (workers).

וְיִקְחוּ אֵלֶיךָ — *That they bring to you . . .* when needed; namely when the oil for the light contributed now to the Sanctuary will be consumed. They are not to think that the commandment to kindle the lamp is only a temporary one involving only this oil (now) offered.

XXVIII

2. לְכָבוֹד — *For honor . . .* for the honor of God, the Blessed One, since they are holy garments for His service.

וּלְתִפְאָרֶת — *And for beauty (glory).* That he be a 'teaching priest' (based on *II Chronicles* 15:3) held in reverence by all them round about him *(Psalms* 89:8), (for) they are his disciples, engraved on his heart and shoulders.

3. וְאַתָּה תְּדַבֵּר אֶל כָּל חַכְמֵי לֵב — *And you shall speak to all that are wise hearted . . .* that they do all that is mentioned above (i.e., the various labors of the Sanctuary).

וְעָשׂוּ אֶת בִּגְדֵי אַהֲרֹן — *That they make Aaron's garments.* And they shall also make Aaron's garments.

NOTES

20. וְאַתָּה תְּצַוֶּה — *And you shall command.* The word וְאַתָּה, *and you,* precedes the command regarding the oil in this verse, as well as the one regarding Aaron (28:1), and that of the wise-hearted workers (28:3). This implies that Moses himself was to attend to these three matters.

XXVIII

2. לְכָבוֹד וּלְתִפְאָרֶת — *For honor and for beauty (glory).* The garments of the priest serve a twofold purpose. Primarily they are for the honor of God, not for the honor of the priest. However, they are also meant to lend dignity to the office of the High Priest so that the people, who are all meant to be his pupils, will revere and respect him. In a subtle manner the *Sforno* indicates that reverence for a teacher is motivated not only by the inherent respect students have for their teacher but also by the concern the teacher shows for them. This is symbolized by the names of the tribes which the High Priest carries engraved on his heart (the breastplate, see verse 21) and his shoulders (the onyx stones, see verse 12).

3-5. וְאַתָּה תְּדַבֵּר אֶל כָּל חַכְמֵי לֵב . . . וְעָשׂוּ אֶת בִּגְדֵי אַהֲרֹן לְקַדְּשׁוֹ . . . וְהֵם יִקְחוּ אֶת הַזָּהָב — *And you shall speak to all that are wise hearted . . . that they make Aaron's garments to sanctify him . . . And they shall take the gold.* When one fulfills a sacred task his intent is most impor-

ד לְקַדְּשׁוֹ לְכַהֲנוֹ־לִי: וְאֵלֶּה הַבְּגָדִים אֲשֶׁר יַעֲשׂוּ חֹשֶׁן וְאֵפוֹד וּמְעִיל וּכְתֹנֶת
תַּשְׁבֵּץ מִצְנֶפֶת וְאַבְנֵט וְעָשׂוּ בִגְדֵי־קֹדֶשׁ לְאַהֲרֹן אָחִיךָ וּלְבָנָיו לְכַהֲנוֹ־לִי:
ה וְהֵם יִקְחוּ אֶת־הַזָּהָב וְאֶת־הַתְּכֵלֶת וְאֶת־הָאַרְגָּמָן וְאֶת־תּוֹלַעַת הַשָּׁנִי
וְאֶת־הַשֵּׁשׁ:
ו וְעָשׂוּ אֶת־הָאֵפֹד זָהָב תְּכֵלֶת וְאַרְגָּמָן תּוֹלַעַת שָׁנִי וְשֵׁשׁ מָשְׁזָר מַעֲשֵׂה
ז־ח חֹשֵׁב: שְׁתֵּי כְתֵפֹת חֹבְרֹת יִהְיֶה־לּוֹ אֶל־שְׁנֵי קְצוֹתָיו וְחֻבָּר: וְחֵשֶׁב אֲפֻדָּתוֹ
אֲשֶׁר עָלָיו כְּמַעֲשֵׂהוּ מִמֶּנּוּ יִהְיֶה זָהָב תְּכֵלֶת וְאַרְגָּמָן וְתוֹלַעַת שָׁנִי וְשֵׁשׁ
ט מָשְׁזָר: וְלָקַחְתָּ אֶת־שְׁתֵּי אַבְנֵי־שֹׁהַם וּפִתַּחְתָּ עֲלֵיהֶם שְׁמוֹת בְּנֵי יִשְׂרָאֵל:
י שִׁשָּׁה מִשְּׁמֹתָם עַל הָאֶבֶן הָאֶחָת וְאֶת־שְׁמוֹת הַשִּׁשָּׁה הַנּוֹתָרִים עַל־הָאֶבֶן
יא הַשֵּׁנִית כְּתוֹלְדֹתָם: מַעֲשֵׂה חָרַשׁ אֶבֶן פִּתּוּחֵי חֹתָם תְּפַתַּח אֶת־שְׁתֵּי
יב הָאֲבָנִים עַל־שְׁמֹת בְּנֵי יִשְׂרָאֵל מֻסַבֹּת מִשְׁבְּצוֹת זָהָב תַּעֲשֶׂה אֹתָם: וְשַׂמְתָּ
אֶת־שְׁתֵּי הָאֲבָנִים עַל כִּתְפֹת הָאֵפֹד אַבְנֵי זִכָּרֹן לִבְנֵי יִשְׂרָאֵל וְנָשָׂא
שני יג אַהֲרֹן אֶת־שְׁמוֹתָם לִפְנֵי יהוה עַל־שְׁתֵּי כְתֵפָיו לְזִכָּרֹן: וְעָשִׂיתָ

לְקַדְּשׁוֹ — *To sanctify him.* Toward that purpose shall they make the garments.

5. וְהֵם יִקְחוּ אֶת הַזָּהָב — *And they shall take the gold.* Just as they have (proper) intent at the time of their labor so they should have (proper) intent when they take the gold.

6. הָאֵפֹד — *Ephod* ... a garment (covering) from a person's hips and down. The upper border (was) made like a belt of skillful work, and with it the wearer of the *ephod* girds the robe, as it says, וַיַּחְגֹּר אֹתוֹ בְּחֵשֶׁב הָאֵפֹד, וַיֶּאְפֹּד לוֹ בּוֹ, *and he girded him with the skillfully woven band of the ephod, and bound it to him with it (Leviticus* 8:7).

7. שְׁתֵּי כְתֵפֹת חֹבְרֹת — *Two shoulder pieces joined* ... matched in the work of their images (pictures or designs).

אֶל שְׁנֵי קְצוֹתָיו — *To the two ends* ... to the two extremities of its width.

וְחֻבָּר — *That it may be joined together.* The *ephod* shall be joined with the shoulder pieces in a manner that it be matched in its work with that of the shoulder pieces (straps).

12. עַל שְׁתֵּי כְתֵפָיו לְזִכָּרֹן — *Upon his two shoulders for a memorial* ... to attain mercy for Israel in their merit.

NOTES

tant. Therefore when the craftsmen receive the gold from the contributors it must be with the express intent of using it for the priestly vestments, and when they make the garments they must have in mind at all times that with these garments the priest will be consecrated to the service of God. Compare the *Sforno's* commentary on verse 21 regarding the stones.

7. שְׁתֵּי כְתֵפֹת חֹבְרֹת ... וְחֻבָּר — *Two shoulder pieces joined ... that it may be joined together.* The *Sforno* interprets the words חֹבְרֹת and וְחֻבָּר as *joined* in the sense of *matched.* Compare to the *Sforno* in 26:3 regarding the curtains of the Sanctuary where the same phrase is used by the Torah.

12. עַל שְׁתֵּי כְתֵפָיו לְזִכָּרֹן — *Upon his two shoulders for a memorial.* The Almighty need not be reminded of aught; *'There is no forgetfulness before Your throne of glory'* (from *Mussaf* of Rosh Hashanah). The phrase לְזִכָּרֹן, *for a memorial,* therefore cannot mean as a memorial to God, but to awaken His

יד מִשְׁבְּצֹת זָהָב׃ וּשְׁתֵּי שַׁרְשְׁרֹת זָהָב טָהוֹר מִגְבָּלֹת תַּעֲשֶׂה אֹתָם מַעֲשֵׂה
טו עֲבֹת וְנָתַתָּה אֶת־שַׁרְשְׁרֹת הָעֲבֹתֹת עַל־הַמִּשְׁבְּצֹת׃ וְעָשִׂיתָ
חֹשֶׁן מִשְׁפָּט מַעֲשֵׂה חֹשֵׁב כְּמַעֲשֵׂה אֵפֹד תַּעֲשֶׂנּוּ זָהָב תְּכֵלֶת וְאַרְגָּמָן
טז וְתוֹלַעַת שָׁנִי וְשֵׁשׁ מָשְׁזָר תַּעֲשֶׂה אֹתוֹ׃ רָבוּעַ יִהְיֶה כָּפוּל זֶרֶת אָרְכּוֹ וְזֶרֶת
יז רָחְבּוֹ׃ וּמִלֵּאתָ בוֹ מִלֻּאַת אֶבֶן אַרְבָּעָה טוּרִים אָבֶן טוּר אֹדֶם פִּטְדָה
יח־יט וּבָרֶקֶת הַטּוּר הָאֶחָד׃ וְהַטּוּר הַשֵּׁנִי נֹפֶךְ סַפִּיר וְיַהֲלֹם׃ וְהַטּוּר הַשְּׁלִישִׁי לֶשֶׁם
כ שְׁבוֹ וְאַחְלָמָה׃ וְהַטּוּר הָרְבִיעִי תַּרְשִׁישׁ וְשֹׁהַם וְיָשְׁפֵה מְשֻׁבָּצִים זָהָב יִהְיוּ
כא בְּמִלּוּאֹתָם׃ וְהָאֲבָנִים תִּהְיֶיןָ עַל־שְׁמֹת בְּנֵי־יִשְׂרָאֵל שְׁתֵּים עֶשְׂרֵה עַל־
כב שְׁמֹתָם פִּתּוּחֵי חוֹתָם אִישׁ עַל־שְׁמוֹ תִּהְיֶיןָ לִשְׁנֵי עָשָׂר שָׁבֶט׃ וְעָשִׂיתָ עַל־
כג הַחֹשֶׁן שַׁרְשֹׁת גַּבְלֻת מַעֲשֵׂה עֲבֹת זָהָב טָהוֹר׃ וְעָשִׂיתָ עַל־הַחֹשֶׁן שְׁתֵּי
כד טַבְּעוֹת זָהָב וְנָתַתָּ אֶת־שְׁתֵּי הַטַּבָּעוֹת עַל־שְׁנֵי קְצוֹת הַחֹשֶׁן׃ וְנָתַתָּה
כה אֶת־שְׁתֵּי עֲבֹתֹת הַזָּהָב עַל־שְׁתֵּי הַטַּבָּעֹת אֶל־קְצוֹת הַחֹשֶׁן׃ וְאֵת שְׁתֵּי
קְצוֹת שְׁתֵּי הָעֲבֹתֹת תִּתֵּן עַל־שְׁתֵּי הַמִּשְׁבְּצוֹת וְנָתַתָּה עַל־כִּתְפוֹת הָאֵפֹד
כו אֶל־מוּל פָּנָיו׃ וְעָשִׂיתָ שְׁתֵּי טַבְּעוֹת זָהָב וְשַׂמְתָּ אֹתָם עַל־שְׁנֵי קְצוֹת הַחֹשֶׁן
כז עַל־שְׂפָתוֹ אֲשֶׁר אֶל־עֵבֶר הָאֵפוֹד בָּיְתָה׃ וְעָשִׂיתָ שְׁתֵּי טַבְּעוֹת זָהָב וְנָתַתָּה
אֹתָם עַל־שְׁתֵּי כִתְפוֹת הָאֵפוֹד מִלְּמַטָּה מִמּוּל פָּנָיו לְעֻמַּת מַחְבַּרְתּוֹ

---

14. מִגְבָּלֹת — *Of plaited thread* . . . matched (lined up) exactly from the end of the shoulder pieces to the end of the breastplate.

21. וְהָאֲבָנִים תִּהְיֶיןָ עַל שְׁמֹת בְּנֵי יִשְׂרָאֵל — *And the stones shall be according to the names of the sons of Israel.* When the donors sanctify them let their sanctification be specifically for the purpose of writing the names of the tribes upon them.

שְׁתֵּים עֶשְׂרֵה עַל שְׁמֹתָם — *Twelve, according to their names.* And they shall be twelve in keeping with their names, neither less nor more.

פִּתּוּחֵי חוֹתָם אִישׁ עַל שְׁמוֹ — *Like the engravings of a signet, every one according to his name.* Also the engraver shall engrave the name on the stone of each one and neither change the stone nor the (original) intent from this to that.

22. גַּבְלֻת — *Plaited (chains).* Not chains which can be made longer or shorter.

27. מִמּוּל פָּנָיו — *In the forepart thereof* . . . (underneath) but not (actually) in the forepart.

NOTES

compassion in merit of the names of Israel inscribed on the onyx stones carried on the High Priest's shoulders. Compare the *Sforno's* commentary on *Genesis* 9:16.

21. שְׁתֵּים עֶשְׂרֵה עַל שְׁמֹתָם — *Twelve, according to their names.* The *Sforno* explains why God had to state specifically, '*twelve, according to their names,*' since it already states *the names of the sons of Israel.* The verse stresses the number twelve to emphasize that although Menasseh and Ephraim had been designated by Jacob as being *his* akin to Reuben and Simeon, this was only regarding the dividing of the Land of Israel, where Levi receives no portion. As for all other areas, including the engraving of the name on the breastplate, only the original twelve sons of Jacob shall appear. Hence the *Sforno* states, 'neither less nor more.' See the commentary of the *Sforno* on *Genesis* 49:28.

פִּתּוּחֵי חוֹתָם אִישׁ עַל שְׁמוֹ — *Like the engravings of a signet, every one according to his name.*

כח מִמַּעַל לְחֵשֶׁב הָאֵפוֹד׃ וְיִרְכְּסוּ אֶת־הַחֹשֶׁן מִטַּבְּעֹתָו אֶל־טַבְּעֹת הָאֵפוֹד
בִּפְתִיל תְּכֵלֶת לִהְיוֹת עַל־חֵשֶׁב הָאֵפוֹד וְלֹא־יִזַּח הַחֹשֶׁן מֵעַל הָאֵפוֹד׃
כט וְנָשָׂא אַהֲרֹן אֶת־שְׁמוֹת בְּנֵי־יִשְׂרָאֵל בְּחֹשֶׁן הַמִּשְׁפָּט עַל־לִבּוֹ בְּבֹאוֹ אֶל־
ל הַקֹּדֶשׁ לְזִכָּרֹן לִפְנֵי־יְהוָה תָּמִיד׃ וְנָתַתָּ אֶל־חֹשֶׁן הַמִּשְׁפָּט אֶת־הָאוּרִים
וְאֶת־הַתֻּמִּים וְהָיוּ עַל־לֵב אַהֲרֹן בְּבֹאוֹ לִפְנֵי יְהוָה וְנָשָׂא אַהֲרֹן אֶת־מִשְׁפַּט
שלישי לא בְּנֵי־יִשְׂרָאֵל עַל־לִבּוֹ לִפְנֵי יְהוָה תָּמִיד׃ וְעָשִׂיתָ אֶת־
לב מְעִיל הָאֵפוֹד כְּלִיל תְּכֵלֶת׃ וְהָיָה פִי־רֹאשׁוֹ בְּתוֹכוֹ שָׂפָה יִהְיֶה לְפִיו סָבִיב
לג מַעֲשֵׂה אֹרֵג כְּפִי תַחְרָא יִהְיֶה־לּוֹ לֹא יִקָּרֵעַ׃ וְעָשִׂיתָ עַל־שׁוּלָיו רִמֹּנֵי תְּכֵלֶת
וְאַרְגָּמָן וְתוֹלַעַת שָׁנִי עַל־שׁוּלָיו סָבִיב וּפַעֲמֹנֵי זָהָב בְּתוֹכָם סָבִיב׃
לד-לה פַּעֲמֹן זָהָב וְרִמּוֹן פַּעֲמֹן זָהָב וְרִמּוֹן עַל־שׁוּלֵי הַמְּעִיל סָבִיב׃ וְהָיָה עַל־
אַהֲרֹן לְשָׁרֵת וְנִשְׁמַע קוֹלוֹ בְּבֹאוֹ אֶל־הַקֹּדֶשׁ לִפְנֵי יְהוָה וּבְצֵאתוֹ וְלֹא
לו יָמוּת׃ וְעָשִׂיתָ צִּיץ זָהָב טָהוֹר וּפִתַּחְתָּ עָלָיו
לז פִּתּוּחֵי חֹתָם קֹדֶשׁ לַיהוָה׃ וְשַׂמְתָּ אֹתוֹ עַל־פְּתִיל תְּכֵלֶת וְהָיָה עַל־
לח הַמִּצְנָפֶת אֶל־מוּל פְּנֵי־הַמִּצְנֶפֶת יִהְיֶה׃ וְהָיָה עַל־מֵצַח אַהֲרֹן וְנָשָׂא אַהֲרֹן
אֶת־עֲוֺן הַקֳּדָשִׁים אֲשֶׁר יַקְדִּישׁוּ בְּנֵי יִשְׂרָאֵל לְכָל־מַתְּנֹת קָדְשֵׁיהֶם וְהָיָה
לט עַל־מִצְחוֹ תָּמִיד לְרָצוֹן לָהֶם לִפְנֵי יְהוָה׃ וְשִׁבַּצְתָּ הַכְּתֹנֶת שֵׁשׁ וְעָשִׂיתָ
מ מִצְנֶפֶת שֵׁשׁ וְאַבְנֵט תַּעֲשֶׂה מַעֲשֵׂה רֹקֵם׃ וְלִבְנֵי אַהֲרֹן תַּעֲשֶׂה כֻתֳּנֹת
מא וְעָשִׂיתָ לָהֶם אַבְנֵטִים וּמִגְבָּעוֹת תַּעֲשֶׂה לָהֶם לְכָבוֹד וּלְתִפְאָרֶת׃ וְהִלְבַּשְׁתָּ

לְעֻמַּת מַחְבַּרְתּוֹ — *Close by the coupling.* Across the coupling, in a straight line opposite the place where the shoulder pieces join the *ephod.*

29. לְזִכָּרֹן לִפְנֵי ה׳ תָּמִיד — *For a memorial before* HASHEM *continually.* That God may remember their merits and be mindful of their children that (there be) peace in their merit.

30. מִשְׁפַּט בְּנֵי יִשְׂרָאֵל עַל לִבּוֹ — *The judgment of the Children of Israel on his heart* . . . that he may pray for them that they be found meritorious in judgment.

32. לֹא יִקָּרֵעַ — *That it be not split.* The neck opening shall not open lengthwise in the front but shall be round. The phrase יִקָּרֵעַ is used to (indicate) something which is open lengthwise, similar to, וְקָרַע לוֹ חַלּוֹנָי, *and he cuts him out windows* (*Jeremiah* 22:14), for the windows were constructed long and narrow.

NOTES

Since each stone was designated for a specific tribe and the donor sanctified it for that tribe they could not be interchanged. This is the meaning of the concluding part of this verse, *every one according to his name.*

29. לְזִכָּרֹן — *For a memorial.* See the note on verse 12.

30. מִשְׁפַּט בְּנֵי יִשְׂרָאֵל עַל לִבּוֹ — *The judgment of the Children of Israel on his heart.* The *Sforno* is referring to the judgment of Heaven. The High Priest prays that his people be vindicated when judged from on High.

32. לֹא יִקָּרֵעַ — *That it be not split.* According to the *Sforno's* interpretation the word יִקָּרֵעַ is not used in its usual sense of *torn.* Rather the Torah is describing the design of the neck opening, that it be round, and not an opening which is cut lengthwise. He supports this interpretation from a similar expression in *Jeremiah* where the meaning is clearly an opening that was *long,* not *torn.*

אֹתָם אֶת־אַהֲרֹן אָחִיךָ וְאֶת־בָּנָיו אִתּוֹ וּמָשַׁחְתָּ אֹתָם וּמִלֵּאתָ אֶת־יָדָם

מב וְקִדַּשְׁתָּ אֹתָם וְכִהֲנוּ לִי: וַעֲשֵׂה לָהֶם מִכְנְסֵי־בָד לְכַסּוֹת בְּשַׂר עֶרְוָה

מג מִמָּתְנַיִם וְעַד־יְרֵכַיִם יִהְיוּ: וְהָיוּ עַל־אַהֲרֹן וְעַל־בָּנָיו בְּבֹאָם ׀ אֶל־אֹהֶל

מוֹעֵד אוֹ בְגִשְׁתָּם אֶל־הַמִּזְבֵּחַ לְשָׁרֵת בַּקֹּדֶשׁ וְלֹא־יִשְׂאוּ עָוֹן וָמֵתוּ חֻקַּת

כט רביעי א עוֹלָם לוֹ וּלְזַרְעוֹ אַחֲרָיו: וְזֶה הַדָּבָר אֲשֶׁר־תַּעֲשֶׂה לָהֶם

ב לְקַדֵּשׁ אֹתָם לְכַהֵן לִי לְקַח פַּר אֶחָד בֶּן־בָּקָר וְאֵילִם שְׁנַיִם תְּמִימִם: וְלֶחֶם

מַצּוֹת וְחַלֹּת מַצֹּת בְּלוּלֹת בַּשֶּׁמֶן וּרְקִיקֵי מַצּוֹת מְשֻׁחִים בַּשָּׁמֶן סֹלֶת חִטִּים

ג תַּעֲשֶׂה אֹתָם: וְנָתַתָּ אוֹתָם עַל־סַל אֶחָד וְהִקְרַבְתָּ אֹתָם בַּסָּל וְאֶת־הַפָּר

ד וְאֵת שְׁנֵי הָאֵילִם: וְאֶת־אַהֲרֹן וְאֶת־בָּנָיו תַּקְרִיב אֶל־פֶּתַח אֹהֶל מוֹעֵד

ה וְרָחַצְתָּ אֹתָם בַּמָּיִם: וְלָקַחְתָּ אֶת־הַבְּגָדִים וְהִלְבַּשְׁתָּ אֶת־אַהֲרֹן אֶת־

הַכֻּתֹּנֶת וְאֵת מְעִיל הָאֵפֹד וְאֶת־הָאֵפֹד וְאֶת־הַחֹשֶׁן וְאָפַדְתָּ לוֹ בְּחֵשֶׁב

ו הָאֵפֹד: וְשַׂמְתָּ הַמִּצְנֶפֶת עַל־רֹאשׁוֹ וְנָתַתָּ אֶת־נֵזֶר הַקֹּדֶשׁ עַל־הַמִּצְנָפֶת:

ז־ח וְלָקַחְתָּ אֶת־שֶׁמֶן הַמִּשְׁחָה וְיָצַקְתָּ עַל־רֹאשׁוֹ וּמָשַׁחְתָּ אֹתוֹ: וְאֶת־בָּנָיו

ט תַּקְרִיב וְהִלְבַּשְׁתָּם כֻּתֳּנֹת: וְחָגַרְתָּ אֹתָם אַבְנֵט אַהֲרֹן וּבָנָיו וְחָבַשְׁתָּ לָהֶם

מִגְבָּעֹת וְהָיְתָה לָהֶם כְּהֻנָּה לְחֻקַּת עוֹלָם וּמִלֵּאתָ יַד־אַהֲרֹן וְיַד־בָּנָיו:

י וְהִקְרַבְתָּ אֶת־הַפָּר לִפְנֵי אֹהֶל מוֹעֵד וְסָמַךְ אַהֲרֹן וּבָנָיו אֶת־יְדֵיהֶם עַל־

יא־יב רֹאשׁ הַפָּר: וְשָׁחַטְתָּ אֶת־הַפָּר לִפְנֵי יהוה פֶּתַח אֹהֶל מוֹעֵד: וְלָקַחְתָּ מִדַּם

הַפָּר וְנָתַתָּה עַל־קַרְנֹת הַמִּזְבֵּחַ בְּאֶצְבָּעֶךָ וְאֶת־כָּל־הַדָּם תִּשְׁפֹּךְ אֶל־יְסוֹד

יג הַמִּזְבֵּחַ: וְלָקַחְתָּ אֶת־כָּל־הַחֵלֶב הַמְכַסֶּה אֶת־הַקֶּרֶב וְאֵת הַיֹּתֶרֶת עַל־

הַכָּבֵד וְאֵת שְׁתֵּי הַכְּלָיֹת וְאֶת־הַחֵלֶב אֲשֶׁר עֲלֵיהֶן וְהִקְטַרְתָּ הַמִּזְבֵּחָה:

יד וְאֶת־בְּשַׂר הַפָּר וְאֶת־עֹרוֹ וְאֶת־פִּרְשׁוֹ תִּשְׂרֹף בָּאֵשׁ מִחוּץ לַמַּחֲנֶה חַטָּאת

טו הוּא: וְאֶת־הָאַיִל הָאֶחָד תִּקָּח וְסָמְכוּ אַהֲרֹן וּבָנָיו אֶת־יְדֵיהֶם עַל־רֹאשׁ

טז הָאָיִל: וְשָׁחַטְתָּ אֶת־הָאָיִל וְלָקַחְתָּ אֶת־דָּמוֹ וְזָרַקְתָּ עַל־הַמִּזְבֵּחַ סָבִיב:

יז וְאֶת־הָאַיִל תְּנַתֵּחַ לִנְתָחָיו וְרָחַצְתָּ קִרְבּוֹ וּכְרָעָיו וְנָתַתָּ עַל־נְתָחָיו וְעַל־

יח רֹאשׁוֹ: וְהִקְטַרְתָּ אֶת־כָּל־הָאַיִל הַמִּזְבֵּחָה עֹלָה הוּא לַיהוה רֵיחַ נִיחוֹחַ

חמישי יט אִשֶּׁה לַיהוה הוּא: וְלָקַחְתָּ אֵת הָאַיִל הַשֵּׁנִי וְסָמַךְ אַהֲרֹן וּבָנָיו אֶת־יְדֵיהֶם

כ עַל־רֹאשׁ הָאָיִל: וְשָׁחַטְתָּ אֶת־הָאַיִל וְלָקַחְתָּ מִדָּמוֹ וְנָתַתָּה עַל־תְּנוּךְ אֹזֶן

אַהֲרֹן וְעַל־תְּנוּךְ אֹזֶן בָּנָיו הַיְמָנִית וְעַל־בֹּהֶן יָדָם הַיְמָנִית וְעַל־בֹּהֶן רַגְלָם

כא הַיְמָנִית וְזָרַקְתָּ אֶת־הַדָּם עַל־הַמִּזְבֵּחַ סָבִיב: וְלָקַחְתָּ מִן־הַדָּם אֲשֶׁר עַל־

הַמִּזְבֵּחַ וּמִשֶּׁמֶן הַמִּשְׁחָה וְהִזֵּיתָ עַל־אַהֲרֹן וְעַל־בְּגָדָיו וְעַל־בָּנָיו וְעַל־בִּגְדֵי

כב בָנָיו אִתּוֹ וְקָדַשׁ הוּא וּבְגָדָיו וּבָנָיו וּבִגְדֵי בָנָיו אִתּוֹ: וְלָקַחְתָּ מִן־הָאַיִל

הַחֵלֶב וְהָאַלְיָה וְאֶת־הַחֵלֶב ׀ הַמְכַסֶּה אֶת־הַקֶּרֶב וְאֵת יֹתֶרֶת הַכָּבֵד וְאֵת

׀ שְׁתֵּי הַכְּלָיֹת וְאֶת־הַחֵלֶב אֲשֶׁר עֲלֵיהֶן וְאֵת שׁוֹק הַיָּמִין כִּי אֵיל מִלֻּאִים

---

41. וּמִלֵּאתָ אֶת יָדָם — *And fill their hands.* Perfect (complete) them in a way that they be complete and worthy to serve (in the) sacred service.

XXIX

22. כִּי אֵיל מִלֻּאִים הוּא — *For it is a ram of consecration.* Therefore the right shoulder of this (sacrifice) was given onto the altar, which was not (the case) with other

כג הוּא: וְכִכַּר לֶחֶם אַחַת וַחַלַּת לֶחֶם שֶׁמֶן אַחַת וְרָקִיק אֶחָד מִסַּל הַמַּצּוֹת
כד אֲשֶׁר לִפְנֵי יהוה: וְשַׂמְתָּ הַכֹּל עַל כַּפֵּי אַהֲרֹן וְעַל כַּפֵּי בָנָיו וְהֵנַפְתָּ אֹתָם
כה תְּנוּפָה לִפְנֵי יהוה: וְלָקַחְתָּ אֹתָם מִיָּדָם וְהִקְטַרְתָּ הַמִּזְבֵּחָה עַל־הָעֹלָה לְרֵיחַ
כו נִיחוֹחַ לִפְנֵי יהוה אִשֶּׁה הוּא לַיהוה: וְלָקַחְתָּ אֶת־הֶחָזֶה מֵאֵיל הַמִּלֻּאִים
כז אֲשֶׁר לְאַהֲרֹן וְהֵנַפְתָּ אֹתוֹ תְּנוּפָה לִפְנֵי יהוה וְהָיָה לְךָ לְמָנָה: וְקִדַּשְׁתָּ אֵת
| חֲזֵה הַתְּנוּפָה וְאֵת שׁוֹק הַתְּרוּמָה אֲשֶׁר הוּנַף וַאֲשֶׁר הוּרָם מֵאֵיל הַמִּלֻּאִים
כח מֵאֲשֶׁר לְאַהֲרֹן וּמֵאֲשֶׁר לְבָנָיו: וְהָיָה לְאַהֲרֹן וּלְבָנָיו לְחָק־עוֹלָם מֵאֵת בְּנֵי
יִשְׂרָאֵל כִּי תְרוּמָה הוּא וּתְרוּמָה יִהְיֶה מֵאֵת בְּנֵי־יִשְׂרָאֵל מִזִּבְחֵי שַׁלְמֵיהֶם
כט תְּרוּמָתָם לַיהוה: וּבִגְדֵי הַקֹּדֶשׁ אֲשֶׁר לְאַהֲרֹן יִהְיוּ לְבָנָיו אַחֲרָיו לְמָשְׁחָה
ל בָהֶם וּלְמַלֵּא־בָם אֶת־יָדָם: שִׁבְעַת יָמִים יִלְבָּשָׁם הַכֹּהֵן תַּחְתָּיו מִבָּנָיו אֲשֶׁר

---

sacrifices, because the right shoulder of an animal corresponds to the right hand of a person, and therefore it was proper that the shoulder of the sacrifice on the altar be symbolic of a hand, to consecrate the right hand of the priest who offered it, for indeed the service of the priest was (exclusively) with the right hand as our Sages say, "Wherever 'finger' and 'priesthood' is said (in the Torah) it means only the right one" (*Menachos* 10a).

24. וְהֵנַפְתָּ אֹתָם — *And you shall wave them.* Behold the תְּנוּפָה (whatever is waved) applies to the priest's portion to indicate that they receive (lit., 'merit') it from the שֻׁלְחָן גָּבֹהַּ, *table of the Exalted One.* Now here (in our case) the portion which was elevated onto the altar was also waved, because it (included) the right shoulder which was fitting for the priest (i.e., belonged to him by right) for it came up onto the altar to consecrate him (lit., 'to fill his hand').

29. וּלְמַלֵּא בָם אֶת יָדָם — *And to be consecrated (lit., to fill their hand) in them.* But his children (successors) will not have to bring the sacrifices of consecration written here (in this chapter).

NOTES

XXIX

22. כִּי אֵיל מִלֻּאִים הוּא — *For it is a ram of consecration. Rashi* in his commentary on this verse states, 'We do not find that burning is prescribed for the right shoulder ... except in this case alone.' He also interprets the word מִלֻּאִים, *consecration,* as having the literal meaning of *full,* synonymous with שְׁלָמִים, *peace offering* and שְׁלֵמוּת, *completeness.* The *Sforno* extends this interpretation to explain why the right shoulder was brought onto the altar in this instance. It was done to symbolize the consecration of the priest's right hand which he uses exclusively during his service at the altar and the Temple service. The *Sforno's* interpretation also clarifies the use of the word כִּי, *because.* The Torah is explaining why this offering requires the burning of the right shoulder. It is *because* this ram is brought to complete the consecration of the priest who serves with his right hand.

24. וְהֵנַפְתָּ אֹתָם — *And you shall wave them.* The ritual of 'waving' a sacred object horizontally and vertically is usually interpreted as indicating that the four corners of the earth, the heaven above and the earth below all belong to God. The *Sforno,* however, explains that when the portion of a sacrifice which was given to a priest was waved, it came to teach that he was given it not as his due but from God's table, granted to him by God. Since this right shoulder belonged to the priest it had to be waved.

29. וּלְמַלֵּא בָם אֶת יָדָם — *And to be consecrated in them.* Only Aaron had to be invested into the office of the High Priesthood through the medium of these sacrifices and the placing of the blood on his ear lobe, thumb and large toe.

לא יָבֹא אֶל־אֹהֶל מוֹעֵד לְשָׁרֵת בַּקֹּדֶשׁ: וְאֵת אֵיל הַמִּלֻּאִים תִּקָּח וּבִשַּׁלְתָּ
לב אֶת־בְּשָׂרוֹ בְּמָקֹם קָדֹשׁ: וְאָכַל אַהֲרֹן וּבָנָיו אֶת־בְּשַׂר הָאַיִל וְאֶת־הַלֶּחֶם
לג אֲשֶׁר בַּסָּל פֶּתַח אֹהֶל מוֹעֵד: וְאָכְלוּ אֹתָם אֲשֶׁר כֻּפַּר בָּהֶם לְמַלֵּא אֶת־
לד יָדָם לְקַדֵּשׁ אֹתָם וְזָר לֹא־יֹאכַל כִּי־קֹדֶשׁ הֵם: וְאִם־יִוָּתֵר מִבְּשַׂר הַמִּלֻּאִים
וּמִן־הַלֶּחֶם עַד־הַבֹּקֶר וְשָׂרַפְתָּ אֶת־הַנּוֹתָר בָּאֵשׁ לֹא יֵאָכֵל כִּי־קֹדֶשׁ הוּא:
לה וְעָשִׂיתָ לְאַהֲרֹן וּלְבָנָיו כָּכָה כְּכֹל אֲשֶׁר־צִוִּיתִי אֹתָכָה שִׁבְעַת יָמִים תְּמַלֵּא
לו יָדָם: וּפַר חַטָּאת תַּעֲשֶׂה לַיּוֹם עַל־הַכִּפֻּרִים וְחִטֵּאתָ עַל־הַמִּזְבֵּחַ בְּכַפֶּרְךָ
לז עָלָיו וּמָשַׁחְתָּ אֹתוֹ לְקַדְּשׁוֹ: שִׁבְעַת יָמִים תְּכַפֵּר עַל־הַמִּזְבֵּחַ וְקִדַּשְׁתָּ אֹתוֹ
ששי לח וְהָיָה הַמִּזְבֵּחַ קֹדֶשׁ קָדָשִׁים כָּל־הַנֹּגֵעַ בַּמִּזְבֵּחַ יִקְדָּשׁ: וְזֶה
לט אֲשֶׁר תַּעֲשֶׂה עַל־הַמִּזְבֵּחַ כְּבָשִׂים בְּנֵי־שָׁנָה שְׁנַיִם לַיּוֹם תָּמִיד: אֶת־הַכֶּבֶשׂ
מ הָאֶחָד תַּעֲשֶׂה בַבֹּקֶר וְאֵת הַכֶּבֶשׂ הַשֵּׁנִי תַּעֲשֶׂה בֵּין הָעַרְבָּיִם: וְעִשָּׂרֹן סֹלֶת
מא בָּלוּל בְּשֶׁמֶן כָּתִית רֶבַע הַהִין וְנֵסֶךְ רְבִיעִת הַהִין יָיִן לַכֶּבֶשׂ הָאֶחָד: וְאֵת
הַכֶּבֶשׂ הַשֵּׁנִי תַּעֲשֶׂה בֵּין הָעַרְבָּיִם כְּמִנְחַת הַבֹּקֶר וּכְנִסְכָּהּ תַּעֲשֶׂה־לָּהּ לְרֵיחַ
מב נִיחֹחַ אִשֶּׁה לַיהוָה: עֹלַת תָּמִיד לְדֹרֹתֵיכֶם פֶּתַח אֹהֶל־מוֹעֵד לִפְנֵי יְהוָה
מג אֲשֶׁר אִוָּעֵד לָכֶם שָׁמָּה לְדַבֵּר אֵלֶיךָ שָׁם: וְנֹעַדְתִּי שָׁמָּה לִבְנֵי יִשְׂרָאֵל
מד וְנִקְדַּשׁ בִּכְבֹדִי: וְקִדַּשְׁתִּי אֶת־אֹהֶל מוֹעֵד וְאֶת־הַמִּזְבֵּחַ וְאֶת־אַהֲרֹן וְאֶת־
מה בָּנָיו אֲקַדֵּשׁ לְכַהֵן לִי: וְשָׁכַנְתִּי בְּתוֹךְ בְּנֵי יִשְׂרָאֵל וְהָיִיתִי לָהֶם לֵאלֹהִים:
מו וְיָדְעוּ כִּי אֲנִי יְהוָה אֱלֹהֵיהֶם אֲשֶׁר הוֹצֵאתִי אֹתָם מֵאֶרֶץ מִצְרַיִם לְשָׁכְנִי
בְתוֹכָם אֲנִי יְהוָה אֱלֹהֵיהֶם:
ל שביעי א־ב וְעָשִׂיתָ מִזְבֵּחַ מִקְטַר קְטֹרֶת עֲצֵי שִׁטִּים תַּעֲשֶׂה אֹתוֹ: אַמָּה אָרְכּוֹ וְאַמָּה

45. וְשָׁכַנְתִּי בְּתוֹךְ בְּנֵי יִשְׂרָאֵל — *And I will dwell among the Children of Israel* . . . to accept their service with favor and to hearken to their prayers.

וְהָיִיתִי לָהֶם לֵאלֹהִים — *And I will be their God.* To direct their affairs without an intermediary. And they will not need fear the heavenly signs, for they will be more honored before Me than the heavens whose conduct (movement) is directed through (the angels) that move them. And as a result (of all this) their eternity is ensured.

XXX

1. מִזְבֵּחַ מִקְטַר קְטֹרֶת — *An altar to burn incense upon.* A small amount of fire will be sufficient for the incense alone and (therefore) it need not be hollow, filled with earth, as was necessary for the altar of the burnt offering (where) a continual fire had to be made on the earth. But the fire on this altar (burnt) on its overlay which was of gold and since the fire was small it did not burn the block of the altar which was of wood. Now this altar is not mentioned with the other furnishings in *Parashas Terumah* for its intent (purpose) was not to cause God, the Blessed One, to

NOTES

Henceforth the successors to this position would be consecrated by putting on the eight garments.

45. וְהָיִיתִי לָהֶם לֵאלֹהִים — *And I will be their God*. God is eternal (נִצְחִי). Israel's destiny and fate is linked to Him. Hence, that which is

ג רָחְבּוֹ רָבוּעַ יִהְיֶה וְאַמָּתַיִם קֹמָתוֹ מִמֶּנּוּ קַרְנֹתָיו: וְצִפִּיתָ אֹתוֹ זָהָב טָהוֹר
ד אֶת־גַּגּוֹ וְאֶת־קִירֹתָיו סָבִיב וְאֶת־קַרְנֹתָיו וְעָשִׂיתָ לּוֹ זֵר זָהָב סָבִיב: וּשְׁתֵּי
טַבְּעֹת זָהָב תַּעֲשֶׂה־לּוֹ ׀ מִתַּחַת לְזֵרוֹ עַל שְׁתֵּי צַלְעֹתָיו תַּעֲשֶׂה עַל־שְׁנֵי
ה צְדָּיו וְהָיָה לְבָתִּים לְבַדִּים לָשֵׂאת אֹתוֹ בָּהֵמָּה: וְעָשִׂיתָ אֶת־הַבַּדִּים עֲצֵי
ו שִׁטִּים וְצִפִּיתָ אֹתָם זָהָב: וְנָתַתָּה אֹתוֹ לִפְנֵי הַפָּרֹכֶת אֲשֶׁר עַל־אֲרֹן הָעֵדֻת
ז לִפְנֵי הַכַּפֹּרֶת אֲשֶׁר עַל־הָעֵדֻת אֲשֶׁר אִוָּעֵד לְךָ שָׁמָּה: וְהִקְטִיר עָלָיו אַהֲרֹן
מפטיר ח קְטֹרֶת סַמִּים בַּבֹּקֶר בַּבֹּקֶר בְּהֵיטִיבוֹ אֶת־הַנֵּרֹת יַקְטִירֶנָּה: וּבְהַעֲלֹת אַהֲרֹן
ט אֶת־הַנֵּרֹת בֵּין הָעַרְבַּיִם יַקְטִירֶנָּה קְטֹרֶת תָּמִיד לִפְנֵי יהוה לְדֹרֹתֵיכֶם: לֹא־
י תַעֲלוּ עָלָיו קְטֹרֶת זָרָה וְעֹלָה וּמִנְחָה וְנֵסֶךְ לֹא תִסְּכוּ עָלָיו: וְכִפֶּר אַהֲרֹן
עַל־קַרְנֹתָיו אַחַת בַּשָּׁנָה מִדַּם חַטַּאת הַכִּפֻּרִים אַחַת בַּשָּׁנָה יְכַפֵּר עָלָיו
לְדֹרֹתֵיכֶם קֹדֶשׁ־קָדָשִׁים הוּא לַיהוה:

---

dwell in our midst, as was the case with the other furnishings as it says, וְשָׁכַנְתִּי בְּתוֹכָם כְּכֹל אֲשֶׁר אֲנִי מַרְאֶה אוֹתְךָ אֵת תַּבְנִית הַמִּשְׁכָּן וְאֵת תַּבְנִית כָּל כֵּלָיו, *that I may dwell among them; according to all that I show you the pattern of the Tabernacle and the pattern of all its furniture* (25:8,9). Nor was it meant to bring down the appearance of His glory (honor) in the House as was the case of the sacrifices as it says, וְנֹעַדְתִּי שָׁמָּה לִבְנֵי יִשְׂרָאֵל, *and there I will meet with the Children of Israel* (29:43); and so Moses our Teacher attested saying, זֶה הַדָּבָר אֲשֶׁר צִוָּה ה׳ תַּעֲשׂוּ וְיֵרָא אֲלֵיכֶם כְּבוֹד ה׳, *This is the thing which HASHEM commanded that you should do, that the glory of HASHEM may appear to you (Leviticus* 9:6). But the purpose of this altar was to honor God, the Blessed One, after He comes to accept with favor the service of His people (through) the morning and evening sacrifices, and to welcome His presence with the offering of incense, similar to, הָבוּ לַה׳ כְּבוֹד שְׁמוֹ שְׂאוּ מִנְחָה וּבֹאוּ לְפָנָיו, *Ascribe to HASHEM the glory of His Name, bring an offering and come before Him (I Chronicles* 16:29).

4. שְׁתֵּי צַלְעֹתָיו — *The two ribs.* Its upper corners.

שְׁנֵי צְדָּיו — *Two sides.* The sides of its width.

NOTES

connected to the Eternal is also granted eternity.

XXX

1. מִזְבֵּחַ מִקְטַר קְטֹרֶת — *An altar to burn incense upon.* In the previous *sidrah (Terumah)* the various furnishings of the Sanctuary were discussed — the Ark, table, menorah, altar — whereas the golden altar is not included among these furnishings. Instead it is introduced at the end of the chapter regarding the priestly vestments. The *Sforno* explains this seeming discrepancy by explaining the unique role played by the golden altar as opposed to the outer altar upon which animal sacrifices were brought. The goal and purpose of sacrifices was a twofold one; to bring about God's dwelling in the Sanctuary and to bring down His glory so that He meet with the Children of Israel. All this is tied in with the various furnishings and vessels as well. The golden altar, however, is only used for incense and its purpose is to honor God. This is the reason that this command is separated from the other furnishings discussed above. The *Tanchuma* puts it very well, 'The incense offering does not come to expiate sin or transgression or guilt. It comes only to bring *simchah* (joy and happiness).'

פרשת כי תשא
Parashas Ki Sisa

יא־יב וַיְדַבֵּר יהוה אֶל־מֹשֶׁה לֵּאמֹר: כִּי תִשָּׂא אֶת־רֹאשׁ בְּנֵי־יִשְׂרָאֵל לִפְקֻדֵיהֶם
וְנָתְנוּ אִישׁ כֹּפֶר נַפְשׁוֹ לַיהוה בִּפְקֹד אֹתָם וְלֹא־יִהְיֶה בָהֶם נֶגֶף בִּפְקֹד אֹתָם:
יג זֶה | יִתְּנוּ כָּל־הָעֹבֵר עַל־הַפְּקֻדִים מַחֲצִית הַשֶּׁקֶל בְּשֶׁקֶל הַקֹּדֶשׁ עֶשְׂרִים
יד גֵּרָה הַשֶּׁקֶל מַחֲצִית הַשֶּׁקֶל תְּרוּמָה לַיהוה: כֹּל הָעֹבֵר עַל־הַפְּקֻדִים מִבֶּן
טו עֶשְׂרִים שָׁנָה וָמָעְלָה יִתֵּן תְּרוּמַת יהוה: הֶעָשִׁיר לֹא־יַרְבֶּה וְהַדַּל לֹא יַמְעִיט
טז מִמַּחֲצִית הַשָּׁקֶל לָתֵת אֶת־תְּרוּמַת יהוה לְכַפֵּר עַל־נַפְשֹׁתֵיכֶם: וְלָקַחְתָּ
אֶת־כֶּסֶף הַכִּפֻּרִים מֵאֵת בְּנֵי יִשְׂרָאֵל וְנָתַתָּ אֹתוֹ עַל־עֲבֹדַת אֹהֶל מוֹעֵד
וְהָיָה לִבְנֵי יִשְׂרָאֵל לְזִכָּרוֹן לִפְנֵי יהוה לְכַפֵּר עַל־נַפְשֹׁתֵיכֶם:
יז־יח וַיְדַבֵּר יהוה אֶל־מֹשֶׁה לֵּאמֹר: וְעָשִׂיתָ כִּיּוֹר נְחֹשֶׁת וְכַנּוֹ נְחֹשֶׁת לְרָחְצָה
יט וְנָתַתָּ אֹתוֹ בֵּין־אֹהֶל מוֹעֵד וּבֵין הַמִּזְבֵּחַ וְנָתַתָּ שָׁמָּה מָיִם: וְרָחֲצוּ אַהֲרֹן
כ וּבָנָיו מִמֶּנּוּ אֶת־יְדֵיהֶם וְאֶת־רַגְלֵיהֶם: בְּבֹאָם אֶל־אֹהֶל מוֹעֵד יִרְחֲצוּ־
מַיִם וְלֹא יָמֻתוּ אוֹ בְגִשְׁתָּם אֶל־הַמִּזְבֵּחַ לְשָׁרֵת לְהַקְטִיר אִשֶּׁה לַיהוה:

---

12. וְנָתְנוּ אִישׁ כֹּפֶר נַפְשׁוֹ — *Every man shall give ransom for his soul.* Since the need to count men of the human (race) is due to the changes (of circumstances) which occur in his personality, (both) positive and negative (lit., 'existence and loss') and this is caused by their sins, as our Sages say, אֵין מִיתָה בְּלֹא חֵטְא, *There is no death without sin (Shabbos* 55a), therefore every counting (census) causes iniquities to be recalled, therefore it is fitting that each one give a ransom for his soul in honor of God, the Blessed One, and *He being merciful atones iniquity* (based on *Psalms* 78:38), as it says, לְכַפֵּר עַל נַפְשֹׁתֵיכֶם, *to make atonement for your souls* (v. 15) and hence it says . . .

15. הֶעָשִׁיר לֹא יַרְבֶּה וְהַדַּל לֹא יַמְעִיט — *The rich shall not give more and the poor shall not give less.* For in this לֹא נִכַּר שׁוֹעַ לִפְנֵי דָל, *the rich is not regarded more than the poor (Job* 34:19).

18. וְעָשִׂיתָ כִּיּוֹר — *And you shall make a laver.* This vessel is also not mentioned above together with the other vessels (and furnishings) for its purpose (lit., 'intent') was not to cause the Divine Presence to dwell in the Sanctuary, as was the intent of those vessels as explained above. But the intent (of the laver) was to prepare the priests for their service.

NOTES

12-15. וְנָתְנוּ אִישׁ כֹּפֶר נַפְשׁוֹ . . . לֹא יַרְבֶּה . . . לֹא יַמְעִיט — *Every man shall give ransom for his soul . . . shall not give more . . . shall not give less.* In Torah perspective counting (a census) of people plays a most significant role. The *Sforno*, at the beginning of *Exodus*, comments regarding the *name* of an individual which he explains reveals the essential personality of that person. Here he tells us that counting is not to be considered simply as a way of determining the quantity of a people but it also is an index to their quality. Each time God ordered a census — when they left Egypt; after the sin of the Golden Calf and now when He is prepared to 'dwell' in the Sanctuary — it indicates, to a degree, a change in their status due to their actions. Hence it is akin to a close examination which may reveal many blemishes and shortcomings. Therefore they are told to bring a 'ransom' for their souls which need an atonement. This being the case the amount collected (half-shekel) is uniform, for certainly in this regard there is no difference between rich and poor.

18. וְעָשִׂיתָ כִּיּוֹר — *And you shall make a laver.* Compare to the *Sforno's* commentary on verse 1, regarding the altar of incense.

כא וְרָחֲצוּ יְדֵיהֶם וְרַגְלֵיהֶם וְלֹא יָמֻתוּ וְהָיְתָה לָהֶם חָק־עוֹלָם לוֹ וּלְזַרְעוֹ
לְדֹרֹתָם:
כב־כג וַיְדַבֵּר יהוה אֶל־מֹשֶׁה לֵּאמֹר: וְאַתָּה קַח־לְךָ בְּשָׂמִים רֹאשׁ מָר־דְּרוֹר חֲמֵשׁ
מֵאוֹת וְקִנְּמָן־בֶּשֶׂם מַחֲצִיתוֹ חֲמִשִּׁים וּמָאתָיִם וּקְנֵה־בֹשֶׂם חֲמִשִּׁים וּמָאתָיִם:
כד־כה וְקִדָּה חֲמֵשׁ מֵאוֹת בְּשֶׁקֶל הַקֹּדֶשׁ וְשֶׁמֶן זַיִת הִין: וְעָשִׂיתָ אֹתוֹ שֶׁמֶן
כו מִשְׁחַת־קֹדֶשׁ רֹקַח מִרְקַחַת מַעֲשֵׂה רֹקֵחַ שֶׁמֶן מִשְׁחַת־קֹדֶשׁ יִהְיֶה: וּמָשַׁחְתָּ
כז בוֹ אֶת־אֹהֶל מוֹעֵד וְאֵת אֲרוֹן הָעֵדֻת: וְאֶת־הַשֻּׁלְחָן וְאֶת־כָּל־כֵּלָיו
כח וְאֶת־הַמְּנֹרָה וְאֶת־כֵּלֶיהָ וְאֵת מִזְבַּח הַקְּטֹרֶת: וְאֶת־מִזְבַּח הָעֹלָה וְאֶת־
כט כָּל־כֵּלָיו וְאֶת־הַכִּיֹּר וְאֶת־כַּנּוֹ: וְקִדַּשְׁתָּ אֹתָם וְהָיוּ קֹדֶשׁ קָדָשִׁים כָּל־הַנֹּגֵעַ
ל בָּהֶם יִקְדָּשׁ: וְאֶת־אַהֲרֹן וְאֶת־בָּנָיו תִּמְשָׁח וְקִדַּשְׁתָּ אֹתָם לְכַהֵן לִי:
לא וְאֶל־בְּנֵי יִשְׂרָאֵל תְּדַבֵּר לֵאמֹר שֶׁמֶן מִשְׁחַת־קֹדֶשׁ יִהְיֶה זֶה לִי לְדֹרֹתֵיכֶם:
לב עַל־בְּשַׂר אָדָם לֹא יִיסָךְ וּבְמַתְכֻּנְתּוֹ לֹא תַעֲשׂוּ כָּמֹהוּ קֹדֶשׁ הוּא קֹדֶשׁ
לג יִהְיֶה לָכֶם: אִישׁ אֲשֶׁר יִרְקַח כָּמֹהוּ וַאֲשֶׁר יִתֵּן מִמֶּנּוּ עַל־זָר וְנִכְרַת
לד מֵעַמָּיו: וַיֹּאמֶר יהוה אֶל־מֹשֶׁה קַח־לְךָ סַמִּים נָטָף | וּשְׁחֵלֶת

---

24. וְשֶׁמֶן זַיִת הִין — *And of olive oil a hin.* Without a doubt this quantity of oil was not sufficient to smear the quantity of all those spices, but they cooked the oil with the water in which the spices had been boiled or they floated it (the oil) on the water in which (the spices) had been steeped until the water evaporated (lit., 'ended') through the cooking or through the minimal heat of the water, while the oil remained, as in the art of a compounder. The dispute between our Sages *(Horayos* 11b) is regarding this (question), whether it was sufficient to cook it (the oil) with the water in which the roots had been boiled or to float it (the oil) on the water in which they were steeped and melt them through minimal heat.

25. רֹקַח מִרְקַחַת — *A perfume compounded ...* (i.e.,) a compound which was compounded. The oil was compounded in the compounded water.

31. יִהְיֶה זֶה לִי לְדֹרֹתֵיכֶם — *Unto Me throughout your generations.* It will not be diminished (lit., 'deteriorate').

34. קַח לְךָ סַמִּים — *Take for yourself sweet spices.* Those mentioned by the

NOTES

24. וְשֶׁמֶן זַיִת הִין — *And of olive oil a hin.* The Talmud *(Horayos* 11b) relates a dispute between R' Meir and R' Yehudah regarding this oil of anointment. The former is of the opinion that the roots (of the various spices) were boiled in the oil to give it fragrance. The latter disagrees for he argues that the amount of oil was insufficient to even *smear* the roots, let alone to be boiled with them and not cook out. He therefore is of the opinion (according to *Rashi)* that the spices were steeped in water, the oil then poured over them and left thus until the oil absorbed the scent, after which they skimmed off the oil. The *Sforno* however interprets the argument of R' Meir and R' Yehudah differently in order to justify the position of R' Meir, who also understood that a *hin* of oil could not suffice to even smear the roots. Hence he interprets R' Meir's position as meaning that the oil was boiled in the *water* in which the roots of the spices had originally been cooked. R' Yehudah, on the other hand, is of the opinion that the oil was floated on the top of the water in which the roots had been steeped, and after evaporation of the water, fragrant oil remained.

31. יִהְיֶה זֶה לִי לְדֹרֹתֵיכֶם — *Unto Me throughout your generations.* The phrase לְדֹרֹתֵיכֶם does not mean that the oil of anointment is to be

לה וְחֶלְבְּנָה סַמִּים וּלְבֹנָה זַכָּה בַּד בְּבַד יִהְיֶה: וְעָשִׂיתָ אֹתָהּ קְטֹרֶת רֹקַח מַעֲשֵׂה
לו רוֹקֵחַ מְמֻלָּח טָהוֹר קֹדֶשׁ: וְשָׁחַקְתָּ מִמֶּנָּה הָדֵק וְנָתַתָּה מִמֶּנָּה לִפְנֵי הָעֵדֻת
לז בְּאֹהֶל מוֹעֵד אֲשֶׁר אִוָּעֵד לְךָ שָׁמָּה קֹדֶשׁ קָדָשִׁים תִּהְיֶה לָכֶם: וְהַקְּטֹרֶת
לח אֲשֶׁר תַּעֲשֶׂה בְּמַתְכֻּנְתָּהּ לֹא תַעֲשׂוּ לָכֶם קֹדֶשׁ תִּהְיֶה לְךָ לַיהוָה: אִישׁ
לא א אֲשֶׁר־יַעֲשֶׂה כָמוֹהָ לְהָרִיחַ בָּהּ וְנִכְרַת מֵעַמָּיו: וַיְדַבֵּר יְהוָה
ב אֶל־מֹשֶׁה לֵּאמֹר: רְאֵה קָרָאתִי בְשֵׁם בְּצַלְאֵל בֶּן־אוּרִי בֶן־חוּר לְמַטֵּה

---

anointing oil; they are myrrh, calamus, cinnamon and cassia. With these (bring) stacte, onycha and galbanum and with them aromatics which are able (lit., 'known') to prepare the aforementioned spices, as for example the perfumers know that corn ears (are used) to prepare *rhubarbiro,* and rocksalt to prepare *agrico* and (other) similar (mixtures). Our Sages *(Kerisos* 6a) had a tradition that spikenard, saffron and costus were used to prepare the spices mentioned above.

וּלְבֹנָה זַכָּה — *Pure frankincense.* Which needed no other preparation (fixing); and so these are the eleven spices which our Sages enumerate for the compounding of the incense *(Kerisos* 6a).

35. רֹקַח — *A compound.* Each of these spices shall absorb from one another, and from all (together) one composition will be made.

מַעֲשֵׂה רוֹקֵחַ — *After the art of the compounder.* Each of these spices was to be pounded (crushed) befitting it, for it was not proper that each one of these spices be crushed in a single (similar) manner.

מְמֻלָּח — *Mixed together.* The spices were to be well mixed together so that none of them (remain) separate.

טָהוֹר — *Pure . . .* (i.e.,) clean of all refuse. This was necessary (to caution us) because the incense was made from the original perfume, but for the oil of anointment this (warning) was unnecessary because there were no particles of spices mixed in with the oil at all.

XXXI

2. רְאֵה קָרָאתִי בְשֵׁם — *See, I have called by name.* See and understand that I call him for good reasons (lit., 'not for nothing') for it is of major import in sacred work that

NOTES

made in each generation. Rather it is to be interpreted as miraculously remaining for all generations. This is based on the Talmud (ibid.).

34. קַח לְךָ סַמִּים — *Take for yourself sweet spices.* The word סַמִּים, *spices* or *aromatics,* appears twice in this verse. Both are not specified. The *Sforno* therefore interprets the first phrase as referring to the spices enumerated in verses 23-24 and the second as referring to spices, well known at that time to those skilled in the art of compounding, as useful in the preparation of the spices specified in this verse. The eleven spices alluded to by the *Sforno* which comprised the incense offered on the golden altar were: balm, onycha, galbanum, frankincense, myrrh, cassia, spikenard, saffron, costus, aromatic bark and cinnamon.

35. מְמֻלָּח — *Mixed together.* The word מְמֻלָּח has (incorrectly) been translated seasoned with salt. In reality, as *Rashi* and *Onkelos* translate, it means *mixed together.* This is also the interpretation of the *Sforno.*

טָהוֹר — *Pure.* The word טָהוֹר usually means *ritually pure.* In the context of this verse it means free from impurity.

XXXI

2. רְאֵה קָרָאתִי בְשֵׁם — *See, I have called by*

ג יְהוּדָה: וָאֲמַלֵּא אֹתוֹ רוּחַ אֱלֹהִים בְּחָכְמָה וּבִתְבוּנָה וּבְדַעַת וּבְכָל־
ד־ה מְלָאכָה: לַחְשֹׁב מַחֲשָׁבֹת לַעֲשׂוֹת בַּזָּהָב וּבַכֶּסֶף וּבַנְּחֹשֶׁת: וּבַחֲרֹשֶׁת אֶבֶן
ו לְמַלֹּאת וּבַחֲרֹשֶׁת עֵץ לַעֲשׂוֹת בְּכָל־מְלָאכָה: וַאֲנִי הִנֵּה נָתַתִּי אִתּוֹ אֵת
אָהֳלִיאָב בֶּן־אֲחִיסָמָךְ לְמַטֵּה־דָן וּבְלֵב כָּל־חֲכַם־לֵב נָתַתִּי חָכְמָה וְעָשׂוּ
ז אֵת כָּל־אֲשֶׁר צִוִּיתִךָ: אֵת | אֹהֶל מוֹעֵד וְאֶת־הָאָרֹן לָעֵדֻת וְאֶת־הַכַּפֹּרֶת
ח אֲשֶׁר עָלָיו וְאֵת כָּל־כְּלֵי הָאֹהֶל: וְאֶת־הַשֻּׁלְחָן וְאֶת־כֵּלָיו וְאֶת־הַמְּנֹרָה
ט הַטְּהֹרָה וְאֶת־כָּל־כֵּלֶיהָ וְאֵת מִזְבַּח הַקְּטֹרֶת: וְאֶת־מִזְבַּח הָעֹלָה וְאֶת־כָּל־
י כֵּלָיו וְאֶת־הַכִּיּוֹר וְאֶת־כַּנּוֹ: וְאֵת בִּגְדֵי הַשְּׂרָד וְאֶת־בִּגְדֵי הַקֹּדֶשׁ לְאַהֲרֹן
יא הַכֹּהֵן וְאֶת־בִּגְדֵי בָנָיו לְכַהֵן: וְאֵת שֶׁמֶן הַמִּשְׁחָה וְאֶת־קְטֹרֶת הַסַּמִּים
לַקֹּדֶשׁ כְּכֹל אֲשֶׁר־צִוִּיתִךָ יַעֲשׂוּ:
יב־יג וַיֹּאמֶר יְהוָה אֶל־מֹשֶׁה לֵּאמֹר: וְאַתָּה דַּבֵּר אֶל־בְּנֵי יִשְׂרָאֵל לֵאמֹר אַךְ
אֶת־שַׁבְּתֹתַי תִּשְׁמֹרוּ כִּי אוֹת הִוא בֵּינִי וּבֵינֵיכֶם לְדֹרֹתֵיכֶם לָדַעַת כִּי אֲנִי
יד יְהוָה מְקַדִּשְׁכֶם: וּשְׁמַרְתֶּם אֶת־הַשַּׁבָּת כִּי קֹדֶשׁ הִוא לָכֶם מְחַלְלֶיהָ מוֹת

---

it be done by one chosen of God who has proper intent in his actions to attain the commanded purpose (and end).

13. אַךְ אֶת שַׁבְּתֹתַי תִּשְׁמֹרוּ — *However, you shall keep My Sabbaths.* Although I have commanded you regarding the work of the Sanctuary nonetheless *you shall keep My Sabbaths* and do not override them for the sake of (the *Mishkan).*

כִּי אוֹת הִוא בֵּינִי וּבֵינֵיכֶם — *For it is a sign between Me and you.* And if you desecrate (lit., 'spoil') this sign there is no purpose in making a Sanctuary for Me to dwell in your midst.

14. וּשְׁמַרְתֶּם אֶת הַשַּׁבָּת — *You shall keep the Sabbath.* And also for another reason it is proper that you not override the Sabbath for the building of the Sanctuary . . .

כִּי קֹדֶשׁ הִוא לָכֶם — *For it is holy unto you . . .* being a positive commandment (מִצְוַת עֲשֵׂה).

מְחַלְלֶיהָ מוֹת יוּמָת — *Every one that profanes it shall be put to death.* (This refers to) the negative commandment (לֹא תַעֲשֶׂה), and it is not proper to override a positive and negative commandment which carries a death penalty, to fulfill the positive commandment of building the Sanctuary.

NOTES

name. The Talmud (*Berachos* 55a) states that there are three things which God Himself announces (מַכְרִיז עֲלֵיהֶם), and they are: hunger; plenty (prosperity); and the designation of a good leader. The Talmud brings as proof to the last statement the appointment of Bezalel. This is the thrust of the *Sforno's* comment as well. God told Moses to observe and appreciate that He had chosen the right man for the task of designing and constructing the *Mishkan,* for not only did Bezalel have the necessary skills but he also understood the symbolism of every object designed.

13-15. אַךְ אֶת שַׁבְּתֹתַי תִּשְׁמֹרוּ . . . וּשְׁמַרְתֶּם אֶת הַשַּׁבָּת . . . שֵׁשֶׁת יָמִים יֵעָשֶׂה מְלָאכָה — *However, you shall keep My Sabbaths . . . You shall keep the Sabbath . . . Six days shall work be done.* God gives four reasons for not overriding the Sabbath for the sake of building the *Mishkan:* (a) since the Sabbath is a sign of the covenant between God and Israel, if you desecrate the sign you defeat the purpose of the Sanctuary; (b) the only reason one might think he is permitted to override the Sabbath is because the building of the Sanctuary is a מִצְוַת עֲשֵׂה, *positive commandment,* but no עֲשֵׂה can set

טו יוּמָת כִּי כָּל־הָעֹשֶׂה בָהּ מְלָאכָה וְנִכְרְתָה הַנֶּפֶשׁ הַהִוא מִקֶּרֶב עַמֶּיהָ: שֵׁשֶׁת
יָמִים יֵעָשֶׂה מְלָאכָה וּבַיּוֹם הַשְּׁבִיעִי שַׁבַּת שַׁבָּתוֹן קֹדֶשׁ לַיהוָה כָּל־הָעֹשֶׂה
טז מְלָאכָה בְּיוֹם הַשַּׁבָּת מוֹת יוּמָת: וְשָׁמְרוּ בְנֵי־יִשְׂרָאֵל אֶת־הַשַּׁבָּת לַעֲשׂוֹת
יז אֶת־הַשַּׁבָּת לְדֹרֹתָם בְּרִית עוֹלָם: בֵּינִי וּבֵין בְּנֵי יִשְׂרָאֵל אוֹת הִוא לְעֹלָם

כִּי כָּל הָעֹשֶׂה בָהּ מְלָאכָה וְנִכְרְתָה הַנֶּפֶשׁ הַהִוא — *For whoever does any work on it, that soul shall be cut off*. Also it is fitting (proper) not to override the Sabbath, for its profanation is punished greatly, in that the soul of the profaner is cut off (from his people), because by so doing he denies the creation (lit., 'newness') of the world, and he has no portion in the Sanctuary nor in He Who dwells therein.

מִקֶּרֶב עַמֶּיהָ — *From among his people* ... from the (spiritual) level of the national souls which are of (similar) quality — for eternal life.

15. שֵׁשֶׁת יָמִים יֵעָשֶׂה מְלָאכָה — *Six days shall work be done*. Behold in the six days of labor you can do the work of the Sanctuary, therefore it is not proper to override the Sabbath for it, (since) there is no *mitzvah* (commandment) which overrides the Sabbath unless it has a set, permanent time, which coincides with the Sabbath, such as Divine service (i.e., the daily and Sabbath sacrifice) and circumcision. But when it is possible to fulfill the commandment on another day, it never overrides the Sabbath.

שַׁבַּת שַׁבָּתוֹן — *A Sabbath of complete rest*. Behold even that which is not included (technically) in the general (list) of (prohibited) labors is prohibited as it says, **וּבַיּוֹם** הַשְּׁבִיעִי תִּשְׁבֹּת, *on the seventh day you shall rest* (23:12). This is (so) in order that it be *holy to HASHEM*, that a person should give up completely his temporal affairs and occupy himself with the affairs of eternal life in honor of his Maker.

כָּל הָעֹשֶׂה מְלָאכָה ... יוּמָת — *Whosoever does any work ... shall be put to death*. Therefore the law is that he who nullifies this intent by doing work shall be put to death.

16. וְשָׁמְרוּ בְנֵי יִשְׂרָאֵל אֶת הַשַּׁבָּת — *The Children of Israel shall keep the Sabbath*. In this world (so as) to observe the Sabbath in the day which (will be) wholly Sabbath.

NOTES

aside an עֲשֵׂה and לֹא תַעֲשֶׂה (positive and negative commandments which apply to one commandment), and the Sabbath is such a מִצְוָה; (c) since the profaning of the Sabbath is so serious that it causes the sinner to be cut off from his people, then he would consequently have no share in the Sanctuary anyway, hence the commandment of building such a place is nullified and consequently there is no force of a *mitzvah* to override the Sabbath; (d) the only precedent for another commandment overriding the Sabbath is when we deal with one that must be performed at a specific time, which coincides with the Sabbath as well, such as circumcision (on the eighth day) and sacrifices that have a set time (such as the daily sacrifice, Sabbath offerings and the *Pesach* lamb), but this does not apply in the case of constructing the Sanctuary, since the six days of the week would suffice.

15. שַׁבַּת שַׁבָּתוֹן — *A Sabbath of complete rest*. *Rashi* comments on the phrase מְחַלְלֶיהָ (verse 14): 'Whoever treats it as חוֹל, *ordinary, secular*, insofar as its sanctity is concerned.' This is the intent of the *Sforno* in his commentary on this verse as well, but he links it to the expression שַׁבַּת שַׁבָּתוֹן, *A Sabbath of complete rest*, which is followed by, קֹדֶשׁ לַה׳, *holy to HASHEM*.

16. וְשָׁמְרוּ בְנֵי יִשְׂרָאֵל אֶת הַשַּׁבָּת – *The Children of Israel shall keep the Sabbath*. The *Sforno's* commentary explains the order and sequence of the verse. Israel is enjoined to keep the

כִּי־שֵׁשֶׁת יָמִים עָשָׂה יהוה אֶת־הַשָּׁמַיִם וְאֶת־הָאָרֶץ וּבַיּוֹם הַשְּׁבִיעִי שָׁבַת
שני יח וַיִּנָּפַשׁ׃ וַיִּתֵּן אֶל־מֹשֶׁה כְּכַלֹּתוֹ לְדַבֵּר אִתּוֹ בְּהַר סִינַי שְׁנֵי
לב א לֻחֹת הָעֵדֻת לֻחֹת אֶבֶן כְּתֻבִים בְּאֶצְבַּע אֱלֹהִים׃ וַיַּרְא הָעָם כִּי־בֹשֵׁשׁ מֹשֶׁה

---

17. וּבַיּוֹם הַשְּׁבִיעִי שָׁבַת — *And the seventh day He ceased.* On it the work was complete and in completion there is tranquility.

וַיִּנָּפַשׁ — *And rested.* Therefore the seventh (day) became the 'owner' of an additional soul, which is an added preparation to attain what God, the Blessed One, intended for him (man) regarding the completeness of this world when He said, 'נַעֲשֶׂה אָדָם בְּצַלְמֵנוּ כִּדְמוּתֵנוּ, *Let us make man in Our image, after Our likeness*' (*Genesis* 1:26).

18. וַיִּתֵּן אֶל מֹשֶׁה כְּכַלֹּתוֹ — *And He gave to Moses, when He ended (speaking).* After relating to us the good which was attained each time at the conclusion of Moses' stay on the mountain forty days, (the Torah) explains the reason why the goal which God, the Blessed One, ordained when the Torah was given, when He said, '*And you shall be to Me a kingdom of priests and a holy people*' (19:6), (and also) when He said, '*An earthen altar make unto Me . . . in every place . . . I will come to you*' (20:21), was not realized. (Instead) they were constrained to make a Sanctuary. (Now) we are told that (all) this happened because of the evil choice (made) by Israel, for indeed after the first forty days the tablets (which were) the work of God were given to sanctify everyone (to be) priests and a holy nation according to the good words He had spoken. (But) they rebelled and corrupted their ways and fell from their exalted level, as (the Torah) testifies, saying, וַיִּתְנַצְּלוּ בְנֵי יִשְׂרָאֵל אֶת עֶדְיָם מֵהַר חוֹרֵב, *And the Children of Israel stripped themselves of their ornaments (crowns) from Mount Horeb* (33:6).

שְׁנֵי לֻחֹת הָעֵדֻת — *Two tablets of the testimony.* Those which were designated when He said, '*And I will give you the tablets of stone*' (24:2), but before He gave (them) the Torah and commandments which He wrote as He (had) designated, they began

NOTES

Sabbath, לַעֲשׂוֹת אֶת הַשַּׁבָּת, *so as to make the Sabbath;* seemingly this latter phrase being a reason for the former injunction. The explanation is that by keeping the Sabbath in this life they will merit to observe the 'day' which is wholly Sabbath, namely in the world to come.

17. וּבַיּוֹם הַשְּׁבִיעִי שָׁבַת וַיִּנָּפַשׁ — *And the seventh day He ceased and rested.* There are two phrases in this verse which if translated literally are seemingly anthropomorphic, as ascribing human attributes to the Deity. They are שָׁבַת, *He ceased,* and וַיִּנָּפַשׁ, *He rested. Rashi* and other commentators attempt to interpret these phrases in a manner which would not attribute to God, Who created the world through His word and Who 'neither faints nor grows weary,' the need to rest or refresh Himself. The *Sforno* in his interpretation of this verse anticipates this problem and explains the verse thus: When God completed His work of creation it brought tranquility, for completion of any task brings with it a great sense of peace and serenity. This is the sense of the word שָׁבַת. (See the *Sforno* on 20:11.) As for the phrase וַיִּנָּפַשׁ, the *Sforno* explains it to mean that the Sabbath was given to expand man's soul (נֶפֶשׁ), and indeed to grant an added dimension to it (נֶפֶשׁ יְתֵרָה), so that he be better prepared to realize the purpose meant for him and to reach the goal of serving God by perfecting his Divine image and likeness. Hence the word וַיִּנָּפַשׁ pertains to the נֶפֶשׁ of man, not of God.

18. וַיִּתֵּן אֶל מֹשֶׁה כְּכַלֹּתוֹ — *And He gave to Moses, when He ended (speaking).* For the explanation of the *Sforno's* commentary on this verse see his commentary on 24:18 and the explanatory notes on that verse.

לָרֶדֶת מִן־הָהָר וַיִּקָּהֵל הָעָם עַל־אַהֲרֹן וַיֹּאמְרוּ אֵלָיו קוּם ׀ עֲשֵׂה־לָנוּ
אֱלֹהִים אֲשֶׁר יֵלְכוּ לְפָנֵינוּ כִּי־זֶה ׀ מֹשֶׁה הָאִישׁ אֲשֶׁר הֶעֱלָנוּ מֵאֶרֶץ מִצְרַיִם
ב לֹא יָדַעְנוּ מֶה־הָיָה לוֹ: וַיֹּאמֶר אֲלֵהֶם אַהֲרֹן פָּרְקוּ נִזְמֵי הַזָּהָב אֲשֶׁר בְּאָזְנֵי
ג נְשֵׁיכֶם בְּנֵיכֶם וּבְנֹתֵיכֶם וְהָבִיאוּ אֵלָי: וַיִּתְפָּרְקוּ כָּל־הָעָם אֶת־נִזְמֵי הַזָּהָב
ד אֲשֶׁר בְּאָזְנֵיהֶם וַיָּבִיאוּ אֶל־אַהֲרֹן: וַיִּקַּח מִיָּדָם וַיָּצַר אֹתוֹ בַּחֶרֶט וַיַּעֲשֵׂהוּ
עֵגֶל מַסֵּכָה וַיֹּאמְרוּ אֵלֶּה אֱלֹהֶיךָ יִשְׂרָאֵל אֲשֶׁר הֶעֱלוּךָ מֵאֶרֶץ מִצְרָיִם:
ה וַיַּרְא אַהֲרֹן וַיִּבֶן מִזְבֵּחַ לְפָנָיו וַיִּקְרָא אַהֲרֹן וַיֹּאמַר חַג לַיהוָה מָחָר:
ו וַיַּשְׁכִּימוּ מִמָּחֳרָת וַיַּעֲלוּ עֹלֹת וַיַּגִּשׁוּ שְׁלָמִים וַיֵּשֶׁב הָעָם לֶאֱכֹל וְשָׁתוֹ
וַיָּקֻמוּ לְצַחֵק:
ז וַיְדַבֵּר יְהוָה אֶל־מֹשֶׁה לֶךְ־רֵד כִּי שִׁחֵת עַמְּךָ אֲשֶׁר הֶעֱלֵיתָ מֵאֶרֶץ מִצְרָיִם:
ח סָרוּ מַהֵר מִן־הַדֶּרֶךְ אֲשֶׁר צִוִּיתִם עָשׂוּ לָהֶם עֵגֶל מַסֵּכָה וַיִּשְׁתַּחֲווּ־לוֹ
וַיִּזְבְּחוּ־לוֹ וַיֹּאמְרוּ אֵלֶּה אֱלֹהֶיךָ יִשְׂרָאֵל אֲשֶׁר הֶעֱלוּךָ מֵאֶרֶץ מִצְרָיִם:
ט וַיֹּאמֶר יְהוָה אֶל־מֹשֶׁה רָאִיתִי אֶת־הָעָם הַזֶּה וְהִנֵּה עַם־קְשֵׁה־עֹרֶף הוּא:

---

the act of the (Golden) Calf, and (He) said to Moses, לֶךְ רֵד כִּי שִׁחֵת עַמְּךָ, *Get you down for your people have dealt corruptly* (32:7).

XXXII

4. אֵלֶּה אֱלֹהֶיךָ יִשְׂרָאֵל — *This is your god, O Israel.* These will be for you 'gods' to whom you shall pray for all your needs, and you will worship (serve) them to attain your desires.

5. חַג לַה׳ מָחָר — *Tomorrow shall be a feast to HASHEM.* And do not mingle His happiness with another god.

8. סָרוּ מַהֵר — *They have turned aside quickly.* Before I completed giving you what I designated to give, namely, הַתּוֹרָה וְהַמִּצְוָה אֲשֶׁר כָּתַבְתִּי, *the Torah and the commandments which I have written* (24:12).

9. וְהִנֵּה עַם קְשֵׁה עֹרֶף הוּא — *And behold it is a stiff-necked people.* Their neck is (like) an iron sinew and they will not turn to listen to the words of any righteous

NOTES

XXXII

4. אֵלֶּה אֱלֹהֶיךָ יִשְׂרָאֵל — *This is your god, O Israel.* The *Sforno* uses language mirroring phrases he used in 20:2 in his interpretation of the first commandment of God on Mount Sinai. Thus he underscores how diametrically opposed the Golden Calf episode is to that of the Revelation. There God commanded them to pray only to Him and worship only Him, while here the leaders of the mixed multitude urged Israel to worship the Golden Calf. Even if their intent was that the calf be an intermediary, this was in contradiction to the word אֱלֹהֶיךָ, *your God,* which the *Sforno* explains to mean 'without any need of an intermediary.'

5. חַג לַה׳ מָחָר — *Tomorrow shall be a feast to HASHEM.* Just as Israel was enjoined from communicating with God through an intermediary, so were they forbidden to serve other gods *together* with *HASHEM* (the second commandment — לֹא יִהְיֶה לְךָ). Aaron, hoping to avoid a confrontation while stalling for time, pleaded with the people to delay their service of the calf, appealing to them not to join their worship of the calf with that of *God's feast* which he declared for the morrow.

8. סָרוּ מַהֵר — *They have turned aside quickly.* The *Sforno* interprets the word מַהֵר, *quickly,* as meaning a hasty act which precluded God's implementation of His original plan. Since the

י־יא וְעַתָּה הַנִּיחָה לִּי וְיִחַר־אַפִּי בָהֶם וַאֲכַלֵּם וְאֶעֱשֶׂה אוֹתְךָ לְגוֹי גָּדוֹל: וַיְחַל
מֹשֶׁה אֶת־פְּנֵי יְהוָה אֱלֹהָיו וַיֹּאמֶר לָמָה יהוה יֶחֱרֶה אַפְּךָ בְּעַמֶּךָ אֲשֶׁר
יב הוֹצֵאתָ מֵאֶרֶץ מִצְרַיִם בְּכֹחַ גָּדוֹל וּבְיָד חֲזָקָה: לָמָּה יֹאמְרוּ מִצְרַיִם לֵאמֹר
בְּרָעָה הוֹצִיאָם לַהֲרֹג אֹתָם בֶּהָרִים וּלְכַלֹּתָם מֵעַל פְּנֵי הָאֲדָמָה שׁוּב
יג מֵחֲרוֹן אַפֶּךָ וְהִנָּחֵם עַל־הָרָעָה לְעַמֶּךָ: זְכֹר לְאַבְרָהָם לְיִצְחָק וּלְיִשְׂרָאֵל
עֲבָדֶיךָ אֲשֶׁר נִשְׁבַּעְתָּ לָהֶם בָּךְ וַתְּדַבֵּר אֲלֵהֶם אַרְבֶּה אֶת־זַרְעֲכֶם כְּכוֹכְבֵי
הַשָּׁמָיִם וְכָל־הָאָרֶץ הַזֹּאת אֲשֶׁר אָמַרְתִּי אֶתֵּן לְזַרְעֲכֶם וְנָחֲלוּ לְעֹלָם:
יד וַיִּנָּחֶם יְהוָה עַל־הָרָעָה אֲשֶׁר דִּבֶּר לַעֲשׂוֹת לְעַמּוֹ:
טו וַיִּפֶן וַיֵּרֶד מֹשֶׁה מִן־הָהָר וּשְׁנֵי לֻחֹת הָעֵדֻת בְּיָדוֹ לֻחֹת כְּתֻבִים מִשְּׁנֵי
טז עֶבְרֵיהֶם מִזֶּה וּמִזֶּה הֵם כְּתֻבִים: וְהַלֻּחֹת מַעֲשֵׂה אֱלֹהִים הֵמָּה וְהַמִּכְתָּב
יז מִכְתַּב אֱלֹהִים הוּא חָרוּת עַל־הַלֻּחֹת: וַיִּשְׁמַע יְהוֹשֻׁעַ אֶת־קוֹל הָעָם בְּרֵעֹה
יח וַיֹּאמֶר אֶל־מֹשֶׁה קוֹל מִלְחָמָה בַּמַּחֲנֶה: וַיֹּאמֶר אֵין קוֹל עֲנוֹת גְּבוּרָה וְאֵין
יט קוֹל עֲנוֹת חֲלוּשָׁה קוֹל עַנּוֹת אָנֹכִי שֹׁמֵעַ: וַיְהִי כַּאֲשֶׁר קָרַב אֶל־הַמַּחֲנֶה

---

teacher in any manner; (hence) there is no hope that they will repent.

11. לָמָה ה׳ יֶחֱרֶה אַפְּךָ בְּעַמֶּךָ — *HASHEM, why are You so angry with Your people?* (This refers to) those that did not sin with the calf.

13. וְכָל הָאָרֶץ הַזֹּאת אֲשֶׁר אָמַרְתִּי אֶתֵּן לְזַרְעֲכֶם וְנָחֲלוּ — *And all this land that I have spoken of I will give to your seed and they shall inherit it.* (Moses spoke of) the fourth generation, as it says, וְדוֹר רְבִיעִי יָשׁוּבוּ הֵנָּה, *And in the fourth generation they shall come back here (Genesis* 15:16). (He said, 'This promise was to include all of Israel) but it will now not be fulfilled except through my seed alone.'

15. וּשְׁנֵי לֻחֹת הָעֵדֻת בְּיָדוֹ — *With the two tablets of the testimony in his hand.* For he thought that when he returned to them they would repent; and if not, he would break them (the tablets) in their sight that *their eyes might fail* (based on *Lamentations* 4:17 and *Psalms* 69:4) so that they would repent.

NOTES

Ten Commandments had already been inscribed, it can only refer to the Torah and *mitzvos* which had as yet not been written.

9. וְהִנֵּה עַם קְשֵׁה עֹרֶף הוּא — *And behold it is a stiff-necked people.* As the *Sforno* says later (verse 30), in knowledge (recognition) of one's sins lies the beginning of repentance. Conversely if one refuses to listen to admonition and is blind to his shortcomings, there is scant chance that he will repent. This is the meaning of the *Sforno's* interpretation of a *stiff-necked people.*

11. לָמָה ה׳ יֶחֱרֶה אַפְּךָ בְּעַמֶּךָ — *HASHEM, why are You so angry with Your people?* This interpretation is called for, else Moses' question is without merit. The children of Israel have sinned in a grievous manner, and God is understandably angry; why then this question? The answer is that Moses is referring to the many who did not transgress. Moses himself eventually grasped the answer, as we see in verse 25, when he realized that although they did not actively sin, nonetheless they were guilty of apathy and they failed to protest against, and oppose, the actions of the sinners.

15. וּשְׁנֵי לֻחֹת הָעֵדֻת בְּיָדוֹ — *With the two tablets of the testimony in his hand.* The *Sforno* explains the reason for bringing down the tablets. Since Israel had sinned and were not worthy to receive them, why not leave them in heaven? The answer is that if they repent *at once* he will give the tablets to them, and if not, the shattering of the tablets will hopefully shock them into repentance.

וַיַּרְא אֶת־הָעֵגֶל וּמְחֹלֹת וַיִּחַר־אַף מֹשֶׁה וַיַּשְׁלֵךְ מִיָּדָו אֶת־הַלֻּחֹת וַיְשַׁבֵּר
כ אֹתָם תַּחַת הָהָר: וַיִּקַּח אֶת־הָעֵגֶל אֲשֶׁר עָשׂוּ וַיִּשְׂרֹף בָּאֵשׁ וַיִּטְחַן עַד
כא אֲשֶׁר־דָּק וַיִּזֶר עַל־פְּנֵי הַמַּיִם וַיַּשְׁקְ אֶת־בְּנֵי יִשְׂרָאֵל: וַיֹּאמֶר מֹשֶׁה אֶל־
כב אַהֲרֹן מֶה־עָשָׂה לְךָ הָעָם הַזֶּה כִּי־הֵבֵאתָ עָלָיו חֲטָאָה גְדֹלָה: וַיֹּאמֶר אַהֲרֹן
כג אַל־יִחַר אַף אֲדֹנִי אַתָּה יָדַעְתָּ אֶת־הָעָם כִּי בְרָע הוּא: וַיֹּאמְרוּ לִי עֲשֵׂה־
לָנוּ אֱלֹהִים אֲשֶׁר יֵלְכוּ לְפָנֵינוּ כִּי־זֶה ׀ מֹשֶׁה הָאִישׁ אֲשֶׁר הֶעֱלָנוּ מֵאֶרֶץ
כד מִצְרַיִם לֹא יָדַעְנוּ מֶה־הָיָה לוֹ: וָאֹמַר לָהֶם לְמִי זָהָב הִתְפָּרָקוּ וַיִּתְּנוּ־לִי

---

19. וַיַּרְא אֶת הָעֵגֶל וּמְחֹלֹת וַיִּחַר אַף מֹשֶׁה — *And he saw the calf and the dancing, and Moses' anger was kindled.* When he saw that they were happy in their disgrace, similar to, כִּי רָעָתֵכִי אָז תַּעֲלֹזִי, *When you do evil then you rejoice (Jeremiah* 11:15), this angered him and he despaired that he would be able to repair the crooked in a manner that they would return to their perfection and be worthy (to receive) those tablets.

21. כִּי הֵבֵאתָ עָלָיו חֲטָאָה גְדֹלָה — *That you have brought a great sin upon them.* They rejoiced in their disgrace with dance because you fixed a feast for them on the morrow, and that is more evil than the transgression and rebellion in making the calf; for this he had to ask mercy even more so (than he did on the mountain — verses 11-13), as it says, אַתֶּם חֲטָאתֶם חֲטָאָה גְדֹלָה, *You have sinned a great sin* (verse 30), and also in his prayer he said, 'אָנָּא חָטָא הָעָם הַזֶּה חֲטָאָה גְדֹלָה', *This people has sinned a great sin'* (v. 31). Also in the order of the thirteen attributes he mentions *iniquity, transgression and sin* (34:7), and also in his prayer there, וְסָלַחְתָּ לַעֲוֹנֵנוּ וּלְחַטָּאתֵנוּ, *and pardon our iniquity and our sin* (ibid. 9). Therefore he said (to Aaron), 'Although they gathered against you and compelled you to make the calf for them, what did they do to you that you (felt it) necessary to fix a feast for them on the morrow? For that was the cause of the dancing which they (did do) to rejoice with the calf — (and this) was worse than the making of it!'

22. כִּי בְרָע הוּא — *That they are set on evil.* They were already inclined to evil, (for they were) attached (joined) to the idolatry of Egypt.

24. וָאֹמַר לָהֶם לְמִי זָהָב — *And I said to them, 'Who has gold?'* I diverted (lit., 'placed') them to the infeasible, for there was no ready gold (at hand).

הִתְפָּרָקוּ וַיִּתְּנוּ לִי — *They removed it and gave it to me.* And they contributed the gold quickly.

NOTES

19. וַיַּרְא אֶת הָעֵגֶל וּמְחֹלֹת וַיִּחַר אַף מֹשֶׁה — *And he saw the calf and the dancing, and Moses' anger was kindled.* One may excuse man for transgressing by rationalizing that he did so in a moment of weakness or passion. However when that is the case, the sinner is contrite after he has sinned. To rejoice, however, is an indication that he is happy in his deviate act; hence there is little hope that he will repent. When Moses saw the dancing he despaired of their eventual penitence and therefore he broke the tablets, for they were not worthy to receive them.

21. כִּי הֵבֵאתָ עָלָיו חֲטָאָה גְדֹלָה — *That you have brought a great sin upon them.* Extending his interpretation on verse 19, regarding the happiness demonstrated by the sinners in their new god, the *Sforno* explains that this was the thrust of Moses' admonition of his brother. Moses felt that the declaration by Aaron of a *feast to God on the morrow* sanctioned the

כה וָֽאַשְׁלִכֵ֥הוּ בָאֵ֖שׁ וַיֵּצֵ֥א הָעֵ֖גֶל הַזֶּֽה׃ וַיַּ֤רְא מֹשֶׁה֙ אֶת־הָעָ֔ם כִּ֥י פָרֻ֖עַ ה֑וּא
כו כִּֽי־פְרָעֹ֣ה אַהֲרֹ֔ן לְשִׁמְצָ֖ה בְּקָמֵיהֶֽם׃ וַיַּעֲמֹ֤ד מֹשֶׁה֙ בְּשַׁ֣עַר הַֽמַּחֲנֶ֔ה וַיֹּ֕אמֶר מִ֥י
כז לַֽיהוָ֖ה אֵלָ֑י וַיֵּאָסְפ֥וּ אֵלָ֖יו כָּל־בְּנֵ֥י לֵוִֽי׃ וַיֹּ֣אמֶר לָהֶ֗ם כֹּֽה־אָמַ֤ר יהוה֙ אֱלֹהֵ֣י
יִשְׂרָאֵ֔ל שִׂ֥ימוּ אִישׁ־חַרְבּ֖וֹ עַל־יְרֵכ֑וֹ עִבְר֨וּ וָשׁ֜וּבוּ מִשַּׁ֤עַר לָשַׁ֙עַר֙ בַּֽמַּחֲנֶ֔ה

וָאַשְׁלִכֵהוּ בָאֵשׁ — *And I cast it into the fire.* I attempted to delay the matter, so I threw the gold into the fire without using any of the goldsmith's devices necessary to melt (and refine) the gold.

וַיֵּצֵא הָעֵגֶל הַזֶּה — *And there came out this calf.* Without my (overt) act, and they did not wait for me to do as they had said (requested); for indeed when it says, וַיַּעֲשֵׂהוּ עֵגֶל מַסֵּכָה, *And make it into a molten calf* (v. 4), it does not refer to Aaron but it means whosoever did make it, similar to, וְסָמַךְ אֶת יָדוֹ . . . וְשָׁחַט, *and he shall lay his hand . . . and he shall slaughter (Leviticus* 3:8) which means: *He who brings the offering shall lay, etc., the one who slaughters shall kill, etc.* and so (the Torah) attests, saying, אֲשֶׁר עָשׂוּ אֶת הָעֵגֶל אֲשֶׁר עָשָׂה אַהֲרֹן, *Who made the calf which Aaron made* (v. 35), i.e., they made the calf from which Aaron had done his work; the fashioning and casting the gold into the fire.

25. כִּי פָרֻעַ הוּא — *That they were uncovered.* The inclination (lit., 'heart') of the (people) to evil was revealed and made known through this (i.e., the calf).

כִּי פְרָעֹה אַהֲרֹן — *For Aaron had uncovered them.* He had revealed that there were no righteous men among them, for if there had been righteous ones there to help Aaron when (the people) gathered against him, Aaron would not have made the calf at all.

לְשִׁמְצָה בְּקָמֵיהֶם — *For a derision among their adversaries.* (They will now be) an ignominy among their enemies, who will (now) say of them that they are not loyal to their covenant and there is not even one among them who does good; nor did they show favor to a prophet or leader in their midst. This (will be said) for although not all, or even the majority of them, rose up against Aaron still they will all be derided because they did not protest against those who did.

27. עִבְרוּ וָשׁוּבוּ מִשַּׁעַר לָשַׁעַר — *Go to and fro from gate to gate.* This will atone for

NOTES

making of the calf thereby precipitating their celebration. It is this rejoicing with idolatry which is called *a great sin,* more serious than the actual making of the calf. In his commentary on 34:7 the *Sforno* explains the word חַטָּאָה, *sin,* as meaning 'additional angering (of God)' which is engendered by rejoicing in one's transgression and iniquity.

24. וָאַשְׁלִכֵהוּ בָאֵשׁ — *And I cast it into the fire.* Aaron attempted to mitigate his involvement in the making of the calf. In verse 4 the Torah tells us that Aaron did *fashion the gold with a graving tool* and cast it into the fire. However, the Torah does not tell us specifically who the subject is of *and made it into a molten calf,* the word וַיַּעֲשֵׂהוּ being indefinite. The *Sforno* feels that verse 35 casts some light on the identity of those who actually made the Golden Calf; they were men *other* than Aaron who did so with the consent of the people, as he states in his interpretation of that verse.

25. כִּי פְרָעֹה אַהֲרֹן — *For Aaron had uncovered them.* As *Rashi* points out the word פָּרֻעַ means to *uncover* (as we find by the *sotah* whose hair is uncovered). However, whereas *Rashi* explains it to mean that the people's shame and disgrace were revealed, the *Sforno* explains it as revealing that there were no righteous men among Israel prepared to rise to Aaron's defense. This lack of support for Aaron would be derided by the enemies of Israel.

27. עִבְרוּ וָשׁוּבוּ מִשַּׁעַר לָשַׁעַר — *Go to and fro from gate to gate.* To counteract the sin of

כח וְהִרְגוּ אִישׁ־אֶת־אָחִיו וְאִישׁ אֶת־רֵעֵהוּ וְאִישׁ אֶת־קְרֹבוֹ: וַיַּעֲשׂוּ בְנֵי־לֵוִי
כט כִּדְבַר מֹשֶׁה וַיִּפֹּל מִן־הָעָם בַּיּוֹם הַהוּא כִּשְׁלֹשֶׁת אַלְפֵי אִישׁ: וַיֹּאמֶר מֹשֶׁה
מִלְאוּ יֶדְכֶם הַיּוֹם לַיהוָה כִּי אִישׁ בִּבְנוֹ וּבְאָחִיו וְלָתֵת עֲלֵיכֶם הַיּוֹם בְּרָכָה:
ל וַיְהִי מִמָּחֳרָת וַיֹּאמֶר מֹשֶׁה אֶל־הָעָם אַתֶּם חֲטָאתֶם חֲטָאָה גְדֹלָה וְעַתָּה

---

the non-sinners who did not protest against (and prevent) those who did sin. This (atonement shall be) since just as they did not protest against the sinners, so they will (now) not protest against (or prevent) those who kill them!

29. מִלְאוּ יֶדְכֶם הַיּוֹם לַה׳ — *Consecrate* (lit., *fill) your hands today to* HASHEM. Attain perfection (completeness) for your hands today that they be prepared to serve Him in His holy House (Temple).

כִּי אִישׁ בִּבְנוֹ — *For every man 'through' his son.* For each one of you already became holy to God through his son by circumcising (him) in the wilderness!

וּבְאָחִיו — *And against his brothers* ... by killing (him) today and thereby *consecrate your hands* by proper (good) intent and complete your preparation in the service of God.

וְלָתֵת עֲלֵיכֶם הַיּוֹם בְּרָכָה — *That He may also bestow upon you a blessing today.* And also consecrate your hands in a manner that *Hashem*, the Blessed One, give you *a blessing today* by making as your aim the keeping of His judgment and covenant, as it says, כִּי שָׁמְרוּ אִמְרָתֶךָ וּבְרִיתְךָ יִנְצֹרוּ, יוֹרוּ מִשְׁפָּטֶיךָ . . . בָּרֵךְ ה׳ חֵילוֹ וּפֹעַל יָדָיו תִּרְצֶה, *For they have observed Your word and keep Your covenant. They shall teach Your ordinances ... Bless,* HASHEM, *his substance and accept the work of his hands* (*Deut.* 33:9-11).

30. אַתֶּם חֲטָאתֶם חֲטָאָה גְדֹלָה — *You have sinned a great sin.* Recognize the greatness of your sin for indeed through such knowledge there will doubtless be repentance, as it says, כִּי פְשָׁעַי אֲנִי אֵדָע, *for I acknowledge my transgressions* (*Psalms* 51:5), and as it says, אַךְ דְּעִי עֲוֹנֵךְ, *only acknowledge your iniquity* (*Jeremiah* 3:13).

NOTES

apathy and the failure to protest the evil action of a large number of their brethren, it was necessary to balance that inaction with a willingness to support the Levites' punishment of the sinners, if only by not interfering with them. That is why this punishment had to be carried out publicly and openly — not stealthily. Hence they were told to *go to and fro from gate to gate*. The phrase *gate* in the Torah implies *in the open*.

29. מִלְאוּ יֶדְכֶם הַיּוֹם לַה׳ — *Consecrate* (lit., *fill your hands) yourselves today to* HASHEM. The expression מִלְאוּ יֶדְכֶם means to prepare one's self to fulfill a certain charge, to devote one's energies and talents to some purpose. This same expression was used above (28:41) regarding the consecration of the priests. Here it is used for the Levites who through their willingness to avenge the honor of *Hashem* will also become consecrated to God's service — replacing the firstborn who had heretofore been entrusted with that responsibility. By responding to Moses's call of *Whosoever is on* HASHEM*'s side let him come to me* (v. 26), the tribe of Levi prepared themselves for the service of *Hashem* and were blessed by Him. The verses from *Deut.* 33:9-11 refer to the episode related here. See the *Sforno* 28:41.

כִּי אִישׁ בִּבְנוֹ — *For every man 'through' his son.* When the command is given in verse 27 to *slay every man his brother* it is interpreted to mean a half-brother who is from the same mother but a different father, hence a non-Levite since *all* the sons of Levi were loyal to God. However, the phrase אִישׁ בִּבְנוֹ, *every man his son*, is most difficult to comprehend, for is not his son also a Levite? The *Sforno* answers this question in a most original manner. This is

לא אֶעֱלֶה אֶל־יהוה אוּלַי אֲכַפְּרָה בְּעַד חַטַּאתְכֶם: וַיָּשָׁב מֹשֶׁה אֶל־יהוה
לב וַיֹּאמַר אָנָּא חָטָא הָעָם הַזֶּה חֲטָאָה גְדֹלָה וַיַּעֲשׂוּ לָהֶם אֱלֹהֵי זָהָב: וְעַתָּה
לג אִם־תִּשָּׂא חַטָּאתָם וְאִם־אַיִן מְחֵנִי נָא מִסִּפְרְךָ אֲשֶׁר כָּתָבְתָּ: וַיֹּאמֶר יהוה
לד אֶל־מֹשֶׁה מִי אֲשֶׁר חָטָא־לִי אֶמְחֶנּוּ מִסִּפְרִי: וְעַתָּה לֵךְ | נְחֵה אֶת־הָעָם
אֶל אֲשֶׁר־דִּבַּרְתִּי לָךְ הִנֵּה מַלְאָכִי יֵלֵךְ לְפָנֶיךָ וּבְיוֹם פָּקְדִי וּפָקַדְתִּי עֲלֵהֶם

---

32. אִם תִּשָּׂא חַטָּאתָם וְאִם אַיִן מְחֵנִי נָא מִסִּפְרְךָ — *If You will forgive their sin — and if not blot me, I pray You, out of Your book.* Whether You agree to forgive their sins or You do not agree to forgive, blot out my merits from Your book and add it to their account so that they will merit forgiveness.

33. מִי אֲשֶׁר חָטָא לִי אֶמְחֶנּוּ מִסִּפְרִי — *Whosoever has sinned against Me, him will I blot out of My book.* Who is there that sinned against Me, that I should erase his merits from My book so that he shall merit forgiveness for sins — this never ever happened! For the law before Me (Divine judgment) is the reverse; indeed each one must bear punishment for his iniquity, and will receive reward for his merits, for אֵין מִצְוָה מְכַבָּה עֲבֵירָה, *a mitzvah cannot extinguish a transgression (Sotah* 21a); how much more so will I not add *your* merits to *their* account!

34. אֶל אֲשֶׁר דִּבַּרְתִּי לָךְ — *To (the place) of which I have spoken to you.* When I said: אַעֲלֶה אֶתְכֶם מֵעֳנִי מִצְרַיִם, *I will bring you up out of the affliction of Egypt* (3:17), אֶל אֶרֶץ טוֹבָה, *unto a good land* (3:8).

וּבְיוֹם פָּקְדִי — *In the day when I visit ...* when they will continue to sin, as (for example) the sin of the spies.

וּפָקַדְתִּי עֲלֵהֶם חַטָּאתָם — *I will visit their sin upon them ...* this sin — and I will no longer continue to forgive it, similar to, וְאִם רָעָה תִּמָּצֵא בוֹ וָמֵת, *but if wickedness shall be found in him, he shall die (I Kings* 1:52). And so He indicated when He said there (the episode of the spies), עַד אָנָה יְנַאֲצֻנִי הָעָם הַזֶּה, *How long will this people despise Me? (Numbers* 14:11); for after they have persisted in their foolishness they are certain to continue their guilty ways, as our Sages state, 'When a man transgresses and repeats his offense it becomes (as if it were) permitted to him' *(Yoma* 86b).

NOTES

not to be understood as being part of the order to slay, but refers to the fact that the tribe of Levi had already established their credentials of sanctity, self-sacrifice and loyalty to God, since they were the only tribe that circumcised their sons in the wilderness. The sense of this phrase is: Because each man had circumcised his son he is worthy to be chosen to serve God, be it to exterminate the wicked or to serve Him in the Temple.

32-33. אִם תִּשָּׂא חַטָּאתָם וְאִם אַיִן מְחֵנִי נָא מִסִּפְרְךָ ... מִי אֲשֶׁר חָטָא לִי אֶמְחֶנּוּ מִסִּפְרִי — *If You will forgive their sin — and if not blot me, I pray You, out of Your book ... Whosoever has sinned against Me, him will I blot out of My book.* Moses did not ask God to erase him from His book if Israel is not forgiven. Rather he suggested that his merits be *transferred* to the credit of Israel in the hope that this would tilt the scales in their favor and they would be forgiven. God answered that when a person is judged from on High he cannot cancel out his transgressions with his merits *(mitzvos)* but each side of his ledger is independent of the other, i.e., he is rewarded for his *mitzvos* and punished for his sins; how much more so is this true of one person's merits (Moses's) and another's sins (Israel's).

34. וּפָקַדְתִּי עֲלֵהֶם חַטָּאתָם — *I will visit their sin upon them.* Our Sages interpret this verse as meaning that 'no punishment comes upon Israel in which there is not a part of payment for the sin of the Golden Calf' *(Sanhedrin* 102a). The *Sforno* however interprets the verse

לה חַטָּאתָם: וַיִּגֹּף יהוה אֶת־הָעָם עַל אֲשֶׁר עָשׂוּ אֶת־הָעֵגֶל אֲשֶׁר עָשָׂה
לג א אַהֲרֹן: וַיְדַבֵּר יהוה אֶל־מֹשֶׁה לֵךְ עֲלֵה מִזֶּה אַתָּה וְהָעָם
אֲשֶׁר הֶעֱלִיתָ מֵאֶרֶץ מִצְרָיִם אֶל־הָאָרֶץ אֲשֶׁר נִשְׁבַּעְתִּי לְאַבְרָהָם לְיִצְחָק
ב וּלְיַעֲקֹב לֵאמֹר לְזַרְעֲךָ אֶתְּנֶנָּה: וְשָׁלַחְתִּי לְפָנֶיךָ מַלְאָךְ וְגֵרַשְׁתִּי
ג אֶת־הַכְּנַעֲנִי הָאֱמֹרִי וְהַחִתִּי וְהַפְּרִזִּי הַחִוִּי וְהַיְבוּסִי: אֶל־אֶרֶץ זָבַת חָלָב
וּדְבָשׁ כִּי לֹא אֶעֱלֶה בְּקִרְבְּךָ כִּי עַם־קְשֵׁה־עֹרֶף אַתָּה פֶּן־אֲכֶלְךָ בַּדָּרֶךְ:
ד וַיִּשְׁמַע הָעָם אֶת־הַדָּבָר הָרָע הַזֶּה וַיִּתְאַבָּלוּ וְלֹא־שָׁתוּ אִישׁ עֶדְיוֹ עָלָיו:
ה וַיֹּאמֶר יהוה אֶל־מֹשֶׁה אֱמֹר אֶל־בְּנֵי־יִשְׂרָאֵל אַתֶּם עַם־קְשֵׁה־עֹרֶף רֶגַע

---

35. עַל אֲשֶׁר עָשׂוּ אֶת הָעֵגֶל אֲשֶׁר עָשָׂה אַהֲרֹן — *Because they made the calf which Aaron made.* With their consent, the one who made the molten calf brought it forth into actuality (from) that object which Aaron had made when he fashioned it and threw it in the fire, as he (Aaron) attested, saying, 'וַיֵּצֵא הָעֵגֶל הַזֶּה, *and there came out this calf*' (v. 24).

XXXIII

2. וְשָׁלַחְתִּי לְפָנֶיךָ מַלְאָךְ — *And I will send an angel before you.* The *captain of the host of* HASHEM who appeared to Joshua *(Joshua* 5:14).

3. אֶל אֶרֶץ זָבַת חָלָב וּדְבָשׁ — *To a land flowing with milk and honey.* Go up from this place which is dry and desolate and (hence) you are dependent upon miracles for your sustenance of which you are unworthy, and go to a land flowing with milk and honey where you can sustain (yourselves) without (need) for miracles.

כִּי לֹא אֶעֱלֶה בְּקִרְבְּךָ — *For I will not go up in your midst.* Therefore I say, *Go up from here, you and the people* (v. 1) and do not wait to camp or journey according to *Hashem's* word (command).

פֶּן אֲכֶלְךָ בַּדָּרֶךְ — *Lest I consume you on the way.* Because when I dwell in your midst the punishment for your iniquities is far greater.

NOTES

thus: Whenever they will sin against Me in a similar vein, i.e., questioning God or the credibility of Moses such as we find in the incident of the spies *(Numbers* 14), I will have to conclude that they will continue to do so on and on. Therefore I will be constrained to punish them at that time for this sin as well. Indeed at that time God decreed that they would not enter the Land of Israel, a punishment not only for the episode of the spies but for the sin of the Calf as well.

XXXIII

2. וְשָׁלַחְתִּי לְפָנֶיךָ מַלְאָךְ — *And I will send an angel before you.* The *Sforno* in his commentary on verses 12 and 16 states that the mission of this angel began with the entrance of Israel into the Land. His role was a military one for the purpose of expelling the seven nations from Canaan. Therefore the *Sforno* identifies this angel as the *captain of the host of* HASHEM who appeared to Joshua as Israel began the conquest of the Land.

3. כִּי לֹא אֶעֱלֶה בְּקִרְבְּךָ פֶּן אֲכֶלְךָ בַּדָּרֶךְ — *For I will not go up in your midst lest I consume you on the way.* Not only the existence of Israel, but their itinerary in the wilderness was totally in the hands of God. Their food and water were provided by Him miraculously and their travel schedule was determined by God. *At the commandment of* HASHEM *the children of Israel journeyed and at the commandment of* HASHEM *they encamped (Numbers* 9:18). This intimate relationship of God with Israel in the wilderness, though beneficial, was also fraught with a certain danger. When the Almighty is constantly present and directly involved, any transgression becomes magnified and the people are more vulnerable to God's wrath. Hence God told Moses that as a result of the sin of the Golden Calf, He would remove Himself from their midst for they

אֶחָד אֶעֱלֶה בְקִרְבְּךָ וְכִלִּיתִיךָ וְעַתָּה הוֹרֵד עֶדְיְךָ מֵעָלֶיךָ וְאֵדְעָה מָה
ו־ז אֶעֱשֶׂה־לָּךְ: וַיִּתְנַצְּלוּ בְנֵי־יִשְׂרָאֵל אֶת־עֶדְיָם מֵהַר חוֹרֵב: וּמֹשֶׁה יִקַּח אֶת־
הָאֹהֶל וְנָטָה־לוֹ ׀ מִחוּץ לַמַּחֲנֶה הַרְחֵק מִן־הַמַּחֲנֶה וְקָרָא לוֹ אֹהֶל מוֹעֵד
ח וְהָיָה כָּל־מְבַקֵּשׁ יהוה יֵצֵא אֶל־אֹהֶל מוֹעֵד אֲשֶׁר מִחוּץ לַמַּחֲנֶה: וְהָיָה
כְּצֵאת מֹשֶׁה אֶל־הָאֹהֶל יָקוּמוּ כָּל־הָעָם וְנִצְּבוּ אִישׁ פֶּתַח אָהֳלוֹ וְהִבִּיטוּ
ט אַחֲרֵי מֹשֶׁה עַד־בֹּאוֹ הָאֹהֱלָה: וְהָיָה כְּבֹא מֹשֶׁה הָאֹהֱלָה יֵרֵד עַמּוּד הֶעָנָן
י וְעָמַד פֶּתַח הָאֹהֶל וְדִבֶּר עִם־מֹשֶׁה: וְרָאָה כָל־הָעָם אֶת־עַמּוּד הֶעָנָן עֹמֵד
יא פֶּתַח הָאֹהֶל וְקָם כָּל־הָעָם וְהִשְׁתַּחֲווּ אִישׁ פֶּתַח אָהֳלוֹ: וְדִבֶּר יהוה אֶל־
מֹשֶׁה פָּנִים אֶל־פָּנִים כַּאֲשֶׁר יְדַבֵּר אִישׁ אֶל־רֵעֵהוּ וְשָׁב אֶל־הַמַּחֲנֶה

---

5. רֶגַע אֶחָד אֶעֱלֶה בְקִרְבְּךָ וְכִלִּיתִיךָ — *If I go up into your midst for one moment I shall consume you.* You mourn My saying, '*I will not go up in your midst,*' but that is for your good, for if I were to go up in your midst, I would consume you, since you are 'a stiff-necked people' that does not attend (lit., 'turn') to the voice of teachers, even though you *are* prepared (to reach) perfection, with the spiritual preparation you attained standing at Mount Sinai.

וְעַתָּה הוֹרֵד עֶדְיְךָ מֵעָלֶיךָ — *Now take off your ornaments from yourself . . .* i.e., that spiritual preparation given to you at that honored (glorious) station (i.e., when you received the Torah), remove it from yourselves, for God, the Blessed One, once He has given a gift, will not recall it from the recipient without his acquiescence, as our Sages say, 'We have learned, once He has given, He will not take back' (*Taanis* 25a).

וְאֵדְעָה מָה אֶעֱשֶׂה לָּךְ — *That I may know what to do to you.* For then you will not deserve to (receive) such a severe punishment.

7. וְקָרָא לוֹ אֹהֶל מוֹעֵד — *And he called it the Tent of Meeting.* To let it be known that God, the Blessed One, met with him there and not in the Israelite camp.

11. פָּנִים אֶל פָּנִים — *Face to face.* Not, נֹפֵל וּגְלוּי עֵינָיִם, *fallen down, yet with opened eyes (Numbers* 24:4), but while in control of his senses.

כַּאֲשֶׁר יְדַבֵּר אִישׁ אֶל רֵעֵהוּ — *As a man speaks to his friend . . .* and not through riddles.

NOTES

were no longer worthy to be sustained miraculously by God nor to have their movements directed by Him. Although this is meant as retribution for their transgression it also is for their own benefit, since their vulnerability to God's anger would now be lessened and they would also go to the Land of Israel where they would live a normal, natural life, earning their own livelihood and determining their own destiny. This was God's intent at this point, but the sin of the spies prolonged their wandering in the wilderness for many more years.

5. וְעַתָּה הוֹרֵד עֶדְיְךָ מֵעָלֶיךָ — *Now take off your ornaments from yourself.* The *Sforno* continues his commentary on verse 3 in this verse. Israel was told to appreciate that God's departure from the camp was for their own benefit, as was the demand that they remove their ornaments. A person and a people are judged by different standards; the greater one's superiority the more stringent the judgment. The *Sforno* interprets the word עֲדִי as a 'spiritual *ornament*,' namely the special gift of spiritual apprehension of God granted to Israel at Sinai. As such, their punishment for iniquity would be extremely severe. Hence they were told to divest themselves of this unique gift and thereby they would be judged more leniently. The *Sforno* stresses that *they* had to remove this ornament themselves, for once God gives a gift, He does not take it back on His own.

11. פָּנִים אֶל פָּנִים — *Face to face.* See the *Sforno's* commentary 19:9 where he states that

וּמְשָׁרְתוֹ יְהוֹשֻׁעַ בִּן־נוּן נַעַר לֹא יָמִישׁ מִתּוֹךְ הָאֹהֶל:
שלישי יב וַיֹּאמֶר מֹשֶׁה אֶל־יהוה רְאֵה אַתָּה אֹמֵר אֵלַי הַעַל אֶת־הָעָם הַזֶּה וְאַתָּה
לֹא הוֹדַעְתַּנִי אֵת אֲשֶׁר־תִּשְׁלַח עִמִּי וְאַתָּה אָמַרְתָּ יְדַעְתִּיךָ בְשֵׁם וְגַם־
יג מָצָאתָ חֵן בְּעֵינָי: וְעַתָּה אִם־נָא מָצָאתִי חֵן בְּעֵינֶיךָ הוֹדִעֵנִי נָא אֶת־

לֹא יָמִישׁ מִתּוֹךְ הָאֹהֶל — *Departed not out of the tent.* To prevent any Israelite from entering since they were all under rebuke then, and that place (the Tent) was predisposed to the resting of the Divine Presence, similar to, אַל תִּקְרַב הֲלֹם, *do not approach near here (Exodus* 3:5), which was said to Moses since he was not sufficiently (spiritually) prepared at that time (to approach) that place.

12. רְאֵה — *See.* Watch (over us) and do not conceal Your face from us regarding this.

אַתָּה אֹמֵר אֵלַי הַעַל אֶת הָעָם הַזֶּה — *You say to me, 'Bring up this people' . . .* when You said to me, לֵךְ עֲלֵה מִזֶּה אַתָּה וְהָעָם, *Depart, go up from here, you and the people* (v. 1).

וְאַתָּה לֹא הוֹדַעְתַּנִי אֵת אֲשֶׁר תִּשְׁלַח עִמִּי — *And You have not let me know whom You will send with me.* When You said, וְשָׁלַחְתִּי לְפָנֶיךָ מַלְאָךְ וְגֵרַשְׁתִּי, *and I will send an angel before you and I will drive out, etc.* (v. 2), it was understood (as applying) to the time when we shall enter the Land, but en route we will have neither Your Presence nor (that of) an angel.

וְאַתָּה אָמַרְתָּ יְדַעְתִּיךָ בְשֵׁם — *And You said, I know you by name.* And perforce when You placed upon me (the task) to lead them (Israel) on the way, it did not mean (that You were) abandoning them, similar to, וָאֹמַר לֹא אֶרְעֶה אֶתְכֶם הַמֵּתָה תָמוּת וְהַנִּכְחֶדֶת תִּכָּחֵד, *Then I said, I will not be your shepherd; that which dies let it die; and that which is to be cut off, let it be cut off (Zechariah* 11:9), but You desired that I be the messenger who goes before the camp of Israel.

13. וְעַתָּה — *Now, therefore.* And since You have agreed that I should be the (מַלְאָךְ) messenger . . .

הוֹדִעֵנִי נָא אֶת דְּרָכֶךָ — *Show me now Your ways.* Show me (inform me) two of Your wondrous ways: one, how through Your knowledge alone You grant existence to all existence, as is demonstrated in fact; second, (given) Your unimpeachable knowledge of the future, how can there be in the nature (of man) the possible (freedom of) choice?

NOTES

all of Israel merited to reach this special level of prophecy at Sinai, and were able to apprehend and comprehend God without suspending their senses. See notes there. Even Balaam, whom our Sages compare to Moses insofar as his prophetic powers were concerned, was only able to see a vision of the Almighty while in a trance, or in a dream through a medium (see *Rashi* verse 17). The expression *face to face* is explained by the *Rambam* in his *Guide* (I:37) as 'a presence to another presence without an intermediary.'

לֹא יָמִישׁ מִתּוֹךְ הָאֹהֶל — *Departed not out of the tent.* The *Sforno* is referring to the middle forty days (see his commentary to 24:18) when he says, 'they were all under rebuke then.'

12. אַתָּה אֹמֵר אֵלַי . . . אֵת אֲשֶׁר תִּשְׁלַח עִמִּי — *You say to me . . . whom You will send with me.* Moses realized that since the angel appointed by God (v. 2) will not assume his responsibilities until they enter the Land of Israel, hence in the absence of the *Shechinah* (Divine Presence), he (i.e., Moses) is to serve as the מַלְאָךְ, *messenger,* during this interim period. As such he feels it necessary to comprehend God more fully, else how can he function as His messen-

יד דְּרָכֶ֗ךָ וְאֵדָעֲךָ֙ לְמַ֣עַן אֶמְצָא־חֵ֣ן בְּעֵינֶ֔יךָ וּרְאֵ֕ה כִּ֥י עַמְּךָ֖ הַגּ֥וֹי הַזֶּֽה: וַיֹּאמַ֑ר
טו פָּנַ֥י יֵלֵ֖כוּ וַהֲנִחֹ֥תִי לָֽךְ: וַיֹּ֣אמֶר אֵלָ֔יו אִם־אֵ֤ין פָּנֶ֨יךָ֙ הֹלְכִ֔ים אַל־תַּעֲלֵ֖נוּ מִזֶּֽה:

וְאֵדָעֲךָ — *That I may know You.* For indeed through knowledge of actions (manifestation) there is some knowledge of the form from which these manifestations (actions) emanate.

לְמַעַן אֶמְצָא חֵן בְּעֵינֶיךָ — *That I may find grace in Your sight.* For this I will find grace and good favor in the sight of God, as it says, כִּי אִם בְּזֹאת יִתְהַלֵּל הַמִּתְהַלֵּל הַשְׂכֵּל וְיָדֹעַ אוֹתִי ... כִּי בְאֵלֶּה חָפַצְתִּי, *But let him that glories glory in this, that he understands and knows Me ... for in these things I delight (Jeremiah 9:23).*

וּרְאֵה כִּי עַמְּךָ הַגּוֹי הַזֶּה — *And consider that this nation is Your people.* For Your Name is known in their midst, and not among the nations, as it says, נוֹדָע בִּיהוּדָה אֱלֹהִים בְּיִשְׂרָאֵל גָּדוֹל שְׁמוֹ, *In Judah, God is known, His name is great in Israel (Psalms 76:2).* And therefore it is improper that You withhold from me that which I requested, because of their sins, as our Sages say, 'Thirty of them were worthy that the Divine Presence come to rest upon them as (it did) for Moses our Teacher' (Baba Basra 134a).

14. פָּנַי יֵלֵכוּ — *My presence shall go with you.* As you journey to *Eretz Yisrael*, My presence shall go before you but not in your midst.

וַהֲנִחֹתִי לָךְ — *And I will give you rest.* I will give you rest from all your enemies about you, in such a manner that you will bring them to the Land securely.

15. אִם אֵין פָּנֶיךָ הֹלְכִים — *If Your presence does not go.* Now, while we are still encamped. If Your presence, which You removed, does not accompany us to dwell in our midst ...

אַל תַּעֲלֵנוּ מִזֶּה — *Carry us not up from here.* Then it would be better for us to dwell in the wilderness than to enter the Land without your *Shechinah* (Divine Presence), for in such a manner we will, without a doubt, be exiled from it quickly.

NOTES

ger? The *Rambam* in his *Guide* (I:54) explains that Moses made two requests. 'One ... to let him know His essence and true reality. The second request ... was that He should let him know His attributes.' This latter request was granted (see v. 19) but the former was not (see v. 20), according to the *Rambam.* The *Sforno,* however, interprets the two requests differently (see v. 13). As for God's answer see the *Sforno* on verses 19, 20 and 23. Also see the *Sforno* on 25:20 and the Notes there for clarification of וְאֵדָעֲךָ, *that I may know You,* and the finding of favor and grace in God's sight through knowledge of Him.

13. וּרְאֵה כִּי עַמְּךָ הַגּוֹי הַזֶּה — *And consider that this nation is Your people.* The Talmud (*Baba Basra* 134a) relates that the Elder Hillel had eighty pupils of whom thirty were so out-

standing that they were worthy to have the Divine Presence rest on them, but since their generation had sinned, this misconduct prevented it from coming to pass. Moses, however, argued that the sin of the people should not prevent God from granting his request, in spite of their transgression, since God's existence and might was only recognized by Israel among all the nations.

14-15. פָּנַי יֵלֵכוּ ... אַל תַּעֲלֵנוּ מִזֶּה — *My presence shall go with you ... Carry us not up from here.* God responded favorably to Moses' request, but only partially. He would go *before* them to prepare the way to *Eretz Yisrael* but He would not be *in* their midst. Moses was not satisfied, for if Israel would enter the Land without God's presence they would not remain there permanently. Unfortunately his-

טז וּבַמֶּה ׀ יִוָּדַע אֵפוֹא כִּי־מָצָאתִי חֵן בְּעֵינֶיךָ אֲנִי וְעַמֶּךָ הֲלוֹא בְּלֶכְתְּךָ עִמָּנוּ
וְנִפְלֵינוּ אֲנִי וְעַמְּךָ מִכָּל־הָעָם אֲשֶׁר עַל־פְּנֵי הָאֲדָמָה׃
רביעי יז וַיֹּאמֶר יהוה אֶל־מֹשֶׁה גַּם אֶת־הַדָּבָר הַזֶּה אֲשֶׁר דִּבַּרְתָּ אֶעֱשֶׂה כִּי־מָצָאתָ
יח־יט חֵן בְּעֵינַי וָאֵדָעֲךָ בְּשֵׁם׃ וַיֹּאמַר הַרְאֵנִי נָא אֶת־כְּבֹדֶךָ׃ וַיֹּאמֶר אֲנִי אַעֲבִיר
כָּל־טוּבִי עַל־פָּנֶיךָ וְקָרָאתִי בְשֵׁם יהוה לְפָנֶיךָ וְחַנֹּתִי אֶת־אֲשֶׁר אָחֹן

16. וּבַמֶּה יִוָּדַע אֵפוֹא — *For with what shall it be known.* Although we will enter the Land, for the angel will drive out the nations, (but) how will it be known that this was a Divine act? In every war it is customary for one nation to overpower another nation and at times expel them.

הֲלוֹא בְּלֶכְתְּךָ עִמָּנוּ וְנִפְלֵינוּ — *Is it not if You go up with us so that we be distinguished?* Similar to, נָחִיתָ בְחַסְדְּךָ עַם זוּ גָּאָלְתָּ נֵהַלְתָּ בְעָזְּךָ . . . שָׁמְעוּ עַמִּים יִרְגָּזוּן, *With kindness You led this people that You redeemed; You have guided them in Your strength . . . The peoples have heard, they tremble* (15:13,14). For when the nations see that You are with us we shall be in their eyes more wonderful and singular in virtue than all other nations, and they will not strive to rise up against us, as Rahab attested when she said, כִּי שָׁמַעְנוּ אֵת אֲשֶׁר הוֹבִישׁ ה׳ אֶת מֵי יַם סוּף . . . וְלֹא קָמָה עוֹד רוּחַ בְּאִישׁ מִפְּנֵיכֶם כִּי ה׳ אֱלֹהֵיכֶם הוּא אֱלֹהִים בַּשָּׁמַיִם מִמַּעַל וְעַל הָאָרֶץ מִתָּחַת, *For we have heard how HASHEM dried up the waters of the Sea of Reeds . . . neither did there remain any more courage in any man because of you; for HASHEM your God is the God of heaven above and on the earth beneath* (*Joshua* 2:10,11).

18. אֶת כְּבֹדֶךָ — *Your glory . . .* (i.e.,) how all existence draws its existence from Yours, considering the great disparity between them (and You) as it says, מְלֹא כָל הָאָרֶץ כְּבוֹדוֹ, *the whole earth is full of His glory* (*Isaiah* 6:3).

19. אֲנִי אַעֲבִיר כָּל טוּבִי עַל פָּנֶיךָ — *I will make all My goodness pass before you.* This (answer) will not be withheld because I am not gracious, for indeed, *I will pass all My goodness before you.*

וְקָרָאתִי בְשֵׁם ה׳ לְפָנֶיךָ — *And I will proclaim the Name of HASHEM before you.* Behold he who calls in the Name of *HASHEM* is one who makes known and teaches the existence of God, the Blessed One, and His ways of goodness. He therefore says, *I will make all My goodness pass before you* in such a manner that were your faculties of discernment (understanding) sufficient in this (area) you would attain all you desire (— but they are not!). Nonetheless, I will teach you a bit of My ways of goodness, for your benefit, and with this knowledge you will gain some knowledge of My essence (being) as it says, *and stood with Him there and proclaimed the Name of HASHEM* (34:5).

וְחַנֹּתִי אֶת אֲשֶׁר אָחֹן — *And I will be gracious to whom I will be gracious.* I will grant to you that grace which I am wont to give all who find favor in My eyes, which is with an abundant flow, without parsimony or miserliness.

NOTES

tory proved him to be right.

16. הֲלוֹא בְּלֶכְתְּךָ עִמָּנוּ וְנִפְלֵינוּ — *Is it not if You go up with us so that we be distinguished?* The *Sforno* underscores that our distinction as a people, which all the nations recognize, lies in the fact that our power and strength is not our own, but emanates from God alone. Otherwise we are no different than other nations and our unique role in the history of man is forfeit. This is the thrust of Moses' argument that God relent and bring Israel into the Land Himself.

כ וְרִחַמְתִּי אֶת־אֲשֶׁר אֲרַחֵם׃ וַיֹּאמֶר לֹא תוּכַל לִרְאֹת אֶת־פָּנָי כִּי לֹא־יִרְאַנִי
כא־כב הָאָדָם וָחָי׃ וַיֹּאמֶר יהוה הִנֵּה מָקוֹם אִתִּי וְנִצַּבְתָּ עַל־הַצּוּר׃ וְהָיָה בַּעֲבֹר
כג כְּבֹדִי וְשַׂמְתִּיךָ בְּנִקְרַת הַצּוּר וְשַׂכֹּתִי כַפִּי עָלֶיךָ עַד־עָבְרִי׃ וַהֲסִרֹתִי אֶת־
כַּפִּי וְרָאִיתָ אֶת־אֲחֹרָי וּפָנַי לֹא יֵרָאוּ׃
לד חמישי א וַיֹּאמֶר יהוה אֶל־מֹשֶׁה פְּסָל־לְךָ שְׁנֵי־לֻחֹת אֲבָנִים כָּרִאשֹׁנִים וְכָתַבְתִּי עַל־

וְרִחַמְתִּי אֶת אֲשֶׁר אֲרַחֵם — *And I will show mercy to whom I will show mercy.* I will have mercy on you that you shall not perish from the lightning flash of My glory, as it is My wont to show mercy to all who are proper and worthy of this (privilege), as it says, וְשַׂכֹּתִי כַפִּי עָלֶיךָ עַד עָבְרִי, *and I will cover you with My hand until I have passed by* (v. 22).

20. וַיֹּאמֶר לֹא תוּכַל לִרְאֹת — *And He said, 'You cannot see.'* This will not be impossible (lit., 'denied you') because of any lack in My manifestation but due to a deficiency in your (ability to) receive, for you will be unable to receive the outpouring of the Light.

21. הִנֵּה מָקוֹם אִתִּי — *Behold there is a place by Me.* A place ready for the vision of God, as our Sages say regarding the cave wherein Moses and Elijah stood. (This cave) is one of the ten things created on the sixth day at twilight (בֵּין הַשְּׁמָשׁוֹת) (*Pesachim* 54a).

23. וְרָאִיתָ אֶת אֲחֹרָי — *And you shall see My back.* You will see the action (manifestation) of that which is lower (inferior) to Me.

וּפָנַי לֹא יֵרָאוּ — *But My face shall not be seen.* But none, beside Me, shall see how the existence of everything draws its existence from My existence, as you requested.

NOTES

19-20. אֲנִי אַעֲבִיר כָּל טוּבִי עַל פָּנֶיךָ . . . וְרִחַמְתִּי אֶת אֲשֶׁר אֲרַחֵם . . . וַיֹּאמֶר לֹא תוּכַל לִרְאֹת — *I will make all My goodness pass before you . . . And I will show mercy to whom I will show mercy . . . And He said, 'You cannot see.'* The sense of the *Sforno's* interpretation of this verse is as follows: God, being gracious, was prepared to comply with the request of Moses — to make *His ways* known to him. However, the limitations of man, including even a Moses, are such that he is not able to grasp *all* that God is willing to reveal. Nonetheless, through the manifestation of His deeds, man can comprehend a bit of God's being and essence. When God agreed to reveal Himself to Moses (albeit minimally) there was also a need for mercy, since the intensity of the Divine light is so great that a human being is endangered by it, hence there was a need for God's 'protective hand.'

21. הִנֵּה מָקוֹם אִתִּי — *Behold there is a place by Me.* The Sages in *Avos* (5:9) list certain things created on the eve of the Sabbath בֵּין הַשְּׁמָשׁוֹת, *at twilight.* That list does not mention the cave where Moses and Elijah both stood to catch a glimpse of the Almighty. However, in tractate *Pesachim* 54a this cave is included among the ten things created at that time.

23. וְרָאִיתָ אֶת אֲחֹרָי וּפָנַי לֹא יֵרָאוּ — *And you shall see My back, but My face shall not be seen.* The *Rambam* in his *Guide* (I:21,38) interprets the phrase פָּנַי *(My face)* as meaning a certain apprehension of God which Moses requested but which was not granted. Rather he was shown a relatively 'inferior' apprehension, which is designated as אֲחֹרָי *(My back).* The *Rambam* also interprets *back* as meaning that which follows from God's will, 'all things created by Me.' The *Sforno* combines these two interpretations of the *Rambam*, interpreting אֲחֹרָי as referring to the actions of God which manifest His being but are not to be understood as His essence, which is far superior. This concept is also found in the *Guide* (I:53) where the *Rambam* states, 'Every attribute (of God) is an attribute of His action and not an attribute of His essence.' The *Sforno*, however, interprets the expression פָּנִים

ב הַלֻּחֹת אֶת־הַדְּבָרִים אֲשֶׁר הָיוּ עַל־הַלֻּחֹת הָרִאשֹׁנִים אֲשֶׁר שִׁבַּרְתָּ: וֶהְיֵה
נָכוֹן לַבֹּקֶר וְעָלִיתָ בַבֹּקֶר אֶל־הַר סִינַי וְנִצַּבְתָּ לִי שָׁם עַל־רֹאשׁ הָהָר:
ג וְאִישׁ לֹא־יַעֲלֶה עִמָּךְ וְגַם־אִישׁ אַל־יֵרָא בְּכָל־הָהָר גַּם־הַצֹּאן וְהַבָּקָר אַל־
ד יִרְעוּ אֶל־מוּל הָהָר הַהוּא: וַיִּפְסֹל שְׁנֵי־לֻחֹת אֲבָנִים כָּרִאשֹׁנִים וַיַּשְׁכֵּם
מֹשֶׁה בַבֹּקֶר וַיַּעַל אֶל־הַר סִינַי כַּאֲשֶׁר צִוָּה יְהוָה אֹתוֹ וַיִּקַּח בְּיָדוֹ שְׁנֵי לֻחֹת
ה־ו אֲבָנִים: וַיֵּרֶד יְהוָה בֶּעָנָן וַיִּתְיַצֵּב עִמּוֹ שָׁם וַיִּקְרָא בְשֵׁם יְהוָה: וַיַּעֲבֹר יְהוָה
׀ עַל־פָּנָיו וַיִּקְרָא יְהוָה ׀ יְהוָה אֵל רַחוּם וְחַנּוּן אֶרֶךְ אַפַּיִם וְרַב־חֶסֶד וֶאֱמֶת:

XXXIV

5. וַיִּתְיַצֵּב עִמּוֹ שָׁם — *And stood with Him there.* Moses stood with God, the Blessed One, as He had said to him, וְנִצַּבְתָּ לִי שָׁם, *and stand there with Me* (v. 2).

וַיִּקְרָא — *And proclaimed.* God, the Blessed One (proclaimed).

בְּשֵׁם ה׳ — *In the Name of HASHEM* . . . a proclamation making known the Divine actions (attributes).

6. וַיִּקְרָא — *And proclaimed.* God, The Blessed One (proclaimed).

ה׳ ה׳ — *HASHEM, HASHEM.* He is the Cause, Who made of 'nothing something' *(ex nihilo)* and He sustains the existence of all that exists, for there is no preservation of any existence except for that which flows (emanates) from His existence.

אֵל — *God* . . . capable of all actions which are according to His will, (this being) the opposite of actions which extend from a natural force which do so out of necessity, not due to free choice.

רחום — *Merciful* . . . to those who are guilty, lightening their punishment when they call out to Him, as it says, פְּנֵי ה׳ בְּעֹשֵׂי רָע . . . צָעֲקוּ וַה׳ שָׁמֵעַ, *The face of HASHEM is against those who do evil . . . they cry out and HASHEM hears (Psalms* 34:17,18). And He (also) sees the affliction of the oppressed, as (we find), *Moreover I have seen the oppression* (3:9).

NOTES

(face) as referring to God's existence from which all existence emanates, and this no man can hope to comprehend.

XXXIV

5. וַיִּתְיַצֵּב עִמּוֹ שָׁם — *And stood with Him there.* Although God is the subject of the verbs וַיֵּרֶד, *and He descended,* and וַיִּקְרָא, *and He proclaimed* or *called,* the subject of וַיִּתְיַצֵּב, *and he stood,* is Moses. The reason for the *Sforno's* interpretation is that the word is identical to that in verse 2 where God specifically commanded Moses to *stand* on the top of the mountain.

6. וַיִּקְרָא ה׳ ה׳ — *And proclaimed, 'HASHEM, HASHEM.'* The Sages tell us that these verses (6-7) comprise the י״ג מִדּוֹת, *thirteen attributes of God.* Each of His names represents a different aspect of His Being as do the various descriptive terms of His actions, such as merciful, gracious, etc. The *Sforno* explains each of these names and terms in his commentary on these two verses. The repetition of *HASHEM, HASHEM,* is explained in a different vein than that of *Rashi* (quoting the Talmud, *Rosh Hashanah* 17) who states 'the attribute of mercy applies before a man sins and after he sins.' The *Sforno* explains the dual usage as indicating two aspects of God's omnipotence — one as the Creator *ex nihilo* and secondly as the One Who grants, in an ongoing fashion, existence to all He has created.

אֵל — *God.* Regarding the name אֵל, *God,* the *Sforno* departs from *Rashi's* interpretation that this name is also one of mercy and compassion. The *Sforno,* as do some other

ז נֹצֵר חֶסֶד לָאֲלָפִים נֹשֵׂא עָוֺן וָפֶשַׁע וְחַטָּאָה וְנַקֵּה לֹא יְנַקֶּה פֹּקֵד ׀ עֲוֺן אָבוֹת

וְחַנּוּן — *And gracious.* He is gracious and good to (i.e., rewards) those who beseech Him even though they are not (fully) deserving.

אֶרֶךְ אַפַּיִם — *Long-suffering* ... to the righteous and to the wicked so that they might repent (*Baba Kamma* 50b).

וְרַב חֶסֶד — *And abundant in loving-kindness.* Tilting (the scale) toward loving-kindness when one is judged, as our Sages say, 'He forgives the very first (sin) and that is (His) attribute' (*Rosh Hashanah* 17a).

וֶאֱמֶת — *And truth.* And abundant truth. He is long-suffering but collects His due (*Midrash Bereishis Rabbah* 67:4), as our Sages say, 'The sin itself is not forgiven' (*Rosh Hashanah* 17a), and as it says, אֲשֶׁר לֹא יִשָּׂא פָנִים, *Who regards not persons* (*Deut.* 10:17); 'Abraham cannot save Ishmael nor can Isaac save Esau' (*Sanhedrin* 104a); וְלֹא יִקַּח שׁוֹחַד, *nor takes bribe* (*Deut.* 10:17); 'A mitzvah does not extinguish a transgression' (*Sotah* 21a).

7. נֹצֵר חֶסֶד לָאֲלָפִים — *Keeping mercy (kindness) to the thousands.* He guards (keeps) the merit of fathers for the sons, to do good for the sons because of their fathers.

נֹשֵׂא עָוֺן — *Forgiving iniquity* ... (a sin committed) with premeditation.

וָפֶשַׁע — *And transgression* ... (a sin committed) as rebellion against the kingdom (of heaven).

וְחַטָּאָה — *And sin* ... provocation added to rebellion, similar to כִּי רָעָתֵכִי אָז תַּעֲלֹזִי, *When you do evil then you rejoice* (*Jeremiah* 11:15). However, the forgiveness of one is not similar to the other, without a doubt, therefore these attributes are enumerated separately.

NOTES

commentators, interprets it as indicating God's infinite power whose every action represents His freedom of will, whereas the natural forces He created function according to the ways ordained by the Almighty at the time of creation, be it the sun, moon, planets, etc., which cannot choose to function or to cease operating.

רַחוּם וְחַנּוּן — *Merciful and gracious.* Mercy (רַחוּם) indicates a disposition to forgive or forbear. Hence it is applicable to one who has sinned and is guilty. He will be punished but God's attribute of mercy will lighten the punishment. The phrase חַנּוּן implies *grace*, the freely given unmerited favor of God; hence it relates to one who is not fully guilty yet not fully deserving of forbearance either.

אֶרֶךְ אַפַּיִם — *Long suffering.* The Hebrew term אַפַּיִם is in the plural, implying that God's patience and forbearance is extended to two categories of people. One is the righteous, who are also in need of this attribute, the second being the wicked — for both are in need of repentance.

וְרַב חֶסֶד וֶאֱמֶת — *And abundant in loving-kindness and truth.* The Talmud (*Rosh Hashanah* 17a) cited by the *Sforno* refers to a בֵּינוֹנִי, *an average person,* whose actions are half *mitzvos* and half transgressions. By removing the first sin from the scale of justice, God causes the scale to tilt in the merit of that individual. However, if the sins still outweigh the merits, then that first sin is placed back on the scale. This is the meaning of וֶאֱמֶת, *and truth,* for the initial transgression is only *set aside* but not *cancelled.* Coupled with God's loving-kindness is His insistence that justice be done. The two are delicately balanced by Him in His infinite wisdom.

7. נֹשֵׂא עָוֺן וָפֶשַׁע וְחַטָּאָה — *Forgiving iniquity and transgression and sin. Rashi,* basing himself on the Talmud (*Yoma* 36), distinguishes between עָוֺן and פֶּשַׁע — the former being a premeditated sin, while the latter implies a sin

ח עַל־בָּנִים וְעַל־בְּנֵי בָנִים עַל־שִׁלֵּשִׁים וְעַל־רִבֵּעִים: וַיְמַהֵר מֹשֶׁה וַיִּקֹּד
ט אַרְצָה וַיִּשְׁתָּחוּ: וַיֹּאמֶר אִם־נָא מָצָאתִי חֵן בְּעֵינֶיךָ אֲדֹנָי יֵלֶךְ־נָא אֲדֹנָי
בְּקִרְבֵּנוּ כִּי עַם־קְשֵׁה־עֹרֶף הוּא וְסָלַחְתָּ לַעֲוֹנֵנוּ וּלְחַטָּאתֵנוּ וּנְחַלְתָּנוּ:

וְנַקֵּה לֹא יְנַקֶּה — *And clear, He will not clear.* Although He will clear those who repent (from a motivation of) love, which is the repentance that 'reaches to the throne of glory' (*Yoma* 86a), as our Sages state, 'iniquities are considered as merits' (*Yoma* 86b), and of whom is said, חָיוֹ יִחְיֶה, *he shall surely live* (*Ezekiel* 33:15), nonetheless *He will not clear* even those who repent, if their repentance (is motivated) only by fear of punishment, as our Sages say, 'sins of premeditation are considered as sins committed in error' (ibid.), as it is written: כִּי כָשַׁלְתָּ בַּעֲוֺנֶךָ, *for you have stumbled in your iniquity* (*Hosea* 14:2).

פֹּקֵד עֲוֹן אָבוֹת עַל בָּנִים — *Visiting the iniquity of the fathers upon the children.* He waits to destroy the wicked of the land until their measure is full. (Now) this fullness comes when their iniquity reaches a level of evil where there is no hope of repentance. This occurs most often when their wickedness persists over successive generations.

עַל שִׁלֵּשִׁים — *Unto the third (generation)* . . . if the later generation is more wicked than their fathers, similar to, וַיַּקְשׁוּ אֶת עָרְפָּם, הֵרֵעוּ מֵאֲבוֹתָם, *but stiffened their neck, they did worse than their fathers* (*Jeremiah* 7:26).

וְעַל רִבֵּעִים — *And unto the fourth (generation).* If they do not add, but persist (in doing evil).

8. וַיְמַהֵר מֹשֶׁה — *And Moses made haste.* An added (dimension of) submissiveness; for indeed (when one) hastens to bow down it indicates the great (importance) of the one to whom he is bowing, as our Sages say, 'When Rav Sheshes bowed (at מוֹדִים) he bowed like a stick' (*Berachos* 12b).

9. כִּי עַם קְשֵׁה עֹרֶף הוּא — *For it is a stiff-necked people.* And they will certainly sin, and even though by accompanying us the iniquity of the generation will be greater,

NOTES

committed with malice aforethought to rebel against God. The word חַטָּאָה, however, is not translated by *Rashi*. The *Sforno*, consistent with his commentary on the sin of the Golden Calf (32:21), interprets this phrase to mean the sin added to iniquity and transgression by rejoicing, rather than regretting one's sinful actions.

וְנַקֵּה לֹא יְנַקֶּה — *And clear, He will not clear.* The Talmud addresses itself to the seeming self-contradictory nature of the phrase — *clear, not clear* — and explains that it depends on the action of the sinner as to whether he repents or not. The *Sforno* elaborates on this interpretation and comments that even if one repents, his motivation is a determining factor. תְּשׁוּבָה מֵאַהֲבָה, *repentance motivated by love*, transforms sins into merits while תְּשׁוּבָה מִיִּרְאָה, *repentance motivated by fear*, can only transform iniquities into שׁוֹגֵג, as though they were non-premeditated, hence the punishment will be lighter.

פֹּקֵד עֲוֹן אָבוֹת עַל בָּנִים עַל שִׁלֵּשִׁים וְעַל רִבֵּעִים — *Visiting the iniquity of the fathers upon the children unto the third (generation) and unto the fourth (generation).* God does not punish the sinner immediately. He waits patiently in the hope that he will repent. When that hope proves to be false, God will still wait until the third or fourth generation to exact retribution. If the descendants add to the wickedness of their ancestors, the third generation will be punished; if they only persist but do not add, God will wait until the fourth generation.

8. וַיְמַהֵר מֹשֶׁה — *And Moses made haste.* A stick descends quickly in one fell swoop. Compare this *Sforno* to *Genesis* 18:2 and 24:20.

9. כִּי עַם קְשֵׁה עֹרֶף הוּא — *For it is a stiff-necked people.* Although Israel will be more vulnera-

ששי י וַיֹּאמֶר הִנֵּה אָנֹכִי כֹּרֵת בְּרִית נֶגֶד כָּל־עַמְּךָ אֶעֱשֶׂה נִפְלָאֹת אֲשֶׁר לֹא־
נִבְרְאוּ בְכָל־הָאָרֶץ וּבְכָל־הַגּוֹיִם וְרָאָה כָל־הָעָם אֲשֶׁר־אַתָּה בְקִרְבּוֹ אֶת־
יא מַעֲשֵׂה יהוה כִּי־נוֹרָא הוּא אֲשֶׁר אֲנִי עֹשֶׂה עִמָּךְ: שְׁמָר־לְךָ אֵת אֲשֶׁר אָנֹכִי
מְצַוְּךָ הַיּוֹם הִנְנִי גֹרֵשׁ מִפָּנֶיךָ אֶת־הָאֱמֹרִי וְהַכְּנַעֲנִי וְהַחִתִּי וְהַפְּרִזִּי וְהַחִוִּי
יב וְהַיְבוּסִי: הִשָּׁמֶר לְךָ פֶּן־תִּכְרֹת בְּרִית לְיוֹשֵׁב הָאָרֶץ אֲשֶׁר אַתָּה בָּא עָלֶיהָ
יג פֶּן־יִהְיֶה לְמוֹקֵשׁ בְּקִרְבֶּךָ: כִּי אֶת־מִזְבְּחֹתָם תִּתֹּצוּן וְאֶת־מַצֵּבֹתָם תְּשַׁבֵּרוּן
יד וְאֶת־אֲשֵׁרָיו תִּכְרֹתוּן: כִּי לֹא תִשְׁתַּחֲוֶה לְאֵל אַחֵר כִּי יהוה קַנָּא שְׁמוֹ אֵל

---

as You said, 'רֶגַע אֶחָד אֶעֱלֶה בְקִרְבְּךָ וְכִלִּיתִיךָ, *If I go up in your midst for one moment I shall consume you'* (33:5), nonetheless it is better for us that You accompany us . . .

וְסָלַחְתָּ לַעֲוֹנֵנוּ — *And pardon our iniquity* . . . for pardon is Yours and we can hope to (receive) Your forgiveness. But let not an angel accompany us, even though the sin of rebellion against him will be lesser; still, there is (also) no hope of pardon with him, as You (Yourself) said, כִּי לֹא יִשָּׂא לְפִשְׁעֲכֶם, *For he will not pardon your transgression* (23:21).

10. הִנֵּה אָנֹכִי כֹּרֵת בְּרִית — *Behold I make a covenant.* To be in your midst, as (our Sages) said, 'They were exiled to Babylonia and the *Shechinah* (Divine Presence) was with them; when they were exiled to Elam the *Shechinah* was with them; they were exiled to Edom and the *Shechinah* was with them' (*Megillah* 29a).

נֶגֶד כָּל עַמְּךָ אֶעֱשֶׂה נִפְלָאֹת — *Before all your people I will do marvels.* When they will pray invoking (lit., 'through') these attributes.

וְרָאָה כָל הָעָם אֲשֶׁר אַתָּה בְקִרְבּוֹ — *And all the people, in whose midst you are, shall see.* However, the awesome work of God in the presence of all the people will only be in the sight of those people in whose midst you (Moses) are, (they alone) will see the *works of* HASHEM.

אֲשֶׁר אֲנִי עֹשֶׂה עִמָּךְ — *That I do with you* . . . in your merit, as it says, כִּי מָצָאתָ חֵן בְּעֵינַי וָאֵדָעֲךָ בְּשֵׁם, *For you have found grace in My sight and I know you by name* (33:17).

11. שְׁמָר לְךָ אֵת אֲשֶׁר אָנֹכִי מְצַוְּךָ הַיּוֹם — *Observe, you, that which I am commanding you this day.* I not only warn you not to *change your glory for that which does not profit (Jeremiah* 2:11), but I also caution you not to allow others to worship (any god) except Me.

14. כִּי לֹא תִשְׁתַּחֲוֶה לְאֵל אַחֵר — *For you shall bow down to no other god.* Therefore you shall break down his altar and show him no favor for you shall honor no other god but Me.

NOTES

ble if God accompanies them, still the advantage of God's presence and His power of forgiveness outweigh the drawbacks. As *Rashi* points out, the word כִּי in the context of this verse is the reason for Moses' request — i.e., precisely *because* they are stiff-necked they need Your presence.

10. וְרָאָה כָל הָעָם אֲשֶׁר אַתָּה בְקִרְבּוֹ . . . אֲשֶׁר אֲנִי עֹשֶׂה עִמָּךְ — *And all the people, in whose midst you are, shall see . . . that I do with you.* Although God will always answer Israel when they invoke the י״ג מִדּוֹת (as we do in our prayers to this very day), the awesome wonders will only be witnessed by Israel in the generation of Moses, for they were performed only in his merit.

11. שְׁמָר לְךָ אֵת אֲשֶׁר אָנֹכִי מְצַוְּךָ הַיּוֹם — *Observe, you, that which I am commanding you this*

טו קַנָּא הוּא: פֶּן־תִּכְרֹת בְּרִית לְיוֹשֵׁב הָאָרֶץ וְזָנוּ ׀ אַחֲרֵי אֱלֹהֵיהֶם וְזָבְחוּ
טז לֵאלֹהֵיהֶם וְקָרָא לְךָ וְאָכַלְתָּ מִזִּבְחוֹ: וְלָקַחְתָּ מִבְּנֹתָיו לְבָנֶיךָ וְזָנוּ בְנֹתָיו
יז אַחֲרֵי אֱלֹהֵיהֶן וְהִזְנוּ אֶת־בָּנֶיךָ אַחֲרֵי אֱלֹהֵיהֶן: אֱלֹהֵי מַסֵּכָה לֹא
יח תַעֲשֶׂה־לָּךְ: אֶת־חַג הַמַּצּוֹת תִּשְׁמֹר שִׁבְעַת יָמִים תֹּאכַל מַצּוֹת אֲשֶׁר

כִּי ה׳ קַנָּא שְׁמוֹ — *For HASHEM's Name is Jealous.* Because His Name indicates a category of an Existent which is inapplicable to any other existent save Him, therefore . . .

אֵל קַנָּא הוּא — *A jealous God is He . . .* (Who) will punish anyone who serves another (god) together with Him.

15. פֶּן תִּכְרֹת בְּרִית — *Lest you make a covenant.* And the reason I said (that) you shall not make a covenant with the inhabitants of the land is because if you are (joined) with him in a covenant you will be misled (to follow) another god, in one of two ways: If he invites you to eat of his sacrifice, you will serve his god together with him, so as to satisfy his desire; (or) you will do it because of love for women, as occurred at Peor (*Numbers* 22:5).

17. אֱלֹהֵי מַסֵּכָה — *Molten gods.* These (refer to) talismen which were made at certain known hours in conjunction with certain stars. They were made molten so that the various parts of those symbols should (combine) together at that moment. Those who made them thought that they would attain their (desired) material and bodily needs (through them). Now perhaps one might think that this (practice) was not a rebellion against God, the Blessed One, since the participant did not accept it upon himself as a god, but (nonetheless) this is indeed contrary to His will, for He does not want His worshipers to turn for help to any god but Him, as it says, וַאֲנַחְנוּ לֹא נֵדַע מַה נַּעֲשֶׂה כִּי עָלֶיךָ עֵינֵינוּ, *We know not what to do, but our eyes are upon You* (*II Chronicles* 20:12).

18. אֶת חַג הַמַּצּוֹת תִּשְׁמֹר — *The Feast of Matzos you shall keep.* After mentioning the prohibition of molten gods, through whom their makers thought to attain their temporal needs (lit., 'life of the hour'), (the Torah) makes mention of those commandments from which various imagined success will result: the ripening, the harvest, the ingathering and matters of possessions. These are arranged in this chapter according to the order that they were (first) given to Israel. The first of them is the Feast of Matzos, at the time appointed in the month of *Aviv* when the ripening is blessed. Second is the subject of the firstborn, through whom the flocks are blessed, and this commandment was after the Feast of Matzos immediately after the exodus from Egypt. Third is the commandment of the Sabbath which was given

NOTES

day. Although God had already prohibited the bowing down to other gods (23:24), the admonition here is not redundant for it adds the warning of not allowing others to do so as well.

17. אֱלֹהֵי מַסֵּכָה — *Molten gods.* A talisman was an object engraved with magical symbols purported to bring luck or protection to its bearer. As the *Sforno* explains, this prohibition was necessary, although God had already cautioned them not to worship other gods, because these objects were not considered deities. Nonetheless they are forbidden for the reason given by the *Sforno.*

18-26. אֶת חַג הַמַּצּוֹת תִּשְׁמֹר . . . לֹא תְבַשֵּׁל גְּדִי . . . — *The feast of Matzos you shall keep . . . You shall not boil a kid . . .* The sequence of these verses is difficult to comprehend. The three

יט צִוִּיתִךָ לְמוֹעֵד חֹדֶשׁ הָאָבִיב כִּי בְּחֹדֶשׁ הָאָבִיב יָצָאתָ מִמִּצְרָיִם: כָּל־פֶּטֶר
כ רֶחֶם לִי וְכָל־מִקְנְךָ תִּזָּכָר פֶּטֶר שׁוֹר וָשֶׂה: וּפֶטֶר חֲמוֹר תִּפְדֶּה בְשֶׂה וְאִם־
כא לֹא תִפְדֶּה וַעֲרַפְתּוֹ כֹּל בְּכוֹר בָּנֶיךָ תִּפְדֶּה וְלֹא־יֵרָאוּ פָנַי רֵיקָם: שֵׁשֶׁת
כב יָמִים תַּעֲבֹד וּבַיּוֹם הַשְּׁבִיעִי תִּשְׁבֹּת בֶּחָרִישׁ וּבַקָּצִיר תִּשְׁבֹּת: וְחַג שָׁבֻעֹת

---

at Marah and through it the days of work are blessed, as it says, שֵׁשֶׁת יָמִים תַּעֲשֶׂה מַעֲשֶׂיךָ, *Six days you shall do your work* (23:12). Together with it (the Torah) speaks of the seventh year which blesses the years, as it says, וְשֵׁשׁ שָׁנִים תִּזְרַע, *And six years you shall sow* (23:10). Fourth is the Feast of Harvest (Shavuos) wherein *the appointed weeks of the harvest are kept for us* (based on *Jeremiah* 5:24). Fifth is the Feast of Ingathering (Succos) through which the ingathering is blessed, as it says, כְּבִרְכַּת ה׳ אֱלֹהֶיךָ אֲשֶׁר נָתַן לָךְ, *according to the blessing of* HASHEM *your God which He has given you (Deut.* 16:17). After all these commandments (the Torah) mentions a commandment which is common to the three festivals, namely, יֵרָאֶה כָּל זְכוּרְךָ, *all your males shall appear* (v. 23). Afterward commandments special to the Feast of Matzos are mentioned: לֹא תִשְׁחַט עַל חָמֵץ, *You shall not offer on chometz, etc.;* and וְלֹא יָלִין, *You shall not leave etc.* (v. 25). Afterward (the Torah) mentions a special *mitzvah* which is mainly connected to the Feast of Harvest, i.e., רֵאשִׁית בִּכּוּרֵי אַדְמָתְךָ, *the choicest first fruits of your land, etc.* (v. 26), as our Sages say, 'From *Atzereth* (Shavuos) until the Feast (Succos) one brings and reads' (*Bikkurim* 1:6). Later (the Torah) mentions a commandment which in the majority of cases is especially linked to Succos, i.e., לֹא תְבַשֵּׁל גְּדִי בַּחֲלֵב אִמּוֹ, *You shall not boil a kid in its mother's milk,* for that is the season of the kids, as some of our Sages say, 'On the first day of Tishrei is the Rosh Hashanah of tithing animals' (*Mishnah, Rosh Hashanah* 1:1).

19. כָּל פֶּטֶר רֶחֶם לִי — *All that opens the womb is Mine.* Among man, clean animals and some unclean ones, but they shall be so in various ways, therefore it says . . .

וְכָל מִקְנְךָ תִּזָּכָר פֶּטֶר שׁוֹר וָשֶׂה — *And of all your cattle you shall sanctify the males, the firstlings of ox and sheep.* That is . . . the firstling of an ox and sheep תִּזָּכָר, it shall be *remembered* as a part of the sacrifices called אַזְכָּרָה, *a remembrance,* as it says, אַךְ בְּכוֹר שׁוֹר אוֹ בְכוֹר כֶּשֶׂב אוֹ בְכוֹר עֵז לֹא תִפְדֶּה קֹדֶשׁ הֵם אֶת דָּמָם תִּזְרֹק . . . וְאֶת חֶלְבָּם תַּקְטִיר, *But the firstling of an ox or the firstling of a sheep or the firstling of a goat you shall not redeem; they are holy, you shall dash their blood . . . and their fat burn* (*Numbers* 18:17).

20. וּפֶטֶר חֲמוֹר תִּפְדֶּה בְשֶׂה . . . כֹּל בְּכוֹר בָּנֶיךָ תִּפְדֶּה — *And the firstling of an ass you shall redeem with a lamb . . . All the firstborn of your sons you shall redeem.* The redemption (being) the established valuation (five *shekels* — see *Numbers* 18:16).

21. שֵׁשֶׁת יָמִים תַּעֲבֹד וּבַיּוֹם הַשְּׁבִיעִי תִּשְׁבֹּת — *Six days you shall work, but on the seventh day you shall rest.* You shall succeed in your six days of work when you rest on the seventh.

בֶּחָרִישׁ וּבַקָּצִיר תִּשְׁבֹּת — *In plowing time and in harvest you shall rest.* Also when you will rest once every seven years from plowing and harvest, which is the

NOTES

festivals are separated by commandments regarding firstlings, the Sabbath and the Sabbatical year, after which we find the verses regarding the commandment to come up to

כג תַעֲשֶׂה לְךָ בִּכּוּרֵי קְצִיר חִטִּים וְחַג הָאָסִיף תְּקוּפַת הַשָּׁנָה: שָׁלֹשׁ פְּעָמִים
כד בַּשָּׁנָה יֵרָאֶה כָּל־זְכוּרְךָ אֶת־פְּנֵי הָאָדֹן ׀ יהוה אֱלֹהֵי יִשְׂרָאֵל: כִּי־אוֹרִישׁ
גּוֹיִם מִפָּנֶיךָ וְהִרְחַבְתִּי אֶת־גְּבֻלֶךָ וְלֹא־יַחְמֹד אִישׁ אֶת־אַרְצְךָ בַּעֲלֹתְךָ
כה לֵרָאוֹת אֶת־פְּנֵי יהוה אֱלֹהֶיךָ שָׁלֹשׁ פְּעָמִים בַּשָּׁנָה: לֹא־תִשְׁחַט עַל־חָמֵץ
כו דַּם־זִבְחִי וְלֹא־יָלִין לַבֹּקֶר זֶבַח חַג הַפָּסַח: רֵאשִׁית בִּכּוּרֵי אַדְמָתְךָ תָּבִיא

Sabbath of years that is also called שַׁבָּת לַה׳, *a Sabbath to HASHEM (Leviticus* 25:2), then you will be successful in your plowing and harvest (the other six years) as it says, שֵׁשׁ שָׁנִים תִּזְרַע שָׂדֶךָ וְאָסַפְתָּ אֶת תְּבוּאָתָהּ, *Six years you shall sow your field ... and gather its produce* (ibid. v. 3).

23. אֶת פְּנֵי הָאָדֹן ה׳ — *Before the Lord, HASHEM ...* Who arranges all your affairs in the natural (material) realm, similar to, וּלְאָדוֹן לְכָל בֵּיתוֹ, *And master of all his house (Genesis* 45:8).

אֱלֹהֵי יִשְׂרָאֵל — *God of Israel ...* Who arranges (controls) the affairs of Israel in spiritual matters which transcend nature, which do not apply except to that which is separated (from matter) and (hence) called *Elohim,* similar to זֹבֵחַ לָאֱלֹהִים יָחֳרָם, *He who sacrifices to the gods shall be utterly destroyed* (22:19), and (also) to אֱלָהִין דִּי מְדָרְהוֹן עִם בִּשְׂרָא לָא אִיתוֹהִי, *the gods whose dwelling is not with flesh (Daniel* 2:11). It is for this (reason) that it is said of the demons, לֹא אֱלֹהַּ, *no-gods (Deut.* 32:17), for they are material beings who are mortal like man, as our Sages have mentioned *(Chagigah* 16a). Expert judges are also called *Elohim* (22:27), for they occasionally judge in an extrasensory (fashion) similar to Solomon of whom it is said, כִּי חָכְמַת אֱלֹהִים בְּקִרְבּוֹ לַעֲשׂוֹת מִשְׁפָּט, *The wisdom of God was in him to do judgment (I Kings* 3:28), and as it says, וְלֹא לְמַרְאֵה עֵינָיו יִשְׁפּוֹט וְלֹא לְמִשְׁמַע אָזְנָיו יוֹכִיחַ, *and he shall not judge after the sight of his eyes, neither decide after the hearing of his ears (Isaiah* 11:3). This is why God, the Blessed One, is called אֱלֹהֵי הָאֱלֹהִים, *God of gods (Deut.* 10:17), Who arranges those affairs which are not in the natural realm but they are separated from matter; (and also) אֲדֹנֵי הָאֲדֹנִים, *the Lord of lords* (ibid.), Who arranges the matters of nature, which are the heavenly causes (phenomena) — therefore (the Torah) says ...

יֵרָאֶה כָּל זְכוּרְךָ — *All your males shall appear ...* to give thanks for all the good which emanates from Him to you in (all) natural matters (in His role as) *Lord of Israel,* and for that which emanates from Him for eternal life as the *God of Israel.*

26. רֵאשִׁית בִּכּוּרֵי אַדְמָתְךָ תָּבִיא — *The choicest first fruits of your Land you shall bring.* And through this you will attain success with (your) fruit, as it says: וְרֵאשִׁית כָּל בִּכּוּרֵי כֹל ... תִּתְּנוּ לַכֹּהֵן לְהָנִיחַ בְּרָכָה אֶל בֵּיתֶךָ, *And the first of all the first fruits of all things ... you shall give to the priest that he may cause a blessing to rest in your house (Ezekiel* 44:30).

NOTES

the Temple three times a year, followed by the laws of the *Pesach* lamb and the first fruits, culminating with the prohibition of mixing milk and meat! The *Sforno* in his commentary on these verses clarifies the sequence.

23. אֶת אֶת פְּנֵי הָאָדֹן ה׳ אֱלֹהֵי יִשְׂרָאֵל — *Before the Lord, HASHEM, God of Israel.* Two expressions are used in this verse — אָדוֹן which means master or lord, and אֱלֹהֵי, *God,* of Israel. The *Sforno* interprets the former appellation (אָדוֹן) as indicating the role of God as our Master guiding the material and physical affairs of Israel, while the latter name (אֱלֹהֵי)

בֵּית יְהוָה אֱלֹהֶיךָ לֹא־תְבַשֵּׁל גְּדִי בַּחֲלֵב אִמּוֹ:

שביעי   כז וַיֹּאמֶר יְהוָה אֶל־מֹשֶׁה כְּתָב־לְךָ אֶת־הַדְּבָרִים הָאֵלֶּה כִּי עַל־פִּי ׀ הַדְּבָרִים
כח הָאֵלֶּה כָּרַתִּי אִתְּךָ בְּרִית וְאֶת־יִשְׂרָאֵל: וַיְהִי־שָׁם עִם־יְהוָה אַרְבָּעִים יוֹם
וְאַרְבָּעִים לַיְלָה לֶחֶם לֹא אָכַל וּמַיִם לֹא שָׁתָה וַיִּכְתֹּב עַל־הַלֻּחֹת אֵת
כט דִּבְרֵי הַבְּרִית עֲשֶׂרֶת הַדְּבָרִים: וַיְהִי בְּרֶדֶת מֹשֶׁה מֵהַר סִינַי וּשְׁנֵי לֻחֹת
הָעֵדֻת בְּיַד־מֹשֶׁה בְּרִדְתּוֹ מִן־הָהָר וּמֹשֶׁה לֹא־יָדַע כִּי קָרַן עוֹר פָּנָיו בְּדַבְּרוֹ
ל אִתּוֹ: וַיַּרְא אַהֲרֹן וְכָל־בְּנֵי יִשְׂרָאֵל אֶת־מֹשֶׁה וְהִנֵּה קָרַן עוֹר פָּנָיו וַיִּירְאוּ
לא מִגֶּשֶׁת אֵלָיו: וַיִּקְרָא אֲלֵהֶם מֹשֶׁה וַיָּשֻׁבוּ אֵלָיו אַהֲרֹן וְכָל־הַנְּשִׂאִים בָּעֵדָה
לב וַיְדַבֵּר מֹשֶׁה אֲלֵהֶם: וְאַחֲרֵי־כֵן נִגְּשׁוּ כָּל־בְּנֵי יִשְׂרָאֵל וַיְצַוֵּם אֵת כָּל־אֲשֶׁר
מפטיר   לג דִּבֶּר יְהוָה אִתּוֹ בְּהַר סִינָי: וַיְכַל מֹשֶׁה מִדַּבֵּר אִתָּם וַיִּתֵּן עַל־פָּנָיו מַסְוֶה:
לד וּבְבֹא מֹשֶׁה לִפְנֵי יְהוָה לְדַבֵּר אִתּוֹ יָסִיר אֶת־הַמַּסְוֶה עַד־צֵאתוֹ וְיָצָא וְדִבֶּר
לה אֶל־בְּנֵי יִשְׂרָאֵל אֵת אֲשֶׁר יְצֻוֶּה: וְרָאוּ בְנֵי־יִשְׂרָאֵל אֶת־פְּנֵי מֹשֶׁה כִּי קָרַן
עוֹר פְּנֵי מֹשֶׁה וְהֵשִׁיב מֹשֶׁה אֶת־הַמַּסְוֶה עַל־פָּנָיו עַד־בֹּאוֹ לְדַבֵּר אִתּוֹ:

... לֹא תְבַשֵּׁל גְּדִי — *You shall not boil a kid . . .* As was the way of the heathens (lit., 'strange sons') who thought they would attain prosperity in their fruit or flocks, by means of this practice.

27. כְּתָב לְךָ אֶת הַדְּבָרִים הָאֵלֶּה — *Write yourself these words.* Although before the sin of the calf I intended to give you אֶת לֻחֹת הָאֶבֶן וְהַתּוֹרָה וְהַמִּצְוָה אֲשֶׁר כָּתַבְתִּי, *the tablets of law, and the Torah and the commandment which I have written* (24:12), now that they sinned and you hewed out for yourself the tablets — (upon which) I will write — I will not give you (now) the Torah and the commandment which I wrote, but you will have to write it yourself.

28. וַיְהִי שָׁם עִם ה' — *And he was there with HASHEM . . .* for the last time.

32. וַיְצַוֵּם אֵת כָּל אֲשֶׁר דִּבֶּר ה' אִתּוֹ — *And he commanded them all that HASHEM had spoken with him . . .* the work of the Sanctuary, its appointments and the offering of the *beka* (half-shekel) for each person (lit., 'per head').

33. וַיְכַל מֹשֶׁה מִדַּבֵּר אִתָּם — *And when Moses had done speaking with them.* But when he still spoke to them it was without the veil, similar to, וְהָיוּ עֵינֶיךָ רֹאוֹת אֶת מוֹרֶיךָ, *your eyes shall see your teacher* (Isaiah 30:20), and as our Sages say: 'And if I saw his face I would be even sharper' (Eruvin 13b).

NOTES

indicates God's role in guiding the spiritual (and historical) destiny of Israel. See the *Sforno* on *Genesis* 1:1 and the note there for an explanation of the term אֱלֹהִים and its application to judges and heavenly forces. When Israel went up to the Temple three times a year, it was to pay homage to God in His dual role as אָדוֹן and as אֱלֹהֵי יִשְׂרָאֵל.

27. כְּתָב לְךָ אֶת הַדְּבָרִים הָאֵלֶּה — *Write yourself these words.* God's original intention was to write the Ten Commandments, the law and

the commandments *Himself*, but after they sinned with the Golden Calf and consequently were no longer worthy of this special honor, Moses is charged with the task of writing all this.

28. וַיְהִי שָׁם עִם ה' — *And he was there with HASHEM.* The third and final time. See 24:18.

33. וַיְכַל מֹשֶׁה מִדַּבֵּר אִתָּם — *And when Moses had done speaking with them* (he placed a veil over his face). Moses' face was not covered by the veil while speaking to God nor when he

NOTES

spoke to the people, communicating the message of God to them. Although his face sent forth rays of heavenly light, and the people after the sin were not really worthy to gaze at this radiance, nonetheless Moses did not cover his face, for Torah can best be transmitted when students see the face of their teacher. The *Maharsha* in *Eruvin* 13b explains that when a student sees the subtle expressions on his teacher's face he can more readily understand him. The Talmud there relates that Rav was a student of R' Meir. In those days students sat in a circle with some sitting in front of their teacher while others sat behind him. Rav is quoted as saying, 'I am sharper than others because I studied under R' Meir, but I was seated behind him. Had I been seated in front and been privileged to see his face I would be even sharper.' The *Sforno* cites this statement to prove his point that Moses showed his face to the people while instructing them.

פרשת ויקהל
Parashas Vayakhel

לה
א וַיַּקְהֵל מֹשֶׁה אֶת־כָּל־עֲדַת בְּנֵי יִשְׂרָאֵל וַיֹּאמֶר אֲלֵהֶם אֵלֶּה הַדְּבָרִים
ב אֲשֶׁר־צִוָּה יהוה לַעֲשֹׂת אֹתָם: שֵׁשֶׁת יָמִים תֵּעָשֶׂה מְלָאכָה וּבַיּוֹם הַשְּׁבִיעִי
ג יִהְיֶה לָכֶם קֹדֶשׁ שַׁבַּת שַׁבָּתוֹן לַיהוה כָּל־הָעֹשֶׂה בוֹ מְלָאכָה יוּמָת: לֹא־
תְבַעֲרוּ אֵשׁ בְּכֹל מֹשְׁבֹתֵיכֶם בְּיוֹם הַשַּׁבָּת:
ד וַיֹּאמֶר מֹשֶׁה אֶל־כָּל־עֲדַת בְּנֵי־יִשְׂרָאֵל לֵאמֹר זֶה הַדָּבָר אֲשֶׁר־צִוָּה יהוה
ה לֵאמֹר: קְחוּ מֵאִתְּכֶם תְּרוּמָה לַיהוה כֹּל נְדִיב לִבּוֹ יְבִיאֶהָ אֵת תְּרוּמַת
ו־ז יהוה זָהָב וָכֶסֶף וּנְחֹשֶׁת: וּתְכֵלֶת וְאַרְגָּמָן וְתוֹלַעַת שָׁנִי וְשֵׁשׁ וְעִזִּים: וְעֹרֹת

XXXV

1. אֵלֶּה הַדְּבָרִים אֲשֶׁר צִוָּה ה׳ — *These are the words which* HASHEM *has commanded.* That which I said above when I commanded you all that God had spoken with me on the mountain of Sinai (34:32), they are the things which He commanded to do (only) on weekdays.

2. וּבַיּוֹם הַשְּׁבִיעִי יִהְיֶה לָכֶם קֹדֶשׁ — *On the seventh day there shall be to you a holy day.* And you shall not do (any work) even the work of the Sanctuary.

כָּל הָעֹשֶׂה בוֹ מְלָאכָה יוּמָת — *Whosoever does any work therein shall be put to death.* Even though it is the work of a *mitzvah* (commanded by God).

3. לֹא תְבַעֲרוּ אֵשׁ — *You shall kindle no fire.* Even though kindling a fire in itself is in most instances destructive (damaging), nonetheless since (fire) is the medium (means) for all, or most, works — it is prohibited on the Sabbath.

5. קְחוּ מֵאִתְּכֶם — *Take from among you.* You shall choose men who will accept from you offerings to God.

כֹּל נְדִיב לִבּוֹ — *Whosoever is of a willing heart.* The officers shall not collect with force.

יְבִיאֶהָ אֵת תְּרוּמַת ה׳ — *Let him bring it with* HASHEM*'s offering.* He shall bring the offering (together) with HASHEM*'s offering* which is not a (voluntary) offering, (namely) the offering of בֶּקַע לַגֻּלְגֹּלֶת, *a half-shekel a head* (38:26).

NOTES

XXXV

1. אֵלֶּה הַדְּבָרִים אֲשֶׁר צִוָּה ה׳ — *These are the words which* HASHEM *has commanded.* The *Sforno* links this verse to the following one which speaks of the Sabbath and the prohibition of doing any work — including that of constructing the *Mishkan* — on the Sabbath. The sense of the verse is: When Moses came down from Sinai he commanded Israel concerning the Tabernacle and the half-*shekel*, as the *Sforno* explained above (34:32). Now he tells them that these labors and contributions shall only be done and collected during the six days of the week, but not on the Sabbath, even though it is a *mitzvah*.

3. לֹא תְבַעֲרוּ אֵשׁ — *You shall kindle no fire.* There are thirty-nine prohibited labors on the Sabbath. There are different reasons given in the Talmud (*Sanhedrin* 35) as to why the Torah here chooses to specify only one, namely that of kindling a fire. The *Sforno's* answer is according to R' Shimon (*Shabbos* 106a). Whereas מְקַלְקֵל, *a destructive, damaging act*, on the Sabbath is normally non-punishable, if it serves a constructive purpose one is liable. As the *Sforno* explains, in conjunction with the construction of the Sanctuary most work required fire, hence it was no longer מְקַלְקֵל but of a positive nature and therefore prohibited.

5. קְחוּ מֵאִתְּכֶם — *Take from among you.* The expression קְחוּ, *take*, in this verse, similar to

ח אֵילִם מְאָדָּמִים וְעֹרֹת תְּחָשִׁים וַעֲצֵי שִׁטִּים: וְשֶׁמֶן לַמָּאוֹר וּבְשָׂמִים לְשֶׁמֶן
ט הַמִּשְׁחָה וְלִקְטֹרֶת הַסַּמִּים: וְאַבְנֵי־שֹׁהַם וְאַבְנֵי מִלֻּאִים לָאֵפוֹד וְלַחֹשֶׁן:
י־יא וְכָל־חֲכַם־לֵב בָּכֶם יָבֹאוּ וְיַעֲשׂוּ אֵת כָּל־אֲשֶׁר צִוָּה יהוה: אֶת־הַמִּשְׁכָּן אֶת־
אָהֳלוֹ וְאֶת־מִכְסֵהוּ אֶת־קְרָסָיו וְאֶת־קְרָשָׁיו אֶת־בְּרִיחָו אֶת־עַמֻּדָיו וְאֶת־
יב־יג אֲדָנָיו: אֶת־הָאָרֹן וְאֶת־בַּדָּיו אֶת־הַכַּפֹּרֶת וְאֵת פָּרֹכֶת הַמָּסָךְ: אֶת־הַשֻּׁלְחָן
יד וְאֶת־בַּדָּיו וְאֶת־כָּל־כֵּלָיו וְאֵת לֶחֶם הַפָּנִים: וְאֶת־מְנֹרַת הַמָּאוֹר וְאֶת־
טו כֵּלֶיהָ וְאֶת־נֵרֹתֶיהָ וְאֵת שֶׁמֶן הַמָּאוֹר: וְאֶת־מִזְבַּח הַקְּטֹרֶת וְאֶת־בַּדָּיו וְאֵת
טז שֶׁמֶן הַמִּשְׁחָה וְאֵת קְטֹרֶת הַסַּמִּים וְאֶת־מָסַךְ הַפֶּתַח לְפֶתַח הַמִּשְׁכָּן: אֵת ׀
מִזְבַּח הָעֹלָה וְאֶת־מִכְבַּר הַנְּחֹשֶׁת אֲשֶׁר־לוֹ אֶת־בַּדָּיו וְאֶת־כָּל־כֵּלָיו אֶת־
יז הַכִּיֹּר וְאֶת־כַּנּוֹ: אֵת קַלְעֵי הֶחָצֵר אֶת־עַמֻּדָיו וְאֶת־אֲדָנֶיהָ וְאֵת מָסַךְ שַׁעַר
יח־יט הֶחָצֵר: אֶת־יִתְדֹת הַמִּשְׁכָּן וְאֶת־יִתְדֹת הֶחָצֵר וְאֶת־מֵיתְרֵיהֶם: אֶת־בִּגְדֵי
הַשְּׂרָד לְשָׁרֵת בַּקֹּדֶשׁ אֶת־בִּגְדֵי הַקֹּדֶשׁ לְאַהֲרֹן הַכֹּהֵן וְאֶת־בִּגְדֵי בָנָיו
שני כ־כא לְכַהֵן: וַיֵּצְאוּ כָּל־עֲדַת בְּנֵי־יִשְׂרָאֵל מִלִּפְנֵי מֹשֶׁה: וַיָּבֹאוּ כָּל־אִישׁ אֲשֶׁר־
נְשָׂאוֹ לִבּוֹ וְכֹל אֲשֶׁר נָדְבָה רוּחוֹ אֹתוֹ הֵבִיאוּ אֶת־תְּרוּמַת יהוה לִמְלֶאכֶת
כב אֹהֶל מוֹעֵד וּלְכָל־עֲבֹדָתוֹ וּלְבִגְדֵי הַקֹּדֶשׁ: וַיָּבֹאוּ הָאֲנָשִׁים עַל־הַנָּשִׁים כֹּל ׀
נְדִיב לֵב הֵבִיאוּ חָח וָנֶזֶם וְטַבַּעַת וְכוּמָז כָּל־כְּלִי זָהָב וְכָל־אִישׁ אֲשֶׁר הֵנִיף
כג תְּנוּפַת זָהָב לַיהוה: וְכָל־אִישׁ אֲשֶׁר־נִמְצָא אִתּוֹ תְּכֵלֶת וְאַרְגָּמָן וְתוֹלַעַת

---

11. אֶת הַמִּשְׁכָּן אֶת אָהֳלוֹ — *The Mishkan, its tent.* That which he had already explained to Israel when he said, וַיְצַוֵּם אֵת כָּל אֲשֶׁר דִּבֶּר ה׳ אִתּוֹ בְּהַר סִינָי, *And he commanded them all that HASHEM had spoken with him in Mount Sinai* (34:32).

22. וַיָּבֹאוּ הָאֲנָשִׁים עַל הַנָּשִׁים — *And the men came with the women.* (Together) with the contributing women came their men (husbands) to confirm their offerings, so that the officers would accept them, since we do not accept (contributions) from women except for small (insignificant) things.

וְכָל אִישׁ אֲשֶׁר הֵנִיף תְּנוּפַת זָהָב — *And every man that brought a waving (offering) of gold.* And together with the women who contributed gold jewelry, men also who offered (gifts) of gold, similar to that which our Sages say, 'A row which was all silver — silver; which was all gold — gold. They were not mingled' (*Pesachim* 64a).

NOTES

that of וְיִקְחוּ in 25:2, is difficult to understand. Would not the word תְּנוּ, *give*, and וְיִתְּנוּ have been more appropriate? The *Sforno*, however, both here and in *Parashas Terumah*, explains the choice of this word as meaning to appoint officers who will *take* (i.e., accept) the offerings from the people.

יְבִיאֶהָ אֵת תְּרוּמַת ה׳ — *Let him bring it with HASHEM's offering.* The word אֵת in this verse means *with*. Therefore the *Sforno* explains that together with the free-will offerings of gold, silver and brass, the officers were to collect the mandatory half-*shekel* from each Israelite. This explains the repetition of the word תְּרוּמָה in this verse; one applies to the contribution and the other to the tax.

22. וַיָּבֹאוּ הָאֲנָשִׁים עַל הַנָּשִׁים ... וְכָל אִישׁ אֲשֶׁר הֵנִיף תְּנוּפַת זָהָב — *And the men came with the women ... And every man that brought a waving (offering) of gold.* The Talmud (*Baba Kama* 119a) states that since what a woman owns belongs to her husband, she can only contribute a small amount of her funds or possessions to charity or any religious cause for we assume that in such a case her husband will not object. When these women were

כד שָׁנִי וְשֵׁשׁ וְעִזִּים וְעֹרֹת אֵילִם מְאָדָּמִים וְעֹרֹת תְּחָשִׁים הֵבִיאוּ: כָּל־מֵרִים
תְּרוּמַת כֶּסֶף וּנְחֹשֶׁת הֵבִיאוּ אֵת תְּרוּמַת יהוה וְכֹל אֲשֶׁר נִמְצָא אִתּוֹ עֲצֵי
כה שִׁטִּים לְכָל־מְלֶאכֶת הָעֲבֹדָה הֵבִיאוּ: וְכָל־אִשָּׁה חַכְמַת־לֵב בְּיָדֶיהָ טָווּ
וַיָּבִיאוּ מַטְוֶה אֶת־הַתְּכֵלֶת וְאֶת־הָאַרְגָּמָן אֶת־תּוֹלַעַת הַשָּׁנִי וְאֶת־הַשֵּׁשׁ:
כו-כז וְכָל־הַנָּשִׁים אֲשֶׁר נָשָׂא לִבָּן אֹתָנָה בְּחָכְמָה טָווּ אֶת־הָעִזִּים: וְהַנְּשִׂאִם
כח הֵבִיאוּ אֵת אַבְנֵי הַשֹּׁהַם וְאֵת אַבְנֵי הַמִּלֻּאִים לָאֵפוֹד וְלַחֹשֶׁן: וְאֶת־הַבֹּשֶׂם
כט וְאֶת־הַשָּׁמֶן לְמָאוֹר וּלְשֶׁמֶן הַמִּשְׁחָה וְלִקְטֹרֶת הַסַּמִּים: כָּל־אִישׁ וְאִשָּׁה
אֲשֶׁר נָדַב לִבָּם אֹתָם לְהָבִיא לְכָל־הַמְּלָאכָה אֲשֶׁר צִוָּה יהוה לַעֲשׂוֹת
בְּיַד־מֹשֶׁה הֵבִיאוּ בְנֵי־יִשְׂרָאֵל נְדָבָה לַיהוה:
שלישי [שני] ל וַיֹּאמֶר מֹשֶׁה אֶל־בְּנֵי יִשְׂרָאֵל רְאוּ קָרָא יהוה בְּשֵׁם בְּצַלְאֵל בֶּן־אוּרִי בֶן־
לא חוּר לְמַטֵּה יְהוּדָה: וַיְמַלֵּא אֹתוֹ רוּחַ אֱלֹהִים בְּחָכְמָה בִּתְבוּנָה וּבְדַעַת
לב-לג וּבְכָל־מְלָאכָה: וְלַחְשֹׁב מַחֲשָׁבֹת לַעֲשֹׂת בַּזָּהָב וּבַכֶּסֶף וּבַנְּחֹשֶׁת: וּבַחֲרֹשֶׁת
לד אֶבֶן לְמַלֹּאת וּבַחֲרֹשֶׁת עֵץ לַעֲשׂוֹת בְּכָל־מְלֶאכֶת מַחֲשָׁבֶת: וּלְהוֹרֹת נָתַן
לה בְּלִבּוֹ הוּא וְאָהֳלִיאָב בֶּן־אֲחִיסָמָךְ לְמַטֵּה־דָן: מִלֵּא אֹתָם חָכְמַת־לֵב
לַעֲשׂוֹת כָּל־מְלֶאכֶת חָרָשׁ ׀ וְחֹשֵׁב וְרֹקֵם בַּתְּכֵלֶת וּבָאַרְגָּמָן בְּתוֹלַעַת
לו א הַשָּׁנִי וּבַשֵּׁשׁ וְאֹרֵג עֹשֵׂי כָּל־מְלָאכָה וְחֹשְׁבֵי מַחֲשָׁבֹת: וְעָשָׂה בְצַלְאֵל
וְאָהֳלִיאָב וְכֹל ׀ אִישׁ חֲכַם־לֵב אֲשֶׁר נָתַן יהוה חָכְמָה וּתְבוּנָה בָּהֵמָּה
לָדַעַת לַעֲשֹׂת אֶת־כָּל־מְלֶאכֶת עֲבֹדַת הַקֹּדֶשׁ לְכֹל אֲשֶׁר־צִוָּה יהוה:
ב וַיִּקְרָא מֹשֶׁה אֶל־בְּצַלְאֵל וְאֶל־אָהֳלִיאָב וְאֶל כָּל־אִישׁ חֲכַם־לֵב אֲשֶׁר נָתַן
יהוה חָכְמָה בְּלִבּוֹ כֹּל אֲשֶׁר נְשָׂאוֹ לִבּוֹ לְקָרְבָה אֶל־הַמְּלָאכָה לַעֲשֹׂת
ג אֹתָהּ: וַיִּקְחוּ מִלִּפְנֵי מֹשֶׁה אֵת כָּל־הַתְּרוּמָה אֲשֶׁר הֵבִיאוּ בְּנֵי יִשְׂרָאֵל

---

26. טָווּ אֶת הָעִזִּים — *Spun the goats' hair . . .* (while it was still) on the goats, as our Sages tell us (*Shabbos* 99a), so that there be added gloss to the spun hair, because many removed (items) are diminished somewhat in quality when they are detached from their place of growth (origin), as it happens with bee honey, cassia (a variety of cinnamon), milk and others.

NOTES

moved to contribute their golden ornaments to the *Mishkan,* it was necessary for their husbands to accompany them and inform the officers that it was with their consent. In this manner the *Sforno* explains the reason why the men came with the women. He also explains the concluding part of this verse as meaning that since those men who brought gold were in the minority, since it was unusual for them to have gold trinkets or jewelry, they came together with the women so as to join those who were contributing that particular precious metal. We see from the selection of the Mishnah cited by the *Sforno* that when the *Pesach* sacrifice (קָרְבַּן פֶּסַח) was brought, the row of priests with gold receptacles was separate from those who stood with silver receptacles (*Pesachim* 64a). This was done for aesthetic reasons; hence the same was true when the Israelites lined up to bring their offerings to the work of the *Mishkan.* The *Ramban* also comments that there were few men who brought gold, and that is why the expression תְּנוּפָה, *waving,* is used, indicating that the officers would wave it so the people should see the generous contribution of that particular donor!

26. טָווּ אֶת הָעִזִּים — *Spun the goats' hair.* The previous verse states, *all the women that were*

לִמְלֶאכֶת עֲבֹדַת הַקֹּדֶשׁ לַעֲשֹׂת אֹתָהּ וְהֵם הֵבִיאוּ אֵלָיו עוֹד נְדָבָה בַּבֹּקֶר
ד בַּבֹּקֶר׃ וַיָּבֹאוּ כָּל־הַחֲכָמִים הָעֹשִׂים אֵת כָּל־מְלֶאכֶת הַקֹּדֶשׁ אִישׁ־אִישׁ
ה מִמְּלַאכְתּוֹ אֲשֶׁר־הֵמָּה עֹשִׂים׃ וַיֹּאמְרוּ אֶל־מֹשֶׁה לֵּאמֹר מַרְבִּים הָעָם
ו לְהָבִיא מִדֵּי הָעֲבֹדָה לַמְּלָאכָה אֲשֶׁר־צִוָּה יהוה לַעֲשֹׂת אֹתָהּ׃ וַיְצַו מֹשֶׁה
וַיַּעֲבִירוּ קוֹל בַּמַּחֲנֶה לֵאמֹר אִישׁ וְאִשָּׁה אַל־יַעֲשׂוּ־עוֹד מְלָאכָה לִתְרוּמַת
ז הַקֹּדֶשׁ וַיִּכָּלֵא הָעָם מֵהָבִיא׃ וְהַמְּלָאכָה הָיְתָה דַיָּם לְכָל־הַמְּלָאכָה לַעֲשׂוֹת
רביעי ח אֹתָהּ וְהוֹתֵר׃ וַיַּעֲשׂוּ כָל־חֲכַם־לֵב בְּעֹשֵׂי הַמְּלָאכָה אֶת־

XXXVI

4. אִישׁ אִישׁ מִמְּלַאכְתּוֹ — *Every man from his work.* The (Torah) relates the trustworthiness of each craftsman and the generosity of Israel regarding all that was necessary for each of the works.

5. לַמְּלָאכָה אֲשֶׁר צִוָּה ה׳ לַעֲשֹׂת אֹתָהּ — *For the work which* HASHEM *commanded to make.* Behold, the contribution of the people is more than what is required for the work which God commanded to make, i.e., without additions or subtractions, for He gave exact measures (requirements) for the *Mishkan* and its furnishings, (and one is) neither to add nor diminish them, unlike the structures of Solomon and Herod (Hordos).

6. אַל יַעֲשׂוּ עוֹד מְלָאכָה לִתְרוּמַת הַקֹּדֶשׁ — *Let none make any more work for the offering of the Sanctuary.* He did not announce that they should not bring voluntary contributions, but he announced that they should not do any more work, such as the spinning work, as it says, וַיָּבִיאוּ מַטְוֶה, *and brought that which they had spun* (35:25), and the preparation work of the wood, as it says, עֲצֵי שִׁטִּים לְכָל מְלֶאכֶת הָעֲבֹדָה הֵבִיאוּ, *acacia wood for any work of the service did they bring* (35:24), and the preparation of the hides, and other (similar work).

7. וְהַמְּלָאכָה הָיְתָה דַיָּם — *And the work was sufficient.* The work (i.e., material) of the donors in all that they contributed was sufficient for the workers of the *Mishkan.*

NOTES

wise hearted, whereas this verse uses the expression *whose heart stirred them up.* Also the expression טָווּ אֶת הָעִזִּים literally translated means *spun the goats;* the word *hair* is not specifically written. For these reasons *Rashi,* quoting the Talmud, comments that the spinning was done while the hair was still on the living animal, which required extraordinary skill. The *Sforno* adds that this was done so that none of the gloss should be lost in the process.

XXXVI

5-7. לַמְּלָאכָה אֲשֶׁר צִוָּה ה׳ לַעֲשֹׂת אֹתָהּ ... אַל יַעֲשׂוּ עוֹד מְלָאכָה לִתְרוּמַת הַקֹּדֶשׁ ... וְהַמְּלָאכָה הָיְתָה דַיָּם ... וְהוֹתֵר — *For the work which* HASHEM *commanded to make ... Let none make any more work for the offering of the Sanctuary ... And the work was sufficient ... and too much.* The *Sforno* explains these three verses in the following manner. Insofar as contributions were concerned there was no objection to the people bringing as much as they wanted. This, however, would in no way change the number of component parts of the *Mishkan,* nor the qualitative manner in which they would be constructed or fashioned, since God had given exact instructions regarding the dimensions and measurements of the structure, the furnishings and vessels. Therefore the announcement was not to do any more work. It was not to cease bringing

הַמִּשְׁכָּן עֶשֶׂר יְרִיעֹת שֵׁשׁ מָשְׁזָר וּתְכֵלֶת וְאַרְגָּמָן וְתוֹלַעַת שָׁנִי כְּרֻבִים
ט מַעֲשֵׂה חֹשֵׁב עָשָׂה אֹתָם׃ אֹרֶךְ הַיְרִיעָה הָאַחַת שְׁמֹנֶה וְעֶשְׂרִים בָּאַמָּה
י וְרֹחַב אַרְבַּע בָּאַמָּה הַיְרִיעָה הָאֶחָת מִדָּה אַחַת לְכָל־הַיְרִיעֹת׃ וַיְחַבֵּר אֶת־
יא חֲמֵשׁ הַיְרִיעֹת אַחַת אֶל־אֶחָת וְחָמֵשׁ יְרִיעֹת חִבַּר אַחַת אֶל־אֶחָת׃ וַיַּעַשׂ
לֻלְאֹת תְּכֵלֶת עַל שְׂפַת הַיְרִיעָה הָאֶחָת מִקָּצָה בַּמַּחְבָּרֶת כֵּן עָשָׂה בִּשְׂפַת
יב הַיְרִיעָה הַקִּיצוֹנָה בַּמַּחְבֶּרֶת הַשֵּׁנִית׃ חֲמִשִּׁים לֻלָאֹת עָשָׂה בַּיְרִיעָה הָאֶחָת
וַחֲמִשִּׁים לֻלָאֹת עָשָׂה בִּקְצֵה הַיְרִיעָה אֲשֶׁר בַּמַּחְבֶּרֶת הַשֵּׁנִית מַקְבִּילֹת
יג הַלֻּלָאֹת אַחַת אֶל־אֶחָת׃ וַיַּעַשׂ חֲמִשִּׁים קַרְסֵי זָהָב וַיְחַבֵּר אֶת־
הַיְרִיעֹת אַחַת אֶל־אַחַת בַּקְּרָסִים וַיְהִי הַמִּשְׁכָּן אֶחָד׃
יד וַיַּעַשׂ יְרִיעֹת עִזִּים לְאֹהֶל עַל־הַמִּשְׁכָּן עַשְׁתֵּי־עֶשְׂרֵה יְרִיעֹת עָשָׂה אֹתָם׃
טו אֹרֶךְ הַיְרִיעָה הָאַחַת שְׁלֹשִׁים בָּאַמָּה וְאַרְבַּע אַמּוֹת רֹחַב הַיְרִיעָה הָאֶחָת
טז מִדָּה אַחַת לְעַשְׁתֵּי עֶשְׂרֵה יְרִיעֹת׃ וַיְחַבֵּר אֶת־חֲמֵשׁ הַיְרִיעֹת לְבָד וְאֶת־
יז שֵׁשׁ הַיְרִיעֹת לְבָד׃ וַיַּעַשׂ לֻלָאֹת חֲמִשִּׁים עַל שְׂפַת הַיְרִיעָה הַקִּיצֹנָה
יח בַּמַּחְבָּרֶת וַחֲמִשִּׁים לֻלָאֹת עָשָׂה עַל־שְׂפַת הַיְרִיעָה הַחֹבֶרֶת הַשֵּׁנִית׃ וַיַּעַשׂ
יט קַרְסֵי נְחֹשֶׁת חֲמִשִּׁים לְחַבֵּר אֶת־הָאֹהֶל לִהְיֹת אֶחָד׃ וַיַּעַשׂ מִכְסֶה לָאֹהֶל

לְכָל הַמְּלָאכָה — *For all the work . . .* (i.e.,) for every aspect of work that was (required) to do it.

לַעֲשׂוֹת אֹתָהּ וְהוֹתֵר — *To make it, and too much.* To do that work and to leave over, in such a manner that they did not have to stint in the method of their workmanship due to any concern that material may be lacking.

8. וַיַּעֲשׂוּ כָּל חֲכַם לֵב בְּעֹשֵׂי הַמְּלָאכָה — *And every wise-hearted man among them who did the work.* The wiser ones among them made the *mishkan* (curtains) which was *the work of skillful workers* (26:1) having different figures on their two sides, as our Sages mention *(Yoma* 72b). Now these curtains were not as thick as the *paroches* (the curtain separating the Holy of Holies from the Holy). The (Torah) repeats in this chapter all that was (already) said in (the form) of a command in *Parashas Terumah,* (in order) to tell us that they made everything with the intent to do the will of Him Who commanded and toward (His) goal (purpose). The Ark, which was singular among the furnishings, was made by Bezalel who was the greatest (craftsman) of them all, as our Sages say, 'Bezalel knew how to combine (or join) the letters with which heaven and earth were created' *(Berachos* 55a).

NOTES

contributions of gold, silver, brass or other materials. The *Sforno* explains verse 7 which seemingly contradicts itself, by first stating דַּיָּם, *sufficient*, and then וְהוֹתֵר, *too much*, by pointing out that only by bringing a bit more than needed was the material sufficient for the worker who did not have to stint or worry that he would not have enough to complete his work.

8. וַיַּעֲשׂוּ כָל חֲכַם לֵב בְּעֹשֵׂי הַמְּלָאכָה — *And every wise-hearted man among them who did the work.* The *Sforno* explains that although both the *mishkan*-curtains and the *paroches* required skillful workmanship the former was more demanding and was executed by wiser ones, for it was made of finer, more delicate material than the veil.

The curtains had figures of Cherubim woven into them, the figure of a lion on the one side and an eagle on the other *(Rashi* 26:1). This is referred to as מַעֲשֵׂה חֹשֵׁב, *skillful work*. This same phrase is used regarding the *paroches* in verse 31 of that chapter.

חמישי כ עֹרֹת אֵלִם מְאָדָּמִים וּמִכְסֵה עֹרֹת תְּחָשִׁים מִלְמָעְלָה׃ וַיַּעַשׂ
כא אֶת־הַקְּרָשִׁים לַמִּשְׁכָּן עֲצֵי שִׁטִּים עֹמְדִים׃ עֶשֶׂר אַמֹּת אֹרֶךְ הַקָּרֶשׁ וְאַמָּה
כב וַחֲצִי הָאַמָּה רֹחַב הַקֶּרֶשׁ הָאֶחָד׃ שְׁתֵּי יָדֹת לַקֶּרֶשׁ הָאֶחָד מְשֻׁלָּבֹת אַחַת
כג אֶל־אֶחָת כֵּן עָשָׂה לְכֹל קַרְשֵׁי הַמִּשְׁכָּן׃ וַיַּעַשׂ אֶת־הַקְּרָשִׁים לַמִּשְׁכָּן
כד עֶשְׂרִים קְרָשִׁים לִפְאַת נֶגֶב תֵּימָנָה׃ וְאַרְבָּעִים אַדְנֵי־כֶסֶף עָשָׂה תַּחַת
עֶשְׂרִים הַקְּרָשִׁים שְׁנֵי אֲדָנִים תַּחַת־הַקֶּרֶשׁ הָאֶחָד לִשְׁתֵּי יְדֹתָיו וּשְׁנֵי
כה אֲדָנִים תַּחַת־הַקֶּרֶשׁ הָאֶחָד לִשְׁתֵּי יְדֹתָיו׃ וּלְצֶלַע הַמִּשְׁכָּן הַשֵּׁנִית לִפְאַת
כו צָפוֹן עָשָׂה עֶשְׂרִים קְרָשִׁים׃ וְאַרְבָּעִים אַדְנֵיהֶם כָּסֶף שְׁנֵי אֲדָנִים תַּחַת
כז הַקֶּרֶשׁ הָאֶחָד וּשְׁנֵי אֲדָנִים תַּחַת הַקֶּרֶשׁ הָאֶחָד׃ וּלְיַרְכְּתֵי הַמִּשְׁכָּן יָמָּה
כח־כט עָשָׂה שִׁשָּׁה קְרָשִׁים׃ וּשְׁנֵי קְרָשִׁים עָשָׂה לִמְקֻצְעֹת הַמִּשְׁכָּן בַּיַּרְכָתָיִם׃ וְהָיוּ
תוֹאֲמִם מִלְּמַטָּה וְיַחְדָּו יִהְיוּ תַמִּים אֶל־רֹאשׁוֹ אֶל־הַטַּבַּעַת הָאֶחָת כֵּן
ל עָשָׂה לִשְׁנֵיהֶם לִשְׁנֵי הַמִּקְצֹעֹת׃ וְהָיוּ שְׁמֹנָה קְרָשִׁים וְאַדְנֵיהֶם כֶּסֶף שִׁשָּׁה
לא עָשָׂר אֲדָנִים שְׁנֵי אֲדָנִים תַּחַת הַקֶּרֶשׁ הָאֶחָד׃ וַיַּעַשׂ בְּרִיחֵי עֲצֵי
לב שִׁטִּים חֲמִשָּׁה לְקַרְשֵׁי צֶלַע־הַמִּשְׁכָּן הָאֶחָת׃ וַחֲמִשָּׁה בְרִיחִם לְקַרְשֵׁי צֶלַע־
לג הַמִּשְׁכָּן הַשֵּׁנִית וַחֲמִשָּׁה בְרִיחִם לְקַרְשֵׁי הַמִּשְׁכָּן לַיַּרְכָתַיִם יָמָּה׃ וַיַּעַשׂ
לד אֶת־הַבְּרִיחַ הַתִּיכֹן לִבְרֹחַ בְּתוֹךְ הַקְּרָשִׁים מִן־הַקָּצֶה אֶל־הַקָּצֶה׃ וְאֶת־
הַקְּרָשִׁים צִפָּה זָהָב וְאֶת־טַבְּעֹתָם עָשָׂה זָהָב בָּתִּים לַבְּרִיחִם וַיְצַף אֶת־
לה הַבְּרִיחִם זָהָב׃ וַיַּעַשׂ אֶת־הַפָּרֹכֶת תְּכֵלֶת וְאַרְגָּמָן וְתוֹלַעַת שָׁנִי וְשֵׁשׁ מָשְׁזָר
לו מַעֲשֵׂה חֹשֵׁב עָשָׂה אֹתָהּ כְּרֻבִים׃ וַיַּעַשׂ לָהּ אַרְבָּעָה עַמּוּדֵי שִׁטִּים וַיְצַפֵּם
לז זָהָב וָוֵיהֶם זָהָב וַיִּצֹק לָהֶם אַרְבָּעָה אַדְנֵי־כָסֶף׃ וַיַּעַשׂ מָסָךְ לְפֶתַח הָאֹהֶל
לח תְּכֵלֶת וְאַרְגָּמָן וְתוֹלַעַת שָׁנִי וְשֵׁשׁ מָשְׁזָר מַעֲשֵׂה רֹקֵם׃ וְאֶת־עַמּוּדָיו חֲמִשָּׁה
וְאֶת־וָוֵיהֶם וְצִפָּה רָאשֵׁיהֶם וַחֲשֻׁקֵיהֶם זָהָב וְאַדְנֵיהֶם חֲמִשָּׁה נְחֹשֶׁת׃

לז

א וַיַּעַשׂ בְּצַלְאֵל אֶת־הָאָרֹן עֲצֵי שִׁטִּים אַמָּתַיִם וָחֵצִי אָרְכּוֹ וְאַמָּה וָחֵצִי רָחְבּוֹ
ב וְאַמָּה וָחֵצִי קֹמָתוֹ׃ וַיְצַפֵּהוּ זָהָב טָהוֹר מִבַּיִת וּמִחוּץ וַיַּעַשׂ לוֹ זֵר זָהָב סָבִיב׃
ג וַיִּצֹק לוֹ אַרְבַּע טַבְּעֹת זָהָב עַל אַרְבַּע פַּעֲמֹתָיו וּשְׁתֵּי טַבָּעֹת עַל־צַלְעוֹ
ד הָאֶחָת וּשְׁתֵּי טַבָּעֹת עַל־צַלְעוֹ הַשֵּׁנִית׃ וַיַּעַשׂ בַּדֵּי עֲצֵי שִׁטִּים וַיְצַף אֹתָם
ה זָהָב׃ וַיָּבֵא אֶת־הַבַּדִּים בַּטַּבָּעֹת עַל צַלְעֹת הָאָרֹן לָשֵׂאת אֶת־הָאָרֹן׃
ו־ז וַיַּעַשׂ כַּפֹּרֶת זָהָב טָהוֹר אַמָּתַיִם וָחֵצִי אָרְכָּהּ וְאַמָּה וָחֵצִי רָחְבָּהּ׃ וַיַּעַשׂ שְׁנֵי
ח כְרֻבִים זָהָב מִקְשָׁה עָשָׂה אֹתָם מִשְּׁנֵי קְצוֹת הַכַּפֹּרֶת׃ כְּרוּב־אֶחָד מִקָּצָה
מִזֶּה וּכְרוּב־אֶחָד מִקָּצָה מִזֶּה מִן־הַכַּפֹּרֶת עָשָׂה אֶת־הַכְּרֻבִים מִשְּׁנֵי
°קְצוֹתָיו ק׳ ט °קצוותו׃ וַיִּהְיוּ הַכְּרֻבִים פֹּרְשֵׂי כְנָפַיִם לְמַעְלָה סֹכְכִים בְּכַנְפֵיהֶם עַל־
הַכַּפֹּרֶת וּפְנֵיהֶם אִישׁ אֶל־אָחִיו אֶל־הַכַּפֹּרֶת הָיוּ פְּנֵי הַכְּרֻבִים׃
י וַיַּעַשׂ אֶת־הַשֻּׁלְחָן עֲצֵי שִׁטִּים אַמָּתַיִם אָרְכּוֹ וְאַמָּה רָחְבּוֹ וְאַמָּה וָחֵצִי
יא־יב קֹמָתוֹ׃ וַיְצַף אֹתוֹ זָהָב טָהוֹר וַיַּעַשׂ לוֹ זֵר זָהָב סָבִיב׃ וַיַּעַשׂ לוֹ מִסְגֶּרֶת טֹפַח
יג סָבִיב וַיַּעַשׂ זֵר־זָהָב לְמִסְגַּרְתּוֹ סָבִיב׃ וַיִּצֹק לוֹ אַרְבַּע טַבְּעֹת זָהָב וַיִּתֵּן
יד אֶת־הַטַּבָּעֹת עַל אַרְבַּע הַפֵּאֹת אֲשֶׁר לְאַרְבַּע רַגְלָיו׃ לְעֻמַּת הַמִּסְגֶּרֶת הָיוּ
טו הַטַּבָּעֹת בָּתִּים לַבַּדִּים לָשֵׂאת אֶת־הַשֻּׁלְחָן׃ וַיַּעַשׂ אֶת־הַבַּדִּים עֲצֵי שִׁטִּים
טז וַיְצַף אֹתָם זָהָב לָשֵׂאת אֶת־הַשֻּׁלְחָן׃ וַיַּעַשׂ אֶת־הַכֵּלִים ׀ אֲשֶׁר עַל־הַשֻּׁלְחָן

אֶת־קְעָרֹתָיו וְאֶת־כַּפֹּתָיו וְאֵת מְנַקִּיֹּתָיו וְאֶת־הַקְּשָׂוֹת אֲשֶׁר יֻסַּךְ בָּהֵן זָהָב
טָהוֹר׃
ששי [שלישי] יז וַיַּעַשׂ אֶת־הַמְּנֹרָה זָהָב טָהוֹר מִקְשָׁה עָשָׂה אֶת־הַמְּנֹרָה יְרֵכָהּ וְקָנָהּ גְּבִיעֶיהָ
יח כַּפְתֹּרֶיהָ וּפְרָחֶיהָ מִמֶּנָּה הָיוּ׃ וְשִׁשָּׁה קָנִים יֹצְאִים מִצִּדֶּיהָ שְׁלֹשָׁה ׀ קְנֵי מְנֹרָה
יט מִצִּדָּהּ הָאֶחָד וּשְׁלֹשָׁה קְנֵי מְנֹרָה מִצִּדָּהּ הַשֵּׁנִי׃ שְׁלֹשָׁה גְבִעִים מְשֻׁקָּדִים
בַּקָּנֶה הָאֶחָד כַּפְתֹּר וָפֶרַח וּשְׁלֹשָׁה גְבִעִים מְשֻׁקָּדִים בְּקָנֶה אֶחָד כַּפְתֹּר
כ וָפָרַח כֵּן לְשֵׁשֶׁת הַקָּנִים הַיֹּצְאִים מִן־הַמְּנֹרָה׃ וּבַמְּנֹרָה אַרְבָּעָה גְבִעִים
כא מְשֻׁקָּדִים כַּפְתֹּרֶיהָ וּפְרָחֶיהָ׃ וְכַפְתֹּר תַּחַת שְׁנֵי הַקָּנִים מִמֶּנָּה וְכַפְתֹּר תַּחַת
שְׁנֵי הַקָּנִים מִמֶּנָּה וְכַפְתֹּר תַּחַת־שְׁנֵי הַקָּנִים מִמֶּנָּה לְשֵׁשֶׁת הַקָּנִים הַיֹּצְאִים
כב־כג מִמֶּנָּה׃ כַּפְתֹּרֵיהֶם וּקְנֹתָם מִמֶּנָּה הָיוּ כֻּלָּהּ מִקְשָׁה אַחַת זָהָב טָהוֹר׃ וַיַּעַשׂ
כד אֶת־נֵרֹתֶיהָ שִׁבְעָה וּמַלְקָחֶיהָ וּמַחְתֹּתֶיהָ זָהָב טָהוֹר׃ כִּכָּר זָהָב טָהוֹר עָשָׂה
אֹתָהּ וְאֵת כָּל־כֵּלֶיהָ׃
כה וַיַּעַשׂ אֶת־מִזְבַּח הַקְּטֹרֶת עֲצֵי שִׁטִּים אַמָּה אָרְכּוֹ וְאַמָּה רָחְבּוֹ רָבוּעַ
כו וְאַמָּתַיִם קֹמָתוֹ מִמֶּנּוּ הָיוּ קַרְנֹתָיו׃ וַיְצַף אֹתוֹ זָהָב טָהוֹר אֶת־גַּגּוֹ
כז וְאֶת־קִירֹתָיו סָבִיב וְאֶת־קַרְנֹתָיו וַיַּעַשׂ לוֹ זֵר זָהָב סָבִיב׃ וּשְׁתֵּי טַבְּעֹת
זָהָב עָשָׂה־לוֹ ׀ מִתַּחַת לְזֵרוֹ עַל שְׁתֵּי צַלְעֹתָיו עַל שְׁנֵי צִדָּיו לְבָתִּים
כח לְבַדִּים לָשֵׂאת אֹתוֹ בָּהֶם׃ וַיַּעַשׂ אֶת־הַבַּדִּים עֲצֵי שִׁטִּים וַיְצַף אֹתָם
כט זָהָב׃ וַיַּעַשׂ אֶת־שֶׁמֶן הַמִּשְׁחָה קֹדֶשׁ וְאֶת־קְטֹרֶת הַסַּמִּים טָהוֹר מַעֲשֵׂה
לח שביעי א רֹקֵחַ׃ וַיַּעַשׂ אֶת־מִזְבַּח הָעֹלָה עֲצֵי שִׁטִּים חָמֵשׁ אַמּוֹת אָרְכּוֹ
[רביעי] ב וְחָמֵשׁ־אַמּוֹת רָחְבּוֹ רָבוּעַ וְשָׁלֹשׁ אַמּוֹת קֹמָתוֹ׃ וַיַּעַשׂ קַרְנֹתָיו עַל אַרְבַּע
ג פִּנֹּתָיו מִמֶּנּוּ הָיוּ קַרְנֹתָיו וַיְצַף אֹתוֹ נְחֹשֶׁת׃ וַיַּעַשׂ אֶת־כָּל־כְּלֵי הַמִּזְבֵּחַ
אֶת־הַסִּירֹת וְאֶת־הַיָּעִים וְאֶת־הַמִּזְרָקֹת אֶת־הַמִּזְלָגֹת וְאֶת־הַמַּחְתֹּת כָּל־
ד כֵּלָיו עָשָׂה נְחֹשֶׁת׃ וַיַּעַשׂ לַמִּזְבֵּחַ מִכְבָּר מַעֲשֵׂה רֶשֶׁת נְחֹשֶׁת תַּחַת כַּרְכֻּבּוֹ
ה מִלְּמַטָּה עַד־חֶצְיוֹ׃ וַיִּצֹק אַרְבַּע טַבָּעֹת בְּאַרְבַּע הַקְּצָוֹת לְמִכְבַּר הַנְּחֹשֶׁת
ו־ז בָּתִּים לַבַּדִּים׃ וַיַּעַשׂ אֶת־הַבַּדִּים עֲצֵי שִׁטִּים וַיְצַף אֹתָם נְחֹשֶׁת׃ וַיָּבֵא
אֶת־הַבַּדִּים בַּטַּבָּעֹת עַל צַלְעֹת הַמִּזְבֵּחַ לָשֵׂאת אֹתוֹ בָּהֶם נְבוּב לֻחֹת
ח עָשָׂה אֹתוֹ׃ וַיַּעַשׂ אֵת הַכִּיּוֹר נְחֹשֶׁת וְאֵת כַּנּוֹ נְחֹשֶׁת

XXXVII

29. וַיַּעַשׂ אֶת שֶׁמֶן הַמִּשְׁחָה קֹדֶשׁ — *And he made the anointing oil holy.* With the intent that it should not be impaired, as it says, קֹדֶשׁ יִהְיֶה זֶה לִי לְדֹרֹתֵיכֶם, *it shall be holy to Me throughout your generations* (30:31).

וְאֶת קְטֹרֶת הַסַּמִּים טָהוֹר — *And the pure incense of the sweet spices.* Spices cleansed of waste as it says, מְמֻלָּח טָהוֹר, *mixed together, pure* (30:35).

NOTES

XXXVII

29. וַיַּעַשׂ אֶת שֶׁמֶן הַמִּשְׁחָה קֹדֶשׁ וְאֶת קְטֹרֶת הַסַּמִּים טָהוֹר — *And he made the anointing oil holy and the pure incense of the sweet spices.* See the *Sforno* on 30:31 and 30:35 and the explanatory notes on those verses.

ט בְּמַרְאֹת הַצֹּבְאֹת אֲשֶׁר צָבְאוּ פֶּתַח אֹהֶל מוֹעֵד: וַיַּעַשׂ אֶת־
י הֶחָצֵר לִפְאַת ׀ נֶגֶב תֵּימָנָה קַלְעֵי הֶחָצֵר שֵׁשׁ מָשְׁזָר מֵאָה בָּאַמָּה: עַמּוּדֵיהֶם
יא עֶשְׂרִים וְאַדְנֵיהֶם עֶשְׂרִים נְחֹשֶׁת וָוֵי הָעַמֻּדִים וַחֲשֻׁקֵיהֶם כָּסֶף: וְלִפְאַת צָפוֹן
מֵאָה בָאַמָּה עַמּוּדֵיהֶם עֶשְׂרִים וְאַדְנֵיהֶם עֶשְׂרִים נְחֹשֶׁת וָוֵי הָעַמּוּדִים
יב וַחֲשֻׁקֵיהֶם כָּסֶף: וְלִפְאַת־יָם קְלָעִים חֲמִשִּׁים בָּאַמָּה עַמּוּדֵיהֶם עֲשָׂרָה
יג וְאַדְנֵיהֶם עֲשָׂרָה וָוֵי הָעַמֻּדִים וַחֲשׁוּקֵיהֶם כָּסֶף: וְלִפְאַת קֵדְמָה מִזְרָחָה
יד חֲמִשִּׁים אַמָּה: קְלָעִים חֲמֵשׁ־עֶשְׂרֵה אַמָּה אֶל־הַכָּתֵף עַמּוּדֵיהֶם שְׁלֹשָׁה
טו וְאַדְנֵיהֶם שְׁלֹשָׁה: וְלַכָּתֵף הַשֵּׁנִית מִזֶּה וּמִזֶּה לְשַׁעַר הֶחָצֵר קְלָעִים חֲמֵשׁ
טז עֶשְׂרֵה אַמָּה עַמֻּדֵיהֶם שְׁלֹשָׁה וְאַדְנֵיהֶם שְׁלֹשָׁה: כָּל־קַלְעֵי הֶחָצֵר סָבִיב
יז שֵׁשׁ מָשְׁזָר: וְהָאֲדָנִים לָעַמֻּדִים נְחֹשֶׁת וָוֵי הָעַמּוּדִים וַחֲשׁוּקֵיהֶם כֶּסֶף וְצִפּוּי
מפטיר יח רָאשֵׁיהֶם כָּסֶף וְהֵם מְחֻשָּׁקִים כֶּסֶף כֹּל עַמֻּדֵי הֶחָצֵר: וּמָסַךְ שַׁעַר הֶחָצֵר
מַעֲשֵׂה רֹקֵם תְּכֵלֶת וְאַרְגָּמָן וְתוֹלַעַת שָׁנִי וְשֵׁשׁ מָשְׁזָר וְעֶשְׂרִים אַמָּה אֹרֶךְ
יט וְקוֹמָה בְרֹחַב חָמֵשׁ אַמּוֹת לְעֻמַּת קַלְעֵי הֶחָצֵר: וְעַמֻּדֵיהֶם אַרְבָּעָה
כ וְאַדְנֵיהֶם אַרְבָּעָה נְחֹשֶׁת וָוֵיהֶם כֶּסֶף וְצִפּוּי רָאשֵׁיהֶם וַחֲשֻׁקֵיהֶם כָּסֶף: וְכָל־
הַיְתֵדֹת לַמִּשְׁכָּן וְלֶחָצֵר סָבִיב נְחֹשֶׁת:

XXXVIII

8. בְּמַרְאֹת הַצֹּבְאֹת — *Of the mirrors of the serving women.* Which were not included in the brass of the offering, as explained in *Parashas Pekudei,* where it says, וַיַּעַשׂ בָּהּ, *and he made with it, etc.* (38:30), but does not mention the laver and the base among those made of it (brass).

אֲשֶׁר צָבְאוּ פֶּתַח אֹהֶל מוֹעֵד — *Who did service at the door of the tent of meeting.* To hearken to the words of the living God, as it says, וְהָיָה כָּל מְבַקֵּשׁ ה׳ יֵצֵא אֶל אֹהֶל מוֹעֵד, *and every one who sought* HASHEM *went out to the tent of meeting* (33:7). Now these women rejected their ornaments, and sanctified their mirrors, (thereby) demonstrating that they no longer needed them.

NOTES

XXXVIII

8. בְּמַרְאֹת הַצֹּבְאֹת אֲשֶׁר צָבְאוּ ... — *Of the mirrors of the serving women who did service ...* In the next *parashah* (38:29) the Torah gives us an exact count of the brass offering and continues with an accounting of the items made from the brass (verses 30 and 31). The laver and its stand, however, which were also made of brass, are not included. The *Sforno* explains that the reason for this omission is that the brass for the laver was not taken from the general brass offerings, but from the mirrors of those women who parted with them and offered them to the *Mishkan.* By so doing they demonstrated their willingness to give up these beauty aids, which they considered of relatively little value, and instead committed them to the service of God.

פרשת פקודי
Parashas Pekudei

כא אֵלֶּה פְקוּדֵי הַמִּשְׁכָּן מִשְׁכַּן הָעֵדֻת אֲשֶׁר פֻּקַּד עַל־פִּי מֹשֶׁה עֲבֹדַת הַלְוִיִּם
כב בְּיַד אִיתָמָר בֶּן־אַהֲרֹן הַכֹּהֵן: וּבְצַלְאֵל בֶּן־אוּרִי בֶן־חוּר לְמַטֵּה יְהוּדָה עָשָׂה

21. אֵלֶּה פְקוּדֵי הַמִּשְׁכָּן — *These are the accounts of the Mishkan.* Each part of the *Mishkan*, written above, were those counted of which are said, וּבְשֵׁמֹת תִּפְקְדוּ אֶת כְּלֵי מִשְׁמֶרֶת מַשָּׂאָם ... בְּיַד אִיתָמָר, *and by name you shall appoint the furnishings (articles) of the charge of their burden ... under the hand of Ithamar (Numbers* 4:32-33). This is because each one of them (the articles counted) was worthy to be considered as important and to be called by its private (individual) name, not only part of a generic group (category). This is certainly justified (regarding) each one of the holy vessels which were carried by the children of Kehath, and therefore they did not deteriorate, as our Sages say, 'Perhaps you will say their hope of restoration is gone and their expectation is frustrated, so it is written, *Acacia wood standing up* (26:15), (this means) which stand forever and ever' *(Yoma* 72a).

They also did not fall into the hands of the enemy, as opposed to what happened to the Temple of Solomon and its articles (furnishings and vessels) as it is explained (regarding) the destruction of the First Temple at the hands of Nebuchadnezzar, (where) none of the articles of the *Mishkan* of our teacher Moses are mentioned *(II Kings* 25:13-17).

מִשְׁכַּן הָעֵדֻת — *The Tabernacle of the testimony.* The (Torah) tells us the virtues of this *Mishkan,* by which (reason) it was worthy to be everlasting and not to fall into the hands of the enemy: first, because it was מִשְׁכַּן הָעֵדֻת, *the Tabernacle of the testimony,* where the tablets of testimony were (deposited); second, אֲשֶׁר פֻּקַּד עַל פִּי מֹשֶׁה, *as they were rendered according to the commandment of Moses;* third, because it was through עֲבוֹדַת הַלְוִיִּם בְּיַד אִיתָמָר, *the service of the Levites by the hand of Ithamar,* for indeed the charge of all the parts of the *Mishkan* were in the hands of Ithamar; fourth ...

NOTES

21. אֵלֶּה פְקוּדֵי הַמִּשְׁכָּן מִשְׁכַּן הָעֵדֻת — *These are the accounts of the Mishkan, the Tabernacle of the testimony.* The *Sforno* established at the beginning of this Book which is called שְׁמוֹת, *Names,* that any person called by name in the Torah is worthy to be recorded by that name. The same is true of the articles of the Sanctuary, be it the component parts or the furnishings and vessels therein. These are all accounted for here in *Parashas Pekudei.* However, it is in the book of *Numbers* that the Torah emphasizes the significance of all these parts and vessels by stating, *by 'name' you shall appoint, etc.* It is for this reason that the *Sforno* cites *Numbers* 4:32 in his commentary here. Now that which is holy and of great import does not deteriorate or decay but is everlasting. Nor does it pass into the possession of any other people save Israel. This was the unique character of 'the *Mishkan* of our teacher Moses,' as the *Sforno* puts it. He gives four reasons for the special role played by this Sanctuary in our history, and its superiority to all the other Temples, enjoying God's special providence: (a) the לוּחוֹת הַבְּרִית, *tablets of the covenant,* were deposited in the Ark, testifying to God's covenant with Israel; (b) only this Sanctuary was constructed by Moses, the master of all prophets, of whom the Torah tells us, *there has not arisen a prophet since in Israel like unto Moses,* and therefore it was worthy of the Almighty's protection; (c) the fact that the service of the Levites in this *Mishkan* was in the hands of Ithamar, Aaron's son, who was an outstanding man of piety and integrity, also contributed to the elevated status of this particular Sanctuary; and (d) the fact that Bezalel was the architect and builder of the *Mishkan* helped to insure its everlasting nature, for the *Mishkan* mirrors the creation of heaven and earth and Bezalel had been blessed with special wisdom and the ability to reflect

כג אֵ֚ת כָּל־אֲשֶׁר־צִוָּ֥ה יְהֹוָ֖ה אֶת־מֹשֶֽׁה: וְאִתּ֗וֹ אׇהֳלִיאָ֞ב בֶּן־אֲחִיסָמָ֛ךְ לְמַטֵּה־דָ֖ן

כד חָרָ֣שׁ וְחֹשֵׁ֑ב וְרֹקֵ֗ם בַּתְּכֵ֙לֶת֙ וּבָֽאַרְגָּמָ֔ן וּבְתוֹלַ֥עַת הַשָּׁנִ֖י וּבַשֵּֽׁשׁ:   כׇּל־ הַזָּהָ֗ב הֶֽעָשׂוּי֙ לַמְּלָאכָ֔ה בְּכֹ֖ל מְלֶ֣אכֶת הַקֹּ֑דֶשׁ וַיְהִ֣י ׀ זְהַ֣ב הַתְּנוּפָ֗ה תֵּ֤שַׁע

כה וְעֶשְׂרִים֙ כִּכָּ֔ר וּשְׁבַ֥ע מֵא֛וֹת וּשְׁלֹשִׁ֥ים שֶׁ֖קֶל בְּשֶׁ֥קֶל הַקֹּֽדֶשׁ: וְכֶ֣סֶף פְּקוּדֵ֣י הָֽעֵדָ֗ה מְאַ֣ת כִּכָּ֑ר וְאֶ֜לֶף וּשְׁבַ֤ע מֵאוֹת֙ וַֽחֲמִשָּׁ֣ה וְשִׁבְעִ֔ים שֶׁ֖קֶל בְּשֶׁ֥קֶל

כו הַקֹּֽדֶשׁ: בֶּ֚קַע לַגֻּלְגֹּ֔לֶת מַֽחֲצִ֖ית הַשֶּׁ֑קֶל בְּשֶׁ֣קֶל הַקֹּ֔דֶשׁ לְכֹ֨ל הָֽעֹבֵ֜ר עַל־ הַפְּקֻדִ֗ים מִבֶּ֨ן עֶשְׂרִ֤ים שָׁנָה֙ וָמַ֔עְלָה לְשֵׁשׁ־מֵא֥וֹת אֶ֖לֶף וּשְׁלֹ֣שֶׁת אֲלָפִ֑ים

כז וַֽחֲמֵ֥שׁ מֵא֖וֹת וַֽחֲמִשִּֽׁים: וַיְהִ֗י מְאַת֙ כִּכַּ֣ר הַכֶּ֔סֶף לָצֶ֗קֶת אֵ֚ת אַדְנֵ֣י הַקֹּ֔דֶשׁ

כח וְאֵ֖ת אַדְנֵ֣י הַפָּרֹ֑כֶת מְאַ֧ת אֲדָנִ֛ים לִמְאַ֥ת הַכִּכָּ֖ר כִּכָּ֥ר לָאָֽדֶן: וְאֶת־הָאֶ֜לֶף וּשְׁבַ֤ע הַמֵּאוֹת֙ וַֽחֲמִשָּׁ֣ה וְשִׁבְעִ֔ים עָשָׂ֥ה וָוִ֖ים לָֽעַמּוּדִ֑ים וְצִפָּ֥ה רָֽאשֵׁיהֶ֖ם וְחִשַּׁ֥ק

כט־ל אֹתָֽם: וּנְחֹ֥שֶׁת הַתְּנוּפָ֖ה שִׁבְעִ֣ים כִּכָּ֑ר וְאַלְפַּ֥יִם וְאַרְבַּע־מֵא֖וֹת שָֽׁקֶל: וַיַּ֣עַשׂ בָּ֗הּ אֶת־אַדְנֵי֙ פֶּ֚תַח אֹ֣הֶל מוֹעֵ֔ד וְאֵת֙ מִזְבַּ֣ח הַנְּחֹ֔שֶׁת וְאֶת־מִכְבַּ֥ר הַנְּחֹ֖שֶׁת

---

22. . . . וּבְצַלְאֵל בֶּן אוּרִי בֶּן חוּר לְמַטֵּה יְהוּדָה עָשָׂה — *And Bezalel the son of Uri, the son of Hur of the tribe of Judah made* . . . the leaders of the craftsmen of the *Mishkan's* work and its articles were noblemen (noble lineage) and the righteous ones of the generation, and therefore the Divine Presence rested on the work of their hands, and it did not fall into the hands of their enemies. But the Temple of Solomon (was built by) workers of the nations of the world (*I Kings 7:13*), and although the Divine Presence did rest there its sections deteriorated and it was necessary to לְחַזֵּק בֶּדֶק הַבָּיִת, *repair the breaches of the house* (*II Kings 22:5*), and eventually it all fell into the hands of the enemy. But the Second Temple, which did not meet even one of these conditions (and) the Divine Presence did not come to rest in it at all, fell into the hand of the enemy for indeed the Second Temple was not *the Mishkan of the testimony* since there were no tablets of testimony in it (at all) and it was Koresh Cyrus who charged (that it be built) (*Ezra 1:2*), and (also) there were no sons of Levi there, as Ezra attested when he said, וָאָבִינָה בָּעָם וּבַכֹּהֲנִים וּמִבְּנֵי לֵוִי לֹא מָצָאתִי שָׁם, *and I inspected the people and the priests but found there none of the sons of Levi* (*Ezra 8:15*), and among those who occupied themselves with the building were Zidonites and Zorites, as is explained in the book of *Ezra* (*3:7*).

24. כׇּל הַזָּהָב — *All the gold.* (The Torah) attests to, and defines the (quantity) of gold, silver and brass included in the work of the *Mishkan*, which was a very small amount compared to the riches of the First Temple, as explained in the Book of *Kings* (*I Kings 6; 20:35 and 7; 48-50*), and even more so were the riches of Herod's temple. Nevertheless the appearance of God's glory was more constantly (found) in the *Mishkan* of Moses than in the First Temple, and was not present at all in the Second Temple. This teaches us that it is not the amount of riches and the size of the

NOTES

God's creative powers.

The *Sforno* adds that not only Bezalel, but all who occupied themselves with the construction of the *Mishkan*, were men of stature, sincerity and piety, as compared to the First and Second Temples which were built by workmen of various peoples, and also did not possess — in some cases — the other factors which gave this *Mishkan* its special status.

24. כׇּל הַזָּהָב — *All the gold.* The *Sforno* is of the opinion that there must be some vital

לא אֲשֶׁר־לוֹ וְאֵת כָּל־כְּלֵי הַמִּזְבֵּחַ: וְאֶת־אַדְנֵי הֶחָצֵר סָבִיב וְאֶת־אַדְנֵי שַׁעַר
לט א הֶחָצֵר וְאֵת כָּל־יִתְדֹת הַמִּשְׁכָּן וְאֶת־כָּל־יִתְדֹת הֶחָצֵר סָבִיב: וּמִן־הַתְּכֵלֶת
וְהָאַרְגָּמָן וְתוֹלַעַת הַשָּׁנִי עָשׂוּ בִגְדֵי־שְׂרָד לְשָׁרֵת בַּקֹּדֶשׁ וַיַּעֲשׂוּ אֶת־בִּגְדֵי
הַקֹּדֶשׁ אֲשֶׁר לְאַהֲרֹן כַּאֲשֶׁר צִוָּה יְהוָה אֶת־מֹשֶׁה:
שני [חמישי] ב־ג וַיַּעַשׂ אֶת־הָאֵפֹד זָהָב תְּכֵלֶת וְאַרְגָּמָן וְתוֹלַעַת שָׁנִי וְשֵׁשׁ מָשְׁזָר: וַיְרַקְּעוּ
אֶת־פַּחֵי הַזָּהָב וְקִצֵּץ פְּתִילִם לַעֲשׂוֹת בְּתוֹךְ הַתְּכֵלֶת וּבְתוֹךְ הָאַרְגָּמָן
ד וּבְתוֹךְ תּוֹלַעַת הַשָּׁנִי וּבְתוֹךְ הַשֵּׁשׁ מַעֲשֵׂה חֹשֵׁב: כְּתֵפֹת עָשׂוּ־לוֹ חֹבְרֹת
ה עַל־שְׁנֵי °קצוותו חֻבָּר: וְחֵשֶׁב אֲפֻדָּתוֹ אֲשֶׁר עָלָיו מִמֶּנּוּ הוּא כְּמַעֲשֵׂהוּ °קְצוֹתָיו ק׳
זָהָב תְּכֵלֶת וְאַרְגָּמָן וְתוֹלַעַת שָׁנִי וְשֵׁשׁ מָשְׁזָר כַּאֲשֶׁר צִוָּה יְהוָה אֶת־
ו מֹשֶׁה: וַיַּעֲשׂוּ אֶת־אַבְנֵי הַשֹּׁהַם מֻסַבֹּת מִשְׁבְּצֹת זָהָב מְפֻתָּחֹת
ז פִּתּוּחֵי חוֹתָם עַל־שְׁמוֹת בְּנֵי יִשְׂרָאֵל: וַיָּשֶׂם אֹתָם עַל כִּתְפֹת הָאֵפֹד אַבְנֵי
זִכָּרוֹן לִבְנֵי יִשְׂרָאֵל כַּאֲשֶׁר צִוָּה יְהוָה אֶת־מֹשֶׁה:
ח וַיַּעַשׂ אֶת־הַחֹשֶׁן מַעֲשֵׂה חֹשֵׁב כְּמַעֲשֵׂה אֵפֹד זָהָב תְּכֵלֶת וְאַרְגָּמָן וְתוֹלַעַת
ט שָׁנִי וְשֵׁשׁ מָשְׁזָר: רָבוּעַ הָיָה כָּפוּל עָשׂוּ אֶת־הַחֹשֶׁן זֶרֶת אָרְכּוֹ וְזֶרֶת רָחְבּוֹ
י כָּפוּל: וַיְמַלְאוּ־בוֹ אַרְבָּעָה טוּרֵי אָבֶן טוּר אֹדֶם פִּטְדָה וּבָרֶקֶת הַטּוּר
יא־יב הָאֶחָד: וְהַטּוּר הַשֵּׁנִי נֹפֶךְ סַפִּיר וְיָהֲלֹם: וְהַטּוּר הַשְּׁלִישִׁי לֶשֶׁם שְׁבוֹ
יג וְאַחְלָמָה: וְהַטּוּר הָרְבִיעִי תַּרְשִׁישׁ שֹׁהַם וְיָשְׁפֵה מוּסַבֹּת מִשְׁבְּצוֹת זָהָב

---

structure which causes the Divine Presence to dwell in Israel, but God desires those who fear Him, and their deeds, in order to dwell in their midst.

XXXIX

1. בִּגְדֵי שְׂרָד — *Crocheted garments.* Garments (covers) which had no precise images (on them) except for a crocheted design; (they were) of sufficient (size) to cover the vessels.

3. וַיְרַקְּעוּ אֶת פַּחֵי הַזָּהָב — *And they beat the gold into thin plates.* The donors who contributed the gold for the priestly garments beat (it) into thin plates, preparing it for the craftsmen to make into threads.

וְקִצֵּץ פְּתִילִים — *And he cut threads.* The craftsman cut threads from the beaten (gold) plates which had been contributed.

NOTES

reason for the Torah to enumerate the quantities of precious metal collected and used in the *Mishkan* of Moses. This is to be understood as telling us how insignificant they were in comparison to the Temples of Solomon and Herod. Nevertheless the *Shechinah* appeared more often in this humbler structure. The Torah, thereby, is teaching us a great moral lesson. It is not the amount of gold one lavishes upon a holy temple which draws the Divine Presence to it, but the obedience of the people to God's will.

XXXIX

3. וַיְרַקְּעוּ אֶת פַּחֵי הַזָּהָב וְקִצֵּץ פְּתִילִים — *And they beat the gold into thin plates and he cut threads.* The phrase וַיְרַקְּעוּ, *and they beat,* is in the plural, whereas the verb וְקִצֵּץ, *and he cut,* is in the singular. The *Sforno* explains the former as referring to the numerous donors who contributed the gold. Their responsibility was to prepare the gold by beating it into plates. The latter task of cutting it into threads was that of each craftsman, hence it is written in

יד בְּמִלֻּאֹתָם: וְהָאֲבָנִים עַל־שְׁמֹת בְּנֵי־יִשְׂרָאֵל הֵנָּה שְׁתֵּים עֶשְׂרֵה עַל־
טו שְׁמֹתָם פִּתּוּחֵי חֹתָם אִישׁ עַל־שְׁמוֹ לִשְׁנֵים עָשָׂר שָׁבֶט: וַיַּעֲשׂוּ עַל־הַחֹשֶׁן
טז שַׁרְשְׁרֹת גַּבְלֻת מַעֲשֵׂה עֲבֹת זָהָב טָהוֹר: וַיַּעֲשׂוּ שְׁתֵּי מִשְׁבְּצֹת זָהָב וּשְׁתֵּי
יז טַבְּעֹת זָהָב וַיִּתְּנוּ אֶת־שְׁתֵּי הַטַּבָּעֹת עַל־שְׁנֵי קְצוֹת הַחֹשֶׁן: וַיִּתְּנוּ שְׁתֵּי
יח הָעֲבֹתֹת הַזָּהָב עַל־שְׁתֵּי הַטַּבָּעֹת עַל־קְצוֹת הַחֹשֶׁן: וְאֵת שְׁתֵּי קְצוֹת שְׁתֵּי
הָעֲבֹתֹת נָתְנוּ עַל־שְׁתֵּי הַמִּשְׁבְּצֹת וַיִּתְּנֻם עַל־כִּתְפֹת הָאֵפֹד אֶל־מוּל פָּנָיו:
יט וַיַּעֲשׂוּ שְׁתֵּי טַבְּעֹת זָהָב וַיָּשִׂימוּ עַל־שְׁנֵי קְצוֹת הַחֹשֶׁן עַל־שְׂפָתוֹ אֲשֶׁר אֶל־
כ עֵבֶר הָאֵפֹד בָּיְתָה: וַיַּעֲשׂוּ שְׁתֵּי טַבְּעֹת זָהָב וַיִּתְּנֻם עַל־שְׁתֵּי כִתְפֹת הָאֵפֹד
כא מִלְּמַטָּה מִמּוּל פָּנָיו לְעֻמַּת מַחְבַּרְתּוֹ מִמַּעַל לְחֵשֶׁב הָאֵפֹד: וַיִּרְכְּסוּ אֶת־
הַחֹשֶׁן מִטַּבְּעֹתָיו אֶל־טַבְּעֹת הָאֵפֹד בִּפְתִיל תְּכֵלֶת לִהְיֹת עַל־חֵשֶׁב הָאֵפֹד
וְלֹא־יִזַּח הַחֹשֶׁן מֵעַל הָאֵפֹד כַּאֲשֶׁר צִוָּה יהוָה אֶת־מֹשֶׁה:
שלישי כב־כג וַיַּעַשׂ אֶת־מְעִיל הָאֵפֹד מַעֲשֵׂה אֹרֵג כְּלִיל תְּכֵלֶת: וּפִי־הַמְּעִיל בְּתוֹכוֹ
[ששי] כד כְּפִי תַחְרָא שָׂפָה לְפִיו סָבִיב לֹא יִקָּרֵעַ: וַיַּעֲשׂוּ עַל־שׁוּלֵי הַמְּעִיל רִמּוֹנֵי
כה תְּכֵלֶת וְאַרְגָּמָן וְתוֹלַעַת שָׁנִי מָשְׁזָר: וַיַּעֲשׂוּ פַעֲמֹנֵי זָהָב טָהוֹר וַיִּתְּנוּ
אֶת־הַפַּעֲמֹנִים בְּתוֹךְ הָרִמֹּנִים עַל־שׁוּלֵי הַמְּעִיל סָבִיב בְּתוֹךְ הָרִמֹּנִים:
כו פַּעֲמֹן וְרִמֹּן פַּעֲמֹן וְרִמֹּן עַל־שׁוּלֵי הַמְּעִיל סָבִיב לְשָׁרֵת כַּאֲשֶׁר צִוָּה יהוָה
כז אֶת־מֹשֶׁה: וַיַּעֲשׂוּ אֶת־הַכָּתְנֹת שֵׁשׁ מַעֲשֵׂה אֹרֵג לְאַהֲרֹן
כח וּלְבָנָיו: וְאֵת הַמִּצְנֶפֶת שֵׁשׁ וְאֶת־פַּאֲרֵי הַמִּגְבָּעֹת שֵׁשׁ וְאֶת־מִכְנְסֵי הַבָּד
כט שֵׁשׁ מָשְׁזָר: וְאֶת־הָאַבְנֵט שֵׁשׁ מָשְׁזָר וּתְכֵלֶת וְאַרְגָּמָן וְתוֹלַעַת שָׁנִי מַעֲשֵׂה
ל רֹקֵם כַּאֲשֶׁר צִוָּה יהוָה אֶת־מֹשֶׁה: וַיַּעֲשׂוּ אֶת־צִיץ נֵזֶר־
לא הַקֹּדֶשׁ זָהָב טָהוֹר וַיִּכְתְּבוּ עָלָיו מִכְתַּב פִּתּוּחֵי חוֹתָם קֹדֶשׁ לַיהוָה: וַיִּתְּנוּ
עָלָיו פְּתִיל תְּכֵלֶת לָתֵת עַל־הַמִּצְנֶפֶת מִלְמָעְלָה כַּאֲשֶׁר צִוָּה יהוָה
לב אֶת־מֹשֶׁה: וַתֵּכֶל כָּל־עֲבֹדַת מִשְׁכַּן אֹהֶל מוֹעֵד וַיַּעֲשׂוּ בְּנֵי
יִשְׂרָאֵל כְּכֹל אֲשֶׁר צִוָּה יהוָה אֶת־מֹשֶׁה כֵּן עָשׂוּ:
רביעי לג וַיָּבִיאוּ אֶת־הַמִּשְׁכָּן אֶל־מֹשֶׁה אֶת־הָאֹהֶל וְאֶת־כָּל־כֵּלָיו קְרָסָיו קְרָשָׁיו

---

5. כַּאֲשֶׁר צִוָּה ה' אֶת מֹשֶׁה — *As HASHEM commanded Moses.* The intent of the craftsmen, in their work, was to fulfill the will of God, the Blessed One, in accordance with His command to Moses.

32. וַתֵּכֶל ... וַיַּעֲשׂוּ בְּנֵי יִשְׂרָאֵל — *Thus was finished ... and the Children of Israel did.* The entire, complete work (project) was done by all of Israel; some of them contributed money while some did the work, (motivated) by the generosity of their heart to fulfill the will of their Maker.

וְכֵן עָשׂוּ — *So they did* ... not less, not more.

33. וַיָּבִיאוּ אֶת הַמִּשְׁכָּן — *And they brought the mishkan* ... the curtains, the work of the skillful workmen (26:1).

NOTES

the singular.

5. כַּאֲשֶׁר צִוָּה ה' אֶת מֹשֶׁה — *As HASHEM commanded Moses.* Compare to the *Sforno's* commentary 36:8.

33. וַיָּבִיאוּ אֶת הַמִּשְׁכָּן ... וְאֶת כָּל כֵּלָיו — *And they brought the mishkan ... and all its*

לד בְּרִיחָו וְעַמֻּדָיו וַאֲדָנָיו: וְאֶת־מִכְסֵה עוֹרֹת הָאֵילִם הַמְאָדָּמִים וְאֶת־מִכְסֵה
לה עֹרֹת הַתְּחָשִׁים וְאֵת פָּרֹכֶת הַמָּסָךְ: אֶת־אֲרוֹן הָעֵדֻת וְאֶת־בַּדָּיו וְאֵת
לו־לז הַכַּפֹּרֶת: אֶת־הַשֻּׁלְחָן אֶת־כָּל־כֵּלָיו וְאֵת לֶחֶם הַפָּנִים: אֶת־הַמְּנֹרָה
לח הַטְּהֹרָה אֶת־נֵרֹתֶיהָ נֵרֹת הַמַּעֲרָכָה וְאֶת־כָּל־כֵּלֶיהָ וְאֵת שֶׁמֶן הַמָּאוֹר: וְאֵת
מִזְבַּח הַזָּהָב וְאֵת שֶׁמֶן הַמִּשְׁחָה וְאֵת קְטֹרֶת הַסַּמִּים וְאֵת מָסַךְ פֶּתַח
לט הָאֹהֶל: אֵת | מִזְבַּח הַנְּחֹשֶׁת וְאֶת־מִכְבַּר הַנְּחֹשֶׁת אֲשֶׁר־לוֹ אֶת־בַּדָּיו וְאֶת־
מ כָּל־כֵּלָיו אֶת־הַכִּיֹּר וְאֶת־כַּנּוֹ: אֵת קַלְעֵי הֶחָצֵר אֶת־עַמֻּדֶיהָ וְאֶת־אֲדָנֶיהָ
וְאֶת־הַמָּסָךְ לְשַׁעַר הֶחָצֵר אֶת־מֵיתָרָיו וִיתֵדֹתֶיהָ וְאֵת כָּל־כְּלֵי עֲבֹדַת
מא הַמִּשְׁכָּן לְאֹהֶל מוֹעֵד: אֶת־בִּגְדֵי הַשְּׂרָד לְשָׁרֵת בַּקֹּדֶשׁ אֶת־בִּגְדֵי הַקֹּדֶשׁ
מב לְאַהֲרֹן הַכֹּהֵן וְאֶת־בִּגְדֵי בָנָיו לְכַהֵן: כְּכֹל אֲשֶׁר־צִוָּה יהוה אֶת־מֹשֶׁה כֵּן
מג עָשׂוּ בְּנֵי יִשְׂרָאֵל אֵת כָּל־הָעֲבֹדָה: וַיַּרְא מֹשֶׁה אֶת־כָּל־הַמְּלָאכָה וְהִנֵּה
עָשׂוּ אֹתָהּ כַּאֲשֶׁר צִוָּה יהוה כֵּן עָשׂוּ וַיְבָרֶךְ אֹתָם מֹשֶׁה:

מ חמישי [שביעי]

א־ב וַיְדַבֵּר יהוה אֶל־מֹשֶׁה לֵּאמֹר: בְּיוֹם־הַחֹדֶשׁ הָרִאשׁוֹן בְּאֶחָד לַחֹדֶשׁ תָּקִים
ג אֶת־מִשְׁכַּן אֹהֶל מוֹעֵד: וְשַׂמְתָּ שָׁם אֵת אֲרוֹן הָעֵדוּת וְסַכֹּתָ עַל־הָאָרֹן
ד אֶת־הַפָּרֹכֶת: וְהֵבֵאתָ אֶת־הַשֻּׁלְחָן וְעָרַכְתָּ אֶת־עֶרְכּוֹ וְהֵבֵאתָ אֶת־הַמְּנֹרָה
ה וְהַעֲלֵיתָ אֶת־נֵרֹתֶיהָ: וְנָתַתָּה אֶת־מִזְבַּח הַזָּהָב לִקְטֹרֶת לִפְנֵי אֲרוֹן הָעֵדֻת
ו וְשַׂמְתָּ אֶת־מָסַךְ הַפֶּתַח לַמִּשְׁכָּן: וְנָתַתָּה אֵת מִזְבַּח הָעֹלָה לִפְנֵי פֶּתַח
ז מִשְׁכַּן אֹהֶל־מוֹעֵד: וְנָתַתָּ אֶת־הַכִּיֹּר בֵּין־אֹהֶל מוֹעֵד וּבֵין הַמִּזְבֵּחַ וְנָתַתָּ
ח־ט שָׁם מָיִם: וְשַׂמְתָּ אֶת־הֶחָצֵר סָבִיב וְנָתַתָּ אֶת־מָסַךְ שַׁעַר הֶחָצֵר: וְלָקַחְתָּ
אֶת־שֶׁמֶן הַמִּשְׁחָה וּמָשַׁחְתָּ אֶת־הַמִּשְׁכָּן וְאֶת־כָּל־אֲשֶׁר־בּוֹ וְקִדַּשְׁתָּ אֹתוֹ
י וְאֶת־כָּל־כֵּלָיו וְהָיָה קֹדֶשׁ: וּמָשַׁחְתָּ אֶת־מִזְבַּח הָעֹלָה וְאֶת־כָּל־כֵּלָיו
יא וְקִדַּשְׁתָּ אֶת־הַמִּזְבֵּחַ וְהָיָה הַמִּזְבֵּחַ קֹדֶשׁ קָדָשִׁים: וּמָשַׁחְתָּ אֶת־הַכִּיֹּר

אֶת הָאֹהֶל — *The tent* ... the curtains of goats' hair (26:7).

וְאֶת כָּל כֵּלָיו — *And all its furniture* ... of the *Mishkan;* for the clasps, boards, bars, pillars, and the sockets were the furnishings of the *Mishkan*.

42. כְּכֹל אֲשֶׁר צִוָּה ה׳ אֶת מֹשֶׁה כֵּן עָשׂוּ בְּנֵי יִשְׂרָאֵל אֵת כָּל הָעֲבֹדָה — *According to all that* HASHEM *commanded Moses, so the Children of Israel did all the work.* In the order that God later commanded Moses (to follow) when erecting the *Mishkan* (40:2-15).

43. כֵּן עָשׂוּ — *So they had done it.* In that same order itself did the craftsmen make (the various articles) and (in that same order) those who brought them did bring them.

NOTES

furniture. The *Sforno,* commenting on 26:1, states that the curtains are called the *mishkan* because within the area enclosed by them are the sacred vessels. Similarly in this verse he translates the word מִשְׁכָּן as meaning the curtains. The concluding part of the verse, וְאֶת כָּל כֵּלָיו, *and all its furniture,* refers to the *Mishkan,* i.e., the Tabernacle, not the curtains, for these are all integral parts of the Tabernacle.

42-43. כְּכֹל אֲשֶׁר צִוָּה ה׳ אֶת מֹשֶׁה כֵּן עָשׂוּ בְּנֵי יִשְׂרָאֵל אֵת כָּל הָעֲבֹדָה ... כֵּן עָשׂוּ — *According to all that* HASHEM *commanded Moses, so the Children of Israel did all the work* ... *So they had done it.* The fashioning of every part of

יב וְאֶת־כַּנּוֹ וְקִדַּשְׁתָּ אֹתוֹ: וְהִקְרַבְתָּ אֶת־אַהֲרֹן וְאֶת־בָּנָיו אֶל־פֶּתַח אֹהֶל

יג מוֹעֵד וְרָחַצְתָּ אֹתָם בַּמָּיִם: וְהִלְבַּשְׁתָּ אֶת־אַהֲרֹן אֵת בִּגְדֵי הַקֹּדֶשׁ וּמָשַׁחְתָּ

יד אֹתוֹ וְקִדַּשְׁתָּ אֹתוֹ וְכִהֵן לִי: וְאֶת־בָּנָיו תַּקְרִיב וְהִלְבַּשְׁתָּ אֹתָם כֻּתֳּנֹת:

טו וּמָשַׁחְתָּ אֹתָם כַּאֲשֶׁר מָשַׁחְתָּ אֶת־אֲבִיהֶם וְכִהֲנוּ לִי וְהָיְתָה לִהְיֹת לָהֶם

טז מָשְׁחָתָם לִכְהֻנַּת עוֹלָם לְדֹרֹתָם: וַיַּעַשׂ מֹשֶׁה כְּכֹל אֲשֶׁר צִוָּה יְהוָה אֹתוֹ

ששי יז כֵּן עָשָׂה: וַיְהִי בַּחֹדֶשׁ הָרִאשׁוֹן בַּשָּׁנָה הַשֵּׁנִית בְּאֶחָד

יח לַחֹדֶשׁ הוּקַם הַמִּשְׁכָּן: וַיָּקֶם מֹשֶׁה אֶת־הַמִּשְׁכָּן וַיִּתֵּן אֶת־אֲדָנָיו וַיָּשֶׂם

יט אֶת־קְרָשָׁיו וַיִּתֵּן אֶת־בְּרִיחָיו וַיָּקֶם אֶת־עַמּוּדָיו: וַיִּפְרֹשׂ אֶת־הָאֹהֶל עַל־

הַמִּשְׁכָּן וַיָּשֶׂם אֶת־מִכְסֵה הָאֹהֶל עָלָיו מִלְמָעְלָה כַּאֲשֶׁר צִוָּה יְהוָה אֶת־

כ מֹשֶׁה: וַיִּקַּח וַיִּתֵּן אֶת־הָעֵדֻת אֶל־הָאָרֹן וַיָּשֶׂם אֶת־

כא הַבַּדִּים עַל־הָאָרֹן וַיִּתֵּן אֶת־הַכַּפֹּרֶת עַל־הָאָרֹן מִלְמָעְלָה: וַיָּבֵא אֶת־הָאָרֹן

אֶל־הַמִּשְׁכָּן וַיָּשֶׂם אֵת פָּרֹכֶת הַמָּסָךְ וַיָּסֶךְ עַל אֲרוֹן הָעֵדוּת כַּאֲשֶׁר צִוָּה

כב יְהוָה אֶת־מֹשֶׁה: וַיִּתֵּן אֶת־הַשֻּׁלְחָן בְּאֹהֶל מוֹעֵד עַל יֶרֶךְ

כג הַמִּשְׁכָּן צָפֹנָה מִחוּץ לַפָּרֹכֶת: וַיַּעֲרֹךְ עָלָיו עֵרֶךְ לֶחֶם לִפְנֵי יְהוָה כַּאֲשֶׁר

כד צִוָּה יְהוָה אֶת־מֹשֶׁה: וַיָּשֶׂם אֶת־הַמְּנֹרָה בְּאֹהֶל מוֹעֵד נֹכַח

כה הַשֻּׁלְחָן עַל יֶרֶךְ הַמִּשְׁכָּן נֶגְבָּה: וַיַּעַל הַנֵּרֹת לִפְנֵי יְהוָה כַּאֲשֶׁר צִוָּה יְהוָה

כו אֶת־מֹשֶׁה: וַיָּשֶׂם אֶת־מִזְבַּח הַזָּהָב בְּאֹהֶל מוֹעֵד לִפְנֵי הַפָּרֹכֶת:

שביעי כז-כח וַיַּקְטֵר עָלָיו קְטֹרֶת סַמִּים כַּאֲשֶׁר צִוָּה יְהוָה אֶת־מֹשֶׁה: וַיָּשֶׂם

כט אֶת־מָסַךְ הַפֶּתַח לַמִּשְׁכָּן: וְאֵת מִזְבַּח הָעֹלָה שָׂם פֶּתַח מִשְׁכַּן אֹהֶל־מוֹעֵד

ל וַיַּעַל עָלָיו אֶת־הָעֹלָה וְאֶת־הַמִּנְחָה כַּאֲשֶׁר צִוָּה יְהוָה אֶת־מֹשֶׁה: וַיָּשֶׂם

לא אֶת־הַכִּיֹּר בֵּין־אֹהֶל מוֹעֵד וּבֵין הַמִּזְבֵּחַ וַיִּתֵּן שָׁמָּה מַיִם לְרָחְצָה: וְרָחֲצוּ

לב מִמֶּנּוּ מֹשֶׁה וְאַהֲרֹן וּבָנָיו אֶת־יְדֵיהֶם וְאֶת־רַגְלֵיהֶם: בְּבֹאָם אֶל־אֹהֶל מוֹעֵד

XL

18. וַיָּקֶם מֹשֶׁה אֶת הַמִּשְׁכָּן — *And Moses raised up the mishkan.* The ten curtains, the work of the skillful workmen, which is called *mishkan*, were raised up before the erection of the boards — either by men holding them or in a miraculous way, as our Sages tell us *(Menachos 99a).* And in this order they were made and brought to Moses. For indeed these ten curtains comprise the principal (part) of the *Mishkan's* structure. The other (items) which were part of that structure, (such as) the sockets, boards, bars, pillars and the tent were only (for the purpose) of supporting and covering the *mishkan* curtains.

NOTES

the Tabernacle, the sequence of bringing every item to Moses, and the order in which he put it together all followed an exact order, as commanded by God to Moses. This is what the *Sforno* stresses in his commentary on these two verses.

XL

18. וַיָּקֶם מֹשֶׁה אֶת הַמִּשְׁכָּן — *And Moses raised*

up the mishkan. As mentioned above Moses erected the *Mishkan* in a precise exact order. As these verses clearly state (18-19) he first raised up the curtains (which are called 'the *mishkan'* as explained in 26:1 and 39:33) followed by the laying of the sockets, the setting up of the boards (which were on the inside of the curtains), the placing of the bars and the spreading of the tent over the Tabernacle. Now the question is, how did the

לג וּבְקָרְבָתָם אֶל־הַמִּזְבֵּחַ יִרְחָצוּ כַּאֲשֶׁר צִוָּה יהוה אֶת־מֹשֶׁה: וַיָּקֶם
אֶת־הֶחָצֵר סָבִיב לַמִּשְׁכָּן וְלַמִּזְבֵּחַ וַיִּתֵּן אֶת־מָסַךְ שַׁעַר הֶחָצֵר וַיְכַל מֹשֶׁה
אֶת־הַמְּלָאכָה:
מפטיר לד־לה וַיְכַס הֶעָנָן אֶת־אֹהֶל מוֹעֵד וּכְבוֹד יהוה מָלֵא אֶת־הַמִּשְׁכָּן: וְלֹא־יָכֹל מֹשֶׁה
לָבוֹא אֶל־אֹהֶל מוֹעֵד כִּי־שָׁכַן עָלָיו הֶעָנָן וּכְבוֹד יהוה מָלֵא אֶת־הַמִּשְׁכָּן:
לו־לז וּבְהֵעָלוֹת הֶעָנָן מֵעַל הַמִּשְׁכָּן יִסְעוּ בְּנֵי יִשְׂרָאֵל בְּכֹל מַסְעֵיהֶם: וְאִם־לֹא
לח יֵעָלֶה הֶעָנָן וְלֹא יִסְעוּ עַד־יוֹם הֵעָלֹתוֹ: כִּי עֲנַן יהוה עַל־הַמִּשְׁכָּן יוֹמָם וְאֵשׁ
תִּהְיֶה לַיְלָה בּוֹ לְעֵינֵי כָל־בֵּית־יִשְׂרָאֵל בְּכָל־מַסְעֵיהֶם:

33-34. וַיְכַל מֹשֶׁה ... וַיְכַס הֶעָנָן — *And Moses finished ... and the cloud covered.* Immediately after Moses finished the work necessary to cause the Divine Presence to dwell, which is the work of the raising and the labors therein, the cloud covered and the *Shechinah* dwelled (therein).

מָלֵא אֶת הַמִּשְׁכָּן — *Filled the Mishkan.* (God's glory) revealed itself in every part of the *Mishkan* (Tabernacle) but not outside of it at all.

35. אֶל אֹהֶל מוֹעֵד — *Into the tent of meeting.* Within the curtains outside the *paroches*.

36. וּבְהֵעָלוֹת הֶעָנָן — *And whenever the cloud went up.* The *Shechinah* was so (firmly) established in the *Mishkan* that it did not depart at all from there until Israel had to journey. (Now) this was not so in Shiloh, nor in the First Temple nor in the Second Temple. But even more than this will be (manifested) in the Third Temple (may it be built and established speedily in our days), as it says: וַאֲנִי אֶהְיֶה לָּהּ נְאֻם ה׳ חוֹמַת אֵשׁ סָבִיב וּלְכָבוֹד אֶהְיֶה בְתוֹכָהּ, *'For I,' says* H*ASHEM*, *'will be to her a wall of fire roundabout, and will be the glory in the midst of her'* (*Zechariah* 2:9).

NOTES

curtains hang prior to the erecting of the boards since they had no support whatsoever? This is what the *Sforno* means when he states that either 'men (the Levites) held them' in place, or they remained suspended 'in a miraculous way.' The selection from the Talmud (*Menachos* 99a) cited by the *Sforno* discusses the principle that in the realm of the sacred מַעֲלִין וְלֹא מוֹרִידִין, *one always elevates but never debases.* The proof brought to the prohibition of debasing something sacred is from the order in which Moses erected the *Mishkan*. *Rashi* explains that since Moses began by raising up the curtains, they could not be allowed to fall while he was putting up the boards for this would constitute debasement of the most sacred part of the *Mishkan*, namely the curtains which are also called the *mishkan*, as explained above! Hence the curtains must have remained in their elevated position, one way or another, as the *Sforno* states, while the sockets, boards and bars were being put into place.

36. וּבְהֵעָלוֹת הֶעָנָן — *And whenever the cloud went up.* The prophet Zechariah saw a man in his vision measuring Jerusalem, who said to the prophet that the city *will be inhabited like unwalled towns because of the multitude of men* in it. The verse quoted by the *Sforno* follows this statement of the man in Zechariah's vision. Based on this verse the *Sforno* states that God's presence in Jerusalem at the time of redemption will be even more pervasive than it was in the time of the *Mishkan* of Moses.